SMITH AND BA
ON
THE MODERN ENGLISH LEGAL
SYSTEM

AUSTRALIA
LBC Information Services
Sydney

CANADA and USA
Carswell
Toronto

NEW ZEALAND
Brooker's
Auckland

SINGAPORE and MALAYSIA
Thomson Information (S.E. Asia)
Singapore

SMITH AND BAILEY
ON
THE MODERN ENGLISH LEGAL
SYSTEM

Third Edition

by

S. H. BAILEY, M.A., LL.B.,

*Professor of Public Law at the
University of Nottingham*

and

M. J. GUNN, LL.B.,

*Professor of Mental Health Law
at De Montfort University
Sometime Head of the School of Law
and Professor of the University of
Westminster*

LONDON
SWEET & MAXWELL
1996

First Edition 1984
Second Impression 1986
Third Impression 1987
Fourth Impression 1988
Second Edition 1991
Second Impression 1992
Third Impression 1994
Fourth Impression 1995
Third Edition 1996

Published in 1996 by
Sweet & Maxwell Limited of
100 Avenue Road, Swiss Cottage, London NW3 3PF
Computerset by Wyvern Typesetting Ltd, Bristol
Printed by Clays Ltd, St Ives plc

A CIP Catalogue Record
for this book is available
from the British Library

ISBN 0 421 50840 X

CONTENTS

PART I: COURTS, PERSONNEL AND SOURCES OF LAW

PART II: SOLVING LEGAL PROBLEMS

PART III: PRE-TRIAL PROCEDURE

PART IV: THE HEARING

PREFACE

The five years since the last edition of this book have seen no slackening in the pace of change in the English Legal System. The role and influence of Community Law has developed. The process of statutory interpretation is coming to terms with the decision in *Pepper (Inspector of Taxes) v. Hart* permitting recourse to legislative materials as an aid to interpretation. The legal profession has continued to change with the times and legal education is in the midst of a major review from the Lord Chancellor's Advisory Committee on Legal Education and Conduct.

The criminal justice process is subject to seemingly endless change, reflecting the tension between concern to prevent further miscarriages of justice and the Government's apparent desire to increase conviction rates and the prison population. The civil justice process has been under scrutiny, again, by Lord Woolf, whose final report is available both in print and on the Internet. The commitment to reform has been enhanced by Lord Woolf's appointment as Master of Rolls. The relationship between the judiciary and the Government in the discharge of their respective responsibilities for the administration of justice and of the courts has been increasingly problematic. All these, and much more besides, have necessitated much rewriting.

The authors wish to acknowledge the assistance of officials of the General Council of the Bar, the Crown Prosecution Service, the Home Office, the Law Society, the Lord Chancellor's Department and the National Association of Citizens' Advice Bureaux, and would like to thank colleagues who have helped on particular points: Robert Abbey, Stuart Barry, Diane Birch, Andy Boon, Richard Card, Michael Grant, Ian Hooker, David Ormerod and Stephen Weatherill. Responsibility for the finished product, however, rests with us.

We wish to thank the publishers for their support and patience, for preparing the tables and index and for all their other work on this edition. We wish publicly to acknowledge the tremendous support and forbearance from our families: Maeve, Benjamin and Christopher; and Diane and Leonara.

We have endeavoured to state the law as at the end of January 1996, but have attempted to incorporate as many later developments as possible at proof stage. One development which could not be noted was the publication of the Government's White Paper on Legal Aid, *Striking the Balance* (Cm. 3305, 1996), but our publishers have kindly allowed us to include the summary of changes in the addition to this preface.

Lord Woolf's final report on access to civil justice was published on July 26, 1996. We are most grateful to our publishers for allowing us to reproduce the press notice from the Lord Chancellor's Department as an addition to this Preface.

S.H.B.   July 1996
M.J.G.   Leicester & Nottingham

Striking the balance: Summary of Changes

GENERAL

Targeting

A.1   Legal aid will, in principle, be capable of providing any help — not just from lawyers — that can either (1) prevent court proceedings or questions that would demand a legal solution from arising, or (2) promote their settlement or other disposal, in accordance with the law and in a way that will produce an enforceable result (paragraph 1.19).

A.2   As now, the Lord Chancellor will be able to make regulations about the types of case and service covered by legal aid, and about financial eligibility and contributions. There are no plans to exercise the power to extend legal aid to provide representation before any more tribunals (paragraph 2.2).

A.3   The Lord Chancellor will allocate separate, pre-determined budgets for criminal, family and civil (non-family) legal aid to the Legal Aid Board (paragraph 2.3).

A.4   Expenditure will be targeted on priority areas as follows:
- the Lord Chancellor will give directions about priorities to the Legal Aid Board;
- the Board, in the light of those directions, will devise and apply a formula to allocate budgets for different categories of case to each region;
- regional budgets will be refined to reflect local need (on which Regional Legal Services Committees, representing local interests, will have advised);
- the Board will then submit the resulting national strategic plan to the Lord Chancellor for his approval (paragraphs 2.4–2.10).

A.5   The Board will also develop an information strategy so that people will know what services are available and can be directed to them (paragraph 2.12).

Contracting

A.6   Most legal aid services will be provided under contracts between the Legal Aid Board and providers in the private or voluntary sectors. But the Board will be able to test and develop other ways of providing services, including grants and the use of directly employed staff (paragraphs 3.1–3.3).

A.7   The Board will seek to get the best price for services that meet its requirements for quality, geographic access and an adequate range of providers (paragraphs 3.7–3.11).

A.8   All contracts will include quality standards. These will build on the Legal Aid Board's franchising initiative, which sets standards for offices' management and checks that appropriate steps are taken in individual cases. In addition, outcomes and other key features of cases under contracts will be monitored (paragraphs 3.12–3.21).

A.9   Payments under contracts will be made in a way that rewards efficiency. The main options are either a single price covering all work that comes forward at a particular place and/or over a particular period, or a set price per case subject to a maximum volume. Prices will include disbursements, including expert reports and the use of barristers or other advocates. But there will be special arrangements for very expensive cases or unexpectedly high demand. Providers will be paid at regular intervals (paragraphs 3.22–3.25).

CIVIL AND FAMILY LEGAL AID

Contracting

A.10   In the civil and family field, the main types of contract will cover:
- initial advice and assistance in particular areas of civil or family law, with special arrangements where more substantial work is needed before or instead of issuing court proceedings;
- representation in particular types of civil or family proceedings;
- mediation in family matters; and
- one-off contracts for expensive cases (paragraphs 3.27, 3.30 & 3.36).

A.11   Franchised advice agencies will be able to get contracts to provide advice and assistance in their areas of expertise. The Legal Aid Board will develop partnership agreements with advice agencies and their existing funders to ensure that the legal aid funding is used to provide additional services and not simply to replace existing grants (paragraph 3.29).

Granting civil legal aid — testing the merits of the case

A.12   Initial advice and assistance will be available on the basis of a quick and simple test, applied by the provider. This will consider whether legal aid is available for the matter, whether it falls within the provider's contract and whether it is reasonable to provide some advice and assistance (paragraph 2.15).

A.13   More substantial help or representation in litigation will require a more detailed test to decide whether the cases deserve a share of the public funds available. The Lord Chancellor will make regulations setting out the criteria (*e.g.* prospects of success, cost-benefit and importance) to be weighed against the level of resources available for cases of that type. The Legal Aid Board will produce a national code containing directions and guidance on how the test should be applied in practice. This will need the Lord Chancellor's approval (paragraphs 2.16–2.17).

A.14   The Board will be able to delegate the test to providers to enable them to grant legal aid out of their own contracts. This approach will be carefully piloted (paragraph 2.18).

A.15 Providers will be able to withdraw legal aid if the circumstances of the case change, but not because a more deserving case has arisen (paragraph 2.21).

A.16 Where legal aid is refused or withdrawn, the applicant will be able to ask the Legal Aid Board to review the decision. There will be a right of appeal (paragraphs 2.20–2.21).

Granting civil legal aid — financial conditions

A.17 Initial advice and assistance will be subject to a simple means test undertaken by the provider. Once legal aid spending is under better control, we hope to match eligibility for initial advice and assistance with that for more substantial help. People claiming Income Support and some other social security benefits would continue to receive free advice and assistance, but all other financially eligible applicants would pay a fixed contribution (paragraphs 4.9–4.11).

A.18 People claiming some benefits will automatically be eligible for more substantial help in civil and family matters, including mediation and representation in litigation. Other people will be subject to a detailed means assessment by the Legal Aid Board. As now, applicants with access to alternative sources of funding, such as legal expenses insurance, will not be eligible for legal aid regardless of their means. In future, the possibility of reaching a conditional fee agreement might also be taken into account (paragraph 4.12).

A.19 As now, applicants whose disposable income and capital are between the lower and upper limits will be required to make contributions related to their ability to pay. In future, contributions from income will continue to be payable after the end of a case until the cost of the case has been met (subject to a ceiling for expensive cases and any time limit). At the same time, we will consider introducing a graduated scale for calculating contributions (paragraphs 4.23–4.25).

A.20 There will also be a minimum contribution payable by *all* assisted persons, including those on any social security benefit, who issue or defend most types of court proceedings. Further minimum contributions might be payable at subsequent stages in proceedings, for example setting down for trial (paragraph 4.26).

A.21 Any costs not recovered from the other party, or already met by way of contributions, will still give rise to a statutory charge on assets preserved or recovered in the proceedings. There will be a single capital allowance, linked to Income Support levels, which applicants can claim once in respect of either the capital contribution or the statutory charge (paragraphs 4.18–4.19).

A.22 The Legal Aid Board will also be able to recover costs from an assisted person who later sells his or her home (paragraph 4.20).

A.23 The assisted person's maximum liability for contributions or the statutory charge will be calculated in advance by reference to bands relating to the stage that a case reaches (paragraph 4.16).

A.24 Whether to award *inter partes* costs will remain in the discretion of the court. How much an assisted person's unsuccessful opponent has to pay will be calculated by reference to the bands (paragraph 4.17).

A.24 The court will treat legally-aided parties in much the same way as other litigants when it considers to award *inter partes* costs. But there will be rules about how far costs orders against assisted persons can be enforced (paragraphs 4.28–4.29).

A.26   If a successful unassisted defendant will suffer financial hardship because he or she cannot enforce an award against the assisted person straight away, the court will be able to order a payment from the legal aid fund. The Board will seek to recover the money from the assisted person (paragraph 4.30).

A.27   Subject to the successful completion of the current trial period, the Government intends to extend the scope of conditional fees to cover most types of civil case involving a financial claim (paragraph 4.31).

A.28   The Government is considering how the Legal Aid Board might develop partnerships with the private sector to offer quality-assured legal services to people who do not qualify for legal aid (paragraph 4.32).

CRIMINAL LEGAL AID

Contracting

A.29   New arrangements for contracting routine criminal cases will be considered and tested. These arrangements would bring together the existing fragmented provision for advice, assistance and representation for suspects and defendants at the police station and in the magistrates' court. Solicitors would have to provide all necessary services to clients who chose them or who were assigned to them at a duty session. So far as possible, contracts would be for a fixed price based on the number of police and magistrates' court duty sessions covered (paragraphs 5.8–5.11).

A.30   People who want help in a criminal case will be able to choose any solicitor whose firm has a contract, or call on the services of the duty solicitor (paragraph 5.10).

A.31   Contracts for more substantial Crown Court work will probably be based on an agreed price per case (paragraph 5.12). There will be one-off contracts for very expensive cases (paragraph 5.18).

A.32   Letting contracts for criminal work will involve a consultative process overseen by Regional Legal Services Committees, in order to take account of sensitivities in local communities (paragraph 5.13).

Granting criminal legal aid — the interests of justice test

A.33   Criminal legal aid services will be available on the same basis as now. In particular, whether a person is entitled to representation in a criminal case will be decided according to the interests of justice (paragraph 5.6).

A.34   If criminal contracting was developed in the way suggested above, the Legal Aid Board would eventually take over responsibility from the courts for determining applications for criminal legal aid. In practice, the function would be delegated to contracted solicitors, but applicants would be able to appeal.

The courts would also be able to ask another solicitor to consider representing an unrepresented defendant (paragraphs 5.15–5.17).

Granting criminal legal aid — financial conditions

A.35   Advice and assistance at a police station and on a person's first appearance at a magistrates' court will remain free, with no means test or contributions (paragraph 5.19).

A.36   Advice, assistance and representation before and during the early stages of a criminal case in a magistrates' court will remain free for those claiming certain social security benefits. All other represented defendants will pay a fixed contribution on their second appearance at court in relation to a particular matter (paragraph 5.20).

A.37   More substantial help will be subject to a detailed means assessment. Responsibility for means assessment will be transferred from the courts to the Legal Aid Board (paragraphs 5.21 and 5.22).

Lord Chancellor's Department Press Notice (232.96), "Access to Justice" — Lord Woolf's final report

Lord Woolf, Master of the Rolls, today published his final report to the Lord Chancellor on access to civil justice. Lord Woolf said it will create a new landscape for civil justice.

A draft of new Civil Proceedings Rules is also published with the final report. "These will harmonise and simplify procedures for all High Court and county court cases and replace the two separate rule books for the Supreme Court and county courts," Lord Woolf said. Publication of the report and draft rules completes the second, and final, stage of a two-year inquiry into civil justice.

Lord Woolf's interim report, published in June 1995, set out a blue print for change. It proposed a new system of case management by the courts to reduce costs and delay in civil litigation. The final report builds on these proposals, and fills in details by:

- setting out a detailed fast track procedure for cases up to £10,000, with a maximum timetable of 30 weeks;
- recommending guideline maximum legal costs at the top of the fast track of £2,500, excluding VAT and disbursements;
- proposing the use of pre-action protocols to encourage a more co-operative approach to dispute resolution and promote fair settlements, avoiding litigation wherever possible; and making detailed proposals to increase access to justice in key areas of litigation (medical negligence, housing, multi-party actions and judicial review).

Commenting on the work of his Inquiry, Lord Woolf said:

"My primary concern has been to improve access to justice, in particular for individuals and small businesses. I believe the key to this is enabling people to resolve their disputes in a more co-operative and less confrontational way than our traditional litigation system allows.

"The Inquiry has paved the way for a more co-operative approach, by including both claimants' and defendants' representatives in the working groups which developed proposals on housing, medical negligence, fast track procedures, pre-action protocols and other specialist jurisdictions.

"The results show that the opposing sides do have a common interest in the creation of an accessible and affordable civil justice system. Tactical delays and the withholding of information benefit no-one — they are not in the interests of justice.

"I am particularly concerned about the level of public expenditure on litigation, especially in medical negligence and housing. Substantial amounts of public money which are now absorbed in legal costs could be better spent on enhanced medical care and on improving standards of public housing.

"The Civil Proceedings Rules, which will govern proceedings under the new system, will be clear and straightforward. They start with new guiding principles which should influence all procedural decisions which the court makes. They emphasise the importance of the need for economy, expedition, and achieving equality between the parties."

ACKNOWLEDGMENTS

The authors and publishers would like to thank the following for permission to reproduce material from publications in which they have copyright.

Crown Copyright. Reproduced with the permission of the Controller of HMSO.

The Green Form Key Card and accompanying notes reproduced by kind permission of the Legal Aid Board.

Extracts from various law reports reproduced with kind permission of the Incorporated Council of Law Reporting for England and Wales.

TABLE OF CASES

TABLE OF STATUTES

TABLE OF STATUTORY INSTRUMENTS

RULES OF THE SUPREME COURT

COUNTY COURT RULES

PART I

**COURTS, PERSONNEL AND
SOURCES OF LAW**

CHAPTER 1

INTRODUCTION

A. THE ENGLISH LEGAL SYSTEM

THE study of the English legal system is a vital part of any law student's course. Not only are the legal institutions and processes integral to every other legal course he or she will study, they are also the subject of necessary scrutiny for assessing how well the law provides solutions to the problems it is intended to meet.

Law students are not always aware of the social context in which the rules of law they learn about will actually operate. Some of their teachers are more enthusiastic than others about ensuring that their study is not directed solely to the rules of law contained in statutes or gleaned from the decisions of the superior courts. In respect of the institutions, processes and people of the English legal system in particular, some students affect impatience at the study of matters which they think are better left to social scientists. Some even have the mis-guided belief that the study of the institutions and processes of our law does not carry the intellectual challenge of other legal subjects. Yet a failure to under-stand the English legal system will make much of what the student learns of those other subjects either incomprehensible or misleading.

For example, those studying the law of negligence need to know the basic elements of the tort and their respective functions. They will discover that until comparatively recently its scope has been confined to cases of physical damage to person or property and that the great majority of cases actually brought arise out of accidents on the road or at work. Liability in tort will be compared with other sources of accident compensation, such as social security, and related to the insurance position. As regards a tort claim, however, the student should not only be aware of the rules which prescribe who has a right to bring a claim for damages, but also of the processes whereby legal rights are actually vindicated, and indeed the enormous practical difficulties that face potential claimants. These processes form an important part of the subject matter of this book.

Almost every aspect of life in the modern state is regulated or affected in some way by law. There are laws which provide for the remedying of defined grievances (*e.g.* by the payment of damages in respect of accidentally inflicted injuries), laws which prohibit anti-social activities and provide for the imposition of penal sanctions for breach (*e.g.* the criminal law of murder or theft), laws which regulate potentially harmful activities by, for example, systems for licens-ing, registration or inspection, usually in conjunction with the prescription of standards (*e.g.* liquor licensing, the protection of health and safety at work), laws which confer state benefits upon individuals (*e.g.* education, highways, social security, national health service) and laws which facilitate private arrangements (*e.g.* marriages, contracts, wills).[1] In a sense, the whole body of English law could be said to constitute the English legal system. However, we use the term in a narrower sense to cover the distinctive legal institutions and processes that come into operation when for some reason there is doubt or disagreement as to how the law applies in a given situation: there may be recourse to a lawyer or some other agency for legal advice, or, usually as a last resort, involvement in litigation before a court or tribunal.

The label "English legal system" is convenient, but has to be treated with a little care. For one thing, it extends to both England and Wales (Scotland, Northern Ireland, the Isle of Man and the Channel Islands have separate systems). For another, it is not as systematically organised as a "system" perhaps should be.

B. SOME BASIC CONCEPTS

There is not room here for an introduction to the theoretical background of the role of law in society.[2] There are, however, certain concepts that will appear at various points in this book and require some explanation here.

1. "COMMON LAW" AND "CIVIL LAW"

The "common law" was the term that came to be used for the laws and customs applied by the royal courts which emerged after the Norman Conquest, and which progressively replaced local laws and customs applied in sundry local courts.[3] As the decisions of these courts came to be recorded and published, so the practice developed whereby past decisions would be cited in argument before the courts, and would be regarded as being of persuasive or even binding authority.[4] The point that decisions of the superior courts are a source of law in their own right is a distinctive feature of "common law systems", the term here being used to distinguish such systems from continental, "civil law",[5] systems based in origin upon Roman law but now upon a series of codes established in the nineteenth and twentieth centuries. The basic elements of English law have become established in a number of Commonwealth countries (most notably Australia, New Zealand and Canada, excluding Quebec) and the United States (except Louisiana).

---

[1] These five legal techniques were distinguished by R. Summers, "The Technique Element in Law," 59 Calif. L. R. 733 (1971). See also J. Farrar and A. M. Dugdale, *Introduction to Legal Method* (3rd ed., 1990), Chap. 2, who distinguish two further techniques: the "constitutive" technique whereby the law recognises a group of people as constituting a legal person (*e.g.* a company), and the "fiscal" technique whereby the government raises money by taxation.

[2] See B. Roshier and H. Teff, *Law and Society in England* (1980); P. S. Atiyah, *Law and Modern Society* (2nd ed., 1995); R. Cotterell, *The Sociology of Law: An Introduction* (2nd ed., 1992).

[3] See below, pp. 34–37 on the growth of the royal courts.

[4] See Chap. 7.

[5] This usage of the term "civil" should be distinguished from its uses "as opposed to (i) ecclesiastical; (ii) criminal; (iii) military": *Osborn's Concise Law Dictionary* (8th ed. 1993).

2. "Common Law" and Statute

Apart from its use as a convenient label for one kind of legal system, the term "common law" is used, in a narrower sense, for one of a number of distinct sources of law that exist within such a system. Laws enacted by the Queen in Parliament ("Acts of Parliament" or "statutes"), or made under delegated powers conferred by statute, have come to be of arguably greater significance than the decisions of the courts.[6] The common law has always been particularly associated with the protection of such matters as personal freedom, rights of property and contract, and individual interests in reputation and bodily security. However, the nineteenth and twentieth centuries have seen a substantial expansion of the accepted role of government to include the pursuit of such collective purposes as the protection of public health and welfare and the direction of the economy. The National Health Service, state education and social security are all examples of services established and regulated by legislation. It has also come to be felt that important changes in areas still dominated by the common law are more legitimately made by statute than by judges, although the vein of judicial creativity is by no means exhausted.[7]

The term "common law" is thus used to denote rules derived from decisions of the superior courts in contrast to those derived from statute. There is, however, one usage that is narrower still. Only some judge-made rules are rules of the common law in this narrower sense—the others are rules of "equity" which are of distinct historical origin.

3. "Common Law" and "Equity"

By the thirteenth century, the Crown had, in effect, delegated its inherent power to dispense justice to the judges of three royal courts: the Exchequer, the Common Bench—or as it came to be known in Tudor times, the Common Pleas—and the King's (or Queen's) Bench.[8] At this time, the Common Bench was by far the busiest court as regards civil cases, with jurisdiction over matters between subject and subject such as disputes over rights to land and actions for debt.[9] Proceedings were commenced by the plaintiff's purchase of a writ from the Chancery.[10] The Chancery was originally the royal secretariat, the place where all kinds of royal documents were prepared and authenticated by the Great Seal. Its head was the Chancellor,[11] whose office came to be one of the

---

[6] See Chaps. 5 and 6.

[7] See pp. 249–258.

[8] See further below, pp. 36–38 on the development of these courts.

[9] The King's Bench shared with the Common Bench cases of "trespass" (the term then simply meaning "wrong" as in the Lord's Prayer) and heard proceedings to correct errors in the Common Bench and local courts. Its main function was to deal with what are now called criminal cases—pleas of the Crown. By the end of the sixteenth century it had by a series of procedural devices obtained a civil jurisdiction comparable with the Common Pleas.

[10] Proceedings in the King's Bench were commenced by a petition known as a "bill" addressed directly to the court by the plaintiff, a simpler and cheaper procedure.

[11] Where a Chancellor was not appointed, the Great Seal could be entrusted to temporary "Keepers of the Seal". Occasionally, a permanent appointment was made to the office of "Lord Keeper of the Great Seal" where it was wished not to make an appointment to the more dignified office of Lord Chancellor; the powers of the two offices were the same.

great offices of state. In medieval times, most Chancellors were bishops and graduates in civil or canon law. Some holders of the office were in effect the King's chief minister.

The plaintiff was obliged to obtain a writ in a form appropriate to the claim. At first, if there was no precedent the Chancery would be prepared to draft a new one, but by the end of the thirteenth century this could no longer be done. Once the writ was obtained it governed the detailed form the action would take: if the wrong one had been chosen, the plaintiff was required to recommence proceedings.

Among the duties of the Chancellor were those of determining questions relating to Crown property, hearing common law actions concerning his clerks, servants and officials, and entertaining "petitions of right" (*i.e.* claims against the Crown). In addition, the Chancellor came to deal exclusively with petitions addressed to the King or the Council in respect of grievances which for some reason were not redressed or redressible by proceedings in the common law courts. This might be because of corruption or undue influence affecting proceedings (*e.g.* the bribery of jurors), or because in a particular case strict common law requirements for proof appeared to lead to injustice, or because the matter did not fall within the scope of writs recognised by the common law. The Chancellor would give relief in particular cases by an order directed to the parties, his intervention being based on the dictates of their consciences judged in accordance with his own view of what was just. Proceedings before the Chancellor were simpler, and were in other respects advantageous when compared with the procedures of the common law courts. Moreover, the Chancellor developed several remedies which were not available in other courts, most notably specific performance and the injunction—an order requiring the person to whom it is addressed to perform or to refrain from performing a stated act. When performing these judicial functions, the Chancellor came to be regarded as constituting a court: the Court of Chancery.

The standard illustration of how the Chancellor operated was provided by the person who borrowed money, acknowledged the debt by entering into a bond under seal, subsequently paid the debt, but failed to have the bond cancelled. For a common law court, the sealed bond provided incontrovertible proof of the existence of the debt: the court would enforce a second payment if proceedings were instituted by the creditor. However, the Chancellor could restrain such unconscionable action on the part of the creditor by an injunction directed to him, and order that the bond be cancelled.

At first it was not thought that there were separate systems of "law" and "equity." The Chancellor was frequently advised by the common law judges, and there were suggestions that the common law courts could take account of matters of conscience. However, tensions developed. The arguments on each side indeed reflected what is an inevitable dilemma in any system of law, the problem of reconciling the competing demands of justice and certainty. The more general a rule, the less likely it is to do justice in all the particular cases to which it applies; moreover, an attempt to construct in advance the qualifications to the rule necessary to do justice in all cases would lead to a system of rules of enormous complexity, even if all the problems could be foreseen. Hence, the need for some means whereby particular cases could be dealt with justly. Ad hoc decision-making can however be unjust if like cases are treated differently and, in any event, tends to be unpredictable.[12] The Chancellors reacted to criticisms from common lawyers and to the need to introduce regularity into the processing of an increasing caseload by developing principles of "equity" or justice from their ad hoc interventions. At times, however, the tensions also reflected personal difficulties between the Chancellor and common lawyers. In the sixteenth century Cardinal Wolsey caused much discontent among common lawyers by his preference for his own robust "common sense" over legal learning, and in the early seventeenth century a dispute between Lord Chancellor Ellesmere and Sir Edward Coke, the Chief Justice of the King's Bench, was settled by King James I in favour of the former. The Chancellor's power to issue injunctions preventing a litigant from suing at common law or enforcing a judgment obtained at law was confirmed.[13] By the end of the century the common lawyers had given up the struggle. By this time it was also the established practice for lawyers rather than ecclesiastics to be appointed to the office of Lord Chancellor,[14] and, indeed, men trained in English common law and equity rather than civil law.

The principles of equity were progressively refined and developed, most notably during the course of the seventeenth and eighteenth centuries. Of fundamental significance was the development of the concept of the "trust," whereby property could be legally owned by one person, but held by that person for the benefit of another, the latter's rights being recognised and enforced by the Court of Chancery. By the nineteenth century the organisation of the Court of Chancery was totally incapable of dealing with the business, and a series of reforms increased the number of judges sharing the work of the court with the Lord Chancellor. It was also obvious that the presence of two systems with separate courts was highly inconvenient for litigants. Further reforms in the middle of the century made some of the procedural devices of the Court of Chancery (discovery of documents, injunctions) available in the common law courts, allowed those courts to consider equitable defences, and empowered the Chancery to decide questions of common law, receive oral evidence, determine issues of fact by jury trial and award damages. One aspect of the general reorganisation of the superior courts by the Supreme Court of Judicature Acts 1873 and 1875[15] was the *procedural* fusion of law and equity. Matters of both law and equity can now be determined in the course of one set of proceedings: if there is any conflict between rules of law and rules of equity, the latter are to prevail.[16] In most instances there are differences between the operation of law and equity rather than conflict. For example, different remedies may be available in respect of what both systems acknowledge to be a wrong (*e.g.* damages (common law) and an injunction (equity) in respect of a nuisance). Equity may impose

---

[12] This point was made in the 17th century by John Selden (*Table Talk*, edited by F. Pollock, 1927)—"Equity is a roguish thing, for law we have a measure, knowing what to trust to. Equity is according to the conscience of him that is Chancellor, and as it is larger or narrower so is equity. It is all one as if they should make the standard for the measure we call a foot to be the Chancellor's foot; what an uncertain measure would this be; one Chancellor has a long foot, another a short foot, a third an indifferent foot; it is the same thing in the Chancellor's conscience." These matters are considered further, below, at pp. 13–15.

[13] See J. H. Baker, "The Common Lawyers and the Chancery: 1616" (1969) 4 Ir. Jur. (N.S.) 368.

[14] It became customary for the Chancellor to be ennobled.

[15] See below p. 37.

[16] 1873 Act, s.25(11). See now the Supreme Court Act 1981, s.49.

additional obligations on a person while recognising his or her rights at common law (*e.g.* by accepting that a trustee is the legal owner of property while requiring him or her to hold it for the benefit of another).

4. "LAW" AND "FACT"

(i) Historical background

Today, English law is expounded to law students as a system of substantive rules, derived from the common law and statute, which confer rights, impose obligations, create immunities, confer legal powers and so on. This is, however, a comparatively modern way of looking at the law.[17]

The earliest methods of conducting a law suit, adopted by royal courts from the practice of local courts, involved the intervention of the Almighty. The plaintiff was required to state his claim in the appropriate form. The defendant would make a formal denial of the claim. One of them, usually the defendant, would then be required to swear on oath that his cause was just, and the oath would be tested, or put to proof. This might be done by "compurgation", whereby a fixed number of persons (eventually 12) swore oaths in his support; by "battle" where a party or a person swearing an oath in his support could be compelled to prove his veracity by successfully defending himself in a fight, it being presumed that God would aid the righteous, or by "ordeal"—

> "we find that the person who can carry red-hot iron, who can plunge his hand or his arm into boiling water, who will sink when thrown into the water, is deemed to have right on his side."[18]

By the thirteenth century all these methods were regarded with disfavour although compurgation lingered on as the method of proof in actions of debt, and detinue (*i.e.* actions to recover money owed or property) for several centuries beyond. In such systems there was comparatively little scope for legal learning outside the forms of writs and the correct formulation of claim and defence.

These modes of proof were replaced in both civil and criminal cases by trial by jury, whereby the sheriff (a local officer appointed by the Crown) was required to bring 12 men before the court to enquire into the disputed matter and state the truth of it. At first the "jurors" might be aware of this matter themselves or might be informed before they came to court, but it came to be the rule that they should only act upon evidence given in open court, and that their verdict should be unanimous. The development of the jury caused an elaboration of legal technique in disputes as to what was the material question to be put to the jury.

In civil cases, the material question would be an issue of fact, alleged in pleadings on behalf of the plaintiff and denied by the defendant, which would decide the case one way or another. The lawyers appearing on behalf of each

---

[17] On the historical background see J. H. Baker, *An Introduction to English Legal History* (3rd ed., 1990), Chaps. 4, 5; S. F. C. Milsom, *Historical Foundations of the Common Law* (2nd ed., 1981), Chaps. 2, 3.

[18] Sir William Holdsworth, *A History of English Law* (7th ed., 1956), Vol. 1, p. 310. The person who sunk in water was of course rescued—this was not a medieval "Catch-22" situation. See also R. Bartlett, *Trial by Fire and Water* (1986).

party could debate with the judges in court the appropriate wording of their pleas before they were formally enrolled in the court records. Furthermore, a party was entitled to admit all the facts alleged by his or her opponent but claim that they did not give rise to a good claim: this process of "demurrer" raised an issue of law for the judges to decide. Again, it was possible for tentative demurrers to be debated in court. These debates provided the opportunity for an increasing level of sophistication in legal argument. The judges were, however, reluctant to commit themselves to formal legal exceptions to general rules. Where possible, parties were encouraged to "plead the general issue", *i.e.* simply to deny all the allegations put forward by the opponent. This form of plea remains the standard form of plea in a criminal trial ("not guilty") but originally it was the norm in civil trials as well. This meant that many matters that today would be reflected in detailed rules of law were left to the jury for it to do justice on the facts of the particular case. The best example was the issue of whether a defendant was liable in trespass if he or she was not at fault. For a long time it was thought that the absence of any legal rule on the point meant that liability was strict—the better view held today is that the jury was entitled to acquit the defendant if he or she was not at fault, but that that was never recorded as it was not then a matter for the lawyers. By contrast "special" pleas were only permitted where there was a serious chance that the jury was likely to go wrong if the "general issue" was left to it. Much of the lawyers' debate in court would, in practice, turn on whether a special plea was permitted in the given situation rather than on the substantive question of which of the parties in that situation ought to "win".

In the sixteenth century, the judges evinced a much greater willingness to refine and determine questions of law. Pleadings became written rather than oral, and were entered before the appearance in court rather than at it. Informal, tentative discussions of pleas before formal enrolment were replaced by procedures that enabled matters of law to be raised at Westminster after the jury trial.[19] These procedures[20] enabled the lawyers to argue and the judges to determine the legal implications of facts that had already been found: there could be, for example, an objection to the opponent's plea or to the direction on the law given by the judge for the guidance of the jury. The court at Westminster could order that the plaintiff or defendant should succeed notwithstanding the jury verdict against him or her. A later development was the power to order a new trial.[21] In the same period demurrers became much more common and the judges permitted greater use to be made of the "special verdict" whereby the jury would answer specific questions of fact put to them rather than return a general verdict for one or other of the parties, and the court would enter judgment in the light of these findings. Formal errors could be corrected by a "writ of error".[22]

The development of procedures such as these enabled attention to be switched from matters of form to matters of the substance of the law. The distinction between matters for the judge and matters for the jury now corresponded much

[19] The jury trial would normally be conducted away from Westminster: see below, p. 37.
[20] The defendant could enter a "motion in arrest of judgment" and the plaintiff a motion *non obstante verdicto*.
[21] This was of wider significance in that the court could quash a verdict that was against the weight of evidence or where there was a misdirection on a point of law.
[22] See below, pp. 38, 916.

more closely to the present day distinction between matters of "law" and matters of "fact".

In the nineteenth century the various procedures whereby decisions could be challenged on procedural or substantive legal grounds were replaced by appeals on points of law (and in some circumstances points of fact) to the High Court, the Court of Appeal and the House of Lords,[23] and as the decisions of these courts constitute precedents for the future,[24] it is in the course of such appeals that common law and equity can be developed.

In criminal cases, special pleading was virtually never permitted, and the general plea of "not guilty" has remained the standard form of pleading for the defendant. Questions of law concerning the indictment or the evidence could be raised informally at the trial, an indictment could be removed on a writ of certiorari into the Queen's Bench where the defendant could challenge it for insufficiency in form, and the trial judge could adjourn a difficult case for discussion in Serjeants' Inn or the Exchequer Chamber. This last procedure was only regularised in the nineteenth century. In 1908 it was replaced by a proper appeal to a Court of Criminal Appeal.[25] The scope for the systematic development of criminal law has thus, until comparatively recent times, been limited.

(ii) The distinction today

A distinction between matters of "law" and matters of "fact" is drawn for a number of different purposes: one of the consequent difficulties is that it is possible for the line between "law" and "fact" to be drawn in slightly different places for each of these purposes. Three areas[26] where the distinction is of importance for the operation of the English legal system are (1) the division of function between judge and jury; (2) the rule that only a decision on a point of law can constitute a precedent that can be cited in future cases; and (3) the question whether a particular point may be raised on an appeal limited to matters of law.

The first of these situations has declined in significance with the dramatic reduction over the last hundred years in the use of the jury in civil cases.[27] In all but a tiny proportion of cases the judge determines the facts in issue, states and applies the law and decides what remedy or remedies should be given. The discursive statement of reasons delivered by the judge may well contain a mixture of factual and legal determinations, and will be arranged for convenience of exposition rather than in clearly separated sections. The components of the mixture will normally, however, be appropriately "labelled", and the precedent status and the scope of any further appeal will of course vary according to the true nature of the particular determination. The judge/jury distinction remains of significance in criminal cases where the mode of trial for the numerically small proportion of contested serious cases is still trial by jury.[28]

Rights of appeal can only be created by statute, and the grounds on which

---

[23] See below, pp. 38, 95–103.
[24] See Chap. 7.
[25] See further below, pp. 95–96.
[26] There are others, *e.g.* the effect of a misrepresentation in contract, estoppel and judicial review of administrative action under the *ultra vires* doctrine.
[27] See below pp. 789–793.
[28] See below, p. 888. A few factual matters are determined by the judge, *e.g.* those relating to admissibility of evidence and those relating to mitigation.

an appeal may be taken are almost invariably expressed in the statute. The commonest pattern is for a person aggrieved by the decision of a court, or, in numerous but certainly not all situations, a public authority, to be given one chance to appeal on a matter of fact but several chances to raise a matter of law.[29] Appeals from tribunals are normally limited to points of law.[30]

Some aspects of the law/fact distinction are fairly clear. An issue is one of fact where its resolution depends on the reliability or credibility of direct evidence such as a witness's testimony.[31] An issue whose resolution depends on probabilities, for example by way of inference from circumstantial evidence, is also one of fact.[32] These issues normally constitute answers to the question "what happened?" By contrast, if there is a dispute as to the existence or exact scope of a rule of the common law or a dispute over the meaning of the words of a statute, it is a dispute concerning a matter of law. This leaves one kind of issue that is difficult to classify: whether facts found fall within a common law rule or statutory description. This kind of question, one of "application",[33] has been variously characterised as "law", "fact", "mixed law and fact", "fact and degree", "degree" or *sui generis*. As a matter of theory it is difficult to resist the conclusion that this is really a question of law.[34] However, there have been many cases in which it has not been so categorised.

A number of arguments have been advanced to support the classification of a question of application as one of fact.

(1) The matter can as well be determined by a layman as by a trained lawyer.[35]
(2) The words to be applied are "ordinary words of the English language". This argument was used by the House of Lords in *Cozens v. Brutus*.[36] Here, the application of "insulting" in section 5 of the Public Order Act 1936, which made it an offence to use threatening, abusive or insulting words or behaviour where that was conducive to a breach of the peace, was held to be a matter of fact for the magistrates. Lord Reid stressed the undesirability of courts providing definitions of "ordinary" statutory words, whether from dictionaries or otherwise:

> "we have been warned time and again not to substitute other words for the words of a statute. And there is very good reason for that. Few words have exact synonyms. The overtones are almost always different."[37]

Similarly, it has been held that whether an appropriation is "dishonest"

---

[29] See generally Chap. 17.

[30] See below, p. 966.

[31] These are sometimes termed "primary facts." Such facts may be admitted, or "judicial" notice of them may be taken (*i.e* the facts are of general knowledge or can easily be ascertained from standard reference works).

[32] These are sometimes termed "secondary facts." An example would be inferring the speed of a vehicle from tyre marks left on the road.

[33] The term used by E. Mureinik, "The Application of Rules: Law or Fact?" (1982) 98 L.Q.R. 587.

[34] *ibid. Cf.* G. J. Pitt, "Law, Fact and Casual Workers" (1985) 101 L.Q.R. 217.

[35] Denning L.J in *British Launderers' Association v. Borough of Hendon* [1949] 1 K.B. 462.

[36] [1973] A.C. 854.

[37] *ibid.* p. 861.

for the purpose of the law of theft is, within certain limits, a question of fact for the jury.[38]

(3) The rule in question sets a standard, such as one of "reasonableness."[39] The best example here is whether a defendant's conduct has been "unreasonable" and accordingly in breach of a duty to take care imposed by the law of negligence. This is clearly regarded as a question of fact.[40]

(4) The question is one of "degree". In *Edwards v. Bairstow*[41] the question was whether a particular transaction was an "adventure in the nature of trade." If it was, the profit was subject to tax. Lord Radcliffe stated that this matter was one "in which the facts warrant a determination either way" and "in which it could not be said to be wrong to arrive at a conclusion either way."[42] It was a question of degree and therefore a question of fact.

Running through all these points is the wish to avoid the multiplication of decisions that can be cited as a precedent, and an increase in the number of decisions that can be taken further on appeal.[43]

The view that some questions of application are to be classified as ones of fact is a classic illustration of the competing requirements of principle and pragmatism. On the one hand it is, for example, difficult to see that there is any clear distinction between matters requiring the attention of a "trained lawyer" and those that do not, or between English words that are "ordinary" and those that are not. The "ordinary English word" argument in particular has occasioned much academic criticism[44] and in practice has been ignored much more often than applied.[45] On the other hand it is equally possible to appreciate the dangers of excessive complexity. It would, for example, cause chaos, even in an age of computerised legal databases, if every decision on whether a defendant had behaved "unreasonably" for the purposes of the law of negligence could potentially be cited as an authority.

Finally, there are two factors which further blur the distinction between law and fact. First, there may sometimes be a tendency for an appellate court, if it is satisfied that the decision on a point is wrong, to classify the point as one of law precisely to enable it to intervene. Secondly, if a decision on an undoubted question of fact is unsupported by any evidence, or is a decision which no reasonable person could have reached, it is regarded as erroneous in point of law.[46] This convenient fiction enables an appellate court to retain control over factual determinations that are palpably wrong.

---

[38] *R. v. Feely* [1973] Q.B. 530; *R. v. Ghosh* [1982] Q.B. 1053. See below, pp. 883–884.
[39] This is described by Glanville Williams as raising a question of "evaluative fact": [1976] Crim. L.R. 472.
[40] See *Qualcast (Wolverhampton) Ltd v. Haynes* [1959] A.C 743, below. p. 415.
[41] [1956] A.C. 14.
[42] *ibid.* p. 33.
[43] See, *e.g.* the statements in *Qualcast (Wolverhampton) Ltd v. Haynes*, below, p. 415, n. 12.
[44] See Glanville Williams, *Textbook of Criminal Law* (2nd ed., 1983), pp. 59–67 and [1976] Crim.L.R. 472, 532; J. C. Smith and B. Hogan, *Criminal Law* (7th ed., 1992) pp., 496, 536–544. These authors point out that many apparently ordinary words have been the subject of judicial definition for the guidance of juries.
[45] See D. W. Elliott, "Brutus v. Cozens: Decline and Fall" [1989] Crim.L.R. 323.
[46] See below, p. 921.

5. "Rules" and "Discretion"

As has already been touched upon, it is inherent in any decision-making process that is required to handle more than a small number of cases (1) that consistency and certainty are likely to be regarded as important objectives (albeit not the only ones) but (2) that their achievement is likely to be at the expense of an individualised consideration of and reaction to the merits of each case. This is as true of the handling of cases by courts and tribunals as it is of programmes established by government for the administration of, for example, state welfare benefits. In each of these situations it can loosely be said that the basic rules are made by Parliament (statute) or under the authority of Parliament (delegated legislation) or by certain senior judges (common law), and then put into effect by others (judges, magistrates, tribunal members, administrators in government offices and so on).[47]

It will be difficult, and usually impossible, for the "rulemaker" to draft a set of rules that covers all the possible cases that may arise and indicate with precision the outcome desired in each of them. The consequence will be that a measure of "discretion" will be conferred on the "implementer": the word "discretion" being used here to mean an ability to choose among alternative courses of action or inaction. The inevitable imprecisions of language will be such that the persons charged with the task of implementation will have to interpret some of the words used and decide whether the words apply to the circumstances before them. Indeed, a measure of flexibility or uncertainty may be created deliberately to enable the rules to be applied to situations not anticipated by the rulemaker. This can be done by the use of words of general rather than particular meaning, or by the incorporation in the rules of a standard such as "reasonable", "fair" or "just". The element of choice that may be present here is limited.[48] The rulemaker may go further and *expressly* confer a discretion upon the implementer. This express discretion may to a greater or lesser extent be hedged around by restrictions or limits set by the rulemaker. It must be emphasised that it is not possible to draw a clear line between rule-based and discretion-based decision-making processes: the implementation of rules tends to involve the exercise of a measure of discretion, and discretions tend to be hedged around by rules. All that can be said is that the element of discretion may be weaker or stronger as the case may be.

These points may be illustrated by some examples, both real and hypothetical. Parliament, at the instigation of the government, has enacted that a person who is injured in an "accident arising out of and in the course of his employment" is entitled to certain welfare benefits.[49] This phrase, which first appeared in the Workmen's Compensation Act 1897, has to be applied by the DSS officer who

---

[47] The two groups overlap in the person of a High Court judge who can propound a rule of the common law and apply it in successive breaths.

[48] It is also less usual, although not incorrect, to use the term "discretion" here than in the situations about to be described.

[49] See Social Security Contributions and Benefits Act 1992, s.94. The range of benefits specially linked to this concept was reduced by the Social Security and Housing Benefits Act 1982 and subsequent legislation.

decides in the first instance whether a particular claim for benefit is made out. The issue then may be taken on appeal to a Social Security Appeal Tribunal, then to a Social Security Commissioner and then to the courts.[50] The application of the phrase has indeed given rise to a vast number of cases.[51] It would clearly be absurd to expect any person to construct a set of rules which would cover in advance all the possible circumstances that might arise where there could be doubts as to the applicability of the phrase: even assuming a perfect set of rules *could* be constructed, it would be equally absurd to expect mere mortals to find their way around them, as the rules would be of great complexity. Moreover, an attempt to spell out in detail what would count as an "accident" and the "course of employment" might prevent the extension of the right to benefit to persons injured in novel ways or when employed in novel kinds of employment, where the extension would have been desired by the rulemaker. Accordingly, a certain measure of judgment has to be exercised by those determining the applicability of the statutory phrase, and in the sense that their task is not simple and mechanical they can be said to exercise a discretion.

It would, however, have been possible for an Act of Parliament to have provided that a sum of money should be allocated to a board, and that the board could "pay such sum as it thinks fit to any person who in the opinion of the board has suffered an accident at work." This would have entailed the delegation of a considerably greater measure of discretion than is inherent in the present statutory scheme. Moreover, the wording of the board's powers could have been varied so as to increase or decrease the area of choice open to it. The area of choice could be increased by, for example, deleting the words "at work." Conversely, it could be decreased by, for example, replacing "may" by "shall," by setting a limit to the sum payable in any one case, by deleting the words "in the opinion of the board" or by listing a number of factors that the board would be required to take into account. The wider the area of choice, the better able the board would be to reach the "right" or "most appropriate" decision in each individual case (according to its own concept of "rightness" or "propriety"). On the other hand, its greater freedom of action would enable it more easily to diverge from the rulemaker's conception of justice. Even if the board were comparatively free of fetters imposed by the rulemaker it might still have wished to develop policies for its own guidance to ensure a reasonable measure of flexibility.

A good example of a discretion-based decision making process concerned the "exceptional circumstances additions" and the "exceptional needs payments" which were formerly part of the supplementary benefits scheme. These provided, respectively, for an increase in the weekly payment, or a lump sum, in "exceptional cases" at the discretion of the Supplementary Benefits Commission. In practice, the Commission produced detailed codes for the guidance of the local officials who determined the claims on a day-to-day basis, although the codes were not published.[52] These arrangements contrasted with the rule-based system of national insurance including those for industrial injuries. Following what was

---

[50] See below, pp. 67–71.
[51] See N. J. Wikely, *Ogus, Barendt and Wikeley's The Law of Social Security* (4th ed., 1994), pp. 306–323.
[52] See generally, J. A. Farmer, *Tribunals and Government* (1974), pp. 89–99; M. Adler and A. Bradley, *Justice, Discretion and Poverty* (1975).

the classic "rules" v. "discretion" debate, these discretions were replaced by a rule-based structure,[53] although, more recently, the introduction of the Social Fund has seen in part a return to a discretion-based approach.[54]

Accordingly, among the advantages[55] of predetermined rules over discretions are that like cases will be treated alike (consistency), that persons will not in effect be punished by rules applied *ex post facto* (predictability), that the rule-maker is more likely than a person exercising a discretion to be accountable to an electorate, that the implementer will have a more limited scope to deviate from the rulemaker's objective by arbitrary decision-making, that such divergent decisions can more easily be challenged, that the rules will normally be open to public criticism and that decision-making processes can more easily be planned and routinised. Conversely, rules can be inflexible, and can "permit unreasoned official behaviour"[56]

The "rules" v. "discretion" issue crops up at a number of points in the English legal system. The original development of equity was a discretionary case-by-case response to the generality or inadequacy of common law rules or procedures.[57] The subsequent development of rules of equity was a response to the arbitrariness of a system which could vary as the length of the Chancellor's foot.[58] The issue also arises in debates as to the extent to which courts and tribunals should be bound by precedent,[59] the comparative merits of different styles of statutory drafting,[60] whether it is proper for a jury to acquit a defendant who would by a strict application of the rules of criminal law be liable to be convicted, and the extent to which the discretion of a criminal court as to sentence should be limited or "structured" by the provision of guidelines.[61] As the widest discretionary powers are allocated to administrative bodies such as ministers, officials and local authorities, the extent to which the courts should control or review exercises or non-exercises of power is an important feature of administrative law[62]; however, analogous principles apply to the control by appellate courts of exercises of discretion by judges.[63] The "rules" v. "discretion" issue does not admit of easy or general solutions: the appropriate balance has to be sought depending upon the precise context in which the issue arises.

---

[53] See Wikely (1994), pp. 594–595. For a spirited defence of discretion see R. Titmuss, "Welfare 'Rights,' Law and Discretion" (1971) 42 *The Political Quarterly*, p. 113; answered by R. White in P. Morris *et al, Social Needs and Legal Action* (1973), pp. 23–32; *cf.* M. Adler and S. Asquith (eds.), *Discretion and Welfare* (1981), especially Chaps. 1, 7, 11.

[54] See below, pp. 70–71.

[55] See generally J. Jowell, "The Legal Control of Administrative Discretion" [1973] P.L. 178, 184–194; the pioneering work in the field is K. C. Davis, *Discretionary Justice, A Preliminary Inquiry* (1969) and see P. P. Craig, *Administrative Law* (3rd ed., 1994), pp. 396–400 and R. Baldwin, *Rules and Government* (1995), Chaps.1–3.

[56] [1973] P.L. 178 at p. 193.

[57] See above pp. 5–6.

[58] See above pp. 6–7.

[59] See below, pp. 249–258.

[60] See below, pp. 272–273.

[61] See below, pp. 887–888.

[62] See below, pp. 970–971.

[63] See below, pp. 956–957.

C. THE BASIC INSTITUTIONS OF THE ENGLISH LEGAL SYSTEM

A number of institutions are of central importance to the creation of law. Statute law is enacted by Parliament; a vast quantity of delegated legislation is made under powers conferred by Act of Parliament.[64] Both processes are heavily dominated by the government of the day; indeed, most of the delegated powers are exerciseable by government departments.[65] Legislative authority has also been accorded to the institutions of the European Communities: the Council of Ministers and the Commission.[66] Decisions of the superior courts may also constitute sources of law.[67]

The administration of the legal system, in the sense of the mechanisms for the provision of legal services, the courts and tribunals established for the resolution of legal disputes and the processes for effecting law reform, is almost entirely a matter for central government. In many countries, responsibility for legal affairs is exercised by a "Minister of Justice". However, in the United Kingdom, responsibility for different aspects of the legal system is divided among separate ministries or departments of state, the main ones being the Lord Chancellor's Department, the Home Office, the Law Officers' Departments and the Treasury.[68]

1. THE LORD CHANCELLOR'S DEPARTMENT[69]

As is mentioned elsewhere,[70] the Lord Chancellor exercises a wide range of disparate functions, including those of judge, Speaker of the House of Lords, cabinet minister and government legal adviser. He also has extensive responsibilities concerning the administration of justice, including making or advising on judicial appointments,[71] arranging judicial business in the House of Lords and Privy Council and acting as chairman of the committees that make procedural rules for the Supreme Court and Crown Court.[72] He is responsible for the unified court service, which provides administrative support for the Court of Appeal, High Court, Crown Court and county courts,[73] and supervises the

---

[64] See Chaps. 5 and 6.
[65] A detailed consideration of Parliament and government may be found in such works as S. A. de Smith and R. Brazier, *Constitutional and Administrative Law* (7th ed., 1994).
[66] See below, pp. 306–310.
[67] See Chaps.2, 7.
[68] For a general survey, see R. Brazier, "Government and the Law: Ministerial Responsibility for Legal Affairs" [1989] P.L. 64. See also G. Zellick (ed.), *Law Reform and the Law Commission* (1988), Appendix 7.
[69] See P. Polden, *Guide to the Records of the Lord Chancellor's Department* (HMSO, 1988), which covers the development of the department from about 1870 (systematic record keeping started in 1889) to November 1951. See also R. B. Stevens, "A View from the Lord Chancellor's Office" (1987) 40 C.L.P. 181, "The Independence of the Judiciary: The View from the Lord Chancellor's Office" (1988) 8 O.J.L.S. 222 and *The Independence of the Judiciary* (1993); Sir D. Oulton, *Counsel*, Michaelmas 1986, p. 3; Lord Mackay of Clashfern, (1991) 44 C.L.P. 241.
[70] See below, pp. 222–223.
[71] See below, pp. 227–233.
[72] See below, pp. 94, 96.
[73] See below, pp. 83–84, 93.

legal aid and advice schemes.[74] Responsibility for overseeing the operations of magistrates' courts was transferred to the Lord Chancellor's Department in 1992.[75] Under the Courts and Legal Services Act 1990, the Lord Chancellor is responsible for the appointment of an Advisory Committee on Legal Education and Conduct, a Legal Services Ombudsman, an Authorised Conveyancing Practitioners Board and a Conveyancing Ombudsman.[76] He is also generally responsible for law reform in civil matters, although other government departments have their own specialised areas of concern. For example, company law is within the province of the Department of Trade and Industry and employment law within that of the Department for Education and Employment. Finally, he has a number of miscellaneous responsibilities, for example for the Land Registry,[77] the Public Record Office and the Official Receiver.

Since the Second World War the Lord Chancellor's Department has grown from a small office of personal assistants and advisers to the Lord Chancellor into a substantial government department employing a staff of about 12,000. It has its headquarters in the House of Lords and at Selborne House, Victoria Street, London. The most senior official holds the offices of Permanent Secretary to the Lord Chancellor and Clerk of the Crown in Chancery. Within the Department, there is a Judicial Appointments Group (appointments and training); a Legal Group (law reform, rules of court, international matters and the Statutory Publications Office); a Policy and Legal Services Group (legal services and agencies, legal aid and family law) and sections dealing with the courts service and establishment and finance.[78] For the purposes of courts administration the country is divided into six areas or "Circuits", each controlled by a Circuit Administrator.[79] The Court Service became an executive agency under the Next Steps programme from April 3, 1995[80]: the Lord Chancellor remains accountable to Parliament for the Service, but decisions on day-to-day running are the responsibility of the chief executive.[81] The Service has adopted the *Court Service Charter for Court Users*, under the Citizens Charter, setting out standards of service users are entitled to expect, and explaining the complaints procedures.[82]

Since 1992 the Department has had a Parliamentary Secretary in the House of Commons,[83] ending the unsatisfactory arrangement whereby the Attorney-

---

[74] See below pp. 491–510, 568–580, 763–772. The Lord Chancellor has been responsible for civil legal aid since its introduction and responsibility for criminal legal aid was transferred from the Home Secretary in July 1980.

[75] See (1992) *The Magistrate* 74.

[76] See below, pp. 130–132, 170–173, 186–187.

[77] Responsible for the compulsory registration of titles to land under the Land Registration Acts 1925–1986 and the maintenance of land charges registered under the Land Charges Act 1972. See National Audit Office, *Review of the Operations of H.M. Land Registry* (1986–87 H.C. 39).

[78] *Civil Service Yearbook 1995*, pp. 460–471.

[79] See below, pp. 83–84.

[80] See LCD Court Service Annual Report 1994–95 (1994–95 H.C. 579), Chap. 13.

[81] The first chief executive is Michael Heubner, previously head of the Court Service at LCD Headquarters. See M. Heubner, *Counsel*, March-April 1995, pp. 27–28; R. Smith, *Legal Action*, May 1995, p. 26.

[82] Published in 1995 and available from any court. See also *The Citizen's Charter: Second Report: 1994* (Cm. 2540), noting improvements in the treatment of witnesses, victims, jurors and court users under the auspices of the Charter (pp. 62–65).

[83] See G. Drewry, (1992) 142 N.L.J. 50; J. Rozenberg, *The Search for Justice* (1994), p. 12. The first holder of the position was John M. Taylor M.P., a solicitor; he was succeeded by Jonathan Evans M.P. in 1995 and then Gary Streeter M.P. in 1996. He has no role in the judicial appointments process: Rozenberg, *op. cit.*

General, although not a member of the Department, acted as spokesman for the
Lord Chancellor. The administrative functions of the Department in relation to
courts and tribunals are now subject to review by the Parliamentary Commissioner for Administration,[84] and the Department's policy, administration and
expenditure now fall within the remit of the Select Committee on Home
Affairs.[85]

As is now *de rigeur* for government departments and, indeed, all public sector
institutions, the Lord Chancellor's Department publishes an annual report summarising both its activities and its strategic plan, which sets out "priorities for
the coming years".[86] The current strategic plan states that the Department's
aim is

> "to ensure that people can uphold their rights and fulfil their obligations
> in particular through efficient and affordable courts and legal services, and
> by developing the civil law to meet society's needs."

In pursuit of this aim, the Department will seek to safeguard the independence
of the judiciary and the judicial process; work closely with other bodies on
matters of common interest, uphold the open government code of practice and
citizen's charter commitments; secure maximum value for money from all its
work and ensure that overall expenditure is controlled; build on its knowledge
base, be committed to equal opportunities; and act as a good employer. The
Department's *strategic objectives* are

"● to continue to improve the arrangements for judicial appointment and
   training;
● to ensure that courts can deal with criminal cases in a just, effective and
   cost efficient manner;
● to ensure that civil law is clear and fair, and that dispute resolution procedures are effective and affordable;
● to provide effective and supportive family dispute resolution procedures;
● to encourage and facilitate improvements in magistrates' courts performance; and
● to encourage the provision of competent and affordable legal and related
   services and, where publicity funded, to ensure that they are targeted to
   areas of greatest need."

It will be noted that these are stated at a high level of generality and are for
the most part self-evidently worthy; nevertheless, the references to controlling
costs are significant. It is made clear that there is a limit to the resources made
available to support the operation of the legal system. Indeed, "proper standards

---

[84] Courts and Legal Services Act 1990, s.110, providing that such functions are to be taken as the
   Department's functions, although there is an exception where action is taken at the direction or
   on the authority of a judicial officer.
[85] This development took place in 1991, having previously been resisted by the government on the
   unconvincing ground that such scrutiny might threaten the independence of the judiciary: see G.
   Drewry, (1983) 133 N.L.J. 959–960.
[86] See, *Departmental Report of The Lord Chancellor's and Law Officers' Departments: The Government's Expenditure Plans 1996–97 to 1998–99* (Cm.3209, 1996). The previous strategic plan
   provided for one, "fundamental aim," one "strategic priority," six "guiding principles" and
   six "key challenges." The simplification is to be welcomed.

of service" are only to be maintained so far as is consistent with the control of public expenditure on legal aid and the courts. The increasingly visible emphasis by the Lord Chancellor's Department on the containment of cost has led to tensions between it and the judiciary, with arguments from leading judges that the quality of justice (and the independence of the judiciary) is threatened.[87]

2. THE HOME OFFICE

The Home Secretary is responsible for the maintenance of law and order, and as a result performs various functions that might be regarded as those of a Minister of Justice. These include[88] overall responsibility for prisons and other aspects of the penal system, and the reform of the criminal law, on which he may be advised by the Criminal Law Revision Committee. The Home Secretary advises the Queen on the exercise of the royal prerogative of mercy to grant a free pardon in respect of a conviction or to remit all or part of a penalty.

3. THE LAW OFFICERS[89]

The Attorney-General and the Solicitor-General are the Law Officers of the Crown for England and Wales.[90] They are members of and the chief legal advisers to the government,[91] and are normally members of the House of Commons. Occasionally the Attorney-General has been appointed to the cabinet. The Law Officers may appear on behalf of the Crown at the International Court in the Hague and the European Court of Human Rights in Strasbourg. In this country they may appear in civil litigation or conduct prosecutions. They may not, however, undertake private work.

In civil matters the Attorney may institute proceedings in the High Court for the enforcement of public rights[92] or on behalf of the interests of charity. His consent is required for the institution of criminal proceedings for a large number of criminal offences,[93] and he may stop trials on indictment by entering a *nolle prosequi*.[94] He superintends the work of the Queen's Proctor, who has certain

---

[87] See below, pp. 244–246.

[88] For a full list see R. Brazier, [1989] P.L. 64, 93.

[89] See J. Ll. J. Edwards, *The Law Officers of the Crown* (1964) and *The Attorney-General, Politics and the Public Interest* (1984); Sir Elwyn Jones, [1969] C. L. J. 43; S. C. Silkin, (1980) 4 Trent L. J. 21; Sir Michael Havers, (1984) 52 Medico-Legal Jo. 98. For a list of the Law Officers' functions see Vol. 67, H. C. Deb., November 12, 1984, col. 63, written answer by the Attorney-General; R. Brazier, [1989] P. L. 64, 94.

[90] Since 1972, the Attorney has been Attorney-General for Northern Ireland (see Northern Ireland Constitution Act 1973, s.10). The Solicitor-General is authorised to act as his deputy (*ibid.*). See Edwards (1984), Chap. 9. There are separate Law Officers for Scotland the Lord Advocate and the Solicitor-General for Scotland: see Edwards (1984), Chap. 10.

[91] The settled constitutional practice that Law Officers' advice to government remains confidential was breached in the Westland affair: see R. Austin, (1986) 39 C.L.P. 269, 277–278; M. Linklater and D. Leigh, *Not With Honour* (1986).

[92] *e.g.* to seek injunction to restrain a public nuisance or to restrain repeated or threatened breaches of the criminal law.

[93] See below, p. 696.

[94] See below, p. 696.

duties in matrimonial cases. He exercises ministerial responsibility for the Director of Public Prosecutions, the Crown Prosecution Service and the Serious Fraud Office[95] and, from 1989, the Treasury Solicitor's Department.[96] The Law Officers are assisted by a small staff of civil servants, the Legal Secretariat to the Law Officers, based in the Attorney-General's chambers in the Royal Courts of Justice, and generally divide the duties between them according to their own preferences.[97] The Attorney is also the head of the Bar.[98]

When taking decisions in respect of criminal matters, the Attorney-General is expected to act independently of the government. While in an appropriate case he may seek the views of ministers as to the consequences of a prosecution, there should be no pressure from them in favour of or against a prosecution: the ultimate decision is his.[99] However, it has been asserted that the position is different where the government is acting as government in civil proceedings and the Attorney is the nominal plaintiff: here a decision whether to proceed is the government's collectively.[1]

4. THE DIRECTOR OF PUBLIC PROSECUTIONS

In 1879 pressure for the introduction of a system of public prosecution led to the establishment of the office of Director of Public Prosecutions.[2] It was originally contemplated that he would be provided with a number of locally based assistants, but this development never took place. The Director and his or her staff have thus always been based in London. The first Director took a narrow view of the scope of his functions, and between 1884 and 1908 the office was combined with that of Treasury Solicitor.

---

[95] See below.

[96] Following the recommendations of the *Review of Government Legal Services* by Sir Robert Andrew (HMSO, 1989). See Vol. 145 H. C. Deb., January 19, 1989, cols.262–263, written answer by the Prime Minister. These departments, together with the Legal Secretariat to the Law Officers, are now collectively known as the Law Officers' Departments.

[97] Technically, the Solicitor-General is the Attorney-General's deputy. He may act in the Attorney's place if that office is vacant, if the Attorney is away ill, or if the Attorney authorises him to act: Law Officers Act 1944.

[98] This caused some difficulty in 1989 when the Bar was severely critical of the Lord Chancellor's proposals for reform of the legal profession: see below, p. 137.

[99] The classic statement of principle was made by Sir Hartley Shawcross in 1951: Vol. 483, H. C. Deb., January 29, 1951, cols.683–684: see Edwards (1964), pp. 220–225 and (1984), pp. 318–324.

[1] Sir Michael Havers (Vol. 106, H. C. Deb., December 1, 1986, cols.619–620), referring to the decision not to seek an injunction to restrain publication of Chapman Pincher's book, *Their Trade is Treachery*, a decision to which he was not a party. Analogous decisions in the *Gouriet (Gouriet v. Union of Post Office Workers* [1978] A. C. 435) and *Crossman Diaries (Att. Gen. v. Jonathan Cape Ltd.* [1976] Q.B. 752) cases had, by contrast, been taken independently by the Attorney: see J. Michael "The Wright Case—The Attorney-General's Role" (1986) 136 N.L.J. 1199.

[2] Prosecution of Offences Act 1879. See generally J. Ll. J. Edwards, *The Law Officers of the Crown* (1964), Chaps.16, 17 and *The Attorney-General, Politics and the Public Interest* (1984), Chaps 1–5; G. Mansfield and J. Peay, *The Director of Public Prosecutions* (1987); J. Rozenberg, *The Case for the Crown* (1987); Thomas Hetherington, *Prosecution and the Public Interest* (1989).

The Director's responsibilities are now set out in the Prosecution of Offences Act 1985. He or she is appointed by the Attorney-General and must be a person who has a 10-year general qualification.[3] Prior to the establishment of the Crown Prosecution Service the Director's main functions were to conduct prosecutions in serious cases and to give advice and assistance to chief officers of police respecting the conduct of other prosecutions. He was assisted by a Deputy Director and Assistant Directors, and had a head-quarters staff of about 60.[4] The Director is now head of the Crown Prosecution Service,[5] which is responsible for the conduct of most proceedings instituted by the police. The Service is organised into 13 Areas,[6] each headed by a Chief Crown Prosecutor.

The Serious Fraud Office was established by the Criminal Justice Act 1987 with powers to investigate any suspected offence involving serious or complex fraud and to institute and have the conduct of any criminal proceedings appearing to relate to such fraud.[7] Its operations extend to Northern Ireland, and are wider than that of the C.P.S., which is only responsible for the conduct of proceedings investigated and instituted by the police. It comprises lawyers and accountants, and works in close co-operation with police officers, seconded from a number of forces, who occupy the same building. There continues to be a Fraud Investigation Group attached to the headquarters of the C.P.S. to deal with fraud cases not taken over by the S.F.O. The S.F.O. has come under considerable criticism following a series of high profile cases where the defendants were acquitted, or only convicted on minor charges.[8] Nevertheless, in 1995 the government accepted the recommendation of a review group headed by Rex Davie that the S.F.O. should not be merged with the Fraud Division of the C.P.S., but that the work should be restructured.[9] Under revised criteria for deciding which cases should go to the S.F.O., the key criterion is whether the suspected fraud was such that the direction of the investigation should be in the hands of those who would be responsible for the prosecution. Relevant factors

---

[3] 1985 Act, s.2, as amended. The current D.P.P. is Barbara Mills Q.C., who was appointed in 1992, having previously been Director of the Serious Fraud Office. Her immediate predecessors were Sir Theobald Mathew (1944–64), Sir Norman Skelhorn (1964–77), Sir Thomas Hetherington (1977–87) and Allan Green Q.C. (1987–92).

[4] See below, pp. 695–696.

[5] Below, pp. 700–707. The C.P.S. is not to become an executive agency but is to operate according to "Next Steps" principles from April 1996: *Department Reports of The Lord Chancellor's and Law Officers' Departments: The Government's Expenditure Plans 1996–97 to 1998–99 (Con.* 3209), p. 45.

[6] Reduced from 31 in 1993; see Annual Report of the Crown Prosecution Service 1993–94 (1993–94 H.C. 444), pp. 9–11 Annex B.

[7] s.1. See further below, p. 707. On the work of the S.F.O., see D. N. Kirk and A. J. J. Woodcock, *Serious Fraud: Investigation and Trial* (1992); M. Levi, *The Investigation, Prosecution and Trial of Serious Fraud* (RCCJ Research Study No. 14, 1993); JUSTICE, *Serious Fraud: Securing a fair trial* (1993).

[8] *e.g.* the failure of the prosecution in the *Blue Arrow* case, the acquittal of George Walker in a case arising out of the affairs of the Brent Walker group and the events that led to the passing of a non-custodial sentence on Roger Levitt: see (1993) 143 N.L.J. 1701. For the argument that the criticisms have been exaggerated, see J. Bayes, (1994) 144 N.L.J. 1508. Over the first seven years of the S.F.O.'s existence, the overall conviction rate on a defendant-by-defendant basis was 62%, with one or more defendants convicted in over 75 per cent of trials: Annual Report of the Serious Fraud Office, 1994–95 (1994–95 H.C.589), p. 14.

[9] Statement by the Attorney-General, Vol.257, H.C.Deb., March 31 1995, cols.1309–1317. Other recommendations for changes in working practices had previously been made in the Review of the Handling of Serious Fraud (the Graham Review, 1994: see S.F.O. Annual Report 1994–95 pp. 21; R. Sarker, (1995) 16 Co.Law 56, 213.

include: cases in the order of at least £1m; cases likely to give rise to national publicity and widespread public concern; cases requiring highly specialised knowledge of, for example, stock exchange practices or regulated markets; cases in which there is a significant international dimension; cases where legal, accountancy and investigative skills need to be brought together; cases which appear to be complex and in which the use of the S.F.O.'s special powers under section 2 of the 1987 Act might be appropriate. None of these factors, taken individually, is necessarily conclusive.[10] A Joint Vetting Committee has been established with the C.P.S. to consider marginal cases referred to either organisation.

The D.P.P. may be directed by the Divisional Court to appear for the prosecution on any criminal appeal to the House of Lords, and by the Court of Appeal (Criminal Division) to appear in appeals to that court from the Crown Court or from it to the House of Lords.[11] She also has the power to intervene in prosecutions.[12] This power is used rarely, for example where private prosecutions are instituted maliciously. It includes the right to discontinue proceedings.[13] Finally, the Director's consent to prosecution is required by statute in certain classes of case.[14]

5. THE TREASURY AND OTHER GOVERNMENT DEPARTMENTS

The Treasury is involved in the administration of justice at a number of points. It has overall responsibilities for government expenditure and the organisation of the civil service. The Parliamentary draftsmen are technically Parliamentary Counsel to the Treasury, reporting to the Prime Minister.[15] The Treasury Solicitor heads a large legal department which does legal work for the Treasury and for other government departments.[16] He also presides over inter-departmental management machinery for civil service lawyers and was for many years and for most purposes the *de facto* head of the civil service Civil Legal Group in England and Wales.[17] In 1989 the government legal service was reorganised following a report by Sir Robert Andrew.[18] The Treasury Solicitor was recognised as head of the service, with the responsibility of advising on the personnel

---

[10] S.F.O. Annual Report, 1994–95, pp. 48–49.

[11] Prosecution of Offences Act 1985, s.3(2)/702(f). See below, p. 698.

[12] *ibid.*, s.6. Below, pp. 696, 703.

[13] *Raymond v. Att.-Gen.* [1982] Q.B. 839, decided under the equivalent provision (s.4) of the Prosecution of Offences Act 1979.

[14] See below, pp. 696, 705.

[15] *The Government's Expenditure Plans 1995–96 to 1997–98: Cabinet Office, Privy Council Office and Parliament* (Cm.2820, 1995), p. 8.

[16] There are separate divisions for the Treasury, the Cabinet Office and Office of Public Service, the Department of National Heritage, the Ministry of Defence, the Department for Education and Employment, and the Department of Transport.

[17] See G. Drewry, "The Office of Treasury Solicitor" (1980) 130 N.L.J. 753 and "Lawyers in the U.K. Civil Service" (1981) 59 *Public Administration* 15; (1992) 136 S.J. 78, 96.

[18] *Review of Government Legal Services* (HMSO, 1989). On the appointment of the enquiry see G. Drewry, "Government Lawyers under Scrutiny" (1988) 138 N.L.J. 219.

management of lawyers across departments and supported by a Lawyers' Management Unit.[19]

The European Division of the Department advises the European Secretariat of the Cabinet Office on Community law issues and conducts on behalf of the United Kingdom all litigation in the Court of Justice of the European Community. Other Divisions undertake litigation, deal with *bona vacantia* (administering the estates of intestates), and advisory work for governmental departments. The Government Property Lawyers was established as a Next Steps executive agency of the Lord Chancellor's Department on April 1, 1993. It is located in Taunton and provides a conveyancing and lands advisory service for all government departments and other public bodies. The rest of the Department is to be established as an executive agency from 1996. [20] Legal services to government departments may be the subject of market testing in accordance with guidelines set by the Attorney-General.[21] For example, market testing by Property Holdings led to the Government Property Lawyers securing half the workload, the rest going to private practice solicitors.[22]

6. THE OFFICIAL SOLICITOR

While the Treasury Solicitor is concerned with the government's legal business, the official solicitor to the Supreme Court heads an office in that court. He is appointed by the Lord Chancellor and must be a person with a 10-year general qualification under section 71 of the Courts and Legal Services Act 1990.[23] His functions broadly fall into five categories[24]; the liberty of the subject (making bail applications for remand prisoners, reviewing the cases of persons committed to prison for contempt of court,[25] investigating applications for leave to issue a writ of habeas corpus); the paternalistic jurisdiction (representing wards of court in wardship proceedings, acting as guardian of a minor's estate, dealing with the affairs of mental patients); the conduct of litigation for children and mental patients; the administration of the estates of deceased persons when there is

---

[19] Vol. 145, H.C.Deb., January 19, 1989, cols.262–263, written answer by the Prime Minister. See M. Mair, (1989) L.S.Gaz. March 22, 1989, pp. 12, 37: interview with the Treasury Solicitor, James Nurshaw.

[20] *Departmental Report of The Lord Chancellor's and Law Officers' Departments: The Government's Expenditure Plans 1995–96 to 1997–98* (Cm.2809, 1995), pp. 60–65.

[21] See (1992) 136 S.J.663. The guidelines state that it is not appropriate to use the private sector for core governmental work where ministers and legal advisers need to maintain a close confidential relationship.

[22] Government Property Lawyers Annual Report and Accounts 1994–95 (1994–95 H.C.558), p. 11.

[23] Supreme Court Act 1981, s.90, as amended by the 1990 Act, Sched. 10, para. 49; on the meaning of "general qualification" see below, p. 212, n.63. See N. Lowe and R. White, *Wards of Court* (2nd ed., 1986), Chap. 9; J. M. L. Evans, (1966) 63 L.S.Gaz. 270, 335; C. Dyer, *The Law Magazine*, June 12, 1987, p. 27; D. Venables, (1990) 20 Fam. Law 53.

[24] M. Hinchliffe, (1989) J. of Child Law, pp. 64–67.

[25] It was in this capacity that the Official Solicitor came into prominence in 1972 in obtaining the release of trade unionists committed to prison for disobedience to orders of the National Industrial Relations Court in the course of a national dock strike: *Churchman v. Joint Shop Stewards Committee* [1972] I.C.R. 222; *Midland Cold Storage Ltd v. Turner, The Times,* July 27, 1972. See N. Lowe, *Borrie and Lowe's Law of Contempt* (2nd ed., 1983), pp. 446–448; B. A. Hepple, (1972) 1 I.L.J. 198; Lord Denning, *The Due Process of Law* (1980), pp. 36–39.

no-one else willing or able to do so; and assisting the court (investigating the conduct of litigation, briefing counsel to appear as *amicus curiae*).

7. THE CRIMINAL JUSTICE CONSULTATIVE COUNCIL

Communication among the various agencies involved in the criminal justice system is promoted by the Criminal Justice Consultative Council, established in 1991 on the recommendation of the Woolf Enquiry into the State of the Prisons. The Council's membership included (in 1995) three permanent secretaries, two judges, the D.P.P., a chief constable, a Q.C., a solicitor, a justices' clerk, a magistrate, a chief probation officer, the Director General of Prisons the Chief Executive of the Court Service and senior Home Office representatives.[26] There are also 24 area committees with a corresponding range of members.

D. LAW REFORM

It is inevitable that any legal system cannot be static: there will always be aspects both of the substantive law and the institutional and procedural features of the system that require change. Many aspects of the common law are developed by the decisions of the superior courts. However, the judges seem generally to hold the view that this power should be exercised with caution, although this caution is from time to time thrown to the winds.[27] Commonly, a distinction is drawn between the application of an existing principle to new circumstances, which is regarded as a legitimate exercise for the judges, and the creation of a new principle, which is regarded as a matter for government and Parliament.[28]

Reform by the judges is further handicapped by the fact that the accidents of litigation may not throw up the right cases, that the precise issues in dispute are formulated by the parties (the opinions of the judges on other matters amounting to *obiter dicta* which are not binding in future cases),[29] and that the judges must normally confine themselves to the arguments and information presented by the parties. The judges cannot in any event commission empirical research and even the information derived from existing research is not admissible in evidence. Judicial reforms tend also to be retrospective in nature and hence potentially unfair.[30] Accordingly, most significant law reforms must be achieved by statute.

There are several mechanisms which exist or have existed to further the cause of law reform by statute, including one permanent body, the Law Commission, several part-time bodies such as the Law Reform Committee and the Criminal

---

[26] *Criminal Justice Consultative Council: Summary of Activities 1994–95*, p. 16. See also Farquharson L.J., (1993) *The Magistrate* 26.
[27] See below, pp. 249–258.
[28] See, *e.g.* Lord Pearson and Lord Salmon in *Launchbury v. Morgans* [1973] A.C. 127, 142, 151.
[29] See below, pp. 416–419.
[30] *Cf.* below, p. 443.

Law Revision Committee, and any number of ad hoc Royal Commissions and departmental committees.

1. The Law Commission[31]

Calls for a permanent law reform institution were answered in 1965 by the establishment of two Law Commissions, one for England and Wales and one for Scotland.[32] This move was associated particularly with Lord Gardiner L.C.[33] The Law Commission for England and Wales comprises five "persons appearing . . . to be suitably qualified by the holding of judicial office or by experience as a person having a general qualification (within the meaning of section 71 of the Courts and Legal Services Acts 1990) or as a teacher of law in a university."[34] In practice, the chairman has been a High Court judge, who works full-time for the Commission and normally subsequently receives promotion to the Court of Appeal. The pattern for the other appointments has become settled with a common law Q.C., a solicitor and two academics. There is a legal secretary, a staff of barristers and solicitors from the legal Civil Service and several parliamentary draftsmen.[35]

The Commission's task is:

"to take and keep under review all the law with which [it is] concerned with a view to its systematic development and reform, including in particular the codification of such law, the elimination of anomalies, the repeal of obsolete and unnecessary enactments, the reduction of the number of separate enactments and generally the simplification and modernisation of the law."[36]

---

[31] See generally on the work of the Law Commission, J. H. Farrar, *Law Reform and the Law Commission* (1974); G. J. Zellick (ed.), *Law Reform and the Law Commission* (1988); N. Marsh, (1971) 13 William and Mary L.R. 263; L. C. B. Gower, (1973) 23 Univ. of Toronto L.J. 257; A. L. Diamond, (1976) 10 L.T. 11, and (1977) 51 A. L. J. 396; Sir Michael Kerr, (1980) 96 L. Q. R. 515; P. M. North, (1985) 101 L.Q.R. 338; S. Cretney, (1985) 48 M.L.R. 493; Sir Ralph Gibson, (1986) 39 C.L.P. 57; Sir Roy Beldam, (1987) 16 Kingston L.R. 21; Brooke J., (1995) 16 Stat. L.R. 1 and [1995] Crim. L.R. 911; Staughton L.J., (1995) 16 Stat. L.R. 7. For a discussion of the Law Commission's use of economic reasoning, see A.I. Ogus, "Economics and Law Reform; Thirty Years of Law Commission Endeavour" (1995) 111 L.Q.R. 407. The Commission reviewed the first 20 years of its operations in its 20th Annual Report, 1984–85 (Law Com. No. 155), Part I: see Editorial, (1986) 136 N.L.J. 201. For a critical account of its operations by a former member of its staff, see R. T. Oerton, *Lament for the Law Commission* (1987). For a proposal for its abolition, see A. Samuels, (1986) 136 N.L.J. 747; response by Oerton, *ibid.*, p. 1071.

[32] Law Commissions Act 1965; Lord Chorley and G. Dworkin, (1965) 28 M.L.R. 675.

[33] He had argued the case for such a body in Chap. 1 of G. Gardiner and A. Martin (eds.), *Law Reform NOW* (1963) and *cf.* (1953) 69 L.Q.R. 46.

[34] 1965 Act, s.1(2), as amended by the 1990 Act, Sched. 10, para. 25.

[35] Sir Michael Kerr, (1980) 96 L.Q.R. 515, 523. Four of the five senior Civil Service legal posts were, however, abolished ((1984) 134 N.L.J. 467), the Law Commission relying instead on commissioning work from academic lawyers, some of whom join it on secondment (see 21st Annual Report, 1985–86 (Law Com. No. 159), pp. 1–2, 17). The Law Commission has also noted difficulties caused by delays in replacing staff who have moved elsewhere: 29th Annual Report, 1994 (Law Com. No. 232), pp. 58–59.

[36] 1965 Act s.3(1).

The topics investigated are either referred to it by the Lord Chancellor or are aspects of one of the programmes for examination of different branches of the law with a view to reform that have been approved by the Lord Chancellor and laid before Parliament.[37] The Commission is also required to provide advice and information to government and other bodies concerned with law reform.[38]

In the course of its existence the Law Commission has dealt with a large number of substantive legal topics and projects for the consolidation of statutes and the repeal of obsolete provisions ("Statute Law Reform").[39] It has also worked on the codification of the law of contract and of the law of landlord and tenant, although these tasks proved too onerous and the work has been suspended indefinitely.[40] The prospects for codification of the criminal law are brighter,[41] a draft code having been produced. However, it has been recognised that "the likelihood of Parliament being able to find time to consider, in a single Bill, a proposal as large as a complete Code is very remote."[42] Accordingly, the Commission aims to "progress in stages towards the long-term objective of the enactment of a complete Code", with further work on particular topics built into the base provided by the draft Code.[43]

A notable feature of the Law Commission's working methods in connection with the reform of a substantive legal topic is the circulation of a "working paper". This consists of a detailed statement of the present law on the topic, an account of the criticisms and supposed defects of the law and a statement of the options for change. The Commission normally states a provisional view as to the option that should be preferred. The paper, in both full and summarised forms, is circulated widely and the views of interested parties sought.[44] Following consultation a final report is produced, which includes a draft bill prepared by the parliamentary draftsmen seconded to the Commission. Overall, chances of implementation are reasonably high, although they have less where the matter falls within the purview of a government department other than the Lord Chan-

---

[37] ibid. ss.3(1)(a)(b), (2). There have been six general programmes (approved in 1965, 1968, 1973, 1989, 1991 and 1995) with major items on criminal law, family law and private international law. The programme arrangements are considered by S. Cretney in Zellick (1988), pp. 3–20. The Commission may also consider reform proposals from other quarters.

[38] The Commission publishes a quarterly bulletin *Law Under Review*, giving details of the progress of government law reform projects.

[39] See below, pp. 265–267.

[40] See A. L. Diamond, (1968) 31 M.L.R. 361; Sir Michael Kerr, (1980) 96 L.Q.R. 515, 527–530.

[41] See J. C. Smith, [1984] Stat.L.R. 17 and [1987] Denning L.J. 137; I. Dennis, (1986) 50 J. of Crim. Law 161; *Codification of the Criminal Law: A Report to the Law Commission* (Law Com. No. 143, 1985); Symposium, [1986] Crim.L.R. 285–323; *Criminal Code for England and Wales* (Law Com. No. 177, 1989).

[42] 27th Annual Report, 1992 (Law Com. No. 210), p. 10.

[43] *Ibid.* For the first steps, see the Reports under the general title *Legislating the Criminal Code, Offences against the Person and General Principles* (Law Com. No. 218, Cm. 2370, 1993); , *Intoxication and Criminal Liability* (Law Com. No. 229, 1995); *The Year and a Day Rule in Homicide* (Law Com. No. 230, 1995; *Involuntary Manslaughter* (Law Com. No. 237, 1996). For a vigorous rebuttal of criticisms of the drafting of the Code by F. A. R. Bennion ((1994) 15 Stat.L.R.108), see J. C. Smith (1995) 16 Stat.L.R.105.

[44] See P. M. North, "Law Reform: the Consultation Process" (1982) 66 Trent L.J. 19 and (1985) 101 L.Q.R. 338–346 (expressing some scepticism as to the effectiveness of consultation). The Commission has not followed the example of the Australian Law Reform Commission and organised public meetings or hearings: see the paper by the A.L.R.C. Chairman, Mr. Justice M. D. Kirby, "Reforming Law Reform: New Methods of Law Reform in Australia", to the 1979 Colloquium of the U.K. National Committee on Comparative Law, summarised in M. Zander, *The Law-Making Process* (4th ed., 1994), pp. 451–455.

cellor's Department (most notably the Home Office and the Department of the Environment).[45] By 1994, of all the Commission's law reform reports, 78 had been implemented, 13 expressly or impliedly rejected and 32 remained outstanding. Of those 32, eight were due for presentation to Parliament in 1994–95, and nine were 1993 or 1994 reports.[46] However, these figures conceal the fact that lack of implementation of reports had reached crisis point by 1993. In that year, the Commission reported that only four of its reports since 1990 had been implemented, for lack of Parliamentary time, with only one forming part of the government's legislative programme.[47] However, the introduction of new procedures and the end of a period of non-co-operation between government and opposition whips has enabled inroads to be made on the backlog, there having been a "sea-change in attitudes."[48]

2. THE LAW REFORM COMMITTEE[49]

A part-time Law Revision Committee was appointed by Lord Sankey in 1934 and produced eight reports between then and 1939, most of which were implemented.[50] It was reconstituted by Lord Simonds in 1952 under the title of Law Reform Committee, and comprised judges, practising lawyers and academics. Its permanent secretariat was provided by the Lord Chancellor's Department, but it lacked research facilities and suffered from the inevitable problems of any part-time body. By 1982 it had produced 23 reports.

3. THE CRIMINAL LAW REVISION COMMITTEE

This committee, the counterpart to the Law Reform Committee, but responsible to the Home Secretary rather than the Lord Chancellor, was established in 1959, and included judges, academics and the D.P.P.[51] Its reports have led to important reforming legislation, most notably the Theft Acts 1968 and 1978. Perhaps the best known report was its 11th Report on Evidence, which aroused a storm of opposition, in part at least, according to its defenders, based on the misrepresentation of some of its recommendations.[52] For the purposes of its review of sexual offences, the Committee was advised by a Policy Advisory Committee compris-

---

[45] See Lord Hailsham, "Obstacles to Law Reform" (1981) 34 C.L.P. 279; P. M. North, (1981) III (I) *Liverpool Law Review* 5 and (1985) 101 L.Q.R. 338, 346–357; Lord Hooson Q.C., "Reform of the Legislative Process in the Light of the Law Commission's Work" (1983) 17 L.T. 67; S. Cretney, (1985) 48 M.L.R. 493; G. Drewry in Zellick (1988), pp. 28–43.

[46] 29th Annual Report, 1994 (Law Com. No.232), Appendix 6.

[47] 28th Annual Report, 1993 (Law Com. No.223), pp. 6–12.

[48] 29th Annual Report, Pt. V; below, p. 275.

[49] See E. C. S. Wade, (1961) 24 M.L.R. 3; J. H. Farrar, *Law Reform and the Law Commission* (1974), pp. 9–14, 133–137; M. C. Blair, (1982) 1 C.J.Q. 64.

[50] For an account of the one that was not (the 6th Interim Report on the Statute of Frauds and the Doctrine of Consideration (Cmd. 5549, 1937)), see J. Beatson, (1992) 45(2) C.L.P.I.

[51] See generally, Glanville Williams, "The Work of Criminal Law Reform" (1975) 13 J.S.P.T.L. 183; J. C. Smith, "An academic lawyer and law reform" (1981) 1 L.S. 119.

[52] See the articles cited in the previous footnote and M. Zander in P. Glazebrook (ed.), *Reshaping the Criminal Law* (1978).

ing five members of the C.L.R.C. and 10 members from other disciplines, including probation officers, a consultant psychiatrist, a social worker and a sociologist. There was here a greater potentional for fundamental disagreement about what it is that the law should be attempting to achieve than there had been on earlier references to the C.L.R.C.[53] The Committee has not been convened since 1985.

4. OTHER BODIES

Other bodies which require mention include the rule committees which make procedural rules for the courts[54] and the newly established committee to consider reforms in the Supreme Court.[55]

5. AD HOC COMMITTEES[56]

Investigations by Royal Commissions and departmental committees have long been a familiar feature of the law reform scene. They have the advantage over part-time advisory committees of a much greater commitment of resources, both of the time of their members and in money for research. They have the disadvantage when compared with permanent bodies that, having accumulated a large amount of information and expertise, their members disperse once the body has done its work. Other points of contrast with the law reform bodies discussed above are that ad hoc committees usually have a majority, or at least a large contingent of non-lawyers, and are more likely than those others to be employed in connection with institutional reforms. Since 1960, there have been five Royal Commissions of particular importance for the English legal system. The Royal Commission on Assizes and Quarter Sessions,[57] chaired by Lord Beeching, made proposals for the reorganisation of the criminal courts (other than magistrates courts) which were speedily implemented.[58] The Royal Commission on Civil Liability and Compensation for Personal Injury reported in 1978.[59] It found the private law system for claiming damages in tort to be too dependent on chance, unduly slow and expensive to operate, but felt unable because of its terms of reference to recommend a comprehensive state scheme for the compensation of all accident victims. Such a scheme would have had serious implications for the large number of lawyers, particularly barristers, who specialise in tort work. In the event, the Commission made a large number of piecemeal proposals for reform, only some of which have been implemented.

---

[53] Criminal Law Revision Committee, 15th Report on Sexual Offences (Cmnd. 9213, 1984), pp. 1, 100.

[54] See below, pp. 60, 79, 94, 96.

[55] See below, p. 94.

[56] A list of major reports of official committees and commissions on law reform is given in G. Zellick (ed.), *Law Reform and the Law Commission* (1988), Appendix 6.

[57] Cmnd. 4153, 1969.

[58] See below, pp. 79–81.

[59] Cmnd. 7054, Chairman: Lord Pearson.

The Royal Commission on Legal Services, chaired by an accountant, Sir Henry Benson, reported in 1979.[60] Its terms of reference were:

"to inquire into the law and practice relating to the provision of legal services in England, Wales and Northern Ireland, and to consider whether any, and if so what, changes are desirable in the public interest in the structure, organisation, training, regulation of and entry to the legal profession, including the arrangements for determining its remuneration, whether from private sources or public funds, and in the rules which prevent persons who are neither barristers nor solicitors from undertaking conveyancing and other legal business on behalf of other persons."

The report was widely regarded as a disappointment.[61] It was criticised for its pedestrian style, its paucity of reasoning, the fact that only a limited amount of research[62] was commissioned and its apparent over-dependence on the information and arguments presented by the legal profession. The *Legal Action Group Bulletin* was tempted to ignore the report: it would certainly be kinder so shaky were its foundations.[63] Professor Zander, who had played a significant role in securing the establishment of the Commission and who had submitted a considerable body of evidence, was more welcoming: he counted well over a hundred recommendations that he thought would amount to valuable changes.[64] The only real enthusiasts were the two branches of the legal profession, which was unsurprising given that on many issues their position was endorsed by the Commission. Aspects of the report will be considered at various points in the book. Many of the recommendations directed at the profession were the subject of action; those directed at the government had little impact, except that responsibility for criminal legal aid was transferred from Home Secretary to Lord Chancellor.[65] Indeed, the government subsequently decided, contrary to the recommendation of a majority of members of the Royal Commission, to end the solicitors' conveyancing "monopoly", and fundamental changes have followed the Lord Chancellor's White Paper, *Legal Services: A Framework for the Future*,[66] many comprised in the Courts and Legal Services Act 1990.

The Royal Commission on Criminal Procedure[67] provided an interesting contrast. It was established in 1978 to consider the powers and duties of the police in respect of the investigation of criminal offences and the rights and duties of suspects and accused persons, the process of and responsibility for the prosecution of criminal offences and related matters. Three features of the report were especially noteworthy. First, the Commission was much more active than

---

[60] Cmnd. 7648.
[61] See C. Glasser, *L.A.G. Bull*, September 1979, p. 201; (1979) 129 N.L.J. 1116–1122, 1131–1135, 1140–1146, 1223–1224; M. Elliott, (1980) J.S.W.L. 1; O. Hanson and J. Levin, (1979) *Yearbook of Social Policy*, Chap. 12; (1980) 43 M.L.R. 543–566; (1981) *Windsor Yearbook of Access to Justice* 121 (T. A. Downes, P. R. Hopkins and W. M. Rees) and 179 (P. A. Thomas); P. A. Thomas (ed.), *Law in the Balance* (1982).
[62] See C. Glasser, *op. cit.*
[63] November 1979, p. 246.
[64] (1980) 33 C.L.P. 33, 50.
[65] See *The Government Response to the Report of the Royal Commission on Legal Services* (Cmnd. 9077, 1983). The Law Society and the Bar also published their responses: see *L.A.G. Bulletin*, December 1983, pp. 3, 6.
[66] Cm. 740, 1989. See below, p. 121.
[67] Cmnd. 8092, 1981.

the Royal Commission on Legal Services in sponsoring research. Second, there was a clear intention to identify basic points of principle to which the specific recommendations were to be related.[68] Third, the report indicated the lines that reform should take leaving the details to be worked out. In consequence, the Police and Criminal Evidence Bill was presented to Parliament in 1983, together with proposals for the establishment of a national prosecution service.

In the following decades, Royal Commissions and departmental committees were conspicuous by their absence. Questions of policy tended to be determined by government, with the use of teams of civil servants, perhaps with an independent chairman or advisers, to work out the details of implementation. Examples in the context of the law included the Civil Justice Review,[69] the Magistrates' Courts Scrutiny[70] and the Working Group on the Right of Silence.[71] The Green Papers on Reform of the Legal Profession were simply published as such. This kind of approach is certainly more convenient for government. It leads to a speedier conclusion, and also avoids the risk of an independent body producing unwelcome recommendations. There are, however, corresponding doubts as to the quality of the reports produced.

Concerns over the series of widely publicised cases where there had been a miscarriage of justice[72] led to the appointment of the Royal Commission on Criminal Justice, chaired by Viscount Runciman. Its terms of reference were

"to examine the effectiveness of the criminal justice system in England and Wales in securing the conviction of those guilty of criminal offences and the acquittal of those who are innocent, having regard to the efficient use of resources"

and in particular to consider whether changes were needed in the conduct and supervision of police investigations, the role of the prosecutor, the disclosure of material, the role of experts, defence arrangements, the "right to silence", the role of trial courts and the Court of Appeal and arrangements for considering allegations of miscarriages of justice. It reported in 1993,[73] and made 352 detailed recommendations, many but not all of which were accepted. It commissioned a substantial body of research.[74] However, the report received a largely critical response from academic commentators, who argued that significant findings of that research were ignored, that the report lacked a coherent or explicit theoretical base and that the thrust of the recommendations seemed to be in facilitating convictions rather than protecting the innocent.[75] Furthermore, by the time of the report, the government's major preoccupation was again the fight against crime, symbolised with the introduction, contrary to the R.C.C.J.'s

---

[68] The Commission applied three standards for judging both the existing system and its own recommendations: are the arrangements, actual or proposed, fair and clear?; are they open, that is, not secret and is there accountability?; are they workable and efficient?

[69] *Report of the Review Body on Civil Justice* (Cm. 394, 1988). See I. Ramsey, (1988) 15 J.L.S. 416.

[70] *Magistrates' Courts: Report of a scrutiny* (HMSO, 1989).

[71] *Report of the Working Group on the Right of Silence* (Home Office, 1989).

[72] See below, pp. 662–663.

[73] Cm.2263, 1993.

[74] It published 22 research studies (see list in Appendix 4).

[75] See below, pp. 775–776.

recommendation, of provisions enabling inferences to be drawn from the silence of the accused, in the Criminal Justice and Public Order Act 1994.[76]

On the civil side, Lord Woolf was invited to conduct an inquiry on access to justice. His interim report, *Access to Justice*, published in June 1995, made 124 recommendations. The key feature was that there should be a fundamental transfer in the responsibility for the management of civil litigation from litigants and their legal advisers to the courts.[77]

E. POSSIBLE INSTITUTIONAL REFORMS

Proposals have regularly been made for the establishment of a Ministry of Justice, performing all the functions concerning justice at present divided among separate ministries.[78] The calls have commonly been associated with demands for a more systematic approach to law reform,[79] and have equally commonly been resisted on the highly dubious ground that the establishment of such a ministry might pose a threat to the administration of justice. In 1918, the Machinery of Government Committee chaired by Lord Haldane[80] proposed a redistribution of functions between Lord Chancellor and Home Secretary. The former would cease to be Speaker of the House of Lords and to sit judicially, but would be responsible for all judicial appointments, would continue as chief constitutional adviser to the Crown and would "watch and master all questions relating to legislation." Other matters concerning the administration of justice would pass to the Home Secretary, who would be redesignated as Minister of Justice, and would probably sit in the Commons. These proposals were supported by the Law Society but opposed by the Bar. Four years later, the case against a Ministry of Justice (albeit a ministry on the continental pattern including responsibility for the judiciary) was powerfully made by Lord Birkenhead.[81] Some of the steam was taken out of the case for a Ministry by the establishment of the Law Commissions in 1965. More recently, the developments in the role of the Lord Chancellor's Department outlined above[82] have rendered it into a Ministry of Justice in all but name, with the significant qualification that the ministerial head does not sit in the House of Commons.

Another proposed development has been the creation of a Legal Services Council of laymen and lawyers to review and carry out research on the provision of legal services, to advise the Lord Chancellor and possibly to carry out some

---

[76] See below, pp. 689–691, 860–862, 914.

[77] See below, pp. 78–79, 86–87, 581, 596–600.

[78] See JUSTICE Conference, *Do we Need a Ministry of Justice?* (1970); G. Drewry, "Ministry of Justice—a Matter of Meaning" (1982) 132 N.L.J. 602–603, "Lord Haldane's Ministry of Justice—Stillborn or Strangled at Birth?" (1983) 61 *Public Administration*, 396, "The Debate about a Ministry of Justice—a Joad's-Eye View" [1987] P.L.502, and "Justice and Public Administration" (1992) 45(2) C.L.P.187.

[79] See, *e.g.* Glanville Williams (ed.) *The Reform of the Law* (1951); *cf.* G. Gardiner and A. Martin (eds.), *Law Reform NOW* (1963); P. Archer and A. Martin (eds.), *More Law Reform NOW* (1983), pp. 15–20.

[80] Cd. 9230.

[81] *Points of View* (1922), Vol. I, p. 112. This was apparently prepared by Sir Claud Schuster, Permanent Secretary to the Lord Chancellor 1915–1944: Drewry (1983) *op. cit.*

[82] See pp. 16–19.

executive functions. This was recommended by the Royal Commission on Legal Services,[83] but rejected by the government. More generally, there is a good case for a permanent body analogous to the Law Commission to concern itself with the reform of civil and criminal procedure and the operation of the legal system.[84]

Lord Woolf has recommended the establishment of a Civil Justice Council, chaired by the Head of Civil Justice, with responsibility for overseeing and co-ordinating the implementation of his proposals, and possibly including procedural rule-making for the courts within its remit.[85]

Finally, it may be noted that unlike the position in some other common law jurisdictions, the judges do not play a major role in supervising the administration of the courts.[86] A strong conception of the independence of judiciary would require the judiciary to assume administrative responsibility for the operation of the courts, including control over court buildings and facilities and the organisation of business. However, while there have been judicial expressions of concern that the decisions of civil servants are having an increasingly direct (and deleterious) effect on the work of the courts, what is sought for the judiciary is a position of greater influence, rather than a full transfer of responsibility.[87] Such a transfer would, moreover, in the opinion of Lord Mackay, be an "extremely retrograde step".[88]

F. INFORMATION ABOUT THE LEGAL SYSTEM

Statistical and factual information about the operation of the English legal system can be gleaned from various official sources. Official publications are grouped into a number of classes.[89] "Command papers" are "Presented to Par-

---

[83] R.C.C.P. Report, pp. 125–170; R.C.L.S., Vol. 1, pp. 62–65. See below, pp. 514–515; *Government Response* (above, p. 29, n. 65) p. 6.

[84] See M. Zander, "Promoting Change in the Legal System" (1979) 42 L.Q.R. 489, 502–505. The suggested model is the Vera Institute of Justice of New York, which has assisted in various reform projects in the U.K. A "complete and systematic review of civil procedure" was instituted by the Lord Chancellor see the *Government Response* (above, p. 29, n. 65) pp. 31–32), but took the form of the *ad hoc Civil Justice Review*.

[85] *Access to Justice* (1995), Chap. 27. This body would be analogous but not identical to the Criminal Justice Consultative Council (above, p. 24) and the Children Act Advisory Committee (below, p. 76).

[86] See I. R. Scott, "The Council of Judges in the Supreme Court of England and Wales" [1989] P.L. 379. Lord Mackay of Clashfern, (1991) 44 C. L. P. 241, 247–250; Mr Justice R. D. Nicholson (1993) 67 A.L.J. 404, 422–424. The judges are responsible for what happens in the court room and for "the administrative penumbra immediately surrounding the judicial process" (Lord Mackay, *op.cit.* at p. 247); presiding judges for each circuit and the senior presiding judge deal with the deployment and performance of the judiciary (below, p. 84). Otherwise, administration is in the hands of the courts service (above, p. 17) and while the Lord Chancellor is ultimately accountable to Parliament for the service he is regarded by at least some of the judges as one of "them" rather than one of "us" for these purposes (below, p. 245).

[87] See below, pp. 244–246.

[88] *The Administration of Justice* (1994), p. 48. Lord Mackay argues that there is no way that a judge with security of tenure can be accountable to Parliament for the way in which money is spent and the courts are administered; as Lord Chancellor, he has no security of tenure: *ibid.*

[89] See generally J. E. Pemberton, *British Official Publications* (2nd ed., 1973); D. Butcher, *Official Publications in Britain* (2nd ed., 1991).

liament by Command of Her Majesty''[90] and include reports of Royal Commissions, departmental committees and the Law Commission. "House of Commons" and "House of Lords Papers" are published on behalf of the respective Houses of Parliament.[91] Other documents are published as ''Non-Parliamentary Publications'' by Her Majesty's Stationery Office[92] or by the department concerned.[93]

Statistical information may be found in the series of *Judicial Statistics* (1856–1922) published by the Home Office and covering both civil and criminal matters; and *Criminal Statistics* (1922 to date) also published by the Home Office. There are also Home Office Statistical Bulletins, which provide regular statistical information on some topics, such as the use of the Prevention of Terrorism Acts, and occasional information on others, such as comparative figures on remands in custody by magistrates' courts in different areas. The Lord Chancellor's Department has published various series: *Civil Judicial Statistics* (1922–1974); *Statistics on Judicial Administration* (1972–1974) and *Judicial Statistics*: *England and Wales* (1975 to date). Information on legal services was given in the Annual Report of the Law Society and the Lord Chancellor's Advisory Committee, first issued in 1951 and from 1974–75 termed the *Legal Aid Annual Reports*, and is now found in the Annual Reports of the Legal Aid Board. The Lord Chancellor is required to publish annual reports on the business of the Supreme Court and county courts,[94] and the Master of the Rolls issues annual Reviews of the work of the Court of Appeal (Civil Division).[95]

G. INTERNATIONAL STANDARDS

There is an increasing awareness that minimum standards for the operation of aspects of the legal system are set by international law, enshrined in treaties to which the United Kingdom is a party. The most important such treaties are the European Convention on Human Rights[96] and the International Covenant on Civil and Political Rights.[97] Key articles of the European Convention include Article 5 on the right to liberty and security of person, Article 6 on the right to a fair trial, Article 7, prohibiting retrospective criminal law, and Article 14, providing that the enjoyment of Convention rights and freedoms shall be secured without discrimination on any ground such as (for example) sex, race, colour,

---

[90] These papers are numbered in series and since 1870 have been prefixed by an abbreviation for "Command": 1st series [1]–[4222] 1833–1869; 2nd series [C.1]–[C.9550] 1870–1899; 3rd series [Cd.1]–[Cd.9239] 1900–1918; 4th series [Cmd.1]–Cmd.9889, 1919–1956; 5th series Cmnd.1–9927, 1956–1986; 6th series Cm.1–, 1986–.

[91] These are numbered in the session of publication (*e.g.* 1983–84 H.C. or H.L. 1).

[92] HMSO also publish Command Papers and Parliamentary Papers: see the daily, monthly and annual HMSO lists.

[93] See the *Catalogue of British Official Publications Not Published by HMSO* (1980–).

[94] Courts and Legal Services Act 1990, s.1(12). See the Annual Report of the Lord Chancellor's Department Court Service, published by HMSO.

[95] See *e.g.* below, p. 97, n. 69.

[96] See below, pp. 109–112.

[97] See S. H. Bailey, "Rights in the Administration of Justice" in D. J. Harris and S. Joseph (eds.), *The United Kingdom and the International Covenant on Civil and Political Rights* (1995), Chap. 6.

language or religion. There have been few successful challenges to the United
Kingdom under these provisions in the context of the administration of justice
in England and Wales,[98] with the significant exception of a series of cases concerning the rights of prisoners,[99] one case of excessive delay in civil proceedings
(nine years)[1], and one concerning the retrospective imposition of a confiscation
order following conviction for drug offences.[1a]. Challenges in high-profile cases
concerning the right to silence[2] and the abolition of the marital exemption from
liability for rape have failed.[3] Nevertheless, it is argued that current trends in
the criminal justice process render the United Kingdom increasingly vulnerable
to challenge.[4]

[98] The lack of a right to legal representation for criminal appeals in Scotland has been held to be
unlawful: *Boner v. U.K.*, A-300-B, Judgment of October 28, 1994; *Maxwell v. U.K.*, A-300-C,
Judgment of October 28, 1994.
[99] Cases on prisoners' correspondence (*e.g. Golder v. U.K.*, A-18, Judgment of February 21, 1975;
Silver v. U.K., A-61, Judgment of March 25, 1983); disciplinary proceedings (*Campbell and Fell
v. U.K.*, A-80, Judgment of June 28, 1984); release of life sentence prisoners (*Weeks v. U.K.*,
A-114, Judgment of March 2, 1987; *Thynne, Wilson and Gunnell v. U.K.*, A-190, Judgment of
October 25, 1990), prisoners in psychiatric detention (*X v. U.K.*, A-46, Judgment of November
5, 1981), and persons detained during Her Majesty's pleasure (*Hussein v. U.K., Singh v. U.K.*,
The Times, February 26, 1996, Judgment of February 21, 1996).
[1] *Darnell v. U.K.*, A-272, Judgment of October 26, 1993.
[1a] *Welch v. U.K., The Times*, February 15, 1995, Judgment of February 9, 1995.
[2] See below, p. 691, n. 15.
[3] See below, p. 253.
[4] See Liberty, *Criminal Justice and Civil and Political Liberties* (1993).

CHAPTER 2

COURTS AND TRIBUNALS

A. INTRODUCTION

THERE are several ways in which a legal dispute (which the parties also characterise as "legal") may be resolved. It may be settled by force or by agreement. The dispute may be referred informally or formally to a third party for him or her to arbitrate. Exceptionally, the dispute may be referred to one of the institutions established by the state expressly for the purpose of resolving such matters. Some of these institutions are termed "courts", others "tribunals." These terms cannot be defined with precision, and, for the most part, little turns on whether a particular institution is labelled a court or a tribunal, or whether an institution, however labelled, falls within the legal definition of a "court".

The term "tribunal" can be used very generally to mean any "judicial assembly",[1] including a court; in the present context it is commonly used for "judicial assemblies" other than courts. If established by the state they are generally described as "administrative tribunals" to distinguish them from "domestic tribunals" established by non-state institutions such as professional and sporting associations and trade unions as part of their disciplinary procedures. The label "administrative" reflects the fact that most such tribunals are established to perform judicial functions as part of the administration of some government scheme or programme.

Finally, it should be remembered that while the settlement of disputes is the main function of almost all courts and most tribunals, it is not the only one: a number of administrative functions have also been allocated to them.[2]

B. COURTS

1. SIGNIFICANCE

Apart from the police, the courts of law are perhaps the most visible feature of the English legal system. Only the courts have power to impose punishment in criminal cases; reports of these, and important civil cases decided by the superior courts, commonly appear in the national and local press, and they may be covered by radio and television. Lawyers, and to an even greater extent, law students and lecturers place great emphasis on the decisions of the superior

---

[1] O.E.D.

[2] *e.g.* the licensing functions of magistrates and the discretionary powers of the High Court in relation to the administration of estates or the supervision of the affairs of children and mental patients; *cf.* below, pp. 87–88.

courts. It is, however, difficult to estimate the significance of the courts in the legal system as a whole. The number of cases determined by the courts is small, and by the superior courts[3] minute, in comparison with the number of disputes settled by other means. Moreover, in a high proportion of the cases dealt with by the magistrates' courts and county courts the proceedings are merely mechanical processes for, respectively, the fining of minor traffic offenders and the collection of debts, with no live issue to be determined.

On the other hand, the courts do have a much wider indirect impact, given, first, that the chances of success in legal proceedings will influence the settlement of disputes,[4] and, secondly, that the decisions of superior courts are a source of law.[5]

2. HISTORICAL BACKGROUND[6]

(a) Courts of common law and equity

As we have said, the main function of almost all courts today is the adjudication of disputes. They can, however, trace their origins to local and central institutions in which no distinctions were drawn between the functions of administration, legislation and adjudication. At the local level in the Dark Ages there were community assemblies or "moots" which, *inter alia*, dealt with disputes according to local custom. These assemblies, apart from the smallest, village, assemblies, came to be based on administrative units established by the Crown, the shires, and their subdivisions, the hundreds and the boroughs. At the centre was the *Curia Regis* (King's Court).

Three related themes in early legal development can be discerned. First, the administration of justice came to be regarded as an adjunct of feudal lordship rather than a matter for the community as a whole. Then there was a further shift whereby it came in particular to be one of the prerogatives of the Crown. Thirdly, the administration of justice came to be differentiated from other functions of government. The strengthening of royal justice at the expense of local, communal, justice was a gradual process, and was neither intended nor planned, but it took place at all levels. This process involved the establishment of distinct royal courts, the placing of royal officials in the localities, whether temporarily or permanently, and the development of the supervisory jurisdiction of the royal courts over local courts.

At the centre, three common law courts evolved at different times out of the *Curia Regis*: the Exchequer,[7] the Common Pleas and the King's (or Queen's) Bench. They sat at Westminster Hall. The jurisdictional lines between these courts were complex. In theory, the Exchequer dealt with matters concerning the revenues of the Crown, the Common Pleas suits between subject and subject in which the Crown had no interest, and the King's Bench "pleas of the Crown" (*i.e.* criminal matters and civil cases involving a breach of the King's peace or some other royal interest). By the eighteenth century a variety of fictions had

---

[3] See below, p. 50.
[4] See below, pp. 554–563.
[5] See below, Chap. 7.
[6] See generally J. H. Baker, *An Introduction to Legal History* (3rd ed., 1990), Chaps.1–7.
[7] As well as a common law jurisdiction, this court had an established equity jurisdiction, which was transferred to the Court of Chancery as late as 1842.

enabled each court to exercise a jurisdiction that was similar in substance although different in form to the others.

Parallel to the development of the common law courts at the centre was that of the Court of Chancery, and in particular its function of dealing with petitions.[8] For a time in the sixteenth and seventeenth centuries a number of "conciliar courts" also assumed importance, being courts established under the prerogative to handle judicial matters that came before the Privy Council but were not dealt with by the Chancellor. These included the Court of Star Chamber, which became notorious towards the end of its life for its handling of political crimes, the Court of Requests and several regional offshoots. They were looked on with suspicion by the common law courts and were abolished in the 1640s. The pattern of superior courts otherwise remained substantially unchanged until the nineteenth century, when some new courts were created, and there was subsequently a general reorganisation under the Supreme Court of Judicature Acts 1873–75.[9] In this reorganisation the various superior courts[10] were replaced by one Supreme Court of Judicature comprising the High Court (in five divisions) and the Court of Appeal. The intention initially was for the appellate jurisdiction of the House of Lords to be abolished, but a successful rearguard action was fought for its retention.[11]

Royal justices from the common law courts were also sent out to travel the country. Originally, they conducted all manner of governmental affairs, but they came to concentrate on judicial proceedings. There were two bases for their jurisdiction. In criminal and some civil cases they were given ad hoc commissions from the Crown. In other civil cases they sat with a jury to try issues that arose in litigation in the superior courts at Westminster: the juries technically were summoned to Westminster "unless before then (*nisi prius*) the King's justices have come" into the country. It was obviously more convenient to try the issues locally and transmit the result to London. The system came to be known as the "assize system" and continued until the 1970s,[12] and even the present arrangements have maintained the concept of High Court judges hearing cases in the provinces, albeit now reinforced by local judges.

The significant development in the handling of criminal cases less serious than those dealt with at the assizes was the appointment by the Crown of justices of the peace and the progressive widening of their criminal jurisdiction from the thirteenth century onwards.[13] Civil cases were heard by the successors of the old community assemblies, a variegated pattern of county, hundred, manorial and borough courts. These courts were subject to the supervisory jurisdiction of the superior royal courts and came to apply the common law. They declined for different reasons and at different times, although many were only formally abolished in the 1970s.[14] The important step in the establishment of a regular

---

[8] See above, pp. 5–6.
[9] This followed the recommendations of the First Report of the Judicature Commission (HMSO, 1869).
[10] *i.e.* the Courts of Chancery, Queen's Bench, Common Pleas, Exchequer, Admiralty (see below, p. 36), Probate (below, p. 37), and Divorce and Matrimonial Causes (*ibid.*). The London Court of Bankruptcy, originally established by an Act of 1831 to relieve the Court of Chancery of some of its business, was incorporated in 1884.
[11] See below, pp. 99–100.
[12] See below, p. 80.
[13] See below, pp. 193–194. The justices also had many administrative responsibilities.
[14] Courts Act 1971, ss.42, 43; Administration of Justice Act 1977, s.23, Sched. 4.

system of local civil courts was the creation of new, statutory, county courts in 1846.[15]

(b) Appeals[16]

Provision for appeals was complex. The record of a court's proceedings could be reviewed for error[17] by another common law court[18] or a special court, a number of which were established by statute at various times to sit in a room at Westminster Hall known as the Exchequer Chamber.[19] Error lay from the Courts of Exchequer Chamber to Parliament, this jurisdiction being exercised by the House of Lords. Another, informal, method of review was the practice of judges to reserve cases for the opinion of their brethren, expressed at meetings held in Serjeants' Inn or the Exchequer Chamber.[20] In Chancery proceedings, a case argued before the Master of the Rolls or a Vice-Chancellor[21] could be re-argued before the Chancellor, and the Chancellor could review his own previous decisions and those of his predecessors. In the seventeenth century it was established that proceedings in error lay from the Court of Chancery to the House of Lords. A Court of Appeal in Chancery with appellate judges (Lords Justices) specially appointed to it was created in 1851 to hear appeals from the Master of the Rolls and the Vice-Chancellors. This became the model for the Court of Appeal established by the Judicature Acts 1873–75. The nineteenth century also saw the replacement of proceedings in error by statutory appeals in the modern form.

(c) Other courts

Apart from the courts of common law and equity there were courts that followed civil law procedure: the High Court of Admiralty,[22] which dealt with maritime matters and the High Court of Chivalry,[23] a court of honour. Canon law was administered by archdeacons' courts, the bishops' consistory courts, each presided over by the chancellor of the diocese, and the archbishops' provincial

---

[15] See below, p. 71: These must not be confused with the old shire or county courts presided over by the sheriff.

[16] See Baker (1990), Chap. 9.

[17] This process was more akin to the modern application for judicial review than statutory appeal: see Chap. 17.

[18] Proceedings in error lay from the Common Pleas to the King's Bench until 1830.

[19] (1) One was established in 1357 to hear error from the Exchequer. This comprised the Chancellor and the Treasurer with judges as assistants. (2) A second was established in 1585 to hear error from the Queen's Bench, this court comprising the justices of the Common Pleas and the barons of the Exchequer. (3) In 1830 a new Court of Exchequer Chamber was established to hear error from each of the common law courts. This comprised all the judges of the superior courts, error from one court being heard by the judges of the other two.

[20] In criminal cases such meetings became formalised with the creation of the Court for Crown Cases Reserved in 1848.

[21] See below pp. 223, 224.

[22] This court became part of the Supreme Court of Judicature in the 1873–75 reorganisation. See F. Wiswall, *The Development of Admiralty Jurisdiction and Practice since 1800* (1971)

[23] This court has sat once since 1737: *Manchester Corporation v. Manchester Palace of Varieties Ltd* [1955] P. 133. See G. D. Squibb, *The High Court of Chivalry* (1959). It has jurisdiction over such questions as the right to arms, precedence and descent. In the 1955 case the corporation claimed successfully that the company should be prevented from using the former's arms in their seal and displayed above the main curtain at the Palace Theatre, Manchester.

courts, the Chancery Court of York and the Court of Arches.[24] Further appeals lay to the Pope or to Papal Delegates. Following the Reformation this jurisdiction passed to the Court of High Commission, which lapsed in the 1640s, and the Court of Delegates. The latter court was replaced by the Privy Council in 1832. The relationship between the ecclesiastical courts and the royal courts was stormy and complicated.[25] The jurisdiction of ecclesiastical courts over marriage, divorce and probate ended in 1857 with the creation of the Court of Divorce and Matrimonial Causes and the Court of Probate.[26] Since then, their jurisdiction has been confined to church matters. The present court structure was introduced by the Ecclesiastical Jurisdiction Measure 1963, which retained the consistory courts, but created an appellate system of gothic complexity, largely replacing the appellate jurisdiction of the Privy Council.[27] Appeals in matters of doctrine, ritual or ceremonial lie from the consistory courts to the Court of Ecclesiastical Causes Reserved, which comprises three bishops and two judges, appointed by the Queen.[28]

C. TRIBUNALS

1. INTRODUCTION

The significant role played by administrative tribunals in the adjudication of legal disputes is a development of the present century, although it is possible to find examples of similar institutions in earlier centuries.[29] For example, the General and Special Commissioners of Income Tax were established in 1799 and 1805 respectively, with both assessment and appellate functions. The Railway and Canal Commission was established in 1873, *inter alia*, to settle disputes between railway companies and between companies and their customers, and subsequently evolved into the Transport Tribunal.

The most important factors behind the expansion of the number of tribunals and the range of their work have been the advent of the welfare state and the development of state economic controls. The National Insurance Act 1911 set up the unemployment benefit scheme. All questions concerning claims to benefit were to be determined initially by an insurance officer. A workman dissatisfied with a determination could have it referred to a "court of referees" consisting of a chairman appointed by the Board of Trade, one member from an "employers' panel" and one from a "workmens' panel." A further right of appeal lay to an "umpire"—a national appellate authority appointed by the Crown. This arrangement proved superior to alternative methods of adjudication

---

[24] So called because it usually sat in the arched crypt of the church of St Mary le Bow in London. Its judge became known as the Dean of Arches.

[25] See Baker (1990), Chap. 8.

[26] These courts became part of the Supreme Court of Judicature in the 1873–75 reorganisation.

[27] See E. Garth Moore, *An Introduction to Canon Law* (1967), Chap. XIV.

[28] The first two cases before this court were *In re St Michael and All Angels, Great Torrington* [1985] Fam. 81 and *In re St Stephen's, Walbrook* [1987] Fam. 146: see J. D. C.Harte, (1988) 2 Ecc.L.J. 22.

[29] See R. E. Wraith and P. G. Hutchesson, *Administrative Tribunals* (1973), Chap. 1.

used in legislation of the period,[30] and was adopted as the general model for many of the new tribunals established in the following decades:

"The extension of governmental responsibility for welfare provision, regulation of the economy, employment policy and resource development has created new statutory rights, obligations and restraints. Consequently, new areas of potential dispute have opened up, the boundaries of which have been progressively extended, and which require legislative provision for adjudication. The tendency, for a variety of reasons, has been to use tribunals rather than ordinary courts for settling disputes of this kind."[31]

This is not to say that there have been clear principles governing either the decision to allocate a particular decision to a tribunal or the details of the machinery established:

"Parliament's selection of subjects to be referred to tribunals and inquiries does not form a regular pattern. Certain basic guidelines can be detected, but the choice is influenced by the interplay of various factors—the nature of the decisions, accidents of history, departmental preferences and political considerations—rather than by the application of a set of coherent principles."[32]

These tribunals commonly determine disputes between the citizen and the state arising out of the administration of a statutory scheme.[33] In addition, some determine disputes between citizens, normally arising out of protective legislation enacted for the benefit of one of the parties.[34]

2. THE FRANKS REPORT

A significant landmark in the development of tribunals was the 1957 report of the Committee on Administrative Tribunals and Enquiries chaired by Sir Oliver Franks.[35] Part of the terms of reference required the Committee to review the constitution and working of tribunals other than the ordinary courts of law, constituted by a minister or for the purposes of a minister's functions.[36] Among the general points made by the Committee were, first, that the special procedures

---

[30] *i.e.* Workmen's Compensation Act 1897: disputes concerning compensation for industrial injuries were supposed to be settled by arbitration but in practice went to county court judges and beyond on appeal; Old Age Pensions Act 1908: pensions were administered by pensions committees of local authorities, which also adjudicated disputes, with an appeal to the Local Government Board; National Insurance Act 1911, Part I: national health insurance was administered by friendly societies with an appeal to one of four Insurance Commissioners.

[31] *The Functions of the Council on Tribunals:* Special Report by the Council (Cmnd. 7805, 1980), p. 1.

[32] *ibid.,* pp. 1–2.

[33] *e.g.* disputes concerning claims to welfare benefits.

[34] *e.g.* disputes between landlord and tenant arising out of rent controls, and between employer and employee concerning allegedly unfair dismissals.

[35] Cmnd. 218.

[36] The other part of the terms of reference concerned public inquiry procedures.

within their terms of reference should be marked by the characteristics of "openness, fairness and impartiality"[37]:

> "In the field of tribunals openness appears to us to require the publicity of proceedings and knowledge of the essential reasoning underlying the decisions; fairness to require the adoption of a clear procedure which enables parties to know their rights, to present their case fully and to know the case which they have to meet; and impartiality to require the freedom of tribunals from the influence, real or apparent, of Departments concerned with the subject matter of their decisions."[38]

Secondly, the Committee noted that tribunals as a system for adjudication had come to stay, and indeed that the tendency to refer issues arising from legislative schemes to special tribunals was likely to grow rather than to diminish.[39]

Thirdly, the Committee recommended the establishment of two permanent Councils on Tribunals, one for England and Wales and one for Scotland, to supervise tribunal and inquiry procedures.

In addition, the report made a whole series of detailed recommendations concerning both the constitution and procedures of tribunals generally and particular tribunals. Most of the proposals were implemented in the Tribunals and Inquiries Act 1958, subsequently consolidated in the Tribunals and Inquiries Acts 1971 and now 1992, and in changes of regulation and departmental practice.

3. THE COUCIL ON TRIBUNALS[40]

The 1958 Act established one Council on Tribunals, with a Scottish Committee. Its functions in respect of tribunals are:

> "(a) to keep under review the construction and working of the tribunals specified in Schedule 1 to the [1992] Act;
> (b) to consider and report on particular matters referred to the Council by the Lord Chancellor and the Lord Advocate with respect to any tribunal other than a court of law whether or not specified in Schedule 1;. . . ."[41]

Thus, its powers are consultative and advisory. It was not given the executive powers recommended by the Franks Report as to the appointment of tribunal members, the review of remuneration and the formulation of procedural codes.[42]

---

[37] Cmnd. 218, p. 5.

[38] *ibid.* p. 10.

[39] *ibid.* p. 8.

[40] See *The Functions of the Council on Tribunals*: Special Report by the Council (Cmnd. 7805, 1980); the Council's Annual Reports; H. W. R. Wade, [1960] P.L. 351; J. F. Garner, [1965] P.L. 321; D. G. T. Williams, [1984] P.L. 73 and (1990) 9 C.J.Q. 27; O. Lomas, (1985) 48 M.L.R. 694; C. Harlow and R. Rawlings, *Law and Administration* (1984), Chap. 6.

[41] Special Report, p. 3. It has similar, although not identical functions in respect of procedures involving inquiries held on behalf of a minister.

[42] It must be consulted before procedural rules are made for Schedule 1 tribunals, but does not make the rules itself: 1972 Act, s.8.

Certainly it has no power to reverse or require reconsideration of specific tribunal decisions. The Council has 15 members appointed by the Lord Chancellor
and the Lord Advocate, and the Parliamentary Commissioner for Administration
is a member *ex officio*. The membership comprises a mixture of lawyers, both
practising and academic, and non-lawyers, with the latter predominating. The
Council's requests for additional powers, put forward in its Special Report of
1980, were generally not accepted, although a code for consultation with government departments has been introduced.[43] The Council has done much useful
work in minor matters, securing, for example, many amendments to draft bills,
rules and regulations, and some changes in tribunal practice. It has published a
Report on Model Rules for Tribunals, a Code of Practice on Access for Disabled
People using the Tribunal System and (with Property Holdings) a Register of
Tribunal Hearing Accommodation.[44] However, its political position is weak, its
resources are inadequate[45] and it "remains an inconspicuous advisory committee."[46] It is still met from time to time by spurious arguments from Departments why a proposed new tribunal should not be placed under its jurisdiction;
it sometimes, but not always, succeeds in overcoming them.[47] Access to the
deliberative stage of tribunal hearings is occasionally denied.[48]

4. ADJUDICATION OR ADMINISTRATION

There has been some debate on whether tribunals are to be regarded as part of
the machinery of justice or part of the machinery of administration. The Franks
Committee stated[49]:

"Tribunals are not ordinary courts, but neither are they appendages of
Government Departments. Much of the official evidence, including that of
the Joint Permanent Secretary to the Treasury, appeared to reflect the view
that tribunals should properly be regarded as part of the machinery of
administration, for which the Government must retain a close and continuing responsibility. Thus, for example, tribunals in the social service field
would be regarded as adjuncts to the administration of the services themselves. We do not accept this view. We consider that tribunals should prop-

[43] See the Council's Annual Reports for 1980–81 (1981–82 H. C. 89), pp. 6–7 and 1981–82 (1982–
83 H. C. 64), p. 8 and Appendix C. The Code was recirculated in 1986 and 1992: Annual Report
for 1991–92 (1992–93 H. C. 316), p. 50 and Appendix I.
[44] See Annual Reports for 1990–91 (1991–92 H. C. 97), pp. 23–24 (and Cm.1434); 1992–93 (1993–
94 H. C. 78), pp. 11–13 and Appendix A; and 1993–94 (1994–95 H. C. 22), pp. 11–12 and
Appendix A. A second edition was published in 1995: Annual Report for 1994–95 (1995–96 H.
C. 64), pp. 44–45.
[45] The Lord Chancellor's Department took over two years to consider and reject a request for
additional staff: Annual Report for 1985–86 (1986–87 H. C. 42), pp. 28–30. In 1989–90 the
Council's expenditure was £568,970, and it had a staff of 12 see Annual Report for 1993–94
(1994–95 H. C. 22), pp. 57, 78.
[46] Sir William Wade and C. F. Forsyth, *Administrative Law* (7th ed., 1994), p. 929.
[47] Annual Reports for 1993–94 (1994–95 H. C. 22), pp. 6–8, 41–42 (supervisory jurisdiction over
Police Appeal Tribunals eventually conceded). The Council's position is helped by the fact that
its current chairman, Lord Archer (formerly Peter Archer Q.C.), is a member of the House of
Lords.
[48] *ibid.*, pp. 9, 24–25 (industrial tribunals in Scotland).
[49] Cmnd. 218, p. 9.

erly be regarded as machinery provided by Parliament for adjudication rather than as part of the machinery of administration. The essential point is that in all these cases Parliament has deliberately provided for a decision outside and independent of the Department concerned, either at first instance (for example in the case of Rent Tribunals and the Licensing Authorities for Public Service and Goods Vehicles) or on appeal from a decision of a Minister or of an official in a special statutory position (for example a valuation officer or an insurance officer). Although the relevant statutes do not in all cases expressly enact that tribunals are to consist entirely of persons outside the Government service, the use of the term 'tribunal' in legislation undoubtedly bears this connotation, and the intention of Parliament to provide for the independence of tribunals is clear and unmistakable.''

The supposed characteristic of independence cannot, however, be taken too far. Clearly it is desirable that the expression of the "departmental view" in an individual case should be confined to the representations made at the hearing itself. However, in many respects the departments retain a general influence over tribunal decision-making. They are responsible for the formulation of the relevant primary legislation and procedural rules, albeit in consultation with the Council on Tribunals, and indeed for the "detailed arrangements" for the working of tribunals.[50] There has, however, been a trend in recent years for the Lord Chancellor's Department to take over (or be given) responsibility for the operation of a growing list of tribunals. The Department is now responsible for the Land Tribunal, the Special and General Commissioners of Income Tax, V.A.T. and Duties Tribunals, the Social Security and Child Support Commissioners, the Transport Tribunal, and the Immigration Adjudicators and administrative responsibility for the immigration appellate authorities. The Council on Tribunals has set out some broad guidelines as to the allocation of administrative responsibility for tribunals, suggesting that the main consideration should be the independence of the tribunal and the public perception of that independence. It was necessary to show that there was real independence, especially where the outcome of a tribunal's hearings would affect the public purse on a policy seen by the government or a department as vitally important. There could be a long term aim for the Lord Chancellor's Department to take over responsibility for all such tribunals, but this would not be realistic for the present. Other relevant factors were the tribunal's size and geographical spread, level and involvement with the law. The Council noted that most of the tribunals currently administered by the Department were relatively senior, relatively closely involved with specifically legal issues, and comparatively small, and only sat in a small number of places.[51]

A further aspect of the role of the Lord Chancellor's Department is that it is involved in the consideration of proposals to create new tribunals and provides advice and guidance to other departments on tribunal matters when so requested.[52]

---

[50] Annual Report of the Council on Tribunals for 1975–76 (1976–77 H. C. 236), p. 3. The Council recognises that it is not always practicable for a tribunal to use non-departmental staff and premises: Annual Report for 1981–82 (1982–83 H. C. 64), pp. 26–27.

[51] Annual Report for 1984–85 (1985–86 H. C. 54), pp. 13–14.

[52] Annual Report for 1986–87 (1987–88 H. C. 42), p. 13.

The Franks view on this point has been criticised in two respects. First, it has been pointed out that some tribunals are "policy-oriented" rather than "court substitute":

> For instance, where there is a dispute about social security entitlement, tribunals are basically used in place of the ordinary courts because the latter have become too expensive, formal and technical in their procedure. On the other hand, many matters of planning, whether in transport, land use, or industrial expertise, are given to tribunals because of the lack of expertise and doctrinal flexibility, or policy consciousness, on the part of the courts. Thus different weaknesses in the courts give rise to different types of tribunals.[53]

Examples of policy-oriented tribunals include the Transport Tribunal[54] and the Civil Aviation Authority.[55]

Secondly, it has been argued that even court-substitute tribunals should be seen as hybrid in nature; not only machinery for adjudication but, as well, "vital components of administration."[56]

5. SUPPOSED ADVANTAGES OF TRIBUNALS AS COURT-SUBSTITUTES

The Franks Committee noted that tribunals have certain characteristics which often give them advantages over the courts: "cheapness, accessibility, freedom from technicality, expedition and expert knowledge of their particular subject."[57] Generally, tribunal proceedings are cheaper, speedier,[58] and more expert than courts of law. However, accessibility is hindered by the great complexity of the system of tribunals and the lack of publicity given to their work. Moreover, the Council on Tribunals has stated that:

> "Significant changes have . . . taken place in the general constitutional and administrative climate. There is, for example, a movement towards greater formalism in procedures for settling disputes. The process started with reforms following the Franks Report which, in general, made tribunals more like courts. . . . Since then the trend towards judicialisation has gathered momentum with the result that tribunals are becoming more formal, expensive and procedurally complex. Consequently they tend to become

---

[53] B. Abel-Smith and R. Stevens, *In Search of Justice* (1968), p. 220; see J. A. Farmer, *Tribunals and Government* (1974), Chap. 8, for an argument in favour of the establishment of more policy-oriented tribunals as an alternative to ministerial decision-making.

[54] Goods vehicle licensing appeals: Transport Act 1968, s.70.

[55] Air transport licensing: Civil Aviation Acts 1971, 1980, 1982: see R. Baldwin, *Regulating the Airlines* (1985). Other possible candidates were the Patents Appeal Tribunal (now the Patents Court), the Lands Tribunal and the Industrial Court (renamed the Industrial Arbitration Board in 1971 and the Central Arbitration Committee in 1976): Abel-Smith and Stevens (1968), p. 225.

[56] K. Hendry, "The Tasks of Tribunals: Some Thoughts" (1982) 1 C. J. Q. 253, 259; *cf.* J. A. G. Griffith, "Tribunals and Inquiries" (1959) 22 M. L. R. 125, 129.

[57] Cmnd. 218, p. 9.

[58] The problem of delays is, however, a frequently recurring theme of Annual Reports of the Council on Tribunals.

more difficult for an ordinary citizen to comprehend and cope with on his own."[59]

Associated with this movement are the Council's arguments in favour of the extension of legal aid to tribunals, the appointment of lawyer chairmen and the extension of rights of appeal to the courts. It has also been pointed out that, despite declarations by tribunals that they are not bound by precedent, the requirements of consistency and predictability of decision lead to the development of general principles and an informal *de facto* system of precedent,[60] especially as the decisions of certain tribunals are systematically reported.

Accordingly, it is perhaps more true today than ever that "such differences as there are between [courts and tribunals] are not in any sense fundamental but at most differences in degree. . . ."[61] In particular, it is not possible to argue that courts administer rules of law while tribunals administer both law and policy:

"[N]o such clear line can or should be drawn. Indeed it was the evolution of this myth which helped establish the tribunal system by convincing the judges of the ordinary courts that they were concerned with legal but not with policy questions. . . . Properly understood, tribunals are a more modern form of court. In some cases they may have more discretion than the courts, and this is particularly true of the policy oriented tribunals. But certainly they have no more discretion than the Chancery Division has in handling trusts, wards or companies."[62]

Other, more pragmatic, reasons for establishing tribunals rather than entrusting matters to courts include the need not to overburden the judiciary,[63] the avoidance of Ministerial responsibility for sensitive decisions and the easing of the workload of government departments.[64]

6. THE TRIBUNALS AND INQUIRIES ACT 1992

Apart from establishing the Council on Tribunals, the 1992 Act makes provision for the selection of chairmen of certain tribunals,[65] requires reasons to be given

---

[59] *The Functions of the Council on Tribunals*: Special Report by the Council (Cmnd. 7805, 1980), p. 21.

[60] J. A. Farmer, *Tribunals and Government* (1974), pp. 174–180 and Chap. 3; below, pp. 444–445.

[61] B. Abel-Smith and R. Stevens, *In Search of Justice* (1968), pp. 224, 228. This is perhaps not true of the policy-oriented tribunals: see Farmer (1974), p. 189.

[62] Abel-Smith and Stevens (1968), pp. 227–228.

[63] Franks Report, Cmnd. 218, p. 9. In evidence the Permanent Secretary to the Lord Chancellor had stated that the wholesale transfer of tribunal work to the courts would necessitate the creation of a large number of additional judges, particularly in the county courts. Much of the work did not need the services of a highly remunerated judge. Moreover, a dilution of the bench was undesirable. Since then, there has been a large increase in the number of such judges, but they have been directed towards criminal and not tribunal work: see below, pp. 81, 218–221.

[64] See K. Hendry, (1982) 1 C.J.Q. 253, 257–58, giving the immigration appeals system as an example. See also J. A. G. Griffith, (1959) 22 M.L.R. 125, 129 in relation to national insurance and rent tribunals: "the truth was that the Department did not wish to be bothered with these decisions. And this for the most obvious of reasons: that the Department did not mind what the decisions were, for no questions of policy were involved."

[65] s.6. See below, pp. 214–215.

by Schedule 1 tribunals,[66] provides in many cases for an appeal on a point of law to the High Court[67] and renders inoperative most clauses in statutes passed before August 1, 1958 purporting to exclude judicial review.[68]

D. THE SYSTEM IN OUTLINE

1. COURTS

The courts structure is shown on pp. 47–48 in diagrammatic form, with a table below showing the current workload. The main courts are considered in detail in section E.

2. TRIBUNALS

There are now approximately 60 types of tribunal within the jurisdiction of the Council on Tribunals,[69] and several others outside it. They may be roughly grouped according to subject matter.[70] The table on pp. 50–54 does not, however, purport to be a comprehensive list. Some tribunals are considered in detail in the next section.

Other tribunals of note that have not been included within the jurisdiction of the Council on Tribunals include the Criminal Injuries Compensation Board, set up under the royal prerogative to consider claims for *ex gratia* compensation from the victims of crimes of violence,[71] and the Housing Benefit Review Boards set up[72] to hear appeals by claimants for rent or rates rebate or rent allowance

---

[66] s.10.

[67] s.11.

[68] Such clauses are not to prevent applications for certiorari or mandamus: see below, p. 974.

[69] An alphabetical list is published as an appendix to each Annual Report.

[70] See R. E. Wraith and P. G. Hutchesson, *Administrative Tribunals* (1973), Chap. 2. See also the table in Sir William Wade and C. F. Forsyth, *Administrative Law* (7th ed., 1994), pp. 956ff.

[71] See the White Paper on Compensation for Victims of Crimes of Violence (Cmnd. 2323, 1964); Annual Reports of the Board; Review of the Criminal Injuries Compensation Scheme: Report of an Interdepartmental Working Party (HMSO, 1978). The Board was due to be reconstituted as a statutory tribunal under Part VII of the Criminal Justice Act 1988, and placed under the Council's jurisdiction, but implementation has been delayed and is not now proposed: see *R. v. Secretary of State for the Home Department, ex. p. Fire Brigades Union* [1995] 2 W.L.R. 464, below, p. 284.

[72] Housing Benefits Regulations 1982 (S.I. 1982, No. 1124): see now the Housing Benefits (General) Regulations 1987 (S.I. 1987, No. 1971), regs.81–87 and Sched. 7.

THE COURTS EXERCISING CRIMINAL JURISDICTION

HOUSE of LORDS

Appeal from the Divisional Court subject to the same conditions attached to appeal from the Court of Appeal.

Appeal from the Court of Appeal subject to the grant of a certificate by that court that a point of law of general public importance is involved, and to the granting of leave by that court or the House of Lords.

COURT of APPEAL
CIVIL DIVISION

Appeal from the Crown Court against conviction on indictment on a question of fact or law or against sentence. The leave of the Court of Appeal is normally needed.

QUEEN'S BENCH DIVISION
DIVISIONAL COURT

Appeal by way of Case Stated by prosecution or defence on a matter of law.

Appeal by way of Case Stated, on a question of law only, arising on appeal from the Magistrates' Court.

CROWN COURT

Appeal from the Magistrate's Court against conviction or sentence on a question of law or fact, or committal for sentence.

Committal for trial on indictment Jury trial in the Crown Court.

MAGISTRATES' COURT

SUMMARY JURISDICTION

Trial of summary offences and other offences triable summarily with the consent of the accused.

COMMITTAL PROCEDURE

Initial procedural steps in respect of cases then committed for trial in the Crown Court.

THE PRINCIPAL COURTS EXERCISING CIVIL JURISDICTION

HOUSE of LORDS

'Leapfrog' appeal direct from the High Court provided:— (i) all parties consent, and (ii) a point of law of general public importance is involved relating to the construction of an enactment or on a point on which the trial judge was bound by precedent. Certificate of trial judge and leave of House of Lords required.

Appeal from the Court of Appeal only by leave of that court or the House of Lords

COURT of APPEAL
CIVIL DIVISION

Appeal from the High Court as of right, save in exceptional cases.

Appeal from the County Court as of right except in certain cases where leave is necessary (e.g. in contract and tort claims where value of appeal does not exceed £5,000)

HIGH COURT

Any division of the High Court may sit at any place in England or Wales, but sittings of the Queen's Bench and Family Divisions are regularly held at the Crown Court first-tier centres.

QUEEN'S BENCH DIVISION

Trial of civil actions relating to:— contract and tort and other matters not within the scope of the Family and Chancery Divisions. Two separate courts within the Division exercise jurisdiction over commercial matters and Admiralty matters. The Division supervises the operation of inferior courts and tribunals on applications for judicial review.

FAMILY DIVISION

Trial of defended matrimonial proceedings, and actions relating to legitimacy, validity of marriage, the Married Woman's Property Act 1882 and other matters relating to matrimonial disputes and children.

Appeals from Family Proceedings Courts (Magistrates' Courts) in family matters, (e.g. orders regarding children)

CHANCERY DIVISION

Trials of actions relating to:— mortgages, deeds, specific performance of contracts for the sale of land, partnerships, companies, bankruptcy, revenue matters and contentious probate business.

Divisional Court has certain limited jurisdiction consisting of appeals from the County Court in bankruptcy and land registration matters.

COUNTY COURT

JURISDICTION INCLUDES

(i) Actions in contract or tort (except defamation);
(ii) Equity matters (trusts, mortgages, partnerships etc.) where the value of the fund does not exceed £30,000;
(iii) Actions for recovering land;
(iv) Undefended and some defended matrimonial cases: proceedings under the Children Act 1989
(v) Bankruptcy.

Workload of the courts: Proceedings commenced
Comparative Tables[73]

	1938	1963	1977	1982	1989	1995
1. Appellate Courts						
Judicial Committee of						
the Privy Council	107	46	48	62	55	82
House of Lords:						
From courts in						
England & Wales	32	21	58	65	51	56
From elsewhere	11	18	6	6	12	16
Court of Appeal						
Civil Division	574	711	1,359	1,627	1,622	1,853
Criminal Division	—	2,065	6,399	6,674	7,076	8,187
High Court	263	484	1,029	1,482	2,535	4,674
2. Crown Court (disposals)						
Committals for trial	—	—	53,118	66,184	101,232	88,985
Committals for sentence	—	—	12,846	14,544	8,267	5,557
Appeals	—	—	15,497	20,775	16,860	26,062
3. High Court						
Chancery Division	9,826	16,137	14,651	17,119	30,813	42,251
Queen's Bench	83,641	123,998	176,128	164,396	288,287	153,624
4. Family matters						
(High Court, County Court						
and Family Proceedings						
Courts)						
Probate (grants issued)	149,752	—	251,703	279,127	231,883	248,947
Wardship	—	—	1,491	2,301	4,327	—
Adoption (orders made)	—	—	10,724	9,102	7,516	5,317
Public Law Applications	—	—	—	—	—	17,136
(Children)						
Private Law Applications	—	—	—	—	—	102,000
(Children)						
Dissolution of marriage	9,970	36,385	170,149	173,452	184,610	173,966
Nullity	263	919	1,095	921	478	881
Judicial separation	71	206	1,980	7,480	2,741	3,349
5. County Courts						
Plaints entered	1,262,402	1,543,324	1,673,966	2,048,568	2,615,508	2,445,248
Judgments on hearing	30,821	34,746	141,950	168,682	179,006	112,647
6. Magistrates' Courts						
Indictable offences	—	—	470,000	539,000	449,000	497,000
Summary offences	—	—	458,000	469,000	568,000	587,000
(excluding motoring)						
Motoring offences	—	—	1,165,000	1,214,000	847,000	863,000
7. Other courts and tribunals						
Restrictive Practices Court	—	33	4	0	10	11
Employment Appeal						
Tribunal	—	—	748	829	615	1,380

[73] Based on *Judicial Statistics 1995* (Cm. 3290, 1996) and earlier volumes, and (for magistrates' courts) *Criminal Statistics: England and Wales 1994* (Cm. 3010, 1995). Magistrates' courts figures are for 1994.

Table of Tribunals

General Subject Matter	Tribunal	Jurisdiction	Cases decided in 1994—England and Wales[74]	Number of Tribunals as at 31.12.94 England and Wales[74]
(a) *Social Administration* (1) Personal Welfare	Social Security Appeal Tribunals	National insurance; industrial injuries; others Income support; family credit; others	35,333[75] 36,634[75]	154[75]
	Social Security Commissioners	see p. 70	4,804	1 Chief Commissioner 14 full-time Commissioners
	Disability Appeal Tribunals	Appeals concerning disablement questions arising in claims for disability working allowance etc.	27,512[75]	139
	Medical Appeal Tribunals	Appeals concerning disablement questions arising in claims for disablement benefit etc.	15,516	36
	Mental Health Review Tribunals	Review of the compulsory admission to hospital of mental patients	6,750	9
	Vaccine Damage Payment Tribunals	Medical Appeal Tribunals specially constituted to review refusals of vaccine damage payments	14	8
	Child Support Appeal Tribunals	Appeals concerning orders to pay child maintenance	1,125	52
	Child Support Commissioners	Appeals from C.S.A.T.s	2	1 Chief Commissioner and 15 full-time Commissioners
(2) Pensions	Pensions Appeal Tribunals	Appeals from decisions of the Secretary of State for Social Security concerning war pensions	2,863	Ad hoc

(3) Education	Education Appeal Committees	Appeals against allocation of school places etc.	26,658	Not available
	Education Appeal Committees for Grant-Maintained Schools	Appeals against admissions or expulsion decisions	3,755	Not available
	Special Educational Needs Tribunal	Appeals in special educational needs cases	1	Not available
	Independent Schools Tribunals	Complaints concerning regulation of independent schools	0	1
(4) Employment	Industrial Tribunals	See pp. 63–66	21,003[76]	11 Regional offices with sittings in other centres as necessary
(5) National Health Service	Family Health Service Authorities and Service Committees	Complaints by patients of practitioner's failure to comply with terms of service	2,647	90 (FHSA) 360 (SC)
	National Health Service Tribunal	Appeals against a decision that a practitioner should be removed from the N.H.S.	2	1
(6) Immigration	Immigration Adjudicators	Appeals against decisions of Immigration Officers	26,774	1 Chief, 1 Deputy Chief, 24 full-time, 91 part-time
	Immigration Appeal Tribunal	Appeals from Immigration Officers and Adjudicators	7,148	1 sitting in 2 divs.
(7) Residential Care Homes	Registered Homes Tribunals	Appeals concerning the registration of residential care, nursing and children's homes	31	Ad hoc, drawn from a panel of 9 chairmen and 13 expert members
(b) *Economic matters* (8) Agriculture	Agricultural Land Tribunals	Disputes between landlord and tenant in respect of notice to quit, bad husbandry and drainage	48	8

Table of Tribunals

General Subject Matter	Tribunal	Jurisdiction	Cases decided in 1994—England and Wales[77]	Number of Tribunals as at 31.12.94 England and Wales[77]
	Arbitrators under the Agricultural Holdings Act 1988	Certain disputes over agricultural tenancies	255	Ad hoc[78]
	Dairy Produce Quota Tribunal	Appeals against milk quota decisions	1	1
	Meat Hygiene Appeal Tribunals	Appeals relating to the licensing of premises	1	1
	Commons Commissioners	Determination of claims in respect of common land	539	1 Chief Commissioner, 2 full-time Commissioners
	Plant Varieties and Seeds Tribunal	Disputes between citizens concerning plant variety rights	0	1
(9) Commerce	Comptroller of Patents	Adjudication in respect of patents, registered designs and trade marks	7,773	3
	Director-General of Fair Trading	Licensing decisions concerning consumer credit and estate agent activities	119	10
	Copyright Tribunal	Disputes between citizens concerning licences for copyright material	1	1
	Financial Services Tribunal[79]	References concerning authorisations to act as a practitioner concerning investment	3	1
	Data Protection Registrar	Registration of data users and computer bureaux	39,589	1
	Data Protection Tribunal	Appeals from the Registrar	0	1

Category	Tribunal	Function	Caseload	Composition
(10) Transport	Traffic Commissioners	Licensing of public service passenger vehicles	13,344	1 senior Commissioner and 6 Commissioners serving 8 regional traffic areas
		Licensing of goods vehicles	35,924	
	Transport Tribunal	Appeals from Traffic Commissioners	29	1
	Parking Adjudicators	Appeals in respect of wheelclamping	1, 247	1
	Civil Aviation Authority	Air transport and travel organisers' licensing; air navigation order appeals	1,494	1
(11) Housing	Rent assessment committees	Appeals concerning rents	14,252	Appointed ad hoc from 13 panels
	Rent Tribunals[80]	Disputes between landlord and tenant relating to the rent or security of tenure of certain dwellings	63	Appointed ad hoc from 13 panels
	Leasehold Valuation Tribunals[81]	Valuation of leaseholds for purposes of the Leasehold Reform Act 1967	148	Appointed ad hoc from 14 panels
(12) Foreign Compensation	Foreign Compensation Commission	Distribution of compensation from foreign governments	0	0
(c) *Revenue*				
(13) Taxation	Special and General Commissioners of Income Tax	Tax appeals	Special: 50 General: 215,000	Special: 1 presiding, 2 full-time, 11 deputy General: 392 Divisions
	V.A.T. and Duties Tribunals	V.A.T. appeals	1,580	2
	Tribunal for Part XVII of the Income and Corporation Taxes Act 1988	Nullification of tax advantages from certain transactions in securities, *e.g.* dividend-stripping	1	1

Table of Tribunals

General Subject Matter	Tribunal	Jurisdiction	Cases decided in 1994—England and Wales[82]	Number of Tribunals as at 31.12.94 England and Wales[82]
(14) Statutory Levies	Levy Exemption Referees	Disputes concerning refusal of industrial training boards to grant certificates of exemption from industrial training levy	0	1
	Betting Levy Appeal Tribunal	Appeals in respect of levy on bookmakers by the Horserace Betting Levy Board	0	1
(15) Property, Valuation and Rating	Valuation Tribunals[83]	Rating and council tax appeals	101,000[84]	Tribunals drawn from 64 panels
	Lands Tribunal	See pp. 94–95	206	1
	London Building Act Tribunal of Appeal	Appeals under the Acts	0	Ad hoc

[74] Figures from Annual Report of the Council on Tribunals for 1994–95 (1995–96 H. C. 64), Appendix E.

[75] These figures include Scotland.

[76] 21,645 cases were withdrawn or settled before a hearing.

[77] Figures from Annual Report of the Council on Tribunals for 1994–95 (1995–96 H.C. 64), Appendix E.

[78] Arbitrators are appointed *ad hoc* by the President of the Royal Institute of Chartered Surveyors (formerly by the Minister of Agriculture) from a panel of 431 members nominated by the Lord Chancellor.

[79] There is also an Insolvency Practitioners Tribunal under the Insolvency Act 1986 (1 case in 1994), a Banking Appeal Tribunal under the Banking Act 1987 (0 cases in 1994) and a Building Societies Appeal Tribunal under the Building Societies Act 1986 (0 cases in 1994).

[80] Under the Housing Act 1980, s.72, the functions of rent tribunals are to be performed by rent assessment committees, although when so acting the committees are to be known as "rent tribunals."

[81] Under the Housing Act 1980, s.142, rent assessment committees are established as leasehold valuation tribunals.

[82] Figures from Annual Report of the Council on Tribunals for 1994–95 (1995–96 H.C. 64), Appendix E.

[83] Formerly, Local Valuation Courts, then Valuation and Community Charge Tribunals.

[84] A further 657,000 cases were settled or withdrawn.

(housing benefit) who remain dissatisfied with their local authority's determination of their claims.[85]

E. PARTICULAR COURTS AND TRIBUNALS

In this section we consider the courts and tribunals that feature most prominently in the English legal system, by virtue either of their status in the hierarchy or their caseload. For reasons of space it is not possible to cover all tribunals in detail. We have not divided this section into "courts" and "tribunals" but have incorporated coverage of certain tribunals approximately in accordance with their position in the overall hierarchy.

1. MAGISTRATES' COURTS

(a) Introduction

Magistrates' courts are the inferior criminal courts. In addition they exercise certain family law, administrative law and minor civil functions. England and Wales is divided into "commission areas": each county,[86] the City of London, and five London commission areas (inner London, north-east London, south-east London, south-west London and Middlesex).[87] Each non-metropolitan county[88] and metropolitan district, the City of London, the inner London area and each outer London borough constitutes a "petty sessions area" unless it is divided into "petty sessional divisions" in which case each division constitutes a petty sessions area.[89] Each petty sessions area has its own "bench" of justices with an elected chairman and one or more deputy chairmen.[90] Each justice is a justice

---

[85] These Boards comprise members of the authority whose officers' decisions are in question. The claim of such Boards to be independent does not seem to be supportable.

[86] Including "preserved counties" (i.e. the counties before reorganisation) in Wales: Local Government (Wales) Act 1994, Sched. 2, para. 10(1), amending the 1979 Act, s.1., and see the Magistrates' Courts (Wales) (Consequences of Local Government Changes) Order 1996 (S.I. 1996 No. 675).

[87] Justices of the Peace Act 1979, ss.1, 2.

[88] Including preserved counties in Wales: see n. 86.

[89] ibid. s.4, as amended by the Local Government Act 1985, s.12. See the Local Government (Petty Sessional Divisions etc.) Order 1973 (S.I. 1973 No. 1593), as amended, and, for London, the Petty Sessional Divisions (Inner London) Order 1964 (S.I. 1964 No. 853), as amended, which divides the Inner London area into nine divisions and the Local Government (Magistrates' Courts etc.) Order 1986 (S.I. 1986 No. 399), which made provision for Outer London following the constitution of the Outer London boroughs as petty sessions areas by the Local Government Act 1985. See also the Petty Sessions Areas (Divisions and Names) Regulations 1988 (S.I. 1988 No. 1698), as amended by S.I. 1992 No. 709 and S.I. 1996 No. 576.

[90] See the Justices of the Peace (Size and Chairmanship of Bench) Rules 1995 (S.I. 1995 No. 971). The Home Office and the Lord Chancellor's Department have produced a joint paper on "The Size of Benches" (1986) 42 The Magistrate 118 (benches should normally have more than 12 justices, and have at least 134 planned sittings a year if they are not to be candidates for amalgamation; where a bench has more than 150 justices or 1,750 planning sittings, a stipendiary appointment (below, p. 211) should be considered).

of the peace for the commission area and not merely for the petty session area in which he or she normally sits.[91]

(b) Criminal jurisdiction

Magistrates' courts are involved in some way in virtually all criminal prosecutions. Proceedings may be commenced by a summons or an arrest warrant issued by a justice of the peace.[92] Magistrates' courts try those offences triable only summarily, and have responsibilities in the procedure whereby persons charged with offences triable only on indictment are transferred for trial in the Crown Court. Where proceedings are brought in respect of the intermediate category of offences "triable either way," the court must decide whether the offence appears more suitable for summary trial or for trial on indictment. Once this is decided, and subject to the right of the accused to insist on trial by a jury, the court proceeds either to summary trial or the transfer for trial procedure.[93]

A magistrates' court must be composed of at least two justices of the peace[94] unless there is express provision for a single justice to act,[95] as there is, for example, in the case of issuing a summons.[96] Stipendiary magistrates[97] normally sit alone.

(c) Criminal proceedings concerning children[98]

(i) Youth courts

A youth court[99] must be composed of not more than three justices, and must normally include a man and a woman.[1] The justices must be drawn from the youth court panel appointed by the justices for each petty sessions area at their

---

[91] 1979 Act, s.6. This facilitates the cross-remanding of cases from one petty sessions area to another within the same commission area: see *R. v. Avon Magistrates' Courts Committee, ex p. Bath Law Society* [1988] Q.B. 409.

[92] Magistrates' Courts Act 1980, s.1. The other methods of commencing proceedings are by an arrest without warrant and by a voluntary bill of indictment: see below, pp. 667–670, 749–750. Only this last method by-passes the magistrates' court. As to the geographical limits of the jurisdiction of magistrates' courts, see the 1980 Act, s.2, as amended.

[93] These proceedings are explained more fully in the chapters on criminal procedure.

[94] The office of justice of the peace is considered below, pp. 192–205.

[95] Magistrates' Courts Act 1980, s.121(1). Normally, three justices sit (three being the maximum: S.I. 1995 No. 971, r.3).

[96] *ibid.*, s.26, substituted by the Criminal Justice and Public Order Act 1994, Sched. 4, para. 38.

[97] See below, pp. 211–213.

[98] For research into the "consumer's" view of the former juvenile justice system see H. Parker *et al., Receiving Juvenile Justice* (1981).

[99] Prior to October 1, 1992, youth courts were known as juvenile courts; the change of name was effected by the Criminal Justice Act 1991, s.70. See generally Home Office Circular 30/1992, *Criminal Justice Act 1991: Young People and the Youth Court.* The main changes were that the youth court, not the magistrates' court, now deals with 17-year-olds, and new sentencing powers were conferred: see B. Gibson, (1992) *The Magistrate* 109 and *The Youth Court* (1992).

[1] The Youth Courts (Constitution) Rules 1954 (S.I. 1954 No. 1711), r.12. References to juvenile courts are to be construed as references to youth courts: Criminal Justice Act 1991, s.70(2).

annual meeting.[2] They must be "specially qualified for dealing with youth cases."[3] Each panel elects a chairman and deputy chairman, one of whom must normally preside over each youth court. Stipendiary magistrates are members of the panel *ex officio* although one may only sit alone if he or she thinks it inexpedient in the interests of justice for there to be an adjournment.[4] A court may be held in buildings set apart for the purpose, or, as is more usually the case, in a courtroom normally used for an adult magistrates' court.[5] However, a youth court may not sit in a room that has been or will be used within an hour by another court.[6]

(ii) Jurisdiction

Criminal proceedings may not be instituted against children who are under 10: it is conclusively presumed that they cannot be guilty of any offence.[7] Where children between 10 and 14 are prosecuted it must be proved that they were children of a "mischievous discretion", *i.e.* that they knew that what they were doing was legally or morally wrong. Young persons of 14 and over are regarded as fully responsible for their acts.

The former juvenile courts had jurisdiction in both criminal cases and care proceedings. However, the Children Act 1989 transferred care proceedings to the family proceedings courts.[8] Criminal proceedings against children and young persons[9] must normally take place in a youth court. The main exceptions are that an adult magistrates' court *must* deal with children or young persons (where they are charged jointly with an adult and *may* do so where different charges are made against an adult arising out of the same or connected circumstances or where either an adult or a child or young person is charged with aiding,

[2] Children and Young Persons Act 1933, Sched. 2. In London, the panels are appointed by the Lord Chancellor. In 1986, the Lord Chancellor, having accepted a recommendation from the Judicial Studies Board (see pp. 238–239), required a minimum of 12 sittings per annum for each panel member, with a suggested target of 15 sittings per annum.

[3] 1954 Rules, r.1. The rules do not specify any qualifications. The Home Secretary has suggested that they "should include some direct practical experience of dealing with young persons (*e.g.* through working with youth organisations, teaching or similar work) and a real appreciation of the surroundings and way of life of the children who are likely to come before courts." The most suitable age for first appointment would be between 30 and 40 and no one should normally be first appointed when over 50: Home Office Circular No. 138/1979, printed in *Clarke Hall and Morrison on Children* (10th ed., 1985), pp. E.390–399. See also Circulars 67/1982 (pp. E.514–523) and 61/1983 (pp. E.699–718).

[4] 1954 Rules, rr.2, 12(2). The growing use of stipendiaries for youth court work in London has been said to be against at least the spirit of this requirement: K. Gledhill, (1994) 138 S.J. 470.

[5] Guidance on the design of juvenile courts was given in Home Office Circular No. 39/1971 (*Clarke Hall and Morrison* (9th ed., 1979), pp. 1154–6).

[6] Children and Young Persons Act 1933, s.47, as amended by the 1963 Act, s.17.

[7] Children and Young Persons Act 1933, s.50, as amended by the 1963 Act, s.16(1). At common law the relevant age was seven. Section 4 of the Children and Young Persons Act 1969 provided for the age to be raised to 14, but was repealed, unimplemented, by the Criminal Justice Act 1991, s.72.

[8] See below.

[9] This term applies to children and young persons under 18. For most purposes under the 1933 Act "child" is defined as a person under 14 and "young person" as a person of 14 or over but under 18. The term "child" is differently defined for other purposes: see *Halsbury's Laws of England* (4th ed.) Vol. 24, para. 403.

abetting, causing, procuring, allowing or permitting the other's alleged offence.[10] The youth court will try the case summarily except (1) where the charge is murder or manslaughter in which case the child or young person *must* be transferred for trial in the Crown Court and (2) where the offence is one which carries a penalty for an adult of 14 years' imprisonment or more and the defendant is over 14, in which event the court *may* proceed to transfer for trial.[11]

Any person may institute criminal proceedings against a child or young person[12], but they must notify the appropriate local authority.[13]

(iii) Procedure

The procedure of youth courts is less formal than for adult magistrates' courts.[14] Only members and officers of the court, the parties, their lawyers, witnesses and other persons directly concerned, press, representatives, and other persons specially authorised may be present.[15] There are strict limits as to what may be reported.[16] In the case of children and young persons dealt with summarily the expression "finding of guilt" must be used instead of "conviction" and the expression "order made upon a finding of guilt" instead of "sentence".[17]

(d) Family proceedings

Magistrates have an extensive jurisdiction in family and child law matters.[18] The list includes powers to make orders for financial provision for, or the protection of, parties to a marriage and children of the family, orders under the Children Act 1989 and the Child Support Act 1991 and adoption orders. Proceedings concerning these matters used to be termed "domestic proceedings" and the courts when hearing them "domestic courts", but they were renamed "family proceedings" and "family proceedings courts" by the Children Act 1989.[19] The justices must be appointed from a family court panel constituted on a similar basis to the youth court panel.[20]

The law relating to child care was substantially altered by the 1989 Act,

---

[10] Children and Young Persons Act 1933, s.46, as extended by the 1963 Act, s.18. Applications for bail or for a remand may be heard by any justice or justices (1933 Act, s.46(2)). The adult magistrates' court will normally try the child or young person summarily but may proceed with a view to transferring him or her for trial in the Crown Court (Magistrates' Courts Act 1980, s.24, as amended) or remit for trial (*ibid.* s.29, as amended) or sentence (Children and Young Persons Act 1969, s.7(8)) in the youth court. Magistrates' Courts Act 1980, s.24, as amended.

[11] This enables the Crown Court to invoke the power under section 53(2) of the Children and Young Persons Act 1933 to impose a long sentence of detention.

[12] The provisions of section 5 of the Children and Young Persons Act 1969 which were to restrict private prosecutions were repealed, unimplemented, by the Criminal Justice Act 1991, s.72.

[13] 1969 Act, s.5(8), (9).

[14] See the Magistrates' Courts (Children and Young Persons) Rules 1992 (S.I. 1992 No. 2071).

[15] Children and Young Persons Act 1933, s.47, as amended by the Children and Young Persons Act 1963, s.17(2).

[16] 1933 Act, s.49, as substituted by the Criminal Justice and Public Order Act 1994, s.49.

[17] *ibid.* s.59.

[18] Magistrates' Courts Act 1980, s.65, as amended.

[19] *ibid.* s.67(1), as amended by the 1989 Act, Sched. 11, Pt. II, para. 8.

[20] *ibid.* s.66(1), as amended by the 1989 Act, Sched. 11, Pt. II, para. 8; the Family Proceedings Courts (Constitution) Rules 1991 (S.I. 1991 No. 1405); the Family Proceedings Courts (Constitution) (Metropolitan Area) Rules 1991 (S.I. 1991 No. 1426).

which re-stated the respective powers and responsibilities of parents, courts and local authorities. The courts have power to grant, *inter alia*, "contact orders" (replacing access orders) and "residence orders" (replacing custody orders) and a variety of emergency orders; the grounds on which care or supervision orders may be granted were simplified and narrowed.[21] The magistrates' courts, county courts and High Courts have concurrent jurisdiction under the 1989 Act and the Adoption Act 1976; the Lord Chancellor has power to make orders specifying the level of court and the description of court at which different classes of proceedings should be commenced, and makes provision for the transfer of proceedings.[22] Proceedings under the 1989 Act are normally to be commenced in the magistrates' court.[23] Most orders will, however, continue to be made in divorce or matrimonial proceedings which are commenced in the county court.[24]

The courts have power to make care or supervision orders in respect of children under 17 (16 if married), if they are satisfied that (a) the child is suffering or likely to suffer significant harm; and (b) this is attributable to (i) the care given to the child, or likely to be given to him or her if the order were not made, not being what it would be reasonable to expect a parent to give; or (ii) the child's being beyond parental control.[25] The welfare of the child is the paramount consideration, and the court must take other specified matters into account.[26] Under a care order, the child is taken into the care of the local authority; a supervision order places the child under the supervision of a designated local authority or a probation officer.[27]

(e) Civil jurisdiction

Apart from family proceedings, magistrates' courts have powers in relation to certain other civil matters, including enforcement of the payment of rates, the council tax, income tax and charges for supplies of gas, electricity and water. They also have an important jurisdiction in respect of the granting of liquor licences to public houses and clubs, and licences for bookmakers, betting offices, and premises for gaming and bingo. Finally, there is a vast number[28] of statutory provisions enabling appeals to be brought against administrative decisions of various kinds.

(f) Appeals[29]

Appeals lie from a magistrates' court either as of right to the Crown Court,[30] where proceedings take the form of a complete rehearing, or to the High Court

---

[21] See below.

[22] Children Act 1989, s.92 and Sched. 11; Courts and Legal Services Act 1990, s.9.

[23] Children (Allocation of Proceedings) Order 1991 (S.I. 1991 No. 1677, as amended by S.I. 1993 No. 624 and S.I. 1994 Nos. 2164 and 3138.

[24] See below, pp. 74–75, 91–92.

[25] Children Act 1989, Part IV.

[26] *ibid.* s.1.

[27] *ibid.* s.31.

[28] D. Price, *Appeals* (1982) pp. 53–96, including appeals against refusal of a petshop licence, of a driving licence or a knacker's yard licence, a notice requiring a fire certificate and a notice requiring that an earth closet be replaced by a water closet. For discussion of the jurisdiction of magistrates to entertain appeals concerned with the licensing of pilots see G. Browne, "The Admiralty Jurisdiction of Inner London Magistrates" (1987) 151 J.P.N. 23.

[29] See generally, Chap. 17, below.

[30] See below, pp. 79–85.

by a procedure whereby the magistrates state a case for the opinion of the High Court on a point of law. In family matters the appeal is heard by the Family Division, otherwise the appeal will lie to the Queen's Bench Division. Any further appeal from the High Court lies to the House of Lords in criminal cases and to the Court of Appeal and House of Lords in civil cases.

(g) Administration

Procedural rules are made by the Lord Chancellor after consultation with a Rule Committee, comprising the Lord Chief Justice, the President of the Family Division, the chief metropolitan stipendiary magistrate, and other persons appointed by the Lord Chancellor, who must include a justices' clerk, and specified lawyers.[31]

The administrative arrangements were substantially reformed by the Police and Magistrates' Courts Act 1994,[32] following the White Paper, *A New Framework for Local Justice.*[33] The previous arrangements were that there was a "magistrates' courts committee" for each non-metropolitan county, metropolitan district and outer London borough, and in Inner London (105 in total). Each committee was responsible for (*inter alia*) the appointment of staff and the provision of courses of instruction; it also determined what accommodation and equipment should be provided, although the actual provision was made by the local authority. The local authority met the committee's expenses, including salary. The responsible Department was the Home Office, which provided an 80 per cent grant. In the 1980s the Home Office took a greater interest in the management of the service and instituted a number of measures to encourage greater economy and efficiency.[34]

There was some debate as to whether magistrates' courts committees would be able to respond to the challenge of improving the management of the service.[35] A Home Office scrutiny[36] concluded that they would not, and recommended that they be replaced by a Magistrates' Courts Agency, an executive agency accountable to, but operationally independent of, the Home Office. The Scrutiny found the present arrangements had led to a service which was highly fragmented, lacked a coherent management structure and failed to deliver value for money. Instead, there should be a national service, funded entirely by the government, but with maximum delegation of managerial responsibility and control of resources to the local level. Overall policy responsibility should rest with government, but the service should not be administered directly by a government

---

[31] Magistrates' Courts Act 1980, s.144, and see also ss.145–146; s.144, as amended by the Courts and Legal Services Act 1990, Sched. 18, para. 25(7), requires the appointment of one person with a Supreme Court qualification under s.71 of the 1990 Act, and one with the right to conduct litigation in the Supreme Court.

[32] ss.69–92.

[33] Cm.1829, 1992.

[34] See generally, J. W. Raine, *Local Justice* (1989), Chap. 5.

[35] J. W. Raine, (1986) 150 J.P.N. 260, 280: J. Bowden and J. W. Raine, (1988) 152 J.P.N. 489, 501, 521.

[36] *Magistrates' Courts: Report of A Scrutiny 1989* (HMSO, 1989 (the Le Vay Scrutiny)). For reactions, see (1989) 153 J.P.N. 489, 553, 627–8, 660–1; T. Kavanagh, *ibid.* p. 589; R. Burriss, *ibid.*, p. 655; W. M. S. Tildesley, *ibid.*, p. 670; J. W. Raine, *ibid.*, p. 684; R. L. Jones, (1990) 154 J.P.N. 538. Coopers & Lybrand Deloitte were commissioned to cost the options for change: *ibid.* p. 666. *Cf.* the less radical proposals of the Justices' Clerks Society: *Administering Magistrates' Courts: The Role of the Justices' Clerk* (1989).

department, so as to minimise the risk of government interference in judicial decision-making.

In the event, the government decided against establishing a national service, in view of the cost and the widespread opposition to the proposal among magistrates and court staff.[37] Instead, the White Paper proposed that responsibility for the service be transferred to the Lord Chancellor's Department (the Lord Chancellor already being responsible for the appointment of magistrates[38]). Magistrates' courts committees should have a more clearly defined management role, with a wider range of membership and effective administrative support. Area services should be combined, moving in due course from 105 to 50 or 60 management units. Committees should also be smaller in size; senior managers should have clearer personal accountability to committees for performance standards, in the context of systematic planning and performance review and a new overall policy framework. Finally, a magistrates' courts inspectorate should be established. Steps already in train were the introduction of cash limits to the grant from April 1992, a major programme of management training, the development of a standard court computer system, the formation of a best practice group to issue guidance and a review of court procedure.[39] Furthermore, committees would be encouraged to produce strategic plans.

The necessary legislative changes were made by the Police and Magistrates' Courts Act 1994.[40] There continues to be a magistrates' court committee for each non-metropolitan county, metropolitan district and outer London borough, the Inner London area and the City of London.[41] However, the Lord Chancellor now has power, after consultation, to combine or otherwise alter committee areas (previously a "joint committee area" of two or more existing areas could be established but only on the application of the committees concerned.)[42]

Each committee is to comprise magistrates for the area to which the committee relates, chosen by a selection panel constituted in accordance with regulations made by the Lord Chancellor.[43] It may also include not more than two other members (who need not be justices) co-opted by the committee with the approval of, or appointed by, the Lord Chancellor.[44] The total number of members must not exceed 12.[45] Each committee is responsible for the efficient and effective administration of the magistrates' courts for its area, including the allocation of administrative responsibilities among the justices' chief executive, the justices' clerks and the committee's staff, and the determination of the administrative procedures. Committees may be given directions by the Lord Chancellor and may be required to submit reports and plans to him.[46] Each

[37] See White Paper, Cm.1829, p. 5.
[38] See below, pp. 194–201.
[39] Cm.1829, pp. 3, 4.
[40] See S. Baker and J. English, *A Guide to the Police and Magistrates' Courts Act 1994* (1994).
[41] Justices of the Peace Act 1979, 19, as amended by the Local Government Act 1985, s.12 and the 1994 Act, Sched. 8, para. 4.
[42] 1994 Act, s.69. The programme of amalgamation has commenced. The first group included Berkshire and Oxfordshire; Bradford, Kirklees and Wakefield; Gwyned and Clwyd; and Mid and South Glanorgan.
[43] See the Magistrates' Courts Committees (Constitution) Regulations 1994 (S.I. 1994 No.2811), made under the 1979 Act, s.21, as amended by the 1994 Act, s.71.
[44] 1979 Act, s.20, substituted by the 1994 Act, s.70.
[45] By S. I. 1994 No.2811, reg. 11. This includes any co-opted or appointed members, unless the Lord Chancellor otherwise directs.
[46] 1979 Act, s.22A, 24C, inserted by the 1994 Act, ss.73, 74.

committee must appoint a justices' chief executive from a short-list of one or more persons approved by the Lord Chancellor to act as clerk to the committee and carry on its day-to-day administration. The committee also appoints one or more justices' clerk.[47]

Fears of a threat to judicial independence were met by the provision that justices' clerks and the staff of magistrates' courts committees are not subject to the directions of the committee or the justices' chief executive (acting as such) in giving advice to justices of the peace in individual cases or exercising functions under magistrates' courts rules.[48]

Financial support is still to be provided by local authorities with an 80% grant from the Lord Chancellor's Department.[49] The "paying authority"[50] or authorities must provide the accommodation, and the goods and services, proper for the performance of the magistrates, or justices' clerks for the area, unless the committee gives notice that it intends to obtain any item(s) otherwise than from the authority (or authorities). The accommodation to be provided, the salaries to be paid and the nature and amount of expenses to be incurred are to be determined by the committee after consultation with the paying authority; a paying authority aggrieved by such a determination may appeal to the Lord Chancellor, whose decision is binding.

The Lord Chancellor may appoint H. M. Inspectors of the Magistrates' Courts Service and has wide default powers.[51] The Inspectorate has commenced its programme of work and early reports have contained many detailed recommendations, most (but not all) of which have been accepted by the committee concerned.[52]

Overall, the way is now open for the government to reinforce its key aims of "enhancing accountability, reducing idiosyncrasy, and increasing efficiency", by adopting the twin strategies of "curbing the autonomy of the professionals" by standardising procedures and "curbing the autonomy of the agencies" by forming them into amalgamated hierarchies and establishing systems of objectives and targets.[53] Whether these developments in fact threaten the quality of justice is a theme to which we will return.

Justices form part of the membership of the probation committees that are responsible, under the overall supervision of the Home Office, for the Probation Service.[54] Probation officers have responsibilities in connection with probation orders, supervision orders for young offenders, suspended sentence supervision orders, community service orders, the after-care of persons released from cus-

---

[47] 1979 Act, ss.24D, 24E, 25, inserted by the 1994 Act, ss.75, 76. See the Justices' Chief Executive and Justices' Clerks (Appointment) Regulations 1995 (S.I. 1995 No.686), and further, below, pp. 205–210.

[48] 1979 Act, s.30A, inserted by the 1994 Act, s.78.

[49] 1979 Act, ss.55, 56, substituted by the 1994 Act, s.83.

[50] i.e. any unitary authority or any county other than a unitary authority whose area comprises all or part of the area to which the committee relates: 1979 Act, s.55(10), as substituted.

[51] 1979 Act, s.62A, inserted by the 1994 Act, s.85; and the 1994 Act, ss.86–88.

[52] See Annual Reports of the Magistrates' Courts Service Inspectorate; reports on individual committees are published. The report on Derbyshire was particularly critical; in return the Committee stated that "there had been inconsistencies of approach among the Inspectors and that the overview had been "unbalanced".

[53] J. W. Raine and M. J. Willson, Managing Criminal Justice (1993), p. 209 and passim.

[54] See the Probation Services Act 1993, ss.1–11; F. V. Jarvis, Probation Service Manual (5th ed., 1993); M. Vizard, (1986) 150 J. P. N. 299; A. Rich and J. Waters, (1989) 45 The Magistrate 77; D. E. R. Faulkner, (1989) 153 J. P. N. 606.

tody and the preparation of pre-sentence reports and reports concerning the custody of children and the selection of prisoners for parole. They also provide a welfare service in family cases, and work in prison establishments. The organisation of the service is in the process of change. The Criminal Justice Act 1991[55] put H. M. Inspectorate of Probation on a statutory footing, introduced a new default power exercisable by the Secretary of State and provided for a single probation area in Inner London. Other decisions have been made to retain the probation service as a local service, to subject current expenditure to a cash limit, to amalgamate probation areas, to reduce the size of probation committees and the proportion of members who are justices, and to improve liaison.[56] These changes are closely analogous to those affecting magistrates' courts committees. One or more probation liaison committees has to be established for each petty sessions area, with the responsibility of reviewing the work of probation officers.[57]

2. INDUSTRIAL TRIBUNALS[58]

Industrial tribunals were first established by the Industrial Training Act 1964 to hear appeals by employers assessed for levy payable to an industrial training board. They were then given jurisdiction over disputes about redundancy pay. The Royal Commission on Trade Unions and Employers' Associations[59] recommended that the tribunal's jurisdiction should be enlarged to comprise, subject to certain limitations, all disputes between the individual worker and employer, the primary aim being to make available "a procedure which is easily accessible, informal, speedy and inexpensive, and which gives them the best possible opportunities of arriving at an amicable settlement of their differences."[60] To an extent this recommendation has been fulfilled and the jurisdiction of industrial tribunals has steadily expanded. In addition to the points already mentioned industrial tribunals have jurisdiction in respect of complaints of unfair dismissal,[61] questions as to terms required to be included in a contract

---

[55] ss.73–75.
[56] See *Organising Supervision of Punishment in the Community: A Decision Document* (Home Office, H M S O, 1991), which followed a Green Paper, *Supervision and Punishment in the Community* (Cm.966, 1990). The Green Paper had put forward for consultation the option of establishing a single, national, centrally run probation service, but the government ultimately decided "that for the time being the service will remain locally structured" noting the overwhelming view of respondents that the service can operate most effectively as a local service: *Decision Document*, pp. 2,3.
[57] Probation Service Act 1993, ss.12, 13. See B. Caddick, "Where Next with Liaison" (1995) 42 *Probation Journal* 135.
[58] See K. Whitesides and G. Hawker, *Industrial Tribunals* (1975); M. J. Goodman, *Industrial Tribunals: Practice and Procedure* (4th ed., 1987); *Sweet & Maxwell's Encyclopedia of Employment Law*, Part A7; JUSTICE Report, *Industrial Tribunals* (1987); L. Dickens, *et al.*, *Dismissed: A Study of Unfair Dismissal and the Industrial Tribunal System* (1987); A. M. Leonard, *Judging Inequality* (Cobden Trust., 1987); Green Paper, *Resolving Employment Rights Disputes: Options for Reform* (Cm. 2707, 1994).
[59] Cmnd. 3623, 1968: Chairman: Lord Donovan.
[60] *ibid.*, para. 572.
[61] Employment Rights Act 1996, ss.94–134.

of employment,[62] claims to equal pay,[63] appeals against improvement notices or prohibition notices served by a health and safety inspector[64] and certain complaints relating to sex[65] and race[66] discrimination. Apart from matters arising between employer and employee, they also handle claims by individuals against trade unions for unreasonable exclusion or expulsion in closed shop situations and claims for compensation in respect of pressure on the employer to take action against an individual by reason of membership or non-membership of a union.[67] An important recent development has been the extension[68] and (long-delayed) implementation[69] of the Lord Chancellor's power to confer jurisdiction on industrial tribunals in respect of claims for damages for breach of or for a sum due under a contract of employment or other contracts connected with employment.[70]

The tribunals sit at over 50 centres, grouped under 13 Regional Offices of Industrial Tribunals and the Central Office of Industrial Tribunals in London. There is a President of Industrial Tribunals (England and Wales) who both sits as a chairman and has important administrative responsibilities in relation to the system.[71] Each tribunal has a legally qualified chairman and two "wing" members.[72]

A common criticism of industrial tribunals has been that they have become increasingly "legalistic":

"First, it is observed that the immense quantity of case law reported and cited in the courts is complicating the work of tribunals. Secondly, statutes, which were intended to be straightforward enactments, are increasingly being subjected to subtle lawyers' reasoning."[73]

Lord Denning M.R. suggested that some limit be placed on the reporting of cases:

"If we are not careful, we shall find the Industrial Tribunals bent down

---

[62] *ibid.* s.11, as amended.
[63] Equal Pay Act 1970, as amended.
[64] Health and Safety at Work etc. Act 1974, ss.21–24.
[65] Sex Discrimination Act 1975, ss.63, 72, 73.
[66] Race Relations Act 1976, s.54.
[67] Trade Union and Labour Relations (Consolidation) Act 1992, ss.146, 150, 160.
[68] By the Trade Union and Labour Relations Act 1993, s.38. The only exclusion is a claim for damages or a sum due in respect of personal injuries.
[69] Industrial Tribunals Extension of Jurisdiction (England and Wales) Order 1994 (S.I. 1994 No.1623). An industrial tribunal may not order the payment of an amount exceeding £25,000: *ibid.* art.10.
[70] Employment Protection (Consolidation) Act 1978, s.131, as amended; see now the Industrial Tribunals Act 1996, s.3.
[71] See the Industrial Tribunals (Constitution and Rules of Procedure) Regulations 1993 (SI. 1993 No.2687).
[72] See below, pp. 215–216. A tribunal may comprise the chairman and one lay member if both parties consent. The chairman may sit alone, *e.g.* to deal with interlocutory matters and certain applications for interlocutory relief; powers to sit alone were extended significantly by the Trade Union Reform and Employment Rights Act 1993, s.36 (see now the Industrial Tribunals Act 1996, s.4) and proposals for further extensions are contained in the Green Paper, *Resolving Employment Rights Disputes: Options for Reform* (Cm.2707, 1994), pp. 41–43 (possibly to require chairmen to sit alone in all cases except those involving discrimination or unfair dismissal, and to give a discretion to sit alone in unfair dismissal cases).
[73] R. Munday, "Tribunal Lore: Legalism and the Industrial Tribunals" (1981) 10 I.L.J. 146, 147.

under the weight of the law books or, what is worse, asleep under them. Let principles be reported, but not particular instances."[74]

On the other hand, it has been suggested that growing "legalism" is inevitable given that the legislation is in fact complex and interpretative difficulties unavoidable, that there is a legally qualified chairman, that legal representation is increasingly common, that in practice litigants require consistency in decision-making, and that there must be a reliable yardstick for the conciliatory procedures incorporated in the legislation to work:

"Naturally, tribunals will continue to dispense with the flummery and much of the procedural and evidential paraphernalia of the law courts—in this sense they are informal and comparatively free. But in most important respects, tribunals do closely resemble courts. Thus, if charges of legalism mean that they interpret the law in legal fashion, one would expect to find these charges fully proven for it is quite impossible to see how else tribunals could be expected to behave."[75]

A JUSTICE Report on Industrial Tribunals[76] made a number of proposals for change. For the vast majority of cases the investigative approach should be improved, so as to reduce the need for representation, while, for a minority of cases, the adversarial system should be improved by providing legal aid for representation and establishing an upper tier Industrial Court, with senior chairmen and members, to hear them. The Industrial Court would also assume the appellate functions of the Employment Appeal Tribunal. The Committee confirmed that industrial tribunals did have a number of advantages over ordinary courts, being more accessible, less formal, more expeditious, less expensive and possessed of special expertise.[77] However, complaints of excessive "legalism" were to an extent justified. One cause was the present state of substantive employment law, which was in need of clarification and consolidation in a comprehensible form. The other main cause was the adversarial system which was a major obstacle to informality in the conduct of hearings.[78] The Committee also noted that research indicated that industrial tribunals were particularly weak in understanding and applying the legislation concerning complaints of sex or race discrimination.[79] Special training was necessary for chairmen and members who dealt with such cases.[80]

Some of those points have been addressed in the government's Green Paper,

---

[74] *Walls Meat Co. Ltd v. Khan* [1979] I.C.R. 52, 57, *cf.* Lawton L.J. in *Clay Cross (Quarry Services) Ltd v. Fletcher* [1979] 1 All E.R. 474, 479.

[75] Munday, *op. cit.* p. 159. On the procedure of industrial tribunals see below, pp. 653–661, 808–809.

[76] Chairman: Bob Hepple (1987). See also R. Lewis and J. Clark, *Employment Rights, Industrial Tribunals and Arbitration* (1993), which argues the case for the introduction of voluntary arbitration as an option for unfair dismissal cases, as one response to the legalism of tribunals. *Cf.* the Green Paper, *Resolving Employment Rights Disputes* (1994), pp. 31–33, developing Lewis and Clark's proposal, incorporating a right of appeal on grounds of perversity on the facts or on the interpretation of the law.

[77] pp. 7–9.

[78] Chap. 2.

[79] V. C. Kumar, *Industrial Tribunal Applicants under the Race Relations Act 1976* (Commission for Racial Equality 1986); A. Leonard, *Judging Inequality* (1987).

[80] pp. 35–38.

Resolving Employment Rights Disputes: Options for Reform.[81] The consolidation of individual employment rights legislation has been promised and developments in training encouraged. However, the main thrust of the proposals (some firm, others for discussion) is the improvement of efficiency in the disposal of an ever-increasing workload.[82] It is also suggested that the tribunals be renamed employment tribunals.

Appeals lie on a point of law[83] in most cases to the Employment Appeal Tribunal,[84] and in the others[85] to the Queen's Bench Division.

3. THE EMPLOYMENT APPEAL TRIBUNAL

The Employment Appeal Tribunal[86] was established by the Employment Protection Act 1975[87] as the successor of the politically controversial National Industrial Relations Court, inheriting the latter's appellate functions. Its membership comprises judges of the High Court or Court of Appeal[88] nominated by the Lord Chancellor, at least one judge of the Court of Session nominated by the Lord President of that court, and lay members appointed by the Queen on the recommendation of the Lord Chancellor and the Secretary of State, being persons who "appear . . . to have special knowledge or experience of industrial relations, either as representatives of employers or as representatives of workers."[89] One of the judges is appointed President. Each appeal is normally heard by a judge sitting with two or four lay members[90] Decisions can be by a majority, and the judge can be outvoted, even on a point of law, by the lay members. The E.A.T. hears appeals from industrial tribunals and from the Certification Officer, who performs various functions in respect of trade unions, mostly on points of law. The Court of Appeal has expressed the view that the E.A.T. has taken too wide a view of what constitutes an error of law and has thus interfered too readily

---

[81] Cm. 2707, 1994. See D. Cockburn, (1995) 24 I.L.J. 285.

[82] *e.g.* by introducing greater powers to dismiss hopeless cases both at a pre-hearing review (below, p. 646) and at the hearing; to decide cases on written evidence where both parties consent. Views were sought on (*inter alia*) the extension of provisions for chairmen to sit alone (n. 72 above) and whether tribunals should have express powers to time-limit proceedings.

[83] Fact or law where the question is whether a person has been unreasonably excluded or expelled from membership of a trade union in a closed shop situation.

[84] See below.

[85] *e.g.* industrial training levy assessments, appeals against an improvement or prohibition notice.

[86] A superior court of record. See Phillips J., "Some notes on the Employment Appeal Tribunal" (1978) 7 I.L.J. 137; Browne-Wilkinson J., "The role of the EAT in the 1980s" (1982) 11 I.L.J. 69; Sir John Waite, "Lawyers and Laymen as Judges in Industry" (1986) 15 I.L.J. 32 Sir John Wood, (1990) 19 I.L.J. 133; and below, pp. 245–246.

[87] See now the Industrial Tribunals Act 1996, ss.20–28.

[88] Only the former have so far been nominated. In 1994 there were nine High Court judges (including the President) and one judge of the Court of Session nominated to the E.A.T.

[89] The lay members do not in practice act in a partisan manner.

[90] Normally, there should be equal numbers of members whose knowledge etc. is as representative of employers or of workers; however, an appeal may be heard by a judge and one or three members with the consent of the parties, and certain appeals may be heard by a judge alone or (in cases of national security), the President alone: Trade Union Reforms and Employment Rights Act 1993, s.37; see now the Industrial Tribunals Act 1996, s.28.

with the decisions of industrial tribunals.[91] It suggested that the E.A.T. should be less ready to lay down "guidelines" for industrial tribunals. For example, whether a dismissal is "fair" should essentially be regarded as a question of fact. The consequent advantage of greater flexibility for industrial tribunals has to be balanced against the consequent inconsistency amongst them.[92]

Appeals lie on a point of law from the E.A.T. to the Court of Appeal,[93] with the leave of either court.

4. SOCIAL SECURITY TRIBUNALS[94]

A variety of cash benefits are available under the Social Security Contributions and Benefits Act 1992. These include contributory benefits (*e.g.* unemployment benefit, incapacity benefit, maternity allowance, widow's benefit, retirement pension); non-contributory benefits (*e.g.* attendance allowance, severe disablement allowance, invalid care allowance, disability living allowance, guardian's allowance); disablement benefit; and income-related benefits (income support, family credit, disability working allowance, housing benefit and council tax benefit).[95] Child benefit is payable under the Child Benefit Act 1975. Several tribunals have been established to determine questions arising in the administration of these benefits.

Two discernible trends in the development of the structure of social security tribunals have been, first, the amalgamation of different tribunal jurisdictions and, secondly, the integration of tribunals within the court system. However most recently there has also been a tendency for the government to restrict rights of appeal to an independent tribunal against decisions concerning benefits.

(a) The position to 1984

Prior to 1984, a distinction was drawn between the schemes based on the insurance principle, where entitlement to benefit depended on the claimant having made appropriate contributions and otherwise falling within the rules of the scheme, and the provision of means-tested benefits involving the exercise of discretion. As regards the former, claims and questions arising under the Social Security Act 1975 and the Child Benefit Act 1975 were determined initially by an insurance officer appointed by the Secretary of State for Social Services or, for unemployment benefit, by the Secretary of State for Employ-

---

[91] See *Retarded Children's Aid Society v. Day* [1978] I.C.R 437; *Methven v. Cow Industrial Polymers Ltd* [1980] I.C.R. 463; *Pedersen v. Camden London B.C.* [1981] I.C.R. 674; *Woods v. W. M. Car Services (Peterborough) Ltd* [1982] I.C.R. 693; and the articles cited in n. 86 above. See also *O'Kelly v. Trusthouse Forte plc* [1983] I.C.R. 728.

[92] See Browne-Wilkinson J., *op. cit.* n. 86, p. 72: ". . . there are signs that . . . Industrial Tribunals are beginning to demonstrate a lack of uniformity in their approach to what constitutes fair industrial practice." His Lordship suggested that it would be desirable to aim for a middle way between the early practice of the E.A.T. and the restrictive approach of the Court of Appeal.

[93] In Scotland, appeals lie to the Court of Session.

[94] See generally N. J. Wikeley, *Ogus, Barendt and Wikeley's, The Law of Social Security* (4th ed., 1995), Chap. 17.

[95] 1992 Act, ss.20, 63, 94, 123.

ment. An appeal lay to a National Insurance Local Tribunal,[96] comprising a legally qualified chairman,[97] the member from a panel representing employers and self-employed earners and one from a panel representing employed earners.[98] As regards the latter, tribunals were first set up in the 1930s and subsequently evolved into Supplementary Benefit Appeal Tribunals. These comprised a chairman appointed by the Secretary of State from a panel drawn up by the Lord Chancellor, one "ordinary member" from a panel appointed by the Secretary of State from people "appearing to have knowledge or experience of conditions in the area to which the panel relates and of the problems of people living on low incomes" and one from a panel "appearing . . . to represent work people.[99] The procedures and decision-making of S.B.A.T.s were contrasted unfavourably with those of N.I.L.T.s.[1]

(b) Social Security Appeal Tribunals

In 1980 the supplementary benefit scheme was reformed, with detailed rules of entitlement replacing discretions, thereby bringing it closer in form to the national insurance scheme.[2] The Health and Social Services and Social Security Adjudications Act 1983[3] provided for the merger of the two adjudication systems. Most claims are now submitted to an "adjudication officer" appointed by the Secretary of State for Social Security (including some officers of the Department of Employment to deal with unemployment benefit).[4] There is a Chief Adjudication Officer, who is required to advise adjudication officers and keep their work under review, and to report annually to the Secretary of State on standards of adjudication.[5]

Appeals lie to a Social Security Appeal Tribunal,[6] which now exercises the jurisdictions formerly exercised by N.I.L.T.s and S.B.A.T.s. S.S.A.T.s are organised in six regions, each headed by a Regional Chairman, and the whole system is headed by the President of Social Security Appeal Tribunals Medical Appeal Tribunals and Disability Appeal Tribunals (now generally known as the President of the Independent Tribunal Service).[7] The President must be a lawyer of not less than 10 years' standing, and the regional and other full-time chairmen of not less than five years' standing. All are appointed by the Lord Chancellor. There is also a panel of part-time chairmen appointed by the Lord Chancellor

---

[96] This term did not appear in the legislation, but was the title commonly used. Another label sometimes found was "Social Security Local Tribunal".
[97] This was not a legal requirement but was the almost invariable practice: see below, p. 215.
[98] Social Security Act 1975, s.97(2): see below, p. 216.
[99] Supplementary Benefits Act 1976, Sched. 4.
[1] See the first edition of this book, pp. 55–57.
[2] Social Security Act 1980, Sched. 2.
[3] Sched. 8: in force from April 23, 1984. See J. Mesher, (1983) 10 J.L.S. 135; M. Partington, "The Restructuring of SSATs: a Personal View" in C. Harlow (ed.), *Public Law and Politics* (1986), Chap. 9.
[4] Social Security Administration Act 1992, ss.20, 21, 38.
[5] *ibid.* s.39 See R. Sainsbury, "The Social Security Chief Adjudication Officer: The First Four Years" [1989] P. L. 323.
[6] *ibid.* ss.22, 40, 41, Sched. 2.
[7] The first President was Judge H. J. Byrt, who held the office from 1984: see J. Fulbrook, (1989) 18 I.L.J. 177; Interview, *Legal Action*, September 1989, p. 7; he was succeeded by Judge Derek Holden (1989–1992), Judge Anthony Thorne (1992–1994) and Judge Keith Bassingthwaite (1994–). On the role of the Independent Tribunal Service see I.T.S., *Appeals: What to expect from our Service* (a booklet for appellants).

or the Lord President of the Court of Session under the Tribunals and Inquiries Act 1992.[8] These must be a lawyer of not less than five years' standing.[9] There is a single panel of members constituted by the President for the whole of Great Britain. Each tribunal comprises a chairman, nominated by the President, and two members. The President is also responsible for assigning clerks to tribunals, and it is the duty of the clerk to summon members from the panel. In practice, arrangements are made by staff at the Regional Chairman's office.

(c) Other adjudicating bodies

Certain questions, including whether a person is an "earner", whether he or she is "employed" or "self-employed" and whether he or she complies with "contribution conditions" necessary for receipt of contributory benefits, are still determined by the Secretary of State: in practice by a member of the DSS Solicitors' Office.[10] The Secretary of State may refer a point of law, and a dissatisfied claimant may appeal on such a point, to the High Court.

Certain questions concerning disablement benefit are determined by "Medical Boards" of two medical practitioners, which also hear certain appeals on medical questions from the decisions of a medical practitioner, or adjudication officers. There is a right of appeal to a Medical Appeal Tribunal, comprising a legally qualified chairman and two doctors of consultant status.[11]

Claims to disability living allowance, disability working allowance and attendance allowance are determined by adjudication officers, with advice on medical questions from doctors employed by the Benefits Agency Medical Service.[12] There is then a right to apply for a review[13], and then to appeal on medical issues ("disability questions") to a Disability Appeal Tribunal[14] or on other matters to a S.S.A.T.[15] A D.A.T. comprises a legally qualified chairman appointed by the Lord Chancellor,[16] and two members appointed by the President, one from a panel of medical practitioners and the other from a panel of persons (not medical practitioners) who are experienced in dealing with the needs of disabled persons in a professional or voluntary capacity or because they are themselves disabled.[17] The President nominates the members of particular tribunals.[18]

Appeals in connection with decisions concerning the maintenance of children go before the Child Support Appeal Tribunals, whose composition is the same as for S.S.A.T.s[19] The structure mirrors that of the social security tribunals, with the President of S.S.A.T.s, M.A.T.s and D.A.T.s also appointed as President of

---

[8] s.6.

[9] By virtue of the Courts and Legal Services Act 1990, Sched. 10, para. 37, the qualifications in England became, respectively, a 10 year (President) and 5 year (Chairmen) general qualification under s.71 of the Act, *i.e.* a right of audience in any part of the Supreme Court or in all proceedings in county courts or magistrates' courts.

[10] Social Security Administration Act 1992, ss.17, 18.

[11] *ibid.* s.50, Sched. 2.

[12] *ibid.*, ss.21(3).

[13] *ibid.*, ss.30–32.

[14] See N. Wikeley, (1992) 11 C. J. Q. 227.

[15] 1992 Act., s.33.

[16] With the same rules for eligibility as chairman of S.S.A.T.s and M.A.T.s.

[17] 1992 Act, s.42.

[18] *ibid.*, s.43.

[19] Child Support Act 1991, ss.20, 21.

the Child Support Appeal Tribunals,[20] and provision for the appointment of a Chief Child Support Commissioner and other Child Support Commissioners.[21] These tribunals are distinctive in that they handle disputes (possibly acrimonious ones) between private individuals.

(d) Social Security Commissioners[22]

The National Insurance Commissioners heard appeals from N.I.L.T.s, and appeals on a point of law from Medical Appeal Tribunals and the Attendance Allowance Board. In 1980, a right of appeal on a point of law was created from S.B.A.T.s to the Commissioner,[23] who were renamed Social Security Commissioners.[24] From April 23, 1984, they have heard appeals from S.S.A.T.s and from 1987 these have been restricted to points of law in all cases.[25] At present there is a Chief Social Security Commissioner and 16 Commissioners.[26] In practice three sit in Edinburgh, the others in London, although they may travel to Cardiff or Liverpool to hear cases. The Chief Commissioner may convene a Tribunal of three Commissioners to hear an appeal involving a point of law of special difficulty. He is also responsible for selecting the decisions that are to be reported. Until 1980, the only further possibility of review was an application for judicial review. There is now a right of appeal on a point of law to the Court of Appeal, with the leave of the Commissioner or the court. From 1985, they have been adminis-tered by the Lord Chancellor's Department. The Social Security Com-missioners have also been appointed as Child Support Commissioners under the Child Support Act 1991.

(e) Limitation of rights of appeal

Reforms to the social security system under Part III of the Social Security Act 1986 included the replacement of lump sum "single payments" and "urgent need payments" under the supplementary benefit legislation by pay-ments from the, cash-limited, Social Fund. In one sense this involved a return to a system of discretionary payments. The payments, most in the form of loans, are made by social fund officers appointed by the Secretary of State. In practice, however, the detailed directions given to the officers by the Secretary of State operate very much in the manner of regulations.[27] Controversially, the government decided that there should be no rights of

---

[20] *ibid.*, Sched. 3, para. 1.

[21] *ibid.*, s.22, Sched. 4.

[22] See R. Micklethwait, *The National Insurance Commissioners* (1976); N. Harris, (1993) 22 I. L. J. 222. Under the 1946 legislation there was a National Insurance Commissioner and an Industrial Injuries Commissioner, each with several deputies. The same man commonly held appointments under both schemes. In 1966, these posts were merged, the National Insurance Commissioner was retitled the Chief National Insurance Commissioner, and the deputies became full Commissioners.

[23] Supplementary Benefits Act 1976, s.15A, inserted by the Social Security Act 1979, s.6. This replaced an appeal from S.B.A.T.s to the High Court that had been created in 1978.

[24] Social Security Act 1980, s.14.

[25] Social Security Administration Act 1992, s.23.

[26] The same qualifications are specified as for appointment as President of S.S.A.T.s, M.A.T.s and D.A.T.s above: *ibid*, s.52.

[27] See *R. v. Secretary of State for Social Services, ex p. Stitt, The Times*, July 5, 1990.

appeal within the tribunals system.[28] The legislation provides instead for internal review by social fund inspectors, who are DSS officials appointed as inspectors by the Social Fund Commissioner. The Commissioner is in turn appointed by the Secretary of State. The inspectors are subject to the guidance and directions issued to the social fund officers.[29]

5. COUNTY COURTS

(a) Establishment

The present county courts were originally established by the County Courts Act 1846. This Act followed a lengthy campaign, which aroused hostility in several quarters, including the Bar and certain large London solicitors' firms.[30] The hostility was based essentially on fears of loss of business to provincial attornies and solicitors. In the case of the Bar there was also resistance to the development of provincial Bars, which were seen to be the only effective way of competing for county court business.[31] The aim of the Act was to set up an effective local court for minor cases, and, in particular, the recovery of small debts: proceedings in the superior courts were prohibitively expensive and civil proceedings at the assizes were prone to delay. It is ironic that similar criticisms of ordinary county court proceedings in recent times have led to the development of new, more informal, procedures for small claims, and arguments that a further tier of small claims courts should be established.[32] Indeed, right from the outset the new courts were much more heavily used by shopkeepers, traders, and other creditors than by ordinary people, their establishment leading to "an infinite expansion of credit".[33]

(b) Organisation

England and Wales is divided into districts and at least one court is held in each district.[34] The districts and locations are specified by the Lord Chancellor.[35] In 1994 there were about 257 county courts; 48 courts had Admiralty jurisdiction, 176 divorce jurisdiction, and 136 bankruptcy jurisdiction.[36] About 80 offered trial facilities under which one or more judges were available on a con-

---

[28] See H. Bolderson, (1988) 15 J.L.S. 279. The Council on Tribunals registered their objections in a Special Report, *Social Security – Abolition of independent appeals under the proposed Social Fund* (Cmnd. 9722, 1986). See generally R. Drabble and T. Lynes, [1989] P.L. 297; Ogus, Barendt and Wikeley (1995), 684–685.

[29] Social Security Administration Act. 1992, ss.64–66. Social Fund (Application for Review) Regulations 1988 (S.I. 1988 No. 34).

[30] See B. Abel-Smith and R. Stevens, *Lawyers and the Courts* (1967), pp. 32–37.

[31] See R. Cocks, *Foundations of the Modern Bar* (1983), pp. 25–26, 56–57.

[32] See below, pp. 592–596.

[33] Lord Westbury L.C., quoted by Abel-Smith and Stevens (1967), p. 35.

[34] County Courts Act 1984, s.1; Civil Courts Order 1983 (S.I. 1983 No. 713), as amended. The county court for the City of London is known as the Mayor's and City of London Court: the name is that of a court of similar jurisdiction abolished by the Courts Act 1971. The court is maintained by the City of London rather than the Department of the Environment.

[35] County Courts Act 1984, s.2.

[36] *Judicial Statistics 1989* (Cm. 1154), p. 37.

tinuous basis to hear trials.[37] In London, the Central London Civil Trial Centre
has been established at Park Crescent in the West End. It has two business lists
and hears more complex cases sent from the other London county courts.[38]

A number of centres have been established to handle work in bulk: the Summons Production Centre, located in Northampton, processes summons requests
received on magnetic media from major plaintiffs[39]; the County Court Bulk
Centre, attached to Northampton Crown Court, processes large volumes of debt
recovery cases[40]; the Parking Enforcement Centre, attached to Cardiff County
Court, handles the enforcement of unpaid parking charges for London (as it
will, in due course, for other local authorities).[41]

(c) Judges

Under the original arrangements the districts were grouped into 60 county court
circuits, each with its own judge appointed by the Lord Chancellor from barristers of at least seven years' standing. On the re-organisation of the criminal
courts under the Courts Act 1971[42] the existing county court judges became
Circuit judges.[43] Every Circuit judge is by virtue of his or her office capable of
sitting as a judge for any county court district and at least one is assigned to
each district by the Lord Chancellor.[44] The regular sittings are normally taken
by the assigned judges. In addition, a District judge is appointed for each county
court district by the Lord Chancellor, and assistant and deputy district judges
may also be appointed.[45] A full-time District judge is barred from legal practice.[46] District judges were formerly called registrars; the change of title reflected
the fact that their functions are now judicial. They are responsible for procedural
steps in court proceedings, this responsibility being analogous to those of Masters and Registrars of the High Court, and they try or arbitrate most small claims.
Their administrative functions have now been transferred to the chief clerk or
some other administrative officer, in accordance with the Lord Chancellor's
directions.[47] County courts are administered by the unified court service.[48] There
are substantial staffs of clerks and bailiffs.

---

[37] Lord Woolf's *Interim Report on Access to Justice* (1995), p. 79. This followed a recommendation
of the Civil Justice Review (Cm. 393, 1988), para. 176.
[38] S. Webster (1994) 138 S.J.515. A nominated Circuit judge may issue *Mareva* injunctions in
relation to proceedings in the List: County Court Remedies (Amendment) Regulations 1995 (S.I.
1995 No.206). The Patents County Court (below, p. 76) has moved to the centre from Wood
Green.
[39] In 1994 it issued 47 per cent of the total default summonses issued; it is deemed to be part of
the court in whose name the summons is issued.
[40] *Judicial Statistics 1994* (Cm.2891, 1995), pp. 39, 44.
[41] L.C.D. Court Service Annual Report 1994–95 (1994–95 H.C.579), p. 52.
[42] See below, pp. 79–85.
[43] See below, pp. 218–221.
[44] County Courts Act 1984, s.5. A judge of the Court of Appeal or the High Court or a recorder
may also sit as a county court judge: *ibid.*
[45] County Courts Act 1984, ss.6–9; Courts and Legal Service Act 1990, s.74 and Sched. 10 para.
57. A deputy District judge is appointed as a temporary measure. The eligibility requirement is
now possession of a seven year general qualification (*i.e.* right of audience in any part of the
Supreme Court or in all proceedings in county courts or magistrates courts); it was formerly
being a solicitor of at least seven years' standing.
[46] Courts and Legal Services Act 1990, s.75 and Sched. 11.
[47] County Court Rules 1981, Ord. 1, r. 3.
[48] See below, pp. 83–84.

(d) Jurisdiction

A county court has jurisdiction in almost the whole range of civil proceedings. In some matters the jurisdiction is exclusive, in others it is exercised concurrently with the High Court. In the latter event there is in some cases a monetary limit to the county court's jurisdiction, the "county court limit," specified by Order in Council.[49] However, the High Court and County Courts Jurisdiction Order 1991,[50] following recommendations in the Civil Justice Review,[51] removed the limits for contract, tort and land law actions.

A county court may hear and determine the following matters—

(i) Contract and tort

An action founded on contract or tort.[52] This head of jurisdiction covers the bulk of cases brought in the county court.

(ii) Actions in respect of land

An action for the recovery of land or in respect of title to any hereditament, or for an injunction or declaration relating to any land.[53]

(iii) Equity proceedings

A variety of equity proceedings where the amount involved is not more than £30,000[54]: these include proceedings for the administration of the estate of a deceased person, for foreclosure or redemption of a mortgage, for the specific performance of an agreement for the sale of property, for the maintenance or advancement of an infant and for the dissolution of a partnership. These correspond to matters that would be dealt with in the Chancery Division of the High Court.

---

[49] Made under section 145 of the County Courts Act 1984. The current limits are set by the County Court Jurisdiction Order 1981 (S.I. 1981 No. 1123 (as amended by the High Court and County Courts Juridisction Order 1991 (S.I. 1991 No. 724) and s.147 of the 1984 Act.

[50] S.I. 1991 No.724. See below, p. 77.

[51] Below, p. 567.

[52] County Courts Act 1984, s.15, as amended by S.I. 1991 No.724. This head does not apply to any action where title to any hereditament is in question or any action for libel or slander: *ibid.* There is a similar jurisdiction in respect of money recoverable under a statute: *ibid.* s.16.

[53] *ibid.* s.21, as amended by S.I. 1991 No. 724.

[54] *ibid.* s.23. In addition, many specific powers under the Trustee Act 1925 and the Law of Property Act 1925 are conferred by the 1984 Act, Sched. 2.

(iv) Admiralty proceedings

A variety of Admiralty matters,[55] such as claims for damage done by or to a ship, for loss or damage to goods carried in a ship, or for salvage, towage or pilotage. The jurisdictional limit is £5,000, except for salvage claims, where it is £15,000. Only some county courts are appointed by the Lord Chancellor to take Admiralty proceedings, most of which are on or near the coast.[56]

(v) Probate proceedings

Contentious matters arising in respect of the grant or revocation of probate or administration of estates where the value of the estate is less than £30,000.[57]

(vi) Jurisdiction by agreement

Matters outside the monetary limits where the parties confer jurisdiction on a county court by agreement.[58]

(vii) Family matters

Any county court which has been designated by the Lord Chancellor as a "divorce county court" has jurisdiction to hear and determine any matrimonial cause,[59] although it only has jurisdiction to try the cause if it is also designated as a court of trial.[60] A divorce county court also has jurisdiction to make orders in relation to financial relief and custody of children ancillary to proceedings for divorce, nullity or separation,[61] and, if designated by the Lord Chancellor, to make orders for financial relief where a marriage has been terminated abroad.[62] The jurisdiction of divorce county courts, so far as is exercisable by judges of such courts, is to be exercised by such Circuit judges as the Lord Chancellor may direct.[63] Every matrimonial cause must be commenced in a divorce county court,[64] and will be heard there unless it is transferred to the

---

[55] County Courts Act 1984, ss.26, 27, as amended.
[56] Civil Courts Order 1983 (S.I. 1983 No. 713), as amended.
[57] County Courts Act 1984, s.32, substituted by the Administration of Justice Act 1985, s.51(1).
[58] *ibid*. ss.18 (Queen's Bench Division matters), 24 (many equity proceedings), 27(6) (most Admiralty proceedings).
[59] *i.e.* an action for divorce, nullity of marriage or judicial separation: Matrimonial and Family Proceedings Act 1984, s.32, as amended by the Family Law Act 1986, Sched. 1, para. 27.
[60] 1984 Act, s.33(1); Civil Courts Order 1983 (SI 1983 No. 713), as amended. In London, the Divorce Registry of the Family Division is deemed to be a county court for this purpose; see the 1984 Act, s.42, as amended by the Courts and Legal Services Act 1990, s.74(7).
[61] Under Parts II and III of the Matrimonial Causes Act 1973: 1984 Act, s.34(1)(*a*).
[62] Under Part III of the 1984 Act: *ibid*, ss.33(4), 34(1)(*b*).
[63] 1984 Act, s.36.
[64] *ibid*. s.33(3).

High Court.[65] There is also provision for the transfer of family proceedings from the High Court to the county court.[66] Principles governing the distribution and transfer of business between the High Court and county courts are set out in Directions given by the President of the Family Division.[67] Other family matters may be dealt with by divorce county courts, or, in some cases, any county court. The Family Homes and Domestic Violence Bill 1995 was intended to create a single unified domestic violence jurisdiction and remedies in all levels of courts, but was dropped because of opposition to some of its provisions by Tory back-benchers. A further attempt to secure this reform[68] in Part III of the Family Law Bill is at the time of writing (April 1996) under consideration by Parliament.

The jurisdiction of the county courts concerning children was remodelled on implementation of the Children Act 1989 in October 1991. There is a concurrent jurisdiction across the family proceedings courts,[69] county courts and the High Court.[70] In the county courts, the business is concentrated on particular centres and particular judges, who receive special "guidance". There are four levels of court centre. Ordinary county courts have no involvement except for domestic violence injunctions; divorce county courts can issue all private law proceedings,[71] but contested matters are transferred to "family hearing centres" for trial; family hearing centres can issue and hear all private law family proceedings whether or not they are contested; "care centres" have full jurisdiction in private and public law[72] matters.[73] As to the judiciary, "designated family judges" have full jurisdiction in public and private law, are based at care centres and chair local Family Court Business Committees and Family Court Forums; "nominated care judges" similarly have full public and private law jurisdiction; "circuit family judges" have full private law jurisdiction;[74] district judges can hear private law family work but have a limited jurisdiction; "nominated care district judges" have increased jurisdiction and can hear uncontested public law

---

[65] Under *ibid.* s.39 (which applies to any family proceedings), or section 41 of the County Courts Act 1984. Prior to April 26, 1986, *all* defended causes had to be transferred to the High Court.

[66] Matrimonial and Family Proceedings Act 1984, s.38.

[67] *ibid.* s.37. See *Practice Direction (Family Division: Distribution of Business)* [1992] 1 W. L. R. 586 replacing an earlier direction. A defect in the transitional arrangements led to thousands of divorces being technically invalid: see *Nissim v. Nissim* (1987) 137 N. L. J. Rep. 1207; N. Wikeley, (1988) 7 C. J. Q. 97. They were retrospectively validated by the Matrimonial Proceedings (Transfers) Act 1988.

[68] Implementing recommendations in the Law Commission Report on *Domestic Violence and Occupation of the Family Home* (Law Com. No. 207)

[69] Above, p. 58.

[70] Below, pp. 91–92.

[71] Above, p. 74.

[72] *i.e.* cases usually brought by local authorities or the NSPCC, including care, supervision and emergency protection orders.

[73] *Judicial Statistics 1994* (Cm.2891, 1995), p. 48; Children (Allocation of Proceedings) Order 1991 (SI 1991 No.1677), as amended, Scheds.1, 2. The Principal Registry of the Family Division is treated as if it were a divorce county court, a family hearing centre and a care centre. The original plan was for 51 combined care and family hearing centres and 51 additional family hearing centres: *LCD Court Service Annual Report 1990–91* (1990–91 H. C. 568), pp. 57–60. A further seven FHCs and two CCs were established from the beginning of 1995: *LCD Court Service Annual Report 1994–95* (1994–95 H. C. 579), p. 55. The 1991 Order also provides for the transfer of cases.

[74] Deputy Circuit judges, recorders and assistant recorders are only nominated for private family law proceedings.

cases.[75] The detailed allocation of work is the subject of a Practice Direction.[76] Family Court Business Committees deal with administrative issues, such as the operation of the criteria for the transfer of cases; the Family Court Forums enable the professions involved in the protection and welfare of children to "discuss issues and air concerns."[77]

(viii) Other proceedings

Jurisdiction in a large number of other matters is conferred by specific statutory provisions, including hire-purchase, consumer credit, the Rent Acts, landlord and tenant, housing and sex discrimination.[78] Designated county courts have jurisdiction in bankruptcy matters,[79] race relations,[80] and patents[81]. Appeals also lie to the county court in a number of administrative matters.[82]

(ix) Jurisdiction of the District judge

District judges have jurisdiction:

(1) to determine interlocutory applications;
(2) to conduct pre-trial reviews;
(3) to hear any action or matter
— where the defendant fails to appear at the hearing or admits the claim;
— where the amount involved does not exceed £5,000[83];
— where jurisdiction is expressly conferred; or
— with the leave of the judge and the consent of the parties;
(4) to hear any action for recovery of land regardless of the value of any

---

[75] *Judicial Statistics 1994*, pp. 48–49.

[76] *Practice Direction: Family Proceedings (Allocation to Judiciary) Direction 1993* [1993] 2 F. L. R. 1008, as amended by [1994] 2 F. L. R. 913.

[77] *LCD Court Service Annual Report 1991–92* (1991–92 H. C.102), p. 40. The local committees relay information to the national Children Act Advisory Committee (*ibid.*). This Committee advises ministers and the President of the Family Division on the progress of Children Act cases through the court system, with a view of identifying special difficulties and reducing avoidable delay, and promotes commonality of administrative practice and procedure in the family proceedings courts and county courts: see (1995) *Litigation* 245.

[78] See the annual *County Court Practice* (the "Green Book"); High Court and County Courts Jurisdiction Order 1991 (S.I. 1991 No. 734), art. 2.

[79] Civil Courts Order 1983 (S.I. 1983 No. 713), as amended.

[80] *ibid.*

[81] A Patents County Court has been established in London under the Copyright, Designs and Patents Act 1988, ss.287–292, "to handle smaller, shorter, less complex, less important, lower value actions" than the Patents Court (below, p. 87): *per* Sir Thomas Bingham M.R. in *Chaplin Patents Holdings Co. plc v. Group Lotus plc, The Times*, January 12, 1994, where the Court of Appeal upheld a decision not to transfer proceedings to the High Court.

[82] D. Price, *Appeals* (1982), pp. 46–49 lists 29 situations.

[83] Raised from £1,000 by the County Court (Amendment No. 2) Rules 1991 (S.I. 1991 No. 1126), r.7.

other claim brought in the same action, including a possession claim by a mortgagee.[84]

Their determinations may be reviewed by the judge. The role of the District judge is particularly significant in family matters,[85] where, *inter alia*, they determine interlocutory applications and applications for ancillary relief,[86] and, in undefended divorces under the special procedure, where they examine the evidence and issue a certificate which enables the judge to pronounce the decree.

Where the amount involved is £3,000 or less, defended claims are referred for arbitration by the District judge unless he or she otherwise orders.[86] There are exceptions for claims including a claim for possession of land or a claim for damages for personal injury valued at more than £1,000.[87]

(e) The boundary between High Court and County Court

The relationship between the jurisdictions of the county court and the High Court was significantly altered by the Courts and Legal Services Act 1990, implementing recommendations of the Civil Justice Review.[88] The aim was to switch an increasing proportion of civil business from High Court to county courts; a significant number of High Court civil cases was in any event being heard by Circuit judges sitting as judges of the High Court or by deputy High Court judges. Section 1 of the 1990 Act enables the Lord Chancellor to make provision by order for the allocation of business between the High Court and county courts; jurisdiction to hear applications for judicial review may not, however, be conferred on the county court. The High Court and County Courts Order 1991[89] provides that where both courts have jurisdiction, proceedings may be commenced in either, except that claims for damages for personal injuries must be commenced in the county court, unless the value of the action[90] is £50,000 or more.[91] In cases of concurrent jurisdiction, either court may try the case.[92] However, each court has power to transfer a case to the other.[93] Indeed, if proceedings are required to be started in the other, it must order a transfer or, if satisfied that the person bringing them knew or ought to have known of

---

[84] County Court Rules 1981, Ord. 21, r.5, as amended.

[85] See W. Barrington-Baker *et al., The Matrimonial Jurisdiction of Registrars* (S.S.R.C., 1977).

[86] *e.g.* financial provision and adjustment of property rights on divorce.

[87] County Court Rules 1981, Ord.19, r.3, as substituted by the County Court (Amendment No. 2) Rules 1992 (S.I. 1992 No. 1965), r.6, and amended by S.I. 1995 No. 2838. This last S.I. raised the general limit from £1,000 in accordance with a recommendation of Lord Woolf's Interim Report. See below, pp. 592–596, on small claims in the county court.

[88] Below, p. 567.

[89] S.I. 1991 No.734, as amended by S.I. 1995 No. 205. This order does not apply to family or Admiralty proceedings: art. 12. See I.R. Scott, (1991) 10 C.J.Q. 282.

[90] *i.e.* normally the amount the plaintiff reasonably expects to receive, or the financial worth of a claim for relief other than a specified sum of money: *ibid.,* arts.9, 10.

[91] *ibid.,* arts.4–6A. Other exceptions are that applications or appeals under the Local Government Finance Act, ss.19, 20 must be commenced in the High Court, and applications under the Access to Neighbouring Land Act 1992 must be commenced in the county court.

[92] *ibid.,* art.7(1).

[93] Transfers to a county court must be to such court as the High Court considers appropriate, having regard to the convenience of the parties and other affected persons and the state of business of the courts concerned.

the requirement, order that they be struck out.[94] Orders may be made on the court's own motion or on the application of any party. The discretion to transfer must be exercised with regard to—

"(a) the financial substance of the action, including the value of any counterclaim;
(b) whether the action is otherwise important and, in particular, whether it raises questions of importance to persons who are not parties or questions of general public interest;
(c) the complexity of the facts, legal issues, remedies or procedures involved; and
(d) whether transfer is likely to result in a more speedy trial of the action."[95]

However, ground (d) is insufficient alone. An action (other than equity or probate proceedings) with a value less than £25,000 must be tried in the county court unless (1) a county court considers that it ought to transfer it to the High Court and the High Court considers that it ought to try it; or (2) it is commenced in the High Court and the High Court considers that it ought to try it. An action with a value of £50,000[96] or more must be tried in the High Court unless (1) it is commenced in the county court and that court does not consider that it ought to be transferred, or (2) it is commenced in the High court and transferred.[97]

A review of the 1991 changes completed in 1993 "indicated that, broadly speaking, the changes had met their objectives." In 1993–94, the number of trials in the Queen's Bench general list which resulted in an award of £25,000 or less fell to 346 (compared with 1,828 in 1990–91); the percentage of trials heard by High Court judges involving an award of £5,000 or less fell to 3.8 per cent (71 per cent in 1990–91).[98] It is also the case that the number of writs issued in the Queen's Bench Division has declined sharply, from over 100,000 in 1991–92 to 35,000 in 1994–95.[99]

In his *Interim Report on Access to Justice*, Lord Woolf recommended that while the High Court and county courts should be retained as separate courts and the separate status of High Court judge preserved, the two levels of court should generally have the same jurisdiction and outside London should be administered together. Proceedings could be commenced in either and then transferred by the court to the appropriate level. There would be a combined

---

[94] County Courts Act 1984, ss.40, 42, substituted by the Courts and Legal Services Act 1990, s.2(1), (3). There is also power for the High Court at any stage to order the transfer of proceedings commenced in (or transferred to) the county court to (or back to) the High Court: s.41, as amended by the 1990 Act, s.2(2). The court is not obliged to strike out an action if satisfied that the applicant "knew or ought to have known of the requirement"; it may instead order transfer: *Restick v. Crickmore* [1994] 1 W.L.R. 420.

[95] S.I. 1991 No.734, art. 7(5). See also *Practice Direction* (*County Court: Transfer of Actions*) [1991] 1 W.L.R. 643, noting that cases involving professional negligence, fatal accidents, fraud or undue influence, defamation, malicious prosecution or false imprisonment and claims against the police "may be considered important".

[96] £200,000 in the case of the Central London County Court Business List.

[97] *ibid.*, art. 7(2)–(4).

[98] *LCD Court Service Annual Report 1993–94* (1993–94 H.C. 568), p. 49.

[99] *LCD Court Service Annual Report 1994–95* (1994–95 H.C. 579), p. 37.

set of procedural rules. The county court should have an increased small claims jurisdiction and deal with "fast track" cases.[1]

(f) Procedural Rules

The County Court Rules are made by a rule committee consisting of eleven persons appointed by the Lord Chancellor (five judges of county courts, two district judges, two lawyers with a Supreme Court qualification, and two lawyers with the right to conduct litigation in the Supreme Court). They are subject to the approval of the Lord Chancellor, either as submitted or after amendment by him.[2] The rules were substantially revised in 1981 and are to be found in the current edition of the *County Court Practice* (the "Green Book").[3]

(g) Register of judgments

A register recording all county court judgments and other specified orders is maintained by a private company, Registry Trust Ltd, by agreement with the Lord Chancellor.[4] It was formerly maintained by the County Courts Branch of the Lord Chancellor's Department.

(h) Appeals[5]

Appeals lie to the Court of Appeal (Civil Division)[6] on questions of fact, law or evidence. The leave of either court is necessary if the matter came to the county court on appeal and in other specified circumstances. In a few cases appeals lie to the High Court.[7]

6. THE CROWN COURT[8]

(a) The Beeching Royal Commission

In 1966 the Royal Commission on Assizes and Quarter Sessions was appointed, under the chairmanship of Lord Beeching, to inquire into the arrangements for

[1] Report (1995), pp. 73–75, 79–81. Proposals for integration were previously considered and rejected by the Gorell Committee on County Court Procedure (1908–09 H.C.71), the Beeching Commission on Assizes and Quarter Sessions (Cmnd. 4153, 1969), p. 73, and the Civil Justice Review (Cm.394), Chap. 3. See Sir Jack Jacob, *The Reform of Civil Procedural Law* (1982), pp. 7–13.

[2] County Courts Act 1984, s.75, as amended by the Courts and Legal Services Act 1990, s.16, Sched. 18, para. 47.

[3] County Court Rules 1981 (S.I. 1981 No. 1687). See R.C.L. Gregory Q.C. "The Genesis of the County Court Rules" (1983) 2 C.J.Q. 1.

[4] County Courts Act 1984 ss.73, as amended, and 73A, inserted by the Administration of Justice Act 1985, s.54; Register of County Court Judgments Regulations 1985 (S.I. 1985 No. 1807), as amended by S.I. 1986 No. 2001, S.I. 1993 Nos. 710, 2173.

[5] See generally, Chap. 17.

[6] See below, pp. 96–98, 944–945.

[7] *e.g.* bankruptcy matters are heard by the Divisional Court of the Chancery Division.

[8] See I.R. Scott, *The Crown Court* (1971); *The Crown Court. A guide to good practice* (four separate guides published under this or a similar title by the LCD, the CPS, the Bar Council and the Law Society.

the administration of justice at assizes and quarter sessions outside London, and to report what reforms should be made for the more convenient, economic and efficient disposal of the civil and criminal business dealt with by those courts. The *assize courts* were presided over by High Court judges sent out "on circuit", a system that could be traced back to the twelfth century and which had changed comparatively little since medieval times.[9] There were seven circuits of assize towns. Assizes had jurisdiction over all indictable criminal offences and exclusive jurisdiction over some, including homicide, serious crimes of violence and rape. In addition, assize courts had the same civil jurisdiction as the High Court sitting in London, although priority was given to criminal cases. There were *courts of quarter sessions* for each of the 58 counties and for 93 boroughs; there were five such courts in Greater London and one for the City of London. The borough quarter sessions were presided over by a part-time Recorder, sitting alone. The county quarter sessions comprised a bench of magistrates normally with a legally qualified Chairman or Deputy Chairman, some of whom were whole-time appointments. These courts had jurisdiction to try many indictable offences with a jury, and to hear appeals from magistrates' courts and from a variety of administrative orders. In London, the *Central Criminal Court* at the Old Bailey was in effect the Assize court for criminal cases. It had a number of full time judges, including the Recorder of London and the Common Serjeant; in addition some cases would be taken by High Court judges. In 1956, new courts known as *Crown Courts* were established for Liverpool and Manchester to deal with both quarter sessions and assize work. A full time Recorder was appointed for each court. Responsibility for providing judges, court staff and court buildings was "as fragmented as the system itself."[10]

The Beeching Report identified many defects of assizes and quarter sessions and recommended a fundamental reorganisation. A number of features which a good court system should provide were identified[11]:

	(a)	Ease of physical access.
	(b)	An early hearing.
Convenience	(c)	The assurance of trial on a date of which reasonable notice has been given.
	(d)	Suitable accommodation.
Quality	(e)	Judicial expertise.
	(f)	Adequate and dependable legal representation.
Economy	(g)	Efficient use of all manpower.
	(h)	Optimum use of buildings.

The restricting factors were cost and the capacity of the Bar. The report's proposals were designed to[12]:

(a) simplify the structure of the courts;
(b) deploy judge power as flexibly as possible;
(c) relate court locations to travelling facilities for the public;

---

[9] See above, p. 37. Additional "Commissioners of Assize", usually senior Q.C.s, could be appointed ad hoc.
[10] Beeching Report, p. 31.
[11] *ibid.*, p. 48.
[12] *ibid.*, p. 64.

(d) secure the efficient administration of all court services;

(e) ensure that courts are built and maintained as economically and efficiently as possible.''

The proposals, which involved the creation of a new superior court of criminal jurisdiction, to be called the Crown Court, were largely accepted. They were enacted in the Courts Act 1971, substantial parts of which were re-enacted in the Supreme Court Act 1981.

(b) The constitution of the Crown Court

The Crown Court is part of the Supreme Court of England and Wales.[13] It is a single court, but sittings may be conducted at any place in England and Wales, in accordance with directions given by the Lord Chancellor.[14] There are at present over 90 permanent centres.[15] The name "Central Criminal Court" has been retained for the Crown Court sitting in the City of London at the Old Bailey. There are three kinds of Crown Court centre: "first-tier" centres are visited by High Court judges, Circuit judges and recorders for the complete range of Crown Court business, and by High Court judges for High Court civil work; "second-tier" centres are the same as first-tier except that no civil business is done; "third-tier" centres are visited only by Circuit judges and recorders. The centres are grouped into six circuits: Midland and Oxford, North Eastern, Northern, South Eastern, Wales and Chester, and Western.[16]

The jurisdiction of the Crown Court is exerciseable by any judge of the High Court, Circuit judge or recorder.[17] In some cases one of these may sit with not more than four justices of the peace[18]: a court must normally be so comprised when hearing an appeal or proceedings on committal for sentence,[19] and may be so comprised for other proceedings, but not cases listed for pleas of not guilty.[20]

(c) Jurisdiction

The Crown Court has exclusive jurisdiction with respect to criminal trials on indictment.[21] It also has an extensive appellate jurisdiction inherited from quarter sessions, including appeals from magistrates' courts in criminal cases and appeals in a wide variety of administrative matters, such as betting, gaming and liquor licensing. Magistrates' courts may also commit convicted persons to the Crown Court for sentence.

---

[13] Supreme Court Act 1981, s.1. Procedural rules can be prescribed by the Crown Court Rule Committee: *ibid.* s.86, as amended by the Courts and Legal Services Act 1990, Sched. 18, para. 36(2).

[14] *ibid.* s.78.

[15] See *Shaw's Directory of Courts in the United Kingdom.*

[16] See H.L. Deb. Vol. 314, col. 948, January 26, 1971; H.L. Deb. Vol. 321, col. 572, July 1, 1971; H.L. Deb. Vol. 343, col. 968, June 14, 1973.

[17] Supreme Court Act 1981, s.8. See below pp. 218–221.

[18] *ibid.* and see below, pp. 210–211.

[19] Supreme Court Act 1981, s.74; Crown Court Rules 1982 (S.I. 1982 No. 1109), as amended, rr.3–5.

[20] See below, p. 83.

[21] Supreme Court Act 1981, s.46.

(d) Distribution of business

The classes of cases in the Crown Court suitable for allocation respectively to a High Court judge, Circuit judge or recorder, and to a court including justices, are prescribed in directions given by the Lord Chief Justice, with the concurrence of the Lord Chancellor.[22] For the purposes of trial in the Crown Court, offences are grouped in four classes.

Class 1

These offences are to be tried by a High Court judge and include any offence carrying the death penalty, murder, genocide and offences under section 1 of the Official Secrets Act 1911. A case of murder may be released by or on the authority of a presiding judge, for trial by a Circuit judge approved for the purpose by the Lord Chief Justice.

Class 2

These offences are to be tried by a High Court judge unless a particular case is released by or on the authority of a presiding judge for trial by a Circuit judge, and include manslaughter, infanticide, abortion, rape, sexual intercourse or incest with a girl under 13, sedition, mutiny and piracy. A case of rape, or a serious sexual offence against a child, may be released by a presiding judge for trial only by a Circuit judge or recorder approved for that purpose by the senior presiding judge with the concurrence of the Lord Chief Justice.

Class 3

These offences may be listed for trial by a High Court judge, or, in accordance with general or particular directions given by a presiding judge, by a Circuit judge, or a recorder. They comprise all offences triable only on indictment other than those in classes, 1, 2 and 4.

Class 4

These may be tried by a High Court judge, Circuit judge, recorder, or assistant recorder. They may not be listed for trial by a High Court judge except with his or her consent or that of a presiding judge, and include all offences triable either way and a number of specific offences including wounding or causing

---

[22] Supreme Court Act 1981, s.75; *Practice Direction* (*Crown Court: Allocation of Business*) [1995] 1 W.L.R. 1083.

grievous bodily harm with intent, robbery and conspiracy to commit a Class 3 or 4 offence.

Presiding judges, with the approval of the senior presiding judge, must issue directions as to the need where appropriate to reserve a case for trial by a High Court judge, the allocation of work between Circuit judges, recorders and assistant recorders, and, where necessary, the devolved responsibility of resident or designated judges for such allocation.[23] Specific provision must be made in these directions for cases in 15 specified categories, including, for example, cases involving death or serious risk to life or the use of loaded firearms, arson or criminal damage with intent to endanger life, a number of offences involving serious violence, cases where the trial may last more than 10 days or involve more than five defendants and cases involving difficult issues of law.

Most other Crown Court proceedings are normally listed for hearing by a court presided over by a Circuit judge or a recorder. Any proceedings listed for hearing by a Circuit judge or recorder, except pleas of not guilty, are stated to be suitable for allocation to a court including justices of the peace.

Appeals and committals for sentence are to be heard by (i) a resident or designated judge; (ii) a Circuit judge, nominated by the resident or designated judge, who regularly sits at the Crown Court centre; (iii) an experienced recorder specifically approved by the presiding judges for the purpose; or, otherwise, (iv) a Circuit judge or recorder selected by the resident or designated judge for a specific case or cases.

The same Practice Direction prescribes the general principles for the distribution of business among the different court centres geographically. Generally, the magistrates committing for trial should select the "most convenient location" of the appropriate tier of Crown Court centre, having regard to the convenience of defence, prosecution and witnesses and the expediting of the trial,[24] and to the location or locations designated by the presiding judge as the normal ones for committals from their petty sessions area. It is possible for the location to be changed.[25] In addition, the "catchment areas" are varied if the work-load at a particular Crown Court centre requires cases to be directed to a less busy centre. Arrangements can be made for a case to be transferred from one circuit to another.[26] Thirty-six centres have been designated for the trial of serious and complex fraud trials,[27] and 40 are equipped with live television link facilities.[28]

(e) Administration

Another important feature of the Beeching Report and the Courts Act 1971 was the establishment of a "unified court service" under the direction of the Lord Chancellor, providing administrative support to the Supreme Court, including

---

[23] These are Circuit judges appointed by the presiding judges to have responsibility, at one or more centres, for seeing to the efficient and orderly running of the lists: *Civil Justice Review* (Cm. 394, 1988), para. 307.

[24] Magistrates' Courts Act 1980, s.7.

[25] Supreme Court Act 1981, s.76.

[26] *Practice Direction (Crown Court: Allocation of Business)* [1995] 1 W.L.R. 1083: Allocation of Business, para. 9.

[27] *Practice Direction (Crown Court: Fraud Trials (No. 3))* [1993] 1 W.L.R. 158.

[28] *Practice Direction (Crown Courts: TV Links)* [1992] 1 W.L.R. 838.

the Crown Court and county courts.[29] The service is organised on a circuit basis. The administration in each circuit is headed by a Circuit Administrator, a civil servant of Under Secretary rank responsible to the Lord Chancellor. Each of these has a small headquarters staff and three or four Courts Administrators working under him or her, each responsible for a particular area.[30] Each court has a chief clerk responsible to one of the Courts Administrators. The Circuit Administrators work closely with the presiding judges and deal with such matters as personnel management, finance and accommodation. The Courts Administrator has responsibility for planning the courts' sittings and ensuring the smooth disposal of business between courts, and is a point of contact for the various parties concerned with the running of the courts.

Two High Court judges are assigned to each circuit by the Lord Chief Justice to act as presiding judges: at least one should be present in the circuit at any given time. Presiding judges have certain functions in relation to the allocation of cases.[31]

Their position has been summarised as follows[32]:

"The presiding judges are the judicial authority for the circuit paralleling the administrative authority of the Circuit Administrators. . . . Where they perform properly (and there is some unevenness) the presiding judges make a substantial effort to control judicial performance on their circuits. They know the capabilities of the Circuit judges and in consultation with the Circuit Administrators they see that these judges are properly assigned and utilised according to skill and expertise."

However, it has also been noted that the presiding judges frequently lack confidence when dealing with their more senior colleagues, that some do not capture the respect of Circuit judges in their circuit, that there is too much doubt as to their proper role, that uncertainty is created by the fact that so much depends on the respective personalities of presiding judge and Circuit Administrator and that the judge's position is weakened by the fact that appointments are only for short periods.[33]

A Lord Justice of Appeal has been appointed as a senior presiding judge who is available for consultation by the presiding judges and relieves the Lord Chief Justice of certain administrative responsibilities.[34] The offices of presiding judge and senior presiding judge now have statutory recognition.[35]

(f) Workload

The workload of the Crown Court has increased very significantly since it was established:

---

[29] Courts Act 1971, s.27. See I. R. Scott, *The Crown Court* (1971), Chap. IV; E. C. Friesen and I. R. Scott, *English Criminal Justice* (1977), pp. 121–5 and I. R. Scott, *Court Administration: The Case for a Judicial Council* (1979).

[30] There is a Courts Administrator responsible for the Central Criminal Court.

[31] See above, p. 83.

[32] Friesen and Scott (1977), p. 124.

[33] Scott (1979), p. 16. An account of Judge James Pickles' relations with presiding judges on his circuit and the Lord Chief Justice is given in his book, *Straight from the Bench* (1987), Chap. 1.

[34] (1983) 133 N.L.J. 732.

[35] Courts and Legal Services Act 1990, s.72.

"It is undoubtedly true to say that in the light of the inexorable increase in caseloads chaos would have ensued but for the implementation of the Beeching Reforms. The number of persons working in the court service is now about 10,000 and the range of quasi-judicial and administrative tasks undertaken by this bureaucracy is far greater much more sophisticated than those attempted under the pre-1971 arrangements"[36]

Between 1979 and 1989 committals for trial received by the Crown Court more than doubled, with an average annual growth rate of over 7 per cent.[37] Since 1989, the number peaked in 1991 (104,754) but has since fallen (to 81,186 in 1995).[38]

Other important factors have been the establishment of the circuit bench and the increase in the number of High Court judges, and the court-building programme. Nevertheless, the increase in workload meant that waiting times increased dramatically.[39]

(g) Appeals[40]

Appeals in relation to trials on indictment and in cases where a defendant has been committed for sentence to the Crown Court lie to the Court of Appeal (Criminal Division).[41] Appeals from an exercise of the Crown Court's appellate jurisdiction lie to the High Court on the same basis as appeals there from the magistrates' court.

7. THE HIGH COURT

(a) Constitution

The High Court of Justice is a court of unlimited civil jurisdiction and also has an important appellate jurisdiction in both civil and criminal matters. It is part of the Supreme Court of England and Wales,[42] and was created as part of the reorganisation of the superior courts under the Supreme Court of Judicature

---

[36] Scott (1979), p. 5.

[37] *Judicial Statistics 1989* (Cm. 1154), p. 67.

[38] *Judicial Statistics 1995* (Cm. 3260), p. 61. The highest total ever was in 1988 (106,524) before reclassification of certain offences as summary only.

[39] In 1973, of the 13,925 defendants disposed of on indictment and who had awaited trial in custody, 74 per cent were dealt with within eight weeks of committal and 96 per cent within 20 weeks. In 1980 the figures were 16,088, 54 per cent and 87 per cent respectively. See generally, I. R. Scott, "Crown Court Productivity" [1980] Crim. L. R. 193, noting the growing proportion of not guilty pleas and the lengthening of hearing times in contested cases. By 1987 of 31,443 defendants in custody, 58 per cent. waited less than eight weeks and 85 per cent less than 16 weeks. Between 1980 and 1983 the average waiting time for all defendants committed for trial fell from 17.3 weeks to 14.2 weeks. It stayed at roughly that figure until 1987 (12.3 weeks), 1988 (12.2 weeks)), the lowest annual average level since 1976, and 1989 (12.4 weeks). The figure rose sharply after 1991 to 16.1 in 1995: *Judicial Statistics 1995*, Tables 6.15 to 6.20. See pp. 747–749.

[40] See generally, Chap. 17, below.

[41] See below, pp. 95–96, 923–942.

[42] The Supreme Court was thus re-titled by the Supreme Court Act 1981.

Acts 1873–75. It sits at the Royal Courts of Justice in the Strand[43] and at 26
first-tier Crown Court centres outside London.[44] There are three divisions: the
Chancery Division, Queen's Bench Division and Family Division,[45] headed,
respectively, by the Vice-Chancellor,[46] the Lord Chief Justice and the President
of the Family Division.[47] Each High Court judge[48] is attached to one of the
divisions, but they may be transferred to one of the others with their consent,
and they may act as an additional judge of one of them at the request of the
Lord Chancellor.[49] Different classes of business are allocated for administrative
convenience to each division by rules of court,[50] although technically all the
jurisdiction of the High Court belongs to all the divisions alike.[51] There have
been two major reorganisations. In 1881 the Exchequer and Common Pleas
Divisions were merged into the Queen's Bench Division,[52] and in 1971 the
Probate, Divorce and Admiralty Division was re-named the Family Division,
with Admiralty business assigned to the Queen's Bench Division, probate business other than non-contentious or common form matters assigned to the Chancery Division, and wardship, guardianship and adoption jurisdiction transferred
from Chancery Division to Family Division.[53] A joint committee of High Court
judges and civil servants has recommended abolition of the three separate divisions of the High Court,[54] but this recommendation was not implemented. A
joint committee of the Bar and the Law Society chaired by Hilary Heilbron
Q.C.[55] recommended the merger of the Chancery and Queen's Bench Divisions
to form a Civil Division, presided over by the Lord Chief Justice. However,
Lord Woolf, in his *Interim Report on Access to Justice*, concluded that merger
was not desirable, noting among other factors the distinctive nature of the
specialist jurisdictions that fall under the Chancery umbrella, the team spirit
among Chancery judges and their special relationship with the Chancery Bar,
and the relatively small number of Chancery judges. However, judges should
be assigned to lists according to their expertise, irrespective of the division to
which the list belongs.[56] A further development should be the appointment of
a senior judge as Head of Civil Justice responsible, *inter alia*, to provide leader-

[43] The Supreme Court moved here from Westminster Hall in 1883. See F. W. Maitland, (1942) 8
    C.L.J. 2; J. Kinnard in P. Ferriday (ed.), *Victorian Architecture* (1963); M. H. Port, "The New
    Law Courts Competition, 1866–67" (1968) *Architectural History* 75–93.
[44] See above, p. 81.
[45] Supreme Court Act 1981, s.5(1). The number of divisions can be altered by Order in Council:
    ibid. s.7.
[46] Technically, the Lord Chancellor is the president and the Vice-Chancellor the vice-president of
    the Chancery Division, but the latter is the effective head.
[47] See below, pp. 223, 224.
[48] See below, p. 221.
[49] Supreme Court Act 1981, s.5(2) (3).
[50] Supreme Court Act 1981, s.61.
[51] *ibid.* s.5(5). Any Division to which a cause or matter is assigned has jurisdiction to grant any
    remedy or relief sought notwithstanding that proceedings for such remedy or relief are assigned
    to another Division: *Practice Direction (High Court: Divisions)* [1973] 1 W.L.R. 627. Cases may
    be transferred between Divisions: see J. Jacob, (1988) 7 C.J.Q. 94; *Barclays Bank v. Bemister*
    and *Pryke v. Gibbs Hartley Cooper Ltd* [1989] 1 All E.R. 10, C.A.
[52] This was done by an Order in Council which was made on December 16, 1880 and which came
    into force on February 26, 1881.
[53] Administration of Justice Act 1970, with effect from August 2, 1971.
[54] Committee on the Deployment of the High Court: *Legal Action*, June 1988, p. 5; (1988) L. S.
    Gaz. May 25, p. 3.
[55] *Civil Justice on Trial—The Case for Change* (1993). See I. R. Scott, (1994) 13 C.J.Q. 9.
[56] Report, pp. 76–78.

ship for the civil justice system. Civil work should be made the express responsibility of one of the two presiding judges on each circuit, and there should be a senior civil judge appointed for each trial centre.[57]

Most High Court work is taken by a single judge sitting alone.[58] This should be in open court, except where under rules of court or in accordance with the practice of the court it is dealt with in chambers.[59] A proportion of the appellate and supervisory work of the High Court is dealt with by "divisional courts," which comprise two or more judges.[60]

The business is mainly conducted by the heads of division and the puisne[61] judges of the High Court. In addition, High Court work may be taken by a deputy High Court judge, a Circuit judge, a recorder, a judge of the Court of Appeal or a former judge of the High Court or the Court of Appeal.[62]

(b) The Chancery Division

The division deals with property, trusts, the administration of estates, bankruptcy, partnership, companies, revenue cases, probate business other than non-contentious common form business, and other matters specifically assigned.[63] The Patents Court established in 1977[64] is part of this division. In addition the judges of the division have been assigned to deal with the management of the property and affairs of mental patients under the Mental Health Act 1983. This work is the responsibility of the "Court of Protection" which is in fact an office of the Supreme Court rather than a court.

The business is at present handled by the Vice-Chancellor and 17 puisne judges, two of whom are nominated to the Patents Court although they are available to help with the other work of the Division. One judge (Parker J.) holds the appointment of Vice-Chancellor of the Duchy of Lancaster.[65] The judges are assisted by five Chancery masters and six registrars in bankruptcy.[66] The work is done in London and at eight centres in the provinces.[67] In the latter the work is done by the Vice-Chancellor of the Duchy of Lancaster, by High Court judges sitting at Bristol and Cardiff and by Circuit judges who specialise

---

[57] *ibid.*, pp. 58–62. Sir Richard Scott V.-C. has been appointed as the first Head of Civil Justice.
[58] There is provision for a judge to sit with assessors who are specially qualified in relation to the proceedings in question: 1981 Act, s.70. They are mainly used in Admiralty proceedings. See below, p. 89.
[59] Supreme Court Act 1981, s.67.
[60] *ibid.* s.66.
[61] See below, p. 221.
[62] *ibid.* s.9. There have been complaints that too many High Court cases have been heard by Circuit judges and recorders sitting as deputy High Court judges. The Civil Justice Review Body thought it excessive that 30 per cent of High Court sittings were by persons who were not High Court judges: their proposals for the transfer of business to the county court (see pp. 77–78) should mean that deputy judges would only be appointed to give them experience or to cover peaks of work or temporary shortages of judge power (Cm. 394, para. 192).
[63] *Ibid.* Sched. 1. The judges who deal with bankruptcy are referred to as the "High Court of Justice in Bankruptcy" and those who deal with company matters as the "Companies Court," but these are not formally constituted as courts under the 1981 Act.
[64] Patents Act 1977. The judge may sit with scientific advisers: Supreme Court Act 1981, s.70.
[65] This office, to which the appointment is made by the Chancellor of the Duchy, was formerly held by a Circuit judge: see p. 219.
[66] See R. E. Ball, "The Chancery Master" (1961) 77 L. Q. R. 331. See generally, E. Heward, *Chancery Practice* (2nd ed., 1990).
[67] Leeds, Liverpool, Manchester, Newcastle-upon-Tyne, Preston, and, as from October 10, 1982, Birmingham, Bristol and Cardiff. See *Supreme Court Practice 1995*, Vol. 2, pp. 169–172.

in Chancery work and who sit for this purpose as judges of the High Court.[68] The Vice-Chancellor of the Duchy and another judge effectively act as presiding judges in relation to Chancery work outside London.[69] Steps have also been taken to transfer less onerous cases to the county court,[70] Chancery expertise for this purpose being concentrated at the Mayor's and City of London County Court.[71]

The administrative arrangements for the Chancery Division were substantially revised in 1982[72] following the Report of the Review Body on the Chancery Division of the High Court.[73] Amongst other matters the changes were designed to produce greater flexibility in the deployment of judges and a new approach to the drafting of orders "which should eliminate their present sesquipedalian pedantry."[74] As from October 1, 1982, orders have been simpler in form and drawn by clerks (known as associates) rather than professionally qualified officers, thus bringing practice more into line with the other divisions.

(c) The Queen's Bench Division

This division deals mainly with claims in contract and tort, and also exercises supervisory and appellate jurisdiction over inferior courts and tribunals. The supervisory jurisdiction includes most applications for habeas corpus and all applications for judicial review.[75] The appellate jurisdiction includes appeals by case stated on a point of law from magistrates' courts and the Crown Court. Also part of this division are the Admiralty Court and the Commercial Court.[76] The work is at present handled by the Lord Chief Justice[77] and 64 puisne judges. The business is done in London and at the 26 first-tier Crown Court centres in the provinces.

In London, the judges are assisted by 13[78] masters of the Queen's Bench Division. A master can perform all the functions of the High Court or a judge in chambers, with certain exceptions, and, with the parties' consent, may try actions.[79] Much of the work involves the determination of interlocutory applications.[80] One master sits each day as the Practice Master, to deal with procedural and practice problems arising in the Central Office and generally to

---

[68] See below, p. 225. They may also take equity work in county courts.

[69] Lord Woolf's *Interim Report on Access to Justice* (1995), p. 61.

[70] Under s.40 of the County Courts Act 1984.

[71] *Practice Direction (Chancery: Transfer of Business)* [1988] 1 W.L.R. 741.

[72] See R.S.C. (Amendment No. 2) 1982 (S.I. 1982 No. 1111); *Practice Direction (Chancery Chambers)* [1982] 1 W.L.R. 1189.

[73] Cmnd. 8205, 1981: report by Oliver L. J. and J. M. Woolf Esq.: see R. Blackford, (1981) 78 L. S. Gaz. 590.

[74] Blackford *op. cit.* p. 590.

[75] Supreme Court Act 1981, s.61 and Sched. 1. See below, pp. 968–976.

[76] Supreme Court Act 1981, s.6.

[77] The Lord Chief Justice's time is mainly spent on appellate criminal work in the Divisional Court of the Queen's Bench Division or the Court of Appeal (Criminal Division). He no longer takes applications for judicial review at first instance.

[78] This figure includes the Master of the Crown Office, who is also Registrar of the Criminal Appeal Office. These offices were combined by the Courts and Legal Services Act 1990, s.78.

[79] See A. S. Diamond, "The Queen's Bench Master" (1960) 76 L.Q.R. 504; Sir Jack Jacob, "The Masters of the Queen's Bench Division" (1971) reprinted in *The Reform of Civil Procedural Law* (1982); R.S.C. Ords.36, 63.

[80] *e.g.* in relation to the extension of time, pleadings, striking out, discovery, summons for directions, summary judgment under R.S.C., Ord. 14: see pp. 600–636.

supervise the work of the office. The right of audience before a master is not limited to barristers; solicitors and their clerks may appear, including unadmitted clerks. The work is normally done in chambers, which lead off from an ante-chamber generally known as "the Bear Garden".

(i) The Admiralty Court

This court has jurisdiction in a wide variety of matters concerning ships and aircraft, including claims arising out of collisions, claims for damage to cargo, for goods supplied and for repairs.[81] When necessary, it also exercises the juris-diction of the High Court as a prize court.[82] From 1993, the practice of the Admiralty has been harmonised with that of the Commercial Court.[83]

(ii) The Commercial Court[84]

There were a number of attempts in the nineteenth century to establish some form of specialised commercial court.[85] A Commercial List was established in the Queen's Bench Division in 1895, partly as the result of dissatisfaction with the handling of a commercial case by Lawrance J.[86] This did not, however, end the drift to arbitration.[87] The list was transformed into a court in 1970.[88] The interlocutory stages are handled by the judge rather than a master and pleadings must be "as brief as possible".[89] A judge of the Commercial Court may be appointed as an arbitrator, provided the Lord Chief Justice agrees that he or she can be made available.[90] Separate lists have been established in the district regis-tries in Liverpool and Manchester in 1991, in Birmingham in 1993 and in Bristol in 1994. Cases set down in them are tried by designated circuit commercial judges sitting as High Court judges.[91]

---

[81] Supreme Court Act 1981, ss.20–24.

[82] *Ibid.* s.62.

[83] *Practice Direction (Admirality Court: Practice)* [1993] 1 W.L.R. 960; *Practice Direction (Admirality Court: Practice)* [1996] 1 W.L.R. 127. The *Guide to Commercial Court Practice* (below) applies, with some exceptions.

[84] Sir Anthony Colman and V. Lyon, *The Practice and Procedure of the Commercial Court* (4th ed., 1995); *Civil Justice Review* (Cm. 394, 1988), Chap. 11.

[85] Colman and Lyon (1995), Chap. 1.

[86] See below, p. 229; (1895–96) 1 Com. Cas. pp. i–x; MacKinnon L.J., (1944) 60 L.Q.R., 324–325; V. V. Veeder, (1994) 110 L.Q.R. 282; Lord Parker C.J., *History and Development of Commercial Arbitration* (1959).

[87] See G. Wilson, *Cases and Materials on the English Legal System* (1973), pp. 31–43; R. B. Ferguson, "The Adjudication of commercial disputes and the legal system in modern England" (1980) 7 B.J.L.S. 141.

[88] Administration of Justice Act 1970, s.3(1).

[89] R.S.C., Ord. 72, rr.2, 7.

[90] Administration of Justice Act 1970, s.4; Colman and Lyon (1995), pp. 174–178. Such appoint-ments are rare: *ibid.*, p. 11.

[91] *Practice Direction (Commercial Lists: Manchester and Liverpool)* [1990] 1 W.L.R. 331, see G. Wingate-Saul, (1990) 140 N.L.J. 539; *Practice Direction (Mercantile List: Birmingham)* [1993] 1 W.L.R.1401, *Practice Direction (Mercantile Court: Bristol)* [1994] 1 W.L.R.1522; see L. Curry, 9(12) *The Lawyer*, p. 15, March 21, 1995; F.Meisel (1994) 13 C.J.Q. 9; I. Garrard, *The Times*, July 26, 1994, p. 35, noting that these courts were cheaper and quicker to use than the Commercial Court in London.

A Commercial Court Committee was established in 1977 to consider and keep under review the working of the Court and the appeal procedures in arbitration proceedings, and to report to the Lord Chancellor.[92] A report of this committee[93] led to the enactment of the Arbitration Act 1979, which was designed to limit rights of appeal to the courts from the decisions of arbitrators, and thereby to halt a decline in the standing of London as a leading centre of international commercial arbitration.[94]

In recent years the caseload of the Commercial Court has increased significantly,[95] although it is still small in relation to the number of arbitrations. Waiting times for trial have increased dramatically.[96] Three features of its work are that in many cases either one or both litigants are foreigners, that a significant part of the court's work comes from London arbitrations, and that it is commonplace for cases to involve millions of pounds.[97]

Concern over waiting times led to the establishment of a working party of practitioner members of the Commercial Court Committee to examine possible reforms.[98] Its report was adopted by the Committee and its recommendations as to improved practice, particularly as to documentation and the conduct of the hearing, commended to court users in a *Guide to Commercial Court Practice*.[99] A new combined Admiralty and Commercial Court Registry was established.[1] The operation of the court was also scrutinised by the Civil Justice Review Body,[2] which made a number of recommendations, including the introduction of a minimum jurisdictional limit of £50,000 (with special exceptions for complex or difficult cases), the provision of extra judge power on a temporary basis, and dealing with formal or uncontested business by consent or by applications on paper. There has been no formal government response to these recommendations. The Commercial Court Committee has, however, expressed strong opposition to the introduction of a lower financial limit.[3]

A crisis in the early 1990s caused by the pressure of business was relieved by the appointment of additional judges: there are now 10 Commercial Court

---

[92] See its Annual Report for 1980 (1981) 78 L. S. Gaz. 100; Colman and Lyon, Chap. 2.

[93] Commercial Court Committee, *Report on Arbitration* (Cmnd. 7284, 1978).

[94] See Ferguson (1980), pp. 151–154; Kerr J., "The Arbitration Act 1979" (1980) 43 M.L.R. 45.

[95] The number of cases heard and disposed of increased from an average of 20 a year between 1946 and 1959 (*Report of the Commercial Court Users' Conference* (Cmnd. 1616, 1962) Appendix G) to a high point of 157 in 1981, declining to 108 in 1986 (*Civil Justice Review*, para. 789), 79 in 1993 and 98 in 1994 (Colman and Lyon (1995), p. 20).

[96] From eight months in 1980 to 24 months in 1984 for a trial due to last longer than three days. In January 1987, trials estimated to last between two and four weeks were being given fixed dates for hearing in October 1990; those estimated at over four weeks were listed for February 1991; *Civil Justice Review*, paras.791, 792. A number of applications for transfer to another division were rejected if the sole ground was to obtain an earlier trial: see J. Jacob, (1988) 7 C.J.Q. 5.

[97] Goff. J., "The Commercial Court—How it Works" (1980) 77 L.S. Gaz. 1035. See generally on the working of the court, Colman and Lyon, *op. cit.*

[98] See F. Meisel, "Commercial Court Reform" (1986) 5 C.J.Q. 196.

[99] The *Guide* was last revised in 1994. *Supreme Court Practice 1995* Vol. 1, paras.72/A1—72/A30. See *Practice Direction (Commercial Court: Practice Guide)* [1994] 1 W.L.R. 1270.

[1] R.S.C. (Amendment) 1987 (S.I. 1987 No. 1423); *Practice Direction (Q.B.D.) (New Admiralty and Commercial Court Registry)* [1987] 1 W.L.R. 1459.

[2] Report, Cm. 394, 1988, Chap. 11. The Review Body commissioned a Factual Study by Coopers & Lybrand, which did not endorse all the assumptions that had been made by the earlier working party: see F. Meisel, "Commercial Court Reform—The Lord Chancellor's Consultation Paper" (1987) 6 C.J.Q. 95.

[3] Colman and Lyon (1995), pp. 16–17, 25–26.

judges, six of whom sit at any one time.[4] The recognition that the court is a "very substantial earner indeed of foreign exchange in the form of invisible earnings"[5] no doubt helped the case for additional appointments. It is anticipated that from the beginning of 1996, three judges at any one time will be trying cases arising out of the Lloyd's litigation.[6]

(d) The Family Division

This division exercises the matrimonial and domestic jurisdiction of the High Court, which includes defended divorce cases, proceedings under the Children Act 1989 and matters relating to the wardship or adoption of children,[7] and deals with non-contentious or common form probate business. It also hears appeals from magistrates' courts in family proceedings.[8] The work is at present handled by the President, 15 puisne judges, and 19 district judges of the principal registry of the Family Division in London and at first-tier Crown Court centres.[9]

Many important aspects of High Court family work are dealt with by the District judges of the principal registry and District judges of the High Court, including decisions on ancillary matters (*e.g.* maintenance, adjustment of property rights and the arrangements for contact with children).

A number of proposals have been made for the establishment of "family courts"[10]. Under the present system, there has been jurisdictional confusion as between magistrates' courts, county courts and the High Court,[11] and there are also discrepancies in the substantive law applied and doubts as to whether a system of accusatorial hearings is appropriate for family matters. The Finer Committee on One Parent Families[12] recommended the establishment of family courts to take over all family matters dealt with in magistrates' courts, county courts and the High Court. The family courts would be organised in tiers, on the analogy of the Crown Court. The lowest tier would comprise Circuit judges and magistrates and sit in county courts: magistrates' court buildings would not be used. There would be facilities for conciliation and support by a professional welfare service. The government was, however, unwilling to provide extra court buildings or add to the workload of the circuit bench. Many of the significant differences between the law applicable by the High Court and county court on the one hand and by magistrates' courts on the other were removed,[13] moves were made to keep the domestic jurisdiction of magistrates' courts separate from

---

[4] M. Heaney, 9(12) *The Lawyer*, March 21, 1995, p. 14.

[5] Lord Mackay of Clashfern L. C., quoted by Heaney, *op. cit.*

[6] Potter, J., interview in 9(12) *The Lawyer*, March 21, 1995, p. 15.

[7] See above, pp. 75–76.

[8] Supreme Court Act 1981, Sched. 1. See above, pp. 58–59.

[9] Most of these have been designated as "divorce towns" for the purpose of hearing defended matrimonial causes and ancillary applications: see *Practice Direction* (*Divorce Towns: Defended Causes*)[1971] 1 W.L.R. 1762; Family Proceedings Rules 1991 (S.I. 1991 No. 1247), as amended, r.2.32. The cases here may be dealt with by High Court judges or Circuit judges sitting as High Court judges.

[10] See B. M. Hoggett and D. S. Pearl, *The Family, Law and Society* (2nd ed., 1987), pp. 628–636; Lord McGregor, (1987) 6 C.J.Q.44; B. M. Hoggett, (1986) 6 L.S.1; D. Allen(ed.), *Family justice—a structure for the family court* (1986).

[11] See *The Overlapping Family Jurisdiction of Magistrates' Courts and County Courts*, Research Report of the Socio-Legal Centre for Family Studies, University of Bristol, June 1987, summarised by J. Graham Hall and D. F. Martin, (1987) 151 J.P.N. 659.

[12] Cmnd. 5629, 1974.

[13] Domestic Proceedings and Magistrates' Courts Act 1978.

criminal proceedings,[14] and steps were taken to widen the jurisdiction of the county court and improve the distribution of business between the High Court and county courts.[15]

The Lord Chancellor's Department began to take a greater interest in the question, issuing consultation documents in 1983[16] and 1986.[17] The Family Courts Campaign, a consortium of major organisations and individuals, began action in 1984. They showed, *inter alia*, that the net costs of reform were not as great as have been thought.[18] Lord Havers and Lord Mackay, who in turn succeeded Lord Hailsham as Lord Chancellor in 1987, showed markedly more enthusiasm for change than their predecessor. The 1986 Review identified three options; (a) to retain the existing structure but with a revised distribution of jurisdiction to eliminate duplication and overlap; (b) to create a unified court within the existing High Court and county court structure; (c) to create a wholly new court with its own structure and judiciary. In the event, however, it was a form of Option (a) which was reflected in arrangements under the Children Act 1989.[19]

(e) Official Referees' business

There are eight Circuit judges nominated by the Lord Chancellor to deal with "Official Referees' business".[20] This is business appropriate to be dealt with by an official referee (as these judges are still commonly known) because (a) it involves a prolonged examination of documents or accounts or a technical, scientific or local investigation, or (b) because that is in the interests of one or more of the parties on grounds of expedition, economy or convenience or otherwise.[21] A matter for trial may either be commenced as official referees' business

[14] See the Justices' Clerks' Society, *Resolving Family Conflict in the 1980s* (1982); "Making the Domestic Proceedings Act Work: A joint declaration by the Magistrates' Association and the Justices' Clerks' Society" (1982) 146 J.P.N. 756–758; C. Latham, "Magistrates' courts and the family jurisdiction: A re-assessment of the Finer Concept of Family Court" (1983) 147 J.P.N. 233–236, 246–247.

[15] See pp. 74–75.

[16] Lord Chancellor's Department, *Family Jurisdiction of the High Court and County Courts, A Consultative Paper* (1983). See J. Levin, *L. A. G. Bull.*, March 1983, pp. 5–6.

[17] Lord Chancellor's Department, *Interdepartmental Review of Family and Domestic Jurisdiction.* For responses, see, *e.g.* (1987) 17 *Family Law* 33–34, 64–66 (Family Courts Campaign), 75–76 (Magistrates' Association); J. S. W. Black, (1986) 150 J.P.N. 422; J. Graham Hall and D. F. Martin, *ibid.* p. 436; N. Wikely, (1986) 5 C.J.Q. 288; C. Yates, (1987) J.S.W.L. 300.

[18] J. Stringer and P. M. Smith, *Family Courts—The Price is Right*, summarised by J. Graham Hall and D. F. Martin, "Family Courts—Analysing the Cost" (1988) 152 J.P.N. 517. See also Graham Hall and Martin, "Towards a Unified Family Court—the Cost Factor" (1983) 4 C.J.Q. 223.

[19] See above, pp. 75–76.

[20] Supreme Court Act 1981, s.68. See E. Fay, *Official Referees' Business* (2nd ed., 1988); F. Meisel, (1984) 3 C.J.Q. 97; (1986) 83 L.S.Gaz. 1294; S. Knafler, *Legal Action*, November 1989, p. 12; J. Newey, (1994) 10 Constr.L.J. 20. The office of Official Referee, first established by the Supreme Court of Judicature Act 1873, was abolished by the Courts Act 1971. Existing holders became Circuit judges: 1971 Act, Sched. 2. On each circuit other than the South Eastern two Circuit judges are appointed to conduct this business, although most is taken in London: see T. Heald, "Official referee's business in the provinces" (1983) Constr.L.J. 91. In London the work is also undertaken by 21 recorders and visiting judges who undertake O.R. work part-time on circuit: Newey, *op. cit.*, p. 20.

[21] R.S.C., Ord. 36, rr., 1, as substituted by S.I. 1982 No. 1111, para. 100.

or transferred to a referee.[22] A matter may also be referred for inquiry and report concerning any issue of fact.[23]

In practice, official referees' business;

"covers a surprisingly wide range of subject matter, but much of it involves very substantial building and civil engineering claims with allied disputes about the provision of materials and services, often including a technical or design element, together with the associated liabilities of architects, engineers, surveyors and other professional men."[24]

An Official Referees' Users Committee and an Official Referees' Bar Association have been established.[25]

(f) Administration

Administrative support for the High Court is provided by officials who are technically part of the unified court service.[26] Apart from the masters and registrars appointed under the Supreme Court Act 1981, the officials are civil servants who are members of the Lord Chancellor's Department.[27] In London, the principal offices are the Central Office of the Supreme Court, Chancery Chambers, the Principal Registry of the Family Division,[28] the Admiralty and Commercial Court Registry and the Accounting Department.

Outside London there are district registries of the High Court in about 130 locations.[29] A District judge[30] is appointed by the Lord Chancellor as District judge of the High Court for each registry,[31] and there is provision for the appointment of deputy and assistant District judges.[32] Writs and originating summonses in the Queen's Bench Division may be issued in any district registry; writs and originating summonses in most Chancery actions may be issued out of eight Chancery district registries[33] and in certain specified cases out of any district registry.[34] The other interlocutory steps are also taken here. Matrimonial causes and most other proceedings in the Family Division may be dealt with at those district registries that have a divorce county court within its district,[35] although they can only be tried at the Royal Courts or one of the divorce towns.[36]

---

[22] *ibid.* rr.2, 3.

[23] *ibid.* r.8.

[24] "Referens," "Official Referee's Business—A New Dawn?" (1983) 80 L.S.Gaz. 478, 479. The author noted a trend away from arbitration to official referees in professional negligence cases.

[25] *ibid.*

[26] The Review Body on the Chancery Division found that the establishment of the service had had little impact on the Division, and were highly critical of the Division's administrative arrangements.

[27] Appointed under the Courts Act 1971, s.27.

[28] Referred to as Principal Probate Registry or the Divorce Registry depending on which branch of the Division's work is concerned.

[29] Supreme Court Act 1981, s.99; Civil Courts Order 1983 (S.I. 1983 No. 713), as amended.

[30] See above, p. 72.

[31] Supreme Court Act 1981, s.100.

[32] *ibid.* ss.102, 103. Formerly they were entitled district registrars.

[33] *i.e.* the district registries for the eight centres mentioned above, p. 87, n. 67.

[34] See R. Blackford and C. Jacque, *Chancery Practice Handbook* (1983), pp. 78–80, 100–101.

[35] See the Family Proceedings Rules 1991 (S.I. 1991 No. (247), r.2 (definition of "district registry" for the purpose of the rules), r.2.32.

[36] Above, p. 74, n. 60.

There are district probate registries in 11 places and sub-registries in 18 others.[37] District probate registrars are appointed by the Lord Chancellor.[38]

(g) Procedural rules

Rules for the purpose of regulating and prescribing the practice and procedure to be followed in the High Court and Court of Appeal may be made by the Supreme Court Rule Committee.[39] Most cases[40] are regulated by the Rules of the Supreme Court.[41] These first appeared in 1885 and the most recent major revision was in 1965. They are regularly amended, and are printed, with extensive annotations, in the current edition of *The Supreme Court Practice* (known as the "White Book"). The rules may not alter any matter of substantive law.[42] In 1982, a Supreme Court Procedure Committee was established by the Lord Chief Justice and the other heads of the divisions, in conjunction with the Presidents of the Senate and the Law Society, to consider and recommend reforms in practice and procedure for saving time and costs. Their recommendations are placed before the Rule Committee.[43]

(h) Appeals[44]

Appeals lie either to the Court of Appeal (Civil Division)[45] or direct to the House of Lords.[46] The appeal lies direct to the House of Lords where the case has reached the High Court on appeal from a magistrates' court or the Crown Court in a criminal matter, or, otherwise, under the "leap frog" procedure.

8. THE LANDS TRIBUNAL

The Lands Tribunal was set up in 1949[47] to take over the jurisdiction of official arbitrators to determine disputes concerning the assessment of compensation for

---

[37] Supreme Court Act 1981, s.104; District Probate Registries Order 1982 (S.I. 1982 No. 379).
[38] Supreme Court Act 1981, s.89, Sched. 2.
[39] Supreme Court Act 1981, ss.84, 85, as amended by the Courts and Legal Services Act 1990, Sched. 18, para. 36(1). The Committee comprises the heads of division, three High Court judges, two lawyers with a Supreme Court qualification and two lawyers with the right to conduct litigation in the Supreme Court. See Sir Jack Jacob, "The Machinery of the Rule Committee of the Supreme Court" (1971) reprinted in *The Reform of Civil Procedural Law* (1982).
[40] There are separate sets of rules for bankruptcy, the winding up of companies, non-contentious or common form probate proceedings, prize matters, certain proceedings under the Mental Health Act 1983 and family proceedings.
[41] The Rules are divided into Orders, rules and paragraphs, and are referred to in abbreviated form as (*e.g.*) R.S.C., Ord 1, r.1.
[42] *e.g.* doubts as to whether certain aspects of the "New Order 53," which introduced the "application for judicial review," were *ultra vires* were settled by the enactment of section 31 of the Supreme Court Act 1981 (see below, p. 973).
[43] (1982) 79 L.S.Gaz. 711; Annual Reports of the committee. The membership includes judges, masters, district judges, barristers and solicitors. There is a sub-committee for each division of the High Court. It is currently chaired by Beldam L.J.
[44] See generally Chap. 17.
[45] See below, pp. 96–98.
[46] See below, pp. 98–101.
[47] Lands Tribunal Act 1949. For its rules of procedure see the Lands Tribunal Rules 1996 (S.I. 1996 No. 1022).

the compulsory acquisition of land. It consists of a President, who must be a person who has held judicial office or a lawyer of at least seven years' standing, a number of members who are lawyers of seven years' standing, and a number who are persons with experience in land valuation (*i.e.* qualified surveyors).[48] All are appointed by the Lord Chancellor, the valuation experts after consultation with the president of the Royal Institution of Chartered Surveyors. The Tribunal's jurisdiction may be exercised by any one or more of its members, as selected by the President, and the selection depends on the nature of the matters at issue. The Tribunal's permanent office and secretariat are in London, although it may sit in the provinces if appropriate, for example to facilitate the inspection of the relevant land and buildings. In addition to the jurisdiction in respect of compensation, it has the power to determine disputes as to the valuation of land for taxation, it hears appeals from valuation tribunals, in matters concerning disputed assessments of land and buildings for rating and disputes concerning the community charge, and from leasehold valuation tribunals, and it has a discretionary power to vary, modify or discharge restrictive covenants under section 84 of the Law of Property Act 1925. An appeal lies to the Court of Appeal by case stated on a point of law. The Lands Tribunal is regarded as having a high status in the court structure, notwithstanding that, unlike the Transport Tribunal and the Employment Appeal Tribunal, it is not constituted under the 1949 Act as a court of record.[49] Its proceedings are conducted fairly formally.

9. THE COURT OF APPEAL (CRIMINAL DIVISION)

The Court of Appeal (Criminal Division) hears appeals from trials on indictment or sentences passed by the Crown Court,[50] and references by the Attorney-General under the Criminal Justice Acts 1972 and 1988.[51] It replaced the Court of Criminal Appeal[52] with effect from October 1, 1966.[53] The Lord Chief Justice is the president of the division, and the Lord Chancellor may appoint a vice-president.[54] The work is done by the Lord Chief Justice, Lords Justices and High Court judges.[55] Circuit judges approved by the Lord Chancellor may also

---

[48] 1949 Act, s.2(2), as amended by the Courts and Legal Services Act, 1990, Sched. 10, para. 7. To be eligible, a lawyer must possess a seven year general qualification under s.71 of the 1990 Act, *i.e.* a right of audience in any part of the Supreme Court or all proceedings in county courts or magistrates' courts.

[49] See *Att.-Gen. v. British Broadcasting Corporation* [1981] A.C. 303, 338 (Viscount Dilhorne). *Cf.* the Annual Report of the Council on Tribunals, 1980–81 (1981–82 H.C. 89), p. 8: "The Lands Tribunal is generally regarded as of High Court standing. . . ."

[50] Criminal Appeal Act 1968, Parts I and II, as amended by the Criminal Appeal Act 1995. See below, pp. 923–933.

[51] See below, pp. 939–940 and 933–935.

[52] Established by the Criminal Appeal Act 1907. This Act for the first time established a right of appeal for the *accused*, as distinct from the discretion of the *judge* to refer a point to his fellow judges (see above, p. 10).

[53] Criminal Appeal Act 1966. This followed the Report of the Committee on the Court of Criminal Appeal (Chairman: Lord Donovan; Cmnd. 2755, 1965).

[54] Supreme Court Act 1981, s.3.

[55] On occasion, one or more of the Law Lords (see below, p. 222) may sit: *e.g. R. v. Husseyn* (Note) (1977) 67 Cr.App.R. 131, "explained" in *Attorney-General's References* (Nos.1 and 2 of 1979) [1980] Q.B. 180, see below p. 940.

sit at the request of the Lord Chief Justice.[55a] For the following purposes, a court of the division must comprise an uneven number of judges not less than three.[56]

  (i) determining appeals against conviction;
 (ii) determining appeals against a verdict of not guilty by reason of insanity;
(iii) determining appeals against a finding of unfitness to be tried because of a disability;
 (iv) determining applications for leave to appeal to the House of Lords;
  (v) refusing leave to appeal in situations (i), (ii), (iii) above except where the application has already been refused by a single judge;
 (vi) determining reviews of sentencing.

Otherwise, matters may be determined by a court comprising two judges.[57] A single judge may grant leave to appeal, grant bail and perform certain other functions.[58] Any number of courts may sit at the same time. The court gives a single judgment unless the judge presiding states that in his or her opinion the question is one of law on which it is convenient that separate judgments should be pronounced by the members of the court.[59] Procedural rules may be made by the Crown Court Rule Committee.[60] The administration of criminal appeals is handled by the Criminal Appeal Office, headed by the Registrar of Criminal Appeals.[61]

Appeals lie to the House of Lords, with the leave of the House or the Court of Appeal, where the Court of Appeal has certified that a point of law of general public importance is involved.[62]

10. THE COURT OF APPEAL (CIVIL DIVISION)[63]

The Court of Appeal was established as part of the Supreme Court by the Supreme Court of Judicature Acts 1873 and 1875. It was reconstituted with

---

[55a] Supreme Court Act 1981, s.9, as amended by the Criminal Justice and Public Order Act 1994, s.52 (implementing a recommendation of the Royal Commission on Criminal Justice (Cm. 2263, para. 10.82). Not more than one Circuit judge may sit on an appeal; a Circuit judge may not act as the single judge; and a court including such a judge may not hear an appeal in a case tried by High Court judge.

[56] Supreme Court Act 1981, s.55, as amended by the Criminal Justice Act 1988, Sched. 15, para. 80.

[57] *ibid., e.g.* appeals against sentence. If the court is equally divided the case must be re-argued before an uneven number of judges not less than three: *ibid.* s.55(5).

[58] Criminal Appeal Act 1968, s.31.

[59] Supreme Court Act 1981, s.59. See *R. v. Head* [1958] 1 Q.B. 132, 137; *R. v. Harz* [1967] 1 A.C. 760, 765.

[60] *Ibid.* s.86, as amended by the Courts and Legal Services Act 1990, Sched. 18, para. 36(2). This comprises the Lord Chancellor and any four of: the Lord Chief Justice, two other judges of the Supreme Court, two Circuit judges, the Registrar of Criminal Appeals, a J.P., two lawyers with a Supreme Court qualification under s.71 of the 1990 Act and two lawyers with the right to conduct litigation in the High Court. See the Criminal Appeal Rules 1968 (S.I. 1968 No. 1262), as amended; *A Guide to Proceedings in the Court of Appeal Criminal Division* [1983] Crim.L.R. 415; D. Thompson and H. W. Wollaston, *Court of Appeal—Criminal Division* (1969); M. Knight, *Criminal Appeals* (1970) and I. McLean, *Criminal Appeals* (2nd ed., 1986).

[61] This office is held in combination with that of Master of the Crown Office. See above, p. 88, n. 78.

[62] See below, pp. 98–101 and 942–944.

[63] For accounts of the working of the Court of Appeal see Lord Asquith, (1947–51) 1 J.S.P.T.L. (N.S.) 350, reproduced in L. Blom-Cooper, *The Language of the Law* (1965); Sir R. Evershed,

Civil and Criminal Divisions in 1966.[64] The jurisdiction of the Civil Division includes appeals from the High Court and county courts in civil matters, and from certain other courts and tribunals.[65] The Master of the Rolls[66] is president of the division, and the Lord Chancellor may appoint a vice-president.[67] The work is mainly done by the Master of the Rolls and the Lords Justices,[68] with occasional assistance from Law Lords, heads of division in the High Court, High Court judges and former judges of the Court of Appeal or High Court.

A court of two judges may hear appeals in interlocutory matters, any other appeal with the consent of the parties, and, as a recent development, certain other appeals, including appeals from county courts.[69] Otherwise the court must comprise an uneven number of judges of three or more.[70] A single judge may determine an application for leave to appeal and deal with other matters arising incidentally.[71]

The work of the division is administered by the Registrar of Civil Appeals. This office was created by the Supreme Court Act 1981,[72] following the report of a Working Party headed by Lord Scarman.[73] The Scarman Committee had identified four main sources of wasted time in the Court of Appeal: (1) failure of parties to an appeal to provide the necessary documentation in a suitable form; (2) the requirement that at least two Lords Justices hear procedural applications; (3) the absence of a flexible and co-ordinated listing system; (4) the length of oral hearings. The Registrar's functions include ensuring that the proper documentation is prepared, advising those unfamiliar with the procedure and practice of the court and the establishment of a co-ordinated listing system. The Scarman Committee considered and rejected a change to the system of written briefs and limitations on the time allowed for oral argument which is the practice, for example, in the Supreme Court of the United States. This system was regarded as alien to the British tradition of oral presentation and argument, and not necessarily less expensive because of the time devoted to preparing highly complex briefs. Instead, arrangements have been made for the pre-reading of documents before the oral hearing begins, and for the submission of "skeleton

---

The Court of Appeal in England (1950); D. Karlen, *Appellate Courts in the United States and England* (1963) Chap. 6; Sir John Donaldson M.R., *The Problems of a Master of the Rolls* (Holdsworth Club Presidential Address, 1985) and "The Court of Appeal" (1985) 53 Medico-Legal Jo. 148.

[64] Criminal Appeal Act 1966.

[65] See below, pp. 944–959.

[66] See below, p. 223.

[67] Supreme Court Act 1981, s.3: for the whole court or for the Division.

[68] See below, p. 222.

[69] Supreme Court Act 1981, s.54; Court of Appeal (Civil Division) Order 1982 (S.I. 1982 No. 543). If a court is evenly divided the case is re-argued before an uneven number of judges not less than three: s.54(5). There were about 12 such rehearings between 1982 and 1986: *Court of Appeal (Civil Division): Review of the Legal Year 1985–86* (1986) 130 S.J. 767, 770. In cases of real difficulty counsel should consider whether an application for a three-judge court should be made: *Coldunell Ltd v. Gallon* [1986] Q.B. 1184, 1202.

[70] Lord Denning M.R. used occasionally to convene courts of five judges "because it was believed in his day that a five-judge court would get out of a precedent set by a three-judge court. That has now been exploded, so there is no point in sitting in a five-judge Court. I do not see any point in it. I have never done it and I have no present intention of doing it": Sir John Donaldson M.R., (1985) 53 Medico-Legal Jo. 148, 161.

[71] *ibid.* ss.54(6), 58.

[72] s.89 and Sched. 2.

[73] *Practice Note* (*Court of Appeal: New Procedure*) [1982] 1 W.L.R. 1312 (Sir John Donaldson M.R.).

arguments'' (*i.e.* an abbreviated note of arguments and other matters which would otherwise be dictated to the court at the oral hearing).[74]

Decisions as to the composition of the courts and the allocation of the cases are made by the Registrar acting in consultation with the Master of the Rolls. In general, the constitution of the civil courts is changed about every six weeks and that of the criminal court every three weeks. Civil courts are ''multi-disciplinary'' rather than ''specialised'' (*e.g.* all former Chancery judges sitting on a Chancery appeal) although, where possible, no appeal on a specialist topic is listed before a court none of whose members are familiar with that speciality.[75] A small team of ''in-house'' lawyers has been appointed, each taking charge of the case management of a group of applications and appeals, defined by reference to subject matter. They will also give procedural advice to litigants in person and, where necessary, provide summaries of the issues raised for the use of judges.[76] The introduction of greater efficiency in the administration of the Court of Appeal proved insufficient to reduce the backlog of appeals; indeed the number of cases outstanding at the end of the year has steadily increased.[77] In response, additional judges have been appointed,[78] the requirements as to documentation have been revised, skeleton arguments are to be produced earlier and exchanged and time limits have been set for oral argument in support of applications for leave to appeal and renewed applications for leave to apply for judicial review.[79] This last step moves the court further towards the American approach.[80] The Lord Chancellor has announced a review of the civil appellate procedure to start in early autumn 1996.[80a]

Appeals lie to the House of Lords, with the leave of the court or the House, on questions of law or fact.[81]

11. THE HOUSE OF LORDS[82]

The House of Lords hears appeals (1) from the Court of Appeal; (2) in certain circumstances, direct from the High Court; (3) from the Court of Session (the

---

[74] *Practice Note (Court of Appeal: skeleton arguments)* [1983] 2 All E.R. 34; *Practice Direction (Court of Appeal: Presentation of Argument)* [1989] 1 W.L.R. 281; *Practice Direction (Court of Appeal: Skeleton Argument Time Limits)* [1990] 1 W.L.R. 794.

[75] Sir John Donaldson M.R., *The Problems of A Master of the Rolls* (Holdsworth Club Presidential Address, 1985), pp. 9–10.

[76] Annual Review by the Master of the Rolls, 1988–89, *The Times*, October 13, 1989. See *Practice Statement (Civil Appeals: Setting Down)* [1990] 1 W.L.R. 1436.

[77] Annual Review, 1992–93, p. 2.

[78] *LCD Court Service Annual Report 1994–95* (1994–95 H.C. 579), pp. 31–32. Three additional judges were authorised in 1994 and three more in 1996.

[79] *Practice Statement (Court of Appeal: Procedural Changes)* [1995] 1 W.L.R. 1188; *Practice Direction (Court of Appeal: Procedure)* [1995] 1 W.L.R. 1191, superseding, *inter alia*, the practice directions mentioned above, n.74.

[80] See Leggatt L.J., ''The future of the oral tradition in the Court of Appeal'' (1995) 14 C.J.Q. 11, noting ominously that ''it is comparatively uncommon for members of the court to change their minds about whether to dismiss or allow an appeal, once they have read the skeleton arguments'' (p. 15).

[80a] LCD Press Notice 79, 96, March 26, 1996.

[81] See below, and pp. 961–963.

[82] See L. Blom-Cooper and Gavin Drewry, *Final Appeal* (1972); R. Stevens, *Law and Politics* (1978); A. Paterson, *The Law Lords* (1982); Lord Fraser of Tullybelton, 1986 S.L.T. 33. Brief

highest civil court in Scotland)[83]; (4) from the Court of Appeal in Northern Ireland; (5) in certain circumstances, direct from the High Court of Justice in Northern Ireland and (6) from the Courts-Martial Appeal Court.[84]

An appeal may not be heard or determined unless at least three from the following list are present: (1) the Lord Chancellor[85]; (2) the Lords of Appeal in Ordinary[86]; (3) any peer who has held one of the high judicial offices of Lord Chancellor, member of the Judicial Committee of the Privy Council, Lord of Appeal in Ordinary, judge of the Supreme Court of England and Wales or Northern Ireland or judge of the Court of Session.[87] Technically, it seems that all members of the House of Lords have the right to vote on appeals, but the practice has fallen into disuse. In the early nineteenth century lay peers were used to make up the necessary quorum but by the 1830s there were sufficient Law Lords[88] for a "professional" court to be possible.[89] In 1844 the convention that lay peers did not vote was established in *O'Connell v. R.*[90] Daniel O'Connell appealed against a conviction for conspiracy. Three Law Lords were in favour of allowing the appeal, two were against it. Several lay peers purported to vote with the minority, but were persuaded to withdraw on the ground that in reality the "Court of Law" in the House was constituted by the Law Lords and interference by lay peers would greatly lessen the authority of the House. The last occasion when a lay peer attempted to vote was in *Bradlaugh v. Clarke*[91] when Lord Denman[92] attended throughout the proceedings and purported to vote with Lord Blackburn against the majority of the Law Lords. His attempt was ignored by the Lord Chancellor and the Law Reports, but was noted by *The Times*.[93] In response to a question in the House of Commons, the Home Secretary stated that as the Appellate Jurisdiction Act 1876 had not excluded lay peers, it had been competent for Lord Denman to sit: had his opinion affected the result, he would have been asked to withdraw his vote on the precedent of *O'Connell's* case.[94]

Under the original arrangements for reorganisation incorporated in the Supreme Court of Judicature Act 1873 the appellate role of the House of Lords was to be abolished. The Court of Appeal was to be the final appeal court for

accounts of the work of the Judicial Office in supporting the Law Lords are found in the *House of Lords Annual Reports and Accounts* published by HMSO (*e.g.* 1993–94 H.L. 86).

[83] There is no right of appeal from the highest Scottish criminal court, the High Court of Justiciary: *Mackintosh v. Lord Advocate* (1876) 3 R. (H.L.) 34; Criminal Procedure (Scotland) Act 1887, s.72. See A. J. Maclean, "The House of Lords and Appeals from the High Court of Justiciary 1707–1887" 1985 J. R. 192.

[84] Appeals in English cases are considered in detail below, pp. 942–944, 961–963.

[85] Above, pp. 16–19; below, pp. 222–223.

[86] Below, p. 222.

[87] Appellate Jurisdiction Act 1876, ss.5, 25; Appellate Jurisdiction Act 1887, s.5. For a current list, see the annual *Waterlow's Solicitors and Barristers Diary*.

[88] The term then covered the Lord Chancellor, the Lord Chancellor of Ireland, former Lord Chancellors, ennobled judges, and occasionally a peer who had held a minor judicial office.

[89] Stevens (1978), p. 29.

[90] (1844) 11 Cl. & F. 155, 421–426.

[91] (1883) 8 App. Cas 354. See R. E. Megarry, (1949) 65 L.Q.R. 22–24.

[92] This was the second Lord Denman, son of the Lord Chief Justice and brother of Denman J., a High Court judge, 1872–1892. "Lord Denman was aged seventy-eight at the time of his fling, and he had been a peer for nearly thirty years and a barrister for fifty, so that his was no mere indiscretion of youth and inexperience" (Megarry (1949), p. 24). He "won notoriety rather from his eccentricities than any eminent qualifications" (D.N.B.).

[93] April 10, 1883, p. 4.

[94] Sir William Harcourt, H.C. Deb. Vol. 278, col. 68, April 12, 1883.

England, and ultimately for Scotland, Ireland and the colonies. However, before the arrangements came into effect opposition developed in several quarters, the appeal to the House was retained and provision was made for the appointment of salaried Law Lords.[95]

Up to 1948, appeals to the House of Lords were heard in the chamber of the House. In that year, the process of repairing the Palace of Westminister caused the House to commit the hearing of appeals to an Appellate Committee meeting in a committee room and this practice has been maintained ever since. The committee hears appeals and reports its conclusions to the House, where judgment is delivered at a judicial sitting.[96] The House, or the Appellate Committee, as the case may be, is presided over by the Lord Chancellor or, as is more usually the case, the senior Lord of Appeal in Ordinary present.[97] The Appellate Committee must be distinguished from the "Appeal Committee" which sits to consider and report on petitions for leave to appeal and other incidental matters and which normally comprises three Law Lords.

Selection of Law Lords to sit on Appeal Committees is done by the Principal Clerk to the Judicial Office: selection of Appellate Committees, although theoretically in the hands of the Lord Chancellor, is delegated to his Permanent Secretary, who consults the Lord Chancellor in cases of difficulty.[98] Normally, the most convenient panel available is chosen; occasionally, special considerations may apply, such as the exclusion of judges with a political background from adjudicating in a case with party-political implications,[99] the strong desirability of one or both of the Scottish Law Lords sitting on an appeal from Scotland and the desirability of the presence of a Chancery judge in a Chancery appeal. The room for manoeuvre is in practice limited.

Procedure on appeals to the House of Lords is regulated by Directions and Standing Orders of the House.[1] Each side must submit a "case", drawn up by counsel, which is a "succinct statement of their argument in the Appeal,"[2] although in practice the oral submissions of counsel and the interchange between them and the Law Lords are of greater significance.[3] The Law Lords are generally expected to confine their propositions of law to matters covered by the argument of counsel, although this view is held today less strongly than for-

---

[95] See Stevens (1979), Chap. 2 and R. Stevens, "The Final Appeal: Reform of the House of Lords and Privy Council, 1867–1876" (1964) 80 L.Q.R. 343.

[96] A morning sitting in the Chamber of the House. Some appeals may be heard in the Chamber, *e.g.* during Parliamentary recesses.

[97] Seniority formerly depended on the date of first appointment to the office: Blom-Cooper and Drewry (1972), p. 179. From 1984, the first and second senior Law Lords have been specifically appointed as such by the Queen: H.L. Deb. Vol. 453, cols.914–919, June 27, 1984: see L. Blom-Cooper, [1984] P.L. 376; A.A. Paterson, 1988 J.R. 235, 251, n. 59. The presiding judge may exert significant influence over the course of proceedings: Paterson (1982), pp. 66–72. The most recent senior Lords of Appeal have been Lord Simonds (1954–1962); Lord Reid (1962–1975); Lord Wilberforce (1975–1982); Lord Diplock (1982–1984); Lord Fraser of Tullybelton (1984–1985); Lord Scarman (1985–1986); Lord Keith of Kinkel (1986–).

[98] See Paterson (1982), pp. 87–89. The selections have to be co-ordinated with those for the Judicial Committee of the Privy Council.

[99] This was done for *Heaton's Transport Co. v. T.G.W.U.* [1973] A.C. 15. See A. Paterson, (1979) 1 B.J.L.S. 118, 126.

[1] See *Supreme Court Practice 1995*, Vol. 2, Part 16, Directions as to Procedure, January 1992.

[2] *ibid.*

[3] See A. Paterson, *The Law Lords* (1982), Chaps.3 and 4.

merly.[4] Moreover, they will not normally consider a point not raised in the courts below,[5]

> "But if [the Law Lords] think it is something that really goes to the root of the thing, if they think the whole thing would be rather a mess if they did not allow it to be argued, then they would probably allow it on terms as to costs."[6]

Informal discussions among the Law Lords take place during the hearing of an appeal.[7] Judgment is invariably reserved. At the conclusion of the hearing there is a conference at which provisional opinions are expressed, and a general discussion follows. If there appears to be general agreement, it may also be agreed that a particular Law Lord should write the major opinion. Occasionally, a second conference may be convened.

Each Law Lord is entitled to write his own opinion,[8] although they attempt to avoid the unnecessary multiplication of opinions. Views differ on the desirability of multiple opinions.[9] Paterson found that of those studied:

> "although in non-criminal common law cases only two active Law Lords generally favoured a single judgment in criminal appeals on a point of statutory construction, probably a majority of the active Law Lords favoured that approach."[10]

The main problem with multiple assenting judgments is that the differences in language may make it difficult to discern the *ratio decidendi*[11]; conversely, the same feature may leave subsequent judges greater scope for developing the law. The main problem with single opinions is that they may reflect an uneasy compromise. Recently, the proportion of cases with a single opinion has increased.[12]

The House of Lords has a limited original, as distinct from appellate, jurisdiction, which includes the power to determine peerage claims and the power to conduct impeachment proceedings.[13] The right of a peer to be tried by his peers in cases of treason, felony or misprison of felony was abolished in 1948.[14]

---

[4] *ibid.* pp. 38–45.

[5] *ibid.* pp. 45–49.

[6] Lord Cross, cited by Paterson (1982), p. 47.

[7] The interaction among the Law Lords is discussed by Paterson (1982), Chap. 5.

[8] Occasionally the presiding judge may press for a single opinion: see *D.P.P. v. Smith* [1961] A.C. 290 and *Heaton's Transport Ltd v. T.G.W.U.* [1973] A.C. 15: *cf.* the position in the Judicial Committee of the Privy Council, below, p. 103.

[9] See Blom-Cooper and Drewry (1972), Chap. V; R. Cross, (1977) 93 L.Q.R. 378; Paterson (1982), pp. 96–109 and 183–187.

[10] *op. cit.*, p. 185.

[11] See, *e.g. Boys v. Chaplin* [1971] A.C. 356; *British Railways Board v. Herrington* [1972] A.C. 877: below, pp. 420–421.

[12] See P. V. Baker, (1983) 99 L.Q.R. 371; Lord Diplock *In re Prestige Group plc* [1984] 1 W.L.R. 335, 338, referring to this as "a frequent practice in this House when dealing with questions of statutory construction"; A. Bradney, "The changing face of the House of Lords" 1985 J.R. 178 (statistical analysis of judgments between January 30, 1974 and March 1, 1984).

[13] The last such cases were those of Warren Hastings (1788–1795: see P. J. Marshall, *The Impeachment of Warren Hastings* (1965)) and Viscount Melville (1806); *cf.* below, p. 235.

[14] Criminal Justice Act 1948, s.30. The last trial was that of Lord de Clifford. See, W. T. West, *The Trial of Lord de Clifford 1935* (1984), and, generally P. Marsden, *In Peril Before Parliament* (1965).

12. The Judicial Committee of the Privy Council

The Judicial Committee of the Privy Council was established in 1833,[15] largely
as the result of the efforts of Lord Brougham.[16] Previously, appeals to the Crown
from the colonies, which arose out of the prerogative right of the Sovereign as
the fountainhead of all justice, were dealt with by a committee of the Privy
Council which did not have a regular judicial composition. The 1833 Act limited
the membership almost exclusively to senior judges. The present position is that
the Committee comprises the Lord President of the Council, the Lord Chancellor, the Lords of Appeal in Ordinary and other members of the Privy Council
who hold "high judicial office",[17] and former holders of these offices.[18] In
addition, privy councillors who hold or have held one of a number of judicial
offices in New Zealand and other Commonwealth countries may also be
members.[19]

The Judicial Committee hears appeals from certain Commonwealth countries,
from the Channel Islands, in certain admiralty and ecclesiastical matters and
from the General Medical Council[20] and other professional bodies.[21] The Commonwealth appellate jurisdiction was formerly regarded as an important unifying
influence: it has now dwindled significantly as an increasing number of Commonwealth countries have abandoned the appeal.[22] For example, Canada and
India abolished appeals in 1949, Sri Lanka in 1971, Malaysia in 1985, Australia
(effectively) in 1986 and Singapore in 1994.[23] The New Zealand government
proposes their abolition,[24] and appeals from Hong Kong will end with the territory's reversion to China in 1997.[25] The Committee's decision takes the form
of advice to the Queen, to which effect is given by an Order in Council.[26] It is

---

[15] Judicial Committee Act 1833.
[16] See P. A. Howell, *The Judicial Committee of the Privy Council 1833–1876* (1979), Chap. 12,
D. B. Swinfen, "Henry Brougham and the Judicial Committee of the Privy Council" (1975) 90
L.Q.R. 396; L. P. Beth, [1975] P. L. 219. See generally D. B. Swinfen, *Imperial Appeal* (1987).
[17] As defined by the Appellate Jurisdiction Acts 1876, ss.5, 25 and 1877, s.5. This extends the
membership of the Committee to the Lords Justices of Appeal, although they rarely sit in practice.
[18] Judicial Committee Act 1833, s.1; Appellate Jurisdiction Act 1876, s.6; Appellate Jurisdiction
Act 1887, s.3.
[19] Judicial Committee Amendment Act 1895, s.1, Sched.; Appellate Jurisdiction Act 1908, s.3. The
list in 1994 included eight from New Zealand and one each from the Bahamas, Eastern Caribbean
and Jamaica: *Waterlow's Solicitors and Barristers' Diary 1994*, p. 1–2. For an account of the
experience of the Chief Justice of New Zealand in sitting on the Privy Council, see Interview
with Sir Thomas Eichelbaum, [1994] N.Z.L.J. 86.
[20] Medical Act 1983, s.40.
[21] *e.g.* dentists, vets, chiropodists and remedial gymnasts: Dentists Act 1984, s.29; Veterinary Surgeons Act 1966, s.17; Professions Supplementary to Medicine Act 1960, ss.1, 9. See, *e.g. Libman
v. General Medical Council* [1972] A.C. 217; *McEniff v. General Dental Council* [1980] 1 W.L.R.
328 (dentist struck off for allowing an assistant and a receptionist to fill teeth after he had completed the drilling); *Le Scroog v. General Optical Council* [1982] 1 W.L.R. 1238 (optician struck
off for advertising).
[22] Dominions were given the power to do this by the Statute of Westminster 1931, ss.2, 3.
[23] Australia Act 1986, s.11.
[24] See B. Brown, [1995] N.Z.L.J. 82; P. J. Downey, [1995] N.Z.L.J. 205; [1995] N.Z.L. J.208–218.
The proposal is generally opposed by the New Zealand legal profession.
[25] See P. Wesley-Smith, (1992) 2 H.K.L.J. 118.
[26] For the republics (The Gambia, Singapore, Trinidad and Tobago) the Committee itself is the
decision-making authority.

binding on the relevant Commonwealth courts.[27] A proportion of the cases heard by the Privy Council raise questions of constitutional interpretation. The handling of these cases has been analysed for guidance as to how the House of Lords might deal with matters arising under a written constitution with a Bill of Rights for the United Kingdom. The consensus appears to be that the judges seem not particularly well suited to handling such issue,[28] although the performance recently has been more impressive.[29]

The Committee sits in London. The recording of dissenting opinions has only been permitted since 1966.[30] There is either one unanimous opinion, or one for the majority and one for the minority. Lord Reid thought that the single opinion rule had led to Privy Council judgments being much inferior to speeches in the House of Lords:

> They are perfectly adequate to decide the particular case but not often of wider importance. Yet the same Law Lords have sat and they have taken just as much trouble. The reason is that a single judgment must get the agreement of at least all in the majority so it tends to be no more than the highest common factor of all the views."[31]

Apart from the appellate jurisdiction, the Judicial Committee may entertain an application for a declaration that a person purporting to be a member of the House of Commons is disqualified by the House of Commons Disqualification Act 1975.[32] Finally, Her Majesty may refer any matter to the Judicial Committee for hearing or consideration.[33]

13. THE COURT OF JUSTICE OF THE EUROPEAN COMMUNITIES[34]

(a) Establishment

This Court is one of the four major institutions created by the Treaties establishing the European Communities. There was originally a Court of Justice for

---

[27] At least while that country retains the appeal to the Privy Council. For example, in *Viro v. R.* (1978) 18 A.L.R. 257, the High Court of Australia held that it was no longer bound by decisions of the Privy Council: see R. S. Geddis, (1978) 9 Fed. L. R. 427.

[28] P. Wallington and J. McBride, *Civil Liberties and a Bill of Rights* (1976), pp. 32–33 "We come away with a rather neutral impression of the talents available"; G. J. Zellick "Fundamental Rights in the Privy Council" [1982] P.L. 344 (criticising the decision in a case concerning the death penalty, *Riley v. Attorney General of Jamaica* [1983] 1 A.C. 719); B. de Smith, "The Judicial Committee as a Constitutional Court" [1984] P.L. 557; N. S. Price, "Constitutional Adjudication in the Privy Council and Reflections on the Bill of Rights debate" (1986) 35 I.C.L.Q. 946, criticising *Robinson v. R.* [1985] A.C. 956; *cf.* M. Zander, *A Bill of Rights?* (3rd ed., 1985), pp. 62–64, who takes a more favourable view. On the role of the Privy Council in developing the common law, see J. W. Harris, (1990) 106 L.Q.R. 574.

[29] See, *e.g. Pratt and Morgan v. Attorney-General of Jamaica* [1994] 2 A.C. 1; M. Grieve, "Life after Death Row," *Counsel*, July/August 1994, p. 16.

[30] Judicial Committee (Dissenting Opinion) Order 1966. See D. B. Swinfen, "Single Judgment in the Privy Council 1833–1966" 1975 20 J.R. 153.

[31] "The Judge as Law Maker" (1972) XII J.S.P.T.L. (N.S.) 22, 29.

[32] See s.7.

[33] Judicial Committee Act 1833, s.4. See D. B. Swinfen, "Politics and the Privy Council: Special Reference to the Judicial Committee" 1978 23 J.R. 126.

[34] S. Weatherill and P. Beaumont, *E.C. Law* (2nd ed., 1995), Chap. 6. T. C. Hartley, *The Foundations of European Community Law* (3rd ed., 1994); L. Neville Brown and T. Kennedy, *The*

the European Coal and Steel Community, but when the treaties establishing the European Economic Community and Euratom were concluded it was agreed that there should be one court for the three communities. The Single European Act of 1986 made provision for the establishment of a Court of First Instance to ease the Court's work load.[35]

(b) Composition

The Court consists of 15 judges,[36] assisted by nine advocates general.[37] It may sit either in "plenary session" (*i.e.* with all the judges entitled to be present) or, where permitted by the Rules of Procedure, in "chambers" of three or five judges. It must sit in plenary session when a Member State or a Community Institutions that is a party to the proceedings so request.[38]

Otherwise, matters may be dealt with by a chamber, as, for example, may cases brought by an official against an institution, matters concerning costs and legal aid, and references for a preliminary ruling or direct actions where the difficulty or importance of the case or the circumstances are not such as to require a decision of the court in plenary session. Only one judgment is delivered by the Chamber or Court and it is not revealed whether the decision was unanimous or reached by a majority.

The function of the advocate general is:

"acting with complete impartiality, and independence, to make, in open court, reasoned submissions on cases brought before the Court of Justice, in order to assist the Court. . . ."[39]

This office has no exact equivalent in any national legal system although it is loosely based on that of *commissaire du gouvernement* in proceedings before French administrative courts, especially the Conseil d'Etat. One advocate general is assigned to each case. He or she sits on the bench, next to the judges, and may put questions to the parties. His or her opinion on the case is normally expressed about three weeks after the submissions of counsel have been heard, and, unlike such submissions on behalf of a client, "the Advocate General speaks for no-one but himself."[40] The opinion sets out the facts and relevant legal provisions, analyses the issues in the light of the case law of the court and suggests the appropriate decision for the court to adopt. It tends to be longer,

---

Court of Justice of the European Communities (4th ed., 1994); J. Usher, *European Court Practice* (1983); K. P. E. Lasok, *The European Court of Justice: Practice and Procedure* (1984); Office for Official Publications of the European Communities, *The Court of Justice of the European Community* (4th ed., 1986); H. Rasmussen, *On Law and Policy in the European Court of Justice* (1986).

[35] See section (f), below.

[36] Art. 165/EC, as amended.

[37] Art. 166/EC, as amended. There are to be eight after October 6, 2000: see Weatherill and Beaumont (1995), p. 155, n.3.

[38] Art. 165/EC, as amended by Art.G(49)TEU. Prior to the amendment by the Maastricht Treaty, Art. 165/EC required plenary sessions for cases brought by a Member State or Community institution, and (unless the Court's Rules of Procedure provided otherwise) preliminary rulings.

[39] Art. 166/EC. See A. A. Dashwood, "The Advocate General in the Court of Justice of the European Communities" (1982) 2 L.S. 202; K. Borgsmidt, "The Advocate General at the European Court of Justice: A Comparative Study" (1988) 13 E.L.Rev. 106.

[40] Dashwood, *op. cit.*, p. 207.

more informative and less bland in style than the judgments of the court. The advocate general does not attend the deliberations of the judges. It is thought that his or her opinion is followed in about 70 per cent of cases, but this may be an overestimate.[41]

The judges and advocates general are chosen by agreement among the governments of the Member States. They have to be:

"chosen from persons whose independence is beyond doubt and who possess the qualifications required for appointment to the highest judicial offices in their respective countries or who are jurisconsults of recognised competence,"[42]

and are appointed for a term of six years. A proportion[43] of the judges and advocates general are replaced every three years. The incumbents are eligible for re-appointment. The judges elect one of their number to be President for a (renewable) three year term. The President's functions are to direct the judicial business and the administration of the court and to preside at hearings. One of the advocates general is designated as first advocate general, and performs certain administrative functions, including the distribution of cases among his or her colleagues.

There is one judge of each of the 15 nationalities.[44] There is one advocate general from each of the five largest states[45] and the remainder from the smaller states by rotation.

(c) Jurisdiction

The jurisdiction of the Court of Justice under the EC Treaty[46] can be classified under four main heads: (i) Applications for preliminary rulings under Article 177/EC in the course of proceedings in a national court or tribunal; (ii) Direct actions against Member States or Community institutions; (iii) Staff cases; (iv) Opinions.

(i) Applications for Preliminary rulings

These are considered in Chapter 17.

---

[41] *ibid.* p. 212.
[42] Art. 167/EC. See also the Protocol on the Statute of the Court of Justice.
[43] Seven or eight judges; four advocates general.
[44] These are not legal requirements but are the consequences in practice of the need for the agreement of all the member states. The U.K. judges have been Lord Mackenzie Stuart; formerly a judge of the Court of Session (1973–1988, President 1984–1988); Sir Gordon Slynn; formerly a High Court judge and then an Advocate General (1988–1992); David Edward: a Scottish Q.C. and Professor of European Institutions at the University of Edinburgh, and then judge of the Court of First Instance, 1989–1992 (1992–)
[45] France, Germany, Italy, Spain and the United Kingdom. Those from the U.K. have been J.-P. Warner (1973–1981); Sir Gordon Slynn (1981–1988); Prof. F. Jacobs Q.C. (1988–).
[46] There are analogous procedures under the other Treaties, with some differences in point of detail between the ECSC and the others.

(ii) Direct actions

(1) *Actions against Member States.*[47] Under Article 169/EC, if the Commission
considers that a Member State has failed to fulfil an obligation imposed by the
Treaty or secondary Community legislation, it must deliver a reasoned opinion
on the matter, after giving the State concerned the opportunity to submit its
observations.[48] If the State does not comply with the opinion within the period
laid down by the Commission, the Commission may bring the matter before
the Court of Justice.[49] Under Article 170/EC a Member State may bring similar
proceedings against another Member State, after bringing the matter to the Commission's attention. If a breach is established the Court will make a declaratory
order to that effect.[50] The Member State is required by Article 171/EC to take
the necessary measures to comply.[51] A majority of cases are settled before they
reach the Court.

Prior to amendments effected by the Maastricht Treaty, the sanctions were
political rather than legal, and there was non-compliance in a significant number
of cases. The position now is that, in such cases, the Commission after giving
the Member State concerned the opportunity to submit observations, may issue
a reasoned opinion specifying the points on which there has been non-
compliance. If the Member State fails to take the necessary measures to comply
with the original judgment within the time limit laid down by the Commission,
the latter may bring the matter before the Court and the Court may impose a
lump sum or penalty payment on the Member State.[52] This is an "important
new power, which greatly enhances the armoury of the Court of Justice."[53]

(2) *Actions against community institutions.* These include (1) actions under Article 173/EC for the annulment of acts of the Council and Commission[54];
(2) actions under Article 175/EC against the Council, the Commission or the
Parliament where it has, contrary to the requirements of the Treaty, failed to
act[55]; (3) actions under Article 172/EC to review penalties or fines imposed by

---

[47] Hartley (1994), Chap. 10; Weatherill and Beaumont (1995), Chap. 7; H. A. H. Audretsch, *Supervision in European Community Law* (2nd ed., 1986); A. Dashwood and R. White, (1989) 14
E.L.Rev. 388.
[48] A reasonable time must be allowed: Case 293/85, *Commission v. Belgium* [1989] 2 C.M.L.R.
527. See A. Arnull, (1988) 13 E.L.Rev. 260.
[49] See, *e.g.* Case 232/78 *Commission v. France* [1979] E.C.R. 2729: French ban on the import of
mutton and lamb from the U.K. held to be an infringement of the Treaty; the dispute was eventually compromised.
[50] Only one case under Art. 170 has proceeded to judgment: Case 141/78 *France v. United Kingdom*
[1979] E.C.R. 2923. *Cf.* the procedure under Art. 93/EC whereby the Commission may require
a state to abolish or alter a state aid that distorts or threatens to distort competition: if the state
does not comply the matter may be referred to the Court.
[51] Although Art. 171 does not specify a time limit within which a judgment must be complied
with, implementation must start immediately and be completed as soon as possible: Case 131/
84, *Commission v. Italian Republic* [1985] E.C.R. 3531 (unreasonable delay in implementing
judgment in Case 91/81, [1982] E.C.R. 2133). Implementation must be by national provisions
of a binding nature, not merely by administrative circulars or practices: Case 168/85, *Commission
v. Italy* [1986] E.C.R. 2945.
[52] Art. 171/EC, as amended by Art. G(51)/TEU.
[53] Weatherill and Beaumont (1995), p. 211.
[54] See below, pp. 346–348. Community legislation is considered below at pp. 305–350, and its
interpretation at pp. 404–412.
[55] See below, pp. 349–350.

the Commission; (4) actions under Article 178/EC for damages based on the non-contractual (including tortious) liability of the Communities.[56]

(iii) Staff cases

The court has jurisdiction under Article 179/EC in any dispute between the Community and its servants within the limits and under the conditions laid down in the Staff Regulations or the Conditions of Employment.

(iv) Opinions

The court may under Article 228/EC give an opinion as to whether an international agreement that the Community proposes to enter is compatible with the Treaty.

(d) Some aspects of procedure

Proceedings before the court are governed by the Rules of Procedure[57] drawn up by the court with the approval of the Council. There are four stages—

(1) Written proceedings. Proceedings are commenced by filing an application specifying the subject matter of the dispute, the grounds, the form of order sought and certain other matters. A defence must be filed within one month, and a reply and rejoinder may follow.

(2) Investigation or preliminary inquiry. The case will have been assigned by the President to one of the six chambers. He will also nominate one of the judges in that chamber to act as rapporteur. After the close of pleadings the judge-rapporteur makes a preliminary report which enables the court to decide whether the submission of any evidence is required, such as the oral testimony of witnesses, an expert's report or the personal appearance of the parties. These matters are dealt with at this stage. The judge-rapporteur then prepares a report summarising facts and arguments.

(3) Oral proceedings. At this stage the parties' lawyers address the court.[58] Interchange between court and advocate is a comparatively recent development. The final step of this stage is the delivery of the advocate general's opinion, which takes place in open court, normally a few weeks later.

(4) Judgment. Proceedings may be conducted in Danish, Dutch, English,

---

[56] Art. 215/EC, provides that "the Community shall, in accordance with the general provisions common to the laws of the Member States, make good any damage caused by its institutions or by its servants in the performance of their duties."

[57] A codified version of the 1974 rules as amended was published in the Official Journal 1982, C.39/1.

[58] Any lawyer entitled to practice before a court of a Member State may appear. Thus, either a barrister or solicitor from the U.K. may appear. A litigant may not normally appear in person. Cf. below, pp. 133–138.

Finnish, French, German, Greek, Irish, Italian, Portuguese, Spanish or Swedish. The language is chosen by the applicant, except where an application is made against a Member State, where the state's language is used, and in applications for preliminary rulings, which are conducted in the language of the referring court or tribunal. In practice, the working language is normally French.

There are no court fees. Costs are normally awarded to the successful party against his or her opponent. The court may grant legal aid: aid for an application for a preliminary ruling is, however, regarded as an aspect of the national proceedings, and aid will only be granted by the court if it is not available in those proceedings.

(e) Administration

This is the responsibility of the Registrar and his staff. There is a Registry, translation, library and documentation and interpretation services and an information office. In addition, three legal secretaries are attached to each judge and advocate general.

(f) The Court of First Instance[59]

From 1974, the European Court pressed for the establishment of a separate administrative tribunal to deal with staff cases and thereby relieve the pressure on the Court. For over 20 years, nothing came of this although changes were made in the Court's procedures, including the greater use of Chambers, and the number of judges and advocates general were periodically increased. Eventually, the Single European Act amended the main Treaties[60] to enable the Council, by a Decision, to establish a Court of First Instance of the European Communities, and amend the Rules of Procedure accordingly. The necessary Decision was made in 1988,[61] and provided for a court of 12 (now 15) members "attached to the Court of Justice of the European Communities"[62] and with its seat at the Court. It normally sits in chambers of three or five judges, but may exceptionally sit in plenary session, in accordance with its Rules of Procedure. The members are appointed by common accord of the governments of the Member States for (renewable) six year terms, and with the membership partly renewed every three years.[63] They must be "chosen from persons whose independence is beyond

---

[59] The background is fully considered by T. Kennedy, "The Essential Minimum: The Establishment of the Court of First Instance" (1989) 14 E.L.Rev. 7. See also H. G. Schermers, (1988) 25 C.M.L.Rev. 541; Select Committee on the European Communities, Fifth Report 1987–88 (1987–88 H.L. 20); O. Due, (1988) 4 Y.E.L. 1; T. Kennedy, (1990) 15 E.L.Rev. 54; A. G. Toth in R. White and B. Smythe (eds.), *Current Issues in European and International Law* (1990), Chap. 2; Brown and Kennedy (1994), Chap. 5.

[60] Art. 168a/EC; Art. 32D/ECSC; Art. 140a/Euratom. The Maastricht Treaty amended Art.168a to provide directly for the establishment of the CFI, specifically excluding only A177 references from the classes of action or proceeding that may be conferred on it by the Council; the original version also excluded actions brought by Member States or Community institutions.

[61] Dec. 88/591/ECSC, EC, Euratom, October 24, 1988, [1988] O.J.L. 319/1 (November 25, 1988), [1989] 1 C.M.L.R. 323, as amended.

[62] *ibid.*, Art. 1.

[63] Art. 168a(3)/EC. The first judge from the U.K. was David Edward Q.C. (1989–1992). He was succeeded replaced by Christopher Bellamy Q.C. (1992–).

doubt and who possess the ability required for appointment to judicial office.''[64] No separate advocates general are appointed, but the judges "may be called upon to perform the task of an advocate general",[65] again in accordance with the Rules of Procedure. A President is elected by the judges for a (renewable) three-year term.[66] The Court also appoints a Registrar.

The Court initially exercised the jurisdiction of the European Court in (1) staff cases[67]; (2) competition cases[68]; and (3) coal and steel cases arising from the application of the ECSC Treaty.[69] Its jurisdiction has since been significantly expanded to include all other actions under Articles 173, 175 and 178/EC and actions under Article 181 (where the court may give judgments under an arbitration clause in a contract concluded by or on behalf of the Community).[70] Notwithstanding these developments, the backlog of cases is increasing in both the Court of First Instance and the Court itself.[71]

The Court of First Instance has established its own Rules of Procedure, in agreement with the European Court and with the unanimous approval of the Council.[72]

An appeal lies to the European Court[73] against final decisions of the Court of First Instance, and decisions disposing of the substantive issues in part only or disposing of a procedural issue concerning a plea of lack of competence or inadmissibility. An appeal may be brought by (1) any unsuccessful party (except that interveners other than Member States or Community institutions may only appeal where the Court's decision directly affects them); and (2) (except in staff cases) any non-intervening Member State or Community institution. The appeal is limited to points of law, including lack of competence of the Court of First Instance, and a breach of procedure which adversely affects the appellant's interests. If the appeal is well founded, the European Court is to quash the decision and either itself give final judgment or remit the case to the Court of First Instance. In the latter event, the European Court's decision on points of law is binding.

14. THE EUROPEAN COURT OF HUMAN RIGHTS[74]

Decisions of the European Court of Human Rights have become of increasing significance for the English legal system in recent years. The Convention for

---

[64] *ibid.*

[65] Dec. 88/591, Art. 2(3).

[66] *ibid.*, Art. 2(2). The first President was appointed as such by the Member States: Art. 11.

[67] Disputes between the Communities and their servants under Art. 179/EC and Art. 152/Euratom.

[68] Actions against Community institutions under Arts.173(2) and 175(3)/EC relating to the implementation of the competition rules applicable to undertakings.

[69] Actions against the Commission under Arts.33(2) and 35/ECSC by undertakings or associations of undertakings concerning individual acts relating to the application of Arts.50, 57–66/ECSC.

[70] Dec. 93/350, amending Dec. 88/591.

[71] Weatherill and Beaumont (1995), pp. 188–190.

[72] Art. 168a(4)/EC; O.J. 1991 L 136/5.

[73] Arts. 50–55 of the Protocol on the Statute of the Court of Justice, as amended by Dec. 88/591/ECSC/EEC/Euratom.

[74] See R. Beddard, *Human Rights and Europe* (3rd ed., 1993); J. E. S. Fawcett, *The Application of the European Convention on Human Rights* (2nd ed., 1987); D. J. Harris, M. O'Boyle and C. Warbrick, *The Law of the European Convention on Human Rights* (1995); S. H. Bailey, D. J. Harris and B. L. Jones, *Civil Liberties: Cases and Materials* (4th ed., 1995), Chap. 12; C. Gearty, "The European Court of Human Rights and Civil Liberties: an Overview" [1993] C.L.J. 89.

the Protection of Human Rights and Fundamental Freedoms of November 4, 1950, generally known as the European Convention on Human Rights, was one of the first achievements of the Council of Europe, an association now of 23 states. It came into force in 1953 and there are now 30 states which are parties to the Convention.[75] Article 1 provides that these parties "shall secure to everyone within their jurisdiction" the rights and freedoms defined in Articles 2 to 18. These are mostly civil and political rights,[76] including the right to life (Art. 2), the right not to be subjected to torture or to inhuman or degrading treatment or punishment (Art. 3), the right to liberty and security of person (Art. 5), the right to a fair trial in both civil and criminal cases (Art. 6), the right to respect for private and family life, home and correspondence (Art. 8), the right to freedom of thought, conscience and religion (Art. 9), the right to freedom of expression (Art. 10) and the right to freedom of peaceful assembly and to freedom of association with others (Art. 11). Further rights are specified in the First Protocol to the Convention.[77] Article 13 requires that persons whose guaranteed rights are violated "have an effective remedy before a national authority."

For the purposes of enforcement the Convention established the European Commission of Human Rights and the European Court of Human Rights, each with one member in respect of each party. Each member is elected by the Consultative Assembly of the Council of Europe and sits in an individual capacity and not as a representative of his or her country.

Alleged breaches of the Convention may be raised either by a state party[78] or, if the state against which the complaint is made has accepted the right of individual petition, by an individual.[79] All applications are made first to the Commission. They must normally be made after all effective domestic remedies have been exhausted and within six months from the date when the final decision was taken.[80] They are investigated by the Commission, which may seek to secure a friendly settlement.[81] If a solution is not reached the Commission draws up a Report on the facts, and also states in the Report its opinion[82] as to whether a breach of the Convention has been established. The Report is sent to the Committee of Ministers of the Council of Europe and the states concerned. If the question is not referred to the Court within three months, the matter is dealt with by the Committee.

A matter may only be referred to the Court if the state against which the complaint is made has accepted the compulsory jurisdiction of the Court,[83] or otherwise consents and may only be referred by (1) the Commission; (2) a state party to the Convention whose national is alleged to be a victim; (3) a state

---

[75] The United Kingdom was the first state to ratify the Convention in 1951. In addition, in 1989 the Convention was ratified by San Marino and signed by Finland.

[76] Economic, social and cultural rights are protected under the European Social Charter 1961: see D. J. Harris, *The European Social Charter* (1984); A. Ph. C. M. Jaspers and L. Betten (eds.), *25 years: European Social Charter* (1988).

[77] In force 1954; all member states except Switzerland and Liechtenstein are parties to the protocol. Twenty-two states, not including the U.K., are parties to the Fourth Protocol.

[78] Art. 24. Few such applications have been made. One example is *Ireland v. United Kingdom.* Eur. Court H.R. No. 25 Series A, Judgment of January 18, 1978.

[79] Art. 25. All the parties have made the necessary declarations: The U.K. first made a declaration on January 14, 1966, and this was renewed for five years from January 14, 1981, 1986 and 1991.

[80] Art. 26. There are other grounds on which an application may be considered inadmissible: Art. 27.

[81] Art. 28.

[82] This may be reached by a majority: Art. 34.

[83] Art. 46. On October 31, 1987 all Members except Turkey had done so.

party which referred the case to the Commission; and (4) a state party against which the complaint has been lodged.[84] The individual concerned has no right to insist on a reference to the Court.[85]

Each case is heard either by a Chamber of the Court composed of seven judges,[86] or by the full or "plenary" Court.[87]

As from January 1, 1983, an individual applicant may be represented by an advocate authorised to practise in any of the party states or any other person approved by the President of the Court, or may be given leave to present his or her own case.[88]

Legal aid may be awarded in respect of proceedings before the Commission and the Court. The official languages are English and French.[89] There is provision for the submission of written documents and an oral hearing.[90] The Court deliberates and votes on its decision in private. A judgment of the Court is prepared: each judge is entitled to annex a separate opinion, whether concurring or dissenting, or a bare statement of dissent.[91] In most cases a declaratory judgment is given. If the Court finds that a decision or measure taken by an authority of a state party is in conflict with the obligations imposed by the Convention, it must "if necessary afford just satisfaction to the injured party."[92] In a number of cases monetary compensation has been awarded as "just satisfaction" covering costs and expenses, pecuniary losses and non-pecuniary loss.

One of the major problems of the Convention arrangements is that it typically takes five years for a case to proceed to a final decision by the Court. The Eleventh Protocol,[93] adopted in 1994, provides for the merger of the Commission and the Court into a new European Court of Human Rights. There will be one judge from each state party to the Convention and the Court will sit in chambers of seven or three, or a Grand Chamber of 17. Other changes are that the Committee of Ministers avenue for a decision will be abolished and the right of individual petition will be compulsory.

As of February 1995, the Court has determined 52 cases[94] involving the United Kingdom. In 31 the Court found there to be violations of one or more

---

[84] Art. 48.

[85] By the end of 1994, the Commissioners had registered over 25,000 individual applications; 2,028 had been admitted for consideration on the merits; judgments had been delivered in 473 cases and friendly settlements reached in over 200: Bailey, Harris and Jones (1995), pp. 746, 747; D. Gomien, *Judgments of the European Court of Human Rights: Reference Charts* (Council of Europe, 1995). The workload of the court has increased sharply in recent years.

[86] Art. 43. The seven must include the President or Vice-President, and the judge who is a national of any state party concerned. If the national judge is unable to sit or withdraws, the relevant state may appoint another member of the court or an ad hoc judge.

[87] See the Revised Rules of Court (adopted on November 24, 1982): Cour. (82) 107 of December 2, 1982, r.50.

[88] *ibid.* r.30: see P. J. Duffy, [1983] P.L. 32–33. Previously, the applicant technically had no independent right to appear although in practice his or her lawyer was permitted to address the Court as part of the Commission's case.

[89] Revised Rules of Court, r.27. Another language may be used at the oral stage, with the leave of the President.

[90] Revised Rules of Court, rr.37, 39, 41–46.

[91] *ibid.* r.52.

[92] Art. 50.

[93] (1994) 17 E.H.R.R.501, (1994) E.H.H.R.206. See A. R. Mowbray, [1994] P.L.54; Harris, O'Boyle and Warbrick (1995), Chap. 26. The Protocol will come into force one year after it is ratified by all parties.

[94] Excluding separate applications under Art. 50 where the merits have already been determined.

articles. Either as a consequence, or in anticipation of these findings,[95] English law has been changed in a number of significant respects.[96] For example, the law of contempt of court was amended following the *Sunday Times* case[97]; the law relating to the correspondence of persons in prisons has been radically altered[98]; the law in Northern Ireland concerning homosexual acts has been brought into line with the rest of the United Kingdom[99]; Isle of Man courts have been advised that birching is contrary to the European Convention[1]; and phonetapping has been regulated by statute.[2] The Convention has also had some influence in statutory interpretation,[3] although judges have emphasised on a number of occasions that it is not part of English law.[4] Incorporation of the European Convention into English law is, however, party policy for the Labour Party and the Liberal Democrats, and is supported by a number of leading judges, although the Conservative Party remains opposed.[5]

[95] There are also some changes that can be traced to friendly settlements or Commission decisions.

[96] See P. J. Duffy, (1980) 29 I.C.L.Q. 585–618; A. Drzemczewski, *European Human Rights Convention in Domestic Law* (1983), pp. 314–322; M. P. Furmston, *et al.*, (eds.), *The Effect on English Domestic Law of Membership of the European Communities and of Ratifications of the European Convention on Human Rights* (1983); F. J. Hampson, "The United Kingdom Before the European Court of Human Rights" (1989) 9 Y.E.L. 121; R. R. Churchill and J. R. Young, (1991) 62 B.Y.I.L. 183; D. Kinley, *The European Convention on Human Rights: Compliance without Incorporation* (1993) (arguing the case for pre-legislative scrutiny in the U.K. to promote compliance)); J. P. Gardiner (ed.), *Aspects of the Incorporation of the European Convention on Human Rights into Domestic Law* (1993).

[97] See *Sunday Times Case*, Series A No. 30, Judgment of April 26, 1979: violation of Art. 10; Contempt of Court Act 1981; S. H. Bailey, (1982) 45 M.L.R. 301. It is not certain that the Act went far enough.

[98] See the *Golder Case*, Series A No. 18, Judgment of February 21, 1975; *Case of Silver and Others*: Series A No. 61, Judgment of March 25, 1983: violations of Arts. 6 § 1 and 3; *Case of Campbell and Fell*, Series A No. 80, Judgment of June 28, 1984; *Case of Boyle and Rice*, Series A No. 131, Judgment of April 27, 1988; G. J. Zellick, [1981] P.L. 435–438, [1983] P.L. 167–169.

[99] *Dudgeon Case*, Series A No. 45 Judgment of October 22, 1981: violation of Art. 8; Homosexual Offences (Northern Ireland) Order 1982.

[1] *Tyrer Case*, Series A No. 26, Judgment of April 25, 1978; G. J. Zellick, [1982] P.L. 4–5. The United Kingdom does not now accept the rights of individual petition in respect of the Isle of Man.

[2] *Malone Case*, Series A No. 82, Judgment of August 2, 1984; Bailey, Harris and Jones (1995), pp. 804–809; Interception of Communications Act 1985 (see annotations in *Current Law Statutes 1985* by D. Foulkes). The Convention has also influenced the law affecting mental patients, children in secure accommodation, immigration, and the right of parents to forbid the imposition by a school of corporal punishment on their children.

[3] See below, p. 388–389; A. Drzemczewski, *European Human Rights Convention in Domestic Law* (1983), pp. 166–187; M. Addo, (1995) 46 N.I.L.Q. 1.

[4] *ibid.* pp. 314–322. See, *e.g. Malone v. Metropolitan Police Commissioner* [1979] Ch. 344; *Att.-Gen. v. B.B.C.* [1981] A.C. 303 (Lord Scarman); *R. v. Secretary of State for the Home Department, ex p. Brind* [1991] 1 A.C. 696.

[5] Bailey, Harris and Jones (1995), pp. 25–26.

CHAPTER 3

LAWYERS

A. INTRODUCTION: THE "LEGAL PROFESSION"

THE title "lawyer" is reserved for those who have achieved the special status of membership of the "legal profession".[1] It is not a straightforward job description: many non-lawyers perform legal tasks, some of them full-time. For example, accountants may specialise in revenue law, trade union officials may appear regularly before industrial tribunals on behalf of their members,[2] and solicitors may delegate work to legal executives and para-legals.[3] Conversely, many of the tasks performed by lawyers are not strictly "legal".[4] Membership of the legal profession in England and Wales involves qualification as either a solicitor or a barrister; it is usual to speak of two branches of the profession although historically it would be more accurate to refer to two professions.[5]

It is significant that lawyers are accepted to be members of a "profession". Much has been written about the supposedly distinctive attributes of professions, and how and why occupational groups seek professional status.[6] Medicine and law have been regarded as classic models, although important differences between them have been perceived.[7] The self-conception of the legal profession was articulated by the Law Society in evidence to the Monopolies Commission in 1968.[8]:

"When a profession is fully developed it may be described as a body of men and women (a) identifiable by reference to some register or record; (b) recognised as having a special skill and learning in some field of activity in which the public needs protection against incompetence, the standards of skill and learning being prescribed by the profession itself; (c) hold themselves out as being willing to serve the public; (d) voluntarily

---

[1] "Barrack-room" lawyers don't count. Law lecturers commonly refer to themselves as "academic lawyers" even if they are not qualified. See M. Partington, "Academic lawyers and legal practice in Britain: a preliminary reappraisal" (1988) 15 J. L. S. 374.

[2] See below, p. 823.

[3] See below, p. 187.

[4] See below, p. 117.

[5] M. Birks, *Gentlemen of the Law* (1960), p. 3. See second edition of this book, pp. 107–113.

[6] See T. J. Johnson, *Professions and Power* (1972), pp. 21–38. For an argument that the concept of "profession . . . obscures more than it reveals about the work people do" see M. Cain, (1979) 7 *International Journal of the Sociology of Law* 331. See generally R. Dingwall and P. Lewis (eds.), *The Sociology of the Professions* (1983), in which Cain's paper is reprinted. See also R. Dingwall and P. Fenn, "A respectable profession?" (1987) 7 Int. Rev. Law and Econ. 51; R. L. Abel, *The Legal Profession in England and Wales* (1988), Chap. 1 "Theories of the professions", and note the extensive bibliography.

[7] D. Rueschemeyer, "Lawyers and Doctors: a Comparison of Two Professions" in V. Aubert (ed.) *Sociology of Law* (1969), pp. 267–277, abridged from (1964) 1 *Canadian Review of Sociology and Anthropology*, 17–30.

[8] Quoted in the Report of the Royal Commission on Legal Services (Cmnd. 7648, 1969) Vol. 1, p. 30.

submitting themselves to standards of ethical conduct beyond those required of the ordinary citizen by law; (e) undertaking to accept personal responsibility to those whom they serve for their actions and to their profession for maintaining public confidence.''

This approach was accepted uncritically by the Royal Commission on Legal Services.[9] They emphasised five main features of a profession: (a) central organisation: a governing body with powers of control and discipline; (b) the primary function of giving advice or service in a specialised field of knowledge; (c) the restriction of admission to those with the required standard of education and training; (d) a measure of self-regulation by the profession; and (e) the paramountcy of the duty owed to the client, subject only to responsibility to the court. A rule of conduct or restriction on practice should ''stând or fall on its capacity to protect the interests of, or to enhance the level of service to the public.'' Thus, in theory at least, ''altruistic service'' is offered subject to self-regulation, in return for considerable autonomy from external control.[10] The Royal Commission, having noted that these features existed, found that they promoted the public interest, subject to points of detail, and proposed no fundamental changes. There was no exploration of other features that have been associated with the ''rise of professionalism''. For example, Larson has described professionalisation as:

''the process by which producers of special services sought to constitute *and control* a market for their expertise . . . a collective assertion of special social status (and) a collective process of upward social mobility.''[11]

Arguments for maintaining standards tend to coincide with arguments for monopolies, restrictions on practice and high rewards.[12] There was also no proper analysis of the ways in which professionalism may impede the expansion of legal services.[13] Thus, problems may be defined in the professional's terms and alternative definitions regarded as irrelevant; outsiders, whether lay people or members of other disciplines, may be ignored on the grounds that they are not competent either to assist or to criticise; ''specialised knowledge'' may be guarded by such means as ''the creation of special forms of jargonised discourse and the fostering of an air of impenetrable mystery''[14]; the emphasis on the individual lawyer-client relationship may inhibit the development of group representation and test-case strategies[15]; the proper advertisement of legal services may be prevented.

Many of these problematic features of professionalism have come under

---

[9] R. C. L. S., Vol. 1, pp. 28, 30. Johnson has mentioned the error made by many sociologists in accepting the professions' own definitions of themselves: Johnson (1972), p. 25. The Commission did not discuss the literature on the sociology of the professions.

[10] Johnson sees professionalism as a form of occupational control rather than an expression of the inherent nature of particular occupations: Johnson (1972), p. 45.

[11] M. S. Larson, *The Rise of Professionalism* (1977), p. xvi.

[12] See below, pp. 129–143.

[13] R. Cotterell, ''Legal Services and Professional Ideology'' (1980) (paper presented at the Conference on Legal Services in the Eighties, University College, Cardiff). P. Fennell, ''Solicitors, their markets and their rignorant public': the crisis of the professional ideal'' in Z. Bankowski and G. Mungham (eds.), *Essays in Law and Society* (1980), p. 1.

[14] Cotterell, *op. cit.*, p. 10.

[15] See below, pp. 468–469.

attack in recent years. The general preference of the Royal Commission to endorse the status quo has not prevailed. What he terms "the decline of professionalism" has been charted by Prof. R. L. Abel, who has written extensively on the English legal profession, applying in particular Weberian theories developed by writers such as Larson.[16] We return to his work at the end of the chapter.[17]

B. THE LEGAL PROFESSION TODAY

1. ORGANISATION

The legal profession is divided into two branches: barristers and solicitors. Both barristers and solicitors are professions held in high regard because of their development of controlling admission and ensuring high-quality education for admission.[18] The Bar has developed from the work of advocates since medieval times being based, primarily, in the fours Inns of Court which still exist today: Lincoln's Inn, Gray's Inn, the Inner Temple and the Middle Temple. Solicitors have developed a line of work in meeting the needs of clients unable to process litigation for themselves. The Bar has been left largely unregulated by government, but has run itself initially through the Inns of Court, which have been dominated by the benchers, and also through the judicial control of practice in the courts. The solicitors' profession has been regulated by government in one way or another since a statute of 1605 subjected solicitors[19] to a measure of control to prevent overcharging and to cut their numbers; only "skilfull" (*sic*) and "honest" men were allowed to practise. In 1728 an Act was passed for the better regulation of solicitors, and introduced a roll of solicitors. In 1831 the Society of Attorneys Solicitors and Proctors and others not being barristers practising in the Courts of Law and Equity in the United Kingdom received a Royal Charter, and changed its name, in 1833, to the Incorporated Law Society of the United Kingdom. The Solicitors Act 1843 provided that the Society was to be the Registrar of Attorneys and Solicitors.[20] The governing body of the Bar is the General Council of the Bar of England and Wales.[21]

---

[16] R. L. Abel "The decline of professionalism?" (1986) 49 M.L.R.1, *The Legal Profession in England and Wales* (1988), and "Between market and state: the legal profession in turmoil" (1989) 52 M.L.R. 285; R. L. Abel and P. S. C. Lewis (eds.) *Lawyers in Society: The Common Law World* (1988). See now R. L. Abel and P. Lewis (eds.) *Lawyers in Society* (1996).

[17] Below, pp. 190–191.

[18] See further, first edition of this book, pp. 107–113.

[19] The regulation was also concerned with attorneys, who performed similar functions to those of solicitors, although were more engaged in litigation.

[20] For a fuller introduction to the development of the profession, see 1st edn. of this book, pp. 107–113.

[21] It has 107 members: 3 officers; 14 ex-officio (the Attorney-General, the Solicitor-General, the D.P.P., leaders of the 6 circuits, chairmen of 5 specialist associations); 12 representatives of the Inns; 12 circuit representatives; 5 association representatives; 45 practising barristers; 12 employed and non-practising barristers; 4 co-opted: The General Council of the Bar, *Annual Report 1994*, p. 23 and C. Frazer, "Governing the Bar" (1994) N.L.J. 1589.

"It fulfils the function of what might be called a ιtrade union,' pursuing the interests of the Bar and expanding the market for the Bar's services and is also a watchdog regulating its practices and activities."[22]

It co-operates with the Inns of Court through the Council of the Inns of Court, which comprises representatives of the four Inns, the Bar Council and the Council of Legal Education. The independence of the Inns has been reduced under the new arrangements; where the Council of the Inns and the Bar Council disagree, the latter's policy is to be implemented provided that it has the support of two-thirds of the profession.

The powers and duties of the Law Society are now derived from the Solicitors Act 1974. Membership of the Society is not compulsory, although it is the governing body for the profession as a whole. Thus the Master of the Rolls may only admit as a solicitor a person certified by the Society to have complied with its training regulations and to be suitable for admission.[23] The Society also issues the "practising certificate" which each solicitor wishing to practise must obtain.[24] Many of its statutory functions relate to the maintenance of standards for the protection of the public. However, it is also the main professional association for solicitors. The inconsistency in these roles has led to concern that neither is performed satisfactorily. The Society was able to point to its success in defending solicitors' interests during the deliberations of the Royal Commission. There have, however, been a number of matters on which the Society has fallen out with sections of the rank-and-file[25] and its success in defending the solicitors' "conveyancing monopoly" proved short lived. The composition of the Council of the Law Society has long been criticised as unrepresentative, with very few members under 35, very few women, few from outside private practice and a disproportionate number from large firms.[26]

The General Council of the Bar and the Law Society are no longer entirely free to arrange their own affairs. Of course, they have always had to work with various government departments, such as the Lord Chancellor's Department on legal aid, but there are now two external bodies which may have a significant impact on their work. The first is the Lord Chancellor's Advisory Committee on Legal Education and Conduct which was established to exercise "a general duty of assisting in the maintenance and development of standards in the education, training and conduct of those offering legal services".[27] It has specific functions in relation to those matters, including giving advice to the General Council of the Bar, the Law Society and other authorised bodies on all aspects of their qualification regulations and rules of conduct, and on specialisation schemes.[28] In pursuing these functions it is, for example, engaged in a major review of legal education.[29] It also has a statutory role in regulating the right

---

[22] General Council of the Bar, *A Career at the Bar* (1988), p. 7.
[23] Solicitors Act 1974, s.3.
[24] *ibid.* ss.1, 9–18.
[25] *e.g.* education and training, the problems of sole practitioners, advertising, compulsory insurance: D. Podmore, "Bucher and Strauss Revisited – the Case of the Solicitors' Profession" (1980) 7 B.J.L.S. 1, 4–11.
[26] R. L. Abel, *The Legal Profession in England and Wales* (1988), pp. 242–245; see also below, p. 191.
[27] Courts and Legal Services Act 1990, s.20.
[28] Courts and Legal Services Act 1990, Sched. 2.
[29] See below, pp. 186–187.

to conduct litigation and the right of audience in the higher courts.[30] A.C.L.E.C., as it is known, comprises a chairman and 16 other members appointed by the Lord Chancellor.[31] The first two chairmen have been Lords of Appeal,[32] but may be a judge of the Supreme Court; of the members, one must be a judge who is or has been a Circuit judge, two practising barristers appointed after consultation with the General Council of the Bar, two practising solicitors appointed after consultation with the Law Society, two law teachers appointed after consultation with such institutions concerned with the teaching of law and such persons representing law teachers as the Lord Chancellor considers appropriate, and nine lay members. There is, therefore, a lay majority, which ensures that interests of the user are foremost in the Committee's deliberations.[33] The independence of A.C.L.E.C. from government is guaranteed by government commitment, the approach of the Committee, funding by grant-in-aid and freedom of staff appointments.[34] Whether these are sufficient is a moot point and awaits a careful assessment of the work of A.C.L.E.C.

The other external body which may be involved in the work of the Bar or the Law Society is the Director General of Fair Trading. Any alteration to qualification, regulations or rules of conduct must, as part of the process of approval through A.C.L.E.C., the designated judges and the Lord Chancellor,[35] also be referred to the Director General to consider whether the amendments "would have, or would be likely to have, the effect of restricting, distorting or preventing competition to any significant effect" and provide advice to the Lord Chancellor.[36]

2. LAWYERS AND THEIR WORK

(a) Introduction

In their study of the legal profession in the United States and England, Johnstone and Hopson identified nineteen different "work tasks" performed by lawyers in the United States: giving advice, both legal and non legal; negotiations; drafting letters and legal documents; litigation, including the preparation of cases and advocacy; investigation of facts; legal research and analysis; lobbying legislators and administrators; acting as broker; public relations; filing submissions to government and other organisations; adjudication; financing; property management; referral of clients to other sources of assistance; supervision of others; emotional support to clients; immoral and unpleasant tasks (taking care of disagreeable matters for clients which the clients could do themselves but prefer to have someone else do); acting as scapegoat; and getting business.[37] Any one

---

[30] Courts and Legal Services Act 1990, ss.27 and 28, and see below, pp. 133–138.

[31] Courts and Legal Services Act 1990, s.19 and Sched. 1.

[32] The first was Lord Griffiths, the second Lord Steyn.

[33] White Paper (Cm.740, 1989), p. 27. This approach has been described as a "needless affront to the legal profession:" M. Zander (1989) 139 N.L.J. 300, 303.

[34] White Paper, p. 27.

[35] See below, pp. 126–138 and 148–149.

[36] Courts and Legal Services Act 1990, Sched. 4, para. 9. The Bar's proposals with regard to validating institutions other than the Inns of Court School of Law to teach the Bar Vocational Course were considered by the Director General, as a result of which there was an agreement that between three and six institutions should be validated in the interests of competition.

[37] Q. Johnstone and D. Hopson, *Lawyers and their Work* (1967), Chap. 3.

lawyer might never perform all these tasks, and some, such as advising and negotiation, were generally more significant than others. The variety of combinations in which these tasks were performed by individual lawyers was "almost endless".[38] Laymen could be found performing any of them. English lawyers may be less likely than their American counterparts to act in some of these areas, but it is difficult to think of any of them that no English lawyer would touch. It has been noted that the expertise of many lawyers may be founded not so much on their mastery of legal technique as on their possession of "worldly knowledge" in "giving economic advice or providing organisational 'know-how' and in their interpersonal skills".[39]

(b) Fusion[40]

The English pattern of work is complicated by the division of the legal profession into barristers and solicitors. It is not possible for anyone to be qualified in both branches at the same time. Traditionally, barristers have had an exclusive right of audience in the superior courts, and have not normally been instructed by a lay client direct without the intervention of a solicitor. There is not, however, any *kind* of work done by barristers which is not also done by solicitors. In the lower courts the advocacy work has been shared between the two branches; in tribunals it also has been shared with non-lawyers. Both barristers and solicitors do drafting work. Both may give legal advice, the solicitor direct to the client, the barrister only if approached for his or her oral or written opinion by a solicitor. This would be done where the solicitor lacks the time or resources to do the work personally, to satisfy a "difficult" client or simply because "counsel's opinion" is often regarded as especially authoritative.

The different emphases in the functions of solicitors and barristers have led to marked differences in their geographical distribution: solicitors' offices may be found throughout the country[41]; over 70 per cent of barristers work from chambers in central London, where the superior courts sit, the rest being spread through over 30 provincial centres.[42] A further difference which affects the way that practices are organised is that each barrister must act on his or her own account, whereas solicitors may form partnerships.[43] Many solicitors' firms have several partners and a large employed staff, including fee-earners. Barristers are generally grouped in chambers, which provide administrative support, but a barrister may not share fees or employ fee-earners.

Over the years, there have been many advocates of fusion of the two branches. The profession was not always divided as it is today.[44] The legal professions of other countries are not normally divided. It was argued in submissions to the Royal Commission that the necessity of employing a solicitor as well as a barrister, where the latter's services are required, causes inefficiency (failures in

---

[38] *ibid.* p. 77.
[39] Rueschemeyer, *op cit.*, p. 113, n. 7, at p. 271.
[40] R.C.L.S., Vol. 1, pp. 187–202; G. Gardiner, "Two Lawyers or One" (1970) 23 C.L.P.1; M. Zander, *Lawyers and the Public Interest* (1968), pp. 271–332, (1976) 73 L.S.Gaz. 882, *Legal Services for the Community* (1978), pp. 170–174; F. A. Mann, "Fusion of the Legal Professions?" (1977) 93 L.Q.R. 367; P. Reeves, *Are Two Legal Professions Necessary?* (1986).
[41] See below, p. 125.
[42] See below, p. 144.
[43] See below, pp. 123–125.
[44] See above, pp. 153–154.

communication, delay and the return of briefs by barristers who are doubled-booked), harms the confidence of clients (barristers being regarded by some clients as too remote or insufficiently prepared) and is more expensive for clients obliged to pay for two lawyers rather than one. Most of the professional bodies who gave evidence, including the Senate and the Law Society, opposed fusion. It was feared that fusion would lead to a serious fall in the quality of advocacy. The leading barristers might join the larger firms of solicitors and so be less accessible. Smaller practices might generate insufficient business to justify partnership with a barrister and find it increasingly difficult to brief a barrister of equal standing to the one retained by an opponent. The drift from smaller to larger firms might increase, with a corresponding reduction in the number of offices in smaller towns and rural areas. Smaller firms might be reluctant to refer a client to a large firm for fear of losing him or her permanently. A reduction in the number of specialist advocates might also contribute to the lowering of standards, and make it more difficult for the Lord Chancellor to make "suitable" appointments to the bench: the numbers for consideration would be increased but the candidates would not be as well known to the Lord Chancellor and his or her senior advisers.

Other arguments against fusion have centred on the English form of court procedure.[45] First, there is heavy reliance on the oral rather than written presentation of evidence and argument. Secondly, hearings are single and continuous, this being designed to make best use of judicial time at the cost of inconvenience to practitioners and clients. Barristers are more easily and more economically organised to meet such inconvenience than solicitors could be. Thirdly, there is the "principle of judicial unpreparedness." The judge relies upon the parties to present the case; he or she has no research or investigative staff, and limited time to do his or her own research. The requirement that the judges have confidence in the advocates appearing before them is particularly acute under such a system.[46]

It was not surprising that the Royal Commission unanimously recommended against fusion, notwithstanding the speculative nature of some of the arguments. They saw that the existing system had its advantages; fusion might lead to some saving, but only in small cases and in larger cases the expense might be greater. Employing two lawyers did not necessarily mean that work was duplicated. Some of the adverse criticisms of the present system could be met by other changes.

(c) The 1990 Reforms

The Royal Commission did not favour substantial changes to the various monopolies and restrictive practices enshrined in part in law and in part in professional rules. However, in 1989, the government began to turn its attention to the legal profession, and indicated its determination to introduce significant reforms designed to open up the market for legal services. It was not its stated aim to secure fusion; the main theme was that of dismantling the various monopolies and restrictive practices operated by the two branches of the profession. The main targets were the restrictions preventing unqualified persons

---

[45] See Mann, *op. cit.* n. 40.
[46] The advocate's "duty to the court" rests on rules of professional conduct: see below, pp. 159–170.

undertaking conveyancing, probate or litigation work for reward (especially the so-called "conveyancing monopoly" enjoyed by solicitors); the prohibition on solicitors entering multi-disciplinary partnerships; and the Bar's exclusive rights of audience in higher courts. How did this radical change come about?

In December 1983, a second reading was given to a Private Member's Bill, the House Buyer's Bill, sponsored by Austin Mitchell M. P., which proposed the introduction of a system whereby licensed conveyancers would be permitted to undertake the conveyancing of "houses" with registered title. In response, the government indicated its intention to promote legislation to establish a system of licensed conveyancers and, moreover, to enable solicitors employed by building societies, banks and other organisations to undertake conveyancing for their employers' clients, whether or not the land was registered. This decision was reached by the cabinet over the objections of the then Lord Chancellor, Lord Hailsham, and was apparently motivated by a desire to see increased competition and lower charges.[47] In the event, a system of licensed conveyancers was established by Part II of the Administration of Justice Act 1985, but the government ultimately decided that banks and building societies should only be permitted to offer conveyancing services where they were not the lending institution. On the latter point it accepted the Law Society's argument that the provision of conveyancing services in conjunction with a mortgage loan would lead to an undesirable conflict of interest.[48]

Concern at the threat to conveyancing incomes led to the wholesale relaxation of the professional rules restricting advertising by solicitors, and the revival of arguments by the Law Society that the Bar's monopoly of rights of advocacy in the higher courts should be removed. The latter led to an acrimonious dispute between the two branches of the profession,[49] which was temporarily put into abeyance by the appointment by them of a Committee under the chairmanship of Lady Marre. The Marre Committee comprised (apart from the chairman), six barristers, six solicitors and six independent members, and was asked to report to the Bar Council and the Law Society on the extent to which the services offered by the legal profession met the needs and demands of the public for legal services; how the services of the profession could be made readily available to meet such needs and demands; and those areas where changes in the present education of the legal profession, and in the structure and practices of the profession, might be in the public interest. It reported in July 1988,[50] and, like the Royal Commission, tended to endorse the *status quo*. Its main recommendation affecting the structure of the profession was that solicitors recommended by a Rights of Audience Board and licensed by the Law Society should have extended rights of audience for all purposes in the Crown Court, and that professions other than solicitors should be permitted direct access to barristers.

Although there were moves to relax certain specific professional rules in each branch of the profession, the likelihood of fundamental changes seemed remote.

[47] M. Zander, *A Matter of Justice* (revised ed., 1989), pp. 9–10.
[48] *ibid.* pp. 15–16. The Building Societies Act 1986, s.21 and Sched. 21 established a structure whereby banks, building societies and other financial institutions would be authorised to undertake conveyancing, subject to restrictions in regulations. These provisions were never brought into force and have been superseded by broader arrangements in the Courts and Legal Services Act 1990, below pp. 000–000.
[49] *ibid.* pp. 24–31.
[50] *A Time for Change: Report of the Committee on the Future of the Legal Profession* (*Chairman: Lady Marre C.B.E.*) (General Council of the Bar, The Law Society, 1988).

The Marre Committee had not proposed anything that could be said to be radical. Lord Hailsham in particular was opposed to changes that might weaken the independent Bar. His immediate successor, Lord Havers, took a similar line during his brief period in office. However, the advent of Lord Mackay of Clashfern as Lord Chancellor, the first whose professional life had been at the Scottish and not the English Bar, made it easier for what may be termed a Thatcherite approach to reform to prevail.

On January 25, 1989, the Lord Chancellor published three Green Papers: *The Work and Organisation of the Legal Profession; Contingency Fees*; and *Conveyancing by Authorised Practitioners.*[51] The Papers were not founded on any form of research exercise, and took a line sharply different from those taken by the Royal Commission and the Marre Committee which, to an extent at least, had been based on research. Four months only were to be allowed for consultation. After consultation, the Lord Chancellor produced a White Paper, *Legal Services: A Framework for the Future,*[52] which took up proposals arising from the Civil Justice Review[53], as well as the Green Papers. The tone of the White Paper differed from that in the Green Papers. The main Green Paper, on *The Work and Organisation of the Legal Profession,*[54] was prefaced by the statement that it was the government's overall objective "to see that the public has the best possible access to legal services and that those services are of the right quality for the particular needs of the client"; and that the government believed that this would be "best achieved by ensuring that:—

(a) a market providing legal services operates freely and efficiently so as to give clients the widest possible choice of cost effective services; and

(b) the public can be certain that those services are being supplied by people who have the necessary expertise to provide a service in the area in question."[55]

The resolve of the responsible section of the Lord Chancellor's Department had apparently been stiffened by the transfer of officials of the Department of Trade and Industry, and the result was a Green Paper "whose style and content paid little concession to the sensitivities of lawyers used to articulating, rightly or wrongly, their restrictive practices in terms of 'the interests of justice' ".[56] The White Paper was more moderate in tone, with more frequent reference to the need to secure the proper and efficient administration of justice.[57] There were some modifications in the content of the proposals to meet objections from

---

[51] Cm. 570, 571 and 572, 1989. See (1989) 139 N.L.J. 140–149; F. Cowper, *ibid.* p. 382; Responses, *ibid.* pp. 601–604; R. Smith, *ibid.* p. 897; (1989) 86 L.S. Gaz., February 1, pp. 2–7; M. Zander, *ibid.* March 1, pp. 14–15, 21; R. Abel, *ibid.* March 22, pp. 14, 18, I. R. Scott (1989) 8 C.J.Q. 202; B. Walsh (1989) P.N. 59.

[52] Cm. 740, 1989. See N. Stewart, (1989) 139 N.L.J. 1035; W. Merricks, *ibid.* p. 1036; I. R. Scott, (1990) 9 C.J.Q. 6; J. P. O'Brien, (1989) 133 S.J. 1046.

[53] Cm. 394, Chap. 3.

[54] Cm. 570, 1989.

[55] *ibid.* para. 1.1.

[56] R. Smith, "The Courts and Legal Services Bill: A View at Half-Time" (1990) 17 J.L.S. 242, 243.

[57] *e.g.* Cm. 740, para. 2.3, in respect of the need to maintain "the standards in the conduct of advocacy and . . . litigation which are required in the interests of the proper and efficient administration of justice," and the intention to remove restrictions on practice "which are not necessary in the interests of justice."

professional bodies, but the fundamentals were for the most part little changed.[58]

The White Paper formed the basis of the Courts and Legal Services Act 1990, which was introduced in November 1989 and received Royal Assent a year later. The main features of Parts II to IV of the Act are—

— the establishment, on a statutory basis, of the Lord Chancellor's Advisory Committee on Legal Education and Conduct;
— the establishment of a Legal Services Ombudsman;
— the extension of rights of audience in all courts and rights to conduct litigation and undertake probate work to suitably qualified persons, whether or not barristers or solicitors;
— the removal of the restriction preventing banks and building societies offering conveyancing services to borrowers, subject to safeguards, including a Conveyancing Ombudsman Scheme.
— provision for new regulations and codes setting qualification standards and practice requirements for advocacy and the conduct of litigation, subject to the approval of the Lord Chancellor, assisted by his Advisory Committee;
— the ending of legal restrictions on multi-disciplinary and multinational partnerships;
— changes to rule of eligibility for judicial appointments to reflect enjoyment of advocacy rights rather than status as a barrister or solicitor;
— the strengthening of the powers of the Law Society to deal with poor service by solicitors.

In addition, the professional bodies' rules and practices will be subject to review under the proposed restrictive practices legislation and, unless approved by the Lord Chancellor, open to prohibition.[59]

We consider these matters at the appropriate stages in the following sections.

(d) Solicitors' practices and their work

(i) Numbers

As at July 31, 1995, there were 66,123 solicitors with practising certificates[60] 53,731 were in private practice, on their own account (4,377) or as a partner (26,319), consultant (2,231) or assistant solicitor (20,804). The main categories outside private practice were local government (2,735), commerce or industry (3,718) and the Crown Prosecution Service (1,654).[61] The numbers have consistently increased, apart from periods of decline in the 1840s and between the

---

[58] See generally R. Smith, *op. cit.*, and F. Cownie, "The reform of the legal profession or the end of civilization as we know it" in F. Patfield and R. White (eds.), *The Changing Law* (1990).

[59] See the White Paper, *Opening Markets—New Policy on Restrictive Trade Practices* (Cm. 727, 1989)

[60] A 4 per cent increase on the previous year and a 16 per cent increase since the second edition of this book appeared in 1991. There were 82,828 solicitors on the Roll: *Law Society Annual Statistical Report 1995*, Table 1.3.

[61] *ibid*, Tables 2.2, 2.7 and 2.8.

wars, and have risen dramatically over the past 30 years.[62] The profession recovered from the inter-war years decline in the 1960s and 1970s,[63] which produced
a fear that too many people were seeking to become solicitors.[64] However, there
then followed a period when there was a considerable increase in the demand
for recruits to the solicitors' profession. Indeed, the demand was such that there
was a recruitment crisis in the late 1980s.[65] Since then it has been much more
difficult for people to enter the profession, although there are signs of concern
that there may be another recruitment crisis in the late 1990's. Although the
total number of solicitors has increased, the rate of increase has been slower
than in the previous period. The number of law graduates has increased from
4,659 in 1985 to 6,499 in 1994.[66] There were 8,997 students admitted to law
degrees in 1993.[67] Non-law graduates and others also enter the profession.[68] This
expansion in the number of people wishing to enter the profession has occurred
at the same time as the recession, which has hit the legal profession.[69] Other
trends in recent years have been a steady increase in the proportion of employed
assistant solicitors in private practice and a slight increase in the proportion of
solicitors outside private practice.

(ii) Solicitors' firms: private practice

At one time the only forms of organisation were sole practice and partnerships.
However, since section 9 of the Administration of Justice Act 1985 came into
force on January 1, 1992 it has been possible for solicitors to incorporate, provided there is compliance with the Solicitors' Incorporated Practice Rules
1988.[70]

There are many kinds of solicitors' practice. The range includes firms which
work in all or most company and commericial areas, based often in the City of
London, niche firms specialising in particular areas of work, *e.g.* shipping law
or entertainment law work, firms specialising in legal aid work, and generalist
firms. In size they range from sole practitioners to very large firms.[71] At July
31, 1995, there were 9,855 private practice firms located in 13,770 separate
offices.[72] Although the Law Society described a "typical firm" as recently as

---

[62] In 1963–64 there were 20,683 practising solicitors, in 1973–74 there were 28,741 and in 1983–
84, 44,837: *ibid*, Table 2.2. See, also, R. L. Abel, *The Legal Profession in England and Wales*
(1988).
[63] In 1967 there was one solicitor per 2,164 of the population, and in 1977 1 per 1,497: Abel (1988),
Table 2.14.
[64] See, *e.g.*, P. A. Leach, (1980) 77 L. S. Gaz 29. The number of law graduates doubled between
1967 and 1977: R.C.L.S., Vol. 2, p. 47.
[65] *The Recruitment Crisis: A Report by the Training Committee of the Law Society* (May 1988).
[66] *Law Society Annual Statistical Report 1995*, Table 9.6.
[67] *ibid*, Table 9.2.
[68] See below pp. 182–186.
[69] Concern about the growth of the profession is expressed in the *Law Society's Annual Statistical
Report 1995*, paras. 6.2–6.4.
[70] See *The Guide to the Professional Conduct of Solicitors* (6th ed., 1993), pp. 90–92 and Annex
3B and 3C.
[71] D. Podmore, "Bucher and Strass Revisited—the Case of the Solicitors' Profession" (1980) 7
B.J.L.S. 1, pp. 22–24 suggests a classification of 14 groups.
[72] *Law Society Annual Statistical Report 1995*, Table 3.5.

1978,[73] this is now a meaningless concept, since firms are organised according to the type and range of work undertaken. In 1995, 95 per cent of firms earning at least £15,000 had no more than 10 principals[74] and 83 per cent no more than four. Some 420 firms had 11 or more partners;[75] 69 of which had 16 to 20 partners and 150 of which had over 20 partners.[76] Many of these very large practices are the product of mergers, which have been a feature of recent years.[77] The overall ratio of principals to assistant solicitors was about 1.5:1; in the small firms it was about 2.5:1 and in firms of 11 or more partners, close to 1:1.[78] Large London firms employ a disproportionate number of assistant solicitors;[79] they also employed a significant number of non-fee earners.[80]

In some areas of work, primarily company/commercial, there has been a trend for the size of practices to increase.[81] At the same time, the number of sole practitioners has increased.[82] Forty-one per cent of firms are sole practitioners, 42 per cent are firms with 2–4 partners, 12 per cent are firms with 5–10 partners[83] and five per cent are firms with 11 or more partners.[84] In 1993–94, sole practitioners earned £421m in gross fees (£123,000 per principal and £88,000 per solicitor); firms with 2–4 partners earned £1,293m (£134,000 per principal and £98,000 per solicitor); firms with 5–10 partners earned £1,220m (£175,000 per principal and £114,000 per solicitor); firms with 11–25 partners earned £976m (£210,000 per principal and £126,000 per solicitor); and firms with 26 or more partners earned £2,721m (£485,000 per principal and £196,000 per solicitor).[85] Size alone is, presumably, an insufficient explanation for this distribution of earnings. The larger firms are engaged in types of work for which greater charges can be made, i.e. company/commercial work, as opposed to legal aid work or other less valued work. Further, it is likely to be the case that the large firms reap benefits of scale and thus are more efficient. In order to achieve some of the advantages of a large firm without losing individual identity and control

[73] Memorandum No. 5 to the Royal Commission on Legal Services; (1978) 75 L. S. Gaz. 422, p. 426.

[74] i.e., sole practitioners and partners (who might be equity or salaried partners).

[75] Law Society Annual Statistical Report 1995, Table 3.11.

[76] ibid., Table 3.14.

[77] Particularly spectacular was the 1987 merger of Clifford Turner and Coward Chance to form Clifford Chance: see P. Brown, (1987) 137 N.L.J. 377. This is still the largest firm, with 1,404 fee earners. There are 237 partners (of whom 229 are equity partners) and 890 assistants: "The Top 100" in The Lawyer April 25, 1995.

[78] Law Society Annual Statistical Report 1995, Table 4.1.

[79] ibid., Table 4.4.

[80] Proportionately they employed the same proportion as sole practitioners but a higher proportion than small or medium-size firms. The firms with 11 or more partners employed 36,997 of the total 91,556 non-fee earning staff employed: ibid., Table 4.3. The fall in the number of non-fee earners was particularly arrested in 1995. There were 99,612 in 1989 and 91,119 in 1994: ibid., Table 4.4 and Law Society Annual Statistical Report 1994, para 6.4.

[81] In 1985 there were 313 firms with 11 or more partners, and in 1995 there were 420, which is an increase of 34 per cent: ibid., Table 4.4. See also Abel (1988), op. cit. n. 62 above, R. G. Lee, "From Profession to Business: The Rise and Rise of the City Law Firm" (1992) 19 J.L.S. 31 and C. Whelan and D. McBarnet, "Lawyers in the Market: Delivering Legal Services in Europe" (1992) 19 J.L.S. 49. See the "Top 100" in The Lawyer (1995), April 25.

[82] In 1985 there were 2,617 sole practitioners and in 1995 there were 3,507, an increase of 34 per cent: Law Society Annual Statistical Report 1995, Table 3.12.

[83] There are fewer of these firms—since 1985 there has been a reduction of 1 per cent: ibid., Table 3.12. The reduction is presumably because they are too large for some work and too small for others.

[84] ibid., Table 3.12.

[85] ibid., Table 5.8.

over work practices, etc., some smaller firms band together to pay for central services covering such matters as recruitment, training and marketing.[86]

The recent recession has hit solicitors. A fairly optimistic note was taken in 1994 when the small increase in the number of firms was noted and it was felt that the profession has been relatively resilient.[87] However, in 1995 it was noted that the increase in turnover of private practice firms was only 3.1 per cent, whereas the number of solicitors had increased by 3.4 per cent and the retail price index only by 1.8 per cent so that the "growth was insufficient to maintain previous levels of earning and profitability. It is ominous that there was no increase in the average of gross fees per fee-earned in 1993–94".[88] The Coopers and Lybrand report emphasises the strength of larger, more business oriented and organised firms, but that for "firms at the lower end of the performance range the message is stark—time is running out".[89] It also seems clear that it is important that firms respond positively and pro-actively to the need for different services.[90] What the future holds is open to speculation. Some view things darkly, unless the financial and other forms of management of firms dramatically improves,[91] others believe the traditional strengths of firms, particularly the London firms, will continue to endure.[92] The Law Society has predicted that few firms will collapse and that solicitors who do have to leave the profession will find it useful to maintain a practising certificate.[93]

Geographically, the spread is uneven.[94] In 1995, 37 per cent of solicitors worked in London, where there are 23 per cent of all solicitors' firms, and where 13 per cent of the population live. This compares with rest of the South East (16 per cent of solicitors, 23 per cent of firms and 21 per cent of population), South West (8 per cent, 9 per cent and 9 per cent respectively), Wales (4 per cent, 6 per cent and 6 per cent), West Midlands (7 per cent, 8 per cent and 10 per cent), East Midlands (5 per cent, 5 per cent and 8 per cent), East Anglia (3 per cent, 3 per cent and 4 per cent), North West (10 per cent, 11 per cent and 12 per cent), Yorkshire and Humberside (7 per cent, 7 per cent and 10 per cent) and North (3 per cent, 5 per cent and 6 per cent).[95] Whilst there are many more solicitors situated in London than elsewhere in England, and in Cardiff than elsewhere in Wales, this is not surprising given the nature of those cities. Further, it is to be expected that solicitors set up practice where the business is to be discovered. Obviously this will tend to be in large connurbations, but it may also be in rural areas, especially given many solicitors' dependence upon

---

[86] e.g. the Norton Rose M5 Group, comprising firms in Manchester, Plymouth, Leeds, Bristol, Norwich, Birmingham and London. Other examples include the Eversheds Group, the Legal Resource Group and Law Net. For sole practitioners, there is the Sole Practitioner's Group. Sole practice has the advantages of control over work and lifestyle and, with increasing support, enables the practitioner to engage in interesting work, see, e.g., The Lawyer (1995), January 24, pp. 15–18. See also, M. Blacksell, K. Economides and C. Watkins, Justice Outside the City (1991), esp. Chap. 4.

[87] Law Society Annual Statistical Report 1994, paras.6.3 and 6.4.

[88] Law Society Annual Statistical Report 1995, para. 6.6.

[89] Quoted at ibid., para. 6.9.

[90] ibid., paras. 6.10–6.29.

[91] As to the import of financial management, see B. Woods-Scawen, "Financial management in law firms" (1994) The Lawyer.

[92] J. Kay, The Competitive Advantage of Law and Accountancy in the City of London (1994).

[93] Law Society Annual Statistical Report 1994, paras.6.3 and 6.10.

[94] See Blacksell, Economides and Watkins (1991), op. cit., n. 86 above, and C. Harding and J. Williams (eds.), Legal Provision in the Rural Environment (1994).

[95] Law Society Annual Statistical Report 1995, Table 3.8.

home ownership and probate work, both of which can be generated by elderly people who do not need to live in connurbations. Rural areas are not necessarily badly served by solicitors, for whom there may be attractions not only of business, but also of lifestyle.[96]

(iii) Solicitors' work

In 1990 it was shown that the work of solicitors in general was divided into certain categories: business affairs 20.6 per cent; commercial property 18 per cent; residential conveyancing 18.5 per cent; family 10.6 per cent; probate, wills, etc., 7.2 per cent; personal injury 7.1 per cent; crime 6.1 per cent; and other 11.3 per cent.[97] Similar results were derived for 1985 from a survey commissioned by the Law Society,[98] other than that the time and effort on domestic conveyancing fell during the intervening period.[99] Since 1989 there have been sharp falls in gross fees from residential conveyancing and commercial property work, off set by increases in commercial work and other main services by high street firms, but no major new services have been developed.[1]

Solicitors are generally much less dependent upon legal aid than barristers.[2] Some firms, however, have specialised in legal aid work and they are under increasing pressure as the profitability of such work declines.[3] The traditional dependency of some solicitors on conveyancing has been affected by the end of their monopoly, the price "war", and the crash in the housing market.[4] For the future, it is anticipated that the volume of wills and probate work will increase, but whilst the current main competition to solicitors is people writing their own wills, there is the prospect of other competition in the near future.[5] Other work trends for the future depend upon the developments proposed by the Government in relation to marital breakdown,[6] the number of business formations and failures and their rate of success, the success of solicitors in

[96] Blacksell, Economides and Watkins, *op. cit.*, pp. 24–44. There is also reasonable provision of CABx, though they may provide a less comprehensive service, but little law centre provision, *ibid.*, pp. 44–48. This work builds upon the pioneering work undertaken by K. Foster, "The location of solicitors" (1973) 36 M.L.R. 153, considered in the first edition of this book.

[97] G. Chambers and S. Harwood, *Solicitors in England and Wales: Practice, Organisation and Perceptions; First Report: Practice, Organisation and Perceptions* (1990), Fig. 6.1. In the Annual Statistical Survey of the Law Society the major areas of work discussed in identifying trends for the future are: conveyancing; wills and probate; marital breakdown; crime; business formation and failures; overseas earnings; and workload of the courts: *Law Society's Annual Statistical Report 1994*, Chap. 6. See also Blacksell, Economides and Watkins, *op. cit.*, Chap. 4.

[98] Peat Marwick Survey of the Structure and Finances of the Profession in Private Practice. January 6, 1986, cited in N.C.C., *Ordinary Justice* (1989), p. 60. For earlier surveys, see R.C.L.S., Vol 2, pp. 486–489 (1976–76) and the Report of the Prices and Incomes Board, *Remuneration of Solicitors* (Cmnd. 3529, 1968).

[99] On the assumption that this is not a product of different research methodologies, the explanation probably lies in the ending of the conveyancing monopoly and the price competition for conveyancing amongst all providers, and see below, pp. 130–133.

[1] *Law Society Annual Statistical Report 1995*, para. 6.11.

[2] In 1993–94 solicitors were paid £963.3m of the £6,622m paid to the profession: *Law Society Annual Statistical Report 1995*, Table 7.11.

[3] See Chap. 9.

[4] *Law Society Annual Statistical Report 1995*, paras.6.17–6.21 and see below, pp. 130–133.

[5] *ibid.*, paras. 6.23–6.26 and see below, p. 138.

[6] See Family Law Bill and Act 1996.

developing overseas markets, and the workload of the courts.[7] So the future of the profession is obviously dependent upon the general economic situation and upon what changes occur in the legal system, and the profession will, therefore, be keenly interested in, for example, the consequences both for itself as well as for society of the work on the civil litigation system.[8]

Rates of remuneration are difficult to ascertain. The figures for gross fees earned by firms, principals and solicitors given above do not give an accurate picture of remuneration levels. Further, the figures leave out those firms earning less than £15,000 per year.[9] The 1994 government *New Earnings Survey* showed that the annual average salary for male solicitors was £32,484 and for women solicitors was £25,512. The solicitors included were only those paid through the PAYE scheme, which excludes all equity partners, but includes salaried partners, assistant solicitors, trainee solicitors and solicitors employed outside private practice.[10] These figures do not indicate what the majority of principals earn. It should be remembered that at July 31, 1994 there were 30,696 principals and 20,804 assistant solicitors.[11] The *Chambers' and Partners Directory of the Legal Profession 1994–95* suggests that assistant solicitors with larger firms who are two years' qualified would, on average, be earning between £31,000 and £35,000 in the City of London; between £26,000 and £30,000 in the West End; between £20,000 and £24,000 in the South East; between £20,000 and £23,000 in the South West; between £21,000 and £24,000 in the Midlands; between £22,000 and £28,000 in Lancashire or Yorkshire; between £21,000 and £25,000 in the North East; and between £19,000 and £23,000 in East Anglia.[12] Those working with smaller firms are likely to be earning much less.

(iv) Specialisation

There has been an increasing tendency for solicitors to specialise. Larger firms will normally have, for example, separate litigation, company and property departments and further more specialised sections. Each solicitor will develop his or her career in a particular area. It has become common for league tables to be published comparing the reputation and workload of the leading firms in different areas of practice.[13] Until 1990, however, it was only in limited circumstances that firms could advertise their specialisms.[14] The Law Society has established five specialist panels covering mental health review tribunals (established in 1983), children (1984), planning (1991), personal injury (1993) and medical negligence (1995). The panels were set up to help clients identify solicitors with particular competence in the relevant area. Solicitors not on the panels may undertake the relevant work. Further, solicitors engaged in certain work have

---

[7] See *Law Society Annual Statistical Report 1995* paras.6.18–6.22.

[8] See below, pp. 626–633.

[9] There were 1,233 such firms in 1995: *ibid.*, Chapter 3.

[10] *ibid.*, para. 6.30.

[11] *ibid.*, Table 2.8.

[12] At p. 8, which also provides information on trainee salaries and other years' qualified for assistant solicitors.

[13] See, *e.g.* Chambers & Partners', *The Legal Profession 1990*; J. Pritchard, *The Legal Five Hundred* (1989).

[14] See below, pp. 141–142.

to have achieved specialist status to undertake that work. A local government diploma was introduced in 1985, the licensing of insolvency practitioners was introduced in 1986 consequent upon sections 388 to 398 of the Insolvency Act 1986, and the certification of solicitors with rights of audience in the higher courts was introduced in 1994 consequent upon the ending of the bar's monopoly of the work.[15]

The advantages of panels include the empowerment of the clients in their otherwise unequal relationships with solicitors, improvement of access and the raising of standards.[16] The law is now so complex that it is impossible for solicitors to be sufficiently expert in all fields to be able to offer general advice, indeed it is unfair not only on the clients but also on the solicitors to have such expectations. Specialisation can, therefore, offer benefits not only to clients, but also to solicitors.[17]

(v) Employed solicitors[18]

At July 31, 1995, of the 66,123 solicitors with practising certificates, 3,718 were employed in commerce and industry, 2,735 were employed in local government, 2,009 in other forms of the public sector and 177 in law centres and CABx.[19] Their work is obviously geared to their employers' needs. Lawyers in industry are particularly concerned with property and planning, contracts, financial services, mergers and acquisitions, company law, debt recovery, employment and pensions law.[20] Lawyers in local government are likely to have to work over the widest range in any given year.[21] Their primary areas of work fall into two categories. The first concerns areas of local authority responsibility, particularly housing, land use planning, highways and transportation, general local government work,[22] and, where the department handles it, social services.[23] The second

---

[15] As at July 31, 1995, there were 1,584 members of the Children Panel, 333 members of the M.H.R.T. Panel, 185 members of the Planning Panel, and 1,976 members of the Personal Injury Panel and 69 members of the medical negligence panel. By that date, 282 people had been awarded the local government diploma, 211 people had become licensed insolvency practitioners, and 458 people had obtained rights of audience in higher courts status: *Law Society's Annual Statistical Report 1995*, Tables 10.22a and 10.22b.

[16] See, *e.g.* N.C.C., *Ordinary Justice* (1989), pp. 144–153. See also A. A. Paterson, "Specialisation and the Legal Profession" (1986) 136 N.L.J. 697, 721.

[17] The benefits of specialisation are indicated in the research which demonstrates their importance for accident victims pursuing damages: H. Genn, *Hard Bargaining* (1987).

[18] This does not include solicitors employed in multi-national partnerships (Solicitor's Practice Rules, r.4(2)), but see below, pp. 140–141.

[19] *Law Society Annual Statistical Report 1995*, Table 2.7. The more detailed breakdown is: commerce and industry—commerce/industry 3,644, national undertaking 74; public sector—C.P.S. 1,654, clerk or assistant clerk to justices 195, CPS Agent 51, government service 83 and judges 26. As regards lawyers in central government, see G. Drewry, (1981) 59 *Public Administration* 15, and Sir Robert Andrew, *Review of Government Legal Services* (1989) and above pp. 22–23.

[20] R. Woolfson, J. Plotnikoff and D. Wilson, *Solicitors in the Employed Sector* (Law Society Research Study No. 13, 1994), Table 4.3, which also indicates that other areas of work are intellectual property, E.C. law, consumer and advertising, building law, personal injury, taxation, natural resources and criminal law.

[21] *ibid.*, p. 23 and Table 4.2.

[22] *i.e.*, all Local Government Act, constitutional and corporate matters not falling under other headings.

[23] *ibid.*, Table 4.4(a), which also indicates that the other areas of work are: environmental health, parks, recreation and tourism, economic development, environmental protection, licensing, waste

concerns general legal work, in particular conveyancing, local planning enquiries, contracts, debt collection, criminal, and, where the department handles it, child care.[24] Compulsory competitive tendering may increase the number of local authorities using outside lawyers and so reduce the number of employed solicitors. The government legal service is by far the largest user of outside legal services.[25] The rules on the kind of work which may be undertaken by employed solicitors were relaxed by the 1990 Solicitor's Practice Rules. Rule 4 now provides that solicitors who are employees of non-solicitors must not as part of their employment do solicitor's work for any person other than their employer, except as permitted by the Law Society's Employed Solicitor's Code.[26] Under the Code, employed solicitors may act, without charge, for their fellow employees in any matter relating to their employment, excluding personal injuries.[27] Solicitors employed by associations[28] may act, without charge, for members in non-contentious matters and, with the association indemnifying the member for costs, in contentious matters.[29] Employees and association members must be free to instruct other solicitors.

(vi) "Monopolies"

Solicitors have long enjoyed certain statutory monopolies.[30] Section 20 of the Solicitors Act 1974 makes it an offence for an unqualified person to act as a solicitor and as such commence or conduct litigation on behalf of another. An unqualified person may not pretend to be a solicitor.[31]

It is also an offence for an unqualified person[32] to prepare (directly or indirectly) any instrument "relating to real or personal estate, or any legal proceedings",[33] to take instructions for a grant of probate or letters of

---

collection, agriculture, arts, libraries and museums, consumer protection, education, fire and rescue, and police.

[24] *ibid.*, Table 4.4(b) which also indicates that other areas of work are: employment (including pensions), third party claims and judicial review.

[25] See *Solicitors in the Employed Sector*, Chap. 4.

[26] The Code is promulgated by the Council of the Law Society with the concurrence of the Master of the Rolls: Solicitor's Practice Rules, r.4(1). The Code is to be found in *The Guide to the Professional Conduct of Solicitors* (6th ed., 1993), pp. 131–135.

[27] Employed Solicitor's Code, para. 2.

[28] The membership of the association must be limited to persons concerned in a particular trade, occupation or activity or otherwise having a community of interest. The latter was added in 1990 to include, for example, groups whose membership is based on sex, ethnic origin, nationality, religion or political affiliation (see (1990) L. S. Gaz. August 22, p. 25). The association must be formed for the benefit of its members: Employed Solicitor's Code, para. 3.

[29] Employed Solicitor's Code, para. 3(c).

[30] A non-lawyer may always act in person in matters affecting him- or herself and many people run litigation themselves, see the Interim Report of the Judges' Council Working Party, *Litigants in Person in the Royal Courts of Justice London* (1995, Chair: Otton L. J.). Some of the "monopolies" were shared with other relatively small groups.

[31] Solicitors Act 1974, s.21. See, *e.g., Carter v. Butcher* [1966] 1 Q.B. 526.

[32] Here the term covers a person who is not a solicitor, barrister or notary public, and there are some other exclusions: *ibid.*, ss.22(2), 23(2). For some purposes Scottish solicitors, licensed conveyancers, trade mark agents, patent agents and certain public officers are exempt.

[33] *ibid.*, s.22. "Instrument" does not include a will, an agreement not under seal, a letter of power of attorney, or a "transfer of stock containing no trust or limitation thereof": s.22(3). Thus a contract for the sale of land is not within the restriction, whereas the deed which effects the conveyance is.

administration, or to prepare papers on which to found or oppose such a grant,[34] unless he or she proves that it was not done for or in the expectation of any fee, gain or reward. An offence is committed even where the unqualified person does not personally receive the fee.[35] No person may bring proceedings to recover costs in respect of anything done by an unqualified person acting as a solicitor.[36] The Royal Commission on Legal Services found these restrictions to be in the public interest.[37] For example, in the context of conducting litigation, it took the view that the responsibility of a solicitor to the court and the professional discipline granted the client guarantees which no one else could provide.[38] However, even in the contentious litigation field, the view that solicitors should have a monopoly has been challenged, so the Courts and Legal Services Act 1990 allows for extension of the right to conduct litigation and of the right of audience. There have also been significant challenges to solicitors' monopolies in non-contentious areas.

(1) *Conveyancing* The economic dependence of many solicitors upon conveyancing, when put alongside criticisms of the low quality of service provided[39] and the level of charges, naturally made the "conveyancing monopoly"[40] one of the most controversial areas before the Royal Commission.[41] A majority[42] of the Commission accepted the Law Society's case that the restrictions were in the public interest in view of the complexity of the law relating to the ownership of land, the complexity of the conveyancing process and the need to protect clients from dishonesty, incompetence and overcharging. The Commission were unanimous that a "free-for-all" would not be in the public interest. By a majority they rejected proposals for a system of licensed conveyancers. Indeed they suggested that the restrictions should be extended to cover the preparation of the contract of sale as well as the final document and that the maximum penalty should be raised for the first time since 1894 from £50 to £500. They did not find that charges were excessive. In order to reintroduce more certainty to charging, they suggested there would be a scale of "standard" charges covering the general run of domestic conveyancing.

As we have seen, however, matters have not rested there. Part II of the Administration of Justice Act 1985,[43] founded on the First Report of the Conveyancing Committee, introduced a system of licensed conveyancers.[44] The Act created a new body, The Council for Licensed Conveyancers, with the responsibility of controlling the discipline, admission, training and professional standards

---

[34] *ibid.*, s.23(1).
[35] *Reynolds v. Hoyle* [1976] 1 W.L.R. 207; *cf. Green v. Hoyle* [1976] 1 W.L.R. 575.
[36] 1974 Act, s.25.
[37] R.C.L.S., Vol. 1, pp. 225–231.
[38] *ibid.*, p. 227.
[39] M. Joseph, *The Conveyancing Fraud* (2nd ed., 1989)—a book by a practising solicitor.
[40] It had been sought by the Society of Gentlemen Practisers and was finally granted by William Pitt in 1804 as a *quid pro quo* for an increase in the tax on practising certificates and articles in the Stamp Act 1804: see Abel-Smith and Stevens (1967), pp. 22–23, Kirk (1976), Chap. 7. It was moved from fiscal legislation to a Solicitors Act in 1932. The change seems to have been agreed because of the need to collect tax, rather than for the public interest.
[41] R.C.L.S., Vol. 1, pp. 243–282. The Commission preferred the expression "closed shop".
[42] A third of the members were unconvinced: R.C.L.S., Vol. 1, pp. 808, 809–812, 813–816.
[43] See annotations by P. Kenny in *Current Law Statutes Annotated 1985*; A. Kenny, (1986) 277 E.G. 262, 394.
[44] (Chairman: Prof. J. T. Farrand) *Non-Solicitor Conveyancers—Competence and Consumer Protection* (HMSO, 1984). See [1984] Conv. 393; R. C. A. White, (1985) P.N. 80.

of the new profession of "licensed conveyancer". The Council was required, *inter alia*, to make training rules, rules for regulating professional practice conduct and discipline, rules requiring compulsory indemnity insurance against civil liability and for setting up a compensation fund for the benefit of the victims of negligence, fraud or other dishonesty on the part of licensed conveyancers and rules for keeping accounts. The structure is similar to that applicable to the solicitors' profession as regulated by the Law Society, with some differences of detail.[45] The first licences were granted on May 1, 1987, and solicitors have been directed to proceed in their dealings with licensed conveyancers on the same basis as with solicitors, in recognition of their status as members of a regulated profession.[46] Whilst some solicitors undoubtedly retain the view that only solicitors should engage in conveyancing, the more recent concern has been with the prices charged by some solicitors. The view taken is that the charges are so low that corners must be cut, thus raising the likelihood of errors thereby affecting the reputation of the profession and raising the indemnity cover. Action is to be attempted at least to set a lower limit for charges for conveyancing. Whether this can really be regarded as action in the public interest depends upon the verifiability of the allegations that conveyancing cannot be done properly for, say, £99. The independent evidence does not yet appear to exist to support the claim.

The numbers of licensed conveyancers are as yet too small to have had much direct impact on the work of solicitors.[47] Their existence, coupled with the threat of institutional conveyancing, has, however, played a part in encouraging greater competitiveness among solicitors, with substantial reductions in charges for domestic conveyancing; the widespread use of advertising once the rules restricting it had been relaxed; decisions by solicitors' firms to undertake estate agency as well as conveyancing work, commonly establishing "solicitors' property centres"[48]; the introduction of TransAction, a new National Conveyancing Protocol designed to make the procedure for house transfer speedier and more efficient[49]; and the establishment by the Law Society of the Solicitors' Financial and Property Services Company, as a source of information and market support for firms wishing to offer clients a fully integrated package of financial services.[50]

By 1989, the government had reverted to the view that competition in the provision of conveyancing services could properly be extended, subject to safeguards. The White Paper[51] proposed that the provision of conveyancing services should be open to any "authorised practitioner." The relevant provisions are

---

[45] For commentaries on the Rules promulgated by the Council of Licensed Conveyancers, see [1987] Conv. 396; P. Kenny, (1987) 131 S.J. 958.

[46] Council statement on dealing with licensed conveyancers in *The Guide to the Professional Conduct of Solicitors* (6th ed., 1993) at Annex 24E.

[47] By 1995, there were about 350 licensed conveyancers actively practising in the market and a further 450 or so in employment, accounting for only a small fraction of the conveyancing market.

[48] See (1989) 86 L.S. Gaz., February 22, pp. 4–5, noting the establishment by two firms of a chain of "property shops" in the London area, and the development of Crawley Solicitors Property Centre, set up by six firms.

[49] See (1990) 87 L.S. Gaz., March 21, p. 3 and March 28, p. 4 on TransAction's launch: the Law Society predicted a 90 per cent take-up; adoption of the Protocol is voluntary but preferred practice; see also L. A. Palmer, (1990) 87 L.S. Gaz., April 4, pp. 24–25.

[50] See K. Aldred, (1989) 86 L.S. Gaz., October 25, p. 26 and November 22, pp. 4–5; J. Ames, (1990) 87 L.S. Gaz., August 29, p. 8.

[51] Cm. 740, Chap. 5.

to be found in the Courts and Legal Services Act 1990, ss.34–52, and Scheds.5–7. The Act establishes the Authorised Conveyancing Practitioners Board,[52] comprising a chairman and between 4 and 8 other members appointed by the Lord Chancellor, who must have regard to the desirability of appointing people who have experience in or knowledge of the provision of conveyancing services, associated financial arrangements and consumer or commercial affairs, and securing a balance between the interests of authorised practitioners and those who use their services. The Board must, *inter alia*, seek to develop competition in the provision of conveyancing services, supervise the activities of authorised practitioners, and consider and report on matters referred by the Lord Chancellor. It has power to obtain information from authorised practitioners and those who act on their behalf, and to investigate and intervene in the affairs of an authorised practitioner.[53] This Scheme is not yet operative.

The restrictions in section 22 of the Solicitors Act 1974 will not apply where conveyancing services are provided by an authorised practitioner *i.e.* an individual or corporate body authorised by the Board.[54] The Board must grant authorisation if it is satisfied that the applicant is "fit and proper," and is of the opinion that the applicant will comply with applicable rules and regulations, will be able to meet claims made in connection with the provision of conveyancing services, will maintain satisfactory complaints procedures and satisfactory arrangements to protect clients in the event of ceasing to operate, and will be a member of the Conveyancing Ombudsman Scheme set up by the Act.[55] An authorisation may be refused, or may be granted subject to conditions, and may be revoked or suspended in accordance with rules to be made by the Board. Appeals lie to a Conveyancing Appeals Tribunal, and from the Tribunal, on a point of law, to the High Court.[56]

The Lord Chancellor may make regulations to secure that authorised practitioners maintain satisfactory standards of competence and conduct, that in providing conveyancing services (and in particular in fixing their charges) they act in a manner which is consistent with the maintenance of fair competition between authorised practitioners and others providing conveyancing services, and that the interests of clients are satisfactorily protected. The regulations may include provisions designed to promote efficiency and to avoid unnecessary delay and conflicts of interest, a requirement that, so far as is reasonably practicable, each transaction is under the overall control of one individual, and provisions as to the supervision of specified classes of work by qualified staff, terms and conditions of service, the information to be given to potential clients, the handling of clients' money and the disclosure of an accounting for commissions.[57] The Act also prohibits "tying-in arrangements": a loan for the purchase of residential property may not be made subject to a condition requiring the borrower to use other services (*e.g.* conveyancing services) provided or

---

[52] Courts and Legal Services Act 1990, ss.34, 35 and Sched. 5. These provisions and s.40 were the only sections in force at the time of writing.

[53] *ibid.* ss.47–52.

[54] *ibid.* s.36.

[55] *ibid.* s.37. For the Conveyancing Ombudsman scheme see s.43, and the rules made thereunder and Sched. 7.

[56] *ibid.* ss.38, 39, 41, 42.

[57] *ibid.* s.40. Further details were set out in the *White Paper*, Cm. 740, paras.5.12–5.14, including a requirement for a personal interview, safeguards against conflict of interest and the prevention of conveyancing services being offered at less than their true cost.

specified by the lender, and vice versa.[58] These provisions take account of the concern expressed by the Law Society that competition in the conveyancing market be placed on an equal footing.[59]

The obvious intended beneficiaries of the new arrangements are banks and building societies, but other professions may also become involved. The actual work will have to be carried out or supervised by qualified staff (*i.e.* solicitors, licensed conveyancers, and (subject to appropriate qualification) barristers and notaries.[60]

(2) *Rights of audience*. An analogous area is that of rights of audience.[61] Prior to the Courts and Legal Services Act 1990, these were limited by the practice of the courts and tribunals concerned rather than by rules of law. Litigants in person have a right of audience throughout the legal system.[62] Barristers enjoyed a virtual monopoly of advocacy before the House of Lords, Court of Appeal and High Court.[63] They also had exclusive rights of audience in all Crown Court cases, except that a solicitor might appear (a) in appeals to the Crown Court from a magistrates' court in civil or criminal proceedings or on committal for sentence, if the solicitor or anyone in his or her firm appeared in the court below[64]; and (b) in a wider class of cases in certain remote areas.[65] Barristers and solicitors had rights of audience in the county courts and magistrates' courts; lay persons might be permitted to appear. For example, by custom magistrates allowed police officers, local government officials and civil servants employed by the D.P.P. to appear. In most tribunals there were no restrictions. Any person might attend a trial as a friend of a party to take notes and give advice but he or she would not be accorded a right of audience.[66]

The Royal Commission considered the question of rights of audience and came down resoundingly in favour of the *status quo*. It rejected suggestions that the rights of audience of lay persons should be extended, stressing, particularly for the higher courts, the importance of proceedings for the individual concerned, the "special skill and expertise" called for, and its other proposals for the extension of financial support for legal services. The existing position of litigants in person and lay persons should not, however, be restricted. In the

---

[58] *ibid.* ss.104–107.

[59] *e.g. the Law Society, Striking the Balance* (1989), pp. 5–8 and Annex A; *White Paper*, para. 5.14.

[60] Cm. 740, para. 5.9.

[61] R.C.L.S., Vol. 1, pp. 203–221. For a summary, see *ibid.* p. 221.

[62] Prosecutions in the Crown Court must be conducted by a barrister. See Judges' Council Working Party Interim Report, *Litigants in Person in the Royal Courts of Justice London* (Chair, Otton L. J.).

[63] Solicitors could appear before the single judge of the Court of Appeal (Criminal Division) sitting in chambers, in certain High Court bankruptcy applications and in any High Court proceedings heard in chambers (before a judge, official referee, master or registrar). Rights of audience before the Judicial Committee of the Privy Council were limited to English and Northern Ireland barristers, Scottish advocates and all advocates duly qualified in countries from which appeals lie to the Privy Council.

[64] *Practice Direction* [1972] 1 W.L.R. 307.

[65] *Practice Direction* [1972] 1 W.L.R. 5. The areas are Caernarvon, Barnstaple, Bodmin, Doncaster and Lincoln.

[66] *McKenzie v. McKenzie* [1971] P. 33; *Merry v. Persons Unknown* [1974] C.L.Y. 3003. There is, however, no right to a McKenzie Adviser: see below, p. 493. A superior court may exceptionally hear persons who technically have no right of audience: *Engineers' and Managers' Association v. A.C.A.S.* [1979] 1 W.L.R. 113 (trade union official).

case of the former this was not because the Commission thought they were any good at advocacy, but because their right of audience was "long-established" and no one had actually proposed its removal. In evidence, there had been some jockeying for position among lawyers. The Bar and the judges resisted solicitors' claims[67] for wider rights of audience, particularly in the Crown Court; the Law Society resisted the claims of legal executives.[68] By and large, the resisters won, apart from proposed minor changes to enable a solicitor to appear in any court to deal with formal or unopposed matters.[69] The Commission thought that any significant changes would lead to a lowering of standards. Crown Court advocacy required different skills (e.g. addressing a jury) or greater expertise (e.g. knowledge of the laws of evidence and experience in cross-examination) than advocacy in the magistrates' courts. The Commission's enthusiasm for solicitor-advocates was markedly lukewarm:

> "Many solicitors make competent advocates in magistrates' courts and some are very good. Some could achieve the same standard in the Crown Court if they could so arrange their professional lives as to enable them to concentrate on the work there."[70]

It thought it unlikely that many solicitors, except in large firms, would be able to have the constant practice in Crown Court advocacy which competence and progressive improvement required. However, it feared that enough solicitors would move into this area to have a "serious and disproportionate impact on the income and capacity of barristers to continue in practice".[71] The fear of fusion was thus in the background.

Again, as we have seen, matters have not stood still. The Law Society again raised the question of rights of audience in 1984,[72] and, in 1985, widespread publicity surrounded the attempt by Cyril Smith M.P. to have the terms of the settlement of a libel action brought against him and Radio Trent by 25 other M. P.s read to the High Court by his solicitor. This act did not require the skills of an advocate, and Mr Smith's solicitor took the view that it would be unnecessarily expensive to brief counsel for the task. Leonard J. held that he had no authority to allow a solicitor to appear before him, save in an emergency, and this was affirmed by the Court of Appeal,[73] on the ground that the public interest required that the High Court's general practices and procedures be known and not changed or departed from in piecemeal fashion by individual judges. However, it was acknowledged that the rule might be changed by the judges of the Supreme Court acting as a collegiate body. Accordingly, on May 9, a Practice Direction was issued on behalf of the judges of the High Court and Court of Appeal permitting solicitors to appear in the Supreme Court in

---

[67] The solicitors were refighting a battle lost when the criminal courts were reorganised in 1971: see the *Royal Commission on Assizes and Quarter Sessions* 1966–69, Cmnd. 4153, Written Evidence Nos.32 and 47.

[68] See R.C.L.S., Vol. 1, pp. 413–415.

[69] Seven members of the Commission favoured some extension of the right of audience of solicitors in the Crown Court, particularly to make pleas in mitigation: Vol. 1, pp. 807, 816–823, 828–829.

[70] R.C.L.S., Vol. 1, p. 212. The competence of barristers was not discussed in the chapter on rights of audience. Their increasing prolixity was discussed in Vol. 1, pp. 307–308.

[71] R.C.L.S., Vol. 1, p. 216.

[72] Annual Statement, 1983–84, pp. 48–49; (1984) 81 L.S. Gaz. 1507.

[73] *Abse v. Smith* [1986] Q.B. 536.

formal or unopposed proceedings, and when judgment is delivered in open court following a hearing in Chambers at which that solicitor conducts the case for his or her client.[74] The Marre Committee subsequently supported, by a majority, the extension of rights of audience in the Crown Court to solicitors approved by a Rights of Audience Advisory Board.[75]

The government's proposals were more radical still.[76] The Courts and Legal Services Act 1990,[77] puts rights of audience in courts and in certain tribunals and inquiries[78] on a statutory footing. A person has a right of audience before a court

(a) where he or she has a right of audience granted by the appropriate authorised body,[79] and that body's qualification regulations and rules of conduct have been approved;

(b) where (a) does not apply but he or she has a statutory right of audience;

(c) where (a) does not apply but he or she has a right of audience granted by the court in question;

(d) where he or she is a party to the proceedings and would have had a right of audience as a party if the Act had not been passed;

(e) where he or she is a solicitor's clerk, or corresponding employee of a recognised body, and the proceedings are being heard in chambers in the High Court.

A right of audience can, however, be denied to a person for reasons which apply to him or her as an individual. Sections 20 and 25 of the Solicitors Act 1974 do not apply in relation to any act done in exercise of a right of audience duly granted under the Act.

Similar rules are to apply to rights to conduct litigation, except that the General Council of the Bar is not specified as an "authorised body".[80]

On the coming into force of section 27 of the 1990 Act,[81] the rights of audience enjoyed by barristers and solicitors, and the right to conduct litigation enjoyed by solicitors, immediately before December 7, 1989, were deemed to have been granted, respectively, by the General Council of the Bar and the Law Society, and the relevant qualification regulations and rules of conduct relating to these rights were deemed to have been approved under section 27.[82]

The procedure whereby other professional bodies may become "authorised bodies", and their qualification regulations and rules of conduct approved for

---

[74] *Practice Direction (Solicitors: Rights of Audience)* [1986] 1 W.L.R. 545. The Royal Commission's recommendation in favour of such a change (Vol. 1, p. 219) had previously been accepted in principle by the government (Government Response, Cmnd. 9077, 1983, p. 19) and the Senate of the Inns of Court and the Bar.

[75] Report of the Marre Committee, pp. 149–157. See J. Hodgson, (1988) 138 N.L.J. 615.

[76] *Green Paper*, Chap. 5, *White Paper*, Chap. 3.

[77] s.27.

[78] The term "court" includes (a) any tribunal under the jurisdiction of the Council on Tribunals (b) any court-martial and (c) a statutory inquiry within the meaning of the Tribunals and Inquiries Act 1971, s.19(1): 1990 Act, s.119.

[79] *i.e.* the General Council of the Bar, the Law Society, and a professional body designated by Order in Council (which may include the Council for Licensed Conveyancers: s.53). The procedures for securing and revoking designation are set out in ss.29 and 30 and Sched. 4.

[80] Courts and Legal Services Act 1990, s.28.

[81] On January 1, 1991: see S.I. 1990 No. 2484.

[82] *ibid.* ss.31–33. Fully in force from April 1, 1991: see S.I. 1991 No. 608.

the purposes of section 27, is set out in Schedule 4, Part I. An application must be sent first to the Lord Chancellor's Advisory Committee (ACLEC) for comment, and then to the Lord Chancellor, who is to consider the advice of the Committee, and that of the Director General of Fair Trading (who is to consider whether the regulations and rules would restrict, distort or prevent competition to any significant extent). The application needs the approval of the Lord Chancellor and each of four "designated judges" (the Lord Chief Justice, the Master of the Rolls, the President of the Family Division and the Vice-Chancellor.) The designated judges too must consider the advice of the Committee and the Director General. The applicant is entitled to written reasons for the decision. A similar procedure applies for obtaining approval for the alteration of the qualification regulations and rules of conduct of any authorised body (including the General Council of the Bar and the Law Society) (Schedule 4, Part II) or for revoking the designation of an authorised body (Schedule 4, Part III).

The grant or refusal of approval under Schedule 4 by the Lord Chancellor and the designated judges is not a matter of discretion: any one of them must refuse approval if satisfied that the application is incompatible with the "statutory objective" or the "general principle" laid down in section 17 of the Act. The former is the general objective of

"the development of legal services in England and Wales (and in particular the development of advocacy, litigation, conveyancing and probate services) by making provision for new or better ways of providing such services and a wider choice of persons providing them, while maintaining the proper and efficient administration of justice."

The latter is the general principle that the question whether a person should be granted a right of audience or to conduct litigation is to be determined only by reference to:

(a) whether he or she is qualified in accordance with the educational and training requirements appropriate to the court or proceedings;

(b) whether he or she is a member of a professional or other body which has rules of conduct which are the subject of an effective enforcement mechanism and are likely to be enforced;

(c) whether, in the case of a body whose members provide advocacy services, the body observes a form of the "cab-rank" principle: *i.e.* a satisfactory provision requiring its members not to withhold those services

  (i) on the ground that the nature of the case is objectionable to him or her or to any section of the public;

  (ii) on the ground that the conduct, opinions or beliefs of the prospective client are unacceptable to him or her or to any section of the public;

  (iii) on any ground relating to the prospective client's source of financial support (*e.g.* legal aid); and

(d) whether that body's rules of conduct are "appropriate in the interests of the proper and efficient administration of justice."

However, rules of conduct which allow advocacy services to be withheld on the ground that a proper fee has not been offered are not to be taken as incompatible with the general principle.[83]

These arrangements are a modification of those which were proposed in the Green Paper,[84] where it was suggested that it would be for the Lord Chancellor to decide on the education, qualifications and training of advocates appropriate for each of the various courts, and to specify principles on which Codes of Conduct regulating advocacy should be based. His decisions on rights of audience would be put into effect by subordinate legislation, following the receipt of advice from the Advisory Committee and after consultation with the judiciary. These proposals were attacked, with varying degrees of vehemence, by the judiciary, the Bar and the Law Society as constituting a serious threat to the independence of the legal profession from government.[85] Such new powers, "in less wise hands, could be exercised so as to damage the legal profession and the judiciary in the interests of political dogma".[86] "There are warning lessons from other countries in the Commonwealth which have ceased to have Judges and legal professions independent of the diktat of Government".[87]

The revised arrangements, proposed in the White Paper and enshrined in the Act, leave a lesser degree of control in the hands of the Lord Chancellor, and have given the designated judges a formal role in the procedure. This reflects the significant concern of the Bar with the extension of rights of audience.[88] The Lord Chancellor's Advisory Committee on Legal Education and Conduct plays a pivotal role in assessing proposals prior to reference to the Lord Chancellor and the judges. Despite the concern of many barristers, A.C.L.E.C., the Lord Chancellor and the four designated judges decided to extend rights of audience in the higher courts to solicitors as from 8 December 1993. This was inevitable in view of the policy decision already made and reflected in the Act itself.

In order to exercise the extended right of audience, a solicitor must seek the Higher Courts (All Proceedings) Qualification or the Higher Courts (Criminal Proceedings) Qualification or the Higher Courts (Civil Proceedings) Qualification, which will be granted to solicitors with practising certificates who either (a) have appropriate judicial or higher court advocacy experience[89] or (b) satisfy the Law Society that they are suitably experienced[90] and qualified[91] to exercise such rights of audience.[92] Of signal importance was the expectation that solicitor-advocates would maintain the high standards of advocacy and independence asserted by the Bar. This is achieved by the Law Society's Code for Advocacy,

---

[83] The practitioner must have reasonable ground to consider that it is not a proper fee having regard to the circumstances of the case, the nature of his or her practice or his or her experience and standing: s.17(5).

[84] *Green Paper: The Work and Organisation of the Legal Profession* (Cm. 570), Chaps.4 and 5.

[85] F. Cownie, *op. cit.*, pp. 220–227; *Quality of Justice, The Bar's Response* (1989), Chap. 14; Council of the Law Society, *Striking the Balance* (1989), pp. 14–15; Lord Ackner, (1990) Bracton L. J. 4.

[86] *Quality of Justice*, para. 14.10.

[87] *ibid.* para. 14.9.

[88] See J. Rozenberg, *The Search for Justice* (1994), pp. 147–153.

[89] See the Law Society's Higher Courts Qualification Regulations 1992, reg.4(a) and Sched. 1.

[90] This involves an assessment of experience against set criteria, see the Higher Courts Qualification Regulations, reg.5 and Sched. 2.

[91] There are tests in Evidence and Procedure to be taken and attendance at and passing either or both the Higher Criminal Courts Advocacy Training Course and the Higher Civil Courts Advocacy Training Course, currently run only by the Law Society, is required.

[92] The Higher Courts Qualification Regulations 1992, reg. 4.

which is largely identical to the barristers' Code of Conduct, except that there is no "Cab Rank" rule[93] and the guidance on contact with witnesses is significantly different.[94] It seems likely that the Bar Council and Law Society will work to minimise the differences.[95]

As yet, A.C.L.E.C. has not been convinced that rights of audience in the higher courts should be granted to employed solicitors or barristers, which particularly affects personnel employed by the Crown Prosecution Service.[96] The independent Bar will be keen to pursue this limitation, but the reasons given for denying the right of audience are unimpressive. There does not appear to be much likelihood of compromise of professional standards or of the inability to exercise independent professional judgment—indeed being employed may make the lawyer freer to exercise that judgment, since the financial consequences for future work may be less rather than greater.[97] It is anticipated that some steps towards extending rights of audience, in limited circumstances, for employed barristers are likely to be taken at least before the end of the century.

(3) *Probate*. Section 54 of the 1990 Act when brought into force will extend the right to perform probate work for reward to banks, building societies, insurance companies and their subsidiaries, provided that they operate a complaints scheme which complies with requirements prescribed by regulations, and to other bodies approved under section 55 and Schedule 9.[98] Possible candidates for inclusion include legal executives, licensed conveyancers,[99] authorised conveyancing practitioners and accountants. The profession is well aware of the potential consequences for business.[1]

(vii) Restrictions on practice

(1) *Multi-disciplinary practices*. A solicitor may employ, but may not form a partnership with, a member of another profession.[2] The Royal Commission was not in favour of any change. Some professions (*e.g.* doctors, engineers, architects, patent agents and actuaries) are used as expert witnesses, and it was thought inappropriate for lawyers preparing a case for trial to be in partnership with them. As regards other professions (*e.g.* estate agents), there was perceived a danger that solicitors would be absorbed into large firms, to the detriment of general practice in small towns and rural areas. It was thought that clients' interests were best served by freedom of choice, and that multi-disciplinary partnerships would inhibit it. However, the Royal Commission did accept the

---

[93] See below, pp. 149–151.
[94] For a note of the differences, discussion of them and recommendations for change to the Code of Conduct, see Bar Standards Review Body, *Blueprint for Change* (1994), paras.39–69.
[95] See, *e.g.* Bar Standards Review Body, *Blueprint for the Bar* (1994), para. 133.
[96] A.C.L.E.C.'s failure to recommend has annoyed many organisations, not least the Law Society, many employed barristers and the government itself (the Government Legal Service is affected by the restriction): see Rozenberg, *op. cit.* n. 88 above, pp. 153–160.
[97] See Rozenberg *op. cit.*, pp. 154–155.
[98] See, the *Green Paper: The Work and Organisation of the Legal Profession* (Cm. 570), Chap. 14, and the *White Paper* (Cm. 740), Chap. 6.
[99] 1990 Act, s.53.
[1] See *Law Society Annual Statistical Report 1994*, p. 45.
[2] Solicitors' Practice Rules 1990, r.7(6). Solicitors may form partnerships with a solicitor, a registered foreign lawyer or a recognised body (that is an incorporated practice).

argument that firms should be able to incorporate. Provision was made by section 9 of the Administration of Justice Act, which has recently been brought into force.[3] Further, solicitors may now share fees with non-solicitor employees, provided such an arrangement is not used to get around the restriction on forming partnerships with other professionals.[4] Also, a solicitor who instructs an estate agent as a sub-agent for the sale of a property my remunerate the estate agent on the basis of a proportion of the solicitor's professional fee.[5]

The debate about multi-disciplinary practices continued after the Royal Commission's Report, with pressure for change coming from the then Director General of Fair Trading, Sir Gordon Borrie, arguing for mixed practices with suitable safeguards[6] and the National Consumer Council arguing for consequential consumer benefits such as of one-stop house transfers, and reduction in duplication, delay and extra costs in fields such as tax planning.[7]

The Law Society has been more cautious. It issued a consultation paper in 1987 setting out both sides of the debate.[8] It emphasised the need to preserve "the solicitor's traditional role as an independent and impartial adviser of integrity enjoying a unique position as an officer of the court who is readily available to the public." Independence would be weakened if a solicitor were employed by a non-solicitor, or the practice was owned wholly or partly by a non-solicitor. Mixed practices might lead to confusion as members of the same firm would be subject to different sets of professional practice rules. The development of large practices might be at the expense of smaller ones and so reduce the number of solicitors' firms available to the public. On the other hand, mixed practices could enable solicitors to respond to a more competitive environment, by offering a broader range of services; overheads could be shared; it would be easier to run intensive training programmes; and there could be economies of scale. Since then the Law Society has been engaged in discussions with other professions. The Marre Committee took the view that any action should await the outcome of these discussions.[9]

The Green Paper[10] proposed, in line with Sir Gordon Borrie's recommendation in 1986, that the statutory inhibitions on multi-disciplinary practices should be removed. In response, the Law Society's attitude hardened.[11] It argued that to allow such practices would undermine the network of solicitors' firms, threaten client confidentiality, create potential conflicts of interest, make it more difficult to pursue a complaint and handicap British firms in Europe. As these problems could not satisfactorily be overcome, the statutory prohibition should be maintained. Its view, however, did not prevail.

Section 66 of the Courts and Legal Services Act 1990 repeals section 39 of the Solicitors Act 1974, while providing that this is not to prevent the Law Society from making rules restricting multi-disciplinary partnerships. The matter

---

[3] See above, p. 123.

[4] Solicitor's Practice Rules 1990, r.7(1)(c).

[5] Solicitor's Practice Rules 1990, r.7(2).

[6] *Restrictions on the kind of organisation through which members of professions may offer their services: A Report by the Director General of Fair Trading*, see (1986) 136 N.L.J. 833.

[7] *Ordinary Justice* (HMSO, 1989), pp. 237–245.

[8] *Multi-disciplinary partnerships and allied topics* (April 1987). For responses, see (1987) 84 L. S. Gaz., 2495, J. Harris, (1987) 131 S. J. 644.

[9] *A Time for Change* (1988), pp. 173–177.

[10] *The Work and Organisation of the Legal Profession* (Cm. 570), pp. 43–47.

[11] *Striking the Balance: The Final Response of the Council of the Law Society on the Green Papers* (1989), pp. 23–28.

will thus be left to professional rules. The *White Paper*[12] states that it is the Government's intention that rules of practice approved by, among others, the Lord Chancellor under the procedure described above,[13] should be excluded from prohibition under the proposed new legislation on restrictive trade practices.[14]

One point stressed by the Law Society, the Marre Committee and the National Consumer Council is that if a practice is called "solicitors" it should have a majority of solicitor partners, should be controlled by solicitors and should be regulated by solicitors' rules as to accounts, insurance and compensation arrangements.[15]

(2) *Multi-national practices.* Prohibitions used to apply to multi-national practices, that is solicitors engaged in practices with one or more registered foreign lawyer.[16] The pressure for change came from the development of commercial operations internationally[17] and in particular the development of the Single Market in Europe and steps towards the mutual recognition of professional qualifications.[18] Section 66 of the Courts and Legal Services Act 1990 repealed the restrictions imposed by the Solicitors Act 1974, s.39. The Law Society Rules follow s.66 and make clear that solicitors may practise in England and Wales in partnership and in incorporated practices with registered foreign lawyers.[19] Multi-national practices are subject to broadly the same regulation as solicitors' practices.[20] It is likely that there will be significant development of such practices, as the globalisation of work and therefore of firms develops and becomes increasingly financially attractive.[21] At July 31, 1995 there were 50 multi-national practices with their head officies in England and Wales.[22] As Lee points out, it is the non-European Union jurisdictions for which multi-national practices are attractive. But firms will set in the balance their likely loss of referral work from other sources.[23] The Single European Market has encouraged greater Europeanisation of law firms, in which case multi-national practices are one option, the other being overseas offices (in which lawyers from the host country may

---

[12] Cm. 740, para. 12.3.

[13] At pp. 135–137.

[14] See the White Paper, *Opening Markets—New Policy on Restrictive Trade Practices* (Cm. 727, 1989).

[15] *Striking the Balance*, p. 27; *A Time for Change*, p. 176; *Ordinary Justice*, p. 243.

[16] As defined in the Courts and Legal Services Act 1990, s.89(9).

[17] Many firms had opened offices elsewhere than in England and Wales, notably many of the large City of London firms. Foreign firms were also opening offices in England, especially to take advantage of the jurisdiction of the commercial courts; see J. Carr and R. Morrissey, (1988) I.F.L.Rev 5.

[18] See H. Adamson, *Free Movement of Lawyers* (1992), Chaps.3 and 8 and below, pp. 000–000.

[19] *The Guide to the Professional Conduct of Solicitors* (6th ed., 1993), Principle 8.01. Registered foreign lawyers are registered by the Law Society under s.89 of the Courts and Legal Services Act 1990. To be registered the foreign lawyer must be a member of a legal profession which is so regulated as to make it appropriate for solicitors to enter into multi-national partnerships with members of it; the foreign rules must not prohibit partnerships with solicitors; the applicant must be in good standing with his or her home body; and there must be no other circumstances making it undesirable to register the applicant: *The Guide*, p. 155.

[20] *The Guide*, Principle 8.02. For a summary of the differences: *ibid.*, p. 156.

[21] An indication of the extent of globalisation may be gleaned from "The Top 100" in *The Lawyer* (1995), April 25.

[22] *Law Society Annual Statistical Report 1995*, Table 3.3.

[23] R. G. Lee, "From Profession to Business: The Rise and Rise of the City Law Firm" (1992) 19 J.L.S. 31, at p. 41.

offer legal services and U.K. lawyers may offer U.K. law services),[24] networks and international legal associations, in particular the European Economic Interest Grouping.[25]

(3) *Other developments*. In the course of the on-going debate as to appropriate structures for solicitors' practices, the Law Society has relaxed some of its other rules. Thus the rules about introductions and referrals have been relaxed[26] and non-legal services may be "hived off" to a separate business.[27] On the other hand, new controls on persons (including solicitors) carrying on investment business were introduced by the Financial Services Act 1986. The concept of "investment business" is wide, and includes dealing in investments, arranging deals in investments, (*e.g.* arranging for a client to take out a life policy in connection with house purchase), managing investments, (*e.g.* as a trustee), and giving investment advice. The Law Society has obtained the status of a Recognised Professional Body under the Act, and so may authorise solicitors' firms to conduct investment business. The conduct of such business is regulated by the Solicitors' Investment Business Rules 1990.[28]

(4) *Advertising*. Advertising by solicitors used to be prohibited.[29] "Touting" was regarded as unprofessional and associated with "trade".[30] Collective advertising by the profession and detailed referral lists were officially acceptable—indeed, the Law Society was responsible for a number of national advertising campaigns.[31] These proved controversial.[32] The introduction of individual advertising, with appropriate restrictions, to provide information to the public but not to drum up business, was recommended by both the Monopolies Commission[33] and the Royal Commission.[34]

The relaxation of the restrictions on advertising was regarded by the Royal Commission not simply as helping to improve access to legal services, but also as a "necessary concomitant" to the retention of the conveyancing monopoly, so allowing the customer to "shop around".[35] The Law Society was spurred

---

[24] As to the rules of recognition of qualifications within Europe, see below pp. 189–190. For a list of overseas offices and connections of the 1,000 largest U.K. firms, see *Chambers and Partners Directory of the Legal Profession 1994–95*, pp. 9–16.

[25] Adamson (1992) and C. Whelan and D. McBarnet, "Lawyers in the Market: Delivering Legal Services in Europe" (1992) 19 J.L.S. 49, at pp. 52–55. For a list of such organisations, see *Chambers and Partners' Directory of the Legal Profession 1994–95*, pp. 17–21.

[26] See below, p. 143.

[27] 1990 Rules, Rule 5; first modified in the 1988 Rules: (1988) 85 L.S.Gaz., February 3, p. 14.

[28] *The Guide to the Professional Conduct of Solicitors* (6th ed., 1993), Chap. 26.

[29] Solicitors' Practice Rules, 1936–72, r.1; see P. Fennell, in P. A. Thomas (ed.) *Law in the Balance* (1982), Chap. 6.

[30] "[P]rofessional ideology is not exclusively anti-entrepreneurial, but . . . incorporates elements of the value systems of both the 'pre-industrial gentleman' and the tradesman:" Fennell (1982), p. 144.

[31] *e.g.*, the "Mr Whatsisname" campaign in 1977, and ones in 1979 and 1980, the latter campaign having the theme "consult a solicitor before problems get out of hand": see R. Neill, (1977) 74 L.S.Gaz. 883; G. Sanctuary, (1978) 75 L.S.Gaz. 267; Anon., (1980) 77 L.S.Gaz. 501.

[32] D. Podmore, (1980) 7 B.J.L.S. 1, 8.

[33] *Report on the supply of services of Solicitors in England and Wales in relation to restrictions on advertising*, 1976 (1976–76, H.C. 557).

[34] Vol. 1, pp. 367–373. There has been a Code of Conduct for Lawyers in the European Community which deals with personal publicity for some time (see *The Guide to the Professional Conduct of Solicitors*, (6th ed., 1993), Annex 10B).

[35] Sir Henry Benson, (1979) 76 L.S.Gaz. 1029, 1030.

into action by the threatened loss of the conveyancing monopoly. It produced a new national Solicitor's Directory, including information as to the categories of work undertaken and 28 regional directories. It also agreed that individual advertising on radio (but not television) and in the national and local press should be permitted, subject to recommended restrictions, and that charges might be advertised.[36] The new rules narrowly survived a ballot of the profession in 1985,[37] but there was a further relaxation in 1987,[38] prompted in part by the establishment of licensed conveyancers and the (albeit limited) proposals in the Building Societies Act 1986 to allow building societies to undertake conveyancing.

The old restrictions on advertising have been replaced. The basic principle governing a solicitor's practice is "that a solicitor should be able to give impartial and frank advice to the client, free from any external or adverse pressures or interests which would destroy or weaken the solicitor's professional independence or the fiduciary relationship with the client".[39] Rule 1 of the Solicitor's Practice Rules states that a solicitor must not do anything in the course of practice or permit another to do anything on his or her behalf to compromise or impair:

"(a) the solicitor's independence or integrity;
  (b) a person's freedom to instruct a solicitor of his or her choice;
  (c) the solicitor's duty to act in the best interests of the client;
  (d) the good repute of the solicitor or of the solicitor's profession;
  (e) the solicitor's proper standard of work;
  (f) the solicitor's duty to the Court."

Rule 2 states that solicitors "may at their discretion publicise their practices, or permit other persons to do so, or publicise the business or activities of other persons, provided there is no breach of [the Practice Rules] and provided there is compliance with a Solicitors' Publicity Code. . . ." Rule 3 states that solicitors may accept introductions and referrals of business from other persons and may make introductions and refer business to other persons, provided there is no breach of the Practice Rules, and there is compliance with the Solicitors' Introduction and Referral Code. These two Codes are promulgated by the Council of the Law Society with the concurrence of the Master of the Rolls.

The Solicitors' Publicity Code 1990 permits advertising provided that it complies with the Practice Rules, cannot reasonably be regarded as being in bad taste, is not misleading or inaccurate, and complies with any statutory requirements (e.g., in regulations under the Consumer Credit Act 1974) and the British Code of Advertising Practice or I.B.A. Code of Advertising Standards and Practice. The publicity may be in any medium (including television), may name clients (with their consent), may include a claim to be a specialist or an expert in a particular field, and may include statements as to charges. It may not refer to a solicitor's success rate, make direct comparison or criticism in relation to the charges or quality of service of any other identifiable solicitor, or refer to

---

[36] (1983) 80 L.S.Gaz. 1797, 3222 and 3223; (1984) 81 L.S.Gaz. 1802–1803, 2583; (1985) 82 L.S.Gaz. 3057.
[37] (1985) 82 L.S.Gaz. 2137.
[38] (1987) 84 L.S.Gaz. 155, 234.
[39] *The Guide to the Professional Conduct of Solicitors*, (6th ed., 1993), Principle 11.01.

a solicitor's judicial appointment. Unsolicited mailshots are permitted, but unsolicited telephone calls or visits are not, except for calls or visits to another professional or to publicise a specific commercial property the solicitor has to sell or let, and calls to current or former clients.[40]

A survey of 796 firms in 1986–87 showed that 45.5 per cent had advertised in the media or in Yellow Pages in the previous six months. This figure concealed wide geographical variations, and a high level of "one-off" as opposed to repeat advertising. A wide variety of methods was employed.[41] Particular examples of advertising methods include local radio, the sponsorship of a football team, advertising on buses and the use of advertising hoardings.[42] A survey of advertisements in the local press and Yellow Pages led the National Consumer Council to conclude that solicitors advertising was a small step in the right direction, telling consumers the type of work a firm is willing to handle and helping to make conveyancing more price competitive. However, it rarely drew attention to legal remedies which people did not know about.[43] It has been suggested that firms are in fact wasting money on poor marketing.[44] It is noticeable that many firms' advertising now does endeavor to tell the client what legal remedies may be available, in particular with regard to personal injuries.

Some concerns about advertising have been raised by the National Association of Citizens Advice Bureaux.[45] For example, it has received a significant number of reports from CABx about solicitors who advertise services, in particular benefit advice, and then provide inadequate or wrong advice.[46]

Rule 3 permits arrangements for the introduction of business, provided there is compliance with the Solicitor's Introduction and Referrals Code 1990. The basic principles are that solicitors must retain their professional independence and their ability to advise their clients fearlessly and objectively. The requirements of an introducer should never undermine this independence.[47] Solicitors may not enter into arrangements with claims assessors for the introduction of personal injury clients,[48] and there are particular limits in the field of investment business.[49] Otherwise, solicitors may make arrangements with introducers, subject to restrictions designed to preserve a solicitor's independence, which include: solicitors should not become so reliant upon a limited number of sources of referrals that the interests of the introducers affect the advice given by the solicitor to clients; each firm should conduct six-monthly reviews; solicitors should not pay introducers commission; and where more than 20 per cent of the firm's income arises from a single source of introduction, the firm should consider whether steps should be take to reduce the proportion.

---

[40] Solicitor's Publicity Code 1990 in *The Guide*, Annex 11A.
[41] L. Farmer *et al*. "Advertising by Solicitors" (1988) 85 L. S. Gaz., October 20, p. 25. See also a survey of 350 firms in 1987: (1987) 131 S. J. 760. In 1989–90, over 1200 firms advertised in Yellow Pages through programmes organised by the Law Society: (1990) 87 L. S. Gaz., May 23, p. 13.
[42] M. Zander, *A Matter of Justice* (revised ed., 1989), pp. 12–14.
[43] N. C. C., *Ordinary Justice* (HMSO, 1989), pp. 138–141.
[44] Study by N. Morgan of 74 firms: (1989) 86 L. S. Gaz., April 26, p. 5. He found that marketing activity tended to be restricted to the responsible person or department operating within a narrow brief; market research was used infrequently; and there was little feedback from customers.
[45] N.A.C.A.B., *Barriers to Justice* (1995), paras. 3.49–3.56.
[46] *Ibid.*, para. 3.50.
[47] Solicitors' Introduction and Referral Code 1990, s.1(1).
[48] Solicitors Practice Rules 1990, r.9.
[49] Solicitor's Practice Rules, r.12.

(e) Barristers and their work

(i) Numbers

At October 1, 1995, there were 8,498 barristers (including 891 Q.C.s) in independent practice in 392 sets of chambers. Some 5,621 were in 225 sets in London, and the rest were in 167 sets in the provinces.[50] In general, the size of the Bar has continuously increased since the early 1960s, although the rate of increase has varied. The Bar doubled in size between 1963 and 1979, and increased by almost a half between 1979 and 1989.[51] It has since grown from 6,645 in 1990 to the current position, an increase of nearly 28 per cent. The proportion of the profession of 10 years' call and under has shown a marked increase: in 1966 there were 769 (34 per cent of the practising Bar), and in 1983, 2,367 (47 per cent).[52] The average size of sets of chambers has increased.[53]

(ii) Work

There is an increasing tendency for barristers to specialise, but many still have a general common law practice (contract, crime, tort (especially personal injury cases), landlord and tenant, family matters). If specialising, a barrister may do so in one of the common law areas, in Chancery work (trusts, land law, conveyancing, wills, company law, revenue matters) or in one of the other specialist areas, some of which are specialisms of more general practice. *Chambers & Partners' Directory of the Legal Profession 1994–95*, in addition to those specialisms already mentioned, lists the following: arbitration, aviation, banking, civil liberties, commercial law, company, computer law, construction law, consumer law, defamation, ecclesiastical, employment, environmental, European Community, family law, financial services, immigration, insolvency, insurance and reinsurance, intellectual property, licensing, media and entertainment, medical negligence, parliamentary, partnership, pensions, personal injury, planning and local government, professional negligence, public administration, revenue law, shipping, and sports law.[54] In London, common law chambers are concentrated in the Temple; Chancery barristers are concentrated in Lincoln's Inn. There is no rule requiring chambers to be in one of the inns of court. Concentration there has been preferred because the inns until recently have charged

---

[50] The General Council of the Bar, *Annual Report 1995*, p. 23. The site of chambers does not necessarily limit where the work is done. Barristers may work in London or one of the Circuits (Northern, North Eastern, Midland and Oxford, Western, South Eastern, and Wales and Chester), or interchangeably between them. Each Circuit has a Leader and Committee.

[51] R.C.L.S., Vol. 2, p. 54; *Annual Report of the Bar Council 1990*, pp. 20–21. See R. L. Abel, *The Legal Profession in England and Wales* (1988), pp. 65–72.

[52] *Annual Statement, 1983–84*, p. 19. In 1988, about half of barristers in independent practice were 12 years or less since call: *Quality of Justice* (1989), p. 53.

[53] Abel (1988), pp. 360–361, Table 1.27.

[54] At p. 1041.

barristers only a proportion of the market rent, for the convenience of access to the courts and because of long tradition.[55]

A "rough guide" to the specialist work done by barristers was given in the Bar's Response to the Green Papers.[56]

Analysis of Barristers' Practices

	0% — 10%	10% — 20%	20% — 30%	30% — 40%	40% — 50%	50% — 60%	60% — 70%	70% — 80%	80% — 90%	90% — 100%	Total
Admiralty	71	3	1	18	6	2	15	0	0	0	116
Commercial	544	204	124	72	89	38	45	45	42	62	1265
Criminal	512	275	268	324	344	268	310	408	431	1026	4166
Defamation	144	15	3	5	4	2	3	5	4	9	194
Employment	880	121	30	16	13	8	4	2	3	2	1079
European	73	9	6	5	2	1	0	3	6	10	115
Family	1131	524	367	212	152	79	58	66	47	65	2701
Immigration	188	24	15	5	5	3	1	7	2	2	252
Insolvency	429	63	22	10	11	4	1	2	2	2	546
International	85	19	13	8	8	2	0	0	1	12	148
Official Referees	541	97	50	31	42	16	10	9	1	2	799
Parliamentary	274	53	19	21	12	12	10	14	17	59	491
Patents	192	15	11	3	3	2	3	6	10	31	276
Restrictive Practices and Monopolies	28	4	7	3	1	3	0	1	1	0	48
Revenue	127	21	13	5	10	1	4	4	7	45	237
Chancery	649	136	73	48	43	43	36	67	57	86	1238
Common Law	1349	810	554	435	288	138	122	102	75	84	3957
Other	258	54	40	26	29	12	13	10	13	109	564

The percentages of gross earnings by area of law for barristers were crime 30 per cent, general civil (common law) 17 per cent, commercial general 13 per cent, family 7 per cent, Chancery 8 per cent, commercial specialist 9 per cent, tax 3 per cent, and 12 per cent, other specialisations.[57]

[55] R.C.L.S., Vol. 1, pp. 449–450. There is a set in Wellington St., Covent Garden, and other sets have opened outside the Inns.
[56] *Quality of Justice: The Bar's Response* (1989), pp. 43 and 44, Fig. 5.2.
[57] *ibid.* p. 45, Fig. 5.3.

In the 1970s there were concerns that the recommendations of the Royal Commissions on Civil Liability and Compensation and on Legal Services might prove a threat to the work of barristers. In the event even the modest, piecemeal, proposals of the former were not implemented, apart from some changes to the law of damages.[58] As we have seen, the Bar's rights of audience were upheld by the latter,[59] and members of the Crown Prosecution Service established by the Prosecution of Offences Act 1985 were not given rights of audience in the Crown Court and above.[60] It seemed that prospects were not as bleak as had been feared. However, the Royal Commission on Legal Services confirmed that barristers were increasingly dependent on public funds,[61] and, since then, the low rates of increase in fees for legal aid work has caused increasing dissatisfaction.[62] The renewed challenge of the Law Society on rights of audience and then the government's proposals for radical reform once again put the Bar on the defensive.[63] As we have seen, its case for preserving its monopoly of rights of audience in the higher courts has not prevailed.

As to remuneration, the Royal Commission concluded that the earnings of barristers were not out of line with those in comparable occupations, except that the earnings of barristers in the early years of practice were low.[64] A report by Coopers & Lybrand in 1985 of the remuneration levels of junior council carrying out publicly funded criminal defence work claimed that fees fell well below what was required to meet the principle of "fair and reasonable reward for work reasonably done", and that an increase of 30–40 per cent was necessary to improve the position.[65] The Lord Chancellor rejected a claim for such an increase, casting doubt on some of the assumptions relied on in the Coopers & Lybrand report, and raised fees by 5 per cent. The Bar challenged the decision in court, proceedings being settled on the agreement of the Lord Chancellor to a

---

[58] Royal Commission on Civil Liability and Compensation (Cmnd. 7054, 1979); Administration of Justice Act 1982. The Royal Commission did not even recommend the introduction of a comprehensive state scheme for compensating accident victims.

[59] Above, pp. 133–138.

[60] Above, p. 138.

[61] In 1976–77, £23m. out of £48m. total gross fees were from public funds: R.C.L.S., Vol. 2, pp. 595–597.

[62] See *Legal Action.*

[63] Illustrated by the substantial report, *Quality of Justice*, produced quickly in response to the Green Paper in 1989.

[64] See R.C.L.S., Vol. 1, pp. 507–542 and Vol. 2, pp. 579–626 (surveys of barristers' earnings). Figures for senior barristers are given in the Reports of the Top Salaries Review Board. Income Data Services Ltd. prepared estimates of barristers' earnings as at April 1988 for the Andrew Review of Government Legal Services (HMSO, 1989), Annex to Chap. VIII (pp. 66–69). The median figure for those with between 15 and 35 years experience was £105,954 (Q.C.s) and £39,415 (juniors). The figures were substantially lower for those concentrating on criminal cases.

SENIORITY	Pupillage	1–5 years	6–10 yrs	10 yrs+	Queen's Counsel
Criminal (£,000s)	7–15	20–35	30–60	40–100	100–200+
Commercial (3,000s)	10–20	20–50	50–175	70–300	200–500+

[65] Annual Statement of the Senate 1985–86, p. 76; (1985) 82 L. S. Gaz. 2636.

binding time-table for negotiations for an increase in fees.[66] The Lord Chancellor eventually awarded an additional 3 per cent, plus another 2 per cent if the Bar would change its working practices.[67] The complaints have not gone away. The result has been an increasing polarisation of the Bar between specialists who can command enormous fees[68] and the large number of barristers who rely on public funds.

The late payment of fees by solicitors has been a serious cause for friction between the professions. In consequence, the General Council of the Bar has authorised terms of work on which barristers offer their services to solicitors and a scheme for the withdrawal of credit.[69] It anticipates that fees will be paid in accordance with the agreement between the solicitor and barrister, but the barrister would submit a fee note not later than three months after the work was done and payment is expected promptly. Where payment has not been made, the barrister may complain to the Chairman of the Bar Council who may put into motion an enforcement procedure which can result in the withdrawal of credit for the solicitor in question.

There are at least as many barristers employed in commerce, industry and central and local government as there are in private practice.[70] Their work compares much more closely with that done by employed solicitors in the same fields than with that done by barristers in private practice. Indeed, in 1976 the Chairman of the Solicitors' Commerce and Industry Group said that:

"Fusion is a word that we in commerce and industry never use in practice, because it is an accomplished fact with us. Barristers and solicitors are almost completely interchangeable. . . ."[71]

The Law Society has expressed the view that people who wish to practise as a solicitor should become a solicitor. It has also been suggested that one reason why such barristers do not change is snobbery.[72] However, the Bar Association for Commerce, Finance and Industry persuaded the Royal Commission that the rules preventing employed barristers from undertaking conveyancing and briefing other barristers in non-contentious matters should be relaxed.[73] The Bar Council acted on this recommendation,[74] much to the displeasure of the Law Society.[75]

Further substantial changes took place in 1989, 1990 and 1991. A barrister may now supply legal services as an employed barrister provided he or she is qualified to practise. He or she is not permitted to offer legal services to the

---

[66] *R. v. Lord Chancellor, ex p. Alexander, The Times*, March 21, 22, 24 and 27, 1986; *Counsel*, Easter Term 1986, pp. 24–25. For the background correspondence see the Annual Statement 1985–86, pp. 27–31, and for the proceedings of an angry extraordinary general meeting of the Bar, which authorised the proceedings, see *ibid*. pp. 32–41.

[67] (1986) 83 L.S. Gaz. 2282–7.

[68] M. Zander, *A Matter of Justice* (revised ed., 1989), pp. 34–35.

[69] *Code of Conduct*, Annex D.

[70] R. L. Abel, *The Legal Profession in England and Wales* (1988), pp. 111–113.

[71] (1976) 73 L. S. Gaz. 369.

[72] R.C.L.S., Vol. 1, p. 237; 'Enobarbus' (1980) 77 L. S. Gaz. 766.

[73] R.C.L.S., Vol. 1, pp. 237–241.

[74] Annual Statement, 1979–80, pp. 52–55.

[75] Anon., "A Road to Fusion?" (1980) 77 L.S. Gaz. 637–8. This issue had previously been a bone of contention between the two branches: Abel-Smith and Stevens (1967) pp. 439–443.

public, but may, only whilst acting in the course of employment, supply legal services to, undertake conveyancing services in compliance with the Conveyancing by Employed Barristers Rules on behalf of, appear as counsel in circumstances where immediately before December 7, 1989 barristers in independent practice did not have an exclusive right of audience[76] on behalf of, brief or instruct a barrister in independent practice in any contentious or non-contentious matter on behalf of his or her employer or another employee or an individual member of an association.[77] A barrister in the Government Legal Service may act on behalf of members of the government and of public service for whom the G.L.S. customarily acts.[78] Despite the many amendments, the position of employed barristers is still significantly different from that of barristers in independent practice. The fears of changing the position further are to do both with the public interest (particularly the desire to enable barristers to work fearlessly for the interests of their client, not constrained by other interests) and the dread of competition (if employed barristers were able to do the whole range of work, primarily offer legal services to the public, the livelihood and style of work of barristers in independent practice would be doomed).

One other development to note is that the Code of Conduct has recognised a further category of barristers, that is the "non-practising barrister" who may advise, for free, members of the public, but who is unable to appear as counsel in any court.[79]

(iii) Practice guidance

The professional conduct of barristers is regulated by the profession itself, subject to the oversight of the Legal Services Ombudsman. It is the duty of every barrister to comply with the Code of Conduct of the Bar of England and Wales. Prior to final adoption, the Lord Chancellor's Advisory Committee on Legal Education and Conduct may give the Bar Council advice in relation to all aspects of rules of conduct, and the Bar Council must have regard to that advice when it relates to rights of audience.[80] Further, the 1990 Act requires the Bar Council, when seeking to be designated as an authorised body in relation to rights of audience, to obtain the approval of A.C.L.E.C. for any alterations to rules of conduct relating to rights of audience.[81]

The general purpose of the Code is "to provide the standards of conduct on the part of barristers which are appropriate in the interests of justice" and, in particular, to require barristers in independent practice "to be completely independent on conduct and professional standing as sole practitioners", to act

---

[76] Unless exempted, an employed barrister can so act only if he or she has completed a first six-months pupillage and is completing a further pupillage, or has completed 12 months pupillage or was an employed barrister before January 1, 1989 and has been an employed barrister for a total period of not less than five years: *Code of Conduct*, para. 402.2.

[77] *Code of Conduct*, para. 402.1.

[78] *Code of Conduct*, para. 404.

[79] *Code of Conduct*, para. 212.

[80] Courts and Legal Services Act 1990, Sched. 2, para. 5(3), (4).

[81] Courts and Legal Services Act 1990, s.29(3) and Sched. 4, Part II. For the Bar's concerns about needing to seek such approval, see General Council of the Bar, *Quality of Justice: The Bar's Response* (1989), p. 194.

only as consultants properly instructed and to "acknowledge a public obligation based on the paramount need for access to justice to act for any client (whether legally aided or not) in cases within his [or her] field of practice".[82] For employed barristers the obligations are the same, taking into account their work in providing legal services only to their employers.[83]

To those ends, a barrister must comply with the Code generally, and, in particular, must satisfy the "fundamental principles." These principles are grouped according to the nature of a barrister's work. There are four groups: all barristers; all practising barristers; all barristers in independent practice; and all non-practising barristers.

All barristers must not engage in conduct which is "dishonest or otherwise discreditable to a barrister" or "prejudicial to the administration of justice" or "likely to diminish public confidence in the legal profession of the administration of justice or otherwise bring the legal profession into disrepute".[84]

All practising barristers have "an overriding duty to the Court to ensure in the public interest that the proper and efficient administration of justice is achieved; [they] must assist the Court in the administration of justice and must not deceive or knowingly or recklessly mislead the Court"; they must "promote and protect fearlessly and by all proper and lawful means [a] client's best interests . . . without regard to [their] own interests or to any consequences to [themselves] or to any other person"; they owe their "primary duty[85] . . . to [their] lay client and must not permit the Legal Aid Fund or [their] professional client to limit [their] discretion as to how the interests of [their] lay client can best be served"; they must act towards both lay and professional clients in good faith; must not discriminate on grounds of race, ethnic origin, sex, sexual orientation, marital status, disability, religion or political persuasion; must "not permit [their] absolute independence and integrity and freedom from external pressures to be compromised" nor compromise their professional standards; are individually and personally responsible for their own conduct and professional work; and they must exercise their professional judgment in all professional activities.[86]

Barristers in independent practice must make practice in England and Wales or in the Courts of the European Community their primary occupation and be willing to render legal services for the public, generally for a fee.[87] Barristers may, in general, only be briefed by a professional client.[88] Most significantly, they must comply with the "cab-rank rule":

"A barrister in independent practice must comply with the 'Cab-rank rule' and accordingly except only as otherwise provided in paragraphs 501 502 and 503 he [or she] must in any field in which he [or she] professes to practise in relation to work appropriate to his [or her] experience and

---

[82] *Code of Conduct*, para. 102.

[83] *ibid.*, para. 102(b).

[84] *ibid.*, para. 201(a). In addition, a barrister must not engage directly or indirectly in any occupation which may adversely affect the Bar's reputation or prejudice the barrister's ability to attend properly to the client's interests: *ibid.*, para. 201(b).

[85] Subject only to compliance to specific provisions of legal aid regulations.

[86] *ibid.*, paras.202–206.

[87] *ibid.*, 208.

[88] See below.

seniority and irrespective of whether his [or her] client is paying privately
or is legally aided or is otherwise publicly funded:

(a) accept any brief to appear before a court in which he [or she] professes
    to practise;
(b) accept any instructions;
(c) act for any person on whose behalf he [or she] is briefed or instructed;

and do so irrespective of (i) the party on whose behalf he [or she] is briefed
or instructed (ii) the nature of the case and (iii) any belief or opinion which
he [or she] may have formed as to the character reputation conduct guilt
or innocence of that person.''[89]

The exceptions to its operation are designed to ensure that a barrister will not
accept any brief or instructions which would cause him or her to be ''professionally embarrassed'', which might arise as a result, *e.g.*, of lack of sufficient
experience or competence, or lack of sufficient time to prepare because of other
professional commitments; or if it is a matter in which he or she will find it
difficult to maintain professional independence or where there is a conflict of
interest; or where there is a risk of breaches of the confidence of another client
or that the new client would have an undue advantage because of the work done
for another client.[90] A barrister in independent practice is not obliged to accept
a brief or instructions, *e.g.*, requiring him or her to work outside their ordinary
working year, other than at a proper fee having regard to the case's complexity,
length and difficulty and to the barrister's ability, experience and seniority, or
where expenses are likely to be unreasonably high in relation to the fee.[91] A
Queen's Counsel is not obliged to accept a brief or instructions to settle alone
any document of a kind generally settled only by or with a junior, or to act
without a junior where he or she considers that a junior should also be
instructed.[92] Further, the Code of Conduct has, since 1991, required a practising
barrister, in the case of each brief, to consider whether ''consistently with the
proper and efficient administration of justice and having regard to'' the case,
his or her practice, ability, experience and relationship with the client ''the best
interests of the client would be served by'' using him or her[93] and advise the
client if not.[94]
   It has been said that the rule ''secures for the public a right of representation
in the court which is a pillar of British liberty''.[95] In the debates on the Courts
and Legal Services Act, Lord Mackay, the Lord Chancellor, stated that it supported a principle of non-discrimination so that an advocate does not decline
any case on the basis that it is ''objectionable or that the conduct, opinions or
beliefs of the prospective client are unacceptable to him or any section of the
public. Equally [he or she] must not decline to act on any grounds relating to

[89] *ibid.*, para. 209.
[90] *ibid.*, para. 501, which also lists other circumstances.
[91] *ibid.*, para. 502, which also lists other circumstances.
[92] *ibid.*, para. 503.
[93] *ibid.*, para. 503A.1
[94] *ibid.*, para. 503A.3. For related guidance where there is more than one advocate, see *ibid.*, para.
503A.2.
[95] R.C.L.S., Vol. 1, p. 31, based on the submission of the Senate of the Inns of Court.

the source of any financial support".[96] Further, it requires a barrister to regard a legal aid fee as an adequate fee. The Bar Standards Review Body took the view that "the present rule in the Code of Conduct is widely flouted and not enforced by the Bar Council".[97] To counter this perception, the Body recommended that the rule be modified to comply with section 17 of the Courts and Legal Services Act 1990, which sets the statutory objective in the delivery of legal services and specifically states that rules of conduct should require members not to withhold advocacy services "(i) on the ground that the nature of the case is objectionable to him or to any section of the public; (ii) on the ground that the conduct, opinions or beliefs of the prospective client are unacceptable to him or to any section of the public; (iii) on any ground relating to the source of any financial support which may properly be given to the prospective client for the proceedings in question ...".[98] Further the Body recommended the removal of the fiction that a legal aid fee is adequate in all cases. The Body anticipated that legally aided clients would still receive advocacy services of sufficient quality from barristers. Once the new rule is adopted, the Body recommended that the Bar Council strenuously enforce it.[99]

Non-practising barristers must not appear as counsel in a court or, without indicating that they are not practising, supply legal services to any person.[1]

A wide range of other matters is dealt with in the detailed provisions of the Code, including the administration of a barrister's practice,[2] advertising and publicity,[3] duties to client and court,[4] and the obligations of employed barristers in so far as they are different from those of a barrister in independent practice.[5]

(iv) Restrictions on practice

(1) *Instructions and direct professional access.* One of the main restrictions has long been the general rule that barristers may only take instructions from a solicitor. There were several long established exceptions, covering such matters as foreign work, the examination of material to be published to check for libel and contempt, and briefing by a patent agent or parliamentary agent. There are special rules covering barristers employed in law centres.[6] The old rule was only settled as regards contentious work in 1888 and non-contentious work in 1955. Significant exceptions were made to enable barristers to compete more effectively for foreign work. The Overseas Practice Rules were introduced in 1973[7] and relaxed many of the basic rules of conduct for barristers: apart from being able to receive instructions direct, barristers may negotiate fees direct,

---

[96] Quoted in Bar Standards Review Body, *Blueprint for the Bar* (1994), para. 40.
[97] Bar Standards Review Body, *Blueprint for the Bar* (1994), para. 44.
[98] Courts and Legal Services Act 1990, s.17(3)(c).
[99] Bar Standards Review Body, *Blueprint for the Bar* (1994), para. 54.
[1] *Code of Conduct*, para. 212.
[2] See below, pp. 153–155.
[3] See below, pp. 152–153.
[4] For an argument that the advocate's duty to justice ought to be enshrined in law and not just rules of professional conduct, see D. L. Carey Miller, (1981) 97 L.Q.R. 127. For the rules, see above, p. 149 and below, pp. 166–170.
[5] See above, p. 149.
[6] See below, pp. 483–488.
[7] Annual Statement of the Bar Council, 1973–74, pp. 33–34. They were subsequently relaxed even further: see *Code of Conduct*, para. 306 and Annex F (Overseas Practice Rules).

accept an annual retainer, a fixed fee or a contingent fee, and enter into partnership with any lawyer other than a solicitor for the purpose of sharing an office or services abroad.

From time to time there were rumblings from the Bar that their "self-denying ordinance" might be withdrawn,[8] but the Senate suggested to the Royal Commission that barristers were not equipped to deal with the office work necessary if they were to deal directly with clients. Having decided that fusion would not be in the public interest,[9] it was inevitable that the Royal Commission would not favour the wholesale removal of restrictions on direct access.

The governing provision in the Code of Conduct now requires that barristers in independent practice provide legal services only if instructed by a "professional client".[10] A solicitor is a professional client, but so also is, *e.g.*, a patent agent, a trade mark agent, a licensed conveyancer (in relation to conveyancing services), the Government Legal Service, the legal department of a local or public authority (if headed by a barrister or solicitor), an employed barrister, a law centre or legal advice centre barrister, an arbitrator (in relation to arbitration law, practice or procedure) and an Ombudsman (if his or her office has been recognised by the Bar Council for the provision of advice on law, practice and procedure falling within its jurisdiction which extends to seven Ombudsmen).[11,12] Since 1989, the list has been further extended by granting access by "members of a recognised professional body in a matter which falls generally within the professional expertise of the members of the recognised professional body and in circumstances complying with the Direct Professional Access Rules".[13] Twenty-five professional bodies, including those of the various accountants and engineers, have been so recognised.[14] The Direct Professional Access Rules[15] require the barrister not to accept the instruction if he or she considers that it is in the lay client's interests that a solicitor be instructed, must not accept a brief to appear in the higher courts, county court or the Employment Appeals Tribunal, and must keep a detailed case record, retain copies of all documents and notes and keep a forward diary of all statutory or other time limits which are applicable to Direct Professional Access matters.

The Bar continues to oppose direct lay access on arguments similar to those put to the Royal Commission.[16] Both the Green Paper and the White Paper stated that questions of access should be left to the profession.[17] In the context of these various changes widening direct access to the Bar, it was inevitable that the Bar's rules restricting advertising would be relaxed.

(2) *Advertising and publicity.* The old and traditional restrictions on advertising

---

[8] R. Hazell, *The Bar on Trial* (1978) pp. 172–173.

[9] See above, p. 70.

[10] *Code of Conduct*, para. 210.

[11] *i.e.*, the offices recognised are those of: Parliamentary Ombudsman, Health Service Ombudsman, the Local Government Ombudsmen for England and Wales, and the Insurance, Banking, and Building Society Ombudsmen: *Chambers & Partners' Directory of the Legal Profession 1994–95* (1995), at p. 1043.

[12] *ibid.*, para. 901.

[13] *ibid.*, para. 901. See A. Thornton, "Direct Professional Access" *Counsel*, March/April 1989, pp. 17–19.

[14] *Chambers & Partners' Directory of the Legal Profession 1994–1995* (1995), at p. 1043.

[15] *Code of Conduct* at Annex E.

[16] *Quality of Justice*, pp. 140–142.

[17] Cm. 570, Chap. 8; Cm. 740, p. 38.

have been replaced by a general rule by which a barrister in independent practice may engage in any advertising or promotion in connection with his or her practice provided it conforms to the British Code of Advertising Practice. It may include photographs and illustrations of the barrister, the name of any client (with their consent) and statements about rates, methods of charging, and the nature and extent of his or her services.[18] The "advertising or promotion must not: (a) be inaccurate or likely to mislead; (b) be likely to diminish public confidence in the legal profession or the administration of justice or otherwise bring the legal profession into disrepute; (c) make comparisons with or criticisms of other barristers or other members of any other profession; (d) include statements about the quality of the barrister's work, the size or success of his [or her] practice or his [or her] success rate; (e) indicate or imply any willingness to accept . . . or restrict [briefs accepted] otherwise than in accordance with [the] Code; (f) be so frequent or obtrusive as to cause annoyance to those to whom it is directed".[19] Whilst such restrictions will no doubt maintain the reputation of the profession, such advertising is unlikely to be of much assistance to lay clients not already in the know about the comparative qualities of barristers.

(3) *Partnerships and Chambers.* A practising barrister may not enter a partnership with another practising barrister.[20] The Bar "is an intensely *individual* profession".[21] The Royal Commission recognised that partnerships might often be advantageous for barristers. An income could more easily be provided for a beginner, work could be distributed more evenly and provision for sickness and retirement would be easier. They concluded, however, that a change would not be in the public interest as it would restrict choice, on the assumption that partners would not be permitted to appear on opposite sides. Problems might be acute at the specialist and provincial bars.[22]

At one time the individualism of a barrister's practice was offset by the requirement that he or she join a set of approved chambers. Most barristers operate from a set of chambers involving more than one barrister,[23] in part because of the significant advantages this has to offer. Work may come into chambers either for a particular barrister, who may need to pass it on to another, or in general and so be available to whoever is free. Association of a junior barrister with a successful and excellent Q.C. or other senior barrister can have a dramatic effect upon her or his career.[24] Further, contributions can be aggregated to enable the development of pleasant and appropriate working surroundings and support. Competition and direct access increasingly demand that barristers operate from premises suitable to impress the client. A sufficient library would be a major drain on an individual's resources, as would the provision of well-qualified support staff and technology. Indeed, this was one of the

[18] *Code of Conduct*, para. 307.1.
[19] *ibid.*, para. 307.2.
[20] *ibid.*, para. 207.
[21] General Council of the Bar, *A Career at the Bar* (1988), p. 2.
[22] R.C.L.S., Vol. 1, pp. 462–465, Vol. 2, pp. 375–392. The case for allowing partnerships is argued in M. Zander, *Lawyers and the Public Interest* (1968), pp. 252–269 and Hazell (1978), pp. 123–129.
[23] In 1984 the average numbers of barristers per set in London was 16.7 and only 3 per cent. of 222 sets had four or fewer members; in the provinces the average number was 12.6 and 8 per cent. of 119 sets had four or fewer members: R. L. Abel, *The Legal Profession in England and Wales* (1988), pp. 360–363.
[24] See R.C.L.S., Vol. 1, p. 452.

advantages of chambers' practice which was identified in evidence to the Royal Commission on Legal Services.[25] A barrister may also obtain the assistance of a colleague in the preparation of paperwork and, with the consent of the instructing solicitor, at a hearing—this is known as "devilling". The evidence to the Royal Commission identified dangers in barristers practising alone, particularly in the criminal courts: pressure to ignore the rules against touting and improper association with clients and witnesses. Chambers' practice would also aid in "controlling backsliders" and maintaining standards.[26] There is now no approval system for chambers, nor must a barrister have a clerk,[27] but a barrister in independent practice must notify the Bar Council of the address and telephone number of the chambers[28] from which he or she will operate, exhibit his or her name outside chambers, and have ready access to adequate library facilities.[29] Chambers administration guidelines are produced and barristers must have regard to them.[30] Further, barristers must take all reasonable steps to ensure that the practice is "efficiently and properly administered" and that "proper records are kept".[31] There may be only the one barrister in such a set, which could be the barrister's home. Sufficient guarantees, therefore, and provided in the public interest. Further, this approach may facilitate the continuation in practice of barristers (particularly women) with young children. Where a barrister is of less than three years post-pupillage call, he or she must practice from chambers of which he or she is not the only member and of which at least one member has at least five years' practice.[32]

The Courts and Legal Services Act 1990 declares that no rule of common law prevents barristers from entering into any unincorporated association with persons who are not barristers, but that this is not to prevent the General Council of the Bar from making rules which prohibit or restrict such partnerships.[33] Such rules will be subject to review under the proposed restrictive practices legislation. The *Green Paper: The Work and Organisation of the Legal Profession*[34] stated the view that barristers should be permitted to operate in partnership if they chose to do so. The risk of diminishing clients' choice was outweighed by the advantages of greater efficiency and easing the entry of new barristers into the profession. Moreover, barristers should be permitted to enter multi-disciplinary partnerships.[35] These suggestions were strenuously resisted by the Bar: choice of advocate and access and competition would be reduced, standards would fall and costs would increase. The idea had been opposed by the Royal Commission, the Director General of Fair Trading and Lord Mackay himself

---

[25] R.C.L.S., Vol. 1, p. 455.

[26] R.C.L.S., Vol. 1, pp. 454, 455.

[27] As to the work of barrister's clerks, see below pp. 188–189.

[28] "Chambers" simply means "the principal place at or from which one or more independent barristers in practice carry on their practices": *Code of Conduct*, para. 901.

[29] *Code of Conduct*, para. 303(a). In addition to personal or chambers materials, library facilities may be available in an Inn of Court or in the Bar's central library in London. As to the equivalent system which has operated for some time in Northern Ireland, Scotland and the Republic of Ireland, see *Quality of Justice* (1989), pp. 214–215.

[30] *Code of Conduct*, para. 303(b). The Chambers Administration Guidelines appear in the *Code of Conduct*, Annex B.

[31] *Code of Conduct*, para. 303(c).

[32] *Code of Conduct*, para. 301(d).

[33] s.66(5), (6). Such rules do apply, see *Code of Conduct*, para. 207.

[34] Cm. 570, p. 40.

[35] *ibid.* pp. 46–47.

when leader of the Scottish Bar. MDPs involving barristers would be in effect
fusion with other professions, removing the benefits of independence and the
cab-rank rule.[36] The White Paper merely stated that "the regulation of how the
members of professional bodies organise themselves to meet their clients' needs
is best left to the professions themselves, subject to a proper scrutiny to avoid
unnecessary or undesirable anti-competitive effects".[37] This was reflected in the
1990 Act.

As a result of the recent growth in numbers, coupled with the lack of space,
young barristers have found it increasingly difficult to obtain a permanent place
("seat" or "tenancy") in chambers, although a number have been allowed to
remain after pupillage as "squatters" or "floaters". Insofar as the problem was
caused by shortage of work, the Royal Commission felt there were no real
remedies, although potential entrants should be informed of the difficulties.[38]
However, the Senate "should adopt a vigorous policy to secure the provision
of more accommodation".[39] The Senate's Accommodation Committee subsequently expressed the opinion that it was doing just that.[40] Since then, the
demand for space has continued.[41] In response, the Inns have adopted a policy
of charging full market rents and accommodation has been secured outside but
in the vicinity of the Inns.[42] Of greater significance is the relaxation in the rules
relating to where a barrister may work referred to above.

(4) *Queen's Counsel and junior barristers.* Another distinctive feature of practice at the bar is the division into two ranks: Queen's Counsel[43] and "junior"
barristers.[44] Appointment as a Q.C. is made by the Queen on the advice of the
Lord Chancellor, and is today a mark of eminence in the profession, rather than
a retainer for Crown work. It is for the juniors who wish to "take silk" (Q.C.s
wear silk gowns) to apply; between 20 per cent and 30 per cent of the applications are successful,[45] and re-applications are permissible.[46] The main difference as regards work done is that Q.C.s do not normally do paperwork, except
in those cases where they are briefed to appear alone: their role is that of the
skilled and experienced advocate or specialist adviser, and they are in a position
to concentrate on heavy cases. After his or her elevation a Q.C. would expect,
or at least hope, to take work that is more remunerative, and to reduce his or
her work load. The change can be something of a gamble,[47] but it may be that

---

[36] *Quality of Justice* (1989), Chap. 15.
[37] Cm. 740, p. 39.
[38] R.C.L.S., Vol. 1, pp. 459–60.
[39] *ibid.* pp. 460–462. Specific rules of conduct might also have to be waived.
[40] Annual Statement, 1979–80, p. 27.
[41] *Counsel*, Michaelmas 1985, pp. 17–18; a survey in 1986 showed that 10 per cent of London
barristers were sharing a desk and that in all there was a demand for over 400 more rooms:
Counsel, Hilary 1986, p. 38.
[42] Hirst J. (Chairman of the Accommodation Committee), *Counsel*, Summer 1986, pp. 15–16; P.
Naughton, "Moving Out" *Counsel*, Summer/September 1987, pp. 12–13; Accommodation Committee, *ibid.* p. 36.
[43] "One of Our Counsel learned in the Law." Q.C.s become K.C.s when there are Kings.
[44] R.C.L.S., Vol. 1, pp. 465–471. All barristers who are not Q.C.s are "juniors". There can be
very senior "juniors".
[45] R.C.L.S., Vol. 1, p. 479. There were 52 appointments in 1981, 56 in 1982, 40 in 1983 and 42
in 1984.
[46] There has been considerable concern about the appointments process.
[47] R. E. Megarry, *Lawyer and Litigant in England* (1962), pp. 90–92: "a great adventure with much
to gain and much to lose."

the risks are not as great as they used to be.[48] Most High Court judges are appointed from among the Q.C.s and there are many other judicial appointments available.

Formerly, there were rules of etiquette which prevented a Q.C. from appearing in court without a junior (the two-counsel rule) and which entitled the junior to a fee of two-thirds that of his or her leader. In 1966 the two-thirds rule was abolished[49]; the junior is now simply entitled to a "proper fee".[50] Ten years later the Monopolies Commission reported that the two-counsel rule was contrary to the public interest.[51] The rule was accordingly abrogated as from October 1, 1977 and the Bar Council issued revised rules.[52] A Q.C. may appear alone but must decline to do so if he or she considers that the interest of the client require that a junior should also be instructed. The change seemed to make little practical difference.[53] In 1988, provision was made enabling solicitors to instruct Q.C.s to appear alone in certain criminal cases (guilty pleas, certain appeals and simple cases "with some sensitive overlay, whether political local or other").[54] This too has been little used.[55] A majority of the Royal Commission favoured continuance of the two-tier system, with minor changes.[56] The Green Paper and White Paper proposed that the two-tier system should be retained, with eligibility extended to all who have rights of audience in the High Court or the Crown Court.[57]

3. QUALITY OF SERVICE[58]

Lawyers have always prided themselves on the quality of service which they provide. Because of increasing consumerism on the part of clients, making them more likely to question the work done for them, and increasing competition for many of the services which lawyers offer, it is becoming necessary to be able to assess it and assure others of its existence. The fact of being recognised as members of a profession would, at one time, have been a sufficient mark and

---

[48] Hazell (1978), pp. 23–34. Q.C.s reliant on public funds may be at risk when there are pressures on public expenditure.

[49] See Zander (1968), pp. 146–152.

[50] Annual Statement of the Bar Council, 1971–72, p. 20.

[51] *Barrister Services: A report on the supply by Her Majesty's Counsel alone of their services,* 1976 (1975–76 H.C. 512).

[52] Annual Statement, 1977–78, pp. 42–45; R.C.L.S., Vol. 1, pp. 480–481; *Code of Conduct,* (1990 ed.), para. 503.

[53] R.C.L.S., Vol. 1, pp. 468–470.

[54] (1988) 85 L.S. Gaz., November 2, p. 6.

[55] (1990) 87 L.S. Gaz., August 22, p. 5 (8 out of 1,700 eligible cases). The scheme also allowed for barristers to appear without a solicitor in Crown Court cases involving guilty pleas, appeals against sentence, and committals for sentence; the figures here were only slightly higher: *ibid.* See "Attendence at the Crown Court with counsel" (1989) 86 L.S. Gaz., January 25, pp. 24–25, 38.

[56] *ibid.* Four members thought that the title should be conferred as a mark of honour only: R.C.L.S., Vol. 1, pp. 823, 829. See A. Samuels, (1984) 134 N.L.J. 503.

[57] Cm. 570, Chap. 9; Cm. 740, p. 15. See *Quality of Justice* (1989), Chap. 17; the Bar suggested that there had been indications of a lack of knowledge in the L.C.D. resulting in the refusal of the title to those of distinction and the grant of the title to those not deserving it; appointment by the Judges rather than a government minister should be considered.

[58] For an approach to quality similar to the approach in the following pages, see S. Fennell, "The quality of solicitors' services" (1992) 8 P.N. 115.

guarantee of quality[59] and it is not surprising that many lawyers find it difficult to accept that anyone should question their work. However, times have changed. Also, there are many more members of the professions and so the likelihood of poor quality work becomes greater. It is important to recognise that most legal work is transacted well and efficiently[60] and that most clients are satisfied with the work of their lawyers.[61] Further, "the public continue to hold an image of solicitors that is generally good but not exceptional.[62] A recent survey showed that 66 per cent were very satisfied and 23 per cent fairly satisfied with the personal business services which they had received from a solicitor. Only 10 per cent were dissatisfied.[63] The reasons for being satisfied revealed demands which were not onerous.[64] The reasons given for dissatisfaction were delays, incompetence, high expense and having to chase the solicitor.[65] However, this perception must be tempered by a lower assessment of quality of work in criminal law[66] and a controversial report undertaken by the Consumers' Association which suggested that quality of work was very variable and that many clients were not satisfied with the work done for them.[67] This survey also revealed concerns about the cost of using a solicitor. A similar point was made by the National Association of Citizens' Advice Bureaux.[68]

As regards barristers, the Royal Commission on Legal Services reported that the general opinion among judges and practising lawyers appeared to be that standards fell in the 1960s and 1970s but were rising again.[69] In general, standards of work appear to be very high.[70] However, dissatisfaction has been expressed, as noted by the Royal Commission on Criminal Justice[71] and in the report of the Bar Standards Review Body in particular with regard to the way some barristers undertake pre-trial work and advocacy.[72]

---

[59] See above, pp. 113–115.
[60] Until recently it has not been possible to begin to measure the quality of work of a lawyer, see below. Thus evidence for this assertion is anecdotal and reliant upon the few reported instances of poor quality work relative to the amount of legal work undertaken.
[61] See J. Jenkins and V. Lewis, *Client Perceptions – Existing and potential clients: experiences and perceptions of using a solicitor for personal matters* (1995), paras.5.9 and 5.10 and Table 23. See also J. Jenkins, E. Skordaki and C.F. Willis, *Public Use and Perception of Solicitors' Services* (1989), pp. 12–13; M. Zander, *A Matter of Justice* (revised ed., 1989), pp. 78–80; and R.C.L.S., Vol. 1, p. 292. This question is separate from whether there is work which lawyers should be doing but are not: see Chap. 8.
[62] Jenkins and Lewis (1995), para. 3.2.
[63] *ibid.*, para. 5.9. This shows a marginal improvement over the position in 1989: *ibid.*
[64] *ibid.*, para. 5.10.
[65] Jenkins and Lewis (1995), para. 5.10. These reasons are not dissimilar from those in the 1989 survey: delay, inefficiency, cost, incompetence and failure of communication: Jenkins, Skordaki and Willis (1989 *op. cit.* n. 57 above,) pp. 12–23. Also similar are the findings of other surveys, see R.C.L.S., Vol. 2, pp. 223–233 and M. Zander, *The State of Knowledge about the English Legal Profession* (1980), pp. 55–57.
[66] See below, p. 772. There are doubts about the methodology of the survey as some people pretended to be clients' and then compared the advice received against a blueprint.
[67] *Which?* magazine (1995), October 8.
[68] N.A.C.A.B., *Barriers to Justice* (1995), paras. 3.3–3.16. As to the question of cost, see p. 467 and Chap. 9 and pp. 537–539 below.
[69] R.C.L.S., Vol. 1, p. 292.
[70] See the impression represented to the Bar Standards Review Body by its consultants that "the best barristers are outstanding, and there are many good practitioners": *Blueprint for the Bar* (1994), para. 3.
[71] Royal Commission on Criminal Justice, *Report* (Cm. 2263, 1993) at p. 139: ". . . a small number of barristers were incompetent, prolix and poorly prepared."
[72] *Blueprint for the Bar* (1994), paras.11 and 90.

What is quality may well lie in the eye of the client. Are they satisfied with the service received? When the legal professional is a barrister, the client is another professional, usually a solicitor. Even here, however, it may be very difficult for the professional client to assess the quality of work of the barrister and so determine whether to use her or him again. This is particularly so in advocacy services, since it is less likely that a solicitor rather than a clerk will be in court who is likely to be, therefore, less able to assess the barrister's work.[73] Usually, therefore, the client is not in a position to assess whether the lawyer (barrister or solicitor) did a good job, as opposed to feeling, for example, disgruntled at losing the case and, of course, outcome is not a particularly good guide to quality of the work.

One of the difficulties in assessing quality has always been the lack of measures which may be applied objectively. Quality can be identified when it is seen, but it cannot be expressed more accurately than this.[74] In the context of franchising for legal aid, an attempt has been made to assess quality so as to determine which firms get and then keep a franchise. In the long run, it would not be surprising if such an approach were to be adopted more broadly throughout the profession. The "transaction criteria" have been developed by Sherr, Paterson and Moorhead.[75] The approach is the identification of criteria by which transactions may be measured to determine whether the solicitor has acted competently. This is achieved by breaking down the transaction into certain essential elements and assessing whether they have been satisfied by a relatively straightforward set of questions which may be assessed from the file and which may be objectively ascertained. The researchers do not claim that this is the only means of assessing quality, but it is one essential element, along with such matters as client surveys. Provided the elements of transactions are isolated carefully, this scheme has been evaluated as being a good one for identifying threshold competence.

Increasingly, client surveys are being used by firms to assess the quality of service. Some solicitors defend their decision not to use them by suggesting, e.g., that they know their clients well enough. Experience in other areas, however, demonstrates that nothing is a suitable alternative to the safety of surveys, which are usually anonymous. The same issue arises with regard to the confidence many barristers and their clerks have in their knowledge of their clients' satisfaction, even though the clients will be professionals, usually solicitors.[76]

Quality assurance is also enhanced by the admission of appropriate, qualified personnel who are provided with adequate training.[77] Quality may also, to some extent, be assured by the professional practice rules and the complaints systems. One example of the former is the solicitors' written professional standard concerned with information on costs for clients. In essence, it demands that clients be given initial information about likely costs and that they continue to inform

---

[73] *Blueprint for the Bar* (1994), para. 119, referring to the Royal Commission on Criminal Justice, *Report* (Cm.2263, 1993).

[74] See the difficulty of identifying what is poor service below, p. 162.

[75] See A. Sherr, R. Moorhead and A. Paterson, *Transaction Criteria* (1992); idem, *Lawyers – The Quality Agenda, Volume One: Assessing and Developing Competence and Quality in Legal Aid – The Report of the Birmingham Franchising Pilot* (1994); idem, *Lawyers – The Quality Agenda, Volume Two: Transaction Criteria* (1994).

[76] Bar Standards Review Body, *Blueprint for the Bar* (1994), para. 00.

[77] See below, pp. 182–187.

the client about the likely costs.[78] Since one of the most frequent complaints is about costs, compliance with this standard is critical. However, the Legal Services Ombudsman continues to be critical about both solicitors and the Solicitors Complaints Bureau in the way in which this standard is complied with and the way breaches are dealt with.[79]

When the activity is advocacy, quality assurance is supported by the role of the judges in considering a barrister's work. Judicial comments can be beneficial or detrimental to a barrister's career; judicial comments may assist the barrister in developing advocacy and trial skills. Further, the Bar Council has sought judicial help in raising standards by using judges to bring attention to a barrister's unsatisfactory performance or conduct. The judge is asked to see the barrister privately at the end of a case. If unsatisfied, the judge may seek a response from the head of the barrister's chambers, and, ultimately, may report the barrister for the imposition of disciplinary proceedings. It seems, however, that the judges are not particularly keen to engage in this particular process.[80]

4. COMPLAINTS AGAINST LAWYERS

(a) Solicitors

When things go wrong, there are a number of avenues open to the client affected, although there may be considerable practical difficulties in following them through. The first step is to raise the matter with the firm.[81] Since 1991, Practice Rule 15: Client Care has obliged all principals in private practice to have a complaints handling procedure which must, amongst other things, ensure that clients are informed whom to approach in the event of any problem with the service provided, and who is responsible for the day-to-day conduct of the matter and its overall supervision. Whilst this rule has engendered improvements in those firms not already sufficiently concerned about client care to have established a means of dealing with complaints, a 1994 survey concluded that more needed to be done by the Law Society by way of expanding the remit of the client care rule, taking a tougher line with those solicitors failing to comply, producing a written guide for clients, carrying out public consultation about the rule, and revising the rule requiring all firms to provide a written outline of their complaints procedures.[82] It was also recommended that surveys be used to assess clients' perception of the service.[83] The National Association of Citizens' Advice Bureaux strongly supports these proposals and suggests that firms should be regularly audited to ensure that they are complying with the complaints procedure.[84] A more recent Law Society Survey discovered that two-thirds of clients were not satisfied with the way the solicitor dealt with a complaint.[85]

---

[78] See *The Guide to the Professional Conduct of Solicitors* (6th ed., 1993), paras.13.04–13.14.
[79] *Fourth Annual Report of the Legal Services Ombudsman 1994*, (H.C. 459, 1994–95), paras. 3.9–3.13.
[80] *Blueprint for the Bar* (1994), paras.121–126.
[81] If a client complains to the Solicitors' Complaints Bureau first, the matter will be referred back to the firm for consideration under Rule 15.
[82] N. Harris, *Solicitors and Client Care* (N.C.C., 1994).
[83] *ibid.*, p. 32 and see above.
[84] N.A.C.A.B., *Barriers to Justice* (1995), paras. 3.27–3.30.
[85] V. Brown, *Complaints against solicitors: the complainants' view* (1996).

In addition to the client complaining to the Solicitors' Complaints Bureau, which may lead to disciplinary action and/or bringing legal action (which are considered below), the client may refuse to meet the lawyer's bill and defend any proceedings for payment brought by the lawyer. Further, a criminal offence such as theft may have been committed.[86]

(b) Regulating solicitor's practice

The Law Society's power to make rules regulating the professional practice, conduct and discipline of solicitors is subject to the concurrence of the Master of the Rolls[87] and, to an extent, subject to review by the Lord Chancellor's Advisory Committee on Legal Education and Conduct. ACLEC may give advice on all aspects of rules of conduct, and the Law Society is expressly required to have regard to that advice when it relates to rights of audience and rights to conduct litigation.[88] Further, when the Law Society seeks to be designated as an authorised body under the Courts and Legal Services Act 1990 for the purpose of rights of audience or rights to conduct litigation,[89] any proposed rules of conduct in relation to those rights must be approved by ACLEC.[90]

The regulatory work of the Law Society is delegated to the Solicitor's Complaints Bureau. The Society's proposals to replace the Bureau with a body more concerned with regulation of practice than complaints are considered below.

The rules are set out and amplified in *The Guide to the Professional Conduct of Solicitors*.[91] We have already set out the basic rules[92] governing a solicitor's general duties, publicity, introductions and referrals, complaints, employed solicitors, and multi-disciplinary partnerships.[93] The rules also prevent solicitors being involved in a business, other than in a solicitor's practice, which offers what may be called solicitor's business,[94] and otherwise limit the extent to which solicitors may work with other professionals unless certain safeguards for the

---

[86] There has been an increase in the number of cases referred by the Legal Aid Board to the Solicitors Complaints Board: Solicitors Complaints Bureau, *Annual Report 1994*, p. 8. Solicitor fraud is clearly a problem, see *The Lawyer* (1994) September 20.

[87] Solicitors Act 1974, s.31(1). In general, the principles and rules governing professional conduct are the responsibility of the Society's Standards and Guidance Committee and Professional Standards Directorate.

[88] Courts and Legal Services Act 1990, Sched. 2, paras. 5(3),(4).

[89] See above, pp. 133–138.

[90] Courts and Legal Services Act 1990, ss.27, 28, 29 and Sched. 4, Part II. The Committee was designed specifically to maintain quality of service in the public interest, see *Legal Services: A Framework for the Future* (Cm. 740, 1989), Part II, esp. para. 7.4.

[91] The latest edition is the sixth 1993. It must be read in conjunction with subsequent amendments published in the *Professional Standards Bulletin*.

[92] The Council of the Law Society may waive the rules in any particular case: Solicitors Practice Rules 1990, r.17. There are no general waivers in force.

[93] See above, pp. 127–143.

[94] Solicitors Practice Rules 1990, r.5. The business referred to in r.5(2) involves the following services: the conduct of any matter which could proceed before any court, tribunal or inquiry, whether or not proceedings are commenced; advocacy before any court, tribunal or inquiry; instructing counsel; acting as executor or trustee; drafting any will; giving legal advice; property selling; investment business as defined in the Financial Services Act 1986; any activity reserved to solicitors by the Solicitors Act 1974 or other statute; drafting any other legal documents. If the only service ancillary to the business' main purpose is the latter, a solicitor may be involved in a management consultancy or company secretarial service: r.5(4).

public are observed[95] and apart from the rules relating to multi-national practices. There is a general rule of professional conduct that a solicitor must not act for two or more clients in conflict.[96] The rules specifically prevent a solicitor acting for both clients in certain land transactions, subject to some exceptions.[97] Further, there is a principle of professional conduct that a solicitor "must not act where his or her own interests conflict with the interests of a client or potential client".[98] The Legal Services Ombudsman has insistently proposed that particularly in matrimonial cases, a solicitor should not continue to act for a client with whom he or she has a sexual relationship rather than merely being required to consider whether to continue to act.[99] Solicitors must ensure that every office where they or their firms practise is and can reasonably be seen to be properly supervised in accordance with certain minimum standards.[1]

The practice rules require solicitors to account to their clients where they receive more than £20 as commission, unless the client agrees that the solicitor may retain it.[2] In addition, solicitors must comply with detailed rules about the holding of client's money and the maintenance of adequate book-keeping and recording systems.[3] Some of the interest on those accounts may go to the client otherwise it will be retained by the solicitor.[4] In many other jurisdictions such interest is used for supporting legal education. Such a step in England and Wales would meet some of the financial problems associated with legal education.

Clients are further protected by solicitors' compulsory indemnity cover through the Solicitors Indemnity Fund Ltd to cover loss for civil liability[5] and the Compensation Fund, set up in 1942 and now run by the Solicitors Complaints Bureau.[6] The Compensation Fund enables payments to be made to those

---

[95] Solicitors Practice Rules 1990, r.5(3). The safeguards for the public are: the name of the business has no substantial element in common with the name of any solicitors' practice; the words "solicitor", "barrister" and "lawyer" are not used in connection with the solicitor's involvement with the business; clients referred by the solicitor to the business and, where business and practice premises are shared, all customers of the business are informed in writing that they do not enjoy the statutory protection attached to a solicitor's clients.

[96] Principle 15 of *The Guide* referred to in Solicitors Practice Rules 1990, r.6(1).

[97] The rules prevent a solicitor acting for both the seller and buyer of land at arm's length, the lessor and lessee on the grant of a lease for value at arm's length or the lender and borrower in a private mortgage at arm's length: Solicitors Practice Rules 1990, r.6(1). The exceptions are to be found in r.6(2).

[98] Principle 15.05 of *The Guide*.

[99] *Fourth Annual Report of the Legal Services Ombudsman 1994*, para. 3.15.

[1] Solicitors Practice Rules 1990, r.13. The minimum standards are to be found in r.13(1). See also Principle 3.02 of *The Guide*. See above, p. 123.

[2] Solicitors Practice Rule 1990, r.10.

[3] The Solicitors Accounts Rules 1991 and the Accountant's Report Rules 1991, see *The Guide*, Chap. 27 (which requires an annual accountant's report). Such rules were first made in 1935 because of a number of frauds by solicitors causing public concern: Abel-Smith & Stevens (1967), pp. 190–192. Despite a detailed set of rules and stringent policing (including Law Society access to a solicitor's books: Solicitor's Account Rules 1990, r.27), errors, both deliberate and accidental, still come to light. It is possible that learning about these rules whilst holding a training contract through a Professional Skills Course (see below, p. 185) rather than on a pre-training contract course may assist young solicitors to have their impact firmly embedded in their professional conscience and practice.

[4] See *The Guide*, Principles 27.52–27.64.

[5] Solicitors Indemnity Rules 1995. See *The Guide*, Chap. 28. The Fund covers loss relating to civil liability, see below, p. 174.

[6] See Solicitors Act 1974, s.36 and Sched. 2 and the Solicitors Compensation Fund Rules 1975. See *The Guide*, Chap. 29.

who have suffered loss by reason of a solicitor's dishonesty or in the event of hardship suffered as a result of a solicitor failing to account for money.[7]

One of the most contentious issues for clients is the question of costs. Many problems would be solved were there greater compliance with the written professional standard about providing information.[8] The jurisdiction of the Law Society, delegated to the Solicitor's Complaints Bureau, is considered elsewhere.[9]

(c) Solicitors: Professional misconduct and inadequate professional services[10]

The Law Society has the power to deal with both professional misconduct and inadequate professional services. Its powers have been delegated to the Solicitors Complaints Bureau (S.C.B.). Professional misconduct is undefined. It may be that it is conduct which other members of the profession would regard as " 'dishonourable' or 'deplorable' ".[11] It is unlikely that any breach of a practice rule is necessarily misconduct,[12] but it would include moral turpitude and commission of serious offences, especially offences of dishonesty. Although the Law Society has always had the power to deal with misconduct, it has only had the power to deal with inadequate professional services since the Administration of Justice Act 1985.[13] "Inadequate professional services" is defined as "the provision by solicitors of services which are not of the quality which it is reasonable to expect of them".[14] A prima facie case of inadequate professional services may exist where there is unreasonable delay in dealing with the client's case, failure to seek or follow instructions, failure to account to the client, failure to advise the client, keep her or him fully informed or otherwise to be poor in communication, and general incompetency or inefficiency not giving rise to a specific allegation of negligence.[15] The failure to account ought more properly to be regarded as a prima facie case of professional misconduct. What the Law Society through the S.C.B. cannot investigate is allegations of negligence.[16] Negligence is conduct of a solicitor falling below that standard which may reasonably be expected and entitling the complainant to damages for any loss caused. The dividing line between negligence and inadequate professional services is extremely difficult to draw and, in effect, the S.C.B. deals with small negligence claims as inadequate professional services.[17] Where there is a matter of negligence, the Bureau may refer the complainant to a solicitor on the "Negligence Panel" for advice about instituting action for negligence in the courts.

---

[7] See *The Guide*, para. 29.01 *et seq.*
[8] See above, pp. 158–159 and below pp. 534–536.
[9] See below, pp. 162–166.
[10] See *The Guide* and F. Silverman, *Handbook of Professional Conduct for Solicitors* (1989).
[11] National Consumer Council, *The Solicitors Complaints Bureau: A consumer view* (1994) [hereafter N.C.C. (1994)], p. 31.
[12] However, it is stated in *The Guide* that the Conduct Unit of the S.C.B. "deals with complaints about breaches of the Solicitors' Practice Rules and other allegations of misconduct": para. 30.15.
[13] See now the Solicitors Act 1974, s.37A and Sched. 1A as replaced by the Courts and Legal Services Act 1990, s.93.
[14] Solicitors Act 1974, s.37A.
[15] *The Guide*, para. 30.11.
[16] See *The Guide*, para. 30.02. As to civil liability, see below, pp. 173–178.
[17] N.C.C. (1994), p. 30. The maximum compensation payable is £1,000; alternatively the bill might be reduced where the complainant is successful, see below.

In the first place, complaints should be dealt with by the solicitor concerned and then the senior partner.[18] Only then should a complaint be directed to the S.C.B.[19] The first step is for the Registry to assess whether the matter is to be considered further at all[20] and, if so, the matter is passed to the Primary Investigation Unit, which will determine whether the solicitor has dealt with it under the client care rule. The solicitor is expected to deal with the matter first,[21] however much the relationship between client and solicitor has broken down.[22] The Primary Investigation Unit will attempt to resolve complaints by local conciliation and this is how most complaints are handled.[23] All complaints of inadequate professional services are initially dealt with by conciliation. Conciliation will be conducted by either a caseworker from the S.C.B. or by a local conciliator, normally a retired solicitor.[24] "After speaking to the complainant (though this does not always happen), the conciliator will contact the solicitor to try and reach an agreement "acceptable to both sides". If an agreement is not reached, the caseworker will decide if further action is required. . . . If a complainant (or solicitor) refuses to accept the solution offered by the conciliator, the latter will write an 'assessment' for the Assistant Director [of the S.C.B.]." The end result is likely to be confirmation of the conciliator's view.[25] The N.C.C. is very critical of the conciliation process on the basis that complainants are not given a choice about whether to use conciliation, complaints are not formally investigated unless the possibilities of conciliation have been exhausted and the conciliator can, effectively, impose a settlement or dismiss the complaint.[26] The S.C.B. believes conciliation to be very successful.

If conciliation does not resolve the problem and the matter is to be pursued by the S.C.B., the Primary Investigation Unit will determine whether the matter is one to be referred as a matter of professional misconduct[27] or inadequate professional services[28] for investigation, which tends to be a paper investigation, including calling in the solicitor's files. Because of the difficulty in defining professional misconduct, it would not be surprising were complaints to be misdirected. The Legal Services Ombudsman has drawn attention to this

---

[18] See above, p. 159.

[19] The leaflet helping complainants is fairly clear, but the National Consumer Council is of the view that it is of little value further on, since it fails to explain the process, "some parts of the leaflet are difficult to follow" and there are serious omissions: N.C.C. (1994), p. 24. There is a telephone helpline, providing practical help for people who believe they have a problem with their solicitor and which S.C.B. regards as a "strong weapon in the Bureau's armoury:" Solicitors Complaints Bureau, *Annual Report 1994*, pp. 8–9.

[20] Of 19,649 complaints received in 1994, 16,482 were passed to the Primary Investigation Unit: *ibid.*, p. 17.

[21] Of the 16,482 complaints received in 1994 in the Unit, 4,944 were resolved through Rule 15: *ibid.*, p. 17. The N.C.C. is of the view that this does not mean that the matter has been satisfactorily resolved.

[22] The National Consumer Council is critical of this automatic reference back, and is of the view that many cases so referred disappear rather than being resolved: N.C.C. (1994), p. 44.

[23] In 1994, the P.I.U. received 16,482 complaints, but only 3,167 were passed on to the next stages. Of the remainder, most were resolved by Rule 15, conciliation, or otherwise: Solicitors Complaints Bureau: *Annual Report 1994*, p. 17. See also N.C.C. (1994), p. 50.

[24] Very few conciliations are dealt with by a local conciliator: N.C.C. (1994), p. 53.

[25] *ibid.*, p. 53.

[26] *ibid.*, p. 57.

[27] In 1994, 1,248 were complaints were referred to the Conduct Unit: Solicitors Complaints Bureau, *Annual Report 1994*, p. 17.

[28] In 1994, 1,919 complaints were passed to either the Professional Service Investigation or Assessment sections: *ibid.*, p. 17.

problem.[29] A matter of professional misconduct will be considered by the Conduct Unit and, if the caseworker believes that there is a case to answer, the Conduct Committee of the Adjudication and Appeals Committee or an Assistant Director will be asked to make a first instance decision.[30] An appeal lies to the Adjudication and Appeals Committee. A matter of inadequate professional services follows a similar procedure through the assessment section, although the burden of proof is a balance of probabilities, rather then beyond a reasonable doubt which applies in misconduct cases.[31]

If an allegation of inadequate professional services is proved, the available steps to be taken are: to reduce the solicitor's costs,[32] to direct the solicitor to rectify an error, to order the solicitor to pay compensation to a maximum of £1,000 or to require the solicitor to take such other action in the client's interests as the S.C.B. may specify.[33] Both the Legal Services Ombudsman and the N.C.C. have advocated raising the maximum level of compensation.[34] The N.C.C. is concerned that at least some of the sanctions are rarely used[35] and the Law Society survey suggests that complainants and of the view that the S.C.B. has insufficient power to force solicitors to take appropriate action.[36]

If an allegation of professional misconduct is proved, the available steps include ordering an inspection of accounts, intervening in a solicitor's practice to protect the interests of clients, intervening to recover a particular file for the client or his or her new solicitor, refusing a practising certificate, imposing conditions on the grant of a practising certificate, prohibiting a solicitor from taking an articled clerk, depriving a firm of its Investment Business Certificate, inviting a solicitor to take certain action such as to obtain a remuneration certificate to assess the fairness of charges made, and imposing sanctions ranging from deprecation of a solicitor's conduct to calling a solicitor to be rebuked personally by the chair of the Appeals and Adjudication Committee.[37] Further, the Committee has the power to order payment out of the Solicitor's Compensation Fund where a person has suffered as a consequence of a solicitor's dishonesty.[38] Finally, the Committee may institute disciplinary proceedings before the Solicitors' Disciplinary Tribunal.

The Solicitors Complaints Bureau has two main Committees. The Appeals and Adjudication Committee exercises the relevant jurisdiction of the Law

---

[29] *Third Annual Report of the Legal Services Ombudsman 1993*, para. 3.18 and N.C.C. (1994), pp. 65–67.

[30] *The Guide*, paras.30.15–30.20 and N.C.C. (1994), p. 69.

[31] *ibid.*, pp. 69–70. In 1994, the Assessment Unit considered 4,296 cases. There were 906 first instance decisions made by the Assistant Director, with findings of inadequate professional services in 481 cases. The Professional Service investigators produced investigations which resulted in 284 first instance decisions with 201 findings of inadequate professional services: Solicitors Complaints Bureau, *Annual Report 1994*, p. 9.

[32] This is the most frequently used sanction: Solicitor's Complaints Bureau, *Annual Report 1989*, p. 12 and N.C.C. (1994), p. 75.

[33] Solicitors Act 1974, s.37A and Sched. 1A.

[34] *Fourth Annual Report of the Legal Services Ombudsman 1994*, paras. 3.22–3.24 (£2,500); N.C.C. (1994), p. 104 (£5,000).

[35] N.C.C. (1994), p. 77.

[36] Brown (1996).

[37] Solicitors Act 1974, ss.12, 13, 31, 32, 35 and Sched. 1. A solicitor's appeal lies to the Master of the Rolls or the High Court, depending upon the step taken. These steps may have significant impact upon solicitors, for whom it has been argued that there is inadequate protection: O. Hansen, "Solicitors' discipline" (1990) 140 N.L.J. 1345.

[38] Solicitors Act 1974, s.36 (as amended).

Society. It has 21 members, of whom 10 are lay members. Its secretary is the Director of the S.C.B. The Policy Advisory Committee takes an overview of the work of the Bureau. It has nine members, six of whom are lay members. Its secretary is the Policy Adviser of the S.C.B.

By delegating its powers to the Solicitors Complaints Bureau, the Law Society avoided following the option of a wholly independent procedure whereby complaints would have been dealt with by an organisation completely outside the Law Society, which would have demanded legislative change. The Law Society adopted a quasi-independent arrangement, which is reflected in the lay composition of the Committees of the S.C.B. and in its increasing distance from the Law Society. Nevertheless, the failure to adopt a wholly independent system has been heavily criticised, both at the time and more recently.[39] The 1994 N.C.C. demand for an independent Legal Services Complaints Council employing several Ombudsmen to investigate complaints has been hotly debated. The S.C.B. itself has made the point that the N.C.C. research methodology is flawed and that it fails to reflect the good work of the S.C.B. Further, the Legal Services Ombudsman has taken the view that the proposals, though important, are premature but demanding serious consideration. It is the view of the Legal Services Ombudsman that the Bureau does not favour solicitors and genuinely tries to investigate complaints impartially.[40] The Law Society survey indicates major complainant concerns with the S.C.B.[41] The fact that not all complainants are satisfied does not determine the effectiveness of a complaints mechanism.

The N.C.C. is of the view that the S.C.B. deals with complaints too slowly.[42] Whilst there is some evidence for this view, it is important to note that the level of upheld complaints about delay by the Legal Services Ombudsman is a very small percentage of complaints handled (0.5 per cent), a point confirmed by its own internal statistics. The Bureau appoints temporary staff to assist in reducing delay.[43] The S.C.B. is concerned with many matters other than complaints and there has been a significant increase in its workload, a factor often forgotten by solicitors who grumble about the S.C.B.[44] Further, whilst recognising the force of some of the points made by the N.C.C., the National Association of Citizens' Advice Bureaux concludes that the S.C.B. does not deserve quite the reputation that it has gained.[45] The major problems identified are delay in dealing with complaints, gaining initial advice and a perception by some clients that it is not sufficiently independent of solicitors.[46]

Nevertheless, there is, at the least, a public relations exercise problem for the S.C.B. It would seem that there will be a major restructuring of the work of the S.C.B. since the Law Society, in its 1995 consultation document *Supervision*

---

[39] See A.L. Newbold and G. Zellick, "Reform of the Solicitors' Complaints Procedures: Fact or Fiction" (1987) 6 C.J.Q. 25, esp. 42–43 and N.C.C. (1994).

[40] *Fourth Annual Report of the Legal Services Ombudsman 1994*, paras.3.18–3.20.

[41] *ibid.*, para. 3.21.

[42] N.C.C. (1994), pp. 71–74. Brown (1996).

[43] Solicitors Complaints Bureau, *Annual Report 1994*, p. 13. See also Brown (1996). This reduces staff continuity with complaints handling to which complainants object: Brown (1996).

[44] S.C.B., *Annual Report 1994*, pp. 5–7 and V. Lowe, "Guess which organisation?" (1995) N.L.J. 861. The S.C.B. has a major function with regard to accounts investigations, Remuneration Certificates (see below, pp. 533–536), intervention in a solicitor's practice, costs in default and the Compensation Fund.

[45] N.A.C.A.B., *Barriers to Justice* (1995), paras. 3.31–3.48.

[46] See also Brown (1996).

of Solicitors: The Next Decade, proposes the replacement of the S.C.B. with an organisation, the Solicitors Supervisory Agency, that will emphasise the role of regulating solicitors, rather than dealing with complaints. But there is not a simplistic answer to reducing cost, unless solicitors improve client care and resolve complaints at firm level, greater preventative work is undertaken by the regulatory authorities and the Law Society is tougher in its enforcement policies. The proposals include matters which are likely to appeal to solicitors: a complaint would only be handled where there was a prima facie case, with a *de minimis* principle. The LSO has warned that the Law Society may lose its complaint function and the S.C.B. is to be re-launched in September 1996 as the office for the Supervision of Solicitors.

(d) Disciplinary proceedings: solicitors

A case may come before the Solicitors' Disciplinary Tribunal[47] through the S.C.B. or from complainants directly. The Tribunal sits in divisions of three, comprising two solicitors and one lay member.[48] Applications are heard in private, but the findings are made public.[49] If a complaint is proved, the Tribunal may exercise one or more of the following powers: strike the solicitor off the Roll (indefinitely or for a specified period), fine the solicitor (not more than £5,000), exclude the solicitor from legal aid work, and reprimand the solicitor.[50] The Tribunal may inform the Council of the Law Society that it is of the view that "steps" in respect of inadequate professional services should be taken.[51] An appeal lies to the High Court[52] and then on a point of law to the Court of Appeal and the House of Lords. The High Court, the Crown Court and the Court of Appeal may also exercise jurisdiction over solicitors as officers of the court.[53]

(e) Barristers

Until 1996, there were few avenues available when things go wrong. Some chambers were able to deal with clients, and the client could seek the instigation of disciplinary proceedings or go to law. However, there was no practice rule until 1996 demanding a complaints handling system in chambers, nor a system at the level of the professional body, the Bar Council. A judge may be involved in discussing a barrister's practice[54] and a wasted costs order may be made

---

[47] The Tribunal was established by the Solicitors Act 1974, s.46.

[48] Solicitors Act 1974, s.4(2)–(8).

[49] Solicitors Act 1974, s.48.

[50] Solicitors Act 1974, ss.37A, 47 and Sched. 1A. Reports of proceedings of the Solicitors Disciplinary Tribunal appear in the *Law Society's Gazette* and other publications such as *The Lawyer*.

[51] Solicitors Act 1974, Sched. 1A, para. 8.

[52] Solicitors Act 1974, s.49. In some cases the appeal lies to the Master of the Rolls (ss.43(4), 47(1)(b)) who makes a final decision.

[53] Solicitors Act 1974, ss.50–53 and *Supreme Court Practice 1995*, Vol.2, Part 11, Section D.1. The jurisdiction to strike off is rarely exercised, in part because of the existence of the Solicitors' Disciplinary Tribunal. The striking off of Glanville Davies and the history of the complaint was a major factor in causing the Law Society to amend its complaints procedures, see R.L. Abel, *The Legal Profession in England and Wales* (1988), p. 255. More frequently exercised is the jurisdiction to order a solicitor to compensate others for neglect or misconduct in proceedings before the court, see *Supreme Court Practice 1995*, Vol. 2, para. 3873. The jurisdiction is not readily exercised.

[54] See above, p. 159.

against a barrister whose poor service has caused loss. It was clear that a complaints system was needed and, although some barristers found it difficult to accept, a complainants system was introduced in 1996.[55]

The Bar Standards Review Body recommended, in 1994, that chambers should have procedures to deal with complaints against barristers and staff.[56] Further, it recommended the establishment of a Barristers Complaints Bureau which would deal with complaints against barristers, referring disciplinary matters to the currently existing machinery. The Bureau would be modelled on the lines of the Solicitors Complaints Bureau. It would be under the direction of a non-lawyer, with both barrister and lay members on decision-making panels. The Bureau would have the power to investigate complaints of poor work or unsatisfactory services and would be able to order the payment of compensation, unless the matter were referred for disciplinary proceedings. If possible, complaints should be resolved by conciliation. Anyone would have right of access to the process, without payment of a fee, and the jurisdiction of the Bureau would include performance in court work, for which barristers have immunity from civil proceedings.[57] A right of appeal would exist for the barrister.[58]

However, the Complaints System Working Party of the Bar Council rejected that proposal because the Bureau would be too far removed from the profession's governing body, it might lack the respect of barristers and would be too expensive.[59] What has been proposed, and which may be adopted as early as mid-1996, is the appointment of a Complaints Commissioner, who would not be a barrister. This option was adopted[60] because there would be minimal disruption to existing administrative systems, it would largely meet the criticism of lack of independence, unjustified complaints would be filtered out at an early stage, consistency in the new power to award compensation would result in the Commissioner's involvement in all such cases, and he or she would be able to engage in conciliation. As the Working Party recognised, the disadvantages of the system are that it is part of the Bar's own systems and barristers are still involved in dealing with complaints.[61] Whilst these criticisms are viewed as being "unrealistic" it is difficult to imagine outside bodies and many clients being satisfied with a system which is not only not independent but which is dominated by barristers, whatever their qualities may be. Every complaint would initially be considered by the Complaints Commissioner who would be able to dismiss it, suggest direct contact with the barrister or chambers, attempt conciliation or have it investigated. If investigated, the Complaints Commissioner would decide whether the matter should be dismissed or considered by the Complaints Committee, consisting of barristers and lay people. If referred to the Committee, a Sponsor Member (a barrister) would make a report for the Committee and the Committee would also have a report from the Complaints

---

[55] Complaints System Working Party, *Report* (1995), paras. 22–29. Criminal barristers were particularly connected about a system retrying defendants.

[56] Bar Standards Review Body, *Blueprint for the Bar* (1994), para. 181. This proposal is being considered by the Bar: The Complaints System Working Group, *Report* (1995), para. 44.

[57] See below, pp. 174–176.

[58] *Blueprint for the Bar* (1994), section 7.

[59] Complaints System Working Party, *Report* (1995), para. 84.

[60] A minimalist option of empowering the existing disciplinary bodies to deal with poor service complaints was rejected because it would not have a filter system to weed out frivolous claims at an early stage, and there would be a perceived lack of independence: Complaints System Working Party, *Report* (1995), para. 83. Also rejected was the N.C.C. model.

[61] *ibid.*, paras. 86–87.

Commissioner, who would be expected to put the complainant's case to the Committee. The Committee would decide whether there was a prima facie case of misconduct and, if so, refer it for disciplinary proceedings, which would be as at present, although the bodies would have the power to make a finding of poor service and require an apology or award compensation. If there is a prima facie case of inadequate professional services, the matter would be considered by an Adjudication Panel[62] which, if finding against the barrister, could require an apology, reduce or require repayment of fees, or award compensation (that is a sum punishing the barrister to a maximum of £2,000[63]).[64] A barrister would have a right of appeal against a decision of an Adjudication Panel to a further body consisting of past and present members of the existing Professional Conduct Committee of the Bar Council.[65] The new system will provide for a formal mechanism to deal with complaints of "inadequate professional services" (or "poor work and unsatisfactory service") in which regard the Working Party has endeavoured to clarify its meaning, recognising the difficulties in doing so.[66] The proposal is that inadequate professional services would best be described "as a failure to act in accordance with the requirements of paragraph 601(a) and/or Annex H to the Code [of Conduct]".[67] Paragraph 601(a) states that a practising barrister must "in all [his or her] activities be courteous and act promptly conscientiously diligently and with reasonable competence and take all reasonable and practicable steps to avoid unnecessary expense or waste of the Court's time and to ensure that professional engagements are fulfilled." Annex H expands somewhat on this statement. The sort of things which would be covered are: avoidable lateness, rudeness, delay and acting without reasonable competence.[68] In addition to concerns about the independence and public acceptability of this system, it should be noted that, contrary to the recommendation of the Bar Standards Review Body, it is proposed that immunity from suit should apply to complaints of inadequate professional services.[69] The arguments against the immunity are more compelling, but this part of the package is a major stumbling block for many barristers.[70]

(f) Professional misconduct: barristers

The Bar deals with disciplinary measures through the jurisdiction in relation to professional misconduct. Not every breach of the Code of Conduct amounts to professional misconduct.[71] The power to discipline barristers, which lies with the Judges and the Council of the Inns of Court, has been delegated to the Professional Conduct Committee of the Bar Council (P.C.C.),[72] which is subject to the overview of the Legal Services Ombudsman. The P.C.C. is dominated

---

[62] The Panel would have lay involvement: *ibid.*, paras. 97–99.
[63] *ibid.*, paras. 51, 52 and 56.
[64] *ibid.*, paras. 88–99.
[65] *ibid.*, paras. 101–102.
[66] *ibid.*, paras. 30–39.
[67] *ibid.*, para. 36.
[68] *ibid.*, para. 39 and Annex G.
[69] *ibid.*, paras. 62–68.
[70] *Blueprint for the Bar* (1994), paras. 206–213 and below, pp. 174–176.
[71] Complaints System Working Party, *Report* (1995), para. 34.
[72] The rules governing the proceedings are to be found in the Professional Conduct Committee Rules, the Disciplinary Tribunal Regulations and the Hearings before the Visitors Rules reproduced in the *Code of Conduct*.

by barristers, but there are always two lay members present, from a panel of nine, when a matter is being considered.[73] Anyone may make a complaint. It is first considered by the Professional Conduct Committee,[74] which decides if there is a prima facie case of misconduct. The Secretary of the Committee enables such decision to be made by making such investigations and inquiries (if any) as appear to be necessary.[75] The complaint will be summarily dismissed if it is thought to be trivial or obviously lacking in validity or it is otherwise expedient to adopt this course of action.[76] Otherwise the Secretary writes to the barrister asking for comments in writing or in person. These comments are then sent to the complainant for reply, and when that has been received it is all sent to the Sponsor Member, a member of the P.C.C., who may order further investigations and then prepares a report of the rival contentions for the P.C.C. Thereafter the P.C.C. considers the complaint and may decide to: dismiss the complaint (but only if all the lay representatives agree); determine that no action should be taken; postpone further consideration of the complaint for further investigation or inquiry; where the matter is "domestic", refer it to the treasurer of the Inn or the Leader of the Circuit of the barrister concerned; where informal treatment is required, draw the matter to the barrister's attention in writing and, if appropriate, require attendance before the Chair of the Committee; where there is a prima facie case of professional misconduct but the matter is not sufficiently serious for it to be referred to a summary hearing or the Disciplinary Tribunal, direct that the barrister attend on the Chair of the Committee or a panel consisting of three members of the P.C.C. to provide an explanation of his or her conduct and, if necessary, to be given advice as to his or her future conduct or be admonished; where there is a prima facie case of professional misconduct, but there is no major dispute as to fact and no possibility of a sentence of disbarment or suspension, direct that the complaint should form the subject of a charge before a summary hearing; where there is a prima facie case of misconduct, and the previously stated conditions do not apply, direct that the complaint should form the subject matter of a charge before the Disciplinary Tribunal; or require the barrister to take a test in oral English.[77] Some 70 per cent of complaints are dismissed or have no further action taken, some 15 per cent are dealt with informally and the remainder go to either a summary hearing or Disciplinary Tribunal.[78] The Secretary of the P.C.C. is to take such steps as are reasonably practicable to inform the complainant of the progress and result of a complaint.[79]

If the matter is referred to either a summary hearing or Disciplinary Tribunal, a member of P.C.C. takes charge of the proceedings on its behalf.[80] A summary hearing[81] panel consists of a Q.C. as chair, a lay representative and between one and three barristers. The procedure is informal, although representation is permitted, and private. If satisfied that a charge is proved it may: suspend a barrister from practice for up to three months, with or without conditions; order

---

[73] Complaints System Working Party, *Report* (1995), para. 7.
[74] For its powers and functions, see Professional Conduct Committee Rules, r.2. For a brief report of its work, see the Annual Report of the Bar Council.
[75] Professional Conduct Committee Rules, r.3b.
[76] *ibid.*, r.3c.
[77] *ibid.*, r.3e.
[78] Complaints System Working Party, *Report* (1995), para. 7.
[79] Professional Conduct Committee Rules, r.5.
[80] *ibid.*, r.6.
[81] See the Summary Procedure Rules extracted in the *Code of Conduct*.

a fine be paid to the Bar Council up to £500; order a barrister to forgo or repay fees; order reprimand by the Treasurer of the barrister's Inn; permanently or temporarily exclude him or her from legal aid work; admonish the barrister; or advise as to his or her future conduct.

A Disciplinary Tribunal must consist of a judge as chair, a lay representative and three barristers.[82] Hearings which are relatively formal, evidence being taken on oath and representation permitted, are normally held in private. If a Tribunal is satisfied that a charge is proved, a barrister may be sentenced[83] as for a summary hearing, except that the barrister may also be disbarred; and suspension can be for any period with or without conditions; and the barrister may be ordered to pay a fine up to £5,000 to the Bar Council.[84]

The Bar Standards Review Body has recommended that Disciplinary Tribunals and summary proceedings should have the same power to award compensation as the proposed Barristers Complaints Bureau, so as to prevent the resource-wasting transfer of matters determined to be complaints rather than disciplinary matters. Disciplinary Tribunals, it proposes, should normally be held in public and the findings of the Tribunal and of summary hearings should be published.[85] The Complaints System Working Party has accepted the proposal that compensation be awardable, and that proceedings be public, although a Tribunal must have the power to exclude the public in some cases.[86]

(g) The Legal Services Ombudsman

The office of the Legal Services Ombudsman (L.S.O.) was created by section 21 of the Courts and Legal Services Act 1990 "to reinforce the existing system with more effective measures for dealing with complaints".[87] The L.S.O. may investigate[88] the way in which certain professional bodies (currently the Law Society, the General Council of the Bar, and the Council of Licensed Conveyancers) have handled complaints to them.[89] Secondly, where an allegation is investigated, the substance of the complaint to the professional body may also be investigated.[90] The second power is rarely exercised, which is not surprising in view of the oversight function ascribed to the L.S.O.[91]

The L.S.O. cannot (1) investigate any allegation while it is being investi-

---

[82] Disciplinary Tribunals Regulations (in the *Code of Conduct*), r.2.

[83] It is reported to the Lord Chancellor, Lord Chief Justice, Attorney-General, President, Chair of the Bar Council, Chair of the Professional Conduct Committee, barrister charged, Treasurer of the barrister's Inn of Call and the Treasurer of any other Inn of which the barrister is a member: *ibid.*, r.21(1), (2). The finding and sentence may also be publicised: *ibid.*, r.25.

[84] *ibid.*, r.18(2)(a).

[85] *Blueprint for the Bar* (1994), paras. 220–224.

[86] Complaints System Working Party, *Report* (1995), paras. 51–56 and 70–71.

[87] *Legal Services: A Framework for the Future* (Cm. 740, 1989), para. 10.13.

[88] The L.S.O. may at any time discontinue an investigation: s.22(3). In conducting an investigation, the L.S.O. may require any person to furnish relevant information and produce relevant documents (s.25(1)). The L.S.O. has the same powers as the High Court with regard to the attendance and examination of witnesses and in respect of the production of documents (s.25(2)). Any person in contempt of the L.S.O. may be referred to the High Court (s.25(4)–(7)).

[89] Courts and Legal Services Act 1990, s.22(1).

[90] Courts and Legal Services Act 1990, s.22(2).

[91] See R. James and M. Seneviratne, "The Legal Services Ombudsman: Form versus Function?" (1995) 58 M.L.R 187, p. 189.

gated by the professional body concerned unless the allegation is that that body has acted unreasonably in not starting an investigation or has failed to complete an investigation within a reasonable time or the L.S.O. believes that an investigation is justified despite the investigation by the professional body,[92] (2) investigate any complaint which has been dealt with by a court, the Solicitors Disciplinary Tribunal or the Disciplinary Tribunal of the Council of the Inns of Court, since the procedures in such tribunals satisfy the need for public accountability.[93]

In 1994, 1,598 complaints were received by the L.S.O., an increase upon previous years of 28 per cent,[94] which perhaps suggests that knowledge of and belief in the efficacy of the L.S.O. is getting through to clients. Where the L.S.O. investigates,[95] upon completion a written report of the conclusions must be sent to the person making the allegation, any person in respect of whom the complaint was made, and the professional body concerned.[96] In 1994, 839 reports were issued, with 454 investigations pending or awaiting final report. Of these, the majority concerned solicitors, which is not surprising since they are, by far, the largest of the three professions.[97] In the report, which must be reasoned, the L.S.O. may make one or more of the following recommendations:[98]

(1) that the complaint be reconsidered by the professional body[99];
(2) that the professional body (or any other relevant disciplinary body) should consider its powers in relation to the person about whom the complaint was made and any person who at the time was connected[1] with him or her;[2]
(3) that the person about whom the complaint was made or any person who at the time was connected with him or her should pay compensation, as specified by the L.S.O., to the complainant for loss suffered or

---

[92] Courts and Legal Services Act 1990, s.22(5) and (6).
[93] Courts and Legal Services Act 1990, s.22(7).
[94] *Fourth Annual Report of the Legal Services Ombudsman 1994* (H.C. 459, 1994–95), para. 2.1. This figure represents 8 per cent of the complaints made to the three professional bodies: *ibid.* James and Seneviratne raised doubts about whether "*all*" complainants are told of" the role of the L.S.O. by the Solicitors Complaints Bureau: R. James and M. Seneviratne (1995) *op. cit.* n. 82 above, p. 195.
[95] In some straightforward cases (where it appears on sifting that there is no merit to the allegation and it is unlikely that there will be a recommendation or where it indicates that the Solicitors' Complaints Bureau has acted too slowly), the allegation will be dealt with by a "fast track" method: James and Seneviratne (1995) *op. cit.*, p. 202.
[96] Courts and Legal Services Act 1990, s.23(1). The same people must be informed if the L.S.O. does not investigate: *ibid.* s.22(4).
[97] *Fourth Annual Report of the Legal Services Ombudsman 1994*, para. 2.2. 1177 were about solicitors, 112 about barristers and 42 about licensed conveyancers: *ibid.*
[98] 177 recommendations were made in 1994: *Fourth Annual Report of the Legal Services Ombudsman 1994*, para. 2.3.
[99] Sixty-eight such recommendations were made in 1994: *Fourth Annual Report of the Legal Services Ombudsman 1994*, para. 2.3. This power is used particularly where an investigation has been incomplete and it can more properly be completed by the professional body or there is a case for imposing disciplinary sanctions, which cannot be done by the L.S.O.: *ibid.* para. 3.25. See James and Seneviratne (1995) *op. cit.*, p. 197.
[1] See Courts and Legal Services Act 1990, s.23(11).
[2] There were 49 such recommendations in 1994: *Fourth Annual Report of the Legal Services Ombudsman 1994*, para. 2.4.

inconvenience or distress caused as a result of the matter about which there was a complaint;[3]

(4) that the professional body concerned should pay such compensation;

(5) that a separate payment be made to the complainant in respect of costs related to the making of an allegation.[4]

These are recommendations only, but they are backed by the requirement that a person to whom a report is sent must "have regard to the conclusions and recommendations set out in the report, so far as they concern that person."[5] Further, the person or body to whom such a recommendation is made must, within three months of the date on which the report was sent, notify the L.S.O. of the action taken or proposed to be taken to comply with the recommendation.[6] Finally, any person or body failing to comply with a recommendation must publicise that failure and the reasons for it in such manner as the L.S.O. specifies.[7] If a person or body fails so to publicise, the L.S.O. may take such steps as considered reasonable to publicise the failure.[8]

The L.S.O. has a further critical role. This is in acting as the monitor of the complaints procedures of the professional bodies. To this end, the L.S.O. may make formal recommendations as to how the professional body deals with complaints,[9] have informal meetings with the professional bodies, and make formal comments in the Annual Report.[10] In 95 cases in 1994, the L.S.O. made no recommendation, but criticised the way in which the professional body had dealt with the complaint[11] and in the Annual Reports has frequently been highly critical of the way the various bodies operate. It appears that these approaches have been meeting with some success.[12]

In a careful examination of the work of the L.S.O. and his staff, James and Seneviratne[13] have concluded that, with minor reservations, the office meets the four criteria essential to the work of ombudsmen, that is "independence of the ombudsman from those whom he has power to investigate; effectiveness; fairness; and public accountability".[14] Their major concern is whether the L.S.O.

---

[3] In 1994 there were 60 such recommendations: 35 for under £500, 15 for £500–£1,000, five for £1,000–£2,000, three for £2,000–£3,000, two for £3,000–£4,000 and one for £59,809: *Fourth Annual Report of the Legal Services Ombudsman 1994*, para. 2.4. For an explanation and critique of the ranges, see James and Seneviratne (1995) *op. cit.*, p. 196.

[4] Courts and Legal Services Act 1990, s.23(2),(2) and (4).

[5] Courts and Legal Services Act 1990, s.23(6).

[6] Courts and Legal Services Act 1990, s.23(7).

[7] Courts and Legal Services Act 1990, s.23(8).

[8] Courts and Legal Services Act 1990, s.23(9). Any reasonable expenses incurred by the L.S.O. may be recovered as a civil debt from the person whose failure has been publicised: *ibid.* s.23(10). Eight firms or people were named in the 1994 Annual Report: *Fourth Annual Report of the Legal Services Ombudsman 1994*, Appendix A.

[9] Courts and Legal Services Act 1990, s.24(1). This is a rarely exercised power; see James and Seneviratne (1995) *op. cit.*, pp. 199–200.

[10] James and Seneviratne (1995) *op. cit.*, p. 199.

[11] *Fourth Annual Report of the Legal Services Ombudsman 1994*, para. 2.5.

[12] See *Fourth Annual Report of the Legal Services Ombudsman 1994*, Chapter 3 and James and Seneviratne (1995) *op. cit.*, pp. 200–201. Some of the points made are referred to above in considering the complaints procedures concerned with solicitors and barristers.

[13] P. James and M. Seneviratne, "The Legal Services Ombudsman: Form versus Function?" (1995) 58 M.L.R. 187.

[14] *ibid.* p. 188.

should not be more regularly, if not always, investigating the complaint at the heart of the allegation.[15]

(h) Legal proceedings against lawyers

(i) Negligence

A lawyer's misconduct or incompetence may give rise to a cause of action against him or her. For example, a client may be able to sue for breach of contract,[16] breach of trust[17] or the tort of negligence.[18] The scope of negligence liability has been wider since the decision of the House of Lords in 1963 in *Hedley, Byrne & Co. Ltd v. Heller & Partners Ltd*[19] where it was established that a special relationship could give rise to a duty of care in the giving of information or advice, and that there would be liability in damages in such cases in respect of losses that were purely economic. In *Midland Bank Trust Co. Ltd v. Hett, Stubbs & Kemp*[20] Oliver J. stated that the case of a layman consulting a solicitor seemed:

"to be as typical a case as one could find of the sort of relationship in which the duty of care described in the *Hedley Byrne* case exists."[21]

His Lordship held that the authorities which indicated that the existence of a contract between a solicitor and client precluded any action in tort[22] were inconsistent with *Hedley Byrne* and should not be followed.[23] In *Ross v. Caunters*[24] Sir Robert Megarry V.-C. took matters a step further. Solicitors failed to warn

---

[15] *ibid.* p. 206.
[16] Until the commencement of the Courts and Legal Services Act 1990, barristers could not have been sued in contract. However, s.61(1) now provides that "Any rule of law which prevents a barrister from entering into a contract for the provision of his services as a barrister is hereby abolished." But s.61(2) goes on to provide that "Nothing in subsection (1) prevents the General Council of the Bar from making rules (however described) restricting a barrister's right to enter into contracts." The *Code of Conduct* provides, at para. 210, that any barrister in independent practice "must not when acting in a professional capacity enter into contractual relations relating to the services to be provided by him with any person other than his professional client." The rules relating to independence of action, withdrawal from a case, etc. would presumably be held to be implied terms of such a contract.
[17] *e.g. Re Bell's Indenture* [1980] 1 W.L.R. 1217.
[18] See R. M. Jackson and J. L. Powell, *Professional Negligence* (3rd ed. 1992), Chaps.4 and 5 and A. M. Dugdale and K. M. Stanton, *Professional Negligence* (2nd ed., 1989), pp. 138–143.
[19] [1964] A.C. 465 and see Jackson and Powell (3rd ed., 1992), *passim*; Dugdale and Stanton (1989), *passim*; W. V. H. Rogers (ed.) *Winfield and Jolowicz on Tort* (14th ed., 1994), pp. 290–706; M. A. Jones, *Textbook on Torts* (4th ed., 1993), pp. 63–78.
[20] [1979] Ch. 384, approved in *Henderson v. Merrett Syndicates Ltd* [1994] 3 All E.R. 506. Solicitors acting for both grantor and grantee of an option (to purchase the freehold reversion of a farm) carelessly failed to register the option. The grantor subsequently sold the reversion to a third party and thereby achieved the desired result of defeating the option. The executors of the grantee recovered damages from the solicitors.
[21] [1979] Ch. 384 at 417.
[22] *Groom v. Crocker* [1939] 1 K.B. 194, C.A.; *Clark v. Kirby-Smith* [1964] Ch. 506 (Plowman J.).
[23] Oliver J. held that the claim in contract succeeded as well as the claim in tort. The duty to register was a continuing one which lasted to the same date. The six year limitation period in tort ran from the time when the damage occurred, *i.e.* the date of the sale which defeated the option.
[24] [1980] Ch. 297.

a client that his will should not be witnessed by a spouse of a beneficiary and failed to notice that this had happened. They were held liable to the disappointed beneficiary whose bequest failed. This decision was upheld in *White v. Jones*[25] by the House of Lords by a narrow majority.

The position of the victims of incompetence is further secured by compulsory indemnity requirements. Every solicitor must contribute to the Solicitors' Indemnity Fund which provides cover for loss by solicitors arising from claims in respect of civil liability.[26] Every barrister in independent practice must be a member of the Barristers Mutual Indemnity Fund providing cover against claims for professional negligence.[27] Lawyers do not object to compulsory insurance, but there have been complaints by solicitors about the fact that it is a centrally controlled scheme[28] and about the high premiums charged.[29]

Even assuming the client has perceived that the lawyer has done his or her work incompetently, which is itself problematic, there are a number of problems facing those who wish to sue lawyers. First, legal assistance is advisable, but someone whose dealings with a lawyer have been unsatisfactory and probably protracted and a source of frustration and annoyance, is unlikely to relish the prospect of involvement with yet more lawyers. Moreover there may be difficulties in finding solicitors prepared to bring negligence proceedings against fellow practitioners. In order to alleviate this problem, the Law Society, with the co-operation of local law societies, established a panel of solicitors prepared to act in such cases (the "Negligence Panel").[30]

Secondly, there is a special immunity from an action for negligence which attaches in respect of acts or omissions in the conduct of litigation. The authorities have concerned barristers, but the immunity was regarded as extending to a solicitor acting as advocate.[31] The matter is put beyond doubt by section 62 of the Courts and Legal Services Act 1990, which states that anyone who is not a barrister but lawfully provides any legal services in relation to any proceedings has the same immunity as a barrister.[32]

The House of Lords in *Rondel v. Worsley*[33] held that a barrister was immune from action in respect of his or her conduct at trial. The immunity was justified by public policy:

---

[25] [1995] 1 All E.R. 691 and see C. Kessel, "Solicitor's professional negligence" (1995) N.L.J. 499 and 537.

[26] Solicitor's Indemnity Rules 1995 made under the Solicitors Act 1974, s.37 and the Administration of Justice Act 1985, s.9. The Fund is administered by Solicitors Indemnity Fund Ltd.

[27] *Code of Conduct*, para. 302.

[28] D. Podmore, (1980) 7 B.J.L.S. 1 at 5–6.

[29] Solicitors are obliged to divulge information about gross fees from which is calculated the premium for an Initial and Supplementary Contribution for each indemnity period in respect of each separate practice of which the solicitor is a principal. The initial contribution, subject to possible adjustments (*e.g.* discounts for more principals or low-risk work or low claims ratios), requires assessment of the gross fee divided by the number of principals and then a percentage of that average gross fee per principal is demanded: Solicitors' Indemnity Rules 1992.

[30] See above, p. 162.

[31] *Saif Ali v. Sydney Mitchell & Co.* [1980] A.C. 198, 215, 224, 227.

[32] If the advocate is immune from an action in negligence, there can be no liability for breach of any contract: Courts and Legal Services Act 1990, s.62(2).

[33] [1969] 1 A.C. 191. Until *Hedley Byrne* and *Rondel v. Worsley* were decided it was thought that a barrister could not be sued as he or she could not enter a contractual relationship with either the instructing solicitor or the lay client. This old rule of law has now been abolished, although it has been replaced by rules of conduct, see n. 16 above.

"mainly upon the ground that a barrister owes a duty to the court as well as to his client and should not be inhibited through fear of an action by his client, from performing it; partly on the undesirability of relitigation as between barrister and client of what was litigated between the client and his opponent".[34]

In *Saif Ali v. Sydney Mitchell & Co.*[35] the House of Lords held that the immunity extended only to pre-trial work which was:

"so intimately connected with the conduct of the cause in Court that it can fairly be said to be a preliminary decision affecting the way that cause is to be conducted when it comes to a hearing."[36]

It was alleged that a barrister negligently gave advice which led to the wrong person being joined as defendant. The House of Lords held that he was not immune as the alleged negligence had prevented the plaintiff's cause coming to court. The exact extent of the immunity is difficult to define, but it does appear to extend, *e.g.*, to advice as to plea in a criminal case.[37]

The arguments in favour of the immunity are (1) that the barrister owes a duty to the court which transcends the duty to the client and that the necessary confidence between Bar and Bench would be undetermined by barristers' fear of suits, (2) that there should be a general immunity from suit for all participants in a trial again because of the adverse effects upon the administration of justice if the situation were otherwise, (3) that the "cab rank rule" would be difficult to enforce if barristers had to take on clients who could then pursue actions against them, (4) that relitigation of cases is undesirable and the correct method of challenge is via an appeal.[38] These arguments can be challenged on two bases: the first that they are inherently unsound and the second that they are based on "dubious, empirical assertions about the legal process".[39] Zander has indicated that the first basis of challenge includes the arguments that it is not probable that barristers would be influenced to do their work much differently by the thought that they might be sued for negligence, that re-opening a case is not necessarily bad if, *e.g.*, someone has gone to prison because of the negligence of the barrister, that there is little prospect of considerable litigation in view of the many barriers facing a potential litigant, and that no barrister is likely to know enough about a client for the prospect of litigation to have any effect upon accepting a brief or instruction.[40] Veljanowski and Whelan deal with the second basis of challenge, pointing out the lack of an empirical basis for the immunity, since there is no evidence to support the suggestion that a rash of suits would follow if there was no immunity, there is no evidence that

---

[34] *per* Lord Wilberforce in *Saif Ali v. Sydney Mitchell & Co.* [1980] A.C. 198 at 212.

[35] [1980] A.C. 198.

[36] *per* McCarthy P. in *Rees v. Sinclair* [1974] 1 N.Z.L.R. 180 at 187, endorsed by Lords Wilberforce, Diplock and Salmon. Lord Russell and Lord Keith favoured a wider test under which immunity would be extended to all work in connection with litigation.

[37] *Somasundaram v. M. Julius Melchior & Co.* [1989] 1 All E.R. 129, C.A. See, further, Jackson and Powell (1992), pp. 273–280; Dugdale and Stanton (1989), pp. 158–162; Winfield (1994), pp. 103–104; Jones (1993), pp. 45–46.

[38] See C. G. Veljanowski and C. J. Whelan, "Professional Negligence and the Quality of Legal Services—An Economic Perspective" (1983) 46 M.L.R. 700, 711–712.

[39] Veljanowski and Whelan (1983), p. 712.

[40] M. Zander, *Legal Services for the Community* (1978), pp. 134–136.

"defensive" practices by barristers would abound, rather there is evidence that good practice might be encouraged, and, while the prospect of relitigation appears to be the strongest argument, it may be that it has outlived its validity since "the very existence of an appellate framework suggests that the value of finality in judicial decisions is not absolute" and "it is hard to accept the proposition that an instrument capable of reducing negligence will bring the administration of justice into disrepute."It is hard to avoid Miller's conclusion that the "immunity is an anachronism maintained by lawyers for lawyers".[41] Nevertheless, in 1979, the Royal Commission on Legal Services did not favour any change in this area[42] and the Government was convinced of the arguments in favour of the immunity not only to preserve it for barristers but to make it clear in the Courts and Legal Services Act 1990 that it extended to all advocates.[43]

Thirdly, it must be remembered that liability in negligence does not attach simply because a lawyer turns out to be wrong or makes an error of judgment. A lawyer is only liable if the error is "such as no reasonable well informed and competent member of that profession could have made".[44]

Fourthly, a solicitor who has done work for a client and remains unpaid has the right to retain the papers concerning the client's affairs and other personal property, that is a "retaining or general lien," and also a "lien on property recovered or preserved," that is a right to seek the court to direct that property, except real property, obtained under a court's judgment should be available to the solicitor to cover the client's costs in relation to that work.[45] This may cause both difficulty and resentment. If the solicitor declines to act further, the client or the new solicitor may obtain a court order for delivery of the papers on an undertaking to hold them without prejudice to the lien and to return them on completion of the matter.[46] If the client justifiably discharges the solicitor, the Law Society may gain possession of the documents.[47]

(ii) Wasted costs order

A wasted costs order may be made against a solicitor or barrister. Such a jurisdiction as applied to solicitors has been available since 1939.[48] The Courts and Legal Services Act 1990 extended the wasted costs order to the "the legal or

---

[41] D. L. Carey Miller, "The Advocate's Duty to Justice: Where Does It Belong" (1981) 97 L.Q.R. 127, 138. The Court of Appeal's support for the immunity in *Rondel v. Worsley* was met with scorn by the press, see Zander (1978), p. 136.

[42] R.C.L.S., Vol. 1, pp. 332–333.

[43] S.62. See, *Legal Services: Framework for the Future* (Cm. 740, 1989), para. 10.10.

[44] *per* Lord Diplock in *Sydney Mitchell & Co.* [1980] A.C. 198, 220. For an example of a "reasonable mistake" see *Jones* v. *Jones* [1970] Q.B. 576. See Veljarawski and Whelan (1983), pp. 712–717.

[45] *Cordery on Solicitors* (1988), Chap. 8 and *Supreme Court Practice 1991*, Vol. 2, Part 11, section D.3.

[46] The Royal Commission recommended that this should be normal practice without a court order where a solicitor is replaced for any reason. No such reform has been introduced, see *Cordery on Solicitors* (1988), pp. 245–247.

[47] Solicitors Act, s.35, Sched. 1. This power is rarely exercised. The Royal Commission recommendation that it should be exercised whether the client would otherwise suffer has not been implemented.

[48] *Myers v. Elman* [1940] A.C. 282.

other representative concerned".[49] "Wasted costs" are those incurred by a litigant "as a result of any improper,[50] unreasonable[51] or negligent act or omission" by any legal or other representative, and the court must consider that it is unreasonable to expect the litigant to pay them.[52] General guidance in civil cases has been provided by the Court of Appeal in *Ridehalgh v. Horsefield*,[53] which it is anticipated will also apply in criminal cases.[54] The court exercises a discretion at two stages: first in determining whether to provide the legal representative with the opportunity to show cause why an order should not be made and further proceedings will not always follow; secondly, even if the criteria are satisfied, the court is not bound to make an order, but would have to give sustainable reasons for not doing so.[55] One major issue[56] was in relation to negligence. The Court decided that negligence is to be understood "in an untechnical way to denote failure to act with the competence reasonably to be expected of ordinary members of the profession".[57] The Court then decided that the immunity of advocates from suit in respect of conduct and management of a case in court, considered above, does not apply to this jurisdiction. However, the public interest considerations on which that immunity is based are relevant in considering the costs jurisdiction and the Court concluded that it "is only when, with all allowances made, an advocate's conduct of court proceedings is quite plainly

[49] Supreme Court Act 1981, s.51, as amended by Courts and Legal Services Act 1990, s.4 (see also ss.111 and 112). See S. Fennell, "Wasted costs after the Courts and Legal Services Act 1990" (1993) 9 P.N. 25.

[50] This includes conduct which would be regarded as a serious breach of professional conduct and also conduct which "according to the consensus of professional (including judicial) opinion can be fairly stigmatised [as improper]": *Ridehalgh v. Horsefield* [1994] 3 All E.R. 848, at p. 861.

[51] It includes conduct which is vexatious or designed to harass the other side, and the motive for such action is irrelevant. Conduct is not unreasonable simply because it leads to the "wrong result". "The acid test is whether the conduct permits of a reasonable explanation": *Ridehalgh v. Horsefield*, at pp. 861–862.

[52] Supreme Court Act, s.51(7).

[53] [1994] 3 All E.R. 848.

[54] *ibid.*, p. 868.

[55] *ibid.*, pp. 867–868.

[56] Other issues, both procedural and substantive, include the following. (1) A legal representative is not to be held to have acted improperly, unreasonably or negligently simply by acting for a party who pursues a hopeless case, because advocates are obliged to follow a client's instructions after advising against pursuing such a case. However, if the advocate crosses that line and lends assistance to proceedings which are an abuse of the court, that is another matter: *ibid.*, p. 863. (2) Courts must bear in mind the peculiar responsibility of a lawyer acting for people assisted by the legal aid scheme: *ibid.*, p. 864. (3) Whilst the representatives of the applicant for an order may anticipate that he or she will relieve the lawyers from their obligations of confidentiality in relation to privileged communications, account must be taken of the fact that this may not be the case for the other side's lawyers, and the other side is not obliged to release the obligation, which would, in effect, be the case for the applicant: *ibid.*, p. 866. (4) There must be a causal link between the conduct of the legal representative and the wasted costs: *ibid.*, p. 866. (5) Simple reliance on the advice of counsel will not avoid the jurisdiction, although it will be more reasonable to do so in the more specialist cases: *ibid.*, p. 866. (6) Threats to apply for an order must not be used as intimidation in litigation, but notice of a view that the other side's conduct could lead to such an order is acceptable: *ibid.*, pp. 866–867, adopting *Orchard v. South Eastern Electricity Board* [1987] Q.B. 565, C.A. (7) In general no application should be made until after the end of the trial: *Ridehalgh v. Horsefield*, *loc. cit.* n. 42 above, p. 867. (8) Whilst normally the applicant will be one of the parties to litigation, the court may initiate the inquiry itself. Guidance is given as to the nature of the inquiry and then the procedure to be adopted: *ibid.*, p. 867.

[57] *Ridehalgh v. Harsefield*, at p. 862. Thus it is not necessary to establish all the criteria under the tort of negligence.

unjustifiable that it can be appropriate to make a wasted costs order against" him or her.[58]

5. SOCIAL BACKGROUND, ENTRY AND TRAINING

(a) Social background

Lawyers predominantly come from middle class homes.[59] The same is true of law students. The Law Student Survey shows that only a minority of students' parents were engaged in working class occupations and that a much greater proportion of them had parents who had been to university or polytechnic than was the case in the general population.[60] There is some evidence that the system of admissions to law degrees perpetuates the class structure of the legal profession.[61] Most lawyers are graduates[62] and so the social imbalance seen at the academic stage of qualification maintains the social imbalance at the professional stage. Educational institutions are meeting the challenge to broaden the basis upon which students are admitted to law schools.[63] However, the financial demands of qualification are such that it is easier for people from a relatively well off background to succeed.[64]

We turn now to consider gender and race issues in the legal professions. It should be noted that the equal opportunities issues which arise (and with which the policies of both the Bar and the Law Society deal) are not concerned solely with discrimination on the grounds of gender and race, but also, *e.g.*, with sexual orientation and disability.[65] The passage of the Sex Disqualification (Removal) Act 1919 made it possible for women to become solicitors, and the theoretical possibility of women being barristers became a reality. However, women did not enter the professions in significant numbers until about 25 years ago. Women are poorly represented in the legal profession as a whole,[66] and are particularly

---

[58] *ibid.*, pp. 864–865.

[59] See R. L. Abel, *The Legal Profession in England and Wales* (1988), pp. 74–76 and 170–172 and Table 1.21; R. C. L. S., Vol. 2, pp. 57–61; D. Podmore, (1977) 74 L. S. Gaz. 611; Podmore (1980), pp. 30–32, 90–93.

[60] D. Halpern, *Entry into the Legal Professions* (Law Society Research Study No. 15, 1994), pp. 21–24. See also, M. Zander, *The State of Knowledge about the English Legal Profession* (1980), pp. 22–23; P. McDonald, "The Class of '81: A Glance at the Social Class Composition of Recruits to the Legal Profession" (1982) 9 J. L. S. 267 and M. King, M. Israel and S. Goulbourne, *Ethnic Minorities and Recruitment to the Solicitor's Profession* (1990), pp. 32–34.

[61] See Abel (1988), Chap. 18, esp. pp. 271–275 and King, Israel and Goulbourne (1990), pp. 32–34 and 37–52. See also McDonald (1982) and R. G. Lee, "Survey of law school admissions" (1984) 18 L. T. 165.

[62] In 1993–94 64 per cent of admitted solicitors were law graduates and 19 per cent non-law graduates who had taken the C.P.E. conversion course: *Law Society Annual Statistical Report 1994*, para. 8.2.

[63] Increasingly, admissions tutors in many Law Schools are happy to consider applications from people with non-traditional (*i.e.* non-A level) qualifications, such as an Access course, BTec, etc. or no formal qualifications at all.

[64] See below pp. 185–186.

[65] See, *e.g.*, D. Harvie, "Minorities in a recession" (1992) N. L. J. 746 and H. Hodge, "Equal and decent treatment" (1995) N. L. J. 303.

[66] In 1995, 30 per cent of the 66,123 solicitors with practising certificates were women: *Law Society Annual Statistical Report 1995*, pp. 5–6. In 1990, the figures were 23 per cent of 54,734. At October 1, 1995, 22.3 per cent of the 8,498 barristers in independent practice were women: the General Council of the Bar, *Annual Report 1995*, p. 23. See also D. Harvie (1992) *op. cit.*, J.

poorly represented at the upper echelons of both branches[67] and even in academic law.[68] Women are, for example, more likely to remain as assistant solicitors than men.[69] The picture is changing, but slowly. Women now form a large part of the entry to the profession[70] and the proportion of women holding practising certificates as solicitors is consistently increasing.[71]

It is not only in terms of recruitment and promotion that women have faced significant problems. Work practices and ethics adopted by the professions have added to the problems. Considerable attention is now being paid to keeping women solicitors in the profession,[72] if not for reasons of valuing employees, at least for the need not to lose skilled and expensively trained workers. Part-time work, career breaks and returns have been encouraged.[73] It is also necessary to examine maternity and paternity benefits[74] and flexible working systems.[75] These may, though, militate against further progression unless adequate

---

Goodsir, "It's still a man's world" (1992) N.L.J. 1588, U.K. Inter-Professional Group Working Party on Women's Issues, *Women in the Professions* (1990), the Law Society, *Equal in the Law* (1988) and C. McGlynn, "Soliciting equality – the way forward" (1995) N.L.J. 1065.

[67] As at July 31, 1995, 4,213 of the 35, 632 solicitors with practising certificates over the age of 40 were women: *Law Society Annul Statistical Report 1995*, Table 2.4, 337 of the 8,122 solicitors who had been admitted for more than 30 years and had practising certificates were women: *ibid.*, Table 2.6. Of the 26,319 partners at July 31, 1995, 3,954 were women and of the 4,377 sole practitioners, 722 were women: *ibid.* Table 2.8. Of solicitors in private practice with 10–19 years' experience, 80 per cent of men but only 56 per cent of women are partners, sole practitioners or consultants: *ibid.* Table 2.9. of the 222 sets of barristers chambers in London, 12 had a woman as head of chambers: Chambers and Partners' Directory of the Legal Profession 1994–95, pp. 1119–1233. Of the judiciary recorded in [1996] 1 All E. R., woman judges are to be found in the Court of Appeal (1 out of 36), the Chancery Division (1 out of 18) the Queen's Bench Division (3 out of 66) and the Family Division (3 out of 16), but there has never been a female Law Lord. Of the 891 Queen's Counsel in independent practice at October 1, 1995, 57 were women: The general Council of the Bar, *Annual Report 1995*, p. 23. As at October 30, 1995, of the 113 members of the Bar Council, 20 were women (six representing Junior Counsel under seven years' call): *ibid.*, pp. 22–23. See also, C. McGlynn, "Soliciting Equality—the way forward" (1995) N.L.J. 1065. See *Women in the Professions* (1990), P. Marks, Solicitors' Career Structure Survey (1988) and the Law Society, *Equal in the Law* (1988): See 2nd edition of this book, p. 167.

[68] The number of women professors has increased significantly since the last edition of the book, but is still a relatively small number. But note that the only academic to be appointed as a High Court judge is a woman: Hale J.

[69] *Law Society Annual Statistical Report 1995*, para. 2.9. See also Marks (1988) *op. cit.* n. 67 above, p. 9.

[70] The number of women entering universities to read for a law degree has steadily increased and stood at 54 per cent of all students in 1994: *Law Society Annual Statistical Report 1995*, Table 9.4. In 1900, 593 men and no women were admitted to the Solicitor's Roll: in 1990, 309 men and 14 women (four per cent); in 1960, 671 men and 40 women (six per cent); in 1970, 1,712 men and 165 women (16 per cent); in 1980, 2,515 men and 1,023 women (43 per cent); in 1989–90, 1,990 men and 1,739 women (46.6 per cent); and in 1994–95, 2,229 men and 2,466 women (52.5 per cent): *Women in the Professions*, p. 57 and *Law Society Annual Statistical Report 1995*, Table 10.17; of the 1,593 people called to the Bar in 1994–95, 694 were women (43.6 per cent): General Council of the Bar, *Annual Report 1995*, p. 23.

[71] In 1985 the proportion was 14.4 per cent; and in 1995 it was 30.1 per cent: *Law Society Annual Statistical Reports 1995, Table 2.3*.

[72] Significantly more women than men leave the professions, see Marks (1988), p. 1 and *Law Society Annual Statistical Report 1995*, Table 1.3 (the proportion of women solicitors on the Roll without practising certificates is higher than for men: 24 per cent as opposed to 18 per cent, suggesting a higher drop-out rate).

[73] See *Equal in the Law* (1988), pp. 20–21.

[74] In 1995 the figures of solicitors on maternity leave were recorded for the first time, being 31: *Law Society Annual Statistical Report 1995*, Table 2.7.

[75] C. McGlynn, "Soliciting equality—the way forward" (1995) N.L.J. 1065.

protection is given to people taking up such options. With barristers, who are self-employed, a different range of problems arises. These can be more difficult because chambers may not accept the view that they are responsible in any way for the life and career choices of their tenants. This is an attitude challenged by the Bar's 1995 *Equality Code*.[76]

According to a 1990 survey, it is the case, at least with regard to the solicitor's profession, that women earn less and that the work they do is different. For example, on average male assistant solicitors earn 9 per cent more than their female counterparts, although there were significant regional variations.[77] Women are more likely to specialise in matrimonial law, probate, wills and trusts, and domestic conveyancing than men, who are more likely to specialise in company and commercial work.[78]

Although there have been few formal complaints of sex discrimination,[79] there is an acceptance that it is a significant problem and woman and ethnic minorities trainees anticipate discrimination of entering the profession, although few were put off becoming solicitors.[79a] Indeed, sexual harassment and discrimination can cost firms dear in damages and in reputation.[80] The Law Society has a principle of professional conduct outlawing discrimination and in 1995 the Anti-Discrimination Rules came into effect, which requires all firms to have an anti-discrimination policy, with the Law Society's Model Policy applying in lieu.[81] The Code of Conduct for the Bar of England and Wales contains provisions designed to prevent sex discrimination by a practising barrister both generally and in particular in relation to pupillage.[82] Further, the Sex Discrimination Act 1975 applies to employment in the solicitor's profession and to the offer of pupillage and tenancies at the Bar.[83] Such has been the response to a questionnaire which made clear that most women barristers are subject to some form of sexual discrimination or harassment, that the Bar proposes to establish means whereby support can be provided to women, in particular in identified chambers, whilst not requiring women to pursue a complaint.[84] Promotion for women barristers is also of real concern.[85] A Working Party of the Law Society recommended that sex discrimination be a disciplinary offence, that interviewing

---

[76] See General Council of the Bar, *Equality Code for the Bar* (1995), Chap. 5.

[77] See M. Chambers (ed.), *The Legal Profession 1990*, p. 21.

[78] See Marks (1988), p. 18 and Chambers (1990), pp. 20–21.

[79] It may be the case that women are afraid of making a complaint: C. Newman (1990) L. S. Gaz., June 27, p. 39.

[79a] M. Shiner and T. Newburn, *Entry in the legal professions* (1995).

[80] McGlynn (1995).

[81] McGlynn (1995).

[82] *Code of Conduct of the Bar of England and Wales*, para. 204.

[83] Relevant amendments were introduced by the Courts and Legal Services Act 1990, s.64.

[84] The Bar has had an Equality Code since September 1995. Barristers in independent practice must have regard to it: *Code of Conduct for the Bar of England and Wales*, para. 303. The Equality Code is concerned with discrimination and victimisation on a wide range of grounds and provides guidance to stop or prevent unlawful and prohibited discrimination and guidance on harassment. It also has detailed provisions in relation to selection procedures for pupils and tenants so that all applications are considered on an equal and non-discriminatory basis. A chambers selection procedure must be followed and it is recommended that chambers join the Bar Council's pupillage admissions and clearing house scheme. The code is also concerned to ensure that there can be equality of opportunity in chambers, so *e.g.* roles and duties of pupils are to be identified and there must be fair methods for distributing briefs and work amongst pupils. Fairness must also apply to the recruitment of tenants. There is also a requirement for monitoring to ensure compliance and a scheme for complaints, with the ultimate sanction of a reference to Professional Conduct Committee (see above, pp. 168–170).

[85] See the General Council of the Bar, *Annual Report 1994*, p. 16.

styles should be amended to take account of the requirements of the legislation and that the implications of the legislation should be publicised generally throughout the profession.[86]

As regards race discrimination, the Royal Commission on Legal Services concluded that the situation was not satisfactory and that the trends were unfavourable.[87] There has always been a significant number of people called to the Bar from ethnic minorities, but they have usually been overseas residents who then practice outside the United Kingdom. A 1989 survey showed that 5 per cent of all lawyers were from an ethnic minority.[88] The problem of racial discrimination has been acknowledged. The Solicitor's Code of Conduct prohibits race discrimination[89] and the Bar Council and its Race Relations Committee continue to take steps to combat racial discrimination and disadvantage at the Bar.[90] However, the option of dealing with discrimination by affirmative action has been rejected.[91] Despite the efforts that have been and continue to be made, it seems clear that greater and continuing efforts need to be made,[92] so the introduction of the Equality Code for the Bar, including the granting of pupillages, could assist ethnic minorities students who appear to have greater difficulty in getting pupillages and tenancies.[93] Ethnic minorities barristers continue to be poorly represented in the upper echelons of the professions. The 1989 survey showed that only 1 per cent of Q.C.s were from an ethnic minority.[94]

There are few ethnic minorities solicitors.[95] Part of the problem has been that

[86] *Equal in the Law* (1988), pp. 8–9, 17 and 23. The other recommendations made by the Working Party were that the Law Society should press for legislation enabling it to set different levels of practising certificate fees to enable women to retain a certificate whilst looking after children; change its procedures on the granting of practising certificates after a lapse of time, so as to make it easier for women to return after having had children; and adopt a policy to request tax relief for child-care expenses for women solicitors who return to work: *ibid.* pp. 8, 14–15, 16.

[87] R.C.L.S., Vol. 1, pp. 501–504.

[88] General Council of the Bar, *Quality of Justice: The Bar's Response* (1989), pp. 267–268.

[89] See para. 204.

[90] See the General Council of the Bar, *Annual Report 1994*, p. 15 which refers to other work, including the concern about the Bar Vocational Course being discriminatory on grounds of race.

[91] R. L. Abel, *The Legal Profession in England and Wales* (1988), p. 78 and see *Quality of Justice* (1989), p. 267.

[92] The problems at the Inns of Court School of Law in relation to the pass rate of black students is merely an indication of some of the problems, see F. Bawdon "Falling pass rates" (1992) N.L.J. 1501, S. Rogers, "Race bias report falls short" (1994) *The Lawyer* April 19 and "Whitewashing legal linen" (1994) N.L.J. 485.

[93] See above, n. 73 and see Abel (1988), pp. 78–79; J. Morton "Racial discrimination in the legal profession" (1990) 140 N.L.J. 1104–1107, 1146–1148 and 1184–1185.

[94] *Quality of Justice* (1989), p. 267.

[95] Abel (1988), p. 172. The Law Society Annual Statistical Reports 1990 and 1995 reveal the following figures in Table 2.11 and 2.12 respectively:

Ethnic origin	Number		Per cent	
	1990	1995	1990	1995
White/European	37,403	52,817	68.3%	83%
Afro-Caribbean	74	202	0.1%	70.5%
Asian	477	1,250	0.9%	2%
Chinese	98	270	0.2%	70.5%
African	20	93	0.0%	70.5%
Other ethnic origin	40	355	0.1%	1%
Unanswered/refused	4,969	4,878	9.1%	8%
Unknown	11,653	3,763	21.3%	6%
Total	54,734	63,628	100.0%	100%

81.2 per cent of the students enrolling with the Law Society 1989–90 were white European and 79.1% in 1993–4: Table 10.5 and 11.5 respectively.

of racial discrimination, which the Law Society's Race Relations Committee constantly has under review.[96] Further, the Law Society's code of practice prohibits racial discrimination.[97] Although steps have been taken to combat racial discrimination, there are still many problems. A 1990 report concerned with ethnic minorities and recruitment to the solicitors' profession[98] did not make the usual assumption that there is equality of opportunity, but examined the validity of that assumption. It examined the tests set at each stage of professional qualification and considered their effects upon people from disadvantaged backgrounds so as to determine what the barriers are and how they might be overcome both by the individual and the "gatekeepers".[99] There are barriers which are particularly difficult for people from ethnic minorities to overcome at all stages of qualification: the academic stage, the professional stage and when seeking employment. One barrier is that created by class and race prejudice, e.g., prejudice in favour of Oxbridge applicants for articles. Further barriers are created by the tests used at various stages, e.g., for admission to universities which are of such a nature that people who have experienced educational disadvantages, but who are talented, have significant problems in satisfying them. Finally, the candidate faces the barrier created by the method of informal, unstructured interviews for articles, which are not the best way to assess a candidate's ability. Numerous recommendations were made, including less reliance on A-level scores and greater reliance on a "Profile Model" for university admission, less reliance on unseen written examinations in the L.S.F. examination and greater concentration on skills acquisition, and the introduction of a Code of Practice or a Model Interview Guide to minimise the influence of racial prejudice upon employment selection decisions.[1]

Further, one way to deal with discrimination may be highly disadvantageous to the legal system as a whole. Goulbourne pointed to this issue when she said, "the segregation of the profession which the Royal Commission warned against in 1979 continues not only because of historical forces but because many black solicitors and barristers believe that all black firms and chambers are the only way in which black lawyers can make progress within the profession".[2]

(b) Entry and training

Entry to both branches of the profession is typically by entry through a qualifying law degree or passage of a Common Professional Examination (C.P.E.) for

---

[96] See, e.g. its publication entitled, The Race Report 1989.
[97] See, The Guide to the Professional Conduct of Solicitors (6th ed., 1993), pp. 144–153.
[98] King, Israel and Goulbourne (1990).
[99] ibid., pp. 23–24. The method of assessing the barriers is to use the model established by Twining which requires the asking of four questions: (1) What are the barriers to progress beyond a particular stage? Do the barriers operate against members of disadvantaged groups? (2) Who controls entry and exit at this stage? (3) From the point of view of the individual, by what means might each barrier be surmounted? (4) From the point of view of the gatekeepers and of those concerned with general strategy, what are acceptable and feasible means of eliminating or circumnavigating the barriers or easing the passage of individual members of disadvantaged groups in the interests of improved access?: ibid. p. 24, adopting the Twining model: W. Twining, "Access to Legal Education and the Legal Profession: A Commonwealth Perspective" (1987) 7 Windsor Yearbook of Access of Justice 157.
[1] King, Israel and Goulbourne (1990), pp. 1–7 and 23–109.
[2] S. Goulbourne, "The Recent History of Black Ethnic Minorities in the Solicitors' Profession" in King, Israel and Goulbourne (1990). See also Abel (1988), p. 79

a non-law graduate,[3] followed by a vocational educational stage and a period of practice. In the joint *Announcement on Qualifying Law Degrees* of January 1995, the General Council of the Bar and the Law Society made a significant change in what they recognise as a qualifying law degree by moving away from core subjects with model syllabi, specified methods of assessment and minimum teaching hours. The new announcement came into effect for the intake of 1995. It requires that law degrees comply with the "seven foundations of legal knowledge" which will provide the basic academic stage upon which the subsequent vocational courses and continuing legal education and professional development may build. The announcement has an expectation that certain "central and essential features" will be covered to provide "a coherent introduction to the fundamental concepts and the social context which shapes the way in which law develops and is practised." There are no requirements as to methods of assessment or minimum teaching hours, but minimum criteria are set as to the proportion of a student's work-load which the foundation subjects must occupy in a degree. The seven foundations are: Obligations 1, Obligations 2, Foundations of Criminal Law, Foundations of Equity and the Law of Trusts, Foundations of the Law of the European Union (which is compulsory for the first time), Foundations of Property Law, and Foundations of Public Law. In addition, Legal Research must form part of the degree. The new announcement has not been universally well received, not least because the "foundations" are no such thing, but are core subjects described differently but with less prescription as to content.[4] It also somewhat surprising that the professional bodies have introduced a new scheme when the Lord Chancellor's Advisory Committee on Legal Education and Conduct was engaged in a thorough review of legal education.[5] The C.P.E. option has come under considerable criticism for being a very limited initial step in legal education and for encouraging a narrowing of approach to English legal science.[6] The changes to the C.P.E. to comply with the new *Joint Announcement* only go a small way to satisfying such criticisms. Lengthening the period over which a C.P.E. or equivalent is studied full-time is not an option which would appeal to many non-law graduates, whom many regard as welcome entrants to the legal profession.

Entry to the Bar is restricted to graduates, mature students and qualified legal practitioners transferring to the Bar.[7] An entrant must join one of the Inns of Court and complete two educational stages.[8] The "academic stage" is satisfied by obtaining either a qualifying law degree or a C.P.E. pass. The "vocational

---

[3] For an institution to offer a course leading to a C.P.E., it must be approved by the Common Professional Examination Board. The C.P.E. developed from the Diploma in Law taught at the University of Westminster (then the Polytechnic of Central London) and City University.

[4] For a strong criticism of this approach emphasising the detrimental effect it will have on English legal science, see P. Birks, "Compulsory Subjects: Will the Seven Foundations Ever Crumble?" [1995] 1 Web J.C.L.I.

[5] See below, pp. 186–7.

[6] See P. Birks (ed.), *Reviewing Legal Education* (1994).

[7] As to graduates and mature students, see the Consolidated Regulations of the Inns of Court, published by the Council of Legal Education, regs.2, 4 and Sched. 2. Transfer by qualified legal practitioners is dealt with in Part IV of the Consolidated Regulations. Qualified legal practitioners are dealt with in three groups: (a) legal practitioners from other E.C. Member States; (b) former solicitors; and (c) other qualified legal practitioners, that is Northern Irish barristers, Scottish advocates, Hong Kong barristers and practitioners in other common law jurisdictions: *ibid.*, reg. 35. There is also a special entry route for teachers of the law of England and Wales: *ibid.*, reg. 55A.

[8] Consolidated Regulations, Part II.

stage'' comprises the Bar Vocational Course at the Inns of Court School of Law. The General Council of the Bar has announced that up to six other institutions will be validated to run this course as from September 1997.[9] This will mean that more students can attend the course and that overseas students will not have to sit the old Bar Finals Examination,[10] which has few practical elements other than drafting. The Bar Vocational Course ran for the first time in 1989–90, and has been amended in the light of comments by students, staff, barristers and researchers.[11] The crucial change is the introduction and enhancement of skills training and practical exercises in addition to knowledge-based subjects.

Students who complete the two stages, and comply with the keeping of terms requirements,[12] are ''called to the Bar''.[13] They are not, however, entitled to practise unless they complete 12 months' pupillage with a barrister of at least five years' standing, and may not accept instructions until the second six months of pupillage.[14] The costs of entry are high, including not only tuition fees[15] and maintenance, but also dining fees and special clothes. Barristers may not earn enough to live on for years, and payments for work done may take some considerable time to be paid. Discretionary grants are rarely available from local education authorities. However, the Council of Legal Education and the Inns of Court award a limited number of studentships, some further awards are made by the Inns of Court and the Bar Council has a Scholarship Trust which makes grants to assist students and pupils. Further, it is the policy of the Bar Council to encourage chambers to move towards funding pupillages to ensure an income. It was controversially proposed that call to the Bar be postponed until after 6 months' pupillage which would mean few overseas students took the course and that the qualification ceased to be of any value to those not wishing to practice.

Entry to the solicitor's profession consists, first, of an academic stage. In 1993–94 64% of entrants were people with a qualifying law degree.[16] Nineteen per cent entered with a non-law degree and a C.P.E. qualification.[17] The remain-

[9] Whether A.C.L.E.C. will approve these changes is not yet clear. The Bar had not originally realised it needed such approval.

[10] Courses leading to the examination are provided at a number of institutions, primarily the University of Westminster and also some private institutions, including B.P.P. Law School.

[11] For a description of the original course, see Hoffmann J., ''Change of Course at the CLE'' (1989) *Counsel*, November, pp. 13–14. For assessment by researchers, see V. Johnston and J. Shapland, *Developing Vocational Legal Training for the Bar* (1990) and J. Shapland, R. Wild and V. Johnston, *Pupillage and the Vocational Course* (1995).

[12] ''Keeping of terms'' demands the attending of 18 term dinners in one of the Inns of Court: Consolidated Regulations, reg.8. There are some exceptions and some educational alternatives (see *ibid.*, regs.8 and 9), however, dining is an anticipated custom. Its purpose appears to be to enable students to learn from qualified and practising barristers. The dining requirements may be satisfied, in part, by dining in a local Circuit mess. For a proposal of abolition, see R.C.L.S., Vol. 1, pp. 641–642.

[13] Consolidated Regulations, reg. 23. To be eligible for call, the student must also be 21, have completed and sighed the Call Declaration, paid the relevant fee, and have had his or her name and description screened in the Hall, Benchers' Rooms and Treasurer's of the relevant Inn on four days in the term of call: *ibid.*

[14] Consolidated Regulations, reg. 43.

[15] As a consequence of moving towards validation, the Inns of Court School of Law has lost its £500,000 annual subsidy from the Inns and the fees increased significantly to over £5,000 in 1995.

[16] *Law Society Annual Statistical Report 1994*, Table 8.6. The qualifying degree is defined above, p. 183.

[17] *ibid.*, Table 8.6.

der, non-graduates, entered the profession as mature students,[18] Fellows of the Institute of Legal Executives,[19] Justices Clerks[20] or through an entry by transfer, that is having been an overseas lawyer, a barrister, or a Scottish or Northern Ireland lawyer.[21]

Secondly, all candidates, who must be student members of the Law Society, must take and pass a Legal Practice Course at one of the institutions validated by the Legal Practice Course Board of the Law Society.[22] The purpose of the course is to enable its graduates to enter training contracts with the necessary skills and knowledge to undertake appropriate and sufficiently challenging tasks under supervision.[23] As with qualifying as a barrister, one of the main hurdles at the vocational stage is financial. Local education authority grants are discretionary and rare.[24] The cost of tuition fees (generally £4,500–£5,000) and maintenance must be met either from the student's own resources via, *e.g.*, a loan or other support,[25] or by financial support from a future employer. Some solicitors' firms, in particular large London firms, offer assistance with funding a L.P.C. This is likely only to be true of the prosperous commercial firms and not true of a legal aid practice.[26]

Finally, a person must obtain a two-year training contract (formerly known as articles) and take and pass a Professional Skills Course.[27] After admission, solicitors are required to undertake continuing professional development, which will, in 1996, be mandatory for all solicitors admitted on or after August 1, 1965.[28]

The financial demands involved in qualification to be either a barrister or solicitor could have a significant impact on the composition of the professions.[29] It could become all but impossible for people from relatively poor backgrounds unless they are exceptionally able or have very little concern for financial risk. In addition, there is a move to reduce the number of L.P.C. places. On the one hand it is easy to argue that offering 6,922 full-time and 954 part-time places on an L.P.C. in 1995–96, when there were only 4,170 traineeships in

---

[18] Two people in 1993–94: *ibid.*, Table 8.8.

[19] In 1993–94, 113 people were admitted through this route: *ibid.*, Table 8.8. See below, p. 000.

[20] 56 in 1993–94: *ibid.*, Table 8.8.

[21] 432, 97 and 80 people respectively in 1993–94: *ibid.*, Table 8.8. The admission of overseas lawyers is likely to increase as it includes European Union lawyers, see below, pp. 000–000.

[22] At June 1995, some 28 institutions (including new and old universities and one private institution) offered Legal Practice Courses on full-time or part-time study bases. The University of Northumbria at Newcastle is the only place at which the degree and the Legal Practice Course are run together as an Exempting Law Degree.

[23] The Law Society, *The Law Degree Route to Qualification as a Solicitor* (1995), p. 20. The curriculum comprises: (a) the compulsory areas (conveyancing; wills, probate and administration; business law and practice; and litigation and advocacy); (b) optional subjects (which vary from institution to institution); (c) pervasive topics (professional conduct; investment business under the Financial Services Act; European Community law; and revenue law); (d) practical skills (practical legal research; drafting; interviewing; and negotiation and advocacy).

[24] See the Law Society's survey in *ibid.*, between pp. 37 and 38.

[25] Some charities are beginning to support such training, *e.g.*, the Leonard Sainer Foundation. See *ibid.* (1995), pp. 32–34.

[26] See J. Rozenberg, *The Search for Justice* (1994), p. 162.

[27] Five modules must be completed: advocacy and oral communication; accounts; investment business; personal work management; and professional conduct.

[28] It has been compulsory for the more junior solicitors for some time.

[29] Many students enter the vocational stage in unavoidable debt, because of the reduction in value of the grant, and the move towards student loans.

1994–95,[30] is unacceptable and that fewer L.P.C. places should be available, to lessen the disappointment and anger at spending so much money and not going further in the profession. On the other hand, if the number of places were to be reduced there is real concern as to the effect this would have on entrants. Would it create another factor in producing a more middle-class profession? A similar concern is being expressed as the Bar moves towards the validation of its Bar Vocational Course: should only such places be provided as to produce enough graduates for the pupillages, or should more people be given a chance to enter the profession of their choice? The idea that the L.P.C. or the B.V.C. are transferable qualifications is, however, a poor argument to support the provision of a large number of places, though both courses do involve the development of skills which are transferable to other professions and careers,[31] and the professional bodies are attempting to convince non-legal employers of their value. In recognition of this problem, the Lord Chancellor's Advisory Committee on Legal Education and Conduct examined questions of funding and access to the professions. It concluded that there should be no restrictions on the numbers seeking to enter the profession through limiting the number of validated places or controlling the number of training contracts or pupillages; realistic information, on the basis of accurate data, should be provided to students about the opportunities in the professions; law schools should review their admissions prices, and should make greater use of non-normal admission criteria; funding provision should be made for students on conversion courses and the professional courses; there should be a review of professional sponsorship of legal education; and there should be a fundamental reassessment of the funding of law teaching in Universities which produces a more appropriate funding basis.[32]

There is a public interest in this matter, not only in the consequences for the composition of the profession, but also the content of the education in view of the importance of the work undertaken by solicitors and barristers. So, a publicly accountable committee, the Lord Chancellor's Advisory Committee on Legal Education, is charged, amongst other things, with the general duty to assist "in the maintenance and development of standards in education [and] training . . . of those offering legal services".[33] More specifically, ACLEC (as it is known) is required to "keep under review the education and training of those who provide legal services", to "consider the need for continuing education and training for such persons and the form it should take", and to "consider the steps which professional and other bodies should take to ensure that their members benefit from such continuing education and training".[34] ACLEC published two consultation papers and presented its report in 1996. The first consultation paper was concerned with the initial stage of legal education, and the second with the vocational stage and con-

---

[30] *Law Society Annual Statistical Report 1995*, Table 10.7 and para. 10.10.

[31] Some institutions recognise an L.P.C. as contributing credits (usually about 80 out of 120) to a professional Masters degree (e.g., De Montford University, Nottingham Trent University and the University of Westminster). Some are having an L.P.C. recognised as contributing to a different professional qualification (*e.g.* towards the Institute of Chartered Secretaries' qualification at De Montfort University).

[32] The Lord Chancellor's Advisory Committee on Legal Education and Conduct, *First Report on Legal Education and Training* (1996), Chap. 3.

[33] Courts and Legal Services Act 1990, s.18(1). See Lord Griffiths, "The Lord Chancellor's Advisory Committee on Legal Education and the Legal Profession" (1994) 28 *Law Teacher* 4. Lord Griffiths was the first chair of the committee.

[34] Courts and Legal Services Act 1990, Sched. 2, para. 1(1).

tinuing professional development. ACLEC's Report is the first major review of a legal education for 25 years and aims to make changes to legal education which will enable the professions to meet the legal needs of the 21st century. In so doing lawyers must be capable of being flexible and diverse in knowledge and skills, able to compete in domestic and global markets. At the same time, lawyers must continue to contribute to fundamental democratic values, including the protection of human rights and providing legal services for disadvantaged sections of society. ACLEC also recognised the dangers of forcing legal specialisation too early in someone's career. There is, therefore, a proposal for initial joint professional training. Before that stage, ACLEC recognises a law degree as an independent liberal education. This enables the view of one member of the Marre Committee that, if only 50 per cent of law graduates go into the law, there is a matter of concern to be consigned, appropriately, to history.[35] ACLEC, therefore recognises a law degree as an academic subject in its own right, taught for its own sake. Legal reasoning skills do have wide application.

In order to endeavour to meet the often difficult tension between professional and academic needs at degree level,[36] ACLEC wishes universities to have greater freedom to determine what is taught and learned, but to identify certain outcomes which should be achieved and requiring that two years of a three year degree course be spent learning law. Further, to be a qualifying law degree, certain quality standards would have to be met. As regards the graduate conversion course, ACLEC recommends a two part course, totalling 46 weeks, which would have to be taken to be admitted as a solicitor or barrister. This will go some way to addressing the concerns expressed above.

For those graduates wishing to qualify, the first stage would be gaining a licentiate in Professional Legal Studies which would involve studying on a course common to intending solicitors and barristers. After that course, lasting about 18 weeks, students would progress to either a Legal Practice Course (for solicitors) or a Bar Vocational Course (for Barristers). Each course would last for 15–18 weeks. Initial qualification would be possible provided the student also had completed a training period. Students could elect to do a six month general training agreement, but would have to complete either a 12 months solicitor's training contract or six months pupillage with a barrister in independent practice. Subsequent to qualification, there would be an obligation to participate in continuing professional development.[37]

6. Unadmitted Personnel

Most solicitors' firm employ people who are not solicitors but do professional work similar to that of many solicitors. Such employees are often referred to as legal executives, but that title is formally reserved to people who are Fellows of the Institute of Legal Executives (ILEX).[38] ILEX had 21,472 members, including students and members, at December 31, 1994.[39] Whilst a formal

---

[35] Marre Committee, *A Time for Change*, para. 13.3.
[36] See also M. Zander, *A Matter of Justice* (1989) pp. 82–83.
[37] ACLEC (1966).
[38] See Solicitors' Publicity Code 1990, para. 7(a)(ii).
[39] ILEX, *Annual Report and Accounts to 31st December 1994* (1995), p. 2.

qualification is not required to work as a para-legal, the best career route is likely to lie for a person with the ILEX qualification. Registration as a student depends upon satisfying the qualifications requirements.[40] The student then takes Parts I and II of the ILEX examinations[41] and, on successful completion, becomes a Member. He or she will become a Fellow provided he or she is 25 years of age and has had at least five years' experience in a legal office, including two years after passing all the examinations. A Fellow, therefore, has a general spread of knowledge and expertise in a more limited area of work than a solicitor. The contribution which a Fellow may make is highly significant; many Fellows will be as well versed as the majority of solicitors in their area of expertise. Fellows are bound to observe a Code of Professional Conduct. Someone may stay as a Fellow. It is also possible to qualify as a solicitor, with Fellowship being regarded as the equivalent of graduate status for entry to a Common Professional Examination course, and exemption from some of the subjects being available as a result of ILEX examinations passed. A Legal Practice Course must be passed and then a Fellow may be admitted as a solicitor, because the previous practical experience allows exemption from a training contract. The professional status of legal executives has been enhanced considerably.[42] The future may see rights of audience extended to Fellows.[43] Further, the move to a National Vocational Qualification (NVQ) may herald significant changes. This will enable a response to increasing changes in the labour market, which is increasingly seeing graduates entering the para-legal field. NVQ allows a more flexible response to the various existing qualifications of people wishing to become para-legals, involving the setting of standards of competence by a lead body (in this case the Law Society) which must be achieved, most likely through work-based assessments, or a portfolio of evidence of competence, but not ruling out the need for examinations in some cases.[44]

Barristers' clerks have the rather different role in chambers of acting as office administrator and accountant for the chambers as a whole, and as business manager and agent for each individual member. The title "clerk" is, therefore, rather misleading; indeed a senior clerk operates more as a chief executive or practice manager.[45] Chambers have clerks, although there has been no professional conduct obligation on barristers to employ a clerk.[46] The obligation is on barristers to ensure that their practice is administered efficiently.[47]

The clerk manipulates the flow of work in chambers by virtue of the functions of negotiating fees and arranging each barrister's timetable, and his or her

---

[40] They are satisfied by educational achievements, or being a mature student, or attaining the Preliminary Certificate in Legal Studies.

[41] Part I involves study of a syllabus introducing the student to most of the areas of law and legal practice which are encountered in the legal profession. Part II is satisfied by studying for and passing examinations in four specialist papers: three in law and one in related legal practice.

[42] This despite the failure to convince the Royal Commission on Legal Services to adopts its proposals for profit-sharing, enhanced pay for executives with ILEX qualifications, compulsory arrangements for day release and payment for courses: R.C.L.S., Vol.1, pp. 406–417. See also R. L. Abel, *The Legal Profession in England and Wales* (1988), pp. 207–210.

[43] A submission had been made in 1994 to the Lord Chancellor's Advisory Committee on Legal Education and Conduct. As to rights of audience, see above, pp. 000–000.

[44] See ILEX, "The National Vocational Qualification" (1995) *Legal Executive Journal*.

[45] Institute of Barristers' Clerks, *A Guide to the Barristers' Clerk*.

[46] See the General Council of the Bar, *Quality of Justice* (1989), p. 217; above, p. 000. For the original recommendation, see R.C.L.S., Col.1, p. 484.

[47] *Code of Conduct*, para. 303.

relationships, built up over many years, with solicitors' firms. Increasingly, clerks are employed on formal contracts and are paid salaries, rather than receiving a proportion of the fees. Indeed, the barrister's Code of Conduct expects that all staff appointed to deal with practice administration should have written contracts setting out their obligations.[48]

7. Lawyers and the European Community

The Lawyers' Services Directive[49] is concerned with the provision of services by lawyers and enables a lawyer from another Community country to provide any service in connection with legal proceedings in the United Kingdom, provided that he or she acts in conjunction with a British lawyer entitled to provide that service.[50] E.C. lawyers may not undertake conveyancing work for remuneration, but may undertake will-writing.[51] The directive is not concerned with the establishment of EEC lawyers in the United Kingdom, nor with the mutual recognition of diplomas. The latter is achieved by the Diplomas Directive.[52] It applies to people who have obtained a diploma as a necessary prerequisite for taking up a regulated profession in a Member State, and who wish to have the diploma recognised in another Member State where they wish to establish and take up the profession in question. The host country is entitled to demand an "adaptation mechanism" from the professional, which may be either an aptitude test or an adaptation period. As regards recognition of legal qualifications, the United Kingdom has demanded the passing of an aptitude test.[53] In consequence, the Law Society has introduced a test under the Qualified Lawyers Transfer Regulations 1990.[54] Lawyers from most E.C. Member States must take all parts of the test, whereas lawyers from common law countries are required to take fewer, but that reflects the similarity of English law with that of common law countries and its difference from that of most E.C. countries.[55]

In October 1988, the Council of Bars and Law Societies of Europe agreed a Code of Professional Conduct to be applied to all cross-border activities by and between lawyers.[56] The Code asserts that the function of a lawyer in society is

---

[48] *Code of Conduct*, Annex B: *Chambers Administration Guidelines*, para. 3(c). Most clerks used not to be employed under contracts: R.C.L.S., Vol.1, p. 477.

[49] Council Directive 77/249/EEC, which was implemented in the U.K. by the European Communities (Services of Lawyers) Order 1978 (S.I. 1978 No. 1910).

[50] European Communities (Services of Lawyers) Order 1978, Art. 5. See H. Adamson, *Free Movement of Lawyers* (1992), Chap. 4. See also D. B. Walters (1978) 3 Eur.L.R. 265, D. Edward, "The Legal Profession in the Community" in St. J. Bates, *et al.*, (eds.) *In Memoriam J. D. B. Mitchell* (1983).

[51] European Communities (Services of Lawyers) Order, Arts. 9 and 8.

[52] Council Directive 89/48/EEC. See Adamson (1992), Chap. 5 and also H. Eidenmuller, (1990) 53 M.L.R. 604, J. Toulmin (1989) 1 I.F.L.Rev., August, pp. 19–21 and (1990) 140 N.L.J. 1309.

[53] European Communities (Recognition of Professional Qualifications) Regulations 1991.

[54] See Adamson (1992), pp. 48–49.

[55] It is in recognition of the need to have precise knowledge of the law that the directive permits the host state to determine whether professionals must pass an aptitude test or satisfy an adaptation period, rather than that choice being made by the professional in question: Council Directive 89/48/EEC, Art. 4.1(b), see Adamson (1992), pp. 44–45.

[56] The Code of Conduct appears in the professional guides for both solicitors and barristers; see *The Guide to the Professional Conduct of Solicitors* (6th ed., 1993), Chap. 10 and the *Code of Conduct*, Annex 1. See Adamson (1992), Chap. 7 and also J. Toulmin, *Counsel*, July/August 1989, p. 8.

not only faithfully to perform what he or she is lawfully instructed to do, but also that a lawyer ''must serve the interests of justice as well as those rights and liberties he [or she] is trusted to assert and defend and it is his [or her] duty not only to plead his [or her] client's cause but to be his [or her] adviser.'' The general principles identified for lawyers are: independence, free from all other influence; because the lawyer is engaged in trust relationships, personal honour, honesty and integrity; the ability to maintain confidentiality; respect for the rules of other Bars and Law Societies; not entering into incompatible occupations; respecting appropriate limitations on personal publicity; and acting in the client's best interests. The Code goes on to deal with the lawyer's relations with clients and the courts and with other lawyers.

For the future, it is possible that further regulations will be introduced opening up yet further the legal markets within the European Union. It will always be the case, however, that the different nature of the laws within the Member States will present problems and, in the public interest, it will always be necessary to ensure that people representing themselves as lawyers in the jurisdiction of a particular Member State have a sufficient knowledge and understanding of the law of that state.

The reality is that the more significant developments are concerned with the developments by lawyers' organisations rather than the activities of individual lawyers. Thus the progress of multi-national partnerships is likely to be of more significance in the opening up of markets and will more appropriately satisfy the obligations within the Treaty of Rome.

8. CONCLUSION

The various threads in the developments outlined in this chapter have been drawn together by Abel in his writings on the legal profession in England and Wales.[57] He notes that both branches have lost much of their control over the production *of* producers to academic legal education; financial barriers to entry to the profession have largely disappeared and all barristers and most solicitors are now graduates. This development has facilitated a dramatic increase in the proportion of women entrants to the profession, although not of entrants from ethnic minorities and without a significant effect on the class composition of the profession. The monopolies and restrictive practices that enable profession to control production *by* producers have also come under serious scrutiny and challenge. Given the increasing difficulties in controlling their market by limiting supply, lawyers ''have turned to the alternative strategy of creating demand'' but ''have done so slowly, reluctantly and ineffectively''.[58] The expansion of demand for legal services fuelled by legal aid and the country's growing economic prosperity did not itself result from the activities of the profession (and is obviously vulnerable to, respectively, the government's wishes to curb legal aid expenditure, and economic recession).

These developments have led to heightened competition, and, in turn, an

---

[57] Above, p. 115, n. 16.
[58] (1986) 49 M.L.R. 1, 21.

increase in the proportion of lawyers who are employed (in private practice[59] or by government, commerce or industry), the growth in the size of sets of chambers and solicitors' firms, and a decline in the authority of the profession's governing bodies, which "have lost significant power over their members, to both the state and the ever-larger and more bureaucratic units of production, such as public and private employers, barristers' chambers, and solicitors' firms."

Writing in 1986, Abel predicted the continuing growth in overall numbers and in the numbers employed by government, commerce and industry; the intensification of competition in private practice; the loss of solicitors' business to lay competitors; that the Bar would find it difficult to resist solicitors' claims to enhanced rights of audience given the similarity of academic education and professional training in the two branches; and the supplanting of collective self regulation "by both direct State control and bureaucratic controls within the units of production".[60] His conclusion is worth quoting in full:

"Professionalism, in the sense in which both champions and critics have used that concept during the last two centuries, will not disappear. It will persist as both a nostalgic ideal and a source of legitimation for increasingly anachronistic practices, although it will lose much of its power to convince. And it still will reflect the experience of a dwindling elite—some profit-sharing partners in solicitors' firms and the handful of more successful barristers—who will remain largely impervious to State control and continue to dominate their markets and govern their professional associations. But for the mass of lawyers, occupational life will mean either employment by a large bureaucracy, dependence on a public paymaster, or competition within an increasingly free market. Whichever they choose, these lawyers no longer will enjoy the distinctive privileges of professionals: control over the market for their services and high social status. The age of professionalism is ending."[61]

Recent developments have reinforced these predictions,[62] although the extent of government regulation in the Green Papers[63] was somewhat reduced in the White Paper and Courts and Legal Services Act 1990.[64]

There is every likelihood that the future will see growing divisions in legal practice. Private practice, with ever-larger firms increasingly devoted to delivering legal services to commercial clients, will move further away from the public sector, which will increasingly turn to the use of employed lawyers to deliver legal services to the poor. Public sector lawyers will enjoy inferior working conditions, lower salaries and higher caseloads than their counter-parts in private practice. There is an obvious risk that only the less able or the altruistic will be attracted.[65]

---

[59] The "more intensive and extensive exploitation of subordinated labour undoubtedly is part of the reason for the higher incomes enjoyed by principals in the larger firms": *ibid.* p. 28.

[60] *ibid.* p. 41.

[61] *ibid.* See also R. L. Abel, *The Legal Profession in England and Wales* (1988), Chap. 19.

[62] R. L. Abel, "Between Market and State: the Legal Profession in Turmoil" (1989) 52 M.L.R. 285; A. Sherr, (1990) 53 M.L.R. 406 (review of Abel (1988)).

[63] Criticised, *e.g.* by Abel in "Contradictions in the green papers" (1989) 86 L. S. Gaz., March 22, p. 14.

[64] See F. Cownie, in F. Patfield and R. White (eds.), *The Changing Law* (1990), Chap. 12.

[65] See A. Sherr, (1991) 53 M.L.R. 406.

Chapter 4

JUDGES

In this chapter we consider the men and women who are appointed to adjudicate upon such disputes as are referred to a court or tribunal for determination. The term "judge" is used in the title of this chapter in its wide sense to cover all such persons. More commonly, however, the term is used in a narrower sense to cover those who are appointed to adjudicate in the House of Lords, the Supreme Court of England and Wales (*i.e.* the Court of Appeal, the High Court and the Crown Court) and county courts. In addition, some judicial functions are performed by officers known as "masters" and "registrars". "Magistrates" or "justices of the peace" sit in the magistrates' courts (and in some cases in the Crown Court[1]). Those persons who sit on tribunals are normally simply referred to as tribunal "chairmen" or "members," although there are some with special designations, such as the Social Security Commissioners,[2] the Special and General Commissioners of Income Tax, Immigration Adjudicators and the Commons Commissioners.

A. MAGISTRATES[3]

1. NUMBERS AND FUNCTIONS

In January 1996 there were 30,326 active part-time lay magistrates or "justices of the peace".[4] There was provision for the appointment of up to 60 full-time, paid, "stipendiary magistrates" in London and up to 40 in the provinces.[5] In the City of London, the Lord Mayor and Aldermen are justices *ex officio*.[6] Magistrates sit in the magistrates' courts[7] and in the Crown Court,[8] perform certain administrative tasks such as the granting of liquor licences, issue arrest and search warrants and sign various forms for members of the public.

---

[1] When they are known as "judges of the Crown Court": Supreme Court Act 1981, s.8(1).
[2] See above, pp. 211–213.
[3] The major studies are Sir Thomas Skyrme, *The Changing Image of the Magistracy* (2nd ed., 1983); E. Burney, *J.P.: Magistrate, Court and Community* (1979); M. King and C. May, *Black Magistrates* (1985).
[4] *Judicial Statistics 1995* (Cm. 3290, 1996), p. 90.
[5] Justice of the Peace Act 1979, ss.13, 31. See below, pp. 211–213.
[6] 1979 Act, s.39.
[7] Above, pp. 55–63.
[8] Above, pp. 79–85; below, pp. 210—211.

2. Historical Origins of Justices of the Peace[9]

The history of the justice of the peace as a judicial officer can be traced to the Justices of the Peace Act 1361, which provided:

"First, That in every County of *England* shall be assigned for the keeping of the Peace, one Lord, and with him three or four of the most worthy in the County, with some learned in the Law, and they shall have Power to restrain the Offenders, Rioters, and all other Barators, and to pursue, arrest, take, and chastise them according to their Trespass or Offence; and to cause them to be imprisoned and duly punished according to the Law and Customs of the Realm, and according to that which to them shall seem best to do by their Discretions and good Advisement; and also to inform them, and to enquire of all those that have been Pillors and Robbers in the Parts beyond the Sea, and be now come again, and go wandering, and will not labour as they were wont in Times past, and to take and arrest all those that they may find by Indictment, or by Suspicion, and to put them in Prison; and to take of all them that be not of good Fame, where they shall be found, sufficient Surety and Mainprise of their good behaviour towards the King and his People, and the other duly to punish, to the Intent that the People be not by such Rioters or Rebels troubled nor endamaged, nor the Peace blemished, nor Merchants nor other passing by the Highways of the Realm disturbed, nor put in the Peril which may happen of such Offenders. . . ."[10]

The Crown had previously appointed keepers or conservators of the peace (*Custodes Pacis*) with powers to arrest suspects and initiate criminal proceedings: the Act of 1361 gave in addition the power to determine proceedings. In 1362 the justices were required to hold formal meetings four times a year: these became known as quarter sessions. Over the ensuing centuries, more and more administrative duties were imposed by statute on the justices, including such matters as the construction and maintenance of fortifications, highways, bridges and gaols, the fixing of prices and the recruitment of soldiers. The list of provisions to be implemented or enforced became lengthy and burdensome.[11] Indeed, until the nineteenth century, the business of local government was largely entrusted to the justices. Different functions were committed to one, two or three justices or to quarter sessions. The informal meetings of two or more justices out of quarter sessions came to be known as "petty sessions," the forerunner of magistrates' courts.

The persons appointed in the counties were generally from the "gentry". In the eighteenth century, the justices came into growing disrepute. The corruption

---

[9] On the historical development of the office see E. Moir, *The Justice of the Peace* (1969); J. H. Gleason, *The Justices of the Peace in England* (1969); L. J. K. Glassey, *Politics and the appointment of Justices of the Peace* (1979); N. Landau, *The Justices of the Peace 1679–1760* (1984).

[10] This is still in force, apart from the words "and also to inform . . . in Times past."

[11] In 1485 Lambard asked, "How many Justices, think you, may now suffice, without breaking their backs, to bear so many, not loads, but stacks of statutes?": 1 *Eirenarchia* (1581), Chap. 7. F. Milton (*The English Magistracy* (1967) gives many examples of statutory provisions, including one forbidding a man who was not a Lord to wear a cloak that did not "cover his privy member and Buttocks (he being upright)" (p. 9).

of the Middlesex Justices, described by Edmund Burke as "generally the scum of the earth", was such that they were replaced for most purposes by metropolitan stipendiary magistrates. Elsewhere, their administration of the Poor Law and the Game Laws attracted much criticism. In the nineteenth century they lost most of their administrative functions to central government departments and the new, elected, local authorities, the process of transfer culminating in the Local Government Act 1888. At the same time, their judicial functions were extended, with more offences becoming triable at petty sessions, and with the establishment and development of their matrimonial jurisdiction.[12]

3. APPOINTMENT

The Commission of the Peace is a document issued by the Crown setting out in very general terms the functions of the justices.[13] There is one Commission for each county in England and preserved county in Wales[14], each of five London commission areas and the City of London.[15] Justices of the peace for any commission area are appointed in the name of the Queen by the Lord Chancellor,[16] or, in Greater Manchester, Merseyside and Lancashire, by the Chancellor of the Duchy of Lancaster.[17]

The only qualification for appointment laid down by statute is that the person resides in or within 15 miles of the commission area for which he or she is appointed.[18] However, the booklet *Justices of the Peace in England and Wales: Their Appointment and Duties Explained*, published on behalf of the Lord Chancellor, makes it clear that the following will not be appointed:

"(a) a person over 60 years of age unless there are exceptional circumstances;
  (b) a person convicted of certain offences, or subject to certain court orders[19];
  (c) an undischarged bankrupt[20];
  (d) a person whose sight or hearing is impaired, or who by reason of infirmity cannot carry out all the duties of a justice;
  (e) a serving member of Her Majesty's Forces; a member of the Police; a traffic warden;
  (f) a close relative of a person who is already a justice on the same bench."

---

[12] From the Matrimonial Causes Act 1878 onwards.

[13] Justices of the Peace Act 1979, s.5; The Crown Office (Forms and Proclamations) Rules 1992 (S.I. 1992 No. 1730).

[14] See above, p. 55.

[15] 1979 Act, s.1, as amended by the Local Government (Wales) Act 1994, s.1(3).

[16] *ibid.* s.6. The appointment of magistrates is dealt with by a section of the Judicial Appointments Group within the Lord Chancellor's Department. The post of Secretary of Commissions is held by the Permanent Secretary to the L.C.D., and the section is headed by the Deputy Secretary of Commissions: G. Norman, (1995) *The Magistrate* 132.

[17] *ibid.* s.68. The policy of the two offices is almost invariably identical: Skyrme (1983), p. 240. The Chancellor of the Duchy has concurrent powers with the Lord Chancellor on the appointment, removal and residence of justices, entry on or removal from the Supplemental List and records. On other matters the Lord Chancellor has exclusive powers.

[18] *ibid.* s.7. The Lord Chancellor can direct that this restriction shall not apply: s.7(2).

[19] The notes on the application/recommendation form say "a serious offence" or "a number of minor offences including fixed penalties."

[20] Justices of the Peace Act 1979, s.63A, inserted by the Statute Law (Repeals) Act 1989, Sched. 2.

The notes on the application/recommendation form state that certain other classes of person will not be appointed: a person who has a mother or father, son or daughter or brother or sister who in that Petty Sessional Division is a police officer, traffic warden or member of a Special Constabulary; or who has a close relative who works for the Crown Prosecution Service and appears before that Division; or who works, or whose spouse works, for a magistrates' court in that Division; or who is an M.P., prospective candidate or full-time party political agent for a constituency any part of which is covered by that Division; or who works for a police force or Special Constabulary other than as a police officer; or "whose work or community activities are of a kind which would conflict or clearly not be compatible with the duties of a justice of the peace." The person must also be a British subject.[21] There is no property qualification[22] and women became eligible in 1919.[23]

The Lord Chancellor's booklet states that justices:

"should be personally suitable in character, integrity and understanding . . . and . . . should be generally recognised as such by those among whom they live and work."

They are appointed on the advice of Advisory Committees. These were first established following recommendations of the Royal Commission on the Selection of Justices of the Peace of 1910[24] in response to complaints that the Benches were dominated by Conservatives.

There are 105 committees with overall about 2,000 members,[25] generally one for each non-metropolitan county and metropolitan district, the City of London, some of the larger urban areas and each London commission area. Most of the county committees have sub-committees or area panels. County committees are normally chaired by the Lord Lieutenant, the London Committees by Circuit judges. Most committees have eight to 10 members, and sub-committees about six to eight. The term of office is normally six years. Appointments to a committee are made by the Lord Chancellor, on the recommendation of the chairman.[26] Members are almost invariably existing magistrates.[27] Each committee has at least one Conservative and one Labour member; most have a Liberal, and some in Wales a member of Plaid Cymru. It is the practice to check with the party headquarters that they are known supporters. Until 1988, the names of the committee members were normally kept secret in order to keep them free from pressure and lobbying,[28] although the name and address of the secretary

[21] This is a policy not a rule of law: Skyrme (1983), p. 50.

[22] This was abolished by the Liberal government in 1906: Justices of the Peace Act 1906, s.1.

[23] Sex Disqualification (Removal) Act 1919. Appointments do not, however, appear to fall within the scope of the Sex Discrimination Act 1975: see Skyrme (1983), p. 51. The proportion of women to men has increased steadily—from 1:3.5 in 1947 to 1:1.1 in 1996.

[24] Cd. 5250.

[25] 94 advising the Lord Chancellor, and 11 the Chancellor of the Duchy of Lancaster: L.C.D. Memorandum of Evidence to the House of Commons Select Committee on Home Affairs, *Judicial Appointments Procedures in England and Wales* (1995), p. 75.

[26] *ibid.*, p. 76; Skyrme (1983), pp. 44–46. See also B. Cooke, (1984) 40 *The Magistrate* 69.

[27] In 1982, only 163 (8.6 per cent) of the then 1,900 or so members serving the Lord Chancellor, and only six of the members in the Duchy of Lancaster were neither serving nor retired magistrates: King and May (1985), p. 26.

[28] The Inner London Advisory Committee was an exception; membership of the Nottingham Committee was revealed in 1966.

was published. In that year, the Lord Chancellor, Lord Mackay, announced that he had asked the committees to take steps to make themselves known. About half would have done so by the end of 1988, and it would be a requirement for all by 1992.[29] A candidate can be recommended to a committee by any person or organisation, or can put himself or herself forward. In turn, the recommendations of the committee can be rejected by the Lord Chancellor.[30]

The main areas of difficulty have been those of politics and social and ethnic background.[31] The problems here are linked. The official position as to politics is stated in the Lord Chancellor's booklet:

"Political views are neither a qualification nor a disqualification for appointment as a justice of the peace. When making appointments the Lord Chancellor has regard to political affiliations only in order that he may ensure that no bench becomes unduly overweighted in favour of any one political party."

As regards politics, there have been a number of separate strands of thought. Firstly, some people have been recommended for appointment as a reward for political services rather than because of their fitness for the office. This was condemned by the Royal Commissions of both 1910 and 1946–48.[32] The latter noted that there were still "political appointments" in this sense, although their extent could not be stated with precision.[33]

Secondly, the 1910 Royal Commission stated unequivocally that "it is not in the public interest that there should be an undue preponderance of Justices drawn from one political party."[34] It is not clear whether this was intended to refer to the position nationally or the composition of particular benches, but the latter view seems to be emphasised today. It was certainly the contemporary preponderance of Conservatives on the bench that led to the appointment of both the Royal Commissions of 1910 and 1946–48, by, respectively, a Liberal and a Labour government. However, overall statistics kept of political affiliation are largely based on the declared position of each justice at the time of appointment and are thus of limited reliability. There is no policy to maintain "proportional representation" on the benches.[35] Conversely, it is not at all unusual for the Lord Chancellor to refuse to accept recommendations because a certain party is under-represented.[36]

[29] Vol. 499, H.L.Deb., July 20, 1988, cols.1311–1313.
[30] In recent years he has rarely rejected a recommendation on the grounds of personal unsuitability, it being unlikely that he would have information about candidates other than that gathered by the Advisory Committee; recommendations have, however, been rejected on grounds of occupational and political balance: King and May (1985), pp. 29–30.
[31] See R. Vogler. "Magistrates' Courts and the struggle for local democracy" in C. Sumner (ed.), *Censure, Politics and Criminal Justice* (1990), Chap. 4.
[32] Note 24, above; *Royal Commission on Justices of the Peace* (Cmd. 7463, 1948).
[33] *ibid.*, para. 20.
[34] Cd. 5250, Summary of Conclusions: quoted in the 1946–48 Report (Cmd. 7463, p. 4).
[35] Skyrme (1983), p. 58. In 1983 the percentages, based on statements at the time of appointment, were Conservative 41, Labour 28, Liberal 11, S.D.P.1, Plaid Cymru 0.3 and "Independent and not known" 18.7: Skyrme (1983), p. 58.
[36] *ibid.* p. 59. It can prove difficult to find suitable candidates with a Labour background. A survey by the Labour Campaign for Criminal Justice showed that in one in three of 140 constituencies studied, people were unwilling to put their names forward because two in three Labour party nominees were not appointed. Of 1,500 J.P.s appointed a year there were 100 Labour party

Thirdly, the attention may be focused on the political affiliation of *new appointees*. This was emphasised by the 1946–48 Royal Commission, which stated that if after preliminary selection on merit:

"it is found that a considerable majority of the proposed new justices are of one political faith, the list should be revised with a view to seeing whether equally good, or better, nominations can be made from among members of political parties. If the answer is that they cannot, then the original list should stand."[37]

Fourthly, some have argued that political opinions should be ignored entirely.[38] This has, however, been regarded as impractical by successive Lord Chancellors.

Both Royal Commissions recommended that justices be drawn from different social backgrounds. The 1946–48 Report stated that:

"Care must be taken to see that there are persons in the commission representative of various sections of the community. It is an advantage that a justice should have knowledge of the way of life of other classes than the class to which he belongs, and it is essential that there should be many among the justices who know enough of the lives of the poorest people to understand their outlook and their difficulties."[39]

Such surveys as there have been are now somewhat dated, but consistently show a preponderance of professional and intermediate occupations and the under-representation of manual workers.[40] There is no reason to think that the position has changed significantly.

Efforts have been made to increase the proportion of wage earners. In 1968, loss-of-earnings allowances were introduced.[41] The Employment Protection (Consolidation) Act 1978[42] provides that an employer must give an employee magistrate reasonable time off.[43] However, as Lord Hailsham pointed out,[44] the 1978 Act does not oblige an employer to give a magistrate a job, or to promote him or her if he or she has one. It provides no immunity from redundancy. Lord Mackay has indicated that he is prepared to appoint people who are over 60 in order to complement the categories of people on the bench:

nominees, although that did not take account of Labour voters who were not members: *The Observer*, February 2, 1983.

[37] Cmd. 7463, para. 84.

[38] See the dissent by Lord Merthyr and two other members of the 1946–48 Royal Commission: Cmd. 7463, pp. 92–95.

[39] Para. 84.

[40] See Minutes of Evidence to the Royal Commission, Appendix 4; R. Hood, *Sentencing the Motoring Offender* (1972), Chap. 3; J. Baldwin, (1976) 16 Brit. Jo. Criminol. 171; Skyrme (1983), p. 64 (showing that in 1977 8.2 percent of the magistrates were manual workers); R. Henham, *Sentencing Principles and Magistrates' Behaviour* (1990), Chap. 5.

[41] Justices of the Peace Act 1968. See now the 1979 Act, s.12.

[42] s.29. See A. Samuels, (1986) 42 *The Magistrate* 58. A refusal to pay the person for the time off may constitute a failure to comply with the duty: see *Corner v. Buckinghamshire County Council* [1978] I.C.R. 836.

[43] Magistrates who are public employees are customarily given 18 days' extra paid leave to enable them to sit. Many large private firms have made similar arrangements.

[44] (1981) 37 *The Magistrate* 166.

"For example, these days it is very difficult to find people who are in levels of manufacturing industry to go on the bench during their working lives. It is important however that people with that kind of background should be on the bench.[45]

These have been proper developments, but they seem to have had relatively little effect.

It is only comparatively recently that the ethnic background of magistrates has begun to be properly investigated. King and May's Cobden Trust report,[46] based on research conducted with the co-operation of the Lord Chancellor's Department, was in many respects critical. They found evidence of racial prejudice among some members of advisory committees and sub-committees, in the form of negative racial stereotyping. There was some evidence of direct racial discrimination, and considerable evidence of indirect discrimination in the procedure adopted and the criteria applied by selectors. There were no Afro-Caribbean and few Asians among the members of advisory committees. The procedures were inefficient and amateurish, with too much emphasis placed on interview performance, and the selection criteria of "suitability" and "balance" unacceptably vague. While in some areas there had been a significant increase in the number of black magistrates appointed, the proportion on the bench in many areas still fell far short of the proportion of black people in the local community. The number of black people coming forward as candidates was small. In the event, there was no discernible official reaction to the report.

The Lord Chancellor's Department has conducted a national survey of the ethnic composition of the magistracy, based on the figures on January 1, 1987.[47] At that date there were 455 (1.92%) black magistrates out of 23,730 active magistrates; 2.49% (338[48]) of male magistrates and 1.15% (117[49]) of female magistrates were black. The estimated proportions of black people in the general population and in the 35–54 age range (within which magistrates are normally appointed) were, respectively, 4.69% and 3.92%. The proportional rate of appointment of blacks had increased steadily from 1.77% in 1980 to 4.57% in 1986.[50] The report also argued that

"the available pool in the black population from which magistrates can be drawn has been, and almost certainly still is, much smaller than the pool in the general population."

This was based on the points that in 1986 less than half of the black population were born in this country; that the first priority of many immigrants would have been "to establish themselves and their families before being ready to take part in public life"; and that "cultural differences, such as those affecting the position of women in some groups, will have prevented many blacks from seeing

---

[45] Vol. 503, H.L.Deb., January 19, 1989, col. 330.
[46] *Black Magistrates: A Study of Selection and Appointment* (1985), reviewed by R. Pearson, (1986) 13 J.L.S. 152.
[47] Published in (1988) 44 *The Magistrate* 77–78.
[48] 128 West Indian, Guyanese, African; 204 Indian, Pakistani, Bangladeshi; six others.
[49] 59 West Indian, Guyanese, African; 57 Indian, Pakistani, Bangladeshi; one other.
[50] The figures for new appointments from an ethnic minority in recent years have been 4.8 per cent (1991), 4.4 per cent (1992), 5.5 per cent (1993) and 5.0 per cent (1994): L.C.D. Memorandum on Judicial Appointments Procedures (1995), p. 81.

themselves as candidates for the magistracy." The report "illustrated the progress being made in the appointment of black magistrates". In an accompanying statement of "The qualities looked for in a justice of the peace", the Lord Chancellor emphasised that the magistracy

"is open to all eligible persons regardless of race, religion, colour, social class, sex or political opinion. These factors have no part to play in determining personal suitability for appointment. But second only to the requirement that candidates must be personally suitable is the desirability that each bench should include men and women from all backgrounds and walks of life throughout the petty sessions area and thereby broadly reflect the local community."

In view of this, the absence in the survey of any local breakdown of the statistics is a significant omission.[51]

That a political and social balance is desirable has generally been assumed or asserted rather than explained. It is possible to detect three considerations: the interests of potential appointees; the need to maintain general public confidence in magistrates' courts; and the interests of defendants. The first factor lay behind the appointment of the Royal Commissions of 1910 and 1946–48, although the Reports played down what was clearly not a respectable consideration and placed more emphasis on the second factor. For example, Lord Loreburn L.C. said in evidence to the 1910 Royal Commission:

"I regard it as an indignity and an injustice that any section of opinion should be, in practice, excluded from a legitimate ambition, and I think that it is contrary to the public interest that the authority of the bench of justices should be weakened by any widespread suspicion that the members of it are not fairly selected."[52]

The subsequent Report[53] simply took up the second strand of this reasoning. The interests of actual defendants came a poor third. It will of course be a matter of "pot luck" whether a working class defendant enjoys the supposed benefit of a court with one or more justices thought to be better able than the others to understand his or her outlook and difficulties. The respective social backgrounds of juries and justices do not seem to figure significantly among the considerations that affect the defendant's choice between summary trial and

---

[51] See N. Dholakia, (1988) 44 *The Magistrate* 119, arguing in favour of regular ethnic monitoring, a proposal which had previously been rejected by Lord Hailsham. The author also proposed that selection panels be clearly informed of selection criteria, given guidance or training on the effects which generalised assumptions and prejudices about race can have, and made aware of possible misunderstandings that can occur in interviews between persons of different cultural backgrounds. The author argued that it was vital that advisory committees should have black people in their membership. The response in letters to the editor was generally critical: see (1988) 44 *The Magistrate* 123, 172, and see pp. 209–210 (A. Allott).

[52] Minutes of Evidence. Lord Loreburn was caught between the pressure imposed by Liberal politicians and his own feelings that appointments should be made on merit without reference to politics: R. F. V Heuston, *Lives of the Lord Chancellors* (1964), pp. 153–158.

[53] Report, p. 8.

trial on indictment.[54] Lord Mackay has welcomed the increasing proportion of black magistrates on the basis that

"In addition to the special knowledge and understanding of sections of the community which black magistrates can bring to the bench, their presence in a judicial capacity can be an important factor in reassuring black defendants, witnesses and others connected with legal proceedings that they will be treated impartially by the courts."[55]

A study[56] of 160 newly appointed magistrates in three English counties suggested that there were no significant differences according to social class in attitudes concerning penal philosophy, sentencing practice, the causes of crime, court procedure, and the role of the magistrate. It was noted. however, that there may have been a tendency to appoint magistrates with particular views, whatever the social class. There were differences in attitude related to different political background, with Conservatives tending particularly to be more punitive in their penal philosophy. The authors concluded that "although the relationship between attitudes and behaviour is a problematic one, there is nevertheless a good prima facie case for arguing that differences in viewpoint expressed here are also likely to be expressed in some way in procedural and sentencing policies."[57] An earlier English study had not, however, found there to be such a correlation.[58] Indeed, the most significant factor seemed to be the general attitudes of the bench to which a particular magistrate belonged. Accordingly, it may well be that social and political background may neither be perceived to be of significance by defendants, nor actually of significance in affecting the way they are dealt with, although the evidence on the latter point is not entirely clear.

A recurrent criticism has been that the processes of selection are shrouded in secrecy. It is certainly true that the *formal* procedure is clearly stated in the booklet published by the Lord Chancellor's Department. It is also true that the detailed deliberations of the committees are kept confidential: rightly so, given that the debate will concern the personal qualities of individuals. What is noticeable, however, is the lack of general research on how the advisory committees operate in practice. Two exceptions have been the work of Elizabeth Burney,[59]

---

[54] A. E. Bottoms and J. D. McClean, *Defendants in the Criminal Process* (1976), Chap. 4. The research did show that defendants in general had a higher opinion of the Crown Court than the magistrates, for a variety of reasons.

[55] (1988) 44 *The Magistrate* 218, 219.

[56] R. A. Bond and N. F. Lemon, "Changes in Magistrates' Attitudes During the First Year on the Bench" in D. P. Farrington *et al.* (eds.), *Psychology, Law and Legal Processes* (1979), Chap. 8.

[57] *ibid.* p. 141. *Cf.* J. Hogarth, *Sentencing as a Human Process* (1971) (survey of magistrates in Ontario); A. K. Bottomley, *Decisions in the Penal Process* (1973), Chap. 4. By contrast, a study based upon simulated sentencing exercises found that differences of sentence could not be explained by the group composition of "benches" in terms of age, political affiliation, education, sex or length of experience: A. Kapardis, (1981) 145 J.P.N. 289–291.

[58] R. Hood, *Sentencing the Motoring Offender* (1972); *Cf.* Hood, *Sentencing in Magistrates' Courts* (1962), where the author's findings suggested that the social composition of a bench, in combination with particular community conditions, might affect the prison rate (pp. 76–78, 119–120).

[59] Burney (1979), Chaps.4 and 5. See also R. Pearson in Z. Bankowski and G. Mungham (eds.) *Essays in Law and Society* (1980), Chap. 5.

and King and May.[60] In her study of six advisory committees or sub-committees Burney found that only 16 per cent of the committee members were "non-aligned" politically, almost all of them were members of the Benches concerned and few were under 40. The selection of members of the committees was in practice normally left to the committee chairman. The local chairman of the bench commonly played a lead role. Some, but not all committees used interviews,[61] which might be conducted by several magistrates, or by the chairman either alone or with the clerk. The two dominant routes to the bench seemed to be through personal recommendation from an existing magistrate or through some form of "voluntary work" background (churches, chambers of commerce, youth organisations, sports associations, political parties, etc.). The selectors would seek to weed out people of "extreme' views by pointed questions about the "Shrewsbury pickets". People who would be likely to "fit in" would be favoured. Burney's overall description was that selection "remains a largely personal and intimate affair, almost entirely dominated by existing magistrates who can too easily turn into self-perpetuating oligarchies."[62]

In recent years steps have been taken to attract applicants through advertisements in the national, local and ethnic minority press, posters in public places, articles in local newspapers and participation by Advisory Committee members and justices in radio and television discussions.[63] The effect of these initiatives is as yet unclear.

4. UNDERTAKINGS ON APPOINTMENT

A person selected to be a justice must give certain undertakings before being appointed. These are to complete the required training, to carry out a fair share of magisterial duties (normally to sit for at least 26 times a year[64]) and to resign if he or she fails to honour these undertakings or becomes unable to perform the duties of a justice through changes of residence, infirmity or any other cause, to inform the justices' clerk if he or she is summoned for or charged with a criminal offence or becomes a party to civil proceedings, and to inform the Secretary of Commissions of any conviction or court order against him or her.

---

[60] King and May (1985). They examined the selection and appointment system from the particular perspective of the appointment of black magistrates, conducting postal surveys and detailed local studies in five areas.

[61] All candidates are now interviewed (normally twice) by panels of Advisory Committee or sub-committee members: L.C.D. Memorandum on Judicial Appointments Procedures (1995), p. 77.

[62] Burney (1979), p. 73. Similar views were expressed by King and May (1985), Chap. 4, emphasising the key roles of committee chairmen and secretaries. They proposed that the advisory committees and sub-committees should be completely independent of the local magistracy, and include people who know about magistrates' courts, the local community and selection techniques; the secretary should be a local court clerk, trained in selection procedures; and those procedures should incorporate a comprehension test (see Chap. 16).

[63] L.C.D. Memorandum on Judicial Appointments Procedures (1995), p. 78.

[64] In practice, J.P.s are expected to sit more frequently: of 57 Petty Sessional Divisions surveyed by King and May, a majority (39) expected an average of between 35 and 50 court sessions: King and May (1985), pp. 72–73; the Lord Chancellor expects an average annual attendance of 35 half-days, perhaps rising to 40 on the busier metropolitan benches: Circular AC(92)5, set out in (1992) *The Magistrate* 158, 172.

5. TRAINING

Since 1953 it has been the duty of every magistrates' courts committee to provide courses of instruction for justices in their area, in accordance with arrangements approved by the Lord Chancellor.[65] All justices appointed since January 1, 1966[66] have been required to attend a course of basic training. The current arrangements[67] require newly appointed magistrates to attend an Induction Course, normally within three months of the date of appointment, before sitting to adjudicate in court. They will be given instruction on the obligations imposed by the judicial oath, human awareness, including awareness of the different ethnic, cultural and religious backgrounds of defendants and witnesses, the structure of the magistrates' courts system, the adversarial nature of the criminal trial, and an introduction to the operation of the criminal process. They will attend court as observers and participate in a series of practical exercises covering a bail application, mode of trial determination, a determination of guilt or innocence, and sentencing. Year 1 of Basic Training comprises sitting in court, visits to institutions (the probation service, an adult prison, a young offenders institution) (6 hours) and further training courses (12 hours). Years 2 and 3 each require four hours' training.

Justices appointed after January 1, 1980 have also been required to undertake Refresher Training.[68] The commitment is for 12 hours' training every three years. There is no complete prescribed syllabus, but there must be training in chairmanship and there is likely to be training for the Crown Court. There is a list of approved topics. In addition there are courses for justices appointed to youth court or family court panels.[69] From 1986, further training (12 hours every three years) has been compulsory for magistrates on each of these panels.[70] From January 1, 1996, no magistrate may take the chair unless he or she has taken a fully recognised Chairmanship Course based on the Judicial Studies Board syllabus within the previous six years.[71]

The organisation of the courses is in the hands of Training Officers who are

---

[65] See now the Justice of the Peace Act 1979, s.63.

[66] See *The Training of Justices of the Peace in England and Wales* (Cmnd. 2856, 1967) (White Paper). The Lord Chancellor was assisted from 1974 by an Advisory Committee on Training, chaired by Boreham J. This replaced a National Advisory Council which had been set up to consider the introduction of compulsory training. The Committee was absorbed into the Judicial Studies Board (see below, pp. 238–239) with effect from 1985. The Board's functions with respect to magisterial training are discharged by its Magisterial Committee (see the *Judicial Studies Board Report for 1991–1995* (1995), Chap 5); its function in this context is to supervise the training, not (except in the case of stipendiary magistrates) to perform it.

[67] See the looseleaf *Handbook for the Training of Magistrates* published by the Judicial Studies Board. The syllabus has been completely revised by the Board's Magisterial Committee.

[68] *ibid.* The requirement is operative to the age of 65, or, for those appointed after January 1, 1990, the retiring age of 70.

[69] For example, there has been a substantial programme of training in respect of the Children Act 1989.

[70] L.C.D. Circular MCC (86) 3 ((1986) 42 *The Magistrate* 124).

[71] (1991) *The Magistrate* 139–142; (1992) *The Magistrate* 86; E. Ralphs and G. Norman, (1995) *The Magistrate* 58. See *R. v. Brent JJ., ex p. Richards, The Times,* December 3, 1992, where a decision that the applicant had failed chairmanship training sessions and would not be allowed to take the chair in court was held to be invalid as being unfair and perverse on the facts.

responsible to the Training Committee of the magistrates' courts committees. Most are justices' clerks, although the net is spread more widely for tutors.[72]

Within the limits laid down by the Lord Chancellor there is in fact considerable scope for local variation.[73] There is no clear picture of the effectiveness of the training provided.[74] The Judicial Studies Board Magisterial Committee is responsible for monitoring training; the Deputy Secretary of Commissions (Training) is an *ex officio* member of the Committee and has the right to visit all Training Committees and report back. However, the Board has stated it does not have the resources to undertake the tasks of monitoring and inspection effectively.[75] The Committee has also produced a series of guidance notes for the use of magistrates on structured decision-making.[76]

The training programmes are not designed to turn magistrates into "experts": the best form of training is regarded as experience on the bench. The work of Bond and Lemon[77] suggests that experience is more likely than training to modify the attitudes of newly-appointed magistrates, although neither has much effect in changing previous attitudes on penal policy.

6. CONDUCT AND REMOVAL

A justice of the peace may be removed by the Lord Chancellor.[78] No grounds are specified in the Act. The Lord Chancellor also has power to direct that a justice be transferred to the "supplemental list" if he is satisfied either:

> "(a) that by reason of the justice's age or infirmity or other like cause it is expedient that he should cease to exercise judicial functions as a justice for that area, or
> (b) that the justice declines or neglects to take a proper part in the exercise of those functions."[79]

Justices are also automatically transferred to the supplemental list on reaching the age of 70, or, in the case of a justice who holds or who has held high judicial office, 75.[80] A justice who is on the list may not act as a justice except to authenticate a signature or written declaration, or to give a certificate of facts within his or her knowledge or of his or her opinion as to any matter.[81] He or she may, however, be authorised by the Lord Chancellor to sit in the Crown Court up to the age of 72.

In practice, a justice would only be removed for good cause. Most who leave office have to do so because they are unable to fulfil their share of the work or

---

[72] J. W. Raine, *Local Justice* (1989), pp. 78–79.
[73] See Burney (1979), Chap. 12.
[74] For a critical view, see Skyrme (1983), p. 80.
[75] *Judicial Studies Board Report for 1991–1995* (1995), pp. 20, 21.
[76] *Judicial Studies Board Report for 1983–1987* (1988), paras.12.8–12.15.
[77] *op. cit.* n. 56 above.
[78] Justices of the Peace Act 1979, s.6.
[79] *ibid.* 8(4).
[80] *ibid.* s.8(2).
[81] *ibid.* s.10.

because they move outside the area.[82] In relation to misbehaviour, the "overriding consideration" is that "public confidence in the administration of justice may be preserved."[83] Justices have been removed if they or a spouse have been convicted of an offence, although a conviction for a minor motoring offence will lead to a reprimand rather than suspension or removal. Convictions for drunken driving have in recent years led to suspension during the period of disqualification rather than removal. Justices have also been removed for refusing to apply a law he or she has found distasteful,[84] and for demonstrating outside her own courthouse in support of a defendant on trial inside.[85] Allegations of incapacity or misbehaviour are normally referred to the local Advisory Committee for investigation: if they conclude that the justice should be removed, that is reported to the Lord Chancellor. If the justice does not accept the committee's finding there is then a further inquiry by the Secretary of Commissions. The justice may be interviewed. A recent case shows, however, that the Committee may not permit the justice to appear before them in person and may act on allegations of which he or she is not fully informed.[86] On three occasions in the 1940s the improper conduct of particular court proceedings led to an inquiry, and on one occasion Lord Dilhorne conducted a private inquiry into a lenient sentence imposed by three magistrates.[87]

7. DISQUALIFICATION

Justices are subject to the same common law rules as to disqualification for interest or bias as other judicial officers.[88] In addition, they are expressly dis-

---

[82] Each year, about 1 per cent of all justices on the active list are required to resign for the first reason, and 1 per cent for the second: Skyrme (1983), p. 153.

[83] *ibid.* p. 154.

[84] Colonel Delmer Davies-Evans, who disapproved of certain regulations governing the use of petrol, was removed in 1947 (see Skyrme (1983), pp. 156–7). A Welsh justice who stated that she was not prepared to impose penalties on people who, non-violently, broke laws which she considered unjust to the Welsh language, resigned in 1972: R. Pearson (*op. cit.* n. 59), pp. 89–90; see also Lord Hailsham, (1972) 28 *The Magistrate* 132–134: in a similar case, Lord Gardiner required a Welsh magistrate to resign. A number of magistrates resigned rather than enforce the community charge.

[85] Her application for judicial review of the decision was rejected: *The Times*, September 25, 1985; (1985) 135 N.L.J. 976; Lord Hailsham, (1985) 41 *The Magistrate* 149.

[86] *L. A. G. Bull.*, April 1983, pp. 9–12 (two magistrates removed on account of an "adulterous association", "conducted indiscreetly in a manner likely to give rise to scandal").

[87] Skyrme (1983), pp. 168–169.

[88] Below, p. 248. For cases concerning justices see *R. v. Altrincham JJ., ex p. Pennington* [1975] Q.B. 549; *R. v. Smethwick JJ., ex p. Hands, The Times*, December 4, 1980 (decision on allegation of statutory nuisance against local authority quashed because one of the justices was the wife of the former chairman of the housing committee); *R. v. Liverpool City JJ., ex. p. Topping* [1983] 1 W.L.R. 119; *R. v. Weston-super-Mare JJ., ex p. Shaw* [1987] Q.B. 640 (magistrates' knowledge of other outstanding charges against the defendant: see R. Stevens, (1986) 150 J.P.N. 788; (1986) 150 J.P.N. 805); *R. v. Metropolitan Stipendiary Magistrate, ex p. Gallagher* (1972) 136 J.P. 80; *R. v. Birmingham Magistrates' Court, ex p. Robinson* (1986) 150 J.P. 1 (see J. N. Spencer, (1986) 150 J.P.N. 307); *R. v. Downham Market Magistrates' Court, ex p. Nudd* (1988) 152 J.P. 511 (see N. A. McKittrick, (1988) 152 J.P.N. 643) (magistrates' knowledge of defendant's previous record); *R. v. Cambridge JJ., ex p. Yardline Ltd and Bird* [1990] Crim.L.R.733 (member of Bench employed as consulting surveyor by local authority conducting prosecution for demolition of listed building); *R. v. Romsey JJ., ex p. Gale* (1992) 156 J.P.567 (notes of concluding remarks prepared before all evidence heard); *R. v. Marylebone Magistrates' Court, ex p. Perry* (1992) 156 J.P.696 (magistrate signed warrants while listening to evidence); *R. v. Eley JJ., ex p. Burgess* (1993) 157 J.P.484; *R. v. Marylebone Magistrates' Court, ex p. Joseph, The Times*, May 7, 1993.

qualified from acting in a case involving a local authority if they are a member of that authority.[89] A celebrated case where a magistrate was sufficiently incautious as to admit actual bias was *R. v. Bingham JJ., ex p. Jowitt*.[90] The chairman of a bench hearing a speeding case, where the only evidence was that of the motorist and a police constable, said:

> "Quite the most unpleasant cases that we have to decide are those where the evidence is a direct conflict between a police officer and a member of the public. My principle in such cases has always been to believe the evidence of the police officer, and therefore we find the case proved."

The conviction was quashed.

8. LEGAL LIABILITY

A justice of the peace (or a justices' clerk exercising the functions of a single justice) enjoys a statutory immunity from any action for damages where he or she has acted in the execution of his or her duty and within jurisdiction. Where a justice (or clerk) has acted outside jurisdiction, but in the purported execution of his or her duty, an action will only lie if he or she has acted in bad faith.[91] The position is now similar to that of judges of superior courts.[92] A justice or justices' clerk may be indemnified out of local funds for the expenses of defending proceedings, including any damages awarded against him or her. A justice or justices' clerk who has acted reasonably and in good faith is entitled to an indemnity.[93]

9. JUSTICES' CLERKS[94]

Traditionally, the justices' clerk was both in charge of the administration of the magistrates' court and its chief legal advisor. Originally the clerks were the

[89] Justices of the Peace Act 1979, s.64, as amended. For the rules relating to disqualification of licensing justices see the Licensing Act 1964, s.193 and *R. v. Barnsley Justices* [1960] 2 Q.B. 167.

[90] *The Times*, July 3, 1974.

[91] Justices of the Peace Act 1979, ss.44, 45, substituted by the Courts and Legal Services Act 1990, s.108. On the previous provisions see L. A. Sheridan, (1951) 14 M.L.R. 267; D. Thompson, (1958) 21 M.L.R. 517; "Suing the Beaks" (1990) 154 J.P.N. 212.

[92] See below, pp. 247–248. The Court of Appeal had stated the law of justices' immunity in similar broad terms in *Sirros v. Moore* [1975] Q.B. 118, but that was disapproved by the House of Lords in *In re McC (A Minor)* [1985] A.C. 528, holding that malice and lack of cause did not have to be established where an act was done outside jurisdiction. Following the award of damages against justices in a series of cases where they had acted outside jurisdiction (*In re McC (A Minor)*; *R. v. Waltham Forest JJ., ex p. Solanke* [1986] Q.B. 983; *R. v. Manchester City Magistrates' Court, ex p. Davies (No. 2)* [1989] Q.B. 631), the Lord Chancellor acceded to pressure from the Magistrates' Association in favour of broadening the immunity.

[93] 1979 Act, s.53, to be amended by the Criminal Procedure and Investigations Bill 1996, cl. 65. This will provide that in criminal matters there is an entitlement to an indemnity unless bad faith is proved.

[94] K. C. Clarke, [1964] Crim. L.R. 620, 697; P. Darbyshire, (1980) 144 J.P.N., 186, 201, 219, 233; P. Darbyshire, *The Magistrates' Clerk* (1984); Justices' Clerks' Society, *Administering Magistrates' Courts: The Role of the Justices Clerk* (1989); H. McLaughlin, (1990) 30 Brit. J. Criminol. 358.

personal clerks to individual justices or benches; subsequently, they came to be appointed by the magistrates' courts committees subject to the approval of the Lord Chancellor. In 1989 there were 285 clerkships in England and Wales. Of the 277 members of the Justices' Clerks' Society, 150 were solicitors, 119 barristers and eight qualified by experience.[95]

Significant changes to the administration of magistrates' courts were effected by the Police and Magistrates' Courts Act 1994.[96] Each magistrates' courts committee must now appoint a justices' chief executive from a short list of one or more persons approved by the Lord Chancellor.[97] A person may not be appointed unless he or she is eligible for appointment as a justices' clerk.[98] The chief executive acts as clerk to the committee, and, subject to the committee's directions, carries on the day-to-day administration of the magistrates' courts for the committee's area; he or she must make arrangements for discussions relating to law, practice and procedure among the justices' clerks for the area.[99] The committee also appoints justices' clerks, from a short list approved by the Lord Chancellor,[1] and more than one may be appointed for any petty sessions area. The Lord Chancellor's approval is also required for any decision to increase the number of justices' clerks in a petty sessions area or to have more than one in a new area, or for the removal of the clerk from an area where the magistrates for the area do not consent.[2] The committee must consult the magistrates for a petty sessions area before the appointment or removal of the clerk for the area.[3] To be eligible for appointment as a justices' clerk, a person must have a five-year magistrates' courts qualification,[4] or then be or have previously been a justices' clerk; or be a barrister or solicitor who has served for not less than five years as assistant to a justices' clerk.[5] Justices' chief executives and justices' clerks are employed under a contract of service, except that existing clerks continue to hold office during the pleasure of the magistrates' courts committee concerned.[6] The committee may employ such other staff on such terms as it thinks fit.[7]

The justices' chief executive is the head of what may be a large staff. This will include one or more justices' clerk and a number of assistants. The functions of a justices' clerk include giving advice to justices on law, practice or procedure; furthermore, rules may be made enabling things authorised to be done by a J.P. to be done instead by a justices' clerk or an assistant.[8] Categories of staff include court clerks, general administrative and clerical staff, staff employed on accounts and financial matters and ushers. As from October 1,

---

[95] (1989) 45 The Magistrate 34.
[96] See above, p. 60–62.
[97] 1979 Act, s.24D, inserted by the 1994 Act, s.75. The procedure is prescribed by the Justices' Chief Executives and Justices' Clerks (Appointment) Regulations 1995 (S.I. 1995 No. 686).
[98] ibid.. See below.
[99] ibid., s.24E, inserted by the 1994 Act, s.75.
[1] See n. 97 above.
[2] ibid., s.25, substituted by the 1994 Act, s.76.
[3] ibid.
[4] i.e. a right of audience in all magistrates' courts for five years: Courts and Legal Services Act 1990, s.71.
[5] 1979 Act, s.26, as amended by the 1990 Act, and the 1994 Act, Sch.8, para. 10.
[6] 1979 Act, s.26A, inserted by the 1994 Act, s.77.
[7] 1979 Act, s.27(6), inserted by the 1994 Act, Sch.8, para. 11(3).
[8] 1979 Act, s.28(1), (1A), (3), (1A) as inserted by the 1990 Act, s.117, and amended by the 1994 Act, Sch.8, para. 12. See below, p. 207.

1980, a person may not act as a court clerk unless he or she possesses one of a series of prescribed qualifications.[9] These include being qualified for appointment as a justices' clerk, being a barrister or solicitor, possessing a certificate of competence or a training certificate granted by a magistrates' courts committee, or holding a "Diploma in Magisterial Law".[10] In 1995, there were about 1,200 court clerks working in some 700 courts.[11]

The introduction of new arrangements for the line management of the courts necessitated an express guarantee of "judicial independence". Section 30A of the 1979 Act[12] provides that when exercising specified legal functions[13] or giving advice to justices of the peace in an individual case, a justices' clerk is not "subject to the direction of the magistrates' courts committee, the justices' chief executive or any other person" and any member of the committee's staff is not subject to the direction of the committee or the chief executive when acting as such. Furthermore, a person may not be appointed both as justices' chief executive and as justices' clerk unless the Lord Chancellor has agreed that he or she may hold both appointments, and where there is a joint appointment, he or she may not exercise any functions as justices' clerk unless authorised by the magistrates' courts committee (either generally or in a particular case).[14] The guarantee of independence as enshrined in the new section 30A of the 1979 Act was criticised in the House of Lords as being too narrow, having no application to such matters as "the training of justices, to bench meetings or even remarks made when justices assemble for a day's duties."[15]

The justices' clerk may grant but not refuse legal aid. Under the Justices Clerks Rules 1970[16] a justices' clerk may perform a number of functions otherwise exercisable by a single justice, such as the issuing of a summons, adjourning a hearing with the consent of prosecutor and accused, asking the accused whether he or she pleads guilty or not guilty and fixing or setting aside a date, time and place for the trial of an information. Similarly, an information may be laid before a justice or a justices' clerk. A clerk may delegate to an assistant most of the matters delegated to him or her.[17]

One of the issues that has caused problems since the 1940s has been the role of the court clerk in magistrates' court proceedings.[18] The clerk's function is to

[9] The Justices' Clerks (Qualifications of Assistants) Rules 1979, S.I. 1979 No. 570, as amended by S.I. 1980 No. 1897 and S.I. 1992 No. 1834.

[10] Courses for such a diploma are run by four universities. The Government has rejected, apparently on financial grounds, a proposal that only those with a professional qualification be permitted to advise in court: (1985) 149 J.P.N. 721; (1987) 151 J.P.N. 1; J.C.S., *Administering Magistrates' Courts* (1989), Chap. 12. Low salaries, particularly in comparison with the Crown Prosecution Service, have led to great difficulties in recruiting and retaining qualified clerks: (1988) 152 J.P.N. 402; C. Clegg, (1988) 44 *The Magistrate* 211.

[11] *Working for Justice: A Career for Professionals in the Magistrates' Courts Service* (LCD, 1995).

[12] Inserted by the 1994 Act, s.78.

[13] *i.e.* functions conferred by rules made under the 1978 Act s.28(1),(1A), above, p. 206.

[14] 1979 Act, s.24D(6), (7), inserted by the 1994 Act, s.75.

[15] See S. Baker and J. English, *A Guide to the Police and Magistrates' Courts Act 1994* (1994), p. 115. for earlier criticism on this point, see M. J. Friel, (1993) 157 J.P.N. 712.

[16] S.I. 1970 No. 231, as amended.

[17] *Ibid.*, r.4, inserted by the Magistrates' Courts (Miscellaneous Amendments) Rules 1993 (S.I. 1993 No. 1183). Previously, judicial functions could not be delegated: *R. v. Gateshead JJ., ex p. Tesco Stores Ltd* [1981] Q. B. 470; *R. v. Manchester Stipendiary Magistrate, ex p. Hill* [1983] 1 A.C. 328. See (1992) 156 J.P.N. 435.

[18] The court clerk has been described as the "key worker in setting the tone of the courtroom atmosphere": H. Parker, M. Casburn and D. Turnbull, *Receiving Juvenile Justice* (1981), p. 48.

advise on law and procedure, but not to participate in the decision on the facts. In *R. v. East Kerrier JJ., ex p. Mundy*[19] Lord Goddard C.J. stated that the clerk should not retire with the justices as a matter of course but should wait to be sent for should advice on a point of law be needed. Otherwise, observers might conclude that the clerk was influencing the justices on questions of fact, and this would constitute a breach of the principle that justice must be seen to be done. This apparently caused "alarm and despondency" in some quarters,[20] somewhat to Lord Goddard's surprise, and this led to some further "clarification,"[21] or back-pedalling (depending on one's point of view). At the same time Lord Goddard C.J. threatened that justices who knowingly disobeyed the Divisional Court's directions would be reported to the Lord Chancellor.[22] Since then the trend has been for emphasis to be placed increasingly on the point that lay justices must be given proper professional advice, and less on the need to avoid the appearance that the clerk might have given an opinion on the facts.[23] A Practice Direction was issued in 1981 by Lord Lane C.J., with the concurrence of the President of the Family Division[24]:

1. "A justices' clerk is responsible to the justices for the performance of any of the functions set out below by any member of his staff acting as court clerk[25] and may be called in to advise the justices even when he is not personally sitting with the justices as clerk to the court.

2. It shall be the responsibility of the justices' clerk to advise the justices, as follows: (a) on questions of law or of mixed law and fact[26]; (b) as to matters of practice and procedure.

3. If it appears to him necessary to do so, or he is so requested by the justices, the justices' clerk has the responsibility to (a) refresh the justices' memory as to any matter of evidence and to draw attention to any issues[27] involved in the matters before the court, (b) advise the justices generally on the range of penalties which the law allows them to impose and on any guidance relevant to the choice of penalty provided by the law, the decisions of the superior courts or other authorities.[28] If no

---

[19] [1952] 2 Q.B. 719.

[20] (1953) 10 *The Magistrate* 65.

[21] *R. v. Welshpool JJ., ex p. Holley* [1953] 2 Q.B. 403 (justices can invite the clerk to join them as they retire to advise on a point of law; the fact that he remains while the facts are discussed not sufficient to invalidate their decision); *Practice Note (Justices' Clerks)* [1953] 1 W.L.R. 1416.

[22] *R. v. Barry JJ., ex p. Nagi Kasim* [1953] 1 W.L.R. 1320, 1322.

[23] N. Crampton, (1979) 129 N.L.J. 208; *R. v. Uxbridge Magistrates' Court, ex p. Smith* (1985) 149 J.P. 620 (no objection where the clerk left court to advise the justices, who had retired, that certain legal submissions had been erroneous: criticised by A. Heaton-Armstrong, (1986) 150 J.P.N. 340, 357); *cf. R. v. Bingham JJ., ex p. Bell*, Unreported, discussed by Heaton-Armstrong, *op. cit.* and *R. v. Eccles JJ., ex p. Fitzpatrick* (1989) 89 Cr.App.R. 324 (certiorari granted where there was a reasonable suspicion of improper influence by the clerk. For the clerk's view, see A. Turner, (1992) 156 J.P.N. 723). See also the joint statement by the Magistrates' Association and the Justices' Clerks' Society: (1975) 31 *The Magistrate* 4.

[24] *Practice Direction (Justices: Clerk to Court)* [1981] 1 W.L.R. 1163. See B. Harris, (1981) 145 J.P.N. 403. Some of these points as to the functions of a justices' clerk are also made in the Justices of the Peace Act 1979, s.28(3); it is stated that this subsection is not exhaustive (subs. (4)).

[25] The implication is that these rules apply to all court clerks.

[26] See, *e.g. R. v. Consett JJ., ex p. Postal Bingo Ltd* [1967] 2 Q.B. 9.

[27] This is regarded as referring to issues of fact and evidence, and not issues of law or mixed law and fact: *R. v. Uxbridge Magistrates' Court, ex p. Smith* (1985) 149 J.P. 620.

[28] See (1976) 140 J.P.N. 496.

request for advice has been made by the justices, the justices' clerk shall discharge his responsibility in court in the presence of the parties.

4. The way in which the justices' clerk should perform his functions should be stated as follows. (a) The justices are entitled to the advice of their clerk when they retire in order that the clerk may fulfil his responsibility outlined above. (b) Some justices may prefer to take their own notes of evidence. There is, however, no obligation on them to do so. Whether they do so or not, there is nothing to prevent them from enlisting the aid of their clerk and his notes if they are in any doubt as to the evidence which has been given.[29] (c) If the justices wish to consult their clerk solely about the evidence or his notes of it, this should ordinarily, and certainly in simple cases, be done in open court. The object is to avoid any suspicion that the clerk has been involved in deciding issues of fact.

5. For the reasons stated in the practice direction of January 15, 1954, *Practice Note (Justices' Clerks)* [1954] 1 W.L.R. 213, which remains in full force and effect, in domestic proceedings it is more likely than not that the justices will wish to consult their clerk. In particular, where rules of court require the reasons for their decision to be drawn up in consultation with the clerk, they will need to receive his advice for this purpose.''

If justices summon the clerk when only issues of fact are involved and the clerk has made no note of evidence, a conviction may well be quashed.[30]

It has been argued that the appearance of justice could only realistically be maintained if advice on points of law were always given in open court.[31] The right to give such advice in private seems, however, to be strongly supported by justices' clerks,[32] and the Home Office and the courts have not been inclined to interfere with it.[33] However, where the justices seek advice from the justices' clerk, as distinct from the court clerk actually present when legal submissions were made, the former is expected also to hear submissions in open court, and not in some corridor or private place.[34]

It has been held that the clerk may ask questions in court in order to clear up ambiguities, so long as it is at the express or implied request of the bench,[35] and that it is proper for the clerk, in the absence of the justices and in conjunction with the prosecutor, to explain to an unrepresented defendant that if he or she attacks a prosecution witness his or her previous convictions can be revealed to the court.[36] However, it is not appropriate to warn the defendant and a defence

[29] This impliedly overrules the statements of Donaldson L.J. in *R. v. Guildford JJ., ex p. Harding* (1981) 145 J.P. 174.

[30] *R. v. Worley JJ., ex p. Nash* [1982] C.L. 1932: see the comment at (1983) 147 J.P.N. 209. *Cf. R. v. Eccles JJ., ex p. Fitzpatrick* (1989) 89 Cr.App.R. 324 (appearance of improper influence of decision to commit for trial) and *R. v. Eccles JJ., ex p. Farelly* (1992) 157 J.P. 77 (clerk spoke to justices after they had returned from their deliberations, and then went with them when they left the court again to reconsider, without any explanation).

[31] A. Heaton-Armstrong, (1986) 150 J.P.N. 340, 357.

[32] (1986) 42 *The Magistrate* 40–41: "the practice would have a disastrous effect upon the relationship between magistrates and their clerk. . . . The relationship . . . is the confidential relationship of the lay client and the professional adviser. . . ."

[33] See Heaton-Armstrong, *op. cit.*

[34] *R. v. Chichester JJ., ex p. D.P.P.* (1993) 157 J.P. 1049.

[35] *R. v. Consett JJ., ex p. Postal Bingo Ltd* [1967] 2 Q.B. 9. In general, clerks should not otherwise take an active part in proceedings, except where an unrepresented party is not competent to examine witnesses properly: Lord Parker C.J. in *Simms v. Moore* [1970] 2 Q.B. 327, 332–333.

[36] *R. v. Weston-super-Mare JJ., ex p. Townsend* [1968] 3 All E.R. 225.

witness of the consequences of giving perjured evidence where such a warning has not been given to prosecution witnesses.[37]

In some areas, clerks rule on questions of the admissibility of evidence in the absence of the justices. This is generally accepted to be irregular as the clerk has no legal authority to rule on such matters. On the other hand it is also accepted that it is undesirable for the justices who are to determine guilt to determine disputed questions of admissibility, which may well involve hearing evidence which subsequently has to be disregarded as inadmissible. There is in fact no reason why the parties should not by agreement submit the issue to the clerk and, once a ruling is made, voluntarily abide by it: the real limitation is that the ruling will not technically be binding. It is likely to be in the defendant's interests for this to be done in the absence of the justices: it is unlikely that the justices could be persuaded to differ from the clerk's view on such a question.

It is also a well established practice for lawyers to refer doubtful points of law to the clerk in advance of the hearing in order to obtain what in practice, although again not in theory, amounts to a ruling.[38]

From time to time, suggestions are made for changing the status of justices' clerks.[39] One possibility would be to appoint them to the bench, so that they would become, in those courts where they presided, a legally qualified chairman. Another possibility would be to give them the formal power to rule on points of law, while leaving the determination of the facts, as at present, to the lay justices.[40] This is virtually the present position. There is a persistent minority of cases in which lay justices exert their power to determine a point of law contrary to the clerk's advice. Lord Widgery C.J., however, warned that if justices fly in the face of their clerk's advice and are subsequently reversed on appeal, costs may be awarded against them.[41]

10. MAGISTRATES IN THE CROWN COURT

The Beeching Committee[42] recommended that magistrates should sit as assessors with Circuit judges in the Crown Court. Before reorganization, justices had participated in quarter sessions in the counties, but not in the assizes or borough quarter sessions. The Courts Act 1971[43] provided that justices may sit with a Circuit judge or recorder when conducting a trial on indictment and must do so when the Crown Court is hearing an appeal or dealing with a person committed there for sentence. Moreover, it provided that the justices would act as judges of the Crown Court and not merely as assessors. Lord Gardiner L.C. and Lord Hailsham L.C. were advised to adopt this course by Sir Thomas Skyrme,[44] who argued, inter alia, that the experience would be of benefit to the justices; that

---

[37] R. v. Richmond & Gilling West Magistrates, ex p. Steel [1993] Crim. L.R. 711.
[38] See P. Darbyshire, (1980) 144 J.P.N. 201.
[39] Here the suggestions are usually confined to the justices' clerk personally and do not extend to his or her assistants.
[40] See, e.g., (1992) 156 J.P.N. 433.
[41] Jones v. Nicks [1977] R.T.R. 72, 76. The advice concerned what might constitute a "special reason" for not imposing an endorsement following a speeding conviction.
[42] Royal Commission on Assizes and Quarter Sessions (Cmnd. 4153, 1969).
[43] See now the Supreme Court Act 1981, ss.8, 74, 75; the Crown Court Rules 1982, rr.3–5.
[44] Skyrme (1983), pp. 125–130.

justices could play a valuable part in sentencing, especially where the judge had no local knowledge; and that they could exercise a useful restriction on any idiosyncrasy of a judge or recorder. However, Skyrme subsequently acknowledged that the differences between the Crown Court and quarter sessions turned out to be greater than expected. Long trials that formerly would have been dealt with at assizes were now conducted by a court including justices at the Crown Court. The Crown Court was in continuous session. Trials might be conducted by judges with no experience of sitting with lay justices. Cases commonly ran over a day and this would cause problems for many lay justices. In some areas only those who could sit for several days were summoned: courts were accordingly composed disproportionately of women and the elderly. On the other hand, Circuit judges had been appointed as "liaison judges", and in some areas they were able to improve relationships.[45]

Dissatisfaction with the role of justices in the Crown Court continued in many places.[46] Eventually, the Lord Chancellor directed that justices no longer sit in contested Crown Court trials.[47]

The Lord Chancellor has asked that no justice should sit in the Crown Court unless he or she had completed basic training and had two years' experience. The justices may outvote the judge, although in the case of a tie the latter has a second and casting vote.[48] This is most likely to happen on a question of sentence, but may occur on other matters, such as the discretion to exclude evidence.[49]

11. STIPENDIARY MAGISTRATES

The Queen may appoint up to 60 "metropolitan stipendiary magistrates" for the inner London area,[50] and up to 40 "stipendiary magistrates" elsewhere.[51] The former can trace their existence back to 1792, when they took over criminal jurisdiction from the largely corrupt lay justices.[52] The Metropolitan Police Courts Act 1839 provided that only barristers were to be eligible for appointment. From 1964, they have shared their duties with lay justices, who, with the passage of time, have been restored to respectability.

In the provinces, stipendiaries were appointed in places where there were not enough justices to cope with the work, and where, at the same time, there was

---

[45] Suggestions that liaison judges hold annual conferences of bench chairmen, sentencing conferences and meetings with justices' clerks have, however, been criticised as going beyond their proper role: see Judge Dyer, (1987) 43 *The Magistrate* 223, and for responses: D. H. Kidner, (1988) 44 *The Magistrate* 51, and (1988) 152 J.P.N. 97.

[46] Skyrme (1983), pp. 125–130. See also G. Hawker, *Magistrates in the Crown Court* (1974): Survey by the Institute of Judicial Administration, University of Birmingham.

[47] *Practice Direction (Crime: Crown Court Business) (No. 2)* [1986] 1 W.L.R. 1041 (see now above pp. 82–83). The change was made with the agreement of the Magistrates' Association: (1987) 43 *The Magistrate* 81, 119 (the suggestion had previously been resisted: see Skyrme (1983), pp. 129–130).

[48] Supreme Court Act 1981, s.73.

[49] *R. v. Smith (Benjamin Walker)* [1978] Crim.L.R. 296.

[50] Justices of the Peace Act 1979, s.31. In 1995 there were 50 in post.

[51] 1979 Act, s.13. In 1995 there were 35 in post.

[52] See generally F. Milton, *The English Magistracy* (1967), Chap. 2. Some of the existing justices managed to secure stipendiary appointments, but ministers in the early nineteenth century took greater care over appointments. See also, R. Bartle, (1986) 54 Medico-Legal Jo. 236.

a resistance to the appointment of men who had acquired wealth through industry or trade. Boroughs might petition the Home Secretary to appoint a stipendiary; alternatively, a local Act of Parliament might provide for an appointment. The role of provincial stipendiaries was to supplement rather than to replace the lay justices. The 1948 Royal Commission noted that the determining factor behind whether a particular area had a stipendiary was "not a rational assessment of the present need but the course of past history."[53] The rationalisation of commission areas, which was a by-product of local government reorganisation, provided the opportunity for the right to take the initiative in the making of new appointments to be transferred from local authorities to the Lord Chancellor.[54] The requirements of each area were assessed by the Lord Chancellor's office.[55] The area of jurisdiction of some stipendiaries was increased to enable the post to be retained. One additional stipendiary was appointed in Sheffield.

The question was further reviewed following the paper produced by the Home Office and the Lord Chancellor's Department on The Size of Benches,[56] which set out criteria for the appointment of stipendiaries. The paper stated that one stipendiary was the equivalent of 36 lay magistrates in terms of judicial resources, but that experience suggested that the average stipendiary works much faster than the average lay bench.[57] The aim of an appointment was to support the lay magistracy, not to supersede it. The work, both interesting and routine, would be fairly shared, although the stipendiary should normally hear cases likely to last several days or involving difficult points of law. Relevant criteria that would trigger consideration of an appointment were (a) excessive delays not remediable by other measures; (b) overloading the lay magistracy; and (c) keeping a lay bench down to a conveniently manageable size. In 1988 the Lord Chancellor announced five additional provincial appointments.[58] Where a bench is temporarily over-burdened, an acting stipendiary magistrate[59] may be assigned to assist.[60] A working party on the role of the stipendiary magistrate was established in September 1994 by the Lord Chancellor.

Appointments are made on the recommendation of the Lord Chancellor.[61] An appointee must be a lawyer[62] of seven years' standing.[63] Metropolitan stipendiar-

---

[53] Cmd. 7463, p. 57.
[54] Administration of Justice Act 1973, s.2.
[55] Skyrme (1983), Chap. 13.
[56] (1986) 42 The Magistrate 118 (see above, p. 55); for comments by the Magistrates' Association, see 67th Annual Report, 1986–87, Appendix II.
[57] Claims that a stipendiary can get through the work three times faster than a lay bench have been doubted: see P. Softley, (1985) 149 J.P.N. 710.
[58] For Portsmouth and Southampton, Brent, Nottingham, Rotherham and Birmingham: (1988) 44 The Magistrate at 219. Further appointments are expected to take the number to the current statutory limit of 40.
[59] See below.
[60] Popularly (or unpopularly) known as "flying stipes": they were, for example, employed in some areas during the miners' strike ((1984) 148 J.P.N. 578). There are panels of acting stipendiaries in parts of the country where there are full-time provincial stipendiaries: L.C.D., Judicial Appointments (3rd ed., 1995), Leaflet No. 5, Metropolitan & Provincial Stipendiary Magistrates.
[61] This requirement is express as regards provincial stipendiaries: 1979 Act, s.14(3).
[62] The appointment of solicitors became possible under the Justices of the Peace Act 1949. The first was appointed in 1957. By 1983 20 solicitors had been appointed, 15 in London and five elsewhere: Skyrme (1983), p. 187.
[63] 1979 Act, ss.13(1), 31(2). The requirement is possession of a seven-year general qualification (i.e. rights of audience in any part of the Supreme Court or in all proceedings in county courts or magistrates' courts) under amendments effected by the Courts and Legal Services Act 1990, s.71, Sched. 10, para. 44.

ies may be removed by the Lord Chancellor for inability or misbehaviour[64];
provincial stipendiaries hold office "during pleasure" but may only be removed
on the Lord Chancellor's recommendation.[65] The retiring age is 70, although
the Lord Chancellor may authorise a stipendiary to continue in office up to the
age of 75.[66] The Lord Chancellor may appoint acting stipendiary magistrates,[67]
and a person will not normally be given a full-time appointment without prior
experience as an acting stipendiary.[68] The current salary is £62,621,[69] stipendiaries being grouped with, *inter alia*, masters and registrars of the Supreme Court
and chairmen of Industrial Tribunals.

Traditionally, appointment to judicial office has been on the understanding
that the appointee will remain in that office. Today there is a growing trend for
judicial officers to be "promoted", although it is still very much the exception
rather than the rule. Stipendiaries may be invited to sit as recorders. Some have
been appointed to the Circuit Bench.

Proposals have been made on a number of occasions for extending the role
of stipendiaries outside Inner London. One possibility would be to replace all
lay justices by stipendiaries. Another would be to require that each bench of
magistrates should comprise one stipendiary sitting with lay justices. A third
would be to increase the numbers so that there is at least one in each area,
operating on a peripatetic basis. The 1948 Royal Commission reported against
any radical change in the system.[70] There would not be sufficient candidates for
appointment. The cost of the salaries would be large. Legal training was not in
fact necessary provided legal advice was available. The present system gave the
citizen a part to play in the administration of the law. The third proposal was
advanced by the Bar to the 1948 Royal Commission. The stipendiary would
visit the various benches and sit as chairman and would be available to take
difficult cases. However, the Royal Commission noted that it was difficult to
predict those cases where guidance from a professional magistrate would be
useful, and that it would be undesirable to dilute the responsibility and authority
of lay justices.

B. TRIBUNAL CHAIRMEN AND MEMBERS

There are several patterns on which the composition of a tribunal may be organised.[71] The variations reflect partly the differences in the kind of work undertaken by different tribunals and partly their diverse historical origins. Full-time
appointments are commonly of similar status to one or other of the ranks of the

---

[64] 1979 Act, s.31(4)(c).
[65] 1979 Act, s.13(1).
[66] 1979 Act, s.14, as amended by the Judicial Pensions and Retirement Act 1993, Sched. 6, para. 19.
[67] 1979 Act, ss.15, 34.
[68] *Judicial Appointments* (3rd ed., 1995), Leaflet No. 5, *Metropolitan & Provincial Stipendiary Magistrates*. Candidates must normally be aged between 38 (acting) or 40 (permanent) and 55: *ibid.*
[69] As from December 1, 1996. Metropolitan magistrates receive £64,699 plus a London allowance of £2,000.
[70] Cmd. 7463, Chap. VIII.
[71] See above, pp. 39–46, 50–54.

judiciary. The Presidents of the Lands Tribunal, the Independent Tribunal Service and of Industrial Tribunals and the Chief Social Security Commissioner receive a higher salary than a Circuit judge; members of the Lands Tribunal and Social Security Commissioners receive the same as a Circuit judge; chairmen of Industrial Tribunals and for the Independent Tribunal Service receive the same as a stipendiary magistrate.[72] Most appointments are part-time. On June 1, 1995, there were 80 full-time chairmen of industrial tribunals (70 men and 10 women) and 42 full-time chairmen of S.S.A.T.s (31 men and 11 women).[73]

It is not possible to consider here the details of appointment and tenure for all tribunals.[74] Some general observations can, however, be made.

1. WHO APPOINTS?

The Franks Committee on Administrative Tribunals and Enquiries[75] reported that appointments to tribunals were usually made by the minister responsible for the legislation under which they operated. They had received no significant evidence that any influence was in fact exerted on tribunal members by government departments, but recommended, nevertheless, that chairmen, whether legally qualified or not, should be appointed by the Lord Chancellor and members by the Council on Tribunals.[76] The position today is that the Lord Chancellor is involved in the appointment of a majority of chairmen. He either appoints the chairman directly[77] or appoints a panel from which a selection is made by the relevant department or President of tribunals.[78] The appointment of members has, however, not been transferred to the Council on Tribunals, and it is not seriously argued that it should be. Most tribunal members are appointed by the relevant government department: some are appointed by the Crown or the Lord Chancellor, and some by the relevant President of tribunals.

2. QUALIFICATIONS FOR APPOINTMENT

The Franks Committee recommended that *chairmen* of tribunals:

"should ordinarily have legal qualifications but that the appointment of

---

[72] Regional chairmen receive the same as Circuit judges.

[73] Vol. 262 H. C. Deb., June 21 1995, col. 243, written answer.

[74] See B. L. Jones, *Garner's Administrative Law* (7th ed., 1989), Chap. 8; R. E. Wraith and P. G. Hutchesson, *Administrative Tribunals* (1973), Chap. 4; L.C.D. Memorandum on Judicial Appointments Procedures (1995), pp. 42–50.

[75] Cmnd. 218, 1957.

[76] Cmnd. 218 pp. 11–12.

[77] *e.g.* the President (and members) of the Lands Tribunal: Lands Tribunal Act 1949, s.2; chairman (and members) of Mental Health Review Tribunals: Mental Health Act 1983, s.65(2), Sched. 2. Some are Crown appointments: for example, the provisions governing the appointment and tenure of Social Security Commissioners (Social Security Administration Act 1992, s.52 and Sched. 2) are very similar to those governing Circuit judges (see below, pp. 218–219). See generally, L.C.D., *Judicial Appointments* (3rd ed., 1995), Leaflet No. 7, *Tribunal Appointments*.

[78] See the Tribunals and Inquiries Act 1992, s.6: examples include the chairmen of industrial tribunals and S.S.A.T.s (see above, pp. 65, 69).

persons without legal qualifications should not be ruled out when they are particularly suitable."[79]

There should be no such requirement for members. The possession of a legal qualification is thought to be desirable not so much for the expertise in handling legal rules as for the qualities necessary for good chairmanship. "Objectivity in the treatment of cases and the proper sifting of facts are most often best secured by having a legally qualified chairman. . . ."[80] Many criticisms of Supplementary Benefit Appeal Tribunals were related to the general lack of legally qualified chairmen. They were regularly contrasted unfavourably with National Insurance Local Tribunals where a legal qualification was in practice required.[81] Not all commentators favoured a change to lawyer-chairmen, but the government indicated in 1977 that there would be a "gradual, but significant move to appoint more legally-qualified chairmen of S.B.A.T.s."[82] Between 1977 and 1980 the overall proportion of lawyer chairmen increased from 12 per cent to 26.4 per cent.[83]

In an increasing number of cases, a legal qualification or legal experience is required by statute[84]: in others it is normally required as a matter of practice.[85] Even here, however, there may be criticism that appointees may not have sufficient (or any) experience in the relevant area.[86] It has also been noted that it has become more common for people to hold part-time appointments to more than one tribunal,[87] or for a full-time chairman to sit in addition as a recorder or assistant recorder in the Crown Court.[88]

The background of *members* will obviously be related to the nature of the tribunal's work. An obvious example is that doctors sit on Medical Appeal

---

[79] Cmnd. 218, p. 12.

[80] *ibid.*

[81] See, *e.g.* Kathleen Bell *et al*, "National Insurance Local Tribunals: A Research Study" (1974) 3 *Journal of Social Policy* 289 and (1975) 4 *Journal of Social Policy* 1; Kathleen Bell, *Research Study on Supplementary Benefit Appeal Tribunals—Review of Main Findings: Conclusions: Recommendations* (1975); J. Fulbrook, *Administrative Justice and the Unemployed* (1978), pp. 209–220.

[82] Annual Report of the Council on Tribunals, 1976–77 (1977–78 H.C. 108), p. 26.

[83] N. Harris, "The Appointment of Legally Qualified Chairmen for S.B.A.T.s" (1982) 132 N.L.J. 495. There were some reports of consequential improvements in the conduct of proceedings.

[84] *e.g.* Social Security Commissioners, (lawyer of 10 years' standing), chairmen of Social Security Appeal Tribunals (from April 23, 1989: lawyer of five years' standing), Lands Tribunal members (either lawyer or qualified surveyor) chairmen of Industrial Tribunals and of Medical Appeal Tribunals (lawyers of seven years' standing), chairmen of Mental Health Review Tribunals (persons of suitable legal experience). References to standing here mean the possession of a general qualification (*i.e.* right of audience in any part of the Supreme Court or in all proceedings in county courts or magistrates' courts) for the appropriate number of years: Courts and Legal Services Act 1990, s.71 and Sched. 10, paras.7, 27, 36, 37, 46.

[85] *e.g.* Immigration Adjudicators.

[86] The JUSTICE Report on *Industrial Tribunals* (1987) notes (p. 47) that most appointees as chairman have little or no previous knowledge and experience of employment law and almost invariably lack industrial experience: it recommends that preference be given to candidates with previous experience in employment law, industrial relations and tribunal work; and that there should be closer links with the Circuit bench. The L.C.D. leaflet (*supra*), states in relation to Independent Tribunal Service tribunals that prior experience of social security law is "desirable, but not essential"; however, the Lord Chancellor seeks to appoint as chairmen of industrial tribunals "individuals who can demonstrate a good knowledge of employment law and who have experience of civil litigation."

[87] Wraith and Hutchesson (1973), pp. 114–115; Fulbrook (1978), p. 212.

[88] JUSTICE, *Industrial Tribunals* (1987), p. 45.

Tribunals. A pattern that has been commonly adopted is that of the "representative panel". For example, in Industrial Tribunals, one "wing" member is taken from a panel representing employers and the other from a panel representing employed persons.[89] Similar arrangements were made for National Insurance Local Tribunals and Supplementary Benefit Appeal Tribunals.[90] However, there is a single members' panel for Social Security Appeal Tribunals, appointed by the President of the Independent Tribunal Service and composed of persons appearing to him "to have knowledge or experience of conditions in the area and to be representative of persons living or working in the area."[91] The change to a single panel was coupled with the intention that the range of organisations consulted about membership should be widened out from Trade Councils, Chambers of Commerce and the like to include, for example, groups representing ethnic minorities, the disabled and one-parent families.[92] In practice, the charge seems to have made little difference.[93]

Comparatively little has been written about the social and political background of tribunal chairmen and members,[94] although, as with the judiciary, women and members of ethnic minorities are seriously under-represented.[95] Part-time appointments are commonly for three years with the possibility of renewal, but there are variations.[96]

3. DISMISSAL

No power of a minister to terminate a person's membership of a tribunal is exercisable except with the consent of the Lord Chancellor.[97]

4. TRAINING

The Council on Tribunals has noted the benefits derived from regular meetings of tribunal chairmen, at which difficulties can be discussed and opinions venti-

---

[89] Industrial Tribunals (Constitution and Rules of Procedure) Regulations 1993 (S.I. 1993 No.2687), regs.3, 7. One panel is appointed by the Secretary of State after consultation with e.g. the T.U.C., the other after consultation with e.g. the C.B.I: see JUSTICE, *Industrial Tribunals*, p. 49.

[90] See the first edition of this book, pp. 151–152.

[91] Social Security Administration Act 1992, s.40.

[92] J. Mesher and P. Wood, *Income Related Benefits: the Legislation* (1994), p. 619; *Social Security Appeal Tribunals: A guide to procedure* (HMSO, 1985), pp. 13–14 (nominations are initially submitted to the appropriate regional chairman: *ibid.*).

[93] J. Baldwin, *et al.*, *Judging Social Security* (1992), p. 135.

[94] See W. E. Cavanagh and G. N. Hawker, "Laymen on Administrative Tribunals" (1974) 52 *Public Administration* 215 (Rent Assessment Panels and S.B.A.T.s) and the study of N.I.L.T.s by Kathleen Bell and others: *op.cit.* n. 80 above, pp. 310–315; L. Dickens *et al., Dismissed* (1985), pp. 52–59 (Industrial Tribunals) and JUSTICE, *Industrial Tribunals* (1987), pp. 45–50; J. Baldwin and S. Hill, (1987) 6 C.J.Q. 130 (Local Valuation Panels); J. Baldwin, *et al., Judging Social Security* (1992), pp. 132–140 (S.S.A.T.s).

[95] See JUSTICE, *Industrial Tribunals* (1987), pp. 46, 47–48, 49–50. JUSTICE proposed positive action to promote their recruitment, involving a more open, accessible and democractic appointments process for members.

[96] Wraith and Hutchesson (1973), p. 109. On the monitoring of the progress of part-time Chairmen, see Judge T. Lawrence, (1995) 2 *Tribunals* 9.

[97] Tribunals and Inquiries Act 1992, s.7. The tribunals to which this applies are specified in Sched. 1.

lated,[98] and has stressed the importance of training for both chairmen and members.[99] In various contexts, shortcomings in the quality of decision-making have been related to the absence of adequate training.[1] There have also been developments in the training of tribunal chairmen, although these have lagged behind developments in the training of magistrates.[2] There has been little provision of training for tribunal members. The President of the Independent Tribunal Service is under an express duty to arrange for such meetings of and training for chairmen and members of tribunals as he thinks appropriate.[3]

A Tribunals Committee has been established as part of the enlarged Judicial Studies Board.[4] Its role is seen as complementary to the Council on Tribunals, and to be that of promoting, encouraging and advising.[5] It has run induction courses for newly qualified chairmen, developing into a series of broader training development seminars, has appointed a Tribunals' Training Co-ordinator and publishes a journal, *Tribunals*.[6]

5. CLERKS TO TRIBUNALS[7]

The Franks Committee noted that the practice

"whereby the majority of clerks of tribunals are provided by the Government Departments concerned from their local and regional staffs seems partly to be responsible for the feeling in the minds of some people that tribunals are dependent upon and influenced by those Departments."[8]

They considered the possibility of establishing under the Lord Chancellor's Department a central corps of clerks for all tribunals, but rejected it on the grounds that it was difficult to see how reasonable career prospects could be held out, that it would be difficult to arrange sittings to ensure that the clerks were fully occupied and that it was in any event desirable for the civil servants

---

[98] Annual Report for 1976–77, pp. 19–20. In 1987, the Council organised the first conference of Presidents and Chairmen of major tribunals falling under its jurisdiction: Annual Report for 1986–87 (1987–88 H.C. 234), pp. 6–7.

[99] *e.g.* Annual Report for 1984–85 (1985–86 H.C. 54), p. 11; for 1986–87 (1987–88 H.C. 234), p. 18; for 1987–88 (1988–89 H.C. 102), pp. 31–32; for 1988–89 (1989–90 H.C. 114), pp. 26–27.

[1] *e.g.* in respect of General Commissioners of Income Tax (Annual Report for 1987–88, p. 6); education appeal committees (*ibid.*, p. 13); industrial tribunals, especially in sex discrimination and equal pay cases (A. Leonard, *Judging Inequality* (1987), pp. 71–72; JUSTICE, *Industrial Tribunals* (1987), pp. 35–38, 48, 50).

[2] For example, there was a system for training S.B.A.T. chairmen (see Annual Report of the Council on Tribunals for 1977–78 (1978–79 H.C. 74), pp. 16–17), and some training courses were held for chairmen of Local Valuation Courts (Report for 1978–79 (1979–80 H.C. 359), p. 18).

[3] Social Security Administration Act 1992, Sched. 2, para. 5. The Regional chairmen assist in this task.

[4] See below, pp. 238–239.

[5] *Judicial Studies Board Report for 1987–1991* (HMSO, 1992), p. 57; *Report for 1991–1995* (1995), Chap. 6.

[6] *ibid.*

[7] See Wraith and Hutchesson (1973), Chap. 5, and pp. 300–306.

[8] Cmnd. 218, p. 13.

in social service departments to spend a period as tribunal clerk.[9] To ensure that clerks did not exert a departmental influence, the Committee stated that their duties and conduct should be regulated on the advice of the Council on Tribunals. The duties of a clerk should generally be confined to secretarial work, taking notes of evidence and tendering advice, when requested, on points connected with the tribunal's functions. He or she should not retire with the tribunal unless sent for to advise on a specific point.

Clerks to Social Security Appeal Tribunals and Medical Appeals Tribunals have from April 1984 been appointed by the President (as now are clerks be Disability Appeal Tribunals), and work from the regional offices of his organisation,[10] thus marking their independence from the Department of Social Security. The role of the clerk does not appear to be problematic.[11] A particularly important task is that of explaining the nature of proceedings to appellants; a recent study found that "tribunal clerks on the whole did a good job in difficult circumstances."[12]

C. THE CIRCUIT BENCH

The Circuit Bench was created by the Courts Act 1971 as part of the reorganisation of the criminal courts following the Beeching Commission.[13] The Queen may appoint Circuit judges and recorders on the recommendation of the Lord Chancellor.[14] Circuit judges are appointed to serve full-time in the Crown Court and county courts, recorders and assistant recorders to serve as part-time judges in the Crown Court.[15] Under the 1971 Act, only a barrister or solicitor of 10 years' standing could be appointed as a recorder. A barrister of 10 years' standing or a recorder who had held office for at least three years could be appointed as a Circuit judge. A solicitor might accordingly reach the position of Circuit judge after time as a recorder. Following changes made by the Courts and Legal

---

[9] *ibid.*, pp. 13–14.

[10] Social Security Administration Act 1992, Sched. 2, paras.3, 4. The organisation was originally known as "OPSSAT" for short: see Judge Byrt (the first President), "Administering Appeals," *Adviser*, Oct.–Nov. 1987, p. 6. It is now known as the Independent Tribunal Service.

[11] Difficulties with clerks to S.B.A.Ts have not been experienced with S.S.A.Ts. see Fulbrook (1978), pp. 229–236.

[12] J. Baldwin, *et al., Judging Social Security* (1992), pp. 168–169.

[13] Royal Commission on Assizes and Quarter Sessions (Cmnd. 4153, 1969).

[14] Courts Act 1971, s.16. On December 1, 1994, there were 514 Circuit judges (including 29 women) and 866 recorders (including 41 women); 63 of the Circuit judges and 78 of the recorders were solicitors: L.C.D. Memorandum on Judicial Appointments Procedures (1995), p. 101. The Lord Chancellor may appoint a former judge of the Court of Appeal or the High Court or a former Circuit judge as a deputy Circuit judge: Courts Act 1971, s. 24, substituted by the Supreme Court Act 1981, s. 146.

[15] And to carry out such other judicial functions as may be conferred on them by statute. A Circuit judge or recorder may be requested to act as a judge of the High Court: Supreme Court Act 1981, s.9 as amended by the Administration of Justice Act 1982, s.58. They are addressed as "Your Honour," unless sitting as a judge of the High Court or at the Central Criminal Court when they are addressed as "My Lord" or "My Lady". Circuit judges are referred to as His (or Her) Honour Judge X and recorders as Mr (or Mrs but not Miss) recorder B: *Practice Direction (Judges: Mode of Address)* [1982] 1 W.L.R. 101.

Services Act 1990,[16] the qualification for the appointment of a practitioner as a Circuit judge, recorder or assistant recorder became the enjoyment of general rights of audience in the Crown Court or the county courts for 10 years. Any person who has been a District judge, or equivalent judicial officer,[17] for at least three years, or who is a recorder, is eligible for appointment as a Circuit judge. The requirement that a solicitor serve three years as a recorder before becoming eligible for a Circuit judgeship was removed.

On reorganisation under the 1971 Act, a number of middle-rank judges automatically became Circuit judges, including the Vice-Chancellor of the County Palatine of Lancaster, the Recorder of London, the Common Serjeant, the Recorders of Liverpool and Manchester, Official Referees, the Additional Judges of the Central Criminal Court, county court judges and the whole-time chairmen or deputy chairmen of quarter sessions.[18] Most of these offices were abolished, but some were retained. The Vice-Chancellor of the County Palatine of Lancaster conducts High Court Chancery business in the North.[19] The Common Serjeant and the Recorder of London[20] sit at the Central Criminal Court. Those appointed to these offices become Circuit judges *ex officio*. In addition, the senior Circuit judges at certain large court complexes (*e.g.*, the Recorders of Liverpool and Manchester[21] and the Senior Circuit judge at Newington Causeway) and the Circuit judges who conduct Official Referees' business in London are regarded as holding appointments more burdensome than that of the ordinary Circuit judge, and are paid higher salaries.[22]

The Lord Chancellor may, if he thinks fit, remove a Circuit judge from office on the ground of incapacity or misbehaviour.[23] In 1983, Judge Bruce Campbell was removed from office following his conviction for smuggling whisky and cigarettes.[24] The retiring age is 70, although the Lord Chancellor may authorise a judge to continue in office up to the age of 75.

---

[16] s.71 and Sched. 10, paras. 31, 32.

[17] *e.g.* Social Security Commissioner, President of Tribunals, High Court masters, stipendiary magistrates: see Part IA of Sched. 2 to the Courts Act 1971, inserted by the 1990 Act, Sched. 10, para. 31(2).

[18] Courts Act 1971, Sched. 2, Part I.

[19] He is appointed by the Chancellor of the Duchy of Lancaster. From 1987, the post has been held by a High Court judge, rather than a Circuit judge: see above, p. 87.

[20] The Recorder is elected by the City, but appointed by the Crown to exercise judicial functions. The Common Serjeant is appointed by the Crown. They are paid by the City of London authorities.

[21] These are honorary recorderships under the Courts Act 1971, s.54. The holders are addressed as "My Lord".

[22] £89,123 as compared with £76,717, as from December 1, 1996. Eight judges are assigned to Official Referees' business: see the Supreme Court Act 1981, s.68, above, pp. 92–93. There have in a number of years been difficulties in recruiting Circuit judges, with in 1987–88 three refusals for every one acceptance: salary was said to be a very important factor, especially for Q.C.s, and other factors included a perceived relative lack of status: *Review Body on Top Salaries*, Report No. 28 (Cm. 581, 1989), pp. 4–5. An additional 10 percent increase was recommended by the Board in 1990 (Cm. 938, 1990), Chap. 5. By 1995, there were "no appreciable difficulties": Review Body on Senior Salaries, Report No. 35 (Cm. 2764, 1995), p. 20.

[23] Courts Act 1971, s.17(4).

[24] *The Times*, December 6, 1983. The fact that he was removed (as distinct from resigning) enabled him to keep his pension: Rozenberg (1994), pp. 111–112. Dismissal was threatened in the case of Judge James Pickles, but not effected: *ibid.*, pp. 112–114 and below, p. 237. In Scotland, Sheriff Thomson was removed in 1977 because of his political activities, and Sheriff Stewart in 1992 because of "inability to perform his judicial function": (1994) 144 N.L.J. 1651, noting the dismissal of the latter's application for judicial review.

The appointment of a person as a recorder specifies the term for which he or she is appointed and the frequency and duration of the occasions when he or she will be required to sit. The term may not last beyond the year in which he or she attains 70 (subject to continuance in office to 75 authorised by the Lord Chancellor). The Lord Chancellor may terminate the appointment on the grounds of incapacity, misbehaviour or a failure to comply with the conditions of the appointment.[25] The general terms and conditions for appointment were set out in a statement by the Lord Chancellor's office.[26] Appointments are normally for three years at a time. Appointments of recorders are not renewed where the Lord Chancellor is not satisfied as to their continuing fitness or suitability.[27] They are expected to sit for not less than four working weeks (20 days) a year. A daily fee, travelling expenses and subsistence allowances are payable.

The Lord Chancellor may appoint any person with a seven year general qualification[28] to the position of District judge or deputy District judge. The latter is a part-time appointment.

Judicial appointments are handled by the Judicial Appointments Group within the L.C.D. and the procedures for appointment summarised in the booklet, *Judical Appointments: The Lord Chancellor's Policies and Procedures*.[29] Candidates for appointment as Circuit judges are expected to have proved themselves first by sitting as assistant recorders and recorders (or as holders of one of the other specified judicial offices), and recorders are not appointed unless they have proved themselves as assistant recorders. If an assistant recorder has not progressed to a full recordership after about three to five years, the appointment will be terminated.[30] A District judgeship is a full-time appointment. Some deputy District judges are on track for such an appointment; others continue to sit for renewable three-year terms as part-timers.[31]

In 1994, the Lord Chancellor, following consultation,[32] introduced new procedures for appointments to Circuit and District judgeships.[33] These involve annual open competitions for vacancies, with advertisements in the national and

---

[25] Courts Act 1971, s.21.

[26] (1971) 68 L. S. Gaz. 303.

[27] "Where possible, the recorder is warned in advance of any cause for concern, so as to give him a chance to improve. However, this cannot always be done": L.C.D., *Judicial Appointments* (1986), p. 13. It was not effectively done in the case of Manus Nunan, whose appointment was not renewed in 1985: see *The Guardian*, 13, 14 and 16 June, and December 2 1986; R Brazier, *Constitutional Practice* (2nd ed., 1994), p. 291; Judge James Pickles, *Straight from the Bench* (1987), pp. 29–41, including notes of the interview between Nunan and Lord Hailsham L.C. The words in question were omitted from the 2nd ed. of the L.C.D. booklet.

[28] *i.e.* a right of audience in relation to any class of proceedings in any part of the Supreme Court or all proceedings in county courts or magistrates' courts (Courts and Legal Services Act 1990, s. 71): County Courts Act 1984, s. 9, as amended by the Courts and Legal Services Act 1990, Sched. 10, para. 57. District judges may sit in the county court or the High Court (see above, pp. 72, 93).

[29] (1995). See below, p. 228.

[30] *ibid.* Leaflet 3, Recorder & Assistant Recorder Appointments.

[31] *ibid.* Leaflet 4, District Judge & Deputy District Judge Appointments. Minimum age limits normally applied in practice are 35 (assistant recorders), 38 (recorders and deputy District judges), 40 (District judges) and 45 (Circuit judges): *ibid.* The performance of newly-appointed recorders and assistant recorders is monitored by judges acting as their pupil masters: *The Times*, July 26, 1994, p. 35.

[32] See L.C.D. Consultation Paper, *Developments in Judicial Appointments Procedures* (May 1994). See D. Wheatley Q.C., (1994) 144 N.L.J. 784, arguing that the changes were of form rather than substance, although a small step in the right direction.

[33] L.C.D. Memorandum on Judicial Appointments Procedures (1995), pp. 51–60.

legal press; the preparation and publication of job descriptions and statements of eligibility and selection criteria[34]; the adoption of application forms designed to seek information enabling applicants to be judged against the published criteria; and an interview with a panel comprising a senior member of the LCD Judicial Appointments Group, a serving judge and a lay person. The first lay people have been chosen from among those involved in interviewing for the magistracy.[35] The stated aim is to "build on the strengths of present arrangements to make the appointments system as efficient, fair and open as possible."[36] The publication of selection criteria is "seen as conducive to a process whereby all candidates are measured against the same requirements."[37] These arrangements are to extend to all assistant recorders appointed from April 1997. It will be interesting to see whether these will provide a model for more senior judicial appointments; the introduction of greater objectivity into the system should encourage more applications from women and members of ethnic minorities.[38] The Law Society maintains that there is still excessive reliance on the views of serving judges, that the requirement of prior part-time service before a full-time appointment is unnecessary and disproportionately difficult for solicitors to comply with.[39]

D. JUDGES OF THE SUPERIOR COURTS[40]

1. THE CLASSES OF JUDICIAL OFFICE

Appointments to the High Court Bench are to the office of *puisne*[41] judge or *Justice of the High Court*.[42] A High Court judge is almost invariably knighted (or made a Dame Commander of the British Empire) upon appointment, but is referred to as, for example, "Mr[43] Justice Swallow".[44] Promotion to the Court

---

[34] The selection criteria cover legal knowledge and experience; skills and abilities (intellectual and analytical ability, sound judgment, decisiveness, communication skills, authority); and personal qualities (integrity, fairness, understanding of people and society, sound temperament, courtesy and humanity, and commitment).

[35] *ibid.*, Appendix 10.

[36] *ibid.*, p. 51.

[37] *ibid.*, p. 58.

[38] See below, p. 232.

[39] Evidence to the Home Affairs Committee: (1995) 145 N.L.J. 878.

[40] See generally, J. A. G. Griffith, *The Politics of the Judiciary* (4th ed., 1991) and *Judicial Politics since 1920* (1993); Lord Mackay, *The Adminstration of Justice* (1994) Chap. 1; D. Pannick, *Judges* (1987); J. Rozenberg, *The Search for Justice* (1994), Chaps.1, 2.; R. Brazier, "The appointment and removal of the lower judiciary" (1986) 15 Anglo-Am. L. R. 173 and *Constitutional Practice* (2nd ed., 1994), Chap. 12. On the appointment, control and extra-judicial activities of the judges between 1945 and the mid-1950s, see R. B. Stevens. "The Independence of the judicary: the view from the Lord Chancellor's Office" (1988) 8 O.J.L.S. 222.

[41] Pronounced as if it were "puny". The two words are related, a puisne judge being a "junior" judge in the superior courts of common law.

[42] See the Supreme Court Act 1981, s.4(2).

[43] Or Mrs. There has not yet been a Miss and may never be a Ms. It has been suggested that an unmarried lady would be referred to as "Mrs Justice": A. Samuels, (1982) 79 L. S. Gaz. 509.

[44] Written as Swallow J. If there are two Swallows on the bench, Christian names are also used.

of Appeal involves elevation to the position of *Lord Justice of Appeal*, which
is normally associated with an appointment to membership of the Privy Council.
"Swallow J." becomes "Lord Justice Swallow".[45] The next step is membership
of the House of Lords as a *Lord of Appeal in Ordinary*,[46] one of the "Law
Lords". Although he will have been addressed in court as "My Lord" from
the time of his appointment as a High Court judge, it is only at this stage (in
the normal course of events) that he actually acquires a life peerage, as, say,
"Lord Swallow of Somerset".[47]

In addition, there are several specific judicial offices. The *Lord Chancellor*[48]
has long been regarded as the head of the judiciary, and has now received formal
recognition as "president of the Supreme Court".[49] He is an *ex officio* member
of the Court of Appeal,[50] and is the president of the Chancery Division[51]
although the effective head of that Division is the Vice-Chancellor. If he sits
as a judge at all it is in the House of Lords or the Privy Council, and only Lord
Hailsham of St Marylebone and Lord Mackay of Clashfern (previously a Lord
of Appeal) of the recent Lord Chancellors have sat at all regularly.[52] The Lord
Chancellor has many administrative functions to perform as head of the
judiciary. For example, he has the effective say in most judicial appointments
and assignments, and various powers to give directions affecting the business
of the courts. He also has general responsibility for the unified court service,[53]
the Law Commissions, the legal advice and assistance and legal aid schemes,[54]
the Land Registry and the Public Records Office. He is normally a Cabinet

---

[45] Written as Swallow L.J. The first woman appointed to this office was Dame Elizabeth Butler-Sloss
in 1988: until 1994 she was referred to as "Lord Justice", this being the designation in the
Supreme Court Act 1981, s.2(3); the usage was then changed to "Lady Justice" in anticipation
of a change to the Act: *Practice Note: Mode of Address: Dame Elizabeth Butler-Sloss* [1994] 1
F.L.R. 866.
[46] "The word 'Ordinary' is a technical term used in law to describe a judge who has jurisdiction
to hear cases by virtue of his office. In contrast to other persons who have jurisdiction only by
being peers": Lord Denning, *The Family Story* (1981), p. 184.
[47] Lord Jenkins of Ashley Gardens apparently had wished to be styled Lord Jenkins of 24 Ashley
Gardens, but was thwarted by the College of Arms.
[48] *i.e.* the Lord High Chancellor of Great Britain. Written as Lord Mackay of Clashfern L.C. Incumbents since 1945 have been Lord Jowitt (1945–1951); Lord Simonds (1951–1954); Lord Kilmuir
(1954–1962); Lord Dilhorne (1962–1964); Lord Gardiner (1964–1970); Lord Hailsham (1970–
1974, 1979–1987); Lord Elwyn-Jones (1974–1979); Lord Havers (1987); Lord Mackay
(1987–). See generally R. F. V. Heuston, *Lives of the Lord Chancellors, 1985–1940* (1964) and
1940–1970 (1987); I. S. Dickinson. "Aspects of appointments to the office of Lord Chancellor"
1988 S.L.T. 41 (which lists those appointed between 1830 and 1987).
[49] Supreme Court Act 1981, s.1. He is paid £2,000 more than the Lord Chief Justice: Ministerial
and other Pensions and Salaries Act 1991, s.3.
[50] *ibid.* s.2.
[51] *ibid.* s.5(a).
[52] See G. Drewry, "Lord Chancellor as Judge" (1972) 122 N.L.J. 855. Until the Second World
War the legislative sittings of the House of Lords commenced at 4.15 p.m., enabling the Lord
Chancellor to sit regularly on appeals during the standard hours of 10.30 a.m. to 4.00 p.m. However, wartime difficulties caused the start of legislative sittings to be advanced to 2.30 p.m. and
the Lord Chancellor was compelled to choose between the two kinds of work: R.F.V. Heuston,
Lives of the Lord Chancellors, 1885–1940 (1964), p. xviii. See also A. Bradney, "The Judicial
Activity of the Lord Chancellor 1946–1987" (1989) 16 J.L.S. 360: this sets out statistics of the
judicial activity of Lord Chancellors and former Lord Chancellors in this period.
[53] Courts Act 1971, s.27(1).
[54] See below, pp. 491–510, 568–580, 763–772.

minister, and is the Speaker of the House of Lords.[55] Lord Gardiner stated that his paperwork was about half political and half judicial administration.[56] He is appointed by the Queen on the advice of the Prime Minister, and, as a political appointment, holds office "during pleasure". He goes out of office with the government of which he is a member, and is, indeed, as subject to dismissal by the Prime Minister as any other minister.[57] There are no formal qualifications for appointment, but all have been barristers. Lord Mackay is the first who has not been a member of the English Bar.[58]

The *Lord Chief Justice of England*[59] takes precedence over all judges other than the Lord Chancellor. He is the president of the Court of Appeal (Criminal Division) and the Queen's Bench Division of the High Court. The office was created as part of the reorganisation of the superior courts under the Supreme Court of Judicature Acts 1873–75. Before then each of the superior common law courts had its own chief: the Chief Justices of the Queen's Bench and the Common Pleas, and the Chief Baron of the Exchequer. The first Lord Chief Justice of England appointed as such was, accordingly, Lord Coleridge,[60] Chief Justice of the Common Pleas from 1873, who took the office in 1880 following the deaths of Sir Alexander Cockburn C.J. of the Queen's Bench Division and Chief Baron Kelly.[61] From that date new incumbents have been ennobled if not already peers. The holder is referred to as Lord Bingham of Corn Hill, Chief Justice or Lord Bingham of Corn Hill, Lord Chief Justice.[62]

The office of *Master of the Rolls*[63] dates from at least the thirteenth century. He was originally the keeper of the rolls or records of the Chancery, but with the passage of time he became recognised as a judge in the Court of Chancery: until 1813 he was the only judge in that court other than the Chancellor. After the reorganisation of the courts under the Judicature Acts 1873–75 he continued as a judge of first instance, but the man appointed in 1873, Sir George Jessel, was such an able lawyer that it was thought appropriate for the Master of the Rolls to become a judge of the Court of Appeal.[64] He is now the president of the Court of Appeal (Civil Division).[65] In view of the large number of important

---

[55] See generally on the functions of the Lord Chancellor: *Halsbury's Laws of England* (4th ed.) Vol. 8, paras.1171–1191; the accounts cited in Heuston (1964), p. xv, n. 1 and (1987), p. 1, n. 1; the addresses by Lord Gardiner (1968) and Lord Hailsham (1972) to the Holdsworth Club (published in B. W. Harvey (ed.) *The Lawyer and Justice* (1978); and Lord Hailsham, *The Door Wherein I Went* (1975), pp. 244–258 and (1989) 8 C.J.Q. 308.

[56] Harvey (ed.) (1978), p. 216.

[57] Viscount Kilmuir was dismissed by Harold Macmillan on the "night of the long knives" in July 1962.

[58] He had previously been Lord Advocate, a judge of the Court of Session and a Lord of Appeal.

[59] See F. Bresler, *Lord Goddard* (1977), Chap. 9.

[60] Lord Parker, (1961) 35 A.L.J. 97. Some Chief Justices of the King's Bench had styled themselves, or had been referred to informally as Lord Chief Justice of England, although this was technically incorrect. A notable example of the former was Sir Edward Coke, whose action was said to have displeased the King and to have been one of the causes of his dismissal.

[61] The opportunity was also taken to amalgamate the three common law divisions. The following have held the office: Lord Coleridge 1880–94; Lord Russell of Killowen 1894–1900; Lord Alverstone 1900–1914; Lord Reading 1914–1921; Lord Trevethin 1921–1922; Lord Hewart 1922–1940; Viscount Caldecote 1940–1946; Lord Goddard 1946–1958; Lord Parker 1958–1971; Lord Widgery 1971–1980; Lord Lane 1980–1992; Lord Taylor 1992–1996; Lord Bingham 1996–.

[62] Written as Lord Bingham of Corn Hill C.J. or Lord Bingham of Corn Hill L.C.J.

[63] See Lord Denning, *The Family Story* (1981), pp. 201–204; Sir John Donaldson, M.R., (1984) 17 Bracton L.J. 19 and *The Problems of A Master of the Rolls* (Holdsworth Club, 1985).

[64] Sir Robert Megarry, (1982) 98 L.Q.R. 370, 395.

[65] Supreme Court Act 1981, s.3(2).

civil cases determined in that court and the power of the Master of the Rolls over the allocation of cases, the holder of that office may exert considerable influence over the development of the civil law. It was for this reason that Lord Denning, then a Lord of Appeal in Ordinary, welcomed the appointment as Master of the Rolls.[66] The holder is referred to as Lord Woolf, Master of the Rolls.[67]

The *President of the Family Division* and the *Vice-Chancellor* head, respectively, the Family and Chancery Divisions of the High Court, and are *ex officio* members of the Court of Appeal. The former office was created in 1970, with the transition from the Probate, Divorce and Admiralty Division.[68] The holder is referred to as Sir Stephen Brown, President.[69] The latter office was created in 1970, the holder to be nominated by the Lord Chancellor.[70] It was made a royal appointment analogous to the other heads of division in 1982.[71] The holder is technically the vice-president of the Chancery Division,[72] but is effectively the head. He is referred to as Sir Richard Scott, Vice-Chancellor.[73] The title "Vice Chancellor of England" was used in the nineteenth century for the judges appointed to assist the Lord Chancellor in the Court of Chancery.[74]

One of the Lords Justices of Appeal is to be appointed as Senior Presiding Judge by the Lord Chief Justice, with the agreement of the Lord Chancellor.[75]

2. MASTERS AND REGISTRARS

There are a number of officers of the Supreme Court below the ranks of the judges, who perform both administrative and judicial tasks, the latter in particular in interlocutory matters arising in the course of litigation. There are, for

---

[66] Lord Denning, *The Family Story* (1981), pp. 172, 197; "the Master of the Rolls is still one of the most coveted posts in the land": *ibid.* p. 204. Lord Denning also found himself "too often in a minority" in the House of Lords: *The Discipline of Law* (1979), p. 287.

[67] Written as Lord Woolf M.R. It is common for the holder of the office to be ennobled, although not necessarily on appointment. Recent holders have been Lord Wright 1935–1949; Lord Evershed 1949–1962; Lord Denning 1962–1982; Sir John Donaldson (Lord Donaldson from 1988) 1982–1992; Sir Thomas Bingham 1992–1996; Lord Woolf 1996–.

[68] See above, p. 86. The old division was also headed by a President. The incumbents have been Sir Jocelyn Simon 1962–1971; Sir George Baker 1971–1979; Sir John Arnold 1979–1988 and Sir Stephen Brown 1988–.

[69] Written as Sir Stephen Brown P. Sir Stephen is the first who was previously a Lord Justice of Appeal.

[70] Administration of Justice Act 1970, s.5.

[71] Supreme Court Act 1981, s.10(1). See generally Sir Robert Megarry, (1982) 98 L.Q.R. 370.

[72] 1981 Act, s.5(1)(a).

[73] Written as Sir Richard Scott V.C. Sir Richard is the sixth of the modern Vice-Chancellors; the others were Sir John Pennycuick 1970–1974, Sir John Plowman 1974–1976, Sir Robert Megarry, 1974–1985, Sir Nicolas Browne-Wilkinson 1985–1991 and Sir Donald Nicholls 1991–1994. The last three holders of the office were previously Lords Justices of Appeal.

[74] 53 Geo III c. 24, 1813. In 1841 two additional Vice-Chancellors were appointed. With the death of the last Vice Chancellor of England (Sir Lancelot Shadwell) in 1850 the words "of England" were dropped. The Vice-Chancellors were transferred to the Chancery Division under the Judicature Act 1873. On their death or retirement their successors were styled as High Court justices. See A. B. Schofield, (1966) L. S. Gaz. 298; Megarry, *op. cit.*

[75] Courts and Legal Services Act 1990, s.72.

example,[76] a number of Masters of the Queen's Bench and Chancery Divisions, District Judges of the principal registry of the Family Division, Taxing Masters and Registrars in Bankruptcy. One of each of these groups is appointed as a "senior" or "chief".[77] Particularly important offices held by individuals are those of Master of the Crown Office and Registrar of Criminal Appeals,[78] and the Registrar of Civil Appeals.[79]

3. ELIGIBILITY FOR APPOINTMENT AND NUMBERS

Prior to the Courts and Legal Services Act 1990, appointments as a judge of the Supreme Court were confined to members of the Bar. The position now is as follows:[80]

Position	Max. Number	Qualification
Puisne judges	98[81]	10 years' High Court qualification[82] or two years standing as Circuit judge[83]
Lords Justices of Appeal	35[84]	10 years' High Court qualification or High Court judge.
Lord Chief Justice Master of the Rolls President of the Family Division Vice-Chancellor	}	10 years' High Court qualification or High Court judge or judge of the Court of Appeal

In order to be qualified for appointment as a Lord of Appeal in Ordinary a person has to have (1) been for 15 years a person who has a Supreme Court

---

[76] Schedule 2 to the Supreme Court Act 1981, as substituted by the Courts and Legal Services Act 1990, Sched. 10, para. 49, lists 12 offices. See also s.89, as amended by the 1990 Act, Sched. 18, paras.37, 38. On the work of the Queen's Bench Masters see A. S. Diamond, (1960) 76 L.Q.R. 504 and Sir Jack Jacob, *The Reform of Civil Procedural Law* (1982), p. 349; on Chancery Masters see R. E. Ball, (1961) 77 L.Q.R. 331.

[77] Supreme Court Act 1981, s.89(3).

[78] These were formerly separate posts, the first carrying responsibility for civil work and appeals in the Queen's Bench Division, the second for appeals to the Court of Appeal (Criminal Division). They were amalgamated by the 1990 Act, s.78.

[79] Supreme Court Act 1981, Sched. 2. This post carries responsibility for appeals to the Court of Appeal (Civil Division).

[80] Supreme Court Act 1981, s.10(3), as amended by the Courts and Legal Services Act 1990, s.71.

[81] *ibid.* s.4(1)(e).

[82] *i.e.*, a person who has a right of audience in relation to all proceedings in the High Court: 1990 Act, s.71(3); see further, above, pp. 133–138.

[83] A person of this standing is eligible for appointment as a deputy High Court judge: *ibid.* s.9(4).

[84] *ibid.* s.2(1). The number of puisne judges and Lords Justices may be increased by Order in Council: ss.4(4) and 2(4). The maximum number of puisne judges was increased from 85 to 98 by the Maximum Number of Judges (No.2) Order 1993 (S.I. 1993 No.1255): see H. L. Deb. vol. 545, May 10 1993, col.1048. The number of Lords Justices was raised from 28 to 29 in 1993; from 29 to 32 in 1994 (Maximum Number of Judges Order 1994 (S.I. 1994 No. 3217): see H. L. Deb., Vol. 559, November 30 1994, col. 686); and from 32 to 35 in 1996 (Maximum Number of Judges Order 1996 (S.I. 1996 No. 1142)). See also below, p. 245.

qualification in England,[85] an advocate in Scotland or a solicitor entitled to appear in the Court of Session and the High Court of Justiciary, or a practising barrister in Northern Ireland; or (2) have held for two years one or more of the "high judicial offices" of Lord Chancellor, or judge of the High Court, Court of Appeal, Court of Session or Supreme Court of Judicature of Northern Ireland.[86] There is a maximum number of 12.[87] By convention, two of the Lords of Appeal are Scots lawyers.[88] Most of the offices below the rank of puisne judge can be held by a person with a seven or 10-year general qualification.[89] These are much in the way of minimum requirements: for example, a barrister can expect to wait much longer than 10 years before becoming a serious candidate for appointment to the High Court.

Prior to the reforms effected by the Courts and Legal Services Act 1990, solicitors were not eligible for appointment to the High Court bench and above.[90] The government argued in resisting change on this point that experience as an advocate in the Supreme Court was necessary for appointment to the bench there.[91] With the extension of rights of audience in the higher courts to appropriately qualified solicitors, the change in eligibility for judicial appointment was irresistable. However, the government also at long last accepted the case that Circuit judges should be eligible for appointment to the High Court. Such judges may be solicitors who have never had a right of audience in the higher courts; nevertheless, a successful period as a Circuit judge would seem, as a matter of common sense, to be a better demonstration of one's judicial qualities than experience as an advocate.[92]

The expansion of eligibility for the highest judicial offices was widely welcomed during consultation on the Green Papers on Reform of the legal Profession.[93] One concern expressed in the course of it was that if members of the Crown Prosecution Service were to be given extended rights of audience they would thereby become eligible for a judicial appointment: it was, it was argued, wrong in principle for a person to be appointed as a judge whose experience was exclusively as a prosecutor. The White Paper[94] pointed out that it was the Lord Chancellor's current practice not to appoint serving civil servants to any paid judicial office which would involve hearing criminal cases. As appointment to a full-time judicial office had in practice to be preceded by part-time judicial experience, a member of any part of the government legal service could not become a judge without first returning to private practice for a substantial period.

---

[85] *i.e.* a person with a right of audience in relation to all proceedings in the Supreme Court: 1990 Act, s.71(3)(a); see above, p. 133–138.

[86] Appellate Jurisdiction Act 1876, ss.6, 25, as amended by the Courts and Legal Services Act 1990, Sched. 10, para. 1.

[87] Administration of Justice Act 1968, s.1. This number may be increased by Order in Council: *ibid.* It was raised from 11 by the Maximum Number of Judges Order 1994, n.83 above.

[88] This has been observed notwithstanding the appointment of a Scots lawyer as Lord Chancellor: Lord Mackay was succeeded as Lord of Appeal by Lord Jauncey of Tullichettle.

[89] Supreme Court Act 1981, Sched. 2, as substituted by the 1990 Act, Sched.10, para. 49. A "general qualification" is a right of audience in relation to any class of proceedings in any part of the Supreme Court, or all proceedings in county courts or magistrates' courts: 1990 Act, s.71(3)(c); see above, pp. 133–138.

[90] See JUSTICE Sub-Committee Report on the Judiciary (1972), pp. 9–20.

[91] See (1981) 131 N.L.J. 273; (1981) 79 L. S. Gaz. 193.

[92] The first solicitor Circuit judge to be promoted was Sachs J. in 1993.

[93] See above, p. 121.

[94] *Legal Services: A Framework for the Future* (Cm. 740, 1989), pp. 42, 43.

In the mean time, steps have been taken to encourage solicitor candidates for appointment to the Circuit bench.[95]

Academic lawyers are not appointed directly to the Bench in the United Kingdom, even if they are lawyers of the requisite standing.[96] Moreover, it seems to have become progressively less common for academic lawyers to be a member of either branch of the profession. It is generally agreed that it would not be appropriate to appoint academic lawyers as trial judges, in view of their lack of experience with the process of ascertaining the facts of cases. It is, however, arguable that academics should be eligible for appointment to the Court of Appeal or the House of Lords.[97] It could not be disputed that there would be candidates with the appropriate qualities of intellect and scholarship; it would also be one method of widening the background, political and otherwise, of members of the judiciary, should that be thought to be desirable.[98]

4. METHOD OF APPOINTMENT[99]

Appointment to the positions of Lord Chief Justice, Master of the Rolls, President of the Family Division, Vice-Chancellor, Lord of Appeal in Ordinary and Lord Justice of Appeal are made by the Queen,[1] acting by convention on the advice of the Prime Minister, who, in turn, will have consulted the Lord Chancellor. The effective voice in all appointments is normally that of the Lord Chancellor,[2] following consultations with members of the judiciary and leading members of the legal profession.[3] Occasionally, the Prime Minister may override

---

[95] H. C. Deb. Vol. 157, col. 1022, July 28, 1989, written answer by the Solicitor-General.

[96] The only reference to "practising" barristers related to eligibility for appointment as a Law Lord, above p. 225: The word "practising" does not appear in the qualification substituted by the 1990 Act. Professor Brenda Hoggett Q.C. was appointed to the Bench as Hale J. after moving from an academic post to a spell of almost 10 years as a Law Commissioner.

[97] The JUSTICE Sub-Committee on The Judiciary favoured this proposal: Report (1972) pp. 21–24.

[98] A number of academics have been appointed as tribunal chairmen or recorders; furthermore, Professor David Pearl has become a Circuit judge and Chief Immigration Adjudicator and John Mesher a Social Security Commissioner.

[99] See L.C.D., *Judicial Appointments: The Lord Chancellor's Policies and Procedures* (3rd ed., 1995) and Memorandum on Judicial Appointments Procedures (1995); Shetreet (1976), pp. 46–84; Lord Hailsham, *The Door Wherein I Went* (1975), pp. 254–258; A. Paterson, "Becoming a Judge" in R. Dingwall and P. Lewis (eds.) *The Sociology of the Professions* (1983), Chap. 12; A. Samuels, "Appointing the Judges" (1984) 134 N.L.J. 85, 107; Sir Robert Megarry, "The anatomy of judicial appointment: change but not decay" (1985) 19 U.B.C. Law Rev. 113; Judge T. Lawrence, (1993) 33 Med. Sci. Law 279.

[1] Supreme Court Act 1981, s.10(1)(2).

[2] The Lord Advocate's influence in the appointment of Scots Law Lords has increased in the post-war period: see A. A. Paterson, "Scottish Lords of Appeal, 1876–1988" 1988 J.R. 235. "In the last 20 years, however, it is generally felt that, with promotion from the Bar being out of fashion and neither Lord President evincing any desire to move south, in the case of most appointments the candidates have almost selected themselves": *ibid.*, p. 241.

[3] The extent and method of consultation depends on the level of the appointment : L.C.D. Memorandum on Judicial Appointments Procedures (1995), pp. 18–22, 24–34. For example, leaders of the relevant Circuit Bar and members of the Council of the Law Society are consulted on recordership appointments (the first rung of the ladder); the Lord Chancellor personally consults the four Heads of Division and the Senior Presiding Judge on High Court appointments, Heads of Division on appointments to the Court of Appeal and the Law Lords, the Lord Chief Justice and the Master of the Rolls on appointments to the House of Lords; and the views of a wider range of members of the judiciary are also sought. Lord Halsbury was exceptional in not consulting the

the Lord Chancellor's view in relation to senior appointments.[4] Records on potential candidates are maintained by the staff of the Lord Chancellor's Department Judicial Appointments Group, and candidates are interviewed. Increasing light has been shed on the appointments process by the publication by the Lord Chancellor's Department of a booklet on *Judicial Appointments*[5] and in the Department's Memorandum of Evidence to the Home Affairs Select Committee.[6] There have been a number of developments in the procedures, although most have to date been in respect of appointments below the level of the High Court.[7]

Appointments to the High Court Bench are normally made from the ranks of Queen's Counsel who have been in practice for 20 to 30 years.[8] Junior barristers may be appointed direct but the only persons normally so appointed are the Junior Counsel to the Treasury, who, indeed, are normally elevated to the bench after their period in that position. From time to time there have been promotions from the positions of Official Referee,[9] county court judge,[10] Recorder of Liverpool or Manchester, Circuit judge[11] and Registrar of the Family Division,[12] but these constitute a fairly small minority.[13] One person has been appointed to the High Court Bench and one to the House of Lords after being an advocate general of the Court of Justice of the European Communities.[14]

Appointments are "on merit".[15] The Lord Chancellor's Department publications[16] in fact say very little on what is looked for in respect of High Court appointments.[17] The qualities looked for would seem to be good character, success as an advocate and if appropriate in, a lower judicial office, the rather mystical quality known as "common sense," and good health. Those appointed are usually in their fifties, although some are appointed in their forties.[18] Brilliance as a technical lawyer is not regarded as a necessary precondition, although greater weight is placed on legal ability when appointments to the Chancery Division or to the appellate courts are considered. It is normal for those appointed to have served previously as a recorder or a deputy High Court judge.

Lord Chief Justice: R. F. V. Heuston, *Lives of the Lord Chancellors, 1885–1940* (1964), pp. 47–48.

[4] *e.g.* the appointment of Sir Ernest Pollock rather than Bankes L.J. as Master of the Rolls in 1923: Heuston, *Lives*, p. 428. *Cf.* Samuels (1984) 134 N.L.J. 85, 86.

[5] 3rd ed., 1995.

[6] L.C.D., *Judicial Appointments Procedures in England and Wales*, Memorandum of Evidence to the House of Commons Select Committee on Home Affairs (1995).

[7] See above, pp. 220–221.

[8] L.C.D. Memorandum on Judicial Appointments Procedures (1995), p. 24.

[9] Sir Edward Ridley (1897). The fact that he held office was regarded as counting against him rather than for him. He was the brother of the Home Secretary, and was subsequently thought to be a poor judge: See Heuston, *Lives*, pp. 49–52.

[10] The first was Sir Edward Acton (1920), the Nottingham county court judge. Ten more were elevated between 1945 and 1971.

[11] 22 were elevated between 1973 and 1994.

[12] Butler Sloss J. (1979).

[13] 26 out of 195 appointments between 1970 and 1994.

[14] Warner J. (1981); Lord Slynn (1992).

[15] See above, pp. 220–221.

[16] Above, pp. 227, n. 99.

[17] "Those appointed are in the forefront of their profession and outstanding in their field: they will have enjoyed a substantial and successful practice and high professional regard": L.C.D. Memorandum on Judicial Appointments Procedures (1995), p. 24.

[18] The youngest in the last 50 years were Lords Hodson and Devlin who were 42 when appointed High Court judges in 1937 and 1948 respectively.

Unlike the position in relation to appointments as recorder or Circuit judge, it is not the practice for those eligible to apply for appointment to the High Court Bench although they may let it be known to the Lord Chancellor's Department that they would be interested in such an appointment. Appointments are made by invitation, and invitation does not depend on application.

Several observers have noted an improvement in the quality of judges.[19] "On the whole, I have no doubt that judges are much better educated, more polite and more patient than they used to be."[20]

Political service was formerly a significant factor in many judicial appointments.[21] Of the 139 judges appointed between 1832 and 1906, 80 were M.P.s at the time of their nomination; 11 others had been candidates for Parliament. Of those 80, 63 were appointed by their own party while in office.[22] Lord Halsbury, Unionist Lord Chancellor for three periods,[23] was criticised for making bad appointments of Tory M.P.s.[24] Lord Salisbury, the Prime Minister for most of Halsbury's time as Lord Chancellor, "would never apologise for the practice of making [legal promotions] a reward for political 'right thinking,' "[25] although he expressed the need for caution following public criticism of some of the early appointments.[26] There was contemporary criticism of the appointments of Grantham, J. C. Lawrance, Bruce, Darling, Ridley and Kekewich, all of whom turned out to be poor judges,[27] although each had his defenders. The first four were Conservative M.P.s at the time of their appointment. Ridley had briefly been a Conservative M.P. nearly 20 years before, although that did not seem to have influenced the choice, and Kekewich had been a Conservative candidate. Heuston argues that the last two appointments were unlucky and that "four dubious appointments out of 30 during a tenure of the woolsack lasting 17 years should not weigh too heavily in the scales when making a final judgment."[28]

Lord Haldane, when Lord Chancellor between 1912 and 1915, introduced a policy of appointing "only on the footing of high legal and professional qualifications",[29] and this position, as regards puisne judgeships, has more or less been maintained since. The only political tradition that took significantly longer to die was the idea that the Attorney-General and Solicitor-General had a special

---

[19] C. P. Harvey Q.C., *The Advocate's Devil* (1958), pp. 33–34, comparing the fifties with the twenties, Lord Devlin, *The Judge* (1979), p. 24; D. Pannick, *Judges* (1987), p. 15.

[20] Lord Hailsham, *The Door Wherein I Went* (1975), p. 257.

[21] See A. Paterson, (1974) 1 B.J.L.S. 118. Party politics continues to play a larger role in the appointment of judges in Scotland. This has given rise to adverse criticism: I. D. Willock, 1969 J.R. 193; C. M. Campbell, 1973 J.R. 254.

[22] H. Laski, (1926) 24 Michigan L. R. 529.

[23] 1885–86; 1886–92; 1895–1905.

[24] See Heuston, *Lives*, pp. 36–66.

[25] G. Cecil (Lord Salisbury's daughter and biographer) cited by Heuston, *Lives* p. 36.

[26] *ibid.* p. 57.

[27] Grantham J. attracted severe criticism in Parliament for his partisan trial of two election petitions in 1906: see H. Cecil, *Tipping the Scales* (1965), pp. 194–208; Darling J. was described by C. P. Harvey as a "real shocker" (*The Advocate's Devil* (1958), pp. 32–33) and renowned for his "jokes"; MacKinnon L. J. wrote that J. C. Lawrance J. was "a stupid man, a very ill-equipped lawyer and a bad judge. He was not the worst judge I have appeared before: that distinction I would assign to Mr Justice Ridley. Ridley had much better brains than Lawrance, but he had a perverse instinct for unfairness that Lawrance could never approach" (1944) 60 L.Q.R. 324).

[28] *Lives*, p. 66.

[29] R. B. Haldane, *An Autobiography* (1929), p. 253.

claim should one of the higher judicial offices fall vacant.[30] The Attorney's claim on the position of Lord Chief Justice was supposed to be particularly strong.[31]

Between 1873 and 1945 only four of the 23 holders of the office of Attorney-General did not go on to hold one of the higher judicial offices.[32] All those appointed Lord Chief Justice, with one exception,[33] were former Attorneys. Nine of the 17 men who were Solicitor-General without becoming Attorney-General also progressed to one of the higher judicial offices.[34]

However, much controversy surrounded the appointment of Sir Gordon Hewert as Lord Chief Justice.[35] In 1921 it was arranged that Lord Reading C.J. was to become Viceroy of India. Hewart, as Attorney-General, pressed his claim to the position of Lord Chief Justice but could not be spared from the Commons. Lloyd George appointed a 77-year-old Queen's Bench judge, A. T. Lawrence J., on the understanding that he would retire when called upon, although neither Lord Birkenhead L.C. nor Hewart approved of the plan. Nevertheless, in 1922 Lord Trevethin (as Lawrence became) read of his own resignation in *The Times*, and Hewart duly succeeded him. To add injury to insult, Hewart proved to be "perhaps the worst Lord Chief Justice of England since the seventeenth century. Although no imputation of corruption or dishonesty could be brought against him, as against Scroggs and Jeffreys, on the bench he rivalled them in arbitrary and unjudicial behaviour."[36]

Since 1945 the position has changed significantly. In 1946, Viscount Caldecote C.J. was succeeded by a Lord of Appeal, Lord Goddard, after the post had been declined by Sir Hartley Shawcross, the Attorney-General.[37] Lord Goddard and his successors have not had political careers.[38] Lord Goddard was followed by Lord Parker,[39] who subsequently commented that the non-political nature of the appointment, made clear by the appointments of Lord Goddard, himself and Lord Widgery, was of "vital importance for the administration of justice in this

[30] J. Ll. J. Edwards, *The Law Officers of the Crown* (1964), pp. 309–334.

[31] Eighteen of the 42 Chief Justices of the Common Pleas between 1600 and 1873 were ex-Attorneys, 16 appointed directly. Between 1725 and 1873 all but two of the Chief Justices of the King's Bench were ex-Attorneys, four appointed directly: Edwards (1964), pp. 320–21.

[32] Lord Chancellor (8), L.C.J. (5), M.R. (2), Lord of Appeal (4), L.J. (4): four held two of these offices. The exceptions were Karslake (1874) who suffered a complete physical break-down in 1875, Walton (1905–8) who died in office and Patrick Hastings (1924), Attorney-General in the first Labour Government, who apparently "had no wish to be made a judge" (Lord Birkett, *Six Great Advocates* (1961), p. 37). Sir Henry James (1880–85) was given a peerage and often sat in the House of Lords.

[33] Lord Trevethin (1921).

[34] Lord Chancellor (4); L.J. (3); President of the P.D.A. (2); Lord of Appeal (1: Lord Davey, promoted from Lord Justice). Of the other eight, four held other ministerial offices (Harcourt (1873–74), Gorst (1885–86), Cripps (1930–31) and Monckton (1945)), three died in office or shortly after leaving it (Lockwood (1894–95), Melville (1929–30) and O'Connor (1936–40)), and the other, Clarke (1886–92), refused the position of Master of the Rolls in 1897.

[35] See R. Jackson, *The Chief* (1959), Chap. 9; J. Campbell, *F. E. Smith, First Earl of Birkenhead* (1983), pp. 479–481.

[36] Heuston, *Lives*, pp. 603–604; Cf. C. P. Harvey, *The Advocate's Devil* (1958), p. 32.

[37] See F. Bresler, *Lord Goddard* (1977), pp. 112–115. Shawcross had opposed the idea that there was a "right" of succession, and preferred a political career.

[38] Goddard had stood unsuccessfully as an Independent Conservative in the 1929 General Election, a brief and "ill-starred political venture": Bresler (1977), pp. 60–62.

[39] The then Attorney-General, Sir Reginald Manningham-Buller, did not actively seek the post, but would apparently have liked to have been asked: Bresler (1977), pp. 295–298.

country."[40] The only Law Officers subsequently appointed to the bench have been Lynn Ungoed-Thomas[41] and Sir Jocelyn Simon,[42] and only three of the others have become Lord Chancellor.[43] The appointment of Lord Chief Justices from amongst the ranks of the judiciary has been generally welcomed.

It has become progressively more difficult to combine membership of the Commons with a successful practice at the Bar. Lord Hailsham regretted that he was unable to appoint a single High Court judge from among M.P.s.[44] There is something of a vicious circle in that the lack of a reasonable prospect of elevation to the Bench may discourage the ablest lawyers from seeking a political career. Political experience has been regarded by some as an asset for an appointee. Lord Simon has argued that:

"although no one would wish to see a predominantly political Bench, a seasoning of judges with experience of politics and administration is far from disadvantageous; constituency duties, for example, are calculated to develop a social awareness which ordinary forensic work is not apt to inculcate."[45]

The social and educational background of the judges has been examined in a number of surveys.[46] These show that the judges are overwhelmingly upper or upper middle class in origin, with over three-quarters having attended public school, and a similar proportion either Oxford or Cambridge University. Only ten women have reached the High Court bench, and no members of the ethnic minorities.[47] A report commissioned by the Bar Council and the L.C.D.[48] concluded that "gender discrimination appears to be institutionally present within the Bar and the judiciary" and identified a series of factors that discouraged women from applying for a judicial appointment, including the lack of role models and the reliance on informed soundings from a majority male group.

[40] Bresler (1977), p. 297.
[41] Labour M. P. 1945–62; Solicitor General 1951; High Court judge 1962–72.
[42] Conservative M. P. 1951–62; Solicitor-General 1959–62; President of the Probate, Divorce and Admiralty Division 1962–71; Lord of Appeal 1971–77. Two previous Presidents had formerly been Solicitor-General: Sir Samuel Evans (1910–1919) and Sir Frank (later Lord) Merriman (1934–1962).
[43] Viscount Dilhorne (formerly, Sir Reginald Manningham-Buller), Lord Elwyn-Jones and Lord Havers. Lord Mackay had previously served as Lord Advocate. Between 1945 and 1990 there have been 18 holders of one or both of the Law Offices.
[44] The Door Wherein I Went (1975), p. 256.
[45] (1965) 81 L.Q.R. 289, 295.
[46] The Economist, December 15, 1956, pp. 946–947; K. Goldstein-Jackson, New Society, May 14, 1970; H. Cecil, The English Judge (revised ed., 1972), Chap. 1; J. Brock (M. Phil. dissertation, quoted in the JUSTICE Sub-Committee Report on the Judiciary (1972)); F. L. Morrison, Courts and the Political Process in England (1973), Chap. 3. The background of the Lords of Appeal appointed between 1876 and 1969 is examined in L. Blom-Cooper and G. Drewry, Final Appeal (1972), pp. 158–169. The results of these surveys are summarised by J. A. G. Griffith, The Politics of the Judiciary (4th ed., 1991), pp. 30–33.
[47] Elizabeth Lane J., Booth J., Butler-Sloss J. (now L.J.) Bracewell J., Ebsworth J., Smith J., Arden J., Steel J., Hale J. and Hogg J. Ebsworth J. was the first appointed to the Queen's Bench Division (followed by Smith and Steel JJ.); Arden J. the first appointed to the Chancery Division. As at December 1, 1994, the numbers of judges known or believed to be of ethnic minority origin were: four Circuit judges (0.8%); 11 recorders (1.3%); 10 assistant recorder (2.5%) and one district judge (0.3%): L.C.D. Memorandum on Judicial Appointments Procedures (1995), p. 139.
[48] Without Prejudice? – Sex Equality at the Bar and in the Judiciary, TMS Management Consultants (1992), cited in Rozenberg (1994), pp. 84–86.

Appointments are formally made "on merit" and "without regard to ethnic origin, gender, marital status, sexual orientation, political affiliation, religion, or (subject to the physical requirements of the office) disability."[49] The Lord Chancellor "does ... encourages greater numbers of women and ethnic minority practitioners to apply" but is against positive discrimination or a fast-track appointment procedure for such candidates.[50] The introduction of greater formality into the Circuit and District judge appoint procedures[51] may prove a suitable model for adoption more broadly.

The process of socialisation at the Bar tends to mean that those from other backgrounds do not seem markedly different, if different at all, from the majority.[52] The extent to which judicial attitudes can be related to the social background of the judges is a large and debatable question.[53] Given the continuance for the foreseeable future of the policy of appointing judges largely from the Bar, it is unlikely that there will be any significant change in the background of the people appointed. What is more plausible is that the attitudes of successive generations may gradually change.[54]

Other countries have adopted different methods of appointment. In civil law systems there is normally a career judiciary, which is part of the general civil service and separate from the legal profession. In the United States there are two basic methods of selection, *appointment* and *election*, although a compromise between the two methods is commonly applied.[55] All federal judges are appointed by the President, subject to confirmation by the Senate.[56] An appointment can in practice be vetoed by one of the candidate's home state Senators and candidates are also evaluated by the American Bar Association's influential Committee on Federal Judiciary, which makes its views known to the President and the Senate. In 1970, 82 per cent of state and local judges were elected, although real contests were rare.[57] In a number of states elections are used to confirm in office judges who have been in office for a limited period following appointment by the governor, a separate Commission, or the two together.[58] It

---

[49] L.C.D. Memorandum on Judicial Appointments Procedures (1995), p. 13.

[50] *ibid.*, p. 61–70. Ethnic monitoring of applicants was started in 1991; other steps to encourage women and ethnic minority applicants are summarised at pp. 67–69.

[51] Above, p. 178–182.

[52] As to the social background of barristers, see above, pp. 220–221.

[53] See below, pp. 249–258.

[54] See P. McAuslan, (1983) 46 M.L.R. 1, 19.

[55] See H. Abraham, *The Judicial Process* (6th ed., 1993), Chap. 2 and *Justices and Presidents* (3rd ed., 1992).

[56] The most recent example of a presidential nominee for the Supreme Court failing to obtain confirmation is Judge Robert Bork: see R. Hodder-Williams, (1988) xxxvi *Political Studies*, 613–637; Essays on the Supreme Court Appointment Process (symposium) 101 Harv. L.R. 1146–1229 (1988).

[57] Abraham (1993), p. 34. In recent years a number of state judges (including Chief Justice Rose Bird and two associate justices of the California Supreme Court) have failed to obtain re-election following sustained political campaigns by opponents: see R. Reidinger, "The politics of judging" A.B.A. Journal, April 1 1987, p. 52.

[58] The "Missouri plan" is favoured by the A.B.A. A non-partisan Commission selects three candidates, one of whom the governor must then appoint. After one year in office he or she must be approved by the electorate, running unopposed in a separate, non-partisan judicial ballot: Abraham (1993), pp. 36–39.

is highly unlikely that any of these methods will be introduced here,[59] although some have favoured the formal establishment of a Judicial Commission to evaluate and advise on appointments.[60]

5. PROMOTION

The traditional view has been that there is no system of "promotion" of judges. The fear is that holders of judicial office might allow their promotion prospects to affect their decision-making; care might be taken to avoid offending the senior judges or the politicians responsible for making or influencing judicial appointments. Nevertheless, the trend seems to be for judges to be elevated from the Circuit Bench more regularly, and for appointments to the House of Lords and Court of Appeal to be made from the court below. Appointments are not now made direct from the Bar to the Court of Appeal[61] or the House of Lords,[62] or direct from the High Court to the House of Lords.[63] Three Lord Chancellors, Maugham, Simonds and Dilhorne, have been appointed Lords of Appeal, but the first two of these were simply reverting to an office previously held. At first, elevation to the Court of Appeal from the High Court carried no increase in salary, although membership of the Privy Council was always conferred. The salary of a Lord Justice is now roughly halfway between that of a High Court judge and a Lord of Appeal, although the differentials are small.[64] Apart from the prestige of a higher judicial office, promotion means that there is no longer the disadvantage of having to spend time away from home on circuit. There is, however, no evidence that judges are affected by "promotion sickness".

[59] An argument that the Law Lords, the Lord Chief Justice and the Master of the Rolls, but not the other judges, should be elected, under a plan similar to the "Missouri Plan" is presented by D. Pannick, (1981) 131 N.L.J. 1064.

[60] Report of JUSTICE Sub-Committee on *The Judiciary* (1972), pp. 30–31, 61; JUSTICE Report on *The Judiciary in England and Wales* (1992), Chap. 6; G. Bindman, (1992) 142 N.L.J. 1035. This Commission would also deal with complaints. The conferral of the power of *appointment* on a Judicial Service Commission is advocated by C. Harlow, in Harlow (ed.), *Public Law and Politics* (1986), Chap. 10, and R. Brazier, "Government and the Law" [1989] P.L. 64, 88–91; Brazier also advocates the establishment of Circuit Judicial Committees to advise on the appointment of the lower judiciary. A Law Society discussion document has made similar proposals: (1991) 88 L. S. Gaz., February 20, pp. 6–7. For a defence of reliance on the individual personal responsibility of the Lord Chancellor, see Lord Mackay, *The Administration of Justice*, (1994), Chap. 1. For a comparative discussion, see B. Harris, (1993) 15 Adelaide L. R. 191.

[61] The only examples have been Slesser L.J. (1929), Scott L.J. (1935) and Somervell L.J. (1946) (all Law Officers), Duke L.J. (1918; Chief Secretary for Ireland 1916–18) and Greene L.J. (1935: leader of the Chancery bar, and subsequently Master of the Rolls). Lord Denning has written that experience as a trial judge is valuable for an appeal judge: *The Family Story* (1981), pp. 169–170.

[62] Eleven examples: five Scots, two English, two Irish. The only two since 1930 have been Lord Reid (1948) and Lord Radcliffe (1949) each of whom was an outstanding judge.

[63] Seven examples: Lords Parker (1913), Tomlin (1929), Wright (1932), Porter (1938), Simonds (1944), Uthwatt (1946) and Wilberforce (1964). Lord Slynn was appointed to the House of Lords (1992) after a period as an Advocate General of the European Community; he had previously been a High Court judge.

[64] See below, p. 241. The introduction of a differential was recommended by the Top Salaries Review Body, "in recognition of the promotion which is involved in appointment to the Court of Appeal from the High Court Bench:" Report No. 6, Cmnd. 5846, 1974, p. 31.

6. Tenure[65]

Every judge of the Supreme Court, other than the Lord Chancellor, who holds office "during the pleasure" of (in effect) the Prime Minister:

> "shall hold that office during good behaviour, subject to a power of removal by Her Majesty on an address presented to Her by both Houses of Parliament."[66]

Similarly:

> "Every Lord of Appeal in Ordinary shall hold his office during good behaviour but he may be removed from such office on the address of both Houses of Parliament."[67]

These arrangements date from the Act of Settlement 1700.[68] Before then judicial tenure was not regulated by statute. The King appointed on his own terms, which were usually, although not invariably, "during pleasure".[69]

The Stuarts removed or suspended a number of judges who did not conform to their expectations, James II being particularly enthusiastic in this regard.[70] From 1688, William III's appointments were made during good behaviour: the Act of Settlement took away the monarch's right to choose otherwise, although it seems that William was reluctant to see the legal position changed.[71]

It is generally accepted that under these provisions a judge may be removed from office either (1) for breach of the requirement of good behaviour or (2) by the Crown on an address by both Houses of Parliament, irrespective of whether he or she has been of good behaviour. The "address" procedure is, theoretically, neither the exclusive procedure for removal, nor restricted to cases of misbehaviour. In cases of misbehaviour, there are indeed a number of alternative procedures for removing a judge, which do not seem to be excluded by the Supreme Court Act 1981 or any of its antecedents:

(1) Proceedings in the Queen's Bench Division commenced by the writ of *scire facias* for the repeal of the letters patent by which the office was granted.
(2) Proceedings in the Queen's Bench Division for an injunction to restrain the judge from continuing to act in an office to which he or she is no longer entitled.[72]
(3) Conviction for a criminal offence.

---

[65] See Shetreet (1976), pp. 1–12, 85–159; Sir Kenneth Roberts-Wray, *Commonwealth and Colonial Law* (1966), pp. 484–491; W. Finnie, 1993 S.L.T. 213.

[66] Supreme Court Act 1981, s.11(3).

[67] Appellate Jurisdiction Act 1876, s.6, as amended.

[68] Section 3. This section was to take effect should the arrangements for ensuring the Protestant succession become operative: accordingly, the section came into operation in 1714 with the accession of George I.

[69] See C. H. McIlwain, *Consititutionalism and the Changing World* (1939), pp. 294–307.

[70] See J. H. Baker, *Introduction to Legal History* (3rd ed., 1990), pp. 189–193; A. Havighurst, (1950) 66 L.Q.R. 62, 229; (1953) 69 L.Q.R. 522.

[71] D. Rubini, (1967) 83 L.Q.R. 343.

[72] S. A. de Smith and R. Brazier, *Constitutional and Administrative Law* (7th ed., 1994), p. 408.

In these cases the "misbehaviour" must either be connected with the perform-ance or non-performance of official duties, or, if not so connected, must involve the commission of a criminal offence of moral turpitude. Furthermore, a judge can be removed on any ground by an Act of Parliament, or for "high crimes and misdemeanours" by impeachment.[73] Neither would be used in preference to an address: the latter, in addition, is regarded as obsolete in the United Kingdom.[74]

Today, it is likely that the address procedure would be used in any case where a judge was to be removed, and, further, that this would only be done in a case of misbehaviour,[75] although a rather wider view might be taken of "misbehav-iour" for this purpose, in particular to include private immoral conduct.[76] There have been many statements to the effect that this would be the "proper" way to proceed, notwithstanding the other possibilities.[77]

Conviction for a criminal offence does not inevitably lead to resignation or removal from office. Eight judges[78] have been convicted of driving with excess alcohol, but have continued in office.

The other methods by which a judge may leave office are:

(1) resignation[79];
(2) reaching the retiring age of 70[80];
(3) under the procedure whereby the Lord Chancellor may remove a judge who is disabled by permanent infirmity from the performance of his or her duties and is incapacitated from resigning his or her office.[81]

A retired judge may be asked to sit as a member of the Judicial Committee of

---

[73] A trial by the House of Lords at the instigation of the Commons. This procedure has not been used since the trials of Warren Hastings (1788) and Lord Melville (1805). Among judges who were impeached were two Lord Chancellors, Bacon (1620) and Macclesfield (1725): see H. Cecil, *Tipping the Scales* (1964), pp. 99–126.

[74] The procedure is not obsolete in the U.S.A.: President Nixon resigned rather than face impeachment.

[75] It seems that the address procedure can be used in cases of incapacity: see Shetreet (1976), p. 274. However, resignation would be secured by informal pressure or a judge would be removed by the Lord Chancellor: see below, n. 81.

[76] *Kenrick's case* (1826): Cecil (1964), pp. 165–170.

[77] See Shetreet (1976), pp. 96–103.

[78] A Lord Justice in 1969, a Circuit judge in 1973, a High Court judge in 1975, two Circuit judges in 1985, a High Court Registrar in 1989 (see R. Light (1989) 139 N.L.J. 783), and a District judge in 1993 (see Rozenberg (1994), p. 117). The Registrar and the District judge were severely reprimanded by the Lord Chancellor: *The Times*, June 17, 1989; Rozenberg, *op. cit.*.

[79] Supreme Court Act 1981, s.11(7); Appellate Jurisdiction Act 1876, s.6.

[80] Supreme Court Act 1981, s.11(2), as amended by the Judicial Pensions and Retirement Act 1993, Sched. 6, para. 4. A retirement age (of 75) was first introduced by the Judicial Pensions Act 1959, but did not apply to those in office on December 19, 1959. (One of those to escape was Lord Denning M. R., who retired in 1982 aged 83). The 1993 Act applies both retropsectively and prospectively. Judges other than High Court judges and above may be asked to continue (in annual steps) to 75: 1993 Act, s.26. A judge may retire on full pension (normally half the salary in the last 12 months of service, index-linked), (1) after 20 years' service (raised from 15 by the 1993 Act to bring it into line with the public and private sectors generally); and (2) after attaining the age of 65, or (3) if he or she is disabled by permanent infirmity; otherwise, pensions are paid pro rata. See, generally, annotations by J. Mesher in *Current Law Statutes Annotated 1993*; W. Finnie, "Judicial Tenure and Judicial Pensions" 1993 S.L.T. 213.

[81] Supreme Court Act 1981, s.11(8)(9). See A. Paterson, "The Infirm Judge" (1974) 1 B.J.L.S. 83.

the Privy Council or the House of Lords, or as a deputy judge, on an ad hoc basis. However, this is no longer possible once he or she has reached 75.[82]

If a judge were, for example, to bury a meat cleaver in someone's head the address procedure for removal from office would work swiftly and surely. Judges, however, do not indulge in acts of misbehaviour that are clearly inconsistent with their remaining in office. Where matters are not clear cut, the address procedure is complex, and uncertain in some matters of detail. Charges have been presented on a number of occasions, but only one judge has been removed as a consequence. Sir Jonah Barrington, a judge of the High Court of Admiralty in Ireland, was removed in 1830 for the embezzlement of sums of money paid into court.

7. DISCIPLINE AND CRITICISM

The mechanisms for disciplining judges who misbehave are more significant in practice than the procedures for removal. Judges may be criticised in Parliament. An extreme case is that of Lord Westbury L.C., who resigned in 1865 following votes of censure passed in both Houses concerning certain appointments he had made.

Judges are often criticised in the press. "Scurrilous abuse" of a judge may, however, be punished as contempt for "scandalising the court."[83] This head of contempt must be distinguished from that concerned with publications likely to interfere with the administration of justice in particular proceedings, by, for example, influencing juries. The former head was thought to be obsolete in 1899.[84] However, proceedings were taken against the editor of the *Birmingham Daily Argus* for a spirited attack on Darling J. (an "impudent little man in horsehair, a microcosm of conceit and empty headedness").[85] He apologised, and was fined £100, with £25 costs. According to Abel-Smith and Stevens[86] "within a decade the criticism of judicial behaviour which had been so outspoken was replaced in the press by almost unbroken sycophantic praise for the judges." Similar proceedings were taken on a number of occasions in the 1920s and 1930s. Since then, press criticism of the judiciary has become more commonplace, without matching the personal insults expressed by Mr Gray. Proceedings against Quintin Hogg (as he then was), arising out of criticisms of the Court of Appeal published in *Punch*, were dismissed.[87] Salmon L. J. said.[88]

---

[82] Judicial Pensions and Retirement Act 1993, s.26(7). Lord Bridge seemed displeased by his forced "second retirement": see *Ruxley Electronics and Constructions Ltd v. Forsyth* [1995] 3 W.L.R. 118, 121 (his last case).

[83] See S. H. Bailey, D. J. Harris and B. L. Jones, *Civil Liberties: Cases and Materials* (4th ed., 1995), pp. 421–427; N. V. Lowe, *Borrie and Lowe's Law of Contempt*, (2nd ed., 1983), pp. 226–247; C. J. Miller, *Contempt of Court* (2nd ed., 1989), Chap. 12; C. Walker, "Scandalising in the Eighties" (1985) 101 L.Q.R. 359.

[84] *McLeod v. St Aubyn* [1899] A.C. 549, 561 (a colonial judge was accused of "reducing the judicial character to the level of a clown," and "being narrow, bigoted, vain, vindictive and unscrupulous." The Privy Council held that this did not require committal for contempt).

[85] *R. v. Gray* [1900] 2 Q.B. 36. The full passage is printed in 82 L.T. 534. *Cf.* above, p. 229, n. 27. Darling was apparently "rather amused by the vigour of its expression": D. Walker-Smith, *The Life of Lord Darling* (1938), p. 122.

[86] *Lawyers and the Courts* (1967), pp. 126–7.

[87] *R. v. Metropolitan Police Commissioner, ex p. Blackburn (No. 2)* [1968] 2 Q.B. 150.

[88] *ibid.* p. 155. Mr Hogg subsequently became Lord Chancellor as Lord Hailsham of St Marylebone.

"The authority and reputation of our courts are not so frail that their judgments need to be shielded from criticism, even from the criticism of Mr Quintin Hogg. . . . [N]o criticism of a judgment, however vigorous, can amount to contempt of court, provided it keeps within the limits of reasonable courtesy and good faith."

Judges are from time to time rebuked in appellate courts. Censure may be coupled with the setting aside of a conviction or the reversal of a judgment. Thus, judges have been censured for excessive interruptions,[89] threatening a jury,[90] improper behaviour on the Bench,[91] falling asleep,[92] incompetence,[93] and disloyalty to the decisions of superior courts.[94] Lord Hailsham has written that there are judges who become subject to "judge's disease, that is to say a condition of which the symptoms may be pomposity, irritability, talkativeness, proneness to *obiter dicta*, a tendency to take short cuts."[95]

There may be complaints from barristers, solicitors or litigants, either expressed in court or in private to the judge personally, or made in some other quarter. Complaints may be made to the Lord Chief Justice or the Lord Chancellor.[96] They may be channelled through a head of chambers, the Chairman of the Bar Council, the Attorney-General, the Law Society,[97] an M.P., or some other intermediary. There is generally a preference for taking action privately. Confrontations in court between counsel and judge may be to the client's disadvantage; it is impossible to assess the extent to which they may also be, or be feared to be, to the barrister's future disadvantage. The upshot may be correspondence or an interview between the Lord Chancellor and the judge,[98] or even, on occasion, a public rebuke.[99]

It has been doubted whether the informal pressures on judges are sufficient. Over the years there have been a few judges whose conduct has often been

---

[89] *e.g. Yuill v. Yuill* [1945] P. 15; *Jones v. N.C.B.* [1957] 2 Q.B. 55. The judge in the latter case was Hallett J., who was seen by the Lord Chancellor and resigned shortly afterwards: Lord Denning, *The Due Process of Law* (1980), pp. 58–62 ("The judge who talked too much"). See generally, A. Samuels, "Judicial Misconduct in the Criminal Trial" [1982] Crim.L.R. 221.

[90] *R. v. McKenna* [1960] 1 Q.B. 411 (Stable J. at Nottingham Assizes threatened a jury that if they did not return a verdict within 10 minutes they would be locked up all night. They returned in six minutes with verdicts of guilty, which were quashed on appeal).

[91] *R. v. Hircock* [1970] 1 Q.B. 67. The judge in a criminal trial made gestures of impatience, sighed, and several times "observed in a loud voice, 'Oh God,' and then laid his head across his arm and made groaning noises" (p. 71). The court did not condone this conduct but declined to quash the conviction as being unsafe and unsatisfactory.

[92] If the judge thereby misses something of importance: *R. v. Edworthy* [1961] Crim.L.R. 325; *R. v. Langham* [1972] Crim.L.R. 457.

[93] *Taylor v. Taylor* [1970] 2 All E.R. 609.

[94] *Cassell & Co. Ltd v. Broome* [1972] A.C. 1027, below, pp. 425–426.

[95] *The Door Wherein I Went* (1975), p. 255.

[96] Court users are invited to send complaints "about the way a judge has personally treated you in court (apart from the decisions made in your case)" to the L.C.D. Judicial Appointments Group: *The Court Service Charter for Court Users* (1995), p. 19.

[97] It seems that the Bar and the Law Society will only act in cases of misconduct towards barristers and solicitors, respectively: JUSTICE, Sub-Committee Report on *The Judiciary*, pp. 49–50.

[98] Or an interview with the Lord Chief Justice: one such is described by Judge James Pickles in *Straight from the Bench* (1987), p. 53–57, arising out of his publication of newspaper articles.

[99] *e.g.* the rebuke administered to Judge Pickles by Lord Mackay L. C. for holding a press conference in a pub, and referring to the then Lord Chief Justice as a "dinosaur". Cf. *R. v. Earnshaw* [1990] Crim.L.R. 53.

criticised, but who have nevertheless remained on the Bench. On the other hand, this small minority seems to have dwindled. The JUSTICE Sub-Committee[1] argued that some form of complaints machinery should be established, probably in the form of a complaints tribunal or judicial commission. Such a reform is unlikely to occur in the foreseeable future, and, on the present evidence, the case for it is not made out.[2] Finally, it must be remembered that criticisms of judges in the popular press are commonly marred by such weaknesses as a failure to report accurately the full facts, a failure to understand basic principles of the conduct of trials and a failure to distinguish defects of the law from the defects of the judge.

8. TRAINING[3]

In the late 1970s certain tentative steps were taken to introduce a measure of compulsory training for newly appointed judges. From 1963 onwards a series of conferences and judicial seminars on sentencing were organised by the Lord Chief Justice and the Lord Chancellor's Office. Attendance at these was voluntary. However a Judicial Studies Board was established in 1979 following the report of a Working Party chaired by Bridge L.J.[4]

From October 1985 the Board was re-established, with enlarged responsibilities beyond the criminal jurisdiction, namely the provision of training in the civil and family jurisdictions and the supervision of training for magistrates[5] and tribunal chairmen and members.[6] Executive functions are delegated to a Criminal Committee, chaired by a Queen's Bench judge; a Civil and Family Committee, jointly chaired by judges of the Queen's Bench and Family Divisions; a Magisterial Committee, chaired by a Circuit judge; and a Tribunals Committee, chaired by the President of the Independent Tribunal Service.[7] An Ethic Minorities Advisory Committee advises on questions involving the treatment of members of ethnic minorities in the judicial system.[8]

---

[1] *op. cit.*, pp. 45–61. The case for a Judicial Performance Commission is also made by D. Pannick, *Judges* (1987), pp. 96–104. A Judicial Commission with responsibilities covering the monitoring of sentences, training and complaints has been established in New South Wales by the Judicial Officers Act 1986, criticised by S. Shetreet, (1987) 10 Univ. of N.S.W. L.J. 4.

[2] It was not endorsed by the JUSTICE Committee on *The Administration of the Courts* (1986), Chap. 4.

[3] See M. Partington, "Training the Judiciary in England and Wales" (1994) 13 C.J.Q. 319; A. Ashworth, *Sentencing and Criminal Justice* (1993), pp. 49–50, 53; Judicial Studies Board: report for 1979–82 (HMSO, 1983), report for 1983–87 (HMSO, 1988) report for 1987–91 (HMSO, 1992), and report for 1991–95 (1995); Glidewell L.J., "The Judicial Studies Board" in C. Munro and M. Wasik, *Sentencing, Judicial Discretion and Training* (1992).

[4] *Judicial Studies and Information* (HMSO, 1978). The Working Party had received "widely felt and strongly voiced objection" to the use in their working paper of the term "judicial training," on the grounds that "training" might represent a threat to judicial independence, that appointees might resent the implication that they need to be "trained" and that the "public image of the judge" would be impaired. The Working Party accordingly adopted the term "judicial studies" and emphasised that their proposals would not involve "indoctrination" or "conditioning" (*ibid.* pp. 2 and 3). Lord Devlin was caustic in his condemnation of the working paper: *The Judge* (1979), pp. 18–53; *cf.* book review by E. J. Griew, [1980] Crim.L.R. 812.

[5] See above, p. 202–203.

[6] See above, p. 216–217.

[7] See *Judicial Studies Board: Reports for 1987–1991*, Chap. 1, and for *1991–1995*, Chaps. 1, 2.

[8] See Brooke. J., (1992–93) *The Magistrate* 194.

Since 1981 it has been essential for a recorder or assistant recorder, before first sitting in a criminal case, to have attended a residential induction course (now normally lasting three and a half days) organised by the Board. They are lectured by experienced judges and experts from other disciplines about their duties, and they take part in sentencing and other practical exercises and a mock trial. Also before sitting on their own they must sit for at least a week (or more if necessary) in court with an experienced Circuit judge and for must visit various penal institutions. Voluntary three-day refresher seminars are held for experienced judges, and it is intended that each recorder and Circuit judge will be invited to one such seminar every five years. Additional refresher seminars are organised on a circuit basis and seminars on accountancy principles have been held in conjunction with the Institute of Chartered Accountants.[9] The Criminal Committee circulates to all judiciary sitting in the Crown Court a set of specimen directions, a "Bench Miscellany", with guidance on problems that can arise at trial, and (three times a year) the *Bulletin of the Judicial Studies Board*.[10] The Civil and Family Committee has established training arrangements on similar lines as for the criminal jurisdiction, the main recurrent activities being induction courses for new deputy district judges, for the 50 per cent or so of new assistant recorders who intended to sit in civil as well as criminal cases and for some other new judges, and refresher seminars for established circuit judges. County Court and District Judges' Bench Books have been distributed and *Guidelines for the Assessment of Damages in Personal Injury Cases*.[11] The Ethnic Minorities Advisory Committee has developed a programme of racial awareness training for judges. Substantial training exercises were held in relation to implementation of the Children Act 1989 and the Criminal Justice Act 1991.

There has undoubtedly been a welcome increase in the scope and effectiveness of judicial training. However, as the Board itself makes clear, extra resources in money, manpower and judge time will be required if its activities are to be developed further. The Royal Commission on Criminal Justice stated that "substantially more resources need to be allocated to judicial training than at present," with reductions in the intervals between refresher training.[12]

9. INDEPENDENCE[13]

Much importance is attached to the independence of the judiciary.[14] By that is meant independence from improper pressure by the executive, by litigants or

---

[9] *Judicial Studies Board: Report for 1983–1987*, pp. 45–46.
[10] *Judicial Studies Board: Report for 1991–1995*, pp. 16–17.
[11] (2nd ed., 1994): see *Report for 1991–1995*, Chap. 3 and p. 38.
[12] Cm. 2263, p. 140. See also the discussion by M. Partington (1994) 13 C.J.Q. 319, 328–336.
[13] See W. Lederman (1956) 36 Can. Bar Rev. 769; G. Borrie (1970) 18 Am.J.Comp.Law 697; Sir Anthony Mason (1990) 13. U.N.S.W.L.J. 173; Justice M. D. Kirby, *ibid.*, 187; R. Stevens, *The Independence of the Judiciary: The view from the Lord Chancellor's Office* (1993); Mr. Justice R. D. Nicholson, "Judicial independence and accountability: can they co-exist" (1993) 67 A.L.J. 404; K. Marks (1994) 68 A.L.J. 173; P. Polden, (1996) 25 Anglo-Am.L.R.I. 1i and for comparative and international perspectives, S. Shetreet and J. Deschênes, *Judicial Independence: The Contemporary Debate* (1985).
[14] Article 6, E.C.H.R. provides that "[i]n the determination of his civil rights and obligations or of any criminal charge against him, everyone is entitled to a fair and public hearing within a

by particular pressure groups. Reasons given in support of judicial independence are "(1) that independence is a condition of impartiality and therefore also of fair trials, and (2) that it makes for a separation of powers which enables the courts to check the activities of the other branches of government."[15] As to the first, it has been emphasised that judges must not only be impartial but appear to be impartial. Public confidence is only bolstered by "ostentatious impartiality."[16] As to the second, it has been noted with concern that the public today seem less satisfied that the judges are completely independent of the government in power.[17] An illustration of the dangers that arise when judges are dismissed where their decisions incur the displeasure of the executive is provided by the crisis in Malaysia in 1988.[18]

The extent to which judicial independence is (and should be) respected has come under increased scrutiny in the 1980s and 1990s. It is generally accepted that the various factors about to be discussed are effective in securing that particular judges in deciding individual cases are protected from improper pressures. However, the relationship between the judiciary collectively and the executive has been problematic over a range of contentious issues.[19] The theme that links these is the tension between the constitutional position of the judges (particularly but not exclusively as perceived by themselves) and the "new managerialism" in the provision of public services that has become increasingly prominent in the administration of justice. We return to this below.[20] First, we consider the factors that are relevant to maintaining judicial independence; it will be noted that several are by no means clear-cut. The appointment and the tenure of judges have already been dealt with. Party political considerations seem to have been eliminated, although this does not mean that the decisions of judges are not "political" in a wider sense:[21]

"Judges are part of the machinery of authority within the State and as such cannot avoid the making of political decisions."[22]

Other relevant factors include the following:

---

reasonable time by an independent and impartial tribunal established by law." See also Art. 14(1), I.C.C.P.R., which is in similar, but not identical terms: see S. H. Bailey, in D. J. Harris and S. Joseph (eds.), *The ICCPR and UK Law* (1995), pp. 210–219.

[15] See T. Eckhoff, (1965) 9 *Scandinavian Studies in Law*, pp. 11–48.

[16] *ibid.* p. 12. It has been argued that this feature has been lacking in the appointment of Scottish judges: see C. M. Campbell, 1973 J.R. 254.

[17] See D. Oliver, "The Independence of the Judiciary" (1986) 39 C.L.P. 237 and "Politicians and the Courts" (1988) 41 *Parliamentary Affairs* 13.

[18] See [1988] N.Z.L.J. 217; F. Narinan, [1988] N.Z.L.J. 266; R. H. Hickling, [1989] P.L. 20; F. A. Trindade, (1990) 106 L.Q.R. 51.

[19] Indeed one commentator has described the proposition that there is independence of the judiciary (as distinct from individual judges) as a "constitutional myth": R. Stevens, (1994) 144 N.L.J. 1620, 1621.

[20] See below, pp. 244–246.

[21] A. Paterson, "Judges: A Political Élite" (1974) 1 B.J.L.S. 118. "Whoever can persuade the members of a society that law is inevitable or to take 'law as a given', and that the legal interpretation of a particular social situation is the only possible one, controls an important if not vital source of power in that society. In my contention British Judges are in precisely this position and that is why it is legitimate to characterize them as involved in the realm of politics": *ibid.* p. 129. See also R. J. Wilson, "British Judges as Political Actors" (1973) 1 Int. Journal of Criminology and Penology 197.

[22] J. A. G. Griffith, *The Politics of the Judiciary* (4th ed., 1991), p. 272.

(a) Remuneration

Judges are paid large salaries,[23] which are a charge on the Consolidated Fund and so not subject to an annual vote in Parliament. The current salaries are as follows: Lord Chief Justice: £132,178; Master of the Rolls, Lord of Appeal: £122,230; President of the Family Division, Vice-Chancellor, Lords Justices: £117,190; High Court judges: £104,431.[24] They can be increased, but not reduced, by the Lord Chancellor, with the consent of the Prime Minister as Minister for the Civil Service.[25] From the time salaries became a charge on the Consolidated Fund,[26] they could only be changed by statute, or, between 1965 and 1973, by ministerial order.[27] Under the National Economy Act 1931, the salaries of "persons in His Majesty's service," which term was taken to include the judges, were reduced by 20 per cent. The need to secure the independence of the judiciary was placed at the forefront of their arguments both that the Act did not apply to them as a matter of interpretation, and that it should not apply in principle.[28] The government restored the cuts in 1934. This argument has, however, not figured so prominently in the recent reports of the Senior (formerly Top) Salaries Review Board on judicial salaries, in which more important considerations seem to have been the need to attract lawyers with the right qualities and experience and the need to maintain the judges' status in the community. Thus the Board has taken into account both barristers' earnings and the salaries payable to Permanent Secretaries as "cross-checks", although there are no formal links with either. The written answer announcing the 1982 increases stated simply that it is "in the national interest to ensure an adequate supply of candidates of sufficient calibre for appointment to judicial office."[29] The Board's recommendations are normally accepted.[30] There have been no serious allegations of corruption against English judges for some centuries,[31] and it is not plausible that it is the level of salary alone that is responsible. Even attempts to bribe judges appear to be rare.

---

[23] Certainly by the standards of Professors of Law, but not by those of leading lawyers in private practice.

[24] H. C. Deb. Vol. 271, cols. 294–296, February 8, 1996, written answer. In effect in full from December 1, 1996. These figures implement the recommendations of the Senior Salaries Review Body: Report No. 37, Cm. 3094, 1996. The Board is conducting a fundamental review of judicial posts which will inform the recommendations in its 1997 report (pp. 22–23). As to pensions, see above, p. 235, n. 80.

[25] Supreme Court Act 1981, s.12.

[26] Judges appointed after 1786. There was no change between 1851 and 1954 (Judges' Remuneration Act 1954).

[27] Judges' Remuneration Act 1965.

[28] See Heuston, *Lives*, pp. 513–519; W. Holdsworth, (1932) 48 L.Q.R. 25 and 173 L.T. 336; E. C. S. Wade, (1932) 173 L.T. 246, 267; Stevens (1993), pp. 50–62. The judges were "in a mutinous mood": Lord Sankey L.C., quoted by Heuston, *op. cit.*, p. 514. However, this "squalid incident . . . had not reflected well on the judges. They had appeared selfish and out of touch with reality . . . [W]hat is striking is the amateur level of argument on both sides": Stevens (1993), p. 63.

[29] H. C. Deb. Vol. 23, cols.257–261, written answer, May 12, 1982.

[30] The average 21 per cent increase recommended by the Review Body in 1992 (Report No. 33, Cm. 2015) has, however, been paid in stages that will not be completed until 1999: see Report No.35, Appendix E. The 1996 increase of 3.9 per cent was staged in April and December that year.

[31] In November 1993, it was announced by the D.P.P. that a police investigation had revealed no evidence to support corruption allegations made against Tucker J., the judge appointed to preside at the trial of Asil Nadir: see Ralph Gibson L.J. in *R. v. Central Criminal Court, ex p. Guney* [1994] 1 W.L.R. 438, 444.

It is an accepted convention that judges may not hold paid appointments such as directorships, or carry on any profession or business. Indeed, the holders of full-time judicial appointments are now expressly barred from legal practice.[32] Even the few cases of judges taking business appointments on leaving the bench have attracted criticism.[33]

(b) Judges and the legislature

Judges of the Supreme Court and Circuit judges are disqualified from membership of the House of Commons.[34] The judges that are members of the House of Lords may contribute to its debates, but by a convention established comparatively recently do not take part in political controversy.[35] They tend to confine their contributions to technical questions of a legal nature. However, serving judges have not felt constrained from speaking on controversial matters where they have concerned the legal system itself. This was starkly illustrated by the criticisms, sometimes expressed in intemperate language, of Lord Mackay's Green Papers on reform of the legal profession.[36] Retired Law Lords are even less inhibited. The position in the twenties was less clear cut. In 1922 Lord Carson attacked the proposals for the establishment of the Irish Free State. He was rebuked for doing so by his former supporter, Lord Birkenhead L.C., but was defended by others.[37]

(c) Judges and the executive

It is generally accepted that judges other than the Lord Chancellor should not hold ministerial office or sit in the Cabinet. Both Lord Mansfield and Lord Ellenborough served in the Cabinet while Chief Justice of the King's Bench, but both cases attracted much criticism. Lord Reading C.J. performed various executive tasks for the government during the First World War, but that can be regarded as an anomalous exception to a well-established principle, which has indeed been strengthened by the recent practice of making non-political appointments to the position of Lord Chief Justice.

One matter that has caused some controversy is the common practice of using judges as chairmen or members of Royal Commissions, Departmental

---

[32] Courts and Legal Services Act 1990, s.75 and Sched. 11.

[33] In 1970, Fisher J. resigned at the age of 52 after two and a half years on the Bench in order to join a merchant bank. This provoked some criticism: see (1970) 114 S.J. 593. On the other hand, it was pointed out that a reluctant judge was unlikely to be a good one. The position of Lord Chancellor is arguably different, given the precariousness of office. Both Lord Birkenhead and Lord Kilmuir were criticised for taking business appointments, although the latter declined to draw the pension to which he was entitled. Lord Birkenhead defended his rights to take the pension, but assigned it to the benefit of certain hospitals (see Heuston, *Lives*, pp. 396–8; J. Campbell, *F. E. Smith, First Earl of Birkenhead* (1983), pp. 812–814). For discussion of this issue in New Zealand, see [1994] N.Z.L.J. 311–312.

[34] House of Commons Disqualification Act 1975, s.1 and Sched. 1. There is no disqualification applicable to recorders. In 1994 there were 9 recorder/M.P.s.

[35] See generally L. Blom-Cooper and G. Drewry, *Final Appeal* (1972), pp. 196–215.

[36] See above, pp. 121–122; G. Drewry, (1992) 45(2) C.L.P. 187, 193–194. An example is Lord Lane's comment that "oppression does not stand on the doorstep with a toothbrush moustache and a swastika armband": H. L. Deb. Vol. 505, April 7 1989, col. 1331.

[37] H. L. Debs. Vol. 49, cols.686–698, March 21, 1922; 715–727, March 22, 1922 and cols.931–974 March 29, 1922.

Committees and Tribunals of Inquiry.[38] Indeed, judges are prominent in the ranks of "the Good and the Great". This is both expected and unexceptionable where "lawyers' law" is concerned. However, the subject matter of an inquiry may well be politically controversial. The judge concerned may be called upon to explain or justify the report, and indeed to argue in public the case for or against reform. The topics covered include public disorders (Red Lion Square,[39] Brixton[40]); security matters (security procedures in the public service,[41] the Vassall case,[42] the Profumo affair,[43] the D Notice affair[44]; mis-management in the public service (the collapse of the Vehicle and General Insurance Company,[45] the Crown Agents[46]); events in Northern Ireland (disturbances in 1969,[47] interrogation methods,[48] legal procedures for dealing with terrorists,[49] the "Bloody Sunday" deaths in Londonderry,[50] the working of anti-terrorist legislation,[51] and police interrogation procedures[52]); the interception of communications[53]; industrial disputes (electricity supply,[54] miners,[55] and Grunwick[56]); prisons;[57] and standards in public life.[58] The Vice-Chancellor, Sir Richard Scott, has presided over a lengthy and highly contentious inquiry into the Matrix-Churchill affair where the conduct of ministers and civil servants came under close scrutiny.[59]

The appointment of a committee is often thought to be a political delaying tactic or a mechanism for shuffling off responsibility for a controversial decision: whether or not either of these criticisms is in fact true, in a particular case it may be unfortunate for a judge to be associated with them. Moreover, the judge may find himself or herself in the midst of political controversy. He

---

[38] See D. G. T. Williams, *Not in the Public Interest* (1965), pp. 188–191; P. Hillyard, (1971) 6 I.J. (N.S.) 93; G. Zellick, [1972] P.L. 1; T. J. Cartwright, *Royal Commissions and Departmental Committees in Britain* (1975); G. Rhodes, *Committees of Inquiry* (1975); Griffith (1991), Chap. 2.

[39] Cmnd. 5919, 1975: Lord Scarman.

[40] Cmnd. 8427, 1981: Lord Scarman (Inquiry under the Police Act 1964).

[41] Cmnd. 1681, 1962: Lord Radcliffe (Departmental Committee). The Security Commission is also headed by a judge; the function of this standing commission, first set up in 1964, is to investigate at the Prime Minister's request, breaches of security in the public service, and to report and advise generally on security arrangements. See I. Leigh and L. Lustgarten [1991] P.L. 215, and Lustgarten and Leigh, *In from the Cold!* (1994), pp. 476–491.

[42] Cmnd. 2009, 1963: Lord Radcliffe (Tribunal of Inquiry).

[43] Cmnd. 2152, 1963: Lord Denning. See Lord Denning, *The Due Process of Law* (1980), pp. 67–73; "It was a best-seller": *ibid.* p. 68.

[44] Cmnd. 3309, 1967: Lord Radcliffe (Committee of Privy Counsellors).

[45] 1971–72 H.C. 133: James J. (Tribunal of Inquiry).

[46] 1981–82 H.C. 364: Croom-Johnson J. (Tribunal of Inquiry).

[47] Cmnd. 566 (N.I.), 1972: Scarman J. (Tribunal of Inquiry).

[48] Cmnd. 4801, 1972: Lord Parker (Committee of Privy Counsellors).

[49] Cmnd. 5185, 1972: Lord Diplock (Departmental Committee).

[50] 1971–72 H.C. 220: Lord Widgery C.J. (Tribunal of Inquiry).

[51] Cmnd. 5847, 1975: Lord Gardiner (Departmental Committee).

[52] Cmnd. 7497, 1979: Judge Bennett (Departmental Committee).

[53] Cmnd. 283, 1957: Birkett L.J. (Committee of Privy Counsellors).

[54] Cmnd. 4594, 1971: Lord Wilberforce (Court of Inquiry under the Industrial Courts Act 1919).

[55] Cmnd. 4903, 1972: Lord Wilberforce (Court of Inquiry).

[56] Cmnd. 6922, 1977: Scarman L.J. (Court of Inquiry).

[57] Cm.1456, 1991, Woolf L.J. (Inquiry)

[58] Cm.2850, 1995, Lord Nolan (standing body).

[59] See I. Leigh, "Matrix Churchill, Supergun and the Scott Inquiry" [1993] P.L. 630; R. Norton-Taylor, *Truth is a Difficult Concept* (1995). While in progress the inquiry's working methods have been the subject of political criticism led by Lord Howe: see Sir Louis Blom-Cooper, [1994] P.L. 1.

or she may be criticised for producing what is perceived by certain sections of the community, rightly or wrongly, to be a "whitewashing report",[60] or by the government for not producing such a report.[61] It is arguable that a judge is a suitable person to preside over a process for ascertaining the facts of particular incidents such as the Aberfan disaster and the Summerland fire disaster on the Isle of Man, the fire at Bradford City Football Club and the Hillsborough disaster, where there are no political overtones. Even here, however, there can be problems.[62]

It is accepted that a judge should not become associated with party political research committees.[63]

A stricter view of the permissible range of extra-judicial activities is taken in the United States of America, where the separation of powers is formally entrenched as a constitutional principle. Even the exceptional cases such as the appointment of Justice Murphy as prosecutor at the Nuremberg trials and Chief Justice Warren to investigate the assassination of President Kennedy were controversial.[64]

Analogous problems have arisen in respect of the appointment of judges as members of the Restrictive Practices Court and the short-lived National Industrial Relations Court (N.I.R.C.). The former court determines whether restrictive agreements are contrary to the public interest.[65] Such determinations involve considerations that are political and economic rather than legal. The functions of the N.I.R.C. were more obviously judicial, but the context was that of industrial relations, where it was, and is, highly controversial whether orthodox legal mechanisms are appropriate in principle and workable. Its successor, the Employment Appeal Tribunal, inherited its less controversial functions.

Finally, a matter of growing controversy is the relationship between the judiciary and the executive in the administration of the courts. Sir Nicolas Browne-Wilkinson in a public lecture[66] expressed concern that the executive, through the mechanisms for controlling public expenditure, was increasingly taking decisions that affected the conduct of cases in court, without consulting the judges. Indeed there was no formal machinery for the resolution of disputes

---

[60] e.g. the adverse reaction to Lord Widgery's report on the Londonderry shootings: K. Boyle, T. Hadden and P. Hillyard, *Law and State* (1975), pp. 126–129.

[61] e.g. the report of the Nyasaland Commission of Enquiry led by Devlin J. (H. Macmillan, *Riding the Storm* (1971), pp. 736–8); and the refusal of Harold Wilson to accept the Radcliffe Report on the D Notice Affair: see the White Paper on the D Notice System (Cmnd. 3312, 1967).

[62] In New Zealand, Mahon J. was appointed as sole member of a Royal Commission to inquire into the Mt. Erebus aircraft disaster. Certain statements in the report were held by the Supreme Court to have been made in excess of jurisdiction, and an order for costs against the airline was quashed: *Re Erebus Royal Commission* (No. 2) [1981] 1 N.Z.L.R. 618. Mahon J. resigned see [1982] N./Z.L.J. 37. An appeal to the Privy Council was dismissed: *Re Erebus Royal Commission* [1984] A.C. 808; see K. Keith, [1984] N.Z.L.J. 35; D. Currie, [1984] N.Z.L.J. 43; A Beck, "Trial of a High Court Judge for Defamation" (1987) 103 L.Q.R. 461.

[63] Lord Avonside, a judge of the Court of Session, resigned from a Conservative Committee on the constitutional position in Scotland following public criticism, e.g. by the Lord Advocate: see *The Times*, July 30, 1968, August 8, 1968; R. J. Wilson, "British Judges as Political Actors" (1973) 1 Int. Journal of Criminology and Penology, 197, 199–20.

[64] See A. T. Mason, (1953) 67 Harv. L.R. 193; (1970) 35 *Law and Contemporary Problems* (Symposium).

[65] See R. B. Stevens and B. S. Yamey, *The Restrictive Practices Court* (1965).

[66] "The Independence of the Judiciary in the 1980s" [1988] P.L. 44. See also I. R. Scott, (1988) 7 C.J.Q. 103. Similar concerns have been expressed by Sir John Donaldson: *The Times*, April 13, 1987.

between the judges and court administrators, below the level of the Lord Chancellor. As a result, the criterion of value for money was not properly balanced against the interests of justice.[67] Since this opening shot, there have been a number of skirmishes, with fire most commonly directed at the Lord Chancellor, Lord Mackay.[68] The publication of the 1989 Green Papers on reform of the legal profession led to judicial criticism both of their content (in particular the perceived threat to the independence of the legal profession and thereby of the judiciary) and of the lack of prior consultation with the judges.[69] The introduction of the requirement that changes to rules concerning qualification and conduct required the assent of four senior judges went some way to assuaging the fears expressed.[70] A second issue has been the number of High Court judges. Arguments from successive Lord Chief Justices and others that more High Court judges should be appointed to handle an increasing workload, so as to reduce delays and excessive reliance on Circuit judges and Q.C.s hearing civil cases as deputies, became increasingly public and pointed.[71] Steps were eventually taken in 1993 to increase the maximum number of judges by 13 and to proceed to make 10 new appointments,[72] but this has not affected the number of deputies used, particularly in the Queen's Bench Division.[73] The hand of the Treasury was seen in the delay; the "energetic support of the Lord Chancellor's Department was really needed to uphold the integrity and standing of the judiciary, support which only too frequently appeared to be lacking."[74]

A further *cause célèbre* was provided by exchanges between Lord Mackay and Sir John Wood, the then President of the Employment Appeal Tribunal. These concerned the extent to which preliminary hearings could and should be held in appeals to the Employment Appeal Tribunal in England and Wales, and were the subject of press coverage leading to a discussion in the House of Lords, where most contributors were critical of the position taken by Lord Mackay.[75] According to the critics,[76] it appeared that Lord Mackay, in view of the growing backlog of work in the E.A.T., had attempted to pressurise Sir John Wood into dropping the use of preliminary oral hearings in cases where it was unclear on the face of the notice of appeal whether a point of law was raised. In one letter,

---

[67] One possible solution was the establishment of a collegiate body of judges responsible for the management of certain functions of court administration.

[68] See Sir Francis Purchas, "The constitution in the market place", The Third Joseph Jackson Memorial Lecture (1993) 143 N.L.J. 1604; "Lord Mackay and the Judiciary" (1994) 144 N.L.J. 527 and "What is happening to judicial independence" (1994) 144 N.L.J. 1306; rejoinder by R. Stevens, "On being nicer to James and the children" (1994) 144 N.L.J. 1620; D. Oliver, [1994] P.L.157.

[69] See above, p. 242.

[70] Sir Francis Purchas, (1993) 143 N.L.J. 1604, 1607–1608; (1994) 144 N.L.J. 1306, 1308–1309.

[71] Maximum Number of Judges (No.2) Order 1993 (S.I. 1993 No. 1255). See H.L. Deb., Vol. 545, May 10 1993, col. 1048.

[72] Purchas, (1994) 144 N.L.J. 1306, 1308–1309.

[73] ibid., p. 1309. Not only has the quality of many deputies been criticised (see ibid.), it is seen as the ultimate objective of civil servants to concentrate work in the hands of Circuit judges "who would be under the control of the Executive and could be dismissed without reference to Parliament": Purchas, (1993) 143 N.L.J. 1603, 1605.

[74] H.L. Deb. Vol. 554, April 27 1994, cols.750–804; see also Vol. 553, March 21 1994, cols.497–500 (question).

[75] See *The Observer*, April 3, 1994; Sir Francis Purchas, (1994) 144 N.L.J. 527, 530: "the approach adopted demonstrated all the unattractive attributes of a Treasury driven policy to achieve savings at any cost."

[76] H.L. Deb., Vol. 554, April 23, 1994, cols.791–804.

Lord Mackay invited him to "consider his position". Such a change in approach would particularly prejudice unassisted litigants and was resisted by Sir John Wood. Lord Mackay's explanation was that he was simply looking for an assurance that preliminary oral hearings would not be used in *hopeless* cases, and that the Registrar's power under the E.A.T.'s statutory rules of procedure in such cases to inform the appellant that the appeal cannot proceed would in fact be used. The reference to "considering his position" was not expressed or intended to be a threat of dismissal (in any event, not a matter for the Lord Chancellor), a threat to use his power to move him from the Presidency of the E.A.T., or an invitation to resign. On this footing, matters were considerably less sinister than the critics suggested. Nevertheless the basis of Lord Mackay's intervention was not made clear in the correspondence (was it as the senior judge or as a member of the executive?). Lord Mackay's subsequent argument that it was as the rule-making authority responsible for the E.A.T.'s procedural rules is constitutionally novel.[77]

Other issues that have given rise to judicial criticism have been changes to judicial pensions,[78] cuts to eligibility limits for legal aid[79] and changes in the administration of the magistrates' court service that were perceived as a threat to judicial independence.[80] The particular vulnerability of Circuit judges has been noted.[81]

Most of these matters are ultimately resource-related. There must be a full and ongoing debate on whether the limits on resources made available by the state lead to an unacceptable dilution in the quality of justice; there is also an issue as to the extent to which the judges should be responsible for (as distinct from consulted about) the administration of the legal system.[82] The rhetoric of judicial independence may obscure rather than illuminate these issues, particularly if it is seen simply as an argument to reinforce judicial status or to resist any change.[83]

(d) Public statements by and about judges

Judges are expected to refrain from making party political statements; it is sometimes said that they should refrain from criticising the policy of Acts of Parliament, but that is too restrictive. Reasoned, responsible criticism is acceptable: disparaging remarks are not. Thus, in 1978, Melford Stevenson J. was reprimanded by the Lord Chancellor, Lord Elwyn-Jones, for referring to the Sexual Offences Act 1967 as a "buggers' charter".[84] Judges were formerly inhibited

---

[77] See Sir Francis Purchas, (1994) 144 N.L.J. 1306, 1310: "Once a law has been enacted . . . the law-making process is *functus*."

[78] Judicial Pensions and Retirement Act 1993, above, p. 235.

[79] Below, pp. 577–580.

[80] Above, p. 62.

[81] Judge Harold Wilson, (1994) 144 N.L.J. 1453, noting, *inter alia*, the offence caused by the sending to all judges by recorded delivery of copies of a letter by the Lord Chancellor setting out examples of misbehaviour that would be incompatible with continuing to sit on the Bench.

[82] Above, p. 32.

[83] See R. Stevens, (1994) 144 N.L.J. 1620; G. Drewry, "Judicial independence in Britain: challenges real and threats imagined" in R. Blackburn (ed.), *Constitutional Studies* (1992), Chap. 10.

[84] *The Times*, July 6, 1978.

by the so-called "Kilmuir rules"[85] from broadcasting on radio or television (except on special occasions, such as charitable appeals). However, these "rules" were relaxed by Lord Mackay on assuming office, judges being left to make their own decisions, after such consultation as they may think necessary.[86] Judges are now much more prepared to speak in public about their own role.[87] It is also now more common for judges, both inside and outside Parliament, to advocate changes in government policy in the legal sphere.[88]

Members of the executive are similarly expected to refrain from attacking judges, unless provoked. It is a rule of parliamentary practice that reflections must not be cast upon a judge's character or motives except on a substantive motion specifically criticising him or her or leading to an address for his or her removal, although reasoned arguments that a judge has made a mistake or was wrong are acceptable.[89] Matters that are *sub judice* cannot be discussed, unless they relate to a ministerial decision or concern issues of national importance, and discussion would not prejudice the proceedings.[90]

(e) Judicial immunity from suit[91]

At common law, every judge of a superior or inferior court is immune from liability in damages for any act that is either (1) within jurisdiction or (2) honestly believed to be within jurisdiction[92]. The protection in (1) is available even where the judge is malicious.[93] He or she is also protected by absolute privilege in the law of defamation. Every judge:

"should be able to do his work in complete independence and free from

---

[85] A letter from the then Lord Chancellor, Lord Kilmuir, to the Director-General of the B.B.C. in 1955, set out at [1986] P.L. 384–386. The Lord Chancellor disclaimed any disciplinary jurisdiction over judges, but stated that it was generally undesirable for judges to broadcast (it would, for example, "be inappropriate for the Judiciary to be associated with any series of talks or anything which could fairly be interpreted as entertainment . . .").

[86] See A. W. Bradley, [1988] P.L. at p. 166.

[87] See Rozenberg (1994), pp. 96–103, noting, *inter alia*, the willingness of Lord Taylor C.J. and others to give press conferences.

[88] See, *e.g.*, the growing judicial support for incorporation of the European Convention on Human Rights into English law (*e.g.* Sir Thomas Bingham, (1993) 109 L.Q.R. 390; Lord Taylor C.J. "The Judiciary in the Nineties", Richard Dimbleby Lecture 1992; and continued opposition to the mandatory life sentence for murder (*e.g.* by Lord Lane, Vol. 527 H.L.Deb., April 18, 1991, cols.1562–1564, and in his chairmanship of a Committee on the Penalty for Homicide set up by the Prison Reform Trust: see Lord Windlesham, [1993] Crim. L.R. 644, 656–657).

[89] *Erskine May's Parliamentary Practice* (21st ed., 1989), pp. 379–380; H.C. Deb. Vol. 865, cols.1092, 1144, 1200. December 4, 1973 (criticisms of Sir John Donaldson as President of the National Industrial Relations Court; H.C. Deb. Vol. 935, cols.1381–4, July 19, 1977; H.C. Deb. Vol 34. cols.123–6, 285–6, December 14, 15, 1982 (description by Mrs Thatcher of a 12 month sentence for the rape of a six-year-old girl as "incomprehensible" ruled to be in order).

[90] *Erskine May*, pp. 377–379. H.C. Deb. Vol. 681 cols.1416–17, July 23, 1963; H.C. Deb. Vol. 839 col. 1627, June 28, 1972; H.C. Deb. Vol. 916 cols.882–4, July 29, 1976.

[91] See A. Olowofoyeku, *Suing Judges* (1993); M. Brazier, [1976] P.L. 397.

[92] *Sirros v. Moore* [1975] Q.B. 118, Lord Denning M.R. and Ormrod L.J. Buckley L.J. held that if an act were outside jurisdiction a judge would only be immune if he or she had so acted as a result of a reasonable mistake of fact. See also *Rajski v. Powell* (1987) 11 N.S.W.L.R. 522. (The attempt of majority of the court in *Sirros v. Moore* to equate the position of judges of inferior and superior courts has been disapproved: see above, p. 205).

[93] *Anderson v. Gorrie* [1895] 1 Q.B. 668.

fear. He should not have to turn the pages of his books with trembling fingers, asking himself: 'If I do this, shall I be liable in damages?' "[94]

The rules also prevent the relitigation of the issues determined by the court.[95]

Deliberate misconduct such as corruption could lead to prosecution for a criminal offence[96] and removal from office.

(f) Disqualification for interest or bias

A judge is disqualified from hearing a case in which he or she has a direct pecuniary or proprietary interest, or in circumstances where there is a real danger of bias on his or her part.[97] This rule applies to judges of the superior courts as much as it does to magistrates and tribunal members. Indeed, the leading case on disqualifying interests[98] concerned decrees made by Lord Cottenham L.C. in favour of a canal company in which he held shares. The House of Lords set aside these decrees. Lord Campbell emphasised that:

"No one can suppose that Lord Cottenham could be in the remotest degree influenced by the interest ... but ... it is of the last importance that the maxim that no man is to be a judge in his own cause should be held sacred."[99]

The matters that may give rise to a danger of bias include personal hostility, friendship, family relationship or acquaintance with a party or with a witness. The parties may waive the objection. Where a judge is not technically disqualified, he or she may well refuse to act in a case where one of the parties raises an objection. Objections, however, are not commonly made. Lord Denning M.R. withdrew from a case concerning the Church of Scientology of California as the Church felt that "there was an unconscious influence operating adversely to it" in Lord Denning's previous judgments.[1] The Church had been before Lord Denning's court on eight previous occasions, and noted that his Lordship had doubted whether it was right to call scientology a "religion" and whether the Church was entitled to call itself a church. Shaw L.J. said that it was almost impossible to resist the application for the appeal to be transferred "even though

---

[94] *per* Lord Denning M.R., in *Sirros v. Moore*, n. 92 above, at p. 136.

[95] *cf.* the immunity of advocates, above, pp. 174–176.

[96] *cf. R. v. Llewellyn-Jones* [1967] 3 All E.R. 225 (misbehaviour in a public office: misuse of funds by a county court registrar).

[97] See *R. v. Gough (Robert)* [1993] A.C. 646; Sir William Wade and C. F. Forsyth, *Administrative Law* (7th ed. 1994), Chap. 14.

[98] *Dimes v. Grand Junction Canal Proprietors* (1852) 3 H.L. Cas.759.

[99] *ibid.* p. 793. Dimes was a "crazy attorney" who had "embarked upon interminable litigation" against the Canal company. Cottenham died before judgment was given in the House of Lords: "it was a common belief that Dimes had killed Lord Cottenham": J. B. Atlay, *The Victorian Chancellors* (1906), Vol. 1, p. 415. *Cf. R. v. Mulvihill* [1990] 1 W.L.R. 438, where the Court of Appeal held that a Circuit judge was not disqualified from presiding over a trial concerning seven robberies of banks and building societies where he held 1,650 shares in one of the banks (the NatWest); there was no direct pecuniary interest and no reasonable suspicion of bias (*a fortiori*, there would be no real danger of bias under the *Gough* test, n. 97 above).

[1] *ex p. Church of Scientology of California, The Times*, February 21, 1978. Lord Lane C.J. stood down in *Moss v. McLachlan* [1985] 149 J.P. 167: Pannick (1987), p. 41. *Cf. Arab Monetary Fund v. Hashim (No. 8), The Independent*, April 30, 1993 (counsel should be satisfied that there is material on which an application for removal of a judge can properly be made).

the grounds were not merely slight but non-existent." Conversely, no objection was taken to Lord Denning's acting in a case concerning the Church Commissioners, he being one of the Commissioners,[2] or to the fact that all the members of the Court of Appeal hearing the appeal in the London Transport "fares" case were both users of public transport in London and London ratepayers.[3]

10. THE JUDICIAL FUNCTION

In the course of legal proceedings, judges may be called upon to perform one or more of the following tasks: presiding over a trial (e.g. controlling the course of proceedings; keeping order; ruling on questions of the admissibility of evidence; deciding when to adjourn for lunch); presiding over an appeal[4]; determining a disputed question of fact; determining a disputed question of law; directing a jury on the evidence and the law; deciding what remedy to award or punishment to impose; and giving reasons for such decisions as are theirs. With the marked decline in the use of the jury in civil cases over the last 60 years, the judicial task of determining disputed questions of fact has correspondingly grown in significance. When considering the "nature of the judicial function," however, it is usual to concentrate on the ways in which judges approach the determination of disputed questions of law. Furthermore, attention is directed in particular to the appeal courts,[5] as a higher proportion of time is spent on such questions, as the arguments are more likely to be evenly balanced, and because the decisions of courts at the top of the hierarchy carry most weight. In Chapters 6 and 7 we consider the principles that are applicable to the interpretation of statutes and the handling of precedent cases. We shall see that there is considerable room for flexibility. Moreover, even where there is no directly relevant precedent and no applicable legislation the judge must still give an answer to any legal questions that arise.

The extent to which a judge is prepared to innovate depends upon the respective weight attached to a number of factors[6]: the need for stability and certainty in law (which suggests consistency with established principles and precedents); the wish to do justice as between the parties; the need not to usurp the role of Parliament; the need to justify a decision by reasoned argument and not merely compromise between the parties; and the need to base a decision on at least

---

[2] *Hanson v. Church Commissioners* [1978] Q.B. 823, 831. The actual management of the estate of the Church Commissioners was vested in a separate board of governors. Various "dignitaries", including the Lord Chief Justice, the Master of the Rolls and the Lord Mayor of London, were "merely titular commissioners".

[3] *Bromley London Borough Council v. Greater London Council* [1983] 1 A.C. 768, 771–777. For an argument that the Lord Chancellor ought not to sit in public law cases, see A. W. Bradley, [1988] P.L. 165.

[4] The president of an appellate court can have a significant influence on the course of proceedings, although his or her role is more muted than that of a trial judge sitting alone: see above, p. 100, n. 97.

[5] There have been three studies of the House of Lords: L. Blom-Cooper and G. Drewry, *Final Appeal* (1972); R. Stevens, *Law and Politics* (1979); A. Paterson, *The Law Lords* (1982). The nature of the judicial function is analysed in J. Bell, *Policy Arguments in Judicial Decisions* (1983).

[6] See Paterson (1982), pp. 122–127.

one of the issues raised by the parties. Differences in approach reflect different weight attached to these factors—in particular the first two.

Debates as to the nature of the judicial function have taken place in two different, but related fields: legal theory and socio-legal studies. Important contributions to the theoretical debate have come from some of our leading judges, speaking both extra-judicially and in decided cases. The judges' own perceptions of the proper judicial role are equally of importance as one of the important influences on judicial decision-making identified in empirical studies.

Historically, the theory that held sway for the longest time was the "declaratory theory" expounded by William Blackstone and others. Blackstone wrote[7] that:

> "it is an established rule to abide by former precedents, where the same points come again in litigation ... [the judge] being sworn to determine, not according to his private sentiments: he being sworn to determine, not according to his own private judgment, but according to the known laws and customs of the land: not delegated to pronounce a new law, but to maintain and expound the old one. Yet this rule admits of exception, where the former determination is most evidently contrary to reason; much more if it be clearly contrary to divine law. But even in such cases the subsequent judges do not pretend to make a new law, but to vindicate the old one from misrepresentation. For if it be found that the former decision is manifestly absurd or unjust, it is declared not that such a sentence was *bad law*, but that it was *not law*, that is, not the established custom of the realm, as has been erroneously determined."

Thus the role of the judge is to declare what the law is, not to make it. This theory was not easy to square with the unconcealed law-making activities of particular judges such as Lord Mansfield,[8] and was abused by writers such as Bentham.[9] Nevertheless, judges in the nineteenth and early twentieth centuries generally maintained (with increasing enthusiasm) the position that their function was not to make law and, indeed, that they were not concerned with the policy implications of their rulings.[10] However, this view was held less strongly in the House of Lords than in the lower courts, some of the Law Lords, with equity or Scottish backgrounds, being more concerned with principles than precedent and more likely to advert to the likely consequences of their decisions.

After 1912, the Law Lords, who tended now to be chosen from the professional judiciary, with less regard for political affiliation:

---

[7] *Commentaries*, Vol. 1, pp. 69–70.

[8] Chief Justice the King's Bench, 1756–1788. See C. H. S. Fifoot, *Lord Mansfield* (1936).

[9] *A Comment on the Commentaries* (eds. J. H. Burns and H. L. A. Hart, 1977), pp. 192–206. Bentham's objections were based in part on his opposition to theories of "natural law". Moreover, he disapproved of law-making by judges, taking the view that this was a matter for Parliament.

[10] See, *e.g.* Parke B. in *Egerton v. Brownlow* (1853) 4 H.L.C. 1, 124: "It is the province of the statesman, and not the lawyer, to discuss, and of the legislature to determine, what is the best for the public good, and to provide for it by proper enactments. It is the province of the judge to expound the law only; the written from the statutes: the unwritten or common law from the decisions of our predecessors and of our existing courts, from text-writers of acknowledged authority, and upon the principles to be clearly deduced from them by sound reason and just inference; not to speculate upon what is the best, in his opinion, for the advantage of the community."

"exhibited an increasing tendency to articulate a declaratory theory of law and to insist that the judicial function, even in the final appeal court, was primarily the formalistic or mechanical one of restating existing doctrines."[11]

At the same time there were still some judges, such as Lord Atkin and Lord Wright, who were prepared to develop private law doctrines significantly while maintaining the facade of the declaratory theory. However, there followed what Stevens terms the "era of substantive formalism" in the House of Lords:

"For the 1940s and for much of the 1950s there were no obvious signs that the Law Lords had developed rules out of broader principles of the common law or the liberal state. Indeed, there was virtually no acceptance of an element of discretion, let alone a utilitarian balancing of interests. The process, at best fell into Karl Llewellyn's category of judicial formalism, with opinions written 'in deductive form with an air of expression of single-line inevitability.'[12] At worst, the process was a restatement of the declaratory theory in such extreme form that it denied any purpose for a second appeal court. Legal rationality became an end in itself. The literal meaning of words was to be the only criterion of statutory interpretation."[13]

Deference to the executive in public law cases was to be expected in wartime: strong judicial challenges to the Labour government elected in 1945 with a large majority would obviously have been unwise. This approach was associated particularly with Lord Jowitt, the Labour Lord Chancellor, and Lord Simonds, a Law Lord between 1944 and 1962, apart from his period as Lord Chancellor from 1951 to 1954. A few judges stood out against this approach, notably Lord Denning,[14] but to little avail. The only developments could come with the application of established principles to novel factual situations.

Since the mid-1950s the position has changed. It has become generally accepted by the Law Lords that they may properly exercise a limited law-making function.[15] Lord Radcliffe argued that it was best if judges went about this task "on the quiet."[16]

"Would anyone now deny that judicial decisions are a creative, not merely an expository, contribution to the law? There are no means by which they can be otherwise, so rare is the occasion upon which a decision does not involve choice between two admissible alternatives.... We cannot run the risk of finding the archetypal image of the judge confused in men's minds with the very different image of the legislator.... [T]he image of the judge, objective, impartial, erudite and experienced declarer of the law that is, lies deeper in the consciousness of civilisation than the image of the lawmaker,

---

[11] Stevens (1979), p. 196.
[12] Karl Llewellyn, *The Common Law Tradition* (1960), p. 38.
[13] Stevens (1979), pp. 319–320.
[14] See below, p. 253.
[15] See generally A. Paterson, *The Law Lords* (1982).
[16] See Lord Radcliffe, *Not in Feather Beds* (1968), pp. 265–277. Professor Atiyah has argued that most of the judges "would prefer to shelter behind the declaratory theory in public, and to confine discussion of the nature and use of the creative judicial function amongst the *cognoscenti*" (1980) 15 Israel L.R. 346, 360.

propounding what are avowedly new rules of human conduct. . . . Personally, I think that judges will serve the public interest better if they keep
quiet about their legislative function. No doubt they will discreetly contribute to changes in the law, because . . . they cannot do otherwise, even if
they would. The judge who shows his hand, who advertises what he is
about, may indeed show that he is a strong spirit, unfettered by the past;
but I doubt very much whether he is not doing more harm to general confidence in the law as a constant, safe in the hands of the judges than he is
doing to the law's credit as a set of rules nicely attuned to the sentiments
of the day.''[17]

The dominant influence in the House of Lords in this period was Lord Reid.
In his well-known address entitled ''The Judge as Law Maker'' he swiftly disposed of the declaratory theory:

''We do not believe in fairy tales any more. So we must accept the fact
that for better or worse judges do make law, and tackle the question how
do they approach their task and how they should approach it.''[18]

Where public opinion was sharply divided, whether or not on party lines, no
judge should lean to one side or the other if it can be avoided; if it cannot:

''. . . we must play safe [and] decide the case on the preponderance of
existing authority. Parliament is the right place to settle issues which the
ordinary man regards as controversial.''[19]

It was also improper for judges to disregard or innovate on settled law in areas
where people rely on the certainty of the law in settling their affairs, in particular
in making contracts or settlements. A problem might be too complex for it to
be appropriate for the judges to change some aspect of it: the only proper way
forward would be for there to be legislation following a wide survey of the
whole field.[20] Nevertheless, there was considerable scope for judges to mould
the development of the common law, which should be done having regard to
''common sense, legal principle and public policy in that order.''[21] The judges
did not have so free a hand when interpreting statutes as when dealing with the
common law.

In the late 1950s and early 1960s there were some indications that the House
of Lords was taking a freer attitude to precedents. These led to the Practice
Statement in 1966 in which the Law Lords announced that they would no longer
regard themselves as bound by their own previous decisions.[22] Since then, the
criteria for exercising the power to overrule have been analysed in some detail.

---

[17] Radcliffe (1968), pp. 271–272, 273.
[18] (1972) 12 J.S.P.T.L. 22. For other important contributions to the debate see Diplock L.J., ''The
Courts as Legislators,'' in B. W. Harvey (ed.), *The Lawyer and Justice* (1978), p. 263; Lord
Edmund-Davies ''Judicial Activism'' (1975) 28 C.L.P. 1; Lord Devlin, *The Judge* (1981),
Chap. 1.
[19] (1972) 12 J.S.P.T.L. 22, 23.
[20] See *Myers* v. *D.P.P.* [1965] A.C. 1001, 1022.
[21] (1972) 12 J.S.P.T.L. 22, 25.
[22] See A. Paterson, *The Law Lords* (1982), pp. 143–153, and below, pp. 438–443.

Lord Reid's views have been especially influential,[23] as they have on the wider issues concerning judicial law-making. Similarly, in the field of statutory interpretation the judges have shown a greater inclination to look at the context of the words in a statute, rather than to adopt a narrow literal approach.

Paterson shows that of the 19 Law Lords who were active between 1967 and 1973 at least 12 considered that the Law Lords had an obligation to develop the common law to meet changing social conditions. An even greater proportion of the sample of barristers interviewed by him shared this view, as did at least three of the six Law Lords appointed between 1973 and 1979.[24] Ten of 11 Law Lords interviewed accepted that they ought to be concerned with the possible social and legal consequences of their decisions, at least within the acknowledged limitations of the information available to them.[25] A majority of the Law Lords considered that there were cases coming to the Lords to which there was no single correct solution on the basis of existing legal rules and principles, and in which they had a measure of choice.[26]

In the same period, the Court of Appeal was dominated by Lord Denning M.R., who showed a greater preference for innovation than the Law Lords, albeit coupled with varying success in persuading colleagues in the Court of Appeal to agree with him.[27]

The approach of appellate judges varies according to the context. For example, continued importance has been attached by the House of Lords to the "certainty" factor in commercial and property cases, and, to a lesser extent, in criminal law cases. Here, the willingness of the House of Lords to set aside the common law rule that a man cannot be guilty of raping his wife[28] may be compared with their refusal to abolish the presumption that a child between 10 and 14 is *doli incapax*,[29] or to develop an additional qualified defence to murder to cover the case of the use of excessive force in self-defence or to prevent crime or effect an arrest, reducing the offence to one of manslaughter.[30] The former was seen as the removal of an anachronistic common law fiction, the

---

[23] See Paterson (1982), pp. 153–169.

[24] Paterson (1982), pp. 173–174. But note the view expressed by Lord Scarman in *McLoughlin v. O'Brian* [1983] 1 AC. 410, that where "principle" requires a decision which entails a degree of "policy risk", the court's function is to adjudicate according to "principle," leaving "policy curtailment" to Parliament. The policy issue as to where to draw the line in "nervous shock" cases is "not justiciable. The problem is one of social, economic and financial policy. The considerations relevant to a decision are not such as to be capable of being handled within the limits of the forensic process": pp. 430–431. See, *contra*, Lord Edmund-Davies, pp. 427–428.

[25] Paterson (1982), pp. 177–178.

[26] *ibid.* pp. 192–195. This runs counter to the theory developed by R. M. Dworkin that there is a right answer in all hard cases and that the judges have no discretion to make law: *Taking Rights Seriously* (1977); "No Right Answer" in P. Hacker and J. Raz (eds.), *Law, Morality and Society* (1977); J. W. Harris, *Legal Philosophies* (1980), Chap. 14; Bell (1983), Chap. VIII.

[27] See Stevens (1979), pp. 488–505; Lord Denning *The Discipline of Law* (1979), Parts 1 and 7.

[28] *R. v. R. (Rape: Marital Exemption)* [1992] 1 A.C. 599. See M. Giles, [1992] Crim.L.R. 407. This decision was challenged before the European Court of Human Rights on the ground that the law was changed retrospectively, contrary to Art, 7., ECHR. However, the court ruled that there was no violation as it was reasonable foreseeable by the applicant that a court might embark on the legitimate adaptation of the ingredients of the crime: (*CR and SW v. U. K., The Times,* December 5, 1995.

[29] *C. (A minor) v. D.P.P.* [1995] 2 W.L.R. 383. The presumption prevents a child being convicted of a criminal offence in the absence of clear positive evidence that the child knew that his or her act was seriously wrong, evidence of the acts amounting to the offences alone being insufficient.

[30] *R. v. Clegg* [1995] 1 A.C. 482.

status of women having changed out of all recognition since the rule was enunciated by Hale in the eighteenth century.[31] the latter points were much more
controversial, the government having stated its intention to maintain the *doli
incapax* presumption as recently as 1990.[32] and having consistently resisted proposals to change the scope of the law of murder or the mandatory life sentence
for that offence.[33] By contrast, there was in the 1970s and early 1980s a marked
extension of liability in such aspects of the tort of negligence as negligent misstatement,[34] omissions,[35] nervous shock,[36] economic loss,[37] and injury to trespassers,[38] although in some of these areas, most notably economic loss, the extension of liability has been followed by retrenchment.[39] The House of Lords has
now expressed a preference for developments in the scope of the tort of negligence to be incremental, by analogy with existing cases, rather than by reference
to broadly-expressed principles.[40] Similarly, in *Cambridge Water Co. Ltd. v.
Eastern Counties Leather plc*[41] the House declined to develop a general principle
of strict liability for extra-hazardous activities, preferring instead to modify the
elements of the *Rylands v. Fletcher*[42] tort.[43] In public law, there has been a
whole series of cases in which the courts have analysed, refined and sometimes
extended the grounds upon which administrative and judicial decisions of
government institutions can be challenged under the *ultra vires* doctrine.[44] In
many of these, the challenges have been successful.[45] Recent high profile cases
have seen the House of Lords hold that ministers of the Crown are subject to the
law of contempt of court.[46] and that the government's revised criminal injuries

---

[31] [1992] 1 A.C. 599, 616, *per* Lord Keith.
[32] White Paper, *Crime, Justice and Protecting the Public* (Cm. 965, 1990), para. 8.4.
[33] See, *e.g.*, H.L. Select Committee Report on Murder and Life Imprisonment (1988–89 H.L. 78);
Lord Windlesham, [1993] Crim. L.R. 644. See also A. T. H. Smith, "Judicial law-making in the
criminal law" (1984) 100 L.Q.R. 46 on the supposed distinction between creating new offences
(which is clearly objectionable) and extending existing offences to cover new situations.
[34] *Hedley Byrne & Co. v. Heller & Partners* [1964] A.C. 465.
[35] *Home Office v. Dorset Yacht Co.* [1970] A.C. 1004; *Anns v. London Borough of Merton* [1978]
A.C. 728.
[36] *McLoughlin v. O'Brian* [1983] 1 A.C. 410.
[37] *Junior Books Ltd v. Veitchi Co. Ltd* [1983] 1 A.C. 520.
[38] *British Railways Board v. Herrington* [1972] A.C. 877.
[39] See, e.g. *Leigh and Sillavan Ltd v. Aliakmon Shipping Co. Ltd* [1986] A.C. 785; *Yuen Kun Yeu
v. Att.-Gen. of Hong Kong* [1988] A.C. 175; *D. & F. Estates Ltd v. Church Commissioners for
England* [1989] A.C. 177; *Murphy v. Brentwood District Council* [1991] 1 A.C. 398 (over-ruling
Anns).
[40] *e.g.* Lord Bridge in *Caparo Industries plc v. Dickman* [1990] 2 A.C. 605, 617–618.
[41] [1994] 2 A.C. 264.
[42] (1868) L.R. 3 H.L. 330.
[43] Adding the requirement that the damage be foreseeable; making it easier for the plaintiff to
establish that the defendant's user of land was "non-natural".
[44] For recent general surveys, see A. Lester Q.C., "English judges as law makers" [1993] P.L. 269
and Lord Woolf, "Droit Public - English Style" [1995] P.L. 57.
[45] *e.g. Ridge v. Baldwin* [1964] A.C. 40 (dismissal of a chief constable held void for breach of
natural justice); *Anisminic Ltd v. Foreign Compensation Commission* [1969] 2 A.C. 147 (decision
of the Commission struck down for misinterpretation of the relevant legislation notwithstanding
a statutory clause purporting to exclude judicial review); *Padfield v. Minister of Agriculture*
[1968] A.C. 997 and *Laker Airways v. Department of Trade* [1977] Q.B. 643 (ministerial
decisions held to be abuses of discretion); *Bromley London Borough Council v. Greater London
Council* [1983] 1 A.C. 768 (substantial cuts in fares held to be *ultra vires*).
[46] *M. v. Home Office* [1994] 1 A.C. 377.

compensation scheme was unlawful.[47] The Divisional Court found that the government allocation of aid to the Pergau Dam project in Malaysia was also unlawful.[48] In others, the judges have shown restraint in circumstances where it was not obvious why restraint was any more appropriate.[49]

It is also interesting to contrast the willingness of Sir Robert Megarry V.-C. to extend the field of liability in negligence for economic loss[50] with his unwillingness to create an "altogether new right" in a case where it was claimed that there was a right to hold a telephone conversation in the privacy of one's home without molestation[51]:

> "No new right in the law, fully-fledged with all the appropriate safeguards, can spring from the head of a judge deciding a particular case: only Parliament can create such a right . . . The wider and more indefinite the right claimed, the greater the undesirability of holding that such a right exists."[52]

There are some apparently formidable arguments in favour of judicial restraint in law-making. The making of new law through the legislative process[53] rather than judicially is often said to be more in accordance with democratic theory[54] and is more likely to be based on a proper examination of all the relevant information. English civil procedure generally prevents anyone but the parties to litigation giving evidence[55] and enables the parties to choose what evidence to present. Moreover, there are difficulties in presenting *evidence* as distinct from *argument* about the possible social and economic implications of decisions. Conspicuous creativity in judicial law making is difficult to square with the "ostentatious impartiality" that is also regarded as desirable.[56] The judges have no written constitution to look to as a source of power.[57]

---

[47] *R. v. Secretary of State for the Home Department, ex p. The Fire Brigades Union* [1995] 2 W.L.R. 464. See above, p. 46.

[48] *R. v. Secretary of State for Foreign and Commonwealth Affairs, ex p. World Development Movement Ltd* [1995] 1 W.L.R. 386.

[49] *R. v. Secretary of State for the Department, ex p. Zamir* [1980] A.C. 930 (but *cf. R. v. Secretary of State for the Home Department, ex p. Khawaja* [1984] A.C. 74); *Bushell v. Secretary of State for the Environment* [1981] A.C. 75; *R. v. Secretary of State for the Home Department, ex p. Brind* [1991] A.C. 696 (declining to hold that the doctrine of proportionality constituted an independent ground of challenge in English administrative law).

[50] *Ross v. Caunters* [1980] Ch. 297.

[51] *Malone v. Metropolitan Police Commissioner (No. 2)* [1979] Ch. 344.

[52] *ibid.* pp. 372, 373. Compare also the extension of police powers of seizure by the Court of Appeal in *Chic Fashions Ltd v. Jones* [1968] 2 Q.B. 299 and *Ghani v. Jones* [1970] 1 Q.B. 693 with the refusal of the court to create a new common law power of search: *McLorie v. Oxford* [1982] Q.B. 1290.

[53] See Chap. 5.

[54] But see Atiyah, (1980) 15 Israel L. R. 362–365.

[55] The rules could, of course, be changed. By contrast, in the United States interest groups are much more able to institute litigation, or to present arguments in cases involving other parties.

[56] See above, p. 240.

[57] Although here it should be noted that the power of judicial review exercised by the Supreme Court in the United States is not expressly created by the Constitution, but is itself judge-made: see *Marbury v. Madison* (1803) 1 Cranch 137. Furthermore, a number of judges have expressed the view extra-judicially that in certain circumstances the courts might decline to give effect to statutes that violate fundamental constitutional principles: Lord Woolf, *"Droit Public* - English style" [1995] P.L. 57 (legislation removing or substantially impairing the High Court's powers of judicial review); Sedley J., "Human Rights: a Twenty-first century Agenda" [1995] P.L. 386, 391 ("obligation of the courts to articulate and uphold the ground rules of ethical social existence which we dignify as fundamental human rights"); Laws J. "Law and Democracy" [1995] P.L.

A more pragmatic reason sometimes advanced in favour of restraint is that:

"if people and Parliament come to think that the judicial power is to be confined by nothing other than the judge's sense of what is right (or, as Selden put it, by the length of the Chancellor's foot), confidence in the judicial system will be replaced by fear of it becoming uncertain and arbitrary in its application. Society will then be ready for Parliament to cut the power of the judges. Their power to do justice will become more restricted by law than it need be, or is today."[58]

Nevertheless, restraint is not the same as complete withdrawal from the field. "Law reform" does not rank high in the list of priorities in the struggle for a place in the legislative timetable: if one always waited for Parliament, one would often wait in vain.

In his book, *The Politics of the Judiciary*[59] Professor Griffith argues that the discussion about how creative judges should be:

"has been and is a somewhat unreal discussion. . . . What is lacking . . . is any clear and consistent relationship between the general pronouncements of judges on this matter of creativity and the way they conduct themselves in court."[60]

Moreover, the appellate judges:

"have by their education and training and the pursuit of their profession as barristers, acquired a strikingly homogeneous collection of attitudes, beliefs and principles, which to them represents the public interest. . . . The judicial conception of the public interest . . . is three-fold. It concerns first, the interests of the State (including its moral welfare); secondly, the preservation of law and order broadly interpreted; and, thirdly, the promotion of certain political views normally associated with the Conservative Party."[61]

They are thus concerned to preserve and protect the existing order, to serve the prevailing political and economic forces, this being generally true of all societies today, whether capitalistic or communist. This is not regarded by Griffith as a matter for recrimination: his main concern is simply to dispel the myth that the judges are "neutral."

72 (protection of fundamental freedoms). These suggestions have been criticised as contrary to principle by Lord Irvine of Lairg Q.C., "Judges and decision-makers: the theory and practice of *Wednesbury* review" [1996] P.L. 59.

[58] *Per* Lord Scarman in *Duport Steels Ltd v Sirs* [1980] 1 All E.R. 529, 551. When Roger Parker Q.C. made a similar prediction in his submissions to the Court of Appeal in *Congreve v. Home Office* [1976] Q.B. 629, Lord Denning M.R. stated "We trust that this was not said seriously, but only as a piece of advocate's licence." Mr Parker subsequently apologised if anything he said had sounded like a threat. (See *The Times*, December 6 and 9, 1975.)

[59] For similar studies of particular areas see J. I. Reynolds, "Statutory Covenant of Fitness and Repair" (1974) 37 M.L.R. 377 (and the rejoinder by M. J. Robinson, (1976) 39 M.L.R. 43); J. Hackney, "The Politics of the Chancery" (1981) 34 C.L.P. 113.

[60] p. 185. Paterson, *The Law Lords* (1982), pp. 187–189, argues that the Law Lords have been more consistent than Griffith suggests.

[61] *ibid.* pp. 275, 278. Previous editions included a reference to "the protection of property rights."

In relation to Griffith's view that the appellate judges have acquired a homogenous collection of attitudes, Lord Devlin commented[62]:

"Since he is writing of men in their sixties and seventies whose working life has given them a common outlook on many questions, by no means all political, I have very little doubt that he is right. I have very little doubt either that the same might be written of most English institutions, certainly of all those which like the law are not of a nature to attract the crusading or rebellious spirit."

However, he suggested that whether one agrees that the application of the law has been distorted depended on whether one:

"looks at them from right or from the left. . . . To my mind none of the evidence, general or specific adds much to the inherent probability that men and women of a certain age will be inclined to favour the *status quo*."[63]

He, and others, have, for instance, pointed out that in many of the cases discussed by Griffith there has been a division of opinion both between the Court of Appeal and the House of Lords, and within each court.[64]

Griffith does not suggest that anything can be done to change judicial attitudes. Lord Devlin notes that for a known bias allowance can be made:

"[W]here novel measures are imposed by a minister or by parliament, they must be expressed in language which is emphatic enough and clear enough to penetrate the bias against them of those who are set in their ways: it is no use praying for the rejuvenation of the elderly."[65]

What these contributions to the debate do seem to suggest is that caution should be used in contemplating any dramatic extension of the powers of the judiciary, such as by the creation of a Bill of Rights on the American pattern with entrenched guarantees of civil liberties, expressed in general language, which override both legislation and administrative action. Moreover, one can be a little sceptical about claims such as those of Lord Denning[66]:

"May not the Judges themselves sometimes abuse or misuse their power? It is their duty to administer and apply the law of the land. If they should divert it or depart from it—and do so knowingly—they themselves would be guilty of a misuse of power. So we come up against Juvenal's question, *'Sed quis custodiet ipsos custodes?'* (But who is to guard the guards themselves?). . . . Suppose a future Prime Minister should seek to pack the Bench with judges of his own extreme political colour. Would they be tools in his hand? To that I answer 'No.' Every judge on his appointment discards all politics and all prejudices. You need have no fear. The Judges of England have always in the past—

---

[62] (1978) 41 M.L.R. 501, 505–506.
[63] *ibid.* pp. 507, 509.
[64] B. Roshier and H. Teff, *Law in Society* (1980), p. 67.
[65] (1978) 41 M.L.R. 501, 511.
[66] *Misuse of Power* (*The Richard Dimbleby Lecture 1980*), pp. 18–19. Reprinted in *What Next in the Law?* (1982).

and always will be vigilant in guarding our freedoms. Someone must be trusted. Let it be the Judges.''

On the other hand, the adoption of a "strongly liberal viewpoint" has been identified in recent public law cases in the House of Lords and the Privy Council,[67] which does provide some corroboration for Lord Denning's view.

---

[67] R. Gordon, "The awakened conscience of the nation," *Counsel*, March/April 1994, p. 8, citing the decisions in *Pepper v. Hart* (below, pp. 390–392); *R. v. Secretary of State for the Home Department, ex p. Doody* [1994] 1 A.C. 531 (developing the obligations of public law decision-makers to give reasons for their decisions); *M. v. Home Office* [1994] 1 A.C.377 (holding that ministers may be subject to injunctions and the law of contempt); *Pratt and Morgan v. Attorney-General of Jamaica* [1994] 2 A.C. 1 (holding that delay in carrying out an execution could amount to a breach of constitutional rights); and *R. v. Secretary of State for Employment, ex p. Equal Opportunities Commission* (below, p. 339).

Chapter 5

LEGISLATION

A. INTRODUCTION[1]

IN medieval England there was no clear distinction between legislation and other forms of governmental action, and there was no settled procedure for enactment that had to be followed. The terminology was confusing: well-known early statutes include the "Constitutions" of Clarendon 1164, the "Great Charter" 1215, the "Statute" of Merton 1235 and the "Provisions" of Oxford 1258:

"A statute in the region of Edward I simply means something established by royal authority; whether it is established by the King in Council, or in a Parliament of nobles, or in a Parliament of nobles and commons as well is completely immaterial."[2]

By the fifteenth century the consent of the Commons to a statute was regarded as necessary and in early Tudor times the procedure for enactment took on something like its modern form:

"Legislation . . . was no longer the Government's vague reply to vaguely worded complaints, but rather the deliberate adoption of specific proposals embodied in specific texts emanating from the Crown or its officers."[3]

In the seventeenth century, Coke wrote that "There is no Act of Parliament but must have the consent of the Lords, the Commons and the Royal assent of the King."[4] The constitutional struggles of that century saw the end of serious attempts by the Crown to assert a legislative competence rivalling that of Parliament.[5] In the *Case of Proclamations*[6] the judges resolved that "the King by his proclamation cannot create any offence which was not an offence before" and "that the King hath no prerogative, but that which the law of the land allows him." However, the courts subsequently upheld the Crown's claim to a power to impose taxation incidentally to the exercise of prerogative powers such as those to conduct foreign affairs, regulate trade and take emergency measures

---

[1] See generally on legislation, D. R. Miers and A. C. Page, *Legislation* (2nd ed., 1990); F. A. R. Bennion, *Statute Law* (3rd ed., 1990); and C. Pick, *Passing Legislation in Britain* (Foreign & Commonwealth Office, 1992). On the history of legislation see J. H. Baker, *Introduction to Legal History* (3rd ed., 1990), pp. 234–243; C. K. Allen, *Law in the Making* (7th ed., 1964), pp. 435–469.

[2] T. F. T. Plucknett, *Concise History of the Common Law* (5th ed., 1956), p. 322.

[3] Plucknett, (1944) 60 L.Q.R. 242, 248.

[4] 4 Coke's *Institutes of the Laws of England*, p. 25.

[5] See S. A. de Smith and R. Brazier, *Constitutional and Administrative Law* (7th ed., 1994), pp. 75–78.

[6] (1611) 12 Co. Rep. 74.

for the defence of the realm,[7] and a power to "dispense" with the operation of
a statute for the benefit of an individual.[8] James II also claimed the power to
"suspend" the general operation of statutes, his target being statutes that dis-
criminated against Dissenters and Roman Catholics. The reassertion of such
claims to prerogative power after the Civil War and the Restoration led to the
"Glorious Revolution" of 1688 and the Bill of Rights. The latter measure,
declared to be a statute by the Crown and Parliament Recognition Act 1689,
provided (*inter alia*).

> "That the pretended power of suspending of laws or the execution of laws
> by regall authority without consent of Parlyament is illegal. . . .
>   That the pretended power of dispensing with laws or the execution of
> laws by regall authorities as it hath been assumed and exercised of late is
> illegall. . . .
>   That levying money for or to the use of the Crowne by pretence of
> prerogative without grant of Parlyament for longer time or in other manner
> than the same is or shall be granted is illegal."

The prerogative powers of the Crown were in general restricted, and not abolished, but it was now clear that they could be modified or extinguished according
to Parliament's wishes. Other possible rivals have also been unable to maintain
any challenge to the dominance of Parliament. The Reformation Parliament
established legislative supremacy over the Church.[9] In more recent times, the
courts have refused to accept that a resolution of the House of Commons may
alter the law of the land.[10]

Certain periods of our history have been noted for increases in legislative
activity, and complaints of the difficulty of keeping abreast of the changes.
Parliament passed 677 statutes in the reign of Henry VIII and these occupied
almost as much space as the whole statute book had done in 1509.[11] Between
1711 and 1811 the annual number of Acts passed increased from 74 to 423.
The bulk of the increase was in the number of local and private Acts. The 1811
figures included one for change of name, two for divorce, six for the settlement
of private estates, 33 for inclosure and about 150 concerning local matters such
as turnpike roads, canals and bridges.[12] The most dramatic increase in legislative
activity has, however, been the product of the vast expansion of the activities
of the state during the nineteenth and twentieth centuries, and associated factors
such as the extensive reforms in the civil service and the administrative machinery, the increasingly representative nature of Parliament, the development of
political parties and the strengthening of the role of the Cabinet. The balance
as regards Acts of Parliament has also shifted from private legislation to public
general legislation.[13]

---

[7] *Case of Impositions: Bate's Case* (1606) 2 St.Tr.371; *Case of Ship Money: R. v. Hampden* (1637)
3 St.Tr.825.
[8] *Thomas v. Sorell* (1674) Vaughan 330; *Godden v. Hales* (1686) 11 St.Tr.1165.
[9] J. H. Baker, *The Reports of Sir John Spelman Vol. II*, Introduction (1978), pp. 64–70.
[10] See *Stockdale v. Hansard* (1839) 9 A. & E. 1, where the Court of Queen's Bench held that the
scope of Parliamentary privilege could not be extended by a resolution; *Bowles v. Bank of England*
[1913] 1 Ch. 57.
[11] See Baker, *op. cit.* n. 9, at pp. 43–46.
[12] S. Lambert, *Bills and Acts* (1971), p. 52.
[13] See below, pp. 262–265.

Having established its legislative supremacy, Parliament was reluctant to delegate its powers.[14] In the eighteenth century, public general Acts tended "to be either overloaded with detail or to be directed to specific instances rather than to general rules."[15] However, some law-making powers had from the time of Henry VIII been entrusted to institutions such as the Commissioners of Sewers and the Justices of the Peace, and new powers were from time to time delegated by Parliament. In the eighteenth century, for example, extensive powers were granted to the Commissioners of Customs and Excise, and the Crown was given almost exclusive disciplinary powers over the Army. The following century saw a significant increase of social legislation, and a related extension of powers delegated to local and central government, but the real explosion of delegated legislation has been in the twentieth century.[16] In addition the accession of the United Kingdom to the European Communities has meant that a large body of Community legislation has become applicable in this country. We consider in turn the various forms of legislation: Acts of Parliament, subordinate or delegated legislation and European legislation.

B. ACTS OF PARLIAMENT

1. PARLIAMENTARY SOVEREIGNTY

One of the distinctive features of the constitution of the United Kingdom is the doctrine of Parliamentary sovereignty.[17] A measure which has received the assent of the Queen, Lords and Commons, that assent being given separately and in the two Houses of Parliament by simple majorities, is accepted to have the force of law as an Act of Parliament. Its validity cannot be questioned in the courts and any earlier inconsistent legislation is repealed. Parliament (strictly the "Queen in Parliament") may pass any kind of law without restriction, except that an attempt to bind its successors either as to the content of legislation or the manner and form of its enactment cannot succeed. Acts of Parliament, thus defined, are the supreme form of law; the rule of judicial obedience to them is the "ultimate *political* fact upon which the whole system of legislation hangs."[18] The definition of "Parliament" can be altered, but the process by which that can be achieved is political rather than legal. For example, there is no reason why the British people should not be able to adopt a written constitution, perhaps incorporating a Bill of Rights, which limits the powers of both government and legislature. What is unclear is how this would be done. The people of the United

---

[14] C. K. Allen, *Law and Orders* (3rd ed., 1965), Chap. 2.

[15] *ibid.* p. 28.

[16] In 1993 there were 52 Public General Statutes (3600 pages: 2598 excluding Consolidation and Scottish Acts); 3 General Synod measures (40 pages); 18 local Acts. In 1992 there were 3349 statutory instruments (8964 pages of those printed).

[17] See S. A. de Smith and R. Brazier *Constitutional and Administrative Law* (7th ed., 1994), Chap. 4; E. C. S. Wade and A. W. Bradley, *Constitutional and Administrative Law* (11th ed., 1993), Chap. 5; Sir William Wade, *Constitutional Fundamentals* (2nd ed., 1989), Chap. 3; C. R. Munro, *Studies in Constitutional Law* (1987).

[18] H. W. R. Wade, [1955] C.L.J. 172, 188.

States did so in 1787–88 by means of a Constitutional Convention whose proposals were ratified by specially elected state conventions; the American "Bill of Rights" was added subsequently as a series of constitutional amendments. The judges would have to be satisfied that such a change was generally accepted; a constituent assembly might provide sufficient evidence. They would look to the realities of the situation, as they did at the commencement and conclusion of the Interregnum in the seventeenth century, when they adjusted first to the absence and then to the restoration of the monarchy.

The foregoing represents the orthodox view of Parliamentary sovereignty. It has of course been argued that the definition of "Parliament" is a matter of law rather than politics, and that as such it can be altered by the existing legislative process. Parliament as at present defined could then bind its successors as to the manner and form of legislation by redefining itself either generally or for specific purposes.[19] This view, however, has had more academic support than judicial. The constitutional adviser to the House of Lords Select Committee on a Bill of Rights clearly preferred the orthodox view,[20] and this seemed to be accepted by the Committee. Moreover, the "new view" suffers from the weakness that it would enable a redefinition of "Parliament" to be effected too easily; in effect by a small partisan majority in the House of Commons.[21] For the present, Coke's definition of an Act of Parliament holds good. One important qualification is, however, that at least while the European Communities Act 1972 is on the statute book the judges are prepared to recognise the primacy of European Community law over inconsistent statutes. The status of an Act of Parliament passed with the intention of overriding Community law but without repealing the 1972 Act has not, however, been tested.[21a]

It should be noted that while the concept of "Parliamentary sovereignty" is a doctrine of great technical legal significance it should not be taken as a guide to the reality of the legislative process. First, there have always been external influences which have imposed practical restraints on the kinds of legislation which can be passed. Second, the legislative process is today dominated by the government and not by members of Parliament acting independently. Legislation is initiated and formulated outside Parliament, the functions of Parliament are limited to those of scrutiny and legitimisation, and governments normally enjoy a secure party majority. Third, within "Parliament" the House of Commons is the dominant element.[22] Finally it must not be thought that legislation is the only method by which the government can secure its aims; much is achieved by, for example, exhortation, bargaining and the exercise of its economic power.[23]

2. PUBLIC AND PRIVATE ACTS

A distinction is drawn between public and private Acts. The former are those measures that are intended to alter the general law or deal with the public rev-

---

[19] See R. F. V. Heuston, *Essays in Constitutional Law* (2nd ed., 1964), Chap. 1.

[20] Evidence, 1977–78 H.L. 276, pp. 1–10 (D. Rippengal); Report: 1977–78 H.L. 176.

[21] Given that the House of Lords can be by-passed and that the royal assent by convention cannot be withheld (see below pp. 275–276).

[21a] See pp. 331–344.

[22] See below, pp. 273–276.

[23] See J. J. Richardson and A. G. Jordan, *Governing under Pressure* (1979), Chap. 6.

enue or the administration of justice.[24] The latter are of local[25] or personal[26] concern. The procedure for enactment differs in some respects[27]; a person who wishes to rely on a private Act in court must produce a Queen's Printer's copy or an examined or certified copy of the original whereas judicial notice is taken of public Acts[28]; and a private Act may be construed strictly against the interest of the promoter, although this approach is not always followed today.[29]

An important class of private legislation is that promoted by local authorities. Section 262 of the Local Government Act 1972 provided that all local legislation (with some exceptions, including protective provisions for the benefit of any person and provisions relating to a statutory undertaking), in force immediately before April 1974, would cease to have effect at the end of 1979 in metropolitan counties and at the end of 1984 elsewhere.[30] These dates were subsequently postponed by, respectively, one year and two years.[31] Local authorities wishing to preserve particular provisions were required to promote Bills to that end. Many authorities did so,[32] although the rationalisation process proved to be less straightforward and more expensive than had been anticipated.[33]

Further work on the rationalisation of local legislation is continuing under the auspices of Law Commission, leading to provisions in the series of Statute Law (Repeals) Acts.[34]

The scope and procedures for enactment of private legislation were considered

---

[24] *Halsbury's Laws of England* (4th ed.) Vol. 34, para. 1223. For a useful analysis of the kinds of public Bills according to their content see I. Burton and G. Drewry, *Legislation and Public Policy* (1981), pp. 32–45. The authors draw a broad distinction between innovatory "policy" Bills and non-innovatory "administration" Bills to remedy anomalies, with further sub-categories of "minor policy" Bills dealing with restricted issues within an area of public policy not otherwise intended to be changed, and "administrative reform" Bills which reorganise administrative support for an existing policy. Session-by-session surveys of legislation by Burton and Drewry have appeared in the journal *Parliamentary Affairs*. Details of the progress of Bills are set out with annual *House of Commons Sessional Information Digests* published by HMSO.

[25] Bills dealing with the constitution or election of local governing bodies must be introduced as public Bills: *Halsbury, ibid.*; below, pp. 279–280. See *e.g.* the London Government Act 1963; the Charlwood and Horley Act 1974.

[26] *i.e.* a "private bill relating to the estate, property, status or style, or otherwise relating to the personal affairs of an individual" (H.L. Standing Order 151). These include Bills affecting estates, and Bills to authorise a marriage between persons within the prohibited degrees of affinity: in the case of the latter, the details are now considered by a Select Committee of the House of Lords, and not on the floor of the House: 2nd Report from the Select Committee on Procedure, 1985–86 H.L. 152, approved by the House (H.L. Deb. Vol. 475, cols.709–711, June 3, 1986).

[27] See below, pp. 263–264 and 279–280.

[28] The line between "public" and "private" Acts is drawn rather differently in this context: see *Halsbury's Laws of England* (4th ed.) Vol. 17, para. 150. For this purpose an Act passed after 1850 is deemed to be a public Act and "to be judicially noticed as such unless the contrary is expressly provided by the Act": Interpretation Act 1978, s.3 and Sched. 2, para. 2. For the definition of "judicial notice" see above p. 11, n. 31.

[29] *Maxwell on Interpretation of Statutes* (12th ed., 1969), pp. 262–3. See, *e.g. Allen v. Gulf Oil Refining Ltd* [1981] A.C. 1001, H.L.

[30] See D. Foulkes, [1976] P.L. 272; E. D. Graham, (1979) XLVII *The Table* 109; R. J. B. Morris, [1987] Stat.L.R. 2.

[31] S.I. 1979 No. 969; S.I. 1983 No. 619.

[32] An alternative approach, permitted in a few cases, was for the Secretary of State for the Environment to exercise the power conferred by s.262(9)(a) to exempt particular provisions from the general cesser: see S.I. 1986 No. 1133; Morris, *op. cit.* pp. 26–27.

[33] Foulkes, *op. cit.*; Morris, *op. cit.*

[34] See 29th Annual Report of the Law Commission 1994 (1994–95 H.C. 244), p. 51. C. S. Phipps, (1991) 22 *The Law Librarian* 60; (1992) 23 *The Law Librarian* 35.

by the Joint Committee on Private Bill Procedure in 1987–88.[35] The committee's recommendations were designed to reduce the range of private legislation by diverting matters that could be pursued by other, non-Parliamentary procedures and included recommendations on matters of detail and procedure. The outcome was the introduction by the Transport and Works Act 1992 of a new procedure for the Secretary of State to make orders in respect of such matters as rail, light rail and light rapid transit proposals and inland waterways and broadening the scope of orders in respect of harbours.[36] Orders in relation to proposals which in the Secretary of State's opinion are of national importance require the approval of both Houses of Parliament. Orders under the 1992 Act are delegated legislation and open to challenge in the courts.[37] In addition, there were some detailed changes to private Bill procedure, including the introduction of requirements as to environmental impact assessment.[38]

Public Bills which are found to affect private interests in a manner different from the way in which they affect other private interests in the same category are known as "hybrid" Bills and are subject to an amalgam of the procedural rules applicable to public and private Bills.[39]

3. GOVERNMENT BILLS AND PRIVATE MEMBERS' BILLS

A separate distinction, within the class of public general statutes, is drawn between government and "Private Members'" Bills.[40] Most of the Bills that are successful are introduced by the government of the day,[41] but Bills may also be introduced by individual M.P.s or "Private Peers". In the House of Commons certain days are set aside for Private Members' Bills and a ballot is held each session to determine which M.P.s may take priority on these days. A list of 20 names is drawn up; those near the top have some chance of success, although in practice a Bill will not get through without the support, or at least the

---

[35] 1987–88 H.L. 97, H.C. 625.; *Private Bills and New Procedures—A Consultation Document— The Government's Response to the Report of the Joint Committee on Private Bill Procedure,* Cm. 1110, 1990.

[36] See J. Durkin, P. Lane and M. Peto, *Blackstone's Guide to the Transport and Works Act 1992* (1992).

[37] 1992 Act, s.22 (a statutory *ultra vires* clause: see below, pp. 967–968).

[38] See Vol. 187 H. C. Deb., March 13, 1991, cols.923–925; Vol. 191 H. C. Deb., May 20, 1991, cols. 721–739.

[39] P. Norton, *The Commons in Perspective* (1981), p. 104. In 1976 problems were caused for the government when the Speaker ruled that the Aircraft and Shipbuilding Industries Bill, which had completed its Committee stage, was prima facie hybrid: I. Burton and G. Drewry, (1978) 31 *Parliamentary Affairs* pp. 151–6. Recent examples include the Cardiff Bay Barrage Act 1993.

[40] On Private Members' Bills see P. G. Richards in S. A. Walkland (ed.) *The House of Commons in the Twentieth Century* (1979), Chap. VI; P. Norton, *The Commons in Perspective* (1981), pp. 99–102; P. G. Richards, *Parliament and Conscience* (1970); D. Marsh and Read, *Private Members' Bills* (1988); J. Gray, [1978] P. L. 242 (case study of the Unsolicited Goods and Services Acts 1971 and 1975); S. M. Cretney, "The Forfeiture Acts 1982—the Private Member's Bill as an Instrument of Law Reform" (1990) 10 O.J.L.S. 289; Sir Henry de Waal, [1990] Stat. L.R. 18.

[41] The number per session has varied between 25 and 52 in the period 1985 to 1994, depending in part on the number of sitting days in the session: see the House of Commons *Sessional Information Digest.*

benevolent neutrality, of the government.[42] There are other methods by which a private member may introduce a Bill,[43] but such Bills rarely proceed because of lack of time.[44] Some important measures have commenced life as Private Members' Bills, including the Public Bodies (Admission to Meetings) Act 1960 (sponsored by Margaret Thatcher M.P.), the Abortion Act 1967 (David Steel M.P.) and the Indecent Displays (Control) Act 1981 (Timothy Sainsbury M.P.). Governments tend to prefer to leave matters of conscience to Private Members' legislation: the risks generally outweigh any possible political advantages. One result is that such legislation, once in place, can become difficult to repeal or reform, as shown by the many unsuccessful attempts over the years by anti-abortionists to secure the amendment of the Abortion Act 1967.[45] A Private Members' Bill that fails may, however, provide the impetus for subsequent public legislation.[46] The special features of "private Acts" mentioned above do not apply to those "public general statutes" that happen to start their life as Private Members' Bills.

4. CONSOLIDATION ACTS AND STATUTE LAW REVISION ACTS[47]

On occasion, the law in a particular area is *codified*; the relevant rules as derived from both case-law and existing statutory provisions are set out afresh in one statute. The leading examples are the Bills of Exchange Act 1882, the Sale of Goods Act 1893 (now consolidated in the Sale of Goods Act 1979) and the Theft Act 1968. The Law Commission's objects include that of the codification of areas of English law, but it found that this kind of work could pose great problems and could require the allocation of resources on a scale which was

---

[42] This point is well known to members, who should be "realistic about the prospects of success": Select Committee on Procedure, (5th Report, 1994–95 H.C. 38, *Private Members' Bills*, p. xxxvii). However, the adoption by the government of procedural tactics to block the Civil Rights (Disabled Persons) Bill 1993–94 (and other Bills) where it had failed to make clear its opposition generated considerable controversy.

[43] (1) After Question Time, on notice given under S.O. No. 58, or (2) under the "ten minute rule", which allows time for brief speeches for and against a Bill. Examples of the former that were ultimately successful include the Protection of Birds (Amendment) Bill 1976 (which went through all its Commons stages in 67 seconds) and the Prohibition of Female Circumcision Bill 1985 (which had been presented and had made some progress in previous sessions: see E. A. Sochart, (1988) 41 *Parliamentary Affairs* 508). Examples of the latter include the Bail (Amendment) Act 1993 and the Local Government (Amendment) Act 1993.

[44] For example, in 1993–94, the numbers of Bills presented (and the number successful) were: government Bills 25 (25); ballot Bills 20 (eight); S.O. No. 58 Bills 37 (two); 10-minute rule Bills 49 (none); Lords' Private Members' Bills 10 (six). (House of Commons *Sessional Information Digest 1993–94* (HMSO). The statistics for 1950–85 are given in *Marsh and Read* (1988), pp. 22–23. In 1995, the Select Committee on Procedure (5th Report on *Private Members' Bills*), 1994–95 H.C. 38) noted that they had not received any conclusive evidence that the balance between government and backbench members had shifted over the last 25 years, and did not recommend any changes in procedure.

[45] See D. Marsh and J. Chambers, *Abortion Politics* (1981); Marsh and Read (1988), Chap. 6.

[46] *e.g.* the Home Buyers' Bill sponsored by Austin Mitchell in 1983–84 (see above pp. 119–120 and Mitchell, (1986) 39 *Parliamentary Affairs* 1).

[47] See Lord Simon of Glaisdale and J. V. D. Webb, [1975] P.L. 285; I. Burton and G. Drewry, *Legislation and Public Policy* (1981), pp. 205–213; Lord Simon of Glaisdale, [1985] Stat. L.R. 352. On the interpretation of consolidation legislation see below, pp. 382–383.

regarded as impossible.[48] Much greater progress has, however, been made by
the project on codification of criminal law.[49]

The *consolidation* of statutory provisions on a particular topic is a process
that is more modest in aim, and much more commonly achieved.[50] Here, the
relevant provisions are re-enacted in one or more consolidating statutes. There
are four kinds of consolidation Bill. First, there are straight consolidation Bills
that simply re-enact the existing texts. Second, Bills presented under the Consolidation of Enactments (Procedure) Act 1949 may include "corrections and
minor improvements",[51] which must be approved by a Joint Committee of both
Houses on Consolidation Bills. Third, improvements designed to facilitate the
satisfactory consolidation, but beyond the scope of the 1949 Act may be proposed by the Law Commission; these are also considered by the Joint Committee.[52] Fourth, consolidation with substantial amendments may be prepared
by an *ad hoc* expert committee, or as an ordinary departmental Bill.[53] Where
the consolidation process requires some amendments of substance these may be
included in an ordinary Bill (normally in a Schedule)[54]; once these "pre-
consolidation amendments" have been passed one of the first three kinds of
consolidation measure can be brought forward.[55] Recent large scale consolidations include those of the Housing legislation and the Companies legislation
in 1985, the Income and Corporation Taxes Act 1988,[56] the Planning legislation
in 1990 and the Water legislation in 1991.

Various Statute Law Revision Acts have been passed at intervals from 1856
for the repeal of statutory provisions that are "obsolete, spent, unnecessary or
superseded." Since 1969 the Law Commissions have prepared Statute Law
(Repeals) Bills for the repeal of enactments that in their opinion are "no longer
of practical utility." These are wider in scope. One was passed each year

---

[48] Law Commissions Act 1965, s.3(1); Law Commission's 13th Annual Report 1977–78 (Law Com.
92), para. 2.34 (codification of the law of landlord and tenant); *cf.* 15th Annual Report 1979–80
(Law Com. 107), para. 1.4 (codification of general principles of liability in criminal law). See
above, p. 260.

[49] See above, p. 26 n. 43.

[50] *Report of a Committee appointed by the Lord President of the Council on the Preparation of
Legislation* (The Renton Report: Cmnd. 6053, 1975), pp. 17–18 and Chap. XIV; F. A. R. Bennion,
Statute Law (3rd ed., 1990), Chap. 6.

[51] *i.e.* "amendments of which the effect is confined to resolving ambiguities, removing doubts,
bringing obsolete provisions into conformity with modern practice, or removing unnecessary
provisions or anomalies which are not of substantial importance, and amendments designed to
facilitate improvements in the form or manner in which the law is stated. . . .": 1949 Act, s.2.

[52] The Law Commission report will also cover any necessary "corrections and minor improvements." Law Commission consolidations are separate from their general law reform proposals.
The Hansard Society Commission (below, p. 271) has recommended that the pace of consolidation should continue to increase and that if necessary the drafting resources of the Law Commission be strengthened to make this possible: Report, pp. 110–111.

[53] For an example of the former see the *Report of the Committee on Consolidation of Highway
Law* (Cmnd. 630) which led to the Highways Act 1959; (the Highways Act 1980 followed the
Law Commission procedure.) For an example of the latter, see the Local Government Act 1972.

[54] Section 116 of the Companies Act 1981 enabled amendments, desirable to enable a satisfactory
consolidation to be produced, to be made by Order in Council on the recommendation of the
Law Commission and the Scottish Law Commission: see 19th Annual Report of the Law Commission 1983–84 (1984–85 H.C. 214), p. 34. This device was used as part of the massive consolidation of companies legislation in 1985.

[55] See, *e.g.* the Limitation Amendment Act 1980 and the subsequent consolidation measure, the
Limitation Act 1980, and the Mental Health (Amendment) Act 1982 and the Mental Health Act
1983.

[56] The longest consolidation produced by the Law Commission and the longest Bill ever introduced.

between 1973 and 1978 (inclusive) and further ones in 1981, 1986, 1989, 1993 and 1995.[57] Statute Law Revision Acts are no longer promoted except in relation to Northern Ireland legislation. Both kinds of Bills are considered by the Joint Committee, and make an important contribution to the tidying up of the statute book.

The main advantage of the kinds of measures considered in this section, other than Bills for consolidation with substantial amendments, is that the Parliamentary stages, apart from consideration by the Joint Committee, are taken without debate on matters of substance.

5. PROVISIONAL ORDERS AND SPECIAL PROCEDURE ORDERS[58]

In the nineteenth century, the Provisional Order procedure was introduced as a short cut to local legislation. Many statutes provided that a Minister could make a Provisional Order granting certain powers to a local authority or statutory body, following the completion of certain prescribed formalities. Where there were objections there would normally be a local inquiry. One or more such Orders would then be placed before Parliament to be ratified by a Confirmation Act. Petitions against a Confirmation Bill could be submitted and they would be dealt with in the same manner as objections to a private Bill.[59] There are still some examples of Provisional Order powers on the statute book,[60] but the device has largely been superseded by the use of Orders subject to "special parliamentary procedure" under the Statutory Orders (Special Procedure) Act 1945.[61] This procedure also involves an opportunity for objections to be the subject of a local inquiry, and for petitions either against an Order generally or for amendment to be submitted to Parliament.[62] However, an Order against which no petitions are received comes into effect without a Confirmation Act; an Act is only required when a joint committee of both Houses amends the Order in a way unacceptable to the Minister or reports against the Order as a whole.[63]

---

[57] Provisions identified by the Law Commission as redundant may alternatively be repealed by ordinary legislation: see the 20th Annual Report of the Law Commission 1984–85 (1985–86 H.C. 247), pp. 15–16; 25th Annual Report, 1990 (1990–91 H.C. 249), p. 12.

[58] C. K. Allen, *Law and Orders* (3rd ed., 1965), pp. 76–81.

[59] See below, pp. 279–280.

[60] See, *e.g.* Local Government Act 1972, ss.240, 254(8), 262(10).

[61] As amended by the Statutory Orders (Special Procedure) Act 1965, and see S.I. 1949 No. 2393; S.I. 1962 Nos.409 and 2791. The operation of the procedure was considered by the Joint Committee on Private Bill Procedure (Report, (1987–88) H.L. 9, H.C. 625), pp. 10, 50–51.

[62] For an example of a case where a minister wrongfully refused to accept a memorial from a local authority objector requiring an order to be subjected to special Parliamentary procedure, see *R. v. Ministry of Agriculture, Fisheries and Food, ex p. Wear Valley D.C.* (1988) 152 L.G. Rev. 849 (the minister held erroneously that the authority was not "adversely affected" by the order).

[63] This has been done twice: the Mid-Northamptonshire Water Board Order Confirmation (Special Procedure) Act 1949 and the Okehampton Bypass (Confirmation of Orders) Act 1985. The latter was especially controversial as the Joint Committee had reported against the Orders: see the Report of the Joint Committee on Private Bill Procedure, *loc. cit.* n. 61 above; H.C. Deb. Vol. 87, cols. 140–224, November 19, 1985, and H.L. Deb. Vol. 468, cols.1412ff, December 5, 1985.

6. GENERAL SYNOD MEASURES[64]

The General Synod of the Church of England may pass legislative proposals ("Measures") concerning the Church. A Measure is considered by the Ecclesiastical Committee,[65] which comprises 15 members of each House nominated, respectively, by the Lord Chancellor and the Speaker. The Committee reports to Parliament. A Measure approved by each House[66] is then submitted for royal assent, and when this is signified the Measure has the force and effect of an Act of Parliament.

7. PREPARATION AND DRAFTING

The process by which proposals for legislation are converted into a form suitable for enactment is complex.[67] A government Bill originates from the relevant ministry or department, although the ideas may be put forward from many sources including party election manifestos, civil servants, reports of official committees and outside interest groups, whether established to defend some sectional interest or promote some cause. Occasionally, a pre-legislative Select Committee may be appointed by one or both of the Houses to examine a subject with a view to legislation. These are, however, uncommon and not particularly successful.[68] There is normally a considerable measure of consultation. The government may issue a "Green Paper"[69] which sets out tentative proposals, and may suggest alternatives. Legislative proposals are occasionally considered by the relevant departmental select committee[70] but the Select Committee on Procedure

---

[64] Church of England Assembly (Powers) Act 1919; Synodical Government Measure 1969. See *Hasbury's Laws of England* (4th ed.) Vol. 14, paras. 399–411.

[65] Established by the 1919 Act, s.2.

[66] Parliament must either accept or reject a Measure: it has no power to amend: *ibid.* s.4. In 1927 and 1928 Parliament rejected proposed Measures for the revision of the Prayer Book: other rejected Measures have been the Incumbents (Vacation of Benefices) Measures 1975 and the Appointment of Bishops Measure 1984 (see H. C. Deb. Vol. 64, cols.126–144, July 16 1984).

[67] See S. A. Walkland, *The Legislative Process in Great Britain* (1968); M. Zander, *The Law Making Process* (4th ed., 1994), Chap. 1; and *A Matter of Justice* (1988), pp. 236–252; D. Johnstone, [1980] Stat.L.R. 67 and *A Tax Shall Be Charged* (HMSO, 1975) (preparation of VAT legislation); Miers and Page (1990), Chaps.2–4; E. A. Dreidger, *The Composition of Legislation* (2nd ed., 1976); G. C. Thornton, *Legislative Drafting* (3rd ed., 1987); A. Graham, [1988] Stat.L.R. 4. See also B. W. Hogwood, *From Crisis to Complacency?* (1987), Chap. 5 (setting the legislative process within the wider context of the shaping of public policy in Britain).

[68] See P. Norton, *The Commons in Perspective* (1981), p. 85; *First Report of the Select Committee on Procedure*, 1977–78 H.C. 588, Vol. 1, p. xiii; Miers and Page (1990), pp. 43–46. The Hansard Society Commission (below, p. 271) has stated that such committees might occasionally be useful where a fuller inquiry is needed and legislation is not required in a hurry: Report, pp. 80–81.

[69] On white paper with green covers.

[70] *e.g.* Abolition of the "sus" law (power under the Vagrancy Act 1824, ss.4, 6 to arrest a "suspected person or reputed thief" loitering in a public place with intent to commit an arrestable offence) following Reports of the Home Affairs Committee, 1979–80 H.C. 559, 744. See S. H. Bailey, D. J. Harris and B. L. Jones, *Civil liberties: Cases and Materials* (2nd ed., 1985), p. 55. The Hansard Society Commission (below, p. 271) believes that more use should be made of departmentally related select committees to examine White and Green papers and other consultative documents: Report, p. 80.

has concluded that these committees should not be used principally for that purpose.[71]

Once the appropriate committee of the Cabinet[72] has approved proposals in principle, and provisionally allotted a place in the legislative programme, "Instructions" to draft are prepared by the departmental lawyers[73] and sent to the Parliamentary draftsmen: the "Parliamentary Counsel to the Treasury." The Parliamentary Counsel's office was established in 1869; there are at present 25 counsel, with chambers in Whitehall.[74] Parliamentary counsel are either barristers or solicitors. They normally work in pairs, each Bill being allocated to one of the Senior Counsel working with a Junior Counsel. As well as the drafts of a Bill, the counsel prepare government amendments and relevant motions, give advice on Parliamentary procedure, and attend conferences with ministers as well as sittings of both Houses and their committees. They may also assist with the drafting of Private Members' Bills supported by the government or otherwise likely to become law.[75] "The hours are unpredictable and the work arduous, but correspondingly rewarding."[76] A Bill may well go through a whole series of drafts before it is presented to Parliament, clauses being revised in the light of consultation between the draftsmen and the department. Other departments including the Treasury and outside groups may also be consulted at this stage. Firm proposals may be incorporated in a government "White Paper", and this may be debated in Parliament. The actual drafts of legislation are not, however, normally circulated outside the Whitehall machine before they have been presented to Parliament.

F. A. R. Bennion, formerly one of the Parliamentary counsel, has identified a number of "drafting parameters" which the draftsman must bear in mind, and which affect the form of Bills.[77] Some of these considerations relate to the process of enactment; others to the operation of the law once it has been enacted. The "preparational" parameters include compliance with the pre-Parliamentary and Parliamentary requirements as to the form of Bills and the stages through which they must pass (*procedural legitimacy*); strict conformity with the government's timetable for legislation and other time pressures such as those imposed by emergency legislation (*timeliness*); *comprehensibility* to members of Parliament; the need to structure a Bill in such a way that the main points of policy

---

[71] First Report, 1977–78 H.C. 588, p. xiii; Second Report, 1984–85 H.C. 49, p. vi.

[72] Currently the Committee on the Queen's Speeches and Future Legislation (FLG); see also Miers and Page (1990), pp. 30–34. This committee currently comprises the Lord President of the Council (Chairman), Deputy Prime Minister, Lord Chancellor, Minister without Portfolio, Lord Privy Seal, Attorney-General, Lord Advocate, Parliamentary Secretary to the Treasury, Financial Secretary to the Treasury and Captain of the Gentlemen-at-Arms: *Ministerial Committees of the Cabinet*, Cabinet Office, July 18, 1995.

[73] Instructions for legislation concerning the Inland Revenue are drafted by an Assistant Secretary.

[74] Five more work with the Law Commission. Some appointments are part-time. On drafting in the nineteenth century see F. Bowers, "Victorian Reforms in Legislative Drafting" (1980) 48 *Revue D'Histoire Du Droit* 329–348. The working of the office in the 1930s and 1940s is described in Sir Harold Kent, *In on the Act* (1979).

[75] Private Bills are generally drafted by Parliamentary Agents. Scottish Bills are drafted by members of the Lord Advocate's Department: see Lord Mackay of Clashfern, [1983] Stat.L.R. 68. In 1995, four private sector contracts were awarded to draft parts of the 1996 Finance Bill; the successful applicants were two city solicitor firms, a set of tax chambers and a former member of the Parliamentary Counsel's office working as a freelance: Treasury Press Release 109/95.

[76] Civil Service Commission, *Lawyers: Civil Service Careers* (1980), p. 27.

[77] *Statute Law* (3rd ed., 1990), pp. 28–40. See also G. Engle, [1983] Stat.L.R. 7.

can be debated in a rational order (*debatability*)[78]; the choice of language that will minimise objections from those involved in the legislative process (*acceptability*)[79]; and *brevity*. The "operational parameters" include the need for the text of the Bill to carry out the government's intentions (*legal effectiveness*); the desirability that the text be open to one construction only (*certainty*)[80]; *comprehensibility* to the users of the statute, who will normally be practising lawyers (judge, barrister or solicitor), public officials or non-legal professional advisers[81]; and legal compatibility with the rest of the statute book, so that inconsistent provisions are specifically repealed and that the same words mean the same thing even though they appear in different statutes.[82] These parameters frequently conflict. The most important are procedural legitimacy, timeliness and legal effectiveness, and these may well take priority over comprehensibility and legal compatibility. "The task of making legislative proposals understood by non-lawyer politicians while securing their legal effectiveness is one of the most formidable faced by the Parliamentary draftsmen."[83]

The report of the Renton Committee on the Preparation of Legislation[84] recognised that draftsmen had to work under pressures and constraints that made it very difficult to produce simple and clear legislation. Many statutes were well drafted, but there was cause for concern that difficulty was being encountered by statute-users. They had received complaints about the use of obscure and complex language, over-elaboration of detail in the quest for "certainty", the illogical structure of some statutes and problems created by the arrangement of the statute book in a chronological series of separate Acts. There was also criticism of the use of the "non-textual" method of amendment, whereby the amending Act set out the substance of the change proposed to be made without altering the text of the Act being amended. The Renton Committee endorsed the recent change in practice whereby statutes were amended "textually" by adding words to or deleting words from the original provision whenever convenience permitted.[85] The "non-textual" method eases the task of members of Parliament when examining an amending Bill, by enabling them to comprehend its meaning without having to "look beyond the four corners of the Bill."[86] Nevertheless, the Renton Committee thought that the needs of the user should be given priority over those of the legislator, particularly now that there was an official "loose-booklet" publication in which statutes are printed as amended (Statutes in Force). It seems that it is now settled practice to make the maximum possible use of textual amendment.[87]

The Renton Committee made a number of other proposals for reform. For example, all available methods should be used to recruit and train more drafts-

---

[78] The government may, however, wish a Bill to be drawn in such a way as to restrict opportunities for debate or amendment, for example by drawing the long title narrowly.

[79] "The red-blooded terms of political controversy are toned down. The prose style is flat." (Bennion (1990), p. 34).

[80] The government may, however, intend a provision to be ambiguous.

[81] Bennion (1990), pp. 37–38.

[82] "Contrary to most people's belief, however, there are no books of precedents in th Parliamentary Counsel's Office." (*ibid.*, p. 39).

[83] *ibid.*, p. 33.

[84] Cmnd. 6053, 1975.

[85] *ibid.* Chap. XIII: Statute Law Society, *Statute Law: the Key to Clarity* (1972), pp. 7–18 and *Renton and the Need for Reform* (1979), pp. 27–40.

[86] Lord Thring, *Practical Legislation* (2nd ed., 1902), p. 8, cited in Bennion (1990), p. 32.

[87] D. Johnstone, [1980] Stat.L.R. 112.

men as a matter of high priority; the use of statements of principle should be encouraged, with additional guidance given where necessary in Schedules; more use could be made of examples showing how a Bill is intended to work in particular situations; statements of purpose should be used where they are the most convenient method of clarifying the scope and effect of legislation; long un-paragraphed sentences should be avoided; a statute should be arranged to suit the convenience of its ultimate users; the typographical production should be improved, and there should be more consolidation. They rejected suggestions that there should be a "crash" programme of consolidation and that it should be on a "one Act, one subject basis".[88] Under the latter proposal, each subject would have a principal Act and future legislation on the subject would be effected by textual amendment to that Act. In 1978, Sir David Renton, in an address to the Statute Law Society entitled "Failure to implement the Renton Report",[89] noted that there had been a small increase in the number of draftsmen and increased momentum in the consolidation process, but that Parliament had continued to pass enormous quantities of legislation, with no diminution in the amount of detail and scarcely any use of statements of purpose. The government's response to the Report had been guarded.[90] The Lord President of the Council (Michael Foot) stated in 1977 that the government regarded the recommendations concerning drafting practice:

"as a comprehensive and valuable summary of the best drafting practice, and they are being taken into account in the drafting of all current Government legislation. It is considered essential, however, that parliamentary draftsmen should retain discretion to apply the recommendations in accordance with the requirements of particular legislation."[91]

Subsequent governments have not shown any greater enthusiasm for further reforms based on the Renton Report.[92]

Most recently, the whole subject has been the subject of a comprehensive review by a Commission appointed by the Hansard Society for Parliamentary Government.[93] Although not an official body, the Commission consulted very widely and generated a considerable body of information from official and other sources. The Commission concluded that "the legislative process in this country has been unsatisfactory for a long time and Ministers have not, up till now, shown a willingness to change it."[94] There was an "overwhelming impression" from the evidence that "many of those most directly affected are deeply dissatisfied with the extent, nature, timing and conduct of consultation on bills as at present practised."[95] The government should "make every effort to get bills in a form fit for enactment, without major alteration, before they are presented

---

[88] Renton Report, Chap. XIV.
[89] Statute Law Society, *Renton and the Need for Reform* (1979), pp. 2–8.
[90] *ibid.*, pp. 97–98.
[91] H.C. Deb. Vol. 941, col. 329 written answer, December 15, 1977.
[92] Lord Simon of Glaisdale, "The Renton Report—Ten Years On" [1985] Stat.L.R. 133; H.L. Deb. Vol. 489, cols.1417–1449, summarised at [1988] Stat.L.R. 1.
[93] *Making the Law: The Report of the Hansard Society Commission on the Legislative Process*, November 1992 (1993) (Chairman: Lord Rippon). See M. Rush, (1993) 14 Stat.L.R. 75.
[94] *ibid.*, p. 138.
[95] *ibid.*, p. 139.

to Parliament.''[96] Consultation practice should be improved and enshrined in government guidelines, including the more frequent use of independent inquiries, and more consultation on draft texts.[97] As to drafting,[98] the Cabinet's Legislation Committee should assume the wider and longer-term role of ensuring that Bills conform with the best constitutional principles and, where appropriate, have been prepared after full and genuine consultation. Ministerial responsibility for the Parliamentary Counsel, including oversight of the drafting methods and scrutiny of the drafting of government Bills, should be assigned to the Attorney-General. The number of draftsmen required should be reviewed. The drafting style adopted should be appropriate for the main users of the legislation; draftsmen should always seek for clarity, simplicity and brevity but with certainty paramount, and note the continued criticisms made by those most directly affected of the style of drafting of statute law. Ministers, civil servants and draftsmen should do all they can to eliminate unnecessary detail; some means should be found of informing the citizens, lawyers and the courts of the intention underlying the words of a statute; notes on sections should be published. The Committee also make recommendations on the Parliamentary process, access to the statute book, the programming and time-tabling of legislation and the impact of E.C. legislation.[99] The government's response to date[1] has pointed to the recruitment of four additional draftsmen and an increase in the number of clauses of draft Bills published in advance for consultation. A detailed response is still awaited.

There is a recurrent debate on the issue whether there should be a move from the British style of "common-law" drafting to the "continental" or "civil law" method of drafting. The latter is said to be more lucid and succinct, with more emphasis on basic principles and purposes and less on detail. Proponents of such a move include Sir William Dale[2] and J. A. Clarence Smith[3]; opponents include F. A. R. Bennion[4] and Geoffrey Kolts.[5] It is claimed that civilian texts are shorter, better arranged and more easily understood by laymen; common law drafting may by contrast be "a writhing torrent of convoluted indigestion."[6] Others have argued that "civilian" texts produce a considerable degree of uncertainty, which then has to be resolved by the judges; in effect legislative power is delegated to non-elected judges and officials. "Civilian" texts can be as lengthy and complex as British statutes, and can be badly drafted.[7] Of course, the

---

[96] *ibid.*

[97] Chap. 3 and pp. 139–140.

[98] Chap. 4 and pp. 141–142.

[99] See pp. 268, 277–278.

[1] Viscount Cranborne, Leader of the House, contributing to a debate on the Commission's report, Vol. 559 H.L. Deb., December 14, 1994, cols.1291ff., at cols.1321–1326. He stated that he was "aware of the drum beat of dissatisfaction in your Lordship's House and elsewhere over the legislative process" (col. 1321) and did state that the government wished "to make a positive contribution towards improving the quality of our legislation" (col. 1326).

[2] *Legislative Drafting: A New Approach* (1977); (1981) 30 I.C.L.Q. 141; [1988] Stat.L.R. 15.

[3] Proceedings of the Ninth International Symposium on Comparative Law (1972), pp. 155–178; [1980] Stat.L.R. 14.

[4] *Statute Law* (1990), pp. 23–26; [1980] Stat.L.R. 61.

[5] Second Parliamentary Counsel, Canberra, Australia, [1980] Stat.L.R. 144.

[6] J. A. C. Smith, *op. cit.* note 3, at pp. 158–9.

[7] See, *e.g.* the criticisms of a proposed directive of the European Commission on commercial agents expressed by the Law Commission in 1977 (Law Com. No. 84). The text was described as badly drafted, unclear, ambiguous and internally inconsistent. *Cf.* the criticisms of M. Cutts "Clearer Timeshare Act 1993" by the draftsman of the Timeshare Act 1992: E. Sutherland, "Clearer Drafting and the Timeshare Act 1992" (1993) 14 Stat.L.R. 163.

ability of each side to point to examples where the other's preferred method has gone astray proves little; generalisations as to virtues and vices are easy to make but difficult to support. It is, however, unlikely in the present climate of opinion that many English judges would wish to deal with legislative provisions that were significantly more open-textured than at present, and equally unlikely that they would be regarded by many in the community as well suited to undertake that role.[8]

8. PARLIAMENTARY PROCEDURE[9]

(a) Public Bills

The legislative timetable of Parliament is managed by the government. Detailed government Bills are examined and placed in the timetable by the Cabinet's Legislation Committee,[10] and may be considered by the full Cabinet or the appropriate policy committee. A Bill may generally be introduced in either the House of Commons or the House of Lords, although money Bills must be introduced in the Commons, and politically controversial Bills are normally introduced there.

A government Bill introduced in the Commons is presented by a minister. It receives a formal *first reading*, when only the title is actually read out, and is ordered to be printed. A day is fixed for the *second reading*. A Bill as printed is accompanied by an "Explanatory Memorandum" which explains in non-technical language the content and object of the Bill. If expenditure is involved a "Financial Memorandum" is also attached. At the second reading stage the principles of the Bill are debated on the floor of the House.[11] If the Bill entails public expenditure or taxation this must be authorised by a *financial resolution*

---

[8] See above, pp. 249–258.

[9] S. A. de Smith and R. Brazier, *Constitutional and Administrative Law* (7th ed., 1994), pp. 294–302; S. A. Walkland (ed.), *The House of Commons in the Twentieth Century* (1979), Chap. V; P. Norton, *The Commons in Perspective* (1981), Chap. 5; I. Burton and G. Drewry, *Legislation and Public Policy* (1981); D. Englefield, *Whitehall and Westminster* (1985), Chap. 7; P. Silk, *How Parliament Works* (2nd ed., 1989), Chap. 6; the following Reports from the Select Committee on Procedure: Second Report, 1970–71 H.C. 538, *The Process of Legislation;* First Report, 1977–78 H.C. 588; Second Report, 1984–85 H.C. 49, *Public Bill Procedure*; Second Report, 1985–86 H.C. 324, *Allocation of Time to Government Bills in Standing Committee*; Second Report, 1986–87 H.C. 350, *The Use of Time on the Floor of the House*; Second Report, 1988–89 H.C. 330, *Private Members' Time*; Report of the Select Committee on *Sittings of the House* (the Jopling Committee), 1991–92 H.C. 20 G. Drewry, (1972) 35 M.L.R. 289, (1979) 42 M.L.R. 80 and [1995] P.L. 203; T. St. J. Bates, [1987] Stat. L.R. 44; D. R. Miers, [1989] Stat. L.R. 26.

[10] The membership of the Legislation Committee (LG) comprises all the members of the Future Legislation Committee (except the Deputy Prime Minister) together with the Secretaries of State for Scotland and Wales, Ministers of State for the Foreign Office and for the Home Office and the Parliamentary Secretary, Office of Public Service: *Ministerial Committees of the Cabinet*, Cabinet Office, July 18, 1995.

[11] Non-controversial Bills may be referred to a Second Reading Committee of between 16 and 50 M.P.s and Scottish Bills to the Scottish Grand Committee (members for Scottish constituencies plus between 10 and 15 others). Subsequent stages may also be taken by standing committees. In 1994–95 it was agreed that, experimentally, Law Commission Bills were to be referred automatically to Second Reading Committees although the government would agree to any reasonable opposition request for de-referral, and that greater use would be made of such committees on other Bills by agreement: Vol. 251 H.C. Deb., December 15, 1994, col.802, written answer; Vol.251 H.C. Deb., December 19, 1994, cols.1456–1510.

moved by a minister.[12] After receiving a second reading[13] the Bill proceeds to
the *committee stage*,[14] either at a Standing Committee of between 15 and 60
M.P.s that reflects the party composition of the House, or in Committee of the
Whole House. The latter step is taken for Bills that are either straightforward or
urgent, or, at the other extreme, politically contentious or of major constitutional
significance. The committee examines the Bill clause by clause, first considering
amendments and then the motion that the clause, as amended, "stand part of the
Bill". Amendments may be proposed by the minister in charge, backbenchers or
the opposition; those to be taken are selected by the chairman. Proposed new
clauses are then taken, followed by the Schedules, proposed new Schedules, the
preamble (if any) and the long title.[15] A recent innovation has been to send
some Bills to a "Special Standing Committee" with the power to question
witnesses and request the submission of evidence.[16] This procedure has been
used on only a few occasions,[17] but virtually all the evidence received by the
Select Committee on Procedure on its operation was enthusiastic[18] and it was
enshrined permanently in Standing Orders from 1986.[19] Next, the House considers the Bill again at the *report stage*.[20] Any aspect of the Bill can be raised
and new clauses and further amendments can be proposed. Debate is, however,
confined to the contents of the Bill. Normally, the *third reading* immediately
follows the conclusion of the report stage. Only minor verbal amendments can
be made; if material amendments are necessary the Bill has to be considered
again in committee.

The Bill then proceeds to the House of Lords where the stages are repeated,
with some minor procedural differences. Any amendment proposed may be
moved; there is no selection. The committee stage, if not dispensed with, is
normally taken by a Committee of the Whole House, although a Public Bills

[12] In the case of some Bills, such as Finance Bills, Ways and Means resolutions are passed before the
Bill is introduced. Private Members' Bills rarely include provisions involving public expenditure.

[13] Only three government Bills have failed at second reading since 1905, although it is more than
a mere formality and ministers do not always approach debates with closed minds; Norton (1981),
pp. 86–87. The bills were the Rent Restrictions Bill in 1924, the Reduction of Redundancy
Rebates Bill in 1977 (during the period of the minority Labour government) and the Shops
Bill in 1986 (following a rebellion by 72 government backbenchers: see P. Regan (1988) 41(2)
Parliamentary Affairs 218).

[14] From 1994–95 it was agreed that, experimentally, the committee stage for consolidation Bills
may be dispensed with on a government motion, and the question on third reading put forthwith:
Vol. 251 H.C. Deb., December 19, 1994, cols.1456–1509.

[15] See below, pp. 281–282.

[16] First Report from the Select Committee on Procedure, 1977–78 H.C. 588, pp. xviii–xix; H.C.
Deb. Vol. 991, cols.716–834, October 30, 1980.

[17] Proceedings in the 1980–81 session on the Criminal Attempts Bill, the Education Bill and the
Deep Sea Mining (Temporary Provisions) Bill; in the 1981–82 session on the Mental Health
(Amendment) Bill; and in the 1983–84 session on the Matrimonial and Family Proceedings Bill.
See H. J. Beynon, [1982] P.L. 193; A. Samuels, [1989] Stat. L.R. 208.

[18] *e.g.* memorandum from Sir Patrick Mayhew, the Attorney-General (Second Report from the
Select Committee on Procedure, 1984–85 H.C. 49–II, Appendix 2); and see generally the Report,
1984–85 H.C. 49–I, pp. viii–x.

[19] See H.C. Deb. Vol. 92, February 27 1986, cols.1083–1136. See Standing Order 91. The increased
use of these committees was commended by the Select Committee on Procedure: 2nd Report,
1989–90, H.C. 19, *The working of the Select Committee System*, para. 315; Government response:
Cm.1532, p. 23 "The government will continue to consider the possible use of this procedure
in appropriate cases where this is compatible with its overall management of its legislative
programme."

[20] There is no report stage if a public Bill considered in Committee of the Whole House is
unamended.

Committee is sometimes used.[21] An important development has been the introduction by the House of Lords of special standing committees (subsequently
renamed special public bill committees) to hear oral and written evidence on
and then consider clause-by-clause, Bills, based on Law Commission reports,
that are "largely devoid of party-political controversy".[22] The position as to
implementation of Law Commission Bills has been markedly transformed.[23] If
amendments are made, the Bill is returned to the Commons for them to be
agreed. The Commons respond with a message to the Lords which either signifies their agreement, gives reasons for disagreement or proposes other amendments.[24] Further messages may be exchanged until either final agreement is
reached, the Bill lapses at the end of a session[25] or the Commons resorts to the
Parliament Acts procedure.[26]

In recent years, significant features of the work of the House of Lords have
included longer hours, a higher regular attendance, an increase in the proportions
of the House's time devoted to legislative business and an increase in the self
confidence of peers.[27] Claims that they have demonstrated a new independence
and a new professionalism[28] have, however, been challenged.[29] Defeats of the
government on important questions are still comparatively unusual.

A Bill passed in its entirety by both Houses is presented for the *royal assent*.[30]
The monarch is expected by convention to give that assent; the last occasion
on which it was refused was in 1707 when Queen Anne refused her assent to
a Militia Bill. Assent may be signified (1) by the monarch in person (this was last

---

[21] An experiment with a Public Bill Committee on the Pilotage Bill in 1986–87 did not lead to a
significant saving of time: *Report by the Group on the Working of the House*, 1987–88 H.L. 9,
pp. 9–10. The use of such a committee on the Charities Bill in 1991–92 was deemed more
successful and the House of Lords Select Committee on Procedure of the House has recommended
continued experimentation with them (Report on *The Committee Work of the House*, 1991–92
H.C. 35–1, p. 40). The Group on Sittings of the House has also recommended experimentation
with informal committees convened by the minister in charge of a Bill, in which civil servants
and other advisers might participate; and committees of the whole House off the floor: *Report
to the Leader of the House*, 1993–94 H.L. 83, pp. 4–6; First Report of the Select Committee on
Procedure of the House, 1994–95 H.L. 9.

[22] See Report from the Select Committee on *The Committee Work of the House* (1991–92 H.L.35–
I), pp. 19–22, 40–41; Select Committee on the Procedure of the House, First Report 1992–93
H.L.11, para. 6; Third Report 1993–94 H.L.81 ("the procedure has already proved a valuable
addition to the scrutiny function of the House." The procedure is not technically restricted to
Law Commission Bills.

[23] See above, pp. 26–27 and 273, n. 11. The Law of Property (Miscellaneous Provisions) Bill was
considered by a special standing committee (Report 1993–94 H.L.62); the Private International
Law (Miscellaneous Provisions) Bill and the Family Homes and Domestic Violence Bill by special public bill committees (Reports, 1994–95 H.L. 36 and 55 respectively). Evidence was taken,
inter alia, from the chairman of the Law Commission and other present and former Commissioners. See 29th Annual Report of the Law Commission 1994 (1994–95 H.C. 244), pp. 61–
69. The Hansard Society Commission (above, p. 271) supported these moves: Report, pp. 118–
119.

[24] The complexities of this process were considered by the Select Committee on Procedure, 2nd
Report, 1990–91, H.C. 157.

[25] Public Bills that have not been passed lapse at the end of the session: private Bills (see below)
may be carried forward.

[26] See below.

[27] N. Baldwin in P. Norton (ed.), *Parliament in the 1980s* (1985), Chap. 5; A. Adonis, "The House
of Lords in the 1980s" (1988) 41 *Parliamentary Affairs* 380; *Report by the Group on the Working
of the House* (1987–88 H.L. 9).

[28] Baldwin, *op. cit.*

[29] Adonis, *op. cit.*

[30] See F. A. R. Bennion [1981] Stat.L.R. 133.

done in 1854); (2) by Lords Commissioners in the presence of both Houses[31]; or (3) as is normally the case today, by separate notification to each House in accordance with the Royal Assent Act 1967. The third method, unlike the others, does not involve the interruption of proceedings in the Commons. The second method is only used where royal assent coincides with prorogation.

The Parliament Acts 1911–1949 lay down special procedures whereby a Bill may be presented for royal assent when it has been passed only by the Commons.[32] A money Bill may be so presented where the Lords have failed to pass it without amendment after it has been before them for one month; a non-money Bill may be presented where it has been passed by the Commons in two consecutive sessions and the Lords have failed to pass it in each of those sessions; one year has elapsed between the Commons second reading in the first session and third reading in the second session; the Bill has been sent to the Lords at least one month before the end of each session and the Speaker certifies that the requirements of the Parliament Acts have been complied with. The certificate is conclusive for all purposes and may not be questioned in a court of law. These procedures may not be employed in respect of Bills to prolong the maximum duration of a Parliament beyond five years, to Provisional Order Confirmation Bills or private Bills. Objections by the House of Lords are normally dropped without the necessity of recourse to the Parliament Acts; the procedure has only been used three times.[33]

For the draftsman, the first publication of the Bill after first reading is an important deadline as changes thereafter have to be made by formal amendments. Indeed most of the amendments that are made are government amendments, and these tend to reflect second thoughts by the civil servants rather than the persuasive arguments of members. Amendments of substance proposed by backbenchers or opposition and actually agreed are few in number, and are more likely to be accepted in the Lords.[34] More amendments than usual were carried against the government during the passage of the Scotland and Wales Bills in 1977–78. These were controversial constitutional measures, and the Labour government was then in a minority in the Commons.[35] "Parliament's exposure

---

[31] Under the Royal Assent by Commission Act 1541; this was originally part of the Bill of Attainder against Catherine Howard, which did not receive the King's assent in person to spare his hearing once more the "wicked facts of the case." The Bill actually received the assent on February 11, 1542. The Reading Clerk reads out the title of the Bill; the Commissioners raise their hats; and the Clerk of the Parliaments pronounces "La Reyne le Veult" In the case of money Bills the expression is "La Reyne remercie ses bons sujets, accepte leur benevolence, et ainsi le veult"; for personal private Acts, "Soit fait comme il est désiré." If assent were refused the expression would be "La Reyne s'avisera."

[32] S. A. de Smith and R. Brazier, *Constitutional and Administrative Law* (7th ed., 1994), pp. 329–332.

[33] Welsh Church Act 1914 (disestablishment); Government of Ireland Act 1914 (Home Rule: the Act was not implemented); Parliament Act 1949; War Crimes Act 1991 (see G. Ganz, (1992) 55 M.L.R. 87).

[34] See J. A. G. Griffith, *Parliamentary Scrutiny of Government Bills* (1974); P. Norton, (1976) 57 *The Parliamentarian* 17. Where the government accepts or is unsuccessful in resisting an amendment, the version proposed in debate is usually replaced at a later stage by one drafted by a parliamentary draftsman: T. Millett, [1988] Stat.L.R. 70.

[35] I. Burton and G. Drewry, "Public Legislation: A Survey of the Sessions 1977/8 and 1978/9" (1980) 33 *Parliamentary Affairs* 173, 174–186. These sessions provided "significant evidence for the power that still belongs to backbenchers in the House of Commons," although "only in a minority Parliament may the fate of Government Bills be in serious doubt. Even then, most legislation, being inevitable whatever the Government in power, is secure, protected by the close rapport between the two front benches" (p. 199).

of the successive Bills' inherent defects and illogicalities was impressive."[36] However, "the debates were poorly attended and the debating was done by a few stalwarts, with most M.P.s (though a smaller proportion than usual) content to live up to their image as lobby fodder."

The pressure on the Parliamentary timetable is such that where legislation is particularly contentious governments may secure the placing of limits on the time available for debate (timetable or "guillotine" motions); this may mean that, as in the case of the Scotland and Wales Bills, important clauses are not scrutinised by the Commons, although they will normally be considered by the Lords.[37] The House of Commons Select Committee on Procedure reported in 1978 that:

> "the balance of advantage between Parliament and Government in the day to day working of the Constitution is now weighted in favour of the Government to a degree which arouses widespread anxiety and is inimical to the proper working of our parliamentary democracy."[38]

The Select Committee on Procedure has made proposals, as yet unimplemented, for the earlier timetabling of controversial Bills in Standing Committee by a Legislative Business Committee[39] or by a business subcommittee of the relevant Standing Committee.[40] Timetabling proposals have also made by other bodies[41] but the government and opposition front benches have not been persuaded that they are workable.[42] Another major change proposed by the Hansard Society Commission[43] is the reference of most Bills to a select committee (a "first reading committee") immediately after presentation for a preliminary examination of the Bill's purpose, meaning and intended application. At this "preliminary briefing stage", evidence could be taken from interested parties and civil servants and improvements could be recommended. This process would leave the House better informed and might reduce the need for long second reading debates. As regards the subsequent stages, after second reading Bills should normally be committed to a special standing committee (able to take direct evidence); Ministers should hold precommittee informal factual briefings on technical or complex Bills (as was the case with the Fisheries Bill 1992); if there are many detailed points to be further debated at report stage, Bills should be re-committed to the special standing committee; minimum intervals between stages should be increased to avoid legislation being unduly rushed.[44] Finally,

---

[36] *ibid*. p. 186.
[37] See G. Ganz, "Recent developments in the use of guillotine motions" [1990] P.L. 496.
[38] First Report, 1977–78 H.C. 588, Vol. 1, p. viii.
[39] Second Report, 1984–85 H.C. 49, Part III: this proposal was defeated in the House of Commons (Vol. 92 H.C. Deb., February 27, 1986, cols.1083–1136; Minutes of Evidence of the Select Committee on Procedure (1985–86 H.C. 324-i)).
[40] Second Report from the Select Committee on Procedure, 1985–86 H.C. 324.
[41] The Hansard Society Commission (above, p. 271), Report pp. 121–123; Select Committee on Sittings of the House (1991–92 H.C. 22) (The Jopling Committee).
[42] See Vol.251 H.C.Deb., December 19, 1994, cols.1459–1460 (Tony Newton M.P., Leader of the House): "the most sensible approach . . . is to rely on voluntary agreements reached through the usual channels."
[43] Above, p. 271.
[44] Report, pp. 81–89.

the Commission has suggested the adoption of a two-year rather than one-year legislative programme.[45]

The apparent limitations on the effectiveness of Parliamentary scrutiny have led to suggestions for the scrutiny of legislation by other bodies particularly from the technical standpoint. Sir William Dale has proposed[46] the establishment of a "Law Council" to advise the government on draft Bills. "Its duty would be to examine them from the point of view of coherent and orderly presentation, clarity, conciseness, soundness of legal principle, and suitability for attaining the Government's objective," a function performed in France by the Conseil d'Etat. It would not concern itself with matters of policy, and its advice could be rejected by the government. Its membership would include judges, lawyers (practising and academic) and laymen. The Renton Committee, however, rejected proposals for formal machinery for the scrutiny of the drafting of Bills, either before or after their formal introduction in Parliament.[47] Before introduction, it was for government departments to decide what advice they should obtain as to the drafting of their Bills; after introduction, a new scrutiny stage would "impose undue strain on a Parliamentary machine which is already under great pressure, and . . . add to the labour of the draftsmen who have more than enough to do as it is to keep pace with the legislative programme."

The Renton Committee did recommend new Parliamentary procedures (1) for incorporating improvements (including the correction of obvious inaccuracies) certified by the Speaker and the Lord Chancellor to be of a drafting nature, after the passage of a Bill by both houses and before royal assent[48]; and (2) for the re-enactment of statutes, in whole or in part, with drafting improvements.[49] In addition they suggested that the Statute Law Committee[50] should keep the structure and language of statutes under continuous review, monitor the implementation of the Renton Committee's recommendations and publish reports. None of these proposals has been accepted, the third being rejected by the Cabinet apparently on the grounds that the Committee was not an "appropriate body" to discharge these functions and that the proposal to keep the statute book under

[45] *ibid.*, pp. 114–118.
[46] *Legislative Drafting: A New Approach* (1977), pp. 336–337. The case for the introduction of pre-legislative scrutiny to promote compliance with the European Convention on Human Rights is argued by D. Kinley, *The European Convention on Human Rights: Compliance without Incorporation* (1993).
[47] Cmnd. 6053, pp. 129–133.
[48] This was endorsed in principle by the House of Commons Select Committee on Procedure, 1977–78 H.C. 588, Vol. I, p. xxvii. A proposed procedure for the correction of errors *after* royal assent did not find favour with the House of Lords (Acts of Parliament (Correction of Mistakes) Bill [Lords], session 1976–77, withdrawn) and was not supported by the Select Committee (*ibid.*). See A. Samuels, "Errors in Bills and Acts" [1982] Stat.L.R. 94. This is to be distinguished from the correction of printing errors in HMSO copies of statutes: see below, p. 287, n. 11.
[49] This would be modelled on the present procedure for consolidation Bills.
[50] A committee appointed by the Lord Chancellor and first established in 1868. Its membership included M.P.s, draftsmen, judges, Permanent Secretaries, the Treasury Solicitor and the Chairmen of the Law Commissions. It met once a year and supervised the Statutory Publications Office, the form of Acts and the production of *Statutes in Force*. Most of its functions in the field of consolidation and statute law revision passed to the Law Commissions in 1965. In 1991 it was replaced by the Advisory Committee on Statute Law, to advise the Lord Chancellor on all matters relating to the publication of the statute book. Its membership now includes the Permanent Secretary to the L.C.D., the Clerk of the Parliaments, the Clerk of the House of Commons, the Chairmen of the Law Commissions, First Parliamentary Counsel (and his counterparts for Scotland and Northern Ireland) the Treasury Solicitor, the Solicitor to the Scottish Office, and representatives of HMSO and the L.C.D.: Vol. 529 H.L.Deb., June 13, 1991, WA 65–66.

continuous review was not "likely to lead to any worthwhile improvements in the drafting of legislation."[51]

(b) Private Bills[52]

Standing Orders of each House lay down a complicated series of procedural requirements that must be observed before a private Bill is introduced, including the giving of public notice. In practice, a promoter needs the professional assistance of a Parliamentary Agent,[53] who drafts the Blll and acts on behalf of the promoter thereafter. Petitions for private Bills must normally be deposited by November 27 each session.[54] A local authority that wishes to promote a Bill must resolve to do so by a majority of the whole number of council members at a meeting of which 30 days' notice has been given in the local press; a second meeting must confirm the decision after the deposit of the Bill in Parliament.[55] The promoters must prove to the two "examiners", one appointed by each of the Houses, that the formalities have been observed, and this may be challenged by opponents of the Bill.

Private Bills normally proceed first in the House of Lords. The first reading is a formality; the second reading is normally so, but may be opposed. A Bill that passes the second reading is regarded as having received the conditional approval of the House. If the Bill passes the second reading opposed clauses are then referred to a Select Committee of five Lords. The House may agree to an Instruction to the Committee to the effect that the Committee should have regard to or be satisfied of certain matters before passing a particular provision. Procedure here is largely modelled on judicial proceedings: the case for and against the clause is put by counsel for the promoters and for the objectors; witnesses may be called and examined on oath; government departments may make representations and previous decisions of the Committee may be cited. Unopposed clauses are normally considered by the "Committee on Unopposed Bills", an informal meeting conducted by the Lord Chairman of Committees or his Counsel. The promoters, usually represented here by a Parliamentary Agent rather than counsel, must prove a need for the clauses. Unopposed clauses in local Bills promoted as a consequence of the Local Government Act 1972[56] were referred instead to more formal Select Committees. These applied the principles (1) that the promoters had to prove a current need in their area that could only be met by legislation; (2) that the legislation would deal effectively with the problem; and (3) that provisions to meet a need common to all or a great number of authorities should not be included in a private Bill where the

---

[51] *Renton and the Need for Reform*, pp. 7–8; H.L. Deb. col. 776, March 7, 1978. The Select Committee supported the third proposal, and urged the government to reconsider its attitude: 1977–78 H.C. 588, Vol. 1, pp. xxvii-xxviii.

[52] F. Clifford, *History of Private Bill Legislation* (1887); O. C. Williams, *Historical Development of Private Bill Procedure* (1948); The Study of Parliament Group, "Private Bill Procedure; A Case for Reform" [1981] P.L. 206; Joint Committee on Private Bill Procedure, 1987–88 H.L. 97, H.C. 625.

[53] See D. L. Rydz, *The Parliamentary Agents: A History* (1979).

[54] Personal Bills can be deposited at any time, are customarily presented first to the House of Lords and are considered by the Personal Bills Committee of the Lords before first reading. The other stages are similar to those for other private Bills.

[55] Local Government Act 1972, s.239. A Bill may not be promoted to change a local government area, its status or electoral arrangements: *ibid.* s.70.

[56] See above, p. 263.

government had given a firm undertaking to introduce general legislation to meet that need.[57]

After the committee stage, the report stage is usually a formality although the Bill may be amended. The Bill is given a third reading and sent to the other House where the various stages are repeated, with some differences in detail.[58]

These procedures have been described as "cumbersome and expensive"; proceedings of private Bill committees "can be casual and their decisions unpredictable" and opposed Bill committees "tend to be legalistic and time-consuming".[59] Generally, private members take little interest in private legislation; when they do take an interest, however, their influence may be greater than in relation to public legislation as the whips are rarely applied and normally the government simply offers advice.[60]

9. ARRANGEMENT OF ACTS OF PARLIAMENT[61]

The elements of a public general statute are normally arranged in the following order.

(a) Short title

This is the title by which the statute is generally known (*e.g.* the "Interpretation Act 1978"). The practice of including a section providing for the citation of an Act by a short title developed in the nineteenth century; the Short Titles Act 1896[62] conferred short titles on many statutes passed before this practice became established.

(b) Year and chapter number

A statute passed today is cited by reference either to its short title or to the calendar year in which it is passed and its "chapter number" within that year. Statutes are numbered in the order in which royal assent is given. Until 1963[63] statutes were regarded as chapters of the legislation passed in the relevant *session* rather than *calendar year*, and were numbered accordingly. Thus the Interpretation Act 1889 can be cited as "52 & 53 Vict. c. 63" (chapter 63 of the session that fell in the fifty-second and fifty-third years of the reign of Queen Victoria) and its replacement, the Interpretation Act 1978 as "1978 c. 30" (Chapter 30 of 1978).

---

[57] See *e.g.* Special Report from the Select Committee on the County of South Glamorgan Bill, 1974–75 H.L. 347, Vol. 366 H.L. Deb., cols. 864–930, and Second Report of the Select Committee, 1975–76 H.L. 132.

[58] There are, for example, separate committees for opposed and unopposed *Bills* rather than *clauses*.

[59] The Study of Parliament Group [1981] P.L. 206, 221. For reform proposals see *ibid.* pp. 218–227; Report of the Joint Committee on Private Bill Procedure, 1987–88 H.L. 97, H.C. 628, debated at H.C. Deb. Vol. 151, cols.474–648, April 20 1989; Government response, Cm. 1110, 1990.

[60] P. Norton, (1977) 30 *Parliamentary Affairs* 356.

[61] See F. A. R. Bennion, *Statute Law* (3rd ed., 1990), Chap. 3.

[62] Replacing the Short Titles Act 1892. See also the Statute Law Revision Act 1948, Sched. 2.

[63] The practice was changed by the Acts of Parliament Numbering and Citation Act 1962.

(c) Long title

This describes the scope of the Act; if a Bill is amended so as to go beyond the long title as printed in the Bill the long title must be amended as well.

(d) Date

The date, given in square brackets, is that on which royal assent was signified.

(e) Preamble

Public Acts former[64] included a preamble, which could be lengthy, explaining why the Act was passed. They are still necessary for private Acts, and begin with the word "Whereas," For example the Parliament Act 1911 includes the following:

> "Whereas it is expedient that provision should be made for regulating the relations between the two Houses of Parliament:
>
> And whereas it is intended to substitute for the House of Lords as it at present exists a Second Chamber constituted on a popular instead of hereditary basis, but such substitution cannot be immediately brought into operation:
>
> And whereas provision will require hereafter to be made by Parliament in a measure effecting such substitution for limiting and defining the powers of the new Second Chamber, but it is expedient to make such provision as in this Act appears for restricting the existing powers of the House of Lords:"

(f) Enacting formula

This normally runs:

> "Be it enacted by the Queen's most Excellent Majesty, by and with the advice and consent of the Lords Spiritual and Temporal, and Commons, in this present Parliament assembled, and by the authority of the same, as follows:—"

The formula is slightly different for money Bills and Bills passed under the Parliament Acts procedures.

(g) Sections and Schedules

The body of an Act is divided into *sections* (equivalent to the *clauses* of the Bill) and *subsections*, a practice introduced by Lord Brougham's Act of 1850.[65] Each section is printed with *a marginal note* indicating its content. Occasionally,

---

[64] Preambles are occasionally found in modern public Acts, particularly those which implement international conventions (*e.g.* the Oil in Navigable Waters Act 1963), public Acts of a local nature (*e.g.* the Towyn Trewan Common Act 1963) or legislation of a formal or ceremonial character (*e.g.* the John F. Kennedy Memorial Act 1964). Another example is the Canada Act 1982, which provided for the patriation of the Canadian Constitution.

[65] Interpretation of Acts Act 1850, 13 & 14 Vict. c. 21, s.2.

errors may creep in. For example in the Married Women (Maintenance in Case of Desertion) Act 1886, a subsection (section 1(2)), which provided that a wife who had committed adultery could not claim alimony where her husband had deserted her, was printed with the marginal note "custody of children". A long Act may be divided into *Chapters* or *Parts*. Sections dealing with related subject matter may be grouped under *headings*. Matters of detail are commonly included in *Schedules* at the end of the Act. Each schedule is linked to one of the preceding sections and may be divided into *Parts*, *paragraphs* and *sub-paragraphs*. There may also be *marginal notes* and *cross-headings*. A *Schedule* may be used to set out the provisions of an earlier Act as amended.[66]

The body of the Act may include the following kinds of provision: "definitions, principal provisions, administrative provisions, miscellaneous clauses, penal clauses, clauses dealing with the making of rules or byelaws, saving clauses, temporary and transitory clauses, repeals and savings, date of coming into operation (if specified)" and the duration of the Act if it is limited.[67] "Common-form" clauses, those dealing with geographical extent, commencement, short title, citation and interpretation, are normally found at the end of the statute.

(h) Extent[68]

There is a presumption that an Act applies throughout the United Kingdom[69] and not beyond.[70] "Extent clauses" are used to negative that presumption,[71] Acts which apply only to Scotland or Northern Ireland usually include the country in brackets in the short title.[72] Statutes may expressly be made to apply to transactions abroad. For example, the English courts may exercise jurisdiction in respect of murders committed by British subjects abroad[73] and some Acts extend to the territorial waters adjacent to the United Kingdom.[74]

(i) Commencement[75]

Until 1793 each Act of Parliament was deemed to come into operation from the first day of the session in which it was passed, unless a commencement date

---

[66] Known as a "Keeling schedule". Examples include the Cinematograph Films Act 1948, Sched. 2; *cf.* Education Act 1980, Sched. 5.

[67] Statute Law Society, *Statute Law Deficiencies* (1972), p. 6. (based on Sir Alison Russell's analysis of the general frame of a Bill.).

[68] See F. A. R. Bennion, *Statutory Interpretation* (2nd ed., 1992), Part V.

[69] *i.e.* England, Scotland, Wales and Northern Ireland but not the Channel Islands or the Isle of Man.

[70] See *R. v. Jameson* [1896] 2 Q.B. 425, 430; *Draper & Son Ltd v. Edward Turner & Son Ltd* [1965] 1 Q.B. 424; *Air-India v. Wiggins* [1980] 1 W.L.R. 815.

[71] Extent clauses normally indicate expressly that an Act applies to Northern Ireland even though this is not strictly necessary.

[72] The Renton Committee recommended that where an Act affects only England and Wales this too should be indicated in the short title: Cmnd. 6053, p. 124. This has not been implemented.

[73] Offences against the Person Act 1861, s.9

[74] *e.g.* Wireless Telegraphy Act 1949, ss.1, 6; Marine, etc., Broadcasting (Offences) Act 1967, s.1; *Post Office v. Estuary Radio Ltd* [1968] 2 Q.B. 740. See generally the Law Commission's *Report on the Territorial and Extraterritorial Extent of the Criminal Law* (Law Com. No. 91, 1978) and *Jurisdiction over Offences of Fraud and Dishonesty with a Foreign Element* (Law Com. No. 180, 1989).

[75] See Bennion (1992), pp. 179–188.

was specified. The element of retrospectivity was seen to be unjust and the rule was changed.[76]; an Act now comes into effect at the beginning of the day on which royal assent is given, unless some other commencement date is specified.[77] Today, it is commonly provided that the Act shall come into effect on a specified date, or on a day to be appointed, and, in the latter event, that different days may be appointed for different provisions, different purposes or different areas. The advantages of delayed commencement are that it gives those affected time to prepare, and gives ministers and departments time to draw up the necessary regulations and orders after due consultation with interested parties. The main disadvantage is that it may be difficult for users to establish whether a particular provision is in force.[78] There may be many commencement orders in respect of one statute,[79] and some provisions may never be implemented, for reasons such as a lack of resources[80] and governmental second thoughts about the desirability of particular provisions.[81] Complaints have been voiced about the present position and various improvements proposed.[82] Governments have been exhorted to refrain from promoting legislation unless its implementation within a reasonable time can be foreseen.

In 1982 the Management and Personnel Office (the successor to the Civil Service Department) issued new guidance on the commencement of legislation.[83] Acts which do not provide for a commencement date to be appointed by order should provide for commencement not less than two months after royal assent (three months for consolidation Acts). Commencement provisions should be grouped at the end of any Bill in which that is practicable, if appropriate in a separate clause or Schedule; alternatively, a full list of commencement provisions should be published with the Act or in a press notice. Commencement dates should be specified in the Act where possible and appropriate; otherwise, every effort should be made to minimise the number of commencement orders and to rationalise their issue and the dates of commencement.

In interpreting statutes there is a presumption that statutes do not operate retrospectively so as to affect an existing right or obligation, except as regards matters of procedure.[84] Parliament may, however, use words in a statute which clearly show an intention that it should so operate.[85]

It was commonly assumed that statutory provisions that were not brought into

---

[76] Acts of Parliament (Commencement) Act 1793.

[77] Interpretation Act 1978, s.4.

[78] A most useful publication with this information is *Is it in force?*, an annual cumulative publication published in conjunction with the 4th edition of *Halsbury's Statutes of England*.

[79] See, *e.g.* the Consumer Credit Act 1974 and the Control of Pollution Act 1974.

[80] Examples include various provisions concerning legal advice and law centres (see below, p. 484).

[81] Examples include the Easter Act 1928, provisions of the Children and Young Persons Act 1969, the Health and Safety at Work etc. Act 1974, s.71 (see J. R. Spencer, (1981) 131 N.L.J. 644) and the Criminal Justice Act 1988 (ss.108–117: a statutory scheme for criminal injuries compensation; see p. 284).

[82] A. Samuels, (1979) *The Magistrate* pp. 173–4; Statute Law Society Working Party on the Commencement of Acts of Parliament, [1980] Stat.L.R. 40.

[83] (1982) 79 L.S.Gaz. 968.

[84] *Re Athlumney* [1898] 2 Q.B. 547, 551–2 *per* R. S. Wright J.; *Att.-Gen. v. Vernazza* [1960] A.C. 965. See below, pp. 399–401.

[85] *e.g.* the War Damage Act 1965, which reversed the decision of the House of Lords in *Burmah Oil Co. v. Lord Advocate* [1965] A.C. 75; the Northern Ireland Act 1972, which retrospectively removed limitations on the power of the Parliament of Northern Ireland to legislate for the armed forces: see S. H. Bailey, D. J. Harris and B. L. Jones, *Civil Liberties: Cases and Materials* (4th ed. 1995), pp. 291–292.

force had no legal status or effect. However, this assumption was challenged in *R. v. Secretary of State for the Home Department, ex p. Fire Brigades Union.*[86] Here, the Criminal Justice Act 1988[87] provided for a statutory criminal injuries compensation scheme to replace the scheme introduced by virtue of the royal prerogative. These provisions were, however, not brought into force. In 1993 the government announced that they would not be implemented and would be repealed in due course;[88] furthermore, the existing scheme would be replaced by a (less expensive) flat rate tariff scheme under the royal prerogative. On an application for judicial review, the House of Lords held (1) (unanimously) that the Home Secretary was under no legally enforceable duty to bring the 1988 Act provisions into force at any particular time;[89] but (2) (by three to two)[90] that while these provisions remained unrepealed it was under a duty to keep the question of implementation under review and it was an abuse or excess of power for him to exercise the prerogative power in a manner inconsistent with that duty. Of these two points, the first has the greater long-term significance, given that reliance on the royal prerogative for such programmes is highly exceptional.

(j) Definitions

Modern statutes commonly include "definition sections" in which the meaning of words and phrases found in the statute are explained, either comprehensively (X "means" ABC) or partially (X "includes" ABC). The qualification "unless the contrary intention appears" is usually added. The Interpretation Act 1978 gives definitions of a large number of words and expressions. These are applicable where the words are found "in any Act, unless the contrary intention appears."[91] For example, "Secretary of State" means "one of Her Majesty's Principal Secretaries of State".[92] The 1978 Act also provides generally that:

"In any Act, unless the contrary intention appears—
(a) words importing the masculine gender include the feminine;
(b) words importing the feminine gender include the masculine;
(c) words in the singular include the plural and words in the plural include the singular."[93]

---

[86] [1995] 2 W.L.R. 464.

[87] ss.108–117 and Scheds.6 and 7.

[88] Lord Browne-Wilkinson was rightly critical of this statement, noting that "It is for Parliament, not the executive, to repeal legislation" (p. 474).

[89] This was "a decision of a political and administrative character quite unsuitable to be the subject of review by a court of law" (*per* Lord Keith at p. 466).

[90] Lords Browne-Wilkinson, Lloyd and Nicholls, Lords Keith and Mustill dissenting.

[91] Interpretation Act 1978, s.5 and Sched. 1. They may also apply to subordinate legislation: see *ibid.* s.23.

[92] Many statutory functions are entrusted to "the Secretary of State". This device enables these functions to be switched between departments without the need for the statute to be amended. Where amendment is necessary, as where a function is given to a particular minister, it is usually effected by a statutory instrument under the Ministers of the Crown (Transfer of Functions) Act 1946. The "Secretary of State" device makes it more difficult to discover where responsibility for a particular function commonly lies.

[93] Section 6. See, *e.g. Annicola Investments v. Minister of Housing and Local Government* [1968] 1 Q.B. 631, where the word "houses" was held to include a single house. Examples of cases where the "contrary intention" has appeared are those where the terms "every man" or "any person" have been held not to include women: *e.g. Chorlton v. Lings* (1868) L.R. 4 C.P. 374; *Bebb v. The Law Society* [1914] 1 Ch. 286.

There are also general provisions covering such matters as references to service by post, distance, time of day and the Sovereign, and the construction of subordinate legislation.[94]

(k) Amendments and repeals

Statutes commonly amend or repeal earlier enactments. Repeals are normally set out in a Schedule, although important changes may be included in the body of the Act. A power may be conferred to repeal or modify Acts of Parliament by statutory instrument. An earlier statute may also be amended or repealed by implication where the provisions of a later Act are so inconsistent that the two cannot stand together, although the courts seek to reconcile apparently inconsistent provisions where possible. At common law a repealed Act was treated as if it had never existed, except in relation to transactions past and closed, but this rule was changed in 1889.[95] For example, where an offence is committed against an existing statutory provision, criminal proceedings may now be instituted even after that provision is repealed, unless the repealing enactment provides otherwise.[96] There was also a common law rule that where statute A was repealed by statute B and statute B was subsequently repealed by statute C, statute A was regarded as reviving unless the contrary intention appeared. This rule was abolished in 1850: repealed statutes stay repealed unless expressly revived.[97] Unlike the Scots, the English have never had a rule that a statute can be disregarded on the ground that it is obsolete[98]; such provisions have to be repealed by a subsequent statute.[99]

10. ENROLLMENT AND PUBLICATION[1]

In medieval times a systematic official record of parliamentary statutes was not kept. An incomplete statute roll was started in the Chancery for internal purposes in 1299 and continued to the middle of the fifteenth century. *Rotuli Parliamentorum* ("Rolls of Parliament") were kept between 1290 and 1503; they contained a general record of parliamentary proceedings, but only included some of the Acts. From 1483 "Inrollments of Acts" (records of each Act

---

[94] 1978 Act, ss.7–11.
[95] Interpretation Act 1889, s.38(2); see now the Interpretation Act 1978, s.16.
[96] See *Bennett v. Tatton* (1918) 88 L.J.K.B. 313; *Postlethwaite v. Katz* (1943) 59 T.L.R. 248; *R. v. West London Stipendiary Magistrate, ex p. Simeon* [1983] 1 A.C. 234 (repeal of the "sus" law held not to affect a prosecution for an offence committed before the repeal came into effect). *Cf. Aitken v. South Hams District Council* [1995] 1 A.C. 262 (notice to abate a noise nuisance under s.58 of the Control of Pollution Act 1974 continues to be effective notwithstanding repeal of s.58 by the Environment Protection Act 1990, by virtue of s.16 of the 1978 Act).
[97] See now the Interpretation Act 1978, s.15. Similarly, the repeal of an Act does not revive anything not in force or existing at the time of the repeal: *ibid.* s.16(1)(a). Hence, if statute B modifies statute A by partial repeal or substitution of words, statute A continues in effect subject to the modification notwithstanding the repeal of statute B.
[98] Under the doctrine of desuetude, Acts of the Scottish Parliament may become obsolete and repealed by a long period of contrary practice by the community: *M'Ara v. Magistrates of Edinburgh* 1931 S.C. 1059; *Brown v. Magistrates of Edinburgh* 1913 S.L.T. 456, 458; *Earl of Antrim's Petition* [1967] A.C. 691.
[99] See above, p. 261.
[1] F. A. R. Bennion, *Statutory Interpretation* (2nd ed., 1994), pp. 136–141.

"engrossed" on parchment) were certified by the Clerk of the Parliaments and delivered to the Chancery; the officers of the Chancery commonly termed them the "Parliament Rolls" although they are distinct from the *Rotuli Parliamentorum*. From the middle of the nineteenth century two copies of each Act have been printed on vellum; one copy is kept in the House of Lords, the other in the Public Records Office.[2]

Lawyers at first relied on private manuscript collections of statutes. These formed the basis of unofficial printed collections that began to appear from 1481 onwards. From 1483 *Sessional Volumes of Statutes* were printed and published; these came to be issued by the King's or Queen's Printer but were not technically an official series published by royal or parliamentary authority. Useful collections of *Statutes at Large* appeared in the late eighteenth century, with various editors (*e.g.* Pickering (1762), Ruffhead and Runnington (1786) and Tomlins and Raithby (1811)). These covered statutes from Magna Carta to date; continuation volumes, sometimes covering several sessions, and based on the King's Printer's copies, were produced in the eighteenth and nineteenth centuries under the titles of *Statutes of the United Kingdom* or *Public General Statutes*. The Controller of Her Majesty's Stationery Office was appointed as the Queen's Printer in 1886. From 1940 the King's or Queen's Printer's copies of statutes have been published on an annual rather than a sessional basis, with *Public General Acts and Measures*[3] issued separately from *Local and Personal Acts*; each Act is also published individually by HMSO.

The first official collection of statutes was the edition of *Statutes of the Realm* prepared by the Record Commissioners and published in nine volumes between 1810 and 1828. This gave texts and translations of statutes between 1235 and 1713, excluding the Commonwealth period,[4] and while a considerable improvement on what was otherwise available, was in various respects incomplete and inaccurate.[5] Later in the century, the Statute Law Committee[6] supervised the publication of the first edition of *Statutes Revised*, which comprised the public Acts in force at the end of 1878, as amended, given in chronological order. Two further editions were produced between 1888 and 1929 and in 1950. This series has been superseded by *Statutes in Force*, which is published in loose booklet form rather than in bound volumes to facilitate the substitution of revised copies of statutes that are heavily amended; there are also regular supplements. The volumes are arranged in 124 groups (131 were originally planned) according to subject-matter.[7] These official collections are supplemented by the *Index to the Statutes* and the *Chronological Table of the Statutes*.[8] As a matter

---

[2] See S. A. de Smith and R. Brazier, *Constitutional and Administrative Law* (7th ed., 1994), p. 92. A third print is made of Measures of the General Synod.

[3] These also appear in the *Law Reports Statutes* series.

[4] As to which see C. H. Firth and R. S. Rait, *Acts and Ordinances of the Interregnum* (1911).

[5] See T. F. T. Plucknett, *Statutes and their Interpretation in the Fourteenth Century* (1922), Chap. II.

[6] See above, p. 278.

[7] The published materials are, however, significantly out of date (P. Clinch, [1994] Stat. L. R. 64) and work on revised material (as distinct from newly enacted Acts) and other tables and indexes has been suspended in order to concentrate on the development of a new statute law database: Lord Mackay L.C., vol. 546 H.L. Deb., June 9, 1993, WA 55.

[8] This covers public and general legislation; editions since 1974 have also recorded the effect of local and personal legislation enacted since then. A limited edition of a *Chronological Table of Local Legislation*, covering the effect on all local legislation passed between 1539 and 1973 of general legislation passed between 1925 and 1973, was distributed in 1985 to those particularly concerned with local statute law, and to selected libraries and record offices (20th Annual Report

of citation, references to another Act in a statute passed after 1889 are, unless the contrary intention appears, to be read as referring to (a) any revised edition of the statutes printed by authority, (b) if it is not printed there, to the *Statutes of the Realm*; or (c) in other cases, to the Queen's Printer's copy.[9] Occasionally it may be necessary to go behind the published version and check its authenticity against the original source.[10] Where through a printing error a statute as printed by HMSO does not reflect the version of the vellum print, the Clerk of the Parliament authorises the issue of a correction slip. This is sometimes done where the vellum print does not reflect the version assented to by Parliament.[11]

There are various departmental compilations of statutes and regulations published by HMSO and regularly revised, such as *The Taxes Acts* (for the Inland Revenue) and several works on the law of social security (for the Department of Social Security). The most important current commercial collections are *Halsbury's Statutes of England* (4th ed.: a revised edition arranged by subject matter) and *Current Law Statutes Annotated* (arranged in chronological order). There are also many collections on particular topics published in loose-leaf encyclopedias. An important advantage of these commercial publications is that the statutes are given in annotated form. Statutes and statutory instruments are included in the *Lexis* database, and work is in hand for the development of an official statute law database, which is due for general release by the end of 1997.

11. VALIDITY

The validity of an Act of Parliament may not be questioned in an English court; there is no Bill of Rights or other constitutional limitation to which legislation must conform as there is, for example, in the United States of America.[12] This point has arisen in cases where it has been claimed that a private Act is invalid on the ground that parliamentary standing orders have not been observed[13] or that Parliament has been misled by fraudulent misrepresentations[14]: such claims have failed. In 1982, a taxpayer argued that the change in the status of M.P.s from self-employed meant that they had become employees of the Crown and so disqualified from membership. As a result, the Social Security Act 1975, which imposed on him certain obligations to pay national insurance

---

of the Law Commission 1984–85 (1985–86 H.C. 247), p. 38). It is to be amalgamated with further work concerning earlier periods (local Acts from 1797 and private Acts from 1539) and with the information concerning local legislation contained in the *Chronological Table of the Statutes* since 1974 (22nd Annual Report of the Law Commission 1986–87 (1987–88 H.C. 319), p. 14). See A. M. Rowland (1991) 22 *Law Librarian* 163 and (1992) 23 *Law Librarian* 35.

[9] Interpretation Act 1978, s.19.

[10] See, *e.g. R. v. Casement* [1917] 1 K.B. 98, 134, in relation to the Treason Act 1351, where the *Rotuli Parliamentorum* and the Statute Rolls were consulted.

[11] F. A. R. Bennion, *Statutory Interpretation* (2nd ed., 1994), pp. 136–138; J. J. Rankin, [1987] Stat.L.R. 53.

[12] See above, pp. 261–262. The question of possible conflict with European legislation is considered below, pp. 331–344. As to whether a court may exercise a jurisdiction to determine whether an *ostensibly* authentic Act of Parliament is *in fact* authentic see S. A. de Smith and R. Brazier, *Constitutional and Administrative Law* (7th ed. 1994), pp. 93–95.

[13] *Edinburgh and Dalkeith Rly. v. Wauchope* (1842) 7 Cl. & F. 710.

[14] *Lee v. Bude and Torrington Junction Railway* (1871) L.R. 6 C.P. 576; *Pickin v. British Railways Board* [1974] A.C. 765.

contributions, was invalid. His argument was emphatically and summarily rejected by Nourse J.: "the court can only look at the Parliamentary roll."[15] Of much more importance was the claim of a group of Canadian Indian Chiefs that the Canada Act 1982 was *ultra vires* on the ground that the consent of the "Dominion" of Canada had not been obtained as required by section 4 of the Statute of Westminster 1931, merely the consent of the Senate and House of Commons of Canada. Sir Robert Megarry V.-C. held[16] that he owed "full and dutiful obedience" to every Act of Parliament, and that the Canada Act 1982 was such an Act. The Court of Appeal held[17] that even on the assumption that Parliament could bind its successors by a provision such as section 4, the application failed as there had been compliance with that section. Attempts to impugn statutes on the ground that they are contrary to international law have also failed.[18]

There were in the seventeenth century dicta that Acts of Parliament "against common right and reason, or repugnant, or impossible to be performed,"[19] or contrary to natural justice by making a man judge in his own cause[20] could be held by the judges to be void. However, these dicta were controversial even at that time, were not acted upon, and are not accepted today: "since the supremacy of Parliament was finally demonstrated by the Revolution of 1688 any such idea has become obsolete."[21] This position was reaffirmed by Lord Scarman in *Duport Steels Ltd v. Sirs*[22]:

> ". . . [I]n the field of statute law the judge must be obedient to the will of Parliament as expressed in its enactments. In this field Parliament makes and unmakes the law: the judge's duty is to interpret and to apply the law, not to change it to meet the judge's idea of what justice requires. Interpretation does, of course, imply in the interpreter a power of choice where differing constructions are possible. But our law requires the judge to choose the construction which in his best judgment meets the legislative purposes of the enactment. If the result be unjust but inevitable, the judge may say so and invite Parliament to reconsider its provision. But he must not deny the statute.... Only if a just result can be achieved without violating the legislative purpose of the statute may the judge select the construction which best suits his idea of what justice requires."

---

[15] *Martin v. O'Sullivan* [1982] S.T.C. 416, 419, affirmed [1984] S.T.C. 258.
[16] [1983] Ch. 77.
[17] *ibid.*
[18] *Mortensen v. Peters* 1906 S.L.T. 227; *Cheney v. Conn* [1968] 1 W.L.R. 242.
[19] *Dr Bonham's Case* (1610) 8 Co. Rep. 114, 118, *per* Coke C.J.; Coke subsequently expressed a different view extrajudicially: 4 *Coke's Institutes* 37, 41.
[20] *Day v. Savadge* (1614) Hob. 85, 87 *per* Hobart C.J.; *cf.* Holt C.J. in *City of London v. Wood* (1701) 12 Mod. 669, 686–8.
[21] *Pickin v. British Railways Board* [1974] A.C. 765, 782 *per* Lord Reid. Cf., however, the extra-judicial statements by a number of judges that particular statutory provisions might not be immune from judicial scrutiny: see above, p. 255.
[22] [1980] I.C.R. 161, 189–190.

C. SUBORDINATE LEGISLATION[23]

1. DELEGATION

Each year the output of subordinate[24] legislation vastly exceeds that of Acts of Parliament. Law-making powers have been delegated by Parliament to a wide variety of public authorities, including the Crown, ministers, local authorities and public corporations. Procedural rules may be made for the courts by Rule Committees consisting of judges and lawyers.[25] In addition, the Crown retains certain powers to legislate by virtue of the royal prerogative. There have been examples of the delegation of rule-making powers by Parliament for as long as Parliament has been acknowledged as the supreme law-making body. However, the nineteenth and twentieth centuries have seen an enormous increase, albeit "wayward and unsystematic",[26] in the extent of delegation, matching the extension of the powers and functions of government. Each of the World Wars saw the creation of a complex system of statutory powers, mostly contained in delegated legislation made, respectively, under the Defence of the Realm Acts 1914–15 and the Emergency Powers (Defence) Acts 1939–40; every aspect of national life was closely regulated.

The developments were at first welcomed on the ground that Parliament was thereby able to deal with the issues of importance while the details could be settled departmentally. Certain judges and academic commentators were less enthusiastic. The most extreme of the criticism was expressed by the then Lord Chief Justice, Lord Hewart, in a book entitled "The New Despotism" (1929). The main objections articulated were that wide powers were given to the executive, and that the safeguards against abuse, particularly Parliamentary safeguards, were inadequate. Some people held the view that the delegation of legislative power was unwise and might be dispensed with altogether. However, it was difficult to disentangle general objections to the extension of state power from objections to the particular form that the extension took. Delegated legislation was one of the issues considered by the Committee on Ministers' Powers, which reported in 1932.[27] The Committee expressed the view that "whether good or bad" the practice of delegation was inevitable[28]:

"the system of delegated legislation is both legitimate and constitutionally

---

[23] See C. K. Allen, *Law and Orders* (3rd ed., 1965); Sir William Wade and C. F. Forsyth, *Administrative Law* (7th ed., 1994), Chap. 22; S. A. de Smith and R. Brazier, *Constitutional and Administrative Law* (7th ed., 1994), Chap. 18; K. Puttick, *Challenging Delegated Legislation* (1988); Cabinet Office (Management and Personnel Office), *Statutory Instrument Practice* (2nd ed., 1987); R. Baldwin, *Rules and Government* (1995), Chap. 4.

[24] Strictly, the term "subordinate" legislation covers "all legislation, permitted as well as authorised, that is inferior to statute law"; "delegated" legislation is that "authorised by Act of Parliament": HMSO, *Access to Subordinate Legislation* (House of Commons Library Document No. 5).

[25] Rules of the Supreme Court; County Court Rules; Crown Court Rules.

[26] Allen (1965), p. 32.

[27] Cmd. 4060. The first chairman was the Earl of Donoughmore; he was succeeded as chairman by Sir Leslie Scott.

[28] *ibid.*, p. 5.

desirable for certain purposes, within certain limits, and under certain safeguards."[29]

It pointed to the pressure on parliamentary time, the technicality of the subject matter of modern legislation, the difficulty of working out administrative machinery in time to insert all the required provisions in the Bill, the flexibility of a system which allowed for adaptation to unknown future conditions without the necessity of an amending Act, and for the opportunity for experiment, and the need on occasion for emergency action. The Committee made a number of suggestions for improving the terminology, publication and scrutiny of delegated legislation. One of the members of the Committee, Ellen Wilkinson M.P., thought that certain passages gave:

"the impression that the delegating of legislation is a necessary evil, inevitable in the present state of pressure on parliamentary time, but nevertheless a tendency to be watched with misgiving and carefully safeguarded."[30]

Nevertheless, since then the constitutional propriety of delegation has not seriously been questioned, although concern has been expressed at the growing tendency in recent years for statutory instruments to deal "no longer . . . with means but with principles."[31]

2. THE FORMS OF SUBORDINATE LEGISLATION

The nomenclature of nineteenth century subordinate legislation was varied and confusing. Different procedures were followed for making and issuing the different kinds of rules. Some kind of regularity was created by the Rules Publication Act 1893, and the position was further improved by its replacement, the Statutory Instruments Act 1946. Today, most subordinate legislation takes the form of *statutory instruments* made under the procedure laid down by the 1946 Act or *byelaws* made under the Local Government Act 1972,[32] although other forms are possible. Different names are still used for different kinds of statutory instruments; these names merely indicate the general nature of the instrument and no longer reflect any difference as to the procedure whereby they are made and promulgated. The selection of a particular title is a matter of departmental practice.

The following are the main kinds of subordinate legislation. *Orders in Council*

---

[29] *ibid.*, p. 51.

[30] *ibid.* p. 137. She felt that in the conditions of the modern state the practice "instead of being grudgingly conceded ought to be widely extended, and new ways devised to facilitate the process."

[31] Andrew Bennett, M.P., Chairman of the Joint Committee on Statutory Instruments, in evidence to the Select Committee on Procedure: Second Report, 1986–87 H.C. 350, *The Use of Time on the Floor of the House*, pp. vii, 6. The Committee noted this view "with concern." Examples of recent legislation where the statute merely creates a framework for regulations include the Legal Aid Act 1988 and the Local Government Finance Act 1988 (on the latter, see the notes by M. Grant in *Current Law Statutes Annotated 1988*, pp. 41–12—41–13). See also K. Puttick, *Challenging Delegated Legislation* (1988), Chap. 3.

[32] See below, pp. 292–297.

are made by the Queen with the advice of the Privy Council (the "Queen in Council"). They may be made under the royal prerogative[33]; more commonly they are made under a statutory power, in which case they are normally statutory instruments. *Proclamations* are notices given by the Queen to her subjects; again, they may be made under the royal prerogative[34] or statute[35] and are published in the *London Gazette*. *Royal Warrants* are made under the royal prerogative and normally concern the pay and pensions of members of the armed forces. *Regulations, Rules, Orders, Schemes* and *Warrants* are usually statutory instruments. The usage of these terms is imprecise although "Rules" are usually[36] the procedural rules of a court or tribunal, and the term "Warrant" is used to describe some Treasury instruments which confer an authority or an entitlement to money. *Directions* may occasionally have to be promulgated as statutory instruments.

3. PREPARATION OF SUBORDINATE LEGISLATION

Subordinate legislation is generally drafted by lawyers in the government department concerned, in the Treasury Solicitor's office where the department has no legal branch, or, in cases of exceptional importance or difficulty, by one of the Parliamentary draftsmen. The "division of labour" between the Parliamentary counsel responsible for statutory drafting and departmental lawyers has been described as "a basic weakness of the system",[37] although any significant change would obviously require a large increase in the number of counsel. The "preparational parameters" mentioned above[38] in relation to statutes are not applicable to nearly the same extent, although the draftsman has to take care to ensure that the instrument is *intra vires*[39]; the "operational parameters" are, however, equally important.[40] Prior consultation between the department and advisory bodies and interest groups is a well established practice[41]; consultation requirements may be imposed in the parent Act.[42] Local authority byelaws are prepared by the authority concerned but must normally conform to the models issued by government departments to stand much chance of being confirmed. Important statutory instruments may be examined by the Cabinet's Legislation Committee.

---

[33] *e.g.* an Order altering the constitution of a colony. An Order in Council under the prerogative may not alter the common law or statute law: *The Zamora* [1916] 2 A.C. 77, 90.

[34] *e.g.* coinage proclamations.

[35] *e.g.* proclamations of a state of emergency under the Emergency Powers Act 1920.

[36] Not invariably: see the Immigration Rules.

[37] F. A. R. Bennion, *Statute Law* (3rd ed., 1990), p. 57.

[38] At pp. 269–270.

[39] See below, pp. 298–302.

[40] Bennion (1990), pp. 57–58.

[41] See J. F. Garner, [1964] P.L. 105; A. D. Jergesen, [1978] P.L. 290.

[42] A statutory duty to consult is regarded as mandatory (see below p. 249). However, a court will not imply an obligation to consult if there is no express provision: *Bates v. Lord Hailsham* [1972] 1 W.L.R. 1373.

4. Procedures for Making Subordinate Legislation

(a) Statutory instruments

The "statutory instrument" procedure applies to delegated legislation (1) made, confirmed or approved under a power conferred on the Crown after 1947 by statute[43] and expressed to be exercisable "by Order in Council"[44]; (2) made, confirmed or approved under a power conferred on a minister after 1947 by statute[45] and expressed to be exercisable "by statutory instrument"[46]; (3) made under a power contained in a statute passed before 1948 to make "statutory rules"[47] within the meaning of the Rules Publication Act 1893,[48] or (4) confirmed or approved under certain powers contained in pre-1948 statutes.[49]

The procedural requirements for statutory instruments are prescribed partly by the parent Acts and partly by the 1946 Act. The parent Act may require that the instrument[50] be laid[51] before Parliament.[52] If it does it has to be laid "before it comes into operation," unless it is essential that it comes into operation sooner, in which case the Lord Chancellor and the Speaker must be informed of the reason.[53] This process merely brings the instrument to the attention of Parliament. An instrument may have to be laid in draft[54] or after it has been made. In addition, the instrument may be made subject to the "affirmative resolution" or the "negative resolution" procedure. Under the former, the instrument can only come into effect if a resolution approving it is passed, within the period (if any) specified in the parent Act. Under the latter, which is a much more

---

[43] Sub-delegated legislation made under a power conferred by statutory instrument is thus not normally within the scope of the 1946 Act.

[44] Statutory Instruments Act 1946, s.1(1).

[45] See n. 43 above.

[46] Statutory Instruments Act 1946, s.1(1).

[47] Provided, in most cases, that the rule is of a "legislative" and not an "executive" character: Statutory Instruments Regulations 1947 (S.I. 1948 No. 1), reg. 2(1).

[48] Statutory Instruments Act 1946, s.1(2). There are certain exceptions: see S.I. 1948 No. 1, reg. 2(3) and Schedule.

[49] Statutory Instruments Act 1946, s.9(1); S.I. 1948 No. 1, reg. 2(2); Statutory Instruments (Confirmatory Powers) Order 1947 (S.I. 1948 No. 2). The rule has to be legislative rather than executive in character and subject to the requirement that it be laid before Parliament.

[50] *i.e.* "any document by which" a power to make orders etc. is "exercised": Statutory Instruments Act 1946, s.1(1). A document referred to in regulations need not be laid provided that it is not part and parcel of the regulations: *R. v. Secretary of State for Social Services, ex p. Camden London Borough Council* [1987] 1 W.L.R. 819; and see A. I. L. Campbell, [1987] P.L. 328.

[51] As to the meaning of "laying", see the Laying of Documents before Parliament (Interpretation) Act 1948. It normally involves delivery of copies to the Votes and Proceedings Office of the Commons and the Office of the Clerk of the Parliaments. Subordinate legislation other than statutory instruments may also have to be laid before Parliament, *e.g.* under the Immigration Act 1971; see *R. v. Immigration Appeals Tribunal, ex p. Joyles* [1972] 1 W.L.R. 1390.

[52] Sometimes just the House of Commons: *e.g.* orders prescribing maximum rates under the Rates Act 1984: *R. v. Secretary of State for the Environment, ex p. Greenwich London Borough Council, The Times,* December 19, 1985; *R. v. Secretary of State for the Environment, ex p. Leicester City Council* (1985) 25 R.V.R. 31 (references in section 4(1) to "Parliament" to be read in context as to a reference to the House of Commons only).

[53] Statutory Instruments Act 1946, s.4(1).

[54] See *ibid.* s.6(1). The instrument may not be made within 40 days, and either House may resolve that it shall not be made.

common requirement,[55] but which is less efficacious in ensuring Parliamentary scrutiny, either House may within 40 days of its being laid resolve that the instrument should be annulled.[56] Since 1973 it has been possible for proceedings on statutory instruments to be taken in Commons Standing Committees rather than on the floor of the House. Indeed, from 1994, all affirmative statutory instruments are automatically referred to a standing committee, unless de-referred on a government motion, and debates on the floor of the House are limited to one and a half hours.[57] Nevertheless, Parliamentary scrutiny of the merits of instruments under these procedures is not particularly effective in either forum.[58]

An instrument may also be scrutinised by the Joint Committee on Statutory Instruments. This committee was first appointed in 1973, and replaced the separate committees of each House that had formerly undertaken this work.[59] The Chairman is an Opposition M.P. The Committee examines instruments laid before either House and subject to either form of resolution procedure, other instruments of a general character and special procedure orders. It may draw the attention of Parliament to a particular instrument on any of a number of specified grounds, or on any other grounds not impinging on the merits of or policy behind the instrument. The specified grounds are that:

   (i) it imposes a charge on the public revenues;
  (ii) it is made under an enactment excluding it from challenge in the courts;
 (iii) it purports to have retrospective effect where the parent Act does not so provide;
 (iv) it has been unjustifiably delayed in publication or being laid before Parliament;
  (v) it has not been notified in proper time to the Lord Chancellor and the Speaker where it comes into effect before being presented to Parliament;
 (vi) it may be *ultra vires*;
(vii) it appears to make an unusual or unexpected use of the powers conferred by the parent Act;
(viii) it requires elucidation as to its form or purport; or
 (ix) it is defective in drafting.

Instruments subject to House of Commons proceedings only are examined by the Commons members of the Joint Committee acting as a Commons Select Committee on Statutory Instruments. No formal steps have to be taken in either House following an adverse report by one of these committees, although such

---

[55] In 1976–77 there were 127 instruments subject to affirmative procedure, 669 subject to negative procedure, 37 general instruments only required to be laid, and 197 general instruments not so required: First Report from the Select Committee on Procedure, 1977–78 H.C. 588 Vol. 1, p. xxxi; an increasing proportion of instruments have been made subject to the first two procedures.

[56] Statutory Instruments Act, 1946 s.5(1). This takes the form of an address to Her Majesty praying that the instrument be annulled, and is commonly termed a "prayer".

[57] This is part of a package of measures designed to reduce late sittings in the House: Eighth Report of the Select Committee on Procedure, 1994–95 H.C. 491, *Sitting hours reform*, pp. vii, xvi-xix; Vol.251 H.C.Deb., December 19, 1994, cols.1456–1509.

[58] See First Report from the Select Committee on Procedure, 1977–78 H.C. 588, Vol. 1, pp. xxix-xxxix; J. Beatson, (1979) 12 Cornell Int. L.J. 199; P. Norton, *The Commons in Perspective* (1981) pp. 95–99; P. Byrne, (1976) 29 *Parliamentary Affairs* 366; A. Beith M.P. (1981) 34 *Parliamentary Affairs* 165.

[59] See the Report from the Joint Committee on Delegated Legislation, 1971–72 H.C. 45, H.L. 184.

reports may be referred to in other Parliamentary proceedings concerning the instruments, and the work of these committees and their predecessors seem to have played a part in reducing delays and improving drafting.[60] A survey published in 1988 concluded that the technical process of scrutiny now appears to work as effectively as a parliamentary committee can be expected to function. Nevertheless, the increasing use of delegated legislation for major policy implementation, the lack of parliamentary time for debate, the increase in decisions taken before the Committee's report is published and the emphasis on political rather than legal points in debates on the merits have led to "the reality that parliamentary scrutiny of delegated legislation is not effective democratic control."[61] The Hansard Society Commission[62] considered the "whole approach of Parliament to delegated legislation to be highly unsatisfactory. The House of Commons in particular should give its procedure for the scrutiny of statutory instruments a thorough review."[63]

A development of some significance that was in the course of being introduced when the Commission reported was the establishment by the House of Lords of a Select Committee on the Scrutiny of Delegated Powers.[64] Its terms of reference are:

"to report whether the provisions of any bill[65] inappropriately delegate legislative power; or whether they subject the exercise of legislative power to an inappropriate degree of Parliamentary scrutiny."

It receives memoranda from the relevant government department and has generally been able to report to the House before the Committee stage. It has been particularly concerned with so-called "Henry VIII clauses", which enable primary legislation to be amended or repealed by subordinate legislation; the appropriate level of scrutiny (*i.e.*, affirmative or negative procedure or no parliamentary control) has been recommended according to the circumstances.[66] The Committee appears to have made a useful contribution, its intervention having led to changes in the legislation proposed on a number of occasions.

---

[60] See S. A. de Smith and R. Brazier, *Constitutional and Administrative Law* (7th ed., 1994), pp. 375–377.

[61] J. D. Hayhurst and P. Wallington, "The Parliamentary Scrutiny of Delegated Legislation" [1988] P.L. 547, 573–576. The conclusions are Professor Wallington's. For proposals for minor procedural changes, see Hayhurst and Wallington, pp. 575–576; Second Report from the Select Committee on Procedure, 1986–87 H.C. 350, *The Use of Time on the Floor of the House*, pp. vi–xi. See also T. St. J. Bates, [1986] Stat.L.R. 114.

[62] Above, p. 271.

[63] Report, pp. 89–90. Particular changes proposed include review of S.I.s by departmentally related select committees; the use of special standing committees on longer or more complicated S.I.s; more meaningful motions for debate on an S.I. in standing committee, including the possibility of suggesting (although not making) amendments (pp. 90–94).

[64] Its establishment was proposed by the (Jellicoe) Select Committee on the *Committee Work of the House* (1991–92 H.L. 35-I). It first conducted a general inquiry into the principles of its work (First Report, 1992–93 H.L. 57) and conducted a review of its work in 1994 (12th Report, 1993–94 H.L. 90). See C.M.G.Himsworth, [1995] P.L.34.

[65] It does not, however, consider Consolidation or Supply Bills.

[66] See 1993–94 H.L. 90, pp. 3–4.

Special arrangements for scrutiny have been introduced in respect of "deregulation orders" made under Part I of the Deregulation and Contracting Out Act 1994.[67] These orders, made by the Secretary of State, amend or repeal statutory provisions passed before the end of the 1993–94 session, in order to remove or reduce burdens on business. The procedure was thought by the government to be necessary because of the difficulty of finding time for primary legislation on such matters; however, the switch to secondary legislation aroused controversy because of the perceived inadequacy of the scrutiny arrangements. Accordingly, after a consultation stage, proposals for deregulation orders are examined by a special Deregulation Committee of the House of Commons and by the House of Lords Select Committee on the Scrutiny of Delegated Powers, which report to their respective Houses. Apart from substantive scrutiny, these committees also perform the functions of the Joint Committee on Statutory Instruments in relation to proposed orders. The committees do not have the power to veto draft orders, but adverse reports will be treated with the "utmost seriousness".[68] Sixty days (excluding recesses) are allowed for "Parliamentary consideration" from the day that the proposed order is laid. Orders are subject to an affirmative resolution by each House. It has been suggested that this procedure may form the basis for improved scrutiny of other legislation.[69]

Once a statutory instrument is made it must be sent to the Queen's Printer and copies must as soon as possible be printed and sold.[70] The requirements as to printing and sale do not apply to instruments classified as "local"[71]; to general instruments otherwise regularly printed and published; to temporary instruments; to schedules whose printing and sale "is unnecessary or undesirable having regard to the nature or bulk of the document" and to any other steps taken to publicize them; and to confidential instruments not yet in operation.[72] The requirements may, however, be imposed by the Statutory Instruments Reference Committee appointed by the Lord Chancellor and the Speaker.[73] The Queen's Printer allocates statutory instruments received to the series for the calendar year in which they are made, and numbers them consecutively as near as may be in the order in which they are received.[74] They are cited by their number and year.[75]

---

[67] ss.1–6. See A. Page, *Current Law Statutes Annotated 1994*; M. Royle, (1994) 15 Stat.L.R.170. The procedures have been the subject of consideration by a number of reports of Select Committees of the House of Commons and House of Lords: see Page, *op.cit.*, p. 40–11. See also Fourth Report from the Select Committee on the Scrutiny of Delegated Powers, *Special Report on Deregulation Orders* (1994–95 H.C.48) and Vol.250 H. C. Deb., November 24, 1994, cols.764–789.

[68] Government response (1993–94 H.C. 404) to the *Fourth Report of the Select Committee on Procedure* (1993–94 H.C. 238), p.viii. "In normal circumstances the Government would expect to submit a revised proposal or to withdraw the proposal altogether": *ibid.*

[69] See M. Ryle, "The Deregulation and Contracting Out Bill 1994—A Blueprint for the Reform of the Legislative Process?" (1994) 15 Stat.L.R.170.

[70] Statutory Instruments Act 1946, s.2.

[71] See generally on local statutory instruments, R. J. B. Morris, [1990] Stat.L.R. 28.

[72] Statutory Instruments Regulations 1947 (S.I. 1948 No. 1), regs.3–8. These matters have to be "certified" by the responsible authority (*i.e.* minister) in each case. This must be done in proper form: *Simmonds v. Newell* [1953] 1 W.L.R. 826.

[73] S.I. 1948 No. 1, reg. 11. The Committee has power to determine certain other questions which may arise as to numbering, publication, classification, etc. It consists of the Lord Chairman of Committees (Lords), the Chairman of Ways and Means (Commons) and six senior officers of both Houses: *Erskine May's Parliamentary Practice* (21st ed., 1989), p. 541.

[74] S.I. 1948 No. 1, reg. 3.

[75] Statutory Instruments Act 1946, s.2(2).

HMSO also publishes (1) periodical lists of the titles of instruments issued; (2) an Annual Edition with full texts of instruments issued, an appendix of prerogative legislation and relevant lists, tables and indices; (3) the annual *Table of Government Orders*, a chronological list showing which instruments are still in force, amended or revoked; and (4) the *Index to Government Orders*, issued every two years, which lists existing powers to make delegated legislation and current exercises of those powers according to subject matter. Butterworths publish *Halsbury's Statutory Instruments*, which lists and summarises delegated legislation in force according to subject matter, gives the annotated text of the "more important orders, rules and regulations, selected on the basis of the likely requirements of subscriber",[76] and includes a regular updating service. Regulations are available on *Lexis* and also normally included in encyclopedias on particular topics.

Rules and Orders made before 1949 are included in the series *Statutory Rules and Orders and Statutory Instruments Revised to Dec. 31st 1948*, which is arranged according to subject matter.[77]

The position as to the commencement of subordinate legislation is unclear. The subordinate legislation in question may expressly provide for its own commencement.[78] If it does not, there is some authority that an order can only come into effect when it is *made known*.[79] In a later case,[80] however, Streatfeild J. directed a jury as follows:

"I do not think that it can be said that to make a valid statutory instrument it is required that all of these stages should be gone through; namely, the making, the laying before Parliament, the printing and the certification of that part of it which it might be unnecessary to have printed. In my judgment the making of an instrument is complete when it is first of all made by the Minister concerned and after it has been laid before Parliament."[81]

The defendant was prosecuted for breach of a schedule to a statutory instrument that had not been printed as required by the Act. Streatfeild J. held that it was not invalid for lack of publication.

Section 3(1) of the Statutory Instruments Act 1946 provides that regulations should be made for the publication by HMSO of lists showing the dates of issue of instruments printed and sold by the Queen's Printer; in any legal proceedings, "an entry therein shall be conclusive evidence of the date on which any statutory instrument was first issued" by HMSO.

Section 3(2) provides that in criminal proceedings for a contravention of "any such statutory instrument" it is:

---

[76] *Halsbury's Statutory Instruments: A User's Guide*, p. 5.

[77] Earlier editions were published in 1896 and 1904. Up to and including 1960 the Annual Editions were also arranged by subject-matter rather than chronologically.

[78] From 1947 all statutory instruments required to be laid before Parliament after being made must show the dates on which they come into operation; this does not, however, cover the whole field as not all instruments must be laid. Where a day is specified, the instrument comes into effect at the beginning of that day: Interpretation Act 1978, ss.4(a), 23.

[79] Bailhache J. in *Johnson v. Sargant* [1918] 1 K.B. 101. *Cf. Jones v. Robson* [1901] 1 Q.B. 673 where a requirement to give *notice* of certain orders was held to be directory (but in this case the order had been published, and the defendant knew of it).

[80] *R. v. Sheer Metalcraft Ltd* [1954] 1 Q.B. 586.

[81] *ibid.* p. 590. (There may of course be no "laying" requirement.)

"a defence to prove that the instrument had not been issued by Her Majesty's Stationery Office at the date of the alleged contravention unless it is proved that at that date reasonable steps had been taken for the purpose of bringing the purport of the instrument to the notice of the public, or of persons likely to be affected by it, or of the person charged."[82]

It is not, however, clear whether this defence is available (1) in respect of any instrument which has not been issued, including those exempted from publication requirements; or (2) in respect of an instrument which has not been issued in breach of a publication requirement; or (3) in respect only of the period between the making of an instrument and its issue in circumstances where such issue does subsequently take place.[83] Moreover, the statutory defence does not apply to subordinate legislation other than statutory instruments. There is much to be said for the principle of *Johnson v. Sargant*:[84] "To bind a citizen by a law, the terms of which he has no means of knowing,[85] is the very essence of tyranny."[86]

(b) Local authority byelaws[87]

District and London borough councils have a general power to make byelaws for the "good rule and government" of the area "and for the prevention and suppression of nuisances" therein;[88] in addition there are numerous specific byelaw making powers.[89] The procedure for making byelaws, to be followed in all cases unless specific provision is otherwise made, is laid down by section 236 of the Local Government Act 1972 Byelaws cannot take effect until they are confirmed by the appropriate minister. Public notice must be given at least one month before application is made for confirmation, and a copy must be available for inspection. The confirming authority may fix the date on which a byelaw is to come into effect; if no date is so fixed, it comes into effect one month after it is confirmed. When confirmed, a copy must be printed and deposited at the authority's offices; it must be open to public inspection without payment at all reasonable hours, and copies supplied on payment of such sum, not exceeding 20p per copy, as the authority may determine.[90]

---

[82] It has been suggested that a similar defence should be created in respect of Acts of Parliament: Statute Law Society Working Party on Commencement of Acts of Parliament, [1980] Stat.L.R. 40, 51–52. The defence failed on the facts in *R. v. Sheer Metalcraft Ltd, loc. cit.* in 80 above.

[83] The difficulty is created by the word "such": see D. Lanham, (1974) 37 M.L.R. 510, 521–523. The *Sheer Metalcraft* case (1) is not inconsistent with the first interpretation, but the point as to whether the defence can apply in respect of *exempted* instruments did not arise as the minister had not certified that the instrument should be exempt; (2) is inconsistent with the second interpretation; and (3) is inconsistent with the third, as there was no suggestion that the schedule was ever published.

[84] [1918] 1 K.B. 101. Lanham (*ibid.*) argues that even where a date of commencement is specified, an instrument can only come into effect when published.; *contra*: A.I.L. Campbell, [1982] P.L. 569; response by Lanham, [1983] P.L. 395.

[85] Ignorance of a published instrument would probably not be regarded as a defence: ignorance of the law is not excuse.

[86] *per* Barwick C.J. in *Watson v. Lee* (1980) 54 A.L.J.R. 1, 3.

[87] Sometimes spelt "by-laws."

[88] Local Government Act 1972, s.235(1).

[89] See C.A. Cross, *Encyclopedia of Local Government Law*, Appendix 6.

[90] Local authorities do not always seem to be aware of these obligations.

5. Arrangement of Statutory Instruments

A statutory instrument is normally arranged in the following order:[91]

   (i) Year and number of the instrument.

  (ii) An indication of the subject matter; this corresponds to the categories in the lists published periodically by HMSO.

 (iii) Title.

 (iv) The dates when the instrument was made, laid before Parliament and is due to come into operation.

  (v) A recital naming the person making the instrument and the relevant enabling powers.

 (vi) The main provisions of the instrument. These are termed *articles* (in an Order), *regulations* or *rules* as the case may be. Subdivisions are called *paragraphs*. The instrument may be divided into *Parts* and may include a *Schedule*. Common form provisions as to title, definitions and commencement are placed at the beginning.

 (vii) An indication of the minister by whom the instrument was signed.

(viii) An "Explanatory Note" stated to be "not part of" the instrument.

6. Validity of Subordinate Legislation[92]

All delegated legislation must conform to the limits laid down expressly or impliedly in the enabling Act; if those limits are exceeded the validity of the instrument[93] may be challenged in the courts.[94] Challenges may be made directly, for example by an action in the High Court for a declaration that the legislation is *ultra vires*; or indirectly, for example by raising the argument that an instrument is *ultra vires* as a defence to enforcement proceedings, such as a prosecution for contravening the instrument.[95] An instrument may be *ultra vires* if there has been a failure to comply with a "mandatory" procedural requirement. Some requirements are merely "directory"; the authorities are "directed" to comply with them, but compliance is not a pre-condition to the validity of the instrument. It is not easy to predict whether a court will hold a particular requirement to be mandatory or directory. In this context the duty to consult

---

[91] See Bennion (1990), pp. 55–57.

[92] See generally Sir William Wade and C. F. Forsyth, *Administrative Law* (7th ed., 1994), pp. 874–889; K. Puttick, *Challenging Delegated Legislation* (1988). Successful challenges to the *vires* of statutory instruments between 1914 and 1986 are summarised by J. D. Hayhurst and P. Wallington, [1988] P.L. 547, 566–573.

[93] Or other form of delegated legislation.

[94] The courts may also ensure that prerogative legislation falls within the scope of an existing prerogative power.

[95] Resort to this latter mode of proceeding is well established and in *R. v. Reading Crown Court, ex p. Hutchinson* [1988] Q.B. 384, D.C. (pet. dis. [1988] 1 W.L.R. 308, H.L.) the Divisional Court affirmed that its availability had not been affected by the principle of *O'Reilly v. Mackman* [1983] 2 A.C. 237 that matters of *vires* should normally be raised directly on an application for judicial review. Arguments that a byelaw is *procedurally* as distinct from *substantively* invalid can, however, only be raised on an application for judicial review: *Bugg v. D.P.P.* [1993] Q.B. 473; I. McLeod, [1994] Crim.L.R. 35.

affected parties has been held to be mandatory,[96] but requirements as to publication[97] and laying[98] have been held to be directory. The scope of a consultation requirement was described as follows by Webster J. in *R. v. Secretary of State for Social Services, ex p. Association of Metropolitan Authorities.*[99]

"... in any context the essence of consultation is the communication of a genuine invitation to give advice and a genuine receipt of that advice. In my view it must go without saying that to achieve consultation sufficient information must be supplied by the consulting to the consulted party to enable it to tender helpful advice. Sufficient time must be given by the consulting to the consulted party to enable it to do that, and sufficient time must be available for such advice to be considered by the consulting party. Sufficient, in that context, does not mean ample, but at least enough to enable the relevant purpose to be fulfilled. By helpful advice, in this context, I mean sufficiently informed and considered information or advice about aspects of the form or substance of the proposals, or their implications for the consulted party, being aspects material to the implementation of the proposal as to which the Secretary of State might not be fully informed or advised and as to which the party consulted might have relevant information or advice to offer."

An instrument may also be quashed if there is unfairness in the consultation process.[1]

An instrument may be *ultra vires* if its subject matter lies beyond the scope of the enabling power. For example, in *Hotel and Catering Industry Training Board v. Automobile Proprietary Ltd*[2] the House of Lords held that a power to make an order establishing a Training Board for persons employed "in any

---

[96] *Agricultural etc. Training Board v. Aylesbury Mushrooms Ltd* [1972] 1 W.L.R. 190.

[97] *R. v. Sheer Metalcraft Ltd* [1954] 1 Q.B. 586; see above, pp. 000–000.

[98] See *Bailey v. Williamson* (1873) L.R. 8 Q.B. 118; *Starey v. Graham* [1899] 1 Q.B. 406, 412; *Springer v. Doorly* (1950) L.R.B.G. 10 (W. Indian Court of Appeal); A.I.L. Campbell, [1983] P.L. 43; but see de Smith, Woolf and Jowell, *Judicial Review of Administrative Action* (5th ed., 1995), p. 275, for the argument that laying requirements should be regarded as mandatory; *cf. Bain v. Thorne* (1916) 12 Tas.L.R. 57 (Sup.Ct. of Tasmania). In 1981 Ronald Biggs escaped extradition from Barbados to the U.K. because the Barbados High Court held that regulations designating the U.K. as a country to which a fugitive could be extradited should have been laid before the Barbados Parliament: *The Times*, April 24, 1981: *Biggs v. Commissioner of Police* [1982 May] W.I.L.J. 121. Note, however, that the decision turned on a provision of the Interpretation Act of Barbados to the effect that the term "shall" [*i.e.* in "shall ... be laid" was "to be construed as imperative" (*ibid.*). In *R. v. Secretary of State for Social Services, ex p. Camden London Borough Council* (unreported, February 26, 1986) Macpherson J. held that a requirement that supplementary benefit regulations "shall not be made" unless a draft had been laid before Parliament and approved by each House imposed a mandatory requirement. On appeal, the Court of Appeal assumed this to be so without deciding the point ([1987] 1 W.L.R. 819).

[99] [1986] 1 W.L.R. 1, 4–5.

[1] *R. v. Secretary of State for Health, ex p. U.S. Tobacco International Inc.* [1992] 1 Q.B.353 (ban on oral snuff quashed where the sole importers were not given the details of the scientific advice on which the ban was based).

[2] [1969] 1 W.L.R. 697. See also *R. v. Customs and Excise Commissioners, ex p. Hedges and Butler Ltd* [1986] 2 All E.R. 164 (power to demand production of the whole of the records of a business (including records concerning non-dutiable goods) held not to be "incidental" or "supplementary" to powers concerning the regulation of excise warehouses and dealings in dutiable goods); *R. v. Secretary of State for Social Services, ex p. Cotton, The Times*, December 14, 1985; *R. v. Inland Revenue Commissioners, ex p. Woolwich Equitable Building Society* [1987] S.T.C. 654.

activities of industry or commerce'' did not enable an order to be made in respect of members' clubs.

The established grounds upon which byelaws may be struck down are usually said to be those of *ultra vires*, uncertainty, unreasonableness and repugnancy to the general law,[3] although the last three grounds may also be regarded as facets of the *ultra vires* doctrine. For example, in *Staden v. Tarjanyi*[4] a district council made a byelaw in respect of a pleasure ground which provided:

> "A person shall not in the pleasure ground . . . take off, fly or land any glider, manned or unmanned, weighing in total more than four kilogrammes. . . ."

The respondent flew a hang glider over the pleasure ground and was prosecuted under the byelaw. It was conceded that "in" meant "in or over". The Divisional Court held that the byelaw was invalid for uncertainty:

> ". . . anyone engaged upon the otherwise lawful pursuit of hang gliding must know with reasonable certainty when he is breaking the law and when he is not breaking the law. . . . [T]o be valid the byelaw must set some lower level below which the glider must not fly."[5]

The leading authority on the meaning of "unreasonableness" in the context of byelaws is *Kruse v. Johnson*[6] where Lord Russell of Killowen C. J. stated[7] that local authority byelaws ought to be supported if possible and "benevolently" interpreted, but might be struck down if unreasonable:

> "But unreasonable in what sense? If, for instance, they were found to be partial and unequal in their operation as between different classes; if they were manifestly unjust; if they disclosed bad faith; if they involved such oppressive or gratuitous interference with the rights of those subject to them as could find no justification in the minds of reasonable men, the Court might well say, 'Parliament never intended to give authority to make such rules; they are unreasonable and ultra vires'. . . . A by-law is not unreasonable merely because particular judges may think that it goes further than is prudent or necessary or convenient, or because it is not accompanied by a qualification or an exception which some judges may think ought to be there."

Successful challenges on this ground are rare. It is not clear whether a statutory instrument, as distinct from a byelaw, can be challenged for unreasonableness. In *Maynard v. Osmond*[8] regulations which did not allow police officers to be legally represented in disciplinary proceedings were challenged on

---

[3] See *Cross on Local Government Law* (8th ed., 1991) paras. 6–06–6–10.
[4] (1980) 78 L.G.R. 614.
[5] *ibid.* p. 623.
[6] [1898] 2 Q.B. 91.
[7] At pp. 99–100.
[8] [1977] Q.B. 240.

this ground[9]; the members of the Court of Appeal did not express any doubt as to the court's jurisdiction to entertain such a challenge, but dismissed the application on the merits.

In *R. v. Secretary of State for the Environment, ex p. Nottinghamshire County Council*,[10] the council challenged the 1985–86 guidance on expenditure limits given by the Secretary of State to local authorities, under section 59 of the Local Government, Planning and Land Act 1980, *inter alia* on the ground of unreasonableness. The guidance was required to be laid before, and approved by resolution of, the House of Commons. Lord Scarman in the House of Lords said[11]

". . . I cannot accept that it is constitutionally appropriate, save in very exceptional circumstances, for the courts to intervene on the ground of 'unreasonableness' to quash guidance framed by the Secretary of State and by necessary implication approved by the House of Commons. . . ."

The challenge failed on the merits. It is to be noted that the possibility of a challenge for unreasonableness was not completely ruled out. Indeed, the suggestion that Parliamentary approval would properly restrict the permissible scope of such a challenge has been doubted.[12] It is clearly the case that Parliamentary approval, other than in an Act of Parliament, does not render delegated legislation immune from challenges based on other aspects of the *ultra vires* doctrine.[13] In *R. v. Secretary of State for the Environment, ex p. Hammersmith and Fulham London Borough Council*[14] the House of Lords unanimously approved Lord Scarman's view, although the list of grounds of challenge said to be permissible is so lengthy[15] that it is difficult to see what kind of challenge is ruled out.[16]

Even where there are grounds for holding delegated legislation *ultra vires*, a

---

[9] The Police (Discipline) Regulations 1965 (S.I. 1965 No. 543); the regulations applicable to Deputy Chief Constables, Assistant Chief Constables and Chief Constables did permit legal representation (S.I. 1965 No. 544). The court did not accept that this constituted "unfair discrimination".

[10] [1986] A.C. 240. *Cf. City of Edinburgh District Council v. Secretary of State for Scotland* 1985 S.L.T. 551.

[11] [1986] A.C. 240, 287.

[12] Sir William Wade and C. F. Forsyth, *Administrative Law* (7th ed., 1994), pp. 30, 404–405, 881; C. M. G. Himsworth, 1985 S.L.T. 369; A.I.L. Campbell, 1986 S.L.T. 101; C. T. Reid, [1986] C.L.J. 169. A provision in the Immigration Rules was held to be unreasonable in *R. v. Immigration Appeal Tribunal ex p. Manshoora Begun* [1986] Imm. A. R. 385. The Rules are "administrative instructions from the Home Secretary to immigration officers and statements of policy and practice" (Wade and Forsyth (1994), p. 230). They are subject to Parliamentary disapproval but are not published as statutory instruments.

[13] *R. v. H. M. Treasury ex p. Smedley* [1985] Q.B. 657, 666–669 (*per* Sir John Donaldson M.R. in relation to an Order in Council); *R. v. Secretary of State for the Environment, ex p. Greater London Council* (Unreported, April 3, 1985): discussed in the articles cited in n. 12 above, and in M. Grant, *Ratecapping and the Law* (2nd ed., 1986), pp. 12–13; *R. v. Secretary of State for the Environment, ex p. Nottinghamshire County Council* [1986] A. C. 240, 247–251 (*per* Lord Scarman).

[14] [1991] 1 A. C. 521, 594–597.

[15] That the exercise of discretion frustrates the policy of the statute, that legally relevant considerations have been ignored or irrelevant considerations taken into account, that there is bad faith, improper motive, or manifest absurdity: see Lord Bridge at pp. 596–579. *Cf.* below p. 971.

[16] A challenge to the merits of an exercise of discretion cannot in any event be based on the *ultra vires* doctrine.

remedy may still be refused in the exercise of the court's discretion.[17] The court may be able to hold that an invalid part of an order can be "severed," leaving the remaining part intact.[18] Finally, the court may in an appropriate case hold that an order is invalid only in so far as it affects a particular applicant.[19]

7. QUASI-LEGISLATION[20]

In recent years, greater attention has been paid to "administrative quasi-legislation"[21]: administrative rules that do not have direct legal force. There has been:

> "an exponential growth of statutory and extra-statutory rules in a plethora of forms. Codes of practice, guidance, guidance notes, guidelines, circulars, White Papers, development control policy notes, development briefs, practice statements, tax concessions, Health Service Notices, Family Practitioner Notices, codes of conduct, codes of ethics and conventions are just some of the guises in which the rules appear.[22]"

(a) Statutory rules

There are many variables in the structure and operation of such rules: the overall picture is arguably more confused than the arrangements for delegated legislation were before the Statutory Instruments Act 1946. These variables include the following:

— By whom they are made: a minister; a non-governmental statutory agency; a non-statutory body.
— To whom they are directed: officials; local authorities; courts and tribunals; private organisations and citizens.
— Whether they are subject to Parliamentary scrutiny: there may be a requirement for a code to be laid before Parliament (in draft or in a final version), subject to affirmative or negative procedures.
— How they are published: by HMSO, by a government department or otherwise.

---

[17] e.g. R. v. Secretary of State for Social Services, ex p. Association of Metropolitan Authorities [1986] 1 W.L.R. 1.
[18] Dunkley v. Evans [1981] 3 All E.R. 285; cf. R. v. Secretary of State for Transport, ex p. Greater London Council [1985] 3 All E.R. 300.
[19] e.g. Agricultural etc. Training Board v. Aylesbury Mushrooms Ltd [1972] 1 W.L.R. 190 (where an order was only held to be invalid in respect of a particular organisation that had not been consulted).
[20] G. Ganz, Quasi-Legislation: Recent Developments in Secondary Legislation (1987); R. E. Megarry, (1944) 60 L.Q.R. 125; Lord Campbell, "Codes of Practice as an Alternative to Legislation" [1985] Stat.L.R. 127; A. Samuels, "Codes of Practice and Legislation" [1986] Stat.L.R. 29; T. St. J. Bates, [1986] Stat.L.R. 114, 120–123; Vol. 469 H. L. Deb., cols.1075–1104, January 15, 1986 (debate on codes of practice); R. Baldwin and J. Houghton, "Circular arguments: The Status and Legitimacy of Administrative Rules" [1986] P.L. 239; R. B. Ferguson, "The Legal Status of Non-Statutory Codes of Practice" [1988] J.B.L. 12; R. Baldwin, Rules and Government (1995), Chap. 4.
[21] A term coined by Megarry, op. cit.
[22] Ganz (1987), pp. 1–2.

— Their legal effect: there are several forms. In the case of some codes, no effect is stated, although it does not follow that they are entirely devoid of legal effect. There may be a requirement that provisions of the code be taken into account, if relevant, by a local authority, tribunal or court. It may be provided that breach of a code may be relied upon as tending to establish civil or criminal liability, and compliance as tending to negative such liability: indeed in one case as establishing liability unless the contrary is proved.

— The content: McCrudden[23] distinguishes four types of codes, although any one code may contain elements of them all:

"Codes may include provisions (i) to codify existing non-legal practice; (ii) to codify the already existing law of the courts and/or the previous legal interpretations on a particular issue of the body making the code; (iii) to set out recommended good industrial practice; and (iv) to interpret independently those statutory provisions for which the body making the code has some responsibility."

An alternative typology is suggested by Baldwin and Houghton,[24] who distinguish: (i) procedural rules; (ii) interpretative guides; (iii) instructions to officials; (iv) prescriptive/evidential rules; (v) commendatory rules; (vi) voluntary codes; (vii) rules of practice, management or operation; and (viii) consultative devices and administrative pronouncements.

Examples include the Immigration Rules,[25] the PACE Codes of Practice,[26] the Code of Guidance concerning Homelessness,[27] the Highway Code,[28] the Sex Discrimination Code of Practice,[29] the Code of Practice on Picketing,[30] and the Approved Documents giving guidance with respect to the requirements of building regulation.[31]

The position as to Parliamentary scrutiny is different in a number of respects from that for statutory instruments. On the one hand, particular codes have been examined by the appropriate departmental select committee, which does not normally happen with other forms of legislation. On the other, the Joint Committee on Statutory Instruments only has jurisdiction to examine documents,

---

[23] (1988) 51 M.L.R., 409, 531.

[24] [1986] P.L. 239, 240–245.

[25] Immigration Act 1971, ss.3(2), 19: made by the Secretary of State, issued as a House of Commons paper, subject to annulment by Parliament and binding on adjudicators and the Immigration Appeal Tribunal, no consultation requirements.

[26] See below, p. 666.

[27] Housing Act 1985, s.71: made by the Secretary of State, published as a Circular, authorities to have regard to guidance, no laying or consultation requirements.

[28] Road Traffic Act 1988, s.38: made by the Secretary of State, who must consult such representative organisations as he thinks fit, issued via HMSO, subject to annulment by Parliament, may be relied on in legal proceedings as tending to establish or negative liability.

[29] Sex Discrimination Act 1975, s.56A: made by the Equal Opportunities Commission (with the approval of the Secretary of State), which must consult appropriate organisations, issued via HMSO, draft subject to annulment by Parliament, to be taken into account by Industrial Tribunal if appears relevant.

[30] Trade Union and Labour Relations (Consolidation) Act 1992, ss.203–208: made by the Secretary of State, who must consult ACAS, draft to be approved by Parliament, to be taken into account by Industrial Tribunal if appears relevant.

[31] Building Act 1984, ss.6, 7: made by Secretary of State or designated body, issued via HMSO, no laying or consultation requirement, breach tends to establish and compliance to negative liability in legal proceedings.

other than statutory instruments, that require Parliamentary approval; there is no provision for the merits to be debated in Standing Committee; and the likelihood of a merits debate in the Chamber is low.[32]

The perceived advantages of codes of practice and the like include the use of informal, non-technical, language; flexibility; and the promotion of uniformity of practice, particularly in the public sector.[33] Their "fundamental rationale" is the adoption of a voluntary approach rather than compulsion.[34]

While there is much to be said for this where codes are based on widespread consultation and consensus, there are nevertheless difficulties.[35] Sometimes they are introduced as an unhappy compromise between statutory regulation and inaction. In some areas the voluntary approach has broken down and compulsion has replaced persuasion. There has been criticism of the use of codes with controversial provisions that go beyond existing legislation,[36] particularly given the limited effectiveness of Parliamentary scrutiny. The haphazard variety of forms and procedures is indefensible. Proposals have been made for the strengthening of Parliamentary scrutiny, a "code of practice regulating codes of practice" and the establishment of a body "to advise on the creation of quasi-legal or voluntary rules instead of legal rules and evolve criteria for their use."[37] In December 1987, the government issued Guidance on Codes of Practice and Legislation, primarily for the use of parliamentary draftsmen, and those framing legislative proposals.[38]

(b) Voluntary guidance[39]

There are many examples of codes of practice, guidance and the like without any statutory backing. In the public sector, for example, guidance may be given by central government departments to local authorities in circulars and other forms of communication, and instructions are commonly given to officials within departments.[40] The effect varies widely: the legal effect may be indirect, but the practical implications of great significance.[41] In the private sector such codes have in some circumstances been adduced as evidence, for example of

---

[32] Baldwin and Houghton, [1986] P.L. 239, at pp. 26–32.

[33] In the public sector, codes of practice and other forms of guidance may be used to provide a framework for the exercise of discretionary powers, so as to promote uniformity in decision-making. However, power to give guidance will not normally authorise the issue of binding directions (*Laker Airways Ltd* v. *Department of Trade* [1977] Q. B. 643) and the recipient of such guidance must not fetter its discretion by regarding it as binding (*R.* v. *Police Complaints Board, ex p. Madden* [1983] 1 W. L. R 447). Conversely, such guidance is likely to be a legally relevant consideration and must at least be taken into account.

[34] Ganz (1987), pp. 96–98.

[35] *ibid.*, pp. 98–108.

[36] Highlighted by the decision of Scott J. in *Thomas* v. *National Union of Mineworkers* [1986] Ch. 20 to limit by injunction the number of pickets outside particular premises to six, in line with a provision of the Code of Practice on Picketing then made under section 3 of the Employment Act 1980.

[37] Ganz (1987), Chap. 6; A. Samuels, [1986] Stat. L. R. 29.

[38] [1989] Stat. L. R. 214.

[39] Ganz (1987), pp. 59–65, 75–95; Ferguson, [1988] J.B.L. 12.

[40] *e.g.* the government's policy to reduce the number of school places in the light of falling school rolls; the use of circulars in town and country planning to state planning policy; extra-statutory tax concessions; standing orders and circular instructions governing the management of prisons.

[41] It has been held that even non-statutory guidance, if erroneous in law, can be challenged on an application for judicial review: *Royal College of Nursing* v. *Department of Health and Social Security* [1981] A.C. 800; *Gillick* v. *West Norfolk Area Health Authority* [1986] A.C. 112.

proper professional or technical standards, and may be incorporated into a con-tract.[42] They may also be recognised as appropriate by government, even without express legislative endorsement.[43] Difficulties as to their accessibility and uncer-tainties as to legal effect are even more pronounced here.

D. COMMUNITY LEGISLATION

1. INTRODUCTION

The accession of the United Kingdom to membership of the European Com-munities (the European Economic Community, the European Coal and Steel Community and the European Atomic Energy Community) meant that the vast and ever-increasing body of Community law became applicable in this country.[44] The system of Community law is founded on the provisions of the various Treaties whereby the Member States agreed to establish the Communities, new members joined ("Accession Treaties") and aspects of the original Treaties were changed, most notably by the Single European Act of 1986[45] and the (Maastricht) Treaty on European Union of 1992.[46] Furthermore, the Maastricht Treaty introduced changes to the structure and nomenclature of the arrangements for European co-operation. The 12 Member States established among themselves a "European Union", making "a new stage in the process of creating an ever closer union among the peoples of Europe in which decisions are taken as closely as possible to the citizen."[47] Its task is "to organize, in a manner demon-strating consistency and solidarity, relations between the Member States and between their peoples." The Union is founded on the European Communities,

---

[42] R. B. Ferguson, [1988] J.B.L. 12.

[43] *e.g.* the codes of practice for residential care homes (Centre for Policy on Ageing, *Home Life* (1984)) and nursing homes (National Association of Health Authorities, *Registration and Inspec-tion of Nursing Homes: A Handbook for Health Authorities* (1985)). The Secretaries of State for Social Services and for Wales asked local authorities to regard *Home Life* "in the same light" as guidance issued under section 7 of the Local Authority Social Services Act 1970 (which suggests that it is not technically guidance under the Act). The codes are in practice taken into account by local authorities, inspectors and registered homes tribunals: see D. Carson, [1985] J.S.W.L. 67, 69–70; R. Brooke Ross, [1985] J.S.W.L. 85; R. M. Jones (ed.), *Encyclopedia of Social Services Law and Practice* (1981), para. D1–303.

[44] See L. Collins, *European Community Law in the United Kingdom* (4th ed., 1990), Chaps.1 and 2; J. Usher, *European Community Law and National Law, The Irreversible Transfer?* (1981); T. C. Hartley, *The Foundations of European Community Law* (3rd ed., 1994).

[45] This had the objectives of "unblocking the Community's decision making process, thereby hast-ening the completion of a genuine common market," enhancing the role of the Parliament in the legislative process, and establishing a formal basis for European Political co-operation: A. Arnull, (1986) 11 E.L. Rev. 358; see also H.-J. Glaesner, (1986) 6 Y.E.L. 283; Symposium, (1986) 23 C.M.L. Rev. 743–840; M. A. McElhenny, (1988) 39(1) N.I.L.Q. 54.

[46] This introduced further major changes, including the establishment of a timetable for progress towards economic and monetary union with a single currency and monetary policy; further changes to legislative procedures; new fields of activity, such as culture, public health and con-sumer protection; and citizenship of the European Union. See D. O'Keefe and P. Twomey (eds.), *Legal Issues of the Maastricht Treaty* (1994); Harmsen, (1994) 45 N.I.L.Q. 109; D. Curtin, (1993) 30 C.M.L.Rev.17.

[47] Treaty on European Union, Title I, Article A.

supplemented by the "implementation of a common foreign and security policy" and the development of "close cooperation on justice and home affairs."[48]

The "European Communities" thus form one part of a broader Union; it is, however, only the Communities that possess legislative powers affecting Member States and citizens. One final complication is that while the term "European Community" has popularly been used to cover the three communities, the ECSC and Euratom no longer having independent roles, the Maastricht Treaty substitutes "European Community" for "European Economic Community" throughout the Treaty of Rome.[49]

The Treaty provisions are sometimes termed the *primary* legislation of the Communities. The Treaties give various powers to the Council and the Commission to make laws by *regulation, directive* or *decision*, the resulting body of law being termed *secondary* legislation. Secondary legislation must conform to the express or implied limits set by the relevant treaty provisions. Under Community law, a further distinction is drawn between laws (both primary and secondary) that have *direct application* or *effect* without any act of implementation by Member States and laws that require such implementation.

Under United Kingdom law, rules of international law such as treaty provisions can only take effect within our domestic legal system if expressly implemented by Act of Parliament. Accordingly, the government secured the passage of the European Communities Act 1972 to enable Community law to take effect within the United Kingdom.

In this section we consider, first, the main Community institutions, second, the different kinds of Community legislation and the extent to which it may be directly applicable or effective, third, the question of the supremacy of Community law, fourth, the implementation of Community law in the United Kingdom, and fifth, the methods by which the validity of Community legislation may be challenged.

2. THE COMMUNITY INSTITUTIONS[50]

The four main institutions of the European Community, established by the Treaties, are the Commission, the Council and the European Parliament (the political institutions) and the Court of Justice. The political institutions will be considered here.[51]

(a) The Commission[52]

The Commission comprises 20 members "appointed by common accord of the governments of Member States." They must be nationals of Member States,

---

[48] *ibid.*, Article B. See below, pp. 310–311.

[49] *ibid.*, Title II, Article G.

[50] See Hartley (1994), Chap. 1; S. Weatherill and P. Beaumont, *E.C. Law* (2nd ed., 1995), Chaps.2–4.

[51] The Court of Justice is considered above, pp. 103–109.

[52] Arts.155–163/EC, as amended by Art.G (48)/TEU and the Act of Accession; these provisions replaced the Merger Treaty (1965), Arts.9–19, providing for the merger of the separate High Authority (ECSC) and Commissions (EEC, Euratom) for the three communities. See G. Edwards and D. Spence (eds.), *The European Commission* (1994); E. Noel, *Working Together* (1993); M. Westlake, *The Commission and the Parliament* (1994).

with either one or two members from each Member State. In practice, the five largest countries (France, Germany, Italy, Spain and the United Kingdom) have two each, the rest one each.[53] Each Commissioner is in effect nominated by his or her national state, but must be acceptable to all the Member States,[54] and is not a "representative" of his or her own country. Article 157 of the EC Treaty provides:

> "The members of the Commission shall, in the general interest of the Community, be completely independent in the performance of their duties.
>
> In the performance of these duties, they shall neither seek nor take instructions from any Government or from any other body. They shall refrain from any action incompatible with their duties. Each Member State undertakes to respect this principle and not to seek to influence the members of the Commission in the performance of their tasks. . . ."

The term of office is five years (increased from four years from 1995), and may be renewed. All the Commissioners retire together. The Member States appoint the President; the Commission may appoint one or two Vice-Presidents.[55] Individual Commissioners can be compulsorily retired by the Court of Justice, on the application of the Council or Commission, if they are guilty of serious misconduct or no longer fulfil the conditions required for performance of their duties. Otherwise, individual Commissioners cannot be dismissed, although the whole Commission must resign if a motion of censure is passed by the Parliament. Each Commissioner is allocated special responsibility for one or more subjects, by agreement amongst themselves. The Commissioners are supported by over 15,000 staff, organised into 23 Directorates General, with a number of specialised services, including a Legal Service.

The main activities of the Commission are:

> "formulating proposals for new Community policies, mediating between the Member States to secure the adoption of these proposals, co-ordinating national policies and overseeing the execution of existing Community policies."[56]

Under the EC Treaty, its task is "to ensure the proper functioning and development of the common market."[57] The Commission meets in private and makes decisions by a simple majority vote. Its commitment to the furtherance of

---

[53] The United Kingdom has adopted the practice of nominating one with a Conservative and one with a Labour political background. The U.K. Commissioners have been Sir Christopher Soames and George Thomson (1973–77); Roy Jenkins (1977–81); Christopher Tugendhat (1977–85); Ivor Richard (1981–85); Lord Cockfield and Stanley Clinton Davis (1985–81); Sir Leon Brittan (1989–); Bruce Millan (1989–95); and Neil Kinnock (1995–). Under Art. 158/EC, as amended by Art. G(48)/TEU, Commissioners appointed in 1993 retired in 1995.

[54] From 1995, a new procedure for the appointment of Commissioners prescribed by Art.158/EC came into effect: the governments first nominate the President of the Commission and then, in consultation with him or her, the other Commissioners; they are then subject as a body to a vote of approval by the European Parliament. In 1995, although not a formal part of the procedure, the Parliament held individual hearings for each nominee.

[55] Art.161/EC, as amended by Art.G(48)/TEU.

[56] Hartley (1994) p. 11.

[57] Art. 155/EC; cf. the broader objectives of the Council: below, p. 308.

Community interests provides a balance to the Council of Ministers, which tends to reflect national interests.

(b) The Council[58]

The Council of the European Union[59] comprises representatives of the Member States, each state sending a minister as its delegate authorised to commit the government of that state. The Presidency is held by each Member State[60] in turn for a term of six months.

The Council is attended by different ministers according to the business to be dealt with. General matters are normally considered by foreign ministers; agriculture matters by agriculture ministers, financial matters by finance ministers and so on. The Council meets periodically, and normally in private.[61] It is supported by a General Secretariat, which is organised on similar lines to the Commission, but is much smaller. The Council's business is prepared by the Committee of Permanent Representatives (COREPER), which itself meets at two levels: COREPER II, comprising the heads of permanent delegations (ambassadors), which deals with matters of political importance, and COREPER I, comprising deputies, which deals with day-to-day business and technical matters. In turn there are many committees and expert working groups. The Council

> "takes the final decision on most EC legislation, concludes agreements with foreign countries and, together with the Parliament, decides on the Community budget."[62]

Under the EC Treaty, its task is "to ensure that the objectives set out in the Treaty are attained," and to that end "ensure co-ordination of the general economic policies of the Member States" and "have power to take decisions."[63] The more important decisions are reserved to the Council rather than the Commission.[64]

The Treaties specify different voting arrangements for different kinds of Council decision. Some acts must be unanimous. Most require a "qualified majority."[65] Here the votes of Member States are weighted:

---

[58] Arts.145–154/EC, as amended by Art. G(43)–(46)/TEU, replacing the Merger Treaty (1965), Arts.1–8 (which provided for the merger of separate Councils for each Community).

[59] The Council adopted this title in 1993: Council Decision 93/591 of November 8, 1993.

[60] The order is prescribed by Art. 146/EC, as amended by Art. G(43)/TEU.

[61] From 1993, it has held some public debates and voting outcomes have been made public, as part of a number of moves to improve the transparency of the institutions' business: *Intergovernmental Conference 1996: Commission Report for the Reflection Group* (1995), p. 39. See Council Decision 93/731/EC on public access to Council Documents, Article 5(1) of which provides that Council deliberations are "covered by the obligation of professional secrecy except in so far as the Council decides otherwise." However, in Case T-194/94, *Carvell v. Council, The Times*, November 2, 1995, the Court of First Instance held that the blanket refusal of access to documents under this provision was contrary to Community law; the Council was required in each case to balance the interests of citizens seeking information against its own interest in preserving secrecy. Whether this will lead to a significant change in practice is uncertain.

[62] Hartley (1994), p. 17.

[63] Article 145/EC.

[64] See further below, p. 312.

[65] Article 148(2)/EC; Act of Accession, Art. 15.

France, Germany, Italy, United Kingdom	: 10 votes each
Spain	: 8 votes
Belgium, Greece, Netherlands, Portugal	: 5 votes each
Sweden, Austria	: 4 votes each
Denmark, Ireland, Finland	: 3 votes each
Luxembourg	: 2 votes

A "qualified majority" is 62 of these 87 votes, where the act is based on a Commission proposal; 62 votes with 10 Member States in favour, otherwise. The arrangements mean that the five largest countries cannot outvote the smaller states.[66]

In many important areas the original requirement specified in the Treaties was for unanimity, the qualified majority regime only coming into effect from January 1, 1966. Even then, a convention developed whereby unanimity would be required as a matter of practice (albeit no longer as a matter of law) where "very important interests" of one or more Member States were at stake.[67] In the 1980s, this convention was applied with less force, and matters are now decided by majority votes. The Single European Act amended various Treaty provisions by substituting a qualified majority procedure for a requirement of unanimity. This process was continued by the Maastricht Treaty.

(c) The European Parliament[68]

The Parliament consists of "representatives of the peoples" of the Member States. In 1994, the members were directedly elected, in the following proportions[69]

Germany	99
France, Italy and the United Kingdom	87 each
Spain	64
Netherlands	31
Belgium, Greece and Portugal	25 each
Sweden	22
Austria	21
Denmark, Finland	16 each
Ireland	15
Luxembourg	6
	626

---

[66] Following the accession of Austria, Finland and Sweden, the "blocking minority" of votes was raised from 23 to 26; however, by virtue of the so-called "Ioannina Compromise", where there are 23 to 25 against a proposal, the Council "will do all in its power to reach . . . a satisfactory solution that could be adopted by at least 65 votes": see Weatherill and Beaumont (1995), pp. 81–82.

[67] This was reflected in the so-called "Luxembourg Accords" of January 1966: a press release enshrining the part agreement/part truce that ended a dispute between France and the, then five, other Member States.

[68] Articles 137–144/EC, as amended by Art. G(39)–(42)/TEU. The Parliament was referred to as the Assembly in the Treaties. It resolved to call itself the "European Parliament" in 1962, and that title was recognised in the Single European Act. See F. Jacobs, et al., The European Parliament (1992); M. Westake, The Commission and the Parliament (1994).

[69] Decision and Act of the Council Concerning Direct Elections 1976, Art. 2, as amended by the Acts of Accession of Greece, Art. 10, and of Spain and Portugal, Art. 10, Council Decisioon 93/81 and Act of Accession of Austria, Finland and Sweden, Art. 11.

This does not reflect populations: in those terms the smaller states are over-represented. Members sit in political groupings rather than by country. Much of the work is done by committees.

The Parliament exercises the powers conferred by the Treaties.[70] These have become more extensive over time.

It puts Questions to the Council and the Commission, and is involved in a consultative capacity in the legislative process, its role here having been strengthened by the Single European Act and the Maastricht Treaty.[71] It now has a veto over the admission of new Member States, the conclusion of association agreements with other states and certain legislative proposals.[72] It has had a progressively greater say in the determination of the Community's Budget.[73] Provisions added by the Maastricht Treaty enable the Parliament to request proposals from the Commission on matters on which it considers that a Community act is required to implement the Treaty and to set up temporary committees of inquiry; require it to appoint an Ombudsman; and entitle EU citizens, and other natural or legal persons resident or with a registered office in a Member State to address petitions to it on Community matters which affect him, her or it directly.[74]

(d) Other institutions

Other organs of the Community include the Economic and Social Committee,[75] with members from each Member State representing employers, workers and others (*e.g.* consumers, farmers and the professions), which advises both Council and Commission; the Court of Auditors,[76] which carries out the audit and assists the Council and the Parliament in exercising their powers of control over implementation of the budget; the Committee of the Regions which represents regional and local bodies within the EC; and the European Investment Bank.

Finally, the arrangements for a common foreign and security policy and for cooperation in the fields of justice and home affairs are found, respectively, in Title V (Art.J) and Title VI (Art.K) of the Maastricht Treaty. Title V replaces provision for European political cooperation that had been recognised in Title III of the Single European Act. The EU is to establish "systematic cooperation between Member States in the conduct of policy" and gradually implement "joint action in the areas in which the Member States have important interests in common;" Member States are to "support the Union's external and security policy actively and unreservedly in a spirit of loyalty and mutual solidarity."[77] The EU is represented by the Presidency in matters within the CFSP, and the Presidency in association with the Commission is responsible for the implementation of common measures.[78] The general principles of and general guidelines

---

[70] Art. 137/EC, as amended by Art. G(39)/TEU. These are no longer described as "advisory and supervisory powers".

[71] See below, pp. 327–329.

[72] Art. O/TEU; Art. 228(3)/EC, as amended by Art. G(80)/TEU; Art. 8a(2)/EC, inserted by Art. G.C/TEU (legislation facilitating the exercise of the right of EU citizens to move and reside freely within the territory of the Member States).

[73] Hartley (1994) pp. 49–53.

[74] Arts.138b, 138c, 138d, 138e/EC, added by Art. G(41)/TEU.

[75] Arts.193–198/EC.

[76] Arts.188a–188c, inserted by Art. G(59)/TEU.

[77] Art. J.1/TEU.

[78] Arts. J.5, J.9/TEU.

for the CFSP are defined by the European Council;[79] decisions necessary for defining and implementing the policy are taken by the Council.[80]

Under Title VI, Member States are to co-ordinate their action in a number of specified areas: asylum policy; external border controls; immigration policy and policy regarding nationals of third countries; drug addiction; international fraud; judicial co-operation in civil and criminal matters; customs co-operation; and police co-operation in respect of terrorism, drug-trafficking and other serious forms of international crime. The Council may adopt joint positions on action and may draw up conventions recommended to Member States for adoption.

At the apex of these structures is the European Council—regular conferences of the Heads of State or of Government and the foreign ministers of the Member States. These were informal meetings, attended by representatives of the Commission, but a regular constitution for them was provided by Article 2 of the Single European Act and now by Article D of the Maastricht Treaty, under which the European Council is to "provide the Union with the necessary impetus for its development" and "define the general political guidelines thereof." When discussing Community matters, the European Council acts as the Council of Ministers, but the two are technically distinct.

3. The Kinds of Community Legislation

(a) Treaty provisions concerning Community legislation

The different kinds of Community acts are described in Article 189 of the EC Treaty[81]:

"In order to carry out their task and in accordance with the provisions of this Treaty, the European Parliament acting jointly with the Council, the Council and the Commission shall make regulations and issue directives, take decisions, make recommendations or deliver opinions.

A regulation shall have general application. It shall be binding in its entirety and directly applicable in all Member States.

A directive shall be binding, as to the result to be achieved, upon each Member State to which it is addressed, but shall leave to the national authorities the choice of form and methods.

A decision shall be binding in its entirety upon those to whom it is addressed.

---

[79] See below.
[80] Art. J.8/TEU.
[81] As amended by Art. 6 (60)/TEU. See also Art. 14/ECSC and Art. 161/Euratom. The terminology of ECSC acts is different:

EEC Euratom	ECSC
Regulations Decisions	Decisions
Directives	Recommendations
Recommendations Opinions	Opinions

The following discussion is generally confined to EC legislation.

Recommendations and opinions shall have no binding force.''

Recommendations and opinions cannot be regarded as legislative as they do not have binding effect; it has also been suggested that decisions directed to individuals, as distinct from Member States, are administrative rather than legislative in character.[82]

The Treaties require that regulations, directives and decisions state the reasons on which they are based and refer to any proposals or opinions that were required to be obtained pursuant to other Treaty provisions.[83] Regulations, directives and decisions adopted by the Parliament and the Council jointly, regulations of the Council and the Commission, and directives of those institutions addressed to all Member States. must be published in the Official Journal. They enter into force on the date specified in them, or, if no date is specified, on the twentieth day following their publication. Other directives and decisions must be notified to those to whom they are addressed and take effect upon such notification.[84]

(b) Legislative powers[85]

Under the EC and Euratom Treaties, the major policy decisions and legislative powers are reserved to the Council; the Commission being involved with (in most cases) the formulation of legislative proposals and with the implementation of decisions. However, the Commission does have some legislative powers conferred upon it by the EC Treaty.[86] Furthermore, its position has been strengthened in two ways.

First, procedures have been developed for the delegation of functions from the Council to the Commission. A distinction is drawn between the laying down of general principles and detailed implementation. Only the latter process may be delegated, but that may involve rule-making by the Commission. Such arrangements were held to be lawful by the Court of Justice.[87] Express authority was provided for them by Article 10 of the Single European Act, amending Article 145/EC. Acts adopted by the Council must confer power for the implementation of the rules laid down therein by the Commission, unless (''in specific cases'') the Council reserves the right to exercise directly implementing powers itself. The Council may impose certain requirements in respect of the exercise of these delegated powers, in conformity with procedures prescribed by a Council Decision. The ''Commitology'' Decision was adopted in 1987,[88] and corresponded for the most part to the previous informal arrangements. Other

---

[82] Case 19/77, *Miller v. Commission* [1978] E.C.R. 131, 161 *per* A. G. Warner.

[83] Art. 190/EC, as amended by Art. G(62)/TEU.

[84] Art. 191/EC, as amended by Art. G(63)/TEU.

[85] See Hartley (1994), pp. 38–48, 110–136; R. Baldwin, *Rules and Government* (1995), Chap. 8.

[86] See T. C. Hartley, (1988) 13 E.L. Rev. 122–123; Cases 88–90/80, *France, Italy and the United Kingdom v. Commission* [1982] E.C.R. 2545.

[87] Case 25/70, *Einfuhr – und Vorratsstelle v. Köster* [1970] E.C.R. 1161; Case 41/69, *Chemiefarma v. Commission* [1970] E.C.R. 661; Case 23/75, *Rey Soda v. Cassa Conguaglio Zuchero* [1975] E.C.R. 1279; *cf.* Case 264/86, *France v. Commission* [1988] E.C.R. 973.

[88] Dec. 87/373, O.J. 1987, L 197/33, reproduced in Westlake (1994), *op. cit.* n. 68 above, pp. 113–115. See K. St. C. Bradley, ''Commitology and the law; through a glass, darkly'' (1992) 29 C.M.L. Rev. 693.

than in the "specific cases" mentioned above, the Council may select one of a series of procedures set out in the Decision.[89]

Each procedure requires the Commission to consult a committee comprising representatives of the Member States, and chaired by a representative of the Commission. The committee must deliver its opinion within a time limit laid down by the Chairman according to the urgency of the matter.

Procedure I involves an "advisory committee". As the name suggests, the Commission must "take the utmost account of the opinion delivered by the committee" but is not bound by it. Procedure II involves a "management committee", which forms an opinion acting by a qualified majority. The Commission may proceed to adopt the measure in question, but where it is not in accordance with the committee's opinion, the Council must be informed. There is then a period within which the Council, acting by a qualified majority, may substitute a different decision: under "Variant (a)", a period, determined by the Commission, not exceeding one month; under "Variant (b)", a period not exceeding three months specified by the Council in the original act. Procedure III involves a "regulatory committee", again acting by a qualified majority. The Commission can only adopt the measures forthwith if they are in accordance with the opinion of the committee. If they are not, or if no opinion is delivered, the Commission has to submit to the Council a proposal relating to the measures to be taken, the Council responding by a qualified majority. Then, under "Variant (a)", if the Council has not acted within a period (not exceeding three months) specified in the original act, the proposed measures are to be adopted by the Commission. "Variant (b)" is the same as "Variant (a)", except that the Council can block the measure acting by a simple majority, without formulating its own measures.

The Commission has expressed reservations concerning these procedures, and has complained that the Council has only infrequently adopted the advisory committee procedure, preferring to use "delegation procedures which allow the national authorities to block legislation."[90] The Parliament sought to have the Decision annulled under Article 173, but the European Court held that it did not have capacity to bring such an action.[91] A temporary *modus vivendi* has been agreed in respect of the application of these procedures to the co-decision legislative procedure, pending further consideration at the 1996 Intergovernmental Conference.[92] Under this, draft implementing acts are also to be referred to the appropriate committee of the Parliament, and, where acts go to the Council, the Council is to take "due account" of an unfavourable opinion of the Parliament. Subject to its reservation concerning the IIIb procedure, the Commission currently believes that these procedures operate satisfactorily, noting that of several thousand committee opinions adopted over the last three years,

---

[89] The Decision also prescribes a procedure that may be applied where the Council confers on the Commission the power to decide on "safeguard measures": Art. 3.

[90] See Commission, 21st General Report on the Activities of the European Communities, 1987, point 4; 22nd General Report, 1988, point 9. The Commission has undertaken never to propose variant III(b), where a simple Council majority can block a decision and safeguard measure (b), where the Council can modify or annul by a qualified majority and failure to act results in no decision being taken: Westlake (1994), p. 71.

[91] Case 302/87, *European Parliament v. Council* [1988] E.C.R. 5615.

[92] O.J. C43, February 20, 1995, p. 37.

six decisions were referred back to the Council and there were no cases where no decision was taken.[93]

The second means by which the Commission's powers have been strengthened is by the recognition by the European Court that it enjoys certain *implied* legislative powers. In *Germany v. Commission*[94] the European Court held that:

> "where an Article of the EEC Treaty—in this case Article 118—confers a specific task on the Commission it must be accepted, if that provision is not to be rendered wholly ineffective, that it confers on the Commission necessarily and *per se* the powers which are indispensable in order to carry out that task."[95]

It then proceeded to hold that the Commission enjoyed all "necessary" powers (rather than "indispensible") and took a generous view of what was "necessary".[96] It has been noted that:

> "Since the EC Treaty confers many tasks on the Commission, including such wide-ranging functions as that of ensuring that the provisions of the Treaty are applied,[97] this judgment is potentially very significant and could herald an era of increased Commission law-making."[98]

(c) Direct applicability and direct effect

A distinction is sometimes drawn between the terms *direct applicability* and *direct effect*.[99] Article 189 of the EC Treaty provides that regulations are "directly applicable" in all Member States; they come into force without any act of implementation by Member States. No other form of Community law is expressly stated in the treaties to be directly *applicable*, and it was at first thought that those other forms of law could only take *effect* within Member States if there was an act of implementation. However, the Court of Justice developed the view that treaty provisions could in principle confer rights and impose obligations directly upon individuals irrespective of any act of implementation. In the *Van Gend en Loos* case[1] the plaintiff claimed before a Dutch tribunal that there had been an increase in import duties which was rendered illegal by Article 12[2] of the EC Treaty. The Court of Justice, on a

---

[93] *Commission Report for the Reflection Group* (1995), p. 31.
[94] Cases 281, 283–285, 287/85, [1987] E.C.R. 3203.
[95] *ibid.*, p. 3253.
[96] T. C. Hartley, (1988) 13 E.L. Rev. 122.
[97] Art. 155/EC.
[98] Hartley (1994), p. 111. See also the "supplementary means of action" available to the Council under Art. 235/EC: *ibid.*, pp. 111–115.
[99] See J. A. Winter, (1972) 9 C.M.L.R. 425; J.-P. Warner, (1977) 93 L.Q.R. 349; A. Dashwood, (1977–78) 16 J. of Common Market Studies 229; J. Steiner, (1982) 98 L.Q.R. 229, (1990) 106 L.Q.R. 144 and (1993) 18 E.L. Rev. 3; P. Pescatore, (1983) 8 E.L. Rev 155; N. Green, (1984) 9 E.L. Rev. 295; D. Curtin, (1990) 15 E.L. Rev. 195 and (1990) 27 C.M.L. Rev. 709; P. Craig, (1992) 12 O.J.L.S. 453; G. De Búrca, (1992) 55 M.L.R. 215; N. Maltby, (1993) 109 L.O.R. 301; Plaza Martin, (1994) 43 I.C.L.Q. 26.
[1] Case 26/62, *Van Gend en Loos v. Nederlandse Administratie Der Belastingen* [1963] E.C.R. 1.
[2] "Member States shall refrain from introducing between themselves any new customs duties on imports or exports or any charges having equivalent effect, and from increasing those which they already apply in their trade with each other."

reference from the tribunal, held that Article 12 was indeed directly effective, and could be relied upon by the plaintiff in this case. The court stated[3]:

"To ascertain whether the provisions of an international treaty extend so far in their effects it is necessary to consider the spirit, the general scheme and the wording of those provisions.

The objective of the EEC Treaty, which is to establish a Common Market, the functioning of which is of direct concern to interested parties in the Community, implies that this Treaty is more than an agreement which merely creates mutual obligations between the contracting states. This view is confirmed by the preamble to the Treaty which refers not only to governments but to peoples. It is also confirmed more specifically by the establishment of institutions endowed with sovereign rights, the exercise of which affects Member States and also their citizens. Furthermore, it must be noted that the nationals of the states brought together in the Community are called upon to cooperate in the functioning of this Community through the intermediary of the European Parliament and the Economic and Social Committee.

In addition the task assigned to the Court of Justice under Article 177, the object of which is to secure uniform interpretation of the Treaty by national courts and tribunals, confirms that the states have acknowledged that Community law has an authority which can be invoked by their nationals before those courts and tribunals.

The conclusion to be drawn from this is that the Community constitutes a new legal order of international law for the benefit of which the states have limited their sovereign rights, albeit within limited fields, and the subjects of which comprise not only Member States but also their nationals. Independently of the legislation of Member States, Community law therefore not only imposes obligations on individuals but is also intended to confer upon them rights which become part of their legal heritage. These rights arise not only where they are expressly granted by the Treaty, but also by reason of obligations which the Treaty imposes in a clearly defined way upon individuals as well as upon the Member States and upon the institutions of the Community."

Article 12 imposed a clear and unconditional negative prohibition, "ideally adapted to produce direct effects in the legal relationship between Member States and their subjects."

In this and subsequent cases the Court of Justice has elaborated the criteria by which those *treaty provisions* that are regarded as directly effective are to be distinguished from those that are not. As more provisions have come before the court for consideration, the overall picture has become clearer.[4] The criteria[5] are:

---

[3] pp. 12–13.

[4] A useful table is given in Collins (1990), pp. 122–126.

[5] As formulated by A. G. Mayras in Case 41/74, *Van Duyn v. Home Office* [1974] E.C.R. 1337, 1354. See *e.g. Application des Gaz v. Falks Veritas* [1974] Ch. 381 (Articles 85 and 86/EC); *Rio Tinto Zinc Corporation v. Westinghouse Electric Corporation* [1978] A.C. 547 (Article 85).

"—the provision must impose a clear and precise obligation on Member States;

—it must be unconditional, in other words subject to no limitation; if, however, a provision is subject to certain limitations, their nature and extent must be exactly defined;

—finally, the implementation of a Community rule must not be subject to the adoption of any subsequent rules or regulations on the part either of the Community institutions or of the Member States, so that, in particular, Member States must not be left any real discretion with regard to the application of the rule in question."

A provision may, exceptionally, be held to have direct effect prospectively only.[6]

The Court of Justice has subsequently invoked these criteria to hold that *decisions* addressed to Member States,[7] *directives*[8] and agreements between the Community and non-Member States[9] can be directly effective. *Van Duyn v. Home Office* concerned Article 48 of the EC Treaty, which provided for the "freedom of movement" of workers, including the right to enter and stay in any Member State "subject to limitations justified on grounds of public policy, public security or public health." The scope of these limitations was further regulated by Council Directive 64/221 which provided in Art. 3(1) that, "Measures taken on grounds of public policy or of public security shall be based exclusively on the personal conduct of the individual concerned." Miss Yvonne Van Duyn, a Dutch national, was refused leave to enter the United Kingdom on the ground that she was intending to work for the Church of Scientology. The government regarded scientology as socially harmful, and although it had no power to prohibit its practice it had decided to take steps, within its powers, to curb its growth. Accordingly it decided that foreign nationals such as Miss Van Duyn should be refused entry. She claimed that the refusal was not based on her "personal conduct" and challenged its validity in the High Court. Several questions were referred to the European Court, which held (1) that Article 48 was directly effective; (2) that the relevant provision of directive 64/221 was also directly effective; but (3) that a Member State was entitled to take into

---

[6] Case 43/75, *Defrenne v. Sabena (No. 2)* [1976] E.C.R. 455. This case concerned the direct effect of Art. 119/EEC (equal pay for men and women). The court stated: "As the general level at which pay would have been fixed cannot be known, important considerations of legal certainty affecting all the interests involved, both public and private, make it impossible in principle to reopen the question as regards the past" (p. 481). See T. Koopmans, [1980] C.L.J. 287; M. Waelbroeck, [1981] 1 Y.E.L. 115. This principle was applied in Case 309/85, *Barra v. Belgium* [1988] E.C.R. 355; Case 24/86, *Blaizot v. University of Liege* [1988] E.C.R. 379; Case C-262/88, *Barber v. Guardian Royal Exchange Assurance Group* [1990] E.C.R. I-1889; A. Arnull, (1988) 13 E.L. Rev. 260.

[7] See Case 9/70, *Grad v. Finanzamt Traunstein* [1970] E.C.R. 325: this concerned a decision which prohibited member states from applying specific taxes concurrently with the common turnover tax (VAT) system due to be implemented by directive.

[8] See Case 41/74, *Van Duyn v. Home Office* [1974] E.C.R. 1337; Case 148/78, *Pubblico Ministero v. Ratti* [1979] E.C.R. 162; Case 102/79, *Commission v. Belgium* [1980] E.C.R. 1473; Case 8/81, *Becker v. Finanzamt Münster-Innenstadt* [1982] E.C.R. 53. In Case 131/79, *R. v. Secretary of State for the Home Department, ex p. Santillo* [1980] E.C.R. 1585, 1610–11, A. G. Warner argued that the conditions for the direct effectiveness of Treaty provisions were subject to some qualification when applied to directives. In particular, there will nearly always be some element of discretion which will not, however, prevent a directive being held to be directly effective. See generally, D. Curtin, (1990) 15 E.L. Rev. 195.

[9] Case 104/81, *Kupferberg* [1982] E.C.R. 3641.

account as a matter of personal conduct that the individual was associated with an organisation whose activities were considered by the state to be socially harmful.

There are, however, limitations:

"the European Court has held that directives can only confer rights on individuals (against the State); they cannot impose obligations on individuals (in favour of the State or other individuals). This means that directives are capable of only 'vertical' direct effect; unlike regulations and Treaty provisions, they are not capable of 'horizontal' direct effect."[10]

The leading case here is *Marshall v Southampton and South West Hampshire Area Health Authority (Teaching)*.[11] Miss Marshall was dismissed by the Authority from her post as a dietician when she was 62, although she wished to continue to 65. It was the Authority's policy that the normal retiring age for its employees was the age at which state retirement pensions became payable. For women, this was 60. (The Authority had waived its policy for two years in respect of Miss Marshall.) The Court held that Article 5(1) of Council Directive 76/207 (the "Equal Treatment Directive") was to be interpreted as meaning that a general policy involving the dismissal of a woman solely because she had attained or passed the qualifying age for state pension, which age was different under national legislation for men and for women, constituted discrimination on the ground of sex, contrary to that directive. It could be relied upon against a state authority acting in its capacity as employer: the principle was not confined to governmental acts. It was for the national court to determine whether the Health Authority was a "state authority" for this purpose, although the Court noted that in the order for reference the Court of Appeal had referred to it as a "public authority." The Court stated that as Art. 189/EEC provided that a directive was binding "upon each Member State to which it is addressed", it followed

"that a directive may not of itself impose obligations on an individual and that a provision of a directive may not be relied upon as such against such a person."[12]

Accordingly, the Court of Justice has held that a Member State cannot base

---

[10] Hartley (1994), p. 217.

[11] Case 152/84, [1986] Q.B. 401, [1986] E.C.R. 723 (*Marshall I*). See A. Arnull, (1986) 35 I.C.L.Q. 939 and [1987] P.L. 383; T. Millett, (1987) 36 I.C.L.Q. 616; N. Foster, (1987) 12 E.L. Rev. 222. In subsequent proceedings, the European Court held that Art.6 of the Equal Treatment directive, which required Member States to introduce measures enabling the victims of unlawful discrimination to "pursue their claims by judicial process", was directly effective, and precluded the imposition of limits to the amount of compensation recoverable or the exclusion of an element for interest: Case C-271/91, *Marshall v. Southampton and South West Hampshire Area Health Authority (No. 2)* [1994] Q.B. 126. Accordingly, the statutory limit to compensation for sex discrimination (Sex Discrimination Act 1975, s.65(2)) was not applicable to claims based on Community Law: see the House of Lords decision in *Marshall (No.2)*, restoring the award of the industrial tribunal: [1994] 1 A.C. 530. Section 65(2) was subsequently repealed and provision made for the award of interest by the Sex Discrimination and Equal Pay (Remedies) Regulations 1993 (S.I. 1993 No. 2798).

[12] [1986] Q.B. 401, 422.

criminal proceedings against an individual on the provisions of an unimplemented directive.[13]

The ruling against "horizontal direct effect" has been criticised as having
"serious consequences for the rights of the individual."[14] It has been suggested
that it can be seen as a compromise between, on the one hand, the desire to
give maximum effectiveness to directives and, on the other, the argument based
on the wording of Article 189 and doubts expressed by courts in France (the
Conseil d'Etat) and Germany (the *Bundesfinanzhof*) to the effect that directives
should not be regarded as having *any* direct effect.[15] In any event, the ruling
has been reaffirmed by the Court of Justice in *Paola Faccini Dori v. Recreb
SrL*,[16] where a consumer in proceedings with a trader sought to rely on the
provisions of a directive on consumer protection.[17] The relevant events[18] took
place in 1989 and the directive was only implemented in Italy in 1992. The
Court held that the relevant provisions were unconditional and sufficiently precise in terms of the direct effect doctrine; however, to extend that doctrine to
relations between individuals

> "would be to recognise a power in the Community to enact obligations
> for individuals with immediate effect, whereas it has competence to do so
> only where it is empowered to adopt regulations."[19]

Instead, private individuals had to rely on the principles of the *Marleasing* and
Francovich cases.[20] In reaching this conclusion the Court declined to follow the
opinion of Advocate General Lenz,[21] who argued that directives should be
accorded horizontal direct effect, albeit only for the future, in the interests of
the effective, uniform application of Community law.

Four further points should be noted. First, it has become necessary to determine what amounts to a "state authority". The English courts initially took a
narrow view, holding that directives could give rise to legal rights

> "in employees of the State itself and of any organ or emanation of the
> State, an emanation of the State being understood to include an independent
> public authority charged by the State with the performance of any of the
> classic duties of the State, such as the defence of the realm or the mainten-
> ance of law and order within the realm."[22]

---

[13] Case 14/86, *Pretore di Salo v. Persons Unknown* [1987] E.C.R. 2545, 2569–2570: A. Arnull,
(1988) 13 E.L. Rev. 40; Case 80/86, *Kolpinghuis* [1987] E.C.R. 3969: A. Arnull, (1988) 13 E.L.
Rev. 42.

[14] Arnull, (1986) 35 I.C.L.Q. 939, 943.

[15] Hartley (1994), pp. 216–218.

[16] Case C-91/92, [1994] E.C.R. I-3325. See W. Robinson, (1995) 32 C.M.L. Rev. 629; J. Coppel,
(1994) 57 M.L.R. 859; D. Kinley [1995] I E.P.L. 79.

[17] Dir.85/577/EEC, concerning protection of the consumer in respect of contracts negotiated away
from business premises.

[18] Ms Faccini Dori sought to rely on the directive in claiming the right to cancel a contract for an
English language correspondence course concluded at Milan Central Railway Station.

[19] p. I-3356, para. 24.

[20] See below, pp. 320–324.

[21] [1994] E.C.R. I-3338–I-3345.

[22] *per* Lord Donaldson in *Foster v. British Gas plc* [1988] I.R.L.R. 354, 356.

This did not cover the British Gas Corporation,[23] and Rolls-Royce plc[24] in the period before privatisation. Conversely, a woman police officer who was a member of the Royal Ulster Constabulary Reserve was entitled to rely on the Equal Treatment Directive (76/207) against the Chief Constable,[25] and a regulatory agency acting on behalf of local authorities was held to be an emanation of the State.[26] The Court of Justice, however, took a broader view. In *Foster v. British Gas plc*[27] it held that the Court had jurisdiction in a preliminary ruling to determine the categories of person against whom the provisions of a directive may be relied on, and that it was for national courts to determine whether a party before them fell into one of the categories so defined. The categories include "a body, whatever its legal form, which has been made responsible, pursuant to a measure adopted by the state, for providing a public service under the control of the State and has for that purpose special powers beyond those which result from the normal rules applicable in relations between individuals".[28] In the light of this ruling, the House of Lords held that British Gas, when a nationalised industry, was an emanation of the state.[29] Conversely, the Court of Appeal confirmed that Rolls-Royce plc was not,[30] concluding that the fact of state ownership of a company was not sufficient where the company was not providing a public service and had no special powers.[31] Furthermore, the Employment Appeal Tribunal has held that the governing body of a voluntary-aided school was not an emanation of the state; although they provided a public service, the service was not under the control of the state and the governing body was not an agency of the state and had no special powers.[32]

Secondly, the Court of Justice has held that Community law precludes Member States in proceedings against them in national courts based on unimplemented but directly effective directive provisions from relying on national procedural rules relating to time limits.[33] However, this does not prevent Member States from setting a time limit to retrospective claims for arrears of benefit based on such provisions, provided that the same time limit applies to claims to benefit arrears under national law and that the rule is not framed so as to render virtually impossible the exercise of rights conferred by Community law.[34]

---

[23] *Foster v. British Gas plc*, above.

[24] *Rolls-Royce plc v. Doughty* [1988] 1 C.M.L.R. 569, E.A.T.

[25] Case 222/84, *Johnston v. Chief Constable of the Royal Ulster Constabulary* [1986] E.C.R. 1651, [1987] Q.B. 129; A. Arnull, (1987) 12 E.L. Rev. 56;

[26] *R. v. London Boroughs Transport Committee, ex p. Freight Transport Association Ltd* [1990] C.M.L.R. 229.

[27] Case C-188/89 [1990] E.C.R. I-3330.

[28] Paras.20, 22 and the ruling. Para.18, by contrast, refers to "organisations or bodies which were subject to the authority of the state *or* had special powers beyond those which result from the normal rules applicable to relations between individuals" (emphasis added).

[29] *Foster v. British Gas plc* [1991] 2 A.C. 306.

[30] *Doughty v. Rolls-Royce* [1992] I.C.R. 538.

[31] Relying on the terms of the ruling of the Court of Justice in *Foster* rather than para. 18, and on the subsequent approach of the House of Lords in the same case: [1991] 2 A.C. 306.

[32] *National Union of Teachers v. Governing Body of St Mary's Church of England (Aided) Junior School* [1995] I.C.R. 317.

[33] Case C-208/90, *Emmott v. Minister for Social Welfare* [1991] E.C.R. I-3723, in respect of the three-month time limit for applications for judicial review in Ireland.

[34] Case C-338/91, *Steenhorst-Neerings v. Bestuur van de Bedrijfsvereniging voor Detailhandel, Ambachten en Huisvrouwen* [1993] E.C.R. I-5475; Case C-410/92, *Johnson v. Chief Adjudication Officer (No. 2)* [1995] All E.R. (E.C.) 258.

Thirdly, it was of course still necessary notwithstanding *Marshall* for the United Kingdom to take legislative steps to implement the directive in question so as to extend its benefits to all employees. This was done by the Sex Discrimination Act 1986,[35] which took effect from November 7, 1987.

Fourthly, the courts have considered whether the unamended U.K. legislation[36] could be interpreted in accordance with the Equal Treatment Directive so as to render differential retirement ages for men and women unlawful. The House of Lords in *Duke v. Reliance Systems Ltd*[37] held that it could not. This point is taken up in the following section.

Overall, Member States have tended to present arguments to the Court of Justice against direct effectiveness; Community institutions have tended, not surprisingly, to argue in favour, given that it strengthens their position at the expense of individual Member States, and helps ensure that Community law applies uniformly throughout the Member States. It enables individuals to take action to enforce the requirements of Community law without having to rely on Community institutions to act. It has also been stressed that it is inappropriate for a Member State that has failed to implement a directive or decision addressed to it to rely, in proceedings between itself and an individual, on its own failure to comply with that directive or decision on the basis that it is not directly effective.[38]

It has been argued that the

"granting of direct effect to directives has probably done more than any other initiative by the European Court to enhance the effectiveness of Community law."[39]

Although a regulation is "directly applicable" by virtue of Article 189, it will not necessarily create rights and obligations which may be enforced in national courts. This depends on the wording of the regulation in question[40]: it has been argued that regulations only have "direct effect" if the criteria applicable to treaty provisions and other kinds of Community secondary legislation are fulfilled.[41]

Finally, it should be noted that in these and other cases in this area the Court of Justice has not been consistent in its use of the *terms* "directly applicable" and "direct effect," but has tended to use them interchangeably.[42]

(d) Indirect effect

The limitations on the direct effect doctrine in the context of directives have focused attention on the extent to which unimplemented directives may have

[35] ss.2, 3. See B. Fitzpatrick, (1987) 50 M.L.R. 934.
[36] Sex Discrimination Act 1975, ss.1, 6.
[37] [1988] A.C. 618. See below, pp. 339–341.
[38] Case 148/78, *Pubblico Ministero v. Ratti* [1979] E.C.R. 1624, 1650: A. G. Reischl; *Marshall* [1986] Q.B. 401, 421–422.
[39] Hartley (1994), p. 215.
[40] Usher (1981) *op. cit.* p. 305, n. 44, pp. 18–19.
[41] A. G. Warner in Case 31/74, *Galli* [1975] E.C.R. 47 and Case 74/76, *Iannelli v. Meroni; Steinike and Weinlig v. Germany* [1977] E.C.R. 557, 583; A. G. Reischl in *Ratti*, n. 38 above.
[42] But see A. G. Warner in *Iannelli v. Merioni* [1977] E.C.R. 557 at 583 and A. G. Slynn in Case 8/81, *Becker* [1982] 1 C.M.L.R. 499, 504–5; in *Ratti*, above, A. G. Reischl argued that the term "direct applicability" should only be used in respect of *regulations*.

"indirect effect". An issue has arisen as to the extent to which national courts should have regard to an unimplemented directive in *interpreting* national legislation. Furthermore, the Court of Justice has held that the failure of a Member State to implement a directive may give rise to a liability in damages.

The Court of Justice has developed its view on the first issue over a series of cases. In *Von Colson and Kamann v. Land Nordrhein-Westfalen*,[43] it stated that even where a directive does not have direct effects,

"in applying the national law and in particular the provisions of a national law specifically introduced in order to implement Directive 76/207, national courts are required to interpret their national law in the light of the wording and purpose of the directive in order to achieve the result referred to in the third paragraph of Article 189."[44]

This is so whether or not the time for implementing the directive has expired.[45] It was suggested by A. G. Slynn in *Marshall v. Southampton and South West Hampshire Area Health Authority (Teaching)*[46] that this principle did not apply to require a national court to interpret legislation so that it accords with a *later* directive, "unless it is clear that the legislation was adopted with a proposed directive in mind."[47] This was criticised as too restrictive an approach,[48] but it was adopted by the House of Lords in *Duke v. Reliance Systems Ltd.*[49] However, in *Marleasing SA v. La Comercial Internacional de Alimentación SA*[50] the Court of Justice adopted a broader view. Marleasing sought an order in the Spanish courts for the annulment of a company (La Comercial) under provisions of the Spanish Civil Code that contracts lacking cause or whose cause is unlawful have no legal effect. It was alleged that La Comercial had been established as part of a scheme to defraud the creditors of another company. However, a subsequent EC directive[51] set out an exclusive list of the cases in which the nullity of a company may be declared, and lack of (lawful) cause was not on the list. The Court of Justice stated[52] that:

"the Member States' obligations arising from a directive to achieve the result envisaged by the directive and a duty under Article 5 of the Treaty to take all appropriate measures, whether general or particular, to ensure the fulfilment of that obligation, is binding on all the authorities of Member States including, for matters within their jurisdiction, the courts. It follows

---

[43] Case 14/83, [1984] E.C.R. 1891, 1909.
[44] This passage appears in the Court's reasoning: the operative part of the judgment refers only to legislation adopted for the implementation of the directive. The principle was invoked in the narrower context in Case 262/84, *Beets-Proper v. Van Lanschot Bankiers N.V.* [1986] E.C.R. 782; A. Arnull (1987) 12 E.L. Rev. 229. However, the Court repeated the wider formulation in Case 80/86, *Kolpinghuis Nijmegen B.V.* [1987] E.C.R. 3969; A. Arnull, (1988) 13 E.L. Rev. 42.
[45] *Kolpinghuis*, above.
[46] [1986] Q.B. 401.
[47] *ibid.*, p. 411.
[48] A. Arnull, [1988] P.L. 313, 317.
[49] [1988] A.C. 618, above, criticised by Arnull, *op. cit.* See also *Organon Laboratories Ltd v. D.H.S.S.* [1990] 2 C.M.L.R. 49.
[50] Case C-106/89 [1990] I-E.C.R.4135. See G. de Burca, (1992) 55 M.L.R. 215; Prechal, (1990) 27 C.M.L. Rev. 451; P. Mead, (1991) 16 E.L. Rev. 490; N. Maltby, (1993) 109 L.Q.R. 301.
[51] First Council Directive 68/151/EEC, March 9, 1968, Art. 11.
[52] At p. I-4159, para. 8.

that, in applying national law, whether the provisions in the decision were adopted before or after the directive, the national court called upon to interpret it is required to do so, as far as possible, in the light of the wording and the purpose of the directive in order to achieve the result pursued by the latter and thereby comply with the third paragraph of Article 189 of the Treaty.''

Accordingly, a national court having a case within the scope of the directive was

"required to interpret its national law in the light of the wording and the purpose of that directive in order to preclude a declaration of nullity of a public limited company on a ground other than those listed in Article 11 of the directive.''[53]

While this is a strong statement, its limits should be noted. It must be remembered that it only arises where there is an issue of *interpretation* of national law. It cannot mean that the directive must be applied irrespective of the wording of national law, for that would be to apply the direct effect doctrine between individuals, a step that the court has consistently refused to take, as in the *Marleasing* case itself.[54] This point is confirmed by the inclusion of the words "as far as possible" in paragraph 8 of the judgment.[55] The *Marleasing* approach has, subject to this understanding, been accepted by the English courts.[56]

Of potentially greater significance was the decision of the Court of Justice in *Andrea Francovich and others v. Italian Republic*.[57] A 1980 EC directive[58] provided, *inter alia*, for specific guarantees of the payment of unpaid wage claims in the event of an employer's insolvency. The deadline for implementation was October 23, 1983; Italy failed to fulfil its implementation obligation.[59] A number of workers unable to recover unpaid wages from their employers brought proceedings against the state, claiming fulfilment of the guarantees by the state or, in the alternative, compensation. The Court of Justice held (1) that the provisions of the directive were not directly effective[60]; but (2) that in order to promote the full effectiveness of Community rules, "it is a principle of Community law that the Member States are obliged to make good loss and damages caused to individuals by breaches of Community law for which they can be held responsible.''[61] A further basis for this obligation was Article 5/EC, under which Member States are required to take all appropriate measures to ensure fulfilment of their obligations under Community law; among these is the obligation to

---

[53] At p. I-4160, para. 13.
[54] At p. I-4158, para. 6.
[55] See N. Maltby, (1993) 109 L.Q.R. 301, "It does not oblige the national court to interpret national law . . . *contra legem*": A.G. Van Gerven in Case C-271/91, *Marshall v. Southampton and South West Hampshire Area Health Authority (No. 2)* [1993] 4 All E.R. 586, 605.
[56] *Webb v. EMO Air Cargo Ltd* [1992] 4 All E.R. 929, below, p. 342.
[57] Cases C-6/90 and C-9/90, [1991] I-5357. See G. Bebr, (1992) 29 C.M.L.R. 557; P. Duffy, [1992] 17 E.L. Rev. 133; R. Caranta, [1993] C.L.J. 272; P. P. Craig (1993) 109 L.Q.R. 595; J. Steiner, [1993] 18 E.L. Rev. 3; C. Lewis and S. Moore, [1993] P.L. 151; M. Ross, (1993) 56 M.L.R. 55.
[58] Dir.80/887/EEC.
[59] Confirmed in Case 22/87, *Commission v. Italy* [1989] E.C.R. 143.
[60] They were sufficiently precise and unconditional as regards the persons entitled to and the content of the guarantee, but not as to the identity of the person liable to provide it.
[61] [1991] E.C.R. I-5357, I-5415, para. 37.

nullify the unlawful consequences of a breach of Community law. The conditions for state liability depended on the nature of the breach of Community law. In the case of failure to implement directives they were:

(1) the result prescribed by the directive should entail the grant of rights to individuals;
(2) it should be possible to identify the content of those rights on the basis of the provisions of the directive;
(3) a causal link must exist between the breach of the state's obligation and the loss and damage suffered by the injured parties.

These conditions gave rise to "a right on the part of individuals to obtain reparation, a right founded directly on Community law."[62] It was on the basis of the rules of national law on liability that the state was to make a reparation and for national law to designate the competent courts and procedures, although the substantive and procedural conditions must not be less favourable than for similar domestic claims. Applying these principles, the national court was required to uphold the rights of the employee to obtain reparation for the state's failure to implement the directive, the state being obliged to make good the loss and damage.

The parameters of the *Francovich* doctrine were explored in the joined cases of *Brasserie du Pêcheur SA v. Federal Republic of Germany* and *R. v. Secretary of State for Transport ex p. Factortame Ltd and others (Factortame III)*.[63] In Brassierie du Pêcheur, a French company claimed compensation for damage caused by German laws that prohibited marketing under the designation "bier" (beer) beers lawfully manufactured by different methods in other Member States and that prohibited the import of beers containing additives. These laws were held to be incompatible with Art. 30/EC. In *Factortame III* Spanish fishermen claimed compensation in respect of losses caused by Part II of the Merchant Shipping Act 1988.[64] Various questions were referred to the Court of Justice by the respective national courts.

Among the points made by the Court of Justice were:

(1) that the *Francovich* doctrine is applicable where the national legislature is responsible for the breach;[65]
(2) that where the legislature was acting is a field in which it had wide discretion to make legislative choices, individuals suffering loss or injury thereby are entitled to reparation where
   (i) the Community law rule breached is intended to confer rights upon them;
   (ii) the breach is sufficiently serious; and
   (iii) there is a direct causal link between the breach and the damage suffered;[66]

---

[62] p. 5415, paras.38–41.
[63] Cases C-46/93 and C-48/93, Judgment of March 5, 1996, [1996] All E.R. (E.C.) 301.
[64] Below, pp. 338–339.
[65] *i.e.* where there is national legislation inconsistent with directly effective Community law, and not just where there is a failure to implement a directive that is not itself directly effective (as in *Francovich*).
[66] These principles are analogous to those established in respect of the non-contractual liability of Community institutions under Art. 215/EC.

(3) that, subject to this, the state must make good the consequences of the loss or damage caused by the breach of Community law in accordance with its national law on liability, although the conditions laid down by the national law must not be less favourable than those laid down for similar domestic claims or framed in such a way as to make it execessively difficult to obtain reparation;[67]

(4) that reparation cannot be made conditional upon fault (intentional or negligent) on the part of the state organ responsible for the breach, going beyond that of a sufficiently serious breach of Community law;

(5) that reparation must be commensurate with the loss or damage sustained and cannot exclude a claim for loss of profits; specific damages such as exemplary damages must be available if they might be awarded pursuant to similar claims founded on domestic law; and

(6) the obligation to make good loss or damage cannot be limited to damage sustained after delivery of a judgment of the court finding the infringement of Community law.

Applied to the facts of the cases involved here, the laws infringed (Articles 30 and 52/EC respectively) were plainly intended to confer rights on individuals. The test for whether the breach of Community law was sufficiently serious was whether the Member State concerned "manifestly and gravely disregarded the limits on its discretion." Relevant factors here included the clarity and precision of the rule breached; the measure of discretion left by that rule to the national authorities; whether the infringement and the damage caused was intentional or involuntary; whether any error of law was excusable or inexcusable; the fact that the position taken by a Community institution may have contributed towards the omission; and the adoption or retention of national measures contrary to Community law. A breach would clearly be sufficiently serious if it had persisted despite a judgment establishing the infringement or a clear preliminary ruling or settled case-law on the point. These matters were for the national courts to determine, although the Court did indicate that it would be difficult to regard the (*Brasserie du Pêcheur*) breach of Art. 30/EC by the marketing prohibition as excusable error given the settled case-law of the Court, and that the nationality condition in *Factortame* was "direct discrimination manifestly contrary to Community law." The way is thereby opened for substantial awards of damages in these cases.[68]

(e) Treaty provisions

The main treaties concerning the Communities are:

(1) the Treaty establishing the European Coal and Steel Community (Paris, 1951);

---

[67] *e.g.* by the conditions required to establish the English tort of misfeasance in a public office.

[68] *cf.* Case C-392/93, *R. v. H.M. Treasury, ex p. British Telecommunications plc*, Judgment of March 26, 1996, where the Court held that the U.K. was not to be held liable in damages where it incorrectly implemented a directive, given that the provision in question was imprecisely worded, and the U.K. had acted in good faith and adopted an interpretation that the provision was reasonably capable of bearing; this was not, accordingly, a "sufficiently serious breach of Community Law" of the kind contemplated by *Basserie du Pêcheur* and *Factortame*.

(2) the Treaties establishing the European Economic Community and the European Atomic Energy Community (Rome, 1957);

(3) the Treaty establishing a Single Council and a Single Commission of the European Communities (Brussels 1965; the "Merger Treaty");

(4) the Treaties amending certain Budgetary Provisions of the Treaties (Luxembourg, 1970 and Brussels, 1975);

(5) the Accession Treaties (Brussels, 1972: Denmark, Ireland, Norway,[69] and the United Kingdom (with effect from January 1, 1973); Athens, 1979: Greece (with effect from January 1, 1981); Madrid and Lisbon, 1985: Spain and Portugal (with effect from January 1, 1986); Corfu, 1994: Norway,[70] Austria, Finland and Sweden (with effect from January 1, 1995);

(6) the Treaty providing for the withdrawal of Greenland[71] (Brussels, 1984 (with effect from February 1, 1985));

(7) the Single European Act (Luxembourg and The Hague, 1986 (with effect from July 1, 1987));

(8) The Treaty on European Union (Maastricht, 1992) (with effect from November 1, 1993);

(9) the Agreement on the European Economic Area (Oporto, 1992; Brussels, 1993).

Several of the treaties have extensive Annexes and Protocols. The treaties are published by the EC and HMSO.[72] and in various unofficial collections. There is also a series of treaties entered by the Community with non-Member States.

(f) Regulations, Directives and Decisions

Regulations are the most important form of Community secondary legislation. Under Article 189 of the EC Treaty they are directly applicable without any act of implementation by Member States. Indeed, such acts of implementation are normally prohibited, in case they have the effect of altering the scope of the regulation in question. Member States may not, for example, enact measures which purport to interpret provisions contained in a regulation[73]; such interpretations might vary from state to state, and the regulation would no longer be uniform in application. This prohibition also ensures that provision of a regulation can clearly be perceived to be of Community origin and so subject to the judicial remedies available under Community law, and avoids any ambiguity as to the date of entry into force.[74] Domestic legislation may, however, make supplementary provision, for example by imposing a sanction for breach of a regulation[75] or by prescribing a limitation period for claims based on Community

[69] Norway subsequently did not ratify the Treaty.
[70] Norway again failed to ratify the Treaty.
[71] Greenland had not been a Member State, but had been part of the Community through its association with Denmark: see F. Weiss, (1985) 10 E.L. Rev. 173.
[72] e.g. Cm. 455, 1988 (Consolidated text of EC Treaties); Cm. 2484, 1994 (TEU).
[73] Case 40/69, Hauptzollamt Hamburg v. Bollman [1970] E.C.R. 69; classification of products (turkey rumps) under an agricultural regulation; Case 34/73, Variola v. Italian Minister of Finance [1973] E.C.R. 981.
[74] Usher (1981), p. 17. Member States may not adopt "any measure which would conceal the Community nature and effects of any legal provision from the persons to whom it applies": Case 50/76, Amsterdam Bulb v. Produktschap Voor Siergewassen [1977] E.C.R. 137, 151.
[75] Amsterdam Bulb case, above.

law.[76] Exceptionally, a regulation may itself expressly require Member States
to introduce implementing measures.[77]

Directives are used where the approximation or harmonisation of national
laws is sought rather than strict uniformity. They may only be addressed to
Member States. Choice of method is left to the Member States, although a time
limit for implementation is commonly set.

Decisions may be addressed to Member States, to corporations or to individuals. The European Court has held that:

> "a decision must appear as an act originating from the competent organis-
> ation intended to produce judicial effects, constituting the ultimate end of
> the internal procedure of this organisation and according to which such
> organisation makes its final ruling in a form allowing its nature to be
> identified.[78]

(g) Preparation of Community secondary legislation[79]

The treaties do not lay down a uniform legislative process to be adopted in all
cases. Community legislation may occasionally be made by the Commission,
but is usually made by the Council or (in accordance with a new procedure
introduced by the Maastrictht Treaty) by the Parliament and Council acting
jointly. Under the basic "consultative procedure" the Commission first formu-
lates a proposal after consulting national officials, experts and representatives
of interest groups (the *avant-projet* stage). The draft proposal is then sent to the
Council; Member States may at this stage refer it to their national parliaments.
A copy is sent to the European Parliament so that a preliminary unofficial study
can be commenced in committee. The Council may, and in some cases must[80]
consult the European Parliament and the European Economic and Social Committee (a consultative body representing the various categories of economic and
social activity, including industry, workers and consumers). The European Parliament debates the report of its committee in plenary session. The opinions of
the Parliament and the E.S.C. are transmitted to the Council. The Council may
consider the proposal in three stages: (1) in a Working Group of national experts
convened by the Council secretariat; (2) in the Committee of Permanent Representatives (COREPER); and (3) in the Council itself. The Commission proposal can be amended only if the council is unanimous.[81] Reconsultation with

---

[76] Case 33/76, *Rewe v. Landwirtschaftkammer Saarland* [1976] E.C.R. 1989. The periods must be
reasonable and non-discriminatory.

[77] See Hartley (1994), pp. 206–210; Case 128/78, *Commission v. United Kingdom* [1979] E.C.R.
419.

[78] Case 54/65, *Compagnie des Forges de Châtillon Commentry et Neuves Maison v. High Authority*
[1966] C.M.L.R. 525, 538.

[79] T. St. J. N. Bates, "The Drafting of European Community Legislation" [1983] Stat.L.R. 24;
Hartley (1994), pp. 38–48; Weatherill and Beaumont (1995), pp. 55–63, 108–130, Chap. 5; A.
Dashwood (1994) 19 E.L.Rev. 343 S. Weatherill, *Law and Integration in the European Union*
(1995), Chap. 3.

[80] A requirement to consult will be regarded as an essential procedural requirement: Case 138/79,
Roquette v. Council [1980] E.C.R. 3333; Case 139/79, *Maizena v. Council* [1980] E.C.R. 3393:
see T. C. Hartley, (1981) 6 E.L. Rev. 181. It is not sufficient that the opinion of the European
Parliament is sought; an opinion must be received, unless the need for the legislation is urgent
and the Parliament fails to respond to a request for an urgent opinion: Case C-65/93, *European
Parliament v. Council*, Judgment of March 30, 1995.

[81] Art.189a/EC.

the Parliament is necessary where the text finally adopted differs in essence from that on which it has been consulted, except where the amendments essentially correspond to its wishes.[82]

The Single European Act[83] introduced a new "co-operation procedure"[84] applicable to some of the instances in which the EC Treaty requires the Parliament to be consulted.[85] This procedure commences at the final stage of the standard legislative process. Instead of adopting the proposal forthwith, the Council takes a "common position", acting by a qualified majority.[86] The proposal is sent to the Parliament for a second time (the "second reading"), and the Parliament (acting within three months[87]) can approve or reject it, or propose amendments.[88] If the proposal is approved, or no action is taken within three months,[89] the act will be adopted by the Council. If it is rejected, the Council (acting within three months[90]) can only adopt it by unanimity. Proposed amendments are considered by the Commission (acting within one month) and then returned to the Council. If they are approved by the Commission, the Council (acting within three months[91]) can adopt them by a qualified majority. Amendments not approved by the Commission, and any Council amendments, can only be adopted by unanimity. These arrangements constituted "a real, though small," increase in the power of the Parliament, in so far as it could, in alliance with a Member State, block a measure; as regards amendments, the arrangement in essence enshrined existing practice in legal form.[92]

The Maastricht Treaty[93] introduced a further legislative procedure, the "co-decision" or "conciliation and veto" procedure. The role of the Parliament is here enhanced still further, the procedure providing for the adoption of legislation by the Parliament and Council jointly. It applies to specified legislative powers, including some formerly subject to the co-operation procedure.[94] Under

[82] Case C-65/90, *Parliament v. Council* [1992] E.C.R. I-4593 (*Cabotage-I*); Cases C-388/92, *Parliament v. Council* [1994] E.C.R. I-2067 (*Cabotage-II*), Case C-280/93, *Germany v. Commission* [1994] E.C.R. I-4973.

[83] Arts.6 and 7. See J. Fitzmaurice, (1988) 26 J. of Common Market Studies 389.

[84] Substituted Art. 149(2)/EC. See R. Bieber, (1988) 25 C.M.L. Rev. 711. The procedure is now governed by Art.189c/EC, inserted by Art.G(61)/TEU.

[85] *e.g.* in respect of rules designed to prohibit discrimination on the ground of nationality (Art. 6/EC); common rules applicable to international transport, the operation of transport services by non-resident carriers and measures to improve transport safety (Art.75/EC, as amended by Art.6(16)/TEU); sea and air transport (Art.84/EC); health and safety of workers (Art.118a/EC, as amended by Art.G(33)/TEU); Community environmental policy (Art.130s/EC, inserted by Art.G(38)/TEU). A full list is given in *Scrutiny after Maastricht* (*op. cit.* p. 345, n.25) Annex A.

[86] No time limit is specified for this, unlike for the later stages.

[87] The period may be extended by up to one month, by common accord between the Council and the Parliament: Art.189c(g)/EC.

[88] The Parliament can only reject or propose amendments by an absolute majority of its members: Art.189c(c)/EC.

[89] See n.82 above.

[90] *ibid.*

[91] *ibid.*

[92] Hartley (1994), pp. 41–44. The evidence "shows that a significant proportion of Parliament's amendments are adopted by the Commission and ultimately by the Council: Weatherill and Beaumont (1995), p. 120. Rejection of the common position is a weapon that has been "used sparingly"; four were rejected in 1992 and two in 1994: *ibid.*, p. 121.

[93] Art.G(61)/TEU.

[94] *e.g.* legislation in respect of free movement of workers (Art.49/EC); freedom of establishment (Art.54/EC); exceptions to the right of establishment on grounds of public policy, public security or public health (Art.56/EC); mutual recognition of diplomas etc. (Art.57(1)/EC); establishment of self-employed persons (Art.57(2)/EC, as substituted by Art.G(13)/TEU); freedom of services

the co-decision procedure the Commission submits a proposal to the Parliament and the Council. The Council, by a qualified majority and after obtaining the Parliament's opinion, adopts a common position. This is communicated to the Parliament, together with a full statement of reasons; the Commission also informs the Parliament of its position. The Parliament (acting within three months[95]) can approve the common position, propose amendments or indicate that it intends to reject it.[96] If the proposal is approved, or no action is taken within three months, the act will be adopted by the Council. If the Parliament indicates an intention to reject it, it must immediately inform the Council, and the Council may convene a meeting of a Conciliation Committee[97] to explain further its position. The Parliament thereafter is either to confirm its rejection (by an absolute majority), in which case the proposal is deemed not to have been adopted, or propose amendments.

Where amendments are proposed, the amended text is sent to the Council and the Commission, and the Commission is to deliver an opinion on them. If the Commission's opinion is favourable, the Council may adopt amendments by a qualified majority; if it is unfavourable, they may be adopted unanimously; if the Council does not approve of the act, the Conciliation Committee must forthwith be convened by the President of the Council, in agreement with the President of the Parliament.

The Conciliation Committee comprises the members of the Council or their representatives and an equal number of representatives of the Parliament. Their task is to reach agreement on a joint text, by a qualified majority on the Council side[98] and a majority on the Parliament side. The Commission is to take part in the proceedings and must take all the necessary initiatives with a view to reconciling the positions of Parliament and Council.[99] If within six weeks[1] of being convened, the Committee approves a joint text, the Parliament, acting by an absolute majority of the votes cast, and the Council, acting by a qualified majority,[2] have a further six weeks[3] in which to adopt the proposal; if either of the two fails to do so, it is deemed not to have been adopted.

If the Committee does not approve a joint text, the proposal is deemed not to have been adopted unless the Council, acting by a qualified majority within six weeks[4] of expiry of the period granted to the Committee, confirms the common position agreed before the conciliation procedure was initiated, poss-

---

(Art.66/EC); consumer protection (Art.129a/EC, inserted by Art.G(38)/TEU); and general environmental action programmes (Art.130s(3)/EC, inserted by Art.G(38)/TEU). A full list is given in *Scrutiny after Maastricht, op. cit.* p. 345, n.25, Annex A. The scope of the procedure may be widened following the intergovernmental conference in 1996: Art.189b(8)/EC.

[95] The period can be extended by up to one month, by common accord between the Council and the Parliament: Art.189b(7)/EC.

[96] The proposal of amendments and an indication of rejection (but not approval) must be by an absolute majority of the Parliament's members.

[97] See below. In these circumstances, the three-month period is automatically extended by two months: Art.189b(7)/EC.

[98] The normal requirement that the Council must be unanimous in amending a Commission proposal does not apply: Art.189(a)(1)/EC, inserted by Art.G(61)/TEU.

[99] The Commission may alter its proposal at any time during the procedure, as long as the Council has not acted: Art.189a(2)/EC.

[1] The period can be extended by a maximum of two weeks by common accord of the Parliament and the Council: Art.189b(7)/EC.

[2] See n.98 above.

[3] See n.1 above.

[4] See n.1 above.

ibly with amendments proposed by the Parliament.[5] In this situation, the act is to be finally adopted unless the Parliament, within six weeks[6] of the date of confirmation by the Council, rejects the text by an absolute majority of members, in which case the act is deemed not to have been adopted.

The significance of this procedure is that the Parliament, acting by an absolute majority, has the power of veto. The initial view of the Commission is that the procedure has worked well.[7]

The other major legislative procedure, the "assent procedure" was extended to legislation outside the budgetary process by the Maastricht Treaty.[8] Here, the assent of the Parliament is required, usually to a proposal adopted unanimously by the Council.[9] The Commission notes that this procedure is "ill-adapted to the legislative field" as Parliament may only accept or reject the instrument as laid before it.[10]

These are the main procedures. Overall, the position is excessively complex, the EC Treaty alone having 22 identifiable decision-making procedures, although not all are strictly legislative.[11] The Commission has identified three major weaknesses: the continued divergence between legislative procedures and the budget procedure; the complexity of the system; and the lack of logic in the choice of the various procedures and the different fields of activity where they apply. The legislative processes "need to be radically simplified, with reference to the concept of a hierarchy of acts."[12]

In 1992, the report of a group appointed by the Commission under the Chairmanship of a former Commissioner, Peter Sutherland, made (inter alia) a number of recommendations to improve the quality of EC legislation.[13] The Commission's response was favourable.[14] Recommendations accepted included the adoption of more restrictive criteria for legislative intervention (the "subsidiarity" principle); better co-ordination between different departments and committees of the Commission; earlier and wider consultation; greater use of

---

[5] It is unclear whether unanimity is required for the approval of amendments in accordance with Art.189a(1)/EC: see Weatherill and Beaumont (1995), p. 125, n.175 (asserting that it is), and Hartley (1994), p. 48, n.152 (point doubtful). The Commission appears to take the former view: *Commission Report for the Reflection Group* (1995), p. 76.

[6] See n.1 above.

[7] *Commission Report for the Reflection Group* (1995), p. 29. So far two measures have failed to progress: one, on voice telephony, was rejected by the Parliament following a failure to agree at the conciliation stage, because of its provisions on implementing procedures; the other, on biotechnology, was rejected by the Parliament notwithstanding agreement at the conciliation stage.

[8] This applies, for example, to "provisions" adopted with a view to facilitating the right of EU citizens to move and reside freely within the Member States (Art.8a/EC, inserted by Art.G.C/TEU); conferral of specific tasks on the European Central Bank in stage three of economic and monetary union (Art.105(6)/EC, inserted by Art.G(25)/TEU); and proposals on a uniform procedure for elections to the Parliament (Art.138(3)/EC, as amended by Art.G(40)/TEU.

[9] The assent of the Parliament is also required to other, non-legislative proposals, such as accession treaties and international agreements that (*inter alia*) have important budgetary implications or entail amendment of an act adopted under Art.189b/EC: Art.228/EC, as amended by Art.G/80/TEU.

[10] *Commission Report for the Reflection Group* (1995), p. 30.

[11] *Commission Report for the Reflection Group* (1995), Annex 8 (pp. 80–83).

[12] *ibid.*, pp. 31–33.

[13] *The Internal Market After 1992: Meeting the Challenge: Report to the EEC Commission by the High Level Group on the Operation of Internal Market* (1992). See R. Wainwright, (1994) 15 Stat.L.R.98.

[14] Follow-up to the Sutherland Report (SEC(92)2277 of December 2, 1992).

consolidated texts; consideration of the use of (directly applicable) regulations rather than directives so that a single text (albeit in different languages) is applicable throughout the Member States; and regular monitoring of the effectiveness of legislation. The subsidiarity principle is now enshrined in Article 3b of the EC Treaty,[15] which provides:

> "The Community shall act within the limits of the powers conferred upon it by this Treaty and of the objectives assigned to it therein.
>
> In areas which do not fall within its exclusive competence, the Community shall take action, in accordance with the principle of subsidiarity, only if and in so far as the objectives of the proposed action cannot be sufficiently achieved by the Member States and can therefore, by reason of the scale or effects of the proposed action, be better achieved by the Community.
>
> Any action by the Community shall not go beyond what is necessary to achieve the objectives of this Treaty."

The principle is now applied both in the formulation of the Commission's legislative programme and in the review of the existing legislative provisions; it has led to the withdrawal of some proposals and the amendment of others.[16] It is expected to involve "a move away from detailed Community law that is directly applicable towards looser measures which have to be implemented and fleshed out by Member States."[17] In order to improve transparency in the institution's business, the Commission now publishes its legislative programme on an annual basis, issues more Green and White Papers, and has promoted measures to recast, simplify and consolidate Community legislation.[18] The Council has passed a resolution on the quality of drafting of Community legislation,[19] calling (inter alia) for the wording of an act to be "clear, simple, concise and unambiguous" with "unnecessary abbreviations, 'Community jargon' and excessively long sentences" avoided. Amendments to existing legislation should be textual.

(h) Publication of Community secondary legislation

Regulations, directives and decisions are published in the *Official Journal of the European Communities* ("L Series").[20] An English edition has been published from January 1973; English texts of pre-1972 secondary legislation were published in Special Editions of the *Official Journal* covering the pre-accession period, and by HMSO in a 42-volume work entitled *Secondary Legislation of*

---

[15] Inserted by Art.G(5)/TEU.

[16] See *Commission Report for the Reflection Group* (1995), pp. 37–38; Weatherill and Beaumont (1995), pp. 13–15; the 1993 Inter-Institutional Agreement on Procedures for Implementing the Principle of Subsidiarity reproduced in Westlake (1994), pp. 145–146.

[17] Weatherill and Beaumont (1995), p. 14.

[18] *Commission Report for the Reflection Group* (1995), pp. 39–40. The Parliament, Council and Commission have established accelerated procedures for consolidation proposals: O.J. C43, February 2, 1995, pp. 41–43. On the 1995 legislative programme, see *Bulletin of the EU*, Supplement 1/95.

[19] Council Resolution of June 8, 1993, O.J. C166, June 17, 1993, p. 1.

[20] Since 1968 the *Official Journal* has appeared in two series, one publishing secondary legislation (the "L Series") and the other giving general information, including drafts of proposed legislation (the "C series").

the European Communities: Subject Edition (1973). HMSO supplemented this series with an annual Subject List and Table of Effects up to the end of 1979. Users must now rely on the monthly and annual indices and lists published as supplements to the *Official Journal*. The European Community also publishes periodically a *Directory of Community Legislation In Force*.[21]

(i) Arrangement and citation of Community secondary legislation

The heading of a regulation indicates the authority by which it is made, the Treaty under which it is made and its number.[22] The date on which it is made is given, followed by an indication of the subject matter. (*e.g.* "Council Regulation (EEC) No. 2194/81 of July 27, 1981 laying down the general rules for the system of production aid for dried figs and dried grapes.")

A *preamble* including an explanation of the purposes of the regulation precedes its main provisions. These comprise numbered *articles*, which may be subdivided into *paragraphs*, and grouped under *Titles*. An *annex* may be attached. Directives and decisions are similar to regulations in form.[23] There is a Manual of Precedents.[24]

The correct forms of citation have changed several times.[25] At present they are as follows: Reg. (EC)93/95; Dec. 95/1/EC; Dir.72/182/Euratom.

4. SUPREMACY OF COMMUNITY LAW[26]

It is well established in terms of Community law that on a matter regulated by binding Community law, that law takes precedence over the municipal law of a Member State.[27] It is immaterial whether the municipal law is enacted before or after the relevant Community law,[28] and whether it forms part of that state's fundamental or constitutional law.[29] Thus in the *Van Gend en Loos* case[30] the Court of Justice spoke of the creation of a "new legal order . . . for the benefit of which the states have limited their sovereign rights."

---

[21] Volume I: Analytical Register; Volume II: Chronological Index; Alphabetical Index. See also Sweet & Maxwell's *Encyclopedia of European Union Law* and the C.C.H. *Common Market Law Reporter*.

[22] From 1958 to 1967 there were separate series of regulations for the EEC and Euratom; from 1968 there has been a single series. Regulations were numbered in a continuous sequence until 1963; from that time a new sequence has been started each calendar year.

[23] From 1968 they have been numbered in a single series with recommendations, opinions and financial regulations.

[24] *Manual of Precedents drawn up by the Legal/Linguistic Experts of the Council of the European Communities* (2nd ed., 1983).

[25] *Secondary legislation of the European Communities: Subject Edition* (HMSO, 1973) Vol. 42, pp. vii-viii.

[26] See Hartley (1994), Chaps.7, 8; Weatherill and Beaumont (1995), Chap. 12; C. Munro, *Studies in Constitutional Law* (1982), pp. 127–132; J. W. Bridge, "Abstract Law and Political Reality in the Post-European-Accession British Constitution" [1987] Denning L.J. 23.

[27] Case 26/62, *Van Gend en Loos v. Nederlandse Administratie der Belastingen* [1963] E.C.R. 1.

[28] Case 6/64, *Costa v. ENEL* [1964] E.C.R. 585.

[29] Case 11/70, *Internationale Handelsgesellschaft v. Einfuhr-und Vorratsstelle für Getreide* [1970] E.C.R. 1125; Case 106/77, *Amministrazione delle Finanze dello Stato v. Simmenthal* [1978] E.C.R. 629.

[30] Above, pp. 314–315.

Costa v. ENEL[31] concerned the nationalisation of Italian electricity undertakings. Costa, a shareholder in one of the undertakings (Edison Volta) refused to
pay an invoice for electricity sent by ENEL, and claimed that the nationalisation
was contrary to prior Community law (various articles of the EEC Treaty).
The European Court, on a reference from the Italian magistrate (the Guidice
Conciliatore of Milan), dealt firmly with the submission of the Italian government that a national court was obliged to apply the domestic law in preference
to Community law[32]:

> "By creating a Community of unlimited duration, having its own insti-
> tutions, its own personality, its own legal capacity and capacity of represen-
> tation on the international plane and, more particularly, real powers stem-
> ming from a limitation of sovereignty or a transfer of powers from the
> States to the Community, the Member States have limited their sovereign
> rights, albeit within limited fields, and have thus created a body of law
> which binds both their nationals and themselves.
>   The integration into the laws of each Member State of provisions which
> derive from the Community, and more generally, the terms and the spirit
> of the Treaty, make it impossible for the States, as a corollary, to accord
> precedence to a unilateral and subsequent measure over a legal system
> accepted by them on a basis of reciprocity. Such a measure cannot therefore
> be inconsistent with that legal system. The executive force of Community
> law cannot vary from one State to another in deference to subsequent dom-
> estic laws, without jeopardizing the attainment of the objectives of the
> Treaty set out in Article 5(2) and giving rise to the discrimination pro-
> hibited by Article 7. . . .
>   The precedence of Community law is confirmed by Article 189, whereby
> a regulation 'shall be binding' and 'directly applicable in all Member
> States.' This provision, which is subject to no reservation, would be quite
> meaningless if a State could unilaterally nullify its effects by means of a
> legislative measure which could prevail over Community law.
>   It follows from all these observations that the law stemming from the
> Treaty, an independent source of law, could not, because of its special and
> original nature, be overridden by domestic legal provisions, however
> framed, without being deprived of its character as Community law and
> without the legal basis of the Community itself being called into question.
>   The transfer by the States from their domestic legal system to the Com-
> munity legal system of the rights and obligations arising under the Treaty
> carries with it a permanent limitation of their sovereign rights, against
> which a subsequent unilateral act incompatible with the concept of the
> Community cannot prevail. Consequently Article 177 is to be applied
> regardless of any domestic law, whenever questions relating to the
> interpretation of the Treaty arise."

In the *Simmenthal* case[33] an Italian judge was faced with a conflict between
a Council regulation and Italian laws, some of which were enacted after the

---

[31] Ente Nazionale Energia Elettrica (National Electricity Board), formerly the Edison Volta
undertaking.
[32] pp. 593–594.
[33] [1978] E.C.R. 629.

regulation. Under Italian law domestic legislation contrary to Community law was unconstitutional. However, only the Constitutional Court had jurisdiction to make such a ruling; the ordinary courts could not. The Court of Justice, on a reference by the judge, held that:

"every national court must in a case within its jurisdiction apply Community law in its entirety and protect rights which the latter confers on individuals and must accordingly set aside any provision of national law which may conflict with it, whether prior of subsequent to the Community rule. . . . [I]t is not necessary for the court to request for or await the prior setting aside of such provisions by legislative or other constitutional means."[34]

The position from the point of view of Community law is thus clear; we now consider it from the standpoint of United Kingdom law. The key provisions of the European Communities Act 1972 are contained in sections 2 and 3:

"2.—

(1) All such rights, powers, liabilities, obligations and restrictions from time to time created or arising by or under the Treaties, and all such remedies and procedures from time to time provided for by or under the Treaties, as in accordance with the Treaties are without further enactment to be given legal effect or used in the United Kingdom shall be recognised and available in law, and be enforced, allowed and followed accordingly; and the expression 'enforceable Community right' and similar expressions shall be read as referring to one to which this subsection applies.

(2) Subject to Schedule 2 to this Act, at any time after its passing Her Majesty may by Order in Council, and any designated Minister or department may by regulations, make provision—

    (a) for the purpose of implementing any Community obligation of the United Kingdom, or enabling any such obligation to be implemented, or of enabling any rights enjoyed or to be enjoyed by the United Kingdom under or by virtue of the Treaties to be exercised; or

    (b) for the purpose of dealing with matters arising out of or related to any such obligation or rights or the coming into force, or the operation from time to time, of subsection (1) above;

and in the exercise of any statutory power or duty, including any power to give directions or to legislate by means of orders, rules, regulations or other subordinate instrument, the person entrusted with the power or duty may have regard to the objects of the Communities and to any such obligation or rights as aforesaid.

In this subsection "designated Minister or department" means such Minister of the Crown or government department as may from time to time be designated by Order in Council in relation to any matter or for any purpose, but subject to such restrictions or conditions (if any) as may be specified by the Order in Council. . . .

(4) The provision that may be made under subsection (2) above includes, subject to Schedule 2 to this Act, any such provision (of any such extent) as might be made by Act of Parliament, and any enactment passed or to

[34] *ibid.* pp. 644, 645–646.

be passed, other than one contained in this Part of this Act, shall be
construed and have effect subject to the foregoing provisions of this section; but, except as may be provided by any Act passed after this Act,
Schedule 2 shall have effect in connection with the powers conferred by
this and the following sections of this Act to make Orders in Council
and regulations.

3.—

(1) For the purposes of all legal proceedings any question as to the meaning
or effect of any of the Treaties, or as to the validity, meaning or effect
of any Community instrument, shall be treated as a question of law (and,
if not referred to the European Court, be for determination as such in
accordance with the principles laid down by and any relevant [decision
of the European Court or any court attached thereto)].[35]

(2) Judicial notice shall be taken of the Treaties, of the Official Journal of
the Communities and of any decision of, or expression of opinion by,
the European Court [or any court attached, thereto][36] on any such question
as aforesaid; and the Official Journal shall be admissible as evidence of
any instrument or other act thereby communicated of any of the Communities or of any Community institution.''[37]

Thus, directly applicable and directly effective Community laws are given
effect in the United Kingdom under section 2(1); other matters are to be dealt
with by statute, or by statutory instruments under section 2(2); any question as
to the meaning or effect of the treaties is to be determined in accordance with
Community law of which judicial notice is to be taken (section 3). There is,
however, no attempt to entrench the European Communities Act itself against
repeal. It is unlikely that a court would accept that the "ultimate political fact"[38]
has been redefined so as to deny effect to a statute deliberately enacted by
Parliament as at present constituted which conflicts with existing Community
law. It is even more unlikely that the courts would decline to recognise the
express repeal of the 1972 Act.[39] Where a provision of a United Kingdom statute
is followed by an inconsistent provision of Community law that is directly applicable or effective, the latter is given precedence by section 2 of the European
Communities Act 1972. The position is less clear where the chronology is
reversed and the U.K. statute is enacted after the inconsistent provision of Community law. If both laws were made before the 1972 Act, Community law is
again given precedence by section 2. If the United Kingdom law is more recent,
there are a number of possible situations and the position appears to be as
follows:

---

[35] Words in square brackets substituted by the European Communities (Amendment) Act 1986,
s.2(a).

[36] Words added by *ibid*, s.2(b).

[37] Section 2(3) authorises the necessary expenditure; section 2(5) concerns Northern Ireland; section
2(6) concerns the Channel Islands, the Isle of Man and Gibraltar. Section 3(3)–(5) makes further
provision for proof of community instruments.

[38] See above, pp. 261–262.

[39] For the contrary argument that there has been a binding transfer of powers see Usher (1981),
pp. 30–38; J. D. B. Mitchell, (1967–68) 5 C. M. L. Rev. 112, (1971) *Europarecht* 97, (1979)
56 *International Affairs* 33. A withdrawal from the Community would, however, be negotiated;
the arrangement would be enshrined in a treaty which could be construed as a transfer back from
the Community of those powers: Usher (1981), p. 38.

(1) The United Kingdom legislation may be unclear, in which case an English court will endeavour to interpret it so as to comply with Community law, given the established presumption that Parliament does not intend the United Kingdom to be in breach of its international obligations (the "interpretation" issue).[40] In *Garland v. British Rail Engineering Ltd*,[41] Lord Diplock said.[42]

> "My Lords, even if the obligation to observe the provisions of article 119 were an obligation assumed by the United Kingdom under an ordinary international treaty or convention and there were no question of the treaty obligation being directly applicable as part of the law to be applied by the courts in this country without need for any further enactment, it is a principle of construction of United Kingdom statutes, now too well established to call for citation of authority, that the words of a statute passed after the Treaty has been signed and dealing with the subject matter of the international obligation of the United Kingdom, are to be construed, if they are reasonably capable of bearing such a meaning, as intended to carry out the obligation, and not to be inconsistent with it. A fortiori is this the case where the Treaty obligation arises under one of the Community treaties to which section 2 of the European Communities Act 1972 applies."

(2) If the United Kingdom legislation is clear and unambiguously conflicts with prior Community law, an English court will then determine whether that conflict was intended by Parliament. In the case of inadvertent conflict, the Community legislation will be given priority. Where conflict is intentional, the courts will give effect to the United Kingdom legislation, and the United Kingdom will be in breach of its Treaty obligations (the "sovereignty" issue).

There have been several judicial statements, some preceding accession, which support the primacy of subsequent inconsistent Acts of Parliament, without drawing a distinction between inadvertent and intentional conflicts.[43] Both the "interpretation" and "sovereignty" issues were subsequently raised in *Macarthys Ltd v. Smith*[44] A man was paid £60 a week for managing a stockroom. Four and a half months after he left a woman was appointed in his place at £50 a week. She claimed that she was entitled to equal pay under provisions of the Equal Pay Act 1970 that had been inserted by the Sex Discrimination Act 1975. The Court of Appeal majority[45] held that Equal Pay Act provisions were confined to cases where a man and a woman were in the same employment at the same time. The words had to be given their natural and ordinary meaning and were clear; the terms of Article 119 of the EEC Treaty[46] could therefore not be

---

[40] See below, pp. 339–344, 386–389, 404–412.

[41] [1983] 2 A. C. 751.

[42] At p. 771.

[43] *e.g.* Salmon L.J. in *Blackburn v. Attorney-General* [1971] 1 W.L.R. 1037, 1041. Lord Denning M.R. left the point open; *Felixstowe Dock and Railway Co. v. British Transport Docks Board* [1976] 2 C.M.L.R. 655, per Lord Denning M.R. at pp. 664–665.

[44] [1979] I.C.R. 785, [1981] Q.B. 180; P. Schofield, (1980) 9 I.L.J. 173; T. R. S. Allan, (1983) 3 O.J.L.S. 22. See also *Shields v. E. Coomes (Holdings) Ltd* [1978] 1 W.L.R. 1408.

[45] Lawton and Cumming-Bruce L.JJ., Lord Denning M.R. dissenting on this point.

[46] "Each Member State shall during the first stage ensure and subsequently maintain the application of the principle that men and women should receive equal pay for equal work. . . ." This was amplified by article 1 of a Council directive (Dir.75/117/EEC).

used as an aid to construction. The question whether Article 119 was so confined was referred to the Court of Justice.

Lord Denning took a different view of the proper approach to construction of the English statute and then considered the sovereignty issue[47]:

"Under section 2(1) and (4) of the European Communities Act 1972 the principles laid down in the Treaty are 'without further enactment' to be given legal effect in the United Kingdom: and have priority over 'any enactment passed or to be passed' by our Parliament. So we are entitled—and think bound—to look at article 119 of the Treaty because it is directly applicable here: and also any directive which is directly applicable here: see *Van Duyn v. Home Office* [1975] Ch. 358. We should, I think, look to see what those provisions require about equal pay for men and women. Then we should look at our own legislation on the point—giving it, of course, full faith and credit—assuming that it does fully comply with the obligations under the Treaty. In construing our statute, we are entitled to look to the Treaty as an aid to its construction: and even more, not only as an aid but as an overriding force. If on close investigation it should appear that our legislation is deficient—or is inconsistent with Community law—by some oversight of our draftsmen—then it is our bounden duty to give priority to Community law. Such is the result of section 2(1) and (4) of the European Communities Act 1972.

I pause here, however, to make one observation on a constitutional point. Thus far I have assumed that our Parliament, whenever it passes legislation, intends to fulfil its obligations under the Treaty. If the time should come when our Parliament deliberately passes an Act—with the intention of repudiating the Treaty or any provision in it—or intentionally of acting inconsistently with it—and says so in express terms—then I should have thought that it would be the duty of our courts to follow the statute of our Parliament. I do not however envisage any such situation. As I said in *Blackburn v. Attorney-General* [1971] 1 W.L.R 1037, 1040: "But, if Parliament should do so, then I say we will consider that event when it happens.' Unless there is such an intentional and express repudiation of the Treaty, it is our duty to give priority to the Treaty."

On the sovereignty issue Lawton L.J. said[48]:

"I can see nothing in this case which infringes the sovereignty of Parliament. If I thought there were, I should not presume to take any judicial step which it would be more appropriate for the House of Lords, as part of Parliament, to take. Parliament by its own Act in the exercise of its sovereign powers has enacted that European Community law shall 'be enforced, allowed and followed' in the United Kingdom of Great Britain and Northern Ireland: see section 2(1) of the European Communities Act 1972, and that 'any enactment passed or to be passed . . . shall be construed and have effect subject to' section 2: see section 2(4) of that Act. Parliament's recognition of European Community law and of the jurisdiction of the European Court of Justice by one enactment can be withdrawn by

---

[47] [1979] I.C.R. 785, at p. 789.
[48] At p. 796.

another. There is nothing in the Equal Pay Act 1970, as amended, to indicate that Parliament intended to amend the European Communities Act 1972, or to limit its application."

Cumming-Bruce L.J. indicated that if

"the terms of the Treaty are adjudged in Luxembourg to be inconsistent with the provisions of the Equal Pay Act 1970, European law will prevail over that municipal legislation. But such a judgment in Luxembourg cannot affect the meaning of the English statute."[49]

The Court of Justice subsequently held that Article 119 was not restricted to cases of contemporaneous employment,[50] and the plaintiff's claim was duly conceded in the English proceedings. The matter came before the Court of Appeal again on the question of costs.[51] Lord Denning M.R. said[52]:

"the provisions of article 119 of the EEC Treaty take priority over anything in our English statute on equal pay which is inconsistent with article 119. That priority is given by our own law. It is given by the European Communities Act 1972 itself. Community law is now part of our law; and, whenever there is any inconsistency, Community law has priority. It is not supplanting English law. It is part of our law which overrides any other part which is inconsistent with it."

The other members of the court agreed that the Community legislation prevailed.[53] Cumming Bruce L.J. emphasised that his comment at the earlier stage[54] had to be read in the context of his view (shared by Lawton L.J.) that the English statute was unambiguous. Had he been of the view that it was ambiguous, it would have been "appropriate to look at article 119 in order to assist in resolving the ambiguity."[55]

Accordingly, it appears that both Lord Denning M.R. and Lawton L.J. distinguish between cases of inadvertent and intentional conflict: it would seem that there is no room in the case of inadvertent conflict for the application of an "implied repeal rule" as there is between two inconsistent statutes, and in the case of intentional conflicts the English statute will prevail. Furthermore, even in the case of intentional conflicts it may be that effect would only be given to the English statute if it amended or repealed the European Communities Act 1972: it would not be sufficient merely that the substantive law prescribed

---

[49] At p. 798.
[50] Case 129/79, [1981] Q.B. 180, E.C.J.
[51] [1981] Q.B. 199, C.A. Cf. Re an Absence in Ireland [1977] 1 C.M.L.R. 5, where a national insurance commissioner allowed a claimant's appeal on two grounds, one of which involved the application of Council Regulation (EEC) No. 1408/71 in preference to the provisions of the Social Security Act 1975. See also Re Medical Expenses Incurred in France [1977] 2 C.M.L.R. 317.
[52] At p. 200.
[53] Professor Hood Phillips suggested that even in cases of inadvertent conflict, an English court should give effect to a subsequent, unambiguous United Kingdom Act of Parliament: (1980) 96 L.Q.R. 31; cf. O. Hood Phillips and P. Jackson, O. Hood Phillips' Constitutional and Administrative Law (7th ed., 1987), pp. 74–79.
[54] Set out above.
[55] [1981] Q.B. 180, 201.

by statute was different from that prescribed by Community law. Lawton L.J., but not Lord Denning M.R., appears to support this view.[56]

As to the issues raised in *Macarthys Ltd v. Smith*,[57] it is arguable that although the Court of Appeal approached them as if there was a *conflict* between the Equal Pay Act 1970 and Article 119, the better view is that there was simply a difference between them.

> "Article 119 is directly effective, and Community law applies in the industrial tribunals; to the extent that it gave rights to Mrs Smith more extensive than the Equal Pay Act 1970 (as amended by the Sex Discrimination Act 1975), there was nothing in the 1970 Act forbidding the court from giving effect to those rights. It should follow that Mrs Smith would be entitled to rely on whichever legal rule, art. 119 or the 1970 Act, gave her more extensive rights."[58]

This approach was echoed by the Court of Appeal in *Pickstone v. Freemans plc*,[59] where it was held that while the relevant provision of the Equal Pay Act 1970[60] was unambiguous and could not be construed in conformity with the requirements of Community law, a claim to equal pay (for work of equal value) could instead be based directly on Article 119.[61] Similarly, the House of Lords in *R. v. Secretary of State for Transport, ex p. Factortame Ltd (No. 2)*,[62] following a reference to the Court of Justice,[63] has accepted that Community law imposes an obligation on national courts to provide an effective interlocutory remedy to protect rights having direct effect under Community law. Accordingly, interlocutory orders should be granted against the Crown disapplying Part II of the Merchant Shipping Act 1988[64] and restraining the Secretary of State from enforcing it and related regulations against the applicants, pending the final determination by the European Court of questions concerning the compatability of these provisions with Community law. This was so notwithstanding that, as a matter of domestic law, interlocutory injunctions could not be granted against the Crown.[65]

---

[56] This view is endorsed in *Halsbury's Laws of England*, 4th ed., Vol. 51, para. 3.14.
[57] *loc. cit.* n. 39 above.
[58] L. Collins, *European Community law in the United Kingdom* (4th ed., 1990), p. 32.
[59] [1989] A.C. 66.
[60] Section 1(2)(c).
[61] The House of Lords took a different approach: see below. See also *Mediguard Services Ltd v. Thame* [1994] I.C.R. 751, E.A.T.
[62] [1991] 1 A.C. 603, H.L.
[63] Case C–213/89, *R. v. Secretary of State for Transport, ex p. Factortame Ltd* [1990] E.C.R. I-2433 (known as *Factortame I* by European lawyers but titled (*No. 2*) by the Law Reports ([1991] 1 A.C. 603).
[64] The 1988 Act and associated regulations (Merchant Shipping (Registration of Fishing Vessels) Regulations 1988 (S.I. 1988 No. 1926) were designed to narrow the conditions under which fishing vessels can be registered as British (and thus entitled to fish against the U.K. quotas): vessels would have to have "a genuine and substantial" connection with the U.K. (1988 Act, s.14(3)). The applicants were Spanish nationals, who controlled companies that owned ships registered as British, and which would lose that registration under the new rules.
[65] *R. v. Secretary of State for Transport, ex p. Factortame Ltd* [1990] 2 A.C. 85, H.L. *per* Lord Bridge at pp. 143–150. See N. P. Gravells, [1989] P.L. 568. The House of Lords in *M. v. Home Office* [1994] 1 A.C. 377 subsequently held that, notwithstanding the views of Lord Bridge in *Factortame (No.1)* the High Court did have jurisdiction to grant injunctions against officers of the Crown.

The European Court subsequently ruled that conditions of the kind imposed by the 1988 Act were indeed contrary to Community law.[66]

The possibility of direct challenge to U.K. legislation was recognised and acted upon by the House of Lords in *R. v. Secretary of State for Employment, ex p. Equal Opportunities Commission*,[67] in granting declarations on the application of the E.O.C. that the differing threshold provisions for full-time and part-time workers' entitlement to unfair dismissal and redundancy payments were incompatible with Community law. The less favourable treatment of part-time workers, the great majority of whom were women, constituted indirect sex discrimination for which no objective justification could be established. The *Factortame* decision provided a precedent acknowledging jurisdiction to grant such a declaration.[68] The House did, however, refuse to make a declaration in terms that the Secretary of State was in breach of the provisions of the Equal Treatment Directive which require Member States to introduce measures to abolish any laws contrary to the principle of equal treatment. This was designed to facilitate actions against the United Kingdom by individuals under the *Francovich* principle,[69] but such proceedings were said to raise different issues.[70] The relevant legislation was subsequently amended to comply with Community law.[71]

Cases since *Macarthys Ltd v. Smith*[72] have for the most part raised the "interpretation issue" rather than the "sovereignty issue." The dictum of Lord Diplock in *Garland v. British Rail Engineering Ltd*[73] cited above[74] has been regarded as endorsing Lord Denning's approach in *Macarthys Ltd v. Smith*[75] rather than that of the majority.[76] Lord Diplock's approach was purportedly followed in two, contrasting, decisions of the House of Lords.

In *Duke v. Reliance Systems Ltd*,[77] Mrs Duke was dismissed by her private sector employers shortly after attaining 60, in accordance with their policy that

---

[66] Case C-221/89, *R. v. Secretary of State for Transport, ex p. Factortame Ltd.* [1991] E.C.R. I-3905 known as *Factortame II* by European lawyers but titled (*No. 3*) in the Law Reports [1992] Q.B. 680). Part II of the Merchant Shipping Act 1988 was amended by the Merchant Shipping Act 1988 (Amendment) Order 1989 (S.I. 1989 No. 2006) to comply with an interim order in Art.169 proceedings against the U.K. (Case C-246/89R, *Commission v. U.K.* [1989] E.C.R. I-3125; Case C-246/89, *Commission v. U.K.* [1991] E.C.R. I-4585). Part II of the 1988 Act was subsequently repealed and replaced by the Merchant Shipping (Registration, etc.) Act 1993. Questions arising out of a claim for damages by the Spanish Fishermen have been referred by the Divisional Court to the Court of Justice as Case C-48/93, *R. v., Secretary of State for Transport, ex p. Factortame Ltd.*: see below, pp. 343–344.

[67] [1995] 1 A.C. 1.

[68] "Although the final result is not reported [following the E.C.J. decision in *Factortame II*], no doubt the Divisional Court in due course granted a declaration accordingly": *per* Lord Keith of Kinkel *cf.* above pp. 323–324.

[69] See above, p. 322.

[70] *per* Lord Keith of Kinkel.

[71] See the Employment Protection (Part-Time Employees) Regulations 1995 (S.I. 1995 No.31).

[72] *Loc. cit.* n. 44 above.

[73] [1983] 2 A.C. 751, 771. This approach applies as much to the interpretation of delegated as to primary legislation: *Ken Lane Transport Ltd. v. North Yorkshire County Council* [1995] 1 W.L.R. 1416, D.C.

[74] At p. 335.

[75] Above.

[76] A. W. Bradley, in J. Jowell and D. Oliver, *The Changing Constitution* (2nd ed., 1989), p. 41 (a point omitted from the 3rd ed., 1994).

[77] [1988] A.C. 618. Applied by the House of Lords in *Finnegan v. Clowney Youth Training Programme Ltd* [1990] 2 A.C. 418.

men should retire at 65 but women at 60. She claimed that this constituted discriminatory treatment under the Sex Discrimination Act 1975, s.6(2), but her claim was dismissed on the ground that section 6(4) preserved the right of the employer to operate discriminatory retirement ages. This said that section 6(2) did not apply to "provision in relation to death or retirement". It was clear that the later Council Directive Dir.76/207/EEC (the Equal Treatment Directive) did outlaw discriminatory retirement ages,[78] but (1) this did not have "horizonal direct effect" between individuals,[79] and (2) the U.K. legislation implementing the directive, the Sex Discrimination Act 1986, did not apply retrospectively so as to apply to Mrs Duke's claim. She argued, therefore, that the expression "provision in relation to . . . retirement" should be interpreted as "provision consequent upon retirement," and therefore not applying to protect discriminatory retirement ages. This would enable English law to conform with the Equal Treatment Directive. The argument was rejected.[80] Lord Templeman, with whom the other members of the House of Lords agreed, said:

> "Of course a British court will always be willing and anxious to conclude that United Kingdom law is consistent with Community law. Where an Act is passed for the purpose of giving effect to an obligation imposed by a decision or other instrument a British court will seldom encounter difficulty in concluding that the language of the Act is effective for the intended purpose. But the construction of a British Act of Parliament is a matter of judgment to be determined by British courts and to be derived from the language of the legislation considered in the light of the circumstances prevailing at the date of enactment."[81]

However, the 1975 Act was not passed in order to give effect to the (later) Equal Treatment Directive, and the words of section 6(4)

> "are not reasonably capable of being limited to the meaning ascribed to them by the appellant. Section 2(4) of the European Communities Act 1972 does not in my opinion enable or constrain a British court to distort the meaning of a British statute in order to enforce against an individual a Community directive which has no direct effect between individuals. Section 2(4) applies and only applies where Community provisions are directly applicable."[82]

It is clearly the case that the 1975 Act was intended at the time to preserve differential retirement ages. Indeed the United Kingdom's position was that the Equal Treatment Directive did not prohibit discriminatory retirement ages, an argument ultimately rejected by the European Court in *Marshall I*.[83]

The reasoning in *Duke* has been cogently criticised by commentators on a

---

[78] Case 151/84, *Roberts v. Tate & Lyle Industries Ltd* [1986] E.C.R. 703, [1986] I.C.R. 371; Case 152/84, *Marshall v. Southampton and South-West Hampshire Area Health Authority (Teaching)* [1986] E.C.R. 723, [1986] Q.B. 401.

[79] *Marshall*, above and see pp. 317–318.

[80] It had previously been rejected by the Employment Tribunal and the Court of Appeal in *Roberts v. Cleveland Area Health Authority* [1978] I.C.R. 370, [1979] 1 W.L.R. 754.

[81] [1988] A.C. 618, 638.

[82] *ibid.*, pp. 639–640.

[83] n. 78 above.

variety of grounds.[84] First, it is not obvious that the narrow reading of "in relation to" was a "distortion": it was certainly a less natural reading, but one that was arguably supportable given the requirements of the directive, and the obligation under Community law (via sections 2(4) and 3(1) of the European Communities Act 1972) to interpret national legislation where possible to conform with relevant directives. Secondly, it was incorrect to say that section 2(4) only applied to Community provisions that were "directly applicable."[85] Third, it gave insufficient weight to the presumed continuing intention of the United Kingdom to comply with the requirements of Community law: it is not clear that this was properly subordinated to the contemporary intention in 1975 to preserve discriminatory retirement ages. It is important, however, to see the *Duke* decision in its context. Had Mrs Duke's argument prevailed, the position would have been as if the Sex Discrimination Act 1986 had retrospective effect, and this would undoubtedly have caused severe practical difficulties. It is to be hoped that the rather doubtful reasoning employed to secure that result is not used in subsequent cases so as to undermine proper implementation by the United Kingdom of the requirements of Community law.

The decision of the House of Lords in *Pickstone v. Freemans plc*[86] is accordingly to be welcomed. Here, the House placed renewed emphasis on the need to interpret English law, where possible, so as to comply with Community law. The context of the case was significantly different from that in *Duke*. Here, the question concerned the interpretation of amendments to the Equal Pay Act 1970 specifically designed to bring English law into conformity with Community law. Prior to amendment, the Act took effect where the woman was employed (a) "on like work" or (b) on work "rated as equivalent" on a job evaluation study, with a man in the same employment.[87] The European Court held that this was inadequate to comply with Article 119/EEC and Council Directive Dir.75/117/EEC (the equal pay directive), which imposed a requirement of equal pay for the same work or *work of equal value*. The latter element was not fully implemented by (b), which depended on the employer having consented to a job evaluation[88] study. Accordingly, the Equal Pay (Amendment) Regulations 1983[89] introduced a new para. (c), which allowed an "equal value" claim to be made "where a woman is employed on work, not being work in relation to which paragraph (a) or (b) above applies. . . ." Mrs Pickstone, a "warehouse operative", made a claim under para. (c), claiming her work was of equal value to that of a man employed as a "checker warehouse operative". There happened to be one man also employed as a "warehouse operative".[90] The industrial tribunal and the Employment Appeal Tribunal accepted the employer's argument that para. (a) applied to Mrs Pickstone's work, and that the words " not

---

[84] E. Ellis, (1988) 104, L.Q.R. 379; A. Arnull, [1988] P.L. 313; N. Foster, (1988) 51 M.L.R 775 and (1988) 25 C.M.L. Rev. 629; B. Fitzpatrick, (1989) 9 O.J.L.S. 336.

[85] The European Court in Case 262/84, *Beets-Proper v. Van Lanschot Bankiers N.V.* [1986] E.C.R. 782 held that national legislation, designed to implement a directive that was *not* directly effective, should be interpreted so as to conform to it: See above, p. 321. This obligation would apply to U.K. courts via ss.2(4) and 3(1) of the 1972 Act.

[86] [1989] A.C. 66. See A. W. Bradley, [1988] P. L. 485. *Cf. J. Rothschild Holdings v. Commissioners of Inland Revenue* [1989] 2 C.M.L.R. 612.

[87] Section 1(2)(a), (b).

[88] Case 61/81, *Commission v United Kingdom* [1982] E.C.R. 2601, [1982] I.C.R. 578; S. Atkins, [1983] P.L. 19 and (1983) 8 E.L. Rev. 48.

[89] S.I. 1983 No. 1794.

[90] [1986] I.C.R. 886.

being work. ...'' accordingly barred her claim under para (c). The Court of Appeal[91] held that this was indeed the position under the Equal Pay Act 1970, but that Mrs Pickstone could base her claim directly on Article 119/EEC. The House of Lords interpreted the 1970 Act in such a way as to allow her claim to proceed under it: the exclusionary words in para. (c) were intended to have effect only where the particular man with whom she sought comparison was employed on the same work. Here, her comparator was employed on different work.

> "The opposite result would leave a large gap in the equal work provision, enabling an employer to evade it by employing one token man on the same work as a group of potential women claimants who were deliberately paid less than a group of men employed on work of equal value with that of the women. This would mean that the United Kingdom had failed yet again fully to implement its obligations under article 119 of the Treaty and the Equal Pay Directive, and had not given full effect to the decision of the European Court in *Commission v. U.K.*[92] It is plain that Parliament cannot possibly have intended such a failure."[93]

A purposive, rather than a literal construction was necessary.[94] There is room for argument how far this result involves a "distortion" of the statutory language.

The proper approach of the English courts to the interpretation of directives in the light of the decision of the European Court in *Marleasing*[95] has been stated as follows by Lord Keith of Kinkel in *Webb v. EMO Air Cargo (U.K.) Ltd*:[96]

> "It is for a United Kingdom Court to construe domestic legislation in any field covered by a Community directive so as to accord with the interpretation of the directive as laid down by the European Court, if that can be done without distorting the meaning of the domestic legislation: see *Duke v. GEC Reliance Ltd.*[97] This is so whether the domestic legislation came after or, as in this case, preceded the directive, see *Marleasing SA v. La Comercial Internacional de Alimentación SA. ...*[98]
>
> As the European Court has said, a national court must construe a domestic law to accord with the terms of a directive in the same field only if it is possible to do so. This means that the domestic law must be open to an interpretation consistent with the directive whether or not it is also open to an interpretation inconsistent with it."

This statement has been cited on a number of occasions.[99] In *Webb* itself, the

[91] [1989] A.C. 66. See A. W. Bradley, [1988] P.L. 485, 489–491.
[92] n. 88 above.
[93] *per* Lord Keith of Kinkel at pp. 111–112.
[94] See below, pp. 355–358.
[95] Above, pp. 321–322.
[96] [1992] 4 All E.R. 929, 939, 940. The other members of the House agreed with Lord Keith. See also *Porter v. Cannon Hygiene Ltd* [1993] I.R.L.R. 329, C.A. (N.I.).
[97] [1988] A.C. 618, 639–640 *per* Lord Templeman.
[98] Case C-106/89, [1990] E.C.R. I-4135.
[99] See, *e.g., R. v. Secretary of State for the Environment, ex p. Greenpeace Ltd* [1994] 4 All E.R. 352.

House proceeded to make a reference to the Court of Justice. In the light of the Court's ruling, the House of Lords was able to interpret the Sex Discrimination Act 1975 to accord with Community law.

The facts were that W was engaged to replace a woman on maternity leave (but employed on an indefinite rather than a short-term contract). She was dismissed when it was discovered that she too was pregnant. Section 1(1) of the 1975 Act provides that

> "a person discriminates against a woman in any circumstances relevant for the purposes of any provision of this Act if—(a) on the ground of her sex he treats her less favourably than he treats or would treat a man."

Section 5(3) provides that

> "a comparison of the cases of persons of different sex ... must be such that the relevant circumstances in the one case are the same, or not materially different, in the other."

The House of Lords held initially[1] that the dismissal here was on the basis of W's unavailability for work at the time when she had been particularly required, and that the reason for that unavailability (pregnancy) was not a relevant circumstance. However, the Court of Justice ruled[2] that Community law[3] precluded dismissal of an employee recruited for an unlimited term, with a view initially to replacing another employee, on the ground of pregnancy. Accordingly, the House of Lords[4] reinterpreted the 1975 Act to clarify the reason for unavailability in such a case (pregnancy) as a "relevant circumstance", pregnancy being a circumstance that could not be present in the case of the hypothetical man. While not the preferred reading, this was properly not regarded as "distortion" of the Act.

Finally, in the *Factortame* litigation[5] it was accepted by both the parties and the courts that if the Court of Justice were to rule finally that the relevant provisions of the Merchant Shipping Act 1988 were incompatible with Community law, English courts would have to give effect to the latter, whether as a matter of interpretation of the 1988 Act[6] or by disapplying it as invalid.[7] The Divisional Court "made an order designed to give effect to [the] Court's judgment in *Factortame II* and, to give detailed particulars of their claim for damages."[8]

---

[1] n. 96 above.

[2] Case C-32/93, *Webb v. Emo Air Cargo Ltd* [1994] Q.B. 718, [1994] E.C.R. I-3567.

[3] Arts. 2,5 of Dir.76/207/EEC (the equal treatment directive).

[4] [1995] 1 W.L.R. 1454.

[5] See above, pp. 338–339.

[6] *per* Lord Bridge in *R. v. Secretary of State for Transport, ex p. Factortame Ltd* [1990] 2 A.C. 85, 140, referring to s.2(1) and (4) of the 1972 Act: "This has precisely the same effect as if a section were incorporated in Part II of the Act of 1988 which in terms enacted that the provisions with respect to registration of British fishing vessels were to be without prejudice to the directly enforceable Community rights of nationals of any member state of the E.E.C." Although this can be labelled as an approach based on interpretation, this would seem to be "interpretation" of a kind more radical than adopted hitherto; the words read into the statute have a very substantial modifying effect.

[7] The Court of Appeal in *Factortame*: [1989] 2 C.M.L.R. 353, 396 (Lord Donaldson M.R.), 403–404 (Bingham L.J.), 408 (Mann L.J.).

[8] Case 48/93, *R. v. Secretary of State for Transport, ex p. Factortame Ltd. and others*, Judgment of March 5, 1996, para. 12.

This led to another reference to the Court of Justice and the ruling in *Factortame III*.[8a]

5. IMPLEMENTATION OF COMMUNITY LAW IN THE UNITED KINGDOM

As has been seen, Community law that is directly applicable or effective takes effect in the United Kingdom under section 2(1) of the European Communities Act 1972.[9] In appropriate cases,[10] such law may give rise to defences that can be relied on in English litigation.[11] Alternatively, it may form the basis of an award of damages, (*e.g.* for breach of statutory duty[12] or the tort of misfeasance in a public office[13]) or the grant of an injunction,[14] as a matter of private law, or the grant of public law remedies against the Crown or other public authority.[15]

Primary legislation has been enacted to give effect to major changes, such as those consequent on the accession of new Member States,[16] major budgetary matters,[17] the Single European Act[18] and the Maastricht Treaty.[19] Specific Com-

---

[8a] Above, pp. 323–324.

[9] Above, pp. 333–334.

[10] See generally J. Steiner, "How to make the action suit the case: domestic remedies for breach of EEC law" (1987) 12 E.L. Rev. 102; P. Oliver, "Enforcing Community rights in the English courts" (1987) 50 M.L.R. 881; N. Green and A. Barav, "Damages in the national courts for breach of Community law" [1986] 6 Y.E.L. 55, 83–114; J. S. Davidson, (1985) 34 I.C.L.Q. 178.

[11] *e.g.* a defence to criminal proceedings: Case 63/83, *R. v. Kirk* [1985] 1 All E.R. 453; Case 121/85, *Conegate v. Commissioners of Customs and Excise* [1987] Q.B. 254; or "Euro-defences" based on EC competition law arising in civil actions: *cf. Lansing Bagnall Ltd v. Buccaneer Lift Parts Ltd* [1984] 1 C.M.L.R. 224; *Ransburg-Gema AG v. Electrostatic Plant Systems Ltd* [1989] 2 C.M.L.R. 712.

[12] *e.g.* for a breach of Art. 86/EC (abuse of a dominant position): *per* Lord Diplock in *Garden Foods Ltd v. Milk Marketing Board* [1984] A.C. 130, 141: see K. Banks, (1984) 21 C.M.L. Rev. 669; F. G. Jacobs, (1983) 8 E.L. Rev. 353; M. Friend and J. Shaw, (1984) 100 L.Q.R. 188; but not a breach of Art. 30 (prohibition of quantitative restrictions on imports and measures having equivalent effect): *Bourgoin S.A. v. Ministry of Agriculture, Fisheries and Food* [1985] Q.B. 716, C.A.; or a breach of Art. 10 of Council Reg. 1422/78: *An Bord Bainne v. Milk Marketing Board* [1988] 1 C.M.L.R. 605, C.A.

[13] An action that lies where loss is caused by *ultra vires* acts committed maliciously (*i.e.* with intent to injure the plaintiff) or with knowledge of its illegality: *Bourgoin*, n. 12 above: the parties settled for £3.5 m. (Vol. 102 H. C. Deb. July 23, 1986, col. 116, written answer). This head of liability must now be seen as subject to the ruling of the Court of Justice in *Factortame III*, above, pp. 323–324.

[14] *Garden Cottage Foods*, n. 12 above; *Cutsforth v. Mansfield Inns Ltd* [1986] 1 C.M.L.R. 1.

[15] *e.g. Van Duyn v. Home Office* [1974] 1 W.L.R. 1107, Ch.D., and Case 41/74, [1985] Ch. 358 E.C.J. (action for a declaration); *R. v. Attorney-General, ex p. I.C.I.* [1987] 1 C.M.L.R. 72 and *R. v. Intervention Board for Agricultural Produce, ex p. The Fish Producers' Organisation Ltd* [1988] 2 C.M.L.R. 661 (applications for judicial review).

[16] European Communities (Greek Accession) Act 1979; European Communities (Spanish and Portuguese Accession) Act 1985; European Union (Accessions) Act 1994 (in respect of Austria, Finland and Sweden, and Norway (who subsequently did not join)).

[17] European Communities (Finance) Act 1985.

[18] European Communities (Amendment) Act 1986.

[19] European Communities (Amendment) Act 1993. The process of enacting this Act was particularly fraught for the government: see discussion by P. Beaumont and G. Moir, *Current Law Statutes Annotated* (1993). A challenge to the legality of ratification of the Treaty by the government was rejected: *R. v. Secretary of State for Foreign and Commonwealth Affairs, ex p. Rees-Mogg* [1994] 2 W.L.R. 115; R. Rawlings, [1994] P.L. 254, 367.

munity obligations may also be implemented by Act of Parliament.[20] Section 2(2) of the 1972 Act[21] authorises the making of subordinate legislation (1) to implement other Community laws that are not directly applicable or effective; or (2) to deal with matters related to Community laws that take effect under section 2(1).[22] Subordinate legislation may not, however, (1) provide for the imposition or increase of taxation; (2) be retrospective; (3) confer the power to enact sub-delegated legislation; or (4) create any new criminal offence punishable with more than two years imprisonment, or three months on summary conviction, or a fine of more than £1,000, or £100 a day.[23] It is subject to the negative resolution procedure.[24]

Arrangements have been made for the scrutiny of Community legislation by the Select Committee of the House of Lords on the European Communities and the Select Committee of the House of Commons on European Legislation.[25] These committees consider draft Community legislation and other documents prepared by the Commission for submission to the Council of Ministers. Detailed explanatory memoranda are prepared by the government. The Commons committee concentrates on political implications, although the merits cannot be considered; the Lords deal more with technical legal and administrative implications.[26] The Lords committee has a number of sub-committees, including one customarily chaired by one of the Law Lords on law and institutions,[27] and each of the rest considering Community proposals within a particular subject area. The committees decide, *inter alia*, whether a particular proposal should be considered further by the respective Houses. In the Commons, a debate may be held on the floor of the House or in a standing committee. In 1990, two European Standing Committees were established in order to shift

---

[20] *e.g.* the Companies Acts 1980 and 1981, which implemented directives on the harmonisation of company law; the Importation of Milk Act 1983, passed in response to a judgment of the European Court which held that U.K. restrictions on the importation of U.H.T. milk were contrary to Community rules on the free movement of goods (Case 124/81, *Commission v. United Kingdom* [1983] E.C.R. 203); the Sex Discrimination Act 1986.

[21] Sections 5 and 6 of the 1972 Act confer subordinate powers to make subordinate legislation concerning customs matters and the common agricultural policy. Statutory instruments implementing Community obligations have been made under other statutes.

[22] Note, however, the limits on such legislation in respect of Community regulations: above, p. 325.

[23] European Communities Act 1972, Sched. 2, as amended by the Criminal Law Act 1977, s.32 and the Criminal Justice Act 1982, ss.37, 40, 46.

[24] *ibid.* See above pp. 292–293.

[25] Established in 1974. See 1972–73 H.C. 143 and 463–I ("Foster Committee": Commons); 1972–73 H.L. 194 ("Maybray-King Committee": Lords). See also the First Report from the Select Committee on Procedure, 1977–78 H.C. 588 Vol. I, pp. xl–Xlvi; First Special Report from the Select Committee on European Legislation 1983–84 (1983–84 H.C. 527): Government response, Vol. 65 H.C. Deb., October 29, 1984, cols.800–802, written answer); Second Special Report 1985–86 (1985–86 H.C. 400): Government observations, Cm. 123, 1987; Fourth Report from the Select Committee on Procedure (1988–89 H.C. 622): Government response, Cm. 1081, 1990; First Special Report from the Select Committee on European Legislation 1993–94 (1993–94 H.C. 99), *Scrutiny after Maastricht*; P. Norton, *The Commons in Perspective* (1981), pp. 160–164; Lord Fraser of Tullybelton in St. John Bates *et al.* (eds.), *In Memoriam J. D. B. Mitchell* (1983), pp. 29–37; T. St. J. Bates in M. Ryle and P. G. Richards (eds.), *The Commons Under Scrutiny* (1988), pp. 205–211; E. Denza, "Parliamentary Scrutiny of European Legislation" [1993] Stat.L.R. 56.

[26] Joint meetings are occasionally held.

[27] The "legal eagles committee": E. Denza, [1993] Stat. L.R. 56, 59.

debates away from the floor of the House.[28] The Procedure Committee concluded that these committees functioned very well, making a useful contribution
to effective scrutiny.[29] The government has undertaken that it will normally[30]
provide time for such consideration where recommended by the Select Committee prior to a proposal being discussed by the Council of Ministers. However,
the scrutiny of European secondary legislation is indirect in effect, given that
Parliament can at best influence only one of the members of the Council,
especially now that more Council decisions are reached by qualified majorities
and that the legislative process is likely to be quicker.[31] Moreover, it can be
difficult to keep abreast of changes in draft proposals as they progress through
the Community legislative process.

6. VALIDITY OF EUROPEAN SECONDARY LEGISLATION

(a) Article 173; the action for annulment

The validity of acts of Community institutions that are binding in law, and
whether legislative or not, may be challenged directly by an *action for annulment* brought in the European Court of Justice[32] under Article 173 of the EC
Treaty[33]:

   "The Court of Justice shall review the legality of acts adopted jointly by
   the European Parliament and the Council, of acts of the Council, of the

---

[28] See 1988–89 H.C. 622 and Cm. 1081, n. 20 above; First Special Report from the Select Committee on European Legislation 1989–90 (1989–90 H.C. 512) and Vol. 178 H. C. Deb., October
24, 1990, cols.375–401.

[29] First Report from the Select Committee on Procedure 1991–92 (1991–92 H.C. 31), *Review of
European Standing Committees*; Third Report 1991–92 (1991–92, H.C. 331), *Government
Response*. Debates "have been of a much more highly focused and objective quality": E. Denza,
[1993] Stat. L.R 56, 58.

[30] The strength of the undertaking has varied from time to time. In 1980, the Commons resolved
that no minister should agree to a proposal for Community legislation recommended by the Select
Committee for consideration by the House before the House had given it that consideration unless
(a) the Committee has indicated that agreement need not be withheld or (b) the Minister decides
there are special reasons; in the latter case the reasons should be explained to the House at the
first opportunity: H.C. Deb. Vol. 991, col. 844, October 30, 1980. Agreement to a common
position under the co-operation procedure is treated as "agreement to a proposal" for these
purposes: First Special Report from the Select Committee on European Legislation 1988–89
(1988–89 H.C. 533), pp. iv, v. This was recognised formally, and the resolution was extended
to include documents awaiting scrutiny by the Select Committee, in a revised version approved
on October 24, 1990: H.C. Deb. Vol. 178, col. 400. Agreement to a common position, to a joint
text and to confirmation of the common position under the co-decision procedure is also regarded
as "agreement to a proposal" for these purposes: see First Report from the Select Committee
on European Legislation 1993–94 (1993–94 H.C. 99), *Scrutiny after Maastricht*; Second Report
(1993–94 H.C. 739) (including government reply).

[31] See the reports on the Single European Act and Parliamentary Scrutiny: First Special Report
from the Select Committee on European Legislation 1985–86 (1985–86 H.C. 264) and the First
Special Report 1988–89 (1988–89 H.C. 533); Twelfth Report from the Select Committee on the
European Communities 1985–86 (1985–86 H.L. 149).

[32] See above pp. 103–109: national courts may not rule acts of Community institutions invalid (Case
314/85, *Foto-Frost v. Hauptzollamt Lübeck-Ost* [1987] E.C.R. 4199). The approach adopted by
the European Court to the interpretation of Community law is considered below pp. 404–412.

[33] As amended by Art. G(53)/TEU. See also Art. 33/ECSC; Art. 146/Euratom, as amended.

Commission and the ECB, other than recommendations and opinions,[34] and of acts of the European Parliament intended to produce legal effects vis-à-vis third parties.[35]

It shall for this purpose have jurisdiction in actions brought by a Member State, the Council or the Commission on grounds of lack of competence, infringement of an essential procedural requirement, infringement of this Treaty or of any rule of law relating to its application, or misuse of powers.

The Court shall have jurisdiction under the same conditions in actions brought by the European Parliament and by the ECB for the purpose of protecting their prerogatives.[36]

Any natural or legal person[37] may, under the same conditions, institute proceedings against a decision addressed to that person or against a decision which, although in the form of a regulation or a decision addressed to another person, is of direct and individual concern to the former.

The proceedings provided for in this Article shall be instituted within two months of the publication of the measure, or of its notification to the plaintiff, or, in the absence thereof, of the day on which it came to the knowledge of the latter, as the case may be."

Thus the range of acts that can be challenged by an individual is narrower than those that can be reviewed under the first three paragraphs of Article 173. First, the act must be a "decision" in that it must have legal effect[38] and must not be a regulation, in the sense of an act which applies to objectively determined situations and has legal effects on classes of persons defined in a general and abstract manner.[39] Second, the act must be of "direct and individual concern" to the applicant.[40] If the action is successful, the act challenged is declared by the Court to be void,[41] and the matter is remitted to the institution concerned.

---

[34] This covers any act intended to have legal effect, and not merely regulations, directives and decisions: Case 22/70, *Commission v. Council (ERTA)* [1971] E.C.R. 263 (action for annulment of a Council resolution concerning negotiations leading to an international agreement between the Member States and third countries); Case C-325/91, *France v. Commission*, June 16, 1993 ("communication" intended to have legal effects annulled; commission should have adopted a directive or a decision).

[35] The express reference to the Parliament was added by the Maastricht Treaty; acts of the Parliament had in any event previously been held to be subject to Art. 173: Case 294/83, *Parti Ecologiste "Les Verts" v. European Parliament* [1986] E.C.R. 1339.

[36] Prior to the changes effected by the Maastricht Treaty, the Court had held, initially, that the Parliament had no standing under Art. 173 (Case 302/87, *European Parliament v. Council* [1988] E.C.R. 5615) and then that it had standing to bring proceedings to safeguard its prerogatives (Case C-70/88, *European Parliament v. Council* [1990] E.C.R. I-2041); the ruling in the latter case is now enshrined in Art. 173.

[37] This term includes a Member State: Case 25/62 *Plaumann v. Commission* [1963] E.C.R. 95.

[38] Cases 8–11/66, *Cimenteries v. Commission* (the *Noordwijks Cement Accoord case*) [1967] E.C.R. 75: a notification by the Commission that certain agreements were prohibited under Art. 85/EEC, which had the effect of removing a temporary immunity from fines, was held to be reviewable even though such fines could only be imposed if further steps were taken by the Commission.

[39] Collins *op. cit.* p. 305, n. 44, pp. 232–234, 236–240. The Court looks to the substance and not the form; the fact that the act has been promulgated as a regulation is not conclusive. See, *e.g.* Cases 113, 118–121/77, *Japanese Ball Bearings Cases* [1979] E.C.R. 1185 where four Japanese ball-bearing manufacturers were held to be entitled to challenge a regulation imposing an import duty in general terms, but which on the facts was aimed at them.

[40] There are a number of cases on this point, which are not always easy to reconcile: Collins, pp. 234–256; Hartley (1994), Chap. 12; R. Greaves, (1988) 11 E.L. Rev. 119.

[41] Art. 174/EC.

Preliminary decisions can only be challenged if they affect the applicant's rights independently of the final decision: otherwise, the applicant must await the final decision and challenge that.[42]

The grounds for challenge are set out in Article 173.[43] Although they are based upon the grounds for review in continental, particularly French, administrative law, arguments may be based on principles of administrative law derived from the legal systems of any Member State. The grounds may overlap in the sense that a particular set of facts may involve infringements under more than one heading.

Lack of competence corresponds to the English concept of substantive *ultra vires*[44] and the French concept of *excès de pouvoir* or *incompétence*. It may not be easily distinguishable from an allegation of *infringement of the Treaties or any rules of law relating to their application*. An example is *Meroni v. High Authority*[45] where certain decisions under the Coal and Steel Treaty were held to be improperly delegated to certain subordinate bodies.

Infringement of an essential procedural requirement corresponds to the English doctrine of procedural *ultra vires* and the French concept of *vice de forme*. Only requirements of substantial importance are mandatory: for example, requirements to hold a hearing,[46] to consult the European Parliament,[47] to give reasons[48] and to state the provision under which the measure is adopted.[49] Minor irregularities are ignored; for example, notification of a decision to a subsidiary rather than to the applicants where the latter had full knowledge of the decision in time to institute proceedings,[50] and the reporting of a decision in the *Official Journal* under an inaccurate title.[51]

Misuse of powers broadly corresponds to the abuse of discretion aspect of the *ultra vires* doctrine and the French concept of *détournement de pouvoir*. It covers, for example, the use of a power for an improper purpose.

---

[42] Compare Case 60/81, *I.B.M. v. Commission* [1981] E.C.R. 2639 (decision to institute proceedings for abuse of a dominant position not separately challengeable) *with Case 53/85, A.K.Z.O. Chemie v. Commission* [1986] E.C.R. 1965 (decision to show documents, claimed by the applicant to contain confidential information, to the complainant, challengeable).

[43] Hartley (1994), Chap. 15.

[44] On the English *ultra vires* doctrine see below, pp. 969–972.

[45] Case 9/56, [1957–8] E.C.R. 133; see also Case 48/69. *I.C.I. v. Commission* (the *Dyestuffs* case) [1972] E.C.R. 619.

[46] Case 41/69, *ACF Chemiefarma v. Commission* [1970] E.C.R. 661; the challenge failed on the merits: see also the *Dyestuffs* case above. A hearing may be necessary even though it is not expressly required by Community legislation: Case 17/74, *Transocean Marine Paint Association v. Commission* [1974] E.C.R. 1063.

[47] See above, p. 326.

[48] See Art. 190 above, p. 312; Case 24/62, *Germany v. Commission* [1963] E.C.R. 63. The reasons must be adequate: the act must "set out, in a concise, but clear and relevant manner, the principal issues of law and of fact upon which it is based and which are necessary in order that the reasoning which has led the Commission to its Decision may be understood" (*ibid.* p. 69). See also Case 166/78, *Italy v. Council* [1979] E.C.R. 2575. A Council directive was annulled where the statement of reasons was altered by the Council's secretariat, in a way that went beyond simple corrections of spelling and grammar: Case 131/86, *United Kingdom v. Council* [1988] E.C.R. 905.

[49] Case 45/86, *Commission v. Council* [1987] E.C.R. 1493; A. Arnull, (1987) 12 E.L. Rev. 448. These cases may also raise questions of competence: see generally K. St. C. Bradley, "The European Court and the Legal Basis of Community Legislation" (1988) 13 E.L. Rev. 379.

[50] *Dyestuffs* case, *loc. cit.* n. 45 above.

[51] Case 6/72, *Europemballage & Continental Can v. Commission* [1973] E.C.R. 215.

(b) Article 184: the plea of illegality[52]

Article 184 of the EC Treaty[53] provides that:

Notwithstanding the expiry of the period laid down in the fifth paragraph of Article 173, any party[54] may, in proceedings in which a regulation adopted jointly by the European Parliament and the Council, or a regulation[55] of the Council, of the Commission, or of the ECB is at issue, plead the grounds specified in the second paragraph of Article 173, in order to invoke before the Court of Justice the inapplicability of that regulation.''

An individual may not challenge a *regulation* under Article 173 (above); if, however, he or she happens to be a party to proceedings before the Court of Justice he or she (and any other party) may do so under Article 184. Article 184 may be invoked where proceedings are brought under some other provision of the Treaty which concern the party making the plea of illegality; it does not give that party an independent cause of action.[56]

(c) Article 175: remedy against inaction[57]

Article 175 of the EC Treaty[58] provides that:

"Should the European Parliament, the Council or the Commission, in infringement of this Treaty, fail to act, the Member States and the other institutions of the Community[59] may bring an action before the Court of Justice to have the infringement established.

The action shall be admissible only if the institution concerned has first been called upon to act. If, within two months of being so called upon, the institution concerned has not defined its position, the action may be brought within a further period of two months.

Any natural or legal person may, under the conditions laid down in the preceding paragraphs, complain to the Court of Justice that an institution of the Community has failed to address to that person any act other than a recommendation or an opinion.

The Court of Justice shall have jurisdiction, under the same conditions, in actions or proceedings brought by the ECB in the areas falling within the latter's field of competence and in actions or proceedings brought against the latter.''

The Court of Justice has built in some limitations to actions under this article. An action can only be brought where the institution in question has failed to

---

[52] Hartley (1994), Chap. 14.
[53] As substituted by Art. G(58)/TEU.
[54] This includes Member States: Case 32/65, *Italy v. Council and Commission* [1966] E.C.R. 389.
[55] But not a *decision*: Case 156/77, *Commission v. Belgium* [1978] E.C.R. 1881. The court again looks to substance rather than form: Case 92/78, *Simmenthal v. Commission* [1979] E.C.R. 77.
[56] Case 31/62, *Wohrmann v. Commission* [1962] E.C.R. 501.
[57] Hartley (1994), Chap. 13.
[58] As substituted by Art. G(54)/TEU.
[59] This includes the Council, the Commission and the Parliament: Case 13/83, *European Parliament v. Council* [1985] E.C.R. 1513: See P. Fennell, (1985) 10 E.L. Rev. 264.

define its position within two months. In *Lütticke v. Commission*[60] the Commission had declined to take action against France on the ground that it had in fact complied with the Treaty, and stated as much within the two months period; the court held that an action could therefore not be brought. An individual may not use Article 175 to circumvent the restrictions that prevent him bringing an action directly against a Member State for breach of a Treaty provision,[61] or an action outside the limits of Article 173,[62] by attempting to bring an action against the Commission (respectively) (1) for failing to take action against the Member State or (2) failing to revoke a decision not in fact open to challenge under Article 173.

(d) Articles 177 and 215

The validity of Community legislation may also be considered by the European Court of Justice on a reference under Article 177 of the EC Treaty,[63] or on an action for damages under Article 215 of the EC Treaty.[64] In such cases the restrictions built in to Article 173 do not necessarily apply.

---

[60] Case 48/65, [1966] E.C.R. 19.
[61] Under Articles 169 and 170/E.C. such actions can only be brought by a Member State or the Commission: See the *Lütticke* case, n. 60 above.
[62] See above, pp. 346–348; Cases 10 and 18/68, *Eridania v. Commission* [1969] E.C.R. 459.
[63] See below, pp. 976–987.
[64] See above, p. 107, n. 56.

CHAPTER 6

STATUTORY INTERPRETATION

A. INTRODUCTION

WHILE the enactment of a statute is the culmination of Parliament's legislative process, it is merely the starting point for what may be many years of existence, in some cases posing problems for generations of users. If it is to have its proper effect it must be read and understood, although there are many other factors which govern the extent to which a particular measure is successful. There are various kinds of statute-user and many matters which may cause them difficulty.[1] It cannot realistically be assumed that all statutes are directed at the general public and are therefore designed to be understood by them. It is argued that statutes are complicated:

"... because life is complicated. The bulk of the legislation enacted nowadays is social, economic or financial; the laws they [*i.e.* statutes] must express and the life situations they must regulate are in themselves complicated, and these laws cannot in any language or in any style be reduced to kindergarten level, any more than can the theory of relativity."[2]

The user tends to be the public official charged with the duty of implementation, the lawyer or the non-legal professional adviser, and statutes tend to be drafted accordingly: by experts for experts. Lay people[3] who wish to use statutes thus have to become acquainted with statute-handling techniques, or rely on explanatory material, such as textbooks or government leaflets, written by experts, or consult an expert personally. This is seen by some as a vicious circle: they doubt whether statutes need to be as complicated as experts who earn a living by explaining them to the rest of us would have us believe.

Some of the problems of the user, even the professional user, relate to the discovery of the relevant provisions and the establishment of an authentic, up-to-date text. The provisions may be spread among a number of statutes and statutory instruments which have to be read together. The uninstructed lay person may well not accomplish even this stage. Once established, the text also has to be understood or "interpreted".[4] The task of interpretation may vary in difficulty. Some provisions can be understood automatically, without the conscious perception of any "problem" of interpretation: some problems may be easy to solve after a moment's thought. At the other extreme, a problem may be highly complex, enough to make the reader weep. Printing or drafting errors can turn a provision into gibberish.

---

[1] See F. A. R. Bennion, *Statute Law* (3rd ed., 1990), Part II (pp. 83–205); *cf.* W. Twining and D. Miers, *How To Do Things With Rules* (3rd ed., 1991), Chaps. 4–6.

[2] E. A. Dreidger, cited in Bennion (1990), pp. 209–210.

[3] Or, indeed, lawyers and other professionals in matters outside their expertise.

[4] The O.E.D. definitions of this term include both "to expound the meaning of" and "to make out the meaning of, explain to oneself."

F. A. R. Bennion[5] has identified a number of factors that may cause doubt. Some of these doubt-factors are inevitable and even desirable: others are avoidable. First, there is what he terms the technique of *ellipsis*. Here, the draftsman refrains from using certain words that he or she regards as necessarily implied: the problem is that the users may not realise that this is the case. The unexpressed words may normally be implied in statutes of a particular kind unless Parliament expressly provides to the contrary: many of the principles of judicial review of administrative action rest on this basis,[6] as do certain principles of criminal liability.[7] Alternatively the implication may arise from the words that actually are used. The judges on occasion exercise a limited power (in practice but not in theory) to rewrite statutes, although it can be difficult to predict in any particular case whether a judge will be prepared to act in that way.[8]

Second, the draftsman may use a *broad term* ("a word or phrase of wide meaning") and leave it to the user to judge what situations fall within it. Most words can be said to have a core of certain meaning surrounded by a penumbra of uncertainty. A standard example is the term "vehicle". This clearly covers motor cars, buses and motor cycles, but it is less clear whether it covers an invalid carriage, a child's tricycle, a donkey-cart or a pair of roller-skates.[9] Examples from decided cases include whether the routine oiling and maintenance of points apparatus on the railway fell within the term "relaying or repairing" the permanent way[10]; whether an accident arose "out of and in the course of [the victim's] ... employment"[11]; and whether a car from which the engine had been stolen and a car which could not move under its own power as parts were missing or rusted were "mechanically propelled vehicles" for which a licence was required.[12] Sir Rupert Cross described this sort of case as "part of the daily bread of judges and practitioners."[13] One difficulty here may be that the meaning of a statutory expression may change with the passage of time.[14] A further technical point that may arise when it has to be decided whether

---

[5] *op. cit.* n. 1 above, Chaps 15–19.

[6] *e.g.* breach of natural justice, abuse of discretionary powers: see below, pp. 970–971.

[7] *e.g.* the effect of mistake and insanity on criminal liability. A major defect of the drafting of many statutes creating offences is that they do not make it clear whether *mens rea* is a necessary ingredient: see, *e.g. R. v. Warner* [1969] 2 A.C. 256. Another common defect is that statutes imposing duties do not indicate whether breach of a duty can give rise to a civil action: see, *e.g., Lonhro Ltd v. Shell Petroleum Co. Ltd (No. 2)* [1982] A.C. 173.

[8] See below, pp. 368–372.

[9] Twining and Miers (1991), pp. 216–219, *cf.* H. L. A. Hart, (1958) 4 J.S.P.T.L. (N.S.) 144–145.

[10] *London and North-Eastern Railway v. Berriman* [1946] A.C. 278.

[11] See, *e.g. R. v. Industrial Injuries Commissioner, ex p. A.E.U. (No. 2)* [1966] 2 Q.B. 31. (accident befalling an employee overstaying a tea-break). There have been many cases on this expression: see N. J. Wikeley, *Ogus, Barendt and Wikely's, The Law of Social Security* (4th ed., 1995), pp. 306–323.

[12] *Newberry v. Simmonds* [1961] 2 Q.B. 345; *Smart v. Allan* [1963] 1 Q.B. 291: the answers were, respectively, yes and no, the main difference being that in the latter case there was no reasonable prospect of the vehicle ever being made mobile again.

[13] J. Bell and Sir George Engle, *Cross, Statutory Interpretation* (3rd ed., 1995), pp. 75–76. Another good illustration is provided by the refusal of Parliament to define "disposal" and "disposition" for the purposes of, respectively, capital gains tax and capital transfer tax: see J. Tiley, *Revenue Law* (3rd ed., 1981), paras. 20–01 and 42–02.

[14] See, for example, the "public good" defence in section 4 of the Obscene Publications Act 1959: *R. v. Jordan* [1977] A.C. 699, 718, *per* Lord Wilberforce: "[the phrase 'other objects of general concern'] is no doubt a mobile phrase; it may, and should, change in content as society changes." *Cf. Dyson Holdings Ltd v. Fox* [1976] Q.B. 503 on whether the term "family" includes a "common law" spouse, criticised by D. J. Hurst, (1983) 3 L.S. 21.

a set of facts conforms to a statutory description is whether that decision is one of fact or one of law. This governs whether it should be decided by the jury (if there is one) or the judge, and the extent to which the decision can be upset by an appellate court.[15]

Third, there may be *politic uncertainty*: ambiguous words may be used deliberately, for example where a provision is politically contentious, or where departments wish to minimise the risk of legal challenge.[16]

Fourth, there may be *unforeseeable developments*. These the draftsman cannot be expected to cover, although he or she may use language that is capable of extension. A well-known example of such extension is *Attorney-General v. Edison Telephone Co.*[17] where the Telegraph Act 1869, passed before the telephone was invented, was held to confer on the Postmaster General certain powers concerning telephone messages. However, extension may not be possible, and fresh legislation may be necessary. For example, new provisions of revenue law are regularly passed to meet novel tax avoidance schemes developed by smart lawyers and accountants precisely to exploit unforeseen loopholes.

Fifth, there are many ways in which the wording may be inadequate. There may be a printing error.[18] There may be a drafting error such as the use of a word with two or more distinct meanings without a sufficient indication from the context or by a definition of which is meant, or grammatical or syntactic ambiguity. Examples of the latter include "ambiguous modification", where it is unclear which words are limited, restricted or described by a "modifier",[19] and the faulty reference of pronouns.[20] There may be an erroneous reference to another statute.[21] The draftsman may be mistaken about the law that is being altered[22] or the factual situation with which he or she is dealing. The statutory

---

[15] See above, pp. 10–12 and below, pp. 953–955.

[16] Bennion (1990), Chap. 17; A. S. Miller, "Statutory language and the purposive use of ambiguity" 42 Va.L.Rev. 23 (1956); V. Sacks, "Towards Discovering Parliamentary Intent" [1982] Stat.L.R. 143, 157 (research on the background to a number of cases of interpretative difficulty showed that "unintelligible legislation was being added to the statute book because the Government either lacked clear objectives, or, had deliberately intended to obfuscate in order to avoid controversy").

[17] (1880) 6 Q.B.D. 244. *Cf. Royal College of Nursing v. DHSS* [1981] A.C. 800.

[18] *e.g.* the presence of the word "upon" at the end of section 6 of the Statute of Frauds Amendment Act 1828: *Lyde v. Barnard* (1836) 1 M. & W. 101; Local Government Act 1972, s.262(12) (reference to subsection (10) rather than subsection (9) in the Queen's Printer's copy, corrected in *Statutes in Force*); the presence of the word "convenient" in the Prescription Act 1832, s.8, apparently a misprint for "easement": Sir Robert Megarry and H. W. R. Wade, *The Law Of Real Property* (5th ed., 1984), p. 885.

[19] G. C. Thornton, *Legislative Drafting* (3rd ed., 1987), pp. 23–29. *e.g.* "public hospital or school" (does "public" modify "school" as well as "hospital"?). A statute of Charles II disqualified those who lacked certain property qualifications "other than the son and heir apparent of an esquire, or other person of higher degree." In *Jones v. Smart* (1784) 1 Term Rep. 44 the court held that the words "son and heir apparent of " governed "person of higher degree" as well as "esquire."

[20] Thornton, pp. 29–32. *e.g.* "and when they arose early in the morning, behold, they were all dead corpses": 2 Kings XIX 35.

[21] *e.g.* War Damage Act 1943, s.66(2)(b), corrected by the Universities and College Estates Act 1964, s.4(1), Sched. 3.

[22] *e.g. Inland Revenue Commissioners v. Ayshire Employers' Mutual Insurance Association* [1946] 1 All E.R. 537.

provision may be narrower[23] or wider[24] than the object of the legislation. The
provision may fail to indicate an important element, such as the time at which
conditions of eligibility for some benefit are to be judged.[25] There may be the
type of error described as "defective deeming, or asifism gone wrong."[26] There
may be conflict within a statute or between different statutes. There may simply
be a slip by the draftsman.[27] Overall, Bennion states that "it is extremely
common for draftsmen to produce a text which raises doubt unnecessarily."[28]

As mentioned already, various people may have to interpret statutes for their
own purposes. Some may take action based on their own view of a statutory
provision. For example, in *R. v. Adams*[29] police officers decided that they could
rely on a search warrant in respect of certain premises which had already been
used once. The statute did not deal expressly with the question whether a warrant
could be used more than once: the court held that it could not. Tax assessments
may well be based on the Inland Revenue's interpretation of a doubtful provision
of tax law: it will be for the Commissioners of Taxes or the courts to rule on
the matter if the Revenue view is challenged. The courts stand in a rather different position from other statute users in that they have the power to resolve
authoritatively disputes concerning the meaning of statutory provisions: their
decisions are binding on the parties and may constitute binding precedents for
the future.

It is notable that the general methods of statutory interpretation are not themselves regulated by Parliament, but have been developed by the judges. The
Interpretation Act 1978, which from its title might seem to fulfil such a function,
has the comparatively unambitious aim of providing certain standard definitions
of common provisions,[30] and thereby enables statutes to be drafted more briefly
than otherwise would be the case. Where Parliament or, more realistically, the
executive has been dissatisfied with judicial interpretation of particular provisions the response has been to pay close attention to the future drafting of
specific provisions in that area rather than to attempt to introduce legislation
giving general directions to the judiciary. In the remainder of this chapter we
consider the general approaches taken by judges to the interpretation of statutes,
various internal and external aids to interpretation, the main presumptions which
may be invoked and proposals for reform.

---

[23] *e.g. Adler v. George* [1964] 2 Q.B. 7: the Official Secrets Act 1920, s.3 prohibited obstruction
"in the vicinity of" a prohibited place; the Divisional Court held that this was to be read as
"in or in the vicinity of."

[24] *e.g.* the Criminal Law Act 1977, ss.1 and 5, which on a literal interpretation preserved a much
wider range of common law conspiracies than was obviously intended; in *R. v. Duncalf* [1979]
1 W.L.R. 918 the Court of Appeal declined to give a literal reading "when the effect of so doing
would be so largely to destroy the obvious purpose of this Act" (*per* Roskill L.J. at p. 923). *R.
v. Duncalf* was approved by the House of Lords in *R. v. Ayres* [1984] A.C. 447. See now the
Criminal Justice Act 1987, s.12.

[25] *Jackson v. Hall* [1980] A.C. 854, concerning the Agriculture (Miscellaneous Provisions) Act
1976.

[26] Bennion (1990), pp. 274–275; R. E. Megarry, *Miscellany-at-law* (1955), pp. 361–362 ("there is
too be much of this damned deeming": *per* (A. P. Herbert's) Lord Mildew).

[27] *cf. R. v. Moore* (1994) 159 J.P. 101, below, p. 393, n. 36.

[28] *ibid.* p. 279.

[29] [1980] Q.B. 575.

[30] See above, pp. 284–285.

B. GENERAL APPROACHES TO STATUTORY INTERPRETATION

Judicial attitudes to legislation have changed with the passage of time. One of the important factors has been the part played by statutes in the general scheme of the law: a related factor has been the conception held by judges as to the proper scope of the judicial function. Three so-called "rules" of statutory interpretation have been identified: the "mischief rule," the "golden rule" and the "literal rule," each originating at different stages of legal history. To call them "rules" is misleading: it is better to think of them as general approaches. They were analysed by Professor John Willis in his influential article "Statute Interpretation in a Nutshell".[31] He suggested that:

"a court invokes whichever of the rules produces a result that satisfies its sense of justice in the case before it. Although the literal rule is the one most frequently referred to in express terms, the courts treat all three as valid and refer to them as occasion demands, but, naturally enough, do not assign any reasons for choosing one rather than another."[32]

Thus, on some occasions the "literal rule" would be preferred to the "mischief rule": on others the reverse would be the case. It was impossible to predict with certainty which approach would be adopted in a particular case.[33] More recently, Sir Rupert Cross suggested that the English approach involves not so much a choice between alternative "rules" as a progressive analysis in which the judge first considers the ordinary meaning of the words in the general context of the statute, a broad view being taken of what constitutes the "context", and then moves on to consider other possibilities where the ordinary meaning leads to an absurd result.[34] This unified "contextual" approach is supported by dicta in decisions of the House of Lords where general principles of statutory interpretation have been discussed. However, generalisations as to what judges actually do are difficult to substantiate: Sir Rupert Cross made it clear that his propositions were stated "with all the diffidence, hesitancy and reservation that the subject demands."[35]

It is important to appreciate that this analysis of the approach of judges to statutory interpretation operates at a high level of generality. It provides a framework for the solution of interpretative problems, but is not and cannot itself provide the solution. Where a problem of statutory interpretation comes before a court, counsel for each side will advance detailed arguments based on such matters as the nuances of language, the purpose of the statute, the particular aids and presumptions discussed below, and previously decided cases in the area. Different readings of the text will be examined to see which fits best into the statutory scheme. The practical consequences of the different possible interpretations will be compared. Indeed, the discussions in the House of Lords

---

[31] (1938) 16 Can. Bar Rev. 1.
[32] *ibid.* p. 16.
[33] This situation can be unkindly described as the "today's a day for the golden rule" approach. The tone of Professor Willis' article was one of scepticism.
[34] The current editors of his book refer instead to "a result which is contrary to the purpose of the statute": see below, p. 362, n. 81.
[35] J. Bell and Sir George Engle, *Cross, Statutory Interpretation* (3rd ed., 1995), p. 48.

of general approaches to interpretation, on which Sir Rupert Cross's propositions were based, are not commonly cited in argument in decided cases.

The most recent major work on the subject is F. A. R. Bennion's *Statutory Interpretation*.[36] In his introduction, the author writes:

"The natural and reasonable desire that statutes should be easily understood is doomed to disappointment. Thwarted, it shifts to an equally natural and reasonable desire for efficient tools of interpretation. If statutes must be obscure, let us at least have simple devices to elucidate them. A golden rule would be best, to unlock all mysteries. Alas, there is no golden rule. Nor is there a mischief rule, or a literal rule, or any other cure-all rule of thumb. Instead there are a thousand and one interpretative *criteria*. Fortunately, not all of these present themselves in any one case; but those that do yield factors that the interpreter must figuratively weigh and balance."[37]

The book comprises a Code, with a critical Commentary, in which various detailed interpretative criteria are enumerated, illustrated, and criticised. It is a valuable source of the many kinds of detailed arguments that might be advanced before a court, and relies to a much greater extent than the established practitioners' manuals[38] on recent case law. This is particularly important "given the changes in judicial attitudes to statutory interpretation that have occurred in the past two-to-three decades. . . ."[39] There is a greater willingness to attempt to identify and to consider the purpose of the provision in question, and much less of (if ever there was) an inclination to adhere strictly to the supposed literal meaning of words irrespective of the context and the consequences of such a reading.[40] This point is strongly reinforced by the landmark decision of the House of Lords in *Pepper* (*Inspector of Taxes*) v. *Hart*[41] that the courts are permitted in defined circumstances to consider Parliamentary material, including statements in debate, as an aid to statutory construction. One of the arguments in favour of relaxing the previous rule that excluded reference to such material was expressed as follows by Lord Griffiths[42]:

"The days have long passed when the courts adopted a strict constructionist view of interpretation which required them to adopt the literal meaning of the language. The courts now adopt a purposive approach which seeks to give effect to the true purpose of legislation and are prepared to look at much extraneous material that bears upon the background against which the legislation was enacted. Why then cut ourselves off from the one source in which may be found an authoritative statement of the intention with which the legislation is placed before Parliament?"

---

[36] (2nd ed., 1992, Supplement, 1993). For full reviews of the first edition, see D. R. Miers, [1986] P.L. 160; J. Bell, (1986) 6 O.J.L.S. 288.

[37] *ibid.*, p. 2.

[38] P. St. J. Langan, *Maxwell on the Interpretation of Statutes* (12th ed., 1969); S. G. G. Edgar, *Craies on Statute Law* (7th ed., 1971). These works are regularly cited in court; Bennion (1992) is now cited with increasing frequency, often in preference to the older works.

[39] D. R. Miers, [1986] P.L. 160, 162.

[40] Below, pp. 359–361.

[41] [1993] A.C. 593; below, pp. 390–394.

[42] [1993] A.C. 593, 617. *Cf.* Lord Browne-Wilkinson's reference to "the purposive approach to construction now adopted by the courts in order to give effect to the true intentions of the legislature" (p. 635).

It is often stated, as by Lord Griffiths in the passage just quoted, that the task of the judge is to discover the "intention of Parliament". This may be as to either the meaning or the scope of a particular word or phrase, or the general purpose that was to be achieved by the statute.[43] This concept causes difficulty for a number of reasons.[44] It cannot mean the intention of "all the members of both Houses" as some may not have been aware of the measure, and others may have opposed it. If it is taken to mean "all the members of both Houses who voted for it" there may be problems in that the majority "will almost certainly have been constituted by different persons at the different stages of the passage of the Bill,"[45] and might have had different views as to its meaning or purpose. A vote in favour of a Bill may reflect loyalty to the party whip rather than an understanding or even half-hearted approval of the measure. Even assuming that there is a "collective intention" it is difficult to see how it could be ascertained. Would it be by reference to the debates or by canvassing the opinions of the legislators individually, possibly years after the event? The former would limit the "sample" to the minority who happened to speak: the latter would be a research task which might just produce usable results in respect of a provision requiring interpretation soon after enactment, but with the passage of time it would rapidly become hopeless. In any event it is questionable whether even if it is possible it would be appropriate for the meaning of a particular provision to be determined by an opinion poll of the original legislators. Given these difficulties, and the rule that prohibited reference to Parliamentary material,[46] it was stated that the best is not the only evidence of the "intention of Parliament" was the wording of the statute:

"We often say that we are looking for the intention of Parliament, but that is not quite accurate. We are seeking the meaning of the words which Parliament used. We are seeking not what Parliament meant but the true meaning of what they said."[47]

The meaning of the "intention of Parliament" must now be seen in the light of the decision in *Pepper (Inspector of Taxes) v. Hart*.[48] Reference may now be made in specified circumstances to Parliamentary material that

"clearly discloses the mischief aimed at or the legislative intention lying behind the ambiguous or obscure words."

In the case of statements made to Parliament,

"as at present advised I cannot foresee that any statement other than the

---

[43] Termed respectively "particular legislative intent" and "general legislative intent" by G. C. MacCallum Jr., (1966) 75 Yale L.J. 754.

[44] See Cross (1995), pp. 23–31; M. Radin, (1930) 43 Harv. L.R. 863, 869–872; J. M. Landis, *ibid.* pp. 886–893; D. Payne, (1956) 9 C.L.P. 96; R. Dworkin, "How to read the Civil Rights Act", *New York Review of Books*, December 20, 1979, pp. 37–43.

[45] Cross (1995), p. 24.

[46] See below, pp. 389–390.

[47] *Per* Lord Reid in *Black-Clawson International Ltd v. Papierwerke Waldhof-Aschaffenburg A. G.* [1975] A.C. 591, 613.

[48] [1993] A.C. 593; below, pp. 390–394.

statement of the Minister or other promoter of the Bill is likely to meet these criteria.''[49]

Thus, ''an authoritative statement of the intention with which the legislation is placed before Parliament''[50] is taken to show which interpretation was ''intended by Parliament.''[51] The theory on which this inference is based is that:

> ''If a Minister clearly states the effect of a provision and there is no subsequent relevant amendment to the Bill or withdrawal of the statement it is reasonable to assume that Parliament passed the Bill on the basis that the provision would have the effect stated.''[52]

This, together with the rejection of the possibility of ''dredging through conflicting statements of intention'' in order to establish ''the true intention of Parliament'',[53] confirms that the ''intention of Parliament'' is a notional device rather than something that actually exists. The House of Lords in *Pepper (Inspector of Taxes) v. Hart*[54] was at pains to confirm the orthodox position as to the separation of powers whereby Parliament legislates and the judiciary interpret; the courts would still be interpreting the words of the Act, albeit with the assistance of a wider range of material.[55]

1. The ''Mischief Rule''

The classic statement of the ''mischief rule'' is contained in the resolutions of the Barons of the Exchequer in *Heydon's Case*:[56]

> ''that for the sure and true interpretation of all statutes in general (be they penal or beneficial, restrictive or enlarging of the common law,) four things are to be discerned and considered:—
>
> 1st. What was the common law before the making of the Act.
>
> 2nd. What was the mischief and defect for which the common law did not provide.
>
> 3rd. What remedy the Parliament hath resolved and appointed to cure the disease of the commonwealth.
>
> And, 4th. The true reason of the remedy; and then the office of all the Judges is always to make such construction as shall suppress the mischief, and advance the remedy, and to suppress subtle inventions and evasions for continuance of the mischief, and *pro privato commodo*, and to add force

---

[49] *Ibid.*, p. 634, *per* Lord Browne-Wilkinson (with whom five of the other six members of the House agreed).

[50] *ibid.*, p. 617G, *per* Lord Griffiths.

[51] *ibid.*, p. 617A, *per* Lord Bridge.

[52] *ibid.*, p. 633, *per* Lord Browne-Wilkinson, summarising the submissions of Anthony Lester Q.C. which he subsequently stated that he accepted (p. 634).

[53] *ibid.*, p. 631, *per* Lord Browne-Wilkinson, referring to another of Mr Lester's arguments.

[54] *ibid.*, p. 639–640, *per* Lord Browne-Wilkinson.

[55] This important constitutional point was emphasised by Lord Scarman in *Duport Steels Ltd* v. *Sirs* [1980] I.C.R. 161, 189–190, above, p. 288.

[56] (1584) 3 Co.Rep. 7a, 7b.

and life to the cure and remedy, according to the true intent of the makers of the Act, *pro bono publico.*''

These resolutions were the product of a time when statutes were a minor source of law by comparison with the common law, when drafting was by no means as exact a process as it is today[57] and before the supremacy of Parliament was firmly established. The ''mischief'' could often be discerned from the lengthy preamble normally included.[58]

The ''mischief rule'' was regarded by the Law Commissions, which reported on statutory interpretation in 1969,[59] as a ''rather more satisfactory approach'' than the other two established ''rules''. This was so even though the formulation in *Heydon's Case* was archaic in language, reflected a very different constitutional balance between the executive, Parliament and the people than would now be acceptable, failed to make clear the extent to which the judge should consider the actual language of the statute, assumed that statutes were subsidiary or supplemental to the common law and predated rules which prevented judges considering certain material which might throw light on the ''mischief'' and the ''true reason of the remedy''.[60] Seemingly, therefore, it was the best of a bad lot.

It came to be accepted that the ''mischief rule'' should only be applied where the words were ambiguous[61]; one of the improvements of the ''contextual approach'' discussed below is that the purpose of the statute should be considered as part of the context of the statutory words, and not merely as a last resort where the words are ambiguous.

2. THE ''LITERAL RULE''

The eighteenth and nineteenth centuries saw a trend towards a more literal approach. Courts took an increasingly strict view of the words of a statute: if the case before them was not precisely covered they were not prepared to countenance any alteration of the statutory language. For example, in *R. v. Harris*[62] a statute[63] which made it an offence for someone ''unlawfully and maliciously'' to ''stab, cut, or wound any person'' was held not to apply where the defendant bit off the end of the victim's nose; the words indicated that for an offence to be committed some form of instrument had to be used.[64]

One of the leading statements of the ''literal rule'' was made by Tindal C. J. in advising the House of Lords in the *Sussex Peerage* case[65]:

---

[57] Some statutes were well drafted, such as the Statute of Uses 1535.
[58] *Black-Clawson International Ltd v. Papierwerke Waldhof-Aschaffenburg A.G.* [1975] A.C. 591 *per* Lord Diplock at pp. 637–638. See below, pp. 374–375.
[59] Law Com. No. 21; Scot. Law Com. No. 11.
[60] *ibid.* pp. 19–20. See below, pp. 389–394.
[61] See the *Sussex Peerage Case*, below, pp. 359–360.
[62] (1836) 7 C. & P. 446.
[63] 9 Geo. IV c. 31 s.12.
[64] The judge indicated that the defendant would be indicted for aggravated assault and thus ''would not escape punishment if she was guilty.'' *Cf. Jones v. Smart*, above, p. 353, n. 19.
[65] (1844) 11 Cl. & Fin. 85, 143.

"My Lords, the only rule for the construction of Acts of Parliament is, that they should be construed according to the intent of the Parliament which passed the Act. If the words of the statute are in themselves precise and unambiguous, then no more can be necessary than to expound those words in their natural and ordinary sense. The words themselves alone do, in such case, best declare the intention of the lawgiver. But if any doubt arises from the terms employed by the Legislature, it has always been held a safe means of collecting the intention, to call in aid the ground and cause of making the statute, and to have recourse to the preamble, which, according to Chief Justice Dyer (*Stowel v. Lord Zouch*, Plowden, 369) is 'a key to open the minds of the makers of the Act, and the mischiefs which they intended to redress.' "

This was taken to mean that the "mischief rule" was only applicable where the words were ambiguous.

The literal rule was favoured on a variety of grounds. It encouraged precision in drafting. Should any alternative approach be adopted, an alteration of the statutory language could be seen as a usurpation by non-elected judges of the legislative function of Parliament,[66] and other statute users would have the difficult task of predicting how doubtful provisions might be "rewritten" by the judges. On the other hand judges were criticised on the ground that:

"they have tended excessively to emphasise the literal meaning of statutory provisions without giving due weight to their meaning in wider contexts. . . ."[67]

"To place undue emphasis on the literal meaning of the words of a provision is to assume an unattainable perfection in draftsmanship; . . . [and] ignores the limitations of language, which is not infrequently demonstrated even at the level of the House of Lords when Law Lords differ as to the so-called 'plain meaning' of words."[68]

Moreover, the literal approach is not helpful where the court is resolving a doubt as to the applicability of a "broad term".

Much has been made of a few post-war cases where literalism has perhaps been taken too far. For example, in *Bourne v. Norwich Crematorium*[69] the question was whether a capital allowance could be claimed in respect of expenditure on a new furnace chamber and chimney tower of a crematorium, as expenditure on "buildings and structures" in use "for the purpose of a trade which consists of the manufacture of goods or materials or the subjection of goods or materials to any process." Stamp J. held that it could not: it would be "a distortion of the English language to describe the living or the dead as goods or materials."[70] However, it is unlikely that either the draftsman or Parliament thought specifi-

---

[66] Conversely, it might be argued that a judge could conceal that his or her role was not as impersonal and objective as he or she would like it to appear by paying lip-service to the literal rule.

[67] Law Com. No. 21; Scot. Law Com. No. 11, p. 5.

[68] *ibid.* p. 17. For example, in *London and North Eastern Railway v. Berriman* [1946] A.C. 278 (below p. 367) members of the House of Lords who came to opposite conclusions on the meaning of "repairing" nevertheless each claimed to be applying the "fair and ordinary" (Lord Macmillan at p. 295) or the "natural and ordinary" meaning (Lord Wright at p. 301).

[69] [1967] 1 W.L.R. 691. See also *L.N.E.R. v. Berriman*, below, p. 367.

[70] *ibid.* p. 695.

cally of cremation in connection with capital allowances and the policy of the provisions on capital allowances would seem to cover the "trade" of cremation.[71]

The "contextual approach" discussed below is based on the literal approach, but requires greater attention to be paid to the context in which the words appear.

3. The "Golden Rule"

Some judges have suggested that a court may depart from the ordinary meaning where that would lead to absurdity. In *Grey v. Pearson*[72] Lord Wensleydale said:

"I have been long and deeply impressed with the wisdom of the rule, now, I believe, universally adopted, at least in the Courts of Law in Westminster Hall, that in construing wills and indeed statutes, and all written instruments, the grammatical and ordinary sense of the words is to be adhered to, unless that would lead to some absurdity, or some repugnance or inconsistency with the rest of the instrument, in which case the grammatical and ordinary sense of the words may be modified, so as to avoid that absurdity and inconsistency, but no farther."

This became known as "Lord Wensleydale's golden rule" following a dictum of Lord Blackburn in *River Wear Commissioners v. Adamson*[73]:

"I believe that it is not disputed that what Lord Wensleydale used to call the golden rule is right, *viz.*, that we are to take the whole statute together and construe it all together, giving the words their ordinary signification, unless when so applied they produce an inconsistency, or an absurdity or inconvenience so great as to convince the Court that the intention could not have been to use them in their ordinary signification, and to justify the Court in putting on them some other signification, which, though less proper, is one which the Court thinks the words will bear."

One controversial aspect of this "rule" was whether it could only apply where the words were ambiguous, or whether it could also be used where the ordinary meaning was clear but "absurd". In so far as it was confined to the former situation it was a statement of the blindingly obvious: that where statutory words are ambiguous an interpretation that is not absurd is to be preferred to one that is. In so far as the "rule" could be applied in the latter situation it was clear that it should be used sparingly.[74] Some judges argued it could not be used in such a case at all. Lord Esher said.[75]

---

[71] See Law Com. No. 21, pp. 5–6; Cross (1995), p. 70. The decision has not, however, been reversed by statute.

[72] (1857) 6 H. L. Cas. 61, 106 (a case concerning the construction of a will). *Cf.* the same judge when he was Parke B. in *Becke v. Smith* (1836) 2 M. & W. 191, 195.

[73] (1877) 2 App. Cas. 743, 764–765.

[74] Lord Mersey in *Thompson v. Goold & Co.* [1910] A.C. 409, 420; Lord Loreburn in *Vickers Sons, and Maxim Ltd v. Evans* [1910] A.C. 444, 445.

[75] *R. v. Judge of the City of London Court* [1892] 1 Q.B. 273, 290. *Cf.* Lord Atkinson in *Vacher & Sons Ltd v. London Society of Compositors* [1913] A.C. 107, 121–122.

"If the words of an Act are clear, you must follow them, even though they lead to a manifest absurdity. The Court has nothing to do with the question whether the legislature has committed an absurdity."

Another point of doubt was whether the concept of "absurdity" was confined to cases where a provision was "absurd" because it was "repugnant" to or "inconsistent" with other provisions of the statute, or whether it extended to "absurdity" for any reason. The Law Commissions noted that the "rule" provided no clear means to test the existence of the characteristics of absurdity, inconsistency or inconvenience. or to measure their quality or extent.[76] As it seemed that "absurdity" was in practice judged by reference to whether a particular interpretation was irreconcilable with the general policy of the legislature "the golden rule turns out to be a less explicit form of the mischief rule.[77] The ideas behind the "golden rule" are reflected in the second and third aspects of the contextual approach discussed below.

4. The Unified "Contextual" Approach

Sir Rupert Cross set out a unified approach to statutory interpretation as follows[78]:

"1. The judge must give effect to the [grammatical and][79] ordinary or, where appropriate, the technical meaning of words in the general context of the statute; he must also determine the extent of general words with reference to that context.
2. If the judge considers that the application of the words in their [grammatical and][80] ordinary sense would produce [a result which is contrary to the purpose of the statute],[81] he may apply them in any secondary meaning which they are capable of bearing.
3. The judge may read in words which he considers to be necessarily implied by words which are already in the statute and he has a limited power to add to, alter or ignore statutory words in order to prevent a provision from being unintelligible or absurd or totally unreasonable, unworkable, or totally irreconcilable with the rest of the statute.
4. In applying the above rules the judge may resort to [certain] aids to construction and presumptions. . . ."

---

[76] Law Com. No. 21; Scot. Law Com. No. 11, p. 19.
[77] *ibid.* Sir Rupert Cross regarded the "golden rule" as a "gloss upon the literal rule": Cross *Statutory Interpretation* (1976), p. 170. *Cf.* E. A. Dreidger, (1981) 59 Can. Bar Rev. 781.
[78] Cross (1976), p. 43; third edition by J. Bell and Sir George Engle (1995), p. 49. The label "contextual" was not attached by Cross, but is used here for convenience of reference. Rules 1 and 2 were expounded by Lord Simon in *Maunsell v. Olins* [1975] A.C. 373, 391; rule 3 by Lord Reid in *Federal Steam Navigation Co. Ltd v. Department of Trade and Industry* [1974] 1 W.L.R. 505, 508–509. The "aids" and "presumptions" are discussed in Chapters 5 to 7 of Cross's book.
[79] These words were added by the editors of the second and third editions of *Cross*.
[80] *ibid.*
[81] These words replace "an absurd result which cannot reasonably be supposed to have been the intention of the legislature" from the first edition. See pp. 89–92 of the third edition for discussion of the change.

(a) Rule 1

Under this approach a broader view is taken of the context than under previous approaches. The importance of context was discussed in *Attorney-General v. Prince Ernest Augustus of Hanover.*[82] A statute of Queen Anne's reign[83] provided that Princess Sophia of Hanover "and the Issue of Her Body and all Persons lineally descending from Her born or hereafter to be born be and shall be . . . deemed . . . natural born Subjects of this Kingdom." The preamble recited that in order that they might be encouraged to become acquainted with the laws and constitutions of this realm "it is just and highly reasonable that they in Your Majesties Lifetime" be naturalised.[84] The respondent, who was born in 1914 and was a lineal descendant of Sophia, was granted a declaration that he was a British subject. The enacting words were clear and could not be restricted by the words in the preamble. Viscount Simonds said[85]:

> "[W]ords, and particularly general words, cannot be read in isolation; their colour and content are derived from their context. So it is that I conceive it to be my right and duty to examine every word of a statute in its context, and I use context in its widest sense which I have already indicated as including not only other enacting provisions of the same statute, but its preamble, the existing state of the law, other statutes *in pari materia*, and the mischief which I can, by those and other legitimate means, discern the statute was intended to remedy. . . .
>
> "[N]o one should profess to understand any part of a statute or of any other document before he has read the whole of it. Until he has done so, he is not entitled to say that it, or any part of it, is clear and unambiguous."

Lord Normand said[86]:

> "In order to discover the intention of Parliament it is proper that the court should read the whole Act, inform itself of the legal context of the Act, including Acts so related to it that they may throw light on its meaning, and of the factual context, such as the mischief to be remedied. . . . It is the merest commonplace to say that words abstracted from context may be meaningless or misleading."

Even after the context had been considered it could not be said that the enacting words were unclear; the preamble itself was ambiguous; three of their Lordships also held that there was no inherent absurdity, judged at the time when the statute was passed, in the fact that all lineal descendants would be naturalised.[87]

That the object of the statute is to be considered as part of the context was

---

[82] [1957] A.C. 436.

[83] 4 & 5 Anne c. 16.

[84] On the death of Queen Anne without issue the Crown of England would descend on Sophia and her heirs: Sophia's son became King George I.

[85] At pp. 461, 463. Lord Tucker expressed his "complete agreement" with Viscount Simonds' opinion (p. 472).

[86] At p. 465. See also Lord Somervell at pp. 473–474.

[87] Most of the royal heads of Europe in the early twentieth century, including the German Kaiser, were lineal descendants of Sophia.

emphasised in *Maunsell v. Olins*.[88] The plaintiff owned the freehold of a farm. The farm's tenant had sublet a cottage to the Olins. If the cottage formed "part of premises which had been let as a whole on a superior letting" the Olins were entitled to the continued protection of the Rent Acts after the tenant's death. The House held by three to two[89] that the word "premises" was to be limited to dwelling-houses[90] and as the Olins were not the subtenants of part of premises in that limited sense they were not protected Lord Wilberforce expressly endorsed Viscount Simonds' dictum in the *Hanover* case.[91] Lord Simon, with whom Lord Diplock entirely agreed, held that the term "premises" was to be construed more widely as in ordinary legal parlance "the subject-matter of a letting" or, more technically, as "the subject-matter of the habendum clause of the relevant lease." He did, however, make certain general observations as to interpretation, which were not controverted in the speeches of the majority[92]:

> "The rule in *Heydon's Case*, 3, Co.Rep. 7a itself is sometimes stated as a primary canon of construction, sometimes as secondary (*i.e.* available in the case of an ambiguity): *cf. Maxwell on the Interpretation of Statutes* (12th ed., 1969), pp. 40, 96, with *Craies on Statute Law*, 7th ed. (1971) pp. 94, 96. We think that the explanation of this is that the rule is available at two stages. The first task of a court of construction is to put itself in the shoes of the draftsman—to consider what knowledge he had and, importantly, what statutory objective he had—if only as a guide to the linguistic register. Here is the first consideration of the 'mischief.' Being thus placed in the shoes of the draftsman, the court proceeds to ascertain the meaning of the statutory language. In this task 'the first and most elementary rule of construction' is to consider the plain and primary meaning, in their appropriate register, of the words used. If there is no such plain meaning (*i.e.*, if there is an ambiguity), a number of secondary canons are available to resolve it. Of these one of the most important is the rule in *Heydon's Case*. Here, then, may be a second consideration of the 'mischief'."

In 1980, Lord Scarman said in a lecture in Australia that, "In London, no one would now dare to choose the literal rather than a purposive construction of a statute: and 'legalism' is currently a term of abuse."[93] Similar statements were made in *Pepper (Inspector of Taxes) v. Hart*.[94] Reference is now frequently

---

[88] [1975] A.C. 373. See also *Stock v. Frank Jones (Tipton) Ltd* [1978] 1 W.L.R. 231, 236, and *Powdrill v. Watson* [1995] 2 All E.R. 65, 79 (Lord Browne-Wilkinson).

[89] Lord Reid, Lord Wilberforce and Viscount Dilhorne; Lord Simon and Lord Diplock dissented.

[90] Viscount Dilhorne thought the term might mean "buildings".

[91] Above.

[92] p. 395. Other examples of interpretation in the light of the mischief include *Marshall v. British Broadcasting Corporation* [1979] 1 W.L.R. 1071; *Maidstone B.C. v. Mortimer* [1980] 3 All E.R. 552 and *Royal College of Nursing of the United Kingdom v. DHSS* [1981] A.C. 800.

[93] (1981) 55 A.L.J. 175. *Cf.* Glanville Williams, "The Meaning of Literal Interpretation" (1981) 131 N.L.J. 1128, 1149, who argues that the primary question should be "What was the statute trying to do?" followed by "Will a particular proposed interpretation effectuate that object" and lastly, "Is the interpretation ruled out by the language?"

[94] [1993] A.C. 593; above, p. 356, below, p. 390.

made by judges to the concept of "purposive"[95] statutory construction. Sometimes the term is used broadly to describe the general approach to the construction of statutes. As such, it is misleading as the legislative purpose is but one of the factors that should be considered as part of the context.[96] More commonly, it is used in a narrower sense, in the course of comparing readings based on the literal or grammatical meaning of words with readings based on a purposive approach. It may be used even more narrowly to denote a construction that involves straining the words of the statute in order to fulfil the legislative purpose.[97] The increased frequency in the use of the term by judges coincides with a discernible change in emphasis,[98] but the magnitude of the change should not be exaggerated.

First, it should not be assumed that a purposive approach will lead to a different result than a literal approach. Indeed, the opposite is normally the case:

"This correspondence is not surprising; indeed it is what we would expect. Parliament, having a certain purpose, naturally seeks to express this in the words used. If it did otherwise to any great extent, the legislature would be using an inefficient method."[99]

Accordingly, in a number of cases a purposive approach to construction has been adopted alongside a literal approach, each being regarded as leading to the same result.[1] The choice between different possible readings of the provision in question will commonly be influenced by a consideration of which reading best fulfils the legislative purpose.[2] On occasion, a purposive approach has been adopted where a literal approach would have led to absurdity or would have clearly defeated the purposes of the Act.[3] However, a purposive interpretation may only be adopted if judges "can find in the statute read as a whole or in material to which they are permitted by law to refer as aids to interpretation an expression of Parliament's purpose or policy."[4] Prior to *Pepper (Inspector of Taxes) v. Hart*[5] there were cases where the judges found it impossible to discern

---

[95] *i.e.* one that will "promote the general legislative purpose underlying the provisions": *per* Lord Denning M.R. in *Nothman v. London Borough of Barnet* [1978] 1 W.L.R. 220, 228, based on the Law Commissions' Report: see below, p. 402.

[96] See above, p. 364.

[97] Bennion (1992), p. 660) suggests that the term "purposive construction" is usually intended by judges to bear this meaning. *Sed quaere.*

[98] Lord Diplock in *Carter v. Bradbeer* [1975] 1 W.L.R. 1204, 1206–1207.

[99] Bennion (1992), p. 665.

[1] *Suffolk County Council v. Mason* [1979] A.C. 705 (by both majority and minority judges): effect of designation of a footpath on a definitive map prepared under the National Parks and Access to the Countryside Act 1949; *Gardner v. Moore* [1984] A.C. 548: Motor Insurers Bureau liable to compensate victim of international criminal act; *Leverton v. Clwyd County Council* [1989] A.C. 706: woman and man employed at different establishments under the same collective agreement held to be employed under "common terms and conditions of employment."

[2] See, *e.g. Bank of Scotland v. Grimes* [1985] Q.B. 1179; *In re Smalley* [1985] A.C. 622; *Greater London Council v. Holmes* [1986] Q.B. 989; *Ferguson v. Welsh* [1987] 1 W.L.R. 1553: see below.

[3] *R. v. Ayres* [1984] A.C. 447, modified in *R. v. Cooke* [1986] A.C. 909; *cf.* Lord Diplock in *Jones v. Wrotham Park Settled Estates* [1980] A.C. 74, 105: *cf.* "rule 2" below.

[4] *per* Lord Scarman in *R. v. Barnet London Borough Council, ex p. Nilish Shah* [1983] 2 A.C. 309, 348 (the test was not satisfied here).

[5] [1993] A.C. 593: above, p. 356; below, p. 390.

the legislative purpose.[6] Recourse to parliamentary material may now help to establish the purpose of a particular provision,[7] but does not always do so.[8] Furthermore, there are limits to the extent to which the courts are prepared to distort the statutory language in order to fulfil the legislative purpose.[9] This point may explain why statements are still made that while "purposive construction to resolve ambiguities of statutory language is often appropriate and necessary", the courts' "traditional approach to construction" gives "primacy to the ordinary, grammatical meaning of statutory language", it remaining the "golden rule of construction that a statute means exactly what it says and does not mean what it does not say."[10]

In a number of cases the task of the court is to determine whether a particular expression, often of some generality, applies to certain facts.[11] The decision may be reached as a matter of common sense, often with the assistance of dictionaries,[12] but here, as elsewhere, consideration of the legislative purpose may be helpful. Recent examples include decisions that discrimination on the ground of nationality was not prohibited as being discrimination on the ground of "national origins",[13] that painting was "construction or maintenance work",[14] that a newspaper competition card was a "literary work",[15] that demolition work falls within the expression "work of construction" for the purposes of the Occupiers' Liability Act 1957,[16] that the provision of a daily continental breakfast constitutes "board" under the Rent Act 1977,[17] that a ship of any size provided by an employer for the purposes of his business constituted "equipment" under the Employer's Liability (Defective Equipment) Act 1969,[18] that a miscellaneous variety of items (including ceramic tiles, creosote, curtain railing, roofing felt and wallpaper) were not "motor accessories"[19] and that the defi-

---

[6] Harman J. in *Re Potters Oil Ltd* [1985] BCLC 203, 207–208; Lloyd L.J. in *Hemens (Valuation Officer) v. Whitsbury Farm and Stud Ltd.* [1987] Q.B. 390, 401 (the House of Lords did not advert to this point on appeal, [1988] A.C. 601); Lloyd L.J. in *I.R.C. v. Mobil North Sea Ltd* [1987] 1 W.L.R. 389, 398, dissapproved on appeal by Lord Templeman [1987] 1 W.L.R. 1065, 1071; Mann J. in *Hadley v. Texas Homecare Ltd* and other cases (1987) 86 L.G.R. 577, 582 (list of items that may be sold on Sunday).

[7] See, *e.g.*, *Pepper (Inspector of Taxes) v. Hart* itself.

[8] See below, pp. 392–393.

[9] *per* Lord Diplock in *Jones v. Wrotham Park Settled Estates*, n. 3 above; cf. "rule 3" below.

[10] *per* Lord Bridge of Harwich in *Associated Newspapers Ltd v. Wilson* [1995] 2 A.C. 454, where a majority of the House of Lords held that giving a pay rise only to those employees who agreed to switch from collective bargaining to individual contracts was not "action . . . taken against" the others preventing or deterring them from being union members (contrary to the Employment Protection (Consolidation) Act 1978, s.23(1)); to extend the relevant provisions to cover omissions as well as action would require substantial recasting. See also his Lordship's remarks in *Holden & Co. v.C.P.S. (No. 2)* [1994] 1 A.C. 22, 33.

[11] See above, pp. 10–12, 352–353.

[12] Below, p. 380.

[13] *Ealing London Borough Council v. Race Relations Board* [1972] A.C. 342.

[14] *Wilkinson v. Doncaster Metropolitan Borough Council* (1985) 84 L.G.R. 257.

[15] *Express Newspapers v. Liverpool Daily Post and Echo* [1985] 1 W.L.R. 1089.

[16] *Ferguson v. Welsh* [1987] 1 W.L.R. 1553, 1560.

[17] *Otter v. Norman* [1989] A.C. 129.

[18] *Coltman v. Bibby Tankers Ltd* [1988] A.C. 276. This was so, notwithstanding a statutory definition of "equipment" to the effect that it "includes any plant and machinery, vehicle, aircraft and clothing" (1969 Act, s.1(3)): this was held to be "for the purpose of clarity" and not to cut down the general meaning of "equipment". The House of Lords could not think of any rational explanation for the exclusion of "ship" from the definition section (although this was probably deliberate: Sir Denis Dobson, [1988] Stat. L.R. 126).

[19] *Hadley v. Texas Homecare Ltd* and other cases (1987) 96 L.G.R. 577.

nition of "gypsies" as "persons of nomadic habit of life" included the requirement that there must be some recognisable connection between the travelling
from place to place and the persons' livelihood.[20]

Cases where a court has had to choose between different "ordinary meanings" include *London and North Eastern Railway Co. v. Berriman*,[21] where the
issue was whether a railwayman was "relaying or repairing" the permanent
way while oiling and cleaning points apparatus. He had been knocked down
and killed by a train. If he had been so engaged, his window was entitled to
damages and the company's failure to provide an adequate warning system
would be a criminal offence. By three to two the House of Lords held that
"relaying or repairing" involved putting right something that was wrong and
not merely maintenance work of the kind the railwayman had been doing. The
object of the statute seemed to cover workmen in this situation, but there was
also a presumption that penal statutes should be strictly construed.[22]

Similarly, a narrow interpretation of the provision that a decision of the Crown
Court on a matter "relating to trial on indictment" cannot be questioned by an
appeal by case stated or on an application for judicial review[23] was preferred
to a broad interpretation in *Re Smalley*.[24] It was not possible to discern any
legislative purpose which would be served by giving the words any wider operation than in respect of decisions "affecting the conduct of"[25] the trial. An order
estreating the recognisance of a surely for a defendant who failed to surrender to
his bail at the Crown Court when committed for trial was not such a decision,
and so could be challenged by judicial review. By contrast, in *Greater London
Council v. Holmes*,[26] a purposive approach to the interpretation of the right to
a home loss payment, following compulsory acquisition of land, was held to be
better served by a broad rather than a narrow interpretation. It should be noted
that it has become increasingly common for judges to duck interpretative difficulties by classifying words as "ordinary English words."[27]

Examples of words used in a statute in a technical rather than an ordinary
sense include "fettling" (trimming up of metal castings as they come from the
foundry rather than "to put into good fettle" generally[28]); "crawling boards"
(special boards with battens rather than simply boards for crawling on[29]); "offer

---

[20] *R. v. South Hams District Council, ex. p. Gibb* [1995] Q.B. 158. The duties towards gypsies in
Part II of the Caravan Sites Act 1968 could not have been intended to apply to those "whose
moves are actuated not by need, but by caprice" *(per* Leggatt L.J. at p. 173).

[21] [1946] A.C. 278.

[22] See further, below, pp. 968–976. *cf. Ealing London Borough v. Race Relations Board* [1972]
A.C. 342, where the House of Lords held by four to one that discrimination on the ground of
nationality was not prohibited as being discrimination on the ground of "national origins".

[23] Supreme Court Act 1981, ss.28(2), 29(3).

[24] [1985] A.C. 622: see below, p. 976. See also *Cooper v. Motor Insurers Bureau* [1985] Q.B. 575.
Contrast the statement by May L.J. in *R. v. Broadcasting Complaints Commission, ex p. Owen*
[1985] Q.B. 1153, 1174.

[25] *per* Lord Bridge at pp. 642–645.

[26] [1986] Q.B. 989. See Oliver L.J. at p. 995. *Cf. Att.- Gen's Reference (No. 2 of 1994)* [1995] 1
W.L.R. 1579 (requirement that notice be give "on taking" a sample read as "on the occasion"
of taking it); *R. v. Lynsey* [1995] 3 All E.R.654 ("common assault" in the Criminal Justice Act
1988, s.40, construed in broad sense to include battery).

[27] See above, pp. 11–12.

[28] *Prophet v. Platt Brothers & Co. Ltd* [1961] 1 W.L.R. 1130: See Harman L.J. at p. 1133. The
word "fettle" has other meanings, as in "Tom offered to ... fettle him over the head with a
brick" quoted in O.E.D.

[29] *Jenner v. Allen West and Co. Ltd* [1959] 1 W.L.R. 554.

for sale" (held not to cover the placing of a flick-knife in a shop window as this was in the law of contract merely an invitation to treat[30]); and "acceptance" (held to be used in its technical, commercial meaning, derived from the Bills of Exchange Act 1882, and not in its ordinary colloquial meaning).[31] Conversely, the majority in *Maunsell v. Olins*[32] preferred what they regarded to be the popular meaning of "premises" to the technical legal meaning.

(b) Rule 2

A court may choose a "secondary meaning" where the primary meaning is productive of injustice, absurdity, anomaly or contradiction or a result contrary to the purpose of the statute.[33] Thus, provisions giving a power of arrest in respect of an "offender" or "a person found committing an offence" have been held to cover *apparent* offenders[34]: police officers had to act on the facts as they appeared at the time and were not to be exposed to the risk of actions for damages merely because the suspect was subsequently acquitted. A provision of the Factories Act 1937 requiring the fencing of dangerous parts of a machine while the parts were "in motion" was held not to apply where a workman turned the machine by hand in order to repair it. The machine could not have been repaired while it was fenced.[35]

A court was held entitled to grant relief to a mortgagor under an endowment mortgage, notwithstanding that the words did not strictly apply to that form of mortgage.[36] The legislative purpose of providing relief to mortgagors in temporary financial difficulties applied whatever the kind of mortgage. The notion of "absurdity" here seems not to be confined to cases where a provision is repugnant to or inconsistent with the rest of the statute.[37]

(c) Rule 3

A judge may read in words necessarily implied by the words actually used.[38] The line between cases of "necessary implication" and cases where the statutory language is modified to prevent an anomaly arising is, however, a fine one.

---

[30] *Fisher v. Bell* [1961] 1 Q.B. 394; *cf. Partridge v. Crittenden* [1968] 1 W.L.R. 1204, *British Car Auctions v. Wright* [1972] 1 W.L.R. 1519.

[31] *R. v. Nanayakkara* [1987] 1 W.L.R. 265.

[32] See above, p. 364.

[33] *cf.* the "golden rule," above, pp. 361–362; *Stock v. Frank Jones (Tipton) Ltd* [1978] 1 W.L.R. 231; *R. v. Pigg* [1983] 1 W.L.R. 6, below p. 904.

[34] *Barnard v. Gorman* [1941] A.C. 378; *Wiltshire v. Barrett* [1966] 1 Q.B. 312; *Wills v. Bowley* [1983] 1 A.C. 57 (but note the strong dissenting speeches of Lord Elwyn-Jones and Lord Lowry, who took the view that it was not proper to depart from the literal interpretation of a statute where that would prejudice the liberty of the subject).

[35] *Richard Thomas and Baldwin's Ltd v. Cummings* [1955] A.C. 321.

[36] *Bank of Scotland v. Grimes* [1985] Q.B. 1179. See also *Paterson v. Aggio* (1987) 19 H.L.R. 551.

[37] See Cross (1995), *op. cit.* p. 362, n. 78 above, pp. 93–105.

[38] *Federal Steam Navigation Co. v. Department of Trade and Industry* [1974] 1 W.L.R. 505, 508–9. *Cf.* the concept of "ellipsis": above, p. 352; *Adler v. George*, above, p. 354, n. 23; *Wiltshire v. Barrett, Barnard v. Gorman*, and *Wills v. Bowley*, n. 34 above. Contrast *R. v. Brent London Borough Council, ex p. Awua* [1995] 3 W.L.R. 215, where the House of Lords held that the term "accommodation" for the purposes of the homelessness legislation should never have been read as meaning "settled" or "permanent" accommodation.

It is clear that such modification should be a rare event. In *Stock v. Frank Jones (Tipton) Ltd.*[39] Lord Scarman said[40];

"If the words used by Parliament are plain, there is no room for the 'anomalies' test, unless the consequences are so absurd that, without going outside the statute, one can see that Parliament must have made a drafting mistake. If words 'have been inadvertently used,' it is legitimate for the court to substitute what is apt to avoid the intention of the legislature being defeated: *per* MacKinnon L.J. in *Sutherland Publishing Co. Ltd v. Caxton Publishing Co. Ltd.*[41] This is an acceptable exception to the general rule that plain language excludes a consideration of anomalies, *i.e.* mischievous or absurd consequences. If a study of the statute as a whole leads inexorably to the conclusion that Parliament had erred in its choice of words, *e.g.* used 'and' when 'or' was clearly intended, the courts can, and must, eliminate the error by interpretation. But mere 'manifest absurdity' is not enough; it must be an error (of commission or omission) which in its context defeats the intention of the Act.''

In the same case Lord Simon said that:

"a court would only be justified in departing from the plain words of the statute were it satisfied that: (1) there is clear and gross balance of anomaly; (2) Parliament, the legislative promoters and the draftsman could not have envisaged such anomaly, could not have been prepared to accept it in the interest of a supervening legislative objective; (3) the anomaly can be obviated without detriment to such legislative objective; (4) the language of the statute is susceptible of the modification required to obviate the anomaly.''[42]

There are a number of cases where the word "and" has been substituted for "or", and (? or) "or" for "and". *Federal Steam Navigation Co. Ltd v. Department of Trade and Industry*[43] concerned section 1(1) of the Oil in Navigable Waters Act 1955, which provided that where oil was discharged from a British ship in a prohibited sea area "the owner or master of the ship shall be guilty of an offence." The House of Lords held that where the owner and the master were separate persons both could be convicted, the provision being treated as if it read "the owner and/or the master". In *R. v. Oakes*[44] the Divisional Court treated section 7 of the Official Secrets Act 1920, which made it an offence where a person "aids or abets and does any act preparatory to the commission

---

[39] [1978] 1 W.L.R. 231.

[40] At p. 239.

[41] [1938] Ch. 174, 201.

[42] [1978] 1 W.L.R. 231, p. 237. See also the similar remarks of Lord Diplock in *Jones v. Wrotham Park Settled Estates* [1980] A.C. 74, 105, applied in *I.R.C. v. Trustees of Sir John Aird's Settlement* [1984] Ch. 382, and note the cautious remarks of Sir John Donaldson M.R. in *Carrington v. Therm-A-Stor Ltd* [1983] 1 W.L.R. 138.

[43] [1974] 1 W.L.R. 505. *Cf. R. F. Brown & Co. Ltd v. T. & J. Harrison* (1927) 43 T.L.R. 394, 633, where the Court of Appeal suggested that "or" could sometimes be construed conjunctively; *cf.* MacKinnon L.J. at first instance and in *Sutherland Publishing Co. Ltd v. Caxton Publishing Co. Ltd* [1938] Ch.174, 201: "That is a cowardly evasion. In truth one word is substituted for another. For 'or' can never mean 'and' ''.

[44] [1959] 2 Q.B. 350.

of an offence" under the Official Secrets Act as if it read "aids or abets *or* does any act preparatory." If read literally the result would have been "unintelligible".[45]

In *Re Lockwood*[46] Harman J. ignored certain words of a provision[47] which would have had the effect on an intestacy of preferring more distant relations to nephews and nieces.

In *R. v. Central Criminal Court, ex p. Francis & Francis (A firm)*,[48] the House of Lords held that files of conveyancing documents in the possession of solicitors were "items held with the intention of furthering a criminal purpose" and therefore not "items subject to legal privilege"[49] protected from production to the police.[50] The solicitors had no such intention, but the majority of the House of Lords[51] held that it was sufficient that the documents were intended by a third party to be used to further the criminal purpose of laundering the proceeds of illegal drug-trafficking. This interpretation accorded with the purpose of the legislation. However, in the view of the minority[52] this could not be the grammatical meaning of the words, and such a widening of the ambit of the subsection could not be justified by any legitimate process of implication of terms.[53]

> "It is one thing to abstain from giving to the language of a statute the full effect of its ordinary grammatical meaning in order to avoid some positively harmful or manifestly unjust consequence. This I would describe as a legitimate process of construction to avoid a positive absurdity. But it is quite another thing to read into a statute a meaning which the language used will not bear in order to remedy a supposed defect or shortcoming which, if not made good, will make the statutory machinery less effective than the court believes it ought to be in order to achieve its proper purpose. Even if the lacuna appears to the court as absurd, this is what I describe, inelegantly but in order to point the contrast, as a negative absurdity. I know of no legitimate principle of construction which permits such a negative absurdity to be remedied by implying words which the court thinks necessary to enhance the operation of the statutory machinery."[54]

Lord Oliver regarded the words as clear, concise, unequivocal and unambiguous: "there is no difficulty about giving the subsection a perfectly sensible operation." It might be said to be "anomalous and incomplete" but was not necessarily "absurd".[55] By contrast, Lord Griffiths regarded an interpretation that confined the application of the exception to cases where the solicitors were party

---

[45] *per* Lord Parker C.J. at p. 354. See also *R. v. Corby Juvenile Court, ex p. M* [1987] 1 W.L.R. 55, where Waite J. indicated *obiter* that he would have been prepared in effect to rectify a drafting error, in the light of the legislation's manifest purpose.

[46] [1958] Ch. 231.

[47] Admininstration of Estates Act 1925, s.47(5), as amended.

[48] [1989] A.C. 346.

[49] Police and Criminal Evidence Act 1984, ss. (10)(1), (2).

[50] Under the Drug Trafficking Offences Act 1986, s.27.

[51] Lords Brandon, Griffiths and Goff.

[52] Lords Bridge of Harwick and Oliver of Alymerbon.

[53] *per* Lord Bridge at pp. 371, 374.

[54] *ibid.*, p. 375.

[55] *ibid.*, p. 389.

to the requisite intention as "such an extraordinary result that I would only adopt such a construction if driven to it."[56]

In some cases, however, defective statutory provisions are regarded as beyond judicial redemption. For example, in *Inland Revenue Commissioners v. Hinchy*[57] section 55(3) of the Income Tax Act 1952 provided that a person who failed to submit an accurate tax return should forfeit £20 plus "treble the tax which he ought to be charged under this Act." Hinchy failed to declare some interest upon which the tax due would have been £14 5s. The Commissioners claimed £438 14s.6d. (three times Hinchy's total tax bill for the year plus £20). The House of Lords upheld their claim; their Lordships recognised that the result was absurd, but the words actually used were not capable of a more limited interpretation. In *Canterbury City Council v. Colley*[58] the House of Lords gave effect to a provision[59] that had the effect of requiring the compensation for revocation of a planning permission to rebuild a house to be calculated on the assumption that planning permission would be granted to rebuild the house. While this undoubtedly caused hardship to the owners, the words were "clear and express".[60] Assuming this was an anomaly, it could only be dealt with by "substantially rewriting the section".[61] This would involve "more than a mere purposive construction" and fell outside the parameters laid down by Lord Simon of Glaisdale in *Stock v. Frank Jones (Tipton) Ltd.*[62]

It may be that judges are less inhibited in reading statutory provisions as if the language were modified where they are contained in subordinate legislation. In *R. v. Stratford-on-Avon District Council, ex p. Jackson*,[63] the Court of Appeal held that the words "an application for judicial review shall be made promptly" in R.S.C. Order 53, s.4(1) were to read as if they referred to the application for leave to apply for judicial review. This was the "only sensible construction"[64] which could be given to the rule, and the construction that had been adopted in practice.[65] Similarly, in *Pickstone v. Freemans plc*[66] the House of Lords held that regulations amending the Equal Pay Act 1970 so as to enable the United Kingdom to comply with European Community law should be interpreted so as to achieve that result.

> "It may be that, in order to . . . [do so], some necessary implication falls to be made into their literal meaning. The precise terms of that implication do not seem to me to matter. It is sufficient to say that the words must be

---

[56] *ibid.*, p. 383. For other examples of "rectification", see *Deria v. General Council of British Shipping* [1986] I.C.R. 172; *McMonagle v. Westminster City Council* [1990] 2 A.C. 716 (words regarded as surplusage to avoid absurd result). *X. v. Morgan Grampian Ltd* [1991] 1 A.C. 1, 55; and *Powdrill v. Watson* [1995] 2 All E.R. 65, 85–86.

[57] [1960] A.C. 748. See also *Inland Revenue Commissioners v. Ayrshire Employers' Mutual Insurance Association Ltd* [1946] 1 All E.R. 637.

[58] [1993] A.C. 401.

[59] Town and Country Planning Act 1971, s.164(4).

[60] *per* Lord Oliver of Aylmerton at p. 409.

[61] *per* Lord Oliver at p. 406.

[62] *ibid.*, and see p. 369.

[63] [1985] 1 W.L.R. 1319.

[64] *ibid.*, p. 1322.

[65] The drafting error was subsequently corrected by S.I. 1987 No. 1423, r. 63, Schedule.

[66] [1989] A.C. 66.

construed purposively in order to give effect to the manifest broad intention of the maker of the regulations and of Parliament."[67]

Lord Oliver agreed:

". . . a construction which permits the section to operate as a proper fulfilment of the United Kingdom's obligation under the Treaty involves not so much doing violence to the language of the section as filling a gap by an implication which arises, not from the words used, but from the manifest purpose of the Act and the mischief it was intended to remedy."[68]

Finally, in *Porter v. Honey*[69] the House of Lords held that the deemed consent conferred by regulations[70] for the display of one estate agent's sale board extended by necessary implication to cover the first board displayed notwithstanding the unlawful display of subsequent boards by other agents. The result suggested by the grammatical construction of the regulation was that the first agent would be guilty of an offence where another agent, without the former's knowledge or consent, placed a second board upon the same property. Such a result would be "unjust and absurd."[71]

"We are dealing here with delegated legislation which does not receive the scrutiny of primary legislation and if in the interests of administrative convenience such an apparently unjust rule is to be introduced it should be in the clearest possible language so that the purport of the legislation can be readily recognised and the need for such a measure can be carefully considered before it is approved."[72]

C. THE CONTEXT: INTERNAL AIDS TO INTERPRETATION

There is a wide range of material that may be considered by a judge both (1) in determining the primary meaning of the statutory words and (2) where there is ambiguity, in pointing the way to the interpretation that is to be preferred. Some of these aids may be found within the statute in question, or in certain "rules of language" commonly applied to statutory texts: others are external to the statute. We deal first with "internal aids".

It is commonly observed that statutes must be read as a whole.[73] It may perhaps be doubted whether every word of a long and complicated statute will be examined with care, but a judge may well be presented with arguments based

---

[67] *per* Lord Keith of Kinkel at p. 112.
[68] *ibid.*, p. 125. *Cf.* Lord Oliver's remarks in the *Francis & Francis* case, n. 48 above. In the *Pickstone* case, his Lordship regarded the words as "reasonably capable of bearing" the secondary meaning contended for [1989] A.C. at p. 128; in *Francis & Francis*, he did not.
[69] [1988] 1 W.L.R. 1420.
[70] The Town and Country Planning (Control of Advertisements) Regulations 1984 (S.I. 1984 No. 421).
[71] *per* Lord Griffiths at p. 1422.
[72] *ibid.*, pp. 1426–1427.
[73] See, *e.g.* pp. 363–364 above.

on (1) a comparison with enacting words elsewhere in the statute or (2) one of the non-enacting parts of the statute listed in the previous chapter.[74] There is an important distinction between these two kinds of aid. Non-enacting words of a statute may be consulted as a guide to the meaning of the provision in question; however, if the words of the provision, considered in their context, are regarded as clear, any conflict between them and any of the non-enacting parts must be disregarded. Where a conflict between enacting words cannot be resolved by interpretation, the later provision takes precedence.

1. OTHER ENACTING WORDS

An examination of the whole of a statute, or at least those Parts which deal with the subject matter of the provision to be interpreted, should give some indication of the overall purpose of the legislation. It may show that a particular interpretation of that provision will lead to absurdity when taken with another section.[75] Moreover, there is at least a weak presumption that a word or phrase is to be accorded the same meaning wherever it appears in the statute. For example, in *Gibson v. Ryan*[76] the court had to decide whether an inflatable rubber dinghy and a fish basket came within the term "instrument" in section 7(1) of the Salmon and Freshwater Fisheries (Protection) (Scotland) Act 1951. It held that they did not in the light of section 10, which drew a distinction "between instruments on the one hand, boats on the other hand and baskets on, if there is such a thing, the third hand."[77] A court may, however, be satisfied that different meanings are intended.[78] There may, of course, be a definition section.[79]

2. LONG TITLE

It became established in the nineteenth century that the long title could be considered as an aid to interpretation,[80] once it was accepted that it could be amended as a Bill passed through Parliament. The long title should be read, as part of the context, "as the plainest of all the guides to the general objectives of a statute"[81] although "it will not always help as to particular provisions."[82]

---

[74] See above, pp. 280–285.

[75] See, *e.g. R. v. Prince* (1875) L.R. 2 C.C.R. 154 and cases establishing that a court could not order the forfeiture of real property used in relation to the commission of criminal offences: *R. v. Beard (Graham)* [1974] 1 W.L.R. 1549 and *R. v. Khan (Sultan Ashraf)* [1982] 1 W.L.R. 1405.

[76] [1968] 1 Q.B. 250.

[77] Diplock L.J. at p. 255.

[78] *e.g.* "whosoever being married, shall marry" in section 57 of the Offences Against the Person Act 1861, considered in *R. v. Allen* (1872) L.R. 1 C.C.R. 367: "being married" meant "being validly married" whereas "shall marry" meant "go through a marriage ceremony".

[79] Above, pp. 284–285.

[80] *Fielding v. Morley Corporation* [1899] 1 Ch. 1, 34.

[81] Not all long titles are as helpful in this regard as Lord Simon's words suggest.

[82] *per* Lord Simon in *Black-Clawson International Ltd v. Papierwerke Waldhof Aschaffenburg A.G.* [1975] A.C. 591, 647.

In *Fisher v. Raven*[83] the House of Lords held that the term "obtained credit" in section 13 of the Debtors Act 1869 (which made it an offence to obtain credit under false pretences) was limited to the obtaining of credit in respect of the payment or repayment of money only and did not extend to cover the receipt of money on a promise to render services or deliver goods in the future. The Act's long title:

> "An Act for the Abolition of Imprisonment for Debt, for the Punishment of Fraudulent Debtors, and for other purposes"

was regarded as supporting the view that the Act concerned debtors in the ordinary sense of the word. However, in *Ward v. Holman*[84] the Divisional Court held that section 5 of the Public Order Act 1936, which made it an offence to use in any public place or meeting, *inter alia*, insulting behaviour likely to cause a breach of the peace, was not restricted to conduct at public meetings, processions and the like, notwithstanding the Act's long title. The relevant part of the long title read:

> "An Act to . . . make . . . provision for the preservation of public order on the occasion of public processions and meetings and in public places"

but the court regarded the enacted words as wide and "completely unambiguous"[85] and, accordingly, applicable to disputes between neighbours. The position appears to be that:

> "once their full context is considered in the light of the purposes of the Act, it is the unambiguous words of a section which will prevail over the long title."[86]

3. PREAMBLE

The use of preambles[87] was considered in *Attorney-General v. Ernest Augustus of Hanover*.[88] The position was summarised by Lord Normand[89]:

> "When there is a preamble it is generally in its recitals that the mischief to be remedied and the scope of the Act are described. It is therefore clearly permissible to have recourse to it as an aid to construing the enacting provisions. The preamble is not, however, of the same weight as an aid to construction of a section of the Act as are other relevant enacting words

---

[83] [1964] A.C. 210. See also *Watkinson v. Hollington* [1944] K.B. 16; *R. v. Wheatley* [1979] 1 W.L.R. 144.

[84] [1964] 2 Q.B. 580.

[85] *per* Lord Parker C.J. at p. 587.

[86] Cross (1995), p. 128; *R. v. Bates* [1952] 2 All E.R. 842, 844, *per* Donovan J.; *R. v. Galvin* [1987] Q.B. 862.

[87] The long title is on occasion referred to erroneously as the preamble.

[88] [1957] A.C. 436, see above p. 363.

[89] At p. 467. See also Viscount Simonds at pp. 462–464, and see *The Norwhale* [1975] Q.B. 589.

to be found elsewhere in the Act or even in related Acts. There may be no exact correspondence between preamble and enactment, and the enactment may go beyond, or it may fall short of the indications that may be gathered from the preamble. Again, the preamble cannot be of much or any assistance in construing provisions which embody qualifications or exceptions from the operation of the general purpose of the Act. It is only when it conveys a clear and definite meaning in comparison with relatively obscure or indefinite enacting words that the preamble may legitimately prevail.''

The preamble cannot prevail over clear enacting words.

4. Short Title

It seems that the short title should not be used to resolve a doubt as it is given ''solely for the purpose of facility of reference'' or as a ''statutory nickname''.[90] Some judges, however, have questioned whether it should always be ignored.[91]

5. Headings

Unlike the previous three parts of a statute, headings, side-notes and punctuation are not voted on in Parliament. They may nevertheless be considered as part of the context. In *Director of Public Prosecutions v. Schildkamp*[92] Lord Reid said:

''The question which has arisen in this case is whether and to what extent it is permissible to give weight to punctuation, cross-headings and side-notes to sections in the Act. Taking a strict view, one can say that these should be disregarded because they are not the product of anything done in Parliament. . . .

But it may be more realistic to accept the Act as printed as being the product of the whole legislative process, and to give due weight to everything found in the printed Act. I say more realistic because in very many cases the provision before the court was never even mentioned in debate in either House, and it may be that its wording was never closely scrutinised by any member of either House. In such a case it is not very meaningful

---

[90] Lord Moulton in *Vacher & Sons Ltd v. London Society of Compositors* [1913] A.C. 107, 128. Section 4(1) of the Trade Disputes Act 1906 was held to confer upon trade unions immunity from tort actions generally and not just in trade dispute cases. See also *R. v. Crisp and Homewood* (1919) 83 J.P. 121, where Avory J. held that the broad enacting words of s.2 of the Official Secrets Act 1911 were not to be altered or limited by reference to the short title (*Cf. R. v. Galvin* [1987] Q.B. 862).

[91] Scrutton L.J. in *Re Boaler* [1915] 1 K.B. 21 40; but *cf.* Buckley L.J. at p. 27. In *British Amusement Catering Trades Association v. Westminster City Council* [1990] 1 A.C. 147, Lord Griffiths stated (at p. 157) that he had ''given weight to the title of the [Cinematograph] Acts'' in holding that a video game was not a ''cinematograph exhibition''. Many other considerations pointed to the same conclusion (see below, p. 384).

[92] [1971] A.C. 1, 10.

to say that the words of the Act represent the intention of Parliament but that punctuation, cross-headings and side-notes do not.

So, if the authorities are equivocal and one is free to deal with the whole matter, I would not object to taking all these matters into account, provided that we realise that they cannot have equal weight with the words of the Act. Punctuation can be of some assistance in construction. A cross-heading ought to indicate the scope of the sections which follow it but there is always a possibility that the scope of one of these sections may have been widened by amendment. But a side-note is a poor guide to the scope of a section, for it can do no more than indicate the main subject with which the section deals.''

This case concerned section 332(3) of the Companies' Act 1948, which makes it an offence knowingly to be a party to the carrying on of a business with intent to defraud creditors or for a fraudulent purpose. However, it appeared among a group of sections grouped under the cross-heading "Offences Antecedent to and in course of Winding-Up", and section 332(1), a parallel provision making the officers of a company personally responsible for its debts in similar circumstances, included the words "in the course of the winding-up." The House of Lords held by a majority that an offence under section 332(3) could only be committed after a winding-up order had been made.[93]

It also seems that reference may be made to a heading to resolve a doubt where the enacted words are ambiguous. However, it may not be used to change the meaning of enacted words where they are regarded as clear. Thus, a woman was convicted of an indecent assault upon a boy notwithstanding that the relevant section appeared under the heading of "Unnatural Offences".[94] The words "any indecent assault" were not regarded as ambiguous so as to justify consideration of the heading.

6. Side-Notes

There is no sensible reason why side-notes should be ignored, as Lord Reid noted in *Director of Public Prosecutions v. Schildkamp*.[95] However, the same judge had stated in an earlier case, *Chandler v. Director of Public Prosecutions*,[96] that "side-notes cannot be used as an aid to construction" as they were inserted by the draftsman, altered if necessary during the passage of a Bill by an officer of the House, and were not considered by Parliament.[97] In *Chandler* the defendants were charged under section 1(1) of the Official Secrets Act 1911, which makes it an offence to approach a prohibited place for a purpose prejudicial to the safety of the state, in respect of a demonstration at a military airfield

---

[93] The effect of this decision was reversed by the Companies Act 1981, s.96 (now the Companies Act 1985, s.458): see *R. v. Kemp* [1988] Q.B. 645.

[94] Offences Against the Person Act 1861, s.62; *R. v. Hare* [1934] 1 K.B. 354. See also *R. v. Surrey (North-Eastern Area) Assessment Committee* [1948] 1 K.B. 28, 32–33.

[95] [1971] A.C. 1, 10: above, p. 375. See also *Stephens v. Cuckfield R.D.C.* [1960] 2 Q.B. 372; *Tudor Grange Holdings v. Citibank NA* [1992] Ch. 53 (permissible to have regard to side-note in considering what is the general purpose of the section and the mischief at which it is aimed).

[96] [1964] A.C. 763.

[97] *ibid.* p. 789.

in favour of nuclear disarmament. The marginal note read "Penalties for spying" and it was accepted that the defendants had not engaged in "spying". Nevertheless, the House of Lords held that the defendants were rightly convicted. In so far as this case indicates that a side-note cannot change the meaning of clear enacted words it is consistent with other cases; in so far as it would prohibit any consideration of a side-note it is inconsistent.

7. PUNCTUATION

Punctuation in statutes was considered by Lord Reid in *Inland Revenue Commissioners v. Hinchy*[98]:

> "[B]efore 1850 there was no punctuation in the manuscript copy of an Act which received the Royal Assent, and it does not appear that the printers had any statutory authority to insert punctuation thereafter. So even if punctuation in more modern Acts can be looked at (which is very doubtful), I do not think that one can have any regard to punctuation in older Acts."

In modern statutes, it does now seem that punctuation will be considered to the same extent as non-enacting words, although it may be altered or ignored where necessary to give effect to the purpose of the statute.[99] In *Hanlon v. The Law Society*[1] Lord Lowry said:

> "I consider that not to take account of punctuation disregards the reality that literate people, such as Parliamentary draftsmen, punctuate what they write, if not identically, at least in accordance with grammatical principles. Why should not literate people, such as judges, look at the punctuation in order to interpret the meaning of the legislation as accepted by Parliament."

D. THE CONTEXT: RULES OF LANGUAGE

There are a number of so-called "rules of language" commonly referred to in the context of statutory interpretation by Latin tags. They are not legal rules, but "simply refer to the way in which people speak in certain contexts."[2] Moreover, they are not as precise in their operation as would be expected from their label as "rules".

---

[98] [1960] A.C. 748, 765.

[99] *Alexander v. Mackenzie* 1947 J.C. 155, 166; *R. v. Brixton Prison Governor, ex p. Naranjansingh* [1962] 1 Q.B. 211; *Luby v. Newcastle upon Tyne Corporation* [1965] 1 Q.B. 214.

[1] [1981] A.C. 124, 198. *Cf.* Lord Reid in *D.P.P. v. Schildkamp* above, pp. 375–376.

[2] Cross, (1995), p. 134.

1. EJUSDEM GENERIS

General words following particular ones normally apply only to such persons or things as are *ejusdem generis* (of the same *genus* or class) as the particular ones. For example, the Sunday Observance Act 1677 provided that "no tradesman, artificer, workman, labourer or other person whatsoever, shall do or exercise any worldly labour, business, or work of their ordinary callings upon the Lord's Day." In a series of cases the prohibition was held to be restricted to "other persons" following callings of a similar kind to those specified.[3] There must normally, and perhaps invariably, be more than one species mentioned to constitute a "genus",[4] and it must be possible to construct a "genus" out of the list of specific words. In *Allen v. Emmerson*[5] it was held that the phrase "theatres and other places of entertainment" in section 33 of the Barrow-in-Furness Corporation Act 1872 did not constitute a genus. Accordingly, a fun fair required a licence under the section even though no charge was made for admission.

The *ejusdem generis* rule may be displaced where the general words should be interpreted widely to accord with the object of the statute. *Skinner v. Shew*[6] concerned a provision which enabled a person to obtain an injunction against someone claiming to be the patentee of an invention who threatened him or her with any legal proceedings or liability "by circular advertisement or otherwise", unless he or she instituted those proceedings promptly. The Court of Appeal held that the desire of Parliament was "that threats of patent actions shall not hang over a man's head" and that it would be wrong to read the section as not applying to threats sent by private letter. In *Flack v. Baldry*[7] the Divisional Court held that electricity, discharged[8] from an electric stun gun, fell within the description "any noxious liquid, gas or other thing" in the Firearms Act 1968.[9] Such a weapon as an electric stun gun came within the mischief of the Act.

2. NOSCITUR A SOCIIS

This tag refers to the fact that words "derive colour from those which surround them".[10] For example, the word "floors" in the expression "floors, steps, stairs, passages and gangways", which were required to be kept free from obstruction, was held not to apply to part of a factory floor used for storage rather than passage.[11] The wider context may, however, negative any such "colouration".

---

[3] Not, therefore, a coach proprietor (*Sandeman v. Beach* (1827) 5 L.J. (o.s.) K.B. 298), farmer (*R. v. Cleworth* (1864) 4 B. & S. 927) or barber (*Palmer v. Snow* [1900] 1 Q.B. 725).

[4] *Alexander v. Tredegar Iron and Coal Co. Ltd* [1944] K.B. 390; *Quazi v. Quazi* [1980] A.C. 744, 807–808 (*per* Lord Diplock): the term "other" in the expression "judicial or other proceedings" was held not to be confined to quasi-judicial proceedings.

[5] [1944] K.B. 362.

[6] [1893] 1 Ch. 413. *Cf.* Lord Scarman in *Quazi v. Quazi*, above, at p. 824.

[7] [1988] 1 W.L.R. 214.

[8] The House of Lords held, overruling the Divisional Court on this point, that the electricity was "discharged": [1988] 1 W.L.R. 393.

[9] s.5(1)(b).

[10] *per* Stamp J. in *Bourne v. Norwich Crematorium Ltd* [1967] 1 W.L.R. 691.

[11] Factories Act 1961, s.28(1): *Pengelley v. Bell Punch Co. Ltd* [1964] 1 W.L.R. 1055.

The "*ejusdem generis* rule" can be regarded as an application of this wider principle.

3. EXPRESSIO UNIUS EST EXCLUSIO ALTERIUS

"Mention of one or more things of a particular class may be regarded as silently excluding all other members of the class. . . . Further, where a statute uses two words or expressions, one of which generally includes the other, the more general term is taken in a sense excluding the less general one: otherwise there would have been little point in using the latter as well as the former."[12]

For example, a provision that imposed a poor rate on the occupiers of "lands", houses, tithes and "coal mines" was held not to apply to mines other than coal mines, although the word "lands" would normally cover all kinds of mine.[13] However, a court may be satisfied that the "exclusio" was accidental, particularly where an application of the maxim would lead to absurdity.[14]

E. THE CONTEXT: EXTERNAL AIDS TO INTERPRETATION

1. HISTORICAL SETTING

A judge may consider the historical setting of the provision that is being interpreted. In *Chandler v. Director of Public Prosecutions*[15] the defendants sought to argue that disarmament would be beneficial to the State, and that their purpose was thus not "prejudicial to the safety or interests of the State". Lord Reid said[16]:

"Even in recent times there have been occasions when quite large numbers of people have been bitterly opposed to the use made of the armed forces in peace or in war. The 1911 Act was passed at a time of grave misgiving about the German menace, and it would be surprising and hardly credible that the Parliament of that date intended that a person who deliberately interfered with vital dispositions of the armed forces should be entitled to submit to a jury that Government policy was wrong and that what he did was really in the best interests of the country, and then perhaps to escape conviction because a unanimous verdict on that question could not be obtained."

The Victorian attitude of sympathy towards insurgents against continental

---

[12] *Maxwell on Interpretation of Statutes* (12th ed., 1969), p. 293. See J. M. Keyes, (1989) 10 Stat.L.R. 1.
[13] Poor Relief Act 1601, s.1: *R v. Inhabitants of Sedgley* (1831) 2 B. & Ad. 65.
[14] *Colquhoun v. Brooks* (1888) 21 Q.B.D. 52, 65; *Dean v. Wiesengrund* [1955] 2 Q.B. 120.
[15] [1964] A.C. 763: see above p. 376.
[16] At p. 791.

governments has been considered as part of the background of the Extradition
Act 1870.[17]

2. DICTIONARIES AND OTHER LITERARY SOURCES

Dictionaries are commonly consulted as a guide to the meaning of statutory
words.[18] As words are to be read in their context, as already discussed, this
should only be a starting point:

> "Sentences are not mere collections of words to be taken out of the sen-
> tence, defined separately by reference to the dictionary or decided cases,
> and then put back into the sentence with the meaning which one has
> assigned to them as separate words so as to give the sentence or phrase a
> meaning which as a sentence or phrase it cannot bear without distortion
> of the English language."[19]

Textbooks may also be consulted.[20]

3. PRACTICE

The practice followed in the past may be a guide to interpretation. For example,
the "uniform opinion and practice of eminent conveyancers has always had
great regard paid to it by all courts of justice."[21] This is the case where the
technical meaning of a word or phrase used in conveyancing is in issue.[22] Commercial usage may also be considered. In *United Dominions Trust Ltd v. Kirk-
wood*[23] the Court of Appeal had to apply the phrase "any person bona fide
carrying on the business of banking."[24] Lord Denning M.R. said[25]:

> "In such a matter as this, when Parliament has given no guidance, we
> cannot do better than look at the reputation of the concern amongst intelli-
> gent men of commerce."

---

[17] *Schtraks v. Government of Israel* [1964] A.C. 556, 582, 583: *R. v. Governor of Pentonville Prison,
ex p. Cheng* [1973] A.C. 931. See now the Extradition Act 1989.
[18] See, *e.g. R. v. Peters* (1886) 16 Q.B.D. 636 (definitions of "credit" in Dr Johnson's and Webster's
dictionaries); *Re Ripon (Highfield) Confirmation Order 1938, White and Collins v. Minister of
Health* [1939] 2 K.B. 838 (definition of "park" in O.E.D.); *Eglen (Inspector of Taxes) v. Butcher*
[1988] S.T.C. 782 (definitions of "infirmity" in O.E.D.: third definition, with connotations of
illness or congenital defect, preferred to first, "a weakness or want of strength", with the result
that a dependent relative allowance could not be claimed under income tax legislation in respect
of a healthy infant).
[19] *per* Stamp J. in *Bourne v. Norwich Crematorium Ltd* [1967] 1 W.L.R. 691, 696.
[20] *e.g. Re Castioni* [1891] 1 Q.B. 149 where Stephen J. referred to his own *History of the Criminal
Law* on the meaning of "political crime"; a work by John Stuart Mill was also consulted.
[21] *per* Lord Hardwicke L.C. in *Bassett v. Bassett* (1744) 3 Atk. 203, 208.
[22] See *Jenkins v. Inland Revenue Commissioners* [1944] 2 All E.R. 491; *cf. Pilkington v. Inland
Revenue Commissioners* [1964] A.C. 612, 634.
[23] [1966] 2 Q.B. 431.
[24] Moneylenders Act 1900, s.6(d).
[25] At pp. 454, 455.

In these cases the usage or practice precedes the enactment of related technical legislation. The *subsequent* practice of those who are involved in the implementation of a statute is not generally regarded as a permissible aid.[26] A different view may be taken in respect of old statutes:

"It is said that the best exposition of a statute . . . is that which it has received from contemporary authority. . . . *Contemporanea expositio est fortissima in lege.* Where this has been given by enactment or judicial decision, it is of course to be accepted as conclusive. But, further, the meaning publicly given by contemporary or long professional usage is presumed to be the true one, even where the language has etymologically or popularly a different meaning."[27]

This principle cannot be applied to modern statutes.[28]

4. OTHER STATUES IN PARI MATERIA

Related statutes dealing with the same subject matter as the provision in question may be considered both as part of the context and to resolve ambiguities.[29] A statute may indeed provide expressly that it should be read as one with an earlier statute or series of statutes. *Later* statutes *in pari materia* cannot be regarded as part of the context of the enactment but may be considered where a provision is ambiguous, "to see the meaning which Parliament puts on the self-same phrase in a similar context, in case it throws any light on the matter."[30]

Occasionally an argument may be based on a comparison with a statute not *in pari materia*, although such a statute will not be considered as part of the context.[31]

Where a later Act amends an earlier Act the position as to interpretation is not clear. In *Lewisham London Borough Council v. Lewisham Juvenile Court*

---

[26] *e.g.* practice notes provided by the Central Land Board for the guidance of its staff in the administration of the Town and Country Planning Act 1947: *London County Council v. Central Land Board* [1958] 1 W.L.R. 1296. Statements in a government circular may be "simply wrong": *R. v. Wandsworth London Borough Council, ex p. Beckwith* [1996] 1 W.L.R. 60, 65, *per* Lord Hoffman.

[27] *Maxwell on Interpretation of Statutes* (12th ed., 1969), p. 264 cited in *R. v. Casement* [1917] 1 K.B. 98, where the court declined to take the Statute of Treasons 1351 "and read it as though we had seen it for the first time." See D. J. Hurst, "The problem of the elderly statute" (1983) 3 L.S. 21, 23–30, who notes that the term *contemporanea exposito* should (1) be confined to exposition by commentators at or near the time of enactment, and (2) be distinguished from continuous usage and custom.

[28] *Campbell College, Belfast (Governors) v. Commissioners of Valuation for Northern Ireland* [1964] 1 W.L.R. 912 (strictly, a case concerning usage rather than *contemporanea expositio*: Hurst, *op. cit.*).

[29] See Viscount Simonds in the *Hanover* case, above, p. 363.

[30] *per* Lord Denning M.R. in *Payne v. Bradley* [1962] A.C. 343, 357; *cf. Re MacManaway* [1951] A.C. 161; *Lewisham London Borough Council v. Lewisham Juvenile Court JJ.* [1980] A.C. 273, 281–2, 291; *Mendip District Council v. Glastonbury Festivals Ltd* (1993) 91 L.G.R. 447, 453.

[31] See, *e.g. R. v. Westminster Betting Licensing Committee, ex p. Peabody Donation Fund* [1963] 2 Q.B. 750.

JJ.[32] Viscount Dilhorne stated[33] that it was wrong to construe an *unamended* section of the earlier Act in the light of amendments made by the later Act, unless there was an ambiguity. Lord Salmon, however, said[34] that:

> "the whole Act as amended should be taken into consideration when construing any section in the Act. A section of an Act, whether or not it is amended, must in my view be construed in the context of the whole Act as it stands."

The other judges did not express their views unequivocally on this point, although Lord Keith seemed to incline to Viscount Dilhorne's position and Lord Scarman to Lord Salmon's.[35] Lord Salmon's view may create difficulties for the draftsman of subsequent amendments if he or she is to be required to judge the effect of the amendments on the interpretation of unamended provisions.

Where a later Act inserts a new provision in an earlier Act, it may be held that this provision is to be interpreted by reference to the later Act.[36]

5. LEGISLATIVE ANTECEDENTS

A slightly different situation from those considered in the previous section arises when the provision in question has been re-enacted in the same or similar form in a succession of statutes. For example, the origins of section 56 of the Law of Property Act 1925[37] were considered in *Beswick v. Beswick*,[38] where the House of Lords held that the term "other property" did not apply to personalty. However, the legislative antecedents should not be considered as part of the context of a consolidation measure, and reference to them should only be made if the words are unclear.[39] In interpreting consolidation Acts there is a presump-

---

[32] [1980] A.C. 273.

[33] At pp. 281–2.

[34] At p. 291.

[35] See pp. 302 and 310.

[36] *R. v. Secretary of State for the Home Department, ex p. Margueritte* [1983] Q.B. 180; see A. Samuels, [1983] Stat. L.R. 111.

[37] "A person may take an immediate or other interest in land or other property, or the benefit of any condition, right of entry, covenant or agreement over or respecting land or other property, although he may not be named as a party to the conveyance or other instrument."

[38] [1968] A.C. 58. See also *Pierce v. Bemis* [1986] Q.B. 384.

[39] *Farrell v. Alexander* [1977] A.C. 59: Lord Wilberforce at pp. 72–73, Lord Simon at pp. 82–85 and Lord Edmund-Davies at p. 97; *R. v. West Yorkshire Coroner, ex p. Smith* [1983] Q.B. 335; *R. v. Heron* [1982] 1 W.L.R. 451; *Champion v. Maughan* [1984] 1 W.L.R. 469; *Prior (Valuation Officer) v. Sovereign Chickens Ltd* [1984] 1 W.L.R. 921; *Di Palma v. Victoria Square Property Co. Ltd* [1986] Ch. 150; *Morton v. The Chief Adjudication Officer* [1988] I.R.L.R. 444 (construction of consolidating regulations); *Sheldon v. R.H.M. Outhwaite (Underwriting Agencies) Ltd* [1995] 2 W.L.R. 570 (no ambiguity or difficulty); *Associated Newspapers Ltd v. Wilson* [1995] 2 A.C. 454 (majority and minority in the House of Lords differed on whether there was a "difficulty" justifying recourse to legislative history and differed on the interpretation of that history). Indeed, "it is particularly useful to have recourse to the legislative history if a real difficulty arises," whatever the form of the consolidation measure (see above, p. 266) (*per* Lord Scarman in *R. v. Heron* [1982] 1 W.L.R. 451, 459, 460; *cf.* Lord Simon at p. 455 who stressed the point that the statute in issue here was not (unlike that in *Farrell v. Alexander*), a "modern consolidation Act", but was a "pure" consolidation, with verbatim reproduction of the existing enactment "with all its blemishes and imperfections"; accordingly, it was more likely to be necessary to look at the legislative history). See generally, A. F. Newhouse, "Constructing and Consolidating" [1980] B.T.R. 102; R. Bramwell, [1992] B.T.R. 69.

tion that Parliament does not intend to alter the existing law.[40] As with all presumptions it may be rebutted by clear language.[41]

Where other statutes are considered, arguments may be based on similarities or dissimilarities in the statutory language itself, or on judicial decisions concerning provisions subsequently re-enacted. It is sometimes suggested that Parliament, or more realistically, the draftsman, must have had such decisions in mind during the preparation of consolidation legislation,[42] that there is at least a rebuttable presumption that re-enactment without alteration amounts to the Parliamentary endorsement of the decisions and that, for example, a decision of a High Court judge thus "endorsed" would have to be applied by the Court of Appeal and the House of Lords.[43] The theory of "Parliamentary endorsement" was doubted by Lord Wilberforce and Lord Simon in *Farrell v. Alexander*.[44] Moreover, in *R. v. Chard*[45] the House of Lords held that there might be such a presumption where the judicial interpretation is well settled and well recognised, but that it would yield to the fundamental rule that the ordinary sense of statutory words should be adhered to unless it led to some absurdity. The re-enactment of words in a consolidation Act subject to one of the special parliamentary procedures precluding debate on the merits would not have an effect on the construction of those words.[46]

In the case of *codifying* statutes,[47] "the proper course is in the first instance to examine the language of the statute and to ask what is its natural meaning, uninfluenced by any considerations derived from the previous state of law."[48] The application of any presumption that the law is unaltered would destroy the utility of codification. However, the previous state of the law may be considered where a technical expression is used or a provision of the code is ambiguous.

6. STATUTORY INSTRUMENTS

The extent to which a regulation may be used in interpreting a provision in the Act under which it was made was considered in *Hanlon v. The Law Society*,[49] where Lord Lowry formulated the following propositions[50]:

---

[40] *R. v. Governor of Brixton Prison, ex p. De Demko* [1959] 1 Q.B. 268, affirmed [1959] A.C. 654.
[41] *e.g. Re A Solicitor* [1961] Ch. 491.
[42] See Lord Evershed in *Ex p. De Demko* [1959] 1 Q.B. 268, 281.
[43] *Re Cathcart, ex p. Campbell* (1869) 5 Ch. App. 603, 706 (James L.J.); *Barras v. Aberdeen Fishing and Steam Trawling Co. Ltd* [1933] A.C. 402, 411–412 (Lord Buckmaster); *E.W.P. Ltd v. Moore* [1992] Q.B. 460.
[44] [1977] A.C. 59, 74, 90–91. See also Denning L.J. in *Royal Crown Derby Porcelain Ltd v. Raymond Russell* [1949] 2 K.B. 417, 429; *R. v. Bow Road JJ. (Domestic Proceedings Court), ex p. Adedigba* [1968] 2 Q.B. 572, 583; E. A. Marshall, (1974) 90 L.Q.R. 170; C. J. F. Kidd, (1977) 51 A.L.J. 256.
[45] [1984] A.C. 279.
[46] See also *Stubbings v. Webb* [1993] A.C. 498, 506–507 (amendment of Limitation Act 1939 in 1975 and consolidation in 1980 no endorsement of Court of Appeal decision in *Letang v. Cooper* [1965] 1 Q.B. 232.)
[47] See above, p. 265.
[48] *Bank of England v. Vagliano Brothers* [1891] A.C. 107, 144, 145 (Lord Herschell); applied in *R. v. Fulling* [1987] Q.B. 426 and *R. v. Smurthwaite* [1994] 1 All E.R. 898, in respect of the Police and Criminal Evidence Act 1984.
[49] [1981] A.C. 124.
[50] At pp. 193–4.

"(1) Subordinate legislation may be used in order to construe the parent Act, but only where power is given to amend the Act by regulations or where the meaning of the Act is ambiguous.

(2) Regulations made under the Act provide a Parliamentary or administrative *contemporanea expositio* of the Act but do not decide or control its meaning: to allow this would be to substitute the rule-making authority for the judges as interpreter and would disregard the possibility that the regulation relied on was misconceived or *ultra vires*.

(3) Regulations which are consistent with a certain interpretation of the Act tend to confirm that interpretation.

(4) Where the Act provides a framework built on by contemporaneously prepared regulations, the latter may be a reliable guide to the meaning of the former.

(5) The regulations are a clear guide, and may be decisive, where they are made in pursuance of a power to modify the Act, particularly if they come into operation on the same day as the Act which they modify.

(6) Clear guidance may also be obtained from regulations which are to have effect as if enacted in the parent Act."

Propositions (3) and (4) were cited by Lord Griffiths in *British Amusement Catering Trades Association v. Westminster City Council*,[51] in the course of holding that a video game was not a "cinematograph exhibition," and that, accordingly, an amusement arcade did not have to be licensed under the Cinematograph Act 1909, s.1. His Lordship noted that relevant safety regulations[52] only made sense

"if the 'cinematograph exhibitions' referred to in the regulations are understood in the sense of a show to an audience; for example, there are frequent references to the auditorium. . . . "[53]

7. OFFICIAL REPORTS

Legislation may be preceded by a report of a Royal Commission, the Law Commissions or some other official advisory committee. This kind of material may be considered as evidence of the pre-existing state of the law and the "mischief" with which the legislation was intended to deal. However, it has been held that the recommendations contained therein may not be regarded as evidence of Parliamentary intention as Parliament may not have accepted the rec-

---

[51] [1989] A.C. 147, 158.

[52] The Cinematography (Safety) Regulations 1955 (S.I. 1955 No. 1129). In *Deposit Protection Board v. Dalia* [1994] 2 A.C. 367, 397, Lord Browne-Wilkinson stated that regulations can only be used as an aid to construction if "roughly contemporaneous with the Act being construed." This is inconsistent with the *British Amusement* case, which was not cited.

[53] [1989] A.C. 147, 158. *Cf.* the unwillingness of Wood J. in *R. v. Bolton Metropolitan Borough Council, ex p. B* (1985) 84 L.G.R. 78 to use the Code of Practice made under s.12G of the Child Care Act 1980 as a guide to the meaning of ss.12A to 12G; and Potts J. in *R. v. Secretary of State, ex p. Greenpeace Ltd* [1994] 4 All E.R. 352, 365: "Primary legislation is not to be construed by reference to general policy statements or departmental guidance."

ommendations and acted upon them.[54] The first of these propositions is generally accepted: the second proposition only survived in the *Black-Clawson* case by three to two. The question was whether a judgment in a German court dismissing the plaintiff's claim for money due, on the ground that it was brought out of time, barred such a claim in an English court. It did not have this effect at common law,[55] and the House of Lords held by four to one that this had not been altered by section 8 of the Foreign Judgments (Reciprocal Enforcement) Act 1933. Section 8 had been enacted in a form identical to clause 8 of a draft Bill attached to the report of a departmental committee of "eminent lawyers", and the report indicated that the draft Bill was not thought to change the common law. Of the majority, Lords Reid and Wilberforce held that the report could not be considered as a guide to Parliament's intention. Lord Reid thought that the rule against the citation of expressions of intention in Parliament excluded *a fortiori* such expressions in pre-Parliamentary reports. Lord Wilberforce stated that if reports were admissible as evidence of the meaning of the enacted words there would simply be two documents to construe instead of one, that it was the function of the courts to declare the meaning of enacted words, and that "it would be a degradation of that process if the courts were to be merely a reflecting mirror of what some other interpretation agency might say."[56] Viscount Dilhorne and Lord Simon of Glaisdale thought, however, that reports should be admissible as a guide to Parliament's intention; at least in a case such as this where a draft Bill had been enacted without material alteration.[57] To forbid this "would be to draw a very artificial line which serves no useful purpose."[58] "Why read the crystal when you can read the book? Here the book is already open; it is merely a matter of reading on."[59] Lord Diplock dissented as to the meaning of section 8 but agreed with Lords Reid and Wilberforce on the use of official reports. The *Black-Clawson* case must now be read in light of the decision in *Pepper (Inspector of Taxes) v. Hart*[60] permitting recourse to Parliamentary materials. Reference to *Hansard* may now make it clear whether a report has been relied upon.

In *J. H. Rayner Ltd v. Department of Trade*,[61] Staughton J. held that Cabinet and department documents from the 1950s, obtained from the Public Record

---

[54] *Eastman Photographic Materials Co. Ltd v. Comptroller General of Patents* [1898] A.C. 571; *Assam Railways and Trading Co. Ltd v. Inland Revenue Commissioners* [1935] A.C. 445; *Black-Clawson International Ltd v. Papierwerke Waldhof-Aschaffenburg A. G.* [1975] A.C. 591; *R. v. Allen* [1985] A.C. 1029; *Arnold v. Central Electricity Generating Board* [1988] A.C. 288; *Hampshire County Council v. Milburn* [1991] 1 A.C. 325 (Royal Commission); *R. v. Horseferry Road Magistrates' Court, ex p. Siadatan* [1991] 1 Q.B. 280 (Law Commission Report); *D.P.P. v. Bull* [1995] Q.B. 88 (Wolfenden Report on *Homosexual Offences and Prostitution*). Cf. *R. v. Gomez* [1993] A.C. 442 where the refusal of the majority of the House to refer to the 8th Report of the Criminal Law Revision Committee led to a decision on the law of theft that "flatly contradicted the intention of Parliament", which had enacted legislation in all material respects identical to the CLRC's draft Bill: Commentary by Sir John Smith, [1993] Crim.L.R. 305. See also *R. v. Anderson* [1986] A.C. 27 (Commentary by J. C. Smith, [1985] Crim.L.R. 651). On examination, the mischief identified in a report may turn out to be narrower than that dealt with by Parliament: *R. v. Kemp* [1988] Q.B. 645.
[55] *Harris v. Quine* (1869) L.R. 4 Q.B. 653.
[56] p. 629.
[57] pp. 621–623 and 651–652 respectively.
[58] Viscount Dilhorne at p. 622.
[59] Lord Simon at p. 652.
[60] Below, pp. 390–394.
[61] [1987] BCLC 667.

Office under the 30-year rule,[62] were not admissible as an aid to the interpretation of Order in Council concerning the International Tin Council.

"It would be quite extraordinary to construe either parliamentary or delegated legislation by reference to the secret deliberations of departmental officials or of the Cabinet. One cannot, after all, even look at the deliberations in Parliament recorded by Hansard, which ought at least in theory to be a more immediate guide to the meaning of legislation than the intentions of ministers and their officials."[63]

8. TREATIES AND INTERNATIONAL CONVENTIONS[64]

Problems of statutory interpretation relating to treaties (or international conventions) may arise in four main ways. In the background are two principles: first, that a treaty cannot have effect in English law unless incorporated by statute; and second, that there is a presumption that Parliament does not legislate in such a way that the United Kingdom would be in breach of its international obligations.

(1) An Act of Parliament may implement a treaty and expressly enact that it shall be part of English law. The text will normally be given in a schedule. Here, a broad purposive construction should be adopted rather than a literal one.[65] Textbooks, dictionaries, expert opinion and the judgments of foreign courts may be consulted[66]; *travaux préparatoires*, such as the proceedings of the conferences at which the treaty was prepared, may also be used, albeit with caution.[67]

(2) An Act of Parliament may implement a treaty by enacting substantive provisions of English law but without expressly incorporating the text of the treaty as part of English law. Three questions may arise concerning the use of the treaty as an aid to the interpretation of the statute.

---

[62] Public Records Act 1958, s.5.

[63] [1988] BCLC 667, 689, *per* Staughton J. The relaxation of the rule against citing Parliamentary material in *Pepper (Inspector of Taxes) v. Hart* (below, pp. 390–394) does not extend to departmental documents.

[64] See F. A. Mann, *Foreign Affairs in English Courts* (1986), Chap. 5; R. Higgins in F. G. Jacobs and S. Roberts (eds.), *The Effect of Treaties in Domestic Law* (1987), Chap. 7; L. Collins (ed.), *Dicey and Morris on the Conflict of Laws* (12th ed., 1993), pp. 8–15; D. L. Mendis, (1992) 13 Stat.L.R. 216; R. Gardiner, (1995) 44 I.C.L.Q. 620, criticising the lack of use by English judges of the rules for interpretation of treaties in the Vienna Convention on the Law of Treaties 1969.

[65] *Stag Line Ltd v. Foscolo Mango & Co. Ltd* [1932] A.C. 328, 350; *James Buchanan & Co. Ltd v. Babco Forwarding and Shipping (U.K.) Ltd* [1978] A.C. 141; *cf.* below, p. 411, n. 64 and R. J. C. Munday, (1978) 27 I.C.L.Q. 450; *Fothergill v. Monarch Airlines Ltd* [1981] A.C. 251; *Rothmans Ltd v. Saudi Airlines* [1981] Q.B. 368; *The Hollandia* [1983] 1 A.C. 565: see F. A. Mann, "Uniform Statutes in English Law" (1983) 99 L.Q.R. 376, who argues that the purposive approach has been carried too far.

[66] See, *e.g., Swiss Bank Corporation v. Brink's M.A.T. Ltd* [1986] Q.B. 853.

[67] See the *Fothergill* case, n. 64 above; *Gatoil International Inc. v. Arkwright-Boston Manufacturers Mutual Insurance Co.* [1985] A.C. 255, 263–265. The material must be "public and accessible" and "clearly and indisputably point to a definite legislative intention" (*ibid.*). Reference to *travaux preparatoires* may not prove helpful: *Hiscox v. Outhwaite (No.1)* [1992] 1 A.C. 562, 593; see R. Gardiner, (1995) 44 I.C.L.Q. 620, 624–626.

(i) Can the treaty only be considered if it is expressly referred to in the Act? The intention to implement the treaty may, for example, be mentioned in the preamble or long title.[68] In *Salomon v. Commissioners of Customs and Excise*[69] the Court of Appeal held that a relevant treaty could be consulted even if not expressly referred to in the statute. *Per* Diplock L.J.:

> "If from extrinsic evidence it is plain that the enactment was intended to fulfil Her Majesty's Government's obligations under a particular convention, it matters not that there is no express reference to the convention in the statute. One must not presume that Parliament intends to break an international convention merely because it does not say expressly that it is intending to observe it."[70]

(ii) Can the treaty only be considered if the words of the statute are on their face ambiguous, or is the treaty to be read as part of the context of the statute *before* it is determined whether the words are ambiguous? The first, more restrictive, approach is supported by authority.[71] However, the courts have not been astute to hold statutory words to be clear, without consideration of the treaty,[72] and, in any event, the better view is that the treaty should be considered as part of the context of the enacting words.[73] This would be in conformity with the modern trend towards a broader view of "context" in statutory interpretation.[74]

(iii) If the enacted words are unambiguous, can they be read as if they were modified, by reference to the treaty? The answer here is clearly no. If the enacted words are unclear, but are reasonably capable of more than one meaning, a meaning that is consonant with treaty obligations is to be preferred to one that is not, in accordance with the presumptions mentioned above.[75] However,

---

[68] See, *e.g.*, Recognition of Divorces and Legal Separations Act 1971; Arbitration Act 1975; State Immunity Act 1978.

[69] [1967] 2 Q.B. 116.

[70] *ibid.*, p. 144. *Cf.* Lord Denning M.R. (in more general terms) at p. 141; Russell L.J. at p. 152. *Re Westinghouse Uranium Contract* [1978] A.C. 547; *Re State of Norway's Application* [1987] Q.B. 433. The decision of the House of Lords in *Ellermann Lines Ltd v. Murray* [1931] A.C. 126 had been thought to support a requirement of express reference, but Diplock L.J. in *Salomon* expressed the view that it was not authority for that proposition: [1967] 2 Q.B. 116, 144.

[71] Diplock L.J. in *Salomon v. Commissioners of Customs and Excise* [1967] 2 Q.B. 116, 145. References to having recourse to the terms of a treaty as aids to the construction of provisions that are "ambiguous or vague" are frequent: *e.g, Quazi v. Quazi* [1980] A.C. 744, 808 (Lord Diplock); *Fothergill v. Monarch Airlines Ltd* [1984] A.C. 251, 299 (Lord Roskill); *Minister of Public Works v. Sir Frederick Snow* [1984] A.C. 426, 435 (Lord Brandon). The principle has been formulated by Lord Diplock without *express* reference to "ambiguities" or "vagueness" but it is unlikely that he intended a different result: *The Eschersheim* [1976] 1 W.L.R. 430, 436; *Garland v. British Rail Engineering Ltd* [1983] 2 A.C. 751, 771.

[72] Brandon J. in *The Annie Hay* [1968] P. 341; Lane J. in *The Banco* [1971] P. 137; Warner J. in *National Smokeless Fuels Ltd v. I.R.C.* [1986] S.T.C. 300 (emphasising that a broad view is to be taken in this context of what constitutes an "ambiguity").

[73] I. Brownlie, *Principles of Public International Law* (4th ed., 1990), p. 49; Bennion (1992), p. 462. Lord Denning M.R. appeared to support this position in *Salomon v. Commissioners of Customs and Excise* [1967] 2 Q.B. 116, 141.

[74] Above, pp. 362–368.

[75] *per* Diplock L.J. in *Salomon's* case, [1967] 2 Q.B. 116, 143; *Post Office v. Estuary Radio Ltd* [1968] 2 Q.B. 740, 757.

"If the terms of the legislation are clear and unambiguous, they must be given effect to, whether or not they carry out Her Majesty's treaty obligations, for the sovereign power of the Queen in Parliament extends to breaking treaties (see *Ellerman Lines Ltd v. Murray*[76]), and any remedy for such a breach of an international obligation lies in a forum other than Her Majesty's own courts."[77]

Statutory words cannot be interpreted in order to produce conformity with a treaty if the words are not reasonably capable of bearing that meaning.[78]

(3) It may be argued that a statute should be interpreted in the light of an international convention such as the European Convention on Human Rights. In *Birdi v. Secretary of State for Home Affairs*[79] Lord Denning M.R. said that if an Act of Parliament contradicted the Convention "I might be inclined to hold it invalid." However, he retracted this in *Ex p. Bhajan Singh*.[80] In *R. v. Chief Immigration Officer, ex p. Salamat Bibi*[81] it was said that a court could look to the Convention "if there is any ambiguity in our statutes, or uncertainty in our law."[82] It clearly cannot prevail over clear words in a statute.[83] However, it has also been held that the Secretary of State is not under any legal obligation to take the Convention into account when exercising statutory discretionary powers,[84] and the fact that a right is protected by the Convention does not itself mean that it will be a "legitimate expectation" protected by principles of English administrative law.[85] It is difficult to square this restrictive approach with more positive dicta elsewhere.[86] Indeed, there is much to be said for encouraging consideration of Convention provisions, given that cases involving alleged breaches of the Convention

---

[76] [1931] A.C. 126. It was not "proper to resort to the draft convention for the purpose of giving to the section a meaning other than that which . . . is its natural meaning" (*per* Lord Tomlin at p. 147).

[77] *per* Diplock L.J. in *Salomon's* case, [1967] 2 Q.B. 116, 143.

[78] *cf.* Lord Diplock in *The Eschersheim* [1976] 1 W.L.R. 430, 436. However, it is not obvious that the courts should not be able in this context to employ their limited power to read statutes as if modified: above pp. 368–372.

[79] Unreported, referred to in *R. v. Secretary of State for the Home Department, ex p. Bhajan Singh* [1976] Q.B. 198.

[80] *ibid.*

[81] [1976] 1 W.L.R. 979.

[82] *ibid.* p. 984 *per* Lord Denning M.R. See, to similar effect, Lord Fraser in *Attorney-General v. B.B.C.* [1981] A.C. 303, 352; Sir Robert Megarry V.-C. in *Trawnik v. Lennox* [1985] 1 W.L.R. 532, 541; Lord Goff in *Attorney-General v. Guardian Newspapers (No. 2)* [1990] 1 A.C. 109, 283: ". . . I conceive it to be my duty, when I am free to do so, to interpret the law in accordance with the obligations of the Crown under this treaty"; *Waddington v. Miah* [1974] 1 W.L.R. 683 and *R. v. Deery* [1977] Crim. L. R. 550, where the presumption against retrospective legislation was reinforced by prohibitions against the retrospective application of criminal penalties contained in the European Convention and the International Covenant on Civil and Political Rights; O. Hood Phillips and P. Jackson, *Constitutional and Administrative Law* (7th ed., 1987), pp. 429–433.

[83] *R. v. Greater London Council, ex p. Burgess* [1978] I.C.R. 991; *Kynaston v. Secretary of State for Home Affairs* (1981) 73 Cr. App. R. 281.

[84] *Fernandes v. Secretary of State for the Home Department* [1981] Imm. A.R. 1 *Cf.* the powerful argument that standards derived, *inter alia*, from the Convention should be used to structure the inherently vague concept of *Wednesbury* unreasonableness: J. Jowell and A. Lester, [1987] P.L. 368.

[85] *R. v. Immigration Appeal Tribunal, ex p. Chundawadra* [1988] Imm. A. R. 161.

[86] See the cases cited in n. 82 above.

can be taken to the European Court of Human Rights.[87] This last consideration was not present in a recent decision in which the Court of Appeal held that a court was entitled to take account of the provisions of a treaty in interpreting a statute, even where the statute was not passed to *implement* any particular treaty obligation:

"The principle . . . requires that domestic legislation should be construed so as to be in conformity with an international obligation of this country if it is clear that the legislation was intended by Parliament to be in conformity with that obligation and if such a construction is one which is and was properly applicable to the terms of the legislation when first enacted. International obligations cannot alter the clear meaning of statutes. They may, however, be permitted to make clear which of more than one reasonable meaning was intended by Parliament."[88]

(4) The special case of the interpretation of Community legislation is considered below.[89]

4. PARLIAMENTARY MATERIALS

It was reaffirmed by the House of Lords in *Davis v. Johnson*[90] that a court may not refer to Parliamentary materials for any purpose whatsoever connected with the interpretation of statutes. The prohibition covered such materials as reports of debates in the House and in committee, the explanatory memoranda attached to Bills and successive drafts of Bills. A number of judges openly disagreed with the rule.[91] References were occasionally made to *Hansard* in the course of particular cases, apparently without objection from other parties and without reference to the prohibition.[92] Some judges admitted to consulting *Hansard* informally.[93] Relaxation of the prohibition was opposed by the Law Commissions in view of doubts as to the reliability and availability of legislative material.[94]

By contrast legislative materials were (and are) used in many foreign jurisdictions, including the United States of America and many European countries, where they tend to be more accessible and concise. There have, however, been criticisms that the practice of referring to legislative history has been abused.[95]

---

[87] Above, pp. 109–112.

[88] *per* Ralph Gibson L.J. in *J. H. Rayner Ltd v. Department of Trade* [1989] Ch. 72, 230–231; see to similar effect, Kerr L.J. at pp. 164–166; with whom Nourse L.J. agreed on this point: p. 222. The court approved a dictum of Scarman L. J. in *Pan-American World Airways Inc. v. Department of Trade* [1976] 1 Lloyd's Rep. 257, 261.

[89] pp. 404–412.

[90] [1979] A.C. 264; *Hadmor Productions v. Hamilton* [1983] 1 A.C. 191, 232–233.

[91] *e.g.* Lord Denning M.R. in the Court of Appeal *Davis v. Johnson* [1979] A.C. 264, 276–277.

[92] *e.g. McVeigh v. Beattie* [1988] Fam.69, 84.

[93] *e.g.* Lord Denning M.R. in *Davies v. Johnson* (n. 91 above).

[94] Law Com. No. 21, Scots Law Com. No. 11 (1969), pp. 31–37.

[95] *ibid.*, pp. 32–34. The rules against reliance on lesgislative materials have been relaxed in Australia (by statute: Acts Interpretation Act (Cwlth) s.15AB, added in 1984) and New Zealand (by the judges: see J. F. Burrows, [1989] N.Z.L.J. 94). See also G. Bale, (1995) 74 Can. Bar Rev. 1, 23–25; Bryson J., [1992] Stat.L.R. 187.

In *Pickstone v. Freemans plc*[96] the House of Lords held that it is permissible to cite the terms in which delegated legislation is presented to Parliament by ministers as a guide to the intention of Parliament in approving the legislation in question, and thus as an aid to the interpretation of the legislation. The regulations in question,[97] as is almost universally the case,[98] were not subject to the Parliamentary process of consideration and amendment in Committee as a Bill would have been. Then, in *Pepper (Inspector of Taxes) v. Hart*[99] the House of Lords significantly relaxed the general prohibition as it related to Acts of Parliament. At issue was the interpretation of the Finance Act 1976, which stated that where a benefit was provided by an employer to higher-paid employees (or their families) the employees would have to pay income tax on the "cash equivalent" of that benefit.[1] The "cash equivalent" was the "cost of the benefit" less so much (if any) as was made good to those providing the benefit; the "cost of the benefit" was "the amount of any expense incurred in or in connection with its provision, and . . . includes a proper proportion of any expense relating partly to the benefit and partly to other matters."[2] The appellants were members of staff of a fee-paying school, Malvern College, whose sons were educated at the school under a concessionary scheme whereby they paid one-fifth of the standard fee charged for other parents. They were assessed on income tax on the basis that the "cost of the benefit" was the relevant proportion of the overall expenditure incurred in providing facilities to all the pupils (the "average cost" basis). The taxpayers claimed that the cost should be the *additional* expenditure incurred in respect of their sons (the "marginal cost" basis). As they were filling spare places at the school, this would come to a small amount in respect of equipment and food, itself more than covered by the concessionary fee paid.

The House of Lords held (1) that without recourse to Parliamentary material, the proper interpretation of section 63 would have supported the "average cost" approach adopted by the Revenue[3]; but (2), the prohibition against reliance on Parliamentary material should be relaxed[4]; and (3) in the light of statements made by Robert Sheldon M.P., the Financial Secretary to the Treasury, at the Committee stage, it was clear that the Bill had been passed on the basis that its effect was to assess such benefits on the marginal cost to the employer, and

---

[96] [1989] A.C. 66, H.L. See A. I. L.Campbell, 1989 S.L.T.137. See also *Conerney v. Jacklin* [1985] Crim.L.R.234, where *Hansard* was cited as a guide to the purpose of regulations, as distinct from their interpretation.

[97] The Equal Pay (Amendment) Regulations 1983 (S.I. 1983 No. 1794), amending section 1(2)(c) of the Equal Pay Act 1976, so as to comply with requirements of Community law.

[98] See above, pp. 292–295, on Parliamentary scrutiny.

[99] [1993] A.C. 593. See above, p. 356, 357. Following argument before five Law Lords, a special Appellate Committee of seven Law Lords was convened under the chairmanship of the Lord Chancellor to hear argument on the exclusionary rule. The decision has spawned a vast literature: see, *e.g.*, Bennion (1992, Supplement 1993); S. D. Girvin, (1993) 22 Anglo-Am.L.R. 475; D. Miers, (1993) 56 M.L.R. 695; D. Oliver [1993] P.L. 5; D. Davies, [1993] B.T.R. 172; T.St.J.Bates, (1993) J.L.S.S. 251, (1993) 14 Stat.L.R. 46 and [1995] C.L.J. 127; B.J. Davenport, (1993) 109 L.Q.R. 149; F.A.R.Bennion (1993) 14 Stat.L.R. 149; J. H. Baker, [1993] C.L.J. 353; S. C. Styles, (1993) 14 J.L.S. 151; Sir Nicholas Lyell Q.C. (1994) 15 Stat.L.R. 1; Lord Lester, *ibid*. p. 10; J. C. Jenkins, *ibid.*, p. 23; G. Bale, (1995) 74 Can.Bar Rev.1.

[1] s.61.

[2] s.63.

[3] Lords Browne-Wilkinson, Keith of Kinkel, Bridge of Harwich, Ackner and Oliver of Aylmerton. Lords Mackay of Clashfern and Griffiths disagreed on this point.

[4] All the members of the House of Lords except Lord Mackay of Clashfern L.C.

section 63 should be construed accordingly.[5] The leading speech was given by Lord Browne-Wilkinson,[6] who stated[7] that "the exclusionary rule should be relaxed so as to permit reference to Parliamentary materials where (a) legislation is ambiguous or obscure, or leads to an absurdity; (b) the material relied upon consists of one or more statements by a Minister or other promoter of the Bill together if necessary with such other Parliamentary material as is necessary to understand such statements and their effect; (c) the statements relied upon are clear.[8] Further than this, I would not at present go."

This step was desirable:

"The courts should not deny themselves the light which Parliamentary materials may shed on the meaning of the words Parliament has used and thereby risk subjecting the individual to a law which Parliament never intended to enact."[9]

It would facilitate the modern purposive approach to statutory construction.[10] It was also logically indistinguishable from the position taken in *Pickstone v. Freemans plc*.[11] There, the court was authorised to look at ministerial statements made in introducing regulations which *could not* be amended by Parliament; here the same would be permitted for statements "made in introducing a statutory provision which, though capable of amendment, was not in fact amended."[12] His Lordship rejected a series of arguments against the change. There was nothing constitutionally improper in relaxing the rule: the courts would still be interpreting Parliament's[13] words and would not be "questioning" the "freedom of speech and debates or proceedings" in Parliament contrary to Article 9 of the Bill of Rights.[14] Although the "practical reasons for the rule (difficulty of getting access to Parliamentary materials and the cost and delay in researching it)" were "not without substance", they could be "greatly exaggerated".[15] Experience in Commonwealth countries where the rule had been abandoned did not suggest that the drawbacks were substantial,

"provided that the court keeps a tight control on the circumstances in which references to Parliamentary material are allowed."[16]

Lord Mackay of Clashfern L.C. was the sole dissenter on this point. He had no objection in principle to the change but was concerned at the "possibility

---

[5] Some commentators argue that the statement made late at night to a standing committee "comprising some eleven future cabinet ministers": Sir Nicholas Lyell, (1993) 14 Stat.L.R.1, 5) were "really describing the effects of pre-existing legislation as interpreted in practice by the Revenue rather than setting out the Government's express policy intentions with regard to new wording" (*ibid*. p. 2); and see Bennion (1992, Supplement 1993), pp.A44–A49.

[6] With whom all but Lord Mackay of Clashfern L.C. expressly agreed.

[7] p. 640.

[8] *i.e.* "clearly discloses the mischief aimed at or the legislative intention lying behind the ambiguous or obscure words": *per* Lord Browne-Wilkinson at p. 634.

[9] Lord Browne-Wilkinson at p. 638.

[10] See above, pp. 364–366.

[11] Above, p. 390.

[12] Lord Browne-Wilkinson at p. 635.

[13] *cf*. above, pp. 356–358.

[14] See also *Prebble v. Television New Zealand Ltd* [1995] 1 A.C. 321, P.C.

[15] Lord Browne-Wilkinson at p. 633.

[16] *ibid*.

at least of an immense increase in the cost of litigation."[17] The evidence from other jurisdictions did not justify the view that there had been no substantial increase in the cost of litigation there, and the Parliamentary processes involved were materially different from those in the United Kingdom.[18]

Much of the comment on *Pepper v. Hart* has been critical.[19] There have been fears that the decision will, as predicted by Lord Mackay, lead to a significant increase in cost. Access to Parliamentary materials can be difficult,[20] as can identifying who are the relevant ministers or promoters and following clauses through changes in numbering in successive prints of a Bill. Lord Browne-Wilkinson himself accepted that in many, if not most cases, there would be no "crock of gold".[21] On the other hand, tables of debates on Bills have been published,[22] published annotations to Acts now commonly include relevant extracts from *Hansard*, and *Hansard* for recent sessions has become available on CD-Rom.

Experience of the application of *Pepper v. Hart* in subsequent cases has been mixed. In very few does reference to Parliamentary material appear to have been decisive in solving an interpretative difficulty. A rare example is *Sunderland Polytechnic v. Evans*,[23] where the Employment Appeal Tribunal declined to follow one of its own previous decisions[24] on the interpretation of a provision of the Wages Act 1986, in the light of a reference to two ministerial statements in debate. Reference to *Hansard* may make clear the general purpose of a particular provision, while throwing little light on the meaning of particular words within it.[25]

More frequently, a reference to *Hansard* merely confirms the view of a question of construction that the judge or court would reach independently,[26] although this confirmation may make a matter that is otherwise debatable "clear

---

[17] p. 615.

[18] *ibid.*

[19] See, *e.g.*, Bates, (1993) 14 Stat.L.R. 46 (welcoming the relaxation in principle but noting ambiguities in Lord Browne-Wilkinson's formulation and criticising the failure to relate it to other aids to interpretation); Miers (1993) 56 M.L.R. 695 discussing, *inter alia*, the implications for parliamentary debate and the relationship between the legislature and the judiciary ("there is a real danger of the courts becoming too close to the executive's intentions" (p. 708)).

[20] Only very few law libraries (including the Houses of Parliament and the Universities of Nottingham and London) hold complete series of Standing Committee debates: see G. Holborn, (1993) 24 *Law Librarian* 141.

[21] [1993] A.C. 593 at pp. 634–635, 637. If, however, a clear statement in Parliament is found, that should obviate the need for further litigation.

[22] *Current Law Statutes Service*, Table of Parliamentary Debates (1950–1994).

[23] [1993] I.C.R. 392

[24] *Home Office v. Ayres* [1992] I.C.R. 175.

[25] *Building Societies Commission v. Halifax Building Society* [1995] 3 All E.R. 193, 209–210.

[26] *e.g.*, *R. v. Warwickshire County Council, ex p. Johnson* [1993] A.C. 583, H.L. (misleading price indication by Dixons electrical goods store manager not given "in the course of a business of his" within the Consumer Protection Act 1987, s.20); *Chief Adjudication Officer v. Foster* [1993] A.C. 754, H.L. (power to make regulations specifying circumstances in which persons were to be treated as being or not being severely disabled not confined to defining the degree of disability); *R. v. Secretary of State for the Home Department, ex p. Mehari* [1994] Q.B. 474 (ministerial statement pointed to a particular construction which in any case was supported by other considerations); *Elf Enterprise Caledonia Ltd v. I.R.C.* [1994] S.T.C. 785, 798; *Botross v. London Borough of Hammersmith and Fulham* (1994) 27 H.L.R. 179. Curiously, reference to Parliamentary material to confirm an interpretation was initially proposed by counsel for the appellants in *Pepper v. Hart* as one of the permitted grounds, but this was abandoned during argument: Lord Lester, (1994) 15 Stat.L.R. 10, 21. It rapidly crept into practice.

beyond peradventure."[27] Conversely, the statements made in Parliament may not be helpful,[28] or sufficiently clear to require any different meaning to be given to the words.[29] There are also cases where reference to *Hansard* has not been regarded as justified, on the ground that there is no ambiguity, obscurity or absurdity,[30] which may be because the point is covered by binding precedent,[31] or where a judicial invitation to counsel to undertake a *Pepper v. Hart* search has been resisted in view of the consequent delay.[32]

The conditions laid down by Lord Browne-Wilkinson have naturally been the subject of further consideration. Thus, ambiguity has been identified where the meaning of a particular phrase is uncertain in its application,[33] or where various judges or courts have differed over a point of interpretation.[34] The rules apply to ambiguity in legislation affecting criminal proceedings, and not just civil proceedings.[35] The concept of ambiguity should also apply to the position that arises where there is an inconsistency between two statutory provisions, although a different view appeared to have been taken in *R. v. Moore*.[36] While most of the statements in Parliament referred to have been those of ministers, reference has also been made to statements by the successful mover of an amendment[37] and a Parliamentary Agent before a House of Commons Committee at the committee stage of a Private Bill.[38] The fact that a statement is made on the advice of a law officer is no reason for it to be excluded.[39] However,

---

[27] *Stubbings v. Webb* [1993] A.C. 498, H.L.; *per* Lord Griffiths at p. 508 (three-year limitation for period from date of requisite knowledge for personal injury actions *inter alia* for "breach of duty" not applicable to trespass to the person; reference to *Hansard* made it clear that Parliament intended to implement a Committee report. Oral argument in this and the *Johnson* and *Foster* cases (n.26 above) had been completed before the decision in *Pepper v. Hart* was announced.

[28] *Massmould Holdings Ltd v. Payne* [1993] S.T.C. 62; *Sheppard v. I.R.C* (No. 2) [1993] S.T.C. 240, 255; *Re Bishopsgate Investment Management Ltd* [1993] Ch. 481, 490, (also no ambiguity, obscurity or absurdity); *Welby v. Casswell* [1994] 2 EGLR 4; *R. v. Registered Designs Appeal Tribunal, ex p. Ford Motor Co.Ltd* [1995] 1 W.L.R. 18; *Denby v. Yeldon* [1995] 3 All E.R. 624.

[29] *Macdougall v. Wrexham Maelor Borough Council* (1993) 69 P.& C.R. 109, 122.

[30] *Islwyn Borough Council v. Newport Borough Council, The Times,* June 28, 1993, C.A.; *R. v. Secretary of State for Foreign and Commonwealth Affairs, ex p. Rees-Mogg* [1994] Q.B. 552, 556–557; *Busby v. Co-operative Insurance Society* [1994] 1 EGLR 136; *R. v. Secretary of State for the Home Department, ex p.Okello* [1994] Imm.A.R. 261; *D.P.P. v. Bull* [1995] Q.B. 88 (term "common prostitute" confined to women, as would have been confirmed by a reference to *Hansard*); *Petch v. Gurney (Inspector of Taxes)* [1994] 3 All E.R. 731; *R. v. Singleton* [1995] Crim.L.R. 236.

[31] *Sheppard v. I.R.C. (No. 2)* [1993] S.T.C. 240, Aldous J.; *Dawkins v. Department of the Environment* [1993] I.C.R. 517, C.A.; *National Rivers Authority v. Alfred McAlpine Homes East Ltd* [1994] 4 All E.R. 286, 296–297, D.C

[32] *R. v. Dorset County Council, ex p. Rolls* (1994) 26 H.L.R. 381.

[33] *Sheppard v. I.R.C. (No. 2)* [1993] S.T.C. 624, referring to Lord Diplock in *I.R.C. v. Joiner* [1975] 1 W.L.R. 1701, 1710.

[34] *Doncaster Borough Council v. Secretary of State for the Environment* (1992) 91 L.G.R. 459, 476–477; *Chief Adjudication Officer v. Foster* [1993] A.C. 754, 772.

[35] *Botross v. London Borough of Hammersmith and Fulham* (1994) 27 H.L.R. 179, 186.

[36] (1994) 159 J.P.101, where the Court of Appeal (Criminal Division) solved a problem caused by defective drafting by refusing to apply the literal meaning of a provision as to do so would "frustrate the plain legislative intent", and reading the words "following provisions" as if they were "preceding provisions". It is difficult in any event to see that there was not "absurdity".

[37] *Chief Adjudication Officer v. Foster* [1993] A.C. 754; *Botross v. London Borough of Hammersmith and Fulham* (1994) 27 H.L.R. 179, 187 (amendment accepted by government minister).

[38] *London Regional Transport Pension Fund Trust Co.Ltd v. Hatt, The Times,* May 20, 1993. The statement was of no help to the court.

[39] *R. v. Secretary of State for Foreign and Commonwealth Affairs, ex p. Rees-Mogg* [1994] Q.B. 552, 566, *per* Lloyd L.J.

reference may not be made to a press release, which is a departmental and not a Parliamentary document.[40] Ministerial statements may cease to be of value where words are re-enacted following court decisions on their interpretation.[41] Reference may not be made to ministerial statements on *other* provisions.[41a] The requirement that a statement be "clear" has not received separate attention, although statements cited may not be regarded as helpful.[42]

The decision in *Pepper v. Hart* has led to changes in practice. Any party intending to refer to *Hansard* must, unless the judge otherwise directs, serve upon all other parties and the court copies of the extracts in question, with a brief summary of the argument intended to be based thereon.[43] It seems that extracts from *Hansard* will be cited in argument and decisions on whether the court is able and willing to rely on them are taken later.

As regards Parliamentary proceedings,

> "If it proves necessary to correct any inadvertent ambiguity or error in a ministerial statement made during the passage of a Bill, the aim is to do this as promptly as possible at an appropriate point during the further consideration of the Bill. The best means of doing so and reading such a correction into the official record will depend on a number of factors, including the stage which the Bill has reached and the nature of the proceedings at that point."[44]

Corrections are no longer left to correspondence with Members.

It is too early to gauge the practical significance of *Pepper v. Hart*. Issues concerning the cost of litigation have been raised with the legal profession.[45] The possibility of reference being made to Parliamentary material has been raised in over 70 cases to date.[46] In each of these, research will have been done at the client's expense; in very few indeed does a "crock of gold" appear to have made a difference to the outcome. What cannot be estimated is the extent to which awareness of that material has influenced the supposed "independent" approach of the judges to questions of interpretation. It is likely, however, that having been opened, the door will be impossible to shut.

F. PRESUMPTIONS

1. PRESUMPTIONS OF GENERAL APPLICATION

There are various presumptions that may be applied in doubtful cases. These are to be distinguished from the "presumptions of general application" whereby

---

[40] *Elf Enterprise Caledonia Ltd v. I.R.C.* [1994] S.T.C. 785, 798. A press release was, however, mentioned by Lord Browne-Wilkinson in *Pepper v. Hart* [1993] A.C.593, 628 although the case turned on ministerial statements.

[41] *I.R.C. v. Willoughby* [1995] S.T.C. 143, 174 *per* Morritt L.J.: "In these circumstances it must be assumed that the original intention, whatever it was, was superseded by acceptance of the decisions of the courts."

[41a] *Melluish v. B.M.I. (No. 3) Ltd.* [1995] 3 W.L.R. 631, 645, *per* Lord Browne-Wilkinson.

[42] See above, n. 28.

[43] *Practice Direction (Hansard: Citation)* [1995] 1 W.L.R. 192.

[44] Vol.239, H.C.Deb., March 14, 1994, written answer by the Parliamentary Secretary, Lord Chancellor's Department, John M. Taylor M.P.

[45] Vol.239, H.C.Deb., March 7, 1994, col.70, written answer by Mr Taylor.

[46] *Lexis* search.

certain basic legal principles are presumed to apply unless excluded by express words or necessary implication.[47] These principles modify even unambiguous provisions. Examples include aspects of the *ultra vires* doctrine, such as natural justice and abuse of discretion, general principles of criminal liability, and the principle that no-one shall be allowed to gain an advantage from his or her own wrong. Striking illustrations of this last principle include *Re Sigsworth*,[48] where Clawson J. held that apparently unambiguous provisions as to the distribution of the residuary estate on an intestacy were not to be applied so as to enable a murderer to benefit from the victim's estate, and *R. v. Secretary of State for the Home Department, ex p. Puttick*,[49] where Astrid Proll, who had achieved a marriage with a citizen of the United Kingdom and Colonies by the crimes of fraud, forgery and perjury, was held not to be entitled to registration as a United Kingdom citizen, notwithstanding the absolute terms of section 6(2) of the British Nationality Act 1948. She had entered the country under a false identity, and she had committed these crimes in satisfying the Registrar General that in her assumed identity she had been divorced and there was no impediment to the marriage, and in obtaining a marriage licence.

2. PRESUMPTIONS FOR USE IN DOUBTFUL CASES

These have been termed "policies of clear statement"[50]; or "in effect announcements by the courts to the legislature that certain meanings will not be assumed unless stated with special clarity."[51] The courts have created a measure of protection for certain values by establishing a requirement that Parliament use clear words if they are to be compromised or overridden. There are many difficulties. The Law Commissions pointed out that there was no established order or precedence in the case of conflict between different presumptions; that the individual presumptions were often of doubtful status or imprecise in scope; that reference to a presumption was unnecessary where a court decided that the words are clear; and that there was no accepted test for resolving a conflict between a presumption, such as the presumption that penal statutes should be construed restrictively, and giving effect to the purpose of a statute, for example the purpose of factory legislation to secure safe working conditions.[52]

It is impossible to produce a definitive list of presumptions which may be applied. As the Law Commissions noted, particular presumptions may be "modified or even abandoned with the passage of time, and with the modification of the social values which they embody."[53] There is room for debate as to why certain values and not others are selected for protection, and differences

---

[47] See above, p. 352.
[48] [1935] Ch. 89.
[49] [1981] Q.B. 767. See also *R. v. Chief National Insurance Commissioners, ex p. Connor* [1981] Q.B. 758 and the Forfeiture Act 1982. *Cf. R. v. Registrar-General, ex p. Smith* [1991] 2 Q.B. 393, C.A. (similar principle applied where enforcement of an apparently clear statutory duty would facilitate crime resulting in danger to life); see A.P. Le Sueur, [1991] P.L. 326, noting that the decision ran counter to views expressed in standing committee on the provision in question.
[50] H. M. Hart and A. M. Sacks, cited in Law Com. No. 21, p. 21.
[51] Law Com. No. 21, p. 21.
[52] *ibid.* p. 22.
[53] *ibid.* p. 21. *Cf.* section (d) below.

of view among the judges as to the strength of the protection that ought to be accorded. For example, the presumptions concerned with protecting the existing property or money of individuals have been contrasted with the absence of any presumptions in favour of individuals claiming state benefits.[54] While there are authorities stressing in general terms the importance of protecting individual liberty,[55] and particular freedoms such as freedom of speech,[56] freedom of assembly[57] and freedom from physical restraint,[58] there are comparatively few cases outside the last of these categories where full effect has been given to these factors.[59] Some of the principles of interpretation that have already been mentioned are sometimes put in the form of a presumption, for example presumptions against "intending what is inconvenient or unreasonable" or "intending injustice or absurdity."[60] On the other hand, it has been suggested that now that there is a greater willingness to adopt a purposive approach to interpretation and that a wider view is taken of the context of particular provisions, "the role of presumptions in interpretation is necessarily less important than in the days of more literal interpretation."[61]

(a) Presumptions against changes in the common law

This is one of the more controversial presumptions, given that modern legislation may often be intended to change the common law or may deal with matters with which the common law was unconcerned, such as the "welfare state." Lord Reid formulated the presumption as follows in *Black-Clawson International Ltd v. Papierwerke Waldhof-Aschaffenburg A.G.*:[62]

"In addition to reading the Act you look at the facts presumed to be known to Parliament when the Bill which became the Act in question was before it, and you consider whether there is disclosed some unsatisfactory state of affairs which Parliament can properly be supposed to have intended to remedy by the Act. There is a presumption which can be stated in various ways. One is that in the absence of any clear indication to the contrary, Parliament can be presumed not to have altered the common law further than was necessary to remedy the 'mischief.' Of course it may and quite often does go further. But the principle is that if the enactment is ambiguous, that meaning which relates the scope of the Act to the mischief should

---

[54] Cross (1995), pp. 194; *Presho v. Department of Health and Social Security* [1984] A.C. 310; *Chief Adjudication Officer v. Brunt* [1988] A.C. 711; *Riley v. Chief Adjudication Officer (Note)* [1988] A.C. 746, C.A.
[55] "Parliament is presumed not to enact legislation which interferes with the liberty of the subject without making it clear that this was its intention": *per* McCullough J. in *R. v. Hallstrom, ex p. W.* [1986] Q.B. 1090, 1104 (in the context of detention for treatment under the Mental Health Act 1983: see M. J. Gunn, [1986] J.S.W.L. 290)).
[56] *e.g.* Lord Reid in *Cozens v. Brutus* [1973] A.C. 854, 862; Scarman L.J. in *Re F. (orse. A.) (A Minor) (Publication of Information)* [1977] Fam. 58, 99.
[57] *Cf. Beatty v. Gillbanks* (1892) 9 Q.B.D. 308; Lord Denning M. R. (dissenting) in *Hubbard v. Pitt* [1976] Q.B. 142, 178–179; *Hirst v. Chief Constable of West Yorkshire* (1986) 85 Cr.App.R. 143.
[58] *e.g. R. v. Hallstrom, ex p. W.*, n. 55 above; *Collins v. Wilcock* [1984] 1 W.L.R. 1172.
[59] Compare the above cases with, *e.g., Duncan v. Jones* [1936] K.B. 218; *Thomas v. Sawkins* [1935] 2 K.B. 249; *Liversidge v. Anderson* [1942] A.C. 206.
[60] See *Maxwell on Interpretation of Statutes* (12th ed., 1969), pp. 199–212.
[61] Cross (1995), p. 190.
[62] [1975] A.C. 591, 614.

be taken rather than a different or wider meaning which the contemporary situation did not call for.''

In *Leach v. R.*[63] a provision that a spouse of a defendant "may" be called as a witness was held not to overturn the common law rule that a wife was not *compellable*; it merely made her a *competent* witness. In *Beswick v. Beswick*[64] the House of Lords refused to interpret section 56 of the Law of Property Act 1925 in such a way as to overturn the doctrine of privity of contract. A more doubtful use of the presumption was made in *Chertsey Urban District Council v. Mixnam's Properties Ltd*[65] where the House held that a power for a local authority to attach "such conditions as . . . [it] may think it necessary or desirable to impose" to a caravan site licence could only be used to impose conditions relating to the use of the land: conditions by which the authority sought to protect the interests of tenants were held to be *ultra vires*.

(b) Presumption against ousting the jurisdiction of the courts

The courts have generally looked with disfavour upon Parliament's attempts to oust their jurisdiction. Such attempts have been particularly common in the administrative law context,[66] where "exclusion clauses" have been construed narrowly[67] or evaded.[68] It is notable that where the courts have given effect to an "exclusion clause" the clause has only purported to oust their jurisdiction after a six-week period.[69]

(c) Presumption against interference with vested rights

If there is any ambiguity it is presumed that, "the legislature does not intend to limit vested rights further than clearly appears from the enactment."[70] There is an associated presumption that proprietary rights are not to be taken away without compensation.[71] It has been suggested that where the words are ambiguous, they should be construed in such a way as will cause less interference with

---

[63] [1912] A.C. 305; Criminal Evidence Act 1898, s.4(1). See now the Police and Criminal Evidence Act 1984, s.80.

[64] [1968] A.C. 58, See above, p. 382.

[65] [1965] A.C. 745.

[66] See de Smith, Woolf and Jowell, *Judicial Review of Administrative Action* (5th ed., 1995), pp. 231–249; Sir William Wade and C. F. Forsyth, *Administrative Law* (7th ed., 1994), pp. 729–742.

[67] *e.g.* where a statute provides that a decision shall be "final", that is read as meaning only that there is no right of *appeal*: the remedy of certiorari is not excluded: *R. v. Medical Appeal Tribunal, ex p. Gilmore* [1957] 1 Q.B. 574; *cf. Ex p. Waldron* [1986] Q.B. 824.

[68] *e.g.* a provision that a "determination by the Commission . . . shall not be called in question in any court of law" was held not to exclude proceedings for judicial review where the "determination" was *ultra vires* and a nullity, and thus not a "determination" at all: *Anisminic Ltd v. Foreign Compensation Commission* [1969] 2 A.C. 147 (Foreign Compensation Act 1950, s.4(4)); *cf. Att.-Gen. v. Ryan* [1980] A.C. 718.

[69] *Smith v. East Elloe Rural District Council* [1956] A.C. 585; *R. v. Secretary of State for the Environment, ex p. Ostler* [1977] Q.B. 122; Wade and Forsyth (1994), pp. 745–749. Rather inconsistently, effect in excluding judicial review has been accorded to a "conclusive evidence" provision: *R. v. Registrar of Companies, ex p. Central Bank of India* [1986] Q.B. 1114.

[70] *Per* Ungoed-Thomas J. in *Re Metropolitan Film Studios Application* [1962] 1 W.L.R. 1315, 1323.

[71] *Belfast Corporation v. O.D. Cars Ltd* [1960] A.C. 490; *cf. Westminster Bank Ltd v. Beverley Borough Council* [1971] A.C. 509.

existing rights notwithstanding that it appears that Parliament intended a more "stringent" meaning.[72]

However,

"judges are bound to administer the law as it is, not as they would like it to be. If Parliament, in its wisdom, chooses to legislate in a way which clearly does infringe individual rights, the court is bound to give effect, however unwillingly, to such legislation."[73]

In *Secretary of State for Defence v. Guardian Newspapers Ltd*[74] the House of Lords unanimously rejected the narrow interpretation of section 10 of the Contempt of Court Act 1981[75] adopted by Scott J., who had held that the section had no application to a case where the order being sought was to enforce a property right. Lord Scarman stated that this was not

"an appropriate guide to the true interpretation of a section which has constitutional significance in that its purpose is to support for the benefit of the public the existence of 'a truly effective press.' Specifically, it is my view that, since it is 'in the interests of all of us that we should have a truly effective press,'[76] rights of property have to yield pride of place to the national interest which Parliament must have had in mind when enacting the section. I would, however, add that there certainly remains a place in the law for the principle of construction which the judge applied, namely, that the courts must be slow to impute to Parliament an intention to override property rights in the absence of plain words to that effect. But the principle is not an overriding rule of law: it is an aid, amongst many others, developed by the judges in their never ending task of interpreting statutes in such a way as to give effect to their true purpose."[77]

(d) Strict construction of penal laws in favour of the citizen

Laws which impose criminal or other penalties are strictly construed, so that if the words are ambiguous and there are two reasonable interpretations, the more lenient one will be given.[78] Thus, the provision that "all lotteries are unlawful"

---

[72] *per* Winn L.J. *obiter* in *Allen v. Thorn Electrical Industries Ltd* [1968] 1 Q.B. 487.

[73] *per* Sir Nicolas Browne-Wilkinson in *E.M.I. Records Ltd v. Spillane* [1986] 1 W.L.R. 967, 973, in the course of holding that the Customs and Excise Commissioners had wide powers under the V.A.T. legislation to require the production of documents, which powers were "distasteful to those trained in the law" (*ibid*).

[74] [1985] A.C. 339.

[75] "No court may require a person to disclose . . . the source of information contained in a publication for which he is responsible, unless it be established to the satisfaction of the court that disclosure is necessary in the interests of justice or national security or for the prevention of disorder or crime."

[76] *per* Griffiths L.J., [1984] Ch. 156, 167.

[77] [1985] A.C. 339, 362–363. The House of Lords (by three to two) dismissed an appeal against an order that the *Guardian* return a leaked document to the Secretary of State, in the interests of national security. The identity of the "leaker", Sarah Tisdall, was thereby discovered.

[78] *per* Lord Esher in *Tuck & Sons v. Priester* (1887) 19 Q.B.D. 629, 638; *R. v. Allen* [1985] A.C. 1029, 1034; *R. v. Clarke* [1985] A.C. 1037, 1048, 1053; but *cf. R. v. Caldwell* [1982] A.C. 341 where the House of Lords majority held that the word "reckless" was to be construed as an "ordinary English word" notwithstanding that this was contrary to: (1) the interests of the defendant; (2) the views of the Law Commission and (3) established decisions of lower courts, and that it would cause great complexity in the law: see J. C. Smith, [1981] Crim. L. R. 393.

was not interpreted as creating a criminal offence.[79] A provision penalising the personation at an election of "any person entitled to vote" was held not to apply to a person who personated a deceased voter.[80] Other examples are *R. v. Harris*[81] and *London and North Eastern Railway Co. v. Berriman*.[82] It has, however, been suggested that while the courts still pay lip service to this principle, it is rarely applied in practice if there are social reasons for convicting.[83] In *Anderton v. Ryan*[84] the House of Lords adopted a restrictive, and purportedly "purposive," reading of section 1 of the Criminal Attempts Act 1981, so that it would not apply to some forms of impossible attempts. In so doing they took insufficient account of the Law Commission Report that led to the 1981 Act,[85] and introduced "confusion and uncertainty".[86] Their Lordships regarded some results of a broad reading of the section as absurd, and Lord Bridge found it surprising that Parliament, if intending to do so, "should have done so by anything less than the clearest express language."[87] Following devastating academic criticism,[88] the House of Lords overruled *Anderton v. Ryan* in *R. v. Shivpuri*.[89]

Statutes giving the police a power of arrest are not regarded as "penal laws" for this purpose[90]:

"no one doubts that a prime factor in the process of construction [of statutes conferring arrest powers] is a strong presumption in favour of the liberty of the innocent subject. But it is clear from the authorities at least that a statute may be held to have rebutted the presumption by something falling short of clear express language."[91]

(e) Presumption against retrospective operation

"Perhaps no rule of construction is more firmly established than this—that a retrospective operation is not to be given to a statute so as to impair an existing right or obligation, otherwise than as regards matter of procedure, unless that effect cannot be avoided without doing violence to the language of the enactment. If the enactment is expressed in language which is fairly capable of either interpretation, it ought to be construed as prospective only."[92]

---

[79] Betting and Lotteries Act 1934: *Sales-Matic Ltd v. Hinchcliffe* [1959] 1 W.L.R. 1005.
[80] Poor Law Amendment Act 1851, s.3: *Whiteley v. Chappell* (1868) L.R. 4 Q.B. 147.
[81] Above, p. 359.
[82] Above, p. 367.
[83] Glanville Williams, *Textbook of Criminal Law* (2nd ed., 1983), pp. 12–18; *cf. Fisher v. Bell* (pp. 367–368, above); *R. v. Ottewell* [1970] A.C. 642, 649; *R. v. Bloxham* [1983] 1 A.C. 109, 114; *Attorney-General's Reference (No. 1 of 1988)* [1989] A.C. 971, 991.
[84] [1985] A.C. 560.
[85] Law Com. No. 102.
[86] J. C. Smith, [1985] Crim. L. R. 504.
[87] [1985] A.C. 560, 583.
[88] Most notably by Glanville Williams, "The Lords and Impossible Attempts or *Quis Custodiet Ipsos Custodes*?" [1986] C.L.J. 33, acknowledged by Lord Bridge in *R. v. Shivpuri* [1987] A.C. 1, 23. See below, pp. 440–441.
[89] [1987] A.C. 1: see J. R. Spencer, [1986] C.L.J. 361; P. R. Glazebrook, [1986] C.L.J. 363 (noting that the decision in *Shivpuri* involved modification of the statutory language).
[90] See above, p. 368, n. 34.
[91] *per* Lord Bridge in *Wills v. Bowley* [1983] 1 A.C. 57, 101. It is difficult to see how such a presumption can be regarded as either "strong" or even much of a "presumption."
[92] R. S. Wright J. in *Re Athlumney* [1898] 2 Q.B. 547, 551–2. See above, p. 283.

Furthermore,

"it seems to me entirely proper, in a case where some retrospective operation was clearly intended, equally to presume that the retrospective operation of the statute extends no further than is necessary to give effect either
to its clear language or to its manifest purpose."[93]

In *L'Office Cherifien des Phosphates v. Yamashita-Shinnihon Steamship Co.
Ltd*,[94] the House of Lords emphasised, however, that the basis of the rule was
"simple fairness". The question to what degree, if any, a particular provision
has retrospective effect was to be determined not by reference to "generalised
presumptions or maxims" but considering

"whether the consequences of reading the statute with the suggested degree
of retrospectivity is so unfair that the words used by Parliament cannot
have been intended to mean what they might appear to say."[95]

This question in turn was to be answered by weighing a series of factors, including the degree of retrospectivity suggested; the value and nature of the rights
affected on which the retrospective legislation will impinge; the clarity of the
language; and the circumstances in which the legislation was enacted. The distinction between substantive and procedural rights was misleading,

"since it leaves out of the account the fact that some procedural rights are
more valuable than some substantive rights."[96]

Moreover, it was doubtful whether it was "possible to assign rights such as the
present unequivocally to one category rather than another." On this approach,
section 13A of the Arbitration Act 1950,[97] which conferred a new power on an
arbitrator to dismiss a claim for want of prosecution where there had been "inordinate and inexcusable delay", was to be interpreted as enabling an arbitrator
to take account of delays before the section came into force.

In *Waddington v. Miah*[98] the House of Lords held that certain offences created

---

[93] *per* Lord Bridge in *Arnold v. Central Electricity Generating Board* [1988] A.C. 228, 275, in the
course of holding that while the Limitation Act 1975 modified retrospectively the position as to
limitation in respect of actions governed by the Law Reform (Limitation of Actions, etc.) Act
1954, as amended, it did not apply so as to defeat a right to plead a time bar that had accrued
under the Limitation Act 1939. See also *Pearce v. Secretary of State for Defence* [1988] A.C.
755.

[94] [1994] 1 A.C. 486, H.L.

[95] *per* Lord Mustill at pp. 524–525. The other members of the House agreed with Lord Mustill's
speech.

[96] *per* Lord Mustill at p. 528. See also *Yew Bon Tew v. Kenderaan Bas Maria* [1983] 1 A.C. 553,
where the Privy Council noted that an apparently "procedural" alteration, such as a change in
limitation period, could affect existing rights and obligations; retrospective effect was denied to
an extension in limitation period so as to affect an accrued right to plead a time bar. For other
examples of cases where retrospective effect has been denied, see *Bonning v. Dodsley* [1982] 1
W.L.R. 279; *Lewis v. Lewis* [1986] A.C. 828; *Plewa v. Chief Adjudication officer* [1995] 1 A.C.
249. Retrospective effect was given to procedural changes in *Thompson v. Thompson* [1986]
Fam. 38 and *R. v. Makanjuola* [1995] 3 All E.R. 730, and, is view of clear words in the statute,
to restrictions on right of appeal against a deportation order in *R. v. Secretary of State for the
Home Department, ex p. Mundowa* [1992] 3 All E.R. 606.

[97] Inserted by the Courts and Legal Services Act 1990, s.102; in force from January 1, 1992.

[98] [1974] 1 W.L.R. 683.

by the Immigration Act 1971 were not intended to operate retrospectively. Lord Reid stated[99] that in view of the prohibitions contained in the Universal Declaration of Human Rights and the European Convention on Human Rights, "it is hardly credible that any government department would promote or that Parliament would pass retrospective criminal legislation."

On the other hand, in *Chebaro v. Chebaro*[1] the Court of Appeal held that the right conferred by the Matrimonial and Family Proceedings Act 1984, section 12(1), to apply for financial relief where a marriage "has been dissolved" by proceedings overseas, applied to a decree pronounced before the commencement of the Act. The meaning of the words used, importing a retrospective effect, was "plain and unequivocal".[2]

(f) Presumption that statutes do not affect the Crown

It is presumed that the Crown is not bound by a statute unless reference is made to it expressly or by necessary implication:

> "Since laws are made by rulers for subjects a general expression in a statute such as 'any person,' descriptive of those upon whom the statute imposes obligations or restraints is not to be read as including the ruler himself."[3]

Questions may arise as to whether a particular institution is a servant or agent of the Crown and so within the "shield of the Crown".[4]

(g) Others

Other presumptions that may be invoked include the presumption that Parliament does not intend to violate international law,[5] and that a statute does not apply to acts committed abroad.[6]

G. REFORM

As mentioned above,[7] Parliament has refrained from intervening to give general directions to the judges as to methods of statutory interpretation. The Law

---

[99] At p. 694.

[1] [1987] Fam. 127.

[2] *per* Balcombe L.J. at p. 131. See also *Williams v. Williams* [1971] P. 271; *Powys v. Powys* [1971] P. 340; *Hewitt v. Lewis* [1986] 1 W.L.R. 444; *Hager v. Osborne* [1992] Fam. 94.

[3] *per* Diplock L.J. in *B.B.C. v. Johns* [1965] Ch. 32, 78; *cf.* Wrottesley J. in *Att.-Gen v. Hancock* [1940] 1 All E.R. 32, 34. *Lord Advocate v. Dumbarton District Council* [1990] 2 A.C. 580 (noted by J. Wolffe, [1990] P.L. 14); O. Hood Phillips and P. Jackson, *Constitutional and Administrative Law* (7th ed., 1987), pp. 613–616. The Crown may rely on any statutory defence that would be available to a private party: Crown Proceedings Act 1947, s.31(1). See generally, P. W. Hogg, *Liability of the Crown* (2nd ed., 1990); P. Jackson, [1990] Denning L.J. 45.

[4] See, *e.g. Tamlin v. Hannaford* [1950] 1 K.B. 18; *Town Investments Ltd v. Department of the Environment* [1978] A.C. 359; *British Medical Association v. Greater Glasgow Health Board* [1989] A.C. 1211.

[5] See above, pp. 386–389.

[6] See above, p. 282.

[7] p. 354.

Commissions saw their report on *The Interpretation of Statutes*[8] as a contribution to the process of educating judges and practitioners, and only proposed a limited degree of statutory intervention. They appended draft clauses, of which these were the first two[9]:

"1.—
(1) In ascertaining the meaning of any provision of an Act, the matters which may be considered shall, in addition to those which may be considered for that purpose apart from this section, include the following, that is to say—

(a) all indications provided by the Act as printed by authority, including punctuation and side-notes, and the short title of the Act;
(b) any relevant report of a Royal Commission, Committee or other body which had been presented or made to or laid before Parliament or either House before the time when the Act was passed;
(c) any relevant treaty or other international agreement which is referred to in the Act or of which copies had been presented to Parliament by command of Her Majesty before that time, whether or not the United Kingdom were bound by it at that time;
(d) any other document bearing upon the subject-matter of the legislation which had been presented to Parliament by command of Her Majesty before that time;
(e) any document (whether falling within the foregoing paragraphs or not) which is declared by the Act to be a relevant document for the purposes of this section.
(2) The weight to be given for the purposes of this section to any such matter as is mentioned in subsection (1) shall be no more than is appropriate in the circumstances.
(3) Nothing in this section shall be construed as authorising the consideration of reports of proceedings in Parliament for any purpose for which they could not be considered apart from this section.
2.—The following shall be included among the principles to be applied in the interpretation of Acts, namely—
(a) that a construction which would promote the general legislative purpose underlying the provision in question is to be preferred to a construction which would not; and
(b) that a construction which is consistent with the international obligations of Her Majesty's Government in the United Kingdom is to be preferred to a construction which is not."

Clause 1 would clarify, and in some respects relax the strictness of the rules which excluded altogether, or excluded when the meaning was otherwise unambiguous, certain internal and external aids from consideration by a court. Clause 1(1)(e) would also encourage the preparation in selected cases of explanatory material for use by the courts, which might "elucidate the contextual assump-

---

[8] Law Com. No. 21; Scot. Law Com. No. 11 (1969).
[9] Clause 3 provided for the application of the first two clauses to subordinate legislation; Clause 4 provided for a presumption that breach of a statutory duty should be actionable at the suit of any person who sustains damage.

tions on which legislation has been passed."[10] Clause 2 emphasised the importance in interpretation of a provision of the general legislative purpose underlying it (clause 2)(a)) and the fulfilment of international obligations (clause 2(b)).[11]

The Renton Committee[12] approved the whole of clauses 1 and 2 except paragraphs (b) and (d) of clause 1: unrestricted admission of such materials would place too great a burden on litigants, their advisers and the courts, would do nothing to make statutes more immediately intelligible to the lay public and might greatly lengthen court proceedings. They doubted the value of clause 1(e) as it was already open to Parliament to do this.[13] Clause 2 was regarded as reflecting current practice. No opinion was expressed on the other two clauses. The Committee proposed in addition the enactment of a provision that "In the absence of any express indication to the contrary, a construction that would exclude retrospective effect is to be preferred to one that would not." It should also be made clear that a court in interpreting legislation intended to give effect to a provision of a Community treaty or instrument should take the relevant provisions of Community law into account.

Lord Scarman, who had been chairman of the Law Commission at the time of the 1969 report, introduced the Commissions' proposals as a draft Bill in 1980. The following year he introduced a Bill based on those proposals modified largely to take account of the Renton Committee's suggestions. The first Bill failed on second reading in the Lords; the second passed the Lords but was the subject of objections on the motion for second reading in the Commons, and as a Private Peer's Bill without government support did not proceed further.[14]

In so far as the proposed provisions reflect current practice they seem superfluous; the few that go beyond it, such as the use of official reports and White Papers, have been controversial, but have been overtaken by the relaxation in the prohibition against reference to Parliamentary materials achieved by the judges.[15] Clause 1(c)[16] would have the effect of disapproving the restrictive approach adopted in *Ellerman Lines v. Murray*,[17] and as such would be useful, but that decision has been largely outflanked, and might well be reconsidered by the House of Lords if the occasion were to rise. Overall, the enactment of these proposals would make little difference in practice.

The Renton Committee's recommendation that the preparation of a new Interpretation Act should be put in hand eventually led to the Interpretation Act 1978, a consolidation measure with minor changes incorporating Law Commission proposals. This is an aid to drafting rather than interpretation.[18] "At the level of general principles . . . the subject does not lend itself to legislation."[19]

---

[10] See above, p. 389.

[11] Law Com. No. 21; Scot. Law Com. No. 11, pp. 49–50.

[12] Cmnd. 6053, 1975 pp. 139–148. See above, pp. 270–271.

[13] Clauses in the Matrimonial Proceedings and Properties Bill 1970 and the Animals Bill 1970, which provided that regard could be had to relevant, specified Law Commission reports, were successfully opposed in the House of Commons.

[14] Interpretation of Legislation Bill (1979–80 H.L. Bill 141); Interpretation of Legislation Bill (1980–81)-HC. Bill 120); F.A.R. Bennion, (1981) 131 N.L.J. 840; Miers and Page (2nd ed., 1990), pp. 176–180.

[15] See above, pp. 389–394.

[16] Clause 1(b) of the 1980–81 Bill.

[17] [1931] A.C. 126; above, p. 387, n. 70.

[18] Above, pp. 284–285.

[19] Cross (1995), p. 191. Courts of Commonwealth countries where declarations of general principles of interpretation have been enacted seem rarely to refer to them in practice: W. A. Leitch, [1980] Stat.L.R. 5, 8.

H. THE INTERPRETATION OF COMMUNITY LEGISLATION

1. METHODS OF INTERPRETATION

Close attention has been paid to the methods of interpretation of Community legislation adopted by the Court of Justice of the European Communities.[20] A number of different techniques have been identified, to which commentators have attached a variety of labels. The Court has consistently shown that it is more likely to be influenced by the *context*[21] and *purposes*[22] of a legislative provision than its exact *wording*[23] or the subjective intentions of those who promulgated the legislation.[24] The extent to which the Court's overall approach differs from the so-called "common law" approach of English judges is debatable. It has also probably been exaggerated.[25] Certainly the ideas underlying the various techniques of interpretation adopted by the Court are more familiar than some of the labels. It should also be noted that the techniques tend to be employed cumulatively rather than as alternatives.[26]

The process of interpretation must obviously commence with an analysis of the text. However, literal interpretation, in so far as that implies an exclusive or predominant concern with wording and grammar, is not favoured. The Court has shown little inclination to hold that words carry one "plain," "ordinary" or "clear" meaning so that considerations of context and purpose are rendered irrelevant. There are several reasons for this.

(a) The method of drafting

Many of the key provisions of the EC and Euratom Treaties are drafted in general terms, and with no "definition sections". For example, Article 9/EC refers to the prohibition between member states of customs duties and "all charges having equivalent effect." Article 86/EC prohibits the "abuse by one or more undertakings of a dominant position within the common market or in a substantial part of it." It gives four examples of an "abuse" but no indication of what is meant by "dominant position". These concepts are left to be developed by the Community institutions, including the Court. The ECSC Treaty and Community secondary legislation are in general more tightly drafted, but they still, inevitably, employ broad terms.

---

[20] See the *Reports of the Judicial and Academic Conference*, Court of Justice of the European Communities, September 27–28, 1976; A. Bredimas, *Methods of Interpretation and Community Law* (1978); L. N. Brown and T. Kennedy, *The Court of Justice of the European Communities* (4th ed., 1994), Chap 14; R. Plender, "The Interpretation of Community Acts by Reference to the Intentions of the Authors" [1982] 2 Y.E.L. 57; T. Millett, [1989] Stat.L.R. 163 S. Weatherill and P. Beaumont, *EC Law* (2nd ed., 1995), pp. 166–182.

[21] "Contextual" or "schematic" interpretation.

[22] "Purposive" or "teleological" interpretation.

[23] "Literal" interpretation.

[24] "Historical" or "subjective" interpretation.

[25] P. Dagtoglou, "The English Judges and European Community Law" [1978] C.L.J. 76.

[26] There is, for example, no place for a "today's the day for the teleological rule" approach.

(b) Languages

The texts of the EC and Euratom Treaties and all Community secondary legislation are published in several languages, each of which is equally authentic.[27] Arguments based on the exact wording of any one version are accordingly less compelling; it can never have been intended that Community law applies differently in different Member States. In cases of doubt it may be necessary to consider all the versions, in the light, as ever of context and purposes. For example, in *Stauder v. City of Ulm*[28] the Court considered a decision of the Commission on the sale of butter at reduced prices to persons in receipt of welfare benefits. The German and Dutch versions provided that the butter had to be exchanged for a "coupon indicating [the recipients'] names." A German citizen argued that this was an infringement of fundamental rights. The Court found that the French and Italian versions referred to a "coupon referring to the person concerned", and preferred this more liberal wording. The objective of the decision could be achieved by methods of identification other than names.

(c) The status of the Court

The Court is in a stronger position in relation to the other Community institutions than a national court in relation to its national parliament. Legislation is not promulgated by an elected body alone, but by the nominated Commission and Council or by the Commission and European Parliament acting jointly. The European Parliament is now directly elected, but its role in law-making is in many areas essentially consultative. The Court is expressly enjoined to "ensure that in the interpretation and application of this Treaty the law is observed"[29] and is expressly empowered to review the legality of acts of the Council and Commission.[30] It is placed on an equal footing with the other institutions in Article 4/EC Moreover, it has proved more difficult than expected for the Council to agree upon legislative proposals placed before it by the Commission. The resultant "legislative short-fall" has compelled the Court to determine questions of interpretation, and to fill gaps, in the light of the general aims of the Community and general principles of law. To an extent it has been forced to adopt a legislative role, and has not felt the need to disguise it.[31]

The Court's position in relation to the Member States is more problematic. There is an inevitable tension between the Community's harmonisation aims and the perceived interests of individual Member States. The Court could have adopted a position of neutrality; instead it has chosen to take a "partisan" line in favour of the achievement of the aims of the Community, as a kind of counterweight to the Council of Ministers, which has tended more to reflect state interests. Member States are indeed expressly required by Article 5/EC to take all appropriate measures to fulfil obligations arising out of the Treaty or

[27] The only authentic text of the ECSC Treaty is French. The other two basic Treaties and the Single European Act are authentic in Danish, Dutch, English, Finnish, French, German, Greek, Irish, Italian, Portuguese, Spanish and Swedish and the secondary legislation in all these except Irish.

[28] Case 29/69, [1969] E.C.R. 419.

[29] Art. 164/EC.

[30] Art. 173/EC. Above, pp. 346–348.

[31] Note, for example, the enunciation of a rule with *prospective* effect only in the second *Defrenne* case: Case 43/75, [1976] E.C.R. 455.

acts of Community institutions, to facilitate the achievement of the Community's tasks and to abstain from any measure that could jeopardise the attainment of the objectives of the Treaty.

(d) Community purposes

The freedom of the Court to adopt a purposive approach is naturally facilitated by the express statement of the Community's aims and objectives included in the Treaties (including their preambles). Articles 2 and 3/EC[32] provide:

ARTICLE 2

The Community shall have as its task, by establishing a common market and an economic and monetary union and by implementing the common policies or activities referred to in Articles 3 and 3a, to promote throughout the Community a harmonious and balanced development of economic activities, sustainable and non-inflationary growth respecting the environment, a high degree of convergence of economic performance, a high level of employment and of social protection, the raising of the standard of living and quality of life, and economic and social cohesion and solidarity among Member States.

ARTICLE 3

For the purposes set out in Article 2, the activities of the Community shall include, as provided in this Treaty and in accordance with the timetable set out therein:

(a) the elimination, as between Member States, of customs duties and quantitative restrictions on the import and export of goods, and of all other measures having equivalent effect;
(b) a common commercial policy;
(c) an internal market characterized by the abolition, as between Member States, of obstacles to the free movement of goods, persons, services and capital;
(d) measures concerning the entry and movement of persons in the internal market as provided for in Article 100c;
(e) a common policy in the sphere of agriculture and fisheries;
(f) a common policy in the sphere of transport;
(g) a system ensuring that competition in the internal market is not distorted;
(h) the approximation of the laws of Member States to the extent required for the functioning of the common market;
(i) a policy in the social sphere comprising a European Social Fund;
(j) the strengthening of economic and social cohesion;
(k) a policy in the sphere of the environment;

---

[32] As substituted by Art. G (2), (3)/TEU. Art. 3a provides for economic and monetary union.

(l) the strengthening of the competitiveness of Community industry;
(m) the promotion of research and technological development;
(n) encouragement for the establishment and development of trans-European networks;
(o) a contribution to the attainment of a high level of health protection;
(p) a contribution to education and training of quality and to the flowering of the cultures of the Member States;
(q) a policy in the sphere of development cooperation;
(r) the association of the overseas countries and territories in order to increase trade and promote jointly economic and social development;
(s) a contribution to the strengthening of consumer protection;
(t) measures in the spheres of energy, civil protection and tourism.''

Moreover, the reasons on which regulations, directives and decisions are based are stated in a preamble. The Court has attached much more importance to these express statements of purpose than to attempts to discern from other sources the subjective intentions of the authors of Community legislation.[33] Indeed, the details of the negotiations leading up to the Treaties and of debates within the Council and Commission concerning secondary legislation have not been published.[34] There have been occasional references by Advocates General to a statement made by the government of a Member State to the national parliament in the course of a ratification debate, but not to the exclusion of other considerations.[35]

In relation to purposive interpretation reference has been made to the so-called "rule of effectiveness" (*règle de l'effet utile*), a concept borrowed from international law. This means that, "preference should be given to the construction which gives the rule its fullest effect and maximum practical value."[36] This concept has been used as a justification for holding that the Community or one of its institutions has certain "implied powers", such as the power to require the repayment of a state aid granted in breach of the Treaty.[37] Similarly, in the *E.R.T.A. Case*[38] it was held that the Community had the implied power to establish treaty relations with non-Member States. The Court argued that it was the "necessary effect" or "consequence" of the making of a regulation on the harmonisation of provisions in the road transport field that the Community assume the exclusive right to conclude international agreements relating to the same subject matter.

---

[33] In case 136/79, *National Panasonic (U.K.) Ltd v. Commission* [1980] E.C.R. 2033, A. G. Warner argued that statements by individual members of the Council, the European Parliament, the Commission or the Commission's staff could not be relied upon for guidance as to the meaning of a Council Regulation (pp. 2066–7). See generally Plender (1982), op. cit. n.20 above.

[34] In Case C-292/89, *R. v. Immigration Appeal Tribunal, ex p. Antonissen* [1991] E.C.R. I-745, the Court held that a declaration made by the Council at the time of adoption of certain secondary legislation, and disclosed by the Council for the purposes of litigation, could not be used for the purposes of interpretation as the content of the declaration was not referred to in the wording of the legislation.

[35] See *e.g.*, Case 6/60, *Humblet v. Belgium* [1960] E.C.R. 559.

[36] H. Kutcher, *Conference Reports* (see p., n. 20 above), I–41.

[37] e.g. Case 70/72, *Commission v. Germany* [1973] E.C.R. 829.

[38] Case 22/70, *Commission v. Council* (E.R.T.A.) [1971] E.C.R. 263.

(e) Context

References by the Court to the purposes of the Community are commonly closely associated with arguments that seek to place the provision to be interpreted in the context of relevant rules of Community law. The Court may refer to the "general scheme of the Treaty", or to other treaty provisions in the relevant Part or to general principles of Community law. In the case of secondary legislation reference will be made to the enabling provisions in the Treaty.

(f) Examples

Striking examples of the Court's dynamic approach to interpretation are provided by its decisions already discussed on the direct effectiveness of treaty provisions and secondary legislation, and the supremacy of Community law.[39] Another good example is the *Continental Can* case[40] A New York company (Continental Can) held, through a German subsidiary (SLW), what the Commission determined to be a dominant position over a substantial part of the common market in meat tins, fish tins and metal closures for glass jars. Subsequently, acting through a Belgian subsidiary (Europemballage), Continental Can acquired a Dutch firm (TDV) which specialised in similar products. The Commission decided that the merger amounted to an abuse of the dominant position mentioned above, as the effect was practically to eliminate competition in the relevant products. The ECSC treaty expressly provided for merger control (Article 66); the EEC Treaty did not. Nevertheless, the Court held that a merger could in principle amount to an abuse of a dominant position contrary to Article 86/EEC, although it did not do so on the facts of the case. In so deciding the Court stated that it was necessary "to go back to the spirit, general scheme and wording of Article 86, as well as to the system and objectives of the Treaty."[41] It referred to the original version of Articles 2 and 3(f)[42], and to Article 85, which prohibited:

> "all agreements between undertakings, decisions by associations of undertakings and concerted practices which may affect trade between Member States and which have as their object or effect the prevention, restriction or distortion of competition within the common market. . . ."

The Court observed:[43]

> "[I]f Article 3(f) provides for the institution of a system ensuring that competition in the common market is not distorted, then it requires *a fortiori* that a competition must not be eliminated. This requirement is so essential that without it numerous provisions of the Treaty would be pointless. Moreover, it corresponds to the precept of Article 2 of the Treaty. . . .
> . . . Articles 85 and 86 seek to achieve the same aim on different levels, that is, the maintenance of effective competition within the common market. The restraint of competition which is prohibited if it is the result

---

[39] The *van Gend en Loos* case, above, pp. 314–316; *Costa v. E.N.E.L.*, above, p. 332.
[40] Case 6/72, *Europemballage Corporation and Continental Can Co. Inc. v. Commission* [1973] E.C.R. 215.
[41] *ibid.* p. 243.
[42] Art. 3(f) is now 3(g): above, p 406.
[43] p. 244.

of behaviour falling under Article 85, cannot become permissible by the fact that such behaviour succeeds under the influence of a dominant undertaking and results in the merger of the undertaking concerned."

In other words, the prohibition of certain acts when done in concert by separate undertakings was not to be evaded by merger of those undertakings.

It is a matter of debate whether the Court has gone too far in its willingness to "fill gaps".[44] It is clearly obliged to make policy decisions given the points already made as to the broad terms of many key Treaty provisions and secondary legislation. It is not so clear that decisions that recognise an inherent jurisdiction in the Court outside the express heads of jurisdiction set out in the EC Treaty[45] that are reached "despite textual indications to the contrary"[46] are justifiable.[47] That there are limits is illustrated by the decisions confirming that directives are not directly effective between private individuals.[48]

(g) Restrictive interpretation

Interpretation in the light of purposes and context does not necessarily mean that such interpretation is "broad" or "liberal." Exceptions to general Community rules and derogations to Treaty obligations are restrictively interpreted. For example, the principle of the free movement of workers is subject to "limitations justified on grounds of public policy, public security or public health."[49] These limitations are strictly construed.[50] Restrictions may not be imposed unless the person's presence or conduct "constitutes a genuine and sufficiently serious threat to public policy",[51] and the requirements of public policy must affect "one of the fundamental interests of society",[52] although it is for the national authorities to determine whether the facts of a particular case fall within these principles.

2. GENERAL PRINCIPLES OF LAW[53]

The Court often refers to "general principles of law" derived from the national laws of Member States.[54] These are regarded as part of "the law" of which the

---

[44] See, e.g., Weatherill and Beaumont (1995), pp. 174–182; H. Rasmussen, *On Law and Policy in the European Court of Justice* (1986) and (1988) 13 E.L.Rev.28.

[45] Case C-2/88/mm., *Zvartveld and Others* [1990] E.C.R. I-3367 and I-4405 (order to Commission to send reports to a national court).

[46] e.g. Case 294/83, *Les Verts v. European Parliament* [1986] E.C.R.1339 (action under Art.173/EEC to review legality of act of Parliament admissible notwithstanding the absence of any reference to Parliament in Art. 173 in its original form; Case C-70/88, *European Parliament v. Council* [1990] E.C.R. I-2041, above, p. 347.

[47] Weatherill and Beaumont (1995), pp. 176–182.

[48] Above, pp. 317–318.

[49] Art. 48(3)/EC; Directive 64/221/EEC.

[50] Case 41/74, *Van Duyn v. Home Office* [1974] E.C.R. 1337, above, pp. 316–317; Case 67/74, *Bonsignore v. Oberstadtdirektor Cologne* [1975] E.C.R. 297; Case 36/75, *Rutili v. French Minister of the Interior* [1975] E.C.R. 1219; Case 30/77, *R. v. Bouchereau* [1977] E.C.R. 1999.

[51] *Rutili* [1975] E.C.R. 1219, 1231.

[52] *Bouchereau* [1977] E.C.R. 1999, 2014.

[53] L. N. Brown and T. Kennedy, *The Court of Justice of the European Communities* (4th ed., 1994), Chap. 15; D. Wyatt and A. Dashwood, *The Substantive Law of the E.E.C.* (3rd ed., 1993), pp. 88–103; T. C. Hartley, *The Foundations of European Community Law* (3rd ed., 1994), Chap. 5.

[54] They may also be derived from Treaty provisions.

Court is to ensure observance.[55] They can be employed in the interpretation of Treaty provisions but cannot override them. In relation to secondary legislation and other acts of the institutions they are not so confined: a challenge to the legality of a measure may be based on breach of one of these principles.[56]

Examples include:

— the principle of *proportionality*, which requires that:
   "the individual should not have his freedom of action limited beyond the degree necessary for the public interest";[57]
— the *audi alteram partem* principle of natural justice, which requires that persons affected by an adverse decision be given an opportunity to make representations[58];
— the principle of *equality*:
   "whereby comparable situations must not be treated differently and different situations must not be treated in the same way unless such treatment is objectively justified"[59];
— the related principles of *legal certainty* and *legitimate expectation*, which require, respectively, that:
   "those subject to the law should not be placed in a situation of uncertainty as to their rights and obligations" and "those who act in good faith on the basis of the law as it is or seems to be should not be frustrated in their expectations."[60]

These "general principles" include respect for "fundamental rights",[61] derived from national constitutions or from international conventions concerning human rights, such as the European Convention on Human Rights.[62] This does not mean that the Convention is part of Community law and so directly enforceable under

---

[55] Art. 164/EC, above, p. 405. See also Article 173/EC, above, p. 347, which provides expressly that a Community act may be annulled for infringement of "any rule of law relating to its application." *Cf.* Article 215(2).
[56] See above, p. 348.
[57] A. G. de Lamothe in Case 11/70, *Internationale Handelsgesellschaft v. EVSt.* [1970] E.C.R. 1125, 1147; *cf. R. v. Secretary of State for the Home Department, ex p. Brind* [1991] 1 A.C. 696, where the House of Lords refused to hold that the proportionality doctrine was part of English domestic law and the *Rutili* case, above (requirement of a *genuine and sufficiently serious* threat to public policy to justify interference with freedom of movement).
[58] Case 11/74, *Transocean Marine Paint Association v. Commission* [1974] E.C.R. 1063; *cf.* Case 136/79, *National Panasonic Ltd v. Commission* [1980] E.C.R. 2033 (no need to give prior warning of an investigation by Commission inspectors).
[59] Wyatt and Dashwood (1993), p. 96. See Case 20/71, *Sabbatini v. European Parliament* [1972] E.C.R. 345 (Council Regulation concerning expatriation allowances for employees of the Parliament held invalid on the ground of sex discrimination.)
[60] Wyatt and Dashwood (1993), p. 91.
[61] T. C. Hartley, (1975–76) 1 E.L.Rev. 54; M. Dauses, (1985) 10 E.L.Rev. 398; S. O'Leary, (1995) 32 C.M.L.Rev. 519; J. Weiler, (1995) 32 C.M.C.Rev. 579 the *International Handels* case (n. 57, above).
[62] Case 4/73, *Nold v. Commission* [1974] E.C.R. 491; the *Rutili* Case (n. 51, above); Case 118/75 *Watson and Belmann* [1976] E.C.R. 1185; Case 136/79, *National Panasonic (U.K.) Ltd v. Commission* [1980] E.C.R. 2033 (no infringement of the right of privacy guaranteed by article 8(1) of the European Convention: an investigation of a company's books without prior warning was held to be justified as "necessary in a democratic society in the interests of . . . the economic well-being of the country," within the one of the exceptions specified in article 8(2)); Case 63/83, *Kirk* [1984] E.C.R. 2689 (application of the principle that penal provisions may not have retrospective effect): see N. Foster, (1985) 10 E.L.Rev. 276.

the European Communities Act 1972: "the European Court does not deal with fundamental rights in the abstract; it only deals with them if they arise under Treaties and have a bearing on Community law questions."[63]

3. INTERPRETATION BY ENGLISH COURTS

The approach that should be taken by English judges was considered by Lord Denning M. R. in *Bulmer v. Bollinger*[64]:

"Beyond doubt the English courts must follow the same principles as the European court. Otherwise there would be differences between the countries of the nine. . . . It is enjoined on the English courts by section 3 of the European Community Act 1972. . . .

No longer must they examine the words in meticulous detail. No longer must they argue about the precise grammatical sense. They must look to the purpose or intent. To quote the words of the European court in the *Da Costa* case[65], they must deduce 'from the wording and the spirit of the Treaty the meaning of the community rules.' They must not confine themselves to the English text. They must consider, if need be, all the authentic texts. . . . They must divine the spirit of the Treaty and gain inspiration from it. If they find a gap, they must fill it as best they can. They must do what the framers of the instrument would have done if they had thought about it. So we must do the same. Those are the principles, as I understand it, on which the European court acts."

The dangers of applying a strict literal interpretation to provisions of Community law are illustrated by *R. v. Henn.*[66] Article 30/EC prohibits the imposition of "quantitative restrictions on imports and all measures having equivalent effect." The Court of Appeal (Criminal Division) held that the ban on the importation of indecent or obscene material imposed by section 42 of the Customs Consolidation Act 1876 did not fall within Article 30 as it imposed a total prohibition rather than a mere restriction "measured by quantity". This view was, not, however, relied upon by counsel on appeal to the House of Lords, or in argument before the Court of Justice, as it was clearly contrary to a number of earlier decisions of the Court of Justice, and inconsistent with the purposes of the Community. As a matter of common sense, a complete prohibition on the free movement of goods is likely to be more questionable under Community

---

[63] *Kaur v. Lord Advocate* 1980 S.C. 319, 333 (Lord Ross, Court of Session (Outer House)).

[64] [1974] Ch. 401, 425–426. See also the similar views expressed by Lord Denning M. R. in *Buchanan & Co. Ltd v. Babco Forwarding & Shipping (U.K.) Ltd* [1977] Q.B. 208, 213–214. His Lordship's attempt to apply the "European Method" of "filling gaps" to the interpretation of an international convention on the carriage of goods by road was resisted by the House of Lords: [1978] A.C. 141, 153 (Lord Wilberforce), 156 (Viscount Dilhorne) and 160 (Lord Salmon); *cf.* above, p. 386. See also the doubts as to the propriety of "gap-filling" expressed by Nolan J. in *Yoga for Health Foundation v. Customs and Excise Commissioners* [1984] S.T.C. 630.

[65] [1963] C.M.L.R. 224, 237.

[66] [1978] 1 W.L.R. 1031, C.A.; [1981] A.C. 850, E.C.J., H.L.; Case 34/79 [1979] E.C.R. 3795.

law than a partial restriction. Lord Diplock said that this showed "the danger
of an English court applying English canons of statutory construction."[67] It is
submitted that the Court of Appeal's interpretation was excessively "literalist"
even by English standards.

---

[67] [1981] A.C. at p. 914. See also *R. v. Licensing Authority, ex p. Smith, Kline & French Laboratories Ltd* [1990] 1 A.C. 64, 75 (Dillon L.J.), 84 (Balcombe L.J.) and 87 (Staughton L.J.) (need
to adopt a purposive and not a semantic approach to the interpretation of EC directives). An
appeal to the House of Lords was dismissed, the matter being determined by reference to English
law: [1990] 1 A.C. 64, 90. See to the same effect the House of Lords in *Litter v. Forth Dry
Dock & Engineering Co. Ltd* [1990] 1 A.C. 546.

CHAPTER 7

JUDICIAL PRECEDENT

A. INTRODUCTION[1]

ONE of the hallmarks of any good decision-making process is consistency: like cases should be treated alike. Consistency is not, however, always appropriate, as, for example, where a case is seen with the passage of time and changes of circumstance no longer to offer a just solution to a recurring problem. Moreover, there are always difficulties in determining whether two cases are truly "like". Nevertheless, unjustifiable inconsistency may lead to a sense of grievance on the part of those affected and to a reasonable suspicion that the people making the decisions do not know what they are about. One of the main functions of the superior courts of law is the authoritative determination of disputed questions of law. A court's decision is expected to be consistent with decisions in previous cases and to provide certainty for the future so that the parties and others may arrange their affairs in reliance on the court's opinion. These considerations are reflected in the English system of judicial precedent.

The decisions of judges must be reasoned, and the reasons will include propositions of law. A judge in a later case is bound to consider the relevant case law and will normally accept the propositions stated as correct unless there is good reason to disagree; in some circumstances he or she is required to accept them even if they are in his or her view obviously wrong. So all relevant precedents are to a greater or lesser extent "persuasive", and some of them may be "binding" under what is termed the doctrine of *stare decisis*.[2] The characteristic that an individual precedent may be binding is distinctive of common law systems. In continental systems based upon codes that are theoretically complete, judicial decisions are not, technically, sources of legal rules. They may, however, carry great persuasive weight, particularly where there is a trend of cases to the same effect, and they have been of great importance in the development of certain areas of the law.[3]

Under the English system, a proposition stated in or derived from case. A is binding in case B if (1) it is a proposition of law; (2) it forms part of the *ratio decidendi* of case A (the reason or ground upon which the decision is based); (3) case A was decided in a court whose decisions are binding on the court that

---

[1] See generally Sir Rupert Cross and J. W. Harris, *Precedent in English Law* (4th ed., 1991); L. Goldstein (ed.), *Precedent in Law* (1987) (note the bibliography at pp. 249–273).

[2] "Keep to what has been decided previously:" Cross and Harris (1991), p. 3. The term is most commonly used to refer to the common law notion of *binding* precedent (Cross and Harris (1991), p. 100: "the general orthodox interpretation of *stare decisis* . . . is *stare rationibus decidendis* ('keep to the *rationes decidendi* of past cases').") Alternative possible usages are (1) broader: referring to the general desirability of conformity with past precedents (*cf.* Cross (1977), p. 4), and (2) narrower: referring to the obligation to follow the *decision* (*i.e.* order of the court) in a past case that is not reasonably distinguishable, as distinct from the principle of law on which the decision was based (Cross and Harris (1991), pp. 100–101).

[3] *ibid.* pp. 10–15. R. David and J. Brierley, *Major Legal Systems in the World Today* (3rd ed., 1985), pp. 133–149; R. David, *English Law and French Law* (1980), pp. 21–26.

413

is deciding case B; and (4) there is no relevant difference between cases A and B which renders case A "distinguishable". A precedent which is not binding may nevertheless be persuasive. These points are developed below. As we shall see, judges faced with a precedent that they do not like have a number of possible escape routes to explore, and there is for the litigant who can afford it the possibility of recourse to a higher court for a bad precedent to be overruled. The system seeks to balance the general benefits of consistency and certainty against the requirement of justice in individual cases.

On one view judges are seen as picking their way through dusty old volumes of law reports and loyally following the precedents without too much regard for the justice of the case. On another they are seen as paying lip service to the system, and "loyally" following all the precedents that they agree with; those that they do not agree with are distinguished on spurious grounds, or just ignored. These views lie at the extremes and contain elements of caricature as well as truth. It is not possible to make a useful generalisation about judicial behaviour in practice; there are variations in approach from judge to judge, and the same judge may even vary his or her position according to the nature of the case to be decided.[4]

The notion that judges ought generally to abide by relevant precedents developed over several centuries.[5] Blackstone wrote in the eighteenth century that it was "an established rule to abide by former precedents, where the same points come again in litigation ... unless flatly absurd or unjust",[6] and Parke J. said in 1833[7]:

"Our common-law system consists in the applying to new combinations of circumstances those rules of law which we derive from legal principles and judicial precedent; and for the sake of attaining uniformity, consistency and certainty, we must apply those rules, where they are not plainly unreasonable and inconvenient, to all cases which arise; and we are not at liberty to reject them, and to abandon all analogy to them, in those to which they have not yet been judicially applied, because we think that the rules are not as convenient and reasonable as we ourselves could have devised."

The practice of relying on precedents in equity was also established by the eighteenth century. The modern strict rules whereby a single precedent can be binding, and precedents can be binding even if "unreasonable and inconvenient", developed in the nineteenth and twentieth centuries. Important factors were the regularisation of and improvements in law reporting following the establishment of the Incorporated Council of Law Reporting[8] and the reorganisation of the courts with a clear hierarchical structure in the latter part of the nineteenth century.[9] The rule that appellate courts are normally bound by their

---

[4] See further above, pp. 249–258.
[5] See C. K. Allen, *Law in the Making* (7th ed., 1964), pp. 187–235, 380–382; T. Ellis Lewis, (1930) 46 L.Q.R. 207, 341, (1931) 47 L.Q.R. 411, (1932) 48 L.Q.R. 230; W. H. D. Winder, (1941) 57 L.Q.R. 245 (precedent in equity); G. J. Postema, "Some roots of our notion of precedent" and J. Evans, "Changes in the doctrine of precedent during the nineteenth century" in Goldstein (1987), Chaps.1, 2.
[6] *Blackstone's Commentaries* 69, 70.
[7] *Mirehouse v. Rennell* (1833) 1 Cl. & F. 527, 546.
[8] See below, pp. 452–453.
[9] See above, p. 37.

own previous decisions was clearly established for the House of Lords in 1898[10] and for the Court of Appeal in 1944.[11]

B. PROPOSITION OF "LAW"

Decisions on questions of fact may not be cited as precedents.[12] The line between "law" and "fact" may, however, be difficult to draw. An issue is one of fact where it turns on the reliability or credibility of direct evidence, or on inferences from circumstantial evidence. For example, the fact that someone was driving at a high speed may be established by the testimony of a witness, or by inference from such evidence as tyre marks. More difficult are cases which raise an issue whether the facts found conform to a legal description. Such issues are sometimes classified as issues of fact. For example, whether conduct is "unreasonable," and so a breach of the duty of care for the purposes of the tort of negligence, is a question of fact. In *Baker v. E. Longhurst & Sons Ltd*[13] Scrutton L.J. stated[14] that "if a person rides in the dark he must ride at such a pace that he can pull up within the limit of his vision. . . ." This was treated as a proposition of law until the Court of Appeal ruled that it was not.[15] In *Qualcast (Wolverhampton) Ltd v. Haynes*[16] the House of Lords held that a county court judge could not be bound by precedent to hold that an employer who failed to give instructions to an employee as to the use of protective clothing had been negligent.

Where a legal description contained in a statute is "an ordinary word of the English language" its application to the facts found is a question of fact, and it may not be the subject of judicial definition or interpretation.[17] The judges are particularly inclined to classify questions as questions of fact where they wish to avoid the proliferation of authorities.[18] However, where words are used in an unusual sense, or a statute has to be "construed" or "interpreted" before it can be applied, a question of law is raised.[19] The construction of particular words in a contract similarly does not give rise to a binding decision on a point of law.[20]

---

[10] See below, pp. 438–443. It was changed in 1966.

[11] See below, pp. 425–438.

[12] *Qualcast (Wolverhampton) Ltd v. Haynes* [1959] A.C. 743. Otherwise, "the precedent system will die from a surfeit of authorities" (per Lord Somervell at p. 758), or the judges might be "crushed under the weight of our own reports" (*per* Lord Denning at p. 761).

[13] [1933] 2 K.B. 461.

[14] At p. 468.

[15] *Tidy v. Battman* [1934] 1 K.B. 319; *Morris v. Luton Corporation* [1946] 1 K.B. 114; Lord Greene hoped that this "suggested principle" would "rest peacefully in the grave" (p. 116). Cf. *Worsfold v. Howe* [1980] 1 W.L.R. 1175.

[16] [1959] A.C. 743.

[17] See above, pp. 11–12.

[18] e.g. *R. v. Industrial Injuries Commissioner, ex p. A.E.U. (No. 2)* [1966] 2 Q.B. 31, 45, 48–49, *per* Lord Denning M.R., in relation to the expression "arising out of and in the course of his employment."

[19] Denning L.J. in *British Launderers' Association v. Borough of Hendon Rating Authority* [1949] 1 K.B. 462, 471–472; Lord Reid in *Cozens v. Brutus*, above, pp. 11–12.

[20] *per* May L.J. in *Ashville Investments Ltd v. Elmer Contractors Ltd* [1989] Q.B. 488, 495 (construction of an arbitration clause); *Clarke v. Newland* (unreported, December 21, 1988)

C. DETERMINING THE RATIO DECIDENDI

1. RATIO AND DICTUM

A proposition of law can only be binding if it forms part of the *ratio decidendi*[21] (commonly shortened to *ratio*) of the case.

Sir Rupert Cross and J. W. Harris, in the leading English monograph on precedent, gives this description[22]:

> "The *ratio decidendi* of a case is any rule of law expressly or impliedly treated by the judge as a necessary step in reaching his conclusion, having regard to the line of reasoning adopted by him, or a necessary part of his direction to the jury."[23]

They also point out that a judge may adopt more than one line of reasoning leading to the same result, in which case there may be more than one *ratio*. A proposition of law stated by a judge that is not necessary for his or her conclusion is termed an *obiter dictum* or *dictum*.[24] It may, for example, be a proposition wider than is necessary for the facts of the case, or a proposition concerning some matter not raised in the case. Statements of law on points which are fully argued by counsel and considered by the judge, but which do not technically play any part in determining the result, are sometimes termed "judicial dicta".[25]

Conversely, where a court *assumes* a proposition of law to be correct without addressing its mind to it, the decision of that court is not binding authority for that proposition.[26]

(interpretation of restrictive covenant in a partnership agreement). In *Customers and Excise Commissioners v. Le Rififi Ltd* [1995] S.T.C. 103, the Court of Appeal held that the same principle applied to the construction of a VAT assessment form.

[21] Usually pronounced "rayshio", although variants may be encountered in practice.

[22] *Precedent in English Law* (4th ed., 1991), p. 72.

[23] *cf.* the narrower definition proposed by N. MacCormick (in L. Goldstein (ed.), *Judicial Precedent* (1987), Chap. 6, p. 170): "A *ratio decidendi* is a ruling expressly or impliedly given by a judge which is sufficient to settle a point of law put in issue by the parties' arguments in a case, being a point on which a ruling was necessary to his justification (or one of his alternative justifications) of the decision in the case." It is narrower in that it refers to a "ruling" by the judge (so as to cover the interpretation of a statute rather than the statute itself where one is involved), and a requirement that it be necessary for the *justification* for the decision, rather than the decision itself.

[24] Not "an *obiter*". The plural is *obiter dicta*. For examples of cases where it has been held that a particular proposition was not necessary for the decision, see *Penn-Texas Corporation v. Murat Anstalt (No. 2)* [1964] 2 Q.B. 647, 661 (Lord Denning M.R.); *Re State of Norway's Application (No. 2)* [1988] 3 W.L.R. 603, 618–620 (May L.J.), 629–631 (Balcombe L.J.), 646–649 (Woolf L.J.); *Rickless v. United Artists Corp.* [1988] Q.B. 40.

[25] Megarry J. in *Brunner v. Greenslade* [1971] Ch. 993, 1002–3.

[26] *per* Warner J. in *Barrs v. Bethell* [1982] Ch. 294, 308, relying on Lord Diplock in *Baker v. The Queen* [1975] A.C. 774, 788 and Russell L. J. in *National Enterprises Ltd v. Racal Communications Ltd* [1975] Ch. 397, 406; *Pritchard v. J. H. Cobden Ltd* [1988] Fam. 22, 38, 49; *re Hetherington* [1990] Ch. 1. This principle, however, is not always observed, *e.g.* in respect of the *Havana* case: see below, pp. 431–432. It has been suggested that the matter turns on whether the court in the earlier case had "turned its mind to the point" and not on whether the point has been argued: *R. v. Charles* (1975) 63 Cr.App. R. 252, 259 (Bridge L.J.); *Meer v. London Borough of Tower Hamlets* [1988] I.R.L.R. 399, 402 (Balcombe L.J.).

2. THE PRINCIPLE ENUNCIATED BY THE JUDGE

The task of determining the *ratio* of a case can be complicated, and writers on the subject are not agreed as to how that task is approached by the judges in practice, or how, in theory, it should be approached.[27] It is impossible to assert with confidence that there is any one method of approach which is invariably adopted by the judges. The obvious starting point is the wording of the judgment in question. A judge in giving the reasons for his or her decision will normally indicate the proposition[28] of law upon which he or she regards the decision as based. He or she will explain why he or she thinks this proposition is correct, usually by referring to earlier authorities and showing that it makes good sense. These "explanations" or "justifications" must be distinguished from the proposition of law which they support, as only the latter can be part of the *ratio*.[29] The proposition as enunciated by the judge has a good claim to be regarded as the *ratio*. For example, the editor of a published law report who endeavours to state the *ratio* in the headnote to the case, will frequently use actual sentences from the judgment. A judge in a later case will commonly summarise the effect of a case by citing a passage from the judgment, and saying that a particular sentence or passage sets out "the *ratio*." In many cases, the judge will be content to leave the matter there. However, it may be necessary for the judgment in the earlier case to be subjected to careful analysis (by academic commentators, by counsel, and ultimately by the judge) for the *ratio* to be determined.

In some cases, the rulings are "so embedded in the reasoning as to require minor grammatical reconstruction in order to obtain more explicitly stated forms of them."[30] There may be differing views as to whether a particular ruling was "necessary for the decision".[31] It may be unclear, where a number of different reasons are given for a decision, whether each is to be regarded as a *ratio*.[32] Further difficulties may arise from the differing levels of generality of language that may be used in the formulation of propositions of law: the *ratio* may subsequently be restated in wider or narrower form.[33]

Then, in "extreme cases, judges may do no more than indicate that it is

---

[27] See, *e.g.* Cross and Harris (1991) Chap. 2; A. L. Goodhart, "Determining the *Ratio Decidendi* of a Case" in *Essays in Jurisprudence and the Common Law* (1931), pp. 1–26; the somewhat acerbic dispute between J. L. Montrose and A. W. B. Simpson: (1957) 20 M.L.R. 124, 413, 587, (1958) 21 M.L.R. 155; A. L. Goodhart, (1959) 22 M.L.R. 117; Simpson, in A. G. Guest (ed.) *Oxford Essays in Jurisprudence* (1961), Chap. VI; N. H. Andrews, (1985) 5 L. S. 205, 209–222; N. MacCormick in L. Goldstein (ed.), *Judicial Precedent* (1987), Chap. 6.

[28] There may be more than one relevant proposition; the singular is used here for convenience.

[29] *cf.* Goodhart (1931), pp. 3–4: "A bad reason may often make good law."

[30] MacCormick (1987), p. 180.

[31] A good example here is provided by a proposition stated by Lord Bridge in *R. v. Secretary of State for the Home Department, ex p. Khawaja* [1984] A.C. 74, 117, to the effect that the Home Secretary could not base a "conductive to the public good" deportation order (Immigration Act 1971, s.3(5)(b)) on a ground arising from the circumstances of the original entry of the person concerned. Divergent views were subsequently expressed on (1) what Lord Bridge meant; (2) whether it was necessary for the ultimate decision in *Khawaja*; (3) whether it should anyway be followed even if *obiter*: compare *In re Owusu-Sekyere* [1987] Imm. A.R. 425, C.A., with *R. v. Immigration Appeal Tribunal, ex p. Patel* [1988] Imm. A.R. 35, C.A. The matter was ultimately resolved by the House of Lords (through Lord Bridge) holding that the proposition was "simply mistaken": *Ex p. Patel* [1988] A.C. 910, 922.

[32] See below, p. 420.

[33] See below, pp. 418–419.

because the facts of the case are certain facts viewed under certain fact-descriptions that the decision ought to be as it is."[34] Here, the method for determining the *ratio* suggested by A. L. Goodhart[35] can be employed: that is, by taking account of (a) the facts treated expressly or impliedly by the judge as material, and (b) the decision as based on them. Other features of Goodhart's theory were (1) that the *ratio* was not found in the reasons given on the rule of law set forth in the opinion (although the opinion might furnish a guide for determining which facts the judge considered material and which immaterial); (2) the inclusion of a series of rules for finding which facts were and were not material; (3) that the judge's view on this question had to be accepted by subsequent courts. The theory was offered as being of general application, and, indeed, as "a guide to the method which I believe most English courts follow."[36] Both claims are doubtful, the first because of the downplaying of the principle as enunciated by the judge,[37] and the second simply because "there seems little or no evidence to support this."[38] Nevertheless, the method remains potentially helpful where; probably through faulty technique, the reasons given for a decision do not include an express indication of the relevant principle of law.

3. THE "INTERPRETATION" OF PRECEDENTS

The judge who is called upon to determine a disputed point of law chooses the generality of the language in which he or she expresses a conclusion. The proposition may be very general, it may be closely tailored to the facts of the case or it may be formulated at some intermediate level. Most, although not all judges are reluctant to make general statements of law, and it is anyway well established that a judgment must be read in the light of the facts of the case in which it was given. In *Quinn v. Leathem*,[39] the Earl of Halsbury L.C. said that:

"every judgment must be read as applicable to the particular facts proved, or assumed to be proved, since the generality of the expressions which may be found there are not intended to be expositions of the whole law, but governed and qualified by the particular facts of the case in which such expressions are to be found."

This point is commonly made where the judge in case B wishes to hold that the *ratio* of case A is narrower than that apparently expounded by the judge or court in case A, and is accordingly not applicable. An example of this is given by the decision of the majority of the Privy Council in *Mutual Life and Citizens'*

---

[34] MacCormick (1987), p. 180.

[35] Goodhart (1931), pp. 1–26.

[36] A. L. Goodhart, (1959) 22 M.L.R. 117, 124.

[37] *Cf.* Cross and Harris (1991), pp. 63–71, criticising Goodhart's "scanty regard to the way in which the case was argued and pleaded, the process of reasoning adopted by the judge and the relation of the case to other decisions" (*ibid.* p. 67).

[38] Lord Lloyd and M. D. A. Freeman, *Lloyd's Introduction to Jurisprudence* (5th ed., 1985), p. 1117 (omitted from the 6th ed., 1994).

[39] [1901] A.C. 495, 506. *Cf.* Diplock L. J. in *Miller-Mead v. Minister of Housing and Local Government* [1963] 2 Q.B. 196, 235–236.

Assurance Co. Ltd v. Evatt,[40] which sought to restrict the scope of liability in tort for negligent misstatement to cases where the defendant was or claimed to be in the business of giving information or advice of the relevant kind. The speeches in the leading case, *Hedley Byrne & Co. Ltd v. Heller and Partners Ltd*[41] were interpreted to support the incorporation of such a condition, notwithstanding the dissent of Lord Reid and Lord Morris of Borth-y-Gest, who had taken part in the *Hedley Byrne* decision and who said that they were "unable to construe the passages from our speeches cited in the judgment of the majority in the way in which they are there construed."[42] Conversely, a proposition stated by a judge may be regarded as too restrictive. A well known example is *Barwick v. The English Joint Stock Bank*,[43] where Willes J. said:

> "The general rule is, that the master is answerable for every such wrong of the servant or agent as is committed in the course of the service and for the master's benefit, though no express command or privity of the master be proved."[44]

It had previously been doubted whether a master was vicariously liable in respect of the fraud, as distinct from the non-deliberate wrongdoing, of a servant. On the facts of the case the master had benefited, albeit unwittingly, from the fraud. Subsequently, in *Lloyd v. Grace, Smith & Co.*[45] the House of Lords held that an employer could be vicariously liable for the fraud of an employee committed in the course of employment, notwithstanding that the employer received no benefit. The reference to the "master's benefit" was not to be regarded as part of the *ratio* of *Barwick's* case in the light of Willes J.'s judgment when read as a whole and of judgments in other cases both before and after *Barwick*. These are examples of the *ratio* of a case being reformulated *by a court not bound by it*. It has indeed been doubted whether courts "exercise any power of correcting statements of law drawn from binding decisions."[46]

4. Cases Where no Reasons are Given

The report of an old case may simply contain a statement of the facts, the arguments of counsel and an order of the court based on those facts. Here, the *ratio* has, if possible, to be inferred, but its authority is understandably very weak.[47] It would be most unusual for such a case to be decisive in modern litigation.

---

[40] [1971] A.C. 793. On the Privy Council and precedent, see below, pp. 433, 433–444.
[41] [1964] A.C. 465.
[42] [1971] A.C. 793, 813. The minority position has been preferred by several English judges: see *Esso Petroleum Co. Ltd v. Mardon* [1975] Q.B. 819, 830 (Lawson J.) and [1976] Q.B. 801, 827 (Ormrod L.J.); *Howard Marine and Dredging Co. Ltd v. Ogden & Sons Ltd* [1978] Q.B. 574, 591 (Lord Denning M.R.), 600 (Shaw L.J.).
[43] (1866) L.R. 2 Ex. 259.
[44] *ibid.* p. 265.
[45] [1912] A.C. 716.
[46] See A. W. B. Simpson, (1959) 22 M.L.R. 453, 455–457.
[47] Cross and Harris (1991), p. 47.

5. Judgments With More than one Ratio

A number of distinct points of law may be at issue in a case, each of which taken separately would be sufficient to determine the case in favour of one side (say the plaintiff). The judge may be content to take one point only, give judgment for the plaintiff, and decline to comment on the other points. Instead, he or she may express an opinion on these points, while making it clear that the decision is to rest on the first point and that the other remarks are *dicta*. Yet again, he or she may state a conclusion on each point without any distinction, resolving them all in favour of the plaintiff. In the third situation, each conclusion is a separate *ratio*, and in principle, each *ratio* is binding.[48]

6. The Ratio Decidendi of Appellate Courts[49]

Determining the *ratio* of the decision of an appellate court where separate judgments are given can be a difficult task. Some principles are reasonably clear. Where all the members of the court are agreed as to the result of the case, any *ratio* that commands the support of a majority is binding.[50] For example, in a three-member court where two judges support ground A and the third ground B, ground A is the *ratio*. If three judges support ground A and two ground B, there are two *rationes*. Where a judge dissents as to the result, his or her views must technically be disregarded for the purpose of ascertaining the *ratio* on the ground that his or her reasons cannot be "necessary" for a decision he or she opposes. Dissenting judgments may, however, carry persuasive weight. Where there is no majority in favour of any particular *ratio*, a later court may hold that the case has no discernible *ratio* which has to be followed, although it may not adopt any reasoning which would show the decision itself to be wrong.[51] In some cases there may be much time and effort spent in the search for a *ratio* which is as elusive as the holy grail.[52]

---

[48] *Jacobs v. London County Council* [1950] A.C. 361, 369 (Lord Simonds); *Behrens v. Bertram Mills Circus Ltd* [1957] 2 Q.B. 1, 24–25 (Devlin J.); *Miliangos v. George Frank (Textiles) Ltd* [1975] Q.B. 487, 502–503 (Lord Denning M.R.); R. E. Megarry, (1958) 74 L.Q.R. 350; *City of Westminster v. Clarke* (1991) 23 H.L.R. 506, *per* Dillon L.J. at p. 515 and Balcombe L.J. at p. 516 (the decision of the Court of Appeal was subsequently reversed by the House of Lords: [1992] 2 A.C. 288). On other occasions Lord Denning argued that the Court of Appeal is not necessarily bound by both or all the *rationes* of an earlier *Court of Appeal* decision: *Hanning v. Maitland (No. 2)* [1970] 1 Q.B. 580; *Ministry of Defence v. Jeremiah* [1980] 1 Q.B. 87. On this he stood alone: see Hazel Carty, (1981) 1 L.S. 68, 71–72.

[49] Cross and Harris (1991), pp. 84–96; G. Paton and G. Sawer, (1947) 63 L.Q.R. 461; A. M. Honoré, (1955) 71 L.Q.R. 196.

[50] *e.g. Amalgamated Society of Railway Servants v. Osborne* [1910] A.C. 87. A statement "I agree" may simply indicate concurrence with the order proposed in the leading judgment and not necessarily all the reasoning: Lord Russell of Killowen (then Russell L.J.), Address to the Holdsworth Club of the University of Birmingham 1968–69, reprinted in B. W. Harvey (ed.), *The Lawyer and Justice* (1978).

[51] See the analysis of the decision of the House of Lords in *Central Asbestos Ltd v. Dodd* [1973] A.C. 518 by the Court of Appeal in *Re Harper v. National Coal Board (Intended Action)* [1974] Q.B. 614.

[52] See, for example, the decision of the House of Lords in *Chaplin v. Boys* [1971] A.C. 356. First-year law students are not recommended to read this case; it should, however, be one of the party pieces of students of conflict of laws.

A further complication arises where the Court of Appeal bases a decision on point A, but the case proceeds to the House of Lords, which (1) dismisses the appeal, but (2) bases its decision on point B, (3) holds that on a proper analysis point A does not arise and (4) expresses no view on the soundness of point A. In *R. v. Secretary of State for the Home Department, ex p. Al-Mehdawi*[53] the Court of Appeal held that the previous decision of the Court of Appeal[54] is no longer binding authority for point A, although it remains of "powerful persuasive influence".[55] Counsel for the Secretary of State had argued that this was so either (1) because point A had been replaced by point B as the *ratio* of the decision, or (2) as an additional exception to the rule in *Young v. Bristol Aeroplane Co. Ltd.*[56] The Court of Appeal seemed to accept the first of these arguments, but did not expressly reject the second.

D. THE HIERARCHY OF THE COURTS AND THE RULES OF BINDING PRECEDENT

Broadly speaking, a court is only *obliged* to follow the decisions of courts at a higher or the same level in the court structure, and there are a number of exceptions even to that requirement. For the purposes of the following discussion it must be assumed that all the other factors mentioned in Section A above are present which combine to make a precedent binding in a particular case.

1. MAGISTRATES COURTS AND COUNTY COURTS

Decisions of these courts are rarely reported outside the pages of local newspapers, but even if they were properly reported they would not constitute precedents binding on anyone. They do not bind themselves, although it is to be expected that an individual magistrate or county court judge will attempt to be consistent in his or her own decision-making. A magistrates' court may also be reminded by the clerk of the practice of the local bench, and other benches in the area. The matter upon which a "local view" may develop will rarely be a point of law; more commonly it will relate to a procedural requirement or the exercise of discretion, as in sentencing or the granting of bail.[57] Magistrates' courts and county courts are bound by decisions of the High Court, Court of Appeal and House of Lords.

---

[53] [1990] 1 A.C. 876.
[54] Here, *R. v. Diggines, ex p. Rahmani* [1985] Q.B. 1109, C.A., on appeal: [1986] A.C. 475.
[55] *per* Taylor L.J., [1990] 1 A.C. 876, 883. Taylor L.J. had, indeed, been a party to the Court of Appeal decision in *ex p. Rahmani*, and ultimately, here, remained of the same opinion. The decision on the point in question was, however, ultimately reversed by the House of Lords: *ibid.*
[56] [1944] K.B. 718. See below, pp. 427–436.
[57] See, *e.g. R. v. Nottingham JJ., ex p. Davies* [1981] 1 Q.B. 38 where the practice of the City of Nottingham bench of refusing to hear full argument on a third or subsequent application for bail, unless there were "new circumstances", was endorsed by the Divisional Court.

2. THE CROWN COURT

Decisions of judges in the Crown Court are reported rather more frequently than those of magistrates' and county courts. This is partly because the judge may be a High Court judge whose pronouncements are inevitably more authoritative, and partly because reports of cases on points of criminal law, even at this level, find an outlet in the pages of publications such as the Criminal Law Review and the Criminal Appeal Reports. However, there is no regular reporting, and it has been suggested that Crown Court decisions are merely persuasive authorities whatever the status of the judge.[58] The Crown Court is bound by decisions of the Court of Appeal and the House of Lords. It has been asserted that it is not bound by decisions of the Divisional Court,[59] but this is hard to square with the rule that Divisional Courts are normally bound by their own previous decisions.[60]

3. THE HIGH COURT

The decision of a High Court judge is binding on inferior courts, but not technically on another High Court judge, and certainly not on a Divisional Court (*i.e.* a court of two or more judges). High Court judges are reluctant to depart from the decisions of other High Court judges,[61] Chancery judges being particularly loath to disagree with their colleagues for fear of upsetting transactions affecting property rights and the like.[62] There are, however, examples of judicial disagreement, one of the most notable in recent years being on the question whether failure to wear a seat-belt in a car can amount to contributory negligence. This had to be settled by the Court of Appeal.[63] However, it has been stated that where there are conflicting decisions of judges of co-ordinate jurisdiction, the later decision should thereafter be preferred, provided that it was reached after full consideration of the first decision: the only, rare, exception would be where the third judge was convinced that the second judge was wrong in not following the first, for example where some binding or persuasive authority had not been cited in either of the first two cases.[64] This view has been cited with approval

---

[58] A. Ashworth, ''The Binding Effect of Crown Court Decisions'' [1980] Crim.L.R. 402–403; *cf.* Cross and Harris (1991), pp. 6, 123. Some cases are reported in the regular law reports: see, *e.g. R. v. Bourne* [1939] 1 K.B. 687, where the summing up of Macnaghten J. on the pre-Abortion Act 1967 law of procuring an abortion was generally accepted as authoritative (*cf.* [1938] 3 All E.R. 615).

[59] *R. v. Colyer* [1974] Crim.L.R. 243 (Judge Stinson).

[60] See below, pp. 423–425.

[61] See *Police Authority for Huddersfield v. Watson* [1947] K.B. 842, 848, where it is explained by Lord Goddard C.J. to be a matter of ''judicial comity''.

[62] There are also many fewer Chancery judges than Queen's Bench judges and so they are more likely to meet each other; whether this boosts ''judicial comity'' is a matter for speculation.

[63] *Froom v. Butcher* [1976] Q.B. 286 answered the question in the affirmative.

[64] *Colchester Estates (Cardiff) v. Carlton Industries plc* [1986] Ch. 80.

on a number of occasions,[65] although it has been emphasised that the matter remains one of judicial comity: there is no new head of binding precedent.[66]

4. DIVISIONAL COURTS

A Divisional Court is bound by decisions of the Court of Appeal and the House of Lords. In *Huddersfield Police Authority v. Watson*[67] and *Younghusband v. Luftig*,[68] Divisional Courts of the King's Bench Division, in each case presided over by Lord Goddard C.J., held that they were bound by previous Divisional Court decisions to the same extent that the Court of Appeal was bound by its own previous decisions.[69]

The matter was reconsidered by the Divisional Court in *R. v. Greater Manchester Coroner, ex p. Tal*.[70] It was held that the position was different where a Divisional Court was exercising the supervisory jurisdiction of the High Court on an application for judicial review,[71] and was faced by a previous decision of the Divisional Court acting in the same capacity. Its position was analogous to that of a judge at first instance faced with a previous decision of another judge of first instance: here, the judge in the later case would follow the earlier decision

"unless he is convinced that that judgment is wrong, as a matter of judicial comity; but he is not bound to follow a judge of equal jurisdiction."[72]

The same principle of *stare decisis* was applicable where two Divisional Court decisions were involved:

"We have no doubt that it will be only in rare cases that a divisional court will think it fit to depart from a decision of another divisional court exercising this jurisdiction."[73]

---

[65] *Taylor Woodrow Property Co. Ltd v. Lonrho Textiles Ltd* [1985] 2 EGLR 120, B. Hytner Q. C., sitting as a deputy High Court judge (in respect of two conflicting decisions of the Court of Appeal); *Elite Investments Ltd v. T. 1. Bainbridge Silencers Ltd.* [1986] 2 EGLR 43, Judge Paul Baker Q.C., sitting as a judge of the High Court; *Glofield Properties Ltd, v. Morley* [1988] 1 EGLR 113, Hutchison J; *Re A. E. Farr Ltd* [1992] B.C.L. 333, where Ferris J. on this basis followed a decision of Vinelott J. in preference to an earlier decision of his own (thus taking judicial comity long way); this course of action was subsequently commended by Dillon L.J. in *Bishopsgate Investment Ltd v. Maxwell* [1993] Ch.1, 14; the Court of Appeal in that case upholding Vinelott J.'s approach; *Chancery plc v. Ketteringham, The Times*, November 23, 1993, David Neuberger Q.C. sitting as a deputy High Court judge.

[66] *Forsikringsaktieselskapet Vesta v. Butcher* [1986] 2 All E.R. 488, Hobhouse J.

[67] [1947] K.B. 842: on an appeal from quarter sessions in a civil case concerning police pensions.

[68] [1949] 2 K.B. 354: on an appeal by case stated from justices in a criminal case.

[69] Under *Young v. Bristol Aeroplane Co. Ltd.*, below, pp. 427–436. The possibility of the Divisional Court applying one of the *Young v. Bristol Aeroplane* exceptions was acknowledged by Lord Goddard in the latter case: [1949] 2 K.B. 354, 361.

[70] [1985] Q.B. 67. See P. Jackson, (1985) 101 L.Q.R. 157.

[71] See below, pp. 968–976.

[72] *ibid.*, at p. 81, *per* Robert Goff L.J., citing *Huddersfield Police Authority v. Watson* [1947] K.B. 842, 848, *per* Lord Goddard C.J.

[73] [1985] Q.B. 67, 81, *per* Robert Goff L.J.

Ex p. Tal was one of these "rare cases",[74] the Divisional Court holding that any error of law made by an inferior court or tribunal caused it to act outside its jurisdiction.[75] It declined to follow *R. v. Surrey Coroner, ex p. Campbell*,[76] where it had been held that this principle applied only to *tribunals*, and not *courts*, such as a coroner's court.[77] The court in *Ex. p. Tal*[78] also expressed doubts, *obiter*, as to whether the strict approach to precedent in cases where the Divisional Court was acting in an appellate capacity was still appropriate. Robert Goff L. J. noted that at the time of *Younghusband v. Luftig*,[79] the Divisional Court was the final court of appeal in criminal cases tried summarily,[80] and the House of Lords, in most cases the final court of appeal, regarded itself as bound by its own previous decisions (subject to narrow exceptions).[81] Neither of these points remained true in 1984. In criminal cases at least, his Lordship[82] could see no reason why the Divisional Court should not adopt the more flexible approach of the Criminal Division of the Court of Appeal,[83] in preference to the narrower approach of the Civil Division based on *Young v. Bristol Aeroplane Co.*[84]

In subsequent cases, the approach to precedent of the Divisional Court in *Ex p. Tal*[85] has been cited with approval on numerous occasions,[86] although some judges seem happier to disregard a previous Divisional Court decision if this can be done by reference to a "*Young v. Bristol Aeroplane Co.* exception".[87] It has also been emphasised that *Ex p. Tal*

"was not intended to provide freedom to parties to re-argue points simply

---

[74] Another is *R. v. Chief Metropolitan Stipendiary Magistrate, ex p. Secretary of State for the Home Department* [1988] 1 W.L.R. 1204.

[75] Under the principle of *Anisminic Ltd v. Foreign Compensation Commission* [1969] 2 A.C. 147.

[76] [1982] Q.B. 661.

[77] In accordance with *dicta* of Lord Diplock in *Re Racal Communications Ltd* [1981] A.C. 374.

[78] n. 70 above.

[79] n. 68 above.

[80] See below, p. 922. It had also been the final court of appeal under the police pensions legislation in *Huddersfield Police Authority v. Watson*, n. 72 above.

[81] See below, p. 438.

[82] [1985] Q.B. 67, 78, 79.

[83] See below, pp. 436–488. A more flexible approach had also been adopted in two nineteenth century Divisional Court cases, both concerning criminal appeals: *Fortescue v. Vestry of St Matthew, Bethnal Green* [1891] 2 Q.B. 170; *Kruse v. Johnson* [1898] 2 Q.B. 91. These cases were not cited in *Huddersfield Police Authority v. Watson and Younghusband v. Luftig.*

[84] Below, pp. 427–436.

[85] n. 70 above.

[86] *Hornigold v. Chief Constable of Lancashire* [1986] Crim. L. R. 792 (appeal in a criminal case); *R. v. Chief Metropolitan Stipendiary Magistrate, ex p. Secretary of State for the Home Department* [1988] 1 W.L.R. 1204 (application for judicial review); *R. v. Metropolitan Stipendiary Magistrate, ex p. London Waste Regulation Authority* [1993] 3 All E.R. 113 (appeal by case stated and application for judicial review); *R. v. Hendon JJ, ex p. D.P.P.* [1994] Q.B. 167 (application for judicial review; D.C. disagreed with a statement made in a previous case "without discussion" (Mann L.J. at p. 179)). *cf. Rogers v. Essex County Council* [1985] 1 W.L.R. 700, where the Divisional Court on an appeal in a criminal case preferred to distinguish an earlier decision (on doubtful grounds: see P. Jackson, (1985) 101 L.Q.R. 486): *Ex p. Tal* was cited for the proposition that as the court was acting in an "appellate capacity" it was "prima facie bound" by a previous decision (p. 706).

[87] *R. v. Plymouth JJ, ex p. Driver* [1986] Q.B. 95, 123–124 (*per incuriam*); *R.v. Plymouth JJ., ex p. Hart* [1986] Q.B. 950 (conflicting decisions); *R.v. Weston-super-Mare JJ., ex p. Shaw* [1987] Q.B. 640, 648 (conflicting decisions): all applications for judicial review; *Shaw v. D.P.P.* [1993] 1 All E.R. 918 (*per incuriam*).

on the ground that they might persuade the Court to reach a different conclusion. Before a point may be re-argued, the party must be able to indicate, at the outset of the argument, specific material on the basis of which it might properly be submitted that the Court may be convinced that the previous decision was plainly wrong.''[88]

Divisional Court decisions are binding on High Court judges sitting alone[89] and inferior courts, but not the Employment Appeal Tribunal.[90]

5. THE COURT OF APPEAL (CIVIL DIVISION)

(a) The general position

Decisions of the Court of Appeal are binding on the Divisional Court, the Employment Appeal Tribunal, High Court judges[91] and inferior courts. The Court of Appeal is bound to follow decisions of the House of Lords. On occasion, the House has felt it necessary to remind the Court of Appeal of this. In 1970, Captain Jack Broome R. N. (retd.) brought a libel action against David Irving and Cassell & Co. Ltd., respectively author and publisher of a book entitled *The Destruction of Convoy P.Q.17*. The case was heard over 17 days by Lawton J. and a jury.[92] The jury awarded £15,000 "compensatory damages" and £25,000 "exemplary damages." The situations in which exemplary damages could be awarded had been listed by Lord Devlin in *Rookes v. Barnard*[93], a decision of the House of Lords, and the principles subsequently applied by the Court of Appeal to the tort of defamation.[94] Not surprisingly, Lawton J. had directed the jury accordingly in the *P.Q.17* case. Both author and publisher appealed against the award of exemplary damages. The Court of Appeal, after a nine-day hearing, rejected the appeal.[95] The case fell within one of the situations in which Lord Devlin had held that exemplary damages could be awarded,[96] the judge's direction had been adequate and the jury's award was not perversely large. The Court of Appeal was not, however, content with that. The members of the court (Lord Denning M.R., Salmon and Phillimore L.JJ.) took the view that the law on exemplary damages as expounded by Lord Devlin was "unworkable." Lord Denning M.R. said that the common law on

---

[88] *Hornigold v. Chief Constable of Lancashire* [1986] Crim. L.R. 792.
[89] *Huddersfield Police Authority v. Watson* [1947] K.B. 842, 848; *Ettenfield v. Ettenfield* [1939] P. 377, 380; *contra: Elderton v. United Kingdom Totalisator Co. Ltd* (1945) 61 T.L.R. 529 where a judge of the Chancery Division declined to follow the decision of a Divisional Court of the Queen's Bench Division.
[90] *Portec (U.K.) Ltd v. Mogensen* [1976] I.C.R. 396, 400; *Breach v. Epsylon Industries Ltd* [1976] I.C.R. 316, 320.
[91] Even an *ex parte* decision of the Court of Appeal: *The Alexandros P.* [1986] Q.B. 464. In *Lane v. Willis* [1972] 1 W.L.R. 326, 332, Davies L.J. rebuked Lawson J. for expressing the opinion, though accepting he was bound by it, that a Court of Appeal decision was wrong.
[92] It survived an interruption by Welsh language demonstrators: *Morris v. Crown Office* [1970] 2 Q.B. 114.
[93] [1964] A.C. 1129. The other members of the House expressly concurred with Lord Devlin's statement on exemplary damages.
[94] *McCarey v. Associated Newspapers Ltd* [1965] 2 Q.B. 86; *Broadway Approvals Ltd v. Odhams Press Ltd* [1965] 1 W.L.R. 805.
[95] *Broome v. Cassell & Co. Ltd* [1971] 2 Q.B. 354.
[96] See W. V. H. Rogers, *Winfield and Jolowicz on Tort* (14th ed., 1994), pp. 635–642.

exemplary damages had been well settled before 1964, that there were two House of Lords cases[97] which had approved that settled doctrine and which Lord Devlin must have "overlooked" or "misunderstood," that *Rookes v. Barnard* had not been followed in Commonwealth courts, and that the new doctrine was "hopelessly illogical and inconsistent." He concluded:

> "I think the difficulties presented by *Rookes v. Barnard* are so great that the judges should direct the juries in accordance with the law as it was understood before *Rookes v. Barnard*. Any attempt to follow *Rookes v. Barnard* is bound to lead to confusion."[98]

Surprisingly, there was no discussion of the question whether Lord Devlin's statement formed part of the *ratio decidendi* of *Rookes v. Barnard*.

Cassells appealed to the House of Lords; a 13-day hearing was held before seven Law Lords. The Court of Appeal's decision to uphold the jury's verdict was affirmed by a majority.[99] Lord Devlin's approach to exemplary damages was endorsed, with varying enthusiasm, by a majority. The approach of the Court of Appeal to *Rookes v. Barnard* was roundly condemned. Lord Hailsham L.C.:

> "[I]t is not open to the Court of Appeal to give gratuitous advice to judges of first instance to ignore decisions of the House of Lords in this way and, if it were open to the Court of Appeal to do so, it would be highly undesirable. . . .
>
> "The fact is, and I hope it will never be necessary to say so again, that, in the hierarchical system of courts which exists in this country, it is necessary for each lower tier, including the Court of Appeal, to accept loyally the decisions of the higher tiers. Where decisions manifestly conflict, the decision in *Young v. Bristol Aeroplane Co. Ltd* offers guidance to each tier in matters affecting its own decisions. It does not entitle it to question considered decisions in the upper tiers with the same freedom."[1]

Other members of the House of Lords added their voices to the chorus of disapproval.[2] They pointed out that the parties had been put to much expense in litigating broad legal issues unnecessary for the disposal of their dispute.[3] Lord Devlin had not overlooked the two House of Lords cases (*Ley v. Hamilton* was discussed at length in his speech) and, on proper analysis, they were not binding authorities on the award of exemplary damages.[4]

The House of Lords similarly found it necessary to assert its authority over the Court of Appeal in *Miliangos v. George Frank (Textiles) Ltd*.[5]

Since the retirement of Lord Denning M.R., the loyalty of the Court of Appeal to decisions of the House of Lords has not been in question.

---

[97] *E. Hulton & Co.* v. *Jones* [1910] A.C. 20 and *Ley v. Hamilton* (1935) 153 L.T. 384.

[98] [1971] 2 Q.B. 354, 381, 384.

[99] *Cassell & Co. Ltd* v. *Broome* [1972] A.C. 1027. It has been described as "what may well be the most hostile *affirmation* of a Court of Appeal decision in our history": Julius Stone, "On the Liberation of Appellate Judges—How not to do it!" (1972) 35 M.L.R. 449.

[1] [1972] A.C. 1027, 1054.

[2] See Lord Reid at pp. 1084, 1091–3; Lord Wilberforce at pp. 1112–1113; Lord Diplock at pp. 1131–1132; Lord Kilbrandon at pp. 1132, 1135.

[3] *cf.* below, p. 961, n. 23.

[4] Viscount Dilhorne dissented on this last point: [1972] A.C. at pp. 1109–11.

[5] [1976] A.C. 443, discussed below, pp. 431–432.

(b) Young v. Bristol Aeroplane Co. Ltd

In *Young v. Bristol Aeroplane Co. Ltd*[6] the Court of Appeal[7] held that it was bound by its own previous decisions, and by decisions of courts of co-ordinate jurisdiction such as the Courts of Exchequer Chamber. Three exceptions were identified. First a decision of the Court of Appeal given *per incuriam* need not be followed. Secondly, where the court is faced by previous conflicting decisions of the Court of Appeal or a court of co-ordinate jurisdiction, it may choose which to follow. Thirdly, where a previous decision of the Court of Appeal, although not expressly overruled, cannot stand with a subsequent decision of the House of Lords, the decision of the House must be followed. Since *Young's* case further light has been thrown on the scope of these three exceptions and suggestions have been made for additional ones. Lord Denning M.R. fought, almost single-handed, against the notion that the Court of Appeal should be bound by its own previous decisions at all. In addition, it has been unclear whether the grounds upon which the Court of Appeal may question one of its own decisions may be employed by a court lower in the hierarchy in respect of a decision of a higher court. These matters are considered in turn.

(c) Accepted exceptions to Young v. Bristol Aeroplane Co. Ltd

(i) Decisions given per incuriam

If interpreted and applied literally the *per incuriam* doctrine could be used to evade the effect of any decision thought to have been reached "through want of care." However, the term in this context is interpreted narrowly. A decision will not be regarded as *per incuriam* merely on the ground that another court thinks it wrongly decided, that it has been inadequately argued[8] or that the decision contains points which are not derived from the arguments of counsel.[9] In *Morelle v. Wakeling*, Sir Raymond Evershed M.R. said that as a general rule the *per incuriam* doctrine could only apply to:

"decisions given in ignorance or forgetfulness of some inconsistent statutory provision or of some authority binding on the court concerned: so that in such cases some part of the decision or some step in the reasoning on which it is based is found, on that account to be demonstrably wrong."[10]

[6] [1944] K.B. 718.

[7] A "full court" consisting of Lord Greene M.R., Scott, MacKinnon, Luxmoore, Goddard and du Parcq L.JJ. Note that it was held in this case a "full court" is bound by previous Court of Appeal decisions to the same extent as a court ordinarily constituted. See further below pp. 437–438.

[8] *Morelle* v. *Wakeling* [1955] 2 Q.B. 379, 406; *Miliangos* v. *George Frank (Textiles) Ltd* [1975] Q.B. 487, 503 (Lord Denning M.R.); *cf. Chief Adjudication Officer* v. *Brunt* [1988] A.C. 711, 724, 726, C.A.

[9] *per* Lord Diplock in *Cassell & Co. Ltd* v. *Broome* [1972] A.C. 1027, 1131.

[10] [1955] 2 Q.B. 379, 406. See generally, P. Wesley-Smith, (1980) 15 J.S.P.T.L. (N.S.) 58. In *Industrial Properties Ltd* v. *A.E.I.* [1977] Q.B. 580 dicta in a Court of Appeal decision were held to have been made *per incuriam* on the ground that the court had misunderstood a decision of the Court of Exchequer Chamber; they had only been referred to an inadequate report of that decision.

In *Dixon* v. *British Broadcasting Corporation*[11] a decision on the construction of a statutory provision was regarded as *per incuriam* on the ground that other relevant provisions which threw light on the words in question had not been brought to the attention of the court. A clearer example is *Bonulami* v. *Home Secretary*.[12] An order was obtained under the Bankers' Books Evidence Act 1879 for the inspection of bank accounts to obtain evidence in criminal proceedings. The Court of Appeal (Civil Division) held that it had no jurisdiction to entertain an appeal as this was a "criminal cause or matter",[13] notwithstanding that in an earlier[14] case it had heard such an appeal: The point as to jurisdiction had not been taken or considered by counsel or any member of the court:

> "Failure to consider a statutory provision is one of the clearest cases in which, on the principles laid down in *Young* v. *Bristol Aeroplane Co. Ltd.*, this court is not bound to follow its own decisions."[15]

The exact scope of the *per incuriam* doctrine has been thrown into some doubt by three judgments of Sir John (subsequently Lord) Donaldson M.R. In *Duke* v. *Reliance Systems Ltd*[16] he put it in narrow terms, as applying where the court *must* (not *might*) have reached a different conclusion had a statute or binding precedent been drawn to its attention. In *Williams* v. *Fawcett*,[17] the Court of Appeal disapproved one of the grounds of a number of decisions[18] in which it had been held that a notice to show cause why the respondent should not be committed to prison for breach of a non-mol-estation order had to be signed by the "proper officer" of the county court. There was no warrant for this requirement in the statute or procedural rules. Sir John Donaldson M.R. recognised the dangers of treating a decision as given *per incuriam* simply on the ground that it could be demonstrated to be wrong, but argued that this was an "exceptional" case for various reasons: (1) the clearness with which the growth of the error could be detected if the decisions were read consecutively; (2) the cases were concerned with the liberty of the subject[19]; (3) they were by no means unusual; and (4) they were "most unlikely to reach the House of Lords, which, if we do not act is alone able to correct the error which has crept into the law."[20]

Subsequently, in *Rickards* v. *Rickards*[21] the Court of Appeal declined to follow its own previous decision in *Podbery* v. *Peak*,[22] in which it had been held that the Court of Appeal had no jurisdiction to entertain an appeal against

---

[11] [1979] Q.B. 546.
[12] [1985] Q.B. 675. See also *White* v. *Chief Adjudication Officer* [1986] 2 All E.R. 905; *Pearce* v. *Secretary of State for Defence* [1988] A.C. 755, 785, C.A.; *Rakhit* v. *Carty* [1990] 2 Q.B. 315.
[13] Supreme Court Act 1981, s.18(1)(a): see below, p. 945.
[14] *R.* v. *Grossman* (1981) 73 Cr. App. R. 302.
[15] *per* Stephenson L. J. at [1985] Q.B. 675, 682.
[16] [1988] Q.B. 108. See above, pp. 339–341.
[17] [1988] Q.B. 604.
[18] *Lee* v. *Walker* [1988] Q.B. 1191 and several unreported decisions.
[19] Although it was noted that the present decision would not be beneficial to the contemnors, who would be deprived of a technical ground of challenge to their imprisonment; *Williams* v. *Fawcett* is therefore not to be equated with the "special exception" recognised in the Criminal Division of the Court of Appeal: see below, pp. 436–438.
[20] [1988] Q.B. 604, 616–617.
[21] [1990] Fam. 194.
[22] [1981] Ch. 344.

the refusal of a judge to grant leave to appeal out of time. The court in *Rickards*, which included Lord Donaldson M.R., was satisfied that the decision in *Podbery v. Peak* was wrong, but noted that in practice it was unlikely that litigants would incur the cost of appealing to the House of Lords on this point.[23] Further considerations that justified treating *Podbery v. Peak* as a decision given *per incuriam* were (1) that it related to a procedural rule rather than substantive law (erroneous decisions as to procedural rules affecting only the parties engaged in the relevant litigation); and (2) that it involved the jurisdiction of the court, errors on matters of jurisdiction being "particularly objectionable".[24] It was stated that this extended approach to the *per incuriam* doctrine should only be adopted in "rare and exceptional" cases.[25]

In more recent cases, the narrowness of the scope of this extension to the *per incuriam* doctrine has been emphasised. In *Re Probe Data Systems (No.3)*[26] the Court of Appeal regarded these authorities as establishing that

"in order to come within this category, it must be shown not only that the decision involved some 'manifest slip or error', but also that to leave the decision standing would be likely to produce serious inconvenience in the administration of justice, or significant injustice to citizens, or some equally serious consequences."[27]

However, in other cases, an apparently broader approach has been adopted. Thus, in *R. v. Parole Board, ex p. Wilson*[28] the Court of Appeal departed from the decision in *R. v. Secretary of State for the Home Department, ex p. Gunnell*[29] in holding that a discretionary life sentence prisoner was entitled to disclosure of the reasons, report or facts adverse to his request for release. This was justified, as "the liberty of the subject was in issue"[30] and he would in any event be entitled to see the information once section 34 of the Criminal Justice Act 1991 was brought into force.

(ii) Conflicting decisions

Decisions in the Court of Appeal may conflict. The decision in case A may not be cited to the court in case B, whereas both cases A and B are cited in case

---

[23] Leave was granted in *Bokhari v. Mahmood* (unreported, 1988) for the point to be taken to the House of Lords, but the appeal was not pursued.

[24] "Either because it will involve an abuse of power if the true view is that the court has no jurisdiction or a breach of the court's statutory duty if the true view is that the court is wrongly declining jurisdiction": *per* Lord Donaldson M.R. at p. 203.

[25] Lord Donaldson M.R. at p. 203 Balcombe L.J. at p. 206; Nicholls L.J. at p.210; *cf.* Lord Donaldson M.R. in *Langley v. North West Water Authority* [1991] 1 W.L.R. 697, confirming that "any departure from previous decisions of this court is in principle undesirable and should only be considered if the previous decision is manifestly wrong. Even then it will be necessary to take account of whether the decision purports to be of general application and whether there is any other way of remedying the error, for example, by encouraging an appeal to the House of Lords." See further below, pp. 430–431.

[26] [1992] BCLC 405.

[27] *per* Scott L.J. at p. 414.

[28] [1991] 1 Q.B. 740.

[29] *The Times*, November 7 1984.

[30] Lord Taylor C.J. at p. 755 citing only this factor from the many mentioned by Lord Donaldson M.R. in *Williams v. Fawcett* [1986] Q.B. 604, 615 and 616.

C^{31}; case A may not have been reported,[32] or may simply have been overlooked. Cases A and B may be decided by different divisions of the Court of Appeal at roughly the same time. Case A may be cited in case B but, in the view of the court in case C, erroneously interpreted. The resulting confusion may be settled by the Court of Appeal choosing which case or line of cases to follow and overruling any cases that conflict.[33] It has been argued that the court should be bound by the earlier case, case A (as the court in case B was not entitled to depart from it[34]) and, alternatively, that it should follow case B (as the later case[35]) but neither argument has prevailed.

(iii) Decisions impliedly overruled by the House of Lords

In *Young v. Bristol Aeroplane Co. Ltd.*[36] Lord Greene M.R. stated that the Court of Appeal was not bound by a previous decision which "although not expressly overruled, cannot stand with a subsequent decision of the House of Lords."[37] This principle was relied upon by Oliver J. in *Midland Bank Trust Co. Ltd v. Hett, Stubbs & Kemp*[38] where he declined to follow the decision of the Court of Appeal in *Groom v. Crocker*[39] on the ground that it was inconsistent with the subsequent decision of the House of Lords in *Hedley Byrne & Co. Ltd v. Heller & Partners Ltd.*[40]

(iv) Decisions on interlocutory appeals

In *Boys v. Chaplin*[41] the Court of Appeal held that it was not bound by a previous decision of the Court of Appeal where that court comprised two Lords Justices hearing an interlocutory appeal. It is the nature of the appeal that is crucial, not the number of members of the court. In *Langley v. North Western Water Authority*[42] the Court of Appeal affirmed, *obiter*,[43] that "the authority of a two judge court should today be regarded as being the same as that of a three judge court." It is not clear whether this is intended to cast doubt on the reasoning of *Boys*

---

[31] See the cases discussed in *Fisher v. Ruislip-Northwood Urban District Council* [1945] K.B. 584. The decision in case B may be regarded as given *per incuriam*: see *W. A. Sharratt Ltd v. John Boromley Church Stratton Ltd* [1985] Q.B. 1038.

[32] *e.g. Cathrineholm A/S v. Norequipment Trading Ltd* [1972] 2 Q.B. 314.

[33] *ibid.; Ross-Smith v. Ross-Smith* [1961] P. 39; *Ashburn Anstalt v. arnold* [1989] Ch. 1; *cf. Midland Bank Trust Co. Ltd v. Hett, Stubbs & Kemp* [1979] Ch. 384.

[34] A.L. Goodhart, (1947) 9 C.L.J. 349.

[35] R. N. Gooderson, (1950) 10 C.L.J. 432.

[36] [1944] K.B. 718.

[37] *ibid.* p. 722.

[38] [1979] Ch. 384. The case concerned the liability of a solicitor for negligence: see above pp. 173–174.

[39] [1939] 1 K.B. 194. Authorities following *Groom v. Crocker* and decided after *Hedley Byrne* were regarded as inconsistent with the decision of the Court of Appeal in *Esso Petroleum Co. Ltd v. Mardon* [1976] Q.B. 801.

[40] [1964] A.C. 465.

[41] [1968] 2 Q.B. 1.

[42] [1991] 1 W.L.R. 697.

[43] *per* Lord Donaldson M.R. at p. 710.

v. Chaplin.[44] Lord Donaldson M.R. noted that, in that case, Lord Denning M.R. and Diplock L.J.[45] relied on "the summary nature of the argument under the then existing practice in the case of interlocutory appeals heard by two judge courts"; he contrasted this with the "present practice", where the division of work between two and three-judge courts was "not determined by whether there will be no need for other than brief argument or the point is of minimal importance other than to the immediate parties."[46] This suggests that this aspect of *Boys v. Chaplin* might be open to reconsideration.

(d) Possible exceptions to Young v. Bristol Aeroplane Co. Ltd

(i) Inconsistency with an earlier House of Lords decision

Lord Greene M.R.'s summary of conclusions in the *Young's* case and the headnotes of most of the reports indicate that a Court of Appeal decision which is inconsistent with *any* House of Lords case, whether prior or subsequent, does not bind the Court of Appeal. The relevant passage from the main body of Lord Greene's judgment,[47] however, includes the word "subsequent." Moreover, in *Williams v. Glasbrook Bros.*[48] Lord Greene expressly asserted that the exception was so limited; if the Court of Appeal misinterprets an earlier House of Lords decision "nobody but the House of Lords can put that mistake right."[49] This position has been supported by Lord Denning M.R.[50] and Lord Simon,[51] and is to be preferred "in the interests of certainty."[52] Against these authorities, and in favour of a more widely drawn exception to *Young's* case, are the decision of the Court of Appeal in *Fitzsimons v. The Ford Motor Co.*[53] and the opinion of Lord Cross in *Miliangos v. George Frank (Textiles) Ltd.*[54]

The *Miliangos* case illustrates some of the difficulties that can arise. In 1960 the House of Lords in the *Havana* case[55] made a decision which was based on the unchallenged assumption that a judgment in an English court could only be given in sterling. The actual point in issue was the date at which a debt payable in U.S. dollars had to be converted to the equivalent in sterling for the purposes of proceedings in England to enforce payment. In *Schorsch Meier G.m.b.H. v. Hennin*[56] the Court of Appeal[57] held (1) that the operation of the *Havana* case had been limited by Article 106 of the EEC Treaty, which was regarded as

---

[44] [1968] 2 Q.B. 1.
[45] At pp. 23 and 35 respectively.
[46] [1991] 1 W.L.R. at p. 710.
[47] Above, p. 427.
[48] [1947] 2 All E.R. 884.
[49] *ibid.* p. 885. If the House of Lords decision had not been cited, the Court of Appeal decision would be *per incuriam*: see above.
[50] *Miliangos v. George Frank (Textiles) Ltd* [1975] Q.B. 416, 502.
[51] *ibid.* [1976] A.C. 443, 478–479.
[52] Sir Rupert Cross, *Precedent in English Law* (3rd ed., 1977), p. 143, a statement omitted from the fourth edition.
[53] [1946] 1 All E.R. 429. This was not cited in *Williams v. Glasbrook Bros.*
[54] [1976] A.C. 443, 496.
[55] *United Railways of Havana and Regla Warehouses Ltd* [1961] A.C. 1007.
[56] [1975] Q.B. 416.
[57] Lord Denning M.R., Lawton L.J. and Foster J.

enabling EEC nationals to obtain judgments in a foreign currency and (2) (Lawton L.J. dissenting) that in any event the *Havana* rule could be disregarded as the fact that sterling was no longer a stable currency meant that the rationale behind the rule no longer stood. On the latter point, the majority founded themselves on the maxim *cessante ratione legis cessat ipsa lex* (if the reason for a law ceases to be valid the law itself ceases). In *Miliangos v. George Franks (Textiles) Ltd* a plaintiff who was not an EEC national sought to take advantage of the second *ratio* of *Schorsch Meier*. Bristow J.[58] held that he was obliged to follow the House of Lords decision in *Havana* in preference to that of the Court of Appeal in *Schorsch Meier*, notwithstanding the fact that it had been cited to the court in *Schorsch Meier*. The *Havana* rule could only be altered by statute or another decision of the House. On appeal, the Court of Appeal[59] then held that *Schorsch Meier* was binding (1) on courts beneath the Court of Appeal in the hierarchy and (2) on the Court of Appeal itself, the relevant exception to *Young v. Bristol Aeroplane Co. Ltd* being confined to inconsistent *subsequent* House of Lords decisions. The House of Lords held (1) that the Court of Appeal had acted incorrectly in *Schorsch Meier* in failing to follow *Havana*; but (2) (Lord Simon dissenting) that the *Havana* case should be overruled. As to the dilemma facing the trial judge and the Court of Appeal in *Miliangos*, Lord Cross[60] took the view that *Schorsch Meier* should not have been followed (endorsing Bristow J.'s approach), Lord Simon[61] thought that the Court of Appeal in *Miliangos* had acted correctly, and the other members of the House of Lords expressed no definite opinion.[62] The position taken by Bristow J. and Lord Cross assumes that:

> "the *Schorsch Meier* majority decision was not law in any proper sense, since it was reached in total disregard of the proper law as it then existed in a rule of the House of Lords, and which . . . bound the Court of Appeal to reach a decision contrary to that actually reached."[63]

However, the analogous argument is not accepted in cases of "horizontal conflict" between decisions in the same court. Thus, where Court of Appeal decisions conflict, the Court of Appeal in a subsequent case may choose which to follow.[64]

More recently, in *Holden & Co. v. Crown Prosecution Service*[65] the Court of Appeal asserted a preference for the broader view, relying on a dictum of Lord Wright in *Noble v. Southern Railway Co.*[66] However, none of the other relevant authorities on the point were cited (except *Young v. Bristol Aeroplane Co. Ltd*[67]

---

[58] [1975] Q.B. 487, 491.
[59] [1975] Q.B. 487, 499.
[60] [1976] A.C. 443, 496.
[61] [1976] A.C. 443, 470.
[62] Professor Cross thought the desirability of contradictory statements on this point to be "highly questionable" and that there was "something to be said for the discreet silence" of the other three members of the House: P. M. S. Hacker and J. Raz (eds.), *Law, Morality and Society* (1977), p. 153.
[63] C. E. F. Rickett, (1980) 43 M.L.R. 136, 141.
[64] See above, pp. 429–430.
[65] [1990] 2 Q.B. 261, *per* Lord Lane C. J. at p. 272.
[66] [1940] A.C. 583, 598.
[67] [1944] K.B. 718.

itself) and the decision on this point might therefore be open to challenge as reached *per incuriam*.

(ii) Inconsistency with a Privy Council decision

In *Worcester Works Finance Ltd v. Cooden Engineering Co. Ltd*[68] Lord Denning M.R. said:[69]

> "Although decisions of the Privy Council are not binding on this Court, nevertheless when the Privy Council disapproves of a previous decision of this Court or casts doubt on it, we are at liberty to depart from the previous decision."

This statement can be seen as part of Lord Denning's battle against the rule that the Court of Appeal is bound by its own previous decisions, and it is not clear whether it is still authoritative in the light of the strictures of the House of Lords in *Davis v. Johnson*.[70]

(iii) Other possibilities[71]

In *B. v. B.*[72] the Court of Appeal held that section 1(1) of the Domestic Violence and Matrimonial Proceedings Act 1976 did not give a county court jurisdiction to grant an injunction excluding a spouse[73] from the from the "matrimonial home" where that spouse had a proprietary interest in the home. A few days later this decision was followed by the Court of Appeal in *Cantliff v. Jenkins*.[74] These cases caused some consternation, as the plain words of the statute seemed to give the county court that jurisdiction. The point was raised again in *Davis v. Johnson*, and a five-member Court of Appeal was assembled.[75] Only Cumming-Bruce L.J. held that the earlier cases were correctly decided. Goff L.J. held that they were binding even though they were wrong. The other three members of the court held that they were wrong, and, on a variety of grounds, not binding. Lord Denning said that:

> "while the court should regard itself as normally bound by a previous decision of the court, nevertheless it should be at liberty to depart from it if it is convinced that the previous decision was wrong."[76]

---

[68] [1972] 1 Q.B. 210.
[69] At p. 217.
[70] Below. On the Privy Council and precedent see further below, pp. 443–444 and 447.
[71] See also *R. v. Secretary of State for the Home Department, ex p. Al-Mehdawi* [1990] 1 A.C. 876, above, p. 421.
[72] [1978] Fam. 26, decided on October 13, 1977 by Bridge, Waller and Megaw L.JJ.
[73] Whether real, or for want of a better expression, "common law".
[74] [1978] Fam. 47, decided on October 20, 1977 by Stamp, Orr and Ormrod L.JJ. The couple were joint tenants.
[75] [1979] A.C. 264. Lord Denning M.R., Sir George Baker P., Goff, Shaw and Cumming-Bruce L.JJ.: described by Lord Denning as "a court of all the talents" [1979] A.C. 264, 271.
[76] [1979] A.C. 264, 278–282.

Either the Court of Appeal should take for itself guidelines similar to those taken by the House of Lords,[77] or this should be regarded as an additional exception to *Young v. Bristol Aeroplane Co. Ltd.*[78] Lord Denning had long argued for such a change,[79] but had been unable to convince either his colleagues or the House of Lords.

Sir George Baker P. was prepared to distinguish *B. v. B.* on the ground that the welfare of a child was not involved as it was in *Davis v. Johnson.* If that distinction were not acceptable,[80] a new exception to *Young v. Bristol Aeroplane Co. Ltd* should be created:

"The Court is not bound to follow a previous decision of its own if satisfied that that decision was clearly wrong and cannot stand in the face of the will and intention of Parliament expressed in simple language in a recent statute passed to remedy a serious mischief or abuse, and further adherence to the previous decision must lead to injustice in the particular case and unduly restrict proper development of the law with injustice to others."[81]

Shaw L.J. suggested a new exception to *Young's* case that was even narrower:

"in some such terms as that the principle of *stare decisis* should be relaxed where its application would have the effect of depriving actual and potential victims of violence of a vital protection which an Act of Parliament was plainly designed to afford to them, especially where, as in the context of domestic violence, that deprivation must inevitably give rise to an irremediable detriment to such victims and create in regard to them an injustice irreversible by a later decision of the House of Lords."[82]

The House of Lords unanimously dismissed an appeal; *B. v. B.* and *Cantliff v. Jenkins* were overruled.[83] However, the House strongly reafffirmed the rule that the Court of Appeal was bound by its own previous decisions, subject to clearly defined exceptions which did not include those advanced in the Court of Appeal. The argument in favour of *Young's* case was summarised by Lord Diplock[84]:

---

[77] See below, pp. 438–443.

[78] [1944] K.B. 718.

[79] *The Discipline of Law* (1979), pp. 297–300; *Gallie v. Lee* [1969] 2 Ch. 17, 37; *Hanning v. Maitland (No. 2)* [1970] 1 Q.B. 580, 587; *Barrington v. Lee* [1972] 1 Q.B. 326, 338. He temporarily conceded defeat in *Tiverton Estates Ltd v. Wearwell Ltd* [1975] Ch. 146, 160–161, but raised the point again in *Davis v. Johnson* and suffered a "crushing rebuff" (*The Discipline of Law* (1979), p. 299).

[80] That this distinction was not acceptable was subsequently conceded in the House of Lords.

[81] [1979] A.C. 264, 290.

[82] [1979] A.C. 264, 308.

[83] Lord Diplock alone thought that *B. v. B.* had been correctly decided, making the overall division of appellate judicial opinion eight all: [1979] A.C. 264, 323. That case had concerned the situation where the man was sole tenant. However, his Lordship held that an injunction could be awarded where both parties were joint tenants: as the facts of *Davis v. Johnson* fell into that category he was in favour of dismissing the appeal.

[84] [1979] A.C. 264, 326. Viscount Dilhorne, Lord Kilbrandon, and Lord Scarman expressly agreed with Lord Diplock's views on precedent: [1979] A.C. 264, 336, 340, 349. See also Scarman L.J. in *Tiverton Estates Ltd v. Wearwell Ltd* [1975] Ch. 146, 172–173 and in *Farrell v. Alexander* [1976] Q.B. 345, 371.

"In an appellate court of last resort a balance must be struck between the need on the one hand for the legal certainty resulting from the binding effect of previous decisions, and, on the other side the avoidance of undue restriction on the proper development of the law. In the case of an inter-mediate appellate court, however, the second desideratum can be taken care of by appeal to a superior appellate court, if reasonable means of access to it are available; while the risk to the first desideratum, legal certainty if the court is not bound by its own previous decisions grows even greater with increasing membership and the number of three-judge divisions in which it sits. . . ."

The argument against is that "the House of Lords may never have an oppor-tunity to correct [an] error; and thus it may be perpetuated indefinitely, perhaps for ever."[85] Litigants may be unable to finance a further appeal; the case may be settled; an insurance company or big employer who wins in the Court of Appeal may "buy off an appeal to the House of Lords by paying ample compen-sation to the appellant."[86] Lord Diplock responded by pointing out that in view of *Cantliff v. Jenkins* there had been no need for anything but the briefest of hearings in the Court of Appeal, and an appeal to the House could have been heard and decided quickly. The argument of delay and expense could also be used to justify any High Court or county court judge in refusing to follow a decision of the Court of Appeal that he thought was wrong. There is also the possibility of using the "leap-frog" procedure under the Administration of Jus-tice Act 1969.[87]

Lord Salmon expressed some sympathy for Lord Denning's views, but said that "until such time, if ever, as all his colleagues in the Court of Appeal agree with those views, *stare decisis* must still hold the field."[88] In view of the large number of Lord Justices, keeping to *stare decisis* might be "no bad thing". He suggested that where the Court of Appeal gave leave to appeal from a decision it felt bound to make by authority and with which it disagreed, it should have the statutory power to order that the costs of the appeal be paid from public funds. This would be a very rare occurrence, and the cost minimal.

According to the Court of Appeal *stare decisis* does not prevent an English court giving effect to a change in a rule of international law notwithstanding the existence of English precedents based on the old rule.[89] It also seems that the Court of Appeal is not bound by its own previous decisions where it is the court of last resort, with no possible appeal to the House of Lords.[90]

---

[85] *per* Lord Denning M.R. in *Davis v. Johnson* [1979] A.C. 264, 278.
[86] *ibid.* p. 278.
[87] See below, pp. 960–961. Lord Diplock [1979] A.C. 264, 324–325.
[88] [1979] A.C. 264, 344.
[89] *Trendtex Trading Corporation v. Central Bank of Nigeria* [1977] Q.B. 529, 554 (Lord Denning M.R.), 579 (Shaw L.J.) (a case on the scope of the doctrine of state immunity). Stephenson L.J. dissented on this point. The Court of Appeal's decision was followed by Robert Goff J. and the Court of Appeal in *I Congreso del Partido* [1978] Q.B. 500 and [1981] 1 All E.R. 1092, and Lloyd J. in *Planmount Ltd v. Republic of Zaire* [1981] 1 All E.R. 1110; but not by Donaldson J. in *Uganda Co. (Holdings) Ltd v. Government of Uganda* [1979] 1 Lloyd's Rep. 481. The House of Lords in *I Congreso del Partido* endorsed the general approach of the Court of Appeal in *Trendtex* but did not advert to the "precedent" aspect: [1983] 1 A.C. 244.
[90] Lord Denning M.R. in *Davis v. Johnson* [1979] A.C. 264, 282.

(e) Can lower tiers rely on the exceptions to Young v. Bristol Aeroplane Co. Ltd?

This question was answered in the negative by Lord Hailsham L.C. in *Cassell & Co. Ltd v. Broome*,[91] but there have been cases where the Divisional Court or a trial judge has declined to follow a decision of the Court of Appeal on the ground that it was inconsistent with a House of Lords decision,[92] and the point cannot be regarded as settled. It is difficult, for example, to see that a trial judge should follow a decision of a higher court given in ignorance of a binding statutory provision. According to Lord Denning M.R., where decisions of the same court conflict, lower courts should follow the later case[93]; Donaldson J. disagreed.[94]

6. The Court of Appeal (Criminal Division)[95]

This court is obviously bound by decisions of the House of Lords. It is also generally bound by its own previous decisions and those of its forerunners, the Court of Criminal Appeal and the Court for Crown Cases Reserved. However, as the liberty of the subject is involved, *stare decisis* is not applied with the same rigidity as in the Civil Division. A decision may not be followed if it falls within one of the established exceptions to *Young v. Bristol Aeroplane Co. Ltd.*[96] An example is *R. v. Gould*[97] where the Court of, Appeal (Criminal Division) followed a decision of the Court of Crown Cases Reserved in 1889[98] in preference to a later conflicting decision of the Court of Criminal Appeal in 1921,[99] on the question whether *mens rea* was an essential ingredient of the offence of bigamy. In addition, Diplock L.J. stated in *Gould* that:

"if upon due consideration we were to be of opinion that the law had been either misapplied or misunderstood in an earlier decision of this court or

---

[91] [1972] A.C. 1027, 1054; above, pp. 425–426. In *Baker v. The Queen* [1975] A.C. 774, 788, Lord Diplock stated that a lower court could not rely on the *per incuriam* rule in relation to the decision of a higher court, but could choose between conflicting decisions.

[92] *R. v. Northumberland Compensation Appeal Tribunal, ex p. Shaw* [1951] 1 K.B. 711, where the Divisional Court declined to follow the decision of the Court of Appeal in *Racecourse Betting Control Board v. Secretary for Air* [1944] Ch. 114 on the ground that it was inconsistent with the views expressed by the House of Lords in *Walsall Overseers v. L.N.W. Ry. Co.* (1878) 4 App.Cas.30 and the Privy Council in *R. v. Nat. Bell Liquors Ltd* [1922] 2 A.C. 128, which cases had not been cited. The *Shaw* case was not cited in *Cassell & Co. Ltd v. Broome*. See also *Midland Bank v. Hett, Stubbs & Kemp*, above, p. 430; *The Alexandros* P. [1986] Q.B. 464.

[93] *Davis v. Johnson* [1979] A.C. 264, 279. See to the same effect *Taylor Woodrow Property Co. Ltd v. Lonrho Textiles Ltd* [1985] 2 EGLR 120, B. Hytner Q.C. (sitting as a deputy High Court judge); Warner J. in *Re Smith (a bankrupt)* [1988] Ch. 457.

[94] *Uganda Co. (Holdings) Ltd v. Government of Uganda* [1979] 1 Lloyd's Rep. 481, 485: a trial judge should "seek to anticipate how the Court of Appeal itself would ... resolve the conflict."

[95] See G. Zellick, [1974] Crim.L.R. 222; R. Pattenden, [1984] Crim.L.R. 592.

[96] [1944] K.B. 718. See above, pp. 427–436. For an example of an application of the *per incuriam* doctrine, see *R. v. Ewing* [1983] Q.B. 1039, disapproving *R. v. Angeli* [1979] 1 W.L.R. 26 on the ground that it could not stand with the decision of the House of Lords in *Blyth v. Blyth* [1966] A.C. 643; and *R. v. El-Gazzar* (1986) 8 Cr.App.(S) 182.

[97] [1968] 2 Q.B. 65. Other examples are *R. v. Preece, R. v. Howells* (1976) 63 Cr.App.R. 28; *R. v. Maginnis* [1986] Q.B. 618.

[98] *R. v. Tolson* (1889) 23 Q.B.D. 168.

[99] *R. v. Wheat* [1921] 2 K.B. 119.

its predecessor, the Court of Criminal Appeal, we should be entitled to depart from the view as to the law expressed in the earlier decision notwithstanding that the case could not be brought within any of the exceptions laid down in *Young v. Bristol Aeroplane Co. Ltd.*"[1]

It has been uncertain whether this power is available wherever the court is convinced that the earlier decision is wrong, as this *dictum* suggests, or only where overruling is in the interests of the defendant. The preponderance of authority supports the latter, narrower view. A clear statement was made by the court in *R. v. Spencer*[2]:

"As a matter of principle we respectfully find it difficult to see why there should in general be any difference in the application of the principle of *stare decisis* between the Civil and Criminal Divisions of the Court, save that we must remember that in the latter we may be dealing with the liberty of the subject[3] and if a departure from authority is necessary in the interests of justice to an appellant, then this court should not shrink from so acting."[4]

This restriction does not apply to decisions on matters of sentencing. In *R. v. Newsome, R. v. Browne*[5] the Court of Appeal (Criminal Division) overruled two earlier decisions of the court[6] to the effect that a judge could not increase a sentence of imprisonment once passed to ensure that it would not be suspended even if this were to be done immediately. Widgery L.J. said[7] that if a court of five members is constituted:

"to consider an issue of discretion and the principles upon which discretion should be exercised, that court ought to have the right to depart from an earlier view expressed by a court of three, especially where it was a matter in which the court did not have the opportunity of hearing argument on both sides."

The view that a "full court"[8] has greater power to overrule than an ordinarily

---

[1] [1968] 2 Q.B. 65, 69.

[2] [1985] Q.B. 771.

[3] The defendant's "liberty" appears not to be at stake where he or she has been fined but not imprisoned: *R. v. Burke* [1988] Crim.L.R. 839, C.A.

[4] *ibid.*, p. 779, *per* May L.J. See, to the same effect, Lord Goddard C.J. in *R. v. Taylor* [1950] 2 K.B. 368, 371 (Court of Criminal Appeal), referring to the "bounden duty" of the court to reconsider an erroneous decision, on the strength of which "an accused person has been sentenced and imprisoned"; Lord Diplock, *obiter*, in *D.P.P. v. Merriman* [1973] A.C. 584, 605: the liberty of the court "to depart from a precedent which it is convinced was erroneous is restricted to cases where the departure is in favour of the accused": this *dictum* was applied by the court in *R. v. Jenkins* (1983) 76 Cr.App.R. 313, 318 (the better view here is that the consideration was irrelevant as the court was choosing between conflicting decisions and not overruling a single decision: J. C. Smith, [1983] Crim.L.R. at pp. 388–389), and in *R. v. Howe* [1986] Q.B. 626, 642.

[5] [1970] 2 Q.B. 711, decided in July 1970.

[6] *R. v. Corr, The Times*, January 16, 1970 and *R. v. Maylam* (unreported) decided on February 26, 1970. In *Newsome and Browne*, the actual sentences were suspended as it was "the only fair thing to do" (a form of prospective overruling: see below, p. 443).

[7] At p. 717.

[8] A term which usually denotes a court of more than the usual number of judges (*e.g.* five or seven for the Divisional Court, five for the Court of Appeal and seven in the House of Lords) and not a court of all the judges eligible to sit.

438   CHAPTER 7

constituted court was also held by the Court of Criminal Appeal,[9] although it has been rejected by the Divisional Court[10] and the Court of Appeal.[11] It seems in practice that a full court is not necessary where one of the exceptions to *Young v. Bristol Aeroplane Co. Ltd* is applied, but is thought appropriate where overruling is contemplated on wider grounds.[12] In *Newsome* Widgery L.J. stressed that the court would be more reluctant to depart from an earlier decision where guilt or innocence was involved as distinct from the exercise of the court's discretion. In practice, the court seems reluctant to depart from its own previous decisions, even where it regards them as doubtful, and overruling would be in the accused's interests. Instead, the matter is left for the House of Lords.[13]

It is uncertain whether the Court of Appeal (Criminal Division) is bound by decisions of the Court of Appeal (Civil Division), and *vice versa*. Before reorganisation the Court of Appeal and Court of Criminal Appeal seemed not to be bound by each other's decisions.[14]

A decision of the court is treated as a binding authority notwithstanding that the appellant who has won the argument on the point of law has had his or her appeal dismissed under the proviso to section 2 of the Criminal Appeal Act 1968.[15]

7. THE HOUSE OF LORDS

Decisions of the House of Lords are[16] binding on courts lower in the hierarchy, including, if not especially, the Court of Appeal. In *London Tramways v. London County Council*[17] the House of Lords held that it was bound by its own previous decisions in the interests of finality and certainty in the law. It was accepted that a decision could be questioned where it conflicted with another decision of the House or was made *per incuriam*.[18] Other exceptions were suggested. How-

---

[9] *R. v. Taylor* [1950] 2 K.B. 368.
[10] *Younghusband v. Luftig* [1949] 2 K.B. 354: curiously, a criminal case.
[11] In the exercise of its civil jurisdiction: *Young v. Bristol Aeroplane Co. Ltd* [1944] K.B. 718, 725.
[12] *Gould* was decided by a three-member court: see Zellick [1974] Crim.L.R. 222, 231–232.
[13] See the cases discussed by R. Pattenden, [1984] Crim.L.R. 592, 599–602. Pattenden's argument that the "special exception" in criminal cases no longer survives predates the reaffirmation of its existence in *R. v. Spencer*, n. 2 above.
[14] See *Hardie & Lane v. Chilton* [1928] 2 K.B. 306, C.A. versus *R. v. Denyer* [1926] 2 K.B. 258, C.C.A. and the statement of Lord Hewart C.J. in the Court of Criminal Appeal at 20 Cr. App. Rep. 185.
[15] As originally enacted; see below, pp. 927–928. Here the distinction between *ratio* and *dictum* is "meaningless in practice": Cross and Harris (1991), p. 80; above, pp. 416–421.
[16] The dismissal by the House of Lords of a petition for leave to appeal against a decision of a lower court does not constitute implied approval of that decision by the House: *Re Wilson* [1985] A.C. 750, 756.
[17] [1898] A.C. 375: not "London Street Tramways" see the list of errata at the start of the [1898] A.C. volume (Cross and Harris (1991), p. 102, n. 22).
[18] See above, pp. 427–430. For an example of a choice by the House of Lords between two conflicting decisions of its own, see *Moodie v. Inland Revenue Commissioners* [1993] 1 W.L.R. 266 (following *Ramsay (W.T.) Ltd v. I.R.C.* in preference to *I.R.C. v. Plummer* [1980] A.C. 896). See J. Tiley, [1991] B.T.R. 402; D. Sandler [1993] C.L.J. 399. Lord Templeman stated (at p. 273): "Faced with conflicting decisions, the courts are entitled and bound to follow *Ramsay's* case because in *Plummer's* case this House was never asked to consider the effect of a self-cancelling scheme and because the principle of *Ramsay's* case restores justice between individual taxpayers and the general body of taxpayers." It is submitted that these are substantive reasons for preferring *Ramsay*, rather than a rule that the later of two conflicting decisions must always be followed.

ever, as the House was the final court of appeal the correction of error was normally dependent on the vagaries of the legislative process. In 1966 Lord Gardiner L.C. made the following statement on behalf of himself and the Lords of Appeal in Ordinary[19]:

"Their Lordships regard the use of precedent as an indispensable foundation upon which to decide what is the law and its application to individual cases. It provides at least some degree of certainty upon which individuals can rely on the conduct of their affairs, as well as a basis for orderly development of legal rules.

Their Lordships nevertheless recognise that too rigid adherence to precedent may lead to injustice in a particular case and also unduly restrict the proper development of the law. They propose, therefore, to modify their present practice and, while treating former decisions of this House as normally binding, to depart from a previous decision when it appears right to do so.

In this connection they will bear in mind the danger of disturbing retrospectively the basis on which contracts, settlements of property and fiscal arrangements have been entered into and also the especial need for certainty as to the criminal law.

This announcement is not intended to affect the use of precedent elsewhere than in this House."

A press notice issued at the same time[20] indicated that the statement was of great importance although it should not be supposed that it would frequently be applied. An example of a case where it might be used would be where an earlier decision was "influenced by the existence of conditions which no longer prevail, and that in modern conditions the law ought to be different." The change would also enable the House to pay greater attention to Commonwealth decisions critical of the House. As predicted the power has been used sparingly. Members of the House seem reluctant to state expressly that an earlier decision is "overruled" even where that appears to be the case.

The decision in *The Aello*[21] on a point of shipping law[22] was overruled in the *Johanna Oldendorff*.[23] As we have seen, the *Havana* case,[24] or at least the assumption upon which it was based, was overruled in *Miliangos v. George*

---

[19] *Practice Statement (Judicial Precedent)* [1966] 1 W.L.R. 1234. Lord Denning M.R. and Lord Parker C.J. were also present. See R. W. M. Dias, [1966] C.L.J. 153; R. Stone, [1968] C.L.J. 35; J. Stone, (1969) 69 Columbia L. R. 1162. The circumstances surrounding the introduction of the Statement and the way in which it has been used are examined by A. Paterson in *The Law Lords* (1982), Chap. 6 and pp. 154–169 and G. Maher, [1981] Stat.L.R. 85. See also below, pp. 445–446.

[20] See M. Zander, *The Law-Making Process* (4th ed., 1994), pp. 192–193.

[21] [1961] A.C. 135.

[22] The test for determining when a ship has "arrived" in port. The expense of delay in discharging cargo from an "arrived" ship caused, for example, by congestion at the berths, normally falls on the charterer and not on the owners of the vessel.

[23] *E. L. Oldendorff v. Tradax Export* [1974] A.C. 479. This was the first occasion when the statement was clearly used. It has been argued that it had already been used in *Conway v. Rimmer* [1968] A.C. 910 and *British Railways Board v. Herrington* [1972] A.C. 879: see Paterson (1982), p. 164. On *Conway v. Rimmer*, see J. Stone, *op. cit.* n. 19 above.

[24] [1961] A.C. 1007: see above, pp. 431–432.

Frank (Textiles) Ltd.[25] The decision in *Congreve v. Inland Revenue Commissioners*[26] was overruled in *Vestey v. Inland Revenue Commissioners (Nos.1 and 2)*[27] on the ground that the earlier decision, on a point of construction of a Finance Act, had led to unforeseen results that were "arbitrary, potentially unjust and fundamentally unconstitutional."[28] The law as to the liability of the occupiers of land towards trespassers was restated by the House, with some differences of formulation among their Lordships, in *British Railways Board v. Herrington.*[29] The law as expounded, more restrictively, by the House in *Robert Addie & Sons (Collieries) Ltd v. Dumbreck*[30] was, according to the headnote in the Law Reports, "reconsidered".[31] Then, the House in *R. v. Secretary of State for the Home Department, ex p. Khawaja*[32] overruled the decision in *R. v. Secretary of State for the Home Department, ex p. Zamir,*[33] holding that a person could only be removed as an "illegal immigrant" if the *court* was satisfied that the entry was illegal: it would no longer be sufficient that the *immigration officer* was satisfied and had some evidence for that belief. The issue concerned the liberty of the subject and did not fall into any of the categories in which the *Practice Statement* indicated the need for special caution.

Most spectacularly, the House of Lords in *R. v. Shivpuri*[34] overruled its earlier decision in *Anderton v. Ryan,*[35] which had misinterpreted the Criminal Attempts Act 1981 in holding that a defence of impossibility in the criminal law had to an extent survived the Act. *Anderton v. Ryan* had been adversely criticised by almost all the academic commentators, most notably by Professor Glanville Williams in an article in the Cambridge Law Journal.[36] Among the grounds for Professor Williams' criticism were that the House disregarded (1) the bulk of the relevant academic literature, (2) the Law Commission report that led to the 1981 Act[37] and (3) the plain words of the Act. Lord Bridge, who had been a party to the decision in *Anderton v. Ryan*, delivered the main speech in *R. v. Shivpuri*. He acknowledged that the earlier decision was wrong, that there was no valid ground on which it could be distinguished, and that it should be overruled, notwithstanding the "especial need for certainty in the criminal law".[38] He was undeterred by the consideration that *Anderton v. Ryan* was recent: "If serious error is embodied in a decision of this house has distorted the law, the

---

[25] [1976] A.C. 443. In the same year the Statement was used in the Scottish case of *Dick v. Burgh of Falkirk* 1976 S.L.T. 21.

[26] [1948] 1 All E.R. 948.

[27] [1980] A.C. 1148.

[28] *per* Lord Wilberforce at p. 1176.

[29] [1972] A.C. 879.

[30] [1929] A.C. 358.

[31] Lord Reid's word at p. 879. Lord Reid (p. 898) and Lord Morris did, however, say that *Addie's* case was "wrongly decided." Lord Pearson regarded the *Addie* formulation as an "anomaly" which "should be discarded" (p. 930). Lord Diplock rejected it "as amounting to an exclusive or comprehensive statement" of the duty owed to a trespasser (p. 941). Lord Wilberforce spoke of "developing" the law in *Addie's* case (p. 921). See now the Occupiers' Liability Act 1984.

[32] [1984] A.C. 74.

[33] [1980] A.C. 930.

[34] [1987] A.C. 1.

[35] [1985] A.C. 560.

[36] "The Lords and Impossible Attempts, or *Quis Custodiet Ipsos Custodes?*" [1986] C.L.J. 33.

[37] *Attempt, and Impossibility in relation to Attempt, Conspiracy and Incitement* (Law Com. No. 102, 1980).

[38] A reference to the 1966 *Practice Statement*, above p. 439.

sooner it is corrected the better."[39] He could not see how anyone could have acted in reliance on *Anderton v. Ryan* in the belief that he or she was acting innocently, and now find that, after all, he or she was to be held to have committed a criminal offence. A decision to follow *Anderton v. Ryan* would "be tantamount to a declaration that the Act of 1981 left the law of criminal attempts unchanged following the decision in *R. v. Smith (Roger)*."[40] He concluded by referring to Professor Williams' article:

> "The language in which he criticises the decision in *Anderton v. Ryan* is not conspicuous for its moderation, but it would be foolish, on that account, not to recognise the force of the criticism and churlish not to acknowledge the assistance I have derived from it."[41]

Nine months later, in *R. v. Howe*[42] the House of Lords again departed from an earlier decision in a criminal law case, overruling *D.P.P. for Northern Ireland v. Lynch*.[43] In *Howe*, it was held that duress can never be a defence to murder: in *Lynch* it had been held that it could be raised as a defence by a principal in the second degree, albeit not the actual killer. Here, the arguments in favour of overruling were significantly weaker than in *R. v. Shivpuri*.[44] Finally, in *Murphy v. Brentwood District Council*,[45] the House overruled its decision in *Anns v. Merton London Borough Council*,[46] and held that a local authority owes no duty of care in tort to protect the purchaser of a house from economic losses caused by defects in the house. *Anns* was contrary to established principle, and overruling would restore certainty to the law.

Other invitations to the House to overrule a past decision have not been accepted. A remarkable example is *Jones v. Secretary of State for Social Services*[47] where four out of seven members of the House held that the earlier decision of the House in *Re Dowling*[48] on a point of national insurance law[49] was incorrect, but only three thought that *Re Dowling* should be overruled.

---

[39] [1987] A.C. 1, 23.

[40] [1975] A.C. 476, also known as *Haughton v. Smith* [1973] 3 All E.R. 1109, H.L. Criticism of this decision had led to the 1981 Act.

[41] [1987] A.C. 1, 23. Professor Williams' campaign on this issue stretched over decades: see P. S. Atiyah, *Pragmatism and Theory in English Law* (1987), pp. 180–183. On *Shivpuri*, see J. R. Spencer, [1986] C.L.J. 361; P. R. Glazebrook, [1986] C.L.J. 363; [1986] Crim.L.R. 536, commentary by J. C. Smith; E. M. Clare Canton, (1987) 137 N.L.J. 491, also commenting on *Howe*, below.

[42] [1987] A.C. 417.

[43] [1975] A.C. 653.

[44] See [1987] Crim.L.R. 480, commentary by J. C. Smith; C. Gearty, [1987] C.L.J. 203; H. P. Milgate, "Duress and the Criminal Law: Another about turn by the House of Lords" [1988] C.L.J. 61; L. Walters, "Murder under duress and judicial decision-making in the House of Lords" (1988) 8 L.S. 61.

[45] [1991] 1 A.C. 398. See J. W. Harris, (1991) 11 O.J.L.S. 416.

[46] [1978] A.C. 728.

[47] [1972] A.C. 944. Alternatively entitled *R. v. National Insurance Commissioners, ex p. Hudson*. See J. Stone, (1972) 35 M.L.R. 449, 469–477.

[48] *R. v. Deputy Industrial Injuries Commissioner, ex p. Amalgamated Engineering Union, re Dowling* [1967] 1 A.C. 725.

[49] Whether a decision by a National Insurance Commissioner (adjudicating a claim for industrial injuries benefit) that injuries were caused by an industrial accident, was binding on a Medical Appeal Tribunal (adjudicating a subsequent claim for industrial disablement benefit).

The main "defector" was Lord Simon of Glaisdale, who stated[50] that the 1966 declaration should be used most sparingly; that a variation of view on a matter of statutory construction would rarely provide a suitable occasion for its use unless it could be convincingly shown that a previous, erroneous, construction was causing administrative difficulties or individual injustice; that the House should be reluctant to encourage litigants to reopen arguments once concluded; that there was much to be said for each side of this case; and that *Re Dowling* was not unworkable and could in any event be altered more appropriately by Parliament.[51] In *Fitzleet Estates Ltd v. Cherry*[52] the House refused to review a 1965 majority decision on a point of tax law, in the absence of any new argument, any change of circumstances or any suggestion that it was productive of injustice. In *Hesperides Hotels Ltd v. Muftizade*[53] the House declined to modify the long established rule that the High Court has no jurisdiction to entertain an action for damages for trespass to land situated abroad.[54] The rule was accepted in other jurisdictions, a change might involve conflict with foreign jurisdictions and there had been no change of circumstances. Finally, in *President of India v. La Pintada Compania Navigacion S. A.*[55] the House declined to depart from an earlier decision[56] that the common law does not award general damages for delay in payment of a debt. Much of the injustice caused by this decision had been removed by a combination of legislative and judicial intervention; Parliament had declined to accept a recommendation from the Law Commission[57] that would have covered the case here, while accepting other recommendations in the area; and reversal of the common law rule would have the effect of overriding restrictions in the statutory provisions that had been enacted.

In other cases, the House may simply be convinced that the earlier decision was correct.[58]

---

[50] At pp. 1024–1025. Lord Wilberforce would not have favoured overruling *Re Dowling* if its *ratio* had been narrowly interpreted (see pp. 995–996). Lord Diplock was in favour of overruling but recognised he was in the minority and so he reluctantly agreed that the appeal should be allowed (p. 1015). *Cf.* Lord Reid in *R. v. Knuller* [1973] A.C. 435, 455–456, where he expressed the view that the House should not overrule *Shaw v. D.P.P.* [1962] A.C. 220, notwithstanding that he had dissented in *Shaw* and still thought that it had been wrongly decided *cf.* Lord Hailsham and Lord Edmund-Davies in *R. v. Cunningham* [1982] A.C. 566, 581, 582. See R. Brazier, [1973] Crim.L.R. 98.

[51] It was so altered: see N. J. Wikeley and others, *Ogus, Barendt and Wikeley's The Law of Social Security* (4th ed., 1995), p. 331.

[52] [1977] 1 W.L.R. 1345. Similarly, in *Paal Wilson & Co. v. Partenreederei Hannah Blumenthal* [1983] 1 A. C. 854 the House declined to overrule the recent decision in *Bremer Vulkan v. South India Shipping Corp.* [1981] A. C. 909, which had "provoked serious disquiet among the whole commercial community" (per Lord Goff in *Food Corporation of India v. Antclizo Shipping Corporation (The Antclizo)* [1988] 1 W.L.R. 603, 606). One point was "the special need for certainty, consistency and continuity in the field of commercial law" (*per* Lord Brandon at p. 913). See B. J. Davenport, (1988) 104 L. Q. R. 493. The House called for the matter to be considered by Parliament and this led to the Courts and Legal Services Act 1990, s.102.

[53] [1979] A. C. 508.

[54] *British South Africa Co. v. Companhia de Moçambique* [1893] A. C. 602.

[55] [1985] A. C. 104. See P.M.N., [1984] 3 LMCLQ 365.

[56] *London, Chatham and Dover Railway Co. v. South Eastern Railway Co.* [1893] A. C. 429.

[57] Law Com. 88 (Cmnd. 7229, 1978) Report on Interest: see the Administration of Justice Act 1982, Sched. 1. The relevant recommendation had indeed been rejected by the government: see P.M.N., *op. cit.*, p. 366.

[58] See, *e.g., Smoker v. London Fire and Civil Defence Authority* [1991] 2 A. C. 502 (*Parry v. Cleaver* [1970] A.C. 1), *R. v. Reid* [1992] 1 W.L.R. 793 (*R. v. Laurence* [1982] A. C. 510).

Harris[59] suggests that an analysis of the case law reveals certain underlying considerations. First, the House must be convinced that it is in a position to substitute a ruling which will make a "net improvement in the law"[60] secondly, the House will normally decline to overrule a decision where there are no new arguments not considered in the earlier case and no material change in circumstances; thirdly, it is a reason not to overrule a decision that people have regulated their affairs in reliance on it; fourthly, importance may be attached to the fact that legislation appears to have been enacted on the assumption that the impugned decision represents the law; fifthly, there is some support for the view that the House should not overrule an earlier decision where the issue is moot, the ruling on it making no difference to the outcome of the present case.

In *Jones v. Secretary of State for Social Services*,[61] Lord Simon of Glaisdale suggested that consideration should be given to the introduction, preferably by statute, of a power for the House of Lords to overrule a decision "prospectively" (*i.e.* for future cases only). Such a power is exercised by the United States Supreme Court[62] and in several states in the U.S.A. This involves the express recognition that the notion that judges do not make law is a fiction, but avoids the undesirable consequences of retrospectively upsetting established arrangements.[63] There are difficulties in choosing the date of transition: for example, should the litigant who has successfully argued that a case should be overruled be entitled to the retrospective effect of that decision, notwithstanding the general determination that the rule should be changed prospectively? If the answer is no, litigants will have little incentive to mount the necessary arguments. Lord Devlin has opposed the general idea of prospective overruling on the ground that it "turns judges into undisguised legislators."[64] The House of Lords changed a rule of *practice* (as distinct from a rule of *law*) prospectively in *Connelly v. D.P.P.*[65]

In practice a decision of the House of Lords on an appeal from Scotland or Northern Ireland will be regarded as binding on English courts lower in the hierarchy on points where the law of the two countries is the same.[66]

8. THE PRIVY COUNCIL

Decisions of the Judicial Committee of the Privy Council are not technically binding on English courts except in respect of matters where an appeal lies from

---

[59] Cross and Harris (1991), pp. 135–143, "Towards principles of overruling—when should a final Court of Appeal second guess?" (1990) 10 O.J.L.S. 135 and (1991) 11 O.J.L.S. See also A. Paterson, *The Law Lords* (1982), pp. 156–167, identifying criteria that reflected the dominant consensus of the Law Lords in the mid-1970s.

[60] Cross and Harris (1991), p. 138.

[61] [1972] A.C. 944, 1026–7. See also his Lordship's statement in *Miliangos v. George Frank (Textiles) Ltd* [1976] A.C. 443, 490, and Lord Diplock, [1972] A.C. 944, 1015.

[62] See, *e.g. Mapp v. Ohio* 367 U.S. 643 (1961); *Linkletter v. Walker* 381 U.S. 618 (1965); *Miranda v. Arizona* 384 U.S. 436 (1966).

[63] See generally W. Friedmann, (1966) 29 M.L.R. 593; M. D. A. Freeman, (1973) 26 C.L.P. 166; A. Nichol, (1976) 39 M.L.R. 542; Cross and Harris (1991), pp. 228–232.

[64] Lord Devlin, "Judges and Lawmakers" (1976) 39 M.L.R. 11, 20: reprinted in *The Judge* (1979), p. 12.

[65] [1964] A.C. 1254.

[66] Cross and Harris (1991), p. 22, *Heyman v. Darwins Ltd* [1942] A.C. 356, 401 (Lord Porter); *Glasgow Corporation v. Central Land Board* 1956 S.C. (H.L.) 1: where the law of "crown

such a court to the Privy Council.[67] They may, however, be highly persuasive.[68] The Privy Council will normally follow its own previous decisions, but is not bound to do so.[69] It is not bound to follow decisions of the House of Lords on common law issues, although the latter have great persuasive authority: the common law may develop differently in different parts of the Commonwealth.[70] A House of Lords decision on the interpretation of recent legislation common to England and another part of the Commonwealth will however, be treated as binding.[71]

9. THE COURT OF JUSTICE OF THE EUROPEAN COMMUNITIES

The decisions of this court on matters of Community law are binding on English courts up to and including the House of Lords.[72] It tends to follow its own previous decisions, although it is not bound to do so.[73] The Court of First Instance is expressly bound by decisions of the Court of Justice on points of law in cases referred back to the Court of First Instance.[74] Otherwise, it will regard itself as bound by decisions of the Court of Justice and will not lightly depart from its own previous decisions.[75]

10. TRIBUNALS

Where there is a hierarchy of tribunals, the decisions of the appellate tribunals will bind lower tribunals. For example, social security appeal tribunals must follow decisions of the social security commissioners (formerly known as the

---

privilege'' was held to be different in the two countries; *Re Tuck's Settlement Trusts, Public Trustee v. Tuck* [1978] Ch. 49, 61 (Lord Denning M.R.).

[67] *e.g.* in ecclesiastical and prize matters: *Combe v. Edwards* (1877) 2 P.D. 354. In *Port Line Ltd v. Ben Line Steamers Ltd* [1958] 2 Q.B. 146, Diplock J. declined to follow a Privy Council decision that was in his view wrongly decided.

[68] See, *e.g.* above, p. 433, below, p. 447.

[69] *Gideon Nkambule v. R.* [1950] A.C. 379; *Fatuma Binti Mohamed Bin Salim v. Mohamed Bin Salim* [1952] A.C. 1; *Baker v. The Queen* [1975] A.C. 774, 787–788.

[70] *e.g.* on the right to punitive damages in tort: the Privy Council in *Australian Consolidated Press Ltd v. Uren* [1969] 1 A.C. 590 did not follow the House of Lords decision in *Rookes v. Barnard* [1964] A.C. 1129; and on the liability of a local authority in respect of the inspection of buildings in the course of construction the Privy Council in *Invercargill City Council v. Hamlin* [1996] 2 W.L.R. 367 did not follow the decision of the House of Lords in *Murphy v. Brentwood District Council* [1991] 1 A.C. 398 (above, p. 441).

[71] *de Lasala v. de Lasala* [1980] A.C. 546.

[72] See above, pp. 331–344; European Communities Act 1972, s.3(1).

[73] Cases 2, 8, 29, 30/62, *Da Costa en Schaake NV v. Nederlandse Belasting-administratie* [1963] E.C.R. 31; L. N. Brown and T. Kennedy, *The Court of Justice of the European Communities* (4th ed., 1994) Chap. 16; T. Koopmans in D. O'Keefe and H. G. Schermers (eds.), *Essays in European Law and Integration* (1982); A. G. Toth, "The authority of judgments of the European Court of Justice: binding force and legal effect" (1984) 4 Y.E.L. 1.

[74] Statute of the Court of Justice, art. 54, second para. (as amended to take account of the establishment of the Court of First Instance).

[75] Brown and Kennedy (1994), pp. 350–352.

national insurance commissioners).[76] Tribunals are not permitted to lay down precedents binding on themselves,[77] the emphasis, in theory at least, being on deciding each case on its own facts. However, the case law of some tribunals is systematically reported[78] and general principles tend to become established,[79] and the "essential differences in practice from, say, the House of Lords or the Court of Appeal . . . are not as marked as one might think."[80] In the context of social security appeals, a Tribunal of Commissioners has held[81] that in determining whether to be bound by a decision of a previous Tribunal, it should adopt and adapt the principles laid down in the 1966 *Practice Statement*[82] concerning the House of Lords, and not the principles laid down in *Young v. Bristol Aeroplane Co. Ltd.*[83]

11. The Nature of Rules of Binding Precedent

Apart from the 1966 *Practice Statement*, propositions as to the binding effects of previous decisions have been contained in the judgments of decided cases. It has been pointed out that such propositions cannot form part of the *ratio* of a case as they are "necessarily irrelevant to the issues of law and fact that have to be decided by the court."[84] Professor Cross[85] argued that this only seems applicable to statements of higher courts about the way in which lower courts should behave,[86] but that in any event statements about the rules of precedent are statements about the courts' own practice which fall outside the *ratio–obiter* distinction. The 1966 *Practice Statement* owed its validity "to the inherent power of any court to regulate its own practice."[87] The possibility that the Court of Appeal might change the rule that it is bound by its own previous decisions

---

[76] *R.(I) 12/75* (Tribunal of Commissioners); N. J. Wikeley, *Ogus, Barendt and Wikely's The Law of Social Security* (4th ed., 1995), pp. 680–681. A single Commissioner should follow a decision of a Tribunal of Commissioners on a point of legal principle unless there are compelling reasons why he should not: *ibid.*; *R.(U) 4/88(T)*.

[77] *Merchandise Transport Ltd v. British Transport Commission* [1962] 2 Q.B. 173, C.A., in relation to the Transport Tribunal.

[78] In the context of social security, the Commissioners have emphasised that adjudicating officers and tribunals are bound by unreported Commissioners' decisions as well as reported: *R.(I) 12/75; R. (SB) 22/86.*

[79] J. A. Farmer, *Tribunals and Government* (1974), Chap. 3, pp. 171–180.

[80] *ibid.* p. 175.

[81] *R.(U) 4/88.*

[82] Above, pp. 438–443.

[83] Above, pp. 427–436.

[84] Glanville Williams, (1954) 70 L.Q.R. 469, 471; *cf.* Diplock L.J. in *Boys v. Chaplin* [1968] 2 K.B. 1,35.

[85] "The House of Lords and the Rules of Precedent" in P. M. S. Hacker and J. Raz (eds.), *Law, Morality and Society* (1977), pp. 144–160. For the contrary argument that pronouncements on precedent do indeed establish rules of law, see P. J. Evans, [1982] C.L.J. 162, criticised by L. Goldstein, [1984] C.L.J. 88, with a reply by Evans, *ibid.* p. 108. For the argument that they establish rules of *customary* law, see P. Aldridge, (1984) 47 M.L.R. 187. For the argument that the 1966 *Practice Statement* established, or modified, a constitutional convention, see Lord Simon of Glaisdale in *R. v. Knuller* [1973] A.C. 435, at p. 485 and A. R. Blackshield, in L. Goldstein (ed.), *Judicial Precedent* (1987), Chap. 5.

[86] *ibid.* p. 154.

[87] *ibid.* p. 157; Salmon L.J. in *Gallie v. Lee* [1969] 2 Ch. 17, 49; Lord Denning M.R. in *Davis v. Johnson* [1979] A.C. 264, 281; Lord Salmon in *Davis v. Johnson* (above p. 435).

by a similar practice statement has been mooted.[88] However, Lord Simon of Glaisdale asserted that any change would require legislation,[89] Cumming-Bruce L.J. accepted loyally that the constitutional functions of the House of Lords include that of declaring with authority the extent to which the Court of Appeal is bound by its previous decisions,[90] and Lord Denning in any event failed to persuade his colleagues that a change would be desirable.[91]

E. PERSUASIVE AUTHORITIES[92]

Precedents that are not technically binding may be cited as persuasive authorities. The extent to which a precedent will be persuasive may depend on a variety of factors including the status of the court, the country in which it was located, the reputation of the judge, whether the relevant proposition formed part of the *ratio*, whether the judgment was considered or *ex tempore*[93] and whether the judge in the later case agrees with it. Thus the attention of the court may be drawn to the *ratio* of a decision of an English court lower in the hierarchy, to *obiter dicta*, to a dissenting judgment, to a decision of the Privy Council or to a court abroad.

Great weight will be attached to considered statements by the House of Lords whatever their technical standing. For example, in *Hedley Byrne & Co. Ltd v. Heller and Partners Ltd*,[94] the House of Lords held that the existence of a special relationship could give rise to a duty to take care in giving information or advice; breach of the duty could in turn lead to an action for damages in respect of purely economic losses. The Court of Appeal had held that such a duty could not arise, following its earlier decision in *Candler v. Crane, Christmas & Co.*[95] The House overruled the *Candler* decision and endorsed the dissenting judgment in that case by Denning L.J. Having found that a duty of care *did* arise as the plaintiffs claimed, the House nonetheless found for the *defendants* on the ground that they had effectively disclaimed responsibility for the statements in question. There was much debate on the issue whether the observations concerning the duty of care were *obiter*.[96] Cairns J. in *W. B. Anderson and Sons Ltd v. Rhodes*[97] regarded such a suggestion as "unrealistic":

"When five members of the House of Lords have all said, after close examination of the authorities, that a certain type of tort exists, I think that a judge of first instance should proceed on the basis that it does exist without

---

[88] *ibid.*

[89] *Miliangos v. George Frank (Textiles) Ltd* [1976] A.C. 443, 470.

[90] *Davis v. Johnson* [1979] A.C. 264, 311.

[91] See above, pp. 433–434.

[92] See R. Bronaugh, "Persuasive precedent" in L. Goldstein (ed.), *Judicial Precedent* (1987), Chap. 8.

[93] Lord Russell of Killowen has suggested that unreserved judgments should be approached with "great caution:" *op. cit.* p. 420, n. 50; *cf.* Lord Reid in *Haley v. London Electricity Board* [1965] A.C. 778, 792.

[94] [1964] A.C. 465.

[95] [1951] 2 K.B. 164.

[96] See W. V. H. Rogers, *Winfield and Jolowicz on Tort* (13th ed., 1989), p. 274, n. 97.

[97] [1967] 2 All E.R. 850.

pausing to embark on an investigation whether what was said was necessary to the ultimate decision."[98]

Similarly, it became accepted that solicitors acting as advocates were entitled to the same immunity from legal action as barristers, notwithstanding that the view had been expressed in decisions of the House of Lords concerning barristers.[99]

The "neighbour principle" expounded by Lord Atkin in *Donoghue v. Stevenson*[1] can be regarded as part of the *ratio* of his speech, but not as part of the *ratio* of the House of Lords as a whole.[2] Nevertheless the principle was influential in subsequent decisions which extended the scope of the tort of negligence,[3] although the most recent decisions in the area have emphasised that it should be used cautiously and is not the sole determinant of the existence of a duty of care.[4] Decisions of the Privy Council may be strongly persuasive, particularly now that membership of the Judicial Committee is mainly drawn from Lords of Appeal.[5] The Privy Council decision in *The Wagon Mound (No. 1)*[6] is accepted to be the leading authority on remoteness of damage in the tort of negligence, and has been applied in preference to the decision of the Court of Appeal in *Re Polemis*.[7]

The desirability of uniformity between Scottish and English courts on points common to both systems has often been stressed, particularly on the construction of statutes and revenue and taxation matters.[8] The citation of overseas authorities seems to be increasingly common.[9] Lord Denning would not, however, in practice have followed a decision of the deputy magistrate of East Tonga in preference to six decisions of the House of Lords.[10] There have been complaints that counsel, particularly in busy appellate courts, cite too many authorities both English and foreign[11]; at the same time, counsel owes a duty to the court to cite all relevant authorities whether for or against him.

---

[98] *ibid.* p. 857.
[99] For the present position, see above, pp. 174–176.
[1] [1932] A.C. 562, 580.
[2] Two of the five members dissented and the other two did not expressly concur with Lord Atkin's formulation: see R. F. V. Heuston, (1957) 20 M.L.R. 1, 5–9.
[3] See, *e.g. Hedley Byrne & Co. Ltd v. Heller and Partners Ltd* [1964] A.C. 465.
[4] See, *e.g. Murphy v. Brentwood District Council* [1991] 1 A.C. 398.
[5] Similarly, decisions of the House of Lords and Court of Appeal are of high persuasive authority in the courts of the Isle of Man, given that the Privy Council is the final court of appeal from a Manx court: *Frankland v. The Queen* [1987] A.C. 576, P.C.
[6] *Overseas Tankship (U.K.) Ltd v. Morts Dock Engineering Co. Ltd* [1961] A.C. 388.
[7] *Re Polemis and Furness, Withy & Co. Ltd* [1921] 2 K.B. 560: see *Doughty v. Turner Manufacturing Co. Ltd* [1964] 1 Q.B. 518, C.A.; *Smith v. Leech Brain & Co. Ltd* [1962] 2 Q.B. 405, 415, where Lord Parker C.J. indicated *obiter* that the *Wagon Mound* case enabled a trial judge to follow other decisions of the Court of Appeal prior to *Polemis*. The test for remoteness is now whether the kind of damage was reasonably foreseeable: the former test was whether the damage was the direct consequence of the defendant's conduct. *Cf.* Robert Goff J. in *I Congreso del Partido* [1978] Q.B. 500, 517–519.
[8] See, *e.g. Abbott v. Philbin (Inspector of Taxes)* [1960] Ch. 27, rvsd. [1961] A.C. 352; *Westward Television Ltd v. Hart (Inspector of Taxes)* [1969] 1 Ch. 201, 212; *Secretary of State for Employment and Productivity v. Clarke, Chapman & Co. Ltd.* [1971] 1 W.L.R. 1094, 1102.
[9] See R. J. C. Munday, (1978) 14 J.S.P.T.L. (N.S.) 201, 203–207.
[10] See the (regrettably) fictional report of *Grenouille v. National Union of Seamen* reproduced in Denning, *The Family Story* (1981), pp. 219–220.
[11] See, *e.g.* Lawton L.J., (1980) 14 L.T. 163, 166.

Textbooks may be cited as authorities although they can never be binding.[12] Some treatises have long been accepted as authoritative guides to the law in previous centuries, including the Abridgments of the Year Books[13] compiled by Fitzherbert and Brooke, the treatise known as "Glanvill" dating from the late twelfth century, Bracton's *De Legibus et Consuetudinibus Angliae* from the thirteenth, Littleton's *Tenures* from the fourteenth, Fitzherbert's *Nature Brevium*, Coke's *Institutes of the Laws of England* first published in 1628, eighteenth century works on criminal law by Hale, Hawkins and Foster[14] and Blackstone's *Commentaries on the Laws of England* first published in 1765–69. These works are not cited often today, the ones on criminal law perhaps being referred to most commonly.[15] It used to be convention that living authors could not be cited as authorities, although their words could be adopted by counsel as part of his or her argument,[16] on the doubtful ground that while alive the author might change his or her mind.[17] This convention is no longer observed,[18] and books and articles by authors both living and dead are commonly cited.[19] In appropriate cases reference may also be made to principles of Roman law, and especially, in that regard, Justinian's *Digest*.[20]

F. DISTINGUISHING

A precedent, whether persuasive or binding, need not be applied or followed if it can be "distinguished:" *i.e.* there is a material distinction between the facts of the precedent case and the case in question. What counts as a "material" distinction is obviously crucial. The judge in the later case is expected to explain why the distinction is such as to justify the application of a different rule. If the distinction is spurious, the judge may be criticised or reversed or, if the case distinguished is generally regarded as a bad precedent, applauded for his or her boldness. There is no test or set of tests for whether a distinction is legally relevant; it all depends upon the circumstances of the case.

An example is provided by *R. v. Secretary of State for the Environment, ex p. Ostler*.[21] In 1956, the House of Lords in *Smith v. East Elloe R.D.C.*[22] ruled

[12] *Cordell v. Second Clanfield Properties Ltd* [1969] 2 Ch. 9, 16: Megarry J. in relation to Sir Robert Megarry and H. W. R. Wade, *The Law of Real Property*.

[13] See below, p. 452.

[14] Sir Matthew Hale, *The History of the Pleas of the Crown*, published posthumously in 1736 but written in the previous century; William Hawkins, *Pleas of the Crown* (1716); Sir Michael Foster, *Crown Cases* and *Crown Law* (1762).

[15] See, *e.g. Button v. D.P.P.* [1966] A.C. 591; *R. v. Merriman* [1973] A.C. 584 (*Hale and Hawkins*).

[16] See, *e.g* Vaughan Williams L.J. in *Greenlands Ltd v. Wilmshurst* (1913) 29 T.L.R. 685, 687.

[17] Lord Reid, (1972) 12 J.S.P.T.L. (N.S.) 22. This convention was the basis of somewhat leaden jokes to the effect that certain celebrated works were "fortunately" not works of authority.

[18] See *Halsbury's Laws of England* (4th ed.) Vol. 26, para. 587.

[19] For example, in criminal law cases references to books by Glanville Williams and Sir John Smith and B. Hogan are frequent; in administrative law, Sir William Wade and C. F. Forsyth, *Administrative Law*, (7th ed., 1994) and de Smith, Woolf and Jowell, *Judicial Review of Administrative Action* (5th ed., 1995) are similarly authoritative. See the splendid story by A. Arden, [1980] Conv. 454, 458 (review of the 4th ed. of *de Smith*).

[20] See, *e.g. Coggs v. Bernard* (1703) 2 Ld. Raym. 909 and *Dalton v. Angus* (1881) 6 App. Cas.740.

[21] [1977] Q.B. 122.

[22] [1956] A.C. 736.

that a provision[23] that the validity of a compulsory purchase order should not be questioned in any legal proceedings, other than a statutory application to quash made within six weeks, meant what it said: an action to impugn an order on the ground of fraud could not be brought some six years later. However, in *Anisminic Ltd v. The Foreign Compensation Commission*[24] the House held that section 4 of the Foreign Compensation Act 1950, which provided that a determination by the Commission "shall not be called in question in any court of law", was not effective to render immune from judicial review a purported determination that was in truth a nullity and thus not a "determination" at all. The decision in *Smith v. East Elloe R.D.C.* was adversely criticised but not overruled. In *Ostler* the Court of Appeal was faced with an ouster clause of the kind at issue in *Smith v. East Elloe R.D.C.*, and it followed *Smith* in preference to *Anisminic*, which was distinguished on a variety of grounds. For example, the point was taken that section 4 of the 1950 Act purported to exclude judicial review altogether whereas the provision in *Ostler* was more akin to a limitation period in that it excluded review only after a six-week period. It was said that *Anisminic* concerned a "judicial" decision and *Ostler* an "administrative" one. Their Lordships were not, however, unanimous as to their reasons, and Lord Denning M.R. subsequently indicated extra-judicially that he no longer regarded most of his own as sound.[25]

G. PRECEDENT AND STATUTORY INTERPRETATION

A decision on a question of the construction of a statute is binding to the same extent as a decision on other kinds of question.[26] Thus it is applicable in cases concerning the same words in the same Act and "in all cases which do not provide substantial relevant differences."[27] The same words appearing in a different statute may be interpreted differently, although a decision on the construction of a particular set of words may be used as a guide when other statutes dealing with the same or a similar subject-matter are considered.[28] If words which have been the subject of construction by a court are re-enacted by Parliament without alteration, a court will be very slow to overrule that decision but not always unwilling to do so.[29] Moreover Lord Wilberforce has stated that[30]:

"Self-contained statutes, whether consolidating previous law, or so doing with the amendments, should be interpreted, if reasonably possible, without

---

[23] Acquisition of Land (Authorisation Procedure) Act 1946, Sched. 1, Part IV, paras.15, 16.

[24] [1969] 2 A.C. 147.

[25] *The Discipline of Law* (1979), pp. 108–109.

[26] *Per* Lord Reid in *Goodrich v. Paisner* [1957] A.C. 65, 88 and *London Transport Executive v. Betts* [1959] A.C. 211, 232.

[27] *Goodrich v. Paisner, ibid.*

[28] *ibid.*; Lord Upjohn in *Ogden Industries Pty Ltd v. Lucas* [1970] A.C. 113, 127; *R. v. Freeman* [1970] 1 W.L.R. 788 (meaning of "firearm" in successive Firearms Acts).

[29] *Royal Crown Derby Porcelain Ltd v. Raymond Russell* [1949] 2 K.B. 417, 429, *per* Denning L. J.; *cf. R. v. Bow Road JJ., ex p. Adedigba* [1968] 2 Q.B. 572.

[30] *Farrell v. Alexander* [1977] A.C. 59, 73. Lord Simon and Lord Edmund-Davies agreed with this approach *cf.* above pp. 382–383.

recourse to antecedents,[31] and that recourse should only be had when there is a real and substantial difficulty or ambiguity which classical methods of construction cannot resolve.''

H. RATIO DECIDENDI AND RES JUDICATA

In its wider meaning the term "judgment" is used to cover the whole of the judge's pronouncement after the arguments of each side have been heard (*e.g.* as in "I will deliver my judgment after lunch"). In its narrower meaning it is used to cover the order of the court as distinct from the reasons for it (*e.g.* "There will be judgment for the plaintiff for £500"). Assuming the order lies within the judge's jurisdiction it is binding on the parties (*res judicata*). They may not reopen the issue that has just been determined, unless a statute has provided for an appeal.[32] Thus the court's *order* is binding on the *parties* under the *res judicata* doctrine; the *ratio decidendi* is binding on other *courts* in accordance with the principles outlined above under the doctrine of binding precedent. A startling illustration of the distinction was provided by the following series of cases. A testator, John Arkle Waring, left annuities to Mr Howard and Mrs Louie Burton-Butler "free of income tax". In 1942 the Court of Appeal in *Re Waring, Westminster Bank Ltd v. Awdry*,[33] on an appeal in which Howard was a party, held that income tax had to be deducted. Louie was not a party as she was in an enemy occupied country. Leave to appeal to the House of Lords was refused. Four years later the House of Lords in *Berkeley v. Berkeley*[34] overruled the *Awdry* case. Subsequently, Jenkins J. held that the *Awdry* case was *res judicata* so far as Howard was concerned notwithstanding that its *ratio* had been overruled in *Berkeley v. Berkeley* and that Louie's annuity would be dealt with in accordance with the latter case.[35]

I. LAW REPORTS[36]

(a) Introduction

Any legal system that is based to any significant extent upon judicial precedent requires an effective system whereby those precedents are reported and indexed. In theory, a case may be cited as a precedent even it if has not been reported.

---

[31] *i.e.* the history of the provisions and the cases decided on them.

[32] See Chap. 17. In the case of courts and tribunals with a jurisdiction limited by statute there is also the possibility of judicial review under the *ultra vires* doctrine where the jurisdiction has been exceeded or abused.

[33] [1942] Ch. 426.

[34] [1946] A.C. 555.

[35] *Re Waring, Westminster Bank v. Burton-Butler* [1948] Ch. 221.

[36] See generally Sweet & Maxwell's *Guide to Law Reports and Statutes* (4th ed., 1962); J. Dane and P. A. Thomas, *How to use a law library* (2nd ed., 1987), Chap. 2; W. W. S. Breem, in E. M. Moys (ed.), *Manual of Law Librarianship* (2nd ed., 1987), Chap. 4: "Primary sources: law reports."

In practice, comparatively few cases are referred to in textbooks or cited in court unless they have been reported in one of the series of published law reports, although such references seem to be becoming more common.[37] Occasionally a judge has referred to an unreported case with which he was concerned as counsel or judge.[38] Indexed transcripts of all unreported cases in the Court of Appeal (Civil Division) are kept in the Supreme Court Library[39] and some are listed in *Current Law* and copies of unreported House of Lords decisions are kept in the House of Lords Records Office. Thousands of unreported cases decided since January 1, 1980, including all decisions of the House of Lords and Court of Appeal (Civil Division), are included on *Lexis*. Until recently, the only condition for admission of a report has been that it has been vouched for by a barrister present during the whole time when the judgment was given.[40] However, in *Roberts Petroleum Ltd v. Kenny Ltd*,[41] the House of Lords stated that in future it would decline to allow transcripts of unreported judgments of the Court of Appeal (Civil Division) to be cited in the House without leave; such leave would only be granted on counsel giving an assurance that the transcript contained some relevant principle of law that was binding on the Court of Appeal and of which the substance, as distinct from the mere choice of phraseology, was not to be found in any judgment of that court that had appeared in one of the generalised or specialised series of reports.

(b) A modern law report

A full law report today commonly includes the following information:
The names of the parties[42]; the court in which the case was decided; the name of the judge or judges; the date or dates of the hearing; the headnote (a summary of the decision prepared by the reporter)[43]; lists of the cases discussed and cited;

---

[37] R. J. C. Munday, (1978) 14 J.S.P.T.L. (N.S.) 201, 207–216.

[38] *e.g. Wilkinson v. Downton* [1897] 2 Q.B. 57, 61; *Harling v. Eddy* [1951] 2 K.B. 739, 746 (Denning L.J.).

[39] From 1951, an official note has been made of all Court of Appeal (Civil Division) decisions (see (1951) 95 S.J. 266). A microfiche edition of the transcripts 1951–1980 is available from HMSO (see V. Tunkel, (1986) 136 N.L.J., 1045). Transcripts of decisions of the Court of Appeal (Criminal Division) from 1960 are held by the Criminal Appeal Office in the Royal Courts of Justice (Breem, in Moys (1987), p. 143). The arrangements for transcribing cases are considered by Breem, *op. cit.*, pp. 144–146, and S. Cole, (1988) 19 *The Law Librarian* 89.

[40] See *Parkinson v. Parkinson* [1939] P. 346, 348, 351–352; *Birtwistle v. Tweedale* [1954] 1 W.L.R. 190n: *Estates Gazette* report not admitted. *Cf. Baker v. Sims* [1959] 1 Q.B. 114 and *Smith v. Wyles* [1959] 1 Q.B. 164. A report by a person who is a solicitor or has a Supreme Court qualification (*i.e.* a right of audience in relation to all proceedings in the Supreme Court) has the same authority as if it had been by a barrister: Courts and Legal Services Act 1990, s.115.

[41] [1983] 2 A.C. 192. See R. J. C. Munday, (1983) 80 L. S. Gaz 1337; N. H. Andrews, (1985) 5 L.S. 205. Note the critical response of F. A. R. Bennion (*ibid.* p. 1635) and N. Harrison (Managing Director of the company which markets *Lexis*), (1984) 81 L. S. Gaz. 257. It is uncertain whether the Court of Appeal will adopt a similar stance, but note the remarks of Sir John Donaldson M.R. in *Stanley v. International Harvester Co. of Great Britain Ltd, The Times*, February 7, 1983. The point is not mentioned in *Practice Direction (Court of Appeal: Citation of Authority)* [1995] 1 W.L.R. 1096, which sets out practice for the Court of Appeal.

[42] Appeals to the House of Lords have since 1974 carried the same title as in the court of first instance: *Procedure Direction* [1974] 1 W.L.R. 305. Previously, the name of the appellant appeared first.

[43] The headnote may be inaccurate (see, *e.g. Young v. Bristol Aeroplane Co. Ltd*, above, p. 431) although modern headnotes are generally reliable. It may include a summary of the facts or simply be the reporter's version of the *ratio decidendi*.

the previous history of the litigation, including a summary of the claims made
and the result of proceedings in lower courts; the facts[44]; the names of counsel;
the arguments of counsel[45]; an indication of whether judgment is reserved by
the inclusion of the expression *Cur. adv. vult*[46]; the judgment or judgments[47];
the order of the court and an indication of whether leave to appeal is granted
or refused; the names of the solicitors; the name of the barrister who reports
the case.

(c) Law reporting[48]

The earliest law reports were contained in the "Year Books" compiled annually
between the thirteenth and sixteenth centuries. These reports concentrated upon
points of procedure and pleading rather than the final decisions of the courts,
and were written first in Norman French and later in "law French" (an amalgam
of English, French and Latin).[49] These are today mainly of interest to legal
historians. Between the sixteenth and nineteenth centuries a large number of
"private" or "nominate" reports appeared. Most were named after the reporter.
They varied widely in their style and content, their accuracy and their reputation.[50] Some, such as those of Coke, Plowden and Saunders were of high
authority. Others were regarded as of little value.[51] Some were in law French;
most were in English. The focus of attention switched from the pleadings to
the Court's decision and the best reports included the full reasons. The first to
be published in more or less the form we have today, although not verbatim
reports, were Burrow's reports of the eighteenth century. The first that regularly
published reports of newly decided cases were Durnford and East's "Term
Reports". The private reports are cited by the name, usually abbreviated, of the
reporter or the reports, the volume and the page.[52] The year is not technically
part of the reference but is normally included.[53] Most of the cases in the private
reports were reprinted in *The English Reports* published in 176 volumes between
1900 and 1930. There was also a series entitled *The Revised Reports* edited by
Sir Frederick Pollock and included such cases reported between 1785 and 1865
as were "still of practical utility".[54]

The patchwork coverage of private enterprise law reports was seen to be
unsatisfactory.[55] In 1865 a council consisting of the Attorney-General, the Solicitor-General, two barristers from each of the inns of court, two sergeants and
two solicitors was formed; in 1870 it was incorporated as "The Incorporated

---

[44] The facts stated in the judgments may be left unedited or the reporter may set out the facts
separately.

[45] These are only regularly printed in a few sets of reports such as The Law Reports and Lloyds'
Law Reports. Interjections from the bench may also be included.

[46] *Curia advisari vult*: "the court wishes to consider the matter."

[47] In full reports these are printed verbatim, in some, such as in the Criminal Law Review and the
Solicitors' Journal, only summaries are given.

[48] See J. H. Baker, *An Introduction to English Legal History* (3rd ed., 1990), pp. 204–214; L. W.
Abbott, *Law Reporting in England 1485–1585* (1973), reviewed by Baker, [1974] C.L.J. 156; P.
Reeves, (1989) 86 L. S. Gaz. July 26.

[49] See J. H. Baker, *Manual of Law French* (1979).

[50] C. K. Allen, *Law in the Making* (7th ed., 1964), pp. 221–232.

[51] *e.g.* Barnardiston: see R. G. Logan, (1987) 18 *The Law Librarian* 87.

[52] *e.g. Coggs v. Bernard* (1703) 2 Ld. Raym. 909 (Lord Raymond).

[53] In round brackets. Where the year is part of a reference it is given in square brackets.

[54] See R. G. Logan, (1982) 13 *The Law Librarian* 23.

[55] See W. T. S. Daniel, *The History and Origin of "The Law Reports"* [1884].

Council of Law Reporting for England and Wales" with as its primary object:

"the preparation and publication in a convenient form, at a moderate price, and under gratuitous professional control of Reports of Judicial Decisions of the Superior and Appellate Courts of England."

The Council is not funded by the state and is non-profit-making.[56] Its reports are semi-official in that judgments appearing in the Law Reports are revised by the judges, and that this series should be cited in preference to any alternative.[57] The corrections may make the report conform to what was actually said; on occasion a report is changed to conform to what the judge meant to say, which is rather more controversial.[58] There have been three series of the Law Reports: the first from 1865 to 1875,[59] the second from 1875 to 1890[60] and the third from 1891 to date.[61] The Incorporated Council also publishes the (unrevised) "Weekly Law Reports" and the "Industrial Cases Reports". There are a number of series of specialist official reports including the "Reports of Tax Cases" published under the direction of the Inland Revenue, the "Reports of Patent, Design and Trade Mark Cases" published by the Patent Office and the "Immigration Appeal Reports" published by HMSO. There are also a number of series associated more obviously with private enterprise, of which the "All England Law Reports" is a general series rivalling the Weekly Law Reports.[62] The trend is for an increasing number of cases to be reported and for new series of reports to be started,[63] with concomitant problems of expense for law libraries and practitioners, duplication[64] and pressure on research time. Brief law reports also appear in an increasing number of daily newspapers.[65] These are usually

---

[56] *Incorporated Council of Law Reporting v. Att.-Gen.* [1972] Ch. 73. The Court of Appeal held that the Council's purposes were charitable.

[57] *Westminster Bank Executors and Trustee Co. (Channel Islands) Ltd v. National Bank of Greece S.A. (Practice Note)* [1970] 1 W.L.R. 1400; *Bray v. Best* [1989] 1 W.L.R. 167, 169; *Practice Direction (Law Reports: Citation)* [1991] 1 W.L.R. 1.

[58] See, *e.g. Ghani v. Jones* [1970] 1 Q.B. 693; R. M. Jackson, [1970] C.L.J. 1, 3; (1969) 119 N.L.J. 1011; (1970) 120 N.L.J. 423.

[59] *e.g. Osgood v. Nelson* (1872) L.R. 5 H.L. 636. A reference to this series normally includes the year of the decision (in round brackets as it is not technically part of the reference); the letters "L.R."; the volume number of the relevant series; the abbreviation for that series (there were 11 in all, running concurrently); and the page number.

[60] *e.g. Huth v. Clarke* (1890) 25 Q.B.D. 391. A reference no longer includes the letters "L.R." and there are six series: one for Appeal Cases and one for each of the five divisions of the High Court (reduced to three in 1888).

[61] *e.g. Ridge v. Baldwin* [1964] A.C. 40. A reference includes the year of the *report*, not the decision, in square brackets; the series (A.C.; Q.B.; Ch.; Fam.) and the page number.

[62] The criteria for the selection of cases for reporting in the Law Reports and the All England Law Reports are considered by N. H. Andrews, "Reporting Case Law" (1985) 5 L.S. 205, 225–231, based on information supplied by the editors of these series. See also, F. D. Cumbrae-Stewart, "The aim and form of law reports" (1985) 59 A.L.J. 616.

[63] R. J. C. Munday, (1978) 14 J.S.P.T.L. (N.S.) 201–203. See also D. Milman, (1987) 8 Co. Law. 242, noting several new series of company law reports.

[64] A glance at Sweet & Maxwell's *Current Law Citator* will confirm this.

[65] *The Times* has printed law reports for over 100 years. It has been joined by the *Financial Times, Guardian, Independent* and *Daily Telegraph*: see M. Findlay, *The Law Magazine*, March 18, 1989, p. 31. These reports are indexed in the *Daily Law Reports Index* published by Legal Information Resources Ltd, which commenced publication in 1988 (with fortnightly, quarterly and annual cumulations).

printed shortly after judgment has been given, and are compiled by barristers and are so citable in court.[66]

The system of law reporting was examined by a committee which reported in 1940.[67] The committee did not favour any radical change, such as giving the Incorporated Council a monopoly of reporting or the licensing of reporters. The majority rejected the proposals of A. L. Goodhart, who wrote a dissenting report, that a shorthand writer should take down the text of every judgment, that a transcript be sent to the judge for correction and that the corrected report be filed in the court records and made available to any reporter or member of the public for a small fee. The reasons put forward were the cost, the extra burden on the judges and the fact that almost every decision of importance was already reported: "What remains is less likely to be a treasure house than a rubbish heap in which a jewel will rarely, if ever, be discovered."[68]

Decisions of the Court of Justice of the European Communities are reported in the *European Court Reports*, an official series, and in the *Common Market Law Reports*, a private enterprise series, which includes in addition reports of the decisions of national courts on Community law matters.

The most significant developments in the near future will be in the field of the computerisation of statutes, statutory instruments and law reports.[69] Butterworths offer the American *Lexis* system, which includes English, Scottish and American materials[70]; and some European and Commonwealth materials. An increasing amount of material is also becoming available on CD-Rom and, particularly in the case of North American and Commonwealth countries, the Internet.

[66] They must be distinguished from summaries of cases in the "news" pages of *The Sun* (etc.).
[67] Report of the Law Reporting Committee (HMSO, 1940).
[68] *ibid.* p. 20.
[69] See generally G. Bull, (1980) 11 *The Law Librarian* 34–40; *Poly Law Review*, Vol. 5, No. 2, Spring 1980; C. M. Campbell (ed.), *Data Processing and the Law* (1984) (introduction); and "Computers in Legal Work" (1988) 39 N.I.L.Q. 1.
[70] (1979) 130 N.L.J. 507.

PART II

SOLVING LEGAL PROBLEMS

CHAPTER 8

PROBLEMS ABOUT PROBLEMS

WE encounter a difficulty at the beginning of this part of the book by directing our attention to the solution of "legal" problems. How should such problems be defined? Are there distinctions to be drawn between legal problems and social problems? How effective are lawyers in solving legal problems? How far should lawyers be "creating" problems by identifying malpractice and abuse and making the victims aware of it? What is a problem?

These are issues which have been the subject of research and discussion in the last few decades reflecting the growing awareness of the existence of an unmet need for legal assistance with problems and the development of law centres and other agencies to meet it. They are central to the debate over the provision of legal services and the response to these issues will affect the formulation of policy.

This chapter explores some of these issues and Chapter 9 assesses the strengths and weaknesses of the major agencies currently involved in giving advice and solving problems. Throughout both chapters we shall be particularly concerned with the role of lawyers.[1]

A great deal of emphasis is placed on the role of courts in settling disputes. The law student learns much of his or her law from decided cases,[2] public attention is inevitably focused upon the adversarial contest, civil and criminal procedure is lengthy and complex, books on the English legal system (including ours) devote a considerable amount of space to litigation, and English procedure tends to individualise grievances and tailor them to the adversarial model.[3] Yet it remains true that only a tiny fraction of legal matters end up in court.[4] If it were otherwise the court system would simply collapse under the strain.

This is partly explained by the lawyer's ability to advise on and negotiate settlements to the mutual satisfaction of the parties to a dispute. In addition, parties to disputes are increasingly looking to alternative methods of resolving disputes and government policy encourages or requires the development and use of methods to resolve disputes other than by litigation in many areas.[5] Alternative dispute resolution is both acceptable and essential. Further, some

---

[1] In the long run such concern may have to change depending upon the effect the Courts and Legal Services Act 1990 has on widening the types of people who provide legal services, see pp. 119–143, 148–156 above.

[2] Through the doctrine of *stare decisis*, see Chap. 7 above.

[3] It is, of course, true that a successful individual action will have an effect on the rights and duties of other people through the definition of the law, but there is no general provision as yet in the English legal system for a group or class action except in matters of company law; as to recent developments, see below, p. 545.

[4] See pp. 555–557, below.

[5] See below, pp. 554–566. The Government intended to require mediation in the process of divorce (*Looking to the Future: Mediation and the Ground for Divorce* (Cm. 2799, 1955)), but has since backed down from requiring it to be mandatory. See, *e.g.*, S. D. Sclater, "A Critical Approach to the White Paper on Divorce Reform" [1995] Web J.C.L.I.). The Government also intends to encourage A.D.R. through its legal aid proposals (*Legal Aid—Targeting Need* (Cm. 2854, 1995)).

matters are non-contentious and rarely result in litigation.[6] Other matters are
resolved on the receipt of information or advice about the law.

However, many legal matters do not emerge for legal assistance, let alone
litigation, because they are never identified as legal problems by the sufferers,
or never reach lawyers, or, having reached lawyers, are not recognised as problems within the lawyer's or the law's purview.[7] This situation is unacceptable
and any scheme to provide public legal services must be judged on its ability
to bridge the gap by involving lawyers or appropriate advisers in the resolution
of all matters that require their assistance.

A. WHAT IS A PROBLEM?

This may appear to be an odd question to pose, but it has a bearing on our
approach to the provision of legal services and the involvement of lawyers.
Does a situation only become a problem when the sufferer identifies it as something about which he or she can do something? If the mood is one of resigned
acceptance, that the situation represents one's life difficulties, that there is no
help to be obtained in dealing with the matter, should we consider that such a
person has a problem?

This is not confined to legal problems (although in many situations there may
be an unrecognised legal problem) but has its effects in other areas as well. The
failure on the part of the sufferer to appreciate that solutions might exist may
be the result of a combination of factors including ignorance,[8] apathy,[9] complexity of the situation,[10] generality of the problem and the extent of financial
or physical resources required to rectify matters.[11] When the need for assistance
is not even recognised, there is considerable difficulty for any advice agency in
providing assistance. The role of the lawyer or adviser in taking the initiative
in identifying problems with which help can be provided becomes important,
and it is in this type of work that the law centres have been particularly success-

---

[6] This is generally true of conveyancing, wills and probate and agreeing contractual relationships.
    Of course there is litigation and, in absolute terms, it may appear that there is a lot, but this is
    not true when compared with the number of such transactions.
[7] This general difficulty has been termed "unmet legal need". See, *e.g.*, R. Abel-Smith, M. Zander
    and R. Brooke, *Legal Problems and the Citizen* (1973); P. Morris, R. White and P. Lewis, *Social
    Needs* and *Legal Action* (1973); Law Society, "Law Society's Memo No. 2—Unmet Need"
    (1976) 73 L. S. Gaz. 1061; A. Byles and P. Morris, *Unmet need: the case of the neighbourhood
    law centre* (1977); H. Genn, *Meeting Legal Needs?* (1982); D. Harris *et al.*, *Compensation and
    Support for Illness and Injury* (1984); The Committee on the Future of the Legal Profession, *A
    Time for Change* (1988), Chair: Lady Marre, Chap. 7 [hereafter, the Marre Committee]; P. Robert-
    shaw, *Rethinking Legal Need: The Case of Criminal Justice* (1991); Legal Action Group, *A
    Strategy for Justice* (1992); R. Smith (ed.), *Shaping the Future* (1995); Legal Aid Board Annual
    Reports 1994–95 (H.C. 526, 1995), Chap. 5; Lord Chancellor's Department, *Legal Aid—Tar-
    geting Need* (Cm. 2854, 1995).
[8] Ignorance of the criminal law does not excuse from liability for its breach—ignorance of the
    civil law on the part of the public seems almost to be assumed. See p. 463 below.
[9] *ibid.*
[10] H. Genn, "Who Claims Compensation: Factors Associated with Claiming and Obtaining Dam-
    ages" in Harris *et al.* (1984), esp. pp. 70–76.
[11] The sufferer may recognise a problem but see no realistic opportunity of solving it, see *ibid.*,
    esp. pp. 73–76. See also the Marre Committee (1988), para. 7.15.

ful. The identification of the problem then is made by the adviser rather than the sufferer and the relationship between the *need* for legal services and the *demands* actually made by clients is exposed.[12]

If the provision of legal services is to be limited to those matters in which the sufferer realises that there is a situation of difficulty for which the law provides a means of solution and with which a lawyer can be of assistance much of the pioneering work of law centres would be nullified.[13]

B. WHEN IS A PROBLEM "LEGAL"?

The attribution of a particular "legal" character to certain problems underlies the research which has been done into "unmet legal need", for it is by no means every problem which requires a lawyer's assistance in its resolution. Equally, not every problem with which a lawyer is asked to deal is a legal one. Traditionally, lawyers have been proud of their reputation as advisers on general financial and property matters.[14] In any event, it would be pointless to define as legal problems only those which are *actually* dealt with by lawyers, for that would exclude all those problems which never reach them, but which should.

Would it be realistic to define legal problems as those with which private practitioners normally deal? There are two factors to this definition: the selection of appropriate problems by potential clients[15] and the lawyer's acceptance of them as appropriate for him or her to handle. The consequence is a range of problems with which solicitors normally deal, and a possible definition of legal problems. However, this is a very restrictive definition. If a client does not identify the landlord's failure to repair a rented house as a legal problem, or if a solicitor viewed it as outside his or her field, it would not be a legal problem. This cannot be right.[16]

There is often, therefore, a narrow perception of the circumstances in which

[12] For an analysis of this particular problem, see Adamsdown Community Trust, *Community Need and Law Centre Practice* (1978), pp. 36–37. The Marre Committee stated that it might be suggested that "... legal services could be divided into those which are needed (and so should, presumably, be guaranteed to all) and those relative luxuries for which there is simply a 'demand'. We do not believe that there is such a distinction. Access to legal services is a pre-requisite of a just society and we believe that this access should be provided to the extent that private and public funding is available to meet it": Marre Committee (1988), para. 7.9.

[13] It can be extremely difficult to draw the line between intervention on behalf of those suffering in the local community and the mounting of "campaigns." This has been one of the most sensitive issues in the development of law centres and is still unresolved. See R.C.L.S., Vol. 1, pp. 83–84 and the Law Centres Foundation, "A response to the Royal Commission on Legal Services" (1980). For the problems encountered by NACAB, see *Review of the National Association of Citizens Advice Bureaux* (Cmnd. 9139, 1983). See below, p. 468.

[14] Their traditional role is affected by regulation in certain areas, *e.g.*, with regard to the giving of financial advice and the impact of the Financial Services Act 1986 on legal practice, and by the increasing difficulty of being able to justify non-fee-paying activity, such as counselling.

[15] Increasing legal awareness through, *e.g.*, advertising by lawyers and legal and rights education in schools, will have its impact on clients' assessments of the legal nature of a problem.

[16] Acceptance of this approach would, by definition, mean that there was no unmet need. The particular area identified where clients need advice but which has not been within the traditional work of the solicitor is that of social welfare law, and recent proposals are intended to address this problem, see *Targeting Need* (1995), Chap. 8 with proposals to meet the need through having social welfare block contracts included in the new legal aid scheme, see below, p. 522.

it is appropriate to approach a solicitor.[17] There have been criticisms of the narrow nature of the work of most solicitors and it is true that the legal advice and assistance scheme was introduced in 1973 to extend the range of work of solicitors. It has not been particularly successful.[18]

Another approach is objectively to define a problem as legal against categories of types of problem. This emphasises those problems with which a solicitor *could* deal. It was this approach which was adopted by Abel-Smith, Zander and Brooke in their research into unmet legal need, published as *Legal Problems and the Citizen*. They chose 17 specific and common situations as the basis of a questionnaire.[19]

An objective definition is open to criticism on the grounds of particular exclusions from, or inclusions in, the categories and the extent of the categories themselves. A more fundamental objection is that it may be *exclusive* rather than *inclusive*, in the sense that our thinking may be confined to those matters which fall within accepted categories rather than accepting that all situations to which the law pertains can give rise to legal problems despite the fact that there is no immediately available legal framework for their solution. In particular, the categories are set by legal specialists rather than the potential clients and so represent a normative ascription of what is a legal problem from the supply side. What the approach fails to achieve is an assessment of what are legal problems from the point of view of a potential client, from the demand side, which has been identified as felt and expressed need. Indeed it is suggested that this is the failing of most approaches to legal need.[20]

A definition of a legal problem as "an unresolved difficulty to which the law is relevant" may appear to be too vague and begging too many questions.[21] However, it may form the basis of a new approach to problems to which lawyers and advisers will not seek to establish the legal nature of the problem and then find the relevant law, but will rather seek to establish the nature of the problems and then contemplate whether any part of the law might be relevant.[22] The

---

[17] See, *e.g.*, J. Jenkins and V. Lewis, *Client Perceptions; Existing and Potential Clients; Experiences and Perceptions of Using a Solicitor for Personal Matters* (1995), Chap. 2; J. Jenkins, E. Skordaki and C. F. Willis, *Public Use and Perception of Solicitors* (1989), Chap. 5; Abel-Smith, Zander and Brooke (1973), pp. 156–160; Research Surveys of Great Britain, *Report on Awareness, Usage and Attitudes towards the Professional Services and Advice Provided by Solicitors* (1986); G. Chambers and S. Harwood, *Solicitors in England and Wales; Practice, Organisation and Perceptions—First Report: The Work of Solicitors in Private Practice* (1990); and G. Chambers and S. Harwood, *Solicitors in England and Wales: Practice Organisation and Perceptions—Second Report; The Private Practice Firm* (1991).

[18] See below, p. 507.

[19] The situations were: taking a lease, repairs undone, attempted eviction of the client (a tenant), attempted eviction by the client (a landlord), buying a house, defective goods, instalment arrears, unpaid debt owed, taken to court for debt, death in the family, making a will, accidents, social security benefits, employment problems, matrimonial problems, court proceedings, and juvenile court proceedings: *Legal Problems and the Citizen*, Chap. 8.

[20] This is the taxonomy developed by J. S. Bradshaw in *Problems and Progress in Medical Care* (1972) and discussed in P. Robertshaw, *Rethinking Legal Need: The Case of Criminal Justice* (1991). Felt need is limited because it is what the client may want without any idea of what may be available, whereas expressed need is " 'felt' need translated into action, or economic demand."

[21] This sort of definition was adopted by the R.C.L.S. (Vol.1, para. 2.2) and the Marre Committee (1988), para. 7.3.

[22] Categorisation is essential for initial teaching, but is not determinative of what the law can do. Thus, the ability to understand tort or contract is of no particular assistance if, *e.g.*, the company involved in international trade or the elderly person seek advice about a matter of concern which ranges over many traditional legal categories.

adoption of such an approach demands an open mind on the part of the lawyer to listen to and offer an acceptable approach to the problem identified by the potential client.

The advantages of this approach are: first, there is less of a risk of inappropriately distinguishing between legal and, say, social problems.[23] It follows that social welfare law issues become as much a matter for private practitioners as for law centres and advice agencies.[24] Secondly, there is an encouragement to clients to make use of legal services, because they can identify lawyers as one of the "correct" agencies to approach.[25] This, then, can assist in overcoming the narrow perception of what lawyers can do. Lawyers are, in any case, active in this development because of the recession causing lawyers to make greater efforts to seek business, so endeavouring to make themselves more attractive to potential clients. Thirdly, a new remedy or novel application of the law may result from the approach, because of the need for imagination on the part of the lawyer, thus again potentially creating greater business.[26]

We have indicated what we consider to be the best working definition of a legal problem, but the discussion will be without practical significance unless an effective means of ensuring that those who have legal problems, however defined, secure legal assistance. It is this problem which is to be addressed in the following pages and which the government appeared to have begun to recognise in its 1995 legal aid proposals.[27]

C. LEGAL PROBLEMS AND THE USE OF LAWYERS

The best people to assist with legal problems are not always lawyers.[28] Trading standards departments have always been a valuable resource for dealing with consumer problems,[29] and Citizens' Advice Bureaux are the major source of advice on a wide range of problems.[30] The reasons for this view include the need for speed, flexibility and informality, particularly in hearings before tribunals, and concerns about the experience of lawyers in particular areas of work, particularly social welfare law.

---

[23] This particular dichotomy is criticised in P. Morris, R. Cooper and A. Byles, "Public Attitudes to Problem Definition and Problem Solving: A Pilot Study" (1973–74) 3 Brit. J. Social Work 301.

[24] Considerable current attention is being paid to this matter, see the Marre Committee (1988), paras. 7.10–7.13; Legal Aid Board Annual Reports 1994–95 (H.C. 526, 1995), Chap. 5; Legal Aid Board, *Franchising Specification* (2nd ed., 1995), para. 3.9 (it is a mandatory requirement that even where a franchisee does not have a franchise for welfare benefits work, "it must have at least one employee suitably qualified to recognise the need for welfare benefits advice"); Lord Chancellor's Department, *Legal Aid—Targeting Need* (Cm. 2854, 1995), esp. Chap. 8.

[25] See, *e.g.* the Marre Committee (1988), para. 7.15 and Chap. 9.

[26] See, *e.g.* the Marre Committee (1988), paras. 7.9–7.14. An example of imaginative use of the law is the application of the law of trusts to give an unmarried partner an interest in a shared home: *Cook v. Head* [1972] 1 W.L.R. 518.

[27] *Targeting Need* (1995), particularly paras. 3.7–3.11 and below pp. 000–000.

[28] Proponents of this view in the early 1970s include R. Titmuss, (1971) 42 *Political Quarterly* 113 and the Consumer Council, *Justice Out of Reach* (1970).

[29] See below, pp. 477–478.

[30] See below, pp. 473–476, where, *e.g.*, the option of advisers providing a "legal" response is identified as an appropriate response to a client's problem.

1. WHO USES SOLICITORS?

The 1994 survey of client perceptions of solicitors services[31] largely confirms the results of earlier surveys[32] which have shown that the range of problems on which solicitors are consulted is quite narrow. "The services most frequently used remain unchanged from the 1989 survey and the main services provided to private clients remain the same as in 1978"[33] On the most recent occasion of using a solicitor, he or she had been used for buying and selling a home (40 per cent), making a will (13 per cent), divorce and matrimonial problems (9 per cent), dealing with someone's estate (8 per cent), compensation for injury (6 per cent) and motoring (4 per cent) and other offences (3 per cent).[34] In responding spontaneously to questions, the public indicated that they are most aware of the conveyancing and property matters (70 per cent), wills, trusts and settlements (48 per cent), divorce (41 per cent) and law and order and criminal convictions (33 per cent) services offered by solicitors.[35] "Following prompting solicitors are also associated with negotiating accident or compensation claims (61%), motor offences (59%) and witnessing signatures (60%). Compared with 1989 some heightened awareness of the availability of advice on pensions is indicated . . . . "[36]

The respondents in the 1994 survey had been made more aware of some solicitor's services, as is witnessed by the increasing awareness of the will-writing role, largely perhaps a product of an advertising campaign, and the availability of pensions advice, which may have been a product of the recent adverse media coverage in relation to occupational pensions.[37] There is probably still a restricted perception of the sorts of matters with which solicitors deal, although the figures are affected by people failing to make use of a solicitor even knowing they could help.[38] Repeat players are most likely to be aware of what services can be provided by solicitors, to accept that solicitors may be valuable over a range of work and to be prepared to use them again, but only providing their previous experience suggests, on, *e.g.*, a personal cost/benefit analysis, that engaging a solicitor is worthwhile.[39]

---

[31] J. Jenkins and V. Lewis, *Client Perceptions — Existing and Potential Clients: Experience and Perceptions of Using a Solicitor for Personal Matters* (1995).

[32] M. Zander, (1969) 66 L. S. Gaz. 174; Morris, Cooper and Byles, (1973–74); Adamsdown Community Trust (1978); R.C.L.S., Vol. 2, s.8, pp. 173–198; Research Surveys of Great Britain (1986); Jenkins, Skordaki and Willis (1989), Chap. 5.

[33] Jenkins and Lewis (1995), para. 2.6. The 1989 survey is Jenkins, Skordaki and Willis (1989) and the 1978 reference is to the Royal Commission on Legal Services.

[34] Jenkins and Lewis (1995), Table 4. We are concerned with private clients, but note that "the purposes for which solicitors had been used in business were primarily buying/selling/renting/letting property (31%), business contracts (23%), setting up a business (18%) and financial services (17%)", *ibid.*, para. 2.7.

[35] *ibid.*, para. 2.14 and Table 5. This is roughly the same in the 1989 survey.

[36] *ibid.* para. 2.15 and Table 5.

[37] *ibid.*, para. 2.15.

[38] There was a fall in the proportion of the public using a solicitor for personal and business purposes between 1989 and 1994, but this may well have been more to do with the recession and other factors affecting ability to pay than lack of awareness or reluctance to use a solicitor for non-financial reasons; *ibid.*, para. 2.4.

[39] Such an analysis will include the assistance of a legally qualified person against the cost and extra time involved, see Robertshaw (1991), Chap. 4.

Potential solicitor clients are increasingly using other people to undertake apparently legal work.[40] Non-solicitors may now undertake conveyancing.[41] The 1994 survey shows that 92 per cent of conveyances were done by solicitors, 4 per cent by licensed conveyancers, 2 per cent by building societies and banks and 2 per cent were own conveyances. Seventy-four per cent of wills were written by solicitors, 10 per cent by other professional will-writers, and 12 per cent were own will-writers.[42]

It seems to be clear that not enough use is made of solicitors for the solution of legal problems. This is particularly so in the case of areas of social welfare law. The reasons for this seem to fall into three categories: ignorance of what solicitors can do on the part of potential clients and a lack of preparedness to pursue legal action, that is apathy; the public image of lawyers; and barriers against use, in particular cost and accessibility.

2. IGNORANCE AND APATHY

In the context of claims for personal injuries, it is clear that ignorance of the law dissuades potential claimants from seeking advice, and most people only seek legal advice after first obtaining advice from other services, which may be ill-informed and thus cause a person with a claim not to pursue it.[43] More generally, the Marre Committee was convinced by the evidence which it received that ignorance was a major cause of people not seeking legal advice when it was appropriate.[44] An aspect of the problem related to ignorance is that of apathy, in the sense that a person says "It's not worth pursuing it", or "Let's just forget about it", or "It's just one of those things." The Oxford Study shows that apathy is a major reason in explaining why people do not seek legal advice.[45]

The Marre Committee suggested that the solutions lie in four areas.[46] First, teaching of legal and rights awareness in schools.[47] Secondly, public relations, by which is meant encouraging good public relations exercises, as opposed to advertising on the part of both individual lawyers and the professional bodies. Thirdly, media advertising by solicitors.[48] Finally, information from the professional bodies directed to specific areas,[49] rather than generalised campaigns, which tend to be expensive and ineffective.

---

[40] As indicated above, this has always been a part of the work of the CAB service, and see below, pp. 473–476.

[41] See above, pp. 130–133.

[42] Jenkins and Lewis (1995), Table 11. The prospect of the introduction of probate practitioners taking more work from solicitors is one of which the profession is acutely aware, see below, p. 138.

[43] Genn (1980), esp. pp. 75–76, 65–67.

[44] The Marre Committee (1988), paras.7.17–7.39.

[45] Genn (1984).

[46] The Marre Committee (1988), paras.7.20–7.39.

[47] Improving general legal education and information is a major theme in R. Smith (ed.), *Shaping The Future* (1995), Part III.

[48] See above, pp. 141–143.

[49] *e.g.* the annual promotional campaign related to will-making, see Jenkins and Lewis (1995), para. 2.14.

3. THE PUBLIC IMAGE

The image of an advice-giving agency is crucial because it is at the stage of the identification of the appropriate agency that most people are obstructed on the way to the solution of their problem.[50] For a repeat player, the major factor is likely to be the impression created by the previous solicitor contact. Where the individual is a first-time player in the legal system, a strong image will assist in agency identification, although it can act negatively also. The Marre Committee made it clear that the image of lawyers is a particular problem, identifying two aspects.

First, there is a fear of lawyers. They are unapproachable because of the inaccessibility of premises and their unwelcoming nature, because their methods of work do not tie in with the needs of clients, and because of a lack of response to the needs of linguistic minorities. Thus they recommended greater use of shop premises, encouraged innovative work practices, emphasised the need for interpreters and encouraged the professional bodies to assist people from ethnic and cultural minorities to become lawyers.[51] Secondly, there is dissatisfaction with lawyers. It did not appear that this was a major problem,[52] but it did exist.[53]

The 1994 Client Perceptions survey discovered that

"the public continue to hold an image of solicitors that is generally good but not exceptional. Of the six professions evaluated, solicitors fall approximately in the middle range while NHS doctors were regarded most highly on all criteria. Estate agents, on the other hand, were the profession held in the least regard. Over a third of respondents held solicitors to be well respected (34%) with doctors being the only profession to have more people attribute them with this characteristic (74%). Bank managers and dentists were equally well respected with associations of 27% and 26% respectively. Only 4% of respondents considered estate agents to be well respected."[54]

The survey goes on to point out that the "findings confirm ... that people evaluate different professions according to perceptions of credibility and of the relationship between costs and service provision."[55] It would seem that the Law Society's Practice Managements Standards and Client Care initiative[56] are having their effect, but that more still needs to be done. For example, "solicitors should examine their own client communication skills in the light of the finding that 16% of recent clients thought solicitors were pompous and have a condescending manner."[57] Further, 17 per cent thought that solicitors were not as

---

[50] Adamsdown Community Trust, *Community Need and Law Centre Practice* (1978), pp. 41–46.
[51] The Marre Committee (1988), paras.7.40–7.47. As to the recruitment of lawyers from ethnic minorities, see above, pp. 181–182.
[52] See above, pp. 156–157.
[53] The Marre Committee (1988), paras.7.48–7.93.
[54] Jenkins and Lewis (1995), para. 3.2.
[55] *ibid*, para. 3.4.
[56] See above, p. 159. See also the qualities demanded of franchisees for legal aid work, see below, pp. 491–492 and 158.
[57] Jenkins and Lewis (1995), para. 3.6.

honest as they might be.[58] A 1995 survey by the *Which? Magazine* has, however, suggested that many clients are not satisfied with the work undertaken and the cost of that work.[59]

Law Centres are not afflicted by such problems, but they have a different agenda and a different attitude to their clients. Further, they do not appear to be burdened with the same difficulties as the private profession, presumably partly because of the different image of the agency involved and the different expectations of the clients involved.[60]

4. BARRIERS

The most notable barriers in the way of those needing legal advice are its cost and its accessibility. In the 1994 Client Perceptions survey, 40 per cent of respondents though that solicitors were "mainly after your money" and 45 per cent thought that solicitors' charges were "too high for the work they do".[61] There is clear research evidence that cost has a deterrent effect upon initially seeking advice and then pursuing a claim.[62] This is exacerbated by the limits upon eligibility for legal aid[63] and continuing ignorance of the scheme.[64]

The second barrier is that of accessibility to lawyers. If there are not enough lawyers or they are not in the right place, knowing that a solicitor may help is of little value.[65]

Simply throwing money at these barriers is an inadequate response, in part because the resources available are limited. Thus, the recommendations, for example, of the Marre Committee, are much more specific in their treatment of the problem. Whilst assistance with cost and redeployment of lawyers is part of the answer to the failure of many people to use lawyers, they are clearly not the whole answer. Indeed, public education about the nature of legal problems and the role of lawyers in solving them might be much more effective in the long run.

D. UNMET LEGAL NEED

It may appear that we consider that every problem with a legal component requires legal assistance, for we have not proposed any other criterion for the provision of legal services than that a legal problem exists. This may seem a

---

[58] *ibid.*, Table 6.
[59] See above, p. 157.
[60] This was the experience of the Adamsdown Community and Advice Centre (1978) and has been one of the strengths of the Citizens' Advice Bureaux — they have a very strong *generalist* image. See also JUSTICE, *Law Centres* (1995), esp. Chaps.7 & 8.
[61] Jenkins & Lewis (1995), Table 6.
[62] R.C.L.S., Vol. 1, pp. 48–49 & Vol. 2, p. 262; Genn (1984), esp. pp. 73–74; the Marre Committee (1988), para. 7.15 and Chaps.8 & 10; *Civil Justice Review* (1989), Chap. 6. See below, Chap 9.
[63] See below pp. 994–996 and 570–576.
[64] Genn (1984), esp p. 67.
[65] See the Marre Committee (1988), paras.7.94–7.108 and see above, pp. 123–127.

profligate approach, yet just as there are difficulties in defining legal problems, so there are difficulties when an individual *needs* assistance. It is obvious that the circumstances, financial resources and personal competence of individuals differ, as will the subjective importance of the matter. How can a general proposition of need be formulated when there are so many personal variables? Should any such proposition even be attempted?

In conducting their pioneering survey,[66] Abel-Smith, Zander and Brooke were faced with this problem. Their solution was to assess, in respect of each category of problems identified,[67] what would constitute "... a risk of substantial loss or disadvantage which would be important for the individual concerned."[68] This standard varies for each category, so no general proposition can be developed. Zander later recognised that this approach was only really valid for research purposes,[69] and others have not made the attempt.[70] On the other hand, Robertshaw attempted a means of identifying legal need which was, for him, intellectually satisfying and an appropriate foundation for assessing the provision of services within the criminal justice system. At the least what he draws attention to is the need to contemplate legal need from the perspective of the potential client, who may find it difficult to identify anything other than a feel that some assistance is required, rather than merely from the suppliers who may have a vested interest in what is identified as work that lawyers can do, but are not providing.[71]

In the context of legal aid, individual need is tested by a combination of the means, merits and reasonableness tests, which rely upon factors such as whether a solicitor would advise a private client to pursue the claim, whether there is sufficient benefit in pursuing the matter and whether the defendant could satisfy a claim.[72] A similar test cannot apply to general legal advice, because it would result in a static approach failing to meet the needs of the clients and, perhaps, failing to admit the developments by the suppliers, that is the lawyers.

The Royal Commission on Legal Services appeared to accept that legal need can be defined by reference to the existence of a legal problem on which an individual wishes to be advised, since it recommended that solicitors should offer free initial half-hour interviews.[73] Certainly, it is important to recognise that the identification by an individual that he or she has a problem which may demand a legal response is an element in determining the extent of legal need. Indeed, the Government commented in the 1995 Consultation Paper on Legal Aid that the "existing scheme tends to channel clients and money to solicitors. It encourages a system of lawyer led services, and delivers what lawyers are best able to supply."[74]

If it be conceded that the need for legal advice arises from the existence of a legal problem, the difficulties in meeting that need would appear to have been exposed earlier in the chapter. However, studies demonstrate that obstructions

---

[66] *Legal Problems and the Citizen* (1973).
[67] The categories are listed at n. 19 above.
[68] *ibid.*, p. 12.
[69] *Legal Services for the Community* (1978), p. 280.
[70] See, *e.g.*, the Marre Committee (1988), para. 7.10.
[71] See P. Robertshaw, *Rethinking Legal Need: The Case of Criminal Justice* (1991). His thesis goes much further than is suggested in the text.
[72] See further, pp. 570–572 below.
[73] R.C.L.S., Vol.1, pp. 134–135.
[74] *Legal Aid—Targeting Need* (1995), para. 3.8.

in the way of obtaining legal advice have different effects on different sorts of people.

The most obvious differential obstruction is cost. Some studies show that those in the higher socio-economic groups use lawyers more often than those in the lower groups.[75] It would appear that poverty is a primary cause for failure to seek legal advice. Even if legal aid were to be effective in overcoming this problem,[76] the less affluent may also suffer the disadvantages of lack of influence, energy and awareness.[77] However, the Oxford Study suggests that people from the higher socio-economic groups are *less* likely to make a claim for damages consequent upon personal injury being suffered.[78] The most important factor in determining whether an accident victim obtained damages was found to be access to advice, both pre-legal and legal, which may be offered without it even being sought.[79] The reality may be that all these factors are true, but their impact may vary. People who are poor are more likely to be eligible for legal aid, thus alleviating some of the cost problems; people who are not poor are more likely to be able to take advantage of the legal advice on offer through access to agencies and knowledge. Other factors are significant and are increasingly being assessed, so the 1994 Client Perceptions study identified that there was little difference between men and women in the frequency of their use of solicitors, but that the elderly used solicitors more rarely than others.[80] The survey also discovered that "ethnic minority respondents had a lower awareness of the services provided by solicitors than the total population."[81] One further development to note is the increasing possibility of lawyers seeking clients, not just through advertising,[82] but also through buying lists of names of accident victims and contacting them direct with an offer of services.[83]

Not only is pre-legal advice essential from various agencies essential,[84] but also public education, easy access to initial information (*e.g.*, the provision in court lobbies of informational telephone kiosks[85]), advice agencies and others who may be able to refer on a person with a potential claim. The development of advice agencies is not the only solution to unmet legal need, but it is important.[86] For the purposes of legal aid provision, the Legal Aid Board is attempting

---

[75] Between 1989 and 1994, use of solicitors by social status was AB-42 per cent; C1–38 per cent; C2–32 per cent; DE-27 per cent; Jenkins and Lewis (1995), Table 2. See also, *e.g.*, Abel-Smith, Zander and Brooke (1973); R.C.L.S., Vol.2, s.8; and Jenkins, Skordaki and Willis (1989), Table 12.

[76] See below, pp. 513–525 and 577–580.

[77] J. Carlin and J. Howard, "Legal Representation and Class Justice" (1965) 12 *U.C.L.A. Law Review* 381.

[78] Genn (1984), esp. p. 51–56, Table 2.6.

[79] *ibid.*, pp. 65–67, 76. The most frequent pre-legal advisers were: trade union, medical, employer, police, potential defendant, AA/RAC, the advisee's own insurance company, workmate or fellow patient, friend, relative: *ibid.*, Table 2.11. See also Jenkins, Skordaki and Willis (1989), p. 19.

[80] Jenkins and Lewis (1995), Table 2. The Oxford Study discovered that women were less likely to seek damages and two other groups were under-represented: the young and the elderly; Genn (1984), esp. pp. 51–56, 58–65, Table 2.12.

[81] *ibid.*, para. 7.5.

[82] See above, pp. 141–144.

[83] As reported in *The Independent*, October 30, 1995.

[84] The Oxford Study identified the following sources in personal injury cases: trade union, medical, employer, police, potential defendant, AA/RAC, the advisee's own insurance company, workmate or fellow patient, friend or relative: *ibid.*, Table 2.11.

[85] See T. Purcell, "Technology's role in access to legal services and legal information" in R. Smith (ed.), *Shaping the Future* (1995), pp. 75–78.

[86] See Chap. 9.

to identify the need for legal services by developing "predictive models of relative need". The Board has models to cover areas of social welfare law, that is housing, debt, welfare benefits and immigration/nationality.[87] These are the areas where the Board believes there is a large unmet need and it is, in part, upon these which the Government has built in recognising some areas into which greater effort has to be put to direct legal resources.[88]

Needless to say, the answer to the problem of unmet legal need does not lie solely in the development of advice agencies. Not all recipients of damages in the Oxford Study received "pre-legal advice". The evidence of the Users' Survey of the Royal Commission on Legal Services suggested that three-quarters of the people who sought legal advice had received no help from people outside their household on the matter in question.[89] Further it suggested that of those people who did not go to a lawyer, a higher proportion had received help from outside the household, and of that group only one-quarter had received advice to go to a lawyer which they had ignored.[90] Such contrary evidence does not denigrate the value of pre-legal advice, but suggests that, as would be expected, it is not the only significant factor in determining whether, and if so why and how, people seek legal advice.

The Oxford Study pointed out other significant factors in assessing the kinds of people who do not seek legal advice for a claim for damages for personal injuries. Of particular interest, is the finding that, proportionately, women were less likely to seek damages, although, if they did, they were more likely to be successful. Two other groups which were under-represented in terms of making such claims were the young and the elderly.[91] The needs here may well be partly dealt with by educational improvements and the importance of changing work practices and the image of lawyers.

It is quite possible that the extent of unmet legal need can never be ascertained and that which can be ascertained cannot adequately be explained. The barriers are clear enough, what remains unclear is why some people are able to surmount them when others fail miserably.

E. INTERVENTION OF LAWYERS—THE "CREATING" OF LEGAL PROBLEMS

The Royal Commission on Legal Services concluded that this sort of work should *not* be part of the responsibilities of the citizens' law centres that were proposed.[92] What was identified as ". . . general community work . . . organising groups to bring pressure to bear . . . becoming a focus in the neighbourhood for campaigns,"[93] was said to be inappropriate for a legal service. The Commission took the view that the responsibility of a legal service was the provision of legal

---

[87] *Legal Aid Board Annual Reports 1994–95* (H.C. 526, 1995), paras. 5.2 and 5.3.
[88] See *Targeting Need* (1995). Whilst many parts of the proposals have been doubted, this commitment has been warmly welcomed, see below, pp. 519–525.
[89] R.C.L.S., Vol. 2, p. 207, para. 8.127.
[90] R.C.L.S., Vol. 2, p. 262, para. 8.395.
[91] Genn (1984), esp. pp. 51–56, 58–65, Table 2.12.
[92] R.C.L.S., Vol. 1, pp. 83–84. See p. 461 below.
[93] *ibid.*, p. 83, para. 8.19.

advice and assistance to individuals, that community action tends to involve only one section of the community, and that the independence of a centre is compromised if it becomes a base for campaigns. Consequently, they recommended that "campaigning" should be funded from elsewhere and not undertaken by law centres.

The Report was published after a very interesting and well-argued case was made by the Adamsdown Community Trust[94] for precisely the sort of intervention which the Report proscribed.[95] Independence was not compromised, it was stated, and although the identification of causes deserving of support and finance from the advice agency might be questionable, in practice only those problems which gave real cause for community concern could be pursued successfully because of the need for public support. It was also noted that interventionist action could include leafletting in the area, talks to local groups and the preparation of kits and materials as well as the organisation of pressure groups and similar activities.

There may be difficulties in particular law centres in finding the right balance between assisting clients in individual cases and taking on group work or projects, but it seems unduly restrictive to deny that the latter was a proper role for lawyers to play.[96]

---

[94] Adamsdown Community Trust (1978).
[95] The projects described in the survey concerned a provisional slum clearance programme and roads and pavements in disrepair in the Adamsdown area.
[96] Non-casewook is a feature of the work of Law Centres, See JUSTICE, *Law Centres* (1995) and below, pp. 483–488.

CHAPTER 9

INFORMATION AND ADVICE SERVICES

By discussing in the preceding chapter the ways in which the public may perceive a problem as a "legal" problem and the steps which the profession might take to assist in the identification of problems which require legal advice for their solution we have already indicated that we are concerned, in the main, with the provision of information and advice by lawyers. However, legal advice is not provided solely by lawyers and it is certainly not restricted to those operating within the professional structure described in Chapter 3.[1] In this chapter we shall deal with the major advice-giving agencies prior to a discussion of the arrangements under which the private profession and the law centres provide legal advice and assistance.

A. THE SPECIAL FEATURES OF INFORMATION AND ADVICE PROVISION

A person may seek advice for one or more purposes and it is important to distinguish those who may need help in establishing whether they have a problem, those who need help in establishing what action they can take and those who need help in pursuing a remedy. Even when the problem has been identified as having a legal perspective it is by no means certain that the client will conclude that a solicitor is the most appropriate source of advice. Different agencies may assist in different situations and lawyers still labour under the handicap of their public image.[2]

1. WHICH AGENCY?

What are the factors which influence the choice of a particular agency? Whilst there may be circumstances which influence individuals in their selection of an adviser,[3] it seems likely that the crucial factors are availability, cost and reputation.

The distribution of advice agencies around the country leaves large areas

---

[1] See particularly pp. 122–156 above.
[2] R.C.L.S., Vol. 1, pp. 33–36, 45 and see above. pp. 464–465.
[3] For example, previous contact with a particular agency; personal knowledge of existing agencies; recommendations from friends.

(especially the rural districts) without some of the basic agencies,[4] and even within urban areas it is unusual to find solicitors, in particular, located in the districts with the greatest density of population.[5] Advice needs to be locally available.

The cost of obtaining advice becomes significant when a client considers using professional agencies. Cost is obviously a factor which is balanced against the need for special skill or expertise, but it was an appreciation of the fears of the public about the financial consequences of visiting a solicitor which led, e.g., the Royal Commission on Legal Services to recommend the "free initial half-hour" despite the possibilities of abuse.[6] Many of the statutory and voluntary agencies provide advice without charge and many solicitors provide a free or cheap initial interview.[7]

The reputation of a particular agency will depend on the public perception of its efficiency, its impartiality, its independence and its approachability. That there is concern over the indifferent public image of the legal profession is evident—other agencies place varying degrees of emphasis upon different features of their reputation, some stressing their independence, others their approachability.

2. What Help?

Information and advice may be different and may require different communication skills on the part of the adviser. Again, advice and assistance may be different with the latter requiring some positive action on behalf of the client. Most of the agencies that we shall be describing in the following sections would claim to offer information, advice and assistance but some are dubious as to the extent to which they *should* take action on behalf of a client[8] and some will refer a matter on to specialists when they reach the limits of their competence. This raises the question of the role of the specialist agency in relation to the generalist and the development of a referral system. Co-ordination of generalist and specialist advice services is of prime importance and the National Consumer Council identified as a fundamental objective of a national advice system:

". . . the achievement of a proper mix of specialist and voluntary services

---

[4] See the maps taken from various sources collected in *The Fourth Right of Citizenship*, a National Consumer Council Discussion Paper (1977), pp. 47–55. For an analysis of the especial problems of rural areas, see *Rural Advice and Information*, NACAB Occasional Paper No. 2, (1978); *36th Legal Aid Annual Reports* (1985–86), pp. 208–214; K. Economides and M. Blacksell, "Access to Justice in Rural Britain: Final Report" (1987) 16 Anglo-Am.L.R. 353 (and associated working papers); M. Blacksell *et al.*, *Legal Action*, April 1986, p. 7 and August 1986, p. 7; M. Slatter and M. Moseley, (1986) 136 N.L.J. 626; E. Kempson, *Legal Advice and Assistance* (1989) (comparative study of services in Cornwall, Oldham and Newham); M. Blacksell, K. Economides and C. Watkins, *Justice Outside the City* (1991); C. Harding and J. Williams (eds.) *Legal Provisions in The Rural Environment*; and see above, pp. 125–126.

[5] See above, p. 125.

[6] R.C.L.S., Vol. 1, pp. 45, 134–135. This recommendation was not accepted by the Government: see p. 515 below.

[7] See below, pp. 488–490.

[8] See, for example, the Chairman's statement in the National Association of Citizens Advice Bureaux Annual Report and Accounts, 1979–80, at p. 5.

and of working links and effective referral systems for the handling of people's problems where more than one agency needs to be involved."[9]

We have already noted that lawyers can be expected to provide a whole range of help which would certainly include information, advice and assistance.[10]

3. GIVEN BY WHOM?

Some agencies we shall be discussing rely solely upon one type of adviser so that there is no dispute about suitability. In others, however, there can be tensions over the relative desirability of volunteers and professionals. Citizens' Advice Bureaux, for example, rely heavily upon volunteers with few paid advisers and it is argued that this gives the organisation a positive strength and a particularly good claim to independence and impartiality. On the other hand, professional advisers (including lawyers) tend to lay emphasis upon the skill and expertise which are supposed to come with professional status and training.

The dispute between the volunteer and the professional is likely to continue[11] but it should not be allowed to obscure the fact that the skills of the good adviser are not necessarily professional skills, nor are they especially lawyerly skills. The client wants an adviser who can interview sympathetically, ascertain the facts, analyse the problem and suggest a course of action. The expertise of the adviser in the particular problem which emerges will doubtless influence the proposed course of action (which might include a referral) but the preliminary *advisory* skills may be possessed by a volunteer as by a professional. We shall return to these points later in the chapter but should now describe the range of information and advice agencies which will offer help with legal problems.

4. THE OVERALL PICTURE

One point clearly illustrated in this chapter is that there is no overall strategy for the provision, co-ordination and funding of advice services. There are many forms that such services may take; there is excessive reliance on the charity of volunteers to provide services that ought in principle to be publicly funded; funding problems seem to be chronic. An attempt to look at the overall picture was made by the Royal Commission on Legal Services: its recommendations were widely criticised and largely ignored.[12] More recently, attention has been

---

[9] *The Fourth Right of Citizenship*, p. 65, cited with approval in R.C.L.S., Vol. 1, p. 72. The National Consumer Council have long expressed concern about the lack of a national policy for generalist advice provision. See *Ordinary Justice* (1989), pp. 108–114.

[10] Above, p. 459.

[11] If only because the evidence in other areas of social work is of increased professional involvement. 90 per cent of the staff of Citizens Advice Bureaux are volunteers: NACAB Annual Report 1994–95. The proportion of paid workers has increased, although only five CABx employ solicitors: JUSTICE, *Law Centres*, p. 8. There can be tensions between paid workers and volunteers: see Citron (*op. cit.*, n. 16 below), pp. 64–66, and disputes about their respective merits: see V. Macnair, *Legal Action*, May 1989, p. 8; responses, June 1989, p. 28; July 1989, pp. 25–26.

[12] See below, pp. 514–515.

focused on the statutory legal advice scheme (and, indeed, legal aid generally), prompted, it seems, more by government concern at rising public expenditure costs than any serious wish that those who need but cannot afford legal services obtain them. In 1986, the Legal Aid Efficiency Scrutiny, conducted by four civil servants from the Treasury and the Lord Chancellor's Department, made radical proposals for change. Some, but not all, of its recommendations were implemented in the Legal Aid Act 1988 (which also consolidated legal aid legislation). The administration of the legal advice and assistance and civil legal aid schemes was transferred to a new Legal Aid Board, whose remit included that of considering fundamental changes in the administration of the schemes.[13] The Government then again turned its attention to the legal aid scheme in its 1995 Consultation Paper: *Legal Aid-Targeting Need.*[14]

The most recent general survey of the provision of legal services was undertaken by the National Consumer Council.[15]

B. GENERALIST AGENCIES OFFERING LEGAL ADVICE

1. THE CITIZENS' ADVICE BUREAUX[16]

It is somehow ironic that the major generalist agency owes its existence to wartime necessity. The CAB service has its origins in the combined operation set up in 1938 by the Ministry of Health, the National Council for Social Service and the Family Welfare Association to provide advice and information in an emergency. The outbreak of war was the emergency and a centrally-funded national service came into being. At the end of the war government assistance was withdrawn and local Bureaux were left to scrape along on what they could glean from local authorities and other sources. Many disappeared.

The service was revived at the beginning of the 1960s by the injection of government funding and was stimulated by honourable mention from two major inquiries. In 1962 the Molony Committee on Consumer Protection declared itself to be strongly in favour of the service and recognised its potential:

"The aggrieved consumer needs an accessible local service to which he can take his troubles and where he will receive a realistic appraisal, a measure of help in presenting his case, or a pointer to the next step. This need cannot be better filled than by the Citizens Advice Bureaux."[17]

In 1980 the Royal Commission on Legal Services reported that it had:

---

[13] See below, pp. 515–519.

[14] Cm. 2854, 1995.

[15] N.C.C., *Ordinary Justice: Legal services and the courts in England and Wales: a consumer view (HMSO, 1989).*

[16] J. Citron, *Citizens Advice Bureaux: For the Community, by the Community* (1989); J. Richards, *Inform, Advise and Support: 50 Years of the Citizens Advice Bureau* (1989).

[17] *Final Report of the Committee on Consumer Protection*, (Cmnd. 1781, 1962), Recommendation 108, relating to paras.481, 491–3.

". . . identified a particular national advice service, provided by the citizens' advice bureaux, which together form the largest and, in our view, the best placed organisation to provide a primary or first tier service."

The central body, the National Association of Citizens' Advice Bureaux was the subject of a review[18] initiated by Dr. Gerard Vaughan, as Minister for Consumer Affairs, which described the CAB service as ". . . an invaluable national asset."

At the present time there are 721 Bureaux[19] in the United Kingdom which are registered with the National Association of Citizens' Advice Bureaux (NACAB). All these Bureaux are required to conform with national standards in their operation and to conform to the training requirements adopted by NACAB. The advantage of membership of the national association is the receipt of the NACAB monthly information service and access to other support services.[20]

The aims of the Citizens' Advice Bureaux service are:

"— to ensure that individuals do not suffer through ignorance of their rights and responsibilities or of the services available; or through an inability to express their needs effectively;
— exercise a responsible influence on the development of social policies and services, both locally and nationally.
The service therefore provides free to all individuals a confidential, impartial and independent service of information, guidance and support, and makes responsible use of the experience so gained."[21]

In 1994–95 the CAB service handled 6,492,983 problems.[22] In the categorisation adopted by NACAB, the greatest number were concerned with benefits (28.4 per cent), consumer and credit (14.8 per cent), housing (11.2 per cent), employment (10.3 per cent), legal (10.0 per cent) and relationships (7.7 per cent).[23] Debt is not categorised separately, but is a significant problem.[24] The main response to these problems is the provision of detailed information and advice, which amounts to 69 per cent of the work and includes "benefit calculations, helping clients understand their rights and responsibilities, providing guidance on legal procedures and the administration of government and private services, helping to draft letters." Seventeen per cent of the work is advocacy and negotiation with external bodies on behalf of clients, 4 per cent involves "preparing clients' cases for representation at county court and tribunals." Indeed, in 86 per cent of CABx the representation work is undertaken by the advisers. Eight per cent

---

[18] *Review of the National Association of Citizens' Advice Bureaux* (the Lovelock report: Cmnd. 9139, 1984). The review dismissed concerns about the alleged party political activities of CAB workers: see Richards (1989), pp. 15–23.
[19] Another 1,006 outlets are attached to them: NACAB Annual Report, 1994–95, inside cover.
[20] See Citron (1989), Chap. 5 The information system is so highly regarded that the House of Commons Library has subscribed to it: NACAB Annual Report, 1994–95, p. 4.
[21] Citron (1989).
[22] NACAB Annual Report, 1994–95, p. 20.
[23] *ibid.*, p. 20.
[24] It is recorded as part of the main categories (see NACAB Annual Report, 1994–95, p. 21) and amounted to 740,618 problems: *ibid.*, p. 22.

of the work is simple requests for information and referrals and 3 per cent involves providing a "listening ear".[25]

So, in relation to those problems which have a legal content, a Citizens' Advice Bureau may adopt one or more strategies. Most obviously advisers are trained at least to provide information and advice, but frequently take on cases in more of an active or representational role. Otherwise, it may refer some cases to a solicitor.[26] It may engage local solicitors in a rota to whom clients are referred for a free interview and many solicitors are very willing to offer their time for such a service. It may even appoint its own solicitor, but is much more likely to use solicitors on a voluntary basis.[27]

The Royal Commission on Legal Services gave a firm indication of how it considered the CAB should resolve the conflict between its generalist role and the inclination to become involved in specialist areas:

"... the functions to be fulfilled by the CAB service [must] be defined with care. There is sometimes a tendency for a generalist service to expand into specialisms with which it is in daily contact. If this were to happen in the case of the CABx, they would have lost their primary purpose as first tier advisory agencies; there would be duplication of effort, waste of public money and, in all probability, deterioration in the quality of specialised advice provided."[28]

The CAB service is keenly aware of this dilemma, in particular with regard to the non-solicitor agency franchising pilot for funding from the Legal Aid Board.[29] The pilot scheme enables the employment of specialists to deal with a range of social welfare law work, but it does not affect the generalist advice service. Indeed, one CAB manager has stated: "The holistic approach to client problems is a strength of the CAB Service which is recognised by the Legal Aid Board. Franchised bureaux will continue to deal with all aspects of problems which clients bring to them, not just the legally aidable ones."[30] The demand for such a service is great, even though the numbers of clients seen fell slightly during 1994–95. The drop was partly caused by the success of the service enticing clients to it, but then putting some off when queues for interviews developed[31] or telephone calls were not answered swiftly.[32] The solution is greater funding, but, at national level, the Department of Trade and Industry froze the grant to NACAB at £12,130,300.[33] Some of that money is used to pump-prime new bureaux, to train volunteers, to maintain quality and to provide the

---

[25] *ibid.*, p. 21. For a fuller indication of the often innovative work of CABx, see *ibid.*, pp. 10–17 and for a profile of a CAB, *ibid.*, 18–19.

[26] There is general guidance as to making referrals, but much is left to the discretion of CAB managers: J. Baldwin, (1989) 8 C.J.Q. 24, 33–36.

[27] Only five CABx employ solicitors: JUSTICE, *Law Centres* (1995), p. 8, referring to *Employment of Solicitors in Bureaux* a report by the Research and Development Department of NACAB.

[28] R.C.L.S., Vol. 1, p. 75. These views were echoed in the Lovelock review (Cmnd. 9139, 1984).

[29] See also below, p. 524.

[30] NACAB Annual Report, 1994–95, p. 8.

[31] Much of the work demands considerable effort on the part of a Bureau, often in long, in-depth interviews: *ibid.*, p. 21.

[32] These are reasons identified by NACAB: *ibid.*, p. 21.

[33] *ibid.*, esp. pp. 24–25.

information service.[34] Local CABx continue to depend on local authority financing, which runs at over £40m. in total and which represents 85 per cent of their funding.[35] However, there are significant regional variations,[36] which necessarily result in different levels of service.[37]

2. NEIGHBOURHOOD ADVICE CENTRES[38]

These are informal groups operating in a wide diversity of localities and conditions, with very different structures and objectives. In general they offer assistance with all types of problem but are often to be found in the areas of urban development and rehousing which are likely to expose housing, welfare benefit and educational problems.[39] About two-thirds provide a generalist advice service, and about one third, general assistance to a specific group of users, (e.g. women, the elderly, ethnic minority communities).[40] These centres may attract finance from a variety of sources, mainly local authorities, and there has been some government funding.[41]

3. YOUNG PEOPLE'S ADVISORY AND COUNSELLING SERVICES

In 1986, there were over 70 generalist agencies providing information, advice and counselling to young people. They were federated nationally to the National Association of Young People's Counselling and Advisory Services

---

[34] The total income to NACAB in 1994–95 was £15,187,700. The DTI provides, therefore, 79.9 per cent of that income, the rest coming from DoE (£248,300), DSS (£7,800), LBGC (£269,600), private sector (£572,200), local and district authorities (£166,200), charitable trusts (£328,600), Information System (£857,100) and other (£607,600). It is spent as follows: field support and quality monitoring (£5,277,780), training (£3,124,290), information services (£2,067,640), member representation, social policy and communication (£1,653,100), finance/administration (£1,570,690), and bureaux development grants (£1,537,100): NACAB Annual Report, 1994–95, p. 25.

[35] *ibid.*, p. 26.

[36] The pence per capita figures reveal dramatic differences, from London Boroughs paying 143.6p to English counties paying 16.2p. Only the Welsh counties froze payments in 1994–95; rates of increase varied from 2.1 per cent by Welsh counties to 11.8 per cent by English counties: *ibid.*

[37] NACAB Annual Report, 1994–95, p. 26.

[38] There is a comparative dearth of material charting the activities of centres of this kind. An early appraisal was contained in Leissner, *Family Advice Centres*, National Bureau for Co-operation in Child Care (1967), and particular studies include Bond, *The Hillfields Information and Opinion Centre—the Evolution of A Social Agency Controlled by Local Residents*, CDP Occasional Paper (1972); *Report, Evaluation and Recommendations from Cumbria CDP*, Dept. of Soc. Admin., York University (1975); N.C.C., *Information and Advice Services in the U.K.* (1983). The Federation of Independent Advice Centres (FIAC) Directory of Independent Advice Centres (ed., A. Thackeray and M. Jones, 1988) lists about 390 such centres in England and Wales. They rely more on paid staff than do CABx. Guidance on the establishment of advice centres is given in C. Thornton, *Managing to Advise* (1989), published by FIAC.

[39] *The Fourth Right of Citizenship*.

[40] R. Berthoud *et al.*, *Standing Up for Claimants* (PSI Research Report 663, 1986), pp. 78–79, based on a survey by E. Kempson.

[41] Notably from the Home Office Community Development Project 1968–78 (hence CDP in n. 38 above): see M. Loney, *Community against Government* (1983).

(NAYPCAS), which had a small secretariat funded by the Home Office. The largest proportion of funds was received through local authorities.[42]

4. The Media

It is impossible to ignore the increasing use of the media as a source of information and advice. Quite apart from the communication of information of all kinds which is the function of radio, television and the press, more and more time is being devoted to the provision of general and specific advice, usually at the request of individuals. This development is not unconnected with the development of local radio, the popularity of the phone-in programme, the introduction of day time television and the proliferation of television channels.

Depending on resources, the media can respond to enquiries in much the same way as any other agency. The particular organisation can build up its own expertise[43]; it can acquire answers which are then relayed[44]; it can refer the enquirer to another agency; it can bring in specialists to answer the enquiries direct.[45] Legal advice frequently forms the basis of specific programmes or articles, no doubt because of the inherent fascination of legal problems for lay people. There is also some credit to be gained by radio, television or the press where an individual's problem is solved and (as it is normally represented) the forces of darkness are vanquished.

C. SPECIALIST AGENCIES OFFERING LEGAL ADVICE TO THE PUBLIC

1. Consumer Advice Centres

The high percentage of enquiries to CABx concerning consumer affairs[46] demonstrates the particular need for specialist advice in the field. Local government has enforcement powers which it exercises through Trading Standards Departments.[47] It also has the power to provide advisory services.[48] Under these powers, 110 consumer advice centres were established by the end of 1976 after a combination of pressure from the Consumers' Association, the introduction of more consumer legislation, the injection of national government funding[49]

---

[42] R. Berthoud, *et al.*, (1986), pp. 79–80.

[43] As where a particular phone-in presenter gains local knowledge and experience, or where a presenter researches problems raised by listeners and makes them into a programme through his or her own investigation.

[44] By getting those who have the answers, for example local authority departments or welfare agencies, to take part in the programme by telephone.

[45] To answer questions on particular topics specified in advance either in print or on radio/television.

[46] See above p. 474.

[47] See B. W. Harvey and D. L. Parry, *The Law of Consumer Protection and Fair Trading* (4th ed, 1992), pp. 46–48.

[48] Under the Local Government Act 1972, ss.137 and 142.

[49] £1.4m. in December 1975 and a further £3m. in November 1976; see National Consumer Council, *Fourth Right of Citizenship* (1977).

and the 1974 local government reorganisation. These centres provided both pre-shopping advice on quality, fitness and "value for money"[50] and a complaints service for disgruntled consumers. In most places, they were closely tied in with Trading Standards Departments, so allowing for close liaison between the advisory and enforcement agencies, to the significant benefit of consumers.

They attracted criticism from a number of quarters[51] and by 1986 only 29 remained, run by the Trading Standards Departments of 20 local authorities.[52] The remainder had fallen victim to political change in central government[53] and local authorities. It is unfortunate that the CACs were seen as a political football and they provide an interesting indication of what might possibly happen were all legal services to be funded from local or central government.[54]

2. HOUSING ADVICE

Housing advice centres were coming into existence at about the time that the first law centre was being opened,[55] and it is not unrealistic to attribute their inception to the generally increased awareness of the need for advice services. However, the direct impetus came from the Seebohm Report[56] in 1968, which recommended the establishment of an official housing advice agency to give assistance with, *inter alia*, landlord and tenant problems, public health legislation and rent fixing. The obligation to provide such a service should rest, it was said, with the local authority.

In the event the first two centres demonstrated the dual approach to much advisory work in that one was set up by a local authority (in Lambeth) and one by voluntary bodies (in South Kensington).[57] That pattern has continued: a majority of the centres now in operation are run by the local authority, and the rest are independent, many either run by or associated with Shelter.[58] Financial assistance from the Urban Aid programme acted as an inducement to many local authorities and Department of the Environment schemes fund some centres directly. One obvious limitation of local authority-run centres is that unlike the independent centres they cannot help local authority tenants and homeless applicants fight legal battles against the authority.[59]

A separate development saw the establishment of a variety of arrangements

---

[50] By comparative testing, with the justification that the consumer can be better protected by buying wisely than by complaining vigorously.

[51] The Nottingham CAC attracted strong criticism when it embarked upon a survey of the level of professional fees. (The criticism came from the professions, not the consumers.)

[52] National Consumer Council, *Ordinary Justice* (1989), pp. 52–53.

[53] In 1979 the new Minister for Consumer Affairs withdrew cash grants to the centres; see Harvey and Parry (1992), p. 49.

[54] *cf.* below, pp. 487–488.

[55] See below p. 484.

[56] *Report of the Committee on Local Authority and Allied Personal Social Services* (Cmnd. 3703, 1968).

[57] The bodies concerned were Shelter and the Catholic Housing Aid Society.

[58] In 1994, there were over 80 organisations providing housing advice and aid which were independent of local authorities. There were 32 Shelter Housing Aid Centres in England and Wales: *Housing Year Book 1995*, pp. 357–371.

[59] Many of the independent organisations providing housing advice and aid do so for a particular local authority area: *ibid.*

offering advice and perhaps representation to defendants to possession actions in the county court. There were about 20 in 1990; they offer a valuable service, and are generally welcomed by the judiciary. Models include a permanent welfare officer available at the county court,[60] rota schemes for duty lay advisers from local advice agencies, and duty schemes staffed by private practitioners.[61] The major stumbling block to the last of these is that solicitors can only be remunerated for advice under the green form scheme. The regulations governing assistance by way of representation (ABWOR) in county courts were tightened in 1989 to exclude arranged schemes.[62]

3. Money Advice Centres

The provision of specialist money advice expanded significantly in the 1980s. In 1982, the National Consumer Council identified 16 money advice centres in Britain.[63] By 1986 there were over a hundred specialist money advice services, all but four in England and Wales, taking the form either of individual advisers within a larger unit or of separate units. The majority were based in CABx, some in local authorities, (e.g. in social services departments or to support rent officers), and there were six voluntary sector money advice centres.[64] NACAB established five Money Advice Support Units, with funding from private sector credit agencies.[65] The establishment of eight Money Advice Support Services will aid the raising of funds and support from the financial sector.[66] A Policy Studies Institute report[67] concluded that specialist money advice was helpful to debtors, particularly multiple debtors. Advisers had skills in negotiating with individual creditors and in planning an overall strategy of negotiation among several creditors, arising out of their knowledge of the legal position, experience of previous negotiations, the ability to communicate in a businesslike way, and their position as independent third parties. The location of money advice services is, however, haphazard. The case for expansion is strong—debt, for instance, was "one of the fastest growing problems of the 1980s",[68] but they are as much a victim of the lack of a coherent overall strategy as other advice services.

---

[60] A. Grosskurth, *Legal Action*, April 1990, pp. 7–8. See also *34th Legal Aid Annual Reports* [1983–84], pp. 348–350; *35th Annual Reports* [1984–85], pp. 230–232; Lee Burrows, *Rent Arrears and the Courts: A Report by the Lay Advisory Service* (1986). The Legal Aid Board has proposed pilot schemes for county court duty advisers: (1990) 87 L.S. Gaz., October 3, 1990, p. 8.

[61] *ibid.*

[62] See below, pp. 495 and 500.

[63] N.C.C., *Money Advice: debt counselling and money advice services training and publications* (1982). The first was the Birmingham Settlement Money Advice Centre established in 1971: see J. Blamire and A. Izzard, *Debt Counselling* (1987).

[64] T. Hinton and R. Berthoud, *Money Advice Services* (PSI Research Report 669, 1988), Chap. 1.

[65] NACAB Annual Report, 1988–89, p. 17. See M. Wolfe, *Legal Action*, November 1989, p. 25, emphasising the need for caution about credit industry funding.

[66] NACAB Annual Report, 1994–95, p. 6.

[67] Hinton and Berthoud (1988), Chap. 7.

[68] N.C.C., *Ordinary Justice* (1989), p. 116. The N.C.C. estimated that there was a need for over 4,000 specialist money advisers compared with the existing 200: *ibid.*, p. 119 and see above p. 474.

4. WELFARE RIGHTS UNITS

In 1995, 37 local authorities, usually in urban areas and Labour controlled, employed specialist welfare rights workers. There might be a single worker employed by the council or a team. Their work comprises the provision of direct advice services to claimants, including casework and tribunal representation, the promotion of benefits through campaigns, publicity and work with local groups, support and training for other advice givers, both among council staff and in the voluntary sector, and influencing the policy and practice of public agencies.[69]

5. CHARITIES AND PRESSURE GROUPS

Organisations with charitable status operating in a particular field often acquire knowledge and expertise which can prove extremely valuable to individuals who may be in need of that sort of advice. The housing charity, Shelter, was in at the beginning of the Housing Advice Centre movement and the Child Poverty Action Group has been extremely active in the field of welfare rights.[70] DIAL (Disablement Information and Advice Lines) give a great deal of assistance to people who are disabled or who have a disabled relative,[71] and Gingerbread, the charity concerned with one-parent families, does much educative and advisory work.

The Claimants Union has been active in the field of social security and welfare benefits and, in some areas of the country, offers advice and representation at tribunals to those in need.

D. SPECIALIST AGENCIES OFFERING LEGAL ADVICE TO MEMBERS

One of the benefits of membership of some organisations is that specialist legal advice is made available, normally connected with the main business of the organisation. This may be done through the employment of lawyers within the organisation or by the engagement of lawyers in private practice at the expense of the organisation. It is not proposed to list all the groups providing this sort of service, merely to select three examples.

---

[69] R. Berthoud, S. Benson and S. Williams, *Standing Up for Claimants: Welfare Rights Work in Local Authorities* (PSI Research Report No. 663, 1986). There has been some debate as to whether welfare rights work has a proper place in social work: see G. Fimister, *Welfare Rights Work in Social Services* (1986) (Fimister argues persuasively that it does).

[70] Especially in publications, notably the *National Welfare Benefits Handbook*, and the monthly *Welfare Rights Bulletin*, and in the establishment of the Citizens' Rights Office handling telephone enquiries from advisers from all over the country.

[71] In 1988 there were 65 centres affiliated to Dial U.K. Some concentrate on a telephone service, others also have a centre where people can call. See N.C.C., *Ordinary Justice* (1989), pp. 49–50.

1. The Trade Unions[72]

Legal services provided through a trade union have been, and remain, a significant factor in the recruitment and retention of members. It appears that most, if not all, trade unions offer some form of legal advice service to members although it is likely to be restricted to those matters which touch directly on employment.[73] The unions have been heavily involved in the development of industrial injuries law; common law claims arising out of accidents at work; employment law; and health and safety standards. Additionally, they provide representation at Social Security Appeal Tribunals and at Industrial Tribunals.

This has placed trade unions in something of a dilemma. Whilst their representatives might wish to see a general extension of legal services in the public sector, they would not wish the value of their own legal services to members to diminish. The TUC evidence to the Royal Commission on Legal Services appeared to place greater emphasis upon the preservation of the union role in advice-giving than on a general expansion of legal services.[74] This position was reaffirmed by the exclusion of employment-related matters from the Unionlaw scheme launched in 1989.[75]

The unions provide advice in a variety of ways, some using legal staff engaged for the purpose and others relying on the general full-time officials supported by recourse to the private practitioner.

The professional associations will normally offer a legal advice service in exactly the same way as trade unions and in the medical profession specific groups have been established to provide insurance cover and assist members who are sued.[76]

2. The Motoring Organisations

The Automobile Association and the Royal Automobile Club provide a variety of benefits for their members which includes legal advice. Naturally, this is

---

[72] See generally, G. Latta and R. Lewis, "Trade Union Legal Services" (1974) XII *British Journal of Industrial Relations* 561; R. Lewis and G. Latta, "Union Legal Services" (1973) 123 N.L.J. 386; M. Zander, *Legal Services for the Community* (1978), pp. 305–308; R. Lewis, "Legal Services in the Trade Unions," in, *Advice Services in Welfare Rights* (ed. Brooke), Fabian research series 329 (1976). Much of the work is based on the survey conducted by Lewis and Latta at the L.S.E. See also D. Harris *et al.*, *Compensation and Support for Illness and Injury* (1984), pp. 66–70, 80–81, 119–120; L. Dickens *et al.*, *Dismissed* (1985), pp. 43–48; and A. Boon "Ethics and Strategy in Personal Injury Litigation" (1995) 22 J.L.S. 353.

[73] Taken from the results of a 1976 questionnaire sent out by the TUC and forming the basis of evidence to the Royal Commission. Of 55 unions who replied, *all* provided advice on employment but only nine provided general legal advice to members.

[74] For a critical analysis of the TUC position, see G. Bindman, "Trade Unions and Legal Services", *LAG Bulletin*, March 1979, p. 56.

[75] (1988) 138 N.L.J. 640; (1990) 87 L.S. Gaz., September 19, p. 6. The scheme, available to members of TUC-affiliated unions, provides access lists to solicitors participating in the scheme, free diagnostic interviews (without use of the green form), free estimates of the cost of further work, fixed priced conveyancing and wills, and a Code of Practice.

[76] The Medical Defence Union, the Medical Protection Society and the Medical Practitioners' Defence Society. The role of these societies has changed somewhat now that damages claims involving the NHS are met wholly by health authorities (from January 1, 1990).

confined to motoring but can include the cost of representation in summary proceedings as well as advice on claims and general motoring law, disputes with garages, and claims arising out of accidents.

The benefits offered by the AA are not as substantial as they may, at first sight, appear since the free legal representation scheme may be withheld altogether at the discretion of the Association; the AA will not negotiate in respect of the defence of claims made against members; the AA cannot give advice or act where the Association or any of its subsidiary companies may be involved.[77] Notwithstanding these limitations, members must be reassured by such a scheme and it must be an aid to recruitment.

3. THE CONSUMERS' ASSOCIATION

The CA began in 1957 as a small group publishing a magazine with the results of the comparative testing of aspirins and kettles and has since then become a multi-million pound operation with influence over manufacturers and retailers as well as those responsible for the formulation of consumer policy.[78]

The information function is performed through the magazine *Which?* available to subscribers but having a general impact because of its availability in libraries and the extent to which it is referred to and talked about. The value of the information lies in its comparative nature and in the reputation for thoroughness which the CA has acquired. Unfavourable mention in *Which?* is regarded as a major problem for well-known manufacturers. This approach was used to consider solicitors' services and published in the October 1995 edition.[79] The researchers sought advice from a number of lawyers and compared that advice with an ideal answer. Provided the comparator is correct, this approach provides an informative assessment of the quality of a solicitor's work. Unsurprisingly, this approach has been criticised by numerous solicitors. More validly, there have been concerns about the accuracy of the comparator and of the assessment of how good was the advice given, since law often does not allow for merely one answer or approach. A retraction in regard to one firm was published in the November 1995 edition.

On the legal advice side, the CA operates a legal service for individual members on payment of a separate subscription. Legal advice, in the form of answers to readers' questions, is also contained in the magazines, and there are statements of law in other CA publications.[80]

---

[77] *Automobile Association Members' Handbook* 1988/89, p. 19.

[78] As exemplified by the critical report of the B.L. Metro in the July 1981 *Motoring Which?* and the responses of the manufacturer and users, *Sunday Times*, June 28, 1981, *The Times*, June 29, 1981.

[79] See above p. 157.

[80] *The Good Food Guide* for instance attempts to set out the law about eating in a restaurant.

E. LAW CENTRES[81]

One of the most significant developments in the provision of legal advice and assistance over the last 25 years has been the emergence of law centres. Drawing some inspiration from the American system of neighbourhood law firms but adapting themselves to local conditions and the rules of the legal profession in this country, the law centres now provide a local base for the dissemination of legal services outside the private profession.

1. THE BEGINNINGS

Some provision was made for the giving of legal advice by salaried solicitors outside the ambit of private practice in the Legal Aid and Advice Act 1949, but the part of the Act which would have established full-time paid solicitors located at the Legal Aid Area Headquarters and travelling to smaller places was never brought into force.[82] An alternative scheme for the provision of advice was proposed and adopted after 10 years of pressure had failed to get the original scheme implemented.[83]

The real origins of the law centre movement are usually attributed to the publication of pamphlets by the lawyers of the Conservative and Labour parties and the individual initiative of pioneers who became impatient at the slowness of the official bodies to respond to the pressure for change. *Justice for All*[84] analysed the unmet need for professional legal services and proposed the establishment of local legal centres in places of deprivation, to be staffed by salaried lawyers and to exist with and be supplemental to the private profession. It was suggested that the type of work undertaken by the centres should be restricted but that they should be free of those rules of professional etiquette (*e.g.*, advertising and touting for business) which would inhibit their work.[85] It is not, perhaps, surprising that the solution of the Conservative lawyers in their pamphlet, *Rough Justice*,[86] to the same problem of unmet legal need was the introduction of subsidies for practitioners operating privately in deprived areas and an extension

---

[81] For a comprehensive survey of the origins and development of the law centre movement, see M. Zander, *Legal Services for the Community* (1978), Chaps.2 and 3; R.C.L.S., Vol. 1, Chap. 8; Law Centres Federation, *The Case for Law Centres* (3rd ed., 1989); R. Widdison, (1988) L.S.Gaz., March 16, pp. 35–37. See also G. Burke and G. Cole, [1985] J.S.W.L. 274 (evaluation of Holloway Neighbourhood Law Centre); J. Morton, "Liverpool, 8: Anatomy of a Law Centre" (1988) 138 N.L.J. 141 L; JUSTICE, *Law Centres* (1995).

[82] s.7 contains the appropriate provisions. The significance of the failure to implement the proposals should not be underestimated. This part of the scheme was, "... an essential part of the total Scheme without which it would lack the necessary impact." The failure to implement it "... was a fatal mistake from which the inevitable consequences are now being reaped": *Legal Aid and Advice, Report of The Law Society* 1973–74 (24th Report), Special Appendix 18, "Legal aid at the cross-roads."

[83] The "statutory" and the "voluntary" scheme introduced in 1959.

[84] A report of the Society of Labour Lawyers, Fabian research series 273 (1968). Quite apart from the well-argued and well-documented proposals the report contains references to most of the written material then available about law centres and a helpful description of the American experience.

[85] *ibid.*, pp. 61–62.

[86] Society of Conservative Lawyers, *Rough Justice* (1968).

of the assistance given by lawyers to voluntary advice agencies. However, they were prepared to countenance the appointment of salaried lawyers as a last resort.

The Law Society was striking various poses in 1968 and 1969,[87] but from apparently implacable opposition to the original scheme of salaried solicitors contemplated in the 1949 Act (to depart from the alternative system adopted in 1959 would be "a serious mistake"[88]) and the proposals of *Justice for All*[89], it moved to acceptance of salaried solicitors as part of its own proposals for an Advisory Liaison Service.[90] This Service would provide legal help to CABx and other social agencies, similar to that hitherto provided by solicitors to CABx on an honorary basis; would establish close liaison between the local profession and CABx and other social services; would provide oral advice for the public in cases that could be readily disposed of; would maintain permanent advisory centres where necessary, offering advice and assistance short of proceedings or representation in court; and would set up permanent local centres offering representation in magistrates' courts and county courts and the conduct of litigation so far as this could not be absorbed by solicitors' firms.

Part II of the Legal Advice and Assistance Act 1972 contained provisions which appeared to be designed to give the Law Society power to carry out these proposals. The Lord Chancellor's Legal Aid Advisory Committee had already indicated that the Law Society should be given these powers,[91] but it, and the Law Society, were then frustrated[92] by the failure of successive governments to bring this part of the Act into force. In fact, the Law Society had minimal involvement in projects connected with the Advisory Liaison Service.[93]

2. DEVELOPMENT

Impatient of the slow progress made through the "official channels", local lawyers and community workers set up a law centre in North Kensington in 1970.[94] After a lapse of three years a variety of centres emerged in 1973/74; by October 1982 there were 38 centres around the country,[95] by 1987–88 there were 61,[96] and by 1995 there were 55.[97]

The struggle for most of the centres has been and still is for funds.[98] "Law

---

[87] These are fully explored and possible explanations offered in M. Zander, *Legal Services for the Community* (1978), pp. 64–76.

[88] *Legal Advice and Assistance*, Memorandum of the Council of The Law Society, February 1968, para. 21.

[89] (1968) 65 L.S.Gaz. 655: Inaugural address of Mr H. E. Sargant.

[90] *Legal Advice and Assistance*, Memorandum of the Council of the Law Society, July 1969.

[91] *Report of the Advisory Committee on the better provision of Legal Advice and Assistance*, (Cmnd. 4249, 1970).

[92] See, *e.g. 23rd and 24th Annual Reports on Legal Aid*, 1972–73 and 1973–74.

[93] *cf.* below, p. 510.

[94] It has managed to survive: see C. Robinson *et al., Coming of Age: North Kensington Law Centre 1970–88*.

[95] *31st Legal Aid Annual Reports* (1980–81), pp. 128–129. The early stages of development are charted in M. Zander and P. Russell, "Law Centres Survey" (1976) 73 L.S. Gaz. 208; R.C.L.S., Vol. 2, Part B, Section 3.

[96] *38th Legal Aid Annual Reports* (1987–88), pp. 102–103.

[97] There are also four in Scotland: JUSTICE, *Law Centres* (1995), p. 4 and Appendix 2.

[98] This is the explanation for the reduction in membership of LCF.

centres are mostly funded by grant-aid from public or charitable funds. . . . For most the major source of support is the local council, but central government, charities and solicitors' firms also contribute in varying degrees." But "funding sources have emerged and grown in an unco-ordinated, sporadic fashion in response to local initiatives."[99] Some funding is available from the Legal Aid Board, which reflects the fact that law centres are undertaking more legal aid work.[1] Block contracting for legal aid may also see greater funding for law centres.[2] Such funds have to be used for casework, so the non-casework may be affected.[3]

The other problem which affected some law centres was the necessity to obtain exemption (a "waiver") from the professional rules of etiquette imposed by the Law Society. The particular rules in question related to advertising and touting and became the focus for the antagonism which some established members of the profession displayed towards the new centres. After much acrimony[4] an agreement was reached in 1977 about the conditions under which the Law Society would grant waivers to law centres and it was thereafter no longer a source of difficulty. The objective of the operation of the power to grant waivers was to produce harmonious relations between all lawyers and to ensure that the roles of the "public" ' and "private" sectors of the profession continued broadly to complement one another.[5]

3. WORK

As there are many centres, so there are many different ways of operating, but in a survey conducted for the Royal Commission[6] an extract from a document prepared by the Legal Action Group was found helpful, not only for the description of law centres, but also for the distinction it drew between their function and that of *legal advice centres*.

"Legal advice centres are staffed by volunteer lawyers (solicitors, barristers and articled clerks) and have limited opening hours. The centres are essentially for advice and usually offer only a limited amount, if any, of further assistance. There is no charge for the service. . . . The telephone, where there is one, may be staffed only during advice sessions. . . .

Law centres employ full-time staff, including lawyers, and will handle a client's case from beginning to end, including representation in court or at a tribunal. The service is free unless the centre explains otherwise. Law centres vary in the services that they provide for individual clients.

---

[99] *ibid.*, p. 17. The North Kensington Law Centre started on charitable funds from the City Parochial Foundation and the Pilgrim Trust; the Urban Programme of the Department of the Environment supported projects in Lambeth, Hounslow, North Manchester, Sandwell and South Islington.

[1] In 1992–93 law centres received £3,099,260 from the Legal Aid Board, of which £2,182,860 was from legal aid and £917,000 in grants to nine law centres and the Law Centres Federation: *ibid.*, p. 17.

[2] See below, p. 522.

[3] See below.

[4] M. Zander, "Waivers—the end of a long story?" (1977) 127 N.L.J. 1236, and *Legal Services for the Community* (1978), pp. 89–93.

[5] For the position of solicitors employed in law centres, see below.

[6] R.C.L.S., Vol. 2, Part B, Section 3.1.

(a) They are all restricted to acting for clients living (or sometimes working) within a limited geographical area round the centre.

(b) They all operate on a very broad restriction against acting for clients who can afford to pay solicitors' fees.

(c) They are restricted in the kind of work they undertake. This varies from centre to centre but most specialise in landlord/tenant, juvenile crimes and care cases, employment and welfare benefits.

(d) Some centres concentrate on group work and do little individual case work.

All centres may be prepared to give preliminary advice to clients falling outside these categories. . . ."[7]

This distinction is also to be seen in the minimum requirements for membership of the Law Centres Federation:

"independence . . .
control by consumers of law centre services . . .
six staff, including two lawyers . . .
a defined catchment area . . .
a non-profit-making structure
capacity to represent clients in court
a commitment to equal opportunities"[8]

It is important to point out the major differences between the work of law centres and that of the private profession. Law centre work is concentrated in areas of social welfare law, including housing, employment and discrimination, social security, immigration and nationality, children's rights, education, and local government law.[9] Prior to 1990 and by agreement with the Law Society, law centres did not work in conveyancing, commercial matters, divorce proceedings, most probate and wills, large personal injury claims and adult crime.[10] However, since 1990 the professional conduct rule has stated that a "solicitor employed by a law centre, a Citizen's Advice Bureau or similar non-commercial organis-ation may, in accordance with paragraph 7 of the Employed Solicitor's Code 1990, advise and act for members of the public. . . ."[11] The Employed Solicitor's Code requires that no funder has a majority representation on the management committee and that the centre must be independent of central and local govern-ment, that no fees are charged except under the legal aid scheme or where the centre indemnifies the client in relation to the solicitor's costs which are not recoverable from another source, that all fees earned and costs recovered by the solicitor are paid to the centre, that the centre is a member of LCF, and that the centre provides indemnity cover through the Solicitor's Indemnity Fund to roughly the same extent as a private practice solicitor.[12] Thus a law centre cannot charge for work such as conveyancing. In view of the precarious financial pos-ition of most centres, it follows that they are likely not to be in competition with private practice, except in so far as they provide a legal aid service. In the

---

[7] LAG directory of legal advice and law centres.
[8] JUSTICE (1995), p. 4 taking the information from the guidelines for membership of the LCF.
[9] *ibid.*, p. 4, which is taken from LCF, *The Case for Law Centres* (1989).
[10] *ibid.*
[11] *The Guide to the Professional Conduct of Solicitors* (6th ed., 1993), Principle 4.08.
[12] *ibid.*, p. 134.

case of the latter, it will be for the centre to determine whether it is to demand the legal aid contribution from the client. If the contribution is not sought, the client gains a significant financial advantage from going to a law centre rather than to a private practice solicitor. It seems unlikely that many law centres cannot afford to demand the contribution and, in any case, many of their clients are likely to be given advice without a contribution.

In addition to casework, law centres are involved in non-casework, which includes education and training, telephone advice, test cases, group litigation, and lobbying local and central government on matters arising from its work.[13] The test case strategy is used where possible because the perception of community need is greater for a centre than private practice and because limited resources may best be deployed through group work.[14] There is no evidence that this activity is politically motivated, as opposed to being motivated by genuine community need.[15]

Despite the potential for conflict, research shows that CABx, law centres and private practitioners tend to establish co-operative and complementary relationships.[16] Indeed the establishment of a law centre may lead to the development of local legal aid solicitors' practices, to some extent relying on referrals from the law centre.[17]

4. THE FUTURE

Client satisfaction with law centres is high. Law centre workers are approachable and accessible.[18] Many organisations, including the political parties, are supportive of the work of law centres.[19] The few evaluations of law centre work tend to indicate good quality work delivered in a different manner from that of private practitioners.[20] Law centres have clearly played a significant part in the provision of legal advice. Nevertheless, their future remains uncertain. As JUSTICE has pointed out, "In practice, law centres have stood or fallen on far cruder assessments of spending priorities by funding bodies and no detailed evaluation of work would have made a difference."[21] This is illustrated by the problems in Wandsworth, where the centre was closed in 1980,[22] resurrected again and then disappeared with the closure of the three Wandsworth law centres in January 1990, despite a supportive and comprehensive review of advice services in 1987 by the Community Information Project.[23] As noted above, the number of law

---

[13] JUSTICE (1995), p. 5.
[14] Adamsdown Community Trust, *Community Need and Law Centre Practice* (1978); R. Campbell, *Legal Action* February 1989, pp. 7–8; *cf.* K. Hatton, *Legal Action*, June 1989, p. 10.
[15] JUSTICE (1995), p. 13.
[16] E. Kempson, *Legal Advice and Assistance* (1989), p. 71; J. Baldwin, "The role of CABx and law centres in the provision of legal advice and assistance" (1989) 8 C.J.Q. 24; JUSTICE (1995), pp. 11–12.
[17] R. Widdison, (1989) 86 L. S. Gaz. 35, 37; and see J. Baldwin (1989) and JUSTICE (1995), p. 12.
[18] L. Hiscock and G. Cole, "Law centre client perceptions of the service they received at the Centres they visited" (1992).
[19] JUSTICE (1995), p. 13.
[20] *ibid.*, p. 15.
[21] *ibid.*
[22] "Wandsworth Law Centre", *LAG Bulletin*, August 1979, p. 177 and January 1980, p. 4.
[23] *ibid.*, pp. 3 and 21. A similar fate had befallen such centres in 1980.

centres has reduced from 60 to 55 as a consequence of financial pressure, and many existing law centres are constantly in search of funding. Nevertheless, new law centres do open. Such vagaries in funding are damaging to law centres and hence to their clients.

Some of the financial problems may be addressed if law centres receive block contracts under the Government's 1995 proposals for legal aid.[24] This support may be very important, in particular because of the desire to support social welfare law work, which is the main thrust of the casework of law centres. However, such funding will not support all the work undertaken by law centres. There is still, therefore, validity in the proposal made by the old Lord Chancellor's Advisory Committee on Legal Aid that law centres should be treated as an essential part of the national network of legal services and that the Lord Chancellor should take on responsibility for their core funding.[25]

F. SOLICITORS IN PRIVATE PRACTICE

For all the varieties of advice agency that have flourished it is still the established legal profession which is the major purveyor of legal advice. The role of the private practitioner has, however, been called into question in respect of two of the requirements of an advice agency discussed at the beginning of this chapter, namely the cost and availability of the service.

Evidence that the cost of a solicitor's advice (together with fear about cost) and the relative inaccessibility of many offices combined to deter large sections of the community from using a solicitor led to speculation about the degree of "unmet legal need" which exists.[26] It was that speculation and accompanying doubts about the ability of the private practitioner to meet this need which led to the rapid growth of interest in alternative means of providing legal advice. Other agencies have already been described—we are now concerned with the response of the private profession to these problems of cost and access.

If clients are able to pay the bill they can get advice from a solicitor as often as they desire and on whatever topic they choose. If they cannot pay the bill they must rely on the services provided voluntarily by solicitors and barristers; or a law centre; or come within the statutory advice scheme; or use another agency; or do without.

1. VOLUNTARY SCHEMES

It is unnecessary to go too far back in history to discover the origins of some of the voluntary schemes for the provision of legal advice which now exist.

---

[24] See below, pp. 522.

[25] *34th Legal Aid Annual Reports* [1983–84], pp. 338–346; *35th Annual Reports* [1984]85], pp. 225–226; *38th Annual Reports* (1987–88), pp. 102–103. See also L.C.F., *The Case for Law Centres* (3rd ed., 1989), pp. 16–17.

[26] The best examination of this problem is to be found in B. Abel-Smith, M. Zander and R. Brooke *Legal Problems and the Citizen* (1973). See also a memorandum of the Law Society, "Unmet Need" (1976) 73 L.S. Gaz. 1061. See further, Chap. 8.

Lawyers have traditionally been generous with their time and talents, more so than any other profession except, perhaps, medicine, and they are accustomed to rendering assistance to those who are genuinely unable to afford professional fees. This help took the form of the poor persons' procedure in litigation[27] but it was realised that procedures were no good unless those who might need them were aware of them. From the beginning of this century there was a growing awareness of the need for legal advice.[28]

However, in 1944 the Rushcliffe Committee[29] were still able to conclude that there was no organised provision for legal advice throughout the country. Amongst the disorganised provision were to be found examples of clients who would never be charged by solicitors; advice-giving by stipendiary magistrates, magistrates' clerks, and county court registrars; a Poor Man's Lawyer service in London and the provinces staffed by volunteers; trade union legal advice and Citizens' Advice Bureaux.[30]

Of these the Poor Man's Lawyer scheme involved the greatest number of solicitors and barristers, having begun at Toynbee Hall in 1893 and spread from there. Cambridge House Legal Advice Centre and Mary Ward Settlement Centre flourished on either side of the Thames. These are the direct forerunners of the legal advice centres now to be referred to and all such centres relied exclusively on volunteer professional legal personnel.

(a) Legal advice centres

These have already been compared with law centres earlier in this chapter[31] and it was noted then that they are staffed by volunteer lawyers, have limited opening hours, offer only advice, and make no charge for the service provided. There have been 100 or so such centres and they can attribute their origins to the individual legal and charitable initiatives of members of the profession.[32] They operate to give advice and to act as a referral agency for the private profession.

(b) Rota schemes

The CAB service has taken the initiative in setting up a system of advisory sessions in which local solicitors, operating on a rota, give free legal advice to clients who have been "booked in" to a special session by a local CAB. These sessions are particularly appropriate where the bureau worker is of the opinion that the problem can be dealt with in one interview with a solicitor, but it is permissible for the solicitor taking the session to accept the interviewee as his or her own client if further advice is needed.[33] More and more

---

[27] Below, p. 568.
[28] See the description in B. Abel-Smith and R. Stevens, *Lawyers and the Courts* (1978), pp. 148–149.
[29] *Report of the Committee on Legal Aid and Advice* (Cmd. 6641, 1945).
[30] *ibid.*, pp. 17–21.
[31] Above, pp. 485–487.
[32] R.C.L.S., Vol. 1, p. 76; LAG Report, *Legal Advice Centres—an explosion* (1972), referred to in *LAG Bulletin*, October 1972, p. 11. The assistance and advice provided through Toynbee Hall, the Mary Ward Settlement and Cambridge House, three London charities, was the model for much of what followed.
[33] This formerly required a waiver from the Law Society in respect of the Solicitors' Practice Rules, rule 1, but all that is required now is compliance with the Solicitors' Introduction and Referral Code 1990.

Bureaux are establishing this arrangement with the consent and encouragement of the Law Society and the goodwill of very many members of the
profession.

The importance of the rota scheme should not be underestimated. It ensures
that the solicitor only sees those clients who have been identified by a volunteer
worker as being in need of professional advice; it provides a free initial interview
to encourage those who may be worried about cost; and it permits the solicitor
to take on those clients who may need more extensive legal assistance. The
drawback, inevitably, is that everything is dependent upon the existence of a
CAB in the area, its willingness to set up the scheme, and the co-operation of
the local profession.

The development of such schemes ought to be assured since they were commended by the Royal Commission,[34] are greatly valued by NACAB[35] and has
the support of the Law Society. However, in 1988 over 300 bureaux still lacked
schemes.[36]

(c) General

Many solicitors and barristers provide their services free to certain clients,
for certain causes or on certain occasions. It is a form of service of which
many people are unaware, but is not insignificant in its impact.[37] One service
is the free initial consultation, which of course is not merely philanthropic
since it may lead to more business. It would be grossly unfair though to
suggest that there is such an economic motive behind all pro bono work.
Until 1993 there was a £5 fixed fee interview scheme, which was abandoned
by the Law Society because it had fallen into disuse—for which lack of
publicity was, in part, to blame.[38] It was replaced by local referral schemes,
but many of these have not worked well and so the National Association of
Citizens' Advice Bureaux has recommended the reintroduction of a national
free or fixed fee interview scheme, with appropriate publicity and leaflets.[39]
There is also an Accident Line service operated by the Law Society, which
is a specialist panel whereby a free first interview is provided for clients
with potential personal injury claims.[40]

---

[34] R.C.L.S., Vol. 1, p. 73.

[35] NACAB Annual Report, 1981–82, p. 8.

[36] NACAB Annual Report, 1988–89, p. 14.

[37] Little research work has been undertaken, so most of the evidence is anecdotal. However, a
survey has been undertaken by R. Abbey and A. Boon of the University of Westminster.

[38] N.A.C.A.B., *Barriers to Justice* (1995), para. 3.67 and J. Baldwin and S. Hill, *The Operation of
the Green Form Scheme in England and Wales* (1988), pp. 19–121.

[39] N.A.C.A.B., *Barriers to Justice* (1995), para. 3.75.

[40] *ibid.*, para. 3.74. Details about Accident Line are available on the Internet. There is considerable
profit in such claims, which is why solicitors are keen to gain business, even in some questionable
forms, such as the purchase of lists of names of accident victims; see *The Independent*, October
30, 1995.

2. THE GREEN FORM SCHEME[41]

The "green form" scheme[42] came into existence with the passing of the Legal Advice and Assistance Act 1972.[43]

(a) Administration

The administration of the scheme passed from the Law Society to the Legal Aid Board on April 1, 1989, under the Legal Aid Act 1988. Whilst there is, therefore, a central administration, the individual practitioner has greater discretion in legal advice than legal aid. If he or she is a franchisee, all questions of eligibility are dealt with by the practitioner.[44] If not, most matters are dealt with by the solicitor and it need only be referred to the Area Director where an extension to the financial limit on the amount of advice that can be given is required.[45]

Franchising

The Legal Aid Board has decided to devolve many of its powers to solicitors, advice agencies and law centres through the franchising scheme and the Non-Solicitor Agencies Franchising Scheme.[46] Franchising will eventually extend to all forms of legal aid work. The first franchise contracts, from August 1994, were concerned with green form work, telephone advice, advice by way of representation and emergency legal aid. The categories of work covered are: matrimonial/family; crime; housing; debt; employment; personal injury; welfare benefits; consumer/general contract; and immigration/nationality. By March 31, 1995, 1,050 solicitors' offices and other organisations were franchised. On average they had franchises in four of the categories of work, and 80 per cent of the franchisees had contracts for both personal injury and matrimonial work.[47]

---

[41] See Baldwin and Hill (1988). For discussion, see Baldwin and Hill, (1986) 5 C.J.Q. 247; Baldwin, (1988) 138 N.L.J. 631, 664, 928, and (1989) 8 C.J.Q. 24 and N.A.C.B., *Barriers to Justice* (1995), paras. 2.1–2.40. See O. Hansen, *Legal Aid in Practice* (3rd ed., 1993), Chap. 2.

[42] The colloquial name derives from the colour of the form. It is formally known as legal advice and assistance.

[43] Now consolidated in the Legal Aid Act 1988, and regulations made thereunder. For a brief consideration of the history, see the second edition of this book, p. 443. A fixed fee interview was introduced in 1977 and abandoned in 1994 as it had fallen into disuse, largely because payment of £5 was derisory.

[44] See below.

[45] Legal Aid Act 1988, s.10(1)(h); Legal Advice and Assistance Regulations 1989, reg. 21.

[46] See below, p. 524. In origin, the Government's intention had been to transfer green form work to advice agencies, but this proved to be impracticable, see J. Rozenberg, *The Search for Justice* (1995), p. 233.

[47] *Legal Aid Board Annual Report (1994–95)* (H.C. 526, 1995), para. 6.3.

The advantages of having a franchise are financial[48] and administrative.[49] The advantages for clients are that, in order to gain a franchise, the firm must convince the Legal Aid Board through the contracting procedure that it meets certain quality standards. Quality of service is assured by compliance with transaction criteria and audit of the handling of cases, so testing

> "whether a case file shows that basic issues necessary to provide a competent service have been addressed,[50] with the Law Society's Practice Management Standards, with competent handling of legal aid accounts, and with demands for accessibility of the advice."

The initial reaction to the franchising proposal was hostile, in part because of the fear of change and in part because it was perceived as a means of the Government reducing the work of solicitors. However, the initial general reaction appears to have been favourable because of the delivery of a quality service at reasonable remuneration levels. More significant advantages to those with franchises will accrue as the scheme develops. The financial advantages will increase, greater decision-making powers will be devolved to the franchisee, it will become more difficult for non-franchised solicitors to undertake legal aid work, and the quality of service to clients and client care guarantees are expected to improve.[51] Nevertheless, there are still real concerns about the scheme, e.g., that "the present wide distribution of legal aid throughout the profession is likely to contract" and there will be "increasing tension manifest in the role of the Legal Aid Board" between its role as the "voice of the consumer" as a purchaser of legal services and its control of the franchisees.[52] Competition will not be abolished, but it is certainly the case that not all solicitors will be able to engage in legal aid work.

(b) Scope

The object of the green form scheme is to make readily available a cheap and effective source of legal advice for those who would otherwise be unable to afford it. To that end, a solicitor may give oral or written advice on the application of English law to any particular circumstances in relation to the person seeking the advice, and on any steps which he or she might appropriately take.[53]

---

[48] Firms are paid on account, thus improving cash flow (see Legal Aid Board, *Franchising Specification* (2nd ed., 1995), para. 2.21), and will be paid more than non-franchised solicitors, which is already true in criminal legal aid cases in the magistrates' courts (see *Franchising Specification*, paras.2.18 and 2.19) and for green form work, see *Legal Aid Board Annual Reports (1994–95)*, para. 6.7.

[49] The objective is to delegate as many decisions as possible to the firms, see *Franchising Specification*, paras.2.10–2.13. Green form extensions can be undertaken without prior authority, see *Franchising Specification*, para. 2.9.

[50] *Legal Aid Board Annual Reports (1994–95)*, para. 4.9. For the detailed requirements as to file management, see Legal Aid Board, *Franchising Specification* (2nd ed., 1995).

[51] See, in part, N.A.C.A.B., *Barriers to Justice* (1995), para. 2.81. As to quality measures and client care, see above, pp. 156–159.

[52] R. Smith, "Lawyers, courts and alternatives" in R. Smith (ed.), *Shaping the Future* (1995), pp. 30–31. It is doubtful whether, especially when set against quality improvements, the reduction in choice, rather than its removal, is likely to be a significant factor.

[53] Legal Aid Act 1988, s.2(2).

The client may also be given "assistance" in taking those steps.[54] If necessary, the solicitor may seek the advice of counsel[55] but this may be difficult because of the financial limits imposed.

It will be observed that, although the range of matters which fall within the scheme is very wide, the solicitor is limited to the giving of advice and assistance and not representation. Since legal aid is also unavailable for representation at the vast majority of tribunals,[56] the scheme was immediately criticised for leaving out of its scope those who needed the services of an advocate at a tribunal. This was alleged to be a very serious omission, and a great handicap to the efficacy of the scheme.

Whilst this omission is still serious, the Legal Aid Act 1979 made special provision for "assistance by way of representation" in certain situations and this development is considered further below.[57] A solicitor's written advice could include a "brief" for the client to read out at a tribunal hearing. Further, "advice and assitance" includes a solicitor advising a client informally in any proceedings as a McKenzie adviser.[58] Thus an extension under the green form scheme may be granted for this purpose.[59]

Another limitation placed upon the scheme is the amount of advice which a solicitor is permitted to give without reference to the Area Director. In respect of advice and assistance at a police station,[60] the general limit is work to the value of £90.[61] In other cases of advice and assistance, the limit is twice the hourly rate laid down in the Legal Aid in Criminal and Care Proceedings (Costs) Regulations, except when it is matrimonial work involving the drafting of a

---

[54] *ibid.*, s.2(3).
[55] *ibid.*, s.2(6). This would involve seeking an extension to the financial limit, see below p. 494.
[56] Below, pp. 569–570.
[57] At pp. 495 and 500. The general question of the desirability of legal representation at tribunals is considered below at pp. 822–835.
[58] *Legal Aid Handbook 1995*, para. 2–23. A McKenzie adviser is an adviser who accompanies a party to proceedings before a court or tribunal and gives advice on the conduct of the case, and is so called as a result of *McKenzie v. McKenzie* [1971] Ch. 33, where an Australian barrister (not called McKenzie) was held to have been wrongly excluded from the hearing of the action. The Court of Appeal adopted the words of Lord Tenterden C. J. in *Collier v. Hicks* (1831) 2 C.A. 663 at p. 669: "Any person, whether he be a professional man or not, may attend as a friend of either party, may take notes, may quietly make suggestions, and give advice; but no one can demand to take part in the proceedings as an advocate, contrary to the regulations of the court as settled by the discretion of the justices." There is, however, no *right* to a McKenzie adviser: *R. v. Leicester City JJ., ex p. Barrow, The Times*, January 9, 1991, in the context of proceedings to enforce payment of the community charge. See O. Hansen, (1991) 141 N.L.J. 122.
[59] Legal Advice and Assistance Regulations 1989, reg.21. The Legal Aid Board has made clear that it would "normally be unreasonable to grant an extension: (a) where full legal aid is available for the proceedings and the client will be better served by being fully represented in such proceedings; (b) unless the solicitor can satisfy the area office that, by reason of either the difficulty of the case or the importance to the client or the inability of the client to act on his or her own without legal help, it is necessary for the client to have the services of a solicitor acting as a McKenzie adviser"; *Legal Aid Handbook 1995*, para. 2–23.
[60] That is advice and assistance to a person who (a) is arrested and held in custody at a police station or elsewhere, or (b) is being interviewed in connection with a serious service offence, or (c) is a volunteer: Legal Advice and Assistance Regulations, reg.6(1).
[61] *Ibid.*, reg.4(1)(a). This may be extended, without justification to the Board, where a crime franchisee exceeds it if the interests of justice require it as a matter of urgency: Legal Advice and Assistance at Police Stations (Remuneration) Regulations 1989 (S.I. 1989 No. 342), reg.5(6) and *Franchising Specification*, para. 2.20.

petition, when the limit is three times the hourly rate.[62] The hourly rate is amended regularly. In 1995, the hourly rate for preparation was £43.25; for advocacy £54.50; for attendance at court where counsel is assigned £29.50; and for travelling and waiting £24.25. For routine letters written and routine telephone calls the rate was £3.35 per item.[63] The rate for franchisees is higher: in 1995, the hourly rate for preparation was £44.25; for advocacy £55.50; for attendance at court where counsel is assigned £30.00; and for travelling and waiting £24.75. For routine letters written and routine telephone calls the rate was £3.45 per item.[64]

Further limitations were introduced in 1989 when considerable restrictions were placed on the use of the scheme for conveyancing and wills. Conveyancing services are now only covered where they are necessary to implement a court order, or an agreement made in matrimonial proceedings, or where the client is proposing to enter a rental purchase agreement or conditional sale agreement. Advice and assistance in making a will can only be given to a client who is over 70, or disabled or suffering from a mental disorder (or a parent or guardian wishing to provide for such a person), or a single parent wishing to appoint a testamentary guardian.[65] The exclusion of wills and conveyancing originated from a recommendation of the Legal Aid Scrutiny that public money should be directed towards the enforcement or defence of rights and not simply to enable clients to arrange their own affairs.[66] The recommendation, and its ultimate partial acceptance, have been criticised on the grounds that lack of legal advice at an early stage may simply lead to disputes later on, to be resolved with the support of legal aid, and that the cost savings were unlikely to be substantial.[67]

(c) Eligibility

Would-be recipients of green form scheme advice must demonstrate their eligibility by complying with a means test. The result of the application of the test will establish entitlement to advice free of charge or disentitlement. Until 1993, there was a middle category of entitlement subject to financial contribution, but that, controversially, has been abolished.[68] The test is administered by the solicitor who will require information about the "disposable capital" ' and "disposable income" ' of the applicant. An applicant in receipt, directly or indirectly, of income support, family credit or disability working allowance is automatically entitled to green form advice, provided that her or his capital does not exceed the prescribed limits.[69] A client whose disposable capital and/or disposable income exceeds the prescribed limits is not entitled to advice or assistance at all. The financial criteria are amended from time to time by regulations. In 1996, the limits were: disposable capital £1,000, and weekly disposable income £75.[70]

---

[62] Legal Advice and Assistance Regulations, reg.4(1)(b),(c).
[63] *ibid.*, Sched. 6, para. 1.
[64] *ibid.*, Sched. 6, para. 2.
[65] Legal Advice and Assistance (Scope) Regulations 1989 (S.I. 1989 No. 550), regs.3, 4.
[66] *Legal Aid Scrutiny* (1986), vol. 2, Pt. IV, para. 24.
[67] *36th Legal Aid Annual Reports* (1985–86), p. 154 (the Law Society); *37th Annual Reports* (1986–87), p. 156 (Lord Chancellor's Advisory Committee); *Legal Action*, December 1988, p. 4 (L.A.G.).
[68] See J. Rozenberg, *The Search for Justice* (1994), pp. 225–232 and N.A.C.A.B., *Barriers to Justice* (1995), paras. 2.12–2.2.37.
[69] Legal Advice and Assistance Regulations, reg. 13(2).
[70] *ibid.*, reg.11(1).

The solicitor calculates entitlement by use of the "Key Card" and the green form itself. The Key Card and the green form are intended to be placed side by side and are reproduced on pages 496–499. The card discloses the financial limits, and the advice given to the solicitor on the completion of the form. One further point to note is that the Legal Aid Board may exercise a statutory charge on any money or property recovered or preserved by the client in respect of unpaid fees.[71] Even though there are both specific and general exemptions from this provision,[72] it is so important to the client that the solicitor must be at pains to explain its effect very carefully to an applicant for legal advice.

(d) Assistance by way of representation

The Legal Aid Act 1979[73] extended the scope of the legal advice and assistance scheme to include "assistance by way of representation" (ABWOR) at certain proceedings. The proceedings for which ABWOR is available have been developed through regulations made by the Lord Chancellor, whose approach has been cautious. ABWOR is available for most civil, particularly domestic, cases in magistrates' courts,[74] proceedings in county courts where a party is not represented and certain conditions are fulfilled,[75] to a person before a Mental Health Review Tribunal,[76] to a prisoner in proceedings before a prison governor who has permitted the person to be legally represented,[77] and to a discretionary life prisoner before the Parole Board.[78]

A financial eligibility test applies to all applicants for ABWOR, except for representation before a Mental Health Review Tribunal.[79] The result of the test is that the applicant is eligible for free representation, is eligible subject to a contribution, or is not eligible at all. In 1996, the limits were: weekly disposable income, £162; disposable capital, £3,000.[80] Weekly contributions are payable if the weekly disposable income exceeds £67 and does not exceed £162. The contribution is one-third of the amount by which the applicant's weekly

---

[71] Legal Aid Act 1988, s.11.

[72] Legal Advice and Assistance Regulations 1989, regs.32 and 33, and Sched. 4. See also below, pp. 574–576.

[73] s.1, amending the Legal Aid Act 1974, s.2. See now the Legal Aid Act 1988, ss.2(4) and 8(2); the Scope Regulations, Part III, and the Legal Advice and Assistance Regulations, regs.5, 5A, 7, 22 and 27.

[74] Scope Regulations, reg. 7 and Sched. This work had originally been entirely covered by the civil legal aid scheme. Where more work needs to be done, civil legal aid may be available. Civil legal aid is not available as an alternative to ABWOR: Legal Aid Act 1988, s.15(3)(b).

[75] The court must be satisfied that the hearing should proceed on the same day, that the party would not otherwise be represented, and that a solicitor in the precincts of the court is available to provide ABWOR: Scope Regulations, reg. 8.

[76] ibid, reg. 9(a). There is a Law Society Panel of solicitors with MHRT experience: see above, p. 127.

[77] ibid, reg. 9(b). This followed the decision in R v. Secretary of State for the Home Department, ex p. Tarrant [1985] Q.B. 251 that Boards of Visitors could allow legal representation. Boards of Visitors no longer exercise disciplinary powers, but the possibility of representation does extend to governor's hearings.

[78] Scope Regulations, reg. 9(c).

[79] This change was introduced by the Legal Advice and Assistance (Amendment) Regulations 1994 (S.I. 1994 No. 808); see now Legal Advice and Assistance Regulations, reg. 5A.

[80] ibid., reg. 11(2).

Green Form

GF 1 Key Card

LEGAL AID BOARD LEGAL AID ACT 1988

To be used by solicitors with NO franchise contract which covers the category of work into which this green form falls

Legal aid account no: _____

Ref: _____

(Copy from extension authority before sending claim)

➤ If you have a franchise contract covering the category of work into which this claim falls, complete form GF7.

➤ If you give advice and assistance about making a will you must submit form GF4 with your claim.

➤ You should keep a copy of the entire green form.

Client's details   *Please use block capitals *Delete the one which does not apply* | Male/Female* |

Surname: _____   First names: _____

Address: _____

_____   Postcode: _____

National Insurance No: [ ][ ][ ][ ][ ]   Date of birth: _____   **[A]**

Capital details   *(give these details even if the client gets income support, family credit or disability working allowance)*

How many dependants (partner, children or other relatives of his/her household) does the client have? _____

Give the total savings and other capital which the client has (and if relevant his or her partner)

Client: £ _____

Spouse (or person living as if a spouse of the client): £ _____

Total: £ _____

Income details   **[B]**

Does the client get Income Support, Family Credit or Disability Working Allowance?

[ ] Yes: ignore the rest of this section   [ ] No: give the total gross weekly income of

The client: | £ _____

The client's spouse (or person living as if a spouse of the client): £ _____

Total: | £ _____

Calculate the total allowable deductions: Income tax: £ _____   **[C]**

National Insurance contributions: £ _____   **[D]**

Spouse (or person living as if a spouse of the client): £ _____   **[E]**

Attendance allowance, disability living allowance, constant attendance allowance and any payment made out of the Social Fund: £ _____   **[F]**

Dependent children and other dependants: *Age   Number*

Under 11 _____ £ _____

11 to 15 _____ £ _____

16 to 17 _____ £ _____   **[G]**

18 and over _____ £ _____

Less total deductions: £ _____

Total weekly disposable income: £ _____

Client's declaration

I confirm that:

➤ I am over the compulsory school-leaving age (or, if not, the solicitor is advising me under Regulation 14(2A) Legal Advice & Assistance Regulations 1989);

➤ I have/have not *(delete whichever one is not correct)* previously received help from a solicitor on this matter under the green form; and

➤ I understand that I might have to pay my solicitor's costs out of any property or money which is recovered or preserved for me.

As far as I am aware, the information on this page is correct. I understand that if I give false information I could be prosecuted.

Signed: _____   Date: ____ / ____ / ____

95/4/18

Green Form or ABWOR 1

ENGLAND and WALES

GREEN FORM AND ABWOR KEY CARD
(NO. 27)

Effective from 10th April 1995

Please see over for further explanatory notes.

If you advise a client who returns to you for further advice on the same matter under a Green Form within 6 months of you submitting your claim for payment, fill in the client's details and the date of your claim only then strike through the rest of the front page. Set out your further claim on the back of the GF1

CAPITAL means the amount or value of every resource of a capital nature.
In computing Disposable Capital disregard
  (i) the value of the main or only dwelling house in which the client resides, and
  (ii) the value of household furniture and effects, articles of personal clothing and tools or implements of the client's trade and
  (iii) the subject matter of the advice and assistance.

A

Maximum Disposable Capital for Financial Eligibility (dependant=partner, child or relative)

Advice and Assistance*	ABWOR**
£1000–client with no dependants	£3000–client with no dependants
£1335–client with 1 dependant	£3335–client with 1 dependant
£1535–client with 2 dependants	£3535–client with 2 dependants
Add £100 for each additional dependant	

* Capital must be assessed for advice and assistance even if client is on income support, family credit or disability working allowance See note 3
** All capital is disregarded if client is on income support See note 3

B

INCOME means the total income from all sources which the client received or became entitled to during or in respect of the seven days up to and including the date of this application.

The capital and weekly income of both partners must be taken into account unless
(a) they have a contrary interest
(b) they live apart
(c) it is inequitable or impractical to aggregate their means

Some types of income are ignored See note 3

C
D
E
F

In computing Disposable Income deduct:-
  (i) Income Tax
  (ii) Contributions paid under the Social Security Acts 1975–88
  (iii) £26.50 in respect of the client's partner (if living together) whether or not their means are aggregated. Where they are separated or divorced, the allowance will be the actual maintenance paid by the client in respect of the previous 7 days.
  (iv) The following payments made under the Social Security Contributions and Benefits Act 1992:
    i) disability living allowance;
    ii) attendance allowance paid under section 64 or Schedule 8 paragraphs 4 or 7(2);
    iii) constant attendance allowance paid under section 104 and 105 as an increase to a disablement pension; or
    iv) any payment made out of the social fund.

These deductions also apply to the partner's income if there is aggregation

G
  v) £15.95 for each dependent child or dependent relative of the household under 11 years of age
  £23.40 for each dependent child or dependent relative of the household of 11 but under 16 years of age
  £28.00 for each dependent child or dependent relative of the household of 16 or 17 years of age
  £36.80 for each dependent child or dependent relative of the household of 18 years of age or over

There is no deduction in relation to a foster child

Where the child or dependent relative is not a member of the household the allowance will be the actual maintenance paid by the client in respect of the previous 7 days.

Maximum Weekly Disposable Income for Financial Eligibility.
Advice and Assistance
Green Form advice and assistance is only available to people who get income support, family credit, disability working allowance or not more than £72 a week disposable income (and who come within the maximum capital limit). They will pay no contribution.
ABWOR
Lower limit £64 a week (no contribution to pay)
Upper limit £156 a week (people with disposable weekly income between the lower and upper limits will be liable to pay a **weekly** contribution (collected by the solicitor) from the date of the ABWOR approval to its withdrawal or the end of the proceedings.
The amount of weekly contribution is calculated as 1/3 of the weekly disposable income over £64.

Note

The green form must be signed by or on behalf of the client at the initial interview as soon as his/her eligibility has been determined except in the case of an authorised postal application.

Attach a completed Form GF3 as proof of every financial extension

---

Category of problem *Please tick the relevant box*

☐ Personal injury *(G)*	☐ Debt *(E)*	☐ Housing *(D)*	☐ Welfare benefits *(H)*

☐ Crime *(C)*   ☐ Immigration *(J)*   ☐ Employment *(F)*

☐ Consumer/general contract *(K)*

☐ Matrimonial/family: *please also tick one of the following boxes:*

☐ Other *(L) specify in the summary*

(A) ☐ Petitioner in divorce or judicial separation

(M) ☐ Respondent in divorce or judicial separation

(N) ☐ Child support assessment

(B) ☐ Other family matters *(please specify in the summary)*

Solicitor charge

Has any money or property been recovered for the client? ☐ No: go on to the next section   ☐ Yes: please give details:

_____

Summary of work

Has a legal aid certificate or order been granted or applied for? ☐ No   ☐ Yes: give the reference: _____

Please give below a brief summary of the work done:

Breakdown of work done

Please give a breakdown of the work done. If an extension has been granted, record below only the carry forward total times spent, and any subsequent work undertaken. Complete in chronological order, continuing on a separate sheet if necessary

FEE EARNER'S INITIALS	DATE D M Y	TRAVEL Hrs Mins	ATTENDANCE Hrs Mins	PREPARATION Hrs Mins
Totals carried forward from any extension(s) granted:	:	:	:
	:	:	:
	:	:	:
	:	:	:
	:	:	: •
	:	:	:
	:	:	:
	:	:	:
	:	:	:

Time old rate	:	:	:
Costs old rate	£	£	£
Time current rate	:	:	:
Costs current rate	£	£	£
Total costs	£	£	£

Letters and Telephone Calls *(not telephone advice calls)*

		Number	£
Letters written	old rate:		
	current rate:		
Telephone calls	old rate:		
	current rate:		
	Total		

Details of disbursements   £   VAT

	£	VAT
Counsel's fees:		
Mileage:		
Other disbursements:		
Totals		

	Claimed	Area office use only Assessed
Profit costs: £		£
VAT on profit costs: £		£
Total disbursements: £		£
VAT on disbursements: £		£
Total claim: £		£

➤ I certify that all the information given in this claim is correct: I have not claimed and will not otherwise claim for the same items from the Legal Aid Fund and I have held a valid practising certificate throughout the conduct of this matter.

Solicitor's personal signature: _____ Date:___/___/___ Sol ref: _____

Name & address of firm/office: _____

May 1995

GREEN FORM AND ABWOR KEY CARD (NO. 27)
EXPLANATORY NOTES

1. General

Your attention is particularly drawn to *The Legal Advice and Assistance Regulations 1989* ("the regulations") as amended and to *The Legal Advice and Assistance (Scope) Regulations 1989* ("the scope regulations") as amended.

2. Conveyancing and Wills

You should note that it is not permitted to give advice and assistance in respect of conveyancing matters or the making of a will except in those circumstances set out in *regulations 3 and 4* of the scope regulations. Form GF4 must be completed in respect of advice and assistance in the making of a will.

3. Financial Eligibility

(a) The responsibility for determining eligibility is placed upon the solicitor under *Schedule 2* of the regulations.

(b) *Schedule 2* of the regulations sets out the method of assessment of resources of the client. The only deductions and allowances which can be made are those referred to in *Schedule 2*. Built-in deductions have already been made for miscellaneous expenditure such as rent, mortgage repayments and hire-purchase repayments etc.

(c) When considering a client's means it may be useful to have the following points in mind:-

(i) If part of the main dwelling is let and the client lives in the remaining part, although the capital value of the main dwelling house should be left out of account in computing capital, the rent should be included in computing income.

(ii) Capital means the amount or value of every resource of a capital nature so that capital derived from a bank loan or borrowing facilities should be taken into account.

(iii) There is no power to disregard income in self-employed cases merely because the client may have incurred unspecified expenses at an earlier date.

(iv) A cohabitee should be treated the same way as a spouse.

(v) Income means the total income from all sources which the client received or became entitled to during or in respect of the seven days up to and including the date of application. It will include child benefit but will not include disability living allowance.

(vi) Fostering allowances received in respect of fostered children should not be taken into account in assessing the financial eligibility of the client.

(vii) Because different income and capital limits apply for advice and assistance and ABWOR, clients may be eligible for ABWOR when not eligible for advice and assistance.

(viii) Clients in receipt of income support will always be eligible for ABWOR regardless of capital but not necessarily for advice and assistance. Clients in receipt of family credit or disability working allowance will always qualify on income for both Green Form and ABWOR but may be out of scope on capital.

(d) From 11 April 1994 ABWOR for mental health review tribunals is available without reference to means.

4. Solicitor and Client relationship

(a) A solicitor may, for reasonable cause, either refuse to accept an application for legal advice and assistance or, having accepted it, decline to give advice and assistance without giving reasons to the client. He may however be required to give reasons to the legal aid area office.

(b) Under ABWOR, once financial eligibility has been established, a client should be told the amount of the weekly contribution due (if any), and arrangements should be made for payment either outright or by instalments to be agreed between the solicitor and the client. Payments should begin from the date ABWOR is approved by the area office. Any contribution paid should be retained on client account until the ABWOR approval is withdrawn or the proceedings concluded.

(c) If the contribution exceeds the costs payable and VAT, the excess should be returned to the client.

(d) If the contribution payable under ABWOR is likely to be more than the costs of giving ABWOR, the solicitor should collect only enough to cover his or her reasonable costs.

5. Remuneration

(a) The initial financial limit of expenditure under Green Form (at present two hours' worth of work, or three hours' worth of work in the case of an undefended divorce or judicial separation petition) is exclusive of VAT as is any financial extension granted.

(b) The financial limit of three hours' worth of work in undefended divorce or judicial separation cases under Green Form is only applicable where a petition has been drafted. It need not, however, have been filed.

(c) The legal aid fund is only responsible for paying to solicitor and counsel such of their costs as are not covered by the client's contribution (ABWOR only), party and party costs awarded and the charge which arises in the solicitor's favour on any property recovered or preserved. *Schedule 4* of the regulations sets out the circumstances when the charge does not apply. Application may be made to the area office for authority not to enforce the charge where (a) it would cause grave hardship or distress to the client, or (b) it could be enforced only with unreasonable difficulty.

(d) Costs for work done under *regulation 7(1) (b)* or *regulation 8* of the scope regulations, should not exceed the usual financial limit. In such cases, only one week's contribution will be payable.

6. Court Proceedings

A solicitor may not take steps in court proceedings unless either approval is given by the legal aid area office for ABWOR in a magistrates' court or a solicitor is acting according to the other conditions detailed in *regulation 7* and *regulation 8* of the scope regulations.

7. Authorities

(a) The authority of the legal aid area office is required before accepting an application from: – a child (unless the child is entitled to conduct the particular proceedings without a next friend or guardian ad litem),

– a person on behalf of a child or a patient (in the case of such person not falling within the categories referred to in regulation 14 of the regulations),

– a person residing outside England and Wales or

– a person who has already received advice and assistance from another solicitor on the same matter.

(b) Where approval of the legal aid area office is required for ABWOR, even if approval is given, the prior permission of the legal aid area office is required to obtain a report or opinion or an expert, to tender expert evidence or to perform an act which is either unusual in its nature or involves unusually large expenditure. The prior permission of the legal aid area office is therefore required before obtaining a blood test (including DNA test) even if it is ordered by the court. Note that the area office may make a payment on account of disbursements under ABWOR.

Printed by LBF

APRIL 1995

disposable income exceeds £67. The contribution is payable throughout the duration of ABWOR support.[81]

ABWOR is significant in those areas where it is available, but as a general
scheme it would only be highly significant if it were to be available to a much
wider range of proceedings, especially those for which legal aid is not available.
One critic expressed fears that it might "... become a new kind of legal aid on
the cheap",[82] yet others were concerned lest it be thought that the green form
was appropriate for anything other than low-cost proceedings. The Law Society
conceded that it might "... be suitable for some tribunal proceedings or even
some criminal proceedings in magistrates' courts," but remained "firmly convinced of the necessity for retaining the [legal aid] certificate procedure for cases
which are likely to be lengthy and costly."[83]

At least the powers are there in the statute and have been used in some
cases. ABWOR is a useful peg for piecemeal extensions of publicly funded
representation.

A solicitor is required to obtain authority to use the green form scheme in
such proceedings.[84] An application must be made to the Area Director, and there
is a right to appeal against a refusal to the area committee.[85] Eligibility depends
on the client's resources.[86] Counsel may be briefed with the approval of the
Area Director; assistance may be withdrawn in certain circumstances; costs may
be awarded out of the legal aid fund to an unassisted party; the statutory charge
operates subject to specified exceptions.[86a] All these provisions indicate the
hybrid nature of assistance by way of representation. Legal advice in form—
legal aid in substance.

(e) Duty solicitor schemes[87]

The first duty solicitor scheme was initiated by the Bristol Law Society in 1972
with the objective of discovering whether there were defendants appearing before
Bristol Magistrates who were in need of legal advice but not receiving it.[88] Experienced solicitors took turns in seeing defendants in custody and those referred to
them by the court so that they could advise (not represent) an appropriate course of
action. This could involve an adjournment for legal aid application, social welfare
report, referral to another solicitor, bail application or simply suggestions for a plea
in mitigation. All those involved in the Bristol scheme (local law society, magistrates, magistrates' clerks and police) expressed themselves to be satisfied with the
result and this scheme provided the model for others which followed.

Since the development of schemes was left to local initiative and was dependent upon the co-operation of the local magistrates' court, national coverage
was patchy and the services offered were variable. By mid-1975 there were 29
duty solicitor schemes operating[89] and the Law Society, in consultation with

---

[81] *ibid.*, reg. 11(2), (3).
[82] Lord Gifford, in the debate on the Legal Aid Act 1979 (H.C.Deb., Vol. 398, col. 919).
[83] *30th Legal Aid Annual Reports* [1979–80], p. 12.
[84] Except in respect of warrants of further detention and the precincts provisions.
[85] Legal Advice and Assistance Regulations 1989 (S.I. 1989 No. 340), regs.22, 26–27.
[86] *ibid.*, regs.23, 25, 27, 32, 33, Sched. 4.
[86a] Except for proceedings before Mental Health Review Tribunals.
[87] A. Blake *et al., The Duty Solicitors' Handbook* (1988).
[88] The pilot scheme was described in (1972) 69 L.S. Gaz 819.
[89] *25th Legal Aid Annual Reports* [1974–75], pp. 6–7.

other interested parties, prepared and published a guide for the assistance of local law societies.[90] This document listed such matters as the functions of a duty solicitor, the scope of the scheme, remuneration,[91] emergency services and waivers.[92]

These schemes were well received and had extended considerably by the end of the 1970s. The Royal Commission on Legal Services described them as ". . . indispensable in a number of ways: they provide pre-trial advice to defendants who are often confused or ignorant and who have not previously obtained it, they encourage the adequate preparation of bail applications and help to reduce the number of ill-advised pleas, whether of guilt or innocence, and the number of remands required."[93]

The Legal Aid Act 1982[94] enabled the Law Society, under scheme-making powers contained in the Legal Aid Act 1974,[95] to formulate a uniform scheme for the provision of duty solicitor services. The first statutory scheme was the Legal Aid (Duty Solicitor) Scheme 1983.[96] This provided for a three-tier committee structure. Overall responsibility was exercised by the Law Society's Legal Aid (Duty Solicitor) Committee.[97] There were 24 regional duty solicitor committees,[98] whose functions included those of deciding at which courts duty solicitors should be in attendance, and establishing and appointing the members of the local committees. Local schemes were run by a local duty solicitor committee,[99] whose functions included that of considering applications from those wishing to act as duty solicitors. Selection criteria were specified, including the requirements that the solicitor's office be reasonably accessible to the appropriate magistrates' court and that the solicitor have sufficient criminal advocacy experience during the previous 18 months.[1] An unsuccessful applicant could appeal to the regional committee.

Under the scheme "advice and representation" was available without a means test or the payment of a contribution. A duty solicitor had an obligation to

---

[90] (1975) 72 L.S. Gaz. 577–579.

[91] The Law Society's Guide advised that neither the green form nor criminal legal aid was ideal, but that the former should where possible be used for advice and the latter for representation.

[92] A waiver of Rule 1 of the Solicitors' Practice Rules was required for voluntary schemes as in law centres and legal advice centres.

[93] R.C.L.S. Vol. 1, p. 93.

[94] s.1.

[95] s.15.

[96] Set out as Appendix 4P to the *34th Legal Aid Annual Reports* [1983–84], pp. 185–197, discussed at pp. 37–43, *ibid.* See S. Hillyard, (1983) 80 L.S. Gaz. 2649 and (1984) 81 L.S. Gaz. 1184. It was replaced, successively, by schemes established first under the Police and Criminal Evidence Act 1984, s.59 (see the Legal Aid (Duty Solicitor) Schemes 1985, 1987 and 1988) and then under the Legal Aid Act 1988 (see now the Legal Aid Board Duty Solicitor Arrangements 1994 and the Legal Aid Board Legal Advice and Assistance at Police Stations Register Arrangements 1994; see *Legal Aid Handbook 1995*, pp. 457–486).

[97] The Law Society's Legal Aid Committee and three nominees of the Lord Chancellor.

[98] Including a representative of each local duty solicitor committee and of the legal aid area committee, a J.P., a justices' clerk, and two lay persons, and perhaps representatives of the probation service, police and prosecuting solicitors and, in London, stipendiary magistrates. A police member became a requirement (following the development of the 24-hour scheme for advice at police stations: see below).

[99] With at least three solicitors with criminal advocacy experience, and perhaps a J.P., a justices' clerk and not more than three lay persons; a *requirement* that there be at least one lay member was introduced in 1987.

[1] Provision was subsequently made for an alternative requirement of 12 months experience with a compulsory interview.

provide advice to persons in custody and, if desired, to make a bail application; he or she had a discretion to provide advice and representation to defendants, whether or not in custody, in cases involving imprisonable offences, and even in connection with non-imprisonable offences in exceptional cases. Representation could not, however, be provided for contested cases or committal proceedings. The Scheme emphasised the right of defendants to choose their own solicitor, and required the duty solicitor to check whether the defendant already had one. Remuneration was claimed from the appropriate area legal aid committee.[2]

The first task of the regional committees was to bring the existing voluntary schemes within the scope of the statutory Scheme and to establish new local schemes so as to secure coverage of "busy" courts.[3] The next stage involved the establishment of schemes for "less busy" courts.[4] For the former, the normal requirement would be for the duty solicitor to attend the court; for the latter the predominant arrangement would be a "call-in" scheme based on either a list or a rota of duty solicitors. Coverage has progressively been extended, with 88 per cent of courts covered by 1990.[5]

A parallel development, which started in 1983 in anticipation of implementation of what became the Police and Criminal Evidence Act 1984, saw the planning and introduction of the "24-hour duty solicitor scheme" for the provision of legal advice to suspects and others in police stations. As we discuss elsewhere,[6] the 1984 Act introduced a new statutory right to legal advice, as part of a detailed legal regime governing the detention and interrogation of suspects. Both this and the 24-hour Scheme were implemented as from January 1, 1986.[7] Administration of this Scheme was passed to the committee structure already established for court duty solicitor schemes, and indeed provided an additional impetus for the establishment of new local court schemes.

Since April 1, 1989, responsibility for the duty solicitor schemes has passed to the Legal Aid Board under the Legal Aid Act 1988. The scheme is now operated on accordance with the Legal Aid Board Duty Solicitor Arrangements 1994. The Duty Solicitor Committee of the Legal Aid Board has delegated to it the duties and powers of the Board. Regional and local committees are responsible to it for their work.[8] Beneath the Duty Solicitor Committee lie the Regional Duty Solicitor Committees. Their membership comprises between 10 and 35 members, including at least one member from each local committee[9] within the region,[10] one or more J.P. nominated by the Magistrates' Association, two lay members, one or more justices' clerk nominated by the Justices' Clerks Society,

---

[2] Initially under the Legal Advice and Representation (Duty Solicitor) (Remuneration) Regulations 1983 (S.I. 1983 No. 1451). Remuneration is based on the time spent at court (plus travel costs where a duty solicitor is called in by the court or attends court at weekends or Bank Holidays). The current regulations are the Legal Advice and Assistance (Duty Solicitor) (Remuneration) Regulations 1989 (S.I. 1989 No. 341), as amended.

[3] Defined as those dealing with more than 1,250 new (non-motoring) defendants per annum or 10 per sitting; there were estimated to be about 225: *34th Legal Aid Annual Reports* [1983–84], pp. 40–41.

[4] *35th Legal Aid Annual Reports* [1984–85], pp. 36–37.

[5] *Legal Aid Board Annual Reports* (1989–90), p. 33.

[6] Below, pp. 677–680, 763–772.

[7] Only just: the revised Legal Aid (Duty Solicitor) Scheme 1985 was only approved on December 10, 1985; much ill-will was generated by the L.C.D.'s delay in providing information, especially about remuneration, until late 1985: see the *36th Legal Aid Annual Reports* (1985–86), pp. 15–19.

[8] For greater detail, see the Duty Solicitor Arrangements 1994, reg.5.

[9] One of these must be an experienced duty solicitor.

[10] There are 15 regions, with some being sub-divided; see *Legal Aid Handbook 1995*, pp. 566–570.

two lay members and one or more police representative as nominated by the chief officers,[11] but the majority of members are to be solicitors.[12] These committees determine in which magistrates' court a scheme is to operate, make arrangements for those courts where there is not to be a scheme, establish local committees to oversee the schemes, and supervise those committees.[13] Similarly, these committees determine what arrangements are to be made to provide duty solicitors at police stations and to appoint committees, which they supervise, to oversee such schemes.[14] The regional committees also must approve the use of duty solicitor representatives in a scheme, and make determinations about whether a person may be on the scheme if he or she lives more than 45 minutes from the station.[15] It is this committee which, e.g., may exclude or suspend solicitors from a scheme, monitors and oversees the schemes, requires improvements where not satisfied with a scheme, hears appeals from solicitors, and investigates complaints about the schemes.[16] Local duty solicitor committees consist of between four and 15 members.[17] The majority of members must be solicitors and a committee's members must comprise at least three experienced duty solicitors and one lay member.[18] The primary role of these committees is to ensure that magistrates' courts schemes or police station schemes are operating as approved by the regional committee.[19]

A local 24-hour scheme can take one of three forms.[20] First, there can be a rota scheme, where all the member solicitors are on duty in turn. During the duty period the solicitor has to be available all the time to provide advice over the telephone or at the police station, and receives a standby payment, up to half of which is deducted if advice is provided up to that level of work. Secondly, there can be a panel scheme where the member solicitors are asked in turn to provide advice; as no one is obliged to give the advice there is no standby payment. Thirdly, there may be a combined rota/panel scheme where a panel normally operates but there is a rota at certain times, such as at night, weekends or bank holidays. Panel schemes are more appropriate where the volume of work is low. The proportion of police stations covered has increased steadily to 95 per cent, the majority of the rest being small stations where there are likely to be few suspects.[21]

It is important to recognise that a suspect may use her or his "own" solicitor.[22] Indeed, "own" solicitors account for two-thirds of all solicitors called in

---

[11] Duty Solicitor Arrangements 1994, reg.7. It may also have on it a member of an area committee, someone from the probation service and Crown Prosecution Service, a stipendiary magistrate and more lay members.

[12] ibid., reg.9.

[13] ibid., reg.13.

[14] ibid., reg.14.

[15] ibid.

[16] ibid., reg. 15.

[17] ibid., reg. 17.

[18] ibid., regs.20 and 18. As to other possible categories of membership, see ibid., reg. 18.

[19] ibid., regs.25, 26 and 27.

[20] See also A. Sanders and R. Young, Criminal Justice (1994), p. 138.

[21] Legal Aid Board Annual Reports (1989–90), p. 33 and see Sanders and Young (1994), p. 129.

[22] Using an "own" solicitor also has been found to present some problems, see Sanders and Young (1994), pp. 129–146; J. Baldwin, The Role of Legal Representatives at Police Stations (Royal Commission on Criminal Justice Research Study No.3, 1992); M. McConville and J. Hodgson, Custodial Legal Advice and the Right to Silence (Royal Commission on Criminal Justice Research Study No. 16, 1993); and see below, pp. 763–767.

to police stations for advice.[23] The police station scheme has been successful in contributing to the increase in the proportion of suspects who receive legal advice at the police station, although that proportion is still relatively low.[24] Some of the problems for suspects accessing legal advice are the product of police practices,[25] but some are the product of the practice of solicitors. Some suspects do not wish to receive legal advice because their previous experience has been poor.[26] The problems created by solicitors have been discovered to include the following.

(1) The unavailability of solicitors even on duty schemes where the schemes have not required someone always to be on duty. Even if a scheme requires someone to be on duty, the scheme may be simply overstretched by demand.[27]

(2) Often the legal advice has been provided not by a solicitor but by a paralegal, who has not always been properly trained to perform the task.[28] One study identified the possible problems of using non-qualified staff as being: lack of legal expertise; lack of confidence; role conflict; and over-identification with the police.[29]

(3) Often advice would be given over the telephone rather than in person, which, except in very clear cases, can lead to poor, inaccurate or detrimental advice.[30]

(4) When a legal adviser is present, he or she often does very little. It has been concluded that

"passivity and compliance on the part of lawyers are therefore the normal, the expected, almost required responses at the police station .... The lawyers' roles in the interview room remains a precarious one, and it is no real surprise to note that the junior staff who mainly turn up to police stations are more inclined to facilitate police questioning than they are to challenge it."[31]

The failure of legal advisers to act is most starkly seen in the case of the "Cardiff Three", where the Court of Appeal commented that "the

---

[23] Royal Commission on Criminal Justice, *Report* (Cm. 2263, 1993); p. 38.

[24] See below, pp. 763–767. The request rates have been: 1988—25 per cent. 1990—24 per cent and 1991—32 per cent and the consultation rates have been: 1988—19 per cent, 1990—18 per cent, 1991—25 per cent: Sanders and Young (1994), p. 130. The Crown Court Study for the Royal Commission on Criminal Justice found that there were far higher rates of requesting (66 per cent) and receiving (53 per cent) legal advice after arrest: Royal Commission on Criminal Justice, *Report* (Cm. 2263, 1993), p. 35, but such a result is understandable: Sanders and Young (1994), p. 130. The variation between police stations is not: D. Brown *et al., Changing the Code: Police Detention under the Revised PACE Codes of Practice* (Home Office Research Study No. 129, 1992) and Sanders and Young (1994), p. 130. Duty solicitors give over one-third of all police station advice: A. Sanders *et al.,* Advice and Assistance at Police Stations and the 24-Hour Duty Solicitor Scheme (1989), p. 185.

[25] Sanders and Young (1994), pp. 130–137 and see below, pp. 763–767.

[26] *ibid.,* p. 137.

[27] *ibid.,* p. 138.

[28] *ibid.,* pp. 138–140 and McConville and Hodgson (1993), pp. 16–37. McConville and Hodgson discovered that in 24.4 per cent of cases which they considered the legal adviser was an admitted solicitor, but in 15.6 per cent of cases it was an articled clerk, in 31.1 per cent of cases it was a clerk on their staff, in 21.1 per cent of cases it was a former police officer, in 4.4 per cent of cases it was a non-staff clerk and in 3.3 per cent of cases it was someone from an outside agency.

[29] McConville and Hodgson (1993), pp. 30–34.

[30] Sanders and Young (1994), pp. 140–142.

[31] Baldwin (1992), p. 52.

solicitor appears to have been gravely at fault for sitting passively through this travesty of an interview'' which clearly contravened the rules against oppression.[32]

Sanders and Young have suggested three reasons why the scheme, and the Police and Criminal Evidence Act 1984, are ineffective:[33]

(1) Enforcement is in the hands of those same officers and solicitors who may not have a vested interest in adhering to the rules. As regards solicitors, this is compounded by the poor rate of pay and the frequently unsociable hours.[34]
(2) Police stations are police territory, but the main suspects for breach of the rules (the police) are also the gatekeepers.
(3) The rules themselves have allowed for bending.

Many of these criticisms have been taken seriously. In addition to making recommendations about improving suspects' chances of requesting legal advice,[35] the Royal Commission in Criminal Justice, whilst not able to recommend a scheme whereby solicitors worked from police stations, recommended that steps be taken to improve the quality of the legal advice made available.

(1) The guidance to solicitors (the Law Society's *Advising Clients at the Police Station*) on their roles should be made more widely known, be better understood, and more consistently acted upon. Specifically, it was recommended that the Law Society actively progress their production of a training video.[36]
(2) Steps should be taken to ensure that the client's own solicitor and their representatives should meet the same standards as duty solicitors. This should be the case even where the solicitor is not working under the legal aid scheme.[37]
(3) The training, education, supervision and monitoring of all legal advisers who operate at police stations should be reviewed.[38]

Endeavours are being made to improve the duty solicitor scheme by tightening the appointment process for duty solicitors and their representatives and clarifying the obligations imposed upon them.[39] The selection criteria for membership of a scheme as a duty solicitor are that the applicant must hold a current practising certificate, be willing to act personally as duty solicitor and to undertake the majority of rota duties allocated, must have a regular criminal practice, have comprehensive experience of defence work, including magistrates' court

---

[32] *R v. Paris, Abdullahi and Miller* (1993) 97 Cr. App. R. 99 at p. 104, and see Commentary by D. Birch at [1994] Crim. L.R. 362 and Sanders and Young (1994), pp. 143–144.

[33] *ibid.*, pp. 145–146.

[34] *ibid.*, p. 145. The Royal Commission also drew attention to this point, though it was outside its remit: *Report* (Cm. 2263, 1993), pp. 38–39.

[35] Royal Commission on Criminal Justice, *Report* (Cm. 2263, 1993), pp. 35–37.

[36] *ibid.*, p. 38.

[37] *ibid.*

[38] *ibid.*

[39] See the Legal Aid Board Duty Solicitor Arrangements 1994 and the Legal Aid Board Legal Advice and Assistance at Police Stations Register Arrangements 1994 in the *Legal Aid Handbook 1995*, pp. 457–486.

advocacy, in the previous 12 months[40] (unless he or she has been employed as a prosecutor for at least 18 months, when six months' defence experience is required) and adequate experience of providing advice to persons arrested and held in custody, and be prepared to act in such a way as not to discriminate on grounds of race, gender, sexual orientation, religion or disability. The solicitor must be competent to provide advice and assistance, and the committee will determine this by having regard to the solicitor's advocacy including an ability to provide advice and representation under time restraints without full preparation, an adequate knowledge of magistrates' court procedure, and an adequate knowledge of the sorts of offences likely to be heard. The solicitor must have attended an advocacy training course, unless he or she has substantial experience of defence advocacy, and have attended a police station advice course, unless he or she has substantial experience of that work. The committee has a discretion not to accept the applicant for good reason.[41] The applicant must possess or have access to appropriate books and periodicals. He or she must live within 45 minutes' travel time of the relevant police station and be prepared to be reasonably accessible when on duty. Finally, the solicitor must agree not to provide money or other gifts to a suspect, except food, drink and smoking materials for immediate consumption.[42]

The selection process is rigorous, involving an interview by a sub-committee of the local committee and approval of the appointment by the local committee. The applicant has a right of appeal to the regional committee.[43] The appointment lasts for five years and a duty solicitor may then be reselected, with the local committee considering any representations as to performance and provided clear criteria are satisfied, including continuing satisfaction of the original appointment criteria and completion of at least six hours' continuing training.[44] The selection process of duty solicitors' representatives involves similarly rigorous criteria and selection process. A representative must, *inter alia*, be employed by one firm of solicitors, have experience of providing advice whilst working for a solicitor's firm, be competent to act as a representative, have received appropriate training, have access to appropriate books and periodicals, and must be registered under the Police Stations Register Arrangements 1994.[45]

The duty solicitor is obliged to accept a case, unless otherwise engaged with another suspect, and must provide initial advice on the telephone.[46] Thereafter the solicitor or representative is obliged to attend the police station where the suspect has been arrested for an arrestable offence[47] and the police intend to interview her or him, where identification is to be resolved by identity parade, group identification or confrontation, or where he or she complains of serious maltreatment by the police.[48] In other circumstances, the duty solicitor has a

---

[40] Absence of up to 12 months for good reason is no bar to satisfying the criteria.
[41] This includes commission of crimes and adverse findings by the Adjudication Committee of the Solicitors' Complaints Bureau or the Solicitors' Disciplinary Tribunal.
[42] Duty Solicitor Arrangements 1994, paras.32(1)(d)–(i), (2)–(5) and 33.
[43] *ibid.*, paras.34–37.
[44] *ibid.*, paras.38–41.
[45] *ibid.*, para. 45. There is an interview procedure and the possibility of reselection: *ibid.*, paras.46–48.
[46] *ibid.*, para. 53.
[47] See below, p. 667.
[48] Duty Solicitor Arrangements, para. 54.

discretion, exercisable with regard to stated criteria, whether to attend the station, and, if so, whether it should be the solicitor or a representative.[49]

(f) Green form usage

It was quite clear in 1973 that the new advice scheme was intended to bring into solicitors' offices problems of a kind which had not hitherto surfaced. The analysis of the unmet need for legal services identified types of problem which were not being dealt with as well as types of people. Since the advice scheme now permitted access to a solicitor on *any* question of English law and the advertising campaign which launched it stressed the "social welfare" problems now within the scheme, it was disappointing that the first evidence of usage showed little deviation from the traditional pattern.[50] The absence of legal aid for tribunal representation was advanced as a reason for the very low percentage of cases concerned with tribunals, as well as the expectation that cases categorised under other headings (*e.g.*, "employment", "landlord and tenant") might have included tribunal work.

The green form scheme and ABWOR are the most widely used of the legal aid schemes. However, there was a reduction in their usage in 1994–95 which meant that they accounted for less than half of all acts of assistance.[51] In 1984–85 the green form scheme and ABWOR accounted for nearly a quarter of all legal aid expenditure, whereas in 1994–95 the proportion was only one-ninth.[52] The pattern of usage has changed over the years. Whilst comparisons are not easy to make, because of the different way in which the statistics are reported, it was at one time possible to suggest that the types of problems dealt with had been remarkably constant since 1973–74: the proportion of family cases had settled at just over 40 per cent, crime at around 22 per cent, landlord and tenant and housing, and hire purchase and debt, at around 6 per cent, each, accidents and injuries at around 5 per cent, employment and consumer at around 2 per cent each, immigration at just under 1 per cent, and the rest around 11 per cent.[53] In 1994–95, the proportion of crime cases was just over 25 per cent, family cases just over 15 per cent, matrimonial cases just over 12 per cent, welfare benefits at nearly 9.5 per cent, landlord and tenant and housing at nearly 8 per cent, hire purchase and debt at just over 6 per cent, accidents and injuries at nearly 5 per cent, immigration and nationality at over 3 per cent, consumer and employment each at just over 1.5 per cent, and the rest at around 12.5 per cent.[54] The explanations for the changes lie in the effects of the Children Act 1989 moving many cases to civil legal aid, the stabilisation in the growth of criminal legal aid through the duty solicitor schemes, increasing awareness of services provided in the areas of social welfare law, increasing preparedness to

---

[49] *ibid.*, para. 55.
[50] *24th Legal Aid Annual Reports* [1973–74], Appendix 4, Part II, 2. The analysis, based on a sample of 10 per cent of claims for payment under the scheme in 1973–74, showed that the largest categories were matrimonial, 60 per cent; criminal, 10 per cent; and landlord and tenant, 5 per cent: the remaining 25 per cent was spread among the remaining categories, with only 1 per cent for tribunals.
[51] *Legal Aid Board Annual Reports 1994–95* (H.C. 526, 1995), p. 83.
[52] *ibid.*
[53] See the second edition of this book at p. 456.
[54] *Legal Aid Board Annual Reports 1994–95* (H.C. 526, 1995), Tables Advice 1 and Advice 2.

go to law in general and in particular in the areas where there has been increased usage of the schemes.[55]

It may be that difficulty in getting people with problems to consult a solicitor is more to do with their perception of the problem and the ability of a solicitor to help than with the cost and availability of the advice service. The Law Society has been left to reflect that "... the types of problem on which advice and assistance was sought during the past year is surprisingly, and perhaps regrettably, consistent with the experience of previous years ... people who are eligible for advice and assistance are still accustomed to consult solicitors for a comparatively narrow range of problems."[56]

Apart from questions of the *pattern* of usage, the overall amount of usage had steadily increased prior to 1994–95,[57] as had the cost.[58] There are, however, considerable regional variations, with variations among solicitors as to their policy in using the green form scheme, and variations in the practice of area offices.[59]

(g) Green form deficiencies

Some would argue that the major deficiency in the green form scheme is that it is administered through solicitors and must, therefore, share the same unattractiveness to some members of the public. The arguments about the location, availability, approachability and cost of the solicitors' offices emerge again in this context. It would appear that, until recently, only the traditional problems have been brought in (see above).

Four other major criticisms of the scheme have been advanced—that the initial limit is too low; that the financial criteria are too strict; that the scheme is not sufficiently well-known to attract those who need it; and that the system is open to abuse by solicitors.

The first of these criticisms was by far the strongest made by solicitors interviewed for their research study by Baldwin and Hill.[60] The consequences of a low initial limit was that a solicitor would either have to stop work at an early stage and wait for an extension to be authorised, which "is time-consuming, causes delay and raises difficulties with clients," or work on without an extension. In any event it might not be worthwhile seeking an extension where the sum over the limit is relatively small. Work might also be unremunerated given the difficulties of extracting contributions from clients.[61] The move to limits based on hours[62] may help, but the periods of two and three hours specified have still been criticised as too low.[63]

The financial eligibility rules are a major source of grievance with the green form scheme. First, the disposable capital limit for advice and assistance

---

[55] See, in part, *ibid.*, p. 83.
[56] *30th Legal Aid Annual Reports* [1979–80], p. 6.
[57] From 438,519 bills in 1979–80 to 1,029,018 in 1989–90, to 1,573,847 in 1994–95.
[58] Payment totalled £12.3m. in 1979–80, compared with £60.4m. in 1987–88, £58.1m. in 1988–89 and £66.5m. in 1989–90.
[59] *e.g.* in deciding whether to pursue a legal aid application or stay with the green form scheme: see Baldwin and Hill (1988), Chap. 2.
[60] Baldwin and Hill (1988), p. 62, Table 14. This criticism was over 10 times more common than complaints that the rates of remuneration were too low.
[61] *ibid.*, pp. 54–64.
[62] Above, p. 493.
[63] *38th Legal Aid Annual Reports* (1987–88), p. 105 (Lord Chancellor's Advisory Committee).

(£1,000) is considerably lower than that for civil legal aid (£3,000), and the weekly disposable income limit for advice and assistance (£75) is very low. Secondly, the rates are harsher than they used to be, so the maximum weekly disposable income was £75 in 1992/93. Thirdly, the abolition of contributory advice and assistance has removed a significant group of people from access to initial advice. Whilst only 10 per cent of bills may have required a contribution, these people no longer are entitled to any support.[64] The savings achieved by this change have, therefore, been minimal.[65] These three factors militate against some people receiving sound initial advice, so some people with a strong case are deterred from proceeding further, and some people with weak cases continue with no real prospect of success. If advice cannot be received from lawyers, this places an additional burden on other advice agencies, such as CABx.[66] It is possible to be eligible for civil legal aid and not for advice and assistance, which exacerbates these problems.[67]

The advertising of the scheme and the consequent level of public awareness has been a constant source of concern. Two targets have been identified. One, the general public, can really only be reached by direct advertising in the media—the other, the "gate-keepers", those who work in the social field and in advice agencies, need to be approached much more selectively. They are the people who can refer clients on to solicitors and it is highly likely that the "Advisory Liaison Service" and the proposed liaison officers[68] could have played a significant part in making and fostering those contacts. In their absence, the information circulating about the green form scheme can be haphazard depending upon the enthusiasm of voluntary and statutory advice agencies and the activities of local law societies. Advertising campaigns have been sporadic and their effect is extremely difficult to assess.[69]

As to abuse of the scheme by solicitors, the research study by Baldwin and Hill[70] found that officials in area legal aid offices "tended to view members of the legal profession with considerable suspicion",[71] but more on the basis that solicitors might make full or excessive use of the scheme[72] than that there was malpractice or dishonesty. The checks that were carried out were not particularly rigorous and did not in fact tend to reveal abuse. Indeed "evidence of serious abuse of the green form scheme has always proved elusive."[73] There was a case for the introduction of much more systematic and thorough random checks: these might detect or deter wrongdoers, although the vast majority of solicitors would be unlikely to risk their livelihoods for trifling amounts; "more

---

[64] About 10 per cent of people would be required to make a contribution prior to the change in April 1993 (which is still working its way through the system: *Legal Aid Board Annual Reports 1994–5*, Table Advice 3).

[65] About £4 m. in 1993/4 and £9 m. in 1994/5: NACAB, *Barriers to Justice* (1995), para. 2.22.

[66] *ibid.*, paras.2.14–2.21.

[67] *ibid.*, paras.2.29–2.34.

[68] Above, pp. 483–484.

[69] Some have been specific, such as that to launch the £25 scheme, in 1973, and that directed at the North-East, others more general, such as the "Don't Trust Whatsisname" campaign. See above p. 000.

[70] Baldwin and Hill (1988), Chap. 4.

[71] *ibid.*, p. 67.

[72] *e.g.* "We found in one firm, for instance, that every client seemed to come out with a will regardless of what the original problem was": statement by an officer cited at p. 68.

[73] *ibid.*, p. 79.

importantly they would ... allay public concern and offical suspicion about improper use of the green form scheme.''[74]

Notwithstanding the various deficiencies, mentioned in this section, the overall view of the green form scheme expressed by Baldwin and Hill was encouraging:

> ''... we have found ourselves at the end of the research thoroughly persuaded of its merits. Notwithstanding the serious criticisms we have made in the report about certain aspects of the scheme, the results, taken as a whole, demonstrate that the green form scheme represents an invaluable social service and provides a source of immediate legal advice to those who need it.... [Many] more people are assisted under the ... scheme than are assisted under all other forms of legal aid put together. This is remarkable given that the ... scheme makes up only about a fifth of the total legal aid budget.''[75]

G. ADMINISTRATION AND POLICY MAKING

(a) Administration

Until 1989, the green form scheme and the duty solicitor scheme were administered by the Law Society, as an adjunct to its responsibilities for civil legal aid.[76] As a part of the general debate about publicly funded legal services,[77] the need for overall co-ordination of the legal aid scheme became apparent. The Legal Aid Efficiency Scrutiny identified pressing need for action in certain areas,[78] which included the need to reorganise the administration of the legal aid system to ensure that the systems were simple, the lines of responsibility were clear and that one organisation had overall responsibility. The Scrutiny team recommended that there should be a nationally based Legal Services Board controlling the system through the existing area offices and through agents in the courts.[79] The ensuing White Paper paid tribute to the Law Society, but proposed the creation of a Legal Aid Board.[80] Some functions (e.g., assessment of means, decisions on the grant of legal aid and some of the determinations of bills now carried out in the courts) were not immediately assigned to it, but it was anticipated that they would eventually fall within the Board's remit.

The Legal Aid Board was established by Part II of the Legal Aid Act 1988.[81] It formally commenced operations in August 1988 after some three months'

---

[74] *ibid.*, p. 80.
[75] *ibid.*, pp. 128, 129. A more sceptical view has been expressed by A. Sanders and L. Bridges, (1990) 140 N.L.J. 85, arguing by analogy with their findings on the 24 Hour Duty Solicitor Scheme (above, pp. 503–506); for a critical response see S. Hill, (1990) 140 N.L.J. 323, reply by Sanders and Bridges, (1990) 140 N.L.J. 496.
[76] Below, pp. 568–569.
[77] Below, pp. 546–548.
[78] These are considered more fully below, see pp. 515–517.
[79] *Legal Aid Efficiency Scrutiny* (L.C.D.) 1986, Vol. 2, Chap. V.
[80] Cm. 118, Chap. 3.
[81] See *Current Law Statutes 1988*, annotations by I. Storey; D. Matheson, *Legal Aid: The New Framework* (1988).

shadow existence, and assumed the Law Society's legal aid and advice responsibilities on April 1, 1989.

It comprises between 11 and 17 members appointed by the Lord Chancellor (one appointed as chairman), with at least two solicitors and two barristers (appointed after consultation with, respectively, the Law Society and the General Council of the Bar).[82] Its general function is that of securing that advice, assistance and representation are available in accordance with the Act and of administering the Act.[83] Some specific functions can only be conferred by an order made by the Lord Chancellor.[84] It has power to secure the provision of advice, assistance and representation by entering into contracts, but only if the Lord Chancellor directs.[85] It is to publish information as to the discharge of its functions, supply information to the Lord Chancellor as and when required, make annual reports, and "have regard, in discharging its functions, to such guidance as may from time to time be given by the Lord Chancellor."[86] A major focus of concern among commentators was how independent of the Lord Chancellor the Board would be.[87]

In June 1995, the Board had 13 members. Its chairman (Sir Tim Chessells) and four of its members had backgrounds in industry or commerce; there were two solicitors, two barristers, two people with an advice agency background, one former civil servant, and one former academic lawyer.[88]

The Board took over the legal aid scheme's administrative structure and most of the staff. It also took over all aspects of the duty solicitor scheme.[89] The Board reported that it had established management objectives and expressed confidence that the introduction of new management techniques, in many cases building on work in hand, would lead to significant improvements in the speed and quality of service and efficiency.[90]

According to its Management Statement, the objectives of the Board are: to act in ways which generally support and further the Lord Chancellor's objectives for legal aid; to operate within the statutory framework; to ensure that the aspects of the scheme for which it is directly responsible are efficiently and effectively managed; to advise the Lord Chancellor as to whether the objectives for the scheme as a whole are being met and whether there is the most effective and efficient use of the resources allocated to legal aid; to consider whether it should acquire within its areas of responsibility those legal aid functions not currently within its remit; to ensure that those receiving legal aid receive a service which meets defined levels of quality at a value for money price; to advise the Lord

[82] Legal Aid Act 1988, s.3(5)–(8). The Lord Chancellor must have regard to the desirability of including members with knowledge of the provision of legal services, the work of the courts and social conditions and management: *ibid.*, s.3(9).

[83] *ibid.*, s.3(2).

[84] *ibid.*, s.3(4): these include determining the costs of representation under civil legal aid; functions as regards representation under criminal legal aid (other than determining costs of representation in magistrates' courts); determining the financial resources of persons for the purposes of the Act.

[85] *ibid.*, s.4(2)(a), (4). As to proposals with regard to block contracting, see below, p. 522.

[86] *ibid.*, s.5.

[87] *e.g.* R. Smith, *Legal Action*, April 1988, p. 6.

[88] *Legal Aid Board Annual Reports 1994–95* (H.C. 526), Appendix 4.

[89] The Council of the Law Society decided by a small majority not to seek to retain responsibility for vetting and appointment of duty solicitors: see *Legal Action*. October 1988, p. 3 and December 1988, p. 5.

[90] Cm. 688, p. 4.

Chancellor on problems with legal aid and undertaking such monitoring as requested; and to ensure the establishment and development of systems to assess an applicant's means and the merits of the case.[91] So the Board has under review its operational strategy and performance by looking more deeply at how it conducts its business, having a greater focus on quality (in particular consistency of decision-making, better communications and more effective handling of complaints), and "maintaining overall standards of time taken performance while extending the areas of work targeted."[92]

(b) Policy-making

Under the old system, the annual reports of the Law Society, and the comments and advice of the Lord Chancellor's Advisory Committee on Legal Aid[93] were a valuable source of information and of recommendations for change in policy (whether accepted or not).

The Greater Manchester Legal Services Committee was established in April 1977. It originally consisted of various types of lawyer and representatives of volunteer and statutory organisations, with the common objective of co-ordinating and improving legal services in Manchester.[94] It extended its boundaries in 1985, becoming the North Western Legal Services Committee, covering Greater Manchester, Cumbria and Lancashire. The progress of the Committee has been charted in the Legal Aid Annual Reports[95] and it has an impressive list of achievements. It has stimulated duty solicitor schemes, including schemes at prisons; encouraged law centres; monitored the grant and refusal of legal aid in magistrates' courts; provided training for volunteer workers at advice agencies; published a leaflet aimed at those who have suffered accidents; produced directories of advice agencies; and taken on other responsibilities connected with the stimulation and co-ordination of legal services. Most importantly, it has shown what advances are possible given enthusiasm, goodwill and a full-time secretary paid for out of the Legal Aid Fund.[96]

A North East Legal Services Committee was established in 1982. To the disappointment of the Law Society and the Lord Chancellor's Advisory Committee, the Lord Chancellor declined to fund a full-time secretariat, claiming that it should be left to local or charitable sources.[97] As a result, its activities have been more limited than its counterpart in the North-West.

Current sources of informed comment are the various national bodies with

[91] *Legal Aid Board Annual Reports 1994–95* (H.C. 526), at para. 2.2.
[92] *ibid.*, Chap. 3, esp. para. 3.3
[93] Since abolished.
[94] The original members included members of both branches of the legal profession, the Legal Aid Area Secretary, the Director of the local law centre, the clerk to the Bury Magistrates and representatives of the C.A.B., the Child Poverty Action Group, the probation services, the local Social Services Department, the local trades council and other groups.
[95] They are mentioned annually. For fuller treatment, see *32nd Legal Aid Annual Reports* [1981–82], pp. 121–124; *36th Annual Reports* (1985–86), pp. 214–218. See also C. Schofield and V. Hereward, *L.A.G. Bulletin*, June 1979, p. 127 and R. Smith, *Legal Action*, October 1987, pp. 6–7.
[96] The full-time official has undoubtedly played a major part in the success of the experiment. This was a liaison officer appointment authorised by the Lord Chancellor and demonstrates how useful the provisions of the Legal Advice and Assistance Act 1972 could have been if applied nationally.
[97] *34th Legal Aid Annual Reports* [1983–84], pp. 54–55, 346–347, and subsequent Reports. There is a project for the establishment of a committee in South Wales, subject to similar funding difficulties: *37th Annual Reports* (1986–87), pp. 26–27; *39th Annual Reports* (1988–89), p. 3.

an interest in legal services: the Legal Action Group, NACAB, the Law Centres Federation, the Advice Services Alliance (an umbrella organisation for advice services), the National Consumer Council and so on. The decisive voice is, as one would expect, that of the Lord Chancellor's Department and the Treasury.

H. REFORM

"In the last analysis, therefore, it is for Parliament to decide the extent to which legal services are to be provided at public expense to meet the needs of the majority of the population. But, unless legal services are provided, the full benefit of our legal rights and safeguards cannot be realised."[98]

The preceding parts of the chapter have shown that the present diversity of sources for legal information and advice has resulted from piecemeal development, partly by lawyers, partly by non-lawyers, without any coherent structure or philosophy. There is legal advice from non-lawyers, from salaried lawyers and from the private profession paid for by the client, the State, local government, charities or provided gratuitously—or a combination of them.

The case for the establishment of a coherent overall strategy for the provision of publicly-funded legal services is overwhelming.[99] An attempt to provide such a strategy was made by the Royal Commission on Legal Services, which reported in 1979.[1] Many of its recommendations were criticised and the government's response was dismissive. Another was made by the Legal Aid Efficiency Scrutiny, a team of civil servants which reported to the Lord Chancellor in 1986. Some of its recommendations were accepted[2] and found their way into the Legal Aid Act 1988. Whilst the Legal Aid Board has responsibility for developing the scheme, is engaged in a wide range of such activities (*e.g.*, franchising and the non-solicitor agencies franchising pilot) and has encouraged proposals for alternative legal services projects,[3] the Government has made further, radical proposals in its 1995 Consultation Paper: *Legal Aid—Targeting Need*.[4] The other source of change in the provision of legal services is the fundamental reform of the legal profession effected by the Courts and Legal Services Act 1990; that is dealt with in Chapter 3.

---

[98] R.C.L.S., Vol. 1, p. 58.
[99] See also Legal Action Group, *A Strategy for Justice* (1992).
[1] Chaired by Lord Benson (Cmnd. 7648, 1979): see above p. 29.
[2] White Paper, *Legal Aid in England and Wales: A New Framework* (Cm. 118, 1987).
[3] Bill and Seargeant have evaluated some of the alternative legal services projects and concluded that funding would be appropriate for them all. The projects reviewed were: second-tier support (where a C.A.B. employs a resource lawyer to whom referrals are made); information work (a self-help park for tenants facing eviction; a computer database in planning and environmental issues; and a travellers' leaflet); telephone helplines (a generalist advice line; and a debt advise service); group work (used in resolving long leaseholders disputes; environmental pollution work; and a compensation for tenants project); and test cases (the community care test project): G. Bull and J. Seargeant, "Alternative methods of service delivery" (1996) *Legal Action*, March, 8.
[4] Cm. 2854.

1. THE ROYAL COMMISSION ON LEGAL SERVICES

(a) Principles[5]

The three basic principles identified by the Commission were all related to the general principle that "... legal services should be available to those who need them but cannot afford to pay for them."[6] Despite the acceptance of this principle the Commission found that a large number of people were not obtaining adequate legal services and set out the principles that should, in future, govern the provision of legal services:

    (i) Financial assistance out of public funds should be available for every individual (not corporations) who, without it, would suffer an undue financial burden in properly pursuing or defending his or her legal rights;

   (ii) All those who receive legal services are entitled to expect the same standard of legal service irrespective of their personal circumstances;

  (iii) The client, whether supported out of public funds or fee-paying, should always have a free choice among available lawyers and should not be required to retain an assigned lawyer.

In turning these principles into the means by which legal services were to be provided the Commission did not recommend any radical departure from the present "mixed economy" in legal advice and information. There would still be a place for amateurs, for salaried professionals and for private professionals, all of them supported in varying degrees by government funds.

(b) Proposals

The Commission's main proposals were

    (i) the establishment of an advisory council for Legal Services to keep under review the provision of all forms of legal services;

   (ii) the establishment of regional committees modelled on the Greater Manchester Legal Services Committee (as it then was);

  (iii) the encouragement of CABx as first-tier generalist advice agencies, with the development of rota schemes; they should not become over-specialised and required adequate government funding;

  (iv) the establishment of a new species of law centre, "Citizens' Law Centres," financed out of public funds, without involvement in general community work such as the mounting of campaigns or political or social work, with clients paying on the same basis as legally-aided clients of private practitioners, managed by a central agency and advised by a local advisory committee;

  (v) assimilation of the green form scheme with legal aid when the levels of eligibility and contribution could be made the same, with eligibility limits raised;

  (vi) provision for a free initial half-hour interview with a solicitor, available irrespective of means.

---

[5] R.C.L.S., Vol. 1, pp. 50–54.
[6] This was said to have been established with the introduction of legal aid in 1950.

(c) Responses

The public response to the Royal Commission Report was largely predictable. Particularly in its treatment of legal services the Report was alleged to be unduly supportive of the private profession and insufficiently imaginative in its proposals for the development of the public sector.

However, the critical response of organisations heavily involved in the current provision of legal services should be noted. The Legal Action Group attacked the Report on all fronts,[7] making particularly strong comment about the failure to recommend significant changes in the private profession and the ineffectual role assigned to the proposed Council for Legal Services. Only a Legal Service Commission with executive powers could do the necessary research and co-ordination job. The Law Centres Federation,[8] not surprisingly, were entirely hostile to the proposed Citizens' Law Centres and their response was directed mainly to that topic. The Federation was especially opposed to the means-testing of clients and the prospect of central control. Following this pattern, the Greater Manchester Legal Services Committee was also critical of the particular proposals which affected its area of concern and took the view that the regional committees proposed in the Report would not achieve what was required. Despite receiving warm commendation from the Commission, the Committee's response was cool with further criticism of the proposals on law centres and practice in deprived areas. The NACAB responses[9] were less strident in tone but contained detailed criticisms of many aspects of the Report, again, with particular reference to its own area of operation. The professions, by contrast, welcomed the majority of the recommendations with more than a hint of relief.

The Government response was belated and almost insulting.[10] The two volumes of the Commission's Report were dismissed in a very short document. In particular:

   (i) the case for the creation of a Council for Legal Services was rejected;
   (ii) the role of generalised agencies was endorsed, but with no additional funding;
   (iii) the recommendations on Citizen's Law Centres were still under consideration;
   (iv) eligibility limits for legal aid were to be retained, and the contributions currently payable are not unreasonable;
   (v) the "free half-hour" of advice would not be introduced;
   (vi) extension to the scheme for assistance by way of representation would be made when necessary.

2. THE LEGAL AID EFFICIENCY SCRUTINY

Following the Benson Report, the Lord Chancellor's Advisory Committee on Legal Aid noted that the government's response to the Royal Commission

---

[7] "Legal Services—A new start" LAG (1980).

[8] *A response to the Royal Commission on Legal Services*, Law Centres Federation (1980).

[9] Memoranda in response to the Report published by NACAB in August 1980 and March 1981.

[10] *The Government Response to the Report of the Royal Commission on Legal Services* (Cmnd. 9077, 1983).

"singularly lacked any commitment to a unified approach" and that "lack of clear ministerial responsibility and direction for legal services is a chronic problem.[11] In January 1986, the government appointed a team of officials "to consider the determinants of expenditure on the legal aid scheme by looking at its operation and administration in practice, and make recommendations." The team reported in June 1986.[12] It concluded that there was a pressing need for action in four main areas:

(i) legal aid procedures for handling applications, contributions and payments needed to be redesigned;

(ii) improved value for money should be obtained by cutting down on unnecessary procedures, (e.g., committals, remand hearings), strengthening controls on the progress of legally aided proceedings, changing listing practices, and restricting legal aid to solicitors who have demonstrated competence by membership of an appropriate panel;

(iii) the arrangements for legal advice represented a wasteful use of resources and did not guarantee a reasonable service to all who need it;

(iv) the administration of the legal aid system should be reorganised to ensure that the systems were simple, that there were clear lines of responsibility and that one organisation had clear overall responsibility for the operation of legal aid and advice.

Many (but not all) of the specific recommendations under (i) and (ii) were accepted and have led to changes in law or practice.[13] They are dealt with, as appropriate, in the sections on legal aid.[14]

The Scrutiny team's proposals for legal advice were the most controversial.[15] Its diagnosis of existing weaknesses was unexceptional, with reference to the lack of co-ordination in the provision of advice agencies, overlap in the service provided by advice agencies and private practitioners and difficulties in obtaining advice in an emergency. The proposals were startling. In essence, the existing green form scheme should be abolished and replaced by a system of advice based on a much greater involvement of advice agencies. Except in criminal areas, initial advice should be given by an advice agency, such as a CAB, rather than a private practitioner, and criminal cases would be limited to one hour's work. Family cases should be only referred to a solicitor where detailed advice and negotiation about the arrangements to be made for financial provision and for the children were needed; other civil cases should only be referred once it was clear that court proceedings should be initiated. The Area Directors should be made responsible for the effective and co-ordinated provision of legal advice and tribunal representation in their areas. The Scrutiny team estimated that this

---

[11] *34th Legal Aid Annual Reports* [1983–84], p. 334.

[12] *Legal Aid Efficiency Scrutiny* (L.C.D., 1986), Vols.1 and 2. There had come and gone, meanwhile, with comparatively little result, a management scrutiny by Coopers & Lybrand, a substantial study of eligibility by the Lord Chancellor's Advisory Committee (*34th Legal Aid Reports* [1983–84], pp. 239–333), and a National Audit Office enquiry (1985–86 H.C. 128) and associated Public Accounts Committee Report (1985–86 H.C. 330).

[13] See Vol. 2, Chaps. II and III of the *Scrutiny*; the White Paper, Legal *Aid in England and Wales: A New Framework* (Cm. 118, 1987), Chaps.5 and 6, and Annex B.

[14] Below, pp. 569–580, 767–772. Pre-trial criminal and remand hearings are considered at pp. 739–742 and 744–749.

[15] Vol. 2, Chap. IV.

would generate a need for an additional 500 lay advisers and 125 lawyers for the advice agencies.

The proposals were widely regarded as unrealistic, with adverse criticism (at varying strengths) from the Law Society, the Lord Chancellor's Advisory Committee on Legal Aid, NACAB, the Legal Action Group and others.[16] The strong reservations of NACAB were particularly noteworthy given the proposal to switch responsibilities to CABx and other generalist advice agencies. The 1986 NACAB AGM overwhelmingly passed a resolution expressing concern that the proposals might change the fundamental character of the CAB sevice and might prejudice its independence, would cut legal services and reduce freedom of choice of legal service to the poor and would damage working relationships between CABx and legal aid practitioners, other advice agencies and law centres.

The White Paper[17] accepted that there was force in some of the objections that had been made, and expressed the belief that the existing Green Form Scheme could be "improved to provide better service at lower cost."[18] The only changes that would be put into effect immediately would be the removal of wills and conveyancing from the ambit of the scheme.[19] The government was, however, "attracted to the principle of using the skills of advice agencies, especially to deal with those areas of work in which their special experience is likely to be greater than that of many solicitors in private practice.[20] The new Legal Aid Board would accordingly be given power to make alternative arrangements for the provision of particular categories of work. For example, the Board might contract with advice agencies for the provision of advice on welfare benefits, which would then be removed from the scope of the green form scheme. However, it would be left to the Board to consider whether and how this might be done. The immediate threat to the green form scheme was thus lifted, with a question mark left hanging over at least aspects of it.

3. THE LEGAL AID BOARD

(a) The future of the green form scheme

Amongst the early tasks indicated for the Board by the Lord Chancellor was to consider whether the best use was being made of resources devoted to advice and assistance, whether better arrangements might be made by using advice

---

[16] See, respectively, *Legal Aid Efficiency Scrutiny: The Law Society's Response* (October 1986); *36th Legal Aid Annual Reports* (1985–86), pp. 198–208 (Lord Chancellor's Advisory Committee); NACAB Annual Report 1986–87, pp. 20–21, 26; *Legal Action*, October 1986, pp. 4–9. See also J. Baldwin and S. Hill, (1986) 5 C.J.Q. 283, indicating that their research project (above, pp. 508–510) provided no evidence to support such a restructuring.

[17] Cm. 118, Chap. 4.

[18] *ibid.*, para. 24. " 'ıt was never a living duck,' said Lord Hailsham of the proposal . . . to transfer green form advice to the voluntary sector": quoted in *Legal Action*, May 1987, p. 4.

[19] Above, p. 494.

[20] Cm. 118, para. 24. This point was taken up in a debate conducted through the pages of *Legal Action* in 1988 as to the desirability of transferring welfare benefit and housing work from solicitors to advice agencies; following an article by A. Blake and D. Beale, *Legal Action*, December 1987, p. 6.

agencies and other organisations, and whether any further exclusions from the green form scheme would be appropriate.[21]

The Board gave indications of its thinking in its first Report to the Lord Chancellor and in a consultation paper issued in May 1989.[22] It was impressed with the usefulness and flexibility of the scheme, but needed to consider whether there could be a more effective use of resources. It confirmed that the scheme should remain demand-led, with payment on a case-by-case basis. Specific ideas on which it sought views were that preparatory advice given before the granting of a legal aid order should be claimed and paid for under that order and not the green form scheme, and that welfare benefit entitlement work[23] should either be limited to a fixed fee or excluded altogether. As to more general options for change, the Board referred to the possibilities of exclusive or semi-exclusive "contracting", and of "franchising". The idea of "contracting", with tendering for contracts, had been floated in the 1987 White Paper. However, the Board was unenthusiastic: there would be either limited or no consumer choice, and restricted access for the public would cause difficulties arising out of conflicts of interest between parties; the Board was "far from satisfied that there is generally a sufficient spread of the skills to make any form of competitive tendering a realistic or worthwhile exercise now or in the near future."[24]

Instead, the favoured option was "franchising". This would involve identifying those who could satisfy criteria or competence and reliability, and encouraging them by removing some of the administrative restrictions now applying.[25] It would be open to any solicitors' firms, and (although there were difficulties, e.g., about funding) advice agencies and law centres, which satisfied the criteria. The green form scheme would continue alongside franchise outlets until the access objective was met, with the aim of concentrating the majority of legal advice work on franchises. Moreover, franchising had the potential of extending beyond the green form scheme to civil and criminal legal aid. There could be two kinds, "general practice" and "specialist" franchises. The former, covering all or most categories of legal aid work, would almost always be provided by solicitors' firms; the latter could be provided by solicitors' firms, law centres, advice agencies and national organisations giving advice to individual clients. Prospective franchisees would need to demonstrate substantial involvement in the relevant work (in the case of general practice franchise, receipt of at least £40,000 p.a. from the Legal Aid Fund). There would be mechanisms to enable the Board to monitor the quality of service provided.

Responses were mixed.[26] There was wide support for the continuation of the scheme, in the light of the endorsements provided by the Baldwin and Hill research project, and that it should operate on a demand-led basis. Contracting

---

[21] Letter from the Lord Chancellor to the Board, cited in the Board's Report, (Cm. 688, 1989, pp. 10–11).

[22] ibid., 4 and Annex C; Second Stage Consultation on the Future of the Green Form Scheme (1989).

[23] Advice and assistance relating to the assessment of an entitlement to benefits, including negotiations with the D.S.S.

[24] Consultation Paper, p. 7.

[25] Delegation of power to exceed the green form limits; a system of monthly payments on account; simplified administration; ability to advertise that a franchise is held.

[26] See the Law Society, Franchising Legal Aid (1989); NACAB, Response to the Consultation Paper on the Future of the Green Form Scheme (1989); N.C.C., Franchising and the Future of the Green Form Scheme (1989); 39th Legal Aid Annual Reports (1988–89), pp. 95–98 (Lord Chancellor's Advisory Committee).

was unanimously rejected.[27] Welfare benefit work should not be excluded from the scheme; on the contrary, it should be accorded a high priority. There was some support for specialist but not for general practice franchising. Respondents other than the Law Society thought that the supposed difficulties of including advice agencies in franchising had been exaggerated; their involvement should indeed be encouraged, and would require additional resources. Any changes should only be introduced after proper research and costing, and after an initial experiment. A number of respondents noted that franchising would probably be as, if not more, suitable for legal aid administration than the green form scheme. The Law Society had greater reservations about franchising than the other bodies, except that it liked the administrative advantages and thought that they should be extended to all legal aid practitioners who satisfied quality control criteria developed by the Board and the Law Society.

Overall, the picture is less gloomy than might have been feared. The flaws in some of the ideas put forward by the Board have been cogently exposed, but it has shown a welcome willingness to take account of criticisms and alter its position accordingly. Franchising is now in place.[28]

4. Legal Aid—Targeting Need

In 1995 the Government, in the form of the Lord Chancellor's Department, issued a Consultation Paper on legal aid: *Legal Aid—Targeting Need,*[29] covering the whole of the legal aid scheme in an integrated approach, and not just the green form scheme. The Government stated that

"the objectives for the provision of publicly funded legal services are: (i) People who cannot afford to resolve their legal problems on their own should have access to publicly funded legal services, which should seek to achieve the most effective, efficient and economical resolution. (ii) Legal aid should be targeted towards those whose need is greatest. (iii) Legally aided services should be of high quality and efficiency. (iv) The overall cost of legal aid has to be affordable and controllable. (v) People should pay towards the cost of legal aid what they can reasonably afford. (vi) The system of remuneration for providing legally aided services should create incentives for effectiveness, high quality and efficiency."[30]

"Legal services" include "all services aimed at resolving legal problems, whether provided by lawyers or other suppliers such as advice agencies."[31] The Government does not consider funding of legal services in isolation, but views this matter in the context of three overall objectives: "To make the law itself simpler and easier to understand;[32] to make the processes of resolving disputes

---

[27] An impressive catalogue of criticisms is set out in the NACAB paper at p. 13.

[28] See above, pp. 491–492.

[29] (Cm. 2854, 1995) (hereafter *Targeting Need* (1995)). The White Paper, *Striking the Balance* (1996) is referred to in the Preface.

[30] *Targeting Need* (1995), para. 1.13.

[31] *ibid.*, para. 1.14.

[32] This echoes a call of the National Consumer Council: *The Cost of Justice* (1994), pp. 7–8 and, it is promised, will result in greater encouragement for the widely respected work of the Law Commission: *Targeting Need* (1995), para. 1.6 and see pp. 25–27.

in court simpler,[33] quicker and more affordable;[34] to encourage alternative ways of resolving disputes[35] so that people do not always have to use lawyers and courts to resolve their disputes.''[36]

The Government states that the ''existing scheme does not deliver legal services in areas where there is a clear need for greater help.''[37] The ''existing scheme'' refers to the five component parts of the legal aid scheme: civil legal aid[38]; criminal legal aid[39]; legal advice and assistance[40]; assistance by way of representation[41]; and duty solicitor schemes.[42] The areas it identifies as not being covered are those not traditionally associated with lawyers,[43] which can be given the umbrella term ''social welfare law''.[44] Not all lawyers in private practice have ignored these areas of work, but the role of law centres[45] and advice agencies[46] is significant in filling the gap. However, such organisations are not directly funded by the Legal Aid Fund and frequently have difficulty in ensuring funding. The Legal Aid Fund provides some funding for Law Centres through the legal aid cases the Centres and, more rarely, advice agencies take on. These are some of the significant limitations of the legal aid scheme, the costs of which, the Government says, are escalating much faster than inflation.[47] There has been a rise in the number of acts of assistance, but this does not fully explain the rise in cost. The Government, whilst essaying guesses at the reasons for the rise, has decided to respond to the call carefully to investigate them.[48]

The Government recognises that three approaches have been tried to control costs: ''alterations to the scope of legal aid; alterations to the rules of eligibility for legal aid; alterations to fees payable to lawyers for legal aid work.''[49] Few recent changes have been made to scope,[50] but eligibility for legal aid was significantly and controversially reduced in April 1993. The changes included:

''the disposable income limits for civil and criminal legal aid [being] reduced to the level of the adult Income Support rate; upper eligibility limits for civil legal aid [being] frozen; the contribution required [being]

---

[33] See below, pp. 567–568, 594–596, 597–600, 626–633.
[34] See below, pp. 542–546.
[35] See below, pp. 554–566.
[36] *Targeting Need* (1995), para. 1.5.
[37] *ibid.*, para. 3.7.
[38] See below, pp. 569–580.
[39] See below, pp. 763–772.
[40] See above, pp. 491–495, 496–499 and 507–513.
[41] See above, pp. 495, 500 and 767.
[42] See above, pp. 500–507 and 763–767.
[43] As to the traditional work of lawyers, see above pp. 126–127 and 459–463, as to the role of lawyers in the recognition of ''legal'' problems, see above, pp. 459–463 and 465–469.
[44] For the Government, this covers ''housing, employment, immigration, debt, and welfare benefits. Consumer issues might also be included'': *Targeting Need* (1995), para. 8.2. The Legal Action Group believes this list to be ''manifestly capricious'' asking why it does not include, *e.g.*, ''the Children Act, medical negligence and education.'' Legal Action Group, ''Green paper: amber light'' (1995) *Legal Action*, October, p. 6.
[45] See above, pp. 483–488.
[46] See above, pp. 473–482.
[47] ''In 1993/94 the scheme cost over £1,200 million. This is five times greater than ten years ago and far outstrips inflation'': *Targeting Need* (1995), para. 3.17, but see below.
[48] *ibid.*, paras. 3.17 and 3.18, responding to such call as that of the National Consumer Council in *The Cost of Justice* (1994), pp. 14–16.
[49] *Targeting Need* (1995), para. 3.23.
[50] The Government recognises that its proposals may lead to an extension in scope: *ibid.*, para. 3.24.

increased from one quarter of disposable income above the lower limit to one third; contributions [being] made payable for the duration of the case; dependant's allowances [being] reduced to the same level as the allowances for people on Income Support: prior to these changes they were 25 per cent higher,[51] contributory legal advice and assistance [being] scrapped[52], [and] the qualifying disposable income limit [being] set at £61 per week (as against £75 per week previously)."[53]

These swingeing cuts in eligibility were highly controversial,[54] having the effect of seeing those households eligible for legal aid reduced to 48 per cent.[55] The Government has listened to the critique to the extent of determining that there should be no further cuts in eligibility.[56]

Of the three approaches, the first two are ill-targeted to cut costs. The latter might have an effect on costs—indeed some believe that the remuneration and work of lawyers is significantly responsible.[57] The introduction of standard fees may well hold down some of the costs of the legal aid scheme.[58] However, little is actually known of the reasons for the cost explosion and it is anticipated that controlling lawyers' fees will have limited effect.[59] Reduction in the remuneration of lawyers has the obvious consequence of making them consider whether to continue with legal aid practice. The legal lobby is a powerful one.

The Government has identified the problem that the current scheme encourages people to seek legal solutions to problems. There is no incentive to seek alternative remedies.[60] Blaming the lawyers is easy, but account must be taken of their need to be paid for work done[61] and of the fact that many lawyers, particularly those dependent on legal aid work, do not make vast salaries.[62]

Thus different solutions are proposed by the Government. It recognises the contribution which partial solutions, that is a contingency legal aid fund,[63] conditional fees,[64] and legal expenses insurance,[65] can make,[66] but seeks a more fundamental approach based on

"four essential principles: funds must be targeted on needs and priorities; the scheme must deliver high quality services and contain incentives for suppliers constantly to improve the quality of those services and to find new and better ways of delivering them; the new scheme must also include incentives for suppliers to provide the most effective and economical

---

[51] For all these, see below, pp. 570–574.
[52] See above, p. 494.
[53] *Targeting Need* (1995), Appendix 1, paras. 32.
[54] See J. Rozenberg, *The Search for Justice* (1994), pp. 224–232 and see below, pp. 577–579.
[55] This is the Government's own assessment, see *Targeting Need* (1995), Appendix 1, para. 33. See below, pp. 577–579.
[56] *ibid.*, para. 3.25.
[57] See, *e.g.*, the Home Affairs Committee, *Legal Aid: The Lord Chancellor's Proposals* (1993) and National Consumer Council, *The Cost of Justice* (1994), pp. 14–15.
[58] See summary in *Targeting Need* (1995), Appendix 1, para. 34.
[59] *ibid.*, para. 3.28.
[60] *ibid.*, paras. 3.29–3.32. As to alternative dispute resolution, see below, pp. 563–566.
[61] Some pro bono work is done, see above, p. 490.
[62] See above, p. 124.
[63] See below, p. 545.
[64] See below, pp. 543–545.
[65] See below, p. 543.
[66] *Targeting Need* (1995), paras. 3.33–3.37.

solutions to problems in the interests of the client and the tax payer; [and] it must operate within an overall fixed budget, for without this there will be no discipline for setting priorities."[67]

The Government's major proposal is the introduction of a system of block contracts, which "is a contract between an agent and a supplier for the provision of legal services to clients for an agreed period and cost."[68] The overall objective is "to improve access to justice by establishing a means of setting priorities for legal aid and for targeting expenditure where there is greatest need. It would assure quality of services and value for money within a predetermined and controlled cost."[69] The contract would cover the type of services to be provided (which would cover all the areas of advice, assistance and representation covered under the present scheme),[70] their quality,[71] volume and price[72] and the geographical accessibility of the service.[73] Further, the Government wishes to ensure that cases would not be taken on where the client did not have a reasonable prospect of success or where the opponent would have no means of satisfying a judgement: "In each case the supplier would be required to consider the importance to the client, the complexity of the case, the need for urgency, whether (if relevant) any recovery was likely and cost/benefit considerations in the use of public funds." Some work might have to be done in some cases to determine these matters. Further, it is intended to ensure that suppliers do not just take on those cases with the highest profit margins, and they would not be allowed to reject cases simply because they were complicated or offered very little return.[74] These are entirely laudable sentiments. Contracts in civil, non-family legal aid[75] would cover three basic elements: "initial fact gathering and problem diagnosis", "basic advice and assistance" and "more detailed problem resolution including court proceedings, representation, alternative dispute resolution."[76] Broadly, the same approach would be taken for contracts for legal aid work on social welfare cases.[77] The most notable factor is the awarding of contracts for such work, hence encouraging solicitors and non-solicitor agencies to develop the work.

---

[67] ibid., para. 4.2.

[68] "There would be different contractual arrangements for different categories of work ... and different types of supplier" and "provisions [would be included] to guard against 'cherry picking' cases, so that suppliers did not only take on cases that were financially advantageous to them": ibid., para. 4.20(g) and (k).

[69] ibid., para. 4.18.

[70] ibid., para. 4.20(c).

[71] The quality control approach draws upon the work done in relation to franchising, see above, pp. 491–492 and 158. Quality will be measured by the use of outcome measures which are being developed by the Legal Aid Board, the effective use of non-court-based solutions, the satisfaction of transaction criteria and management standards and an audit of complaints: ibid., paras.6.42–6.48.

[72] ibid., paras. 6.23–6.32.

[73] This means that geographical situation could be of importance in the granting of a contract (ibid., paras. 6.17 and 6.18).

[74] ibid., paras. 6.39–6.41.

[75] The approach would be slightly different in legal aid for family cases by reason of the nature of the work, so there would be the possibility of suppliers offering the following services: preliminary advice and assistance (which could be carried out also by non-solicitor agencies); advice and assistance from lawyers; mediation; representation by solicitors either in negotiations or litigation: ibid., para. 9.3.

[76] ibid., para. 7.12.

[77] ibid., para. 8.5.

In legal aid for criminal cases, the government proposes to link advice and assistance and representation together, so contracts would cover all three.[78] The present requirements effectively mean that it is difficult to provide one form of criminal legal support, say a duty solicitor scheme, and not another, say representation in court. A client would be able to instruct a solicitor who did not have a contract for a police station duty solicitor scheme, but would then not be eligible for legal aid.[79] Block contracts would also be available to participate in court duty solicitor schemes.[80] Representation would be available on the same basis as under the present scheme,[81] and the purpose of block contracts would, therefore, be to encourage the most effective use of the money available. The existing tests for eligibility in the interests of justice would continue to apply, but options for change are set out regarding not only the administration of the test, but also changes to it. There has been considerable concern over whether magistrates' courts are performing their duties properly in granting legal aid, primarily in relation to the question of financial eligibility, but also with regard to the interests of justice test, so whilst one option is to leave the matter with the courts, another option is for the solicitors to assess the interests of justice test (which would impose a considerable burden on them). A further option is for the criteria to be assessed by the Legal Aid Board (but whether this could be done efficiently is open to doubt). A final option "would be to develop a different set of criteria for determining the interests of justice that would be simpler, easier to apply and to audit." The Government is of the view that the availability of legal aid does not need to be extended and that it cannot be restricted from the present position because of the requirements of Article 6 of the European Convention on Human Rights. One possibility for consultation is that legal aid would be granted where "(a) the applicant was charged with an offence which was either indictable or triable either way; (b) the applicant may be unable to understand the proceedings or to state his [or her] own case because of his [or her] inadequate knowledge of English, mental illness or other mental or physical disability; (c) there is an allegation of serious abuse of power by the police." Whether it would really be easier for a solicitor to apply this test rather than the current one is one of real doubt.[82]

As regards financial eligibility, the Government makes the following proposals, many of which will be welcomed by those concerned about the disintegration of financial support for those seeking legal help

(i) Civil diagnostic work would be non-contributory.[83]
(ii) As regards non-family civil legal aid,[84] all advice and assistance in social welfare cases would be means tested, but free to those who qualify. Advice and assistance for other non-family civil legal aid cases would be means tested and contributory, along the lines of the existing green form scheme. The statutory charge would not apply. A full means test would apply to representation, and it would be contributory with the statutory charge and recovery of costs applying. Assessment of means

---

[78] *ibid.*, para. 10.3.
[79] *ibid.*, para. 10.5.
[80] *ibid.*, para. 10.6.
[81] For the present scheme as to representation, see below, pp. 768–771.
[82] *ibid.*, paras. 10.11–10.18.
[83] *ibid.*, para. 12.5.
[84] For the proposals in relation to family legal aid, see paras. 12.10–12.14.

would not be carried out by solicitors, but by a specialised assessment organisation.[85]

(iii) Both duty solicitor schemes would operate on a non-contributory basis.[86]

(iv) Despite the cost of criminal legal aid,[87] the Government does not intend to alter the current test, but intends to make the assessment arrangements efficient and effective.[88]

Block contracts would guarantee income to the supplier, provided that the contract conditions were met. Payment would be in the form of regular predetermined sums, rather than case by case.[89] Block contracting builds upon two current initiatives of the Legal Aid Board—franchising[90] and the non-solicitor agencies franchising pilot.[91]

Block contracting would operate within priorities for legal aid which would be set by the Government, subject to Parliamentary scrutiny.[92] The setting of priorities, both locally and nationally, would mean that the contracts would be targeted to meet those needs. The setting of priorities would initially, for family legal aid and criminal legal aid, reflect existing demand since it is assumed that is as accurate an indicator as can be made available. In civil legal aid, the intention is to build upon the predictive modelling being developed by the Legal Aid Board to assess need.[93] This will enable a more accurate and fairer allocation of funds.

The contracts would "be let within an overall predetermined budget for legal services."[94] Note that a reserve would be held by the Legal Aid Board for "major unforeseen events", including "major disasters, new multi-party actions and exceptionally high cost cases."[95]

It is not surprising to discover that one of the major objection to these proposals has been the setting of a predetermined budget. The Legal Action Group describes it as "the crudest possible method for controlling expenditure" and "it is inherently illogical to divorce the level of expenditure on a service from fluctuations in demand."[96] Similar views are expressed by the CAB Service[97] and the Law Centres Federation.[98] The Legal Aid Board has suggested that, as regards criminal legal aid, this approach may be contrary to Article 6 of the European Convention on Human Rights.[99] The concern is not only about the iniquity of such a system, which may make meeting demand dependent upon factors other than the merits of a case and could lead to cases in certain areas not being supported,[1] but also that the huge expansion in cost of the system has

[85] *ibid.*, paras 12.6–12.9.
[86] *ibid.*, para. 12.15.
[87] i.e. £450m: *ibid.*, para. 12–16.
[88] *ibid.*, paras. 12.16–12.19.
[89] *ibid.*, para. 4.6.
[90] See above, pp. 491–492.
[91] *ibid.*, paras. 4.13–4.17.
[92] *ibid.*, paras. 4.19 and 5.6.
[93] *ibid.*, paras. 5.11–5.16. The current models exist in four areas of social welfare law (housing, debt, welfare and immigration).
[94] *ibid.*, para. 4.27.
[95] *ibid.*, para. 4.20(m).
[96] Legal Action Group, "Green paper: amber light" (1995) *Legal Action*, October, p. 6.
[97] N.A.C.A.B., *Legal Aid—Targeting Need: Response of the CAB Service* (1995), section 4.
[98] L.C.F., *Advancing Law for the People: Annual Report 1994–95* (1995), p. 4.
[99] *The Times*, November 28 1995.
[1] NACAB (1995), pp. 8–9.

been halted. There has been an underspend since the 1993 eligibility cuts, which may suggest that it is too soon to make such dramatic changes to the system and it would be better to learn the outcome of the research into the causes of the rise in expenditure.[2] Further concerns are whether the Government has accurately ascertained the problems with the current system. The Legal Action Group is concerned that being selective about what is supported will not lead to areas currently within the scheme losing support; does not accept that unmeritorious cases are pursued; accepts that some cases should be diverted from legal resolution, but with great care; and accepts that quality is not as high as it could be.[3] The CAB Service, in addition to addressing the proposals as a whole, is pleased to have its highly regarded work recognised by the Government, but is concerned that, if cases are to come its way under block contracting, this should not affect the ethos of the service, which is to treat clients holistically and not simply deal with the legal problem presented, nor should it affect the existing funding arrangements of the Service.

5. CONCLUSION

We conclude this chapter as we started it. It does not seem that we are any nearer the integrated approach to legal services long advocated by the Lord Chancellor's Advisory Committee. In recent years, the Committee has noted, with disappointment, that the new Legal Aid Board was not "a Legal Services Board with overall responsibility for legal aid and legal services"[4]; that the present system could not be said to constitute a "comprehensive system of legal services offering good early advice"[5]; and that in considering reform to the legal profession, there had been a failure by government "to examine the place that lawyers' services should occupy in the field of legal services as a whole."[6] The Committee has expressed concern that these reforms, particularly those concerning conveyancing and the Bar, may lead to a breakdown in the network of solicitors' offices, especially in rural areas, and a diminution in the quality of service to legally aided clients.[7]

There are blueprints available for the comprehensive provisions of legal services. One is provided by the National Consumer Council in its report *Ordinary Justice*, with a proposed network of general advice centres with access both to specialist advice agencies, with salaried staff and volunteers, and the legal profession.[8] In the end, it comes down to resources. The argument is often heard that problems are not necessarily solved by throwing money at them; how are they solved if you don't?

---

[2] See NACAB (1995), pp. 6–7 and Legal Action Group (1995), p. 6.
[3] Legal Action Group (1995), p. 6.
[4] *37th Legal Aid Annual Reports* (1986–87), p. 155.
[5] *38th Legal Aid Annual Reports* (1987–88), p. 98.
[6] *39th Legal Aid Annual Reports* (1988–89), p. 100.
[7] *ibid.*, pp. 98–101.
[8] (HMSO, 1989), Chap. 4. The Council had previously issued a discussion document (*Good Advice for All* (1986)) setting out guidelines on standards for local advice services. These were adopted by the Advice Services Alliance (which includes NACAB, the Federation of Independent Advice Centres, the Law Centres Federation, DIAL, Shelter and U.K.I.A.S.) in its "Go for Advice" manifesto in 1987 (but note the comments of R. Smith, *Legal Action*, August 1987, p. 6).

PART III

PRE-TRIAL PROCEDURE

CHAPTER 10

FEATURES OF LITIGATION

IN Part II we looked at advice and information. Now we begin a Part called Pre-trial Procedure and it may appear that we are progressing inexorably towards the courtroom. Yet between the recognition of a dispute which may end in a trial and its actual arrival before the judge lies a lengthy period of negotiation before or during the operation of the formal pre-trial procedure. An understanding of the significance of these negotiations, which may sometimes more accurately be described as bargaining, and the resulting settlements is fundamental to civil litigation. We concentrate on civil matters, even though in the criminal context there is the analogous feature of "plea bargaining".[1] The other two topics we consider in this chapter, costs and delay, have significance in both civil and criminal litigation, and are interrelated with pre-trial negotiations.

Influencing both civil and criminal procedure before and at trial, the English *adversarial* approach permits the parties to dictate the issues to be resolved and to settle the pace of the action. In civil cases, the court has had no role in directing the course of the proceedings except on the application of one or other party. It has always been able to impose penalties on parties who break the rules without permission, by the award of costs against them,[2] but it has not been able to enforce the rules of its own volition. This is all changing with moves towards court management of litigation.[3]

The parties select the issues on which to fight and the evidence with which to support their case. Whilst it may be in the interests of the court and a "fair result" for as much as possible to be disclosed in the early stages so that the matters really in dispute can be identified and the strength of the evidence assessed, it will often be in the interests of the parties to conceal what they know. For them, negotiation, in the form of bargaining, can proceed more effectively through a process of bluff and ambush, which is inimical to the demands of justice. Consequently, there are demands for greater openness in pre-trial procedure.[4]

---

[1] "Plea bargaining" is dealt with in Chapter 16 on the Criminal Trial. On the point of comparison between criminal and civil matters, see H. Genn, *Hard Bargaining* (1987), esp. at Chap. 2.
[2] See below, p. 000. There are other possible sanctions, see Sir Jack I. H. Jacob, *The Fabric of English Civil Justice* (1987), Chap. 2.
[3] See below, pp. 581 and 597–600.
[4] See below, pp. 630–632.

A. COSTS

1. CIVIL CASES[5]

The costs involved in civil litigation are of the utmost importance to the parties—they may prevent an action ever being brought,[6] they may render a victory in court Pyrrhic when damages are swallowed up in costs,[7] they may prevent a meritorious appeal, and they will always be a factor in the risk of litigation.[8]

Costs have to be looked at in two respects, first, the costs which may be ordered to be paid by one of the parties to the other in litigation, and, secondly, the costs which a client is obliged to pay the solicitor. It is not necessarily the case that the successful party will receive costs from the losing party which will cover the whole of the solicitor's bill.

(a) Costs payable in litigation

In deciding whether to begin or continue litigation, one major factor is whether a party will have to pay the costs or be able to recover them from the other party.

The principles in relation to the taxation of costs[9] after a trial do not prevent the parties reaching their own agreement about costs where a settlement is effected before trial. Indeed, in the majority of cases costs are agreed between the parties. Nevertheless the taxation rules remain significant in providing the framework within which the parties can negotiate.[10]

The steps are, first, that the judge must decide who should pay costs and on what basis, and, secondly, a "taxing officer"[11] must determine exactly what costs are to be paid. The basic rule is that "costs follow the event," that is to say the successful party can expect the judge to order the loser to pay some or all of his or her solicitor's bill.[12]

---

[5] This topic is dealt with more fully in J. O'Hare and R. N. Hill, *Civil Litigation* (6th ed., 1993), Chap. 23 and D. Barnard and M. Houghton, *The New Civil Court in Action* (1993), Chap. 15. See also *The Supreme Court Practice 1995*, pp. 1042–1159; *The County Court Practice 1995*, pp. 1595–1696.

[6] See pp. 562–563 above.

[7] See pp. 539–541 below.

[8] See pp. 546 and 563 below.

[9] *i.e.* the procedure whereby the exact sum to be paid is determined.

[10] Since the taxation of costs is both expensive and time consuming, O'Hare and Hill (1993), p. 566, recommend that solicitors should, where possible, try to avoid taxation by agreeing costs with each other.

[11] A "taxing officer" is a taxing master (or, in minor matters, a principal clerk of the taxing office) in the High Court in London; a district judge of the High Court outside London; and a district judge in the county court.

[12] The award of costs is a discretionary matter: Supreme Court Act 1981, s.51; R.S.C. Ord. 62, r. (4), but the discretion is exercised within the rules that have been established: R.S.C. Ord. 62, which impose no real limit on the exercise of judicial discretion: *Aiden Shipping Ltd v. Interbulk Ltd* [1986] A.C. 965. A successful plaintiff who receives more than nominal damages should, in normal circumstances, be granted a costs order against the defendant: *Gupta v. Klito, The Times*, November 23, 1989. In some cases it is known that costs do not follow the event: R.S.C. Ord. 62, r. 6. Certain matters must be taken into account in exercising the discretion, such as payments into court, and "Calderbank" letters: R.S.C. Ord 62, r. 9, below pp. 536–537. See, further, O'Hare and Hill (1993), pp. 541–549 and Jacob (1987), pp. 45–46, 275–276. The costs of and

A judge may order that costs are to be taxed on one of two bases.

(a) *Standard basis*, where "... a reasonable amount in respect of all costs reasonably incurred" is allowed. Any doubts as to questions of reasonableness in either respect are resolved in favour of the paying party.[13] As the terminology suggests, this is the usual basis upon which costs will be taxed.

(b) *Indemnity basis*, where "all costs ... except insofar as they are of an unreasonable amount or have been unreasonably incurred" will be allowed. Any doubts as to questions of reasonableness in either respect are to be resolved in favour of the receiving party.[14]

Thus it is only in cases of debate about the reasonableness of costs incurred that the different bases of taxation produce any difference in the actual costs received. From the point of view of the receiving party, the indemnity basis is the preferred basis, since then the burden of establishing that the expenditure was unreasonable lies upon the other party. It appears that costs are awarded on the indemnity basis only in exceptional cases, for example "major test cases" and "cases in which the paying party's conduct is considered to have been wholly unmeritorious, oppressive or in contempt of court"[15] and the court must expressly direct that costs be awarded on such a basis.[16]

The subsequent procedure is for the solicitor to compile a bill of costs and send it to the appropriate officer of the court for "taxing."[17] The preparation of a bill of costs for a taxation hearing is a very skilled and detailed task.[18] Specialists exist who undertake the drafting of the bill, usually for a commission calculated on the total amount of the bill or for a salary if employed by a large firm of solicitors. This payment is allowable on taxation and so may be recoverable from the losing party.[19]

The taxing officer hears the parties and decides any issues in dispute,[20] either allowing the item in the bill to stand or disallowing or reducing it. The total arrived at by this process is the total of "taxed costs" and is that amount which the loser is required to pay.[21] Taxation is designed to ensure that the losing

---

incidental to all proceedings in a county court are at the discretion of the court: C.C.R., Ord. 38, r. 1(2). The issue of costs is an example of the complexity produced in civil procedure by two sets of rules and is why the Civil Justice Review recommended that there be a common core of procedural rules: *Civil Justice Review* (1988), paras.277–280. This proposal is also made by Lord Woolf: Lord Woolf, *Access to Justice: An Interim Report* (1995); and See D. Greenslade, "A Fresh Approach: Uniform Rules of Court" in A. A. S. Zuckerman and R. Cranston, (eds.) *Reform of Civil Procedure* (1995). See also Jacob (1987), p. 50–67, 260.

[13] R.S.C. Ord. 62, r. 12(1); C.C.R. Ord. 38, r. 19A.
[14] R.S.C. Ord. 62, r. 12(2); C.C.R. Ord. 38, r. 19A.
[15] O'Hare and Hill (1993), p. 542.
[16] R.S.C. Ord. 62, r. 3(4); C.C.R. Ord. 38, r. 1.
[17] "Taxing" is the term given to the procedure which is conducted by a taxing officer, see n. 11 above.
[18] See the specimen bill of costs reproduced in O'Hare and Hill (1993), pp. 555–564.
[19] R.S.C. Ord. 62, r. 27; C.C.R., Ord. 38, r. 2.
[20] Where a hearing is held.
[21] In some circumstances, in addition to there being agreed costs between the parties, which avoids this process, there might also be "assessed costs" that is a fixed sum specified by the court at trial: R.S.C. Ord. 62, r. 7; C.C.R. Ord. 38, r. 19; or "fixed costs": R.S.C. Ord. 62, Appendix 3; C.C.R., Appendix B; see, O'Hare and Hill (1993), pp. 566–567; *County Court Practice 1989*, pp. 246–247.

party only has to pay those expenses properly incurred and is not saddled with the cost of unnecessary or unduly expensive work. The taxing officer must consider the directions of the court.

In a High Court action, the taxing officer, in exercising his or her discretion must have regard, amongst other factors, to the complexity, difficulty and novelty of the case, the skill, specialised knowledge and responsibility required of, and the time and labour expended by, solicitor and counsel, the number and importance of documents, the importance of the matter to the client, and the amount of money or value of property involved.[22] In a county court action, on the other hand, the amount of costs awarded is determined by the application of one of three scales.[23]

The costs which may be ordered to be paid are limited to "fees, charges, disbursements, expenses and remuneration and, in relation to proceedings . . ., also . . . costs of or incidental to those proceedings."[24] Such costs are unlikely to cover all the work that a solicitor has undertaken on behalf of a client.[25]

There are some circumstances in which costs are *not* awarded to the successful party. For example, in the various stages of pre-trial procedure the party who is ultimately successful may have caused undue delay or not followed the proper procedure and been penalised at that time by the award of costs against him or her in respect of a particular hearing.[26] These will eventually be disallowed on taxation.

Two other related matters should be mentioned. First, the successful unassisted party in an action where the opponent is legally aided may be awarded costs against the Legal Aid Board where certain statutory conditions are met.[27] Secondly, people who conduct their own litigation are entitled to costs in respect of their own time and effort spent preparing and presenting the case.[28] In addition to costs incurred by such a person which would also have been incurred by a solicitor acting on his or her behalf, the court can allow on taxation a sum not more than two-thirds of that which a solicitor would have been allowed for profit costs. If the litigant in person has not actually suffered pecuniary loss in the preparation of the case (which this sum would compensate) the court will only allow up to £8.25 per hour for the time reasonably spent in preparation.[29]

The Woolf Report has expressed some concerns about the damage produced

---

[22] R.S.C. Ord 62, Appendix 2, Part 1, para. 1.

[23] (1) Where the sum of money involved is greater than £25 but less than £100, the lower scale applies. This is rarely applied in practice, since most such cases go to arbitration rather than trial. (2) Where the sum of money is greater than £100 but less than £3,000, scale 1 applies. (3) Where the sum of money is greater than £3,000, scale 2 applies. It adopts the High Court rules, so there is a single costs regime for such cases. In default actions, the district judge sets the costs as thought fit: C.C.R. Ord. 38, r. 4(7): O'Hare and Hill (1993), p. 543. This adopts a proposal of the Civil Justice Review (at paras. 287–293) so as to avoid complexity, as introduced via the Courts and Legal Services Act 1990, s.4. A more radical approach would have been to introduce scales of costs into the High Court: Jacob (1987), p. 275.

[24] R.S.C. Ord. 62, r. 1(4) and see O'Hare and Hill (1993), p. 540.

[25] See *ibid.* As to the bill which a solicitor may present to a client, see below.

[26] *e.g.*, the failure to observe specified time limits, see below, p. 60.

[27] See below, pp. 576–577.

[28] The Litigants in Person (Costs and Expenses) Act 1975. This is one of those rare statutes which started life as a Private Member's Bill. See R.S.C. Ord. 62, r. 18; C.C.R., Ord. 38, r. 17 and Judge's Council Working Party, *Litigants in Person in the Royal Courts of Justice London* (Interim Report, 1995).

[29] R.S.C. Ord. 62, r. 18; C.C.R., Ord. 38, r. 17. In 1993, 91 bills were taxed in the Queen's Bench Division for litigants in person.

by the adversarial approach[30] and has considered the argument that the rule that costs normally follow the result (the "costs indemnity" rule) can induce a "win at all costs mentality [which] is supported by some research which indicates that the existing rule has the tendency to increase expenditure on cases when compared with a system where each party bears its own costs."[31] However, the rule tends only to support meritorious cases where there are greater expectations of success. The arguments for the rule were identified in the Woolf Report. (1) "It is fairer that a party who has succeeded in litigation should at least be able to recover the major proportion of his [or her] own costs from his [or her] unsuccessful opponent." (2) "The rule deters unmeritorious litigation and encourages earlier settlement." It also identified the arguments against the rule. (1) "It may deter meritorious as well as unmeritorious claims." (2) "It favours the wealthy litigant over the less wealthy." (3) "It can so increase the costs at stake that parties feel impelled to go on, thus making it impossible to reach a settlement."[32] The fear of the nuisance action will be limited by Woolf's proposals for case management.[33] No person bringing litigation should be immune from the financial risk factor, because of the burdens imposed on society and the courts of taking such a step, and so Woolf concluded that the rule should stay,[34] but recommended that the rule be made more effective, particularly to encourage co-operative and discourage unco-operative conduct by the parties.[35]

(b) Costs payable to solicitor

The successful party will often receive money in payment of costs from the losing party. However, this will not necessarily cover the costs which the successful party must pay to his or her solicitor. If the matter, as usual, does not end up in court, the agreed costs may also not cover all expenditure.

The solicitor is obliged to represent a bill within a reasonable time of concluding the work.[36] The client's contractual obligation is to pay the bill presented by the solicitor.[37] Ultimately, the solicitor is entitled to sue the client for "proper costs".[38] What costs are proper may ultimately be determined independently by the process of "taxation", but this is a highly unusual step for a solicitor to take; the better approach would be a simple debt action.[39]

The concern for the client is whether the solicitor is overcharging.[40] It is difficult for the client to assess whether the costs are appropriate for the service

---

[30] See below, p. 567.
[31] Woolf Report (1995), p. 201. See A. A. S. Zuckerman," "Reform in the Shadow of Lawyers' Interests" in Zuckerman and Cranston (1995).
[32] Woolf Report (1995), pp. 202–203.
[33] ibid., p. 203, As to case management, see below, pp. 581 and 597–600.
[34] ibid., pp. 203–204.
[35] ibid., p. 204, so the courts should have the full discretion granted under the Supreme Court Act 1981 which is curtailed by R.S.C. Ord. 62, r. 3(3).
[36] The Guide to the Professional Conduct of Solicitors (6th ed., 1993), Principle 14.05.
[37] The initial bill must identify the work to which it relates and the period covered: ibid., Principle 14.06. A more detailed bill than the initial brief one may be demanded: Solicitors Acts 1974, s.64.
[38] See O'Hare and Hill (1993), p. 576.
[39] ibid., p. 578. If taxation is the route adopted by the solicitor against a defaulting client, the client pays the costs of taxation, unless one-fifth of the bill is taxed off: ibid.
[40] In 1995 concern about solicitors' costs was revealed in the controversial Which? survey (see above, p. 157.) and also by commercial clients through a Focus Consultancy survey.

received.[41] A solicitor is obliged to provide information as to costs by a Written Practice Standard which provides that at the outset the solicitor should give "the best information possible about the likely cost of the matter," say how a fee is to be calculated,[42] discuss how various charges are to be met, and consider whether insurance may cover costs. When confirming the client's instructions, the solicitor should confirm in writing what, if any, fee has been agreed, tell the client what other payments may have to be made and when, and confirm the oral estimates. Where the client is paying privately, the solicitor must inform the client that a limit may be set on the costs, explain that estimates cannot always be provided in advance, and inform the client of the approximate costs every six months. If the private paying client is receiving advice in a contentious matter, the solicitor must also, both at the outset and at appropriate stages thereafter, inform the client that he or she will be responsible for the solicitor's costs whatever the outcome of the litigation may be, that he or she may well have to pay the other side's costs if they lose, that if they win, the costs from the loser may well not cover all their costs, and that if the opponent is legally aided costs may not be recoverable even if they win.[43] Where the client is legally aided, he or she must be informed of the effect of a statutory charge, that if they lose there may still be a contribution to the winner's costs despite the legal aid, that if they win they may not get an order for all costs and, in any case, they may not be paid, and of their obligation to pay the assessed contribution.[44] Finally, in all cases the solicitor should "consider with clients whether the likely outcome will justify the expense or risk involved."[45]

If solicitors always complied with the Written Practice Standard, many of the consequent problems with clients would disappear. The client would have a clearer idea of what the bill could be expected to amount to and so would not be surprised at its ultimate size, and the client would be aware of the risks involved in litigation. It is not surprising that the Legal Services Ombudsman has stated that "Full compliance by solicitors with the written professional standard is ... an absolutely essential safeguard for clients, and very much in the

---

[41] This is true for commercial as well as private clients.

[42] The options include: an hourly rate plus mark-up, and a percentage of the value of the transaction. The following tables, taken from *Chambers and Partners' Directory of the Legal Profession 1994–95*, p. 7. gives an indication of hourly rates:

Table A: Partner—£/hour

	Company/Commercial			Commercial Litigation			Private Client		
	Low	average	High	Low	Average	High	Low	Average	High
London	130	240	325	160	180	295	80	165	255
Provinces	65	115	210	65	105	200	60	90	170

Table B: Assistant solicitor—£/hour

	Company/Commercial			Commercial Litigation			Private Client		
	Low	average	High	Low	Average	High	Low	Average	High
London	90	140	220	80	120	210	65	110	135
Provinces	50	85	140	50	75	120	50	70	110

[43] The costs rule was considered above.

[44] See below, pp. 572–576.

[45] The Written Practice Standard is to be found in *The Guide to the Professional Conduct of Solicitors*, Principle 13.04, with further explanation at pp. 282–288.

interests of solicitors themselves if they are to avoid complaints about costs."[46] The National Association of Citizen's Advice Bureaux noted that complaints about costs are a major area of CAB work and that there is poor compliance with the standard.[47] Research sponsored by the National Consumer Council has concluded that "a significant minority [of clients] do not always receive the kind of information on costs required by the ... standards."[48] In consequence, NACAB recommends: (1) that the standard "be amended so as to require solicitors to agree with clients a timetable for regular updates on costs, and to confirm that agreement in writing"; (2) that there be a "requirement that throughout the lifetime of the case solicitors keep under review the possibility of costs outweighing the benefit of any action, and report to the client accordingly"; and (3) that leaflets in English and other languages should be produced to provide information about costs.[49] The National Consumer Council recommends: (1) that there be tougher and more frequent enforcement of the existing standard; (2) that the standard become a practice rule; (3) that a written guide about costs be provided for clients.[50]

Solicitors "must not take unfair advantage of the client by overcharging for work done or to be done."[51] So, if a solicitor deliberately overcharges, disciplinary action would follow.[52] If a client believes that he or she has been overcharged, the matter can be dealt with by the Solicitor's Complaints Bureau[53] which will "if there is a *prima facie* case . . ., investigate the matter, examine the file, allow the solicitor to comment, allow the client to comment on the solicitor's comments, and then reach a decision."[54] The disciplinary action to follow depends on the outcome of that decision.[55]

Assessing the propriety of costs will depend upon whether they relate to a *contentious* matter, which term applies only once an action has begun.[56] If a client objects to the bill submitted by the solicitor in such a matter an application may be made to the High Court for an order for taxation of the bill.[57] If granted,[58] taxation is carried out on the "indemnity basis" but it is presumed that the costs (a) have been reasonably incurred, if they were incurred with the express or implied approval of the client; (b) have been reasonable in amount, if their amount was expressly or impliedly approved by the client; (c) have been unreasonably incurred, if in the circumstances of the case they are of an unusual nature, unless the solicitor satisfies the taxing officer that prior to their being

---

[46] *Fourth Annual Report of the Legal Services Ombudsman 1994* (H.C. 459, 1995), para. 3.12.
[47] NACAB, *Barriers to Justice* (1995), paras. 3.6–3.15. See also J. Jenkins and V. Lewis, *Client Perceptions—Existing and potential clients: experiences and perceptions of using a solicitor for personal matters* (1995).
[48] N. Harris, *Solicitors and Client Care* (1994), p. 22.
[49] N.A.C.A.B. (1995), paras. 3.9, 3.14 and 3.16.
[50] Harris (1994), p. 31.
[51] *The Guide to the Professional Conduct of Solicitors*, Principle 14.10.
[52] See S. Fennell, "The quality of solicitors' services" (1992) 8 P.N. 115, at p. 121 and see above, pp. 159–166.
[53] This is another example of the width of the jurisdiction of the S.C.B., see above, pp. 162–165.
[54] Fennell (1992), at p. 122.
[55] As to disciplinary action against solicitors, see above, pp. 159–166.
[56] The definition is to be found in the Solicitors Act 1974, s.87 and see O'Hare and Hill (1993), p. 577.
[57] Solicitors Act 1974, s.70.
[58] An order must be granted if the request is made within one calendar month of delivery of the bill, otherwise the court has a discretion: Solicitors Act 1974, s.70, and see O'Hare and Hill (1993), p. 578.

incurred the client was informed that they might not be allowed on taxation of costs.[59]

As we have seen, where the business is contentious, the client is assisted in paying what is owed to the solicitor if he or she wins, since costs are then likely to be obtained from the losing party.

In *non-contentious* civil matters, the client may have the fees reviewed by the Law Society, a jurisdiction delegated to the Solicitor's Complaints Bureau, by seeking a remuneration certificate.[60] The client may then be charged such sum as is fair and reasonable having regard to all the circumstances of the case and, *inter alia*, its complexity, the skill and responsibility involved, the time spent, the property involved, and the importance of the matter to the client.[61] Fennell has identified the advantages of this system as being that it is free and the client is not personally involved. The disadvantages are that the client may be unaware of the system because the solicitor is only obliged to inform the client of a right to a certificate before bringing proceedings to recover fees or before charging interest, and not when the bill is delivered;[62] the Solicitors' Complaints Bureau may not be perceived as sufficiently impartial;[63] and the courts have been prepared to uphold a compromise on a bill prior to the client being advised of his or her rights and so the client loses the right to a certificate, whereupon the client would have to challenge the compromise in court.[64] If still unsatisfied, the client has the right to apply to the High Court for an order to have the bill taxed.[65] If granted, the taxing officer assesses the costs on the same basis as in a contentious case. Fennell points out that this process will involve the client paying the costs of taxation unless the bill is reduced by at least one-fifth; it is a formal, litigious procedure; and the client is not informed of this right on delivery of the bill but only prior to the solicitor suing for the fees.[66]

(c) Costs and settlement

The doubts as to whether costs will be available to a party and the possibility that what costs are payable by the other party will not cover the full costs of seeking legal assistance are powerful factors in decisions as to whether and when to settle.[67]

There are also two procedures which may place the plaintiff in further difficulties. The first procedure is the *payment into court*.[68] At any stage in an action for

---

[59] R.S.C. Ord. 62, r. 15(2); C.C.R. Ord. 38, r. 19A and see O'Hare and Hill (1993), p. 579.

[60] Solicitors Remuneration Order 1972, art.3(1). A client may not seek a remuneration certificate after the expiry of one month from the date on which the client was given information under art.3(2), see below, after a bill has been delivered or paid, or after High Court taxation: *ibid.*, art.3(3).

[61] *ibid.*, art.2.

[62] Solicitors Remuneration Order 1972, art.3(2).

[63] Fennell was writing about the Law Society, but the perception of impartiality point is still valid according to the National Consumer Council, *The Solicitor's Complaints Bureau* (1994), see above, p. 165.

[64] Fennell (1992), p. 122.

[65] Solicitors Act 1974, s.70.

[66] Fennell (1992), p. 122.

[67] See below, pp. 562–563.

[68] For the place of payment into court in pre-trial procedure, see below, p. 626; for its effect in the settlement process, see below, p. 562). The procedure is considered in some detail in O'Hare and Hill (1993), pp. 352–370 and N. Andrews, *Principles of Civil Procedure* (1994), pp. 393–401.

debt or damages in either the High Court or a county court, the defendant may make a payment into court in satisfaction of the plaintiff's claim. The plaintiff may accept the payment in settlement of or may continue the action. If a sum greater than that paid in is not recovered at the trial, the plaintiff will be liable for the defendant's taxed costs from the time of the payment in, even though he or she has "won" the action. The judge in making an award of damages will know that a payment into court has been made, but will not know how much and so cannot set the damages to ensure that the payment is or is not beaten. The rule is open to considerable criticism as being a "blunt instrument" to achieve its objective and as operating unfairly on the plaintiff to capitulate without trial under the burden of great financial pressure.[69] It adds considerably to the risk element in litigation.[70] Whilst it may be of advantage to the defendant to force a reluctant plaintiff to settle, it is only available to the defendant and is limited to causes of action, rather then specific issues, such as liability.[71]

The second procedure is the use of *Calderbank* letters.[72] The defendant makes a written offer to compromise the claim, making that offer "without prejudice save as to costs". It is available in actions where a payment into court is not available,[73] which largely limits it to matrimonial proceedings.[74] The court is unaware of the offer until the question of costs falls to be decided.

In his review of civil procedure, Lord Woolf proposes that payments into court should be ended and that *Calderbank* offers should be available in all cases. One advantage is that there are then no moneys for which the court is responsible. It would be possible for a plaintiff as well as a defendant to make an offer. Offers to settle, as they would become, would be possible for individual matters and could be made before the commencement of proceedings.[75]

2. CRIMINAL CASES[76]

To what extent can the "loser pays costs" rule apply in criminal matters? This rule is of lesser significance because of the existence of criminal legal aid[77] and because prosecutions brought by the Crown Prosecution Service are funded by government.[78] Further, the defendant does not have the option of minimising cost by deciding not to go ahead with the case! The defendant does, though, have the right to plead guilty and/or to bargain about charge and plea,[79] either

---

[69] Andrews (1994), pp. 400–401. See also P. Cane, *Atiyah's Accidents, Compensation and the Law* (5th ed., 1993), pp. 231–233.

[70] See below, pp. 562–563.

[71] Woolf Report (1995), p. 194.

[72] So called after the Court of Appeal decision in *Calderbank v. Calderbank* [1976] Fam. 93 and now codified in R.S.C., Ord. 22, r. 14; C.C.R., Ord. 12, r. 10. See O'Hare and Hill (1993), pp. 370–374 and Andrews (1994), p. 402.

[73] R.S.C., Ord. 62, r. 14(2); C.C.R., Ord. 12, r.10(2).

[74] Woolf Report (1995), p. 194.

[75] *ibid.*, Chap. 24 and see R. Cranston, " 'The Rational Study of Law': Social Research and Access" in Zuckerman and Cranston (1995), pp. 44–49.

[76] The governing statute is the Prosecution of Offences Act 1985; see *Halsbury's Laws of England*, Vol. 11(2), paras.1527–1540 and P. Murphy (ed.), *Blackstone's Criminal Practice 1996*, paras. D26.33–D26.47.

[77] See below, pp. 763–772.

[78] See below, pp. 701–704.

[79] See below, pp. 839–841, 850–851, 856–858.

of which might reduce the costs involved in a trial. Criminal courts, though, have powers to make orders about costs in various circumstances.

A *defendant's costs* order may be made in favour of an acquitted defendant by the Crown Court or a magistrates' court.[80] These costs are awarded out of central funds. The award covers what the court considers is reasonably sufficient to compensate the party for expenses properly[81] incurred in the proceedings and directly related to them.[82] In both the magistrates' court and the Crown Court, an order should normally be made whether or not an *inter partes* order is made, unless there are positive reasons for not making an order. The examples given of such reasons are: (a) the defendant's conduct brought suspicion on himself or herself and so misled the prosecution into thinking the case was stronger than it was; and (b) the defendant is acquitted on a technicality, when there was ample evidence to support a conviction.[83] A defendant's costs order may be made by (a) a magistrates' court where an information has been laid but not proceeded with, or where the court decides not to commit the accused for trial, or where, on summary trial, the court dismisses the information;[84] (b) the Crown Court where a person is not tried for an offence for which he or she was indicted, or has been acquitted, it may exercise its discretion where a person is convicted on some counts but not others (in which case only part of the costs may be ordered to be paid), and it may also make an order in favour of a successful appellant.[85] There are also circumstances in which the Divisional Court and the Court of Appeal may make defendant's costs orders: by the Divisional Court on determining proceedings in a criminal cause or matter; and by the Court of Appeal (exercising its discretion on the same principles as the Crown Court) when it allows an appeal against conviction or sentence, on appeal against a preparatory hearing order or ruling, to cover the costs of representation where there is an Attorney-General's reference on law or sentence, and on determining an application for leave to appeal to the House of Lords.[86]

Costs may be awarded to a successful *private prosecutor*[87] out of central funds[88] in relation to proceedings for an indictable offence and before the Divisional Court in respect of a summary offence.[89] Costs are not awardable in summary trials. Costs are awarded, save where there is good reason for not doing so, which would be, for example, where a prosecution was instituted without good cause.[90] The costs awardable are those which are just and reasonable.[91]

---

[80] Prosecution of Offences Act 1985, s.16(1),(2) and *Practice Note* [1991] 2 All E.R. 924. See *Halsbury's Laws of England*, Vol. 11(2), para. 1527 and *Blackstone's Criminal Practice 1996*, paras. D26.34–D26.36.

[81] A requirement of the Prosecution of Offences Act 1985, s.16(6). Costs not properly incurred include those in respect of work unreasonably done, or costs wasted by failure to conduct proceedings with reasonable competence and expedition (note that in such cases a wasted costs order may be made, see above, pp. 176–178): *Practice Note* [1991] 2 All E.R. 924, at para. 5.1.

[82] Prosecution of Offences Act 1985, s.21(1) & 16(6) and *Practice Note* [1991] 2 All E.R. 924, at para. 1.5, and see paras. 1.6–1.8.

[83] *ibid*, at para. 2.2, applied to magistrates' courts by *ibid*., para. 2.1.

[84] *ibid*., para. 2.1.

[85] *ibid*., paras. 2.2–2.4.

[86] *ibid*., paras. 2.5–2.8.

[87] *i.e.*, not a public authority or a person acting on behalf of a public authority: Prosecution of Offences Act 1985, s.17(2).

[88] Prosecution of Offences Act 1985, s.17 and see *Halsbury's Laws of England*, Vol. 11(2), para. 1528 and *Blackstone's Criminal Practice 1996*, paras. D26.39.

[89] *Practice Note* [1991] 2 All E.R. 924, at para. 3.1.

[90] *ibid*., at para. 3.1.

[91] Prosecution of Offences Act 1985, s.17(2).

An award of costs may be made *against a convicted defendant*.[92] The costs awarded will be those that the court considers just and reasonable.[93] The judge has a discretion to exercise in determining whether to make such an order, taking account of whether the defendant chose to contest a strong case against him or her and if the defendant must have known the real truth of the matter.

3. Tribunals

We shall repeat elsewhere that it is difficult to generalise about tribunals. Broadly, the parties to a dispute which is settled by a tribunal will bear their own costs, subject to any specific rules applicable to a particular tribunal. We can merely give a number of examples.

In Social Security Appeal Tribunals,[94] the claimant will receive only compensation for loss of earnings (if any) and travelling expenses. These are payable whatever the outcome of the hearing. No costs can be awarded against the claimant.

In Industrial Tribunals, the tribunal will not normally make an award of costs. There is a power to make an award only where a party has acted frivolously, vexatiously, abusively, disruptively or otherwise unreasonably, either for a fixed sum or for taxed costs.[95]

In the Lands Tribunal, costs are within the discretion of the tribunal[96] and it is interesting to note that of the 21 Lands Tribunal bills taxed in 1995, the average amount allowed on taxation was £17,123.[97]

The last example is highly unusual. Legal aid is not generally available for tribunals,[98] they are intended to be cheap and both sides are clearly expected to bear their own costs.[99]

4. Civil Proceedings—What do they Actually Cost?

The Woolf Inquiry into the civil justice system concluded in the interim report[1] that "excessive cost deters people from making or defending claims" and that the "problem of disproportionate cost occurs throughout the system. It is most

---

[92] Prosecution of Offences Act 1985, s.18, and see *Halsbury's Laws of England*, Vol. 11(2), para. 1529 and *Blackstone's Criminal Practice 1996*, paras. D26.40–D26.42.

[93] Prosecution of Offences Act 1985, s.18(2) and see also *Practice Note* [1991] 2 All E.R. 924, at para. 6.1.

[94] The same rules apply to appeals to the Social Security Commissioners: Social Security Administration Act 1992, Sched. 2 para. 7.

[95] Industrial Tribunals (Constitution and Rules of Procedure) Regulations 1993 (S.I. 1993 No. 2687), Rules of Procedure, Rule 12. Similar provisions apply to the Employment Appeal Tribunal.

[96] Lands Tribunal Rules 1996 (S.I. 1996 No. 1022), r.52.

[97] *Judicial Statistics 1995* (Cm. 3290, 1996), Table 10.1, p. 94. The figure is quite startling in comparison with the much lower figure for actions in the Queen's Bench Division, see p. 540, below.

[98] See below, pp. 569–570.

[99] There are some examples of money being made available to agencies providing a representation and advice service for those using tribunals, *e.g.* government grants are made to specialist advice services, by virtue of Immigration Act 1971, s.23. The Royal Commission on Legal Services advocated that this approach should be adopted more widely.

[1] Woolf Report. (1995).

acute in smaller cases where the costs of litigation, for one side alone, frequently equal or exceed the value of what is at issue."[2] The Woolf Inquiry requested research by the Supreme Court Taxing Office with the assistance of Professor Hazel Genn, which gave information about average costs, confirmed the view that disproportionate cost is a significant problem and provided fascinating information as to the components of the costs.

There is a difference in average costs allowed by the taxing office between different types of case: "medical negligence cases had the highest average costs at £38,252, followed by commercial cases at £29,418, and official referee/breach of contract/libel, other Q.B. cases at £25,786. Medical negligence cases also had the highest minimum costs bill at £5,369, followed by commercial cases at £4,904."[3] Wills/chancery cases, and bankruptcy/companies cases generally have lower costs on average and the more expensive case types were medical negligence, official referee/breach of contract, and commercial cases.[4]

"In *one-half of the lowest value cases* the costs on one side alone were close to, or exceeded the total value of the claim."[5] It must be noted that, "in just under half of the cases in the sample (47 per cent) costs did not exceed 30 per cent of the claim value, and in over a third of cases (36 per cent) costs did not exceed 20 per cent of claim value." However, "in a substantial proportion of cases . . . the *costs on one side alone exceeded* the value of the claim by a substantial amount. Some 16 per cent of bills were the equivalent of 100 per cent or more of claim value, with 6 per cent of these bills representing 200 per cent or more of the claim value."[6] Further study of these latter cases showed that in many the case was relatively light and the claim value was relatively low.[7]

"When costs as a proportion of claim value are analysed by case weight we find that *the more straightforward the case, the higher the costs relative to the value of the claim*", as can be seen from the figure below which the survey produced.[8]

The conclusion as to disproportionate cost is confirmed, according to the

Mean costs as proportion of case value – by case weight

A = most complex   *Assessment of weight of case – exc. seven cases*

[2] *ibid.*, p. 9.
[3] *ibid.*, p. 252.
[4] *ibid.*, p. 253.
[5] *ibid.*, p. 255.
[6] *ibid.*, p. 256.
[7] *ibid.*, p. 257.
[8] *ibid.*, fig. 3.1 on p. 258.

Woolf Report, by various other surveys[9] and is also reflected in the Inbucon Study undertaken as part of the Civil Justice Review.[10] The Woolf Survey also examined the components of costs and produced the following information in tabular form: [11]

Components of bills by case type

	Type of case						
Amount of costs	Bankruptcy companies court & partnership N=61	Wills & Chancery, other N=72	Official Referees breach of contract, libel & QB other N=238	Breach of copyright injunction declaration N=32	Medical negligence N=43	All personal injury N=181	Commercial N=46
Average costs sllowed £	14,792	15,860	25,786	25,031	38,252	20,413	29,418
Counsel fees average – settling pleadings £	633	560	627	1,158	877	274	699
Conferences £	687	502	777	1,045	1,965	741	1,002
Briefs/refresh £	2,182	2,164	3,590	3,745	5,230	2,734	4.492
Written advice £	133	353	301	172	700	336	264
Total counsel fee allowed £	3,636	3,579	5,276	6,121	8,773	4,086	6,457
Counsel fees as % of bill	25%	22%	20%	21%	18%	15%	20%
Expert fees average – total fees £	543	479	3,396	443	5,658	2,624	141
Expert fees as % of bill	9%	5%	16%	7%	15%	13%	4%
Discovery average value £	121	102	483	265	180	226	264
Average % bill	5%	6%	6%	4%	2%	3%	5%
Documents average value £	4,809	4,839	7,364	8,274	9,955	4,901	10,855
Average % bill	30%	31%	31%	35%	27%	25%	40%
Four components as % bill	58%	55%	59%	58%	60%	53%	61%

[9] *ibid.*, p. 10.
[10] Inbucon International Consultants, *Civil Justice Review: Study of Personal Injury Litigation* (1986), and the second edition of this book at pp. 479–480.
[11] Woolf Report (1995), Table 3.7 on p. 259.

5. CIVIL PROCEEDINGS—CAN LITIGATION BE AFFORDABLE?

Clearly civil litigation is often very expensive. In some circumstances, litigation should be avoided, and there is increasing encouragement for parties to a dispute to look to alternative methods of resolution.[12] For many people the costs of litigation are difficult, impossible or off-putting.[13] When litigation is necessary, it is important, if a system of civil justice is to be fair, that litigants must "have an equal opportunity, regardless of their resources, to assert or defend their legal rights."[14] There are broadly three possible approaches to make civil litigation affordable.

(a) Jurisdictional, procedural and administrative reforms

The first is to address the problems in civil procedure so as to reduce the cost of litigation. Lord Woolf concluded that the current level of costs is not an inevitable or necessary feature of litigation and that the current attitudes to litigation are a major factor in creating high costs and costs uncertainty.[15] Clearly cost cannot be the only concern. Lord Woolf identified certain basic principles which must be met by a civil justice system: it must be just in the result it delivers, it must be fair and seen to be so, its procedures must be proportionate to the natures of the issues involved, cases should be processed with reasonable speed, it must be understandable to those who use it, it must be responsive to its users' needs, it should provide such certainty as the disputes allow, and it should be effective in delivering on those principles.[16] On the basis of these principles, radical proposals for change have been made.[17] Undoubtedly the final report, expected in 1996, will show many changes as a consequence of the consultation exercise, and not all the recommendations will eventually be introduced. Nevertheless, reform is essential. Broadly speaking, the proposals are receiving support. Whether they have any effect will depend upon the support and commitment of the professions and, more significantly, whether there will be sufficient input of resources for case management by the courts to work.

(b) Parties enabled to pay more easily

The second approach is by examining ways in which the parties pay. One method is through the support of an organisation. The typical organisations which provide such support are trade unions, which often provide general legal

---

[12] See below, pp. 563–566.

[13] As to the effect of costs on seeking legal action, see p. 465 above.

[14] This is one of the basic principles which should be met as identified by Lord Woolf: Woolf Report (1995), p. 3.

[15] *ibid.*, pp. 10–12. See R. Cranston, " 'The Rational Study of Law': Social Research and Access"; D. Greenslade, "A Fresh Approach: Uniform Rules of Court", both in Zuckerman and Cranston (1995). For a more radical view of procedural reform, see A. A. S. Zuckerman, "A reform of civil procedure—rationing procedure rather than access to justice" (1995) 22 J.L.S. 155.

[16] *ibid.*, pp. 2–3. The *Civil Justice Review* (1989) also made many proposals to reduce delay, cost and complexity, not all of which have been introduced. The need to improve the system is a clear and pressing one, as also identified by the Independent Working Party set up by the General Council of the Bar and the Law Society in its report, *Civil Justice on Trial – The Case for Change* (1993) (hereafter The Heilbron/Hodge report, so named after its chair and vice-chair).

[17] See below, pp. 626–633.

support,[18] and pressure groups, which usually provide support for a particular issue and will support litigation where it furthers the objectives of the group.

It is possible that a litigant may have legal expenses insurance which is "payment of an annual premium to carry cover, in given categories of cases, for a claimant's legal costs (including any costs awarded against him) up to a limit of indemnity."[19] A policy is either personal or commercial and a personal policy is either a "stand-alone" policy or an "add-on-policy" (that is added on to household or motor insurance).[20] The market is currently very small and the premiums are high,[21] but the government is keen to encourage its development, and is contemplating encouraging its extension through employment packages.[22]

A further insurance option is "after the event" insurance, whereby a victim in a personal injury case may buy the insurance after the accident and before the commencement of legal proceedings. The insurance company pays the costs where the victim loses, but a solicitor would not advise a case to be commenced or insurance purchased unless confident in the chances of success.[23]

A fourth method is through a fixed costs scheme, proposed by the Law Society in 1987.[24] Zander describes this scheme as meaning that solicitors would pay a premium to an insurance company and the client would pay a fixed amount to cover the costs in the event of the case being lost.[25]

The fifth method is the contingency or conditional fee system, whereby a lawyer agrees to act for a client on the basis that he or she will receive an agreed proportion of any damages recovered. If no damages are recovered, there is no fee. This is the system of support in many accident cases in the United States. In Scotland there is a long tradition of lawyers acting on a "speculative" basis.[26] At one time, such agreements amounted to the common law offence of champerty,[27] but from the time of the Criminal Law Act 1967, s.13 until 1995, such agreements were not an offence but were unenforceable contracts and were contrary to the professional rules of conduct.

The arguments in favour of such a system include: it allows litigation which would otherwise not be brought; the lawyers involved act more conscientiously on behalf of their client; and it is a simpler method of payment.[28] The arguments against include: it is an open invitation to unprofessional conduct;[29] lawyers will

---

[18] See A. Boon, "Ethics and Strategy in Personal Injury Litigation" (1995) 22 J.L.S. 353 and Supreme Court Procedure Committee, *Guide for use in Group Actions* (1991), p. 27. See above, p. 481.

[19] Lord Chancellor's Department, "Review of the Financial Conditions for Legal Aid: Eligibility for Civil Legal Aid; A Consultation Paper" (1991) quoted in N. Rickman and A. Gray, "The Role of Legal Expenses insurance in Securing Access to the Market for legal Services" in Zuckerman and Cranston (1995), p. 305.

[20] V. Prais, "Legal Expenses Insurance" in Zuckerman and Cranston (1995), p. 434.

[21] Richman and Gray (1995), pp. 313–315.

[22] *Legal Aid—Targeting Need* (Cm. 2854, 1995), paras. 3.36–3.37.

[23] This account is taken from J. Rozenberg, *The Search for Justice* (1994), pp. 187–188.

[24] Law Society's Contentious Business Committee, *Improving Access to Justice* (1987), see M. Zander, *A Matter of Justice* (1989), pp. 56–57.

[25] *ibid.*, p. 57.

[26] *Royal Commission on Legal Services in Scotland* (Cmnd. 7846, 1980), but this is not a contingency fee system: (1989) 139 N.L.J. 138.

[27] See J.W.C. Turner, *Kenny's Outlines of Criminal Law* (18th ed., 1962), para. 475.

[28] R.C.L.S. Report, p. 176.

[29] This is most graphically illustrated by the "ambulance-chasing" lawyers, see Zander (1989), pp. 55–56. *The Independent* reported on October 30, 1995, that solicitors were being sold the names and addresses of persons involved in accidents.

refuse to take on weaker cases; there is increased pressure to win and so accept an early settlement (when costs are relatively low) rather than run the risk, at heavier cost, of going to trial. The arguments against were convincing for the Royal Commission on Legal Services.[30] Michael Zander was very sceptical about this rejection, refusing, in particular, to believe that professional standards would be abandoned so completely.[31] The Civil Justice Review reopened the matter and recognised the paucity of legal aid funding of litigation, the major advances in regulation policy of the professions and, on the basis of competition, considered that it might be more desirable to devise a limited scheme under which lawyers would have a stake in the outcome of a case as an incentive.[32] It recommended that the prohibition on contingency fees and other forms of incentive should be re-examined.[33]

The outcome of that re-examination has been, first, section 58 of the Courts and Legal Services Act 1990, which provided the statutory framework to allow for the introduction of conditional fee agreements (CFA). It defined a CFA as an agreement in writing between a person providing advocacy or litigation services and a client, which is not concerned with certain matrimonial and children proceedings; which provides for that person's fees and expenses, or part of them, to be payable only in specified circumstances; which complies with any requirements imposed by the Lord Chancellor; and which is not a contentious business agreement.[34] The legal status of such agreements is resolved by section 58(3), which provides that they are not unenforceable by reason only of being conditional fee agreements. Secondly, the Lord Chancellor issued a consultation paper in 1993 which proposed that the lawyer would be paid nothing if the case was lost, but would be entitled to a 20 per cent uplift of the normal fee. The uplift was clearly insufficient to cause conditional fee agreements to be concluded and so the uplift was increased to 100 per cent.[35] Thirdly, the Law Society introduced new rules of professional conduct which came into force on July 5, 1995 to end the professional conduct restriction on entering such agreements. Finally, the Lord Chancellor issued two statutory instruments. The first, the Conditional Fee Agreements Order 1995,[36] came into force also on July 5, 1995. The Order means that CFAs may only be entered into in specified proceedings, that is: for personal injuries; by companies in administration or winding up or by their administrators or liquidators and by trustees in bankruptcy; and before the European Commission and Court of Human Rights; but a CFA may not be concluded where the client has legal aid.[37] The maximum uplift of fees is confirmed as 100 per cent. The second statutory instrument, the Conditional Fees Agreement Regulations 1995,[38] prescribes the requirements to be satisfied

---

[30] R.C.L.S., Report, at p. 177. See also the majority in *Wallersteiner v. Moir (No. 2)* [1975] Q.B. 373. Lord Denning M.R., in the minority, put in a strong plea for the contingency fee in a particular type of company law action brought by a shareholder.

[31] M. Zander, *Legal Services for the Community* (1978), p. 218. For an even more spirited defence, see R. White, "Contingent Fee: A Supplement to Legal Aid?" (1978) 41 M.I.R. 286.

[32] *Civil Justice Review* (1989), para. 389.

[33] *ibid.*, paras. 384–389.

[34] The excluded proceedings are listed at s.58(10). A "contentious business agreement" is defined in the Solicitors Act 1974, s.59.

[35] J. Rozenberg, *The Search for Justice* (1994), pp. 186–187.

[36] S.I. 1995, No. 1674.

[37] Indeed the Government does not see CFAs as a substitute for legal aid in general, but as a useful supplement: *Legal Aid—Targeting Need* (Cm. 2854, 1995), para. 3.35.

[38] S.I. 1995, No. 1675.

for an agreement to be a CFA. The agreement, which must be in writing,[39] must state the particular proceedings or parts of them to which it relates; the circumstances in which the lawyer's fees and expenses or part of them are payable; what, if any, payment is due upon partial failure of those circumstances to occur, irrespective of those circumstances occurring, and upon termination of the agreement; the amount payable and whether the amount is limited by reference to the damages recovered on behalf of the client; and that certain matters have been drawn to the client's attention (the availability of legal aid, what are the payments to the lawyer in accordance with the agreement, when the client may be liable to pay the other side's costs, and when taxation of the lawyer's fees and expenses may be sought). As Rozenberg points out, there are drawbacks to the scheme: CFAs are no use where no damages are recoverable from the other side (*e.g.*, in matrimonial or criminal cases), the unsuccessful client will still have to pay the other side's costs, the client will have to pay up to twice as much as normal, and the proceedings for which a CFA may be concluded are very limited. Further, the defendant who wins may not receive anything, since a CFA is likely to be used by a plaintiff who has little or no resources. This may encourage speculative or fraudulent claims.[40]

A sixth method is the establishment of a contingency legal aid fund.[41] The fund is financed by contributions from successful litigants. It would pay lawyers on a normal basis but recoup costs on a contingency basis. The lawyer, therefore, would be paid whatever the outcome of the case.[42] Zander, whilst seeing some merit in the proposal, indicated that the major problem is the initial funding, particularly if the Fund were to be established on a voluntary basis.[43]

The seventh method is by amending the rules which limit multi-party actions to representative actions which could not result in an award of damages.[44] Whilst these rules have not yet been changed but are under consideration, the courts endeavour to take steps to assist such actions[45] and the Legal Aid Board has introduced new arrangements.

The Board had been encouraged by the Government to investigate how to fund multi-party actions through legal aid. The result of this investigation was the Legal Aid Board Multi-Party Action Arrangements 1992. A multi-party action is defined as "any action or actions in which 10 or more assisted persons have causes of action which involve common issues of fact or law arising out of the same cause or event."[46] These actions generally fall into two categories,

---

[39] See the Law Society Model Conditional Fee Agreement.

[40] Rozenberg (1994), p. 187.

[41] Such a proposal is currently under consideration: *Legal Aid—Targeting Need* (Cm. 2854, 1995), para. 3.34.

[42] Such a Fund was proposed by JUSTICE in *Trial of Motor Accident Cases* (1966), criticised by R.C.L.S., Report, pp. 177–178. JUSTICE reiterated the call in its *Memoranda on the Green Papers issued by the Lord Chancellor's Department: Contingency Fees* (1989). See also N.C.C., *Ordinary Justice* (1990), pp. 191–193. The Law Society's Contentious Business Committee put forward a similar proposal: *Improving Access to Justice* (1987).

[43] Zander (1989), p. 56.

[44] R.S.C. Ord. 15, r.12.

[45] *e.g.*, in a case involving over 900 claims arising from the Hillsborough stadium disaster, the court took over the management of the case: *Chapman v Chief Constable of South Yorkshire* (1990) 134 S.J. 726.

[46] Legal Aid Board Multi-Party Action Arrangements 1992, para. 3.

that is, claims arising out of a specific event, such as a disaster, and claims based on a common cause, such as a harmful drug.[47]

(c) Public funding of litigation

There is little, if any, current support for litigation to be financed from public funds irrespective of the means of the parties. Whilst there are obvious objections on the grounds of overall cost and whether it is fair that public moneys should be used to support people who can readily afford litigation, it is the case that there is some litigation which is unavoidable, but involves the parties in cost, and which should be supported. The costs of litigation thrown away as a result of the death or illness of a judge in the course of a trial can be covered by public funds, if the Lord Chancellor thinks it fit to do so.[48] Ensuring these costs are funded publicly is part of a broader proposal for a suitor's fund to indemnify litigants against the cost of a successful appeal and the determination of an unsettled point of law of public importance.[49]

The possibility of funding actions which determine important points of law is particularly interesting, since civil justice has two possibly opposed objectives. First, it is to assist people to resolve their disputes as easily as possible[50] and, secondly, it should enable the making or declaring of law that applies in those disputes.[51] Considerable service is done by the taking of an action which resolves points of law, but public officials can rarely bring actions[52] and the legal aid scheme will not support an action unless the case passes the merits and reasonableness tests.[53] Support for such a fund goes back to the Evershed Committee in 1953,[54] which recommended that a fund should be available for actions at first instance and on appeal, certified by the Attorney-General as raising a question of law of exceptional public interest which it is in the public interest to clarify. The Committee further proposed that the Attorney-General should be able to act on his or her own initiative and apply to intervene in an action or to pursue an appeal even where the parties had settled their differences. The Royal Commission on Legal Services supported these proposals, with the proviso that the judge at trial or on appeal should also be able to determine eligibility in cases where the point at issue does not emerge until later.[55]

In general these proposals have not been implemented, indeed the Government has stated that it is not convinced that it is right to fund litigation out of public funds, other than through the legal aid scheme, where points of law

---

[47] *Legal Aid Handbook* 1995, para. 16–01. See Woolf Issue Paper, *Multi-Party Actions* (1996).
[48] Administration of Justice Act 1985, s.53.
[49] R.C.L.S., Report, p. 179 and JUSTICE, *A Proposal for a Suitors' Fund* (1969).
[50] See the basic principles identified in the Woolf Report, below, pp. 567 and 626–627. Note that this principle may best be satisfied by not going to court, see below, pp. 554–566.
[51] Jacob draws attention to this dichotomy in his Hamlyn Lectures, *The Fabric of English Civil Justice* (1987); see, *e.g.*, p. 8.
[52] The Attorney-General has limited powers, see J.L.J. Edwards, *The Attorney General, Politics and the Public Interest* (1984), Chap. 6 and above, p. 19 and below, p. 974.
[53] The difficulty of determining whether to support cases where the law is very unclear are considered below, pp. 571–572 and 580.
[54] *Committee on Supreme Court Practice and Procedure* (Cmnd. 8878, 1953), Chair: Lord Evershed M.R. For similar proposals, see the Law Society, "The Indemnity Rules", in its *Annual Report*, 1963–64.
[55] This modification was suggested in a JUSTICE report, *Lawyers and the Legal System* (1977).

of general importance are involved.[56] There have, however, been three related developments. The Administration of Justice Act 1969 introduced the leap-frog appeal so that cases could go straight from first instance to the House of Lords, when the Court of Appeal would be bound by precedent, thereby saving considerable costs.[57] The Criminal Justice Act 1972 provides for the Attorney-General to be able to refer a case to the Court of Appeal when he or she is concerned with the law applied by the Crown Court, without affecting the defendant's acquittal.[58] The Equal Opportunities Commission and the Commission for Racial Equality are empowered by the Sex Discrimination Act 1975[59] and the Race Relations Act 1976[60] to render assistance, including the provision of legal services, to individuals alleging discrimination. Similar assistance is given to those who might become involved with Immigration Appeals Tribunals by UKIAS, which receives government money for the purpose.[61]

The JUSTICE report, *A Proposal for a Suitors Fund*, advocates a more radical reform by suggesting that public funds should be used to indemnify litigants against "faults in the system" amongst which it included appeals on fact or law. At the moment it is the ultimate loser who pays the costs, even if he or she happens to have won at first instance and in the Court of Appeal. The report suggested that it was not the ultimate loser's fault that the judge at first instance and the Court of Appeal did not get the right answers, and that the loser should not be liable for the appellate costs. The loser should remain liable for the first instance costs, which would have been incurred in any event. This proposal was rejected outright by the Royal Commission, primarily on the grounds that the risk of a decision being overturned on an appeal is a risk inherent in all litigation and "should be taken into account by all who embark on it."[62]

The current method of funding is the *civil legal aid* scheme which supports litigants who fall within its financial and other limits. It is discussed at the beginning of the following chapter.[63] It alleviates the burden of costs by providing financial assistance to litigants who can satisfy a means test,[64] a merits test and a reasonableness test,[65] and, if necessary, make a contribution towards their own costs.[66] This scheme does not always divert costs away from the assisted litigant to the Legal Aid Fund—far from it. More often it works as a way of postponing the cost to the successful assisted litigant until damages are received from the opponent. The costs incurred by the Fund on behalf of a successful assisted party are defrayed from costs awarded against the loser.[67] Any further outstanding amount is taken from the contribution levied on the assisted party (if any), and any amount still outstanding will normally be taken from any

---

[56] Cmnd. 9077, 1983, p. 19.
[57] ss.12, 13. As to leap-frog appeals, see below pp. 960–961.
[58] s.36, see below pp. 939–940. The Criminal Justice Act 1988, s.36 provides a similar power where the sentence imposed is thought to be too lenient.
[59] s.75.
[60] s.66.
[61] By virtue of the Immigration Act 1971, s.23.
[62] R.C.L.S., Report, p. 180.
[63] See below, pp. 568–580.
[64] Taking into account both the income and capital of the applicant, see below, pp. 570–571.
[65] *i.e.* is there good reason for bringing the action, see below, pp. 571–572.
[66] See below, pp. 572–574.
[67] *i.e.* taxed costs on the usual basis (see above, pp. 530–531). It may not be actually possible to recover such costs.

damages awarded in the action.[68] In the end the successful assisted party probably often pays, one way or another, the same amount as a private client would
have done.

The benefits of the scheme are two-fold. The responsibility for payment is
assumed by the Fund, and if the total costs of the assisted party cannot be
covered by costs awarded, contribution and damages, the liability of that party
to the Fund is nonetheless limited to the original assessed contribution. More
importantly, liability is similarly limited in the event of the assisted party being
unsuccessful.[69] The Legal Aid Fund bears the costs risk, rather than the litigant.[70]

Thus the legal aid scheme permits those eligible to take the risk of litigation
at the possible expense of the Fund. People who could not afford litigation
(because they could not pay the difference between their costs and the taxed
costs recoverable) or who could not afford the risk of litigation (because costs
awarded might not be recoverable or because they might lose) might be assisted
by the scheme. However, the three substantial hurdles which protect the Fund
mean many people will not benefit. If an applicant fails to satisfy the means
test, he or she will be totally ineligible, and the applicant must satisfy the Area
Director both that the case merits assistance and that it is reasonable to pursue
it. The 1993 changes in eligibility have dramatically reduced the number of
households financially eligible, and the spiralling costs have raised major concerns about the future of the civil legal aid scheme. Although these costs seem
now to have been controlled, the scheme faces some major changes in the
future.[71] It is quite clear that many other forms of support for litigation need to
be considered, although it is likely that for people sufficiently poor to satisfy
the financial criteria, legal aid will remain the major source of support.[72]

B. DELAY

Delay causes problems in both civil and criminal matters despite the existence
of time-limits which are intended to expedite cases. The reasons for delay differ
in civil and criminal procedure, not least because in civil matters the conduct
of the action lies in the hands of the parties, who may agree through their
lawyers to delays in proceedings. It is largely for the problems of delay that
the Civil Justice Review and the Woolf Report recommended greater court
involvement through court management of litigation.[73]

1. Civil Matters

"There are four areas in which delay or a lengthy timescale is a matter
for concern:

---

[68] The "statutory charge" on the proceeds of the action, see below, pp. 574–576.
[69] An order for costs may be sought against an unsuccessful assisted party, but is unlikely to be
worth pursuing because that party is unlikely to have any resources because he or she must have
been poor enough to qualify for legal aid.
[70] As to the risk of the Board, therefore, only backing winners, see below, p. 580. Note that it is
rare for costs to be awarded against the Fund, see below, pp. 576–577.
[71] See below, pp. 577–580 and above, pp. 519–525.
[72] See Legal Aid—Targeting Need (Cm. 2854, 1995).
[73] See below, pp. 581 and 597–600.

- the time taken to progress a case from the initial claim to a final hearing;
- the time taken to reach settlement;
- delay in obtaining a hearing date; and
- the time taken by the hearing itself."[74]

The reasons for the slow progress of actions at these stages are diverse. At the outset, the plaintiff may be slow to contact a solicitor;[75] negotiations for a settlement may drag on;[76] where relevant, the extent of the plaintiff's injuries may not become clear until the end of a lengthy period of treatment;[77] investigations may have to be carried out to ascertain the evidence; expert opinions may have to be obtained;[78] communication and action by both sides may be poor and slow; the advice of counsel may be taken; the length of time spent waiting for the trial to begin can be substantial;[79] errors may be made by the professionals involved;[80] the developing litigation ethos may necessitate the lengthening of the process before trial for tactical reasons.[81] The problem of delay tends to be

---

[74] Woolf Report (1995), p. 13. The *Civil Justice Review* (1989), para. 49, identified delay occuring "at three main stages, namely: (i) before proceedings are commenced; (ii) between the commencement of proceedings and the point where the case is either settled or is ready for trial; and (iii) between readiness for trial and the trial itself." One study showed that, in cases where writs or summons were issued, the major component of elapsed time was the period between issue of writ or summons and the settlement or trial: Inbucon (1986), para. 4.2. That study also revealed that in personal injury litigation the three principal causes of delay were: (i) the medical circumstances of the case; (ii) the long wait for trials in the Royal Courts of Justice and provincial trial centres; and (iii) a lack of clear or prompt response from the other side: *ibid.*, para. 4.8.1.

[75] The time taken for an incident causing personal injury to advice first being sought was found in the Inbucon Study to be, expressed as medians (that is half the cases took more than the time and half took less), 3.4 months for cases ultimately at the Royal Courts of Justice, 1.6 months for cases ultimately at District Registries (for provincial High Court cases) and 1.9 months for county court cases: Inbucon (1986), Appendix 1. The figures only relate to those cases where writs or summons were actually issued. The reasons why people may take so long to see a solicitor are, in part, explored in Chap. 8 above.

[76] The Inbucon Study showed that the median period from incident to settlement, where a writ or summons had been issued, for the various types of case, were 43.7 months (Royal Courts of Justice cases), 37.5 months (District Registry cases) 22.0 months (county court cases): Inbucon (1986), Appendix 1. For a consideration of the settlement process, see below, pp. 559–563. Woolf notes that settlement often occurs at a very late stage in proceedings, involving the parties in substantial additional costs. Personal injuries cases often take 4–6 years to settle: Woolf Report (1995), p. 14.

[77] This is often said to be a good reason for delay, but, as Lord Woolf points out, "even in such cases it should be possible to dispose of issues of liability, and to award interim damages": Woolf Report (1995), p. 13.

[78] Lord Woolf identifies the problems associated with some expert evidence in detail and concludes that it is indeed a significant contributor to "avoidable delay": Woolf Report (1995), p. 38. As to his proposals, see below, pp. 626–633.

[79] Lord Woolf noted that, in part because of late settlement of cases, and thus late withdrawal, there is overlisting at the courts in order to ensure full use of the judges' time; this of necessity produces wastage. The Winn Committee on Personal Injuries Litigation drew attention to this problem in 1968 (Cmnd. 3691) and regarded it as deplorable. The Inbucon Study found that the mean waiting periods from setting down until trial were 10.2 months for Royal Courts of Justice cases, 5.1 months for District Registry cases and 1.9 months for county court cases: Inbucon (1986), Appendix 1.

[80] See J. Hern, "Court v. solicitor errors" (1990) L. S. Gaz., May 2, p. 32. It is only recently that specialisation requirements have begun to apply to personal injury litigators, so there is no specific guarantee of litigation expertise, other than the general legal qualification which barristers and solicitors have (see above, pp. 127–128).

[81] Delay is compounded by high usage of interlocutory processes which can sometimes be doubtfully appropriate, *e.g.*, pleadings, discovery and interlocutory injunctions (some of the possibilities

greater with regard to High Court proceedings, whether at the Royal Courts of Justice or not, than county court proceedings.

Delay created by these reasons, both human and procedural, can prove to be extremely frustrating to the parties, most particularly to the plaintiff who will feel that delay amounts to a denial of justice.[82]

The complexities of the law itself can add to the amount of time taken to resolve a case. *Saif Ali v. Sydney Mitchell and Co.*[83] provides an example of a remarkably prolonged action, complicated by the expiry of the limitation period.[84] It is clearly an unusual case, but there was still a considerable lapse of time while the normal procedures were being followed. The timetable was as follows:[85]

March 26, 1966	Mr Saif Ali, a passenger in a car driven by his friend Mr Akram, was injured in a collision with a car driven by Mrs Sugden.
October 16, 1966	Mrs Sugden was convicted of driving without due care and attention.
1967	Mr Ali and Mr Akram consulted a solicitor with a view to making a claim. The solicitor took counsel's opinion.
October 1968	The solicitor instructed the barrister to draft the pleadings and to advise.
November 14, 1968	A writ and statement of claim was issued claiming damages against Mr Sugden only, alleging that his wife was driving as his agent at the time of the accident. Mr Sugden was the owner of the car and he had insured it.
Later	A meeting was held between Mr Ali's solicitor and the insurance company at which the company indicated that the agency question might be disputed, and that contributory negligence might be alleged against Mr Akram.
March 26, 1969	The limitation period expired[86] without any amendment to the writ, and without Mr Ali issuing proceedings against either Mr Akram or Mrs

---

are considered below in Chap. 11): Woolf Report (1995), pp. 14 and 150–179 and see R. Cranston " 'The Rational Study of the Law': Social Research and Access" in Zuckerman and Cranston (1995).

[82] Because the onus is very largely on the plaintiff to keep the action moving, it is he or she who is most likely to become frustrated by delay. Various writers refer to a recognisable medical condition, "litigation neurosis", which can afflict those enmeshed in an unfinished action; see below, p. 561.

[83] [1978] Q.B. 95, C.A.; [1980] A.C. 198, H.L.

[84] Jacob states that the Limitation Acts have "operated in a sort of blind, mathematical way without regard to the merits of the claim or the circumstances of the parties or any other consideration": Jacob (1987), p. 268. He makes certain recommendations for reform: *ibid.* pp. 269–270.

[85] The timetable is culled from the judgments in both the Court of Appeal and the House of Lords. There are, unfortunately, some discrepancies in the dates given in the two courts—naturally, the House of Lords' version has been accepted!

[86] In a personal injuries action such as this, the writ must be issued within three years of the cause of action arising.

	Sugden, the actual drivers in the collision.[87]
August 29, 1969	The writ was served on Mr Sugden.
October 16, 1969	Mr Sugden entered a defence denying his wife's agency.
November 1969	The barrister advised that Mr Ali should be separately represented.[88]
June 24, 1971	Mr Sugden amended his defence and admitted that his wife *was* acting as his agent.
January 21, 1972	Mr Sugden applied to the court for leave to withdraw his admission of agency with consent of the plaintiff's solicitors. Leave was granted.
May 9, 1972	The House of Lords decision in *Launchbury v. Morgans*[89] led Mr Ali's advisers to believe that it was impossible to continue the action.
April 22, 1974	The action against Mr Sugden was discontinued and Mr Ali's impregnable claim had disappeared.
September 19, 1974	Freshly advised, Mr Ali issued a writ against the solicitors who had represented him until November 1969 alleging negligence.
May 29, 1975	The defendant solicitors issued a third party notice[90] against the barrister whose advice they had taken, asking that he should indemnify them on the grounds that they had acted on his advice.
July 26, 1976	The barrister successfully applied to have the third party notice struck out on the grounds that it disclosed no cause of action.
February 24, 1977	The solicitors successfully appealed to Kerr J. and the third party notice was restored. The barrister successfully appealed to the Court of Appeal and the third party notice was again struck out.[91]
November 2, 1978	The solicitors successfully appealed to the House of Lords and the third party notice was restored.[92] *N.B.* The third party action between the solicitors and the barrister did not decide that he *was* negligent merely that *if* he was negligent he *would* be liable to the solicitors. The question of whether he *was* negligent remained for trial if disputed by the barrister.

Prior to the Woolf Inquiry, which considered the problem of delay generally in

---

[87] There would appear to have been good cases against both the actual drivers—presumably, Mr Ali was advised to proceed against Mr Sugden because he was the insured person, and Mr Akram was his friend.

[88] It was perceived too late that Mr Ali's interests and Mr Akram's interests were not identical!

[89] [1973] A.C. 127. A case in which the House of Lords held that a husband who had borrowed his wife's car to go on a "pub-crawl" was not her agent for the purpose of fixing her with liability for his negligent driving.

[90] *i.e.* joining the barrister in Mr Ali's action.

[91] [1968] Q.B. 95. The court relied heavily on *Rondel v. Worsley* [1969] A.C. 191, see above, p. 174.

[92] [1980] A.C. 198.

civil proceedings in the context of a review of civil justice, two official committees[93] had considered the incidence and causes of delay with particular reference to personal injuries litigation and the Civil Justice Review had considered
the general problem of delay in the civil justice system.[94]

One clear approach to deal with delay is to increase the role of the courts in
the management of litigation, and this lies at the heart of the proposals in Lord's
Woolf's Interim Report, *Access to Justice* (1995). Certain steps have already
been taken which are intended to reduce delay, as well as assisting in satisfying
the other basic principles associated with a civil justice system. In 1988 a High
Court judge was given charge of the general list cases of the Queen's Bench.
Cases which had been settled or withdrawn were removed from the list and
sanctions for non-compliance were introduced. Non-personal injury cases
involving claims below £20,000 were identified for transfer to the county court
and three extra Circuit judges sat in the High Court for three months to take
Queen's Bench cases.[95] It appears that in relation to non-jury trial cases these
steps had some success.[96]

As a consequence of the Civil Justice Review further steps have been taken.
The first was a re-examination of the relationship between the High Court and
the county court, to increase the number of cases heard in the county court[97]
and to commence the harmonisation of the procedural rules. These proposals
have had some effects, although delay is still a problem, even though the number
of cases in both the High Court and the county court has recently been dropping.[98] Lord Woolf has recognised delay as one of the main concerns in the
civil justice system, and his proposals are aimed, in part, at eliminating avoidable
delay.[99]

2. CRIMINAL MATERS

Although the delay in criminal cases is of a different order of magnitude, it still
gives rise to concern. The concern is expressed on behalf of defendants in custody because they may ultimately be acquitted or given non-custodial sentences,
and on behalf of defendants on bail because of the uncertainty and unpleasant-
ness of a pending criminal trial. In addition there are difficulties associated with
trials relating to incidents which happened in times long gone by. Witnesses
forget.

There is, in theory, an eight-week time limit between committal and trial on
indictment,[1] but that rule may be dispensed with by the Crown Court and the
following figures indicate the present position. In England and Wales in 1995,

---

[93] *Report of the Committee on Personal Injuries Litigation* (Cmnd.3691, 1968), Chair: Winn L.J.;
    Report of the Personal Injuries Litigation Working Party (Cmnd. 7476, 1979), Chair: Cantley J.
    For a brief consideration of their proposals, see the first edition of this book, pp. 376–387.
[94] *Civil Justice Review, Report of the Review Body on Civil Justice* (Cm. 394, 1989).
[95] So summarised in the *Civil Justice Review* (1989), para. 55.
[96] *Listing Statement (Queen's Bench Non-Jury and Judge in Chambers Lists), The Times*, November
    24, 1990.
[97] For the jurisdiction points, see above, pp. 77–79.
[98] *Judicial Statistics 1995*, pp. 25 and 35.
[99] For a consideration of his proposals, see below, pp. 567, 597–600 and 626–633.
[1] See below, p. 747.

of the 110,463 defendants committed for trial,[2] 39 per cent were dealt with in less than eight weeks; of the 62,388 who pleaded guilty, 50 per cent were dealt with in less than eight weeks;[3] and of the 22,310 who pleaded not guilty, only 19 per cent were dealt with in less than eight weeks. Indeed, of this latter group ("not-guilty pleas"), 14 per cent had to wait longer than 16 weeks for trial.[4]

Delays for defendants in trials on indictment were giving cause for concern as long as 1975, when the James Committee reported, but at that stage over 70 per cent. of cases were disposed of within eight weeks.[5] The overall figure for 1995 is 39 per cent.[6]

Those defendants awaiting trial in custody might seem to be the most seriously disadvantaged by delay and they do tend to take priority. In 1995, 51 per cent of this group waited less than eight weeks for trial, and 77 per cent less than 16 weeks. The figures for those defendants on bail were 35 per cent and 62 per cent respectively.[7]

The situation differs around the country and the *average* length of time between committal and trial for those pleading not guilty varies from 13.2 weeks on the Wales and Chester circuit to 27.1 weeks on the North Eastern Circuit. The national average is 21.3 weeks. For those pleading guilty, the *average* length of time varies from 8.5 weeks on the Wales and Chester Circuit to 16.3 weeks on the Northern Circuit. The national average is 12.9 weeks.[8] All these figures have deteriorated significantly since the second edition of this book was published in 1991[9] although there has been a noticeable improvement since 1994.

One of the problems with trial at Crown Court[10] is with producing lists of cases which are accurate enough to enable prediction of the timing of the case for the benefit of the defendant and counsel and the most efficient use of judicial and court time. The Royal Commission on Criminal Justice had "no solution to the listing problem and, despite all the complaints made to us about it, no different system was suggested to us that was obviously better than the present case."[11] A survey of delay at the Crown Court subsequent to the Royal Commission was able to make a number of proposals which might address the problem, but are to be regarded as an agenda for discussion and collaboration. It is not surprising that the contributory factors are multi-faceted, involving the Lord Chancellor's Department, solicitors, barristers, the Crown Prosecution Service and the judiciary, so it is not surprising that there is no simple remedy.[12]

As regards delay at magistrates' courts, the *Criminal Statistics* now produce information which makes interesting reading.[13] As regards indictable offences

---

[2] For the difficulties of developing new pre-trial procedure, see below, p. 745.
[3] *Judicial Statistics 1995*, Cm. 3290, Tables 6.15 and 6.16.
[4] *ibid.*, Table 6.16.
[5] *The Distribution of Criminal Business between the Crown Court and the Magistrates' Courts*, Cmnd. 6323 (1975), para. 23.
[6] *Judicial Statistics 1995*, Table 6.15.
[7] *ibid.* Table 6.17.
[8] *ibid.* Table 6.18.
[9] See pp. 492–493.
[10] The pre-trial procedure itself has the potential to produce delay for a variety of reasons; see below, Chap. 13.
[11] The Royal Commission on Criminal Justice, *Report* (Cm. 2263, 1993), para. 40.
[12] J. Plotnikoff and R. Woolfson, *From Committal to Trial: Delay at the Crown Court* (1993).
[13] At the time of the second edition of this book, there was little such evidence available; see p. 493.

(including offences triable either way), in 1994 the average number of days from offence to completion was 128, from offence to charge or summons was 43, from charge to summons or first listing was 25 and from first listing to completion was 60. The percentage of defendants dealt with on first court appearance was 20, the average number of times a case was listed in court was 3.5, the average length of adjournment was 24 days, the percentage of defendants pleading guilty was 50 and the number of defendants in the sample was 22,000. As regards summary non-motoring offences in 1994, the average number of days from offence to completion was 137, from offence to charge or summons was 81, from charge to summons or first listing was 37 and from first listing to completion was 20. The percentage of defendants dealt with on first court appearance was 68, the average number of times a case was listed in court was 1.6, the average length of adjournment in days was 32 and the percentage of defendants pleading guilty was 47. The number of defendants in the sample was 9,200.[14] In both categories of offences these figures represent a significant deterioration since 1985. The figures suggest also that, as with Crown Court delay, the causes are multi-faceted. It is possible that a thorough examination of the causes might well suggest that more rigorous control by the judges and greater commitment to speed by the professionals might be worthy proposals. If so, this would mirror an identification of solutions recommended by Lord Woolf for implementation in the civil justice system.[15]

C. SETTLEMENT

Cost and delay are just two of the factors which persuade the great majority of those in dispute to effect a compromise and settle their differences without trial. The then Lord Chief Justice in 1980 commented that, "If it were not that a high proportion of cases are compromised long before they reach court the administration of justice would soon grind to a halt; the courts would be overwhelmed by the volume of work."[16] This sentiment is still true and posits a fundamental dilemma in civil procedure: are settlements fair? The courts have had little role in the procurement of settlements, but now have the obligation to encourage them.[17] Their role in the ratification of settlements has been limited to those involving minors and people under a disability.[18] Lord Woolf recommends the replacement of payments into court with a power to make an offer

---

[14] *Criminal Statistics 1994* (Cm. 3010, 1995), Table 6.3. Statistics are also provided for summary motoring offences.

[15] See below, pp. 626–633.

[16] In the course of the foreword to the first edition (1980) of D. Foskett, *The Law and Practice of Compromise* and still appearing in D. Foskett, *The Law and Practice of Compromise* (3rd edn., 1991), p. ix.

[17] The Commercial Court encourages alternative dispute resolution (ADR): *Practice Note* [1994] 1 All E.R. 34 and the case management practice requires the parties to consider ADR: *Practice Note* [1995] 1 All E.R. 385. Such a power was proposed by Jacob (1987), p. 267.

[18] R.S.C. Ord. 80; C.C.R. Ord. 10, r. 10; see N. Andrews, *Principles of Civil Procedure* (1994), para. 13–024.

to settle, thus encouraging settlements once litigation has been commenced, but in circumstances more conducive to agreement.[19]

1. WHO SETTLES WHEN?

The settlement of a dispute is achieved by an agreement between the parties to abandon any further claim in respect of the subject of the dispute. It takes the form of a legally binding contract and the normal rules of contract apply to establish the existence, meaning and effect of the agreement.[20] In general the parties are completely free to negotiate the terms of the settlement.[21] A settlement may be arrived at more usually before proceedings have begun, but may also be arrived at after proceedings have begun.[22] Once agreement is reached, the settlement is just as final as a judgment and, unless the agreement has been improperly procured, the issues of fact and law raised in the original claim may not be the subject of further litigation.[23]

There is no source of official information on settlements, since court formalities are rare, and thus deductions have to be made from the information available in the judicial statistics, supported by the available research.

(a) Information from the judicial statistics

The judicial statistics inevitably provide an incomplete picture since the only information available relates to matters where a writ has been issued and many disputes may already have been settled by then.[24]

The following figures are taken from the *Judicial Statistics* for 1995.[25] and relate to the Queen's Bench Division. A total of 153,624 writs and originating summons were issued in 1994. Of these, 31,737 were issued by the Central Office in London and 121,887 by district registries. This is a 27 per cent overall reduction since 1993 which in part reflects the impact of the changes increasing the jurisdiction of the county courts.[26] As the number of proceedings instituted in the county courts has also gone down, other factors are at work. Further information is given in relation to those cases for the Royal Courts of Justice:

WRITS ISSUED	31,737
JUDGMENT GIVEN WITHOUT TRIAL	13,241
CASES SET DOWN FOR TRIAL	4,717
CASES DISPOSED OF WITHOUT COURT ATTENDANCE	2,850

---

[19] Woolf Report (1995), As to payments into court, see below, p. 626. See S. Roberts, "Litigation and Settlement" in Zuckerman and Cranston (1995).

[20] Foskett, Chap. 3.

[21] There are some exceptions, e.g. settlements involving infants and persons under disability: Foskett, Chap 21.

[22] Usually a court order is not necessary, although it may, in some circumstances, be thought to be a good idea, see O'Hare and Hill (1993), pp. 35–39 and 382–384.

[23] Foskett (1985), Pt. I.

[24] See below, p. 557.

[25] Cm. 3290, Chap. 3.

[26] *ibid.*, p. 25 and Table 3. 1.

Comprising:
Settled with consent order before hearing   910
Withdrawn before hearing, settled without court
order, or struck out   1,940
CASES DISPOSED OF AFTER ATTENDING
COURT   1,530
Comprising:
Determined after trial   700
Settled during trial or hearing   130
Approval of prior settlement   290
Settlement without notice after court attendance   410

Clearly these figures are not entirely comparable because they relate to cases at different stages in the procedure. Most of the cases determined after a trial would have been begun by a writ issued in 1993 or 1994. However, the figures do give an indication of the proportion of cases resolved by settlement rather than trial.

It will be seen that a high proportion of cases disappear after the issue of a writ, presumably they are either settled or discontinued. A high proportion end in a swift judgment because the defendant is in default or has no real defence.[27] About one case in seven goes through all the pre-trial procedure and is set down for trial. Even then, a large proportion are withdrawn, many settled, before a hearing. A surprisingly high number of cases are settled ''at the door of the court'' with the parties in attendance ready for trial.[28] A number of settlements require the formal approval of the court.[29] A high proportion of trials which begin will end in settlement rather than judgment. As regards the Royal Court of Justice of every 21 writs that were issued in 1995, one case was determined by trial.

These statistics relate to all actions in the Queen's Bench Division. A slightly different picture emerges if we sift out the figures relating to *personal injury negligence actions alone*—the category most discussed in relation to the efficacy of settlements. Again from the Judicial Statistics 1995[30] the table now looks like this:

WRITS ISSUED   1,224
JUDGMENT GIVEN WITHOUT HEARING   Not specified
CASES SET DOWN FOR TRIAL   Not specified
CASES DISPOSED OF WITHOUT COURT   2,200
ATTENDANCE
Comprising:
Settled with consent order before hearing   730
Withdrawn before hearing, settled without court
order, or struck out   1,420
CASES DISPOSED OF AFTER ATTENDING   1,040
COURT:

---

[27] See pp. 601 and 606 below for judgment in default and ''Order 14'' procedure.
[28] The prospect of immediate trial concentrates the minds of the parties and the advisers wonderfully. The action brought by four firemen who attended the King's Cross fire against London Underground was settled just before their claims were to be heard: *The Times*, December 19, 1990.
[29] *e.g.* settlements involving infants and people under a disability.
[30] Cm. 3290, Tables 3.2, 3.4 and 3.5.

Comprising:

Determined after trial	330
Settled during trial or hearing	140
Approval of prior settlement	250
Settlement without notice after court attendance	240

From these figures we can see that a high proportion of the cases disposed of in 1995 were personal injury actions (3,290 out of 4,380), hence the attention paid to this category of cases.

(b) Research information

The Winn Committee reported in 1968[31] that "... of all personal injury claims asserted about 20–25 per cent reach the stage of proceedings being started, and only about 10 per cent of these reach the doors of the court, of which between one-third and one-half are then settled without trial." In the 1989 figures, 56,219 actions were started, 2,760 reached the doors of the court of which 1,610 were settled. The studies conducted for the Pearson Commission produced figures of 86 per cent of cases settled without proceedings being started.

The Oxford Study[32] reveals that of 169 people who reported receiving damages as a consequence of an accident suffered, only four received them as a result of a court order. Of the 165 cases in which damages were received without a court order, 104 were on the basis of the acceptance of the first offer that was made.[33]

We should by now have demonstrated to your satisfaction the enormous importance of the process of settlement. It is the normal procedure in the vast majority of cases. Is it fair?

2. NEGOTIATIONS FOR A SETTLEMENT

"The settlement process is very much a matter of bargaining, and it is bargaining of a difficult and expensive character. As economists would say, the case involves a bilateral monopoly, since the plaintiff has to 'sell' his claim to one potential buyer—the insurer—and the insurer has to 'buy' the claim from only one potential seller—the plaintiff."[34]

Having taken pains in Part II to point out that there are a number of non-legal sources of advice and assistance, we do not now wish to give the impression that the negotiation of settlements is exclusively the province of lawyers. Other agencies are quite heavily involved, some in the capacity of, e.g., mediator or

---

[31] *Report of the Committee on Personal Injuries Litigation* (Cmnd. 3691, 1968), para. 59.

[32] D. Harris *et al.*, *Compensation and Support for Illness and Injury* (1984).

[33] D. Harris. "Claims for Damages: Negotiating, Settling or Abandoning" in Harris *et al.* (1984), Table 3.3. The same study shows that the vast majority of accident victims do not make a claim at all, a factor supported by the Pearson Commission.

[34] Cane (1993), p. 226.

arbitrator,[35] others representing the interests of members in a more specialised field.[36]

Settlements can be examined by considering personal injury claims, in which they play a major role, and which have been the subject of research and critical assessment.[37] It is clear that the analysis in the first paragraph holds good, whoever the parties actually are. The plaintiff cannot shop around for the best offer, the two parties must deal with each other and strike an acceptable bargain through their own negotiating skill.

The defendant in a personal injuries action is likely to be represented by an insurance company, which takes complete control of and financial responsibility for the claim.[38] If the defendant is not insured, he or she is not likely to be worth suing.[39] The staff in the claims department of an insurance company will be skilful and experienced negotiators, with adequate resources to deal with claims.[40]

The plaintiff in a personal injury action is the person hurt as a result of an accident. He or she is unlikely to have any skill or previous experience in seeking compensation for injury and is, therefore, largely dependent on the legal advice sought and received.[41] The routes to seeing a solicitor vary.[42] Some accident victims seek legal advice through an agency, such as their trade union, who will place them in touch with an experienced solicitor.[43] Other plaintiffs will adopt the common, often haphazard, methods of seeking legal advice, which may result in a plaintiff seeing a solicitor who is not experienced in the field.[44]

Once the plaintiff has found a solicitor, the problems that may face the plaintiff in the initial stages of negotiation must be discussed. Two questions arise: first, the liability question, *i.e.* is the defendant liable in law? secondly, the quantum question, *i.e.* if the defendant is liable, how much should the damages be?[45]

Proving liability will depend, if it is denied by the defendant, upon three factors. First, the information which the client has about the accident. It is likely

---

[35] See below pp. 563–566.

[36] Primarily the trade unions, but also the motoring organisations, see above pp. 481–482 and Cane (1993) pp. 219. Advice agencies also involve themselves on behalf of clients, from time to time taking an active part in negotiation and settlement.

[37] See, in particular, Harris *et al.* (1984); H. Genn, *Hard Bargaining* (1987); see also Cane (1993). We consider claims by individuals, but group actions are becoming increasingly significant and present different issues, see Cane (1993), pp. 227–230.

[38] Indeed an action would be unlikely otherwise to proceed, see e.g. the criteria for the award of legal aid, below, pp. 570–572.

[39] Unless rich, either personally or because the defendant is a large company or other organisation (*e.g.*, considerable sums of health service finance fund legal actions against health authorities and their employees).

[40] Experienced negotiators backed by the resources of the company are stilled in negotiating settlement for the bought of the organisation, see Genn (1988), pp. 7–8 and 50–52, 63.

[41] See H. Genn, ''Who Claims Compensation: Factors Associated with Claiming and Obtaining Damages'' in Harris *et al.* (1984), p. 76.

[42] *ibid.* pp. 65–67.

[43] It is clear from the evidence about trades unions' solicitors provided in *ibid.* that there is considerable value in seeing a solicitor through this route since the solicitors engaged by trades unions are experienced in the field of personal injury litigation.

[44] As to seeking legal advice, see Chap. 9, above.

[45] The separateness of these issues is reflected in the fact that is is possible for split trials to be ordered so that, e.g., liability can be established whilst waiting for the medical condition of the plaintiff to be diagnosed adequately and before the quantum issue is determined: R.S.C. Ord. 33, r. 4(2A); C.C.R. Ord. 13, r. 2(2A) and see *Civil Justice Review* (1988), para. 452.

that the client will see the solicitor some time after the accident, when memory may already have begun to fade. Indeed there is evidence which shows that the longer the delay in seeing a solicitor, the less likely damages will be obtained.[46] Secondly, more may be discovered about the accident. Research has shown that it is often the case that a plaintiff's solicitor either does not have the resources to undertake investigations or is loath to seek out all available reports.[47] On the other hand, much information may be available, from accidents reports and other sources.[48] Some help is given by section 33 of the Supreme Court Act 1981. This section establishes a procedure whereby a plaintiff may seek an order requiring a defendant to disclose any documents which may become the subject matter of subsequent proceedings.[49] Unfortunately, the plaintiff must specify the documents believed to be in the possession of the defendant, but the power is still useful in assisting the plaintiff to evaluate the case. Thirdly, there is the question of how good the witnesses will be when, and if, it comes to establishing a case in court. Any witnesses will need to be contacted and the quality of their evidence assessed. Overall, it may be difficult to discover whether there is enough evidence to pursue a claim.[50] If a possible action does emerge from the evidence available, an attempt will be made to put a monetary valuation on the injuries suffered by the plaintiff. At this stage negotiations are likely to begin.

The defendant, however, may well be in a much better position to assess liability, because insurance companies are often able to anticipate possible claims and have considerable resources available to investigate the circumstances of an accident fairly soon after its occurrence.[51]

To establish the possible quantum of damages, it is necessary to obtain as much information as possible about the injuries which the client suffered, and the future effect of such injuries, in particular upon the client's earning capacity. The client will, therefore, need a medical report.[52] Evaluating quantum is particularly difficult. In an American experiment, 20 pairs of practising lawyers negotiated on identical information about a case. The highest outcome was $95,000; the lowest $15,000; and the average was just over $47,000![53] Since negotiation over figures is difficult, a practical suggestion is to "[l]eave it to the insurers to put forward figures in settlement. . . . [T]he defendant's representative . . . should be left to initiate the discussions, for it is not the plaintiff's role to make settlement proposals."[54] One main reason for the difficulties considered here is that a settlement usually involves payment of one lump sum in the same way that damages consequent upon a successful court action are also paid in a lump sum,[55] although an interim award can now be made.[56] It is, however, possible for the injured party and the insurance company to agree on a "structured settlement". Under such a scheme sums of money are paid over

---

[46] D. Harris, "Claims for Damages: Negotiating, Settling or Abandoning" in Harris *et al.* (1984), p. 104 and Table 3.7.

[47] Genn (1987), pp. 67–69.

[48] See, on methods recommended to solicitors for investigating a claim, J. Pritchard and N. Solomon, *Personal Injury Litigation* (7th ed., 1992), Chap. 4.

[49] R.S.C. Ord. 29, r. 7A; and see Pritchard and Solomon (1986).

[50] See also Genn (1987), p. 72–75. For the role of the Bar, see *ibid.* pp. 78–81.

[51] *ibid.* pp. 62–66.

[52] *ibid.* pp. 75–78. For the role of the Bar, see *ibid.* pp. 78–81.

[53] G. R. Williams, *Legal Negotiation and Settlement* (1983), referred to in Genn (1987), p. 77.

[54] Pritchard and Solomon (1992), p. 30.

[55] See below, p. 795.

[56] See Andrews (1994), pp. 234–239.

periodically either for a fixed period or until the death of the injured party. These sums can then be varied over time to reflect changes consequent upon the damage caused to the injured party.[57]

The orthodox view of civil pre-trial procedure, and that to which Lord Woolf subscribes,[58] is that the more the two parties know about the real issues between them the more likely it is that a "realistic" settlement can be reached.[59] In the early stages, however, it may not be in the plaintiff's interests to disclose too much. As good a bargain must be struck as possible. In setting out general guidelines for a solicitor negotiating on behalf of a plaintiff, Pritchard and Solomon counsel caution. Do not provide too much detailed information[60] do not indicate the financial status of the client or his or her willingness and ability to litigate. This advice, along with other hints,[61] emphasises that negotiations are conducted in an atmosphere of pressure. The danger of this approach is an over aggressive, adverserial approach which is often inimical to the interests of the parties.[62]

The desire not to reveal too much information to the other side is, however, a major reason for delay in the civil justice system,[63] as well as causing expense. Consequently, the Civil Justice Review and the Woolf Report make a number of recommendations which will ensure greater openness in pre-trial proceedings.[64]

Thus, the quality of the negotiators and their approach play a significant role in the settlement that is achieved. Insurance company representatives are almost invariably skilled, but the levels of skill and experience of the plaintiff's solicitor varies considerably, and the research evidence suggests that this is a highly significant factor in the settlement process.[65] Further, there is a debate as to whether the best method of approach by the plaintiff's solicitor is confrontation or co-operation. On the whole, the evidence[66] and advice[67] suggests that a combative approach is best, making clear that the plaintiff is prepared to litigate, and doing so swiftly by the issue of proceedings, but this is contrary to the already noted view of Lord Woolf.

Clearly there is considerable pressure on the various parties to the negotiations. Since the plaintiff is a prime contributor, it must be realised that whilst

---

[57] The payments are financed by the purchase of an annuity by the liability insurer, and, by an Inland Revenue concession, are not taxable as income. See M. A. Jones, *Textbook on Torts* (4th ed. 1993), pp. 380–381; R. Lewis, (1988) 15 J.L.S. 392; D. K. Allen, (1988) 104 L.Q.R. 448.

[58] Woolf Report (1995).

[59] This is the especial function of pleadings, see below, pp. 613–620; discovery, see below pp. 621–626; and interrogatories, see below, p. 621. All these procedures take place well after the start of the action and, as we have already seen, a considerable time after the accident.

[60] However, disclosure rules do require revelation of information at an early stage: Pritchard and Solomon (1992), p. 30.

[61] Ask for an interim payment before proceedings commence, leave it to the insurers to put forward the settlement figure, the time to negotiate is when the other side is under pressure and, in particular do not reveal the weaknesses in a case at an early stage. Pritchard and Solomon (1992), pp. 29–31.

[62] Woolf Report (1995).

[63] See above, p. 549.

[64] See below, pp. 626–633.

[65] See Genn (1987), *passim*. Increasingly, skills training forms a part of legal professional education, see above, pp. 183–187, and see N. Gold, K. Mackie and W. Twining, *Learning Lawyers' Skills* (1989), Chap. 7, which is concerned with negotiation.

[66] See Genn (1987), esp. pp. 46–50, 53.

[67] See Pritchard and Solomon (1992), pp. 29–31.

it is important to utilise what advantages are possessed, there is considerable pressure on him or her as well.

3. PRESSURES

The pressure to conclude a settlement is almost always on the plaintiff who is placed at a considerable disadvantage against the skilled defendant.[68] Broadly, the pressures are attributable to delay, cost and the risk of litigation.

We have considered the *delay* likely to occur in a personal injury action which goes to trial in the High Court.[69] The incentive to settle and clear the matter up quickly is significant. The plaintiff may be urgently in need of the money. It is he or she who will be incurring additional expenses as a result of the accident and whose earning power may have been impaired. Social security payments are unlikely to be adequate compensation for loss of earnings and injuries. Interest is payable on damages from the date of the cause of action to the date of judgment in all personal injury cases (unless there are special reasons to the contrary) and the court *may* order interest on that basis in other cases,[70] but the plaintiff may still prefer to have the money in hand. An interim payment may be ordered by the court on application, but an order will only be made when it is clear that the defendant will be held liable at trial.[71]

There is some evidence that delay and associated anxiety can cause a recognisable psychological state of "litigation neurosis",[72] a complaint which disappears on the resolution of the dispute. It is almost inevitable that the circumstances associated with a legal dispute will cause worry and upset, but long delays weaken the spirit as well as the claim.[73]

The plaintiff has little to gain by delay. It may be that the injuries are such that their full effects will not become apparent for some time and a hasty settlement might lead to an underestimation of the damage,[74] but generally delay is on the side of the defendant. Apart from the interest charges involved, the longer

---

[68] Whilst the defendant is skilled if represented by an insurance company (see above), the company may be under pressure not to stretch out negotiations too far, especially when it becomes obvious that the plaintiff has a strong case.

[69] See above pp. 548–552, see also Genn (1987), pp. 100–108.

[70] Supreme Court Act 1981, s.35A (and County Courts Act 1984, s.69).

[71] Supreme Court Act 1981, s.32. An order may be made after an interlocutory hearing if the Master is satisfied that the defendant has admitted liability *or* the plaintiff has obtained judgment with damages to be assessed *or* the plaintiff will win on liability at trial without substantial contributory negligence AND the defendant is insured *or* a public authority *or* has the means to pay: R.S.C. Ord. 29, r.11, see also C.C.R., Ord. 13, r. 12.

[72] See the material cited by P. Cane, *Atiyah's Accidents, Compensation as the Law* (4th edn., 1987), p. 151 and footnotes thereto.

[73] The circumstances of the plaintiff are also important. An elderly, infirm person might want to receive money quickly in order to enjoy it.

[74] The problem is alleviated by the power of the court to award provisional damages in an action for personal injuries in which there is proved or admitted to be a chance that in the future the injured person will develop some serious disease or suffer some serious deterioration caused by the wrongful act or omission of the defendant: Supreme Court Act 1981 s.32A. This power is unlikely to assist the *settlement* process, since it only applies to judgements. Indeed, it may encourage plaintiffs to go to court to take advantage of the power. It will not be possible to reopen settlements on this account so that the plaintiff will now have an additional choice to make in deciding on settlement or action. On the other hand, it may give the plaintiff greater bargaining power with the defendant, since a settlement may now be in the defendant's interests.

a defendant can spin out the negotiations the better. American evidence cited by Phillips and Hawkins demonstrates that delay can be used as a deliberate tactic either against unmeritorious or unreasonable claims, or to alleviate the cash-flow problems of smaller insurance companies.[75]

Plaintiffs have cash-flow problems as well. It is cash flowing on *costs* as the case progresses which provides another incentive to settle. We need not elaborate on our earlier discussion of costs,[76] save in two respects. The rule that costs follow the event is important in negotiations because it adds another factor to the equation. The more unsure the plaintiff is about winning the case, the more significant the possibility of a costs claim becomes,[77] and the calculation of costs which would ultimately be awarded to the successful party complicates the estimation of the total value of the claim. Secondly, the costs pressure can be greatly increased by a judicious payment into court.[78] The mechanics of the payment in have been explained.[79] The tactical advantages to the defendant are considerable. They accrue mainly from the uncertainty which surrounds the calculation of damages. Solicitors and barristers experienced in personal injury litigation will have to estimate a sum for loss of amenity and pain and suffering based on awards in similar cases, their own practice and the published awards contained in specialist books.[80] A rather gruesome list emerges which indicates the value of a leg, arm or toe—but not a precise value. The figure is almost always expressed as a range which will expand according to the seriousness of the injury.[81] When pecuniary losses are added the outcome of an assessment of the plaintiff's damage may be that it is worth, say, between £8,000 and £10,500. If the defendant makes a payment into court of £8,250, the gamble is obvious. Either the plaintiff will receive £8,251 + costs (if the judge's estimate tallies with that of the plaintiff's advisers) or a much lower figure (if it does not, and he or she has to pay costs). Clearly this procedure could impose considerable pressure on plaintiffs.

Zander found that a large number of payments in were accepted and that it was a tactic well used by defendants.[82] However, the Oxford Study showed that in many cases it was not a factor, since very little use was made of this procedure, despite its obvious advantages to the defendant.[83]

Does a payment in place unfair pressure on a plaintiff? Both sides are gambling because the defendant may be paying more than a judge would award at trial. The plaintiff is playing with higher stakes because the cost penalty is likely to be bigger than the amount by which the defendant might overestimate the claim.

Even if it is not used much the trenchant criticisms of it would appear to

---

[75] J. Phillips and K. Hawkins, "Economic aspects of the settlement process" (1976) 39 M.L.R. 497 at pp. 502–503. There is also some English evidence, see *Report of the Committee on Personal Injuries Litigation* (Cmnd. 3691, 1968), paras. 46–62.

[76] Above pp. 530–537. See also, Genn (1987), pp. 109–119.

[77] *ibid.* Chap. 5 and pp. 109–119.

[78] See above, pp. 536–537.

[79] Above, p. 537.

[80] *Kemp and Kemp on the Quantum of Damages.* The monthly parts of *Current Law* also contain details of the latest awards categorised anatomically.

[81] The more serious the injury, the more difficult the estimate. One of the highest damages award in a personal injury action is the £1,571,282 awarded to J. Lambert, 42, an airline pilot injured in a motorcycle accident, see *The Independent*, July 28, 1990.

[82] M. Zander, "Payment into Court" (1975) 125 N.L.J. 638.

[83] Genn (1987), pp. 111–113.

demand reform, as it appears to be a blunt instrument which "should be honed down to produce a greater quality of justice."[84] Although the Civil Justice Review recommended no change, since the evidence suggested that, despite its bluntness, most people were broadly satisfied with payments into court,[85] the Woolf Report has recommended significant changes to produce a more suitable and fairer system.[86]

The third factor is the *risk* of litigation. The onus lies on the plaintiff, if the dispute goes to trial, to prove the case on a balance of probabilities.[87] Uncertainties abound. It may be unsettled whether the defendant is liable at law for the plaintiff's damage.[88] In the absence of a settlement the parties have to litigate to find out. Even if the law is clear, the case may be difficult because of lack of evidence.[89] Evidence depends upon witnesses and, to some extent, their credibility is dependent upon their performance in the witness box.[90] Some witnesses perform very badly. Some witnesses are unavailable at the time of trial.[91] Assuming the case is proved, the judge's estimate of the injuries and the consequent amount of the award is uncertain. After trial, there could be *two* appeals.[92] Looming large over all these doubts is the spectre of costs.

The plaintiff as an individual will feel the pressures much more keenly than the defendant, backed by the insurance company.

No one can be surprised that only one writ in 66 to 100 comes to trial.

D. ALTERNATIVE DISPUTE RESOLUTION

Methods of solving disputes other than going through a process of adjudication have become increasingly popular. Organisations designed to support this approach have become established in the past few years.[93] More significantly,

---

[84] Jacob (1987), p. 118. The Winn Committee described it as, ". . . rather a hit-and-miss affair; it is not sufficiently discriminating to achieve the object which it sets out to achieve; and it may work injustice.": *Winn Committee* (1968), para. 512.

[85] *Civil Justice Review* (1988), paras. 271–273.

[86] See above, pp. 626–633.

[87] This is the standard of proof in a civil action. It means, "Is it more likely than not?"

[88] The case of the unborn children injured by the drug thalidomide illustrates the difficulty. At the time it was by no means certain that there was any liability towards unborn children. That point has now been resolved by the Congenital Disabilities (Civil Liability) Act 1976 for children born after July 22, 1976.

[89] See above pp. 558–559. The plaintiff is aided by discovery and other pre-trial procedures, but it is still up to him or her to find the evidence. The evidence may no longer exist, *e.g.*, the alleged defective machine may no longer exist, or the allegations may be hard to prove, *e.g.*, the witnesses may not give accurate or complementary evidence as to how the road traffic accident happened, and expert evidence to support a claim, *e.g.*, to establish for how long someone will be unable to work or work less well, is expensive.

[90] Any inherent difficulties will be greatly exacerbated by the problem of delay. Witnesses are often giving evidence about incidents which happened some years before the trial.

[91] Abroad, ill, dead. All things are possible.

[92] Creating further delay and potential costs.

[93] IDR (Europe) Ltd was established in 1989 to offer private mediation: S. Roberts, "Alternative Dispute Resolution and Civil Justice: An Unresolved Relationship" (1993) 56 M.L.R. 452, at p. 456. The Centre for Dispute Resolution (CEDR) was more recently established and has met an increasing demand; see J. Harris, (1990) 134 S.J. 1427.

alternative dispute resolution now forms one plank in proposals for reform of the civil justice system (see below).

Settlement is a form of ADR, since it avoids the necessity of adjudication. Settlement also indicates some of the problems which, potentially, face all forms of ADR. Settlement is a contractual matter. There is often an imbalance of power between the contracting parties. One wonders what can be done in order to remedy that balance of power. In part, this may be achieved by seeking the advice of expert lawyers. Where the dispute centres upon a personal injury matter, the plaintiff would be advised to seek the help of a member of the Personal Injury Panel.[94] A further complication is met. There is a significant literature on the most appropriate approach to take to negotiation leading to settlement and there is wide disagreement on the efficacy and ethics of the various approaches. One simple dichotomy is between those who advocate a "litigation-first" approach and those who advocate a more conciliatory approach designed to achieve a compromise.[95] Very different approaches may be achieved as a result of settlement.[96] It is, therefore, too simplistic to assume that ADR is the cure of all the ills of civil justice system.

There are various forms of ADR in addition to settlement. Arbitration has a long and dignified history.[97] Arbitration is used in the resolution of construction disputes. A recent survey of this area indicates some of the problems which may be associated with ADR: Flood and Caiger[98] concluded that some arbitrators felt that the lawyers representing the parties to a dispute actually ran the show, often determining the outcome prior to the involvement of the arbitrator. This is less of a problem where the arbitrator is experienced, particularly when he or she is legally qualified.[99] The viewpoint that merchants are best able to resolve their disputes has a long history, but lawyers are looking for other work and so are "invading" areas in which they have not previously been involved: "lawyers are in a strong position to effect colonisation because of their power over the discourse of legalism. They have the power of appropriation."[1] ADR, therefore, does not necessarily avoid the use of lawyers, even lawyers with an adversarial approach; some methods of arbitration simply put in place a different form of adjudication, which will become little different from a court procedure when more lawyers become involved in representing the parties. The lawyerisation of ADR is also reflected in the profession's response to it by claiming particular expertise, not only in representing clients through it, but also in undertaking the third party work.[2]

---

[94] As to specialisation by lawyers, see above, pp. 127–128.

[95] For a review, see A. Boon, "Ethics and Strategy in Personal Injury Litigation" (1995) 22 J.L.S. 353. See also, e.g. Genn (1987) and C. Menkel-Meadow, "Lawyer Negotiations: Theories and Realities – What We Learn From Mediation" (1993) 56 M.L.R. 361 and the literature references therein.

[96] See above, p. 559.

[97] The Chartered Institute of Arbitrators is a long-standing organisation supporting through it and providing a qualification for arbitrators. A particular form of arbitration is also used in small claims, see below, pp. 802–804.

[98] J. Flood and A. Caiger, "Lawyers and Arbitration: The Juridification of Construction Disputes" (1993) 56 M.L.R. 412, at p. 439.

[99] Arbitration is often a source of income for retired judges, etc.

[1] ibid., at p. 440.

[2] See, e.g., S. Roberts, "Alternative Dispute Resolution and Civil Justice: An Unresolved Relationship" (1993) 56 M.L.R. 452, referring to and considering the reports by the Bar and the Law Society concerned with the professional involvement in ADR: Report of the Committee on Alternative Dispute Resolution (1991) and Alternative Dispute Resolution: A Report Prepared

Two other important forms of ADR are conciliation and mediation. These terms are often used interchangeably and do not have an accepted meaning for all writers. What they reflect is the involvement of a third party in the resolution of a dispute who may be more or less active in proposing solutions. Mediation ordinarily refers to the process of enabling the individuals to identify their own solutions, whereas conciliation often involves more active work on the part of the conciliator. Conciliation is one means used in the resolution of industrial disputes by the Advisory, Conciliation and Arbitration Service.[3] Mediation is often made available to divorcing couples, for which there are many models, reflecting the range of involvement of the mediator.[4] There are different perspectives from which he or she may be operating, so some see themselves in a therapeutic role, which others regard as a role conflicting with that of mediation.[5] The function of the impartial mediator or conciliator may be described[6] as to act as a catalyst to ensure that negotiation does take place and that the issues are confronted, and as a facilitator to enable an agreement which both parties can perceive to be fair. Andrews has identified the advantages of conciliation as opposed to resolution by adjudication as the following:

(1) "*secrecy:* the parties can keep their dispute and negotiations private and confidential";[7]
(2) "*avoidance of acrimony:* a conciliated settlement can be reached without the bitterness associated with litigation";[8]
(3) "*flexibility:* . . . it is possible to settle matters which lie beyond the compass of the law or legal judgment";
(4) "*multiple parties*";
(5) "*saving face:* a conciliated settlement enables the parties to avoid the 'winner takes all' aspect of most judgments";
(6) "*continuing associations:* the consensual resolution of a dispute will be valuable when the parties are not merely casually connected by a single transaction . . ., but have a continuing relationship";
(7) "*achieving a reconciliation:* conciliations' greatest potential benefit is that it might bring about a complete reconciliation between the parties."[9]

The advantages of ADR are such that the Government proposes including mediation as an important, if not essential, element in its new divorce law proposals. There are significant arguments against making it compulsory, which Ingleby identifies as: definitional arguments, since mediation is supposed to be

---

by Henry Brown for the Courts and Legal Services Committee of the Law Society (1991) respectively. See also C. Glasser, "Civil Procedure and the Lawyers – The Adversary System and the Decline of the Orality Principle" (1993) 56 M.L.R. 307, at pp. 318–324.

[3] See, *e.g.*, I. T. Smith, Sir J. C. Wood and G. Thomas, *Industrial Law* (5th ed., 1993), pp. 31–38.

[4] See The University of Newcastle upon Tyne, Conciliation Project Unit, *Report to the Lord Chancellor on the Costs and Effectiveness of Conciliation in England and Wales* (1989), S. Roberts, "A Blueprint for Family Conciliation?" (1990) 53 M.L.R. 88.

[5] See S. Roberts, "Alternative Dispute Resolution and Civil Justice: An Unresolved Relationship" (1993) 56 M.L.R 452, at p. 466, and references therein.

[6] See M. Roberts, *Mediation in Family Disputes* (1988), Chap. 6.

[7] This is of particular interest to many large firms, especially construction firms, and also where revelation of the matter in dispute could be embarrassing or financially damaging.

[8] Litigation can cause each side to dig in and so fail to be flexible, as is indicated in the Woolf Report (1995), *passim*.

[9] Andrews (1994), pp. 407–408.

entered into on the volition of the parties and is not normally institutionalised; lack of justification, since the arguments for compulsory mediation are based upon unwarranted extrapolations from the information about voluntary mediation; and the rule of law concerns about decisions being made, *e.g.*, in the absence of publicly stated rules.[10]

Lord Woolf makes proposals about ADR as a part of his initial ideas about reform of the civil justice system.[11] Woolf proposes that international developments be monitored so as to use best practice in England and Wales. He also proposes the further development of private ombudsmen schemes, for example, in the retail sector.[12] Woolf proposes greater judicial involvement in the encouragement of the use of ADR, so he proposes that the courts should encourage and, further, facilitate mini-trials; the courts should use the expertise of practitioners in various fields to enable the resolution of disputes; the courts should encourage ADR where this would be of advantage to litigants, including the judges quizzing the litigants on whether ADR has been discussed, and, if not, why not.[13] The particular concerns surround the involvement of judges in ADR. Judicial and ADR functions are significantly distinct and it is not clear that it is easy to move from being, say, a mediator to being an adjudicator. Further the judge may have information as a mediator which he or she would not have as an adjudicator, and so the process of adjudication is significantly altered. So juridification has potentially important consequences for civil procedure.

ADR has significant consequences not only for procedure, but also for the substantive law. The more disputes, and the more difficult they are, which are resolved by ADR, the less those disputes are resolved in a publicly accountable environment. Further, the disputes may be resolved without full consideration of the legal imperatives. Finally, ADR means that fewer cases are before the courts, so the courts have fewer opportunities to develop the law and provide appropriate legal solutions to the many problems which arise. So ADR is not a side-effect-free cure-all. It is important that it be used and its development be backed by the Government only for the right reasons. The saving of money alone is an insufficient reason. The objective must be the improvement of access to justice.

---

[10] R. Ingleby, "Court Sponsored Mediation: The Case Against Mandatory Participation" (1993) 56 M.L.R. 441.

[11] The Woolf Report (1995) is considered at a number of points, see above, and below, 597–600 and 626–633.

[12] ADR is on oft-used approach in such disputes. See R. Thomas, "Alternative Dispute Resolution – Consumer Disputes" (1988) 7 C.J.Q. 206. However, some of the difficulties with the support for customers (see above, pp. 802–804) suggests the importance of further approaches.

[13] Woolf Report (1995), Chap. 18.

CHAPTER 11

PRE-TRIAL CIVIL PROCEDURE

AT this stage, we move from a comparative approach, taking account of civil, tribunal and criminal procedure, and concentrate on civil procedure. The procedures which must be followed before a trial in the High Court or county court should be used by the parties to expose the real area of difference between them and concentrate attention upon it. Issues which are not in dispute should be eliminated and the scope of the disagreement narrowed. Using the procedures in this way has the dual effect of preparing the case as precisely as possible for the trial judge and of encouraging a settlement by revealing to the parties the exact nature of their dispute. It has been equally possible to operate the procedures in such a way as to leave all the issues open and so reveal very little to the other party about the case he or she would have to meet. Such obstructionism is a major contributor to delay and the high cost of litigation.

The complexity of pre-trial procedure, particularly in the High Court, has been said to act not only as a deterrent to all but the most determined litigant, but also as a weapon for the recalcitrant defendant who may manipulate it so as to place the pressure of delay upon the plaintiff. Indeed, Lord Woolf identified the adversarial culture, for which lawyers and the system are responsible, as creating an environment in which "questions of expense, delay, compromise and fairness may have only low priority. The consequence is that expense is often excessive, disproportionate and unpredictable; and delay is frequently unreasonable."[1] The need to redress such problems associated with civil procedure has been long recognised.[2] The problems of delay, cost and complexity remain "the key problems facing civil justice to-day."[3] It has even been said that "civil justice is in a state of crisis. . . ."[4] Whilst many of the reforms proposed in the *Civil Justice Review* (1989) have been introduced,[5] there is still a clear need for further reform.[6] Lord Woolf published his interim report in June 1995[7] and it is anticipated that the final report will appear in summer 1996.

In the meantime, procedural complexities remain and continue to necessitate

---

[1] Lord Woolf, *Access to Justice: An Interim Report* (1995) (hereafter Woolf Report (1995)), p. 7. It is available on the Internet. The Lord Chief Justice, in announcing a new *Practice Direction* ([1995] 1 All E.R. 385) which sets out new requirements for case management, said, "The aim is to try and change the whole culture, the ethos, applying in the field of civil litigation." As to case management, see below pp. 581 and 597–600.

[2] For example, the creation of the county courts in 1846; see below p. 580, and *Report of the Review Body on Civil Justice* (Cm. 394, 1989) (hereafter *Civil Justice Review* (1989)). See, also, J. Rozenberg, *The Search for Justice* (1995), pp. 171–182.

[3] Woolf Report (1995), p. 7. See also *Civil Justice on Trial—the Case for Change: Report by the Independent Working Party set up by the General Council of the Bar and the Law Society* (1993) (Chair: H. Heilbron, Vice Chair: H. Hodge) (hereafter, *Heilbron/Hodge Report* (1993)); see above, Chap. 18.

[4] C. Glasser, "Solving the Litigation Crisis" (1994) quoted in Woolf Report (1995), p. 5.

[5] See Rozenberg (1995), pp. 173–174.

[6] The continuing serious flaws resulted in the establishment of the Working Party leading to the *Heilbron/Hodge Report* (1993) and the Woolf Inquiry Team, as well as exercising not only the Government, but also the Opposition (see Labour Party, *Access to Justice* (1995)).

[7] See above, n.1.

the services of a lawyer or other person providing the appropriate legal service[8] in the pursuit of a claim. The legal advice scheme may be invoked for initial advice and assistance,[9] but the litigant who requires the services of a lawyer in civil proceedings must rely on the provisions of the representation element of the legal aid scheme or meet the cost himself or herself. Since many people are unable to meet the costs of litigation from their own resources, the availability of representation under the legal aid scheme will often be the crucial factor in deciding whether the case goes on at all. Therefore, we consider first the operation of the legal aid scheme.

A. OBTAINING LEGAL AID REPRESENTATION

1. THE DEVELOPMENT OF THE CIVIL LEGAL AID SCHEME[10]

The modern legal aid scheme, which provides financial assistance (subject to eligibility) in connection with proceedings in most of our civil courts, has come a long way since 1495 when statute provided for poor people, at the discretion of the Lord Chancellor, to sue without payment to the Crown, and to have lawyers assigned to them without fee.[11] A more formal Poor Persons Procedure was established in 1914[12] and was put under the control of the Law Society in 1925.[13] The Law Society provided the necessary administrative structure. Further, its involvement made more likely the necessary free provision by solicitors of their services. Government money was only made available to meet the cost of the administrative work involved.

The Poor Persons Procedure, dependent upon the charity of the legal profession, could not cope with the increasing pressure of work in the 1930s and was supplemented in 1942 by a Services Divorce Department. This department, consisting of salaried solicitors employed by the Law Society with government funds, dealt with the matrimonial problems occasioned by the Second World War. It must have been in the minds of the members of the Rushcliffe Committee as they took evidence. The committee was set up, with Lord Rushcliffe in the chair, in 1944, to review the provision of professional help for those who were unable to afford it, in both civil and criminal matters. The Committee's report[14] provided the basis upon which the Law Society was invited by the Lord Chancellor to undertake the task of organising a legal aid scheme, which resulted in the Legal Aid and Advice Act 1949 and the regulations made thereunder.

---

[8] See Chap. 3.

[9] As discussed above at p. 491.

[10] For a full consideration of the origins of the legal aid scheme, see S. Pollock, *Legal Aid, the first 25 years* (1975), and R. Egerton, "Historical Aspects of Legal Aid" (1945) 61 L.Q.R. 87.

[11] An Act to admit such persons as are poor to sue *in forma pauperis*.

[12] Described as ". . . the first regular scheme for legal aid in the Supreme Court": H. Kirk, *Portrait of a Profession* (1976), p. 164.

[13] After it had fallen into complete chaos and on the recommendation of a committee under Mr Justice P. O. Lawrence (The Poor Persons' Rules Committee (Cmd. 2358, 1925)).

[14] *Report of the Committee on Legal Aid and Advice* (Cmd. 6641, 1945). This report also contains a good review of the then existing facilities for legal aid and advice.

The legislation, later amended by the Legal Aid Act 1974, relied heavily upon the decisions of the Rushcliffe Committee. Subsequently, the major concern perceived with the system of legal aid was that confusion and inefficiency were created by too many people having the ability to decide whether or not to grant help.[15] Consequently, the administration of the scheme has been removed from the Law Society and placed in the hands of the Legal Aid Board by the Legal Aid Act 1988.[16] The 1988 Act otherwise maintains the same basic structure, but with some reforms.

2. THE SCOPE OF THE SCHEME[17]

The scope of civil legal aid is restricted in five respects. It only applies in specified *courts*, for specified *proceedings*, to those who fall within the *financial conditions*, to those who met the *merits test* and whom it is *reasonable* to support. If all the requirements are fulfilled, civil legal aid consists of *representation* for the purposes of proceedings, and it includes all such assistance as is usually given by a solicitor or counsel in the steps preliminary or incidental to any proceedings and all such assistance as is usually given by a solicitor or counsel in civil proceedings arriving at or giving effect to a compromise to avoid or bring to an end any proceedings.[18] The cost of such representation is met by the Legal Aid Fund, which is administered by the Legal Aid Board,[19] although a contribution may be required from the assisted party in accordance with the rules discussed below.

Taking the first two restrictions, section 14 and Schedule 2 of the Legal Aid Act 1988 prescribe the courts and the proceedings for which representation is available. Representation is currently available for almost all cases[20] in the House of Lords, the Court of Appeal, the High Court and county courts; the Employment Appeal Tribunal; the Lands Tribunal; the Commons Commissioner; the Restrictive Practices Court;[21] and certain proceedings in a magistrates' court.[22] The excepted proceedings, which are specified,[23] are actions in defamation, relator actions, certain proceedings for the recovery of a penalty,[24] election petitions, actions relating to judgment summons in the county court, actions in the county court where the only question is the time and mode of payment of a debt, proceedings for a decree of divorce judicial separation unless

---

[15] See *Legal Aid Efficiency Scrutiny* (Lord Chancellor's Department, 1986), followed by the White Paper, *Legal Aid in England and Wales: A New Framework* (Cm. 118, 1987). See pp. 515–517.

[16] See above, pp. 517–519.

[17] For further information, see *Legal Aid Handbook* 1995.

[18] Legal Aid Act 1988, s.2(4).

[19] *ibid.*, s.6.

[20] In addition to proceedings in the courts mentioned, representation will be available in contempt proceedings where it appears to the court to be desirable to provide it in the interests of justice: Legal Aid Act 1988, s.29.

[21] When the proceedings in that court are taken under the Fair Trading Act 1973, Part III.

[22] *e.g.*, proceedings under the Children Act 1989: Legal Aid Act 1988, s.14, Sched. 2. Part I, para. 2, as amended by the Children Act 1989, Sched. 13.

[23] Legal Aid Act 1988, Sched. 2, Part II.

[24] *i.e.* where those proceedings may be taken by anybody and the penalty is payable to whoever happens to take the proceedings.

the cause is defended or the petition is to be heard in open court[25] and any incidental proceedings. Civil legal aid is also available for all proceedings under the Children Act 1989. Although in general the usual means and merits tests apply, some legal aid is non-means and non-merit tested (*i.e.*, free legal aid) and some is means-tested-only legal aid.[26]

Representation is not available for most tribunals. However, the advice and assistance scheme can be extended to provide some form of representation through the *advice by way of representation scheme* (ABWOR) which extends to certain domestic proceedings in a magistrates' court, urgent court applications, and other proceedings, that is hearings before Mental Health Review Tribunals and prison governors.[27]

3. MAKING APPLICATION—THE MEANS, MERITS AND REASONABLENESS TESTS

The overall administration of the legal aid scheme rests with the Legal Aid Board. The Board operates through 15 areas, each with an area director and an area committee.[28] An application for a representation certificate is made to an area director.[29] It is recommended that a solicitor should assist in the completion of the appropriate application form, for which green form assistance[30] is available.

The assessment of the applicant's resources, which determines financial eligibility for representation, is undertaken by an "assessment officer" in the Legal Aid Assessment Office of the Benefits Agency.[31] The two significant assessments are of the applicant's *disposable income* and *disposable capital*. These

---

[25] For the full, see Legal Aid Act 1988, Sched. 2, Part II, para. 5A.

[26] See *Legal Aid Handbook 1995*, pp. 75–85.

[27] Legal Advice and Assistance (Scope) Regulations 1989 (S.I. 1989, No. 550), regs.7, 8, 9 [hereafter "the Scope Regulations], and see pp. 000–000 above.

[28] Area committees hear appeals from application refusals by a Director. Where there is a franchising contract, the franchisee exercises certain of an Area Director's powers: see Civil Legal Aid (General) Regulations 1989 (S.I. 1989, No.339), reg. 4 (hereafter "the General Regulations"). As to franchising, see pp. 000–000. The Legal Aid Board's management structure below the Board involves a chief executive and five group managers. Group managers are responsible for two or three area offices. Area offices are divided into a number of sections to ensure that enquiries get a prompt and proper response. As to the administration of the scheme, see *Legal Aid Board Annual Reports (1994–95)* (H.C. 526, 1995).

[29] That is the director where the applicant lives in the United Kingdom: the General Regulations, reg. 10(a). However, the application may be passed on to another area office, if it appears to the area director who received it that it "could, without prejudice to the applicant, be more conveniently or appropriately dealt with" elsewhere: *ibid.* reg. 17. As to applications by people resident outside the United Kingdom, see *ibid.*, reg. 10(b). The relevant form for an application for a representation certificate is CLA1; for matrimonial proceedings—CLA2; for an emergency certificate—CLA3. Because of the different scheme for Children Act proceedings, there is a separate range of appropriate forms, see *Notes for Guidance* in *Legal Aid Handbook 1995*, paras. 7.01–7.24.

[30] See pp. 000–000 above.

[31] See "Civil Legal Aid: Guide to Assessing Financial Eligibility" in *Legal Aid Handbook 1995*, pp. 506–508. The Legal Aid Board has not yet requested to exercise the power to assess resources by its own staff: Legal Aid Act 1988, s.3(4)(d). In 1994–95, the Benefits Agency received 234,182 new applications and determined 220,040 claims, deciding that 89.5 per cent were eligible; see *Legal Aid Board Annual Reports (1994–95)*, Table Civil 8. The National Audit Office has recommended more verification of applicants' means, thus introducing a tighter system: National Audit Office, *Civil Aid Means Testing* (H.C. 242, 1996).

are calculated by reference to the regulations[32] and allowance is made for certain items, including dependent children, income tax, national insurance, housing costs, certain disability benefits and work expenses.[33] If a person is on income support, he or she is deemed to have a disposable income making him or her eligible for civil legal aid.[34] As from April 8, 1996, the levels of eligibility for actions other than personal injury cases[35] were as set out in the following table:

	Disposable income	
(a)	More than £7,403 p.a.	: Ineligible
(b)	£2,498–£7,403 p.a.	: Eligible subject to a monthly contribution of 1/36th of the excess of disposable income over £2,498 throughout the case
(c)	Less than £2,498 p.a.	: Eligible without contribution
	Disposable capital	
(a)	More than £6,750	: Ineligible, if it appears that the applicant could afford to proceed without legal aid
(b)	£3,000–£6,750	: Eligible, subject to a contribution not greater than the sum by which the disposable capital exceeds £3,000
(c)	Less than £3,000	: Eligible without contribution

The applicant must be eligible both in respect of income and capital. The figures appear in the Assessment of Resource Regulations, not in the Act, and can be changed relatively easily. The significant reduction in eligibility made in April 1993 was, and remains, very controversial.[36]

If an applicant is financially eligible, the area director must further be satisfied that he or she "has reasonable grounds for taking, defending or being a party to the proceedings."[37] The *merits* test means that the area director must be satisfied that there is a case to be "put before a court for a decision." Certainty of outcome is not needed, otherwise no "cutting edge" case would ever be supported, nor cases where the decision is relatively clear. Care must be taken not to waste public money, which would occur if hopeless cases were supported. One way of approaching this question is to ask whether a solicitor would advise a private client to take or defend proceedings.[38]

Finally, the area director must be satisfied that it is reasonable to support the

---

[32] *i.e.* the Civil Legal Aid (Assessment of Resources) Regulations 1989 (S.I. 1989, No.338) as amended (hereafter known as "the Assessment of Resources Regulations").

[33] See the Assessment of Resources Regulations, reg. 4 and Scheds. 2 and 3.

[34] Assessment of Resources Regulations, Sched. 2, para. 5. Where a person is in receipt of income support, the case is not referred to the Benefits Agency. In 1993/94 it would appear that some 191,000 claimants were in receipt of income support, that is about 45 per cent of the total number, see *Legal Aid Board Annual Reports (1994–95)*, Tables Civil 3 and Civil 8.

[35] Where the subject matter of the dispute includes a claim in respect of personal injuries, legal aid is available to a person whose income does not exceed £8,158 a year, but a person may be refused legal aid where his or her disposable capital exceeds £8,560 and it appears to the area director that he or she could afford to proceed without legal aid: Assessment of Resources Regulations, reg. 4.

[36] See below, pp. 578–579.

[37] Legal Aid Act 1988, s.15(2).

[38] "Notes for Guidance", para. 6–06 in *Legal Aid Handbook 1995*, pp. 58–9.

applicant.[39] Legal aid is likely to be refused on this ground if [40] (a) the applicant has an illegal motive or conduct which would be unacceptable to the court; (b) the proceedings are not likely to be cost effective;[41] (c) the applicant has other rights and facilities thus not needing legal aid,[42] which support would come from another organisation such as a trade union or finance from an estate;[43] (d) compensation is available from the Criminal Injuries Compensation Board; (e) a solicitor would not normally be employed in the type of case;[44] (f) a lower court should be used; (g) ABWOR[45] is available and more appropriate; (h) the defendant could satisfy no judgment against him or her; (i) the applicant would get no personal benefit from the proceedings; (j) the circumstances of the application make grant unreasonable;[46] and (k) the applicant's previous legal aid history indicates that grant is unreasonable.[47]

4. THE REPRESENTATION CERTIFICATE AND THE APPLICANT'S CONTRIBUTION

If the application is approved by the area director, a representation certificate is issued, subject to the acceptance by the applicant of any conditions attached to it. The certificate is likely to specify the extent of the aid available and will often be limited to the taking of particular steps in the action. In the first instance, the certificate may be limited to the taking of counsel's opinion and another application may have to be made to the area director to amend the certificate for further action if counsel's opinion appears to warrant it. In this way, the area director can keep an action under review at all the crucial stages.[48]

If the application is successful and no contribution is payable, the area director issues a representation certificate to the applicant's solicitor, and a copy is sent to the applicant, now known as the "assisted person." If the applicant is successful but there are conditions attached or there is a contribution to pay, an offer of a certificate, with a requirement to accept the conditions or pay the

---

[39] Legal Aid Act 1988, s.15(3).

[40] The following is a summary of most of the guidance in "Notes for Guidance" paras. 6–07 and 6–08 in *Legal Aid Handbook 1995*, pp. 59–62.

[41] The General Regulations, reg.28(a). What may outweigh the cost effectiveness factor are matters such as the importance of the case to the applicant, especially where there is a "negative equity situation" or where, in divorce proceedings, the outcome may affect residence and finance (*N.B.* in a true cost/benefit analysis, this would form part of the costs). Cases which are not likely to be cost effective are, *e.g.*, those where the amount claimed is small, the costs are likely to exceed the benefit to the applicant, the only matter at stake is stature, dignity or reputation, and neighbour disputes: *Legal Aid Handbook 1995*, pp. 59–60.

[42] The General Regulations, reg. 30.

[43] Other sources include: the Commission for Racial Equality, the Equal Opportunities Commission, and AA/RAC: *Legal Aid Handbook 1995*, p. 60.

[44] The General Regulations, reg. 28(b).

[45] See pp. 495–496 above.

[46] *e.g.*, where a company has assigned its action to a director who is eligible for legal aid: *Legal Aid Handbook 1995*, p. 62.

[47] *e.g.*, the applicant previously has failed to co-operate in a means assessment or an earlier certificate has been revoked: *ibid.*, p. 62.

[48] In particular, certificates in matrimonial and personal injury proceedings are likely to be limited to part of the proceedings: see the General Regulations, reg. 46. "Notes for Guidance" sections 8–10 in *Legal Aid Handbook 1995*.

contribution, is made. The applicant has 28 days in which to signify acceptance of any conditions attached. He or she must also make any capital contribution, which is normally payable forthwith, and pay the first instalment of any contribution from income, such contributions being payable throughout the case.[49] Once payment is confirmed, a crtificate is issued and forwarded to the solicitor.

The contributions payable are significant financial burdens, particularly for an applicant towards the top end of the financial eligibility range. In addition, where the contribution is payable from disposable income, the limits set out above apply strictly, whereas there is a discretion to permit the grant of a certificate even if the applicant's disposable capital is over the financial eligibility limit. "Curiously for a legal aid system, this may favour the person with capital as against the person with income, the wage earner."[50] Given that the level of eligibility for free legal aid is so low, it is interesting to note that in 1994–95, 86 per cent of the certificates issued granted legal aid without any contribution.[51] This figure appears to suggest that the requirement of a contribution acts as a serious deterrent to people applying for legal aid. The analysis of maximum contributions determined during 1994–95 contained in the Legal Aid Board Annual Report contains the following figures relating to High Court, county court and magistrates' court proceedings:[52]

	Number	%
Contribution required		
Nil	330,977	85.8
Under £150	8,675	2.2
£159–£299	9,763	2.5
£300–£499	10,625	2.8
£500 and over	25,915	6.7
Total	385,955	100

Once a certificate has been issued there are wide powers vested in the area director to amend it.[53] The area director also has power to discharge or revoke it upon the happening of specified events including a request from the applicant so to do, or where the aid has been abused, or where the applicant is in arrears with contributions, or where the applicant's financial position improves so that he or she is able to afford to fund legal action.[54]

There is a right of appeal to an area committee against a refusal to grant a representation certificate or upon discharge or revocation of a certificate.[55]

---

[49] The General Regulations, reg. 45 and The Assessment of Resources Regulations, reg 4(4).

[50] D. Burrows, Civil Legal Aid (1989), para. 5.22; see also 16th Legal Aid Annual Reports, 1965–66, p. 30.

[51] Legal Aid Board Annual Reports 1994–95, Table Civil 9. The percentage was between 77 and 81 from 1984–85 to 1990–91, since when it moved to 83.9 in 1991–92, and to 85.8 in 1992–93, where it has stayed: ibid.

[52] ibid.

[53] The General Regulations, Part VII and see Legal Aid Handbook 1995, pp. 93–94.

[54] The General Regulations, Part X and see Legal Aid Handbook 1995, pp. 101–104.

[55] The General Regulations, regs. 35–39, 81(2). As to appeals against refusal to remove a limitation upon application to amend, see Legal Aid Handbook 1995, pp. 74 and 94, and see Burrows (1989), para. 6.31. In 1994–95, 55.8 per cent of the 47,766 appeals against the refusal of legal aid were successful: Legal Aid Board Annual Reports 1994–95, Table Civil 4.

Obviously there may be circumstances in which the normal procedure of application and issue cannot be followed because of the urgency of the matter and a procedure exists for obtaining an emergency representation certificate in such cases.[56]

5. The Liabilities of the Assisted Client

When the provision of legal services for those who could not afford the normal fees was dependent upon the charity of the profession, the relationship between client and lawyer must have been somewhat awkward. The object of the legal aid scheme is to ensure that the relationship between solicitor and assisted client is on exactly the same basis as that between solicitor and private client.[57] To that end, a client's financial obligations are to the Legal Aid Fund and the solicitor receives payment from the Fund.[58]

The full financial obligations of an assisted party will, inevitably, depend upon the outcome of the case. As has been seen, the assisted party is usually under no obligation to pay any costs to the solicitor whatever the result; but may be under a liability to pay costs to a successful opponent.

If the assisted party is *successful*, costs may be payable by the opponent in the normal way.[59] These costs are paid straight into the Legal Aid Fund and go to defray the actual costs of the action in the accounts rendered to the Fund by solicitors and counsel acting for the assisted party.[60] If the costs recovered are *not* sufficient to cover the cost to the Fund, the difference is recouped if possible from the contribution made by the assisted party. Any balance remaining from the contribution is returned.[61]

However, where the contribution, if any, is not sufficient to make up the difference, the Legal Aid Board has a first charge on any property, including money, recovered or preserved by the assisted party in the proceedings.[62] This is the "statutory charge." The charge means that the Board is entitled to recover the shortfall on its expenditure out of the property that has been recovered or preserved by the assisted party in the proceedings. Consequently, the assisted party will not receive the full amount of a money award, the Board retaining sufficient to cover the shortfall,[63] or other property will come subject to a charge,

---

[56] The General Regulations, Part III, and see *Legal Aid Handbook* (1994), pp. 52–55. In 1994–95 10.4 per cent of certificates issued for non-matrimonial proceedings were first issued as emergency certificates: *Legal Aid Board Annual Reports 1994–95*, Table Civil 7.

[57] Legal Aid Act 1988, s.31.

[58] To that end a solicitor or barrister may not take any payment for work except from the Board in relation to work covered by the certificate: Legal Aid Act 1988, ss.15(6), 31(3); the General Regulations, r.64; see *Littaur v. Steggles Palmer* [1986] 1 W.L.R. 287, *Legal Aid Handbook* 1995, pp. 104–123.

[59] For an explanation of costs, see above, pp. 530–537, 539–541.

[60] In 1994–95 in civil legal aid cases, £215,864,000 was recovered in costs, significantly reducing the cost to the Exchequer. *Legal Aid Board Annual Reports 1994–95* Table General 4 and n. 68 below.

[61] The General Regulations, reg. 92.

[62] Legal Aid Act 1988, s.16(6). See *Legal Aid Handbook 1994*, pp. 120–135. The charge on property can be registered so as to prevent anyone taking the property without notice of the charge, and so ensuring that the Legal Aid Fund can obtain the money unless the charge is transferred to the new property.

[63] The General Regulations, reg. 92.

which may be enforced by the Board.[64] However, the charges on both money and other property may be postponed or other property substituted, especially where the money or property is required to provide somewhere for the assisted person to live.[65] It is, therefore, very important to establish whether the property was recovered or preserved in the proceedings, since only then does the statutory charge apply. The Legal Aid Board will be concerned to resist any attempt to defeat the charge.[66] Further, there are certain exceptions to the charge, the best known being the first £2,500 recovered or preserved in certain matrimonial proceedings.[67]

The charge helps to reduce the cost to the Exchequer of legal aid.[68] Indeed the statutory charge, along with costs recovery, is more significant, for funding purposes, than contributions.[69] In 1994–95, a statutory charge was imposed in 5,968 non-matrimonial cases, resulting in £10,937,181 being retained to satisfy the net liability of the Legal Aid Fund. The average sum retained was £1,832.64, which, on average, was 1.9 per cent of the award made to the successful assisted party.[70] In matrimonial cases in 1994–95, a statutory charge was imposed in 18,667 cases, resulting in £36,646,899 being retained to satisfy the net liability of the Legal Aid Fund. The average sum retained was £1,963.19, which, on average, was 9.6 per cent of the award made to the successful assisted party.[71]

The statutory charge can be harsh.[72] It was justified in the *Legal Aid Handbook 1990* as "an important and essential part of a publicly funded legal aid system to prevent unreasonable conduct of legally aided litigation and to prevent assisted persons profiting at the expense of public funds."[73]

Whilst this justification may still exist,[74] its harshness has been partially recognised since, in the proposals for reform, it will not apply in green form work,[75] but will continue to apply in civil legal aid.[76] This may well be because the cost to the Exchequer of such change is small. In 1993–94 "the recovery by way of

---

[64] The General Regulations, reg. 95.
[65] The General Regulations, regs. 90, 96, 97, 98. See *Legal Aid Handbook* 1995, pp. 125–130, and see also *Hanlon v. Law Society* [1981] A.C. 124. Postponement extending to money removes the effect of *Simpson v. Law Society* [1987] A.C. 861.
[66] As to whether property has been recovered or preserved, see *Legal Aid Handbook 1995*, pp. 127–128; *Hanlon v. Law Society* [1981] A.C. 124 (property is recovered or preserved if it was in issue in the proceedings, recovered by the claimant if the subject of a successful claim, preserved by the respondent if the claim fails); *Curling v. Law Society* [1985] 1 W.L.R. 470 (property recovered where possession of property obtained through proceedings); see also *Van Hoorn v. Law Society* [1985] Q.B. 106. Burrows' example, at paras. 9.24–9.26, is particularly instructive. As to the castigation by the courts of any attempts to defeat the charge, see *Manley v. Law Society* [1981] 1 W.L.R. 335 and Burrows (1989), paras. 9.57–9.59.
[67] See the General Regulations, reg. 94; *Legal Aid Handbook 1995*, pp. 128–129.
[68] In civil legal aid cases, expenditure on matrimonial cases was £357,255,000, which was reduced, by contributions retained (£11,440,000), costs recovered (£6,822,000) and damages retained (£42,369,000), to £286,624,000 and on other civil cases was £537,122,000, which was reduced, by contributions retained (£7,618,000), costs recovered (£209,042,000) and damages retained (£15,475,000), to £286,624,000: *Legal Aid Board Annual Reports (1994–95)*, Table General 4.
[69] Lord Chancellor's Department, *Legal Aid—Targeting Need* (Cm. 2854, 1995), para. 12.4.
[70] *Legal Aid Board Annual Reports (1994–95)*, Table Civil 16.
[71] *ibid.*, Table Civil 15.
[72] See, *e.g.*, National Consumer Council, *Ordinary Justice* (1989), pp. 92–94.
[73] Legal Aid Board, *Legal Aid Handhook 1990*, p. 51.
[74] It does not appear in the 1995 Handbook, although a similar, less clear sentiment is expressed, see *Legal Aid Handbook 1995*, para. 15–01.
[75] See above, p. 523.
[76] Lord Chancellor's Department, *Legal Aid—Targeting Need* (Cm 2854, 1995), paras.12.7–12.9.

the statutory charge and costs for all green form work was only £1.8 million.''[77]

If the assisted party is *unsuccessful*, his or her liability to the Legal Aid Board is limited to the amount of his or her contribution and, in that respect, the Board bears the financial risk of litigation. However, it is possible for the court to order an assisted party to pay the opponent's costs in the action. The court must first consider whether, on normal grounds, an awards for costs should be so made.[78] If an award should be made, it can only order the assisted party to pay such of those costs as are reasonable having regard to all the circumstances, particularly the financial resources of the parties and their conduct in connection with the dispute.[79] This is not likely to be an especially serious problem for the assisted party, since if no contribution has been expected, he or she is not likely to be able to pay much in the way of costs to the opponent. This leaves successful unassisted parties in a rather unfortunate position.

6. The Costs of Successful Unassisted Parties

It is only since 1964 that a successful unassisted party has been able to obtain costs from the Legal Aid Fund at all. It is not easy to obtain such an award. Section 18 of the Legal Aid Act 1988 permits a court, on the application of a successful unassisted party;[80] to award costs to be paid by the Legal Aid Board if:

   (i) an order for costs would be made on normal principles;
  (ii) the proceedings are finally decided in favour of the unassisted party;[81]
 (iii) it is just and equitable that provision for those costs should be made out of public funds;
 (iv) as respects the costs incurred in a court of first instance, the proceedings were instituted by the assisted party;[82]
  (v) the court has considered the personal liability for costs of the assisted party; and
 (vi) with regard to first instance proceedings, the unassisted party would otherwise suffer severe financial hardship.

The initial approach of the courts was to adopt a highly restrictive interpretation of these provisions, meaning that trifling sums were awarded in costs.[83] It took

---

[77] *ibid.*, para. 12.7. Contributions are no longer made to green form work, see above, p. 494.
[78] See pp. 530–532 above.
[79] Legal Aid Act 1988, s.17(1).
[80] As to the detailed provisions relating to the making of an application, see the General Regulations, regs.134–147.
[81] This requirement is satisfied if that party has substantially succeeded in the action: *Kelly v. London Transport Executive* [1982] 1 W.L.R. 1055.
[82] The meaning of "court of first instance" and of "proceedings" can cause trouble, see *Megarity v. Law Society* [1982] A.C. 81; *R. v. Leeds City Council, ex p. Morris & Morris; Legal Aid Board Annual Reports* (1989–90), p. 151 and see Burrows (1989), paras.10.31–10.33, 10.41–10.43.
[83] See *Nowotnik v. Nowotnik* [1967] P. 83. The fact that the husband had not had to restrict his activities on account of his solicitor's bill led the court to conclude that there was no severe financial hardship. The costs awarded were, according to the court in *Hanning v. Maitland* [1970] Q.B. 580, at p. 587: 1964–5, £74; 1965–6, £838; 1966–7, £243; 1967–8, £251; 1968–9, £239.

a bold decision of the Court of Appeal in *Hanning v. Maitland (No. 2)*[84] to admit the error of the earlier interpretation and relax the application of the conditions. In that case, Lord Denning M. R. said that the "severe financial hardship" condition, applying to courts of first instance only, should not be construed so as "to exclude people of modest income or modest capital who find it hard to bear their own costs."[85] The courts have gone further than might be suggested by this statement. They accept that, in principle, it is possible for private and public companies to suffer severe financial hardship.[86] The courts look at the effect that costs will have on that person's financial position and decide on the facts whether severe financial hardship will be suffered.[87]

In all cases, whether in courts of first instance or not, an award of costs must be "just and equitable". The courts have found that this requirement was satisfied by a building society,[88] a person indemnified by the Automobile Association,[89] an insurance company[90] and a county police authority.[91]

This relaxation of attitude has led to a significant increase in the annual amount paid out of the fund to the successful unassisted parties,[92] but it still remains perilous to be sued by an assisted person. This places an additional responsibility on an area director in deciding whether an applicant for legal aid has reasonable grounds for bringing an action as plaintiff—the director may be protecting unassisted defendants as well as the public purse.

7. THE CIVIL LEGAL AID SCHEME—A CRITIQUE

The civil legal aid scheme, indeed the operation of the whole scheme, is kept under constant review by the Legal Aid Board, which is required to report annually to the Lord Chancellor on the discharge of its functions. Since the creation of the Board, the Lord Chancellor has decided that he no longer needs advice from the Lord Chancellor's Legal Aid Advisory Committee, which has been abolished. It had been critical of many of the recent steps taken with regard to legal aid and recently had been largely ignored by the Government.[93]

Two main issues in relation to the civil legal aid scheme are whether the

---

[84] [1970] Q.B. 580. *Nowotnik v. Nowotnik* was also a Court of Appeal decision.

[85] *ibid.* p. 588.

[86] *Kelly v. London Transport Executive* [1982] 1 W.L.R. 1055; *Thew (R. & T.) Ltd v. Reeves* [1982] Q.B. 1283.

[87] As in *Adams v. Riley* [1988] Q.B. 372 where the spouse's income was not simply aggregated to that of the successful unassisted party in determining whether he would suffer severe financial hardship, but regard was had to the wife's means only to the extent that they diminished his financial responsibilities; and see *Legal Aid Handbook 1995*, p. 124.

[88] *Gallie v. Lee (No. 2)* [1971] A.C. 1039.

[89] *Lewis v. Averay (No. 2)* [1973] 1 W.L.R. 510.

[90] *Davies v. Taylor (No. 2)* [1974] A.C. 225.

[91] *Maynard v. Osmond (No. 2)* [1979] 1 W.L.R. 31. The observations by the Court of Appeal on the procedure to be adopted by the court in the case of an application by a successful unassisted party must be read in the light of *Din v. Wandsworth London Borough Council (No. 2)* [1982] 1 All E.R. 1022, H.L.

[92] From the Annual Reports, it can be seen that the payments to successful unassisted parties have been: 1983–84, £232,130; 1986–87, £280,092; 1989–90, £524,381; 1993–94, £1,269,000; 1994–95, £61,053,000.

[93] See J. Rozenberg, *The Search for Justice* (1994), pp. 268–269. The last report of the Committee was its paper, *Underlying Principles of Publicly Funded Legal Services*.

financial conditions for eligibility are too restrictive, and the scheme's cost.[94] Clearly these are interrelated issues. In April 1993 the Lord Chancellor made radical changes to the eligibility levels, which significantly reduced the numbers of people eligible for legal aid,[95] at a time when many commentators have pointed out that the poor had got poorer and the rich richer.[96] The Government's own estimate was that at least 8 per cent of households lost the right to legal aid.[97] The extent of people affected was hotly disputed.[98] In 1995 "around 48% of households qualified",[99] compared with some 77 per cent of households in 1980.[1] These changes, and the changes to eligibility for green form work (particularly the abolition of contributory green form work),[2] met with a storm of protest.[3] The Legal Action Group said that it was an "unspoken assault on one of the fundamental principles that has underlain legal aid since 1945—the idea that legal aid should be available to all those who could not otherwise afford lawyers and not just to those normally classed as poor".[4] The National Association of Citizen's Advice Bureaux has recommended that "free (non-contributory) civil legal aid be restored to pre-1993 levels."[5] The difficulty with this debate is in knowing what is the "right" level at which to pitch free legal aid. The arguments are largely based upon assertions and are rarely predicated upon a sound theoretical or empirical basis. Nevertheless the assumption that too many people are excluded from pursuing their rights through the courts by the recent eligibility cuts seems to be recognised even by the Government that made them, since it has recognised that the "aim was to contain growth in legal expenditure," and has accepted that "further cuts in eligibility would not be consistent with the objective of targeting those whose need is greatest."[6]

It is not only the level of free legal aid which gives rise to concern. The number of people paying a contribution has always been relatively small. However, the proportion of people accepting the obligation to pay a contribution if they wish to qualify for support has reduced since the eligibility cuts of 1993, not increased as was expected.[7] A less well off group is being expected to pay a contribution.[8] As concluded above, it seems to be the case that paying a contribution is a major disincentive to applying for and continuing a case with

[94] As to the costs of the scheme and proposals for reform, see above, pp. 519–525.

[95] Eligibility limits had tended to rise roughly in line with inflation, but in 1993 the disposable income level for free advice was cut from £3,060 the previous year to £2,294. The changes to dependants' allowances also ensured that there was a tie-in with free legal aid and entitlement to income support. As regards contributory legal aid, the maximum disposable income was frozen at £6,800 for all but personal injury cases, for which it was frozen at £7,500; see, e.g., Rozenberg (1994), pp. 224–225.

[96] See R. Smith, "The changing nature of legal aid" in R. Smith (ed.), *Shaping the Future* (1995), pp. 17–20.

[97] See Rozenberg (1994), p. 225.

[98] Some estimates suggested that 14 million adults would be affected, see *ibid.*, pp. 226 and 267–268.

[99] *Legal Aid—Targeting Need* (1995), Appendix 1, para. 33.

[1] Smith (1995), Table 2.5.

[2] See above, p. 494.

[3] The proposals had a very rough ride through Parliament; see Rozenberg (1994), pp. 229–230 and were even subject to an application for judicial review, see *ibid.*, pp. 230–232.

[4] R. Smith in a speech on 14 November 1992 about what were then proposals and quoted in Rozenberg (1994), p. 226.

[5] NACAB, *Barriers to Justice* (1995), para. 2.45.

[6] *Legal Aid—Targeting Need* (1995), para. 3.25, and see above, p. 521.

[7] For the relevant statistics, see above, p. 521, n.55. See also N.A.C.A.B., *Barriers to Justice* (1995), para. 2.44.

[8] *Barriers to Justice* (1995), paras. 2.42–2.59.

legal aid support. This effect is exacerbated by the increase in the contribution obligation through the new method of payment of the contribution throughout the life of the certificate. In consequence, NACAB recommends "that contributions for civil legal aid are once again limited to a quarter of disposable income"[9] and that the time limit for payment of civil legal aid contributions should be the length of the case or two years, whichever is the shorter.[10] In considering the appropriate levels at which to demand contributions and what contributions to demand, some important questions tend to be left unasked and unanswered. What are the causes of the low level of legal aid with contributions? Is it because only the very poor contemplate seeking support, or that solicitors only draw its attention to that category of client,[11] or some other reason? Is the level of contributions set too high or is it the case that people do not want to pay a contribution which is a reasonable one taking into account that individual's disposable income—i.e., what priority is given to pursuing legal action in an applicant's financial outlays? It might be thought that anyone wishing to take legal action should expect to have to afford some form of financial outlay, provided it is not so great as to deny access to justice.[12]

No one doubts that society cannot afford an excessively high cost legal aid scheme. But since the eligibility cuts in 1993, the scheme has not been spending over budget, indeed it has been underspending.[13] An examination of why legal aid costs had been escalating is still very important, because those savings were made at the expense of eligibility. The Legal Aid Board is attempting to reduce costs through the franchising scheme,[14] through management efficiency,[15] combating fraud[16] and investigating the grant of legal aid to the wealthy.[17] The time is ripe for a reassessment of the costs of legal aid and that is being undertaken by the Government,[18] which is a welcome development.[19]

Concerns have been expressed about the consistency of decision-making.[20] The Board has engaged in considerable efforts to ensure consistency of decision-making, which are reflected in the various "standards." These "standards" are essentially lengthy check-lists directed to such questions as whether to grant civil legal aid.[21] It appears that success is gradually being achieved.[22]

---

[9] *ibid.*, para. 2.47.

[10] *ibid.*, para. 2.52.

[11] NACAB has expressed some concerns about the lack of familiarity of some solicitors with the legal aid scheme and the possibility that this means that many potentially eligible clients do not make an application and concludes that the Law Society should require "solicitors acting on behalf of private clients . . . to confirm in writing to every client at the outset of the case that they have considered whether the clients was eligible for legal aid and the outcome of those considerations:" *Barriers to Justice* (1995), paras. 2.73–2.75. As to the written practice statement on information about costs, see above, p. 534.

[12] This matter is pursued further above, Chap. 10.

[13] NACAB, *Barriers to Justice* (1995), para. 2.92.

[14] See above, pp. 491–492.

[15] See above, pp. 511–512.

[16] The problem of fraud is apparently greatest in green form applications (see above p. 508) and in criminal legal aid granted through the magistrates' courts, but saving money in one part of the scheme helps the financing of all aspects of the scheme.

[17] See *Legal Aid Board Annual Reports 1994–95*, Appendix 3 and see Regulations laid before Parliament in 1996.

[18] See above, pp. 519–525.

[19] *Barriers to Justice* (1995), para. 2.92–2.97.

[20] See, *e.g.*, National Consumer Council, *Ordinary Justice* (1989), pp. 81–82.

[21] *Legal Aid Handbook 1995*, pp. 63–72.

[22] *Legal Aid Board Annual Reports 1994–95*, paras. 3.21–3.23.

It is also questionable whether the grant of legal aid is too conservative. There has to be a reluctance to support too many "cutting edge" cases. But, whilst finance is a limitation upon all litigation,[23] the Legal Aid Board must be careful not to prevent the development of new rights by imposing barriers to such litigation, other than the question whether a solicitor would advise a private client to pursue the case.

The latest series for proposals which addresses the problems facing the legal aid scheme are to be found in the Government's 1995 Consultation Paper, *Legal Aid—Targeting Need*. The proposals for civil legal aid are not sensibly distinguishable from the proposals for the other elements of the legal aid scheme as a whole, and so are considered above.[24]

B. THE COUNTY COURT[25]

The county court has a wide jurisdiction.[26] Its jurisdiction now is synonymous with that of the High Court in many instances.[27] Most of the actions in the county court are claims based upon contract and tort. In 1994 2,658,416 plaints were entered, 2,487,377 (93.5 per cent) of which were "money" plaints.[28] A further 205,708 other proceedings were started in 1994.[29]

It would appear that the prediction that the county court would take cases from the High Court has proved true. In 1991 there was a significant decrease in the work of the Queen's Bench Division of the High Court and an increase in the work of the county courts.[30] Since 1991 there has been a downturn in the work of the Queen's Bench Division, but also 1991 was a peak in the work of the county courts, followed by a reduction such that by 1995 its work was at approximately the level of work in 1989.[31] There is, therefore, some, equivocal, evidence that the High Court has indeed become more of a specialist court.

Despite the harmonisation reforms, there are still jurisdiction questions to be assessed in determining in which court to commence an action, but transfer

---

[23] See above, Chap. 10.

[24] See pp. 519–525.

[25] *The County Court Practice 1995*. See also R. Blackford, *County Court Practice Handbook* (10th ed., 1992) and N. Andrews, *Principles of Civil Procedure* (1994), Chap. 20.

[26] See Chap. 2.

[27] As a consequence of recommendations in the *Civil Justice Review* (1989) introduced by the High Court and County Courts Jurisdiction Order 1991 (S.I. 1991, No.724) meaning that there is no upper limit on actions which might be tried in the county court; see further pp. 73–79 above. There has been greater, though not complete, harmonisation of remedial jurisdiction, see County Courts Act 1984, s.38, as amended.

[28] *Judicial Statistics 1994*, Cm.2891, Table 4.1. Of the money plaints, 2,448,303 were default actions and the rest fixed-date actions: *ibid.*, Table 4.2. The remaining 171,039 plaints were entered for the recovery of land: *ibid.*, Table 4.1.

[29] These comprise: 26,736 bankruptcy petitions, 1,743 winding up petitions under the Companies Act, 6,266 family matters, and 171,963 divorce, nullity and judicial separation petitions: *ibid.*, Table 4.2.

[30] *ibid.*, Charts 3 and 4.

[31] *ibid.* During 1994, in the county courts, claims fell by just over 11 per cent, proceedings concluded by arbitration fell by almost 17 per cent, the number of mortgage possession orders fell by almost 27 per cent, company winding-up petitions fell by just over 27 per cent, and bankruptcy petitions fell by just over 15 per cent: *ibid.*, p. 37.

between the courts has been improved. Penalties now exist to enforce this, which might even result in cases being struck out.[32] County court procedure is easier to follow for the lay person than High Court procedure, but the only circumstances in which a lay person finds it relatively easy to pursue litigation unaided is through the small claims process.[33] A county court is likely to provide a quicker hearing (the average waiting period for a trial in the county courts was 79 weeks[34]) and one which is more convenient to the parties than a High Court hearing.[35]

While there may still be a feeling that a High Court writ will have a greater threatening effect on a recalcitrant defendant than a county court summons, inducing him or her to settle the claim, the changes to the costs rules and the harmonisation of remedies have lessened the perceived disadvantages of a county court action.[36] It is likely that higher damages will be awarded in the High Court and that the enforcement procedures of that Court will still present advantages for High Court rather than county court litigation.

1. Court Management of Litigation

There has not as yet been much progress in court management of litigation, although the Civil Justice Review (1989) recommended it, and it is now at the heart of the proposals in the Woolf Report (1995).[37] Automatic directions exist in the county court, cases are automatically struck out if a hearing has not been requested after 15 months and some judges have experimented with various means of not leaving complete control of the case to the parties and their lawyers.

2. Commencing an Action

A county court action is classified as a fixed date action or a default action, depending upon the nature of the claim. A claim for any relief other than the payment of money must be brought as a fixed date action—any claim for money as a default action.[38] The procedure for the two actions, though initially similar, is different, so it is important to observe the distinction.

To begin either action, the plaintiff must file at the court office a formal request to the "proper officer" to issue a summons to commence the action

---

[32] The jurisdiction is discretionary; see County Courts Act 1984, s.40(1)(b) and *Restick v. Crickmore* (1993) *The Times*, December 3.

[33] See below, pp. 592–594. There has been a noticeable increase in litigation handled by litigants in person; see Lord Woolf, *Access to Justice* (1995, Interim Report) (hereafter the Woolf Report (1995)) and Judges' Council Working Party, *Litigants in Person in the Royal Courts of Justice, London* (1995, Interim Report).

[34] *Judicial Statistics* 1995, Cm. 3290, p. 35.

[35] Most county court actions can be instituted in the court of the plaintiff's choice.

[36] See above, pp. 530–533 and below pp. 794–802.

[37] See below, pp. 597–600.

[38] C.C.R., Ord. 3, r.2.

together with the particulars of claim.[39] There are different forms of the request available from the county court depending upon the nature of the action.[40] The forms require information to be provided which will establish that the court has jurisdiction. There is no specific form for the particulars of claim, even though the object of the particulars is to inform the defendant with sufficient particularity of the claim against him or her. The plaintiff must supply them. If legal help is sought, the lawyer is likely to rely on the precedents which are published.[41] A summons is completed by the plaintiff and checked by the court office before being sent to the defendant. A summons in the (imaginary) case of *Wilkinson v. Walkertronic Super Hi-Fi-Vid Ltd* follows, with the basic particulars of claim. Where the plaintiff is a litigant in person, the documentation will be less formal, but the information upon which the claim is based must appear clearly so that the defendant knows what is the case against him or her.

IN THE NOTTINGHAM COUNTY COURT

CASE NO.

Between

CYRIL JACK WILKINSON   *Plaintiff*

and

WALKERTRONIC
SUPER HI-FI-VID LTD   *Defendant*

PARTICULARS OF CLAIM

1. The Plaintiff purchased for the sum of £75.00 from the Defendant on February 1st 1995 at the Defendant's place of business, a Magivid electronic football game ("the game") for use in conjunction with a television owned by the Plaintiff.
2. At all material times the Defendant was an electrical retailer and the game was sold in the course of the Defendant's business.
3. It was an implied term of the agreement ("the agreement") that the goods supplied to the Plaintiff would be of merchantable quality.
4. Further, or alternatively, the Defendant was aware of the Plaintiff's purpose in purchasing the game, namely for use in conjunction with the Plaintiff's television and it was an implied term of the agreement that the game would be fit for such purpose.
5. The Plaintiff used the game on three occasions, but whilst in use on February 5th 1995 it exploded ("the explosion") causing damage to the Plaintiff's television and setting fire to a pair of curtains. Decorations in the same room were damaged by smoke and scorching.
6. The explosion was caused by the Defendant's breach of contract.
7. In breach of the contract the goods supplied to the Plaintiff were not of merchantable quality and/or were not fit for their purpose.

---

[39] C.C.R., Ord. 3, r.3; Ord 6, r.1.
[40] *ibid.*, Ord. 6.
[41] *Atkin's Encyclopedia of Court Forms in Civil Proceedings* (2nd ed., 1983).

PARTICULARS

(When operated the game malfunctioned causing it to explode.)

8. By reason of matters aforesaid the Plaintiff has suffered loss and damage.

9. Further the Plaintiff claims interest pursuant to section 69 of the County Courts Act 1984 on the amount found to be due to the Plaintiff at such rate and for such period as the Court thinks fit.

PARTICULARS OF SPECIAL DAMAGE

1.	refund of price paid	£75.00
2.	value of the television	£250.00
3.	replacement of curtains	£60.00
4.	redecoration	£390.00

AND the Plaintiff claims:

(1) Damages

(2) The aforesaid interest pursuant to section 69 of the County Courts Act 1984.

Dated this .... day of 1995

To the Registrar of the
Nottingham County Court and
to the Defendant

Popp, Lees and Stone,
Solicitors,
Haltergate,
Nottingham
where they will accept service of
proceedings on behalf of the Plaintiff

County Court Summons

| Case Number | Always quote this | 95/1234567 |

In the   NOTTINGHAM

County Court

The court office is open from 10 am to 4 pm Monday to Friday

(1)
Plaintiff's full name address.

CYRIL JACK WILKINSON
24 ACACIA AVENUE
NADDLEBOROUGH
NOTTINGHAM

(2)
Address for service (and) payment.
(if not as above)
Ref/Tel no.

POPP, LEES AND STONE
23 HALTERGATE
NOTTINGHAM
Solicitor's Ref. No. SP123

Telephone:

Seal

(3)
Defendant's name address.

WALKERTRONIC SUPER HI-FI-VID LTD
37 GRIDLING STREET
NOTTINGHAM

This summons is only valid if sealed by the court.
If it is not sealed it should be sent to the court.

What the plaintiff claims from you

Brief description of type of claim

Price of Goods Supplied not of
merchantable quality and/or fit
for purpose, and consequent damage
to television, curtains and redecoration.

Particulars of the Plaintiff's claim against you

SEE ENCLOSED PARTICULARS OF CLAIM

Amount claimed	£875	00
Court fee	£ 65	00
Solicitor's costs	£115	00
Total amount	£1055	00

Summons issued on

What to do about this summons

You can

- **dispute the claim**
- **make a claim against the Plaintiff**
- **admit the claim in full and offer to pay**
- **pay the total amount shown above**
- **admit only part of the claim**

For information on what to do or if you need further advice, please turn over.

Keep this summons, you may need to refer to it.

Signed
Plaintiff('s solicitor)
(or see enclosed particulars of claim)

N1   Default summons (fixed amount) (Order 3, rule 3(2)(b))

You have 21 days from the date of the postmark to reply to this summons
(A limited company served at its registered office has 16 days to reply.)

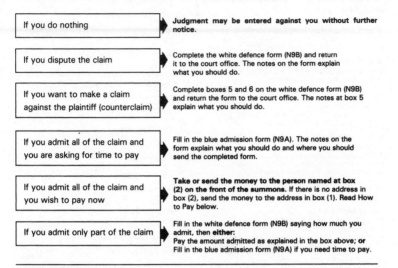

If you do nothing	**Judgment may be entered against you without further notice.**
If you dispute the claim	Complete the white defence form (N9B) and return it to the court office. The notes on the form explain what you should do.
If you want to make a claim against the plaintiff (counterclaim)	Complete boxes 5 and 6 on the white defence form (N9B) and return the form to the court office. The notes at box 5 explain what you should do.
If you admit all of the claim and you are asking for time to pay	Fill in the blue admission form (N9A). The notes on the form explain what you should do and where you should send the completed form.
If you admit all of the claim and you wish to pay now	**Take or send the money to the person named at box (2) on the front of the summons.** If there is no address in box (2), send the money to the address in box (1). Read How to Pay below.
If you admit only part of the claim	Fill in the white defence form (N9B) saying how much you admit, then **either:** Pay the amount admitted as explained in the box above; **or** Fill in the blue admission form (N9A) if you need time to pay.

Interest on Judgments

If judgment is entered against you and is for more than £5,000, the Plaintiff may be entitled to interest on the total amount.

Registration of Judgments

If the summons results in a judgment against you, your name and address may be entered in the Register of County Court Judgments. **This may make it difficult for you to get credit.** A leaflet giving further information can be obtained from the court.

Further Advice

You can get help to complete the reply forms and information about court procedures at any county court office or citizens' advice bureau. The address and telephone number of your local court is listed under "Courts" in the phone book. When corresponding with the court, please address forms or letters to the Chief Clerk. Always quote the whole of the case number which appears at the top right corner on the front of this form; the court is unable to trace your case without it.

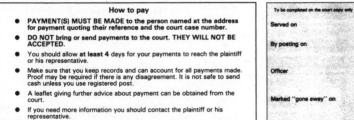

How to pay	To be completed on the court copy only
● **PAYMENT(S) MUST BE MADE to the person named at the address for payment quoting their reference and the court case number.**	Served on
● **DO NOT bring or send payments to the court. THEY WILL NOT BE ACCEPTED.**	By posting on
● You should allow **at least 4** days for your payments to reach the plaintiff or his representative.	
● Make sure that you keep records and can account for all payments made. Proof may be required if there is any disagreement. It is not safe to send cash unless you use registered post.	Officer
● A leaflet giving further advice about payment can be obtained from the court.	
● If you need more information you should contact the plaintiff or his representative.	Marked "gone away" on

OYEZ The Solicitors' Law Stationery Society Ltd, Oyez House, 7 Spa Road, London SE16 3QQ   1991 Edition
7.96 F29961

County Court N1   5039008
* * *

Admission

When to fill in this form
- Only fill in this form if you are admitting all or some of the claim **and** you are asking for time to pay
- If you are disputing the claim or you wish to pay the amount claimed, read the back of the summons

How to fill in this form
- Tick the correct boxes and give as much information as you can. **Then sign and date the form.**
- Make your offer of payment in box 11 on the back of this form. **If you make no offer the plaintiff will decide how you should pay.**
- You can get help to complete this form at **any** county court office or citizens' advice bureau.

Where to send this form
- **If you admit the claim in full**
  Send the completed form to the address shown at box (2) on the front of the summons. If there is no address in box (2) send the form to the address in box (1).
- **If you admit only part of the claim**
  Send the form **to the court** at the address given on the summons, together with the white defence form (N9B).

What happens next
- **If you admit the claim in full and offer to pay**
  If the plaintiff accepts your offer, judgment will be entered and you will be sent an order telling you how and when to pay. If the plaintiff does **not** accept your offer, the court will fix a rate of payment based on the details you have given in this form and the plaintiff's comments. Judgment will be entered and you will be sent an order telling you how and when to pay.
- **If you admit only part of the claim**
  The court will tell you what to do next.

How much of the claim do you admit?

☐ I admit the full amount claimed as shown on the summons   **or**

☐ I admit the amount of   £ _____

---

1 Personal details

Surname	WALKERTRONIC SUPER HI-FI-VID LTD.

Forename _____

☐ Mr   ☐ Mrs   ☐ Miss   ☐ Ms

☐ Married   ☐ Single   ☐ Other *(specify)* _____

Age _____

Address _____

Postcode _____

In the

NOTTINGHAM   **County Court**

Case Number	*Always quote this*	95/1234567

Plaintiff *(including ref.)*   CYRIL JACK WILKINSON
Ref. No. SP 123

Defendant   WALKERTRONIC SUPER HI-FI-VID LTD.

---

2 Dependants   *(people you look after financially)*

Number of children in each age group

under 11 ☐   11-15 ☐   16-17 ☐   18 & over ☐

Other dependants
(give details)

3 Employment

☐ I am employed as a _____

My employer is _____

Jobs other than main job *(give details)* _____

☐ I am self employed as a _____

Annual turnover is..................... £ _____

☐ I am not in arrears with my national insurance contributions, income tax and VAT

☐ I am in arrears and I owe.......... £ _____

Give details of:
(a) contracts and other work in hand
(b) any sums due for work done

☐ I have been unemployed for   years   months

☐ I am a pensioner

4 Bank account and savings

☐ I have a bank account

☐ The account is in credit by .... £ _____

☐ The account is overdrawn by.... £ _____

☐ I have a savings or building society account

The amount in the account is .... £ _____

5 Property

I live in   ☐ my own property   ☐ lodgings

☐ jointly owned property   ☐ council property

☐ rented property

N9A Form of admission and statement of means to accompany Form N1 (order 9, rule2) (1.95)   N9A 266   *Printed by Satellite Press Limited*

6 Income

My usual take home pay *(including overtime, commission, bonuses etc)*	£	per
Income support	£	per
Child benefit(s)	£	per
Other state benefit(s)	£	per
My pension(s)	£	per
Others living in my home give me	£	per
Other income *(give details below)*		
	£	per
	£	per
	£	per
Total income	**£**	**per**

8 Priority debts *(This section is for arrears only. Do not include regular expenses listed in box 7.)*

Rent arrears	£	per
Mortgage arrears	£	per
Council Tax/Community Charge arrears	£	per
Water charges arrears	£	per
Fuel debts: Gas	£	per
Electricity	£	per
Other	£	per
Maintenance arrears	£	per
Others *(give details below)*		
	£	per
	£	per
Total priority debts	**£**	**per**

7 Expenses

(Do not include any payments made by other members of the household out of their own income)

I have regular expenses as follows:

Mortgage *(including second mortgage)*	£	per
Rent	£	per
Council Tax	£	per
Gas	£	per
Electricity	£	per
Water charges	£	per
TV rental and licence	£	per
HP repayments	£	per
Mail order	£	per
Housekeeping, food, school meals	£	per
Travelling expenses	£	per
Children's clothing	£	per
Maintenance payments	£	per
Others *(not court orders or credit debts listed in boxes 9 and 10)*		
	£	per
	£	per
	£	per
Total expenses	**£**	**per**

9 Court orders

Court	Case No.	£	per
Total court order instalments		**£**	**per**

Of the payments above, I am behind with payments to *(please list)*

10 Credit debts

Loans and credit card debts *(please list)*

	£	per
	£	per
	£	per

Of the payments above, I am behind with payments to *(please list)*

11 Do you wish to make an offer of payment?

- *If you take away the totals of boxes, 7, 8 and 9 and the payments you are making in box 10 from the total in box 6 you will get some idea of the sort of sum you should offer. The offer you make should be one you can afford.*

☐ I can pay the amount admitted on

or

☐ I can pay by monthly instalments of £

12 Declaration   I declare that the details I have given above are true to the best of my knowledge

Signed   Dated

Position
(firm or company)

Defence and Counterclaim

In the

Nottingham

County Court

Case Number   *Always quote this*

Plaintiff *(including ref.)*

Defendant

The court office is open from 10am to 4pm Monday to Friday

60 CANAL STREET

When to fill in this form
• Only fill in this form if you wish to dispute all or part of the claim **and/or** make a claim against the plaintiff (counterclaim)

How to fill in this form
• Please check that the correct case details are shown on this form. You must ensure that all the boxes at the top right of this form are completed. You can obtain the correct names and numbers from the summons. The court cannot trace your case without this information.
• Follow the instructions given in each section. Tick the correct boxes and give the other details asked for.
• If you wish only to make a claim against the plaintiff (counterclaim) go to section 5.
• Complete and sign section 6 before returning this form.

Where to send this form
• Send or take this form immediately to the court office at the address shown above.
• If you admit part of the claim and you are asking for time to pay, you will also need to fill in the blue admission form (N9A) and send **both** reply forms to the court.
• Keep the summons and a copy of this defence; you may need them.

Legal Aid
• You may be entitled to legal aid. Ask about the legal aid scheme at any county court office, citizen's advice bureau, legal advice centre or firm of solicitors displaying the legal aid sign.

What happens next
• If you complete box 3 on this form, the court will ask the plaintiff to confirm that he has received payment. If he tells the court that you have not paid, the court will tell you what you should do.
• If you complete box 4 or 5, the court will tell you what you should do.
• If the summons is not from your local county court, it will automatically be transferred to your local court.

2 Arbitration under the small claims procedure
How the claim will be dealt with if defended

If the claim is for £1,000 or less it will be dealt with by arbitration (small claims procedure) unless the court decides the case is too difficult to be dealt with in this informal way. Costs and the grounds for setting aside an arbitration award are strictly limited. If the claim is for £1,000 or less and is not dealt with by arbitration, costs, including the costs of a legal representative, may be allowed.

If the claim is for over £1,000 it can still be dealt with by arbitration if either you or the plaintiff asks for it and the court approves. If the claim is dealt with by arbitration in these circumstances, costs may be allowed.

Please tick this box if the claim is worth over £1,000 and you would like it dealt with by arbitration. ☐

(go on to section 3)

3 Do you dispute this claim because you have already paid it? *Tick whichever applies*

☐ **No** *(go to section 4)*

☐ **Yes I paid** £ _____ **to the plaintiff**

on _____ *(before the summons was issued)*

Give details of where and how you paid it in the box below *(then go to section 6)*

1 How much of the claim do you dispute?

☑ **I dispute the full amount claimed** *(go to section 2)*

or

☐ **I admit the amount of** £ _____

If you dispute only part of the claim you must **either**:

• pay the amount admitted to the person named at the address for payment in box (2) on the front of the summons or if there is no address in box (2), send the money to the address in box (1) (see How to Pay on the back of the summons). Then send this defence to the court.

or

• complete the blue admission form and send it to the court with this defence.

Tick whichever applies

☐ I paid the amount admitted on _____

or

☐ I enclose the completed form of admission

(go to section 2)

N9B – Form of defence and counterclaim to accompany Form N1 (Order 9, rule 2) (1.95)   N9B 266   Printed by Satellite Press Limited

Case No. [   ]

4 If you dispute the claim for reasons other than payment, what are your reasons?

Use the box below to give full details. *(If you need to continue on a separate sheet, put the case number in the top right hand corner.)*

[   ]

5 If you wish to make a claim against the plaintiff (counterclaim)

If your claim is for a specific sum of money, how much are you claiming? £ [   ]

- If your claim against the plaintiff is for more than the plaintiff's claim against you, you may have to pay a fee. Ask at your local court office whether a fee is payable.

- You may not be able to make a counterclaim where the plaintiff is the Crown (e.g. a Government Department). Ask at your local county court office for further information.

What are your reasons for making the counterclaim?

- Use the box opposite to give full details. *(If you need to continue on a separate sheet, put the case number in the top right hand corner.)*

(go on to section 6)

[   ]

6 Signed *(To be signed by you or by your solicitor)* [   ] **Position** *(firm or company)* [   ]

Give an address to which notices about this case can be sent to you [   ] **Dated** [   ]

Post Code [   ]

Once the request and the particulars of claim have been filed and the appropriate fee paid,[42] the district judge must enter a plaint in the court record and, for a fixed date action, fix a return day on which the pre-trial review is to take place or the action is to be heard.[43] The proper officer must also prepare and issue a summons, together with the particulars of claim, and this is normally served by a court officer on the defendant. Service of the summons does not have to be effected in person; postal service is likely to be sufficient and there are special rules for violent or threatening defendants![44]

Together with the summons, the defendant receives a form for admission, defence and counterclaim[45] which must be returned to the court within 14 days of service. In a default claim and some fixed date actions, failure to submit a defence will permit the plaintiff, on submission of the appropriate form, *to have judgment entered against the defendant immediately*.[46] Therein lies the advantage of the default action. If the defendant in a default action does submit a defence in the prescribed time, the district judge fixes a date for the preliminary hearing, and the action proceeds in the same way as a fixed date action. The defendant in a fixed date action is permitted to submit a defence at any point before the return day,[47] but if it is outside the 14 day period he or she may have to meet any costs incurred as a result of the delay.[48]

3. The Defence

A defendant to any action may wish to dispute all or part of the liability asserted by the plaintiff, or may disagree with the amount claimed whilst admitting liability, or may wish to dispute the claim and make a counter-claim against the plaintiff.[49] The form served on the defendant permits all these possibilities and is much easier to follow than the old forms, which were criticised as being too complicated. It is not necessary to use the form to make a defence, the defendant only needs to submit some document indicating that the claim is disputed.[50]

The district judge must send a copy of the defence to the plaintiff.[51] The case will then proceed to pre-trial review. As already mentioned, the defendant[52] may submit a defence up to the return day and even at the pre-trial review if he or she is prepared to risk costs being awarded against him or her. However, if a defendant delays submitting a defence unduly, the court has power to order him

---

[42] On a scale in proportion to the amount of damages claimed, see *County Court Practice 1995*, pp. 1698–1699. Where the claim is relatively small it will be advantageous to place a limit on the amount of general damages claimed so as to minimise the court fee.

[43] See below, p. 591. The date must be notified to the defendant along with the summons, but if it is inconvenient an application may be made for adjournment.

[44] C.C.R., Ord. 7, r.5.

[45] The form does not have to be used in making a defence.

[46] C.C.R., Ord. 9, r.6 and 4A.

[47] Or the day on which judgment was entered for failure to submit a defence.

[48] *ibid*. Ord. 9, r.9.

[49] It is possible that the defendant's only dispute will be with either the mode of payment of the damages claimed by the plaintiff or with the quantum, the total amount of damages. These possibilities are not dealt with in the text, see the works on county court practice at n. 25 above.

[50] *ibid*. Ord. 9, r.2(1).

[51] *ibid*. Ord. 9, r.2(2).

[52] *i.e.* a defendant where the plaintiff does not seek a judgment in default upon failure by the defendant to submit a defence.

or her to deliver a defence or risk being debarred from defending the action at all.[53]

The defendant may request further and better particulars of the claim and the court has the power to require the plaintiff to supply them on pain of having the action dismissed.[54]

In our imaginary case, Walkertronic needs no further information and indicates an intention to defend in the following terms. The case will now proceed to pre-trial review.

4. The Pre-Trial Review

This stage of county court procedure was introduced in 1972 and was part of the response to criticism that the county court did not cater adequately for the resolution of small claims.[55] The review can be used either (i) to give judgment for the plaintiff if the district judge thinks fit where the defendant admits the plaintiff's claim[56] or fails to appear,[57] or (ii) to give instructions for the future conduct of the action.[58]

The function of the pre-trial review is made clear by the instructions to the district judge whereby he or she is required to "... give all such directions as appear to be necessary or desirable for securing the just expeditious and economical disposal of the action or matter."[59] Also, the district judge should "... endeavour to secure that the parties make all such admissions and agreements as ought reasonably to be made by them...."[60] Further, the notice to the parties in relation to the pre-trial review indicates that the hearing is informal and in private and that "its purpose is to:

(a) make sure that all the parties and the court understand what the case is about;

(b) see if there is any possibility of settling the dispute, and if not, decide how it is going to be heard and how long the hearing will last;

(c) decide what documents or other evidence is needed from both sides."[61]

The approach of the district judge at this stage of the proceedings is clearly crucial, although, whatever approach may be adopted in practice towards the parties, the review does at least give them the opportunity to meet and survey the relative strength of their cases. Applebey[62] concluded that, whilst useful to

[53] C.C.R., Ord. 9, r.11; Ord. 13, r.2(2).
[54] C.C.R., Ord. 6, r.7; Ord. 13, r.2(2).
[55] The criticisms were most cogently expressed in Consumer Council, *Justice Out of Reach* (HMSO, 1970) and T. G. Ison, "Small Claims" (1972) 35 M.L.R. 18.
[56] C.C.R. Ord. 17, r.6.
[57] Provided also the defendant has not delivered either an admission or a defence: C.C.R., Ord. 17, r.7. Where the defendant has delivered a defence but fails to appear, judgement can be given for the plaintiff, on proof of facts entitling him or her to relief: Ord. 17, r.8.
[58] *ibid.* Ord., 17, rr.1, 9; Ord. 19, pp. 2, 7. This function of the district judge is similar to that of a master in the High Court on a summons for directions.
[59] *ibid.* Ord. 17, r.1.
[60] *ibid.* Ord. 17, r.2.
[61] Practice Form N. 233, see *County Court Practice 1995*, p. 1919.
[62] G. Applebey, *Small Claims in England and Wales* (1978).

lawyers, the pre-trial review in the county court civil action has not been of enormous assistance to the ordinary person trying to conduct his or her own case.

The plaintiff or defendant may, at the pre-trial review, ask for any necessary interlocutory order or any other direction or may request arbitration rather than trial.[63]

As soon as practicable after the pre-trial review, a date for trial is fixed,[64] if a hearing is necessary.

5. SPECIAL PROCEDURES FOR SMALL CLAIMS

About 78 per cent of proceedings where the claim was for below £1,000 were disposed of by arbitration in 1995.[65] It is hardly surprising that special procedures have been devised to make provisions for claims of this size, and that the way in which the county courts handle such claims has been the subject of close scrutiny and criticism, not least during the Civil Justice Review and by the Woolf Inquiry Team.[66]

The county courts owe their establishment to the cost and complexity of civil procedure, which persuaded the government of the day to introduce the County Courts Act 1846 against much opposition from parts of the legal profession.[67] With an original jurisdiction of £20, the court was intended to provide a cheap, accessible and simple forum for the recovery of small debts and demands. It was the criticisms of the costs and complexity in small claims, put most convincingly by the Consumer Council in *Justice Out of Reach*, which led to the procedural reforms of the early 1970s. Further published evidence and public pressure have provoked more change in recent years, with more to come as a consequence of the Woolf Report.[68]

The objective of the changes over the past 20 years has been to make the procedure more attractive to the litigant in person and less expensive than before. Action seeking to meet these objectives has included introducing pre-trial reviews,[69] making arbitration the normal method of resolution,[70] making a preliminary appointment prior to arbitration a rarity,[71] introducing new rules of

---

[63] Except in cases where a sum not exceeding £1000 is involved (see below) the case cannot be referred to arbitration unless both parties agree.

[64] C.C.R., Ord. 17, r.9.

[65] *Judical Statistics* 1995, Cm. 3290, Table 4.7.

[66] See below, pp. 594–596.

[67] The Bar was particularly strongly opposed, mainly on the grounds that it was proposed to give solicitors the right of audience in the new court: see R. Abel-Smith and R. Stevens, *Lawyers and the Courts* (1967) and W. Holdsworth, *History of English Law*, Vol. 1. pp. 187 ff.

[68] See Appleby (1978), National Consumer Council/Welsh Consumer Council, *Simple Justice* (1979), *Civil Justice Review* (1989) and Lord Woolf, *Access to Justice* (1995).

[69] It was introduced in March 1972. "The pre-trial review was designed primarily to help small climants and their opposite numbers, the defendants to small claims, particularly litigants in person whether plaintiffs or defendants": from a speech by Lord Hailsham L. C. made on March 2, 1973 at the opening of Wandsworth County Court. See J. N. Turner, "Small Claims and the County Court in England – a contrast to the Australian approach" (1980) 9 Anglo-Am. L. R. 150 at pp. 160–162.

[70] The first step was the *Practice Direction* [1973] 1 W.L.R. 1178, followed by the County Court (Amendment No. 3) Rules 1980 (S. I. 1980 No. 1807). See below, pp. 802–804.

[71] C.C.R., Ord. 19, r.6(4) introduced in 1992.

conduct for arbitrations to make the process more informal,[72] establishing automatic directions so lessening the need for parties to understand the detailed procedure,[73] enabling and encouraging an interventionist approach by the arbitrator[74] and introducing a "no costs" rule,[75] so making less likely the use of solicitors. Raising the jurisdictional level is important to maintain access to this system, and the upper limit for small claims was raised to £1,000 consequent upon the Civil Justice Review.[76] As from January 8, 1996, the limit is raised to £3,000,[77] consequent upon the recommendation of the Woolf Inquiry into Civil Justice.[78]

The plaintiff must follow the initial procedure outlined above. If the claim[79] is for less than £3,000, the district judge will automatically refer the matter to arbitration, unless there are good reasons why the matter should go to trial instead.[80] In some cases a preliminary appointment will be held.[81] Normally the case goes straight to arbitration before an arbitrator, who will usually be a district judge but may be a Circuit judge[82] or an "outside arbitrator".[83] Prior to the hearing, notice of it is given to the parties, the parties are ordered to supply each other, at most 14 days before the hearing, with copies of all documents in their possession on which they will rely in the case. The parties will also be ordered to supply each other, not less than seven days prior to the hearing, with any expert report on which a party will rely and a list of witnesses to be called at the hearing.[84]

Representation under the legal aid scheme is not available for an arbitration hearing[85] although the plaintiff and defendant may obtain legal advice and assistance if the criteria are met.[86] It is expected that the parties will appear in person

---

[72] See G. Appleby, "Small Claims in Birmingham County Court" (1985) 4 C.J.Q. 203, at p. 204.

[73] C.C.R., Ord. 19, r.6 introduced in 1992.

[74] See below, pp. 802–804.

[75] The rule was introduced in 1973 and further amended in 1981 and 1984. For the current rule, see below. For the rationale, see *Hobbs v. Marlowe* [1978] A. C. 16 and Appleby (1978).

[76] *Civil Justice Review* (1989), para. 162. Other changes consequent upon the Review were introduced in 1992.

[77] The announcement was made on November 6, 1995.

[78] Woolf Report (1995), p. 103.

[79] The Court of Appeal in *Joyce v. Liverpool City Council* (1995) *The Times*, May 2, held that the small claims jurisdiction is not confirmed to monetary claims and includes the power to grant an order under the Housing Act 1985, s.11 requiring a landlord to carry out repairs; see also the Woolf Report (1995), p. 111. Further, the Court of Appeal held in *Afzal* that personal injurities claims for less than £1,000 claims fell within the smll claims jurisdiction. This is a controversial decision (see the Woolf Report (1995), pp. 114–117). Lord Woolf proposes that personal injuries claims for less than £10,000 be dealt with in the fast track, including those cases which might appear to fall within the small claims jurisdiction.

[80] C.C.R. Ord, 19, r.3, see below. A defence to the claim must have been entered by the defendant.

[81] C.C.R., Ord. 19, r.6(1). Such an appointment will only be held if either specific directions prior to a hearing need to be given in the presence of the parties or to enable the judge to dispose of the case because it is ill-founded or there is no reasonable defence. In so deciding, the judge will wish to keep to a minimum the number of court attendances: C.C.R., Ord. 19, r.6(4).

[82] It will be a Circuit judge only by or with the leave of the judge: C.C.R. Ord. 19, r.5(2).

[83] For a reference to an outside arbitrator, the parties must consent: C.C.R. Ord. 19, r.5(3). An "outside arbitrator" is neither a judge nor a district judge (C.C.R., Ord. 19, r.1), but is some suitable person. Outside arbitrators are rarely used. As to a debate of the value of using non-lawyers, see below, pp. 802–804.

[84] C.C.R., Ord. 19, r.6(2) and (3).

[85] Since it is not a proceeding in the county court, for which, in general, representation is available: Legal Aid Act 1988, s.14 and Sched. 2, Part I, para. 1(a).

[86] See above, pp. 492–494.

at a hearing, but legal representation is not prohibited. No costs, including a solicitor's charges and sums allowed to a litigant in person in lieu, are allowed in an arbitration except for those stated on the summons, those incurred in enforcing the award, and those incurred through the unreasonable conduct of the opposing party.[87] (If the case goes for trial rather than arbitration, solicitor's costs *will* be allowed, subject to the normal rules.) A lay representatives scheme has been introduced to allow greater support for litigants, without the necessity for legal representation.[88]

The object of providing for arbitration rather than trial in small claims is to allow litigants to represent themselves at a hearing where their ignorance of procedure and adversarial techniques will not be a handicap.[89] Automatic reference to arbitration may be rescinded. The district judge may order trial in court, on the application of either party of her or his own motion, if satisfied that a difficult question of law or exceptionally complex questions of fact are involved, that fraud is alleged, that both parties agree to trial, or that it would be unreasonable to order arbitration in the particular case having regard to the subject matter, the size of any counterclaim, the parties' circumstances or the interests of other persons likely to be affected by the claim.[90]

Pepper v. *Healey*[91] shows that arbitration may not always be the ideal solution in small claims and provides an example of an arbitration being rescinded.

In that case, Mrs Pepper alleged that Mrs Healey had driven into her car causing damage amounting to £133. Mrs Healey denied that there had been any collision and proposed to call expert evidence to prove that any damage to the plaintiff's car could not have been done by her car. Mrs Healey, comprehensively insured, would have had her legal expenses met by her insurance company. Mrs Pepper, insured only against third-party claims, would not. The registrar rescinded the automatic reference to arbitration on the grounds that the plaintiff needed legal representation in order to present her case properly and the costs burden on her in an arbitration would therefore be unfair. Because the insurance company was paying the defendant's costs, the contest would be unequal. The Court of Appeal upheld this view. (It may seem ironical that the initial question of whether the case should go to arbitration or trial involved three hearings—two in the county court and one in the Court of Appeal.)

6. REVIEW OF SMALL CLAIMS PROCEDURE

The small claims procedure is designed to ensure a relatively informal, inexpensive and speedy form of resolving civil disputes. Reviews of the process taking into account these criteria were undertaken by both the Civil Justice Review and the Lord Woolf Inquiry.

---

[87] C.C.R., Ord. 19, r.4. If a reference to arbitration is rescinded, costs incurred thereafter are recoverable. These provisions do not preclude the award of witnesses' allowances: C.C.R., Ord. 19, r.6(3).

[88] C.C.R., Ord. 19, r.1 and the Lay Representatives (Rights of Audience) Order 1992 (S.I. 1992 No. 1966) made in pursuance of the Courts and Legal Services Act 1990, s.11.

[89] See below, pp. 802–804.

[90] C.C.R., Ord. 19, r.3(2). Where minded to act on own motion, the district judge is obliged to involve the parties: C.C.R., Ord. 19, r.3(3).

[91] [1982] R.T.R. 411.

Many of the recommendations of the Civil Justice Review[92] relied upon the results of a factual study undertaken by Touche Ross Management Consultants.[93] Whilst the factual study produced considerable valuable information, there are gaps and some errors in methodology which mean that its conclusions cannot be relied on exclusively in an assessment of the present procedure.[94] On the positive side, the factual study indicated that, in general, the small claims procedure provided a suitable forum for use by the general public, although the comments on the procedure tended to be about details rather than an overall critique.

On the face of it, the *Judicial Statistics* suggest that the small claims procedure is extensively used. Of the 112,647 proceedings dealt with by hearing in 1995, 88,170 were dealt with by arbitration for cases under £1,000.[95] In 1989, 1,574,130 money plaints valued under £500 (the then small claims limit) were entered.[96] Research has shown that it is not only private citizens who are using the procedure, but also "large organisations"[97] and other "small litigants"[98] make extensive use of it.[99] Lord Woolf noted the concerns expressed about the use of the procedure by such organisations, but concluded that there are no significant disadvantages in it being used by such businesses, provided the district judge is adept at holding the ring in both pre-hearing and hearing procedures.[1] What is more important is that the information might suggest that the private citizen is insufficiently aware of the jurisdiction and so its awareness should be drawn to general attention more successfully.[2]

It has been said that private citizens have considerable difficulty in using the small claims jurisdiction because they have difficulty in understanding the forms supplied by the court and in understanding and knowing how they should be filled in, and also have difficulty with the hearings, which can be very legalistic.[3] There is also some evidence that comprehension of the various aspects of small claims procedures is quite high.[4]

A number of specific problems have been identified which suggest that the objectives are not attained fully or consistently. One of the criticisms is of the variations in approach adopted by the various county courts, court staff and

---

[92] *Civil Justice Review* (1988), Chap. 8.

[93] *Civil Justice Review: Study of The Small Claims Procedure* (1986).

[94] For a critique see C.J. Whelan, "The Role of Research in Civil Justice Reform: Small Claims in the County Court" (1987) 6 C.J.Q. 237. See also Applebey (1987), pp. 216–218.

[95] *Judicial Statistics 1995* (Cm. 2891, 3290), Table 4.7.

[96] *Judicial Statistics 1989* (Cm. 1154, 1990), Table 4.1. This information is no longer recorded in the annual statistics.

[97] *i.e.* large and medium companies, banks, building societies, hire-purchase companies, national or public bodies, and public utilities: Touche Ross Management Consultants (1986), at p. 18.

[98] *i.e.* small businesses and local professional companies: *ibid.*, at pp. 18–19. Unfortunately, for most purposes the research failed to distinguish between private citizens and other small litigants; see Whelan (1987), at pp. 243–244 noting the consequent weaknesses of the research.

[99] Touche Ross Management Consultants (1986), p. 20, shows that, in their sample, 38 per cent of plaintiffs were private citizens and 58 per cent of defendants were private citizens. Such extensive use was made of the small claims procedure by one large organisation, Severn Trent Water Authority, in Birmingham County Court that special provision was made in 1982: Applebey (1987), at p. 205.

[1] Woolf Report (1995), pp. 106–107. Since the major part of his concern is with the quality of the judges' work at arbitrations; see below, pp. 802–804.

[2] See, Woolf Report (1995), pp. 105–106.

[3] See, *e.g.*, Applebey (1987), pp. 225, 227–228, 233.

[4] Touche Ross Management Consultants (1986), p. 84.

district judges, resulting in a difficulty in providing advice of a consistent nature.[5] On the other hand, there may be real value in divergence of approach not only in terms of flexibility, but also in encouraging experimentation which may lead to overall advances being made, which might otherwise not be possible.[6]

Consequently, it must be questioned, with Sir Jack Jacob, whether the present small claims procedure provides "a procedure which is simple, inexpensive and fair".[7] Is it simple? The experience of the Birmingham County Court when it established a separate office to deal with litigants in person would suggest that the answer is that it is not. The office was established because court staff found it extremely time-consuming to assist litigants in person with processing a claim, and, in particular, with providing help with summonses.[8]

Lord Woolf considered this evidence and the evidence supplied to him at various seminars and concluded that the basic problem with the small claims jurisdiction was that the judges needed to exercise more consistent control over pre-hearing and hearing procedure.[9] For example, with regard to pre-hearing procedures, he concluded that this "is an area where a robust judicial approach is required to curtail and disallow adversarial delaying tactics and to ensure speedy progress, the avoidance of unnecessary expense and above all fairness".[10] In consequence, Lord Woolf proposes improvements in the training of the judges to ensure a more consistent approach which should improve the reputation of the procedure and thus remove some of the concerns of those wondering whether to risk its use and other changes concerned with the process of county court arbitration.[11] Lord Woolf also proposes that the discretion to transfer complex cases out of the jurisdiction should be widened by removing the requirement that the complexity must be "exceptional", hence improving flexibility.[12] Small claims he proposes should be dealt with at a single hearing and if clarification is required from the parties this should be done by correspondence or telephone.[13] Combined with his proposals about greater information provision[14] and the courts charter initiative, these may well deal with the problems identified.

C. THE HIGH COURT

The process of settlement or compromise referred to in Chapter 10 may continue throughout a civil action in the High Court, so that the procedural steps neces-

---

[5] See, *e.g., Civil Justice Review* (1988), para. 509, and Applebey (1987), p. 221.
[6] Applebey (1987), p. 234, quoting from National Center for State Courts, *Small Claims Courts: A National Examination* (1978).
[7] Opening Address to the "Reforming Small Claims" conference organised by the Institute of Judicial Administration, University of Birmingham held in 1987, reported in Applebey (1987), p. 227.
[8] See Applebey (1985), p. 206. The evidence showed that the changed administrative procedure also produced costs savings, improved relationships with users who understood the procedure and in training for court staff. See also *Ordinary Justice* (1989), pp. 296–297.
[9] Woolf Report (1995), Chap. 16.
[10] Woolf Report (1995), p. 107.
[11] See below, pp. 802–804.
[12] Woolf Report (1995), pp. 104 and 118.
[13] Woolf Report (1995), p. 118.
[14] Woolf Report (1995), Chap. 18.

sary to bring an action to trial may be taken in the knowledge that a hearing may yet be averted. Indeed, some parts of pre-trial High Court procedure have the effect of increasing the possibilities for compromise by encouraging,[15] imposing pressure for,[16] or facilitating[17] settlement. Much of the court involvement in pre-trial procedures is through Masters or district judges, rather than judges.[18]

1. COURT MANAGEMENT OF LITIGATION

Since the Civil Justice Review there has been a move to see court, rather than party, control of litigation, so as thereby to reduce delay and, it is hoped, the cost of civil litigation.[19] It is a theme which has been picked up by the judicial managers and in the Woolf inquiry into civil justice.[20] Practice Notes have been introduced dealing with case management in civil litigation in both the Queens' Bench and Chancery Divisions[21] and the Family Division[22] of the High Court. The *Practice Note* for the Queen's Bench and Chancery Divisions makes clear that the purpose is to reduce the cost and delay of civil litigation, and this will be achieved by first instance judges asserting "greater control over the preparation for and conduct of hearings than has hitherto been customary". The responsibility of practitioners will be to conduct cases economically with a reminder of the costs jurisdiction of the courts, including the possibility of making a wasted costs order.[23] The consequent areas targeted for the courts to limit are discovery, the length of oral submissions, the time allowed for examination and cross-examination, the issues on which the court wishes to be addressed, and reading aloud from documents and authorities. So, witnesses' statements are to be evidence-in-chief; the requirement that pleadings are to be of facts not evidence[24] is to be strictly enforced and there should be a real attempt by the parties to agree the main issues and to reduce or eliminate the expert issues; requirements in relation to the documents used in court are to be strictly controlled;[25] a pre-trial review is to be held where a case is expected to last more than 10 days;[26] a pre-trial check-list should be lodged by each party

---

[15] See *Practice Note* [1985] 1 All E.R. 385, below.

[16] *e.g.*, the costs indemnity rule (see pp. 530–532 above) and payments into court (see below, p. 626); see N. Andrews, *Principles of Civil Procedure* (1994), pp. 393–402.

[17] *e.g.*, without prejudice communications, expert witness meetings, unused witness statements, pre-trial disclosure, and provisional adjudication; see Andrews (1994), pp. 402–405.

[18] See J.I.H. Jacob, *The Fabric of English Civil Justice* (1987), pp. 109–114 and O'Hare and Hill (1993), pp. 4–5.

[19] See *Civil Justice Review* (1988), paras. 220–228. Its proposals are discussed in the second edition of this book at pp. 536–537.

[20] Woolf has identified that case management is a process being applied in many jurisdictions; see Woolf Report, pp. 30–31 and I. R. Scott, "Caseflow Management in the Trial Court" and R. Cranston, " 'The Rational Study of Law': Social Research and Access in A. A. S. Zuckerman and R. Cranston (eds.), *Reform of Civil Procedure* (1995).

[21] *Practice Note* [1995] 1 All E.R. 385.

[22] *Practice Note* [1995] 1 All E.R. 586.

[23] See above, pp. 176–178.

[24] R.S.C. Ord 18, r.7; see below, p. 613.

[25] See R.S.C. Ord 34, r.10(2)(a). Documents are to be in A4 format if possible, filed properly and securely, and lodged with the court at least two clear days before the hearing.

[26] It should be held between eight and four weeks before the trial and the trial advocates should attend.

with the court at least two months before the trial date;[27] skeleton arguments, which should be as brief as the issues allow and should not exceed 20 sides of double-spaced A4 paper, must be lodged with the court at least three clear days prior to trial; opening speeches must be succinct and then other parties may briefly amplify their skeleton arguments, and written submissions may be required in conjunction with final speeches in heavy cases.

The *Practice Notes* and the earlier recommendations of the *Civil Justice Review* are predicated on the need to solve the same problem as that identified in the 1995 report by Lord Woolf on the civil justice system, *Access to Justice*.[28] Despite the detailed procedural rules with timetables, he identified that

> "In the absence of any effective control by the court itself, however, the timetable is frequently ignored, and the lack of firm supervision enables the parties to exploit the rules to their own advantage. Such exploitation is endemic in the system. . . . All too often, such tactics are used to intimidate the weaker party and produce a resolution of the case which is either unfair or is achieved at a grossly disproportionate cost or after unreasonable delay."[29]

Barristers have found this degree of responsibility difficult to accept and, whilst there are often good reasons for litigation practice, it is impossible to avoid accepting that Lord Woolf is, in general, right. Of course, it also applies to solicitors, who run most litigation, often, but not always, until a very late stage. For Lord Woolf one resolution in case management which

> "involves the court taking the ultimate responsibility for progressing litigation along a chosen track[30] for a pre-determined period during which it is subjected to selected procedures which culminate in an appropriate form of resolution before a suitably experienced judge. Its overall purpose is to encourage settlement of disputes at the earliest appropriate stage; and, where trial is unavoidable, to ensure that cases proceed as quickly as possible to a final hearing which is itself of strictly limited duration."[31]

Provided appropriate resources are made available to enable such case management, it is difficult to quibble with such a proposal on principle. Some people

---

[27] The pre-trial check-list covers: short title of action; folio number; trial date, party lodging check-list; name of solicitor; name(s) or counsel for trial (if known); and then information must be supplied: (a) whether the action has been set down; (b) whether amendments to the pleadings will be made and, if so, when; (c) whether interrogatories are outstanding and upon whom they are to be served; (d) whether all orders in relation to expert, factual and hearsay evidence have been complied with and, if not, what remains to be done; whether any further reports or statements will need to be served; whether orders in relation to oral evidence have been complied with or any further such requirements, what factual and expert witnesses are to be called and if interpreters are needed; whether discovery orders have been complied with and what might be outstanding; whether document bundles will be properly supplied at least seven days prior to trial; whether and when a pre-trial review has been ordered and, if not, whether there should be one; what is the estimate of the trial's length; and whether alternative methods of resolving the dispute have been discussed.

[28] Woolf Report (1995).

[29] Woolf Report (1995), p. 27. For issues relating to settlement of disputes, see above, pp. 554–563.

[30] As to Woolf's proposals for different tracks for cases, see below, pp. 626–633.

[31] Woolf Report (1995), p. 16.

have raised concerns about it raising the cost of litigation, that it is premature to make yet further changes to the system and that there is a lack of supportive research evidence for the approach. The Woolf Report rejects each concern, the first out of hand, the second on the basis of a different judgment, and the third on the basis of partial acceptance, recognition of some research and a recommendation that the proposals be introduced on a staged and monitored basis.[32]

The Woolf proposals involve a recognition that there are different types of civil litigation, and so a three-tier system is proposed: "(a) an increased small claims jurisdiction; (b) a new fast track, for cases at the lower end of the scale; and (c) a new multi-track, covering both the High Court and the county court."[33] The approach would allow cases to be handled appropriately "from the simplest and least expensive to the most complex, important and financially weighty."[34] The proposals build on the move towards county court procedures as a result of amendments introduced after the Civil Justice Review. In fact, in addition to that shift, there has been a reduction in the use of both the county and High Courts.[35] Woolf also recognises that costs of cases are out of proportion to the amounts at issue.[36] Thus, Woolf recommends the introduction of a fast track to provide a quicker and more proportionate means of dealing with lower value and simpler cases which are too big to be dealt with by the small claims court.[37] Above the fast track, Woolf proposes a multi-track approach involving hands-on management by the courts. So, in addition to proposing the encouragement of a more co-operative approach between the parties, there would be a focus on eliminating, at an early stage, those issues which can be so determined, through an enlarged summary procedure.[38] Further, in all cases where a defence is received, there will be an examination by procedural judge and the case will be allocated to the appropriate track. In multi-track cases a decision would be made as to whether the case required full hands-on judicial control, more limited judicial case management or whether it could be dealt with by standard directions on a standard timetable. The criteria for determining which form of management would be

"(a) what is needed in order to achieve a just result; (b) the need to achieve that result in a time and at a cost which is reasonable having regard to the nature of the issues involved and the means of the parties; (c) the desirability of the parties being able to conduct litigation, so far as possible, on fair and equal terms; (d) the wishes of the parties to the litigation; and (e) the need to prevent any one case being conducted in a way that interferes with the resolution of other disputes and wastes the resources of the court."[39]

The courts would have the ultimate responsibility for the allocation of a case

---

[32] *ibid.* pp. 32–33.
[33] *ibid.* See N. Armstrong, "Making Tracks" in A.A.S. Zuckerman and R. Cranston, *Reforming Civil Procedure* (1995). The proposal is to be given priority.
[34] *ibid.*
[35] See above, p. 555.
[36] See above, pp. 532–533 and see the Costs Issue Paper (1996).
[37] Woolf Report, pp. 35–36 and Chap. 7. It would be used for cases from the small claims limit to £10,000 and involve district judges in having greater jurisdiction.
[38] See below, pp. 626–633.
[39] Woolf Report, (1995) pp. 38–39.

to the appropriate track, but that allocation need not be permanent. Flexibility is important. After considering the papers, the procedural judge would "issue appropriate directions including a timetable appropriate to meet the needs of the particular case; fix a case management conference; if necessary, transfer the action to the appropriate court; in specialised and complex cases, arrange for the papers to be considered by a judge of the appropriate seniority".[40] This detail makes quite clear that the proposals mean that the judge will be in control of the management of the case, rather than the parties or their legal representatives. Not only will adequate resourcing be necessary, but Woolf also identifies that effective judicial case management will require: "(a) continuity of management; (b) management and trial by judges at an appropriate level, but who are no more senior than is necessary; and (c) flexible and efficient deployment of the judiciary."[41] Rather than achieving this by allocation of each case to a particular judge, Woolf recommends the development of judicial teams to manage and try civil proceedings, thus combining an appropriate degree of continuity and flexibility.[42]

2. Commencing an Action

We concentrate on the plaintiff beginning an action by way of writ of summons, rather than an originating summons, originating motion or petition.[43] A writ is a formal document containing details of the parties, the plaintiff's claim, an instruction to the defendant to acknowledge the writ within a specified time and a warning to the defendant that he or she must acknowledge the summons and indicate an intention to contest the case or risk the plaintiff proceeding directly to a judgment.[44]

On the back of the writ the plaintiff must set out ("indorse") the nature of the claim against the defendant either in a brief, general statement (a "general indorsement")[45] or in a full statement (a "special indorsement").[46] If the writ contains a general indorsement and the defendant wishes to contest the case, a full statement of claim by the plaintiff will become a necessary part of the pleadings which will follow in due course and then the defendant will at least know the outline of the case against him or her.[47]

The plaintiff (or solicitor) must draw up the writ. The writ must then be "issued" and "served". The "issue" of the writ is the process by which it is made a formal document with the authority of the court. This is achieved by the presentation of sufficient copies of the writ to allow one to be filed at the

---

[40] ibid., (1995) Woolf Report, p. 39, and further embellished in Chaps.7 and 8.

[41] ibid., p. 40.

[42] The necessary changes in judicial deployment and information technology are considered further respectively at ibid., Chaps.11 and 13. For the other related and detailed proposals, see ibid., Chaps.7–14 and (in relation to practice, procedure and costs), Chaps.19–26.

[43] R.S.C. Ord. 5. The originating summons is used where there are no issues of fact arising, but law and documentation interpretation (see J. O'Hare and R. N. Hill Civil Litigation (6th ed., 1993), p. 125). Motions and petitions are very specialised (see ibid., p. 125).

[44] Every writ must be in the established form: R.S.C., Ord. 6, r.1. See generally as to issue and service of a writ, O'Hare and Hill (1993), pp. 207–208, 213–219.

[45] See, e.g. Hacker v. Reliable Nag Supply Stables, below.

[46] See, e.g. Maserati v. Lagonda, below. Special indorsement would normally only be used where the claim is for a liquidated sum, that is a specific sum of money due, in this case, to the plaintiff, or the plaintiff is very anxious to hurry the matter along.

[47] See below, p. 615.

Writ Department of the Central Office of the High Court,[48] one, the "original," to be kept by the plaintiff and one to be served on each defendant. Forms of Acknowledgements of Service for each defendant must also be handed in. The court officer stamps the writs and assigns a reference number, that is a year, letter and number to the action.[49]

"Service" of the writ must take place within four months of the date of issue of the writ.[50] Service is normally effected by sending it by first-class post to the usual address of the defendant or to his or her solicitor who will accept service on the defendant's behalf.[51] Personal service, where the plaintiff or his or her agent actually gives to or leaves with the defendant a copy of the writ, is still possible, but postal service is obviously less onerous.[52]

The following (pp. 602–605) are two examples of a writ of summons. The first, in the imaginary case of *Hacker* v. *Reliable Nag Supply Stables* (a firm) is a claim for damages for breach of contract, the writ being generally indorsed. The second in the imaginary case of *Maserati* v. *Lagonda*, is a claim for the price of goods sold and delivered, the writ being specially indorsed.

3. The Acknowledgement of Service—and the Consequences of Failure[53]

As noted, the plaintiff is required to serve on the defendant, as well as a writ, a form on which service of the writ can be acknowledged. Normally an acknowledgement is required within 14 days. The acknowledgement must indicate whether the defendant intends to contest the claim.[54] If the claim is to be contested and the writ has been specially indorsed, a defence must be served on the plaintiff within 14 days after the time for acknowledging service.[55] If the writ is generally indorsed, a defence need not be served until after a full statement of claim has been served by the plaintiff.

The defendant may wish to contest the claim and the form makes provision for that response. If the defendant simply fails to indicate an intention to contest the action (by not acknowledging service at all) the plaintiff is entitled to enter *final* judgment for the amount claimed, interest and costs, if the claim is for a liquidated amount[56] and *interlocutory* judgment, if the claim is for an unliquidated amount;[57] both known as default judgments. In the latter case the defendant will still be able to appear and dispute the amount of damages when they fall to be assessed by a master prior to final judgment being entered for the plaintiff.

---

[48] Or at a convenient District Registry.

[49] *e.g.* 1995-A-No. 789, where A is the initial of the plaintiff's surname or family name.

[50] R.S.C., Ord. 6, r.8(3). Exceptions are permitted to this rule: *ibid*. The period was reduced from 12 months following the Civil Justice Review.

[51] R.S.C., Ord. 10, r.1 and Ord. 65, r.5.

[52] Postal service was introduced in 1980 and was described in the 1988 White Book as ". . . a landmark in the procedure and practice of the Chancery and Queen's Bench Divisions of the High Court"; *Supreme Court Practice 1988*, para. 10/1/6. Thus there is now little scope for the athletic and ingenious defendant to avoid service of the writ by keeping out of the way of the plaintiff.

[53] See O'Hare and Hill (1993), pp. 219–234.

[54] See example in the text, question 2 on the Acknowledgment of Service.

[55] *ibid*. Directions for Acknowledgment of Service.

[56] R.S.C., Ord. 13, r.1. A "liquidated" amount is where the damages claimed is a specified sum.

[57] R.S.C., Ord. 13, r.2.

COURT FEES ONLY

Writ indorsed
with Statement
of Claim
[Unliquidated
Demand]
(O. 6, r.1)

IN THE HIGH COURT OF JUSTICE
Queen's Bench Division

19 94 . $^{\underline{H}}$.—No. 179

[NOTTINGHAM **District Registry]**

Between

PETER GEORGE MARTIN HACKER Plaintiff

AND

RELIABLE NAG SUPPLY STABLES (sued as a firm)

Defendant

(1) Insert name. **To the Defendant** (¹) RELIABLE NAG SUPPLY STABLES

(2) Insert address. of (²) THE WIDE PADOCKS, LEAK AVENUE, GROATHAM, NOTTINGHAMSHIRE

This Writ of Summons has been issued against you by the above-named Plaintiff in respect of the claim set out on the back.

Within 14 days after the service of this Writ on you, counting the day of service, you must either satisfy the claim or return to the Court Office mentioned below the accompanying **Acknowledgment of Service** stating therein whether you intend to contest these proceedings.

If you fail to satisfy the claim or to return the Acknowledgment within the time stated, or if you return the Acknowledgment without stating therein an intention to contest the proceedings, the Plaintiff may proceed with the action and judgment may be entered against you forthwith without further notice.

(3) Complete
and delete as
necessary

Issued from the (³) [Central Office] [Admiralty and Commercial Registry] [NOTTINGHAM District Registry] of the High Court this FIRST day of DECEMBER 1994.

NOTE:—This Writ may not be served later than 4 calendar months *(or, if leave is required to effect service out of the jurisdiction, 6 months)* beginning with that date unless renewed by order of the Court.

IMPORTANT
Directions for Acknowledgment of Service are given with the accompanying form.

Statement of Claim

The Plaintiff's claim is for

Damages for breach of an implied term in the contract for sale of a piebald gelding by the Defendant to the Plaintiff on the 25th day of June 1994 and for the interest thereon.

(Signed)   GEORGE WASHINGTON

(1) If this Writ was issued out of a District Registry, this indorsement as to place where the cause of action arose should be completed.

(2) Delete as necessary.

(3) Insert name of place.

(4) For phraseology of this indorsement where the Plaintiff sues in person, see *Supreme Court Practice*, Vol. 2, para. 1.

(¹) [(²) [The cause] [one of the causes] of action in respect of which the Plaintiff claim   relief in this action arose wholly or in part at (³) in the district of the District Registry named overleaf.]

(⁴) **This Writ** was issued by POPP, LEES AND STONE

of 23 HALTERGATE, NOTTINGHAM

[Agent   for

of   ]

Solicitor   for the said Plaintiff   whose address   (²) [is] [are]

19 LONG ROAD, PEGWORTH, NOTTINGHAMSHIRE

Solicitor's Reference MB 456   Tel. No: 0115 900 0000

OYEZ The Solicitors' Law Stationery Society Ltd, Oyez House, 7 Spa Road, London SE16 3QQ   12 94 F28483
5044043
★ ★ ★

High Court A3A

COURT FEES ONLY

**Writ indorsed
with Statement
of Claim
[Liquidated
Demand]
(O.6, r. 1)**

IN THE HIGH COURT OF JUSTICE

19 94 .-M .—No. 792

Queen's Bench Division

[NOTTINGHAM   **District Registry]**

Between

ALFONSO FREDERICO MASERATI   Plaintiff

AND

WILLIAM DANIEL HENRY LAGONDA

Defendant

(1) Insert name.

To the Defendant (¹) WILLIAM DANIEL HENRY LAGONDA

(2) Insert address.   of (²)   23 TALBOT GARDENS, MORGAN-CUM-MIDGET,
NOTTINGHAMSHIRE

This Writ of Summons has been issued against you by the above-named Plaintiff in respect of the claim set out on the back.

Within 14 days after the service of this Writ on you, counting the day of service, you must either satisfy the claim or return to the Court Office mentioned below the accompanying **Acknowledgment of Service** stating therein whether you intend to contest these proceedings.

If you fail to satisfy the claim or to return the Acknowledgment within the time stated, or if you return the Acknowledgment without stating therein an intention to contest the proceedings, the Plaintiff   may proceed with the action and judgment may be entered against you forthwith without further notice.

(3) Complete
and delete as
necessary.

Issued from the (³) [Central Office] [Admiralty and Commercial Registry]
[NOTTINGHAM
District Registry] of the High Court
this FIRST   day of DECEMBER   19 94

NOTE:—This Writ may not be served later than 4 calendar months *(or, if leave is required to effect service out of the jurisdiction, 6 months)* beginning with that date unless renewed by order of the Court.

IMPORTANT

Directions for Acknowledgment of Service are given with the accompanying form.

Statement of Claim

The Plaintiff's claim is for

the sum of £4000 being the price of goods sold and delivered to the Defendants and interests amounting to [£   total by date of writ] and continuing at a rate of [£   ] per day until payment or judgment.

Particulars

A motorcar, registered number ABC 123, sold to the Defendant under contract contained in letters dated the 29th day of June 1994 and delivered to the Defendants at his house by the Plaintiff on the 30th day of June 1994.

(Signed)   GEORGE WASHINGTON

If, within the time for returning the Acknowledgment of Service, the Defendant pay   the amount claimed and £   300   for costs and, if the Plaintiff obtain   an order for substituted service, the additional sum of £ 10.00   , further proceedings will be stayed. The money must be paid to the Plaintiff ,   his Solicitor   or Agent.

(1) If this Writ was issued out of a District Registry, this indorsement as to place where the cause of action arose should be completed.

(2) Delete as necessary.

(3) Insert name of place.

(4) For phraseology of this indorsement where the Plaintiff sues in person, see *Supreme Court Practice,* vol. 2, para 1.

(1) [(2) [The cause] [One of the causes] of action in respect of which the Plaintiff claim s   relief in this action arose wholly or in part at (3) MORGAN-CUM-MIDGET in the district of the District Registry named overleaf.]

(4) **This Writ** was issued by   POPP, LEES AND STONE of   23, HALTERGATE, NOTTINGHAM

[Agent for
of

Solicitor   for the said Plaintiff   whose address   (2) [is] [are]
    423, TALBOT GARDENS, MORGAN-CUM-MIDGET, NOTTINGHAMSHIRE]

Solicitor's Reference   MB 456   **Tel. No:** 0115 900 0000

OYEZ   The Solicitors' Law Stationery Society Ltd, Oyez House, 7 Spa Road, London SE16 3QQ   5 94 F27254

High Court A2A   5044027
     * *

In both cases, the judgment in favour of the plaintiff can, by order of the court, be set aside[58] if the defendant has a reasonable excuse for the default and also has some merit in his or her case.[59] If a judgment is set aside in this way, the defendant is likely to bear some penalty in costs.

Acknowledgments of service to the two writs are set out below (pp. 607–612). The stables wish to dispute the claim, Mr Lagonda does not.

4. SUMMARY JUDGMENT[60]

It would obviously be an unacceptable delaying tactic for a defendant to indicate an intention to defend when there was no real defence, thus gaining time in which to pay a debt or damages which could not seriously be disputed. The procedure by which a plaintiff is permitted to request the court to enter judgment for him or her summarily is clearly very important, but it is equally important to ensure that a power given to a judge or Master to award a case to the plaintiff who can show that there is no real answer to the claim should not be exercised lightly. The provisions of Order 14 of the Rules of the Supreme Court seek to achieve this balance.[61]

A plaintiff may apply to the court to enter judgment on his or her behalf for the whole or part of the claim if the application can be supported with an affidavit swearing the truth of the facts of the case and stating that the plaintiff believes there to be no defence to the claim.[62] The defendant may be given leave to seek to refute the plaintiff's contention by affidavit or otherwise[63] and demonstrate, at least, that there is an issue to be tried, but he or she is not obliged to prove a defence.[64]

At the hearing, the Master has the task of balancing the rights of plaintiff and defendant, but must allow the defendant to go on if the issue is triable, even if the defendant's chances of success are thought to be slender. However, there are a number of options open to the Master and conditions may be attached to the leave to defend.[65] Conditions may have the effect of discouraging the defendant, or at least inducing careful consideration of the strength of the case. The Master may give judgment for the plaintiff and thus greatly speed up the process of litigation.

---

[58] R.S.C., Ord. 13, r.9.

[59] This is not the only ground for setting aside the judgment, there may have been formal irregularities.

[60] See Jacob (1987), pp. 122–124 and O'Hare and Hill (1993), pp. 234–236, 240–247.

[61] The summary judgment procedure is commonly referred to as "Order 14 procedure". This procedure is not available in certain actions, including defamation, false prosecution and false imprisonment, all of which are triable by jury as of qualified right: R.S.C., Ord. 14, r.1(2), and see pp. 000–000, below. A court may, at any stage in proceedings, determine a question of law or construction of a document where the matter can be suitably and finally determined: R.S.C., Ord. 14A.

[62] R.S.C., Ord., 14, r.2.

[63] It is, however, unusual to allow oral examination of the parties at an Order 14 hearing.

[64] R.S.C., Ord., 14, rr.3, 4.

[65] The order most favourable to the defendant is an order for unconditional leave to defend, but the Master may require money to be paid in by the defendant, or only give leave to defend as a "short cause" (a special list to cater for actions which can be tried in a short time—up to four hours).

**Acknowledgment of Service of
Writ of Summons**

Guidance notes for the Defendant

Read these notes carefully

They will help you to fill in the form attached and tell you what other steps you need to take.

Act quickly

You have only a limited time to return the form. If you do not return the form promptly, the Plaintiff may obtain a court order that you pay what is being claimed immediately (called "entering judgment by default").

Help and advice

You can get help and legal advice from:

- a solicitor (who can fill in the form and return it to the court for you) or
- a Citizen's Advice Bureau.

They will also tell you if you qualify for help with your legal costs ("legal aid").

Staff at any District Registry or office in the Royal Courts of Justice (Strand, London) will help you to fill in the form.

Time for returning the form

You have **14 days** from the day you receive the writ of summons to **return the completed form to the court**. The day on which the 14 day period begins depends on how you received the writ (how it was "served" on you).

If the writ was:

- handed to you personally, the 14 days begins on the day you were given the writ;
- delivered by post, the 14 days begins 7 days from the date of the postmark;
- put through your letterbox, the 14 days begins 7 days from the day this was done.

If you are a limited company and the writ was delivered by post, the 14 days begins:

- on the second working day from the date of the postmark if first class post was used;
- on the fourth working day from the date of the postmark if the second class post was used.

If the writ was served on you at an address outside England and Wales, the writ will tell you how long you have to return the acknowledgment form.

Filling in the form

Read these notes carefully.

They will help you to fill in the form opposite and tell you what other steps you need to take.

> You can use the same form of acknowledgment for two (or more) defendants provided the form makes this clear and they all wish to reply in the same way.

If you are **under 18 or a mental patient** ("under a disability") you must ask an **adult** to act for you. The adult, who is called a "next friend" or "guardian ad litem", can be any friend or relative who is not a co-defendant in the same claim. But they must act on your behalf with the help of a solicitor. **The solicitor must fill in the form of acknowledgment.**

Part 1   Write in your full name. If your name was incorrect on the writ, add the words "sued as" followed by the name stated on the writ.

       If you are: • a person trading in a name other than your own, write in your name followed by the words "trading as" and the name under which you trade;

                 • a partner in a firm, write in your name followed by the words "partner in the firm of" and the name of the firm. **If you are sued as a partner but are not, say so.**

                                                            ⟶

Part 2   Tick the appropriate box to show whether you intend to contest all, or part, of the claim. **If you contest any part of the claim, read note 2 below on preparing your defence.**

                                                            ⟶

Part 3   **Should only be filled in if the Plaintiff is claiming a fixed amount of money and you do not contest the claim.**

Part 3   Tick the appropriate box to show whether you intend to ask the court to make an order preventing the Plaintiff from enforcing any order for you to pay the amount claimed (called asking for a "stay of execution"). A stay of execution will allow you to pay the debt, perhaps by instalments. **If you wish to apply for a stay of execution, read note 3 below. This tells you how to make your application.**

                                                            ⟶

Part 4   **can only be filled in:**

         • **if the writ of summons was <u>not issued</u> in the Royal Courts of Justice or the District Registry for the area where you live, carry on business or have your registered office, <u>and</u>**

         • **the cause of the Plaintiff's action, or part of it, did not arise in that area.**

Part 4   Tick the appropriate box to show whether you wish the case to be transferred to the Royal Courts of Justice (London) or to another District Registry. If you are unsure which is the District Registry for your area, staff at the District Registry which issued the writ will tell you. If the case is transferred, you will be told when this has happened and what your new case number is. The Plaintiff may object to the transfer; if so, there may be a hearing.

                                                            ⟶

Part 5   Unless your solicitor is filling in the form on your behalf, you must sign the form and give an address to which court documents should be sent, and any reference, telephone or fax numbers. If you are being sued as an individual (that is in your own name rather than that of your firm or company) the address you give must be one in England and Wales. If you are a **limited company**, the form may be filled in by an **authorised officer** who must state his position in that company, or a solicitor. A solicitor may give his firm's address; an authorised officer must give the registered or principal office of the company.

                                                            ⟶

What to do when you have filled in the form.

1. Return the form

Detach these guidance notes and send or take the acknowledgment form to the office in the Royal Courts of Justice or District Registry which issued the writ.

2. Preparing the defence

If you contest the Plaintiff's claim, you must set out your reasons for doing so in writing (called a "defence"). You must send or take a copy of your defence to the Plaintiff (or the Plaintiff's solicitor). The time in which you have to do this will depend on whether you were given full particulars of the Plaintiff's claim (called a "statement of claim") with the writ.

If a statement of claim was **included** in the writ, or **accompanied it**, you must serve your defence within 14 days after the time for acknowledging service of the writ.

If a statement of claim is served on you **after** you received the writ, you must serve your defence 14 days from the date you received the statement of claim.

3. Applying for a stay of execution

If you agree that you owe the Plaintiff the amount of money claimed but want a stay of execution to allow you time to pay, you must issue a summons asking the court to make this order. Your summons must be accompanied by a sworn statement (an "affidavit") setting out details of your income and liabilities and any offer of payment you are making, for example, by instalments.

Copies of the form of summons and affidavit can be obtained from any firm of law stationers.

You must issue your summons at the appropriate office within 14 days of the court receiving your form of acknowledgment of service.

Acknowledgment of Service of Writ of Summons

In the High Court of Justice   **19** 94   **No.** 179

                  Division

                  District Registry   Use black ink and capital letters

Plaintiff   PETER GEORGE MARTIN HACKER

Defendant   RELIABLE NAG SUPPLY STABLES
              (sued as a firm)

Part 1 (Your) (Defendant's)
         full name

> ALICE MARY ARKLE, partner in the firm
> of RELIABLE NAG SUPPLY STABLES

Part 2 (Do you) (Does the Defendant)
         intend to contest:

the whole of the Plaintiff's claim? ☐

part of the Plaintiff's claim? ☐

none of the Plaintiff's claim? ☐

Part 3 If you have said that you do not intend to contest the
whole, or part, of the Plaintiff's claim will you (the
Defendant) be asking the court for a stay of execution?   Yes ☐   No ☐

Part 4 (Do you) (Does the Defendant) wish to have the case transferred to:

the Royal Courts of Justice?   Yes ☐   No ☐

another District Registry?   Yes ☐   No ☐

If to a District Registry, say which one

Part 5 I acknowledge that (I have) (the Defendant has) been served with a copy of the Writ of
Summons

Signed ALICE MARY ARKLE   Date 5th December 1994

Defendant (Solicitor for the Defendant) (Authorised officer) in person

Address to which papers about this case should be sent:

> The Wide Paddock
> Leak Avenue
> Groatham
> Nottinghamshire

Solicitor's
Ref.   Telephone
No.   Fax
No.

When completed this form should be returned to:

Plaintiff's (Plaintiff's solicitor's) details

Address to which papers about this case should be sent:

POPP, LEES AND STONE
23 HALTERGATE
NOTTINGHAM

Solicitor's Ref.	Telephone No.	Fax No.
MB 456	0115 900 0000	0115 900 1000

OYEZ The Solicitors' Law Stationery Society Ltd, Oyez House, 7 Spa Road, London SE16 3QQ

1995 Edition
9 95   F30386
5044217
* * * * *

High Court E22

Acknowledgment of Service of Writ of Summons

In the High Court of Justice   **19** 94   **No.** 792

QUEEN'S BENCH   **Division**
                District Registry   Use black ink and capital letters

Plaintiff

ALFONSO FREDERICO MASERATI

Defendant

WILLIAM DANIEL HENRY LAGONDA

Part 1 (Your) (Defendant's) full name

WILLIAM DANIEL HENRY LAGONDA

Part 2 (Do you) (Does the Defendant) intend to contest:

the whole of the Plaintiff's claim? ☐
part of the Plaintiff's claim? ☐
none of the Plaintiff's claim? ☑

Part 3 If you have said that you do not intend to contest the whole, or part, of the Plaintiff's claim will you (the Defendant) be asking the court for a stay of execution?   Yes ☐   No ☐

Part 4 (Do you) (Does the Defendant) wish to have the case transferred to:

the Royal Courts of Justice?   Yes ☐   No ☐
another District Registry?   Yes ☐   No ☐

If to a District Registry, say which one

Part 5 I acknowledge that (I have) (the Defendant has) been served with a copy of the Writ of Summons

Signed FURLONG AND Co.   Date 5th December 1994
Defendant (Solicitor for the Defendant) (Authorised officer)

Address to which papers about this case should be sent:

43 BRIDLE LANE
NOTTINGHAM

Solicitor's Ref.   Telephone No.   Fax No.

When completed this form should be returned to:

Plaintiff's (Plaintiff's solicitor's) details

Address to which papers about this case should be sent:

```
POPP, LEES AND STONE,
23 HALTERGATE,
NOTTINGHAM.
```

| Solicitor's Ref. | MB456 | Telephone No. | 0115 900 0000 | Fax No. | 0115 900 1000 |

OYEZ The Solicitors' Law Stationery Society Ltd, Oyez House, 7 Spa Road, London SE16 3QQ

1995 Edition
9 95 F30386
5044217
★ ★ ★ ★ ★

High Court E22

5. THE PLEADINGS[66]

Since the adversarial system depends upon the two parties selecting the issues for resolution and acquiring the evidence to support them, it is necessary that the parties should communicate to each other the elements of their case. The system of pleadings amounts to a formal exchange of allegations so as to define with clarity and precision the matters which are in dispute. They also reduce the possibility of one party being surprised by the case of the other at trial.[67] Pleadings can offer an opportunity to narrow down the issue between the parties. The way in which the pleadings are conducted is largely a matter for the parties, although this aspect of pleadings is constantly being eroded in an effort to produce a fair and efficient system of civil justice.

If the plaintiff has served a generally indorsed writ on the defendant, the first document to be prepared and served is the statement of claim. In the statement of claim the plaintiff's claim against the defendant must be set out, with the facts which will be relied upon for support, the injury/loss that has been suffered and the remedy which is sought.[68] The statement needs to be sufficiently full to allow the defendant to ascertain the case against him or her and to prepare a defence.

The basic rule governing all pleading is contained in R.S.C., Ord., 18, r. 7(1):

". . . [E]very pleading must contain, and contain only, a statement in a summary form of the material facts on which the party pleading relies for his claim or defence, as the case may be, but not the evidence by which facts are to be proved, and the statement must be as brief as the nature of the case admits."

The art of drafting pleadings is therefore very important. Pleadings must state facts only, not law or evidence, they must state only the material facts and those material facts must be pleaded with sufficient detail but without excessive detail. Drawing that latter balance is where the real skill lies.[69]

In *Hacker* v. *Reliable Nag Supply Stables*[70] the statement of claim could be set out as follows.

---

[66] See Jacob (1987), pp. 87–92 and O'Hare and Hill (1993), pp. 248–252.
[67] See, further, Jacob (1987), p. 90.
[68] R.S.C., Ord. 18, r.15.
[69] See O'Hare and Hill (1993), Chap. 9.
[70] The imaginary case which we began by writ of summons at p. 601 above.

IN THE HIGH COURT OF JUSTICE   1994 H. No. 179
QUEEN'S BENCH DIVISION
NOTTINGHAM DISTRICT REGISTRY.
WRIT ISSUED THE 1st DAY OF DECEMBER 1994

Between

PETER GEORGE
MARTIN HACKER   *Plaintiff*
and
RELIABLE NAG SUPPLY
STABLES   *Defendants*
(SUED AS A FIRM)

STATEMENT OF CLAIM

1. The Plaintiff and the Defendants entered into an oral contract ("the contract") on June 25th 1994 at the Defendant's place of business for the sale of a piebald gelding, known as Skipper, ("the horse") by the Defendants to the Plaintiff for the price of £65,000 which was paid by the Plaintiff to the Defendants on that day.
2. At all material times the Defendants were horse traders and the horse was sold in the course of the Defendant's business.
3. The Plaintiff took delivery of the horse from the Defendant on June 26th 1994.
4. There was an implied term in the contract that the horse was sound and in good health.
5. Further or alternatively the Plaintiff made known to the Defendants before and at the time of the contract that he required the horse for general hacking and for jumping at the local gymkhanas and accordingly it was an implied term of the said contract that it would be fit for such purposes.
6. In breach of the contract the horse supplied by the Defendants to the Plaintiff was not of merchantable quality and/or was not fit for its purpose.

PARTICULARS

The horse was found to be suffering from Bastard Strangles and in consequence thereof was entirely useless and worthless to the Plaintiff.
7. By reason of the matters aforesaid the plaintiff has suffered loss and damage.

PARTICULARS OF SPECIAL DAMAGE

Cost price of horse	£65,000
Fees paid to Sutton Riding Enterprises for the care	£290
of alternative horse from July 1st to August 20th	

8. Further the plaintiff claims interest pursuant to section 35A of the Supreme Court Act 1981 on the amount found to be due to the Plaintiff at such rate and for such period as the Court thinks fit.

AND the Plaintiff claims:

(1)   Damages
(2)   The aforesaid interest pursuant section 35A of the Supreme Court Act 1981.

Served this 12th day of January 1995
by Popp, Lees and Stone, 23 Haltergate, Nottingham.
Solicitors for the Plaintiff.

The defendant may consider that the information given in the statement of claim is defective, or insufficient to allow a defence to the claim to be prepared. The defendant is entitled to request from the plaintiff any further information required and this is done by way of request for what are known as "further and better particulars."[71] This procedure may be used in different ways—it may be a genuine request for information so that the defendant may better understand the case, or it may be another delaying tactic designed to increase the pressure on the plaintiff who is anxious to get damages. In the case of *Hacker*, the defendant wishes to know more . . .

IN THE HIGH COURT OF JUSTICE   1994 H. No. 179
QUEEN'S BENCH DIVISION
NOTTINGHAM DISTRICT REGISTRY

Between

PETER GEORGE
MARTIN HACKER   *Plaintiff*
and
RELIABLE NAG SUPPLY
STABLES   *Defendants*
(SUED AS A FIRM)

REQUEST BY THE DEFENDANTS FOR FURTHER AND BETTER
PARTICULARS OF THE STATEMENT OF CLAIM

The Plaintiff and Defendant entered into an oral Contract on June 25th 1994 at the Defendant's place of business for the Sale of a piebald gelding, known as Skipper, by the Defendants to the Plaintiff for the price of £65,000 which was paid by the Plaintiff to the Defendant on that day.
Under paragraph 1

Give full particulars of all facts and matters relied on in support of the allegation that an oral contract was made between the Plaintiff and the Defendants on June 25th 1994

Under paragraph 5

Give full particulars of all facts and matters relied upon in support of the allegation that the Plaintiff made known to the Defendants that he required the horse for general hacking and jumping at local gymkhanas,

[71] R.S.C., Ord. 18, r.12. See O'Hare and Hill (1993), pp. 199–202.

and of the allegation that there was an implied term that the horse would
be fit for such purpose.

Under paragraph 6

State at which time it is alleged that the said horse was discovered to be
suffering from Bastard Strangles and for how long it is alleged that the
condition had existed.

Under paragraph 7

Give full particulars of the stabling provided for the alternative horse at
Sutton Riding Enterprises and a detailed analysis of the fees charged.

Martin Martinson

Served this 18th day of February 1995

By Furlong and Co., 43 Bridle Lane, Nottingham
Solicitors for the Defendants.

In due course the defendant must serve a defence on the plaintiff.[72] There are
specified time limits for the conduct of pleadings,[73] but these are often dispensed
with by the consent of the parties or by order of the court.[74] The possibility of
creating delay in the whole procedure will be lessened by the introduction of
the overall timetable.

Having been given the necessary information about the plaintiff's case, the
defendant must settle on his or her tactics. In the defence, he or she may choose
to refute the whole of the plaintiff's claim and the facts on which it is based,[75]
or may admit the whole case whilst pleading an explanation which allows liability to be avoided,[76] or may admit the whole case but object that it discloses
no cause of action,[77] or may adopt a combination of these approaches, or may
adopt them as alternatives.[78] Naturally, the wider the defence, the wider the
issues that remain for resolution at the trial and the greater must be the plaintiff's
preparations. If the defendant is not prepared to admit any of the facts pleaded
by the plaintiff they may all have to be proved in court with a consequent
increase in the length and cost of the case. However, either party may serve
notice under R.S.C., Ord. 27 requiring the admission of facts with a penalty in

[72] And every other party to the action who may be affected thereby: R.S.C., Ord. 18, r.2.
[73] Contained in the provisions of Ord. 18. Technically the current time limit, which is often not
observed by agreement, is 14 days.
[74] R.S.C., Ord. 3, r.5. The advantage of obtaining the consent of the other party to an extension of
time limits is that it saves the cost of an application to the court.
[75] Known as a "traverse".
[76] Known as a "confession and avoidance".
[77] Known as "objection in point of law".
[78] Pleadings in the alternative can sometimes appear extremely confusing. Hence, "(1) The Defendant denies that she was present at the time alleged and that she hit the plaintiff (traverse); (2)
If, which is not admitted, the defendant was present and did hit the plaintiff, she did so in
self-defence (confession and avoidance); (3) If, which is not admitted, the defendant was present
and hit the plaintiff and did not act in self-defence, the statement of claim discloses no cause of
action (objection in point of law)."

costs for refusal.[79] If the defendant does make substantial admissions, the defence will have the effect of disclosing and narrowing the issue between the parties so that they are both aware of precisely what remains in dispute. In order that the pleadings should disclose clearly what remains in dispute, any issue of fact in a pleading must be specifically denied or it will be deemed to have been admitted.[80]

So far we have omitted consideration of one important possibility. The defendant may wish to make a claim against the plaintiff in addition to defending the plaintiff's claim. It is not necessary to begin a separate action. It is possible to add a *counterclaim*[81] to the defence. Set out below is the defence and counterclaim of the Reliable Nag Supply Stables.

IN THE HIGH COURT OF JUSTICE   1994 H. No. 179
QUEEN'S BENCH DIVISION
NOTTINGHAM DISTRICT REGISTRY
Between

PETER GEORGE
MARTIN HACKER   *Plaintiff*
and
RELIABLE NAG SUPPLY
STABLES   *Defendants*
DEFENCE AND COUNTERCLAIM

DEFENCE

1. It is admitted that by a contract made on June 25th 1994, the Defendants sold to the Plaintiff a piebald gelding for the price of £65,000, which price was paid by the Plaintiff. Save as aforesaid the first paragraph of the Statement of Claim is denied.
2. Paragraphs 2 and 3 of the Statement of Claim are admitted.
3. It is admitted that the said horse was found to be suffering from Bastard Strangles after it had been delivered to the Plaintiff. Save as aforesaid, the implied terms and each and every fact and matter alleged in the fourth, fifth, sixth and seventh paragraphs of the Statement of Claim are denied, and it is denied that the Defendants were in breach of contract as alleged or at all.
4. Further or alternatively, it was an express term of the said agreement that the Defendant would exchange the said horse for another if the same should within 14 days prove unsuitable to the Plaintiff.
5. By a further agreement made at or about the beginning of July 1994 between the Defendants and the Plaintiff, pursuant to the express term referred to in paragraph 4 hereof, the Plaintiff agreed to exchange the said horse for another and to take delivery of a suitable bay mare owned by the Defendants pending his decision to retain the said piebald gelding or the said bay mare.
6. In breach of contract, the Plaintiff failed to make any decision as to which

---

[79] R.S.C., Ord. 27 has amended in line with the recommendations of the *Civil Justice Review* (1988), para. 236, in an attempt to encourage openness in pre-trial procedure to reduce delay and cost.
[80] R.S.C., Ord. 18, r.13. Since the aim is to produce the real controversy between the parties which requires to be determined, there are liberal powers of amendment: R.S.C., Ord. 20, r.8.
[81] R.S.C., Ord. 18, r.18.

of the said horses he would retain, and, on or about August 21st 1994 returned the said bay mare to the Defendants thereby repudiating the said agreement.

7. If and to the extent, if at all, which is denied, that the Defendants are liable to the Plaintiff they will seek to set off the damages and sums counter-claimed herein to extinguish or diminish such liability.

8. The Defendants repeat paragraphs 1 to 6 of their defence herein.

9. It was an implied term of the agreement pursuant whereto the Defendants delivered the said bay mare to the Plaintiff that the Plaintiff would take reasonable care of the said bay mare whilst in his custody.

10. In breach of the said implied term the Plaintiff failed to take reasonable care of the said bay mare.

PARTICULARS

When the Plaintiff returned the said bay mare to the Defendants its ribs were protruding, its hooves were broken, its coat was dull and ungroomed, 3 shoes were missing and it was in poor health.

11. By reason of the said breaches and each of them, the Defendants suffered loss and damage.

12. Further the Defendant claims interest pursuant to section 35A of the Supreme Court Act 1981 on the amount found to be due to the Plaintiff at such rate and for such period as the Court thinks fit.

PARTICULARS OF DAMAGE

(1)	Loss of profit on the sale of a horse	300.00
(2)	Transport costs on delivery and collection	50.00
(3)	Veterinary costs for said bay mare	120.00
(4)	Farrier's fees for said bay mare	90.00
(5)	Loss of value of said bay mare	400.00
		960.00

AND the Defendants counterclaim
 (1)   Damages under paragraph 12 hereof.
 (2)   The aforesaid interest pursuant to section 35A of the Supreme Court Act 1981.

William Naseby

Dated this 28th day of March 1995

Where a defence raises new facts the plaintiff may wish to enter a reply[82] and where a counterclaim has been made it is usual for the plaintiff to enter a defence. These can conveniently be combined and will usually be the final document in the pleadings. The defendant is, however, permitted to seek the leave of the court[83] to enter a *Rejoinder*, the plaintiff a *Surrejoinder*, the defendant a *Rebutter*, the plaintiff a *Surrebutter*. Despite these delightful names, the White Book comments "None of these names for pleadings occurs in the former or

[82] R.S.C., Ord. 18, r.3.
[83] R.S.C., Ord. 18, r.4.

present rules. All except rejoinder are rare to the point of extinction; and even rejoinder is seldom seen.''[84] In the light of the development of court management of litigation, especially in relation to delay, they could become extinct.[85]

Below we set out a reply and defence to counterclaim in *Hacker's* case:

IN THE HIGH COURT OF JUSTICE   1994 H. No. 179
QUEEN'S BENCH DIVISION
NOTTINGHAM DISTRICT REGISTRY

Between

PETER GEORGE
MARTIN HACKER   *Plaintiff*
and
RELIABLE NAG SUPPLY
STABLES   *Defendants*
(SUED AS A FIRM)

REPLY AND DEFENCE TO COUNTERCLAIM

REPLY

1. The Plaintiff joins issue save insofar as paragraphs 1 to 3 of the Defence and Counterclaim are concerned.

DEFENCE TO COUNTERCLAIM

2. It is admitted that the further agreement referred to in paragraph 4 of the Defence and Counterclaim was made, but it is denied that the Defendants offered a suitable horse in exchange.

3. The Plaintiff paid employees of Sutton Riding Enterprises to attend to the said substitute horse and informed the Defendants at all times of the poor condition of the said horse.

4. The Plaintiff denies that the said horse was in the condition described in paragraph 10 of the Defence and Counterclaim.

5. Whereas the Plaintiff had been informed and believed that the said horse was ill when returned to the Defendants the said illness was a direct result of the poor condition of the said horse at the time of its delivery to the Plaintiff by the Defendants.

6. Each and every claim for damages in paragraph 12 of the Defence and Counterclaim is denied by the Plaintiff.

George Washington

Dated this 25th day of April 1995

---

[84] *Supreme Court Practice 1995*, para. 18/4/1.
[85] See above, pp. 597–600.

"It has become fashionable in these days to attach decreasing importance to pleadings, and it is beyond doubt that there have been times when an insistence on complete compliance with their technicalities put justice at risk. ... But pleadings continue to play an essential part in civil action ... the primary purpose of pleadings remains and it can still prove of vital importance. That purpose is to define the issues and thereby to inform the parties in advance of the case they have to meet and so enable them to take steps to deal with it."[86]

6. THE SUMMONS FOR DIRECTIONS[87]

Within one month of the close of pleadings, the plaintiff must take out a "summons for directions".[88] This procedure is designed to bring the action before a Master who may give directions to resolve any outstanding matters between the parties which should be dealt with by an interlocutory application and directions about the future course of the action designed to "secure the just, expeditious and economical disposal thereof."[89] The summons can, therefore, operate as a time-saving and cost-saving device in that its object is to ensure that the action is fully prepared for trial. It may also provide an opportunity for the parties to indicate to the Master and to each other that points formerly in issue will not be pursued at trial. In that way, like the preliminary hearing in the county court, it may serve to assist the process of settlement and compromise.

Prior to the Civil Justice Review, in theory different directions were given dependent upon the particular action. In fact, as Jacob pointed out, the general summons for directions had become "virtually a non event", with the Master knowing little or nothing about the case, except what was revealed in the pleadings. Consequently, "in summons after summons, the orders and directions follow[ed] substantially the same pattern, with more repetition than variation."[90]

In consequence a system of automatic directions is being introduced. Currently, automatic directions are provided for in personal injury actions[91] and in county court actions.[92] In the future standard directions will be provided for High Court actions, but it will be open to the parties to apply to the court for additional or different directions, for a general stock-taking and for directions as to the conduct of the case.[93] Where, exceptionally, no standard directions have been devised there should be a summons for directions.

---

[86] *Per* Lord Edmund Davies in *Farrell v. Sec. of State for Defence* [1980] 1 W.L.R. 172 at p. 179. See also observations on the importance of pleadings by Scarman L. J. in *Fulham v. Newcastle Chronicle* [1977] 1 W.L.R. 651 at 659c and Megaw L. J. in *Commission for Racial Equality v. Ealing London Borough Council* [1978] 1 W.L.R. 112, at pp. 117–118. See also Jacob (1987), p. 90.

[87] See Jacob (1987), pp. 102–109 and O'Hare and Hill (1993), pp. 468–482.

[88] R.S.C., Ord. 25, r.1. If the plaintiff fails to take out the summons, the defendants may do so or apply to have the action dismissed.

[89] R.S.C., Ord. 25, r.1(1)(b).

[90] Jacob (1987), p. 104.

[91] R.S.C., Ord. 25, r.8 and see O'Hare and Hill (1993), pp. 482–499.

[92] See C.C.R. Ord 17, r.11 and see *Civil Justice Review* (1988), paras.255–260.

[93] *Civil Justice Review* (1988), paras.237–254.

7. Discovery and Inspection of Documents[94]

So that each party may be aware of documents relating to issues in the case, rules requiring "discovery" of those documents place an obligation on the litigants to disclose their existence and, possibly, to disclose their content.[95] Discovery is automatic in actions where the pleadings are closed, with the possibility of using the summons for directions to require additional information.[96]

Each party must produce a list of documents ". . . which are or have been in his possession, custody or power relating to any matter in question . . . in the action."[97] The list must be in a prescribed form[98] and the documents are divided into three categories—those which the plaintiff or defendant has in his or her possession, custody or power and is willing to produce; those which he or she has, but is not willing to produce; and those which he or she has had, but has no longer. Objections to the production of documents for inspection will be based on one or more of the privileges[99] to which a litigant is entitled.

A list of documents in *Hacker* v. *Reliable Nag Supply Stables* is set out at pp. 622–625.

The objects of discovery are further assisted by the procedure known as "discovery by interrogatories".[1] Interrogatories are methods of eliciting information relevant to the action. Some interrogatories may be served without a court order, that is those relating to any matter in question between the parties which are necessary either for disposing fairly of the case or for saving costs.[2] Further, a party may apply to the court for an order giving him or her leave to serve any interrogatories on the other party relating to any matter in question between the parties.[3] Interrogatories are to be answered within 28 days of service.[4]

Objections may be made to such requests for information. The person on whom interrogatories without order are served may apply to the court within 14 days of service to have them varied or withdrawn, the court on such an application making whatever order it thinks fit.[5] A copy of the proposed ordered interrogatories must be served on the other party with the summons by which the application is made.[6] It is at the stage of hearing objections that issues relating to privilege will be considered. If the answers to the interrogatories are provided, but are insufficient, the request can be renewed. If an order is not complied with, the court has the power, if it thinks fit, to order that the action is dismissed or that the defence is struck out and judgment entered accordingly.[7]

A new power was given to the courts in 1970 to assist a party who wished

---

[94] See Jacob (1987), pp. 92–102 and O'Hare and Hill (1993), Chap. 18.
[95] R.S.C., Ord. 24.
[96] *ibid.* r.2.
[97] *ibid.* r.2(1).
[98] See below.
[99] There are certain recognised privileges—the legal professional privilege; the privilege against self-incrimination; "without prejudice" documents; Crown privilege or public interest immunity: see *Supreme Court Practice 1995*, paras. 24/5/5–24/5/8.
[1] R.S.C., Ord. 26.
[2] *ibid.* r.1(1).
[3] *ibid.* r.1(2).
[4] *ibid.* r.2(1).
[5] *ibid.* r.3(2).
[6] *ibid.* r.4(1).
[7] *ibid.* r.5, 6.

List of
Documents
(0.24 r.5)

IN THE HIGH COURT OF JUSTICE   19 94.—H .—No. 179

QUEEN'S BENCH **Division**

NOTTINGHAM DISTRICT REGISTRY

Between

PETER GEORGE MARTIN HACKER

                                                                        Plaintiff

AND

RELIABLE NAG SUPPLY STABLES (sued as a firm)

                                                                        Defendant

LIST OF DOCUMENTS

         The following is a list of the documents relating to the matters in question in this
action which are or have been in the possession, custody or power of the above-
named(¹)   Plaintiff PETER GEORGE MARTIN HACKER

(1) Plaintiffs (or
Defendant(s)) A.B.

and which is served in compliance with Order 24, rule 2 [or the order herein dated the
                        day of   , 19].

(2) Plaintiff(s) or
Defendant(s).

         1. The (²) Plaintiff   has in his possession, custody or power the
documents relating to the matters in question in this action enumerated in Schedule 1
hereto.

         2. The (²) Plaintiff   objects to produce the documents enumerated
(3) State ground of in Part 2 of the said Schedule 1 on the ground that (³) they are
objection.   privileged documents as between solicitor and client.

         3. The (²) Plaintiff   has had, but has not now, in his
possession, custody or power the documents relating to the matters in question in this
action enumerated in Schedule 2 hereto.

         4. Of the documents in the said Schedule 2, those numbered 1 and 2
(4) Plaintiff's or   in that Schedule were last in the (⁴) Plaintiff's possession, custody
Defendant's.   or power on (⁵) 14th May 1993   and the remainder on (⁵)
(5) State when.
(6) Here state   (⁶) They are now in the possession of the defendant's solicitors
what has become
of the said docu-
ments and in
whose possession
they now are.

         5. Neither the (²) Plaintiff nor his Solicitor nor any other person
on his behalf, has now, or ever had, in his possession, custody or
power any document of any description whatever relating to any matter in question in
this action, other than the documents enumerated in Schedules 1 and 2 hereto.

SCHEDULE 1.—Part 1.

(Here enumerate in a convenient order the documents (or bundles of documents, if of the same nature, such as invoices) in the possession, custody or power of the party in question which he does not object to produce, with a short description of each document or bundle sufficient to identify it.)

Description of Document	Date
1. Copy of letters between Plaintiff's solicitors and Defendant's solicitors	Various
2. Receipts for £100 signed by Aline Arkle	25th June 1994
3. Account of Sutton Riding Enterprises	22nd August 1994
4. Letter from Plaintiff to Defendants	20th August 1994
5. Letter from Defendants to Plaintiff	21st August 1994
6. Copy letter from Plaintiff to Defendants	3rd September 1994

SCHEDULE 1.—Part 2.

(Here enumerate as aforesaid the documents in the possession, custody or power of the party in question which he objects to produce.)

Description of Document	Date
Correspondence between Plaintiff's solicitor and Plaintiff. Notes and documents related solely to the preparation of the Plaintiff's case.	

SCHEDULE 2.

(Here enumerate as aforesaid the documents which have been, but at the date of service of the list are not, in the possession, custody or power of the party in question.)

1. Copy letters to Defendant's solicitors

2. Copy letters from Plaintiff's to Defendants   20 August 1994

Dated the 20th   day of May   , 19 95

NOTICE TO INSPECT

Take notice that the documents in the above list, other than those listed in Part 2 of Schedule 1 [and Schedule 2], may be inspected at [the office of the Solicitor of the above-named (7) POPP, LEES AND STONE, 23 HALTERGATE, NOTTINGHAM

(7) Plaintiff(s) *or* Defendant(s) *(insert address) or as may be.*

]

(8) Defendant(s) *(or* Plaintiff(s) C.D.

on the   20th   day of June   19 95, between the hours
of 5.00 pm   and

To the (8) Defendant   ⎱ Served the 20th   day of May   , 1995
                              ⎰ by POPP, LEES AND STONE
                                 of 23 HALTERGATE, NOTTINGHAM
and his Solicitor   Solicitor for the Plaintiff

19 .— .—No.

IN THE HIGH COURT OF JUSTICE

Division

Dated 19 .

List of Documents

Solicitor

OYEZ The Solicitors' Law Stationery Society Ltd., 10 92 F23322
Oyez House, 7 Spa Road, London SE16 3QQ 5048071

High Court B9

to discover whether or not he or she had a case by acquiring information from the potential defendant. Now contained in the Supreme Court Act 1981 s.33(2), this provision permits a person who appears to be likely to be a party to a personal injuries claim to request the court to order discovery of any documents relevant to the issue held by another potential party.[8]

As a result of proposals in the Civil Justice Review, R.S.C., Ord. 38, r.2A now requires that the court should direct all parties to serve on the other parties to an action commenced by writ, written statements of the oral evidence which each party intends to use at the trial. Failure to comply with the rule means that the party will not be able to introduce that evidence at the trial. The statement will stand as evidence in chief. The introduction of this process has been thought by some to be the most important recent change in civil procedure, since it encourages a cards-on-the-table approach to litigation.[9]

8. PAYMENT INTO COURT[10]

At any stage of the action after the issue of a writ, a defendant may pay money to the court in attempted satisfaction of the plaintiff's claim. The plaintiff may then choose whether to accept the amount paid in and discontinue the action, or carry on the action in the hope of obtaining a greater sum at trial. The penalty for the plaintiff is that he or she will normally bear all the costs of the action from the date of the payment in unless awarded a sum in excess of the amount the defendant has paid in.[11]

This is a very useful procedure for a defendant who may use it either to protect himself or herself from a zealous plaintiff who wants to have the "day in court" or to apply pressure to accept a sum in settlement rather than risk a heavy bill in costs. It is important to stress two points. First, that the plaintiff must "take it or leave it"—the sum cannot be accepted and the action continued. Second, the judge is not told of the payment in until the questions of liability and damages have been settled.[12]

In the case of a claim for a liquidated sum, the plaintiff's decision is not likely to be difficult. Where the sum is unliquidated the inherent uncertainties of the value of the claim, the difficulties of proof, the desirability of money in hand will all combine to make the choice much harder.

D. CIVIL JUSTICE REFORM

Concern about and interest in the civil justice system has been growing for some time. There has been much interest in personal injury litigation,[13] and increas-

---

[8] Further, plaintiffs in personal injuries actions must have provided with their statement of claim a medical report and a statement of the special damages claimed: R.S.C., Ord. 18, r.12.

[9] See C. Glasser, "Civil Procedure and the Lawyers – The Adversary System and the Decline of the Orality Principle" (1993) 56 M.L.R. 307, at p. 314.

[10] See pp. 536–537 and 562 above; Jacob (1987), pp. 117–119 and O'Hare and Hill (1993), Chap. 16.

[11] The matter of costs is within the discretion of the court, see above, p. 530.

[12] R.S.C., Ord 22, r.7. If the judge is told inadvertently he or she must decide whether to continue the case or order a retrial.

[13] See above, pp. 555–563.

ingly an interest in the civil justice system as a whole. There have been three major reviews of the system in recent times: the Civil Justice Review,[14] the Heilbron/Hodge Report,[15] and the Woolf Inquiry, which is on-going.[16] The civil justice system is increasingly a subject of critical consideration.[17]

Lord Woolf asserts that a "system of civil justice is essential to the maintenance of a civilised society," and identifies certain basic principles:

"(a) It should be *just* in the results it delivers. (b) It should be *fair* and be seen to be by:—ensuring that litigants have an equal opportunity, regardless of their resources, to assert or defend their legal rights;—providing every litigant with an adequate opportunity to state his [or her] own case and answer his [or her] opponent's;—treating like cases alike. (c) Procedures and cost should be *proportionate* to the nature of the issues involved. (d) It should deal with cases with reasonable *speed*. (e) It should be *understandable* to those who use it. (f) It should be *responsive* to the needs of those who use it. (g) It should provide as much *certainty* as the nature of particular cases allows. (h) It should be *effective*: adequately resourced and organised so as to give effect to the previous principles."[18]

On the basis of these principles, Woolf identifies areas where there are problems and makes proposals for change and reform. One theme, which is not entirely new, is the concern with party, or at least lawyer, control over litigation, which may be inimical to the fair and speedy solution of disputes. The solution is greater judicial involvement and control prior to trial.[19] The dangers inherent in this are the difficulty for a judge of moving from the different roles inherent in procedure and trial. This is illustrated by the concerns expressed about judicial involvement in resolving disputes other than by adjudication.[20] More significantly, these concerns express the view that greater judicial involvement strikes at the inherent attributes of the civil justice system: the adversarial system and orality of argument. The dangers have been outlined by Jacob and Glasser[21] and include affecting the court's role as, "representing the wider public interest in the peaceful resolution of disputes, [it] remains neutral and inactive towards the parties, regulating the way in which the disputants must proceed if they are to obtain finality in the action and responding only to interlocutory applications

[14] *Report of the Review Body on Civil Justice* (Cm. 394, 1989), see second edition of this book, *passim* and, *e.g.*, Swanton, [1994] C.L.P. 111.
[15] *Civil Justice on Trial—the Case for Change*, the Report by the Independent Working Party set up jointly by the General Council of the Bar and the Law Society (1993) Chair: H. Heilbron; Vice-Chair: H. Hodge.
[16] Lord Woolf, *Access to Justice, An Interim Report to the Lord Chancellor on the civil justice system in England and Wales* (1995) (Woolf Report) (1995)). The final report will be published in 1996.
[17] See, *e.g.*, Sir Jack I. E. Jacob, *The Fabric of English Civil Justice* (1987), N. Andrews, *Principles of Civil Procedure* (1994), A. A. S. Zuckerman and R. Cranston (eds) *Reform of Civil Procedure* (1995) and *The Civil Justice Quarterly*.
[18] Woolf Report (1995), pp. 2–3.
[19] This has clearly been a development since the Civil Justice Review; see, *e.g.*, C. Glasser, "Civil Procedure and the Lawyers—The Adversary System and the Decline of the Orality Principle" (1993) 56 M.L.R. 307, at pp. 310–317.
[20] See above, pp. 563–566.
[21] See C. Glasser, "Civil Procedure and the Lawyers—The Adversary System and the Decline of the Orality Principle" (1993) 56 M.L.R. 307 drawing upon Jacob (1987).

made to it and the necessity to deliver judgment after a trial has taken place."[22] The advantages of the movement towards greater judicial involvement include a reduction in costs and delay and a more open system producing more appropriate resolutions. Despite the pull of tradition, these may seem to be laudable aims to pursue, provided they are objectives in their own right and not reflective of a desire simply to reduce the expensive call of the courts on the Government purse.

The problems identified by Woolf have also been noted in the context of our review of litigation: the adversarial environment; the expense of litigation, often involving excessive and unaffordable cost, disproportionate cost, uncertainty as to cost and uncompetitive costs; delay in processing claims; complexity in the system; the unavailability of legal assistance and advice; and the low priority for civil justice.[23] In determining what approach to take, Woolf identified the following as the primary problems demanding resolution: the unrestrained adversarial culture of the present system;[24] the lack of control over litigation; inadequate system attention to costs, delay and equality between the parties; complexity; and the lack of judicial responsibility for the efficient use of resources.[25] In consequence, Woolf proposes that the management of litigation be moved from litigants to the courts, which we consider above.[26] This and his other proposals are designed to achieve the working objectives which he lays down.

"(a) In so far as this is practicable, the parties to a dispute should be able to obtain information and advice to enable them to resolve that dispute in an economic, expeditions and practical manner and if this is not possible to conduct satisfactorily the appropriate litigation.

(b) The parties should:
   i) whenever it is reasonable for them to do so settle their disputes (either the whole dispute or individual issues comprised in the dispute) before resorting to the courts;
   ii) where it is not possible to resolve a dispute or an issue prior to proceedings, then they should do so at as early a stage in the proceedings as is possible.

(c) Where there exists an appropriate alternative dispute resolution mechanism which is capable of resolving a dispute more economically and efficiently than court proceedings, then the parties should be encouraged not to commence or pursue proceedings in court until after they have made use of that mechanism.

(d) Prior to commencing and throughout the course of proceedings the parties should be able to be, and should be, kept fully informed of the likely

---

[22] Glasser (1993), at p. 307.

[23] Woolf Report (1995), pp. 7–17.

[24] It is not surprising that solicitors and barristers have found this view hard to accept. But it should also be noted that solicitors and barristers are, in general, very adept at responding to change and ensuring that they expand their offer of skills to cover such new areas; indeed the lawyerisation of alternative dispute resolution is often a matter of some concern—see above, pp. 564–565—and it is clear that lawyers are responding to the general trend in civil justice towards greater control of litigation by the courts; see Glasser (1993), pp. 318–324.

[25] Woolf Report (1995), p. 18.

[26] At pp. 597–600.

costs and consequences of the proceedings and any alternative methods of resolving those proceedings.

(e) Proceedings should be conducted and disposed of in a manner, at a cost and within a timescale which is appropriate, taking into account the nature of the issues involved and the means of the parties.

(f) Whenever this is practical, proceedings and the issues in the proceedings should be disposed of summarily.

(g) Whenever practical and to the extent possible, evidence and facts should be agreed and the issues identified between the parties prior to the hearing.

(h) Legal proceedings and trials should be subject to pre-determined timetables.

(i) From an early stage in any proceedings, the probable and, whenever possible, the actual date of each significant step in proceedings, including the trial, should be known and the parties should only be allowed to depart from that date for good reasons.

(j) The maximum length of any trial should be pre-determined and that length should only be exceeded for good reason.

(k) In considering whether there is good reason for permitting the parties to depart from the predetermined dates, and for extending the length of trial, the courts should take into account the effect of doing so not only upon the parties involved in the proceedings but also on other proceedings awaiting a hearing and the resources of the courts.

(l) Only such discovery should take place, and only such evidence should be before the court, as is necessary for the just and appropriate disposal of the proceedings, and the evidence should be in a form which is most appropriate in all circumstances.

(m) The court's rules of procedure should give effect in a simple, clear and non-technical manner to the preceding aims.

(n) The court system should be provided with the resources and the judicial and administrative structure necessary to fulfil these aims.''[27]

Lord Woolf identified a number of areas in which significant improvements can be made so as to enable the civil justice system more fully to satisfy the principles he identified.

(1) Case management should be transferred from the litigants to the courts.[28]

(2) Judicial responsibility for the system should fall to a new Head of Civil Justice, supported by a Presiding Judge for each Circuit, two Chancery judges overseeing also the business and mercantile lists, and senior civil judges at each trial centre and its satellite courts. The Court Service should appoint officials to support the responsible judges.[29]

(3) The judiciary's skills, time and expertise should be utilised more effectively.[30]

(4) There should be as much harmonisation of the High Court and county courts as possible without amalgamating them, thus advancing further an approach commenced through the *Civil Justice Review* Lord Woolf

---

[27] *ibid.*, pp. 19–21.
[28] This matter has been considered above, pp. 597–600.
[29] See above, pp. 86–87.
[30] Woolf Report (1995), pp. 63–72.

proposes that it should be possible to commence proceedings in any court, the responsibility being with the court to ensure that it is dealt with by the appropriate court.[31] In so doing, the court would have the responsibility of allocating the case to the appropriate "track". There would be three tracks: small claims, fast track and multi-track (which latter would have different levels of judicial involvement). These tracks would operate within the existing High Court and county court structure, but with much greater alignment of the jurisdiction of those courts. In broad outline, there would be new unified rules providing a common procedure for the conduct of civil business. The new multi-track would straddle both the High Court and the county courts. This has the advantage of retaining some of the advantages of the High Court in terms of the special expertise of High Court judges and of the special expertise of the Queen's Bench and Chancery Divisions[32] at the Royal Courts of Justice in London. Small claims and fast track cases would be dealt with by the county courts. There would, therefore, be a network of courts with designated major civil trial centres outside London.[33]

(5) Small claims procedures in the county courts should be improved.[34]

(6) There should be a full examination of the role which information technology can play, which would include the support for case management and litigation generally which it can provide. Woolf has in mind not just the value of computers, but also video recording and viewing facilities and video and telephone conferencing.[35]

(7) Further assistance should be offered to litigants in person. In outline, the proposals involve a commitment to providing information and support to litigants, through attitudinal changes on the part of all players including the judges, as well as a more interventionist role in the hearing, the provision of court-based advice services, access to court libraries, the use of information technology kiosks, the provision of private facilities in courts for litigants, the development of a duty advice scheme, court hearings at more convenient times for litigants and information being provided in appropriate minority languages as well as in English.[36]

(8) Alternative approaches to dispensing justice should be developed.[37]

(9) There should be a new ethos of co-operation on the part of litigants and lawyers and so the professional bodies should draw up guidelines for lawyers' pre-proceedings conduct.[38]

---

[31] If successful, it may be that the old causes of action will finally no longer be ruling civil procedure from their grave.

[32] Lord Woolf decided not to propose the amalgamation of these two Divisions, contrary to the proposals of the Heilbron/Hodge Committee, because the Chancery Division enables the development of an umbrella organisation for a number of specialist jurisdictions, the judges may develop procedures not available to the Queen's Bench Division, and there is a particularly efficient disposal of work because of the effective working relationship between the small number of Chancery judges and the small Chancery Bar. Also the other proposals would lessen the need for an amalgamation: Woolf Report (1995), pp. 76–77.

[33] ibid., Chap. 12.

[34] See above, pp. 594–596.

[35] ibid. Chap. 13.

[36] ibid. Chap. 17. See also the Interim Report of the Judges' Council Working Party, Litigants in Person in the Royal Courts of Justice (1995).

[37] See above, pp. 563–566.

[38] Woolf Report (1995), pp. 150–152.

(10) Reforms to certain procedural rules should be given a priority. Woolf identifies that there are a number of problems associated with *pleadings*:

"(a) they often fail to set out the facts clearly and so impede identification of the issues; (b) they concentrate too much on causes of action and defences, rather than on facts, which in turn contributes to over-use of alternative positions; defences in particular are deliberately framed to keep all options open for as long as possible; (c) affirmative defences are not pleaded; (d) longwindedness; and (e) the original pleadings get out of date as they are superseded by amendments and further and better particulars; after the exchange of witness statements, they become less relevant for the purpose of the trial agenda."[39]

These problems are compounded, according to Woolf, by the failure of the courts to impose adequate sanctions, so there is little court scrutiny of pleadings against what is required by the rules of court. Woolf proposes that there must be greater judicial scrutiny and that the objective of pleadings—to state facts—must be restored. Thus major changes are proposed to the system. First, there would be proper judicial scrutiny of pleadings.

"(a) The claimant and the defendant each set out in a single document all the material matters on which they rely. (b) The claim and defence are considered by the procedural judge after the defence is filed. (c) The procedural judge forms a view as to whether the issues can readily be identified. He [or she] then has the following options: (i) He [or she] gives directions, standard or tailor-made, according to the track to which the case is assigned and the particular circumstances of the case. Directions could include instructions to clarify particular points in the claim or defence. (ii) Alternatively, where the factual allegations are so unclear that the matters in dispute cannot be properly identified, he [or she] will hold a case management conference. This will only be done where it is not possible to proceed under option (i). If the case was on the fast track, the conference would usually be on the telephone. (d) In cases where there is a case management conference, whether specifically because the pleadings are unclear or simply as a consequence of the case being assigned to a particular track, a major aim will be to produce an agreed statement of the issues in dispute. This will be the responsibility of the parties (normally the claimant). The statement of issues will effectively take over from the pleadings. Except where the state of the pleadings prevents this, the parties will produce a provisional list of issues (agreed if possible) before the case management conference. This will give a proper focus to the case management conference (the lack of which has contributed to the failure of previous attempts to introduce a robust summons for directions) and enable its purpose to be achieved in a relatively short hearing."[40]

Further, there would be fresh guidance on the content of a claim empha-

[39] *ibid.*, pp. 153–154.
[40] *ibid.*, pp. 155–156.

sising the need for a succinct statement of the facts entitling the claimant to a remedy (the statement of facts being the basic function of pleadings), the remedy claimed, any matters of law arising which entitle the claimant to succeed, and the legal nature of the claim where it would not otherwise be clear. Renewed guidance on defences would also be issued so that it would contain the parts of the claim admitted and not admitted, the defendant's version of the facts in so far as it differs from that of the claimant, specific defences and grounds for denying the claim or remedy, and, where the defendant does not know the truth of the claimant's case, demanding that he or she prove the case. A reply would be permissible, but no further pleadings.[41]

As regards *discovery*, Woolf noted that until recently discovery has presented no major concerns. The Heilbron/Hodge Report in 1993, however, identified discovery as the cause of much of the prohibitive expense associated with civil proceedings and many of the submissions to Woolf identified discovery as a significant problem. The solution is not to abolish discovery but "the benefits of a system of discovery will only outweigh the disadvantages if substantially greater control over the scale of discovery is exercised than at present." The solution lies in both the case management approach to litigation and in ensuring that the parties accept and fulfil their responsibilities "only to seek discovery when it is justifiable to do so." Woolf proposes that distinctions be drawn between categories of documents: parties' own supportive documents; adverse documents; relevant documents; and train of inquiry documents. The first two comprise "standard discovery" documents, the latter two "extra discovery" documents. No recommendations are made with regard to small claims cases, just cases on the fast or multi-tracks. On the fast track, there would normally only be discovery of standard discovery documents, thus limiting the current level of discovery which is responsible for many of the problems of overburdening the case with documentation. Further discovery would be possible, but only by showing "very strong grounds indeed". The multi-track cases are thought to cause greater difficulty, because of the wide range of cases involved. Normally, discovery of documents would be ordered during case management by the procedural judge.[42] Woolf also makes recommendations in relation to *offers to settle*.[43–44]

In addition to the proposals in relation to procedural matters relating to pleadings, discovery and offers to settle dealt with above, Woolf identifies two other major contributors to the cost and complexity of litigation. First, the exchange of witness statements, introduced to encourage a more open approach to litigation, has not proved to be as beneficial as was intended. Indeed, Woolf reports that the Commercial Court Users' Committee took the view that it was having a "devastating effect on costs", because of the precision that parties were seeking in their preparation. Woolf appropriately endorsed the principle of exchange of such statements as ensuring that parties may be fully aware of the strengths and weaknesses of the case to be met, thus encouraging settlement in

[41] *ibid.*, pp. 162–163.
[42] *ibid.*, Chap. 21.
[43–44] See above, p. 537.

some case, alternative dispute resolution in others, and limiting the issues for resolution via litigation. In order to ensure that their advantages are secured, Woolf recommends that, on the fast track, exchange of witness summaries should take place and that, on the multi-track, only witness identity and the issues to be covered should be exchanged prior to a case management conference, after which there may be exchange of witness statements. Once at trial, a witness should be limited to the statement, except with the leave of the judge, and cross-examination would also only be permitted with the judge's leave. A practice guide, along the lines of the existing Chancery Courts guide, would be issued and the costs allowed for them should reflect the fact that they are not intended to be elaborate documents.[45] Secondly, Woolf discovered that there is considerable concern about the use and role of expert witnesses; indeed it was the "subject which caused most concern". It seems that the "need to engage experts was a source of excessive expense, delay and, in some cases, increased complexity through the excessive or inappropriate use of experts." In making recommendations, Woolf bore in mind the wide-ranging roles which experts may play in litigation and proposed that the calling of expert evidence "should be subject to the complete control of the court", which could involve the use of assessors rather than witnesses.[46]

(11) For the future and to maintain the pace of change there should be a Civil Justice Council.[47]

Broadly speaking, these proposals have been received well. Of course, if there is concern about the principle of judicial control of litigation,[48] many of the proposals will be unwelcome. The major concern is whether sufficient resources would be made available to ensure that these reforms operate as the package intended by Lord Woolf. It is likely that accepting some and not others will fail to achieve the objectives of the proposals as a whole. The likelihood of introducing reforms must be considered in the context of the reduction in the number of cases in both the Queen's Bench Division of the High Court and in the county courts.[49] Whilst the pressure on the courts is reduced, it must be recognised that pressure of work is still present and Lord Woolf's proposals are by no means merely limited to improving the throughput of cases.

E. PRE-TRIAL REMEDIES[50]

Pre-trial remedies are "designed to deal with the position of the parties pending the trial, to maintain as far as possible the *status quo ante* and to preserve,

---

[45] Woolf Report (1995), Chap. 22.
[46] *ibid.*, Chap. 23, which contains many more detailed proposals.
[47] *ibid.*, pp. 220–221.
[48] See above, p. 599.
[49] See above, p. 555.
[50] See Jacob (1987), pp. 132–147, O'Hare and Hill (1993), Chap. 14 and Andrew (1994), Chaps.8 and 9.

protect and where necessary enhance the rights and interests of the parties in the inevitable interval between the start of the proceedings and the trial."[51] There are many remedies available, but perhaps the three most significant are the interlocutory injunction, the Mareva injunction and Anton Piller orders.

(a) Interlocutory injunction[52]

The significance of the interlocutory injunction is not only that it is a speedy and effective method of preserving the *status quo* prior to a trial, but also that the decision of the judge on the granting of an injunction is often taken by the parties as an indication of what the trial judge would do, and therefore the proceedings may go no further.[53]

An interlocutory injunction is usually negative in form, that is to restrain the defendant from doing something, rather than mandatory, that is requiring an act to be done.[54] It is effective because a breach of an injunction is a contempt of court, which is punishable by imprisonment, fine and sequestration of property, as appropriate. Further, the injunction does not just affect the parties to the action, it also applies to anyone knowing of it and its terms. Third parties then are under an obligation to observe its terms at least so that steps amounting to a breach are not taken, under the penalty of contempt of court.[55]

Such an injunction can be granted in either High Court or county court proceedings.[56] It is usually applied for on the basis of the other party being informed and thus able to challenge the issue of the injunction. However, in an emergency it may be applied for and granted *ex parte*.[57]

An interlocutory injunction will be granted if the principles laid down in *American Cyanamid Co. v. Ethicon Ltd*[58] are satisfied. First the plaintiff must establish that there is a good arguable claim to the right which is to be protected. Secondly, the plaintiff must show that there is a serious question to be tried. Thirdly, the grant depends upon which way the balance of convenience lies.[59]

---

[51] Jacob (1987), p. 132. Interlocutory procedures do not always operate fairly. In particularly use of the *Mareva* injunction can lead to procedural bias, see A.A.S. Zuckerman, "Interlocutory Remedies in Quest of Procedural Fairness" (1993) 56 M.L.R. 325.

[52] The jurisdiction for the grant of such an injunction arises under the Supreme Court Act 1981, s.37, and see R.S.C., Ord. 29. Such an injunction may even, in accordance with European Community Law, be issued to suspend a U.K. Statute; see *Factortame v. Secretary of State for Transport (No. 2)* [1991] 1 A.C. 603.

[53] See O'Hare and Hill (1993), p. 308.

[54] *Bonner v. G. W. Railway* (1883) 24 Ch.D. 1; *Locabail International Finance Ltd v. Agro-export* [1986] 1 All E.R. 901.

[55] *Hubbard v. Woodfield* (1913) 57 S.J. 729; *Seaward v. Paterson* [1897] 1 Ch. 545.

[56] Supreme Court Act 1981, s.37; County Court Act 1984, s.38; R.S.C., Ord. 29; C.C.R., Ords.13, 29. The procedure in county court cases is slightly different from that in the High Court.

[57] R.S.C., Ord. 29, r.1(1), (2). An injunction can usually only be applied for after the issue of a writ, except in cases of urgency: R.S.C., Ord 29, r.1(3).

[58] [1975] A.C. 396.

[59] The balance of convenience means that: (1) if damages are an adequate remedy and the defendant is able to pay them, no injunction will be granted; (2) if the plaintiff's undertaking as to damages, that is the promise to pay the opponent's expenses if he or she fails to establish a right to the injunction, is adequate and payable by the plaintiff, the injunction will be granted; (3) the court will desire to maintain the status quo, thus an injunction may well issue; (4) the court will take other factors, including social and economic factors, into account in determining whether it is appropriate to grant an injunction; (5) the relative strength of the parties' cases is a factor of last resort: see O'Hare and Hill (1993), pp. 310–311. There are exceptions to the principles established in *American Cyanamid*, see *ibid.* pp. 311–315.

(b) Mareva injunctions

The Mareva injunction[60] is a specialised form of interlocutory injunction used to prevent not only a foreign defendant transferring assets abroad and thus out of the jurisdiction and defeating an action, but also to prevent a defendant within the jurisdiction transferring assets abroad or concealing them in England and Wales.[61]

The injunction is effective because it is swift and secret and not only does it act against the defendant, who would be in contempt of court for breach, but also against innocent third parties. The main advantage of this is that it applies to banks through which transfer of assets is most likely to take place, especially in an age of the computerised transfer of funds.[62] The third party has a right to be entitled to be paid all reasonable expenses and costs, thus having a right of set-off in connection with an account which has become the subject of a Mareva injunction.[63]

Such an injunction may be granted in either the High Court or the county court.[64] A Mareva injunction is usually applied for *ex parte*, so that the opponent cannot defeat its effect consequent upon notice of an application. The plaintiff must then show a good arguable case, must make full and frank disclosure of all the facts that the judge will need to know, including in particular information of the existence of assets that are desired to be the object of the injunction, and must make clear the grounds for believing that without an injunction there is a real risk of any judgment in his or her favour not being satisfied. As with all injunctions, the plaintiff must provide an undertaking as to damages, that is the ability to cover the expenses of the defendant should the plaintiff's case ultimately fail.[65]

(c) Anton Piller orders

The Anton Piller order,[66] which is a special form of mandatory injunction, derives from the inherent power of the court to make an order for the detention or preservation of property which is the subject matter of a cause, and of documents and articles relating to it.[67] The order often empowers the plaintiff to enter the defendant's premises and search for and seize material documents and articles, but, as it is not a search warrant,[68] no force may be used in entering premises. The sanction for failure to obey is contempt of court.

Such an order may be granted in High Court or county court proceedings. The application is *ex parte*, that is without notice to the defendant, for obvious

---

[60] So called after the second case in which it was granted: *Mareva Compania Naviera S.A. v. International Bulk Carriers S.A., The Mareva* [1975] 2 Lloyd's Rep. 509.

[61] *The Supreme Court Practice 1995*, para. 29/1/20, and Jacob (1987), pp. 136–138, at 137. It may be issued post-trial.

[62] For the full effect, see *The Supreme Court Practice 1995*, para. 29/1/22.

[63] Jacob (1987), p. 138.

[64] Supreme Court Act 1981, s.37; County Courts Act 1984, s.38; R.S.C., Ord. 29; C.C.R., Ords, 13, 29; see also Matrimonial Causes Act 1973, s.37.

[65] O'Hare and Hill (1993), p. 309.

[66] So called after the case which approved the order: *Anton Piller K.G. v. Manufacturing Processes Ltd* [1976] Ch. 55.

[67] *The Supreme Court Practice 1995*, pp. 535–540, at p. 516 and Jacob (1987), pp. 139–141, at p. 139 and see R.S.C., Ord. 29, rr.2, 3; C.C.R., Ord. 13, r.7.

[68] See below p. 671.

reasons. The plaintiff must provide evidence describing the premises and the relevant property or documents and showing some strong evidence that serious harm or serious injustice will be done if the order is not made.[69] As usual, the plaintiff must make an undertaking as to damages.

(d) Other pre-trial remedies

Other remedies include[70] the High Court power to make interlocutory receivership orders,[71] the High Court or county court power to make interlocutory orders relating to property relevant to an action,[72] the limited power to prevent a defendant leaving the jurisdiction,[73] and the High Court or county court power to make an order requiring an interim payment on account of any damages, debt or other sum which a defendant may be held liable to pay.[74]

---

[69] O'Hare and Hill (1993), p. 309.
[70] For further remedies, see Jacob (1987), pp. 143–147 and O'Hare and Hill (1993), pp. 328–342.
[71] Supreme Court Act 1981, s.37, see O'Hare and Hill (1993), pp. 329–330.
[72] As mentioned as part of the jurisdictional background to Anton Piller orders, see R.S.C., Ord. 29, rr.2, 2A, 3; C.C.R., Ord. 13, r.7.
[73] See Jacob (1987), pp. 141–142.
[74] O'Hare and Hill (1993), pp. 333–339; Jacob (1987), pp. 142–143.

CHAPTER 12

PRE-HEARING: TRIBUNALS

IN the preceding chapter we used the actions in the county court and the Queen's Bench Division as examples of civil procedure. For this chapter there is no standard model. Generalisation about tribunal procedure is almost impossible in the face of widely divergent practice in different tribunals[1] and there is no accepted pattern. However, there are certain common principles and objectives in tribunal adjudication and there are common procedural problems to be solved. This chapter sets out to a examine these objectives and the way in which they influence procedure prior to a tribunal hearing; the common problems which procedural rules must attempt to solve; the amount of legal advice or help which is available; and finally, the pre-hearing procedure adopted in two particular tribunals as illustrative of the various solutions designed to meet the needs of individual claimants and individual tribunals.

A. THE COMMON OBJECTIVES

The starting point of any discussion must be the Franks Report[2] and its assertion that tribunals should display three common characteristics: openness, fairness and impartiality.[3] It is clear that the attainment of each of these objectives will have implications for the procedural rules adopted.

In requiring that tribunals should be open, the Committee intended that the proceedings should be given sufficient publicity so that they were known to those who might need to make use of them. In addition, it was stated that the essential reasoning underlying decisions should be made known to the parties.[4]

Openness means more than the adoption of a rule of procedure that, save where the personal interests of the claimant would be prejudiced, tribunal hearings should be conducted in public. It signifies rather a notion of availability or accessibility—that tribunal adjudication is open to all those who might have a problem lying within the jurisdiction of a particular tribunal. In order that a tribunal is *accessible* to the public, each citizen needs to be aware of his or her right to use the tribunal where appropriate[5]; the information given in official publications and forms must be comprehensible; tribunal hearings need to be conveniently located; advice and assistance needs to be available either through the legal advice scheme or through other agencies; and the procedure to be followed both prior to and during the hearing should be sufficiently clear that the claimant can follow it and understand the implications of seeking a tribunal

---

[1] The various types of tribunal and their jurisdiction are discussed above, pp. 39–46, 50–54.
[2] Report of the Committee on Administrative Tribunals and Enquiries (Cmnd. 218, 1957).
[3] *ibid.* In particular, paras.23–25, 41–42.
[4] *ibid.*, para. 98.
[5] This goes back to the question of ensuring that problems are recognised and identified accurately; see Chap. 8.

hearing. Establishing the right procedural rules is but one aspect of making tribunals accessible to the public.

The objectives of fairness and impartiality are closely linked, and are especially important to a system which does not have the weight and authority enjoyed by the courts in the public esteem. Naturally, the claimant must be assured that the adjudication is even-handed or she will dismiss the whole proceedings as unfair but the procedure to be followed is also crucial. Every claimant will judge the fairness of the tribunal (and hence assess its credibility and reputation) by reference to the way in which the case has progressed and the extent to which he or she has been able to put his or her own side of the argument in the knowledge of the case that has to be met. Procedural fairness – the feeling induced in the claimant that he or she has had "a fair crack of the whip" – is absolutely essential and according to the Franks Committee depends upon, ". . . the adoption of a clear procedure which enables parties to know their rights to present their case fully and to know the case which they have to meet."[6]

As well as displaying these three characteristics, tribunals are also expected to offer informal, cheap and quick adjudication, providing a contrast to the procedures of the High Court.[7] The problem lies in achieving an acceptable standard of decision-making based on adequate information and argument, without rendering tribunals as formal, expensive and slow as the civil courts.

Before a tribunal case reaches a hearing it must be prepared for adjudication and the parties must be in a position to participate fully at the hearing. There are, broadly, three stages in pre-hearing procedure which might be termed, "knowing your rights", "knowing the ropes", and "knowing the case".

B. "KNOWING YOUR RIGHTS"—IDENTIFYING THE TRIBUNAL

Courts do not have to advertise. There is a general awareness that civil courts are the venue for settling disputes, (although there may be some difficulty for individuals in perceiving that they have a problem capable of legal settlement), and as to criminal courts, defendants have little choice about whether they wish to avail themselves of the court's jurisdiction. In respect of tribunals, the first difficulty for the parties may lie in realising that there is a body with jurisdiction over their grievance whose assistance might be invoked. The various tribunals need to be sufficiently well publicised so as to alert people to their existence and powers.

In general, individuals may take their case to a tribunal as a result of a decision of a Government department which affects them (a citizen/state dispute), or as a result of experiencing an event or series of events which the law places within the jurisdiction of a particular tribunal (normally a citizen/ citizen dispute). Into the former category would fall appeals to Social Security

---

[6] Franks Report (1957) para. 42.
[7] For a comparison between courts and tribunals, see R. E. Wraith and P. G. Hutchesson, *Administrative Tribunals* (1973), Chap. 10. *Cf.* above, pp. 44–45.

Appeal Tribunals[8]; to the General Commissioners of Income Tax[9]; to Vaccine Damage Tribunals[10]; to the Immigration Appeal Tribunal[11] and many others Into the latter category would fall applications to an Industrial Tribunal[12]; to a service committee of a Family Health Services Authority[13]; or to a Rent Assessment Committee.[14] This division is significant because in a citizen/state dispute the individual concerned may be notified of the existence of the tribunal and of the right of appeal at the time that the decision is notified. Thus, the claimant knows of the right of appeal and, usually, how to make application. He or she may not know what are the implications of an appeal or precisely how to go about preparing the case, but he or she is given a start.

In respect of citizen/citizen disputes it is for the applicant to realise that if he or she is unfairly dismissed, or maltreated by a doctor, or the rent is too high, that there is an opportunity to pursue the grievance in a tribunal. Some tribunals must, therefore, give special consideration to how they can make the public aware of their jurisdiction.

1. THE AVAILABILITY OF LEGAL ADVICE

With very limited exceptions, legal aid is not available for *representation* at tribunal hearings.[15] The legal advice scheme, however, was intended to provide a source of advice for the public on matters relating to tribunals and how to use them.[16] The legal advice scheme has already been considered in detail,[17] but it will be recalled that a solicitor is permitted to give advice under the scheme to any suitably qualified applicant, "on the application of English law to any particular circumstances which have arisen in relation to the person seeking the advice and as to the steps which that person might appropriately take. . . ."[18]

It was a source of regret to the Lord Chancellor's Advisory Committee on Legal Aid that the green form scheme was not used more extensively for advice on tribunal matters,[19] but that is part of the wider problem of encouraging those

---

[8] Where the original decision is made by an adjudication officer at the Department of Social Security, see above, pp. 68–69.

[9] Against an income tax assessment, the tribunal being arranged in accordance with the Taxes Management Act 1970.

[10] Against the decision of an adjudication officer that the claim of a person under the Vaccine Damage Payments Act 1979 is disallowed.

[11] Either against the decision of an immigration adjudicator or, in certain cases, directly against decisions of an immigration officer under the Immigration Act 1971.

[12] See above, pp. 63–66.

[13] Where complaints may be made about services provided by a general practitioner to his or her patients.

[14] Rent Assessment Committees exercise jurisdiction under Part I of the Housing Act 1988 in determining rents for assured periodic tenancies; this is to replace its jurisdiction under the Rent Act 1977 to review the decisions of rent officers as to fair rents for protected tenancies (such tenancies can only exceptionally come into existance since 1988). They have also exercised the jurisdiction formerly exercised by rent tribunals: Housing Act 1980, s.72

[15] See above, pp. 569–570.

[16] In 1969, the Law Society asserted that the introduction of a legal advice scheme would encourage solicitors to operate in areas of unmet legal need and ensure that adequate legal services would be provided. See also, above, p. 434.

[17] In Chap. 9, above, pp. 491–510.

[18] Legal Aid Act 1988, s.2(2).

[19] See, *e.g. 26th Legal Aid Annual Reports* [1975–76], p. 58.

who could benefit from the green form scheme to get along to a solicitor's office.[20] There was some evidence that claims for payment by solicitors who had undertaken welfare benefits work on the green form scheme were refused by officials in some legal aid areas offices.[21] The Attorney-General subsequently confirmed that matters affecting entitlement to welfare benefits were matters of law to which the scheme applied.[22]

It is difficult to quantify precisely the number of tribunal cases dealt with by solicitors under the green form scheme. The study by Genn and Genn of representation at tribunals found that solicitors were consulted by 4 per cent of appellants before Social Security Appeal Tribunals, 27 per cent of appellants to Immigration Adjudicators, 36 per cent of applicants to Industrial Tribunals and over 60 per cent of patients applying to Mental Health Review Tribunals.[23] It is Social Security Appeal Tribunals that have by far the highest case load,[24] and the contribution of solicitors here under the green form scheme or otherwise is clearly very limited.

2. OTHER SOURCES OF ADVICE

The agencies discussed in Chapter 9 (CABx, independent advice centres, neighbourhood law centres, Trade Union, etc.) are available to offer help to individuals, but their work has been supplemented by the growth of specialist groups. Some of these are attached to large, generalist agencies, some exist independently.[25]

Although Citizens Advice Bureaux have been prominent in developing tribunal assistance and representation, no standard pattern of organisation has emerged. Instead, individual schemes have grown up according to the particular circumstances in different parts of the country. Inevitably, the availability of resources has had a great influence on the type of provision made and its effectiveness. In the West Midlands, a specially funded scheme set up an individual tribunal unit independent of the bureaux in the area, but offering training and support to them and their clients.[26] In Newcastle upon Tyne, a smaller unit was situated within the bureau dealing specifically with cases referred on to it through the bureau. In Chapeltown, Leeds a Tribunal Assistance Unit offered

---

[20] See above, pp. 507–508.

[21] *LAG Bulletin*, July 1983, pp. 1, 5.

[22] H. C. Deb. Vol. 45, col. 604, July 11, 1983; *LAG Bulletin*, August 1983, p. 5. See *Legal Aid Handbook 1990*, p. 32.

[23] H. Genn and Y. Genn, *The Effectiveness of Representation at Tribunals* (L.C.D., 1989), pp. 15, 30, 39, 56. See further on this study, below, pp. 641–642, 822–835.

[24] See above, pp. 52–54.

[25] A survey of some of these specialist groups is contained in R. Lawrence, *Tribunal Representation, The Role of Advice and Advocacy Services* (1980).

[26] The original project was jointly funded by the National Association of Citizens Advice Bureaux and the EEC Action Against Poverty Programme. The report on the project and its significance for tribunal advice and advocacy services generally is E. Kessler, *et al.*, *Combatting Poverty: CABx, Claimants and Tribunals* (1980). The unit now acts as a specialist support unit for CABx, organises training courses and provides a national information service through a telephone hotline, *The Adviser* magazine and the Lawtel data base: see J. Citron, *Citizens Advice Bureaux* (1989), pp. 54–56. It acts in a consultative capacity, but occasionally offers representation.

a service to claimants through the local bureau.[27] In other areas, salaried welfare rights workers have been appointed to provide expertise for a group of bureaux. The universal experience has been that contact with any form of expertise, however provided, has raised the general level of advice-giving in respect of tribunal matters by the ordinary volunteer in the bureau.[28] This, together with the greatly increased demand for assistance with social security and employment problems, has enhanced the value of the CAB service to the general public.

The Free Representation Unit[29] is an independent group, now based in offices on Bedford Row, London WC1, which offers an advocacy service in cases referred to it by advice agencies. In fact, this Unit may not be involved at the pre-hearing stage and may rely heavily on the referring agency for the initial advice to the claimant and preparation of the case. The Unit employs two salaried case workers, one for social security cases and one for employment cases, and there is a solicitor, and an administrative assistant, the funding coming from the Bar Council (33 per cent), the Inns of Court (26 per cent) individual barristers (20 per cent), referral agencies, who pay a small annual income, and training days.[30] These support a hundred or so volunteer representatives, many of whom are Bar students or pupil barristers, some qualified lawyers.[31] In 1994, 3,489 cases were referred to the Unit and representation was provided in 1,682 of those cases.

Other independent groups[32] have based themselves in advice centres offering a service to clients of that centre and those referred by other statutory or voluntary agencies.

The advice available is, therefore, dependent partly upon local initiatives and there is certainly no national coverage.

3. SEEKING ADVICE

A study of tribunal representation conducted for the Lord Chancellor's Department[33] looked at the proportion of appellants before four tribunals (Social Security Appeal Tribunals, Immigration Adjudicators, Industrial Tribunals and Mental Health Review Tribunals) who sought advice before the hearing. From

---

[27] *Tribunal Assistance, the Chapeltown Experience* (NACAB Occasional Paper No. 14, 1982), describes and evaluates the scheme.

[28] See Lawrence, *op. cit.* at p. 75. *Chapeltown Citizens' Advice Bureau, Leeds, Tribunal Assistance Unit, Progress Report – First Two years* (NACAB Occasional Paper No.6. 1979), at pp. 7–8.

[29] *FRU Prospectus,* see also the FRU's Annual Reports; M. Westgate, *Counsel,* Vol. 2, No. 1, Michaelmas/Autumn 1986, p. 12; H. Brooke Q.C. and P. Leaver, *ibid.* p. 13; General Council of the Bar, *Quality of Justice: The Bar's Response* (1989), pp. 72–76 (indicating the Bar Council's wish for FRU services to be expanded); N. Lieven, *Counsel,* February 1991, p. 22; D. Conn, *Legal Action,* December 1993, p. 9; M. Pennycook, *Counsel,* March/April 1994, pp. 23–24. FRU work has also been developed in Birmingham.

[30] Pennycook, *op.cit.*

[31] A chambers scheme aims to encourage more *pro bono* work by qualified barristers: *ibid.*

[32] *e.g.* Birmingham Tribunal Representation Unit; Walsall Advice and Representation Project; South Wales Anti-Poverty Action Centre.

[33] H. Genn and Y. Genn, *The Effectiveness of Representation at Tribunals* (L.C.D., 1989), discussed by R. Young (1990) 8 C.J.Q. 16 and T. Mullen (1990) 53 M.L.R. 230.

information drawn from case files,[34] it appeared that only 22 per cent[35] of S.S.A.T. appellants sought advice before the hearing.[36] The corresponding figures for the other three were much higher: 80 per cent for Immigration Adjudicators,[37] 70 per cent for Industrial Tribunals,[38] and 64 per cent for M.H.R.T.s,[39] again with regional and other variations The study suggested that failure to seek advice (or representation) often stemmed from ignorance about the nature of appeals (ranging from over-confidence to bewilderment). In other cases, appellants who recognised a need for advice either did not know where to go or could not obtain or pay for representation.[40]

C. "KNOWING THE ROPES"—MAKING APPLICATION TO A TRIBUNAL

Rules of procedure begin to take effect when an applicant decides to invoke the jurisdiction of the tribunal by making an application for a hearing. Prior to that he or she may have tried to effect a settlement of the grievance in the same way as would have been done in a civil matter, but because a significant proportion of tribunal matters concern the correctness of a decision made by a government department or agency the scope for settlement may be fairly limited.[41] The means of expressing disagreement with such a decision is not to complain about it to the individual responsible but to commence an appeal to the appropriate tribunal. In other cases, particularly where an application to an Industrial Tribunal may be in prospect, there are pre-hearing procedures expressly designed to secure a mutually acceptable resolution of the problem.[42]

In relation to the making of an application there are three procedural aspects to be considered. What form should the application take? What information should it contain? Within what time limit, if any, should it be made? These are questions which have been considered and answered in the civil courts, and they are obviously questions which are common to all tribunals. It would be tempting to assume that a Code of Procedure could be devised to encompass all tribunal sand make specific provision for these and other points. The Franks

[34] Likely to understate the position.

[35] Of these, 31 per cent went to a C.A.B., 16 per cent to a solicitor, and the rest went to a wide variety of sources including trade unions, tribunal units, law centres, welfare rights centres, social workers, general advice centres, unemployment centres, pressure groups and church groups.

[36] Genn and Genn (1989), pp. 13–15. There were considerable variations according to region and type of case: *ibid.* pp. 15–18.

[37] *ibid.* pp. 29–32; the main sources were U.K.I.A.S. and solicitors.

[38] *ibid.* pp. 38–43; the main sources were solicitors and trade unions (appellants), outside or in-house lawyers (respondents).

[39] *ibid.* pp. 56–57; dominated by solicitors.

[40] *ibid.* pp. 59–62, 221–222.

[41] This is dependent upon the procedures of the Department concerned. In social security matters an application to a tribunal ensures an initial review of the decision by an adjudication officer, and there is some evidence to suggest that the intervention of an advice agency can get "mistakes" straightened out without recourse to a tribunal: Chapeltown Tribunal Assistance Unit, *Progress Report—First Two Years* (see above, n. 28), at pp. 11, 12; Genn and Genn (1989), pp. 136–137; J. Baldwin, N. Wikeley and R. Young, *Judging Social Security* (1992), Chap. 3.

[42] In the Industrial Tribunal procedure, emphasis is placed upon conciliation and the mediating role of the Advisory Conciliation and Arbitration Service, although this usually occurs after the application has been made.

Committee[43] moved towards this position with a recommendation that a Council on Tribunals should formulate the procedural rules for each tribunal, based on principles common to all tribunals but tailored to suit the needs of the particular tribunal.[44] In the event, the Tribunals and Inquiries Act 1958 merely provided that the Council on Tribunals (established by the Act) should be consulted when procedural rules were made in respect of certain specified tribunals.[45]

What form should an application to a tribunal take? Many tribunals require the completion of a printed form—a method of application which can either assist or hinder the applicant. He or she may be deterred from pursuing the case by the complexity or unintelligibility of the questions, but will at least be shown the information required and sometimes directed towards a source of help and advice.[46] Again, the nature of the dispute may have an effect on procedure in that in citizen/state disputes the jurisdiction is likely to be automatic and the applicant will not have to show the grounds which bring the matters within the tribunal's jurisdiction. In citizen/citizen disputes the applicant's first job will be to establish that the case falls within the tribunal's jurisdiction and a printed form with appropriate questions will be helpful both to tribunal and applicant.

The different procedural approaches of Social Security Appeal Tribunals and Industrial Tribunals are illustrated later in the chapter.[47] In many cases the applicant has the opportunity of including matters for the consideration of the tribunal in the application, or in a subsequent statement. Ultimately, he or she may make representations at the hearing (if one is held)[48] and it is likely to be the style and conduct of the hearing which determines how much advance information is required by the tribunal.

All tribunals find it necessary to impose time limits within which an application must be submitted, and some impose limits on later stages of the procedure.[49] The balance has to be struck between allowing a tribunal to make a speedy determination in a dispute (based on evidence which is not too far distant in time) and ensuring that an applicant is not unduly prejudiced by the limit. The Council on Tribunals has taken a particular interest in this matter and has welcomed the extension of time limits in some tribunals.[50] In addition it is desirable that there should be a procedural rule allowing for applications to be made out of time where there is good cause.[51]

---

[43] Report of the Committee on Administrative Tribunals and Enquiries (Cmnd. 218, 1957).

[44] *ibid.*, paras.63–64.

[45] Now Tribunals and Inquiries Act 1992, s.8. Procedural rules are normally contained in a statutory instrument made by the Minister whose Department is responsible for the particular tribunal. The Council has published Model Rules of Procedure (Cm. 1434, 1991) for the guidance of those who draft such rules.

[46] *e.g.* the form of originating application to an Industrial Tribunal states that a Trade Union or C.A.B. may be able to give advice, information, and help in filling the form. D.S.S. and S.S.A.T. leaflets include similar advice (see Leaflets N.I. 246, *How to Appeal* and N.I. 260, A *Guide to Reviews and Appeals*).

[47] See below, pp. 647–661.

[48] Not all tribunals will hold an oral hearing. The Social Security Commissioner may determine an appeal without a hearing, as may a Rent Assessment Committee.

[49] An application to a Social Security Appeal Tribunal must be made within three months of the decision appealed against (to 1986 it had been 28 days); an application to an Industrial Tribunal in respect of unfair dismissal within three months of dismissal. Unfortunately there are no time limits on the hearings and the Council on Tribunals has regularly expressed disquiet at the long backlog of cases awaiting hearing by various tribunals.

[50] Annual Report of the Council on Tribunals, 1980–81, at p. 23.

[51] *e.g.* for industrial tribunals, the claim can be presented "within such further period as the tribunal considers reasonable in a case where it is satisfied that it was not reasonably practicable for the

D. "KNOWING THE CASE"—THE PRE-HEARING EXCHANGE OF INFORMATION

"... citizens should know in good time the case which they will have to meet, whether the issue to be heard by the tribunal is one between citizen and administration or citizen and citizen.... We do not suggest that the procedure should be formalised to the extent of requiring documents in the nature of legal pleadings. What is needed is that the citizen should receive in good time beforehand a document setting out the main points of the opposing case. It should not be necessary ... to require the parties to adhere rigidly at the hearing to the case as previously set out, provided always that the interests of another party are not prejudiced by such flexibility.[52]

The amount of pre-hearing activity and the precision with which the parties are required to formulate and disclose their respective cases can vary very considerably from tribunal to tribunal. Before 1984, the applicant was given the greatest latitude in Social Security Appeal Tribunals. He or she was not required to produce any specific grounds of appeal or indicate what his or her argument might be. This was then changed, and the appeal now must "contain particulars of the grounds on which it is made or given".[53] It is not clear how much detail is necessary.[54] The applicant will receive from the adjudication officer a full statement of facts, submissions, statutory authorities and Commissioner's decisions.[55] This document will also be sent to members of the tribunal and is likely to form the basis of the hearing. There is a power for the tribunal chairman to require the applicant to furnish such further particulars as may reasonably be required.[56]

The parties before a Rent Assessment Committee are more likely to have had a full opportunity of finding out about the case.[57] Where the issue concerns the determination of a fair rent for a protected tenancy, before the matter can come before a Rent Assessment Committee, application must be made to a rent officer. This application can be made by either landlord or tenant or both jointly, but if the application is not joint, the other party is invited to take part in consultations with the rent officer and the applicant to consider what rent should be registered.[58] Only if one party is dissatisfied with the rent which is registered can he or she appeal to the Rent Assessment Committee, who then invite both parties to make written or oral representations. By the time of the hearing, both

---

complaint to be presented before the end of the period of three months": Employment protection (Consolidation) Act 1978, s.67(2). See, e.g. Palmer v. Southend-on-Sea Borough Council [1984] I.C.R. 372 (question what is reasonably practicable essentially one of fact for the tribunal); Machine Tool Industry Research Association v. Simpson [1988] I.C.R. 558.

[52] Report of the Committee on Administrative Tribunals and Enquiries (Cmnd. 218, 1957), at pp. 17–18.

[53] Social Security (Adjudication) Regulations 1995 (S.I. 1995 No. 1801), reg. 3(5). It must also include sufficient particulars to enable the decision appealed against to be identified: ibid.

[54] See C.P.A.G.'s Income-Related Benefits: The Legislation, Commentary by J. Mesher and P. Wood (1994), p. 694. Mesher notes that "the instructions given to Adjudication Officers are that if some reasons, however poorly expressed, are given for an appeal it should be accepted." If the claimant refuses to do so, the matter is put before a chairman of tribunals.

[55] See below, p. 648, where an example is reproduced.

[56] 1995 Regulations, reg. 3(6).

[57] See generally R. E. Megarry, The Rent Acts (1988), Vol. 1, Chaps.24 and 25, Vol. 3, Chaps.16 and 17; J. E. Martin, Residential Security (2nd ed., 1995), Chaps.10 and 14.

[58] Rent Act 1977, Sched. 11, para. 3, as amended.

parties will have had the opportunity to familiarise themselves with all the circumstances and the representations made by each of them. Subject to a few exceptions, no new protected tenancies can be granted after the commencement of the Housing Act 1988. The Rent Assessment Committee does, however, have jurisdiction under Part I of the Act to fix the rent of an assured tenancy where the landlord proposes a rent increase.[59] Here, the tenant applies directly to the committee, and the committee then serves a notice on both parties specifying a period of not less than seven days during which either written representations or a request to make oral representations may be made by that party to the committee. The committee may make such inquiry (if any) as it thinks fit.[60] The tenant must complete an application form providing factual details about the premises,[61] but there is no requirement for the tenant to indicate why he or she objects to the proposed rent increase. Accordingly, the parties here may be less well-informed by the time of the hearing than in cases where the committee's function is that of reviewing the decision of a rent officer.

A third approach is adopted in the Industrial Tribunal.[62] The forms by which an applicant makes the application and the respondent indicates an intention to defend the case, require a certain minimum amount of information. In particular, the applicant is required to state "the grounds, with particulars thereof on which relief is sought."[63] This ensures at the outset that both sides will have some idea of the case to be met. Thereafter there are opportunities for both formal and informal exchange of information.

Formal procedures exist whereby the tribunal may, at the request of one of the parties or of its own volition, require either side to provide further particulars of its case or risk losing the case.[64] These formal procedures reinforce informal requests for information which either party may make of the other. In addition, the tribunal has the power to order discovery of documents.[65] In race and sex discrimination cases there is a "question-and-answer procedure," analogous to interrogatories in civil procedure.[66] Standard questionnaires are available for the purposes of this procedure.[67] The 1993 Regulations introduced a new general power for the tribunal to require a party to provide a written answer to any question if it considers that the answers may help to clarify any issue likely to arise in the proceedings, and it would be likely to assist the progress of the

---

[59] Housing Act 1988, s.13(4)(a), 14. There are certain other matters also within its jurisdiction under Part I.

[60] Rent Assessment Committee (England and Wales) Regulations 1971 (S.I. 1971 No. 1065), reg. 2A, inserted by S.I. 1988 No. 2200.

[61] Prescribed by the Assured Tenancies and Agricultural Occupancies (Forms) Regulations 1988 (S.I. 1988 No. 2203), as amended.

[62] For procedure in Industrial Tribunals generally see, I. T. Smith and Sir John Wood, *Industrial Law* (5th ed., 1993), Chap. 8, pp. 293–324; M. J. Goodman, *Industrial Tribunals' Practice and Procedure* (4th ed., 1987); *Tribunal practice and procedure* (I.D.S. Employment Law Handbook, Series 2 No. 4 (1994)).

[63] Rules of Procedure, r.1; The Rules of Procedure appear as Sched. 1 to the Industrial Tribunals (Constitution and Rules of Procedure) Regulations 1993 (S.I. 1993 No. 2678). Strictly speaking, there is no requirement that the printed forms be used so long as the required information is given in another form, *e.g.* a letter. However, it is crucial that the grounds and particulars are given, so the form is usually regarded as helpful.

[64] Rules of Procedure, r.4(1)(a).

[65] *ibid.* r.4(1)(b).

[66] Sex Discrimination Act 1975, s.74; Race Relations Act 1976, s.65.

[67] Sex Discrimination (Questions and Replies) Order 1975 (S.I. 1975 No. 2048); Race Relations (Questions and Replies) Order 1977 (S.I. 1977 No. 842).

proceedings for it to be available before the hearing.[68] Copies of answers are sent to the other party or parties.

A new procedure was introduced in 1980 which had the effect of disclosing information to the parties. The "pre-hearing assessment" was an attempt to reduce the number of cases going to a hearing by bringing the parties together, without witnesses, to undergo a review of the application. This operated to expose the case to both sides and although there was no power to strike out an unworthy case there was a possible penalty on costs at the hearing if the tribunal indicated, at the pre-hearing assessment, that there was no reasonable prospect of a successful application or defence.[69] These procedures owe more to the High Court and county court than to other tribunals, but overall did not prove to be a success.[70] They have been replaced by "pre-hearing reviews" which include a power for the person or tribunal conducting the review to require a party to pay a deposit of £150 if he or she wishes to continue the proceedings, in respect of contentions that have no reasonable prospect of success.[71] This last step was opposed by the Council on Tribunals, without success.[72] It is now proposed that tribunals should be empowered to dismiss a hopeless case at a pre-hearing review, and where no notice of appearance is lodged, to dismiss a case without a hearing.[73]

Informally, there may be an exchange of information because of the involvement of conciliation officers. All applications and subsequent documents are sent to ACAS[74] and a conciliation officer is under an obligation to attempt a conciliation either at the request of one of the parties, or of his or her own volition.[75] This conciliation may be rejected by the parties but it is likely to lead to some informal exchange of information unless the conciliation officer never even gets his foot in the door. Could this process usefully be adapted to assist settlements in the High Court?

These examples of pre-hearing procedure, necessarily selective, are intended to illustrate three different approaches to the objective set out by the Franks Committee. Full obligatory disclosure by one side; opportunity to disclose by both sides, but no obligation and no penalty for non-disclosure; limited obligatory disclosure by both sides, with opportunities for further disclosure supported by sanctions.

---

[68] Rules of Procedure, r.4(3).
[69] *ibid.*, r.6.
[70] See Smith and Wood (1993), pp. 317–318. There was a decline in their use; they could make conciliation more difficult.
[71] Employment Act 1989, s.20, giving the Secretary of State power to make regulations for pre-hearing reviews; Rules of Procedure, r.7.
[72] Annual Report of the Council on Tribunals for 1987–88 (1988–89 H.C. 102), pp. 36–38; Annual Report for 1988–89 (1988–90 H.C. 114), pp. 33–34.
[73] Green Paper, *Resolving Employment Rights Disputes: Options for Reform* (Cm. 2707, 1994), pp. 37–38.
[74] The Advisory Conciliation and Arbitration Service.
[75] Industrial Tribunals Act 1996, ss.18, 19. See Smith and Wood (1993), pp. 315–317; L. Dickens *et. al.*, *Dismissed* (1985), Chap. 6. In 1992, 63 per cent of applications notified to conciliation officers were settled or withdrawn without a hearing: ACAS Annual Report 1992.

E. PRE-HEARING PROCEDURE IN TWO TRIBUNALS

We have already contrasted some of the procedural aspects of social security tribunals and industrial tribunals in making general points about procedure. Below we set out two cases which illustrate the progress of a case towards a hearing in a Social Security Appeal Tribunal and an Industrial Tribunal. It was noted at the outset that it is difficult to produce "typical" tribunals for consideration, and it is no easier to produce "typical" cases from a single tribunal. One of the alleged virtues of the tribunal system is its flexibility in dealing with differing circumstances. These examples at least demonstrate the documentation involved and indicate the normal procedure.

1. A SOCIAL SECURITY APPEAL TRIBUNAL

Facts: Mr Edward Jones made a claim for a Funeral Payment from the Social Fund in respect of the funeral expenses for his deceased mother, Margaret. His claim was rejected and he appealed to the Gumby Social Security Appeal Tribunal. The Schedule of Evidence (Form AT47) prepared for the hearing comprised—

(1) Form SF 200 on which Mr Jones claimed the Funeral Payment.
(2) Form SF 203 on which the Manager of the Gumby Office of the Benefits Agency requested further information (answers to certain questions on Form SF 200).
(3) Form AT2, which set out the full facts and the Adjudication Officer's decision.

A set of the documents was sent to Mr Jones in September (Form AT6). This letter also asked him to indicate by returning an Enquiry Form whether he wished to withdraw the appeal (no); intended to come to the hearing (yes); whether someone would be coming to speak on his behalf (no); whether he wished the case to be heard in private (yes); whether he was willing to have the appeal heard if the tribunal were incomplete (yes); and whether he had any further comment or evidence (no). He also was asked for any dates in the following three months when he would not be available, and warned that if he did not return the form within 14 days it would be assumed that he did not wish to proceed and consideration would be given to striking it out. Finally, the letter included notes on travelling expenses, subsistence allowance, compensation for loss of earnings, child minding and similar expenses.

At the hearing, the Tribunal rejected Mr Jones' appeal. The record of proceedings was made by the chairman on Form AT3 which, for convenience, is reproduced here rather than in Chapter 15 on the Tribunal Hearing.

We reproduce Forms AT2 and AT3 below.

SOCIAL SECURITY APPEAL TRIBUNAL

IN CONFIDENCE

Appeal or Reference to Appeal Tribunal

For hearing on
Appeal Register Number
Sheet   Line

Benefit: Income Support   Tribunal: **GUMBY**

FULL NAMES OF PERSONS CONCERNED	National Insurance Number				
Name of claimant (Surname) (Other names)	AA	01	02	03	A
*(Mr/Mrs/Miss) JONES EDWARD					
Address 3 WORTLEY STREET,	Benefit reference number				
GUMBY					

___

1

*Reference dated .... for decision whether

*Appeal received on ....10.10.95.... against the following decision of the
Adjudication Officer

which was issued on ....15.9.95.... Appeal written on ....12.10.95....

ADJUDICATION OFFICER'S DECISION

The claimant is not entitled to a payment for funeral expenses because it is not considered reasonable for the responsible person i.e. Edward Jones to accept responsibility for those costs.

___

2

Provisions in Acts and Regulations considered by the Adjudication Officer to be relevant

Section 138 of the Social Security (Contributions and Benefits) Act ("the Act") Regulation 7, 8, and 9 of the Social Fund Maternity and Funeral Expense (General) Regulations, ("The General Regulations").

___

3

Reported decisions of the Commissioner considered by the Adjudication Officer to be relevant

None

Person(s) concerned EDWARD JONES ....

___

4

Claimant's grounds of appeal dated   10.10.95
(Appeal cases only)

I am writing to appeal against a claim I made for funeral expenses. My mother died on August 24 1995 aged 93. I am the eldest son and am responsible for the funeral expenses.

I am at the moment unemployed and claiming income support. My insurance number is AA 01 02 03 A

Thank you.

                              Delete as necessary

5

SUMMARY OF FACTS

1. Mr Jones is a single man aged 59.
2. On 1 September 1995 he made a claim for funeral expenses in respect of Margaret Jones who died on 24 August 1995. The funeral took place on 4 September 1995.
3. Mr Jones stated on the claim form that he was responsible for the costs of the funeral, was in receipt of income support, had no savings and had two brothers, John and Peter. John lived in the same household.
4. The funeral account, from F. J. Brown & Co showed the total cost of the funeral to be £1076.00.
5. On 4 September 1995 a request for more information was issued to Mr Jones, concerning the financial position of John Jones.
6. Mr Jones forwarded a reply into the Gumby Office on 12 September 1995. He stated that Mr John Jones was in full-time employment.
7. Mr Jones appealed the decision not to pay any funeral costs, on the grounds that he was the eldest brother and consequently responsible for the funeral costs.

6

ADJUDICATION OFFICER'S DECISION

1. Section 138(1) of the Act provides as far as is relevant, that payments can be made out of the Social Fund in accordance with this part of the Act—

   a) of prescribed amounts, whether in respect of prescribed items or otherwise, to meet in prescribed circumstances, maternity expenses and funeral expenses; and
   b) ....
      c)
      the claim is made within the period specified for such a claim in regulation 19 of, and Schedule 4 to, the Social Security (Claims and Payments) Regulations 1987.

2. Subject to regulation 8 and Part IV of these Regulations, the amount of a funeral payment shall be an amount sufficient to meet any of the following essential expenses which fall to be met by the responsible person—

   a) the cost of any necessary documentation;
   b) the cost of an ordinary coffin and, in the case of cremation, the cost of an ordinary urn;
   c) the cost of transport for the coffin and bearers and one additional car;
   d) the reasonable cost of flowers from the responsible person;
   e) undertaker's fees and gratuities, chaplain's organist's and cemetery or crematorium fees for a simple funeral;
   f) the cost of any additional expenses arising from a requirement of the religious faith of the deceased, not in excess of £75;
   g) where the death occurred away from the deceased's home, the costs of transporting the body within the United Kingdom to that home or to the undertaker's premises or to a chapel of rest; and
   h) the reasonable travelling costs of one return journey within the United Kingdom by the responsible person in connection with either the arrangement of or attendance at the funeral.

Deductions from an award of a funeral payment

There shall be deducted from the amount of any award which would, but for this regulation, be made under regulation 7 the following amounts:

   a) the amount of any assets of the deceased which are available to the responsible person (on application or otherwise) or any other member of his family without probate or letters of administration having been granted;

3. Regulation 7(1) of the general Regulations provide that—

1) Subject to regulation 8 and Parts IV and V of these Regulations, a social fund payment to meet funeral expenses (referred to in these regulations as a "funeral payment") shall be made only where—

   a) the claimant or the claimant's partner in respect of the date of the claim for a funeral payment—

      i) has been awarded income support, family credit, disability working allowance, housing benefit or council tax benefit where, in the case of council tax benefit, that benefit is awarded by virtue only of the claimant or his partner having fulfilled the conditions of entitlement specified in section 131(3) to (5) of the Social Security Contributions and Benefits Act 1992, (entitlement to the appropriate maximum tax benefit); . . . and

   b) the claimant (in this Part of these Regulations referred to as "the responsible person") accepts responsibility for the costs of a funeral and—

      i) the responsible person was the partner of the deceased; or

      ii) where the responsible person or that person's partner was a close relative of the deceased, it is reasonable for the responsible person to accept responsibility for those costs and there is no other person who was equally or more closely related to the deceased whom, on comparing that other person's income and capital with that of the responsible person and taking account of the nature and extent of that other person's contact with the deceased, it is reasonable to expect to meet those costs; or

      iii) where neither head (i) nor (ii) applies, it is reasonable in view of the extent of the responsible person's or partner's acquaintanceship with the deceased for that person to accept responsibility for those costs; and

   c) the funeral takes place in the United Kingdom; and

   d) the amount of any lump sum due to the responsible person or any other member of his family on the death of the deceased by virtue of any insurance policy, occupational pension scheme, or burial club or any analogous arrangement;

   e) the amount of any contribution which has been received by the responsible person or any other member of his family from a charity or a relative of his or of the deceased, but only to the extent that that amount or, if more than one contribution has been received, the aggregate of such amounts exceeds the cost of any funeral expenses other than those specified in regulation 7(2);

   f) the amount of any funeral grant, made out of public funds, in respect of the death of a person who was entitled to a war disablement pension.

4. I submit therefore that the questions for determination by the Tribunal are as follows:-

   1) Is the claimant in receipt of a Qualifying Benefit at the date of claim for the funeral payment?

      This is not in dispute. The claimant was in receipt of income support.

   2) Is the claimant the "responsible person" in accordance with paragraph 7(1)(b) of the Social Fund General Regulations?

      The claimant accepts responsibility for the funeral costs. However the adjudication officer does not consider that it is reasonable in the circumstances that the claimant accepts responsibility for the funeral costs.

Mr John Jones is equally and as closely related to the deceased. He is engaged in employment and consequently comparing his income with that of the claimant, it is reasonable to expect him to meet the funeral costs. Regulation 7(1)(b)(ii) therefore precludes payment.

5. I submit, therefore that no award of funeral expenses can be made because it is not considered reasonable for the responsible person, i.e. Edward Jones to accept responsibility for those costs.

IN CONFIDENCE **Form AT3**

Record of proceeding of GUMBY Social Security Appeal Tribunal
held on 12 DECEMBER 1995

Full name of Appellant	(Surname) JONES	(other names) EDWARD	Case List No:
Local Office:	GUMBY		Tribunal Regional No: 4/01/95/1700

Appellant notified of hearing on: 28 November 1995

CONSTITUTION OF TRIBUNAL

Names of Tribunal Chairman and Members: MR A. GREEN
MISS B. WHITE
MR I. JENKINS

NAMES OF OTHERS PRESENT (WRITE 'NONE' WHERE APPROPRIATE)

Appellant: PRESENT	Presenting Officer: MR F. WILKINS
Appellant's representative: (*state organisation if any*) NONE	
Witness(es): MR P. JONES (BROTHER)	Others: (*state capacity*) MISS N. ROBINSON (CLERK)

1. Chairman's note of evidence (*i.e. concise details of all oral and written details put before the tribunal including medical advice given by the Medical Assessor*)

Mr E. Jones attended, unrepresented but accompanied by his father, Mr J. Jones.

Mr Wilkins represented the Adjudication Officer.

Tribunal noted documents listed on form AT47.

Chairman introduced all in room, explained functions and tribunal's independence.

Chairman mentions: change in regulation 7, Social Fund Maternity and Funeral Expenses (General) Regulations 1987, with effect from 5 June 1995. That change is not reflected in the Adjudication Officer's submission.

Mr. Wilkins: I was not aware of the changes in regulation 7.

Chairman produces Statutory Instrument[76]

---

[76] The key change was the addition of paras. (1A) and (1B) to reg. 7(1): "(1A) Whether it is reasonable for a person to accept responsibility for meeting the expenses of a funeral shall be determined by the nature and extent of that person's contact with the deceased.

(1B) In a case where the deceased had one or more close relatives and the responsible person is a person to whom paragraph (1)(b)(ii) applies, if on comparing the nature and extent of any such close relative's contact with the deceased and the nature and extent of the responsible person's contact with the deceased, any such close relative was—

(a) in closer contact with the deceased than the responsible person; or

(b) in equally close contact with the deceased and neither that close relative nor his partner, if he has one, has been awarded a benefit to which paragraph (1)(a) refers; or

(c) in equally close contact with the deceased and possesses, together with his partner, if he has one, more capital than the responsible person and his partner and that capital exceeds,

(i) where the close relative or his partner is aged 60 or over, £1,000; or

(ii) where the close relative and his partner, if he has one, are both aged under 60, £500, the responsible person shall not be entitled to a funeral payment under these Regulations in respect of those expenses."

Mr. Wilkins: requests short adjournment: parties leave room.

Parties return.

Mr Wilkins: suggests basis of decision should have been, under amended regulation, that Mr Edward Jones had equally close contact as did Mr John Jones with their late mother. Mr Edward Jones: my brother Mr John Jones was in equally close contact with my late mother as I was. We lived in the same flat, with mother. At the date of claim he was in full-time work and not in receipt of a qualifying benefit.

I am happy for tribunal to proceed today, in spite of me not being aware of changes in regulation explained by the chairman today.

2. Findings of Tribunal on questions of fact material to decision (*i.e. the relevant facts accepted from the evidence available*)

1. Mrs M. Jones, mother of Mr E. Jones, Mr J. Jones and Mr P. Jones, died on 24 August 1995 and her funeral took place on 4 September 1995.
2. On 1 September 1995 Mr E. Jones made a claim for funeral expenses.
3. Mr E. Jones and Mr J. Jones, both single, had lived with their mother until the time of her death at a flat, 3 Wortley Street, Gumby.
4. Mr P. Jones, lived with his wife, at 23 Broad Street, Borchester.
5. Mr P. Jones and his wife used to visit Mrs M. Jones on occasions.
6. Mr E. Jones and Mr J. Jones were in equally close contact with their mother, prior to her death.
7. At the date of the claim for a payment in respect of funeral expenses, Mr E. Jones was in receipt of income support. Mr J. Jones, at that time, was in full-time employment and was not in receipt of income support, family credit, disability working allowance, housing benefit or council tax benefit.

3. Full text of unanimous decision on the Appeal (*including amounts and effective date(s) as appropriate*)

The appeal does not succeed.

Mr E. Jones is not entitled to a payment for funeral expenses in respect of his late mother, Mrs M. Jones.

4. Reasons for decision (*i.e. an explanation of why, when applying the facts to the statutory provisions and case-law, a particular conclusion is reached. And why, if it is not clear from Box 2, certain evidence has been accepted or rejected*)

The tribunal, in this case, is satisfied that Mr E. Jones has not been prejudiced by the tribunal continuing today, even though the Adjudication Officer's written submission did not contain the amended wording (effective from 5 June 1995) of regulation 7 of the Social Fund Maternity and Funeral Expenses (General) Regulations 1987.

The amended wording was fully explained orally to Mr Jones during the hearing by the tribunal chairman and Mr Jones satisfied the tribunal that he fully understands the effect of the amended wording.

It is clear, on that amended wording, that in this case the crucial matters are the degree of contact which Mr E. Jones and Mr J. Jones had with their late mother. Mr E. Jones explained that he and Mr J. Jones lived in the same flat as their mother and in his view had equally close contact.

Consequently, the tribunal is satisfied that regulation 7(1B)(b) applies. As a result, as Mr J. Jones was not, at the date of claim, in receipt of a qualifying benefit, it follows that Mr E. Jones (although he was in receipt of income support at that time) is not entitled to a funeral payment.

Date: 12 DECEMBER 1995	Chairman's Signature:
For clerk's use only	System noted　　　　　　　　[ ]
SSAT decision notified to	Typing checked　　　　　　　[ ]
parties to the proceedings on	
AT3A issued	
Chairman's Direction issued ....Initials	
	Date 19

2. AN INDUSTRIAL TRIBUNAL[77]

Facts: Mr Seamer had been employed by Convoy Carriers as a lorry driver for nearly 10 years. One day in May 1995 he was called into the office of the Managing Director where there were four bottles of gin on the table. The Managing Director said that they had been found in Mr Seamer's car and accused him of stealing them. In the presence of Mr Seamer he telephoned the Police and reported the alleged theft. An argument ensued in which Mr Seamer protested his innocence. Both men lost their temper and abused each other. Eventually, the Managing Director told Mr Seamer that he was sacked, with immediate effect, and that he could collect a week's wages from the Accounts Department.

Mr Seamer subsequently went to the Employment Service Offices where he obtained an application form to send to the Industrial Tribunal. He filled in the form and sent it off, having been told by a friend that his Union might help him.

Mr Seamer submitted the form to the Central Office of the Industrial Tribunals. To help him he was given an explanatory leaflet and a small booklet, "Industrial Tribunals Procedure".[78]

On receipt of an application (Form IT1) the Central Office attempts to ensure that it discloses a cause of action within the jurisdiction of the tribunal.[79] Given that the information on the form can be very sparse this is not always an easy job. If it appears that there is no jurisdiction, the application is returned to the applicant,[80] otherwise it is sent to the respondent with Form IT2, "Notice of Originating Application", which requires the respondent to enter an appearance within 14 days. In this case the company wishes to dispute the application. It gives "notice of appearance," by completing and returning Form IT3. Forms IT1 and IT3 are reproduced below.

---

[77] The jurisdiction of the tribunal is set out above, pp. 63–66. The rules of procedure governing the tribunal are to be found in the Industrial Tribunals Constitution and Rules of Procedure Regulations 1993 (S.I. 1993 No. 2687), as amended.

[78] (ITL1 England and Wales, Revised ed., 1994). Prepared by the Industrial Tribunals, and available free.

[79] This is done by a vetting section at the Central Office.

[80] With a letter pointing out why it appears that the application is outside the jurisdiction. This does not prevent the applicant making a further application and, if it is accepted, the original defective application is not disclosed to the respondent.

I N D U S T R I A L
T R I B U N A L S
ENGLAND AND WALES

Application to an Industrial Tribunal

If you think you have a case for an Industrial Tribunal to consider:

- Read booklet ITL1 (E&W).
  It tells you about:
    - the Industrial Tribunal procedure;
    - what type of complaint they can consider;
    - which law covers your complaint;
    - which booklet describes your complaint more fully.

- Read the booklet which describes your complaint.
  It tells you about:
    - who to contact if you need advice or representation;
    - **qualifying periods** - how long you have to work for an employer before you can apply to an Industrial Tribunal to consider a complaint;
    - **time-limits** - you must send us your application form within the time allowed for your complaint.

You can get the booklets free from any Employment Service Office.

If we do not receive your application within the time-limit stipulated for your type of complaint, we may not be allowed by law to deal with it. If you are in doubt, please contact the Advisory Conciliation and Arbitration Service *(ACAS) (booklet ITL1 gives addresses and telephone numbers)*, or contact your local Employment Service Office.

If you need advice or help to complete your application, you can seek help from, for example, your Trade Union or local Citizens Advice Bureau.

You can present the case yourself or have a representative to act for you. If you name a representative, all further communications will be sent to them and not to you. Please arrange for them to keep you informed of the progress of the case.

If your complaint concerns equal pay or sex discrimination you may wish to contact the Equal Opportunities Commission for advice about representation.

If you are disabled and need any special arrangements when visiting an Industrial Tribunal, please inform the staff at the office dealing with your case who will do all they can to help.

If you have a question about the Industrial Tribunal procedure and cannot find the answer in the booklets, please ring Industrial Tribunal Enquiry line on 0345 959775. *(All calls are charged at local rate).*

Use this form for proceedings in **England and Wales**
*(For proceedings in **Scotland**, use IT1 (SCOT))*

- Please answer all of the questions on the application that apply to your complaint.

- Keep pages 1 and 2.

- Then post **or** fax pages 3 and 4 to:

> The Secretary of the Tribunals,
> Central Office of the Industrial Tribunals,
> Southgate Street,
> Bury St Edmunds,
> Suffolk,
> IP33 2AQ.

> **Telephone:** 01284 762300

> **Fax:** 01284 766334

☞ ***Note:*** • *If you **fax** the form, **do not** post a copy as well*
• *If you **post** the form, take a copy for your records*

Data Protection Act 1984
We may put some of the information you give on this application onto a computer. This helps us to monitor progress and produce statistics. We may also give information to:

- the other party in the case;

- other parts of the Department of Trade and Industry or organisations such as ACAS, the Equal Opportunities Commission or the Commission for Racial Equality.

		For Office Use	
Received at COIT	Case Number		
	Code	UDL	
	Initials	HPB	ROIT 11

INDUSTRIAL TRIBUNALS
ENGLAND AND WALES

Application to an Industrial Tribunal

0446/1

● This form has to be photocopied. If possible, please use BLACK INK and CAPITAL letters
● Where there are tick boxes, please tick the one that applies

1 Please give the type of complaint you want the tribunal to decide *(for example: unfair dismissal, equal pay)*. A full list is given in booklet ITL1. If you have more than one complaint please list all of them.

Unfair Dismissal

2 Please give your details.

Mr ☐ Mrs ☐ Miss ☐ Ms ☐

Surname — Seamer

First Names — Barry

Date of Birth — 23.9.50.

Address

23 Wood Lane
Darbyville
Notts
Postcode

Telephone

Daytime Telephone
(If we or ACAS need to contact you)

Please give an address to which we should send documents, if different from above.

Postcode

3 If a representative is acting for you, please give details.

Name — Not yet, but I am going to the Union

Address

Postcode

Telephone

Reference

IT1(E/W)

4 Please give the dates of your employment.

From

To

5 Please give the name and address of the employer, other organisation or person against whom this complaint is being brought.

Name of employer, organisation or person

Convoy Carriers plc

Address

23 London Road
Darbyville
Notts

Postcode

Telephone

Please give the place where you worked or applied to work, if different than above.

Name of employer, organisation or person.

Address

Postcode

6 Please say what job you did for the employer *(or what job you applied for)*. If this does not apply, please say what your connection was with the employer.

Driver (HGV)

3 — Over ▶

7 Please give the number of normal basic hours worked each week.

45	**hours per week**

9 If your complaint is **not** about dismissal, please give the date when the action you are complaining about took place.

8 Please give your earning details.

Basic wage/salary

£	150	:	00	**p**	per	week

Average take home pay

£	175	:	00	**p**	per	week

Other bonuses/benefits

£ 20.00 night allowance	per	week

10 Unfair dismissal applicants only

Please indicate what you are seeking at this stage, if you win your case:

☐ **Reinstatement:** to carry on working in your old job as before. *(An order for reinstatement normally includes an award of compensation for loss of earnings)*

☐ **Re-engagement:** to start another job or new contract with your old employer. *(An order for re-engagement normally includes an award of compensation for loss of earnings)*

☐ **Compensation only:** to get an award of money

11 Please give details of your complaint.
   If there is not enough space for your answer, please continue on a separate sheet and attach it to this form.

My boss (Mr Hacker) told me that some bottles of gin that were missing from the depot had been found on the back seat of my car. The car was at the depot. He told me not to come back to work and gave me a week's wages. He called me a thief. I told him that I hadn't pinched the gin and that I had been fitted up, but he did not believe me. I did not pinch the gin. I have been interviewed by the Police, but they have not told me whether they will prosecute me.

12 Please sign and date this form, then send it to the address given on page 2.

Signed	*B. Seamer*	Date	1 June 1995

THE INDUSTRIAL TRIBUNALS
NOTICE OF APPEARANCE BY RESPONDENT

In the application of

Case Number
(please quote in all correspondence)

* This form has to be photocopied, if possible please use Black Ink and Capital letters
* If there is not enough space for your answer, please continue on a separate sheet and attach it to this form

1. Full name and address of the Respondent:

CONVOY CARRIERS PLC

23 LONDON ROAD
DARBYVILLE
NOTTS

Post Code:

Telephone number:
DARBYVILLE 1249

2. If you require documents and notices to be sent to a representative or any other address in the United Kingdom please give details:

POPP, LEES AND STONE

83 MAIN STREET
GUMBY
NOTTS

Post Code:

Reference:

Telephone number:

3. Do you intend to resist the application? (Tick appropriate box)

YES [✓]   NO [ ]

4. Was the applicant dismissed? (Tick appropriate box)

YES [✓]   NO [ ]

Please give reason below

Reason for dismissal:

5. Are the dates of employment given by the applicant correct? (Tick appropriate box)

YES [✓]   NO [ ]

please give correct dates below

Began on

Ended on

6. Are the details given by the applicant about wages/salary, take home or other bonuses correct? (Tick appropriate box)

YES [✓]   NO [ ]

Please give correct details below

Basic Wages/Salary	£	per
Average Take Home Pay	£	per
Other Bonuses/Benefits	£	per

PLEASE TURN OVER

for office use only
Date of receipt   Initials

Form IT3 E&W - 1/95

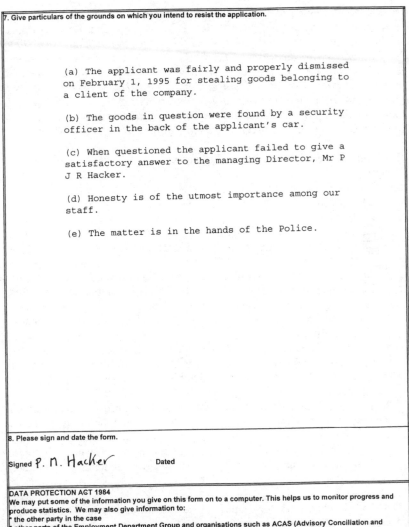

7. Give particulars of the grounds on which you intend to resist the application.

(a) The applicant was fairly and properly dismissed on February 1, 1995 for stealing goods belonging to a client of the company.

(b) The goods in question were found by a security officer in the back of the applicant's car.

(c) When questioned the applicant failed to give a satisfactory answer to the managing Director, Mr P J R Hacker.

(d) Honesty is of the utmost importance among our staff.

(e) The matter is in the hands of the Police.

8. Please sign and date the form.

Signed *P. M. Hacker*   Dated

Please post or fax this form to : The Regional Secretary Southgate Street, Bury St Edmunds, Suffolk, IP33 2AQ.

* IF YOU FAX THE FORM, DO NOT POST A COPY AS WELL
* IF YOU POST THE FORM, TAKE A COPY FOR YOUR RECORDS

Form IT3 E&W - 1/95

At the same time as the originating application is sent to the respondent it is also sent to a conciliation officer.[81] *He receives a copy of the notice of appearance in due course. He is obliged to assist the parties in reaching a conciliation if he is requested to do so, or if he thinks there is a reasonable prospect of success.*[82] *In this case he sees both parties individually. Mr Seamer wants his job back. Convoy Carriers will not give it to him. Mr Seamer has sought the assistance of his Union and they ask the company for more information. The company refuses but is ordered to give further particulars after an application to the Tribunal by the applicant. A standard form direction would be:*

Regional Office of the Industrial Tribunals
(address)
To: Convoy Carriers PLC,
    23 London Road,
    Darbyville,
    Notts.
Case No. 12345/95 Seamer v. Convoy Carriers PLC

1. An application has been received from the Applicant for further particulars of the grounds on which you rely. This application has been referred to the Chairman of Tribunals who by virtue of the powers conferred upon him under rule 4(1)(a) of the Rules of Procedure has granted an order as follows.
2. The particulars requested in the letter dated September 4, 1995 (copy enclosed) should be furnished to Mr D. York, National Union of Lorrymen, York Row, Darbyville by October 30, 1995 and a copy sent to this office.
3. Your attention is drawn to the fact that rule 4(7) provides that if an order under rule 4(1)(a) is not complied with, a tribunal, before or at the hearing, may, strike out the whole or part of the originating application, or, as the case may be, of the notice of appearance and, where appropriate, direct that a respondent shall be debarred from defending altogether.

A. Bowler
Dated 1, October 1995 Assistant Secretary of the Industrial Tribunals
Mr York (Mr Seamer's Union representative) had asked for further particulars of the company's normal security procedures; a list of other employees dismissed on the grounds of dishonesty in the preceding five years; and reasons why the company considered it reasonable to dismiss Mr Seamer immediately without awaiting the outcome of police investigations. The necessary information was supplied. No pre-hearing review was held[83] *and the case was listed for hearing on December 10, 1995. Mr Seamer lost.*

This example demonstrates a relatively straightforward case where the issue between the parties is clear and unlikely to be resolved in advance of the hearing. Much more documentation can be generated, but this is essentially under the

---

[81] An employee of ACAS.
[82] The evidence points to a considerable number of cases settled without a tribunal hearing (see above, p. 51). The conciliation officer is in a position to assist in negotiations leading to any result—compensation, reinstatment or the withdrawal of the application.
[83] See above, p. 646.

control of the parties and is dependent upon the amount of information that is requested. This is in contrast with the Social Security Appeal Tribunal where the appellant receives the full documentation whether he or she wants it or not. Again, even in this simple case, the advisability of securing skilled assistance can be appreciated.

CHAPTER 13

PRE-TRIAL CRIMINAL PROCEDURE

IN this chapter we consider the stages in the process of dealing with those suspected of having committed criminal offences that take place before trial. A trial (whether contested or not) is a necessary pre-condition for the imposition of a formal criminal sanction.[1] However,

"[t]here are few who would now propound the view that the centrepiece of the English criminal process is the trial, and that the few earlier procedures are merely designed to ensure that no one is put on trial unless there is a good case against them and that dangerous people are kept in custody before trial."[2]

This change of view has resulted from research into the operation of the criminal justice system, which has developed particularly strongly from the 1970s onwards.[3] Attention has been paid to the various pressures that lead to pleas of guilty and the avoidance of contested trials. "It has become a commonplace that early decisions in the criminal process seem strongly associated with and determinative of later decisions. . . ."[4] For example, a confession made by a suspect to the police may well be crucial, given the difficulties that will thereafter arise in challenging it or explaining it away in court.[5] A defendant who is remanded in custody will have to overcome a host of practical problems in the organisation of a defence that do not arise if bail is granted.[6] Moreover, the whole system would break down were it not that a very high proportion of those who are prosecuted for an offence plead guilty. In 1994–95, there were guilty pleas in 77.2 per cent of cases handled by the Crown Prosecution Service in the Crown Court, and 81.3 per cent of cases in the magistrates' courts.[7] Accordingly the outcome of the vast majority of cases is determined by the processes considered in the present chapter, and only a minority by the trial process considered in Chapter 16. The recognition in the 1990s that there had been

---

[1] Which is why fixed penalty charges for certain motoring offences do not technically constitute "fines".

[2] A. Ashworth, "Criminal Justice and the Criminal Process" (1988) 28 Brit. J. Criminol. 111, 112.

[3] For general surveys see A. Ashworth, *op. cit* and *The Criminal Process* (1994); A. Sanders and R. Young, *Criminal Justice* (1994); S. Uglow, *Criminal Justice* (1995) and N. Padfield, *Text and Materials on the Criminal Justice Process* (1995).

[4] Ashworth, *op. cit.* n. 2, p. 113.

[5] See below, pp. 680–691.

[6] See below, pp. 731–744.

[7] *Annual Report of the Crown Prosecution Service 1994–95* (1994–95 H.C. 472), pp. 25, 28 The proportion of guilty pleas in all Crown Court cases is given in the *Judicial Statistics* Annual Volume.

miscarriages of justice in a series of high profile case[8] has led to a wealth of discussion of the aspects of the system that had contributed to them. Many related to the pre-trial stages, including the fabrication of evidence by the police, mistaken identification, unreliable work by forensic scientists, unreliable confessions, and non-disclosure of evidence.[9] These matters were the subject of consideration by the Royal Commission on Criminal Justice[10] which was appointed in 1991. However, by the time the Commission reported in 1993 the government's central concern appeared to have reverted from the prevention of miscarriages of justice to the control of crime; and the RCCJ's Report itself, influenced as it was by the terms of reference drafted by government,[11] did not have the prevention of miscarriages as its central organising theme.

The material in the present chapter falls into three broad parts. First, we consider the process of investigation of offences (section A); secondly, the process whereby a decision is taken whether a prosecution should be instituted (sections B and C); and thirdly, the pre-trial procedures in criminal cases (sections D to J). We conclude with an attempt to evaluate some of the basic features of the system (section K).

A. INVESTIGATION

1. THE ROLE OF THE POLICE

Only a small proportion of the criminal offences committed lead ultimately to a criminal prosecution. Many offences will be undetected, or if detected not reported to the police,[12] or if reported not recorded as an offence by the police.[13] Of the offences that do come to the attention of the police, it seems that about 85 per cent are reported by members of the public and only about 15 per cent

---

[8] See the "chronology of *Causes Célèbres*' ": Walker in C. Walker and K. Starmer (eds.), *Justice in Error* (1993), pp. 6–13, including references to the Guildford Four, the Maguire Seven, the Birmingham Six, Judith Ward, the Tottenham Three (Silcott, Raghip and Braithwaite), Stefan Kiszko, the Darvell bothers, and the Cardiff Three (Paris, Abdullahi and Miller), and cases arising out of the activities of the West Midlands Police Serious Crimes Squad.

[9] *Ibid.*, pp. 13–15. Other issues concern the conduct of the trial, the presentation of the accused in a prejudicial manner and appeal procedures (*ibid.*). See also the JUSTICE *Report on Miscarriages of Justice* (1989).

[10] See above, pp. 30–31; below, pp. 773–776.

[11] See below, p. 773.

[12] The *British Crime Survey* (H.O. Research Study No. 76, 1983, p. 10) suggested that less than a quarter of offences are reported. The 1992 British Crime Survey gave an overall reporting rate of 43 per cent with considerable variations according to the offence (*e.g.* 99 per cent of theft of motor vehicles, 73 per cent of burglaries, 20 per cent of common assaults; relevant factors include the seriousness of the incident, the presence of a link between victim and perpetrator, fear of reprisals, and insurance: W. E. Skogan, *Contacts between Police and Public* (H.O. Research Study No. 134, 1994), Chap. 4.

[13] See generally A. K. Bottomley and K. Pease, *Crime and Punishment: Interpreting the Data* (1986), pp. 34–41.

discovered by the police themselves.[14] About a third of the "members of the public" are in fact organisations, store detectives or security firms.[15]

Once offences have come to the attention of the police,

"the clear message that emerges from practically all recent empirical studies . . . is that the police are rarely faced with the classic situation of detective fiction, that of the search for the unidentified perpetrators of known offences."[16]

In most cases the process of detection is straightforward as the offender is, for example, caught red-handed, identified by the victim or other witnesses or found by the police at or near the scene of the crime, or is one of a few people with ready access or an obvious motive, or gives himself or herself up.[17] In a significant number of cases an offence is admitted during an interview concerning other offences,[18] or the offender is identified as such following a search of his or her property, or by someone in police custody.[19] In only a minority of cases[20] are special detection skills used (e.g. involving informants, fingerprint search, local police knowledge, police records). Given the limitations on police manpower and increases in the crime rate, it is unsurprising that most effort will be directed on investigations where a result is most likely, and on the more serious cases.[21]

The arrangements for the supervision of police investigations were one of the matters specified in the RCCJ's terms of reference.[22] They were "less satisfied" with arrangements for supervising routine police enquiries than those in major investigations; indeed research found that supervision as such scarcely applied in most of the cases studied.[23] A "new approach to supervision" was needed throughout the police service, with improved training in supervision at all levels, and detective training and training in investigation should be overhauled. Police

---

[14] A. Ashworth, *The English Criminal Process: a Review of Research* (1984), p. 12, based, *inter alia*, on D. Steer, *Uncovering Crime* (RCCP Research Study No. 7, HMSO, 1980); A. K. Bottomley and C. Coleman, *Understanding Crime Rates* (1981); J. Burrows, "How Crimes Come to Police Notice," H.O. Research Bulletin No. 13, pp. 12–15 (1982). A 1992 survey found that only 5 per cent of recorded crimes come to notice as a result of police patrols or observations: M. Maguire and C. Norris, *The Conduct and Supervision of Criminal Investigations* (RCCJ Research Study No. 5, 1992), p. 8 n. 5.

[15] Burrows, *op. cit.*

[16] Bottomley and Pease (1986), p. 46, based on R. Mawby, *Policing the City* (1979) and Steer (1980).

[17] In Steer's study (1980) of indictable offences dealt with by the Oxford police, these accounted for 47 per cent of a random sample and 71 per cent of a sample of serious cases: p. 73, Table 3.4. See generally pp. 71–78, 96–116.

[18] Many offences thereby come to the attention of the police for the first time. Such admissions may be made with a view to the other offences being "taken into consideration" during sentencing. See below, p. 886. Since PACE TICs have declined considerably in number, with increasing use being made of interviews in prison: M. Maguire and C. Norris (1992), p. 9.

[19] 41 per cent and 20 per cent respectively: *ibid.*

[20] 13 per cent and 11 per cent respectively: *ibid.*

[21] *ibid.* pp. 71–72.

[22] See below, p. 773; Cm.2263, pp. 18–23.

[23] J. Baldwin and T. Moloney, *The Supervision of Police Investigations in Serious Criminal Cases* (RCCJ Research Study No.4, HMSO, 1992); M. Maguire and C. Norris, *The Conduct and Supervision of Criminal Investigations* (RCCJ Research Study No.5, HMSO, 1992); B. Irving and C. Dunningham, *Human Factors in the Quality Control of CID Investigations* (RCCJ Research Study No.21, HMSO, 1993).

performance should be assessed on the basis of other factors besides arrest and conviction rates.[24] New guidelines already introduced for the supervision of serious crime squads were welcomed, particularly in the light of the activities of the West Midlands Police Serious Crime Squad.[25] As regards major enquiries, the RCCJ endorsed moves to introduce external case reviews conducted by H.M. Inspectorate of Constabulary, the opening of policy files for all major inquiries and debriefing following major investigations. The government accepted all the recommendations except that for case reviews (on which there would be further discussion).[26]

A fundamental point emphasised by the RCCJ was that:

> "the police should see it as their duty when conducting investigations to gather and consider all the relevant evidence, including any which may exonerate the suspect . . . . A greater emphasis, such as the police service now advocates, on thorough investigation will not only help to ensure that innocent people are not convicted of crimes which they did not commit but also that fewer guilty people are acquitted because the evidence against them fails when tested in court."[27]

The adoption, once the view is taken that a particular suspect is guilty, of a blinkered approach that concentrates on the construction of a case against him or her and which downplays (or conceals) evidence that points to a different conclusion, has been a recurrent criticism of the police approach to investigations.[28] The rhetoric is now changing[29]; it is too early to assess the effect on outcomes.

To facilitate the process of investigation, the law provides the police with a series of powers to interfere with the legal rights of members of the public: powers of arrest and detention, powers to enter and search land and buildings and to search persons, and powers to seize property. The law also establishes a framework for controlling the exercise of such powers by setting conditions as to who may exercise the power and the circumstances in which it may be exercised, and by providing for supervision or periodic reviews. It also provides remedies for a breach of legal requirements. Given that most police powers authorise the commission of what would otherwise be torts or crimes (*e.g.* assault, false imprisonment, trespass to land, trespass to goods), exceeding the limits of a particular power may well expose the officers concerned (and the chief constable, who is vicariously responsible in tort[30]) to an action for damages or a criminal prosecution. The police are also subject to disciplinary regulations which may be contravened even where no tort or crime is committed.

---

[24] The RCCJ welcomed the developments in appraisal that should lead to officers being assessed on the basis of their skills, abilities and attitudes: H.O. Circular 104/1991.

[25] Civil Liberties Trust, *Unsafe and Unsatisfactory* (1991); Police Complaints Authority, *Report on the Investigation in the West Midlands Police Serious Crime Squad* (1991).

[26] RCCJ Interim Government Response, L.C.D, Home Office, Law Officers' Department, February 1994, p. 7.

[27] Cm.2263, p. 10.

[28] See below, p. 681; M. McConville, *et al. The Case for the Prosecution* (1991).

[29] See, *e.g.*, below, p. 688 on changed approaches to interviewing and *cf.* the rise and (partial decline) of requirements as to the disclosure of prosecution evidence (below, pp. 750–756).

[30] Police Act 1964, s.48.

The key statute in this area is the Police and Criminal Evidence Act 1984.[31] This Act extended the formal powers of the police in certain significant respects but narrowed them in others. It also strengthened the controls over the exercise of police powers in general and clarified and strengthened the rights of defendants in custody. Many of these controls are, however, found not in the Act itself but in Codes of Practice made by the Secretary of State.[32] The sanctions for breach of a Code tend to be more indirect than for breach of the substantive law.[33] The intention was to strike a satisfactory balance between police powers and the rights of subjects, but it remains controversial whether that has been achieved.[34] There is not the space here for more than a brief survey.[35]

2. POLICE POWERS

(a) Arrest

Powers of arrest can be grouped in five categories.

(i) Arrest with a warrant

In some cases an arrest is authorised by a warrant issued by a justice of the peace under section 1 of the Magistrates' Courts Act 1980, as an alternative to the issue of a summons.[36] The issue of an arrest warrant or a summons follows the laying of an information on oath to the effect that the person named has, or is suspected of having, committed an offence. A warrant should not be issued

---

[31] This followed the Report of the Royal Commission on Criminal Procedure (Cmnd. 8092, 1981) but differed in some important matters from its recommendations. See below, pp. 667–692.

[32] Under ss.66, 67. There are at present five codes: Code A on Powers of Stop and Search; Code B on Search and Seizure; Code C on the Detention, Treatment and Questioning of Persons; Code D on the Identification of Persons; and Code E on Tape Recording. Codes A to D were issued in 1985, and revised with effect from April 1, 1991; Code E was issued in 1988; revised versions of all five codes were issued with effect from April 10, 1995.

[33] Breach of a Code by a police officer may also constitute a disciplinary offence; prior to an amendment made by the Police and Magistrates' Courts Act 1994, s.37 (not in force at the time of writing), breach of the Code was *per se* a disciplinary offence. Other persons who investigate offences must have regard to any relevant provision (See *R. v. Twaites and Brown* (1990) 92 Cr. App. R. 106 (Ladbrokes investigators); *R. v. Bayliss* (1993) 98 Cr. App. R. 235 (store detective) and the Codes are admissible in evidence and if relevant to civil or criminal proceedings are to be taken into account by the court or tribunal. However, breach of a Code by a person does not of itself render him or her liable to any civil or criminal proceedings (s.67(8)–(11)). Breach of a Code may give rise to the exclusion of evidence: see below, pp. 686–688.

[34] For a sceptical view, see A. Sanders, "Rights, Remedies and the Police and Criminal Evidence Act" [1988] Crim.L.R.802.

[35] For fuller treatment see R. Clayton and H. Tomlinson, *Civil Actions Against the Police* (2nd ed. 1992); V. Bevan and K. Lidstone, *Investigation of Crime: A Guide to Police Powers* (2nd ed., 1996); M. Zander, *The Police and Criminal Evidence Act 1984* (3rd ed., 1995); D. Feldman, *The Law of Entry, Search and Seizure* (1986); R. T. H. Stone, *Entry, Search and Seizure* (2nd ed., 1989); H. Levenson and F. Fairweather, *Police Powers: a practitioner's guide* (3rd ed., 1996); Symposia, [1985] P.L. 388ff, [1985] Crim.L.R.535ff and [1990] Crim.L.R.452ff.

[36] See below, pp. 728–731.

where a summons would be equally effectual, but may, for example, be employed where the defendant fails to answer to a summons.[37]

(ii) Arrest without a warrant for "arrestable offences"

Section 24 of the Police and Criminal Evidence Act 1984 gives the police and members of the public general powers to arrest without a warrant in respect of the more serious offences classified as "arrestable offences".[38] These are:

— offences for which the sentence is fixed by law (murder, treason, piracy with violence and genocide);
— offences for which a person of 21 or over (not previously convicted) may be sentenced to five years' imprisonment;
— certain other offences specified in section 24(2) that would not otherwise be arrestable offences (e.g. some offences under the Customs and Excise Acts, offences under the Official Secrets Act 1989, indecent assault on a woman, taking a motor vehicle without authority) and related offences (conspiracy, attempt, aiding and abetting etc.).

The offences may be in the present, the past or the future. Thus, any person may arrest anyone who is in the act of committing an arrestable offence or whom he or she has reasonable grounds for suspecting to be committing such an offence. Where an arrestable offence has been committed, any person may arrest anyone who is guilty of it, or whom he or she has reasonable grounds for suspecting to be guilty. (Here, the offence must have been committed by someone.[39]) Where a constable has reasonable grounds for suspecting that an arrestable offence has been committed, he or she may arrest anyone whom he or she has reasonable grounds for suspecting to be guilty of it. A constable may arrest anyone who is about to commit an arrestable offence or whom he or she has reasonable grounds for suspecting to be about to commit such an offence. It will be seen that the powers of the police here are wider than those of private citizens.

(iii) Arrest without a warrant by virtue of "general arrest conditions"

A novel feature of the 1984 Act was the introduction in section 25 of general arrest powers exercisable by the police in respect of all offences other than arrestable offences. These are available where for some reason or another an arrest is necessary notwithstanding that the offence in question is comparatively trivial. Where a constable has reasonable grounds for suspecting such an offence has been or is being committed or attempted, he or she may arrest the relevant

---

[37] ibid.
[38] This replaced similar provisions in the Criminal Law Act 1967, s.2, which in turn had replaced common law powers of arrest for felonies.
[39] See *Walters v. W. H. Smith & Son Ltd* [1914] K.B. 595 (common law); *R. v. Self* [1992] 3 All E.R. 476 (s.24 (5)).

person "if it appears to him [or her] that service of a summons is impracticable or inappropriate because any of the general arrest conditions are satisfied." The "general arrest conditions" are:

    (a) that the name of the relevant person is unknown to, and cannot readily be ascertained by the constable;

    (b) that the constable has reasonable grounds for doubting whether a name furnished is the real name;

    (c) that the relevant person has failed to furnish a satisfactory address for service, or the constable has reasonable grounds for doubting whether an address furnished is a satisfactory one;

    that the constable has reasonable grounds for believing that an arrest is necessary

    (d) to prevent the relevant person causing physical injury to himself or herself or any other person; suffering physical injury; causing loss of or damage to property; committing an offence against public decency; or causing an unlawful obstruction of the highway; or

    (e) to protect a child or other vulnerable person from the relevant person.

(iv) Arrest without warrant under specific statutory powers

The 1984 Act repealed many specific statutory powers of arrest, while preserving powers under some 21 Acts listed in Schedule 2. These include powers under the Immigration Act 1971 and the Mental Health Act 1983. Other specific powers have been created since.[40]

(v) Arrest at common law

At common law, there is a power to arrest for breach of the peace where a breach of the peace is taking place or reasonably anticipated.[41] This power is not confined to constables and was not modified by the 1984 Act.

(vi) Common requirements

There are a number of conditions that must be fulfilled for an arrest to be valid, apart from the existence of a relevant power of arrest. Some are derived from

---

[40] *e.g.* Sporting Events (Control of Alcohol etc.) Act 1985, s.7(2); Public Order Act 1986, s.3(6) (affray), 4(4) (fear or provocation of violence), 5(4) (harassment, alarm or distress), 12(7), 13(10) and 14(7) (processions and assemblies); Prevention of Terrorism (Temporary Provisions) Act 1989, s.15; Criminal Justice and Public Order Act 1994, s.61 (power to remove trespassers from land), s.63 (raves) and s.68 (aggravated trespass).

[41] *R. v. Howell (Erroll)* [1982] Q.B. 416, D. C.; *Albert v. Lavin* [1982] A.C. 546. The court in *Howell* stated that "there is breach of the peace whenever harm is actually done or is likely to be done to a person or in his presence to his property or a person is in fear of being so harmed through an assault, an affray, a riot, unlawful assembly or other disturbance" (*per* Watkins L.J. at p. 427).

the common law and some from statute. Very commonly, the arrestor is required to have "reasonable grounds" to believe or suspect the arrested person to be guilty of an offence. If the validity of the arrest is challenged in legal proceedings the onus lies on the arrestor to establish to the satisfaction of the court that objectively reasonable grounds existed: it is insufficient that the arrestor honestly believed that he or she had such grounds.[42] The concept of reasonable suspicion lies between that of suspicion without any proof and that of prima facie proof based on admissible evidence (*i.e.* evidence that if not controverted would be sufficient for a conviction).[43] Whether it exists in a particular case is a question of fact not law, and it is unusual for an arrest to be held unlawful for lack of reasonable grounds.[44] As well as possessing the requisite reasonable grounds, the arrestor must in fact suspect the arrestee.[45]

The arrestor must make it clear that the arrestee is under compulsion either by physical means, such as taking him or her by the arm, or by using words of compulsion to which the arrestee accedes.[46] The arrestee must be informed that he or she is under arrest, and of the ground for arrest, at the time of the arrest or as soon as practicable thereafter,[47] except where the arrestor is a private citizen and the fact or ground of arrest is obvious. There is a further, general, exception where it is not reasonably practicable to impart the information before the arrestee escapes from arrest.[48] The arrestor must regard his or her action as an arrest in the sense of a possible first step in the criminal process: if, for example, he or she simply detains someone for questioning with no thought of arrest it cannot be a valid arrest.[49] Finally, as the power is a statutory discretion exercisable (normally) by a public official, a particular exercise may be challenged as an *ultra vires* abuse of discretion.[50]

(vii) The effects of PACE

Statistics on arrest are maintained separately by police forces and collated by H.M. Chief Inspector of Constabulary. In 1986 there were 1.31 million arrests

---

[42] *R. v. Inland Revenue Commissions, ex p. Rossminster Ltd* [1980] A.C. 952, 1011, *per* Lord Diplock.

[43] *Dumbell v. Roberts* [1944] 1 All E.R. 326; *Hussein v. Chong Fook Kam* [1970] A.C. 942.

[44] See generally S. H. Bailey and D. J. Birch, [1982] Crim.L.R.475–477. An arrest may be based on hearsay evidence: *Erskine v. Holland* [1971] R.T.R. 199; *R. v. Evans* [1974] R.T.R. 232. See also the *Code of Practice for the Exercise by Police Officers of Statutory Powers of Stop and Search* (HMSO, 1995) (Code A), paras.1.6–1.7A.

[45] *Castorina v. Chief Constable of Surrey* (1988) 138 N.L.J. 180; *Chapman v. D.P.P.* (1988) 153 J.P. 27.

[46] *Alderson v. Booth* [1969] 2 Q.B. 216.

[47] See *Nicholas v. Parsonage* [1987] R.T.R. 199 (arrest under s.25); *D.P.P. v. Hawkins* [1988] 1 W.L.R. 1166 (arrest not retrospectively unlawful if the ground is not given when it first becomes practicable); *Abbassy v. Commissioner of Police of the Metropolis* [1990] 1 W.L.R. 385 (no need to specify a particular crime or give a technical definition of the offence; sufficient to use commonplace language).

[48] Police and Criminal Evidence Act 1984, s.28. The requirements as to giving the ground of arrest were based on the common law: *Christie v. Leachinsky* [1947] A.C. 573. See *Gelberg v. Miller* [1961] 1 W.L.R. 153; *R. v. Telfer* [1976] Crim.L.R.562.

[49] *Kenlin v. Gardiner* [1967] 2 Q.B. 510; *R. v. Brown* (1976) 64 Cr. App.R. 231.

[50] *Holgate-Mohammed v. Duke* [1984] A. C. 437 (where the challenge failed on the merits); *Plange v. Chief Constable of South Humberside Police, The Times*, March 23, 1992 (arrest where officer

and this increased by over one-third to 1.75 million in 1994. Of these, under 600,000 were found guilty or cautioned for indictable offences; on the assumption that arrests are mainly used for the more serious offences, the gap is significant and alarming.[51] Research on the immediate effects of PACE suggested that the level of initial evidence on which arrests were based had become stronger, with a greater emphasis on independent evidence, although there was still a proportion of suspects who were arrested on limited evidence.[52]

(b) Stop and search

The 1984 Act extended the general powers of the police to stop and search persons and vehicles. Under section 1 a constable may stop and search a person or vehicle in a public place if he or she has reasonable grounds to believe he or she will find stolen goods, an offensive weapon, articles adapted for use in burglay, theft, obtaining by deception or taking a vehicle without authority, or a knife or other bladed or sharply pointed article.[53] There are similar powers under other statutes, authorising searches, for example, for drugs, for firearms and for intoxicating liquor at sporting events.[54] All these powers are now subject to the safeguards set out in section 2 of the 1984 Act, which, *inter alia*, require the constable, before commencing a search, to give his or her name and that of his or her police station, the object of the proposed search, the grounds for the search, and, if out of uniform, documentary evidence that he or she is a constable. The person searched may not be required to remove any clothing in public other than an outer coat, jacket or gloves, and only a constable in uniform may stop a vehicle. A record must be made of the search unless it is not practicable to do so.[55]

The exercise of stop and search powers has been controversial, particularly in the light of evidence that black people are more likely to be stopped and searched than white.[56] The Home Secretary has issued a Code of Practice under the 1984 Act regulating their use, emphasising, *inter alia*, that a person's colour, dress or hairstyle can never itself be a reasonable ground for suspicion,[57] but it is still doubted whether the reasonable ground standard is generally met.[58]

The figures for stop-searches have steadily increased, in part due to more

---

knew that there was no possibility of a charge would be unlawful as the officer had acted on an irrelevant consideration or for an improper purpose): *cf.* below, p. 971.

[51] *Statewatch*, July-August 1995, p. 19.

[52] B. L. Irving and I. K. McKenzie, *Police Interrogation: the effect of the Police and Criminal Evidence Act 1984* (1989), pp. 64–66, 145–147, 193. Here, Irving's 1979 study of practice in Brighton (RCCP Research Study No. 2, 1980) was replicated in 1986 and again in 1987). *cf.* K. Bottomley, *et al.*, *The Impact of PACE: Policing in a Northern Force* (1991), Chap. 4, where research in the period 1987–88 suggested that the changes in arrest powers had comparatively little effect on day-to-day policing on the streets, although the view of most police officers was that there had been a significant reduction in the previous practice of arresting suspects "on a hunch".

[53] Police and Criminal Evidence Act 1984, s.1, as amended by the Criminal Justice Act 1988, s.140.

[54] See the list in Annex A to the *Code of Practice for the Exercise by Police Offices of Statutory Powers of Stop and Search* (HMSO, 1995) (Code A).

[55] 1984 Act, s.3.

[56] C. F. Willis, *The Use, Effectiveness and Impact of Police Stop and Search Powers* (H. O. Research and Planning Unit Paper 15, 1983); M. McConville, [1983] Crim.L.R.605.

[57] 1984 Act, s.66; Code A 1.6–1.7A.

[58] D. Dixon *et al.* "Reality and Rules in the Construction and Regulation of Police Suspicion" (1989) 17 Int. Jo. Sociology of Law 185.

comprehensive recording.[59] The proportion leading to an arrest has at the same time declined.[60]

There is also a power to carry out general road checks on the authority of police superintendent.[61] The aim must be to find a person who has committed or is intending to commit an offence, a witness to an offence or a person unlawfully at large.[62] In each case the offence must be a "serious arrestable offence". This concept is defined in section 116 of the 1984 Act, and is employed in respect of several of the powers in the Act. It covers (1) a group of arrestable offences that are always "serious", and (2) any other arrestable offences that have led or are intended or likely to lead to specified consequences.[63]

Section 60 of the Criminal Justice and Public Order Act 1994 introduced a new power to "stop and search in anticipation of violence". Where a police superintendent (or above) reasonably believes that incidents involving serious violence may take place and that it is expedient to do so to prevent their occurrence, he or she may authorise that the section 60 powers shall be exercisable "at any place within the locality for a period not exceeding twenty four hours." These powers enable a uniformed constable to stop any pedestrian or vehicle and search for offensive weapons or dangerous instruments[64]; what is significant here is that the constable need not reasonably suspect that the pedestrian or vehicle is carrying such an item.

(c) Entry, search and seizure

The police have a wide variety of powers to enter and search premises, and seize property, either with or without a warrant. A large number of statutes enable a judge or magistrate to issue a warrant authorising the entry to and search of specified premises. For example, warrants may be granted to search for stolen goods, obscene publications, drugs and a host of other items.[65] The 1984 Act introduced a new general power for justices of the peace to issue warrants authorising entry and search for evidence relating to a serious arrestable

---

[59] Rising from 109,800 in 1986 to 576,000 in 1994 (H. O. Statistical Bulletin No. 16/95, Table A).

[60] From 17.2 per cent to 12.2 per cent (1994): *ibid* Doubts as to the reliability and helpfulness of the official statistics are, however, expressed by A. Sanders and R. Young, *Criminal Justice* (1994), pp. 57–62, given the absence of figures for stops as distinct from stop-searches and uncertainties in the categorisation of *voluntary* stop-searches.

[61] 1984 Act, s.4. The annual figure for road checks lay between 200 and 400 to 1992 (445), rising to 3,560 in 1993 and 3,003 in 1994; most of the increase was due to checks in the City of London following the Bishopsgate bomb explosion in 1993.

[62] These are specified in Sched. 5 and include, *inter alia*, treason, murder, manslaughter, rape, kidnapping, certain sexual offences, certain firearms offences and causing death by reckless driving. They also include drug trafficking offences: see Drug Trafficking Act 1994 1(3)(a) to (f).

[63] 1984 Act, s.116(6), (7). Serious harm to the security of the State or public order; serious interference with the administration of justice or the investigation of offences; death; serious injury; substantial financial gain or serious financial loss to any person (loss being serious if "having regard to all the circumstances, it is serious for the person who suffers it"). See *R. v. McIvor* [1987] Crim.L.R. 409 (Sheffield Crown Court) (theft of 28 beagles worth £880, collectively owned by a hunt, held not to involve serious financial loss); *R v. Eric Smith* [1987] Crim.L.R. 579 (Stafford Crown Court) (robbery of two video recorders and £116 cash held not to be a SAO).

[64] *i.e.* instruments which have a blade or are sharply pointed.

[65] Theft Act 1968, s.26; Obscene Publications Act 1959, s.3; Misuse of Drugs Act 1971, s.23; for a full account, see R. T. H. Stone, *Entry, Search and Seizure* (2nd ed., 1989), Chap. 4.

offence,[66] other than "items subject to legal privilege"[67] "excluded material"[68] or "special procedure material".[69] Existing powers to grant search warrants were thereafter also subject to the restriction that they could not authorise searches for such material.[70] Instead, an order granting access to excluded material or special procedure material may be granted by a Circuit judge, in limited circumstances. The material must either (1) relate to a serious arrestable offence or (2) apart from the restriction mentioned, fall within the scope of an existing search warrant power.[71] In the last resort, a Circuit judge may issue a warrant authorising a constable to enter and search for such material.[72] The 1984 Act also clarified and strengthened the safeguards governing the issue and execution of all search warrants.[73]

The 1984 Act also set out a series of powers for the police to enter premises without a warrant; to execute an arrest warrant; to arrest for an arrestable offence or certain other specified offences; to pursue and recapture a person unlawfully at large;[74] to save life or limb or prevent serious damage to property.[75] The constable must have reasonable grounds for believing that the person sought is

---

[66] 1984 Act, s.8.

[67] *ibid* s.10: generally, communications involving legal advice between professional legal adviser and client, communications concerning legal proceedings, and items enclosed with or referred to in such communications. Items held with the intention of furthering a criminal purpose are not covered (s.10(2)), regardless of whether the intention is that of the holder or another person (*R. v. Central Criminal Court, ex p. Francis & Francis* [1989] A.C. 346); although such items are likely to be special procedure material: *R. v. Guildhall Magistrates' Courts, ex p. Primlaks Ltd* [1990] 1 Q.B. 261 (see below)).

[68] *ibid.* s.11. This covers confidential personal records, human tissue or tissue fluid taken for medical purposes and confidential journalistic material ("personal records" and "journalistic material" being further defined in ss.12 and 13). Excluded material can, however, be disclosed voluntarily by the holder: *R. v. Singleton* [1995] 1 Cr. App. R. 431 (dental records).

[69] *ibid.* s.14. This covers confidential and journalistic material falling outside the definition of "excluded material."

[70] *ibid.*, s.9(2).

[71] *ibid.*, s.9(1) and Sched. 1. Excluded material is more sensitive than special procedure material and only accessible under (2): see *R. v. Central Criminal Court, ex p. Brown, The Times*, September 7, 1992. Non-compliance with an order is a contempt of court. The application is made *inter partes*, prior notice being given to the person holding the material. The material in question must be specified, either in the notice of application or otherwise: *R. v. Central Criminal Court, ex p. Adegbesan* [1986] 1 W.L.R. 1292; *R. v. Manchester Crown Court, ex. p. Taylor* [1988] 1 W.L.R. 705; but the evidence on which the application is based need not: *R. v. Inner London Crown Court, ex p. Baines & Baines* [1988] Q.B. 579. The suspect need not be notified if he or she is not the holder of the material: *R. v. Leicester Crown Court, ex p. D.P.P.* [1987] 1 W.L.R. 1371. The judge may hold the hearing in open court or in chambers: *R. v. Central Criminal Court, ex p. D.P.P., The Independent*, March 31, 1988. See generally R.T. Stone, [1988] Crim.L.R. 498 and A. S. Zuckerman, [1990] Crim.L.R. 472.

[72] *ibid.*, Sched. 1, paras.12–14. This is available, *e.g.* where use of the order procedure might seriously prejudice the investigation.

[73] ss.15,16. See also the *Code of Practice for the Searching of Premises by Police Officers and the Seizure of Property found by Police Officers on Persons or Premises* (HMSO, 1995) (Code B). For example, entry and search must be within one month of the date of the warrant; it must be at a reasonable hour and the officer in charge must first attempt to communicate with the occupier, unless it appears that would frustrate the object of the search; before the search commences (not before entry: *R. v. Longman* (1988) 88 Cr. App. R. 148), the officer must identify him- or herself and state the purpose of the search and the grounds for undertaking it; the warrant must be shown and a copy of the warrant must be given to the occupier or left at the premises. Breach of these last requirements was held to render the search and seizure unlawful in *R. v. Chief Constable of Lancashire, ex p. Parker* [1993] Q.B. 577.

[74] Pursuit must be almost contemporaneous with entry: *D'Souza v. D.P.P.* [1992] 4 All E.R. 545.

[75] s.17.

there. All common law powers of entry were abolished, save that of entry to deal with or prevent a breach of the peace.[76]

Where a person is arrested by a constable away from a police station, that person may be searched on arrest if the constable has reasonable grounds to believe that he or she may present a danger to self or others, or has something which might be used to assist an escape, or which might be evidence relating to an offence. In addition, the constable may enter and search any premises in which the person was at the time of or immediately before the arrest, for evidence relating to the offence in question, if he or she has reasonable grounds to believe that such evidence is there.[77] In the case of arrestable offences, a constable may be authorised by an officer of the rank of inspector or above to enter and search any premises occupied or controlled by a person under arrest if the constable has reasonable grounds to suspect that there is evidence relating to the offence in question or a similar or related arrestable offence.[78]

(d) Detention[79]

Part IV of the 1984 Act introduced for the first time detailed arrangements regulating the length of time persons may be kept in custody by the police before a court appearance. The provisions replaced[80] had merely required the police to bring detainees to court "as soon as practicable". If this was not practicable within 24 hours, the police had to consider whether to grant bail, and had indeed to grant bail unless the offence appeared to be "serious" (a term that was not defined). Under the new arrangements, a person arrested by a constable must be taken to a police station as soon as practicable.[81] This should normally be a "designated police station" (*i.e.* one of the stations designated by the chief officer of police as having enough accommodation for detained prisoners[82]). In some circumstances any station may be used, but no-one may be kept longer than six hours at a non-designated station.

(i) *The Custody Officer*

An important feature of the arrangements is the division of function between the "custody officer" and the officers concerned with the investigation. One or more custody officers (usually sergeants) must be appointed for each designated police station,[83] and a variety of duties are imposed directly on that officer once

---

[76] As to which see *Thomas v. Sawkins* [1935] 2 K.B. 249; *McLeod v. Metropolitan Police Commissioner* [1994] 4 All E.R. 553.

[77] 1984 Act, s.32.

[78] *ibid.* s.18. This power, unlike s.32, is not limited to cases where the person was there at the time of or immediately before the arrest. The authorisation must be contained in an independent document: a record of oral authority included in a notebook is insufficient: *R. v. Badham* [1987] Crim.L.R. 202 (Wood Green Crown Court).

[79] See generally D. Feldman, [1990] Crim.L.R.452.

[80] Magistrates' Courts Act 1980, s.43(4)

[81] 1984 Act, s.30.

[82] *ibid.* s.35.

[83] There is a *duty* to appoint one and a *discretion* (which must be exercised reasonably) to appoint more: *Vince v. Chief Constable of the Dorset Police* [1993] 2 All E.R. 321. The custody officer is not debarred by the statute from participating with other officers in a ploy involving placing suspects in a bugged cell: *R. v. Bailey and Smith* [1993] 3 All E.R. 513 (not the original authors).

a person has been brought to the station. Subject to a few exceptions, the custody officer must not be involved in the investigation.[84]

Thus,

— The custody officer (CO) must determine, as soon as practicable, whether there is sufficient evidence to charge the person arrested (D);

— If in the CO's view there is not sufficient evidence, D must be released (with or without bail), unless the CO has reasonable grounds for believing that D's detention without charge is necessary to secure or preserve evidence relating to an offence for which D is under arrest, or to obtain such evidence by questioning him or her. In that case the CO may authorise D to be kept in police detention, and, if this is done, must open a "custody record" in respect of D, *i.e.* a written record of the various stages and incidents of the period in detention;

— If in the CO's view there is sufficient evidence, D must be (1) charged or (2) released without charge, either with or without bail;[85]

— If at any time the CO becomes aware that the grounds of detention have ceased to apply, and he or she is not aware of any other grounds on which continued detention under the Act could be justified, he or she must order D's immediate release. This is to be without bail unless it appears to the CO (1) that there is need for further investigation of any matter in connection with which D was detained, or (2) that proceedings may be taken against D in respect of any such matter;[86]

— Once D is charged with an offence, the CO must order his or her release (with or without bail[87]) unless (1) D's name and address cannot be ascertained satisfactorily; or the CO has reasonable grounds for believing (2) that D will fail to appear in court to answer to bail; or (3) that where D is arrested for an imprisonable offence, D's detention is necessary to prevent him or her from committing an offence; or (4) that where D is arrested for a non-imprisonable offence, D's detention is necessary to prevent him or her causing physical injury to another or loss or damage to property; or (5) that D's detention is necessary to prevent him or her from interfering with the administration of justice or the investigation of offences (or an offence); or (6) that D's detention is necessary for his or her own protection. In any of these circumstances, the CO may authorise D to be kept in police detention;[88]

— The CO also has general responsibilities for the welfare of those in detention (including ensuring that the requirements of the Act and the Code of Practice governing Detention are observed) and for maintaining the custody records.[89]

---

[84] *ibid.* s.36. An officer of any rank may perform the functions of a custody officer if such an officer is not readily available: s.36(4).

[85] *ibid.* s.37.

[86] *ibid.* s.11.

[87] Bail cannot be granted in certain cases: Criminal Justice and Public Order Act 1994, s.25; below, p. 733.

[88] *ibid.* s.38, as amended by the 1994 Act, s.28(2). In the case of an arrested juvenile (generally persons between 10 and 17) there is a further ground; i.e. that the CO has reasonable grounds for believing that D ought to be detained in his or her own interests: s.38(1)(b).

[89] *ibid..* s.39. See the *Code of Practice for the Detention, Treatment and Questioning of Persons by Police Officers* (HMSO, 1995) (Code C).

These various responsibilities may lead a CO into conflict with an officer of higher rank involved in the investigation. Such matters must be referred to an officer of the rank of superintendent or above.[90]

(ii) *Periodic reviews*

Provision is made for there to be periodic reviews of a person's continued detention in custody. Thus a "review officer" (the CO if D has been arrested and charged, otherwise an inspector or above not directly involved in the investigation) must carry out a review not later than six hours after the detention was first authorised, and then at intervals not longer than nine hours, although these can in some circumstances be postponed. If D has not been charged by the time of the review, the review officer considers again the matters considered by the CO when initially processing D. If D has been charged by then, the review officer performs the functions of the CO arising after an arrested person is charged. Before authorising D's continued detention the review officer must give D (unless asleep), or any solicitor representing D who is available, an opportunity to make representations about the detention.[91]

(iii) *Time limits for detention without charge*

As to the periods of detention, a person cannot be kept in police detention for more than 24 hours without being charged. The "detention clock" normally starts (the "relevant time") when D arrives at the first police station to which he or she is taken after arrest, or, if D is arrested at a police station after attending voluntarily, at the time of arrest. There are special provisions governing persons brought from another police area or outside England and Wales. After the 24-hour period, a person who is not charged must be released, either with or without bail.[92] Exceptionally, however, a longer period of detention without charge may be authorised. This requires the authority of an officer of the rank of superintendent or above, who must have reasonable grounds of believing that D's continued detention is necessary to secure or preserve evidence relating to the offence for which D is under arrest, or to obtain such evidence by questioning him or her; that the offence in question is a serious arrestable offence; and that the investigation is being conducted diligently and expeditiously. The period of detention can be extended by a further 12 hours beyond the initial 24. Authorisation cannot be given by the superintendent after the expiry of the 24-hour period or before the second review.[93]

Detention can only be extended beyond the 36 hour period on the authority

---

[90] *ibid.* s.39(6).

[91] *ibid.* s.40.

[92] *ibid.* s.41. The time the "clock" starts is termed the "relevant time" by s.41(2) and time limits are generally calculated from then.

[93] *ibid.* s.42. In 1994, 465 people were detained for more than 24 hours and subsequently released without charge: H.O. Statistical Bulletin 16/95.

of a warrant of further detention granted by a magistrates' court.[94] The criteria for the grant of a warrant are the same as for authorisation of continued detention by a superintendent. D must be brought before the court and is entitled to legal representation. The application must be made within the 36-hour period, or, if it is not practicable for a court to sit at the expiry of 36 hours, within six hours thereafter.[95] The warrant may extend the detention for such period as the court thinks fit, up to a maximum of 36 hours.[96] Fresh applications may be made to the court, on the same basis, for the warrant to be extended for further periods not exceeding 36 hours, up to a maximum of 96 hours.[97] If an application for a warrant or an extension is refused, and in any event at the expiry of the 96 hour period, D must be charged or released, with or without bail. Release may, however, be postponed until the expiry of any period of detention that has already been authorised.[98] Full details of the various steps involved in extending periods of detention must be entered in the custody record.

(iv) Detention after charge

Where D is kept in detention after charge, he or she must be brought before a magistrates' court as soon as is practicable. If this is to be a local court this must be on the day D is charged or the following day; if this is to be a court in a different petty sessions area, D must be removed to that area as soon as practicable and brought before the court on the day of his or her arrival in the area or the following day. If necessary, the clerk to the justices must make special arrangements for a court to sit.[99]

(v) The effects of PACE

Considerable variations have been found[1] in the length of detention without charge from station to station, this being strongly linked with the seriousness of the crime in question, but also perhaps with differences in custody officers' approach to PACE. The mean length of detention was just over five hours and the median three hours, 19 minutes. By 24 hours, only 1 per cent were still being held without charge. Pre-PACE comparisons suggested that detention

---

[94] i.e. a court of two or more justices sitting otherwise than in open court: s.45(1). In 1994, warrants of further detention were sought in 250 cases and granted in 246: H.O. Statistical Bulletin 10/95.

[95] If an application is made after the 36-hour period, the court must dismiss it if it appears that it would have been reasonable for the police to make it within that period: s.43(7); see R. v. Slough Magistrates' Court, ex p. Stirling (1987) 151 J.P. 603.

[96] 1984 Act, s.43.

[97] ibid. s.44.

[98] e.g. by a superintendent where a warrant of further detention is refused (see s.43(15), (16)), or by a warrant if an extension is refused (see s.44(7)(8)).

[99] ibid. s.46. The clerk has a discretion to arrange for a local court or for a court in another division, in accordance with the wishes of the local justices: R. v. Avon Magistrates' Courts Committee, ex p. Broome [1988] 1 W.L.R. 1246.

[1] D. Brown, Detention at the Police Station under the Police and Criminal Evidence Act 1984 H.O. Research Study No. 104, 1989). This covered just over 5,500 custody records from three or four stations in each of 10 forces.

times were now shorter in some more serious crimes, but slightly longer for less serious offences. Some 18 per cent of those charged were detained in custody, the mean length of detention being nearly 16 hours.[2] Powers available to the police in respect of serious arrestable offences were used infrequently.[3] The detainee's premises were searched in 7 per cent of the sampled cases (4 per cent under section 18, 3 per cent with consent). Strip searches were less common (1 per cent of the sample) and intimate searches and non-consensual fingerprinting rare (seven and five cases in the sample).

It seems that at least the initial authorisation of detention by the custody officer (based on reasonable grounds for believing that detention is necessary to secure or preserve evidence or obtain evidence by questioning) is in practice a formality. Initial refusals are almost unknown.[4] Furthermore, "the review process (at least at 6 and 15 hours) tends to become routinised, with little heed paid to representations.[5]

The RCCJ[6] noted that the police were "not entirely comfortable" with the custody officer role" and that "performance of it, though improving, still leaves something to be desired." They recognised that it might also be unrealistic to expect a custody officer to take an independent view of a case investigated by colleagues.[7] Nevetherless, the role should remain with the police rather than be handed to the CPS or an independent body. Steps should be taken to develop and strengthen performance of the role, including the delegation of clerical and administrative tasks to civilians under the custody officer's control; refresher-training; the centralisation of custody officer functions within forces wherever practicable and their provision as a separate specialist service; the introduction of computerisation of the custody record process to a national standard; continuous video-recording (including sound-track) of all the activities in the custody office, the passages and stairways leading to the cells and, if feasible, the cell passage and doors of individual cells.

(e) Treatment of persons in custody

Part V of the 1984 Act and the Code of Practice on Detention (Code C), give the police certain powers to obtain evidence from persons in custody but, more importantly, make detailed provisions as to the conditions in which such persons are kept.

The Custody Officer (CO) must make a record of everything the person detained (D) has with him or her and if necessary D may be searched to enable

---

[2] B. L. Irving and I. K. McKenzie, *Police Interrogation: the effects of the Police and Criminal Evidence Act 1984* (1989), pp. 81–84, 194–196; Brown, *op. cit.*, pp. 61–67. See also M. Maguire (1988) 28 Brit.J. Criminol. 19, 22–27, 194–196; K. Bottomley *et al.*, *The Impact of PACE* (1991), pp. 121–136.

[3] Brown, *op. cit.*, pp. 47–51: detention without charge over 24 hours (46 cases out of 5,519); warrants of further detention (11 cases); extension of warrant (3 cases); delayed legal advice (55 cases); delayed notification (53 cases); intimate samples (20 cases); non-intimate sample without consent (5 cases). See further below, p. 679.

[4] I. McKenzie, R. Morgan and R. Reiner, [1990] Crim.L.R. 22, 23–27.

[5] Bottomley, *et al.*, (1991), pp. 91–92.

[6] Cm. 2263, pp. 30–34.

[7] Researchers have, however, observed instances of conflict between custody and investigating officers over detention before charge and other matters: Bottomley *et al.* (1991), Chap. V.

this to be done.[8] An officer of the rank of superintendent or above may authorise an intimate search if he or she has reasonable grounds for believing D may have concealed on him or her anything which he or she could use to cause physical injury, or a Class A drug (possessed with criminal intent).[9] Such an officer may also authorise D's fingerprints to be taken without consent if he or she has reasonable grounds for suspecting D's involvement in a criminal offence and that the fingerprints will tend to prove or disprove that involvement.[10] He or she has a similar power to authorise a "non-intimate sample"[11] to be taken without consent.[12] An "intimate sample"[13] may only be taken in such a case if there is *both* authorisation by a superintendent *and* written consent.[14] Provision has now been made to enable samples to be checked against records (particularly significant in the case of DNA samples), for samples of hair (other than pubic hair) to be taken by cutting or plucking, and for a constable to require a charged or convicted person to attend a police station to have a sample taken.[15]

A person held in custody is normally entitled to have someone informed[16]

---

[8] *ibid*. s.54, as amended by the Criminal Justice Act 1988, s.147 and the Criminal Justice and Public Order Act 1994, Sched. 10, para. 55. Clothes and personal effects may only be seized if the CO (a) believes that D may use them use them to cause injury or damage, to interfere with evidence or to assist him or her to escape, (b) has reasonable grounds for believing that they may be evidence relating to an offence: s.54(4). D may be searched at any time in order to ascertain whether he or she has anything which could be used for the purposes set out in (a). The Code of Practice on Detention only permits the CO to order a strip search if he or she considers it necessary to remove an article which D would not be allowed to keep: Code C, Annex A.

[9] *ibid*. s.55, as amended by the 1988 Act, Sched. 15, para. 99. Items may be seized on the same grounds as those set out in s.54(4): s.55(12). In 1994, 77 persons were subjected to an intimate search: H.O. Statistical Bulletin 16/95.

[10] *ibid*. s.61. No such authorisation is necessary if D has been charged with, informed that he or she will be reported for, or convicted of, a "recordable offence" (*i.e.* an offence specified in the National Police Records (Recordable Offences) Regulations 1985 (S.I. 1985 No. 1941): all imprisonable offences and a few others). Fingerprints may be taken at any time with consent. Broadly similar provisions govern the photographing of persons arrested: Code D. 4.

[11] *i.e.* a sample of hair other than pubic hair; a sample taken from or from under a nail; a swab taken from any part of the body including the mouth but not any other body orifice; saliva; or a footprint or similar impression of any part of the body other than a part of the hand: s.65, definitions substituted by the 1994 Act, ss.58, 59(1). The 1994 Act reclassified samples from mouth swabs as non-intimate, in accordance with a recommendation by the RCCJ (Cm. 2263, pp. 14–15). This will assist DNA profiling: see B. Steventon, (1995) 59 Jo. Crim. Law 411.

[12] *ibid*. s.63, as amended by the 1994 Act, s.55: prior to the 1994 Act, this power was confined to suspected serious arrestable offences; the RCCJ (Cm. 2263, pp. 14–16) merely recommended extension of sampling powers to assault and burglary.

[13] *i.e.* a sample of blood, semen or any other tissue fluid, urine or pubic hair, a dental impression, or a swab taken from a person's body orifice other than the mouth: s.65, definitions substituted by the 1994 Act, s.58. The reference to dental impressions was added on the recommendation of the RCCJ (Cm. 2263, p. 15).

[14] *ibid*. s.62, as amended by the 1994 Act, s.54. A court or jury may draw such inferences as appear proper from a refusal without good cause, and a refusal may constitute corroboration: s.62(10). For the destruction of fingerprints and samples after use, see *ibid*. s.64, as amended by the 1988 Act, s.148 and the 1994 Act, s.57 (enabling samples to be retained for statistical purposes).

[15] 1984 Act, s.63A, inserted by the 1994 Act, s.56.

[16] *ibid*. s.56. This replaced the Criminal Law Act 1977, s.62. In addition, the person responsible for the welfare of an arrested child or young person must, if practicable be informed: Children and Young Persons Act 1933, s.34(2)–(11), substituted by the 1988 Act, s.57.

when arrested and to have access on request to legal advice.[17] The latter comprises a right to consult a solicitor[18] privately at any time. Delay in the exercise of these rights can only be authorised by an officer of the rank of superintendent and above in respect of a person in custody for a serious arrestable offence: the officer must have reasonable grounds for believing that exercise of the right will lead to interference with evidence connected with a serious arrestable offence; interference with or injury to other persons; or the alerting of others suspected of such an offence but not yet arrested; or will hinder the recovery of any property obtained as the result of such an offence, or the value of the suspect's proceeds of drug trafficking.[19] In any event, D must be allowed to exercise these rights within 36 hours of the "relevant time".[20]

Code C sets out in some detail requirements as to the physical conditions in which detainees are kept,[21] the handling of any complaints[22] about treatment in custody and medical treatment,[23] the welfare of detainees being the basic responsibility of the custody officer.

Maguire reported that the levels of complaints about treatment by the police in the charge room or cells were said to have fallen dramatically in three of the four areas studied, and that conditions in charge rooms and cells, although not fully satisfactory, had clearly improved. He was surprised by the relaxed and even polite manner in which the procedures were often carried out.[24] Irving and McKenzie noted that the custody officer role and the record-keeping requirements "have, in Brighton at least, eliminated casual infringement of suspects' welfare rights." Moreover, "the system is now so constituted that if a serious

---

[17] *ibid.* s.58. This express legal right replaced the much weaker statement in the Preamble to the Judges Rules that a person under investigation should be able to consult a solicitor privately, even if he or she was in custody, provided no unreasonable delay or hindrance was caused to the investigation or the administration of justice. This was not a legal requirement: in practice few suspects asked to see a solicitor and many requests were refused: see below, pp. 763–764. In *R. v. Chief Constable of South Wales, ex p. Merrick* [1994] 1 W.L.R. 663, D.C., the court recognised a common law right of access to a lawyer of a person on remand in custody at a magistrates' court (s.58 of PACE was not applicable).

[18] This extends to cover a trainee solicitor, a duty solicitor representative or an accredited representative on a register maintained by the Legal Aid Board; other representatives are to be admitted unless an officer of the rank of inspector or above considers that such a visit will hinder the investigation of crime: Code C.6.12. See *R. v. Chief Constable of the Avon and Somerset Constabulary, ex p. Robinson* [1989] 1 W.L.R. 793.

[19] "will" not "might": *R. v. Samuel* [1988] Q.B. 615: see below, p. 686.

[20] 1984 Act, ss.56(2)–(9); 58(5)–(11), as amended by the Drug Trafficking Offences Act 1986, s.32; Code C, Annex B(A). Access may not be delayed on the ground that the solicitor might advise the person not to answer any questions: *ibid.* Part (A).3. Access may only be delayed by reference to the specific circumstances of the case: general fears that solicitors will unwittingly carry out messages etc. will not be sufficient: *R. v. Samuel*, above; *cf. R. v. Alladice* (1988) 87 Cr.App.R. 380.

[21] C. 5, covering, *e.g.* visits, provision of writing materials, and giving an additional right to make one telephone call; C. 8., covering, *e.g.* the heating, cleanliness and ventilation of cells, bedding, toilet facilities, clothing, meals, exercise and hourly visits.

[22] C. 9.1. Complaints must be dealt with by an officer of at least the rank of inspector not connected with the investigation.

[23] C. 9.2–9.6. Special provision is also made for the treatment in custody of the mentally ill, the handicapped, and overseas nationals: C. 1.4, 1.6, 3.6–3.14.

[24] (1988) 28 Brit. J. Criminol. 19, 41.

breach of the rules governing the welfare of prisoners does occur, a serious conspiracy would now be necessary to avoid its detection.[25]

(f) Questioning

Detailed provision is made in Code C governing the questioning of persons in custody. This replaced the non-statutory Judges' Rules and Administrative Directions to the Police, which had previously provided guidance as to the proper conduct of interrogations.[26] A central feature of the position of a person under interrogation (at least in theory) has until recently been the so-called "right to remain silent" or "right of silence".

In general, the police may ask any person such questions as they think appropriate. However, the person asked is normally under no duty to answer.[27] A mere refusal to answer cannot constitute the offence of obstructing a police officer in the exercise of his or her duty.[28] The position at common law was that the jury at trial could not normally be expressly invited to draw any adverse inferences from the silence of the accused before the trial (although they could not be stopped from doing so in the privacy of the jury room).[29] Code C required a suspect normally to be cautioned before questioning and on arrest in the terms: "You do not have to say anything unless you wish to do so, but what you say may be given in evidence", or other words to the same effect.[30]

In practice, only a minority of suspects questioned by the police relied on their right of silence.[31] Indeed, commentators noted the considerable psychological pressures on suspects:

---

[25] B. L. Irving and I. K. McKenzie, *Police Interrogation: the Effects of the Police and Criminal Evidence Act 1994* (1989), pp. 196–198.

[26] The Judges' Rules originated in 1906, with revised versions issued in 1964 and 1978 together with related Administrative Directions from the Home Office. Compliance with the Rules would tend to ensure that a confession was admissible. Breach of a particular Rule or Direction might, but in practice normally did not, render the confession inadmissible.

[27] There are some exceptions where a refusal to give information is itself an offence: *e.g.* the Companies Act 1985, ss.434–436 (investigation of the affairs of a company); Financial Services Act 1986, ss.105 (investigation of investment business) and 177–178 (investigation of insider dealing); Criminal Justice Act 1987, s.2(2) (refusal to answer questions put by the Serious Fraud Office). The last of these was found by the Commission to be contrary to Art.6 of the ECHR: *Saunders v. U.K., The Independent*, September 30, 1994; J. D. Jackson, (1994) 57 M.L.R. 270; S. Nash and M. Furse, [1995] Crim.L.R. 854; below, p. 707. Under s.2(2) the answers cannot be used against the person who gave them unless they change their story; the RCCJ rejected the suggestion that this restriction should be lifted (Cm.2263, pp. 56–57). However, documents produced when required by the Director under section 2(3) of the 1987 Act are not subject to this restriction: *Re Arrows Ltd (No.4)* [1994] 3 All E.R. 814, H.L. Moreover, a refusal to give name and address by a suspect may lead to an arrest under the general arrest conditions—or detention in custody; see above, pp. 667, 674.

[28] If the refusal is combined with positive acts that obstruct the police, such as abuse, threats or misleading answers the position may be different: *e.g. Ricketts v. Cox* (1981) 74 Cr.App.R. 298 (abuse: although the case is doubtful on its facts: see S. H. Bailey, D. J. Harris and B. L. Jones, *Civil Liberties: Cases and Materials* (4th ed., 1995), p. 60).

[29] See J. A. Andrews and M. Hirst, *Criminal Evidence* (1987), paras. 8.10–8.12, 19.86–19.95.

[30] C. 10 (1991 edition).

[31] This was confirmed in the Report of the Royal Commission on Criminal Procedure (Cmnd. 8092, 1981), pp. 83–84, based on research it had commissioned: see P. Softley (Research Study No. 4: confession or admission made by 61 per cent of the 187 suspects in the study); B. Irving (Research Study No. 2: admissions made by 65 per cent of the 60 suspects observed). See also J. Baldwin and M. McConville, Research Study 5 (*Confessions in Crown Court Trials*) and

"To remain silent in a police interview room in the face of determined questioning by an officer with legitimate authority to carry on this activity requires an abnormal exercise of will."[32]

It was a matter of some debate how important confessions or admissions were in establishing the prosecution case. The police certainly regarded interrogation as a central feature of their work, a very high proportion of suspects who made confessions subsequently pleaded guilty, with, *inter alia*, a consequent saving of police time, and only a very small proportion of those who confessed were ultimately acquitted.[33] On the other hand, the research concerning Crown Court cases conducted by Baldwin and McConville for the RCCP indicated that the prosecution's case would only have been fatally weakened had the accused's statement not been adduced in about 20 per cent of cases.[34] Furthermore, false confessions and police misconduct, usually in the form of the inventing of confessions, were identified by JUSTICE as two of the five common threads through most of the allegations of miscarriages of justice made over the years.[35]

In various ways, the arrangements under the 1984 Act were designed to encourage exercise of the right of silence and to improve the reliability of confessions. Thus, a person who asks for legal advice may not be interviewed[36] until he or she has received it unless

(1) exercise of the right of access to such advice can properly be delayed[37]; or

(2) an officer of the rank of superintendent or above has reasonable grounds for believing that

— delay will involve an immediate risk of harm to persons or serious loss of or damage to property;[38]

Courts, Prosecution and Conviction (1981), Chap. 6; J. Vennard, Research Study No. 6. (*Contested Trials in Magistrates' Courts*) and H.O. Research Study No. 71 (1982); M. Zander, [1979] Crim.L.R. 203; B. Mitchell, [1983] Crim.L.R. 5.

[32] Irving, *op. cit.* p. 153. On the psychology of the interrogation process, see B. Irving and L. Hilgendorf, Research Study No. 1 (*Police Interrogation: The Psychological Approach*); B. Irving and I. K. McKenzie, *Police Interrogation: the effect of the Police and Criminal Evidence Act 1984* (1989), pp. 17–25, 235–240; G. H. Gudjonsson, *The Psychology of Interrogations, Confessions and Testimony* (1992).

[33] M. McConville and J. Baldwin, *Courts, Prosecutions, and Convictions* (1981), Chap. 5, esp. pp. 106–114.

[34] *ibid.* Chap. 6. Evaluations of case papers were made by independent assessors. Research concerning contested magistrates' court cases suggested that confession evidence was most influential in cases based on circumstantial rather than direct evidence: Vennard (1980) and (1982).

[35] JUSTICE, *Miscarriages of Justice* (1989), p. 4. The point is reinforced by the presence of unreliable confessions at the heart of many of the high profile miscarriage of justice cases: Walker in C. Walker and K. Starmer (eds.), *Justice in Error* (1993), p. 14, citing the Guildford Four, the Birmingham Six, Judith Ward, Tottenham Three and Cardiff Three cases.

[36] The definition of "interview" has caused particular difficulty (see H. Fenwick, [1993] Crim. L.R. 174; S. Field, (1993) 13 L.S. 254). The current definition is "the questioning of a person regarding his involvement in a criminal offence or offences which ... is required to be carried out under caution" (Code C.11.1A).

[37] Above, pp. 678–679.

[38] It is only on this ground that a person heavily under the influence of drink or drugs can be interviewed at all or an arrested juvenile or a person who is mentally ill or mentally handicapped, a person who has difficulty in understanding English or a hearing disability can be interviewed in a police station in the absence, respectively, of an appropriate adult or of an interpreter: Code C. 11.14, 12.3, 13.2, 13.5, and Annex C. Interviews outside the police station are permitted in limited circumstances: Code C. 11.1. See *D.P.P. v. Blake* [1989] 1 W.L.R. 432 (estranged father

— or awaiting the arrival of the solicitor would cause unreasonable delay
to the process of investigation; or

(3) the solicitor nominated cannot be contacted or refuses to attend (and D
declines to ask for a duty solicitor or the duty solicitor is unavailable); or

(4) D agrees in writing or on tape that the interview may be started at once.[39]
In situations (3) and (4), an officer of the rank of inspector or above must
agree for the interview to proceed.

If D is allowed to consult a solicitor, and the solicitor is available, D must
be allowed to have him or her present during the interview. The solicitor may
only be required to leave the interview if his or her conduct is such that the
investigating officer is unable properly to put questions to the suspect, and then
only on the authority of an officer of the rank of superintendent or above.[40]

Code C prescribes that an accurate record must be made of each interview
with a suspect.[41] Interviews must normally take place at a police station[42] and
the record must normally be made during the course of the interview, which
implies either tape recording the interview or making contemporaneous notes.
Eight hours must normally be allowed in any period of 24 hours free from a
questioning, travel or other interruptions, if possible at night. Interview rooms
must be adequately heated, lit or ventilated. Breaks must normally be made at
recognised meal times and at two-hour intervals. Full details must be recorded
of the periods and of incidents of the interrogation. Written statements under
caution must be taken in accordance with Annex D to the Code.

All interviews by police officers at police stations with a person suspected
of an indictable offence (other than terrorism and espionage offences) must now
be tape-recorded in accordance with the *Code of Practice on Tape Recording*
(PACE Code E).[43] The RCCJ "unreservedly welcome[d] this advance."[44] The
main practical difficulties have concerned the preparation by the police of written summaries.[45] This has proved very time-consuming for the police; on the

---

of juvenile not an "appropriate adult": see Note for Guidance *1C*). On the role of the "appropriate adult", see B. Littlechild, [1995] Crim. L.R. 540.

[39] Code C. 6.6.

[40] Code C. 6.8–6.11. The Notes for Guidance state (*6D*) that a solicitor may challenge an improper
question or the manner in which it is put or advise the client not to reply to particular questions;
cf. ibid. Annex B(A)3, above, p. 679, n. 20.

[41] Code C. 11. The Code (from the 1991 revision) makes it clear that a written record must be kept
of all interviews and other comments by suspects, and, unless impracticable, shown to the suspect.

[42] Following a decision to arrest, the suspect may not be interviewed about the relevant offence
except at a police station unless the consequent delay would be likely to lead to interference
with or harm to evidence or other people or lead to the alerting of other suspects not yet arrested;
here, interviewing must cease once the relevant risk has been averted or the necessary questions
put: Code C.11.1. Research studies for the RCCJ showed that questioning outside the police
station still occurred in a significant proportion of cases (10% in one study, 8% in another); it was,
however, impossible to estimate the frequency of pre-interview "discussions" between police and
suspect, possibly with the use of inducements or threats: Cm.2263, pp. 26–27. On the recommendation of the RCCJ any "significant" statement or silence which occurred before arrival at the
station must be put to the suspect at the start of any interview there: Code C.11.2A.

[43] Police and Criminal Evidence Act 1984 (Tape-recording of Interviews) (No.1) Order 1991 (S.I.
1991 No. 2687) and (No.2) Order 1992 (S.I. 1992 No. 2803). On the protracted process by which
this was achieved, see P. Mirfield, *Confessions* (1985), pp. 19–40 and J. Baldwin, [1985]
Crim.L.R. 695.

[44] Cm. 2263, p. 39.

[45] Originally required by Code E.5.3.

other hand, research found that in less than a third of the cases examined could the summaries be said to provide an accurate and succinct record of the interview.[46] The latest version of Code E merely requires that a written record be made in accordance with national guidelines approved by the Secretary of State.[47] Research is proceeding on the advantages and disadvantages of video-taping of interviews.[48]

In addition to these changes to the regime of police interrogation, there has been an important change in the law governing the admissibility of confessions and admissions in evidence. At common law, the test was whether a confession was "voluntary, in the sense that it has not been obtained from him by fear of prejudice or hope of advantage, exercised or held out by a person in authority, or by oppression."[49] The case law was directed more to the technicalities of this definition than the realities of the reliability of confessions.[50]

The key provisions are now section 76 of PACE, which relates to confessions, and section 78, which concerns the exclusion of all kinds of evidence. The basic test is found in s.76(2):

"(2) If, in any proceedings where the prosecution proposes to give in evidence a confession[51] made by an accused person, it is represented to the court that the confession was or may have been obtained—

(a) by oppression[52] of the person who made it; or

(b) in consequence of anything said or done which was likely, in the circumstances existing at the time, to render unreliable any confession which might be made by him in consequence thereof, the court shall not allow the confession to be given in evidence against him[53] except in so far as the

---

[46] J. Baldwin, *Preparing the Record of Taped Interview* (RCCJ Study No.2, HMSO, 1992). In the view of the Home Office, improvements followed the issue of further guidance in H.O.Circular 21/1992: Cm. 2263, p. 39.

[47] Note for Guidance 5A.

[48] See RCCJ, Cm. 2263, pp. 39–40; J. Baldwin, *Video Taping Police interviews with Suspects: A National Evaluation*, Police Research Series Paper No.1, Home Office, 1992; H.O.Circular 6/1993. Baldwin found that there were additional benefits to video- over audio-taping in some 20 per cent of the cases studied, although showing such recordings to jurors and magistrates might have some prejudicial effect (*e.g.* symptoms of nervousness might be mistaken for symptoms of guilt; a powerful visual impact might distract from what was said). Others are more sceptical: see A. Leonard, (1991) 141 N.L.J. 1512; M. McConville, [1992] Crim.L.R. 532 and (1992) 142 N.L.J. 960 and 1120; *cf.* J. Baldwin, (1991) 141 N.L.J. 1512 and (1992) 142 N.L.J. 1095.

[49] Para. (e) of the preamble to the Judges' Rules, based on *Ibrahim v. R.* [1914] A.C. 599, 609 (basic test for "voluntariness") and see *R. v. Prager* [1972] 1 W.L.R. 260 and *R. v. Hudson* (1980) 72 Cr.App.R. 163 (oppression).

[50] See, generally, RCCP Report (1981), pp. 91–95.

[51] This "includes any statement wholly or partly adverse to the person who made it, whether made to a person in authority or not and whether made in words or otherwise" (s.82(1)); it therefore covers any admission, not just a full confession. However, it seems not to apply to statements which are intended to be exculpatory, but which become damaging at the trial, *e.g.* by then being shown to be evasive or false or inconsistent with the maker's evidence at the trial: *R. v. Sat-Bhambra* (1988) 88 Cr.App.R. 55, criticised by D. J. Birch, [1989] Crim.L.R. 95, 114–116.

[52] This "includes torture, inhuman or degrading treatment, and the use or threat of violence (whether or not amounting to torture)": s.76(8). See below, p. 780.

[53] If a confession is put before the jury and the judge subsequently has doubts about oppression or reliability, it is too late for exclusion under s.76, although the judge could discharge the jury or direct the jury to disregard the statement under the common law: *R. v. Sat-Bhambra*, above.

prosecution proves to the court beyond reasonable doubt that the confession (notwithstanding that it may be true) was not obtained as aforesaid.''[54]

Section 78(1) provides:

"In any proceedings the court may refuse to allow evidence on which the prosecution proposes to rely to be given if it appears to the court that, having regard to all the circumstances including the circumstances in which the evidence was obtained, the admission of the evidence would have such an adverse effect on the fairness of the proceedings that the court ought not to admit it."

This is applicable to confessions as well as other kinds of evidence.[55]

The courts have employed these sections to exclude confession evidence rather more vigorously than had been anticipated.[56]

The first hurdle is that of "oppression," to which the Court of Appeal in *R. v. Fulling*[57] accorded its dictionary meaning as the

"Exercise of authority or power in a burdensome, harsh or wrongful manner; unjust or cruel treatment of subjects, inferiors etc., the imposition of unreasonable or unjust burdens."

The court noted, with apparent approval, a quotation in the dictionary under this definition: "There is not a word in our language which expresses more detestable wickedness than oppression," and continued: "We find it hard to envisage any circumstances in which such oppression would not entail some impropriety on the part of the interrogator."[58] This definition is narrower than the concept of "oppression" at common law,[59] but wider than that suggested by the definition section.[60] To date there are very few decisions[61] in which a confession has been excluded on this ground. It seems clear that breaches of the law or Codes on the part of the police will not necessarily constitute

---

[54] The court may require this to be proved of its own motion: s.76(3). Facts discovered in consequence of an inadmissible confession are themselves admissible, but evidence that they were discovered as a result of the confession is not unless adduced by D: s.76(4)–(6).

[55] *R. v. Mason* [1988] 1 W.L.R. 139. The court's common law powers to exclude evidence were preserved by s.82(3). The ambit of these powers was uncertain, although they clearly included power to exclude evidence whose probative value was outweighed by its prejudicial effect: *R. v. Sang* [1980] A.C. 402. In *Matto v. Wolverhampton Crown Court* [1987] R.T.R. 337, Woolf L.J. indicated that s.78 was if anything wider than the common law (p. 346).

[56] See generally, D. J. Birch, "The Pace Hots Up: Confessions and Confusions under the 1984 Act [1989] Crim.L.R. 95.

[57] [1987] Q.B. 426.

[58] *ibid.* p. 432. See also *R. v. Hughes* [1988] Crim.L.R. 545, C.A. (no police misconduct, so not oppression where, through a misunderstanding, D did not see the Duty Solicitor).

[59] "something which tends to sap, and has sapped, that free will which must exist before a confession is voluntary" (*per* Sachs L.J. in *R. v. Priestly* (1967) 51 Cr.App.R. 1); *cf.* Edmund Davies L.J. in *R. v. Prager* [1972] 1 W.L.R. 260, 266.

[60] See n.52, above. The term "includes" in the definition suggests that it was not intended to be exclusive.

[61] *R.v. Davison* [1988] Crim.L.R. 442 (Central Criminal Court). See further D. J. Birch, Commentary, [1988] Crim.L.R. 444 and [1989] Crim.L.R. 95, 102; *R. v. Ismail* [1990] Crim.L.R. 109 *R. v. Beales* [1991] Crim.L.R. 118 (Norwich Crown Court) (officer deliberately misstated evidence in order to pressurise suspect).

oppression;[62] conversely, it is unlikely that oppression will be found in the absence of such breaches. In *Fulling*[63] itself, D confessed while (so she claimed) in distress following the revelation by the interrogator that her boyfriend had for some three years been having an affair with the woman currently held in the next cell: this was held not to constitute oppression. The most notorious case where oppression has been found is *R. v. Paris, Abdullahi and Miller*[64] (the "Cardiff Three"), where the Court of Appeal (Criminal Division) quashed the convictions of the three appellants for murder. Miller had been interviewed for some 13 hours. Having denied involvement over 300 times, he was finally persuaded to make admissions. Lord Taylor C.J. stated that each member of the court had been "horrified" by what they heard in the tape recording of one interview:

> "Miller was bullied and hectored. The officers ... were not questioning him so much as shouting at him what they wanted him to say. Short of physical violence, it is hard to conceive of a more hostile and intimidating approach by officers to a suspect."[65]

Moreover, Miller's solicitor

> "appears to have been gravely at fault for sitting passively through this travesty of an interview."[66]

Attempts have subsequently been made to address the defects of interviewing techniques illustrated by cases such as this.[67]

The second hurdle is that of "unreliability" and has been invoked more frequently. This has been done where a child has been interviewed in the absence of an "appropriate adult";[68] where there have been doubts about the reliability of a confession by a person of low intelligence;[69] where proper records of the confession have not been kept;[70] where there has been an improper

---

[62] *cf. R. v. Samuel* [1988] Q.B. 615, C.A.; *R. v. Hughes* [1988] Crim. L.R. 545, C.A.

[63] n. 57 above.

[64] (1992) 97 Cr. App. R. 99. *Cf. R. v. Emmerson* (1990) 92 Cr. App. R. 284; *R. v. Heaton* [1993] Crim.L.R. 593; *R. v. L.* [1994] Crim.L.R. 839, where pressure applied (*e.g.* raised voice) did not amount to oppression. Moreover, officers are "not required to give up after the first denial or even after a number of denials": *per* Lord Taylor C.J. in *Paris* at p. 104.

[65] p. 103.

[66] p. 104.

[67] Below, p. 688.

[68] *D.P.P. v. Blake* [1989] 1 W.L.R. 432, C.A.

[69] *R. v. Harvey* [1988] Crim.L.R. 241 (Central Criminal Court): (psychopathic woman of low intelligence may have confessed after hearing her lover confess in order to protect her); *R. v. Everett* [1988] Crim.L.R. 826, C.A. (man of 42 with mental age of 8: judge had taken no account of his mental condition); *R. v. Delaney* (1988) 88 Cr. App. R. 338, C.A. (D educationally subnormal and proper records not kept); *R. v. Raghip, The Times*, December 9, 1991 (psychological evidence of mental condition admissible and court not bound by whether D's I.Q. was above an arbitrary figure for the mentally defective); *R. v. Kenny* [1994] Crim.L.R. 284, C.A. In a number of cases, the confessions of a mentally handicapped suspect have been quashed by the Court of Appeal as unsafe and unsatisfactory, irrespective of any question as to their admissibility: see *R. v. Moss* (1990) 91 Cr. App. R. 371; *R. v. Mackenzie* (1992) 96 Cr.App.R. 98; *R. v. Brine* [1992] Crim.L.R. 122; *R. v. Wood* [1994] Crim.L.R. 222.

[70] *R. v. Doolan* [1988] Crim.L.R. 747, C.A.; *R. v. Delaney*, above; *R v. Waters* [1989] Crim.L.R. 62 (W was also wrongly questioned after charge); *R. v. Chung* (1990) 92 Cr. App. R. 314, C.A.; *R. v. Joseph* [1993] Crim.L.R. 205, C.A. In the absence of a proper record, the prosecution may

inducement;[71] and, in one case, where a drug addict was held in custody for 18 hours without being allowed the prescribed rest periods.[72] In principle, this hurdle is not limited to breaches of the law or of the Codes, but as most of the requirements are designed to promote reliability, breaches of them are a common factor to many of the cases. One limitation is that the unreliability must arise from something "said or done", and this has been held not to include anything said or done by D himself.[73]

By far the largest number of cases in which confessions have been excluded fall under section 78. This has been employed where the police have denied access to a solicitor in breach of D's rights under section 58;[74] where D has not been advised of the right to legal advice;[75] where a proper record of the interview has not been made;[76] where a young person has been interviewed in the absence of an appropriate adult[77] and where there is a breach of a requirement to caution.[78] The Court of Appeal has emphasised that "not every breach or combination of breaches would justify exclusion . . . : they must be significant and substantial."[79] However, "if the police have acted in bad faith, the court will have little difficulty in ruling any confession inadmissible under section 78,

be unable to discharge its onus of proving reliability beyond reasonable doubt: see D. J. Birch, Commentary on *Delaney* [1989] Crim.L.R. 139.

[71] *R. v. Phillips* (1987) Cr.App.R. 18, C.A. (statement that if D confessed, offences could be taken into consideration rather than prosecuted); *R. v. Howden-Simpson* [1991] Crim.L.R. 49 (threat to pursue more than two charges; *R. v. Barry* (1991) 95 Cr.App.R. 384, C.A. (prosecution unable to prove beyond reasonable doubt that statement was not made in response to offer of assistance in obtaining bail).

[72] *R. v. Trussler* [1988] Crim.L.R. 446 (Reading Crown Court).

[73] *R. v. Goldenberg* (1988) 88 Cr.App.R. 285, C.A. (D's argument that his confession was unreliable as his motive was to obtain bail, or credit for helping the police, held not to fall within s.76(2)); *R. v. Crampton* (1990) 92 Cr.App.R. 369 (doubtful whether merely holding an interview with a suspect undergoing withdrawal symptoms is something "done" within the meaning of s.76(2))

[74] *R. v. Samuel* [1988] Q.B. 615, C.A. (confession excluded: "the appellant was denied improperly one of the most important and fundamental rights of a citizen," D would probably not have made incriminating admissions had he had legal advice); *R. v. Parris* (1989) 89 Cr.App.R. 68, C.A. (superintendent's order that D be kept incommunicado under s.56 wrongly assumed to exclude access to a solicitor under s.58); *R. v. Walsh* (1989) 91 Cr.App.R. 161, C.A.; *cf. R. v. Alladice* (1988) 87 Cr.App.R. 380, C.A. (confession not excluded: D was fully aware of his rights and the interviews were found to have been conducted with propriety); *R. v. Dunford* (1990) 91 Cr.App.R. 150, C.A. (D aware of his rights); *R. v. Oliphant* [1992] Crim.L.R. 40, C.A. (presence of solicitor would have added nothing to what O knew of his legal rights); *R. v. Andrews* [1993] Crim.L.R. 447, C.A. (even if solicitor had been present and advised silence, A would not have acted on such advice).

[75] *R. v. Absolam* (1988) 88 Cr.App.R. 332, C.A. (see also n. 76, below); *R. v. Beycan* [1990] Crim.L.R. 185.

[76] Commonly, neither contemporaneous notes nor other notes made after the interview and shown to D: *R. v. Absolam*, above (no caution before questioning, no proper record), *R. v. Keenan* [1990] 2 Q.B. 54, C.A. (officers unaware of Code C); *R. v. Walsh*, above; *R. v. Ismail*, n. 61 above; *R. v. Canale* [1990] 2 All E.R. 187; *R. v. Bryce* [1992] 4 All E.R.567, C.A. (interview after tape recorder switched off at D's request; no fresh caution and no contemporaneous record); *R. v. Cox* (1992) 96 Cr.App.R. 464, C.A. (questioning before arrival at police station held to be "interview" to which Code C.11 requirements applied); *R. v. Joseph* [1993] Crim.L.R. 206, C.A. (interview away from police station after arrest not shown to be necessary; accordingly, no justification for absence of contemporaneous notes); *R. v. Goddard* [1994] Crim.L.R. 46 (*cf. R. v. Matthews, Dennison and Voss* (1989) 91 Cr.App.R. 43; *R. v. Scott* [1991] Crim.L.R. 56 (Code breaches, but confession led to discovery of other evidence)).

[77] *R. v. Weekes* (1992) 97 Cr.App.R. 222, C.A.

[78] *R. v. Absalom*, above; *R. v. Hunt* [1992] Crim.L.R. 582, C.A.; *R. v. Bryce*, above; *R. v. Okafor* [1994] 3 All E.R. 741, C.A. (proviso applied).

[79] *R. v. Keenan*, above; *R. v. Parris*, above; *R. v. Walsh*, above.

if not under section 76."[80] The court has also stated that the main object of section 58 and the Codes is to achieve fairness to a suspect and to the Crown and its officers; that if there were significant and substantial breaches then, prima facie at least, the standards of fairness would not have been met, and to admit evidence thus obtained could not but have an adverse effect on the fairness of proceedings; but that it would still be necessary to consider whether there would be *such* an adverse effect that justice required exclusion of the evidence.[81]

A case which seems to have caused the judges considerable consternation is *R. v. Mason (Carl)*,[82] where D confessed to arson after the interrogators falsely told him, and his solicitor, that they had found at the scene a fragment of a bottle which had contained inflammable liquid and that D's fingerprint was on the fragment. This was described as "reprehensible":

"we hope never again to hear of deceit such as this being practised on an accused person, and more particularly possibly on a solicitor whose duty it is to advise him, unfettered by false information from the police."[83]

There are, however, tricks and stratagems that the police may legitimately use. Thus, in *R. v. Christou and Wright*[84] the Court of Appeal declined to exclude evidence of transactions concerning stolen property conducted at a "shady" jeweller's shop ("Stardust Jewellers") run for three months by under-cover police officers. The transactions were recorded by cameras and sound recording equipment. The court noted that "the trick was not applied to the appellants; they voluntarily applied themselves to the trick",[85] and held that admission of the evidence was not unfair. Furthermore, the requirements of Code C did not apply as the appellants were not being questioned by police officers acting as such. While the undercover officers had asked questions about the areas to be avoided in selling the goods, this was at least partly to maintain their cover. However, where it is established that undercover officers have used their pose in order to circumvent the requirements of the Code, the evidence will be excluded.[86] The line is not necessarily easy to draw.[87]

The courts' willingness to exclude confessions for breaches of the Act or the Codes does much to make their requirements effective.[88] However, it remains

---

[80] *per* Lord Lane C.J. in *R. v. Alladice* (1988) 87 Cr.App.R. 380, 386.

[81] *R. v. Walsh*, above.

[82] [1988] 1 W.L.R. 139.

[83] *ibid.* p. 144.

[84] [1992] 1 Q.B. 979. *Cf. R. v. Smurthwaite, R. v. Gill* [1994] 1 All E.R. 898 where the Court of Appeal declined to exclude the evidence of recordings of conversations in which the defendants solicited police officers posing as contract killers to kill their respective spouses.

[85] *per* Lord Taylor C.J. at p. 989.

[86] *R. v. Bryce* [1992] 4 All E.R. 567 (court excluded answers to questions that were not necessary to maintain cover and were not contemporaneously recorded).

[87] See discussion by G. Robertson Q.C., "Entrapment Evidence" [1994] Crim.L.R. 805. Covertly-recorded conversations to which police officers are not party, but in situations set up by them, have been admitted in a number of cases: see *R. v. Jelen, R. v. Katz* (1989) 90 Cr.App.R. 456; *R. v. Ali (Shaukat), The Times*, February 19, 1991; *R. v. Bailey and Smith* [1993] 3 All E.R. 513 (conversation between B and S placed together in a police cell, with connivance of custody officer, after charge and remand by magistrates); *R. v. Parker* [1995] Crim.L.R. 233, C.A.

[88] See, *e.g.* a general instruction issued by the deputy chief constable of Avon, in part responding to case law, set out in *R. v. Chief Constable of the Avon and Somerset Constabulary, ex p. Robinson* [1989] 2 All E.R. 15, C.A.

the case that the courts have failed to articulate the principles upon which their decisions are based.[89]

Most recently, the debate has focused upon two linked issues. First, there has been the question of the effectiveness of the PACE regime in protecting the interests of suspects under interrogation, and in minimising the risk of false confessions. Secondly, the government has taken the view that the safeguards were now sufficient to justify inroads on the "right of silence", to the extent of permitting the jury or magistrates in certain circumstances to draw adverse inferences from silence.

On the first of these issues, the formal position of the suspect is now considerably enhanced by comparison with the pre-PACE position. However, effectiveness of the formal structure is undermined by such factors as the poor quality of much legal advice in the police station.[90] Furthermore, access to taped records of interviews has demonstrated the very poor quality of much of the interviewing conducted by police officers.[91] In response,

> "the police service, on an official level at least, has been stressing of late that questioning a suspect is only part of the process of investigation – and a decreasingly important part."[92]

A Home Office Circular[93] has laid down Principles of Investigative Interviewing, emphasising, *inter alia*, the points that the role of interviewing should be to obtain accurate and reliable information in order to discover the truth about matters under police investigation, that interviewing should be approached with an open mind, that when questioning anyone a police officer must act fairly and that vulnerable people must be treated with particular consideration at all times. These developments were welcomed by the RCCJ[94] but are at an early stage.[95] The RCCJ (by a majority) rejected proposals that a conviction should never be based solely on an uncorroborated confession, and (unanimously) rejected proposals that no confession should be admissible unless made or confirmed in the presence of a solicitor. However, they did recommend (unanimously) that the judge at trial should warn the jury that great care is needed before convicting on the basis of a confession alone.[96]

A majority of the RCCJ concluded that no change should be made to the right to silence in the police station.[97] They believed that

---

[89] See D. J. Birch, [1989] Crim. L.R. 95. The relevant principles have been helpfully analysed by commentators, and include, apart from reliability and fairness, the protection of rights and the deterrence of police misconduct. See A. Ashworth, "Excluding Evidence as Protecting Rights" [1977] Crim.L.R. 723.

[90] Below, p. 766.

[91] J. Baldwin, "Police Interview Techniques" (1993) 33 Brit. J. Criminol 325. *Cf.* the observations of the Court of Appeal in *R. v. Paris, Abdullahi and Miller*, above, p. 685.

[92] *ibid.*, pp. 325–326.

[93] 22/1992. H.O. Circular 7/1993 announced a new national training package for basic interviewing skills.

[94] Cm. 2263, pp. 11–14.

[95] T. Williamson, "Reflections on Current Police Practice" in D. Morgan and G. M. Stephenson, *Suspicion and Silence* (1994), Chap. 7, noting (at p. 111) that the principles of investigative interviewing were not yet widely understood.,

[96] Cm. 2263, pp. 57–68.

[97] *ibid.*, pp. 50–55, endorsing the position of the RCCP on this point (see Cmnd. 8092, para. 4.50).

"the possibility of an increase in the convictions of the guilty is outweighed by the risk that the extra pressure on suspects to talk in the police station and the adverse inferences invited if they do not may result in more convictions of the innocent."

They recognised the frustration of the police caused by exercise of the right to silence, but thought that experienced professional criminals who wished to remain silent were likely to continue to do so and to justify their position by stating at trial that their solicitors had advised them to say nothing until the allegations against them had been fully disclosed. Research evidence[98] suggested that between 6 per cent and 10 per cent of suspects outside the Metropolitan police district and between 14 per cent and 16 per cent inside exercised their right of silence to some extent;[99] that the right is exercised more often by suspects detained for serious crimes; and that most who are silent in the police station either plead guilty later or are subsequently found guilty. The majority did, however, accept that the position should be changed as regards defence disclosure after disclosure by the prosecution.[1]

Two members of the RCCJ disagreed and thought that it should be possible at trial for adverse inferences to be drawn from silence in the police station; the right to silence offered little or no protection to the vulnerable and safeguards could be strengthened in other ways. The Government, noting the disagreement within the RCCJ, rejected the majority's view and introduced legislation to permit adverse inferences to be drawn at trial from silence in specified circumstances. Changes along these lines had previously been recommended by the Criminal Law Revision Committee[2] and, indeed, adopted as government policy,[3] but then, respectively, dropped in consequence of the storm of opposition aroused[4] and postponed, probably in view of the concern generated by certain widely publicised miscarriages of justice.[5] They were, however, introduced in Northern Ireland.[6]

The Criminal Justice and Public Order Act 1994 now provides that "such inferences as appear proper" may be drawn at various stages of the trial process

---

[98] Summarised by the RCCJ at pp. 53–54.
[99] D. Brown, *The Incidence of Right to Silence in Police Interviews: The Research Evidence Reviewed* (H.O.R.P.U., unpublished).
[1] See below, pp. 756–758. As to silence at trial, see pp. 860–862.
[2] 11th Report, *Evidence (General)* (Cmnd. 4991, 1972). See generally D. J. Galligan, (1988) 41 C.L.P. 69.
[3] H.C.Deb., Vol. 133, May 18, 1988, col. 466 (announcement by the Home Secretary). How the changes were to be effected was the subject of the *Report of the Working Group on the Right of Silence* (Home Office, 1989).
[4] See M. Zander, (1974) 71 L. S. Gaz. 954 and "The Right of Silence in the Police Station and the Caution" in P. Glazebrook (ed.), *Reshaping the Criminal Law* (1978), pp. 344–363.
[5] The issue was included in the terms of reference of the RCCJ. There was also considerable opposition to the Working Group's proposals: see A. A. S. Zuckerman, "Trial by Unfair Means" [1989] Crim.L.R.855; J. Wood and A. Crawford, *The Right to Silence: The case for retention* (1989); S. Greer (1990) 53 M.L.R.709; B. Irving and I. McKenzie, (1990) 1 Jo. of Forensic Psychiatry 167. For arguments in favour of change, see G. Williams, [1988] Crim.L.R.97. For further contributions to the general debate see S. Greer and R, Morgan (eds.), *The Right of Silence Debate* (1990); S. M. Easton, *The Right to Silence* (1991); R. Leng, *The Right to Silence in Police Interrogation: A study of some of the issues underlying the debate* (RCCJ Research Study No. 10, HMSO, 1993); D. Morgan and G. Stephenson, *Suspicion and Silence* (1994).
[6] Criminal Evidence (Northern Ireland) Order 1988 (S.I. 1988 No.987). See J. D. Jackson, (1989) 40 N.I.L.Q. 105, [1991] Crim.L.R. 404, (1993) 44 N.I.L.Q. 103 and [1995] Crim.L.R. 587.

by a court or jury (and in some circumstances, a judge) in four situations.[7] By
section 34(1), the first is

> "where, in any proceedings against a person for an offence, evidence is
> given that the accused –
> (a) at any time before he was charged with the offence, on being ques-
>   tioned under caution by a constable trying to discover whether or by
>   whom the offence had been committed, failed to mention any fact
>   relied on in his defence in those proceedings; or
> (b) on being charged with the offence or officially informed that he might
>   be prosecuted for it, failed to mention any such fact,
> being a fact which in the circumstances existing at the time the accused
> could reasonably have been expected to mention when so questioned,
> charged or informed. . . .

Section 36 enables adverse inferences to be drawn from the failure of an accused
to account for objects, substances or marks found on arrest on him or her or
his or her clothing or footwear[8] or in his possession or in any place in which
he or she is at the time of arrest. The arresting or investigating officer must
reasonably believe that the object etc. may be attributed to the suspect's participation in the commission of an offence specified by the officer, who must inform
the suspect that he or she so believes. The constable must also inform the suspect
in ordinary language of the effect of the section should he or she fail to comply
with the constable's request. Similar provisions apply to an accused's failure to
account for his or her presence at a place at or about the time the offence for
which he or she was arrested is alleged to have been committed (section 37).
Finally, inferences may now be drawn from silence at trial (section 35[9]).
    In consequence of the introduction of section 34, the caution has been changed
to the following[10]:

> "You do not have to say anything. But it may harm your defence if you
> do not mention when questioned something which you later rely on in
> court. Anything you do say may be given in evidence."

It will be noted that while this caution has to be administered (*inter alia*) on
arrest,[11] the questioning of a suspect should normally only take place in a police
station, where the safeguards of access to legal advice and recording requirements apply.[12]
    The new arrangements came into effect on April 10, 1995, and it is impossible
as yet to gauge their effect. The introduction does, however, seem premature,
given the continuing concerns over the effectiveness of safeguards for suspects

---

[7] See I. Dennis, [1995] Crim.L.R. 4, 9–18; R. Pattenden, [1995] Crim.L.R. 602; P. Mirfield, [1995]
Crim.L.R. 612. On implications for legal advisers, see H. Fenwick, [1995] Crim.L.R. 132 and
D. Roberts, [1995] Crim.L.R. 483.
[8] Or the condition of the clothing or footwear.
[9] See below, pp. 860–862.
[10] PACE Code C.10.4. The special warnings under sections 36 and 37 are dealt with in Code
C.10.5A-5C.
[11] Code C.10.3.
[12] See above, pp. 681–683.

at the police station[13] and the lack of research evidence to support police claims that exercise of the right to silence in a significant number of cases seriously impedes the investigation of offences. Also unfortunate is the lack of reference to the operation of similar provisions in Northern Ireland[14] and the introduction of changes notwithstanding the possibility that they may, at least in some circumstances, infringe the European Convention on Human Rights and the International Covenant on Civil and Political Rights.[15] The Government maintains that there is no violation as the right of silence is not itself withdrawn, there being no sanction attached directly to its exercise.[16]

(g) Identification evidence

Identification evidence is recognised as one of the kinds of evidence that must be treated with especial caution:

"Identification, whether by sight or hearing, is evidence which can seem immensely convincing and compelling to a jury but can also, notoriously, be mistaken."[17]

There are, accordingly, special arrangements governing the gathering of such evidence and how it is dealt with at the trial.[18]

The former is now governed by the *Code of Practice for the Identification of Persons by Police Officers* (Code D) made under PACE. The methods for establishing identifications include, in order of preference, formal identification parades, where the suspect is seen by the witness with others of similar appearance; group identifications, where he or she is simply viewed in an informal group of people, commonly in a public place; video film identifications, where he or she is filmed with others of similar appearance; and confrontations, where the suspect alone is confronted by the witness. These are arranged by an "identification officer", not involved in the investigation and at least of the rank of inspector. A parade must be held whenever a suspect disputes an identification

---

[13] Below, p. 766.

[14] See JUSTICE, *The Right of Silence Debate: The Northern Ireland Experience* (1994). The details of the Northern Ireland provisions have been amended to bring them into line with sections 34 to 38 of the 1994 Act.

[15] In *Funke v. France* (A256-A, Judgment of 25 February 1993), the European Court of Human Rights found the right of silence to be embodied in the Art.6 right to a fair trial, and to have been violated by convictions for refusing to disclose bank statements and other documents to customs officials. In *John Murray v. U.K., The Times*, February 9, 1996, the court accepted that the right to remain silent under police questioning and the privilege against self-incrimination were generally recognised international standards which lay at the heart of the notion of a fair procedure under Art. 6. However, the drawing of adverse inferences from the defendant's refusal, at arrest, during police questioning and at trial to explain his presence at a house where an IRA informer had been held captive was held not to infringe Art. 6; these were reasonable inferences to draw in all circumstances of the case.

[16] See *Fourth Periodic Report by the U.K. to the Human Right Committee under Article 40 of the ICCPR* (1994), paras.320–328. The Court of Appeal has stated that "the right of silence remains" and that the burden of proof has not been "watered down", in the course of rejecting an argument that section 35 should only be relied upon in exceptional circumstances: *R. v. Cowan* [1995] 3 W.L.R. 818, C.A.

[17] JUSTICE Report on *Miscarriages of Justice* (1989), p. 10. Well-known cases of miscarriages of justice based on identification evidence include those of Laslo Virag and Luke Dougherty, which led to the Devlin Committee on *Evidence of Identification in Criminal Case* (1975–76 H.C. 338).

[18] On the latter, see below, p. 884.

and consents to a parade, unless the circumstances justifying a group or video identification are present. A parade may also be held if the investigating officer considers that it would be useful and the suspect consents. Furthermore, a parade need not be held if the identification officer considers that, whether by reason of the suspect's unusual appearance or otherwise, it would not be practicable to assemble sufficient people who resemble him or her to make it fair. Group identifications may take place with the suspect's consent, or covertly where he or she refuses to co-operate with a parade or group identification or has failed to attend. A group identification may also be arranged if the investigating officer considers, whether because of the witness's fear or otherwise, that that would be more satisfactory than a parade. Video identifications are permitted if the investigating officer considers that would be more satisfactory. Confrontations do not require the suspect's consent but may only take place if a parade or group or video identification is impracticable, for example as a result of the suspect's non-co-operation.[19] A video or colour photograph must be taken of each parade or group identification.[20]

The courts seem willing to exclude identification evidence under section 78 of PACE where the identification officer has concluded too readily that a parade is impracticable[21] or where there have been other breaches of Code D.[22]

3. Forensic Evidence

In a significant minority of cases, the police seek the assistance of forensic scientists.[23] Their work may give rise to a wide range of admissible prosecution evidence,[24] of which DNA profiling, the analysis of blood specimens and drugs,

---

[19] Code D2 and Annexes A (parades and group identifications), B (video identifications) and C (confrontations). Identification from photographs, photofits etc. is confined where possible to the process of investigation: see Annex D. JUSTICE (above) were informed that formal parades are usually held in about 80 per cent. of cases where such evidence was possible (p. 10).

[20] This requirement was introduced into the 1995 version of Code D on the recommendation of the RCCJ (Cm. 2263, p. 11). Other changes introduced in line with RCCJ recommendations were that a record must be made of the description of the suspect as first given by a potential witness, before the witness takes part in a parade etc., and a copy given to the suspect's solicitor before any parade etc. (Code D.2.0). The RCCJ also encouraged that the establishment of purpose-built suites be extended to all major urban areas.

[21] *R. v. Gaynor* [1988] Crim.L.R. 242 (Liverpool Crown Court); *R. v. Brittain and Richards* [1989] Crim.L.R. 144 (Leeds Crown Court); *R. v. Nagah* (1990) 92 Cr. App. R. 344, C.A. (street identification inadmissible as parade was practicable).

[22] *R. v. Gall* (1989) 90 Cr.App.R. 64, C.A. (investigating officer took part in the conduct of a parade); *R. v. Conway* (1990) 91 Cr.App.R. 143, C.A. (parade not held although requested: no good reason); *Powell v. D.P.P.* [1992] R.T.R. 270, D.C.; *R. v. Finley* [1993] Crim.L.R. 50, C.A.; *R. v. Hope, Limburn and Bleasdale* [1994] Crim.L.R. 118, C.A.; *R. v. Allen* [1995] Crim.L.R. 643, C.A.; *cf. R. v. Quinn* [1990] Crim.L.R. 581 (evidence of identification of Q while on trial in a Dublin court admitted); *R v. Grannell* (1989) 90 Cr.App.R. 149 (breach of Code D, but no unfairness).

[23] The literature is rapidly expanding. See, *e.g.*, C. Jones, *Expert Witnesses* (1994); P. Roberts, "Science in the Criminal Process" (1994) 14 O.J.L.S. 469, "Forensic Science Evidence after Runciman" [1994] Crim.L.R.780 and "What Price a Free Market in Forensic Science Services" (1996) 36 Brit.J.Criminol. 37; RCCJ (Cm. 2263), Chap. 9 and RCCJ Research Studies Nos.6 (G. Robertson, *The role of police surgeons*), 9 (B. Steventon, *The ability to challenge DNA evidence*), 11 (P. Roberts and C. Willmore, *The role of forensic science evidence in criminal proceedings*); C. Walker and R. Stockdale, "Forensic Evidence and Terrorist Trials in the UK" [1995] C.L.J. 69.

[24] See below, p. 751–756, 873–874.

and tests for the presence of explosives are merely some of the best-known illustrations. Police forces tend to rely on the laboratories of the Forensic Science Service (established as a "Next Steps" executive agency of the Home Office in 1991), the Metropolitan Police Forensic Science Laboratory, the Laboratory of the Government Chemist (an executive agency of the Department of Trade and Industry, whose forensic science work mainly involves illicit drugs and documents suspected of being forged) and the Defence Research Agency (an executive agency of the Ministry of Defence which covers forensic investigation for the illegal use of explosives). The FSS and MPFSL have been merged with effect from April 1, 1996. Police authorities may also run their own in-house laboratories for more routine work and employ Scenes of Crime Officers or (civilian) Examiners (SOCOs) who examine scenes of crime for traces that can be sent for forensic examination. Defence lawyers tend to use experts in private practice, who normally act as "defence examiners". They

> "advise defence lawyers about the strength of prosecution evidence, suggest alternative avenues for scientific investigation or alternative interpretations of prosecution data and results, and assist generally in the development of case management strategies."[25]

The defence increasingly have had access to the services of the FSS and other public sector laboratories.

Errors in the performance and evaluation of forensic tests and non-disclosure of forensic evidence were a feature of a number of the high profile miscarriage of justice cases.[26] This has led to a reconsideration of the arrangements for quality control within the FSS and the larger public sector laboratories[27] and the extension of disclosure requirements.[28] Furthermore, the RCCJ recommended that a Forensic Science Advisory Council should be set up to report to the Home Secretary on the performance of both public sector and private sector laboratories and experts.[29] Its responsibilities would include continuing review of the effectiveness of the organisation of the public sector laboratories, the devising of arrangements for external inspection and assessment of both public and private sector laboratories and oversight of the developments of a code of practice. At the time of writing (April 1996) no decision had been announced on this proposal. The RCCJ endorsed developments already under way for the public sector laboratories to introduce charges on a commercial basis, but relied on the proposed Council to "ensure that undue competitiveness does not lead to a diminution in standards."[30] Finally, the RCCJ proposed that there should be a pre-trial discussion between the two sides in all cases in which scientific evidence is being lead; the defence should give advance notice of any grounds on which they intend to dispute prosecution expert evidence; prosecution and defence expert witnesses should produce a written account of what is agreed and what is in dispute, with a preparatory

---

[25] P. Roberts, (1994) 14 O.J.L.S. 469, 489.
[26] See C. Jones, *Expert Witnesses* (1994), Chap. 10 and Walker and Stockdale, *op. cit.*; the cases of the Birmingham Six, Judith Ward and the Maguire Seven.
[27] P. Roberts (1996) 36 Brit.J.Criminol. 37, 52.
[28] RCCJ (Cm. 2263), pp. 149–150.
[29] *ibid.*, pp. 150–151.
[30] *ibid.*, p. 148. For a powerful argument that a market approach to forensic science services is flawed in principle, see P. Roberts, (1996) 36 Brit.J.Criminol. 37.

hearing held in cases of substantial disagreement.[31] Some of these points are subsumed in the general proposals for defence disclosure and preparatory hearings.[32]

B. THE RESPONSIBILITY FOR INSTITUTING PROSECUTIONS[33]

The historical development of the English prosecution process placed emphasis upon the role of the private individual as prosecutor. As the police forces grew so they began to assume the responsibility for bringing prosecutions (but only exercising individual rather than statutory rights); and practice diverged from that in Scotland where a public prosecutor (the procurator fiscal) became established and the right of private prosecution diminished. In fact, for many years the theory of the private prosecution in England no longer matched the reality of the situation, not only because of the powers of the Director of Public Prosecutions,[34] but also because of restrictions placed by statute upon private prosecutions for many offences.[35] In practice, the majority of prosecutions were brought by the police and almost all the balance by other public agencies. Truly private prosecutions were highly unusual.[36] Furthermore, from 1986 the conduct of most classes of criminal proceedings has been taken over by the Crown Prosecution Service established by the Prosecution of Offences 1985. The fiction that the prosecution is acting in a private capacity is here not maintained.

1. PROSECUTION ARRANGEMENTS BEFORE THE PROSECUTION OF OFFENCES ACT 1985

(a) Police Prosecutions

Prior to the establishment of the Crown Prosecution Service, the responsibility of deciding whether or not to prosecute suspects and the conduct of proceedings for less serious offences were regarded as two of the main functions of the police, as aspects of their general duty to enforce the law.[37]

The procedure adopted varied according to the practice of the force concerned but the initial steps were normally taken in the name of the officer who had

---

[31] For discussion, see P. Roberts, [1994] Crim.L.R. 780, 785–788.

[32] See below, pp. 756–760.

[33] See generally, J. Sigler, "Public Prosecution in England and Wales" [1974] Crim. L.R. 642; *The Royal Commission on Criminal Procedure* (Cmnd. 8092, 1980); JUSTICE, *The Prosecution Process in England and Wales* (1970); P. Devlin, *The Criminal Prosecution in England* (1960); M. McConville, "Prosecuting Criminal Cases in England and Wales: Reflections of an inquisitorial adversary" (1984) VI(1) Liverpool L.R. 15; K. de Gama, "Police Powers and Public Prosecutions: Winning by Appearing To Lose?" (1988) 6 Int. J. Sociology of Law 339.

[34] See below, pp. 695–696.

[35] By requiring the consent of the D.P.P., the Attorney-General, a High Court judge or some other authority, to the proposed prosecution. See below, pp. 695, 696.

[36] See further, below, pp. 708–709.

[37] Final Report of the Royal Commission on the Police (Cmnd. 1782, 1962), para. 59.

decided on the prosecution.[38] If there was any legal difficulty, for example in deciding the appropriate charge or assessing the weight of the evidence on a particular charge, the police were able to take advice either from a prosecuting solicitors' department established by the police authority or from a private firm employed for that purpose. The growth of prosecuting solicitors' departments had a significant effect on police prosecutions, but that effect was haphazard since the constitution, size and operation of such departments was entirely a matter for local decision and varied from force to force.

By the 1980s, 31 of the 43 police forces in England and Wales were able to draw on the expertise of their own prosecuting solicitors' department for legal advice and for representation in court.[39] It was clear that a prosecuting solicitor acted on instructions from the police and was merely an adviser in a solicitor/client relationship, but the line of authority, the budgetary controls, the amount of advocacy undertaken and the degree of "independence" enjoyed varied greatly from force to force.[40]

If the police *did* decide on a prosecution it was quite possible for a police officer to present the case in the magistrates' court. The Royal Commission on the Police suggested that it was undesirable for police officers to act as prosecutors save in minor cases.[41] In practice, the police could not conduct cases in the Crown Court and only prosecuted in the magistrates' court in straightforward cases.[42] In some areas, *all* prosecutions were undertaken by prosecuting solicitors. In serious cases, a measure of control was exerted by the Director of Public Prosecutions and the Law Officers.

(b) The Director of Public Prosecutions and the Law Officers[43]

The basic functions of the D.P.P. have always included those of undertaking prosecutions of particular importance or difficulty and advising chief officers of police. Indeed, prior to the establishment of the C.P.S. and the D.P.P.'s new role as head of the service, these were his main functions. Regulations 6 and 7 of the Prosecution of Offences Regulations 1978 (which are still in force[44]) required cases in a number of classes to be referred to the D.P.P. These gave the D.P.P. an important co-ordinating function in these cases, which cases tended to be of a serious or sensitive nature. In addition, two further devices strengthened his position.

First, many statutes provided that prosecutions could only be brought in respect of certain offences with the consent of the D.P.P. This had become a popular provision where the offence was controversial, or the statutory provision slightly ambiguous, or public policy considerations were involved, or mitigating

---

[38] Sometimes in the name of the Chief Constable, more often in the name of the head of the appropriate division or subdivision.

[39] The Metropolitan Police and the City of London force had their own special arrangements, leaving 10 forces to rely on private practitioners to provide the necessary service. See *Royal Commission on Criminal Procedure, The Investigation and Prosecution of Criminal Offences in England and Wales: The Law and Procedure* (hereafter RCCP I) (Cmnd. 8092–1, 1980), Appendix 22.

[40] An analysis of the system is to be found in *The Prosecution System, Survey of Prosecuting Solicitors, Departments*, RCCP Research Study No. 11 (HMSO, 1980).

[41] Cmnd. 1782, para. 381.

[42] RCCP I, paras.144–145.

[43] For a general description see above pp. 19–22.

[44] See below, p. 703.

factors might be present or where vexatious or trivial private prosecutions might be brought.[45]

Secondly, there was a general power vested in the D.P.P. by sections 2 and 4 of the 1979 Act to take over criminal proceedings and then to deal with them as he wished, including the offering of no evidence if he so chose. This power was equally applicable to private prosecutions and was used, for example, to discontinue a private prosecution brought against a person to whom the D.P.P. had given a promise of immunity from proceedings in return for giving evidence for the prosecution at another trial.[46] In that case it was held that the court had no power to interfere with the Director's exercise of discretion in how he conducted proceedings taken over by him.

All these powers taken together gave the D.P.P. a significant amount of control over prosecution policy in relation to serious criminal offences.

The two important provisions relating to the Attorney-General were his power to enter a *nolle prosequi* in proceedings on indictment[47] and the requirement of his consent to the prosecution of certain offences.[48] (These remain after the Prosecution of Offences Act 1985.)

The grant of a *nolle prosequi* by the Attorney-General stops proceedings on indictment immediately and is entered on the court record. It does not actually amount to an acquittal, so the accused may be indicted again on the same charge,[49] but another *nolle prosequi* may then be granted. A request for such a grant may be made by any person and the exercise of the power is equivalent to the D.P.P. taking over proceedings and offering no evidence or a prosecutor offering no evidence, except that in both the latter cases the effect would formally be an acquittal.

The requirement of consent by the Attorney-General to prosecution was to be found in 39[50] statutes at the time of the Royal Commission on Criminal Procedure and included in that category were offences under the Public Order Act 1936,[51] the Hijacking Act 1971 and the Suppression of Terrorism Act 1978. These indicated that the primary responsibility of the Attorney-General in deciding whether to give consent was to weigh factors of national and public significance, conscious that he was the Minister answerable in Parliament for all matters connected with the conduct of criminal proceedings. However, it was clearly established that the Attorney-General's decision should be made on quasi-judicial and not on political grounds.[52]

---

[45] See the evidence of the D.P.P. to the RCCP, part of which is reproduced at RCCP I, para. 159.

[46] *Turner v. D.P.P.* (1978) 68 Cr. App.R. 70. See also statements about the circumstances in which it is proper to grant such immunity in *R. v. Turner* (1975) 61 Cr.App.R. 67 (no relation). The matter was further considered in *Raymond v. Att.-Gen.* [1982] Q.B. 839, where the Court of Appeal confirmed that the power to "conduct" proceedings under s.4 included the power to discontinue them, pointing out that control was exercised over the D.P.P. by the Attorney-General who was, in turn, accountable to Parliament.

[47] This is a common law power not subject to any control by the courts: *R. v. Comptroller of Patents* [1899] 1 Q.B. 909.

[48] *cf.* the powers of the D.P.P. referred to earlier.

[49] Archbold, *Criminal Pleading, Evidence and Practice* (43rd ed.), para. 1–122, relying on *Goddard v. Smith* (1704) 3 Salk. 245.

[50] D.P.P.'s evidence to the RCCP, Appendix 11.

[51] Including that created by the Race Relations Act 1976, of incitement to racial hatred, then s.5A of the 1936 Act.

[52] Statement by the Prime Minister to the House of Commons, February 16, 1959 (H.C. Deb., Vol. 600, col. 31), part of which is cited in RCCP I, para. 164. Questions can be asked in the House and, in one celebrated case, led to the downfall of the first Labour Government following the

(c) Criticisms

These arrangements were subjected to close scrutiny, first by JUSTICE in 1970, and then by the Royal Commission on Criminal Procedure in 1982. JUSTICE[53] argued that the responsibility for prosecutions in all but trivial cases should be taken out of the hands of the police and given to a national prosecuting authority. In support of this recommendation it was said that:

(a) a police officer might convince himself of the guilt of a suspect and become psychologically committed to a prosecution;

(b) public policy and the circumstances of the individual were relevant considerations in the decision to prosecute;

(c) the English system was unique in Europe in allowing the whole process from interrogation to prosecution to be effectively under the control of the police in the majority of cases;

(d) investigators found it difficult to achieve the necessary detachment in taking what is essentially a "judicial-type" decision whether or not to prosecute;

(e) police involvement might influence the conduct of the prosecution in deciding appropriate charges or otherwise "bargaining" with a suspect, or in putting pressure on counsel at trial to take a particular line;

(f) police officers were not trained as lawyers or advocates and those tasks involving the expertise of lawyers or advocates should not be undertaken by the police.

The RCCP's approach was to analyse and establish the standards for judging the adequacy of a prosecution system; to measure the existing system by those standards; and then to recommend any changes necessary to achieve the standards. Put briefly, the RCCP decided that the system should be judged on fairness, openness and accountability, and efficiency.

"Is the system fair; first in the sense that it brings to trial only those against whom there is an adequate and properly prepared case and who it is in the public interest should be prosecuted (that is, tried by a court) rather than dealt with in another way (by cautioning, for example), and secondly in that it does not display arbitrary and inexplicable differences in the way that individual cases or classes of case are treated locally or nationally? Is it open and accountable in the sense that those who make the decisions to prosecute or not can be called publicly to explain and justify their policies and actions as far as that is consistent with protecting the interests of suspects and accused? Is it efficient in the sense that it achieves the objectives that are set for it with the minimum use of resources and the minimum

---

withdrawal of a prosecution for incitement to mutiny against J.R. Campbell, editor of a Communist publication, *Workers Weekly*: see J.Ll.J. Edwards, *The Law Officers of the Crown* (1964), Chap. 11 and *The Attorney-General, Politics and the Public Interest* (1984), pp. 310–318; F. H. Newark, (1969) 20 N.I.L.Q. 19; N. D. Siederer, (1974) 9 *Jo. of Contemporary History* 143; J. F. Naylor, *A Man and an Institution* (1984), pp. 140–149, 156–157 (biography of Sir Maurice Hankey). The independent role of the Attorney-General is fully considered in the two works by Edwards.

[53] *The Prosecution Process in England and Wales* (1970). See also, J. Sigler, [1974] Crim. L.R. 642; A. S. Bowley, [1975] Crim. L.R. 442.

delay? Each of these standards makes its own contribution to what we see as being the single overriding test of a successful system. Is it of a kind to have and does it in fact have the confidence of the public it serves?''[54]

In considering the question of *fairness* in existing arrangements the Commission concentrated on the issues of whether the ''right'' people were brought to trial, and in a way which demonstrated ''consistency'' in policy and practice in the various police forces.

On the former issue, the RCCP discussed the extent to which it was possible or desirable to separate the role of the investigator from that of lawyer in the prosecution process. In an analysis of the respective functions of the United States District Attorney, the Scottish Procurator Fiscal and the Canadian Crown Counsel, the RCCP considered that the two roles there had not been entirely separated.[55] The District Attorney used his staff in an investigative capacity both to improve the quality of cases presented by the police and to deal with major fraud, corruption and ''white-collar'' crime.[56] The Procurator Fiscal was directly involved in the investigation of violent deaths and in the most serious cases would see and take statements from police and witnesses before deciding whether to prosecute.[57] By contrast, in the provinces of British Columbia and Ontario, Crown Counsel were responsible entirely for the conduct of prosecutions *once the police had decided to bring a person to trial*. Crown Counsel had no investigative function, but the police retained a part of the lawyer's function in the initial decision to prosecute. The RCCP concluded that if any of these systems were more effective in putting the ''right'' people on trial it was not because they had succeeded in separating the functions of investigator and prosecutor. On the same issue the RCCP considered the evidence of acquittal statistics which indicated that a high proportion of acquittals ordered and directed by the judge at the Crown Court were the result of insufficient prosecution evidence.[58] The failure of prosecution witnesses at trial accounted for many of these cases, but there were clearly some cases where it should have been foreseen that the evidence would be inadequate. The lack of fairness demonstrated by such cases was only mitigated by their relative infrequency.[59]

Statistics contained in the Report showed that there was, indeed, a degree of inconsistency in prosecution policy and practice,[60] and that there was no effective machinery for achieving conformity.[61] Although this created unfairness the

---

[54] RCCP Rep., para. 6.8.

[55] *ibid.*, paras.6.30.–6.39

[56] See further, J. Sigler, *An Introduction to the Legal System* (1968), p. 79 *et seq.*; H. Mueller, ''The Position of the Criminal Defendant in the U.S.A.'' in J. A. Coutts (ed.), *The Accused* (1966), at pp. 102–104.

[57] The role and powers of the Procurator Fiscal are described in *Criminal Procedure in Scotland and France* (HMSO Edinburgh, 1975), and by Lord Kilbrandon, ''Scotland: Pre-Trial Procedure,'' in *The Accused, op cit.* See also S. R. Moody and J. Tombs, *Prosecution in the Public Interest* (1982).

[58] RCCP Rep., para. 6.19. See also M. McConville and J. Baldwin, *Courts Prosecution and Conviction* (1981).

[59] The RCCP Report suggested that one-fifth of directed acquittals might fall into this category. However, directed acquittals only formed 7 per cent, of all cases disposed of by the Crown Court and the Crown Court only dealt with approximately 15 per cent. of all indictable offences. See RCCP Rep., para. 6.22.

[60] *ibid.* para. 6.40. Inconsistency was primarily evident in the statistics relating to the use of the caution for both adults and juveniles.

[61] See above, p. 695.

RCCP concluded that it was not the main focus of public concern and that the solution, the strengthening of central control or a national prosecution service, could find better justification on the ground of openness and accountability than on the ground of improved fairness.

The question of *accountability* was complicated because of the implications for the defendant of any public scrutiny of the exercise of the discretion to prosecute. Questioning the decision of the prosecutor after an acquittal might amount to a "retrial" if the prosecutor attempted to defend the decision. If the prosecutor was required to defend a decision not to institute proceedings, unwarranted doubts might be cast on the suspect without the suspect having an opportunity to defend him- or herself.

However, the RCCP considered that those problems could be overcome by generalising the issue involved, and that accountability in the "explanatory and co-operative mode"[62] to a local supervisory authority was desirable. Additionally, a prosecution agency would clearly be accountable to the body providing it with funds for its economic efficiency and organisation. There was an obligation on the Attorney-General to answer in Parliament questions on the exercise of discretion, and the courts had some limited degree of control, but there was no real local supervision.[63]

The *efficiency* of a prosecuting system was not to be judged solely in terms of the efficient use of resources. Delays in preparation causing adjournments and inadequate preparation causing the collapse of cases certainly cost money, but could also cause injustice, inconvenience and frustration to all those concerned in the process.

At the same time, the concept of efficiency was notoriously difficult to use in relation to the criminal justice system; objectives were hard to define in precise terms and it was accordingly difficult to measure whether they had been achieved. The best the RCCP could propose was uniformity in prosecution arrangements, which would make possible the detection of inefficiencies in the system, and assist in achieving nationally such consistency in the application of general prosecution policies as was thought desirable.[64]

The RCCP concluded that ". . . there is a case for some change. Indeed, not a single witness who has addressed this part of our terms of reference in detail has argued that there should be absolutely no change made. The areas of debate are on the direction and extent of change.[65]

Obviously impressed with the Canadian experience, the RCCP recommended that the police should retain sole responsibility for the investigation of offences and the initial decision whether to prosecute, and that thereafter the prosecutor should take over the conduct of the case and decide whether to proceed as charged, or modify or withdraw the charges.[66] The major advantage of this proposal appeared to be that it indicated a reasonably clear demarcation of function,

---

[62] The Commission adopted terminology coined by G. Marshall, "Police Accountability Revisited" in Butler and Halsay (eds), *Policy and Politics* (1978). The "explanatory and co-operative mode" is described as a type of accountability in which the supervisory authority has no power to bind or to reverse executive decisions, but where a means is provided for challenge, for the requirement of reasoned explanation and the communication of advice and recommendation. RCCP Rep., para. 6.50.

[63] See pp. 695–696 above for the then current controls.

[64] RCCP Rep., para. 6.64.

[65] *ibid.*, para. 6.65.

[66] *ibid.*, Rep., paras. 7.5. *et seq.*

but it also would serve to maintain the primary responsibility of the police for investigation whilst enhancing the independent status of the prosecutor. The RCCP proposed that the prosecutor should be designated "Crown prosecutor" and that the organisation should be locally based drawing heavily upon the existing prosecuting solicitors' departments. Obviously, every police force would need to have such a department (which would then also offer an advice service to the police) and, consistent with the RCCP'S declared standards, a local supervisory authority would need to be designated for the purposes of accountability. After examining various possibilities,[67] a majority of the RCCP favoured the development of existing police authorities into police and prosecutions authorities with additional powers to supervise the functioning of the prosecution service. Central involvement in the prosecution process should continue in the form of the D.P.P.; ministerial responsibility for the new prosecution service should rest either with the Home Secretary or the Attorney-General, and the Minister should be empowered to set national standards for staffing and performance.[68]

These proposals had a mixed reception,[69] but were broadly accepted by the government, with the exception that the new prosecution service was to be nationally and not locally based.[70] Accountability of a prosecutor to a local body would not be "a proper or efficient arrangement." In matters of prosecution policy the service should be required to conform to guidance from the Attorney-General and not from local authorities; and "to give local authorities responsibility for finance and manpower alone would be to divorce control over policy from control over resources, which would not be conducive to sensible and efficient management of the new service."[71]

2. PROSECUTION ARRANGEMENTS UNDER THE PROSECUTION OF OFFENCES ACT 1985[72]

(a) The Crown Prosecution Service

The 1985 Act established the Crown Prosecution Service. It is headed by the D.P.P., who is now appointed by the Attorney-General and not the Home Secretary.[73] The D.P.P. and the headquarters staff continue to be based in London. England and Wales are divided by the D.P.P. into Areas (in practice based on police areas or combinations of areas).[74] Staff are appointed by the D.P.P. Any

---

[67] *ibid.* paras. 7.21 *et seq.*

[68] *ibid.* para. 7.60.

[69] See generally, A. F. Wilcox, [1981] Crim. L.R. 482.

[70] *An Independent Prosecution Service for England and Wales* (Cmnd. 9074, 1983). The White Paper included, as an Annex, the report of an inter-departmental Working Party on Prosecution Arrangements.

[71] Cmnd. 9074, p. 9.

[72] See the symposium in [1986] Crim. L.R. 3–44; K. W. Lidstone, (1987) 11 Crim. L.J. 296.

[73] 1985 Act s.2. The D.P.P. must possess a 10 year general qualification under the Courts and Legal Services Act 1990, s.71 (*i.e.* a right of audience in any part of the Supreme Court or all proceedings in county courts or magistrates' courts).

[74] There were originally 31 Areas, grouped in four Regions (Northern, Midland, London & South East, South & West: see *Crown Prosecution Service Annual Report for 1987–88* (1987–88 H.C. 563), p. 45. These were reduced to 13 in 1993, including a new unified London area. The aim was to enhance the role and responsibilities of Chief Crown Prosecutors and to provide a shorter

member of the C.P.S. who has a "general qualification" may be designated by him or her as a Crown Prosecutor. The D.P.P. must designate a Chief Crown Prosecutor for each Area, who is responsible to him or her for supervising the operation of the Service in that Area.[75] Crown Prosecutors, whether barristers or solicitors, are accorded the limited rights of audience enjoyed by solicitors holding practising certificates.[76]

Accordingly, the C.P.S. must normally brief counsel in private practice to appear in the Crown Court and higher courts. The C.P.S. also employs unqualified staff.

Arrangements may be made for proceedings to be conducted on behalf of the C.P.S. by any person with a "general qualification," appointed by the D.P.P. Such lawyers have all the powers of a Crown Prosecutor, but exercise them subject to any instructions given by a Crown Prosecutor.[77]

(b) Functions of the Crown Prosecution Service

The 1985 Act is phrased in terms of a set of functions conferred on the D.P.P., acting under the superintendence of the Attorney-General. However, it is also provided that every Crown Prosecutor shall have all the powers of the D.P.P. as to the initiation and conduct of proceedings, acting under his or her direction.[78] Section 3(2) of the 1985 Act provides that it is the duty of the D.P.P.—

"(a) to take over the conduct of all criminal proceedings, other than specified proceedings, instituted on behalf of a police force (whether by a member of that force or by any other person);

(b) to institute and have the conduct of criminal proceedings in any case where it appears to him that—

  (i) the importance or difficulty of the case makes it appropriate that proceedings should be instituted by him; or

  (ii) that it is otherwise appropriate for proceedings to be instituted by him;

(c) to take over the conduct of all binding over proceedings instituted on behalf of a police force (whether by a member of that force or by any other person);

(d) to take over the conduct of all proceedings begun by summons issued under section 3 of the Obscene Publications Act 1959 (forfeiture of obscene articles);

(e) to give, to such extent as he considers appropriate, advice to police forces on all matters relating to criminal offences;

---

and more direct means of communication and accountability: *Annual Report of the C.P.S for 1993–94* (1993–94 H.C. 444), Chap. 2.

[75] 1985 Act, s.1, as amended by the 1990 Act, Sched. 10, para. 61(1).

[76] *ibid.* s.4(1). See above, pp. 133–138. The Lord Chancellor was given power to give additional rights of audience to Crown Prosecutors: s.4(3). Sir Robert Andrew in his *Review of Government Legal Services* (H.M.S.O., 1989) recommended that this power should be exercised in respect of suitably qualified members of the C.P.S. (pp. 51–53). See now, s.4(1)–(3E) substituted by the 1990 Act, Sched. 18, para. 51. The D.P.P.'s proposals for extended rights of audience have not yet been accepted: see p. 138.

[77] *ibid.* s.5, as amended by the Courts and Legal Services Act 1990, Sched. 10, para. 61(2).

[78] 1985 Act, s.1(6). Similarly, where the consent of the D.P.P. is required by statute, that consent can be expressed by a Crown Prosecutor: s.1(7).

(f) to appear for the prosecution, when directed by the court,[79] [on appeals to the Court of Appeal or the House of Lords in criminal cases, and appeals against orders under section 12 of the Contempt of Court Act 1981 (contempt of magistrates' courts)]; and

(g) to discharge such other functions as may from time to time be assigned to him by the Attorney-General in pursuance of this paragraph.''

The key provision governing the relationship between the C.P.S. and the police is section 3(2)(a). The usual task of the C.P.S. is to take over proceedings instituted by the police. Proceedings are ''instituted'' for these purposes when an information is laid before a justice of the peace before the issue of a summons or arrest warrant, or when a person charged with an offence after being taken into custody without a warrant is informed of the particulars of the charge, or when a voluntary bill of indictment is preferred before the court.[80] In these cases, the question for the C.P.S. is whether proceedings should be continued or discontinued.[81] Express provision for the discontinuance of proceedings is made by section 23.[82]

In the case of a person taken into custody without a warrant and charged, but where no magistrates' court has been informed of the charge, the prosecutor may discontinue proceedings by giving notice to the person concerned. Where proceedings have otherwise been instituted, but are still in their ''preliminary stages'' (*i.e.* before the court commences to hear evidence at a summary trial, or before transfer for trial), the prosecutor may discontinue them by giving notice, with reasons, to the clerk of the court. The accused must also be informed, but need not be given reasons, and has the right to require the proceedings to continue. The discontinuance of proceedings under section 23 does not prevent the institution of fresh proceedings in respect of the same offence.[83] If the prosecutor wishes to discontinue at a later stage, the court's consent may be necessary.[84]

There is a limited range of offences which can still be prosecuted to conclusion by the police. These are the ''specified proceedings'' mentioned in section 3(2)(a), and comprise a number of less serious road traffic offences,[85] some commonly dealt with by the fixed penalty procedures. They remain ''specified'' provided that there is a written plea of guilty. If the case is contested, it must then be dealt with by the C.P.S. Apart from these offences, *all* proceedings instituted by the police must be taken over by the C.P.S. It is uncertain whether

---

[79] Defined in s.3(3).

[80] s.15(2). If more than one of these is applicable, the earliest time is taken.

[81] s.15(3) provides that reference as to the conduct of any proceedings include references to their being discontinued.

[82] As amended by the Criminal Justice and Public Order Act 1994, Sched. 4, Pt. II, para. 62.

[83] *ibid.* s.23(9).

[84] At the Crown Court, the approval of the judge is necessary: *R. v. Broad* (1979) 68 Cr.App.R. 281, but at committal proceedings, the consent of the justices is *not* required: *R. v. Canterbury and St Augustine's JJ., ex p. Klisiak* [1982] 1 Q.B. 398. The RCCJ recommended (Cm. 2263, p. 77) that the C.P.S. should be given power to discontinue proceedings up to the beginning of the trial in both the magistrates' court and the Crown Court.

[85] Prosecution of Offences Act 1985 (Specified Proceedings) Order 1985 (S.I. 1985 No. 2010, as amended by S.I. 1988 No. 1121); J. N. Spencer, (1988) 152 J.P.N. 691. See also (1989) 139 N.L.J. 1739.

proceedings are "instituted" by the police where their only involvement is that the suspect is charged by the custody officer.[86]

Section 3(2)(b) preserves the right of the C.P.S. to institute proceedings in serious or difficult cases. Regulations made by the Attorney-General under section 8 require the police to inform the D.P.P. whenever there is a prima facie case that offences in a list set out in the regulations have been committed.[87] These include offences in which a prosecution requires the consent of a Law Officer or the D.P.P., homicide offences (except causing death by reckless driving), abortion, treason or sedition offences, offences which may be subject to an application for extradition and offences where it appears to the chief officer of police that the D.P.P.'s advice or assistance is desirable.

In addition, the D.P.P. may specify other cases which the police are to report to him or her.[88] These include some conspiracies concerning drugs or contravention of immigration laws, criminal libel, certain obscenity cases, and all cases raising questions of Community law.[89]

The 1985 Act also preserves the right of private prosecution by providing that nothing in Part I shall preclude any person from instituting any criminal proceedings, or conducting any proceedings which the D.P.P. is not under a duty to take over.[90] The D.P.P. does, however, still have power to take over private prosecutions at any stage.[91] If a prosecution is taken over, the prosecutor may of course exercise the power to discontinue under section 23.

Crown Prosecutors are given guidance as to the exercise of their powers by the Code for Crown Prosecutors issued by the D.P.P. under section 10.[92]

One organisational problem has concerned the use of unqualified staff within the C.P.S. to review certain categories of cases (most summary offences) to decide whether a prosecution should proceed. A case would only be passed to a Crown Prosecutor where the "case screener's" view was that there was insufficient evidence or a prosecution would be against the public interest, or if he or she considered that that would be helpful. The Divisional Court held that this arrangement was *ultra vires*, there being no express or implied power to delegate such decisions to persons other than Crown Prosecutors and qualified agents.[93] An appeal was taken to the Court of Appeal but the case was settled by agreement. Under that agreement, case examiners will vet a more limited

---

[86] Yes: *R. v. Ealing Magistrates' Court, ex p. Dixon* [1990] 2 Q.B. 91 (prosecution for breach of the Copyright Act 1956 held to be wrongly left to the copyright owners' federation); No: *R. v. Stafford JJ., ex p. Commissioners of Customs and Excise* [1991] 2 Q.B. 339 (held that the Customs and Excise Commissioners could continue a prosecution after charge by the police). The court in *R. v. Stafford JJ* held that the former case was wrongly decided. *R. v. Stafford JJ* was followed in *R. v. Croydon JJ., ex p. Holmberg* (1993) 12 Tr.L.R. 10 (local authority entitled to act as prosecutor in proceedings under the Trade Marks Act 1985).

[87] Prosecution of Offences Regulations 1978, as amended by S.I. 1978 No. 1846 and S.I. 1985 No. 243, regs.6(1), 7. These were made under previous legislation but are thought to take effect under s.8: *Halsbury's Statutes of England*, Vol. 12 (Reissue), p. 940.

[88] 1978 regs, reg. 6(2).

[89] See Archbold, *Criminal Pleading, Evidence and Practice* (43rd ed.), para. 1–124.

[90] Thus a private prosecution may be brought where the D.P.P. has decided not to exercise the power under s.3(2)(b) of the 1985 Act (above, p. 701): *R. v. Bow Street Stipendiary Magistrate, ex p. South Coast Shipping* [1993] Q.B. 645 (private prosecution for manslaughter arising out of the collision between the *Bowbelle* and the *Marchioness* on the River Thames in 1989).

[91] 1985 Act, s.6.

[92] See below.

[93] *R. v. Director of Public Prosecutions, ex p. Association of First Division Civil Servants* (1988) 138 N.L.J. 158.

range of cases, and a decision whether or not to proceed will always be taken by a lawyer.[94] Law clerks were also used to respond to bail applications in the Crown Court and High Court, but this practice was stopped in the light of legal advice that it was unlawful in the absence of express authority in the Prosecution of Offences Act 1985.[95] The necessary authority is now provided by section 74 of the Court and Legal Services Act 1990. The C.P.S. has also considered the idea that minor summary cases might be presented by unqualified staff, after appropriate training.[96] Legislation would be necessary for such a change.

(c) Relationship between the Crown Prosecution Service and the police

As has been mentioned, the crucial feature of this relationship is that in most cases it is still a matter for the police to determine whether proceedings should be *instituted*. They may obtain the advice of the C.P.S. before so deciding, but this is only done in a minority of cases.[97] As a result, the C.P.S. normally has no involvement in cases where the police decide not to prosecute, including the cases where the caution procedure is adopted. This makes it more difficult for a rational prosecution policy to be worked out,[98] although it might be thought unlikely that the police will drop a case that the C.P.S. would have been prepared to prosecute.

Furthermore, doubts were expressed as to the effectiveness in principle of a system of review after the initial decision to prosecute has been taken. It was argued that there is a natural tendency for the police, once satisfied as to who is responsible, to consider as mistaken any material that points in another direction,[99] this tendency being present in a number of notorious miscarriages of justice.[1] The prosecutor would be constrained by the information provided by the police, and

"it would be irrational and indefensible in most cases if the prosecutor did *not* endorse police action, because the file is constructed in order to leave this as the only proper option."[2]

Accordingly, any satisfactory reform would require changes to the investigation process. The prosecutors might be given some powers of direction over investi-

---

[94] *Annual Report of the Crown Prosecution Service for 1988–89* (1988–89 H.C. 411), pp. 17–18.
[95] Evidence of the C.P.S. to the Home Affairs Committee (1989–90 H.C. 118–i), p. 28.
[96] *ibid.* pp. 28–29.
[97] In 1987–88, 1,444,212 defendants' cases were finalised in the magistrates' courts, of which 108,000 were discontinued. The C.P.S. advised the police before charge in 55,760 cases: National Audit Office, *Review of the Crown Prosecution Service* (1988–89 H.C. 345), p. 10. A survey of 13 branches in the last quarter of 1991 found that advice was sought in, on average, 4.3 per cent of cases finalised (ranging from 0.7 per cent to 13.9 per cent for particular branches: D.Crisp and D.Moxon, *Case Screening by the Crown Prosecution Service: How and Why Cases are Terminated* (H.O. Research Study No.137, 1994), p. 7.
[98] *cf.* M. McConville, (1984) VI(1) Liverpool L.R. 15, 28.
[99] McConville, *op. cit.* pp. 28–32; A. Sanders. "Constructing the Case for the Prosecution" (1987) 14 J.L.S. 229.
[1] The Evans, Virag and Dougherty and Confait cases: see L. Kennedy, *Ten Rillington Place* (1961); Devlin Report on the *Evidence of Identification in Criminal Cases* (HMSO, 1976); Fisher Report on the Confait Case (HMSO, 1977). See also the case of Bruce Lee: below, p. 927.
[2] McConville, *op. cit.*, p. 30. *Cf.* A. Sanders, [1986] Crim.L.R. 16, 27, who argues that the structure gives the prosecutors power to drop cases but little incentive to do so; and K. W. Lidstone, (1987) 11 Crim.L.J. 296, 310–312.

gations and the decision to prosecute might be removed altogether from the police.[3]

In practice, the C.P.S. has shown greater independence than might have been anticipated. Its operation is considered further below.[4]

(d) Role of the Attorney-General and the D.P.P. under the new arrangements

Mention has been made earlier in this chapter[5] of the various powers and duties of the D.P.P. and Law Officers that provided a measure of central co-ordination and control under the old arrangements, including requirements for cases to be reported to the D.P.P., consents to prosecution,[6] the D.P.P.'s general power to take over prosecutions, and the *nolle prosequi*. These all still exist, but are obviously no longer the main vehicle for exerting central control or influence over prosecutions. They may, however, still be of importance in respect of prosecutions brought other than by the police. Requirements that proceedings may only be instituted by or with the consent of the Attorney-General or the D.P.P. do not prevent an arrest or the remand in custody or on bail of a person charged with an offence.[7] Accordingly a prosecution may get to the stage of a charge by the police and an initial court appearance without reference to the Attorney-General or the D.P.P. However, a summons should not be issued by a justice of the peace, clerk to the justices or authorised delegate unless he or she is satisfied, *inter alia*, that any necessary authority to prosecute has been obtained.[8] This is the only procedure open to non-police prosecutors, unless the police are prepared to charge on their behalf.[9]

When the consent of the D.P.P. to the prosecution is required, that may now be expressed by a Crown Prosecutor.[10] There are internal arrangements within the C.P.S. governing which cases are to be referred to headquarters.[11]

(e) C.P.S. Operations

It is generally agreed that the C.P.S. got off to a bad start, many of its problems stemming from a lack of resources.[12] Its official complement for staff was inad-

---

[3] See McConville, Sanders and Lidstone, *ops. cit.* above.

[4] Pp. 705–707.

[5] Above, pp. 695–696.

[6] Some of the consent requirements mentioned above (p. 696) have been re-enacted: see now, *e.g.* Public Order Act 1986, s.27(1) (incitement to racial hatred offences); Aviation Security Act 1982, s.8(1) (offences against safety of aircraft); Official Secrets Act 1989, s.9 (most offences under the Act).

[7] Prosecution of Offences Act 1985, s.25, re-enacting s.6 of the 1979 Act: see *R. v. Elliott* (1985) 81 Cr.App.R 115 (the Attorney-General's consent to a prosecution under the Explosive Substances Act 1883 was given eight weeks after charge: it was held that, in view of s.6 of the 1979 Act, the proceedings were instituted at the defendant's first court appearance); *cf. R. v. Whale and Lockton* [1991] Crim.L.R. 692.

[8] *R. v. Gateshead JJ., ex p. Tesco Stores Ltd* [1981] Q.B. 470, 478.

[9] See below, p. 728.

[10] Prosecution of Offences Act 1985, s.1(7).

[11] See *Annual Report of the C.P.S. 1986–87* (1987–88 H.C. 14), Chap. 8.

[12] National Audit Office, *Review of the Crown Prosecution Service* (1988–89 H.C.345); Second Report of the Committee of Public Accounts, *Review of the Crown Prosecution Service* (1989–90 H.C.164); Fourth Report of the Home Affairs Committee (1989–90 H.C.118). The story of the establishment of the C.P.S. is told from the point of view of its first head in Sir Thomas

equate for the work it had to do and it was unable to recruit up to its complement. Private practice lawyers were employed as agents in a higher proportion
of cases than planned or thought desirable, and this added to the expense of the
operation as a whole. A recurrent theme in the criticism of the Service was the
inadequate preparation of cases, particularly less important cases being handled
by inexperienced staff, leading to the late service of papers, delays and the
unnecessary discontinuance of cases. Relations between the C.P.S. and the
police were too often strained, the former criticising the quality and late delivery
of files, the latter complaining that cases were discontinued unnecessarily and
that the C.P.S. demanded a higher standard of file preparation than had been
the norm. Others drew attention to instances both of the dropping of winnable
cases and of the continuation of cases doomed to failure.

A range of steps has been taken in response to these difficulties. A combination of higher salaries, major recruitment initiatives and the recession has
enabled the C.P.S. to recruit substantially to its complement and reduce reliance
on agents.[13] A number of initiatives have been taken or supported to improve
liaison at national and local levels.[14] Internal administrative arrangements have
been reorganised, including the reduction in the number of C.P.S. areas,[15] the
introduction of National Operational Practice, concerned with the development
and introduction of quality of service standards, and the Standard Case Operations (SCOPE) computer system to automate the processing of case administration, the establishment of arrangements for internal audit and for casework
quality assurance,[16] and the introduction of a team approach.[17] Under the auspices of the Working Group on Pre-Trial Issues, a Manual of Guidance for the
preparation and presentation of prosecution files to the C.P.S. by the police was
produced jointly in 1992.[18] The quality of C.P.S. decision-making is considered
below.[19]

The RCCJ endorsed ''the unambiguous separation of the roles of investigator
and prosecutor.''[20] They were encouraged by what they saw as the ''improving

---

Hetherington, *Prosecution and the Public Interest* (1989); *cf.* J. Rozenberg, *The Case for the Crown* (1987), Chap. 4.

[13] From 38 per cent of magistrates' courts sittings at the start of 1990–91 to 13.4 per cent in 1994–95; the target is 10 per cent: *Annual Reports of the C.P.S., 1990–91*, p. 25 and *1994–95*, p. 23.

[14] Including trilateral meetings with the L.C.D. and the Home Office, participation in the work of the Working Group on Pre-Trial Issues and the Standing Commission on Efficiency (*Annual Report of the C.P.S., 1990–91*, pp. 17, 19–20), and more recently, the Criminal Justice Consulta-tive Council and its area committees (above, p. 24).

[15] Above, p. 700.

[16] *Annual Report of the C.P.S., 1992–93*, pp. 8–10.

[17] *Annual Report of the C.P.S., 1994–95*, pp. 15–16. By the end of 1996, each branch is to have a number of integrated teams comprising prosecutors and caseworkers who will be wholly respon-sible for cases throughout their duration wherever they are tried; previously, staff worked princi-pally on either magistrates' courts or Crown Court cases.

[18] See Efficiency Scrutiny, *Administrative Burdens on the Police in the Context of the Criminal Justice System* (June 1995), Chap. 3. ''Full'' files are to be produced where the defendant (or one of the defendants) has been charged with assault, an indictable-only offence or an either-way offence likely to be committed to the Crown Court; has elected trial in the Crown Court; was likely to deny an either-way offence to be tried summarily or a summary-only offence; or has pleaded not guilty in a case to be heard by the magistrates. Otherwise, an ''abbreviated'' file is to be submitted unless the C.P.S. asks for a full file. A new-style abbreviated file requiring even less documentation is to be used experimentally for a year. An inter-agency Trial Issues Group has been established to take this work forward.

[19] pp. 717–718.

[20] Cm. 2263, p. 69.

performance of the C.P.S., although we noted that it may still remain patchy in some areas.''[21] They did not recommend that the C.P.S. should supervise police investigations: C.P.S. staff did not possess the appropriate skills and experience and there would be a serious confusion of roles.[22] However, the police were encouraged to seek the advice of the C.P.S. in appropriate cases in accordance with agreed guidelines. Furthermore, it would not be practicable to give the C.P.S. responsibility for framing the initial charge (C.P.S. staff could not be posted to all police stations.)[23]

The RCCJ thought the police should undertake to meet all reasonable requests from the C.P.S. to make further inquiries, but fell short of recommending that the D.P.P. be given power to require this to be done.[24]

3. THE SERIOUS FRAUD OFFICE

The Serious Fraud Office[25] was established by the Criminal Justice Act 1987, following the Report of the Roskill Committee on Fraud Trials.[26] Its jurisdiction covers England, Wales and Northern Ireland. The Director of the Serious Fraud Office is appointed by the Attorney-General, and acts under his super-intendence.[27] Staff are appointed by the Director.[28] The Director may (i) investigate any suspected offence which appears to him or her on reasonable grounds to involve serious or complex fraud; (ii) institute and have the conduct of any prosecutions which appear to him or her to relate to such fraud; and (iii) take over the conduct of any such proceedings at any stage. He or she may designate any member of the office who is a barrister or solicitor to exercise the Director's powers for the purposes of (ii) and (iii), and such persons have the same rights of audience as Crown Prosecutors.[29] Where the Director has the conduct of a case, the D.P.P.'s responsibilities cease.[30] The main distinctive feature of the Office's work is that it extends to the investigation as well as the prosecution of offences, and it has wide powers to require the person under investigation and any other person whom the Director has reason to believe has relevant information to answer questions or otherwise furnish information, and to require the production of documents.[31] It concentrates on a comparatively small number of the most serious cases: the prosecution of other serious fraud cases continues to be handled by the Fraud Investigation Group within C.P.S. headquarters.

---

[21] ibid., p. 70.

[22] ibid., pp. 22–23, 71–72.

[23] ibid., p. 72–73. Notwithstanding this, pilot schemes for C.P.S. lawyers to work in police stations and police administrative support units have been established in a number of areas (C.P.S. Press Notice, January 26, 1996).

[24] ibid., p. 73–74.

[25] J. Wood, "The Serious Fraud Office" [1989] Crim.L.R. 175; Criminal Justice Act 1987 (Current Law Statutes 1987: Annotations by I. Leigh); P. Carey, (1989) 139 N.L.J. 1629 (comments on some of the S.F.O.'s early cases); above pp. 21–22.

[26] HMSO, 1986.

[27] Criminal Justice Act 1987, s.1.

[28] 1987 Act, Sched. 1, para. 2.

[29] ibid. s.1.

[30] ibid., Sched. 1, para. 5. Statutory requirements for the consent of the D.P.P. to a prosecution are not to prohibit the taking of any step by the Director: ibid. para. 4

[31] ibid., s.2. These powers continue to be available after the suspect has been charged: R. v. Director of Serious Fraud, ex p. Saunders, The Independent, July 29, 1988.

4. OTHER AGENCIES

There are a considerable number of other bodies who institute prosecutions and who should not be left out of account. Government departments, local authorities, nationalised industries and other public bodies may all have cause to institute prosecutions within their particular field. A survey was undertaken on behalf of the Royal Commission on Criminal Procedure[32] which concentrated on particular courts and identified the Post Office, the British Transport Police, the Department of the Environment and local authorities as contributing almost 70 per cent of the non-police prosecutions in those courts.[33]

5. PRIVATE PROSECUTIONS

"This historical right which goes right back to the earliest days of our legal system, though rarely exercised in relation to indictable offences, and though ultimately liable to be controlled by the Attorney-General (by taking over the prosecution and, if he thinks fit, entering a *nolle prosequi*) remains a valuable constitutional safeguard against inertia or partiality on the part of authority."[34] Lord Wilberforce thus stated the traditional view of the private prosecution.

In fact, the growing practice of requiring the consent of the D.P.P. or Attorney-General to prosecution, the establishment of the C.P.S. and the considerable cost of mounting a private prosecution now combine to minimise the significance of this historical right. We have already noted the requirement of consent,[35] but cost is an even more discouraging factor. Legal aid is not available to a private prosecutor who must meet the cost of investigation, preparation and representation[36] out of his or her own pocket. A court may award costs to a successful private prosecutor[37] but he or she also runs the risk of having them awarded against him or her if he or she is not successful. In addition, if the prosecution was vindictive, the prosecutor risks the possibility of an action in malicious prosecution.[38] A private prosecutor has no right of access to documents, such as police statements, reports and photographs, held by the C.P.S.[39]

There have, of course, been some notable private prosecutions,[40] but they

---

[32] *Prosecutions by Private Individuals and Non-Police Agencies*, RCCP Research Study No. 10 (HMSO, 1980). See also A. Samuels, [1986] Crim.L.R. 33.

[33] *ibid.*, Table 2.3 at p. 15.

[34] *Gouriet v. Union of Post Office Workers* [1978] A.C. 435 at p. 477.

[35] At pp. 695–696 above.

[36] The Crown Court can allow a private prosecution to be conducted in person: *R. v. Southwark Gown Court ex p. Tawfick* (1995) 7 Admin. L.R. 410 (by virtue of the Courts and Legal Services Act 1990, s.27(2)(c)).

[37] Prosecution of Offences Act 1985, s.17: costs can only be awarded in respect of proceedings for an indictable offence, and proceedings in the Divisional Court or the House of Lords in respect of a summary offence. They cannot cover investigation expenses. See further pp. 538–539.

[38] See W.V.H. Rogers, *Winfield and Jolowicz on Tort* (14th ed.), pp. 572–580.

[39] *R. v. Director of Public Prosecutions, ex p. Hallas* (1987) 87 Cr.App.R. 340.

[40] Two cases brought by Mrs Mary Whitehouse aroused interest—*R. v. Lemon* [1979] A.C. 617, where the accused was convicted of blasphemous libel and the Crown subsequently took over the case on appeal; and *Whitehouse v. Bogdanov*, where the accused was acquitted on a charge of procuring an act of gross indecency between males contrary to section 13 of the Sexual Offences Act 1956 which resulted from his producing a play (*The Romans in Britain*), containing

have been generally confined to offences of shoplifting and common assault.[41] In some areas supermarkets and other large concerns are encouraged by the police to conduct their own prosecutions for shoplifting. Section 42 of the Offences Against the Person Act 1861 dictated a private prosecution in the majority of cases where common assault occurred,[42] but this section was repealed by the Criminal Justice Act 1988.[43]

C. THE EXERCISE OF DISCRETION IN PROSECUTIONS

Not every criminal offence is prosecuted. The courts could not possibly cope with the workload and, in any event, prosecution may not always be the most effective means of dealing with a violation of the criminal law. If some offenders are to be "let off" whilst others are brought before the courts it is important to know when such a decision may be made, by whom and on what principles. The exercise of this particular discretion has attracted increasing attention.[44]

1. THE POLICE

A choice exists as soon as a police officer discovers that a criminal offence may have been committed. Should an investigation be started if the situation is unclear? If the facts are already clear should action be taken to ensure that the offence is formally considered for prosecution? This problem is faced by every police officer present at an incident and it must be resolved on individual initiative and/or in accordance with instructions received from a superior officer. Although it may be the officer's inclination to warn a motorist driving without lights not to repeat the offence, the Chief Constable may have decided, as a matter of policy, to prosecute all such offenders and issued instructions accordingly. The discretion exercised in this way by the officer concerned is otherwise

a scene of intercourse between males (one non-consenting). The prosecution was discontinued after the judge had ruled that there was a case to answer and the Attorney-General eventually entered a *nolle prosequi*. See [1982] P.L. 165. In Scotland, private prosecutions are extremely rare, but not obsolete: see *X. v. Sweeney* 1982 J.C. 70; R. Harper and A. McWhinnie, *The Glasgow Rape Case* (1983). An individual aggrieved by the decision of the procurator fiscal not to prosecute must obtain authority to prosecute from the High Court by petitioning by Bill for Criminal Letters. A recent example in England is the prosecution of young men accused of the murder of Stephen Lawrence mounted by the victim's family following the dropping of charges by the C.P.S.: see E. Saunders, (1995) 145 N.L.J. 1423, noting the successful outcome of committal proceedings, and rehearsing the difficulties of such prosecutions. The prosecution ultimately failed.

[41] RCCP Research Study No. 10 (see above, n. 32), Chap. 5.

[42] The section specified that in cases of common assault the prosecution should be brought "by or on behalf of the party aggrieved."

[43] Common assault and battery were made summary offences by s.39 of the 1988 Act.

[44] The literature is expanding. See A. F. Wilcox, *The Decision to Prosecute* (1972); N. Osborough, "Police Discretion not to prosecute Juveniles" (1965) 28 M.L.R. 179; D. Steer, *Police Cautions— A Study in the Exercise of Police Discretion* (1970); D. G. T. Williams, "Prosecution, discretion and the accountability of the police" (in R. Hood (ed.) *Crime, Criminology and Public Policy* (1974)), and the works cited in nn.66 and 67 below.

generally uncontrolled, except where failure to take action may itself amount to a criminal offence or neglect of duty.[45]

Two cases have explored the exercise of discretion at a senior level which would affect the way that the officer on the spot carries out his or her duties. In *R. v. Metropolitan Police Commissioner, ex p. Blackburn (No. 1)*,[46] Mr Raymond Blackburn applied for an order of mandamus directed to the Commissioner requiring him to enforce the provisions of the Betting, Gaming and Lotteries Act 1963 in London gaming clubs. It appeared that the Commissioner had sanctioned a force order which effectively stopped observation in gaming clubs by the police and prevented any attempt to enforce the Act.[47] The Court of Appeal held that, whilst the police had a discretion not to prosecute, it was not proper to take a policy decision that certain offences would *never* be prosecuted since that was to negate the exercise of discretion and would amount to a failure in their duty to enforce the law. However, the courts will not interfere in cases where it is alleged that the police are not paying *enough* attention to particular offences or prosecuting in sufficient numbers. Mr. Blackburn again sought an order of mandamus in *R. v. Metropolitan Police Commissioner, ex p. Blackburn (No. 3)*[48] this time in respect of the Obscene Publications Act 1959, but the court would not grant it. Whereas in the first case the police had deliberately decided not to prosecute, in this case they were hampered by lack of resources and the uncertainty of the law. "It is no part of the duty of this court to presume to tell the (Commissioner) how to conduct the affairs of the Metropolitan Police, nor how to deploy his all too limited resources. . . ."[49]

Given that an individual officer may be under instructions about how to deal with particular offences and will also have received training for this task, what considerations are likely to be taken into account in the exercise of discretion? Naturally, the gravity of the offence is likely to be uppermost but the officer may also think about the evidence likely to be available in a prosecution; the degree of certainty that the offence has been committed; the attitude of the victim; the personal circumstances of the offender and the efficacy of a prosecution compared with other ways of dealing with the problem. These are, on a local level, not dissimilar to the considerations appropriate to the decisions of the C.P.S. on whether to continue a prosecution.[50] In this case, however, the decision will need to be taken quickly and often without the help and advice of colleagues. If the officer decides not to arrest or report for prosecution he or she might issue a warning to the offender, attempt a conciliation between offender and victim, or even take the offender into preventive arrest.[51]

Assuming that an officer has arrested an offender or reported him or her for

---

[45] By virtue of the Police (Discipline) Regulations 1985 (S.I. 1985 No. 518), Sched. 1, para. 4. See also *R. v. Dytham* [1979] Q.B. 722 (criminal offence of wilful neglect of duty).

[46] [1968] 2 Q.B. 118. As to judicial review of C.P.S. decisions not to discontinue proceedings, see below, pp. 719–720.

[47] The terms of the relevant instructions are set out in the judgment of Lord Denning M.R. at pp. 134–135. In the event, the instructions in question were withdrawn before the appellate hearing and the Commissioner, through counsel, gave an undertaking to that effect.

[48] [1973] Q.B. 241. For a further instalment in the drama see *R. v. Metropolitan Police Commissioner, ex p. Blackburn, The Times*, March 6, 1980. Mr Blackburn referred to the Master of Rolls in the course of that case as, "the greatest living Englishman"—Lord Denning is reported to have replied, "Tell that to the House of Lords."

[49] *per* Roskill L.J. at p. 262.

[50] See below, pp. 712–718.

[51] Discussed by Wilcox, *op. cit.* at p. 106.

prosecution the decision will pass to a more senior officer. At this stage the police may decide to prosecute, to caution, to administer an informal warning or to take no further action (n.f.a.). They may have the benefit of advice from the C.P.S. If the decision is to prosecute, there is also an exercise of discretion in selecting the particular charge.

The practice differs according to the method of procedure adopted: arrest and charge, or summons. Under the former, the person is arrested (either outside or at the police station) and charged at the police station. After charge the suspect will either be kept in custody and brought by the police before magistrates' court,[52] or, as is more usual, released on bail subject to a duty to attend a magistrates' court on a specified date. Here a decision to charge is made initially by the investigating officer, but must be approved by the custody officer, who must be satisfied that there is sufficient evidence.[53] Where a person is reported for summons, the investigating officer prepares a file and passes it to a more senior officer, who decides whether a prosecution should be instituted. Where a decision not to prosecute is contemplated, the case must be passed up the hierarchy, usually to a Detective Superintendent; a decision to prosecute can be taken at the level of Detective Inspector or Detective Chief Inspector.[54] Overall, the arrest and charge procedure is the normal method used in respect of indictable offences, and the summons procedure the normal method for summary offences,[55] but police forces vary considerably in the respective proportions in which they are used.[56]

The caution, a formal warning issued by the police in circumstances where they are satisfied that the offence is capable of proof but do not intend to prosecute, has only rarely received statutory mention[57] and its use has developed by practice rather than by law. Until 1994 it was government policy, enshrined in a series of Home Office Circulars,[58] to encourage the increasing use of cautions, diverting offenders from the prosecution process. Cautioning was much more frequently used in respect of juveniles than adults; indeed, there was a presumption that a first-time juvenile offender would be cautioned. The numbers of offenders cautioned grew dramatically from 190,000 in 1984 to 321,000 in 1992,

---

[52] In accordance with the requirements of s.46 of the Police and Criminal Evidence Act 1984: above, p. 676.

[53] 1984 Act, ss.37(1)(7); *Code of Practice on Detention etc.* C. 16.1. The equivalent step prior to PACE was the decision of the charge sergeant whether to accept a charge, on the basis of an oral report from the investigating officer. In practice refusals were rare; "charge sergeants (uniformed officers) do not see CID work as their business, so accepting a CID charge is often a mere formality": A. Sanders, "The prosecution process" in D. Moxon (ed.), *Managing Criminal Justice* (1985), pp. 72–73.

[54] Sanders, *op. cit.*, pp. 70–72.

[55] See *Criminal Statistics England and Wales 1994* (Cm. 3010, 1995), Table 8.1 (summons used for 10 per cent of indictable offences, 76 per cent of summary (non-motoring) offences and 85 per cent of summary motoring offences. The proportions in the first two groups have been declining).

[56] See R. Gemmill and R. F. Morgan-Giles, *Arrest, Charge and Summons* (RCCP Research Study No. 9) (HMSO, 1986), based on figures for 1976 and 1978; R. Tarling, P. Jones and A. Sanders, "Police Bail" (1986) 21 H.O.R.B. 52, 54–55, based on figures for 1980.

[57] The Street Offences Act 1959 s.2; the Children and Young Persons Act 1969, s.5(2) (not in force).

[58] H.O. Circulars 70/1978, 14/1985 and 59/1990. The 1985 Circular encouraged the wider use of cautioning for adults. The percentage of 18–21-year-old male offenders cautioned increased from 4 per cent in 1984 to 33 per cent in 1994 (indictable offences) and from 9 per cent to 29 per cent (summary offences excluding motoring offences): *Criminal Statistics 1994*, Table 5.3.

the percentage of all offenders cautioned increasing from 23 per cent to 41 per cent. There have been wide variations in the cautioning rates in different police areas.[59] Other informal warnings must also be carefully distinguished from a formal caution and cannot be referred to in subsequent proceedings. Motoring offences are dealt with differently by the administration of a written caution which is not dependent upon an admission by the offender and may not be referred to in subsequent proceedings for another offence.[60]

In 1994, revised National Standards for cautioning were issued.[61] The main features remain the same. Thus, there must be evidence of guilt sufficient to give a realistic prospect of conviction; the offender must admit the offence; and the offender (or a juvenile's parents or guardian) must understand the significance of a caution and give informed consent to being cautioned. Consideration should be given to whether a caution is in the public interest, taking account of the public interest principles set out in the *Code for Crown Prosecutors*.[62] Thus, the "interests of a youth" must be taken into account when deciding whether to caution. However, there is no longer an express presumption in favour of cautioning a first-time juvenile offender. Furthermore, the Circular makes clear that cautions should never be used for the most serious indictable-only offences such as murder or rape,[63] and multiple cautioning should only be used where the subsequent offence is trivial or there has been a sufficient lapse of time since the first caution to suggest that it had some effect.[64] The views of the victim should be sought but should not be regarded as conclusive. The number of cautions fell in 1993 and 1994.[65]

2. The Code for Crown Prosecutors

Prior to the establishment of the C.P.S., as we have seen, the decision to prosecute would in most cases be taken by the police, in some cases with the advice of a prosecuting solicitor, or by a member of the D.P.P.'s office, It was clear that the police did not adopt a blanket policy of prosecutions, and did take other factors into account, but there was comparatively little formal did, evidence of

---

[59] H.O. Circular 18/1994. See also G. Laycock and R Tarling, "Police force cautioning: policy and practice" in Moxon (ed) (1985), Chap. 6; H. Giller and N. Tutt, [1987] Crim. L.R. 367 and 587; C. Wilkinson and R. Evans, [1990] Crim.L.R. 165 and (1990) 29 *Howard Journal* 155; R. Evans, [1993] Crim. L.R. 572.

[60] R.C.C.P. I, Para. 153.

[61] H. O. Circular 18/1994. See R. Evans, "Cautioning: Counting the Cost of Retrenchment" [1994] Crim. L.R. 566.

[62] See below, pp. 714–716.

[63] Cautions in such cases were previously "discouraged", but were nevertheless used.

[64] Multiple cautioning was said by politicians to have brought the system into disrepute: see R. Evans, [1994] Crim. L.R. 566, 567. However, in general juveniles *are* prosecuted after receiving two cautions, and it is estimated that a move to prosecuting most juveniles after one would increase the numbers of juveniles going into the youth courts by 36 per cent: *ibid.*, p. 569.

[65] To 311,300 in 1993 and 308,400 in 1994: see *Criminal Statistics 1994*, pp. 93–97. The full effects of the 1994 Circular were not likely to be observed until 1995. Nevertheless, there were large falls in cautioning in 1994 for most indictable offence groups, although cautioning for drugs offences continued to rise.

what those factors were.[66] More was known of the approach of the D.P.P., particularly through his evidence to the Royal Commission on Criminal Procedure.[67] In February 1983, the Attorney-General issued *Criteria for Prosecution*,[68] setting out the approach of the Attorney and the D.P.P. to the institution of prosecutions in cases for which they were responsible. The intention was, however, that they be taken into account by all those responsible for prosecutions. The *Criteria* subsequently formed the basis of the *Code for Crown Prosecutors* issued by the D.P.P.

Section 10 of the Prosecution of Offences Act 1985 requires the D.P.P. to issue a Code for Crown Prosecutors giving guidance on general principles to be applied by them in determining whether to institute or discontinue proceedings, what charges should be preferred and what representations should be made about mode of trial. The D.P.P. may make alterations in the Code, and the Code, and any alterations, must be published in an Annual Report of the C.P.S.[69] A third edition was published in June 1994, the aim of the revision being to simplify and improve the language and to set out the evidential test and the public interest factors with greater clarity.[70] It contains less detail than previous versions. It was accompanied by an *Explanatory Memorandum*[71] for the use of Crown Prosecutors, which was originally regarded as a confidential document but subsequently made available to the public. Further details are found in internal manuals which remain confidential.[72]

The Code is to be applied by the C.P.S. "so that it can make fair and consistent decisions about prosecutions." The duty of the C.P.S. is "to make sure that the right person is prosecuted for the right offence and that all relevant facts are given to the court." Crown Prosecutors must be "fair, independent and objective." Their key task is to review cases sent by the police to make sure they meet the tests set out in the Code. This is a "continuing process" so that prosecutors can take account of any change of circumstances.[73] The decision to prosecute is approached in two stages: (1) the *evidential test* and (2) the *public interest test*.[74] As to the first stage, Crown Prosecutors "must be satisfied that

[66] See, however, the account by a former chief constable: A. F. Wilcox, *The Decision to Prosecute* (1972), and the research project conducted by A Sanders between 1980 and 1983: Sanders, [1985] Crim. L.R. 4, and "The Prosecution Process" in D. Moxon (ed.), *Managing Criminal Justice* (1985), Chap. 7.

[67] A useful extract from the evidence submitted is to be found at R.C.C.P. I, Appendix 25. See generally G. Mansfield and J Peay, *The Director of Public Prosecutions* (1987), the report of a research project on the operation of the D.P.P.'s Office prior to the Prosecution of Offences Act 1985: the case samples studied dated from 1982 and 1983.

[68] (1983) 147 J.P.N. 223; Home Office Circular 26/1983. See A. Sanders, "Prosecution Decisions and the Attorney-General's Guidelines" [1985] Crim. L.R. 4: he doubted that the *Criteria* would generally have much effect in reducing "inconsistency, weak cases and shady practice," but noted that they had led to changes in at least two forces (*ibid.* pp. 17, 18).

[69] The Code, as amended, is published in the C.P.S. Annual Reports.

[70] *Annual Report of the Crown Prosecution Service 1994–95* (1994–95 H.C. 472), p. 6. See "The New Code for Crown Prosecutors": (1) A. Ashworth and J. Fionda, "Prosecution, Accountability and the Public Interest" [1994] Crim. L.R. 894; (2) Response by R. K. Daw *ibid.*, p. 904. On previous versions of the Code, see A. Ashworth, "The 'Public Interest' Element in Prosecutions" [1987] Crim. L.R. 595; R. K. Daw, (1989) Jo. Crim. Law 485.

[71] C.P.S., June 1994.

[72] The "reduction in proper accountability" caused by the "removal of important matters out of the public area into the C.P.S. manuals" is criticised by Ashworth and Fionda, [1994] Crim. L.R. 894, 902–903.

[73] Code, para. 3.

[74] Code, paras.5 and 6.

there is enough evidence to provide a 'realistic prospect of conviction' against each defendant on each charge'', taking account of what the defence case may be. There is a "realistic prospect of conviction" where a properly directed jury or bench of magistrates is more likely than not to convict.[75] Crown Prosecutors must consider whether the evidence can be used and is reliable. Relevant considerations are whether any evidence may be excluded by the court, for example, because of the way it was gathered; whether it is likely that a confession is unreliable, for example, because of the defendant's age, intelligence or lack of understanding; whether a witness's background is likely to weaken the prosecution case, as where he or she has a dubious motive or relevant previous conviction; and whether evidence of identification is strong enough (if identity is in issue). Crown Prosecutors should not ignore evidence because they are not sure on these points; they should, however, "look closely at it when deciding if there is a realistic prospect of conviction."

If the evidential test is passed, Crown Prosecutors must then consider if a prosecution is needed in the public interest.[76] "In cases of any seriousness, a prosecution will usually take place unless there are public interest factors tending against prosecution which clearly outweigh those tending in favour."[77] These must be balanced "carefully and fairly" and those that can affect the decision to prosecute "usually depend on the seriousness of the offence or the circumstances of the offender." The Code provides non-exhaustive lists of common public interest factors for and against prosecution.[78] As regards factors in favour, it is noted that "the more serious the offence, the more likely it is that a prosecution will be needed in the public interest." A prosecution is likely to be needed if:

"(a) a conviction is likely to result in a significant sentence;
 (b) a weapon was used or violence was threatened during the commission of the offence;
 (c) the offence was committed against a person serving the public (for example, a police or prison officer, or a nurse);
 (d) the defendant was in a position of authority or trust;
 (e) the evidence shows that the defendant was a ringleader or an organiser of the offence;
 (f) there is evidence that the offence was premeditated;
 (g) there is evidence that the offence was carried out by a group;
 (h) the victim of the offence was vulnerable, has been put in considerable fear, or suffered personal attack, damage or disturbance;

---

[75] The test is objective: Crown Prosecutors should not take into account any perceived local views of juries or magistrates: *Explanatory Memorandum*, para. 4.10. Furthermore, they "should resist the temptation to define the evidential test as 'a 51% rule' . . . weighing evidence (and the public interest) is not a precise science" (*ibid.*, para. 4.14). "On the other hand, it is not unreasonable to talk of a conviction being 'more likely than not' " (*ibid.*).

[76] The D.P.P., and now the C.P.S., are guided by a statement made by a former Attorney-General, Lord Shawcross, in the course of a House of Commons debate. "It has never been the rule in this country—I hope it never will be—that suspected criminal offences must automatically be the subject of prosecution: H. C. Deb. Vol. 483. col. 681, January 29, 1951.

[77] In previous versions of the Code, prosecutors had to consider "whether the public interest requires a prosecution." This *could* be interpreted as suggesting a presumption *against* prosecution. The revised version makes it clear that there is a presumption *in favour* of prosecution.

[78] The *absence* of a factor is not to be taken as a factor tending in the opposite direction: *Explanatory Memorandum*, para. 4.26.

(i) the offence was motivated by any form of discrimination against the victim's ethnic or national origin, sex, religious beliefs, political views or sexual preference;

(j) there is a marked difference between the actual or mental ages of the defendant and the victim, or if there is any element of corruption;

(k) the defendant's previous convictions or cautions are relevant to the present offence;

(l) the defendant is alleged to have committed the offence whilst under an order of the court;

(m) there are grounds for believing that the offence is likely to be continued or repeated, for example, by a history of recurring conduct; or

(n) the offence, although not serious in itself, is widespread in the area where it was committed.''

On the other hand, a prosecution is less likely to be needed if:

''(a) the court is likely to impose a very small or nominal penalty;

(b) the offence was committed as a result of a genuine mistake or misunderstanding (these factors must be balanced against the seriousness of the offence);

(c) the loss or harm can be described as minor and was the result of a single incident, particularly if it was caused by a misjudgment;

(d) there has been a long delay between the offence taking place and the date of the trial, unless:
   - the offence is serious;
   - the delay has been caused in part by the defendant;
   - the offence has only recently come to light; or
   - the complexity of the offence has meant that there has been a long investigation;

(e) a prosecution is likely to have a very bad effect on the victim's physical or mental health, always bearing in mind the seriousness of the offence;

(f) the defendant is elderly or is, or was at the time of the offence, suffering from significant mental or physical ill health, unless the offence is serious or there is a real possibility that it may be repeated. The Crown Prosecution Service, where necessary, applies Home Office guidelines about how to deal with mentally disordered offenders. Crown Prosecutors must balance the desirability of diverting a defendant who is suffering from significant mental or physical ill health with the need to safeguard the general public;

(g) the defendant has put right the loss or harm that was caused (but defendants must not avoid prosecution simply because they can pay compensation); or

(h) details may be made public that could harm sources of information, international relations or national security.''

While the Code lists these competing factors, it is also made clear that prosecutors must not simply add up the number of factors on each side: they

''must decide how important each factor is in the circumstances of each case and go on to make an overall assessment.''

They must also always

"think very carefully about the interests of the victim, which are an important factor, when deciding where the public interest lies."

Where the defendant is a youth, prosecutors must also consider his or her interests; the stigma of a conviction can cause very severe harm to his or her prospects and young offenders can sometimes be dealt with without going to court.
However, prosecutors

"should not avoid prosecuting simply because of the defendant's age. The
seriousness of the offence or the offender's past behaviour may make prosecutions necessary."[79]

Finally, where necessary, Crown Prosecutors should apply the Home Office
guidelines on cautioning and tell the police it they think a caution would be
more suitable than a prosecution.

As to charges,[80] Crown Prosecutors should select charges which (a) reflect
the seriousness of the offending; (b) give the court adequate sentencing powers;
and (c) enable the case to be presented in a clear and simple way. Thus they
may not always continue with the most serious charge and should not continue
with more charges than are necessary. Indeed, they should never go ahead with
more charges than are necessary, or a more serious charge, in order to encourage
a defendant to plead guilty to some, or a less serious charge. They should not
change the charge simply because of the mode-of-trial decision.

As to mode of trial,[81] Crown Prosecutors must apply the national guidelines.[82]
Speed must never be the only reason for asking for summary trial, but prosecutors
should consider the effect of any likely delay if a case is sent to the Crown Court
and any possible stress on victims and witnesses if the case is delayed.

Crown Prosecutors should only accept a guilty plea if they think the court is
able to pass a sentence that matches the seriousness of the offending, and never
just because it is convenient.[83]

If the C.P.S. tells a suspect or defendant that there will not be a prosecution or
that the prosecution has been stopped, that is normally the end of the matter. However, a prosecution may be re-started (a) in rare cases where the original decision
was clearly wrong; (b) where the prosecution has been stopped so that more evidence which is likely to become available in the fairly near future can be collected
(here, the prosecution will tell the defendant that the prosecution may well start
again); or (c) in other cases where more significant evidence is discovered later.[84]

Finally, the Code makes clear that

"police officers should take account of the principles of the Code when
they are deciding whether to charge a defendant with an offence."[85]

---

[79] This is much weaker than the provisions in the previous version that "the youth of the offender"
was a public interest factor against prosecution and that juveniles should not be prosecuted unless
exceptional circumstances dictated otherwise.
[80] Code, para. 7.
[81] Code, para. 8.
[82] Below, p. 725.
[83] Code, para. 9.
[84] *ibid.*, para. 10.
[85] *ibid.*, para. 11

In many respects the Code seems eminently reasonable, albeit at a high level of generality: what is important is how it is applied in practice. One aspect that has been controversial is the "realistic prospects of conviction" test.[86] It has been argued that this weighs too heavily against prosecution.[87] To promote consistency in decision-making, the Service has issued internal manuals giving guidance on policy and practice. These documents are not published. Statements on prosecution policy for particular offences or situations have been published from time to time.[88]

The RCCJ gave some consideration to the quality of decision-making by the C.P.S., noting criticisms of decisions to prosecute cases that might have been discontinued on public interest or evidential grounds.[89] In 1994–95, the overall discontinuance rate in magistrates' courts cases was 11.7 per cent.[90] At the Crown Court, in 1995, of all the defendants who were acquitted on all counts, 47 per cent were discharged by the judge, 17 per cent acquitted on the direction of the judge and 36 per cent acquitted by the jury.[91] Research into the reasons for discontinuance[92] found that 58 per cent of non-motoring and 47 per cent of motoring cases were discontinued on evidential grounds; and 35 per cent and 24 per cent respectively on public interest grounds; and the remainder on grounds including the impossibility of tracing the defendant (5 per cent and 24 per cent respectively) or refusal of an adjournment by a court (3 per cent). As is to be expected, the C.P.S. is less likely to drop serious cases on public interest grounds. Only 5 per cent of terminated cases were dropped before the first court appearance and in 37 per cent of cases the defendant had no advance notification. This research was available to the RCCJ. They regarded the fact that

---

[86] This test originally appeared as a "reasonable prospect of conviction" test in the Attorney-General's *Criteria for Prosecution* (above, p. 713), and became a "realistic prospect" in the first *Code for Crown Prosecutors*. The latter does not appear to import a higher standard (A. Ashworth, *The Criminal Process* (1994), p. 163). However, it is more stringent than the "prima facie" standard previously applied by the police; under this test, there had to be "enough admissible evidence to prove all the necessary elements of the offence and evidence that does not appear so manifestly unreliable that no reasonable tribunal could safely convict upon it": RCCP paras.6–10. It was reformulated following criticism by G. Mansfield and J. Peay, *The Director of Public Prosecutions* (1987), pp. 52–54, 217–225.

[87] G. Williams "Letting off the Guilty and Prosecuting the Innocent" [1985] Crim.L.R. 115, criticised by P. Worboys, [1985] Crim. L.R. 764. Prof. Williams proposed that the prosecutor should consider (1) whether he or she believes the suspect to be guilty; (2) whether a prosecution would have a fair chance of success; (3) whether considerations of humanity or public policy stand in the way of proceedings; and (4) whether he or she has the resources to justify bringing a charge.

[88] See A. Ashworth and J. Fionda, [1994] Crim. L.R. 894, 902 citing "A Statement of Prosecution Policy: Domestic Violence" (C.P.S., 1993), annexed to the Government Reply (Cm. 2269) to the Third Report from the Home Affairs Committee (1992–93 H.C. 245), *Domestic Violence*; and *Charging Standards: Offences against the Person* (C.P.S., 1994) (see [1994] Crim.L.R. 777; this is the first in a series). Driving offences charging standards took effect on March 4, 1996. Statements on conspiracy to commit a statutory offence, conspiracy to defraud and sexual offences were removed from the third version of the Code but still reflect C.P.S. policy (see R.K. Daw, [1994] Crim. L.R. 904, 905).

[89] Cm. 2263, pp. 74–78.

[90] *Annual Report of the C.P.S., 1994–95*, p. 25. The discontinuance figure fell from 12.5 per cent in 1993–94 and 13.5 per cent in 1992–93.

[91] *Judicial Statistics 1995*, p. 65. Discharge by the judge occurs before the jury is empanelled and reflects the absence of a C.P.S. power to discontinue after committal for trial (above, p. 702); acquittal at the direction of the judge occurs at a later stage.

[92] D. Crisp and D. Moxon, *Case Screening by the Crown Prosecution Service* (H.O. Research Study No. 137, HMSO, 1994), based on a sample of cases in 1991. See also the C.P.S.'s own surveys, *e.g. Annual Report of the C.P.S., 1994–95*, pp. 7–8.

only 5 per cent of cases were discontinued before the first court appearance as "disappointingly small". However, they found that this research also indicated that the public interest criteria were being appropriately applied.[93] Other research, on ordered and directed acquittals,[94] found that of 100 case files studied, 45 acquittals were unforeseeable (over half because the victim or key witness disappeared or refused to testify); 27 were foreseeable and 28 possibly foreseeable; in 25 of the cases, the evidential weakness was present and foreseeable before, at or just after committal; at a minimum, 15 should have been discontinued or manifest deficiencies in the evidence rectified. There were instances of inadequate advice from prosecuting counsel. The RCCJ's response was to recommend that counsel's advice should be sought and given in good time.[95] Consultation with the police about discontinuance appears to be improving.[96]

3. PROSECUTIONS BY OTHER AGENCIES

Most of the prosecutions brought by non-police agencies arise out of the enforcement of regulatory legislation in the context of business, including legislation concerning protection of the health and safety of employees,[97] trading standards[98] and protection of the environment.[99] Those who enforce this kind of legislation tend to prefer other methods of securing compliance, such as advice, negotiation and warning, with prosecution as a last resort. The internal decision-making arrangements tend to make prosecution more difficult than non-prosecution.[1] It has been noted that the potential defendants tend to be middle class (companies, managers, self-employed) rather than working class (who comprise the majority of those dealt with by the police).[2] However, it has been argued that the class bias exhibited by the prosecution patterns arises not from deliberate bias on the part of the law enforcers, but reflects more fundamental

---

[93] Cm. 2263, pp. 76–77. Trials with Public Interest Case Assessment Schemes in which probation officers prepare reports on defendants in selected cases for prosecutors have been generally welcomed by those involved, have led to increases on the proportion of public interest discontinuances, but have not generated savings sufficient to cover their costs: D. Crisp *et al., Public Interest Case Assessment Schemes* (H.O. Research Study No. 138, HMSO, 1995).

[94] B. Block, C. Corbett and J. Perry, *Ordered and Directed Acquittals in the Crown Court* (RCCJ Research Study No. 15, HMSO, 1993) and [1993] Crim. L.R. 95.

[95] Cm. 2263, pp. 77–78. The RCCJ also welcomed the introduction of team working (above, p. 706).

[96] *Annual Report of the C.P.S., 1994–95* p. 8: police consulted in 99 per cent of cases where consultation was possible (74 per cent of all cases discontinued); police objections were put forward in 4 per cent of cases. See also Crisp and Moxon (1994), Chap. 4.

[97] See W. G. Carson, "White collar crime and the enforcement of factory legislation" (1970) 10 Brit. J. Criminol. 383, and *The Other Price of Britain's Oil* (1982); D. Kloss, [1978] Crim. L.R. 280.

[98] R. Cranston, *Regulating Business* (1979) (enforcement of trading standards); B. Hutter, *The Reasonable Arm of the Law* (1988) (environmental health officers); H. Croall, (1988) 15 J.L.S. 293 and (1989) 29 Brit. J. Criminol. 157.

[99] See G. Richardson, A. Ogus and P. Burroughs, *Policing Pollution* (1982); K. Hawkins, *Environment and Enforcement* (1984); M. Weatt, (1989) 29 Brit. J. Criminol. 57.

[1] See A. Sanders, "Class Bias in Prosecution" (1985) 24 *Howard Journal* 176, comparing the "institutional propensity to prosecute" of the police with the "propensity not to prosecute" of the Factory Inspectorate.

[2] Sanders, *op. cit.*

economic and social differences between different types of "crime" and "criminal".[3] A similar contrast can be drawn between the rarity of prosecutions for tax evasion by the Inland Revenue and the much more common use of prosecutions for social security frauds.[4]

4. JUDICIAL REVIEW AND THE DECISION TO PROSECUTE

Decisions of the police or another enforcement agency to prosecute and of the C.P.S. not to discontinue a prosecution are open to challenge on an application for judicial review, but this is only rarely likely to succeed. The possibility of judicial review of police decisions was recognised (as regards a decision not to prosecute) in *R. v. Metropolitan Police Commissioner, ex p. Blackburn (No.1)*[5] and (as regards a decision to prosecute and not caution a juvenile) in *R. v. Chief Constable of the Kent County Constabulary, ex p. L.*[6] Decisions whether to prosecute or not discontinue a prosecution against an adult have also been held to be subject to judicial review.[7] However, most of the applications to date have failed. In *ex p. L*[8] the Divisional Court upheld a decision to prosecute L (aged 16) for breaking another boy's nose and kicking him in the head, where all the criteria for cautioning were satisfied apart from the question of seriousness of the offence. In *ex p. B*,[9] the same court upheld a decision to prosecute B (aged 12) for theft of a bag. Here, there was no question of a caution as B denied the offence. The court held that allegations that the investigation into, *inter alia*, B's home and social circumstances had been inadequate were not made out on the facts. By contrast, in *R. v. D.P.P., ex p. C.*[10] the Divisional Court quashed a decision of the C.P.S. to discontinue a prosecution of a man for buggery of his wife. The prosecutor reasoned that although consent was no defence to buggery of a woman, there was insufficient evidence that (as she claimed) she did not in fact consent. Considering it as a case of consensual buggery, the public interest did not require a prosecution, the matter being more appropriately dealt with in a matrimonial court. The Divisional Court held, however, that the prosecutor had failed "to bring his mind fully to bear on whether the evidential sufficiency criteria were satisfied in relation to non-consensual buggery." In

---

[3] *ibid.* pp. 194–197

[4] See M. Levi, [1982] B.T.R. 36; Report of the Keith Committee on the *Enforcement Powers of the Revenue Departments* (Cmnd. 8822, 1983); S. Uglow, "Defrauding the Public Purse" [1984] Crim.L.R. 128; R. Smith, "Who's Fiddling? Fraud and Abuse" in S. Ward (ed.) *DHSS in Crisis* (1985); D. Cook, *Rich Law, Poor Law* (1989). The approach of both the police and other agencies to the investigation and prosecution of fraud is considered by M. Levi, *Regulating Fraud* (1987).

[5] Above, p. 710.

[6] [1993] 1 All E.R. 756.

[7] *R. v. General Council of the Bar, ex p. Percival* [1991] 1 Q.B. 212 (disciplinary proceedings against a barrister); *R. v. Inland Revenue Commissioners, ex p. Mead* [1993] 1 All E.R. 772 (Inland Revenue decision to prosecute for tax evasion. Stuart-Smith L.J. held that judicial review was available in principle but Popplewell J. disagreed; both judges agreed that the application failed on the merits); *R. v. D.P.P., ex p. C* [1995] 1 Cr.App.R. 136 (C.P.S. decision to discontinue proceedings); *cf. R. v. D.P.P., ex p. B* [1993] 1 All E.R. 756 (heard with *ex.p. L*, above) (C.P.S. decision not to discontinue proceedings against a juvenile).

[8] n. 6 above.

[9] n. 7 above. In *ex p. Mead*, n. 7 above, the court upheld the selective prosecution policy of the Inland Revenue.

[10] n. 7 above.

particular, he had assumed too readily that the husband's "line of defence" would have been consent and not a denial that he had buggered her. There was ample medical corroboration on the latter point. Accordingly, he had failed to "have regard to any lines of defence which are plainly open to . . . the accused" as required by para. 4 of the Code.[11] The matter was remitted to the C.P.S. for reconsideration.

The possible grounds for a successful challenge were summarised in *R. v. D.P.P., ex p. C*[12] as being where a decision was reached

"(1) because of some unlawful policy (such as the hypothetical decision in *Blackburn* not to prosecute where the value of goods stolen was below £100); or

(2) because the D.P.P. failed to act in accordance with her own policy as set out in the Code; or

(3) because the decision was perverse. It was a decision at which no reasonable prosecutor could have arrived."

The removal of detailed provisions in the current version of the Code[13] makes a successful application for judicial review even more unlikely. Similarly, the court in *ex.p. L* and *ex.p. B*[14] recognised that it would be very difficult in practice to establish that the authorities had made a decision "regardless of or clearly contrary to" a settled policy of the D.P.P., such as the policy of cautioning juveniles or the (more general) policy of giving special consideration to the interests of juveniles in determining whether the public interest required a prosecution. The weakening of these policies by the 1994 changes to the Code for Crown Prosecutors and to the cautioning guidelines must make the task virtually impossible.

Decisions of the Attorney-General not to prosecute are, by contrast, not open to judicial review, because of his "unique constitutional position."[15] Furthermore the C.P.S. does not owe a duty of care in negligence in the conduct of its prosecution of a defendant.[16]

D. THE CLASSIFICATION OF OFFENCES

If a decision is taken to prosecute an offender, the Crown Prosecutor must decide on the appropriate charge.[17] The selection of the charge is important because it

---

[11] The equivalent in the current draft of the Code is that the prosecution "must consider what the defence case may be": para. 5.1.

[12] [1995] 1 Cr.App.R. 136, 141. The court left open the argument that the C.P.S. had adopted an unlawful policy.

[13] Above, p. 712.

[14] n. 7 above.

[15] *R. v. Att.-Gen., ex p. Taylor, The Independent*, August 3, 1995 (application by T and her sister for judicial review of the Attorney-General's decision not to prosecute certain newspapers for contempt of court in respect of prejudicial coverage of their murder trial, following the quashing of their convictions).

[16] *Elguzouli-Daf v. Commissioner of Police of the Metropolis; McBrearty v. Ministry of Defence* [1995] Q.B. 335, C.A.

[17] He or she can, of course, substitute a different charge for that originally preferred by the police, and can add further charges.

may determine the court in which the case will be tried and, hence, the mode of trial. We have already recorded that both the magistrates' court and the Crown Court have original criminal jurisdiction and the work is divided between them according to the seriousness of the charge. In the Crown Court, the trial is "on indictment" with a judge and jury, and in the magistrates' court the trial is summary and conducted by the magistrates. Criminal offences are classified according to the way in which they are to be tried and the number of categories was reduced to three by the Criminal Law Act 1977,[18] which was based upon the report of the James Committee on the Distribution of Criminal Business between the Crown Court and the Magistrates' Courts.[19]

Section 14 of the 1977 Act provided that there should be offences triable only on indictment; offences triable only summarily; and offences triable either way.[20] A fourth category has been added by section 40 of the Criminal Justice Act 1988, which provides that, in certain circumstances, a summary offence may be added to an indictment tried at the Crown Court.[21]

1. OFFENCES TRIABLE ONLY ON INDICTMENT

All offences at common law were triable on indictment. The other two categories are the creatures of statute and, therefore, in the absence of any specific provision an offence will be triable on indictment. In practice, this category is reserved for the most serious offences including murder, manslaughter, rape, robbery, causing grievous bodily harm with intent, blackmail and riot. Some offences were "downgraded" by the Criminal Law Act 1977, Schedule 2[22] so as to be triable either way, in recognition of the fact that, *inter alia*, appearing to be the keeper of a bawdy house;[23] not providing apprentices or servants with food;[24] assaulting a clergyman at a place of worship[25] and bigamy[26] were no longer regarded as the gravest of offences.

2. OFFENCES TRIABLE ONLY SUMMARILY

Magistrates actually deal with the vast majority of trials in this country and they have exclusive jurisdiction in summary trial. Summary offences must be created

[18] The pertinent parts of this Act were re-enacted in the Magistrates' Courts Act 1980.
[19] (Cmnd. 6323, 1975). The Committee was chaired by James L.J.
[20] Section 14 was repealed by the Magistrates' Courts Act 1980 and *not* re-enacted but it is a convenient statement of the three categories. The procedures hereafter stated apply to adults. In the case of juveniles summary trial is almost always the mode of trial, even for indictable offences: see Magistrates' Courts Act 1980, s.24. The crucial date is the date of D's appearance before the court on the occasion when the court makes its decision as to the mode of trial. If the defendant is over 18 on that date he or she has the right to jury trial: *R. v. Islington North Juvenile Court, ex p. Daley* [1983] 1 A.C. 347; *R. v. Nottingham JJ. ex p. Taylor* [1992] Q.B. 557 (when these cases were decided the crucial age was 17).
[21] See below, p. 727.
[22] Now to be found in Magistrates' Courts Act 1980, Sched. 1.
[23] Disorderly Houses Act 1751, s.8.
[24] Offences Against the Person Act 1861, s.26.
[25] *ibid.* s.36.
[26] *ibid.* s.57.

by statute and the designation of an offence as summary prevents a jury trial. It was the proposed reclassification of certain offences as triable only summarily which caused much heated criticism of the James Report.[27] The Criminal Law Act 1977 subsequently made provision for the "down-grading" of certain offences which might previously have come before a jury,[28] and no strenuous objection was taken to allocating a number of road traffic offences (including driving with a blood-alcohol concentration above the prescribed limit[29]), assaulting a police constable,[30] threatening behaviour in public places[31] and other offences to the magistrates alone. The major controversy was caused by a proposal about theft.

"We think that small thefts should not be triable on indictment. . . . In the last analysis society has to choose between two conflicting aims. On the one hand is the existing right of the citizen to be tried by a judge and jury on any charge of theft or criminal damage, however small the amount involved. On the other is the right, especially important to anyone defending a serious charge, to be tried as soon as possible. . . . At present, defendants on serious charges are suffering the injustice of long-delayed trial, while the time of the Crown Court is partly occupied with minor cases of low monetary value."[32] The Committee went on to recommend that where a person was charged with theft or a related offence where the value of the property involved did not exceed £20, that offence should be triable only summarily.[33] That was included in the Criminal Law Bill.

This raised squarely the question of what sorts of offence should entitle a defendant to trial by jury and the reactions to the proposal were emotional.[34] The Bill was introduced into the House of Lords and by the time it reached the House of Commons the clause which would have enacted the proposal had been withdrawn by the government. It is interesting to note that a similar proposal relating to criminal damage where the value of the property damaged is less than £200 was accepted and such an offence is now triable only summarily.[35] The crucial difference was said to be the element of dishonesty inherent in the offence of theft: ". . . people lose a lifetime's reputation for probity by a single action of dishonesty of a material triviality. . . . [Small thefts] remain offences which are serious in the eyes of all honest men."[36]

The offences of taking a motor vehicle without consent and driving while

---

[27] *The Distribution of Criminal Business between the Crown Court and Magistrates' Courts* (Cmnd. 6323, 1975).

[28] 1977 Act, s.15 and Sched. 1.

[29] Now the Road Traffic Act 1988, s.5.

[30] Police Act 1964, s.51(1). Concern was expressed about these changes: see E. J. Griew, *Current Law Statutes Annotated 1977*, General Note to ss.15–17.

[31] Public Order Act 1936, s.5, as substituted by Race Relations Act 1965, s.7: see now the Public Order Act 1986, ss.4, 5.

[32] James Committee Report (see n.29 above), para. 87.

[33] *ibid.* para. 100.

[34] See the speeches of members of the House of Lords during the debate on the second reading of the Criminal Law Bill, H. L. Deb. Vol. 378, cols.801–873, December 14, 1976.

[35] Magistrates' Courts Act 1980, s.22, as amended, and Sched. 2. The limit was subsequently raised to £400 then to £2,000 and most recently to £5,000 by the Criminal Justice and Public Order Act 1994, s.46; s.22 of the 1980 Act sets out a special procedure to be adopted in these cases, on which see *R. v. Salisbury Magistrates' Court, ex p. Mastin* (1986) 84 Cr.App.R. 248; *R. v. Braden* (1987) 152 J.P. 92.

[36] *per* Lord Edmund-Davies in the debate referred to in n. 34, above.

disqualified[37] were changed from triable either way to summary offences by the Criminal Justice Act 1988.[38] Common assault and battery were also made summary offences.[39] The pressure to reclassify other offences, such as small thefts, as summary only, has continued.[40]

3. Offences Triable Either Way

This category is now comprised of (1) those offences specifically mentioned in the First Schedule to the Magistrates' Courts Act 1980;[41] (2) all other offences which prior to the 1977 Act were triable either on indictment or summarily and which were not redesignated;[42] and (3) all offences established since 1977 as triable either way. Amongst the important offences triable either way are all indictable offences under the Theft Acts 1968 and 1978 (save for robbery, blackmail, assault with intent to rob and some burglaries); most of the offences under the Criminal Damage Act 1971, including arson; and certain offences under the Perjury Act 1911, the Sexual Offences Act 1956, the Forgery and Counterfeiting Act 1981, and the Public Order Act 1986.

In respect of offences triable either way it is, of course, necessary to provide a procedure for determining the mode of trial. Save where the prosecution is being carried on by the Attorney-General, the Solicitor-General or the D.P.P. and trial on indictment is required by him,[43] the accused may opt for summary trial or trial on indictment. The court may impose trial on indictment, but may not insist on summary trial if the defendant[44] objects. The procedure to be followed by the magistrates is as follows[45]:

(i) the charge is written down and read to the accused;

---

[37] Theft Act 1968, s.12; Road Traffic Act 1972, s.99 (now re-enacted in the Road Traffic Act 1988, s.103).

[38] s.37. Penalties greater than the maximum applicable in the magistrates' court had been imposed in only a small number of cases: *Consultative Paper on the Distribution of Business between the Crown Court and the Magistrates' Court* (Home Office, 1986), paras.17–20.

[39] *ibid.* s.39. It was formerly triable either way, unless, anomalously, the prosecution was brought by or on behalf of the victim, in which case it was triable summarily or on indictment *at the discretion of the justices*: see *R.v. Harrow JJ., ex p. Osaseri* [1986] Q.B. 589; E.J. Griew, [1983] Crim. L.R. 710.

[40] See, *e.g.* D. Wolchover, "The Right to Jury Trial" (1986) 136 N.L.J. 530, 576 (critical of the proposal); N. A. McKittrick, "Curbing the Right to Jury Trial" (1988) 152 J.P.N. 515. In 1989, an internal L.C.D. study found that 11–12 per cent of the Crown Court caseload would be saved if theft and handling offences in respect of goods below £100 in value and similar offences were made summary only: RCCJ Report, p. 88. The Home Office sought views on the reclassification of minor thefts, possession of an offensive weapon, and some other offences as summary-only (Home Office, *Mode of Trial: A Consultation Document* (Cm. 2908, 1995), pp. 2–4; the government was, however, aware of the objections to these changes.

[41] Re-enacting Sched. 3 to the Criminal Law Act 1977.

[42] Magistrates' Courts Act 1980, s.17.

[43] *ibid.* s.19(4). The D.P.P. must obtain the consent of the Attorney-General: *ibid.* s.19(5) inserted by the Prosecution of Offences Act 1985, Sched. 1, Pt. 1, para. 2

[44] In the case of joint defendants, if one consents to summary trial and the other elects for jury trial, the justices are not obliged to commit both for trial. *R. v. Brentwood JJ., ex p. Nicholls* [1992] 1 A.C. 1

[45] *ibid.* ss.19–21.

(ii) the court listens to any representations from the prosecutor and the accused about the most suitable mode of trial;

(iii) the court proceeds to decide on the more suitable mode of trial, taking into account the nature of the case, whether the circumstances make the offence one of serious character, whether the limited powers of punishment of a magistrates' court would be adequate, and any other relevant circumstances;

(iv) if the court considers summary trial more appropriate, that should be explained to the accused, and that he or she need not consent to summary trial but can opt for trial by jury, and that after a summary trial the magistrates have power to send him or her to the Crown Court for sentence[46];

(v) if the accused consents to summary trial, the case proceeds;

(vi) if the accused opts for trial on indictment, the magistrates proceed with committal proceedings[47];

(vii) if the court considers that trial on indictment is more appropriate it will proceed with committal proceedings and the accused effectively has no choice in the matter.

Finally, it is important to stress that the magistrates must give proper consideration to all the factors and should not be persuaded by the accused (or prosecutor) to allow a summary trial where the offence ought really to be tried on indictment. There are a number of examples of magistrates' courts being severely criticised for allowing serious cases to be tried summarily.[48] The justices are aided somewhat by a provision that they may, during a trial (before the conclusion of the prosecution evidence),[49] decide to change the mode of trial to indictment if the prosecution case reveals the offence to be more serious than might at first have appeared.[50] The reverse change is possible, from committal proceedings to summary trial, subject, in this case, to the consent of the accused.[51]

The defendant should be permitted to change his or her election if he or she has not properly understood the nature and significance of the choice of the mode of trial.[52] In the absence of bad faith on the part of the prosecutor or of unfairness or prejudice to the accused, the prosecutor may substitute a summary

---

[46] Under the Magistrates' Courts Act 1980, s.38, as amended. See below, p. 844.

[47] See below, pp. 744–749.

[48] See e.g. *R. v. Coe* [1968] 1 W.L.R. 1950; *R. v. Northamptonshire Magistrates' Court ex p. Customs and Excise Commissioners, The Independent,* February 23, 1994 (decision to try £200,000 VAT fraud summarily quashed).

[49] Not after a plea of guilty has been accepted: *R. v. Dudley JJ., ex p. Gillard* [1986] A.C. 442, H.L.; *R. v. Telford JJ., ex p. Darlington* (1987) 87 Cr.App.R. 194; and not prior to the commencement of summary trial: *R. v. Southend Magistrates' Court, ex p. Wood* (1986) 152 J.P. 97; *R. v. St. Helens Magistrates' Court, ex p. Critchley* (1987) 152 J.P. 102. See R. Stevens, (1987) 151 J.P.N. 848.

[50] Magistrates' Courts Act 1980, s.25(2), to be amended by the Criminal Procedure and Investigation Bill 1996, Sched. 1. Not merely because co-accused have been committed for trial: *R. v. Chorley Magistrates' Court, ex p. Darbyshire* [1994] C.L.Y. 997; *R. v. Wigan Magistrates' Court, ex p. Layland* (1995) 160 J.P. 223.

[51] *ibid.*, s.25(3), (3A), (4), as amended by the Prosecution of Offences Act 1985, Scheds.1, 2. See *R. v. Liverpool JJ., ex p. C.P.S.* (1989) 90 Cr. App. R. 261

[52] *R. v. Birmingham JJ., ex p. Hodgson* [1985] Q.B. 1131, D.C. (unrepresented defendants had been under the misapprehension that they had no defence; earlier authorities considered); see B. Gibson, (1985) 149 J.P.N. 67. See also *R. v. Forest Magistrates' Court, ex p. Spicer* (1988) 153 J.P. 81; *R. v. Bourne JJ., ex p. Cope* (1988) 153 J.P. 161.

offence for an either-way offence even if the purpose is to deprive the accused of the right to jury trial.[53]

In the 1980s there was a steady increase in the number and proportion of triable-either-way cases committed to the Crown Court.[54] Home Office research has indicated that a high proportion, over 60 per cent, were committed at the discretion of the magistrates rather than at the insistence of the defendant, and that there were considerable variations in practice among the courts surveyed.[55] Guidelines were formulated in some areas to enhance consistency[56] and magistrates were encouraged to retain more cases within their jurisdiction.[57] National guidelines were published in October 1990.[58] These set out some general considerations, based on the case law, but concluding with the proposition that in general either-way offences should be tried summarily unless the court considers that one or more of the features specified in the guidelines for particular offences is present and that its sentencing powers are insufficient. Examples of these (aggravating) features are, for burglary in a dwelling: entry in the daytime when someone is present or at night when the house is normally occupied; the alleged offence is one of a series of similar offences; soiling, ransacking, damage or vandalism occurs; the offence has professional hallmarks; or the unrecovered property is of high value. For theft and fraud, the features include breach of trust by a person of substantial authority; offences committed or disguised in a sophisticated manner, or by an organised gang, or where the victim is particularly vulnerable (e.g. the elderly or infirm), or where the unrecovered property is of high value. The guidelines also state directly that some offences should generally be committed for trial: these include violent disorder and supply or possession with intent to supply of a Class A drug. Where cases involve complex questions of fact or difficult questions of law, the court should consider committal.

Research into defendants' reasons for choosing between summary trial and trial by jury (where a choice is permitted) suggests that the major factor was the intended plea: defendants intending to contest the case commonly regarded trial by jury in the Crown Court as offering a fairer hearing and a better chance of acquittal, in comparison with the magistrates' courts which were said to be biased in favour of the prosecution. A significant number of defendants intending to plead guilty also wished to be dealt with in the Crown Court, notwithstanding its larger sentencing powers, given their greater confidence in

---

[53] R. v. City of Liverpool Stipendiary Magistrate, ex p. Ellison (1988) 153 J.P. 433.

[54] From 55,000 to 93,500 between 1979 and 1987, an increase from 15 per cent to 21 per cent of all defendants proceeded against for either-way offences, falling to 67,200 (17 per cent) in 1994: Criminal Statistics 1979, Table 4.5; 1989, Table 6.4; 1994, Table 6.5. This has been coupled with an increase in the numbers (to 1988) remanded in custody, the percentage remaining at c.22 per cent in most years: Criminal Statistics 1994, Table 8.8.

[55] C. Hedderman and D. Moxon, Magistrates' Court or Crown Court? Made of trial decisions and sentencing (H.O. Research Study No. 125, HMSO, 1992). See also studies by A. E. Bottoms and J. D. McClean, Defendants in the Criminal Process (1976), Chap. 4; C. R. Searle, (1989) 153 J.P.N. 526; and D. Riley and J. Vennard, Triable-Either-Way Cases: Crown Court or Magistrates' Court? (H.O. Research Study No. 98, 1988).

[56] N. A. McKittrick, "Considerations in determining mode of trial" (1987) 151 J.P.N. 468, setting out guidelines formulated by the liaison judges in the East Midlands. A revised version is set out at (1989) 153 J.P.N. 314. Cf. the study by Searle, op. cit., of cases in Nottingham.

[57] cf. letter from the Home Office to the Magistrates' Association summarising the research and suggesting that it was unlikely that the increase in committal rates was accounted for by an increase in the level of the seriousness of offences: (1989) 45 The Magistrate 65.

[58] Practice Note (Mode of Trial: Guidelines) [1990] 1 W.L.R. 1439.

sentencing by a judge rather than by magistrates. Reasons cited most frequently for those choosing summary trial were to get the case to court quickly, the chance of a lighter sentence, to avoid lengthy court proceedings and the triviality of the case.[59]

The most recent research[60] brings out some apparent oddities in the exercise of choice by both defendants and magistrates. Thus, magistrates' sentencing powers would have been sufficient to deal with 62 per cent of cases where they had declined jurisdiction; most defendants who elected Crown Court trial were influenced by the prospects of acquittal, but 82 per cent ended up pleading guilty to all charges on which they were convicted; while more than half of those who elected jury trial said that the possibility of a lighter sentence influenced their decision, in fact the Crown Court made far more use of custody than the magistrates, irrespective of area.

The RCCJ recommended that in the light of the research, changes should be made to introduce a more rational division of either-way cases between magistrates' courts and Crown Court. If prosecution and defence were agreed on venue, that would be decisive; otherwise, the matter would be determined by the magistrates, the defence no longer having the right to insist on jury trial. This would be likely to lead to fewer cases being sent to the Crown Court. The Commission noted that "trial in a magistrates' court is many times cheaper." Beliefs that trial in the Crown Court would be fairer or offer a better chance of acquittal were not relevant. As to the first point, magistrates' courts "conduct over 93% of all criminal cases and should be trusted to try cases fairly."[61] The RCCJ appeared undisturbed by the absence of research on the quality of criminal justice in the magistrates' court.

The government issued a consultation document[62] seeking views on the possible reclassification of certain offences as summary only,[63] removing the defendant's unfettered right to elect for jury trial[64] and obliging the defendant to enter a plea *before* the mode of trial decision is made. The third of these is to be implemented,[65] and is aimed at "reserving Crown Court trial for those who are not admitting the offence with which they are charged and those whose offence is so serious that, despite a plea of guilty, the Crown Court is the only appropriate form for dealing with it."[66]

Finally, it should be noted that further exhortations to magistrates drawing attention to the research findings appear to have had some effect.[67]

---

[59] Hedderman and Moxon (1992) and Riley and Vennard (1988), confirming earlier surveys by Bottoms and McClean (1976) and J. Gregory, *Crown Court or magistrates' court?* (HMSO, 1976).

[60] Hedderman and Moxon (1992).

[61] Cm. 2263, pp. 85–89.

[62] Home Office, *Mode of Trial: A Consultation Document* (Cm. 2908, 1995).

[63] See above, pp. 722–723.

[64] The government was "mindful of ... the strong arguments against" this proposal: Cm. 2908, p. 4.

[65] Criminal Procedure and Investigations Bill 1996, cl.47, inserting new ss. 17A–17C in the Magistrates' Courts Act 1980.

[66] Cm. 2908, p. 5.

[67] *ibid.*, p. 2. The proportion of triable-either-way cases committed to the Crown Court fell from 20 per cent in 1990 to 16 per cent in 1993, rising to 17 per cent in 1994: *Criminal Statistics England and Wales 1994*, Table 6.5. However, the proportion committed at the direction of magistrates rose from 47 per cent in 1987 to 65 per cent in 1993 and 1994: *ibid.*, p. 132.

4. Summary Offences in the Crown Court

The position is further complicated by sections 40 and 41 of the Criminal Justice Act 1988.[68] Under section 41 where a magistrates' court commits a person to the Crown Court for trial of an either-way offence, it may also commit him or her for trial of any summary offence which is (a) punishable with imprisonment or disqualification from driving, and (b) arises out of circumstances which appear to be the same as or connected with those giving rise to the either-way offence.[69] A decision to exercise this power cannot be questioned on appeal or on an application for judicial review. If the defendant is convicted on the indictment, and then pleads guilty to the summary offence, the Crown Court can deal with it then and there, although it can only exercise the sentencing powers that the magistrates' court would have had. If the defendant pleads not guilty, the matter has to be remitted for trial in the magistrates' court, unless the prosecution state that they would not wish to offer evidence in which case the Crown Court must dismiss the charge. If the Court of Appeal allows an appeal against conviction for the associated either-way offence, it must set aside the conviction for the summary offence, and it may direct that no further proceedings be taken in relation to it.

Section 40[70] applies to a narrower range of summary offences, but enables them to be added to the indictment and actually tried in the Crown Court. The offences are those which were made summary only by sections 37 to 39 of the 1988 Act,[71] and any other offence punishable by imprisonment or a driving disqualification and specified by the Secretary of State. A summary offence in one of these categories can be added to the indictment if it is (a) founded on the same facts or evidence as a count charging an indictable offence, or (b) part of a series of offences of the same or similar character as an indictable offence which is also charged.[72] In either case, the relevant facts or evidence must be disclosed in the committal papers. The offence is tried as if it were an indictable offence, but if the person is convicted, the Crown Court (as under section 41) may only exercise the sentencing powers that the magistrates' courts would have had. Where a person is committed for trial for a summary offence under section 41, and the offence falls in one of the section 40 categories, it may be dealt with at the Crown Court under that section rather than under section 41. These sections provide a more convenient procedure for

---

[68] See D. Tucker, (1989) L.S. Gaz., 15 March, p. 23.

[69] This procedure is not available in conjunction with an indictable-only offence: *R. v. Miall* [1992] Crim. L.R. 71.

[70] To be amended by the Criminal Procedure and Investigations Bill 1996, Sched. 1.

[71] Common assault, taking a motor vehicle without authority, driving while disqualified, criminal damage not exceeding £2,000. Assaulting a prison custody officer (Criminal Justice Act 1991, s.90(1)) or a secure training centre custody officer (Criminal Justice and Public Order Act 1994, s.13(1)) were added by the 1994 Act, Sched. 9, para. 35.

[72] *cf.* the Indictment Rules 1971, r.9: below, p. 849. It is insufficient that a summary offence is linked to another summary offence on the indictment by virtue of s.40: *R. v. Callaghan* [1992] Crim. L.R. 191. Misjoinder of a summary offence does not render the whole indictment invalid: *ibid.*; *R. v. Simon* [1992] Crim. L.R. 444 (*obiter*). In *R. v. Lewis* (1991) 95 Cr. App. R. 131, a count alleging common assault on a police officer at the police station after L's arrest for threatening to kill his former girlfriend and another man was held not to be founded on the same facts on evidence or to be part of a similar series of offences as counts based on the threats. The decision of the court in *Lewis* that misjoinder rendered the whole indictment a nullity was inconsistent with the decision in *Callaghan* (above), which was not cited, and disapproved, *obiter*, in *Simon* (above).

dealing with cases involving both summary and indictable offences but at the cost of adding to the complexity of the law.

E. GETTING THE ACCUSED INTO COURT

If an accused is to be prosecuted for an offence, he or she must actually be brought before a court to have the charge tried or at least to have it determined how and when the trial process should begin. As we have already seen there are two basic methods by which this can be done: by arrest (without warrant) and charge, or by summons.[73] A variant of the second method involves issue of a warrant for the arrest of the accused rather than a summons; these both depend upon the decision of a magistrate after the laying of an information by a named person.[74] The police may be willing to charge a person on behalf of a private prosecutor.[75]

An information is merely a statement of the suspected offence and offender, either written or verbal, in terms specified by the Magistrates Courts Rules 1981,[76] which is placed before a magistrate or the justices' clerk[77] so that a summons or warrant may be issued. If a warrant is required the information must be in writing and on oath,[78] so requiring the attention of a magistrate since a clerk may not act where the information is on oath.[79] A typical information would be set out as follows.[80]

NOTTINGHAM MAGISTRATES COURT

DATE: March 1st 1995

ACCUSED: Henry Frederick Smailey

ADDRESS: 32 Woodland Hall Grove, Cripston, Nottingham.

ALLEGED OFFENCE: Henry Smailey on February 27th 1995, at the Department of Law, University Park, Nottingham, dishonestly stole £5, the property of N. P. Gravells, Esq., contrary to section 1 of the Theft Act 1968.

---

[73] See above, pp. 666–667. Not all persons originally arrested without warrant and subsequently proceeded against are charged: a proportion are reported for summons instead. Powers of arrest without a warrant are considered above, pp. 667–670.

[74] Not, *e.g.* in the name of a police force: *Rubin v. D.P.P.* [1990] 2 Q.B. 80 (although the information here was not held invalid as the identity of the relevant constable could easily have been ascertained and the defendant had suffered no injustice).

[75] *R. v. Stafford JJ., ex p. Commissioners of Customs and Excise* [1991] 2 Q.B. 339.

[76] S.I. 1981 No. 552, and the accompanying Magistrates' Courts Forms Rules 1981 (S.I. 1981 No. 553).

[77] Justices of the Peace Act 1979, s.28(1).

[78] Magistrates' Courts Act 1980, s.1(3).

[79] Justices' Clerks Rules 1970 (S.I. 1970 No. 321), r.3.

[80] Magistrates' Courts (Forms) Rules 1981, Form. 1.

THE INFORMATION OF:	Gavin Edmunds, Police Constable 1234
ADDRESS:	Cripston Police Station, Jug Road, Cripston, Nottingham.
TELEPHONE:	9999999

WHO UPON OATH STATES THAT THE ACCUSED COMMITTED THE OFFENCE OF WHICH PARTICULARS ARE GIVEN ABOVE.

TAKEN AND SWORN BEFORE ME

Cordelia Lear

JUSTICE OF THE PEACE

JUSTICES' CLERK

The information procedure does not seem to be used very often to procure a warrant[81] (the conditions for the grant of which are, in any event, carefully prescribed[82]). On the grant of a summons the magistrate, the clerk or the clerk's delegate[83] should satisfy him- or herself that the offence is known to the law; that it is not out of time; that the court has jurisdiction and that the informant has the requisite authority to prosecute.[84] Furthermore, he or she should consider all the relevant circumstances, which may include information beyond that supplied by the informant.[85] A warrant should only be issued if it appears that a summons will be ineffective.[86] The summons, if issued, will not look very different from the information.[87]

NOTTINGHAM MAGISTRATES COURT

DATE:	March 1st 1995
TO THE ACCUSED:	Henry Frederick Smailey
OF:	32 Woodland Hall Grove, Cripston, Nottingham

YOU ARE HEREBY SUMMONED TO APPEAR ON May 18th 1995, AT

---

[81] RCCP I, para. 179.

[82] By the Magistrates' Courts Act 1980, ss.1(4), 13(2). Broadly speaking, the alleged offence must be indictable or punishable with imprisonment, or the accused must have failed to respond to a summons, or his or her address is not sufficiently known for a summons to be served.

[83] See above, p. 207.

[84] *R. v. Metropolitan Stipendiary Magistrate, ex p. Klahn* [1979] 1 W.L.R. 933.

[85] *R. v. Tower Bridge Metropolitan Stipendiary Magistrate, ex p. Chaudhry* [1993] 3 W.L.R. 1154 (magistrate entitled to refuse to issue summons alleging causing death by reckless driving arising out of incident in respect of which C.P.S. had already laid informations alleging driving without due care and attention and other minor offences); cf. *R. v. Bingley Magistrates' Court, ex p. Morrow, The Times*, April 28, 1994 (magistrates entitled to refuse summons for murder against doctor for removing life support from a patient where a civil court had granted a declaration that this could be done without incurring civil or criminal liability).

[86] *O'Brien v. Brabner* (1885) 49 J.P.N. 227.

[87] Magistrates' Courts (Forms) Rules 1981, Form 2.

10.30 a.m. BEFORE THE MAGISTRATES' COURT at the Guildhall, Nottingham to ANSWER TO THE FOLLOWING INFORMATION

ALLEGED OFFENCE: You on February 27th 1995 at the Department of Law, University Park, Nottingham dishonestly stole £5, the property of N. P. Gravells, Esq., contrary to section 1 of the Theft Act 1968.

PROSECUTOR: Trevor Gunn, Chief Inspector of
                                         Police
ADDRESS: Cripston Police Station, Jug Road,
                                         Cripston, Nottingham.

                                                        Cordelia Lear
                                         JUSTICE OF THE PEACE

The accused should then respond to the summons and attendance at court on a specified day has therefore been secured. The process can be continued on that day. If he or she fails to respond, a warrant may then be appropriate.

In general, magistrates cannot try a summary offence unless the information was laid within six months from the time when the offence was committed.[88] The information is regarded as laid when it is received at the office of the clerk to the justices in the relevant area. For this purpose it is not necessary for it to be considered personally by a justice or justices' clerk; such consideration is only a necessary pre-condition for the issue of a summons or warrant on the basis of the information.[89] The laying of an information before a decision to prosecute has been taken, in order to comply with the time limit, may constitute an abuse of the process of the court, causing the court to decline jurisdiction,[90] as may excessive delay before issuing a summons.[91]

If the accused has been arrested by warrant or without warrant it is the duty of the police then to procure his or her attendance at court. He or she will have been given bail by the police or by the warrant to appear on an appointed day or will have been brought to court in custody. If the accused is in custody after arrest without a warrant he or she must be brought before a magistrates' court in accordance with the requirements of the Police and Criminal Evidence Act 1984.[92]

Technically, when an accused is arrested without warrant and charged at the police station an information is laid when the charge sheet is remitted by the police to the justices' clerk for inclusion on the court list,[93] but this is in reality a fiction and offenders who are brought to court in this way will never have the facts initially scrutinised by a magistrate.

(The RCCP concluded that the summons and warrant procedure was a virtual dead letter since the consideration given to the decision to prosecute by the

---

[88] Magistrates' Courts Act 1980, s.127.
[89] R. v. Manchester Stipendiary Magistrate, ex p. Hill [1983] 1 A.C. 328, 342–343, disapproving dicta in R. v. Gateshead JJ., ex p. Tesco Stores Ltd [1981] Q.B. 470. Informations fed into a computer system within the time limit although printed out after were held to be properly laid in R. v. Pontypridd Juvenile Court, ex p. B. (1988) 153 J.P. 213.
[90] R. v. Brentford JJ., ex p. Wong [1981] Q.B. 445.
[91] R. v. Fairford JJ., ex p. Brewster [1976] Q.B. 600.
[92] See above, p. 676.
[93] The process is described and commented on in RCCP I, para. 182.

justices' clerk or magistrate was minimal. It was proposed that there should, in future, be a single procedure for getting an accused to court, the making of a formal "accusation" by the police fixing the date and time of the first court appearance.[94] This recommendation was not accepted.)

Where an accused is arrested the question will arise at what stage, if at all, he or she should be released before trial.

F. BAIL OR CUSTODY?[95]

To deprive an accused[96] of liberty pending trial may be to keep in custody an innocent person or one who, though convicted, ultimately receives a non-custodial sentence. To allow an accused liberty pending trial may be to permit him or her to disappear, commit further offences, or interfere with witnesses and obstruct the course of justice. It is a difficult decision. The issue is raised as soon as a person is taken into custody and remains live until trial and, indeed, between conviction and appeal. The procedure by which the accused is released subject to a requirement to surrender to custody again at a specified time and place is termed the granting of bail. Bail may be granted by the police, the magistrates' court, the Crown Court, the High Court and the Court of Appeal under a variety of statutory and common law provisions,[97] but the granting of bail in all criminal proceedings must be in accordance with the principles set out in the Bail Act 1976.

This Act, which came into force in the Spring of 1978, was a response to the widespread disquiet about the operation of the system of bail and resulted from the Report of a Home Office Working Party[98] which had been established in 1971 "to review practice and procedure in magistrates' courts relating to the grant or refusal of bail and to make recommendations."[99] Before considering the general principles it is helpful to define two important terms.

A *surety* is a person who is willing to undertake to secure the surrender of the accused to custody. The grant of bail may be made conditional upon the accused finding a suitable surety or sureties.[1] Whoever is willing to be a surety must enter into a *recognizance*, which is a formal acknowledgment that he or she will owe the Crown a specified sum of money if the accused fails to surrender to

---

[94] RCCP Report, para. B.4.
[95] See generally, M. King, *Bail or Custody*, Cobden Trust (1971); A. K. Bottomley, *Decisions in the Penal Process* (1973), pp. 93–105, and "The Granting of Bail: Principles and Practice" (1968) 31 M.L.R. 40; M. Zander, "Bail: A Reappraisal" [1967] Crim.L.R. 25, 100, 128; A. Ashworth, *The English Criminal Process: a Review of Empirical Research* (1984), Chap. 5; M. Winfield, *Lacking Conviction* (1984); C. Chatterton, *Bail: Law and Practice* (1986); E. Cape, *Legal Action*, October 1989, p. 11 and November 1989, p. 21; N. Corre, *Bail in Criminal Proceedings* (1990); R. Morgan and S. Jones, "Bail or Jail?" in E. Stockdale and S. Casale, *Criminal Justice under Stress* (1992) Chap. 2; P. Cavadino and B. Gibson, *Bail: The Law, Best Practice and the Debate* (1993).
[96] We use the term "accused" throughout this section to include those arrested, those on trial, and those convicted.
[97] See below, pp. 738–742.
[98] *Bail Procedures in Magistrates' Courts*, Report of the Home Office Working Party (1974).
[99] Although the terms of reference of the Working Party referred specifically to magistrates' courts the provisions of the Bail Act 1976 actually went somewhat wider.
[1] Bail Act 1976, s.3(4).

custody. No money is payable by the surety unless the accused actually absconds.[2] The amount of the recognizance is a matter for the police officer or court granting bail.

Statutory criteria are now fixed for determining the suitability of persons who may offer to be sureties where the grant of bail is conditional upon finding sureties.[3] In considering the suitability of a proposed surety, regard may be had, *inter alia*, to financial resources, character and any previous convictions, and "proximity" to the accused.[4] If a court or police officer considers a proposed surety to be unsuitable there is provision for appeal.[5]

Prior to the Bail Act it was quite common for the accused to be required to enter into a personal recognizance, but this has now been abolished[6] and the only circumstances in which the accused may be required to provide security is if it appears likely that he or she will leave Great Britain.[7]

1. General Principles Relating to the Grant of Bail

The Bail Act introduced a general right to bail for accused persons and certain others subject to exceptions specified in a Schedule to the Act. In fact, the exceptions are substantial and this has led commentators to speak of a "presumption in favour of bail" rather than a "right to bail". In addition the Act focused attention upon the need for information about the accused to be available to the court so that the bail decision could be an informed one, and required reasons to be given to the accused where bail was not granted so that he or she might more effectively conduct an appeal against the decision.

Section 4 of the Bail Act 1976 creates the *right to bail*:

"(1) A person to whom this section applies shall be granted bail except as provided in Schedule 1 to this Act.

(2) This section applies to a person who is accused of an offence when—

(a) he appears or is brought before a magistrates' court or the Crown

---

[2] The recognizance may not be forfeited if the surety has made every effort to secure the appearance of the accused and acted with all due diligence, but the obligation is upon the surety to satisfy the court that all or part of the sum should not be forfeited. Only in exceptional cases will the court order that the recognizance should not be forfeited: Magistrates' Courts Act 1980, s.120; *R. v. Southampton JJ., ex p. Green* [1976] Q.B. 11; *R. v. Waltham Forest JJ., ex p. Palfrey* (1980) 2 Cr.App.R.(S.) 208; *R. v. Knightsbridge Crown Court, ex p. Newton* [1980] Crim.L.R. 715; *R. v. Ipswich Crown Court, ex p. Reddington* [1981] Crim. L.R. 618; *R. v. Wells Street Magistrates' Court, ex p. Albanese* [1982] Q.B. 333; *R. v. Uxbridge JJ., ex p. Heward-Mills* [1983] 1 W.L.R. 56; *R. v. Inner London Crown Court, ex p. Springall* (1986) 85 Cr.App.R. 214; *R. v. York Crown Court, ex p. Coleman and How* (1987) 86 Cr.App.R. 151; *R. v. Reading Crown Court, ex p. Bello* [1992] 3 All E.R. 353; *R. v. Maidstone Crown Court, ex p. Lever* [1995] 1 W.L.R. 928. The courts appear to be becoming more willing to remit the whole or part of the sum due where the surety has acted reasonably or has not been informed of a change in bail conditions; however, lack of culpability does not *entitle* the surety to remission of the whole or any part of the sum.

[3] Bail Act 1976, s.8(2). See generally J. Morton, "Sureties" (1985) 135 N.L.J. 981.

[4] "Proximity" to the accused includes consideration of kinship, place of residence or other matters.

[5] Bail Act 1976, s.8(5).

[6] *ibid*. s.3(2).

[7] *ibid*. s.3(5).

> Court in the course of or in connection with proceedings for the
> offence, or
> (b) he applies to a court for bail [or for a variation of the conditions of
> bail] in connection with the proceedings.''

There are additional categories brought within the entitlement and some which are excepted.[8] By virtue of section 25 of the Criminal Justice and Public Order Act 1994, bail *cannot* be granted where a person is charged with a homicide offence or rape or attempted rape after having previously been convicted of such an offence or culpable homicide (and, in the case of manslaughter or culpable homicide only, been sentenced to imprisonment or long-term detention). It is important to note that section 4 applies to the grant of bail by courts only. The grant of bail by the police, considered below, is not subject to this provision.

Schedule 1 of the Act creates the *exceptions to the right to bail*, and distinguishes between defendants accused or convicted of offences punishable with imprisonment[9] and those not punishable with imprisonment.[10] In respect of the imprisonable offences the accused need not be granted bail if the court is satisfied that there are substantial grounds for believing that the accused would, if released on bail:

(a) fail to surrender to custody, or
(b) commit an offence while on bail, or
(c) interfere with witnesses or otherwise obstruct the course of justice.[11]

The accused also need not be granted bail if

(a) the offence is indictable or triable either way; and
(b) it appears to the court that he was on bail in criminal proceedings on the date of the offence.[12]

The accused need not be granted bail where the court is satisfied that it has not been practicable to obtain sufficient information since the proceedings were instituted to make a proper decision on bail.[13]

---

[8] Within the entitlement—a person remanded for reports after conviction (Bail Act 1976, s.4(4)); a person brought before the court for breach of a probation, community service, combination or curfew order (s.4(3)). Excluded from entitlement—a person convicted of the offence charged (unless remanded for reports) (s.4(2)); a fugitive offender (s.4(2)); a person who the court is satisfied should be kept in custody for his or her own protection or (if a child or young person) his or her own welfare (Sched. 1, Part I, para. 3; Part II, para. 3); a person charged with treason (s.4(7)); a person arrested for absconding or breach of bail granted (Sched. 1, Part I, para. 6; Part II, para. 5).

[9] Sched. 1, Part I.

[10] Sched. 1, Part II.

[11] Sched. 1, Part I, para. 2.

[12] *ibid.*, para. 2A, inserted by the Criminal Justice and Public Order Act 1994, s.26. The addition of this ground was justified by reference to the large number of crimes said to be committed by persons on bail (estimated to be *c.*10 per cent–12 per cent of those remanded on bail, *c.*50,000 in 1991: see P. M. Morgan, *Offending while on bail: a survey of recent studies* (H.O.R.P.U. Paper. No.65, 1992). The overall number had increased from *c.*35,000 in five years; however, the *proportion* of those on bail committing offences appears to have remained constant, the increase arising from an increase in the total number remanded on bail: Morgan and Jones (*op cit.* n.95, above), pp. 41–45.

[13] *ibid.* para. 5.

This last point emphasises that the court must have access to information about the defendant because it is required to have regard to specified matters (as far as they appear relevant) including:

(a) the nature and seriousness of the offence (and the probable method of dealing with it);
(b) the character, antecedents, associations and community ties of the defendant;
(c) the defendant's record in respect of any previous grants of bail;
(d) the strength of the evidence against him or her.[14]

In respect of non-imprisonable offences the defendant may only be denied bail if it appears to the court that he or she has previously failed to surrender to bail and that the court believes that, if released, he or she would again fail to surrender to custody.[15]

The court, if it is to refuse bail, must be "satisfied that there are substantial grounds for believing" that one of the specified situations exists. This formulation of the standard of proof is a compromise reached after much debate both in the House of Commons and the House of Lords. The original draft was "satisfied that it is probable"; an amendment in the Lords substituted, "satisfied that there is an unacceptable risk";[16] and the eventual compromise was thought to pitch the standard of proof somewhere between the two.[17]

If bail is refused by the court or conditions are imposed on the grant of bail in respect of anyone to whom section 4 of the Act applies, the court must give reasons for withholding bail or imposing the conditions with a view to enabling the accused to make application to another court.[18] This is a logical provision, given that the courts are now directed towards specific considerations in the refusal of bail. The accused is entitled to know in what respect he or she is considered unsuitable for bail. Furthermore, reasons must now be given where the court grants bail to an accused charged with murder, manslaughter, rape, attempted murder or attempted rape.[19]

The court may attach conditions necessary to secure that he or she

(a) surrenders to custody;
(b) does not commit an offence while on bail;
(c) does not interfere with witnesses or otherwise obstruct the course of justice;
(d) makes him- or herself available for the purposes of enabling enquiries, or a report to be made to assist the court in dealing with him or her for the offence.[20]

---

[14] ibid. para. 9.
[15] Sched. 1, Part II, para. 2.
[16] See the speech of Lord Hailsham, H.L. Deb., April 6, 1976, Vol. 369, col. 1544 et seq.
[17] H.C. Deb., November 2, 1976, Vol. 918, col. 1323–4, Mr Brynmor John, then Minister of State, Home Office.
[18] Bail Act 1976, s.5(3).
[19] ibid. Sched. 1, Part I, para. 9A, inserted by the Criminal Justice Act 1988. This provision was passed in view of public concern about bail being too readily granted in cases of serious alleged violence.
[20] ibid. s.3(6), Sched. 1, para. 8(1). The power to attach conditions extends to both imprisonable and non-imprisonable offences (see R. v. Bournemouth Magistrates' Court, ex p. Cross (1988) 89 Cr. App. R. 90). For the argument that a surety of good behaviour might be imposed as a

In this context, it is not necessary that the court has "substantial grounds": it is sufficient that it perceives "a real and not fanciful risk" of, for example, an offence being committed.[21] In the case of a person accused of murder, the court must, unless it considers that satisfactory reports of his or her medical condition have already been obtained, impose bail conditions requiring that he or she undergo examination by two medical practitioners to enable such reports to be prepared.[22]

The imposition of conditions on the grant of bail can be a very serious matter. It is not uncommon for the magistrates to require the accused to report regularly to a police station as a condition of bail, or to observe a curfew, or to reside in or keep away from particular places. In serious matters the accused may be required to surrender his or her passport.[23] It is arguable that the conditions attached ought to relate primarily to securing the attendance of the accused in court but they can also be used to curtail potentially criminal activities pending the trial of the alleged offence.[24]

2. APPLICATION OF THE PRINCIPLES

It seems that the Bail Act has not made a substantial difference to the practice of the courts. There were, indeed, two significant reductions in the number of prisoners on remand[25] but such research as there is shows little general change.[26] The most significant factors influencing remand decisions in the magistrates' courts are whether the police have granted bail, the seriousness of the offence and court policy.[27] Furthermore, Home Office statistics indicate significant vari-

---

condition of bail under the court's binding-over powers, see N. Corre, [1986] Crim.L.R.162. See also B. P. Block, (1990) 154 J. P. N. 83; P. W. H. Lydiate, *ibid.* p. 132.

[21] *R. v. Mansfield JJ., ex p. Sharkey* [1985] Q. B. 613.

[22] Bail Act 1976, s.3(6A), 96(B), inserted by the Mental Health (Amendment) Act 1982, s.34. The grant of bail without complying with this requirement is a nullity: *R. v. Central Criminal Court, ex p. Porter* [1992] Crim.L.R. 121.

[23] Guidance was given by the Home Office in Circular 206/1977 of November 18, 1977. Courts were, *e.g.*, requested to be especially selective in requiring regular reporting to a police station as this can be burdensome for the police and also raise identification problems.

[24] During the 1984–85 miners' strike, striking miners charged with criminal offences were frequently granted bail subject to conditions prohibiting picketing at premises other than the defendant's own place of work: the practice was controversial (see S. McCabe and P. Wallington, *The Police, Public Order, and Civil Liberties* (1988), pp. 97–98), but held to be lawful by the Divisional Court (*R. v. Mansfield JJ., ex p. Sharkey* [1985] Q. B. 613). See also *R. v. Bournemouth Magistrates' Court, ex p. Cross* (1988) 89 Cr. App. R. 90 (bail conditions prohibiting defendants charged with disturbing a fox hunting meet from attending another hunt meeting held valid).

[25] One after the Home Office Circular 155/1975 which urged the courts to take a more liberal view on bail, and the other after the Bail Act 1976.

[26] See below, pp. 743–744 and M. Zander, "The Operation of the Bail Act in London Magistrates' Courts" (1979) 129 N. L. J. 108. See also, R. Vogler, "The Changing Nature of Bail," *LAG, Bulletin*, February 1983, 11; R. East and M. Doherty, "The Practical Operation of Bail," *LAG Bulletin*, March 1984, 12; R. Morgan, "Remands in Custody" [1989] Crim.L.R.481. The annual number of remands in custody is still lower than it was before the bail reforms of the 1970s: NACRO Briefing 32, *Remands in Custody – Some Facts and Figures* (1993), p. 2.

[27] P. Jones, "Remand decisions in magistrates' courts" in D. Moxon (ed.), *Managing Criminal Justice* (1980), Chap. 10. See also P. M. Morgan and R. Pearce, *Remand Decisions in Brighton and Bournemouth* (H. O. R. P. U. Paper 53, 1989); P. M. Morgan, (1990) 29 H. O. R. B. 18

ations in the use of custodial remands among different petty sessional
divisions.[28]

An issue which initially concerned the courts was the procedure to be adopted
on successive applications for bail. The magistrates' court is given power, prior
to the commencement of the hearing, to remand an accused person in custody
for a period not exceeding eight clear days[29] and this may be appropriate where
the prosecution are not yet ready to proceed with the case. In complex cases
this meant a court appearance every eight days for a considerable length of
time.[30] At every appearance the accused was entitled to request bail and would
normally appear before differently constituted courts each time.[31] In Nottingham,
the City justices adopted a policy under which after a second application[32] for
bail they would not consider on subsequent applications matters previously
before the court unless there had been a change in circumstances.[33] In effect,
remand in custody became automatic. A group of Nottingham solicitors organised an application for mandamus by Clive Edgar Davies, charged with various
offences of criminal damage and rape, directing the justices to hear the full facts
supporting an application for bail made on April 10, 1980[34] and determine it
accordingly. In *R. v. Nottingham JJ. ex p. Davies*[35] the Divisional Court refused
the application.

It was argued on behalf of Davies that he had a right to bail which was only
defeasible on the specified grounds; that the court has a duty to consider the
grant of bail on every occasion on which the accused appears; and that the fact
of a previous remand could not, of itself, satisfy the justices that one of the
specified grounds still existed. The court did not accede to the argument and
Donaldson L.J. based his judgment primarily upon a notion of *res judicata*.[36]
The finding of the original court that Schedule 1 circumstances existed, "... is
to be treated like every other finding of the court. It is *res judicata* or analogous
thereto. . . . It follows that on the next occasion when bail is considered the
court should treat, as an essential fact, that at the time when the matter of bail
was last considered, Schedule 1 circumstances did indeed exist. Strictly speaking, they can and should only investigate whether that situation has changed

---

[28] Jones, *op. cit.* above. Home Office Statistical Bulletin 7/87, discussed by B. Gibson (1987) 151
J.P.N. 520 and B. Rowland, (1987) 151 J.P.N. 651. The Home Office has emphasised the need
for consistency: Home Office Circular 25/1988: (1988) 44 *The Magistrate* 173.

[29] Magistrates' Courts Act 1980, s.128(6).

[30] This can clearly be oppressive since the accused is being held in custody without trial, but it is
well established that an unreasonable delay on the part of the prosecution will be a good reason
for granting bail: *R. v. Nottingham Justices, ex p. Davies* [1981] Q.B. 38, at p. 44.

[31] At the time of Davies' application (see note above) the Nottingham bench consisted of 320
justices, with up to 25 courts sitting each day. The chance of getting the same justices two weeks
running was negligible.

[32] After the *second* application, because the first is usually made by a duty solicitor (see above, p.
502) who may not be fully briefed so as to make a proper application. On the second application
the accused will normally be legally aided and represented by his or her own solicitor who should
then be in a position to place all relevant matters before the court.

[33] A policy apparently inspired by certain remarks made by Ackner J. to a meeting of justices'
clerks and reported in (1980) 36 *The Magistrate* 34, 97. The actual wording of the Nottingham
policy is contained in the report of *Davies*, [1981] Q.B. 38, at p. 41.

[34] The date was significant because that was Davies' third application for bail.

[35] [1981] Q.B. 38.

[36] A final judgment already decided by a competent court on the same question.

since then.''[37] The court also indicated that the position of the accused is safeguarded by the provision for an application to a High Court judge for bail.[38]

This decision excited both favourable[39] and unfavourable[40] comment, and was in certain respects in need of clarification.[41] It has now been codified by section 154 of the Criminal Justice Act 1988.[42] This provides:

"(1) If the court decides not to grant the defendant bail, it is the court's duty to consider, at each subsequent hearing while the defendant . . . remains in custody, whether he ought to be granted bail.

(2) At the first hearing[43] after that at which the court decided not to grant the defendant bail[44] he may support an application for bail with any argument as to fact or law that he desires (whether or not he has advanced that argument previously).

(3) At subsequent hearings the court need not hear arguments as to fact or law which it has heard previously.''

This makes it clear that while the court is not obliged to hear repeated arguments, it has a discretion to do so; the position is, accordingly, a little more flexible than that suggested by Donaldson L.J. in *ex p. Davies*.

The position has also been affected to some extent by the provisions of section 59 and Schedule 9 of the Criminal Justice Act 1982.[45] This enables the court to remand an accused in his or her absence for up to three successive remand hearings provided that he or she consents and is legally represented. This alleviates the problem of constant weekly journeys for the accused who does not wish to contest the remand, but *ex p. Davies* still applies to prevent the non-consenting accused from seeking bail on every remand appearance. Section 155 of the Criminal Justice Act 1988[46] authorised the introduction of a new power for the court to remand in custody for a period up to 28 days without the accused's consent. This is exercisable where the accused has previously been remanded

---

[37] [1981] Q.B. 38 at p. 44.

[38] See below, p. 742.

[39] Anon. "Bail Applications" (1980) 144 J.P.N. 319; Editorials in (1980) 36 *The Magistrate* 97, 135; K. Polak, "Applications for Bail" (1980) 144 J.P.N. 525.

[40] M. Hayes, "Where Now the Right to Bail" [1981] Crim.L.R.20. In "Bail—a Suitable Case for Treatment" (1982) 132 N.L.J. 409, J. Burrow analyses other less predictable effects of the decision.

[41] See S. Holdham, (1985) 135 N.L.J. 471; P. W. H. Lydiate, "Bail procedure in magistrates' courts: basic procedures" (1987) 151 J.P.N. 164, 181. See also *R. v. Reading Crown Court, ex p. Malik* [1981] Q.B. 451 and *R. v. Slough JJ., ex p. Duncan and Embling* (1982) 75 Cr. App. R. 384 (different views expressed on whether as a general rule reaching the stage of committal for trial would constitute a change in circumstances: Donaldson L.J. in the *Reading* case indicated *obiter* that it would; Ormrod L.J. in the *Slough* case that it would not necessarily do so).

[42] Inserting a new Part IIA in Sched. 1 to the Bail Act 1976.

[43] Occasions when a person is remanded in his or her absence (see below) are not "hearings": *R. v. Dover and East Kent JJ., ex p. Dean* (1991) 156 J.P. 357.

[44] A decision that it has not been practicable to obtain sufficient information to decide to grant bail (above, p. 733) is not a "decision not to grant bail" for these purposes: *R. v. Calder JJ., ex p. Kennedy* (1992) 156 J.P. 716.

[45] Inserting s.128(1A)–(1C), (3A)–(3E) of the Magistrates' Courts Act 1980, to be amended by the Criminal Procedure and Investigations Bill 1996, cl. 50. See C. May, *Remands in the absence of the accused* (H.O.R.P.U. Paper No. 34, 1985), estimating a saving of 2 per cent on total escort costs.

[46] Inserting s.128A of the Magistrates' Courts Act 1980.

in custody for the same offence and the court has set a date for the next stage in the proceedings.[47]

3. POLICE BAIL[48]

The Police and Criminal Evidence Act 1984 establishes a number of situations in which a person in police custody may be released on bail. The decision in most cases is taken by the custody officer. Where the custody officer orders a person's release under section 34, this must be without bail unless it appears to the custody officer (1) that there is need for further investigation of any matter in connection with which he or she was detained, or (2) that proceedings may be taken against him or her in respect of any such matter: if it does so appear, the person must be released on bail. In other situations, there is a discretion to release with or without bail, as where a person is released before charge (section 37); after charge (section 38); after 24 hours detention (section 41); after 36 hours detention (section 42); or where a warrant for further detention is refused or expires (sections 43, 44).[49] In each case a release on bail "shall be a release on bail granted in accordance with sections 3, 3A, 5 and 5A of the Bail Act 1976 as they apply to bail granted by a constable",[50] and shall be subject to a duty to appear before a magistrates' court or to return to the police station as directed by the custody officer, who must specify the time and place.[51] The option of requiring the accused to return to the police station can be employed to give the police time to continue their enquiries, and to decide whether they wish to prosecute and if so on what charges.

Where an accused is released on police bail after being charged, the custody officer now has the power to attach conditions (other than a condition requiring residence in a bail hostel or that the accused makes himself available for enabling inquiries or a report to be made).[52] Where the custody officer has granted police bail, he or she or another custody officer at the same police station may vary the conditions at the request of the person on bail, and may impose conditions or more onerous conditions.[53] Conditions may only be imposed (or varied) if it appears to the officer necessary to do so for the purpose

---

[47] The provision was first introduced experimentally in specified areas, but now extends to all petty sessions areas: Magistrates' Courts (Remands in Custody) Order 1991 (S.I. 1991 No. 2667). This followed a Home Office report which concluded that there was "little evidence" to support the concerns expressed during the passage of the 1988 Act that this "would cause an increase in the time spent in custody": P. F. Henderson and P. Morgan, *Remands in custody for up to 28 days: the experiments* (H.O.R.P.U. Paper No. 62, 1991). The Prison Reform Trust was, however, critical of this conclusion: see Cavadino and Gibson (1993), Chap. 11

[48] See R. Tarling, P. Jones and A. Sanders, "Police Bail" (1986) 21 H.O. Research Bulletin 52; J. Wadham, "Bail from Police Stations" *Legal Action*, December 1988, pp. 24–25.

[49] See ss.37(2), (7)(b), 38(1); 41(7); 42(10); 43(15)(18); 44(7).

[50] *Ibid.* s.47(1), as amended by the Criminal Justice and Public Order Act 1994, s.27(1)(a). These sections comprise general provisions (s.3), conditions of police bail (s.3A) and supplementary provisions (ss.5, 5A).

[51] *ibid.* s.47(3).

[52] Police and Criminal Evidence Act 1984, s.47(1A), inserted by the Criminal Justice and Public Order Act 1994, s.27(1)(b); Bail Act 1976, ss.3(6), 3A, as amended and inserted by *ibid.*, s.27(2)(3). Section 3A applies section 3 with modifications to conditions in the case of police bail. The introduction of this power was recommended by the RCCJ, Report, para. 5.22.

[53] Bail Act 1976, s.3A(4), applying s.3(8) in different terms to cases of police bail.

of preventing that person from failing to surrender to custody, committing an offence while on bail or interfering with witnesses or otherwise obstructing the course of justice.[54] The custody officer must give reasons for imposing or varying conditions, and these must be included in the custody record.[55] Where a custody officer grants bail and imposes conditions, or varies conditions, a magistrates' court on the application by or on behalf of the person on bail may grant bail or vary the conditions.[56] The police now have an express power of arrest for failure to answer to police bail.[57]

In the case of indictable or either-way offences, the prosecution may apply to the appropriate magistrates' court for the grant of police bail to be reconsidered, and the court may vary or impose conditions or withhold bail. An application must be based on information not available to the custody officer when the decision was taken.[58]

If the accused is in police custody as the result of a warrant issued by a magistrate or the Crown Court, then the warrant itself will dictate the granting of bail and the previous provisions will not apply. Either the warrant will be "endorsed for bail"[59] in terms which must be observed by the police, or it will require the police to bring the accused before the court immediately.[60] In this case, of course, the grant of bail is, strictly speaking, made by the court and not the police.

The use of police bail is substantial. In 1994, 831,000 persons were arrested and charged of whom 732,000 (88 per cent[61]) were bailed and the remainder, 99,000 (12 per cent) held in custody. In general, the more serious the offence, the higher the proportion of those arrested who are held in custody. Research in the 1980s found that the the highest proportion was in respect of robbery (57 per cent); and burglary, sexual offences and criminal damage all exceeded the average.[62]

4. BAIL FROM THE MAGISTRATES' COURT

If the accused has been arrested without warrant, and has not been bailed by the police, or arrested with a warrant which is not endorsed for bail, he or she must be brought before a magistrates' court and will then have an opportunity to request bail. Indeed, the court is under an obligation to consider the question

---

[54] *ibid.*, s.3(A)(15); cf. s.3(6), p. 734, above *supra.*
[55] *ibid.*, s.5A(2), (3), inserted by the 1994 Act, Sch. 3, para. 2, applying s.5(3)(4), in different terms to cases of police bail.
[56] Magistrates' Courts Act 1980, s.43B, inserted by the 1994 Act, Sch.3, para. 3.
[57] Police and Criminal Evidence Act 1984, s.46A, inserted by the 1994 Act, s.29.
[58] Bail Act 1976, s.5B, inserted by the 1994 Act, s.30.
[59] *ibid.* s.117. The magistrate issuing the warrant will state on the warrant that the person arrested is to be released subject to a duty to appear at a specified court and time.
[60] See the form of warrant set out as Form 4, the Magistrates' Courts (Forms) Rules 1981 (S.I. 1981 No. 553).
[61] *Criminal Statistics England and Wales* 1994, Table 8.3.
[62] See R. Tarling, P. Jones and A. Sanders, "Police Bail" (1986) 21 H.O.R.B. 52, Table 2, based on 1980 figures.

of bail even if no application is made.[63] Only comparatively minor cases can be disposed of at one appearance in the magistrates' court. The court accordingly has express power to adjourn

(1) an inquiry as examining justices, either before or during the inquiry;[64]
(2) a summary trial, either before or during the trial;[65]
(3) proceedings to determine mode of trial in the case of offences triable either way;[66] and
(4) the hearing, where the court has begun to try an offence triable either way, but decides to discontinue summary trial and proceed to inquire as examining justices.[67]

On these occasions, the court may, and sometimes must, remand the accused, which simply means a direction that he or she should be held in custody for a specified period, or that he or she should be released on bail with an obligation to appear again before the court on a specified date.[68] The court *must* remand in situation (1); in situations (2) and (3) where the offence is triable either way and either the accused initially attends the court in custody or has at any time been remanded;[69] and where it commits the accused for trial[70] or sentence[71] in the Crown Court. Otherwise the court may either remand the accused or simply adjourn the hearing without remanding, although the latter step is normally only taken in minor cases, usually road traffic matters.[72]

Under section 5B of the Bail Act 1976[73] the prosecutor may apply to the magistrates' court for a grant of bail by it to be reconsidered on the same basis as a grant of police bail may be reconsidered.[74]

In deciding whether to remand on bail or in custody the magistrates must have regard to the provisions of the Bail Act but may take advantage of section 154 of the Criminal Justice Act 1988[75] to lessen the burden of continuing applications. The position is further eased by the provision for extended remands in custody.[76]

---

[63] Because of the provision in the Bail Act 1976, s.4(1) that a person to whom the Act applies *shall* be given bail except where Schedule 1 applies. See J. N. Spencer, (1986) 150 J.P.N. 724; P. H. W. Lydiate, (1987) 151 J.P.N. 25.

[64] Magistrates' Courts Act 1980, s. 5(1).

[65] *ibid.* s.10(1). This power may be exercised after conviction and before sentence, to enable inquiries to be made: s.10(3). There is also a power to adjourn a trial to enable a medical examination and report to be made; this power is available where the offence is punishable with imprisonment and the court is satisfied that the accused did the act or made the omission charged: s.30.

[66] *ibid.* s.18(4).

[67] *ibid.* s.25(2), to be amended by the Criminal Procedure and Investigations Bill 1996, Sched. 1, imposing a duty to adjourn.

[68] *ibid.* s.128(1).

[69] *ibid.* ss.10(4), 18(4).

[70] *ibid.*, s. 6(3).

[71] *ibid.* s.38. Or adjourns for medical reports under. s.30.

[72] Emmins (1995), p. 426.

[73] Inserted by the 1994 Act, s.30.

[74] See above, p. 739.

[75] Above, p. 737

[76] Above, pp. 737–738. Adjournments under ss.10(3) and 30 (see n.65 above) may be for not more than four weeks at a time (if the accused is on bail) or three weeks at a time (if he or she is in custody); and the accused may be remanded for the period of the adjournment: s.128(6)(b). Remands on bail may be for longer than eight days if the accused and the other party consent: s.128(6)(a). The accused may be further remanded if he or she is unable to appear by reason of

5. Bail from the Crown Court

The Crown Court may grant bail to an accused who is in custody pending a hearing in the Crown Court (after committal for trial or sentence); or pending an appeal against conviction or sentence by the magistrates; or pending the completion of the hearing in the Crown Court; or pending the statement of a case for the High Court or the outcome of an application for judicial review; or pending an appeal to the Court of Appeal where the Crown Court has given a certificate under the Criminal Appeal Act 1968.[77]

If, in any of those cases, the accused is actually before the court then application is made orally to the judge, otherwise the application is in writing in a specified form and the accused is not entitled to be present at the hearing.[78] The jurisdiction of the court is quite separate from that of the justices and the High Court, and prior applications to either of those courts will not diminish the obligation of the Crown Court judge to consider the application on its merits and exercise discretion.[79] However, the accused may not make repeated applications to the Crown Court unless there is a change in circumstances.[80]

An important addition to the powers of the Crown Court is the power to grant bail on an application by a person who has been refused bail by a magistrates' court.[81] The application may only be made where the magistrates have heard full argument before refusal.[82] Legal aid is available for the application.[83] This reform was a response to criticism that there was no effective appeal against refusal of bail by the magistrates other than an expensive and difficult application to the High Court. Furthermore, by virtue of the Bail (Amendment) Act 1993, the prosecution now has the right to appeal to the Crown Court against a decision by a magistrates' court to grant bail. This only arises where (1) the accused is charged with or convicted of an offence punishable by five years' imprisonment or more; (2) the prosecution is conducted by the C.P.S.[84]; and (3) the prosecution made representations against bail before it was granted. The matter is reheard and the Crown Court judge may remand the accused in cus-

---

illness or accident: 129(1): see *R. v. Liverpool City JJ., ex p. Grogan* (1990) 155 J.P. 450 (magistrates must have solid grounds for finding this to be established).

[77] Supreme Court Act 1981, s.81, as amended, *inter alia*, by Criminal Justice Act 1982, s.29 and the Criminal Justice and Public Order Act 1994, Sched. 9, para 19, Sched. 10, para. 48. See also, *Practice Direction* [1983] 1 W.L.R. 1292. There is also inherent jurisdiction to grant bail during a trial on indictment and for the period of adjournment for reports following conviction. See *Practice Note* [1974] 1 W.L.R. 770.

[78] Crown Court Rules 1982, r.19.

[79] *R. v. Reading Crown Court, ex p. Malik* [1981] 1 Q.B. 451.

[80] There is no specific provision in the Crown Court Rules to this effect, but the Divisional Court in the *Reading* case (above) indicated that simultaneous or immediately consecutive applications to more than one Crown Court judge will not be permitted.

[81] Criminal Justice Act 1982, s.60, amending the Supreme Court Act 1981, s.81. See also, *Practice Direction* (1983) 77 Cr.App.R. 69.

[82] For the certification procedure to be adopted see Criminal Justice Act 1982, s.60(3), inserting new subsections 5(6A), (6B), (6C) in the Bail Act 1976 (s.5(6A), as amended by the Criminal Justice and Public Order Act 1994, Sched. 4, Pt. II, para. 23(b)).

[83] Criminal Justice Act 1982, s.60(4), amending the Legal Aid Act 1974, s.30: see now the Legal Aid Act 1988, ss.19, 20.

[84] Or a person prescribed by order: the Bail (Amendment) Act 1993 (Prescription of Prosecuting Authorities) Order 1994 (S.I. 1994 No. 1438) lists the S.F.O., the D.T.I., Customs and Excise, the D.S.S., the Post Office and the Inland Revenue.

tody[85] or grant bail with or without conditions. C.P.S. guidance states that the number of appeals under these provisions should be small and should only be instituted in cases of grave concern; relevant factors include risk to victims, the lack of established identity or any community ties and a strong indication that the accused may abscond.[86]

6. Bail from the High Court

A judge of the High Court may exercise both the inherent jurisdiction to grant bail and the statutory powers vested in the High Court by the Criminal Justice Act 1967.[87] The application for a writ of habeas corpus has now largely been superseded by a bail application. The ability of the accused to make application to the High Court was specifically mentioned in the *Davies* case[88] as a check on the accuracy of magistrates' decisions, and an additional safeguard is provided by the application to the Crown Court set out above. Application to the High Court was always a difficult operation because legal aid was rarely granted, forcing applicants to rely on the Official Solicitor.[89]

The accused must apply to a judge in chambers either through his or her own solicitor by summons and affidavit, or by giving written notice to the judge that he or she wants bail.[90] In the latter case, the judge will then appoint the Official Solicitor to act on the accused's behalf. The Official Solicitor will not actually represent the applicant at a hearing in chambers (as his or her own lawyer would) but merely prepares a set of papers for the judge to consider, along with the police submissions. This is widely regarded as an unsatisfactory form of procedure and research demonstrates that the success rate in bail applications made by the Official Solicitor is much lower than in applications made by a lawyer instructed by the applicant.[91] The legally-aided right of appeal referred to above ought to obviate this problem.

7. Breach of Bail

The Bail Act 1976 replaced the defendant's personal recognizance with a new criminal offence of failing to surrender to custody without reasonable cause.[92]

---

[85] The judge should indicate that the period of remand in custody should not exceed eight days from the date when the applicant last appeared before the magistrates: *Re Bone* [1995] C.O.D. 94.

[86] Emmins (1995), p. 442; *Blackstone's Criminal Practice* 1995, para.D5, 38.

[87] s.22, as amended by the Bail Act 1976. The court also has jurisdiction under the Criminal Justice Act 1948, s.37, to grant bail where the accused is applying for certiorari to quash a decision of a magistrates' court or the Crown Court, or appealing by case stated from the Crown Court.

[88] *R. v. Nottingham JJ., ex p. Davies* [1981] Q.B. 38, see above, pp. 736–738.

[89] It is civil legal aid which is appropriate for these applications and the evidence suggests that it has generally been refused on the basis that applicants can rely on the assistance of the Official Solicitor in presenting a case. See the Law Society's criticisms of the Official Solicitor procedure in a paper, *Report on Legal Aid for Bail Applications* (January 1972), and comment in *LAG Bulletin*, January 1980, p. 28.

[90] R.S.C., Ord. 79, r.9(4), (5).

[91] N. Bases and M. Smith, "A study of bail applications through the Official Solicitor to the judge in chambers" [1976] Crim.L.R. 541.

[92] Bail Act 1976, s.6(1). Appearance at the arraignment necessarily involves surrendering to custody: *R. v. Central Criminal Court, ex p. Guney* [1996] 2 W.L.R. 675, H.L. (in respect of the departure to Northern Cyprus of Asil Nadir). *Cf. D.P.P. v. Richards* [1988] Q.B. 701 (compliance with court's procedure requiring D to report to inquiry counter sufficient to surrender to bail).

If a defendant has reasonable cause for failure to surrender to custody at the appointed time and place, he or she must surrender as soon as reasonably practicable thereafter, or be guilty of an offence.[93] Powers of arrest are attached to the offence.[94] The accused may be fined or imprisoned on summary conviction, or by the Crown Court, where the offence is dealt with as if it were a criminal contempt of court.[95] Where the accused has failed to surrender to bail granted by a magistrates' court, proceedings are initiated by the court by its own motion, following an invitation by the prosecutor, the proceedings then being conducted by the prosecutor.[96] Where the accused has failed to surrender to police bail, proceedings should be commenced by charge or the laying of an information.[97]

In the event of failure to surrender, any personal security given by the accused under the limited powers in the Act[98] may be forfeited, as may the sums of money promised by the sureties. Normally those sums would be forfeited in full, but the court must exercise a proper discretion as to whether any part of the sum should be remitted on account of the sureties' behaviour, responsibility or means.[99]

8. NUMBERS OF REMAND PRISONERS

In magistrates' courts the number of persons remanded in custody in respect of indictable offences increased between 1979 (37,900) and 1985 (44,900), fell in 1986 to 36,300, and then rose to 42,900 in 1988; thereafter, the figure varied between 42,900 and 40,400, but rose again to 46,600 in 1994.[1] The numbers committed for trial in custody also increased from 13,000 to 20,000 in the same period.[2] There are indications of increases in committal rates for offences such

---

[93] *ibid.* s.6(2).

[94] *ibid.*, s.7.

[95] The maximum penalties are three months imprisonment or a fine not exceeding level 5 on the standard scale; 12 months imprisonment or a fine at the Crown Court (the offence does not constitute a contempt of court (although treated as such), and so the two years' maximum penalty under the Contempt of Court Act 1981 is inapplicable: *R. v. Reader* (1986) 84 Cr.App.R. 294). Bail Act offences should be dealt with separately from the other substantive matters and put clearly to the defendant: *R. v. Boyle* [1993] Crim.L.R. 40; *R. v. How* [1993] Crim.L.R. 201.

[96] *Practice Direction (Bail: Failure to Surrender)* [1987] 1 W.L.R. 79. This "clarified" the decision of the Divisional Court in *Schiavo v. Anderton* [1987] Q.B. 20, which had raised the possibility of the proceedings being conducted by the justices' clerk rather than the prosecutor (see B. Gibson, (1986) 150 J.P.N. 212; G. J. Bennett and B. Hogan, All E.R. Rev. 1986, p. 112, and note the criticisms expressed in *Murphy v. D.P.P.* [1990] 1 W.L.R. 601). As the proceedings are not commenced by laying an information, the six-month time limit in the Magistrates' Court Act 1980, s.127 does not apply: this is helpful where the accused absconds abroad and remains there for some years, as in *Schiavo v. Anderton*, above.

[97] Failure to surrender here is not tantamount to defiance of a court order.

[98] *i.e.* any security taken where it appears likely that the accused will leave Great Britain: Bail Act 1976, s.3(5).

[99] See above, p. 732, n. 2.

[1] *Criminal Statistics England and Wales 1989* and *1994* Table 8.5. The percentage of persons proceeded against for indictable offences who were remanded increased from 43 per cent in 1979 to 65 per cent in 1994, but the percentage of the remands that were remands in custody fell from 17 per cent to 12 per cent in the same period. (Tables 8.4, 8.5).

[2] *ibid.* Table. 8.7. Between 1984 and 1994, the figure fluctuated between 19,800 (1990) and 24,000 (1987), settling in 1991–1994 at 20,000 or 21,000. The percentage of all those committed for trial has varied between 19 per cent (1980) and 23 per cent (1993, 1994).

as burglary, theft and handling, which are kinds of offences more likely to involve a remand in custody, and in the rate at which bail is refused in certain kinds of case, especially burglary and drugs.[3]

The increase in the number of remand prisoners has caused severe problems of overcrowding in conditions less favourable than those of convicted prisoners, sometimes involving detention in police, rather than prison, custody.[4] Apart from the Bail Act change to a presumption in favour of bail, other contributions to reducing the pressure have been the establishment of more bail hostels[5] and schemes for the collection of information about the accused that would justify release on bail.[6] New schemes are subject to approval by a Bail Practice Committee of the Association of Chief Officers of Probation. A National Steering Group, chaired by the Home Office, advises on strategic and policy considerations.[7] The schemes have the support of all the agencies concerned (probation service, C.P.S., police, Home Office) and monitoring over a six month period showed an overall trend in favour of bail of 13 per cent where bail information sheets are presented to the C.P.S. compared with cases were they are not.[8] Consideration is being given to the involvement of the private sector.[9] There have also been experiments with electronic monitoring ("tagging") schemes, in which the defendants are remanded on bail subject to conditions prescribing periods of curfew, their continued presence at home during these periods being monitored by means of an electronic device.[10]

G. COMMITTAL PROCEEDINGS

Before an accused can be tried on indictment there must normally be a preliminary inquiry into the case conducted in the magistrates' court. The

---

[3] R. Pearce, *Waiting for Crown Court trial: the remand population*, H.O.R.P.U. Paper No. 40 (1987), based on 1980–84 data.

[4] Authorised for periods not exceeding three clear days by the Magistrates' Courts Act 1980, s.128(7), (8). See (1987) 151 J.P.N. 433.

[5] Under the Criminal Justice Act 1982, s.53. See H. Lewis and G. Mair, *Bail and Probation Work II: the use of London probation bail hostels for bailees.* H.O.R.P.U. Paper No. 50 (1988); Cavadino and Gibson (1993), Chap. 7: in July 1993 there were 30 approved bail hostels (659 places) and 84 approved combined probation and bail hostels (1,193 places, 69 per cent occupied by people on bail). National Standards were issued by the Home Office in 1992. Bail support schemes, mostly for juveniles, have been introduced in some areas with Home Office funding: *ibid.*, p. 116.

[6] (1987) 151 J.P.N. 433, 523; G. Mair, *Bail and Probation Work: the ILPS bail action project*, H.O.R.P.U. Paper No. 46 (1988). By July 1993 there were 179 court-based and 31 prison-based bail information schemes: Cavadino and Gibson (1993), pp. 94, 100.

[7] *Bail Information*: Report of the Bail Practice Committee on the expansion of Bail Information Schemes in 1988–89 (1990).

[8] *ibid.*; (1990) 46 *The Magistrate* 35. See also C. Fiddes and C. Lloyd, (1990) 29 H.O.R.B. 23. See also C. Lloyd, *Bail information schemes: practice and effect* (H.O.R.P.U. Paper No.69, 1992) (confirming that bail information "succeeds in influencing remand decisions, and thereby diverting defendants from remands in custody" (p.iii)). Other surveys are summarised by Cavadino and Gibson (1993), Chap. 6.

[9] *Private Sector Involvement in the Remand System* (Green Paper, Cm. 434, 1988).

[10] G. Mair and C. Nee, *Electronic Monitoring: The Trials and Their Results* (H.O. Research Study 120, 1990). The results were not encouraging (the scheme was expensive and over half the 50 people monitored offended or broke conditions while on bail). Nevertheless, provision for electronic monitoring in support of curfew orders imposed after conviction was introduced by the Criminal Justice Act 1991, s.12.

magistrates, referred to in this context as "examining justices," are required to decide whether to commit the accused for trial at the Crown Court, or whether to call a halt to the proceedings at that point if there is not "sufficient evidence to put the accused on trial for any indictable offence".[11] However, if the accused is discharged by the magistrates at the end of the committal proceedings this is not the equivalent of an acquittal at trial. He or she may be charged again with the same offence, and be required to undergo committal proceedings again, whereas an acquittal at trial effectively prevents any further proceedings for the same offence.[12] The only alternative to committal, outside serious or complex fraud cases and cases concerning child abuse, is for the prosecution to seek a voluntary bill of indictment which permits the case to be taken straight to the Crown Court. This procedure is discussed further later in this section.

Until 1968 there was only one form of committal proceedings. This procedure is termed a "full," "conventional," "long" or "old-style" committal to contrast it with the alternative form introduced by section 1 of the Criminal Justice Act 1967, now termed a "paper" or "new-style" committal.

Full committal proceedings consist of the oral presentation of evidence for the consideration of the court. The prosecution must call sufficient of its witnesses to establish a prima facie case against the defendant (although there is no obligation to call every potential prosecution witness) and they will be subject to cross-examination and re-examination, with the whole of their evidence written down, read back to them and authenticated ("depositions"). At the close of the prosecution case, the defence may submit that the evidence given discloses no prima facie case. If the court accedes to the submission it will discharge the defendant; if it does not, the defence will then choose whether to offer any evidence. If it does, which is unusual, the witnesses called and their evidence will be treated in exactly the same way as for the prosecution. The court must make its decision on all the evidence. If the defence does not offer evidence, the magistrates will commit for trial immediately.

The full oral procedure was varied somewhat by provisions which permit the court to accept written evidence subject to specified conditions.[13] This could lead to a marginally shorter hearing, but old-style committals tended to take a long time and were regarded as wasteful of resources. It was, therefore, a welcome relief when the Criminal Justice Act 1967 provided an alternative procedure.

The *paper committal* permits the magistrates to commit a case for trial at the Crown Court without giving any consideration to the prosecution (or defence) evidence provided that certain conditions are fulfilled. So long as all the evidence is in the form of written statements tendered to the court in accordance with section 102 of the Magistrates' Courts Act 1980, the court may commit

---

[11] Magistrates' Courts Act 1980, s. 6(1).

[12] If he or she is discharged after committal proceedings the plea of *autrefois acquit* (below, p. 851) is not available because there has been no trial for the offence. The prosecutor will have to choose whether to abandon the prosecution, or seek further evidence with a view to beginning proceedings again, or invoke the voluntary bill procedure discussed at p. 749 below. Repeated use of committal proceedings may in an appropriate case be restrained as vexatious or an abuse of process: *R.* v. *Manchester City Stipendiary Magistrate, ex p. Snelson* [1977] 1 W.L.R. 911.

[13] Criminal Justice Act 1967, s.2. Now Magistrates' Courts Act 1980, s.102. The conditions are that the statement is signed; that it contains a declaration that it is true to the best of the maker's knowledge; that a copy is given to the other party; that no party objects..

for trial without considering the contents of the statements unless the accused is not legally represented or the defence submits that the statements disclose insufficient evidence.[14] In effect, if the prosecution request a committal under this procedure, the defendant may simply choose to be committed for trial without further ado.

The value of committal proceedings has long been questioned.[15] The RCCJ recommended their abolition, noting that only 7 per cent of committals were old style and that they did not act as an effective filter.[16] The Criminal Justice and Public Order Act 1994[17] provided for the introduction of new arrangements for the transfer of cases from the magistrates' court to the Crown Court, modelled on the provisions applicable in serious and complex fraud cases and child abuse cases.[18] However, following consultation, it emerged that these arrangements would prove expensive and unworkable. Accordingly, the Criminal Procedure and Investigations Bill 1996 provides for the repeal of the transfer provisions of the 1994 Act.[19] It also makes the major change of abolishing the option of old-style committal proceedings.[20]

On committing a person for trial in the Crown Court, the magistrates' court must specify the place at which he is to be tried.[21] In selecting the place of trial the court must have regard to (a) the convenience of the defence, the prosecution and the witnesses, (b) the expediting of the trial; and (c) any direction given by or on behalf of the Lord Chief Justice on the allocation of business.[22-27]

The place of the trial is determined mainly by the nature of the charge on which the accused is committed. Criminal offences triable on indictment are divided into four classes according to their seriousness[28] and the classes are distinguished by stipulations about the seniority of the judge required to try the case. In the light of these, the magistrates must specify the most convenient location of the Crown Court. In practice, each magistrates' court is informed by the presiding judge for the circuit of the location to which proceedings should normally be transferred.[29]

An accused or the prosecutor may make an application to a High Court judge to substitute another place of trial[30] and such applications are usually made in

---

[14] See now the Magistrates' Courts Act 1980, s.6(2), as amended. "Legally represented" means merely that the accused has a legal representative acting for him or her, not necessarily present in court.

[15] See the second edition of this book, pp. 657–661, 692–694. Abolition was, for example, recommended by the RCCP (Cmnd. 8092, para. 8.30).

[16] Report, para. 6.26.

[17] s.44 and Sched. 4.

[18] Below, pp. 760–763.

[19] clause 43.

[20] clause 45 and Sched. 1, which *inter alia*, inserts new ss. 5A–5C and substitutes a new s.6(1),(2) in the Magistrates' Courts Act 1980.

[21] Magistrates' Courts Act 1980, s.7. As to powers to remand in custody or on bail, see above, p. 740.

[22-27] See the Practice Direction (Crown Court: Allocation of Business) [1995] 1 W.L.R.1083, above, pp. 82–83.

[28] *ibid.*

[29] *Blackstone's Criminal Practice 1996*, D6.26.

[30] Supreme Court Act 1981, s.76.

cases where it is feared that local prejudice and hostility will endanger the prospects of a fair trial.[31]

Reporting restrictions apply to committal proceedings.[32] After considerable controversy, the Criminal Justice Act 1967 placed a ban on the full reporting of proceedings where the accused is committed for trial, so as to minimise the risk of publicity prejudicial to the accused.[33] However, the accused (or any of the accused if there is more than one) may apply for the restrictions to be lifted.[34] The court must accede to the application, subject to the requirement where one of two or more accused objects to the lifting of restrictions that it is in the interests of justice to do so.[35] In all cases, certain basic items of information are exempt from the restrictions, including the identity of the court and the names of the justices; the names, addresses[35a] and occupations of the parties and witnesses and the ages of the accused and witnesses the charges (or a summary); the court's decision; the names of legal representatives; the date and place to which proceedings are adjourned; arrangements as to bail and legal aid. Breach of the restrictions is a summary offence. These restrictions are in addition to any other restrictions imposed by an enactment.[36]

The Crown Court Rules provide that the trial should not normally begin before the expiration of 14 days or after the expiration of eight weeks from transfer.[37]

A much more complex scheme of time limits for the "preliminary stages" of proceedings for an offence is established by regulations made under section 22 of the Prosecution of Offences Act 1985. "Custody time limits" may be imposed to govern the period for which a defendant may be kept in custody before the start of summary trial; and, in cases of trial on indictment, for specified "preliminary stages" before arraignment in the Crown Court. "Overall time limits" may be set for the same stages. The effect of expiry of a custody

---

[31] For example, the trial of Brady and Hindley, the Moors Murderers, was held in Chester rather than the more likely location in Manchester, and the trial of those convicted of the Birmingham pub bombings was held in Lancaster. Prejudice is not the only ground for altering the venue, see *Halsbury's Laws of England* (4th ed.) Vol. 11(2), para. 938.

[32] Magistrates' Courts Act 1980, s.8.

[33] See the previous edition of this book, pp. 663–664.

[34] 1980 Act, s.8(2).

[35] 1980 Act, s.8 (2A); this was added by the Criminal Justice (Amendment) Act 1981, s.1, changing the position that any one defendant could have restrictions raised contrary to the wishes of co-defendants. The magistrates must weigh the balance of interest between defendants who disagree over the reporting of proceedings: *R. v. Leeds JJ., ex p. Sykes* [1983] 1 W.L.R. 132. All the co-defendants must have the chance to make representations: *R. v. Wirral District Magistrates' Court, ex p. Meikle* (1990) 154 J.P. 1035.

[35a] The reference to addresses is to be removed by the Criminal Procedure and Investigations Bill 1996, Sched. 1.

[36] 1980 Act, s.8(7). It is possible for magistrates to lift reporting restrictions but forbid publication of particular matters under s.4(2) of the Contempt of Court Act 1981: *R. v. Horsham JJ., ex p. Farquaharson* [1982] Q.B. 762. However, it has been held that magistrates should be slow to impose restrictions under s.4(2) *in addition* to those applicable to committal proceedings: *R. v. Beaconsfield JJ., ex p. Westminster Press Ltd, The Times*, June 28, 1994.

[37] Supreme Court Act 1981, s.77; Crown Court Rules 1982, r.19. This requirement is, however, directory and not mandatory: in an appropriate case the Crown Court may grant an extension of time, even after the eight-week period has expired: *R. v. Governor of Spring Hill Prison, ex p. Sohi and Dhillon* (1987) 86 Cr.App.R. 382

time limit is release on bail[38]; and of an overall time limit that the defendant is
treated as acquitted. However, the court[39] may extend a time limit if it is satisfied
that there is good and sufficient cause for doing so[40] and the prosecution has
acted with all due expedition.[41] The scheme has been introduced progressively,
on an area-by-area basis, and so far is confined to custody time limits and indictable and either-way offences. The standard limits have been are 70 days between
first appearance and commencement of committal proceedings or summary trial
and 112 days between committal and arraignment.[42] Where a defendant is

---

[38] See, e.g., R. v. Sheffield JJ., ex p. Turner [1991] 2 Q.B. 472 (magistrates bound to release on
bail on expiry of limit notwithstanding that application for extension had been deferred by consent; however, expiry of limit between first appearance and committal does not prevent the
accused lawfully being detained in custody for up to the specified period between committal and
trial); R. v. Croydon Crown Court, ex p. Lewis (1994) 158 J.P. 876 (automatic release on bail
lasts to arraignment, not trial). Custody periods begin at the close of the day during which D
was first remanded and expire at relevant midnight thereafter: R. v. Governor of Canterbury
Prison, ex p. Craig [1991] 2 Q.B. 195.

[39] The Crown Court if the defendant has been committed for trial or indicted; otherwise the magistrates' court. A decision of a magistrates' court to grant or refuse an extension may be taken on
appeal to the Crown Court (s.22(7)(8)); such a decision of the Crown Court may be the subject
of an application for judicial review (see s.22(13)). The matter cannot be raised on any appeal
against conviction (s.22(10)). An extension order must be announced in clear terms and not left
to be inferred: In re Ward, Ward and Bond (1990) 1155 J.P. 181.

[40] Which may include the defence's need for time: McKay White v. D.P.P. [1989] Crim.L.R. 375;
or the lack of a court or a trial judge (probably provided that arraignment will occur reasonably
soon after expiry of the time limit): R. v. Norwich Crown Court, ex p. Cox (1992) 97 Cr. App.
R. 145; cf. R. v. Norwich Crown Court, ex p. Stiller (1992) 156 J.P. 624; or the need to protect
the complainant from the risk of serious bodily harm from the applicant: R. v. Luton Crown
Court, ex p. Neaves (1993) 157 J.P. 80; but not the seriousness of the offence or the shortness
of the period of the extension: R. v. Governor of Winchester Prison, ex p. Roddie [1991] 1 W.L.R.
303; or the fact that the accused would be otherwise entitled to bail: R. v. Guildford Crown
Court, ex p. Fraser [1995] C.O.D. 316. The standard of proof in these matters is on the balance
of probabilities: R. v. Governor of Canterbury Prison, ex. p. Craig [1991] 2 Q.B. 195. See A.
Turner, (1993) 76 Archbold News.

[41] Chronic staff shortages are reasons for a lack of "due expedition" and not the basis for a finding
that the prosecution had acted with all due expedition: ex p. Roddie, above; see also R. v. Central
Criminal Court, ex p. Behbehani [1994] Crim.L.R. 352 (lack of due expedition in that copies of
crucial tape recordings should have been served on the defence earlier).

[42] Prosecution of Offences (Custody Time Limits) Regulations 1987 (S.I. 1987 No. 299), as
amended by S.I. 1988 No. 164, S.I. 1989 Nos. 767 and 1107 and S.I. 1995 No. 555. An indication
by counsel at a preliminary hearing of the intended plea does not constitute the hearing an
"arraignment": R. v. Bristol Crown Court, ex p. Commissioners of Customs and Excise [1990]
C.O.D. 11. Arraignment is not to be used as a mechanism for defeating the right to bail: R. v.
Maidstone Crown Court, ex p. Hollstein, The Times, November 4, 1994; R. v. Maidstone Crown
Court, ex p. Clark [1995] 1 W.L.R. 831 (arraignment quashed where D was unable to enter
informed pleas in view of the service on the day of additional material by the prosecution). The
"preliminary stage" in relation to any proceedings is to be redefined the Criminal Procedure
and Investigations Bill 1996, cl. 66: it is not to include any stage after start of the trial and this
is to be when a jury is sworn, a guilty plea accepted or a preliminary hearing commences (for
trials on indictment), or when a magistrates' court begins to hear prosecution evidence or accepts
a guilty plea (for summary trials). A survey of four areas indicated that compliance was generally
high, although variable according to area: P. Morgan and J. Vennard, Pre-Trial Delay: the implications of time limits (H.O. Research Study 110, 1989). Voluntary guidelines for the timing of
the various stages of the trial process have also been set by the Working Group on Pre-Trial
Issues; these are not confined to custody cases, and the guidelines for such cases are more
demanding than the statutory limits. Their effect is to be monitored: Fourth Periodic Report of
the UK to the Human Rights Committee Under Art. 40 of the ICCPR (1994), para. 307.

charged with more than one offence at different dates, a separate limit applies in respect of each offence.[43]

If the accused is intending to rely on an alibi defence he or she must notify the prosecution of the particulars of the alibi not later than seven days after the transfer of proceedings to the Crown Court. If he or she fails to give the requisite notice the alibi defence can only be relied upon at trial with the special permission of the court.[44]

A decision to commit or refuse to commit for trial cannot be the subject of an appeal by case stated to the High Court, as it is not a "final" decision.[45] It may be challenged on an application for judicial review,[46] but such an application will only be successful where the magistrates have acted without jurisdiction.[47] Judicial review is not available simply on the ground that the examining justices have acted on evidence that will or may be inadmissible at trial; however, misreception of evidence may lead to the quashing of a committal where there was "a really susbtantial error leading to a demonstrable injustice."[48]

2. THE VOLUNTARY BILL PROCEDURE[49]

It is convenient to deal with the voluntary bill a procedure at this point since it is a way of getting an indictable offence tried *without* committal by the magistrates. A bill of indictment must be preferred against a defendant as a preliminary to the trial. A bill may only be preferred if proceedings against the defendant have been committed for trial, or as directed by the Court of Appeal (*e.g.* where ordering a new trial) or by a High Court judge.[50]

---

[43] *R. v. Wirral District Magistrates' Court, ex p. Meikle* (1990) 154 J.P. 1035; *R. v. Waltham Forest Magistrates' Court, ex p. Lee* (1993) 157 J.P. 811. The preferral of new charges solely to defeat custody time limits will, however, be an abuse of process (*ibid.*; *cf. R. v. Great Yarmouth Magistrates, ex p. Thomas, Davis and Darlington* [1992] Crim.L.R. 116).

[44] Criminal Justice Act 1967, s.11; s. 11 is to be replaced by the Criminal Procedure and Investigations Bill 1996, cl. 5: below, p. 758. See *R. v. Fields and Adams* [1991] Crim.L.R. 38; *R. v. Johnson* [1994] Crim.L.R. 949.

[45] *Atkinson v. U.S. Government* [1971] A.C. 197 and *Cragg v. Lewes District Council* [1986] Crim.L.R. 800; *Streames v. Copping* [1985] Q.B. 920 (decision that information was not bad for duplicity).

[46] See below, pp. 969–976.

[47] *e.g.* where the offence is summary only: *cf. R. v. Hatfield JJ., ex p. Castle* [1981] 1 W.L.R. 217.

[48] *Neill v. North Antrim Magistrates' Court* [1992] 1 W.L.R. 1220, *per* Lord Mustill at p. 1233. Lord Mustill left open the possibility that the court could also intervene where it was quite obvious that the committal proceedings disclosed no offence (p. 1233). Examining justices do not have the discretion to exclude legally admissible evidence that is available to trial judges: *R. v. Highbury Corner Magistrates' Court, ex p. Boyce* (1984) 79 Cr.App.R. 132. Exceptionally, they are required by s.76(2) of the PACE (see above, p. 683) to rule, if requested, on the admissibility of a confession (s.76(2) being applicable to "any proceedings"), although failure to do so will not normally lead to the quashing of proceedings: *R. v. Oxford City JJ., ex p. Berry* [1988] Q.B. 507; similarly, the discretion to exclude evidence under s.78 of PACE (see above, p. 684) is available to them, but should only be exercised "in the clearest case and in exceptional circumstances": *R. v. King's Lynn JJ., ex p. Holland* [1993] 1 W.L.R. 324. These principles presumably apply to applications for discharge.

[49] See C. M. Chatterton and P. K. Brown, *Committals for Trial to the Crown Court* (1988), pp. 232–241; C. Lewis (1981) 78 L.S. Gaz. 1442; *Practice Direction (Crime: Voluntary Bills)* [1990] 1 W.L.R. 1635; (1991) 155 J.P.N. 83.

[50] Administration of Justice (Miscellaneous Provisions) Act 1933, s.2(2), to be amended by the Criminal Procedure and Investigations Bill 1996, Sched. 1. The 1933 Act abolished the grand

Any person may make a written application to a High Court judge for consent to the preferring of a bill of indictment and must state reasons for the application. If committal proceedings have been taken, the application must be accompanied by depositions and certain statements of belief about the truth of the case.[51] The defendant has no right to a hearing, although the judge, may in the exercise of discretion, entertain written or, perhaps, in very exceptional circumstances, oral representations.[52] The decision of a judge to issue a voluntary bill is not susceptible to challenge on an application for judicial review.[53]

This procedure allows an accused to be put on trial at the discretion of a High Court judge and is rarely used, but could be effective in circumventing committal proceedings where unusual problems arose.[54] The use of the voluntary bill procedure can be controversial. Three prison officers were put on trial for murder in this way after a stipendiary magistrate discharged them after committal proceedings, and 15 youths charged variously with murder, affray and riotous assembly were put on trial by voluntary bill after committal proceedings had been in progress for nearly three weeks with no sign of finishing.[55] Both cases excited considerable comment. The preferment of a voluntary bill may however amount to an abuse of process.[56-57]

H. DISCLOSURE OF EVIDENCE

In a civil case, the pre-trial procedure can be operated so as to allow each party to discover the essentials of the case to be met and to discover the basic issues

jury, which had had to find a bill of indictment to be a "true bill" before the accused could stand trial: the decision in the case of bills preferred following committal proceedings or with the consent of a High Court judge was a formality; the presentation of a bill by a private person was a rarity. See also below, pp. 931–932.

[51] The Indictments (Procedure) Rules 1971 (S.I. 1971 No. 2084) govern the procedure. To be valid, the bill must be signed by a proper officer of the court certifying compliance with the requirements: *R. v. Morais* (1988) 87 Cr.App.R. 9; *R. v. Laming* (1989) 90 Cr.App.R. 450. The applicant (unless the D.P.P. or a Crown Prosecutor: *R. v. Liverpool Crown Court, ex p. Bray* [1987] Crim.L.R. 51) must file an affidavit in support of the application. An indictment preferred by a voluntary bill may be amended on the same basis as an indictment resulting from committal or transfer: *R. v. Wells* (1994) 159 J.P. 243.

[52] *R. v. Raymond* [1981] Q.B. 910, criticised by G. Harrison, (1986) J. Crim. Law 383, but approved by the Privy Council in *Brooks (Lloyd) v. D.P.P. of Jamaica* [1994] 1 A.C. 568. The *Practice Direction* (n. 49 above) refers only to the possibility of written representations.

[53] *R. v. Manchester Crown Court, ex p. Williams and Simpson* (1990) 154 J.P. 589; *contra, R. v. I.R.C., ex p. Dhesi, The Independent*, August 14, 1995.

[54] *e.g.* where the defendant disrupted committal proceedings (*R. v. Paling* (1978) 67 Cr.App.R. 299); or to prefer an indictment against two defendants, one of whom has already been committed for trial (see *Blackstone's Criminal Practice 1995*, D7.5).

[55] The three men were charged with the murder of Mr Barry Prosser, a prisoner, in Winson Green prison, Birmingham. One of the accused had been the subject of *two* unsuccessful committal proceedings on the same charge. This case provides another example of change of venue, the trial being transferred to Leicester Crown Court because of all the publicity that had been generated. The charges against the youths arose out of the death of Terence May, a motorcyclist, in Thornton Heath, South London.

[56-57] *Brooks (Lloyd) v. D.P.P. of Jamaica* [1994] 1 A.C. 568: The preferment of a bill of indictment following a finding of no case to answer in committal proceedings was said to be justified only in "excepional circumstances"; however, the court had to have regard to the "interests

in dispute between the parties. In a criminal matter, the two sides have much less scope for selecting the ground on which they wish to fight and all issues may be left in dispute until the trial.[58] However, it can be a considerable advantage to prosecution, defence and court if by the time of the trial the two sides have some indication of the evidence to be given and the arguments to be raised. The RCCJ made proposals for greater disclosure by the defence, with some restriction on the prosecution's disclosure duties. At the time of writing (April 1996) the Government's own proposals on disclosure have appeared in the Criminal Procedure and Investigations Bill. Before we consider these, we set out the present position.

1. DISCLOSURE BY THE PROSECUTION

Whether the committal is "full" or "paper" the prosecution is required to supply the defence with copies of the depositions or written statements as the case may be.[59] As a result, for trials on indictment the defence should know the total of the prosecution evidence.

The extent to which the prosecution has to disclose other information has developed over time. Some requirements were clear, including that of notifying the defence of, at least, the name and address of a witness who could give material evidence but would not be called by the prosecution;[60] making expert and technical evidence available; giving the defence a copy of any statements made by a prosecution witness which conflict with the evidence given at trial;[61] making known any convictions affecting the credibility of prosecution witnesses.[62] In 1981, the Attorney-General issued guidelines setting out the additional material which must be made available to the defence, with exceptions for especially prejudicial or sensitive information.[63] The Direction extended to all witness statements and documents not included in the committal bundles, the statements of any witnesses to be called at committal and documents referred to therein, and the unedited version(s) of any edited statements or composite statement included in the committal bundle.[64]

of the Crown acting on behalf of the community" as well as the interest of the accused (Lord Woolf at p. 581, citing Gibbs and Mason JJ. in *Barton v. R.* (1980) 147 C.L.R. 75, 101).

[58] Although there is a procedure whereby formal admissions can be made under Criminal Justice Act 1967, s.10, thus eliminating the necessity for undisputed evidence to be given orally at trial.

[59] Magistrates' Courts Act 1980, s.102. To be replaced by ss. 5A—5C, inserted by the Criminal Procedure and Investigations Bill 1996.

[60] There was disagreement between Lord Denning M.R. and Diplock L.J. in *Dallison v. Caffery* [1965] 1 Q.B. 348 on the extent of the obligation. The Master of the Rolls was of the opinion that prosecuting counsel should make the witness' statements available to the defence. Diplock L.J. thought it was enough to make the witness available by notifying a name and address. (*cf. R. v. Bryant and Dickson* (1946) 31 Cr.App.R. 146; *R. v. Lawson* (1989) 90 Cr.App.R. 108).

[61] *R. v. Howes*, March 27, 1950, C.C.A. (unreported), cited in Archbold, *Criminal Pleading, Evidence and Practice* (43rd ed.), para. 4–179.

[62] *R. v. Collister and Warhurst* (1955) 39 Cr.App.R. 100.; *R. v. Paraskeva* (1982) 76 Cr.App.R.162. The same principle applies to disciplinary findings against police officers: *R. v. Edwards* [1991] 1 W.L.R. 207, and the request by a prosecution witness for a reward: *R. v. Rasheed, The Times,* May 20, 1994.

[63] *Practice Note* [1982] 1 All E.R. 734.

[64] Prosecuting counsel were required to consider whether statements had been disclosed in accordance with the guidelines: Code of Conduct (1990 edn.), Annex H, para. 11(4)(d) (Professional Standards Applicable to Criminal Cases).

The guidelines have now been overtaken by cases reconsidering the extent to which the common law requires disclosure.[65] The leading case is *R. v. Ward*[66] where the Court of Appeal on a reference from the Home Secretary quashed the convictions of Judith Ward for complicity in a series of bombings in the 1970s. The Court of Appeal found that the non-disclosure of a series of items of evidence[67] constituted material irregularities. The requirements of the law today were summarised as follows.[68]

(1) Where the prosecution have taken a statement from a person whom they know can give material evidence but decide not to call him or her as a witness, they are under a duty to make that person available as a defence witness. "Material evidence" means evidence which tends either to weaken the prosecution case or to strengthen the defence case.[69]

(2) Unless there are good reason for not doing so, the duty should normally be performed by supplying copies of witness statements or allowing the defence to inspect and make copies. Where there are good reasons for not supplying copies, the duty can be performed by supplying the witness's name and address.

(3) The defence are entitled to be supplied with copies of statements recording relevant interviews, subject to a claim of public interest immunity.

(4) The requirement for the disclosure of expert evidence[70] extend to *all* relevant experiments and tests, including those which tend to cast doubt on the opinion ultimately expressed by the expert.

(5) There is an exception to the general duty of disclosure in respect of claims to public interest immunity.[71] However, such a claim has to be

---

[65] The guidelines do not have legal force and are now no longer authoritative in so far as they conflict with the case law: *R. v. Brown (Winston)* [1994] 1 W.L.R. 1599.

[66] [1993] 1 W.L.R. 619. See also *R. v. Reilly* [1994] Crim.L.R. 279; *R. v. McCarthy* (1994) 158 J.P. 283.

[67] Including material experimental data that might have cast doubt on the evidence of forensic scientists called by the prosecution; statements made to police officers withdrawing confessions made to other officers; other statements by W which cast doubt on her reliability as a witness.

[68] pp. 679–681. A similar approach had previously been adopted by Henry J. at the trial of Ernest Saunders and others (unreported, August 29, 1989) and in *R. v. Maguire* [1992] Q.B. 936.

[69] The test is *materiality* not *admissibility*: *R. v. Preston* [1994] 2 A.C. 730. "Material" documents are those which are (1) relevant or possibly relevant to an issue in the case; or (2) raise or possibly raise a new issue whose existence is not apparent from the evidence the prosecution proposes to use; and (3) hold out a real (as opposed to fanciful) prospect of providing a lead on evidence which goes to (1) or (2): *R. v. Melvin* (unreported, December 20, 1993), approved by the Court of Appeal in *R. v. Keane* [1994] 1 W.L.R. 746, 752. The term "issues in the case" must be given a "broad interpretation": *R. v. Brown (Winston)* [1994] 1 W.L.R. 1599, 1606.

[70] See pp. 692–693.

[71] *i.e.*, a claim that material should not be disclosed in the public interest, the court having to balance that interest against the interests of justice. In a criminal case touching on personal liberty "the weight to be attached to the interest of justice" is plainly very great indeed": *R. v. Governor of Brixton Prison, ex p. Osman (No.1)* [1991] 1 W.L.R. 281, 288. "If the disputed material may prove the defendant's innocence or avoid a miscarriage of justice, then the balance comes down resoundingly in favour of disclosing it": *per* Lord Taylor C.J. in *R. v. Keane* [1994] 1 W.L.R. 746, 751–752 (disclosure was not ordered here as the court was satisfied that the material would not have assisted the defence at all). However, applications for disclosure of details of informants should be scrutinised "with very great care" to see that they are "essential to the running of the defence": *R. v. Turner* [1995] 1 W.L.R. 264, *per* Lord Taylor C.J. (here, disclosure should have been ordered). Similar principles apply to the disclosure of the position of observation posts: *Blake v. D.P.P.; Austin v. D.P.P.* (1993) 97 Cr.App.R. 169.

the subject of a ruling by the court[72] and the defence must always be notified that it has been made; if the prosecution are not prepared to have the issue determined by the court, the prosecution will have to be abandoned.[73]

(6) Nothing in the Attorney-General's Guidelines[74] can derogate from these legal rules.

The ruling on point (5) was subsequently reconsidered by the Court of Appeal in *R. v. Davis, Johnson and Rowe*.[75] The position was modified so that now where the prosecution wishes to rely on public interest immunity or the sensitivity of the material,[76] *whenever possible* it must give notice to the defence and indicate at least the category of the material it holds, and the defence must have the opportunity to make representations to the court. However, where to disclose even the category of the material in question would be in effect to reveal the material itself, a different procedure applies. Here, the prosecution must notify the defence that an application is to be made, but the category of material need not be specified and the application is made *ex parte* by the prosecution.[77] If the court considers that the normal approach should have been followed, it will so order. If not, it will rule on the *ex parte* application. In a highly exceptional case, the prosecution may make an *ex parte* application to the court *without* notifying the defence. Where an application for non-disclosure is successful the issue should be kept under review by the court in the light of developments at trial. The situation may change so that the public interest in non-disclosure may now be eclipsed by the interest in securing fairness to the defendant, in which case the prosecution will either have to disclose or drop the case.

The same principles apply to the disclosure of other kinds of evidence.[78] The obligation to disclosure does not depend on any prior request by the defence.[79]

This expansion of disclosure obligations was met with considerable criticism from the police, who claimed that the balance between defence access and preserving sensitive sources had swung too far towards the accused, and noted that

---

[72] The matter cannot be dealt with by an application for judicial review of a C.P.S. decision to refuse disclosure; the matter is for the Crown Court, not the magistrates at the committal (now transfer) stage: *R. v. C.P.S., ex p. Warby* (1994) 158 J.P. 190. On the other hand, the prosecution are entitled to *disclose* material within a class that ordinarily would attract PII with the approval of the Treasury Solicitor: *R. v. Horseferry Road Magistrates' Court, ex p. Bennett (No.2)* [1994] 1 All E.R. 289.

[73] cf. *R. v. Langford* [1990] Crim.L.R.653, where the prosecution offered no evidence following the judge's ruling that the name and address of an informer, who was "a witness of very great importance" should be disclosed.

[74] See above.

[75] [1993] 1 W.L.R. 613.

[76] The Attorney-General's Guidelines indicated that special procedures applied to "sensitive material". However, in *R. v. Brown (Winston)* [1994] 1 W.L.R. 1599 the Court of Appeal held that there was no room for such a concept outside where a PII claim could be made.

[77] An *ex parte* application may not be made by the defence: *R. v. Turner* [1995] 1 W.L.R. 264, 267.

[78] *R. v. Livingstone* [1993] Crim.L.R. 597 (a building society manual which bore out the defendant's explanation of building society procedure rather than that of a prosecution witness); *R. v. Phillipson* (1989) 91 Cr.App.R. 226 (material relevant to relationship between D and her boyfriend whom she alleged to have placed her under duress). The duty extends to oral as well as written statements: *R. v. Brown (Winston)* [1994] 1 W.L.R. 1599, but not to matters affecting the credibility of defence as distinct from prosecution witnesses: *ibid.*

[79] *R. v. Livingstone*, above.

vast quantities of information now had to be examined and disclosed.[80] The RCCJ[81] thought that the arrangements as to sensitive material were satisfactory,[82] although these cases should be dealt with by High Court judges or nominated Circuit judges. However, they accepted that, otherwise, the burden on the prosecution had gone "beyond what is reasonable", and they made recommendations for change. The Government subsequently published a Consultation Document[83] setting a more detailed scheme that in its view would reduce the burdens on the prosecution to a greater extent than proposed by the RCCJ. Thus, the investigator would be under a duty to preserve material gathered or generated during the investigation; copies of specified categories of the material would be made available to the prosecutor with a schedule of the remainder. The prosecutor would be under a duty to serve any material on which the prosecutor intended to rely, including anything relevant said in interview. In addition there would be "primary prosecution disclosure" of specified categories of unused material or any other material drawn to the prosecutor's attention, which (in either case) *in his or her view* might undermine the prosecution case.[84] This would be followed by "defence disclosure"[85] of sufficient particulars of its case to identify the issues in dispute before the trial. There would then be "secondary prosecution disclosure" of unused material which might assist the particular line of argument disclosed by the defence. Disputes about whether the disclosure duties had been complied with would be resolved by the court before trial; the criteria used by the court would focus on the issues properly identified by the defence or which might reasonably be expected to be raised. Sensitive material would be subject to the procedure set out in *R. v. Davies, Johnson and Rowe*.[86] The Government claimed that this scheme would significantly reduce the volume of material that must be disclosed for no good purpose but not increase the risk of a miscarriage of justice. Critics have suggested that it will merely "accept the risk of further miscarriages as the cost of achieving economy",[87] and it is important to recall that non-disclosure of evidence by the police and others to the prosecutor or the prosecutor to the defence have been recurrent themes in many of the high-profile miscarriage of justice cases.[88]

Provisions on disclosure are contained in the Criminal Procedure and Investigations Bill 1996.[89] The prosecutor is to make "primary disclosure" of any

---

[80] See *e.g.* C. Pollard, [1994] Crim.L.R.42 (Mr Pollard was Chief Constable of the Thames Valley Police).

[81] Cm. 2263, pp. 91–97. These recommendations are considered by J. Glynn, [1993] Crim.L.R. 841.

[82] On the understanding that the procedure outlined in *Davies* did indeed extend to sensitive material falling outside the scope of public interest immunity (contrary to the subsequent decision in *Brown*, p. 753, n.78 above).

[83] *Disclosure: A Consultation Document* (Cm.2864, 1995).

[84] *cf.* the broader requirement proposed by the RCCJ that the prosecution's initial duty should be to give copies of "all material relevant to the offence or to the offender or to the surrounding circumstance of the case", and lists of everything else (pp. 95–96).

[85] See below, p. 757.

[86] n.75 above, p. 753.

[87] R. Leng, [1995] Crim.L.R.704, 708.

[88] See C. Walker in C. Walker and K. Starmer, *Justice in Error* (1993) p. 14, referring to, *inter alia*, the Guildford Four, the Maguire Seven, the Darvell brothers and Judith Ward in particular. Other examples include Stefan Kiszko.

[89] Clauses 1–20.

prosecution material[90] not previously disclosed which in the prosecution's opinion might undermine the case for the prosecution. However, this does not apply if the court upholds a PII claim or the material has been intercepted under a warrant issued under section 2 of the Interception of Communications Act 1985 or indicates that such a warrant has been issued or interception made. The prosecutor must also serve a document indicating the nature of other prosecution material prescribed by the code of practice under Part II and which has not been disclosed, other than material covered by PII or the 1985 Act. Secondary prosecution disclosure is to follow compulsory or voluntary disclosure by the accused. If the accused has reasonable cause to believe that undisclosed prosecution material "might reasonably be expected to assist" the defence as disclosed by the defence, a court order may be sought. The prosecutor is to be under a continuing duty to keep disclosure issues under review. Comments may be made and inferences may be drawn if the defence does not serve a statement (at all or in time) or sets out inconsistent defences.

In respect of summary trials, requirements as to disclosure have until recently been narrower. The rule about notification of witnesses with material evidence has applied,[91] and the procedure for pleading guilty by post requires the accused to be given a concise statement of the facts.[92] The identity of the complainant should be revealed at an early stage.[93] Section 48 of the Criminal Law Act 1977[94] provided for the adoption of rules requiring advance disclosure in summary trials, but even partial implementation was delayed until 1985. The Magistrates' Courts (Advance Information) Rules 1985[95] provide that, in the case of offences triable either way, the prosecution must upon request provide the defence either with copies of the prosecution witnesses' written statements or with a summary of the facts and matters of which the prosecutor proposes to adduce evidence. The request should be made before the mode-of-trial hearing and complied with as soon as practicable. The court at the mode-of-trial hearing must satisfy itself that the accused is aware of the right to advance information. If a request is not complied with, the proceedings must be adjourned unless the court is satisfied that the conduct of the case will not be substantially prejudiced.[96]

Prior to the introduction of the rules a wide variety of informal disclosure practices had developed in different areas.[97] There was optimism that such prac-

---

[90] *i.e.* material in the prosecutor's possession acquired in connection with the case or which he or she has been allowed to inspect under the code of practice governing the recording of information obtained in the course of criminal investigations made by the Secretary of State under Pt. II of the 1996 Bill (clauses. 21–26).

[91] Failure to notify the defence, if it is a gross failure, can lead to the decision of the court being quashed: *R. v. Leyland JJ., ex p. Hawthorn* [1979] Q.B. 283.

[92] Magistrates' Courts Act 1980, s.12: see below, pp. 838–839.

[93] *Daventry District Council v. Olins* (1990) 154 J.P. 478 (the context was a prosecution for selling food unfit for human consumption).

[94] Following recommendations of the James *Committee on the Distribution of Criminal Business* (Cmnd. 6323, 1975), pp. 95–103.

[95] S.I. 1985 No. 601; criticised by J. Pugh, (1985) 149 J.P.N. 327 and Anon., *ibid.*, p. 499.

[96] Failure to comply will only exceptionally amount to an abuse of process: *King v. Kucharz* (1989) 153 J.P. 336.

[97] See J. Baldwin, *Pre-Trial Justice* (1985) and (1985) 149 J.P.N. 179; F. Feeney, "Advance disclosure of the prosecution case" in D. Moxon (ed.), *Managing Criminal Justice* (1985), Chap. 9 (describing two pilot schemes established by the Home Office); J. Baldwin, [1987] Crim.L.R. 315 and 805, [1987] 151 J.P.N. 409 and J. Baldwin, (1988) 152 J.P.N. 2596 (on the role of case summaries prepared by the police).

tices led to more guilty pleas, fewer elections for trial and other savings.[98] In practice, although improving the fairness of proceedings, the 1985 Rules were not as successful in this regard as hoped, and, indeed, were commonly regarded as increasing delays.[99]

The position has now been transformed by decisions that the common law principles set out in *Ward* and *Davis*[1] apply to summary trials.[2] The requirements of natural justice apply with equal force to the magistrates' courts as to the Crown Court. In the case of the former, fairness also requires that normally, where a bench of magistrates has examined material and ruled that it should not be disclosed, trial should then take place before a differently constituted bench.[3] In anticipation of these decisions, procedures for disclosure had already been established by the C.P.S. applying to every case for summary trial[4] following entry of a not guilty plea as well as in cases committed for trial.[5]

2. Disclosure by the Defence

The defence is at present entitled, very largely, to reserve the whole of the defence for the trial and to say nothing about their case until then. The only exceptions to this principle are the requirements to disclose an alibi defence[6] and any expert evidence intended to be adduced[7] on a trial on indictment and to give notice of certain specific defences in minor regulatory offences. The standard form returned by the defence to the Crown Court listing officer (with a copy to the prosecution) requires the intended plea to be indicated.[8]

The RCCJ concluded[9] that there were "powerful reasons for extending the obligations on the defence to provide advance disclosure." This would encourage earlier and better preparation of cases, and might result in the prosecution being dropped in the light of defence disclosure, an earlier resolution through a plea of guilty, or an earlier trial date. The length of the trial could be more readily estimated, leading to a better use of time both of the court and of those involved in the trial. Cases where the defendant withholds the defence to the last possible moment "in the hope of confusing the jury and evading investigation of

---

[98] *ibid.*
[99] J. N. Spencer, (1986) 150 J.P.N. 356; J. Morton, (1988) 152 J.P.N. 104.
[1] Above, pp. 752–753.
[2] *R. v. Bromley Magistrates' Court, ex p. Smith; R. v. Wells Street Magistrates' Court, ex p. King* [1995] 1 W.L.R. 944.
[3] *R. v. South Worcestershire Magistrates, ex p. Lilley* [1995] 1 W.L.R. 1595, D.C. (pet dis., [1996] 1 W.L.R. 481, H.L.), not following on this point a statement in *ex p. Smith, ex p. King*, above.
[4] Except non-imprisonable summary-only traffic cases, where the principles are accepted to be applicable but no formal procedures are thought necessary.
[5] *ex p. Smith, ex p. King*. n. 2 above, pp. 948–950. These procedures were described as "perfectly satisfactory" by Simon Brown L.J. (at p. 949).
[6] Criminal Justice Act 1967, s.11. See above, p. 749.
[7] Crown Court (Advance Notice of Expert Evidence) Rules 1987 (S.I. 1987 No. 716); Home Office Circular 35/1987. The obligation applies to both prosecution and defence, but the prosecution would be obliged to disclose the evidence anyway.
[8] See *The Crown Court. A guide to good practice* (1990) published by the Law Society, Appendix I; and p. 8 of the equivalent *Guide* published by the L.C.D. (HMSO, 1990).
[9] pp. 97–100.

a fabricated defence" ("ambush defences"[10]) would be kept to a minimum. The disclosed defence should be kept from the jury until it or an alternative is advanced at trial (and so could not form part of the prosecution case). Defence disclosure should only be on the basis of the "fullest possible disclosure of the prosecution's case." Furthermore, it should not extend to the names and addresses of defence witnesses. At trial, adverse inferences could be drawn where appropriate from any change from the disclosed defence. On the assumption[11] that full prosecution disclosure is required only in the Crown Court, these proposals should only apply there. Michael Zander dissented from these recommendations[12] on the ground that it was "contrary to principle for the defendant to be made to respond to the prosecution's case until it has been presented at the trial." Given that the burden of proof lies throughout on the prosecution, "it is not the job of the defendant to be helpful either to the prosecution or to the system. His task, if he chooses to put the prosecution to the proof, is simply to defend himself." Furthermore, ambush defences were in fact rare and when they occur "usually do not pose much of a problem."[13] The majority's proposals would in fact "cause extra delay, cost and general inefficiency in the system— to little, if any, purpose", given the general nature of the defence disclosure requirement.

The government subsequently accepted the majority's diagnosis of the "problem", but its provisional proposals[14] involved less onerous "primary prosecution disclosure"[15] and more onerous defence disclosure, requiring the defence to "provide sufficient particulars of its case to identify the issues in dispute between the defence and the prosecution before the commencement of the trial." These would include the names and addresses of defence witnesses, written expert evidence and any evidence which might support a defence. Such disclosure "is in the interest of justice and should assist the better management of trials." Disputes as to whether there has been compliance would be settled at a preliminary hearing. The sanction for non-compliance would be the possible drawing of adverse inferences by the court. Professor Zander's objections applied with even greater force to these proposals.[16] Furthermore the Consultation Document did not suggest that the police should be inhibited from interviewing the defence witnesses: this is particularly objectionable given the opportunity it provides for the police to "deconstruct or tamper with the defence case."[17] In the event, the Criminal Procedure and Investigations Bill 1996 only provided for the defence to be required in the case of indictable offences tried at the Crown Court to give a "defence statement" to the prosecution. This

---

[10] The Crown Court Study (RCCJ Research Study No. 19, by M.Zander and P. Henderson) showed that "ambush defences" were considered by prosecution counsel to have occurred in 7 per cent of contested cases, by the C.P.S. in 10 per cent and by the police in 26 per cent. They were considered by the C.P.S. to have caused "serious problems" in 3 per cent of contested cases and by the police in 8 per cent. See also R. Leng, [1995] Crim.L.R. 704, 706–707. The RCCJ asserted that the consequences in the minority of cases (said without supporting evidence, to be "often the most serious") were unacceptable (p. 98).

[11] Subsequently shown to be false: see above, p. 756.

[12] Cm. 2263, pp. 221–223.

[13] See above, n. 10.

[14] *Disclosure: A Consultation Document* (Cm. 2864, 1995), pp. 15–16.

[15] Above, p. 754.

[16] See R. Leng, [1995] Crim.L.R. 704; *Disclosure: A consultation paper: The JUSTICE Response* (1995).

[17] *ibid.*, p. 710; A. Sanders and R. Young, *Criminal Justice* (1994), p. 373.

would set out "in general terms the nature of the accused's defence", and indicate "the matters on which he takes issue with the prosecution" and the reasons
for doing so.[18] Defence statements may be given voluntarily in other cases.

3. A PRE-TRIAL REVIEW

There have for many years been arrangements for a hearing between committal
and trial designed to enable the judge to make orders that may be necessary to
secure the proper and efficient trial of the case in the light of intended plea
and other information provided by each side.[19] Rules for such a hearing were
promulgated for the Central Criminal Court in 1977,[20] and provided the model
for rules adopted at Crown Court centres in other circuits. One limitation on
their effectiveness is that such a review does not have the force of law and
nothing decided at one is enforceable at the trial.

> "Counsel are expected to honour promises and undertakings given in the
> course of the review; but if they receive contrary instructions from clients
> thereafter, they must follow them unless circumstances demand withdrawal
> from the case."[21]

Moreover, nothing said or done at the pre-trial review can be used in evidence
at the trial without the consent of the party affected.[22]

The Roskill Committee on Fraud Trials noted that there had been no qualitat-
ive or quantitative research into the effects of pre-trial reviews, but had the
impression that they operated sensibly and efficiently in many but not all of the
cases in which they were conducted.[23] They recommended a more formal procedure for serious fraud cases.[24]

Recent developments are following two lines. Firstly, revised rules have been
promulgated for *pleas and directions hearings* in the Crown Court.[25] These
apply to all cases (other than serious fraud) in Crown Court centres which have
notified the magistrates' courts that PDHs have been introduced. At a PDH,
pleas are taken, and in contested cases "prosecution and defence will be
expected to assist the judge in identifying the key issues, and to provide any
additional information required for the proper listing of the case." The advocate
briefed in the case should appear in the PDH "whenever practicable." Before
the PDH, where the defendant intends to plead guilty to all or part of the indict-

---

[18] Clause 5. Provisions for disclosure of alibi evidence are retained (superseding s.11, Criminal
Justice Act 1967, above, p. 749).

[19] See A. Samuels, (1982) 146 J.P.N. 677, 686.

[20] See Archbold, *Criminal Pleading, Evidence and Practice* (43rd ed.), para. 4–43. They also appear
in Appendix 27 of RCCP I, together with the rules adopted on the North Eastern Circuit.

[21] *Per* Watkins L.J. in *R. v. Hutchinson* (1985) 82 Cr.App.R. 51, 56.

[22] *R. v. Hutchinson* (1985) 82 Cr.App.R. 51.

[23] *Report on Fraud Trials* (HMSO, 1986), pp. 79–86.

[24] *ibid.* pp. 87–113; below, pp. 761–762.

[25] *Practice Direction (Crown Court: Plea and Directions Hearings)* [1995] 1 W.L.R. 1318. This
replaced Practice Rules published on October 25, 1994 (*Blackstone's Criminal Practice 1995*
D11.13), and is based on Recommendation 92 of the Report of the Working Group on Pre-Trial
Issues (1990). The Working Group comprised representatives of the L.C.D., the Law Officers'
Department, the Home Office, the Justices' Clerks Society and the C.P.S.

ment, the defence must notify the probation service, the prosecution and the court as soon as this is known. This will enable the defendant to be sentenced at the PDH "whenever possible". In contested cases, prosecution and defence are expected to inform the court of a series of matters including the issues in the case, the number of witnesses, admitted facts, exhibits and schedules, alibis, points of law and evidence expected to arise, the estimated length of the trial, witness and advocate availability. The judge can make "such order or orders as lie within is or her power as appear to be necessary to secure the proper and efficient trial of the case." A standard questionnaire, agreed if possible between prosecution and defence, should be given to the judge. These hearings are typically short, and a pilot study showed a reduction in both the number of cases listed and the number of "cracked" trials.[26]

The second development has been the introduction of *preparatory hearings* in serious fraud cases.[27] Building on these, the Government proposes that judges should have the power to make binding rulings in all cases on any question as to the admissibility of evidence and any other question of law, at any point after the committal of a case to the Crown Court. These would take place at a PDH or another preliminary hearing. Furthermore a pilot study should be conducted on the question whether a scheme of preparatory hearings on the model of those for serious fraud cases might also be established for other complex or potentially lengthy cases. At these hearings, the judge, apart from the power to make binding rules on issues of law or evidence, would have other powers to identify, simplify and narrow the issues in dispute.[28] Save in exceptional circumstances, the same judge should conduct both the preparatory hearing and the proceedings in front of the jury. These powers are to be conferred by the Criminal Procedure and Investigation Bill 1996, Parts III (Preparatory Hearings) and IV (Rulings). Reporting restrictions are to apply to preparatory hearings.

In the magistrates' court the same problem occurs before summary trial, but the number of cases in which a formal pre-trial review is beneficial may be more limited. Prior to implementation of section 48 of the Criminal Law Act 1977, the Nottingham justices' clerks instituted a scheme on their own initiative which was alleged to save money as well as reducing delay and frustration caused by the repeated adjournment of trials where the defence had been caught unprepared by the prosecution.[29] In approximately 20 cases each week, prosecution and defence met at an appointed time for "an informal but candid discussion" without a magistrate present. The benefits of such a scheme were said to include a saving of court time by inducing "realistic" pleas; early notification of points of law that may arise; a reduction in the length of contested cases; confirmation of readiness for trial and a general tidying-up to ensure that the

---

[26] *i.e.*, cases listed for trial before a jury but where, often on the day, the trial is abandoned, *e.g.* because the defendant pleads guilty or no evidence is offered. See Home Office, *Improving the Effectiveness of Pre-Trial Hearings in the Crown Court: A Consultation Document* (Cm. 2924, 1995).

[27] See below, pp. 761–762.

[28] Cm. 2914, 1995. The RCCJ's proposals took a different form with provision for the exchange of papers sufficient in less complex cases and the possibility of binding rulings confined to preparatory hearings that would take place in a minority of cases: Cm. 2263, pp. 101–109. Professor Zander dissented, favouring the development of PDHs: pp. 223–233.

[29] The scheme is glowingly described and commended in A. Debruslais, "Pre-Trial Disclosure in Magistrates' Courts: Why Wait?" (1982) 146 J.P.N. 384, and was the subject of a study by J. Baldwin: *Pre-Trial Justice* (1985).

case can go ahead when listed. About a dozen other courts introduced similar schemes, some short-lived, and with differences in the details of the arrangements.[30] The schemes were indeed perceived to have advantages in promoting the efficient disposal of cases, but there were doubts as to the adequacy of the safeguards for the accused (who in most schemes was not permitted to be present)[31] and the Law Society emphasised that any disclosure of the defence case could only be done with the express or implied authority of the client.[32] The introduction of the requirements for advance disclosure of the prosecution case led to modifications to most although not all of the schemes that remained.[33] The reviews are no longer required as a vehicle for disclosure by the prosecution, and "tend to be held in fewer cases and often are confined to those cases that present particular procedural or evidential difficulties."[34] A recent survey suggested that PTRs had "much to commend them", particularly by facilitating earlier settlements of cases.[35]

I. SPECIAL ARRANGEMENTS FOR FRAUD AND CHILD ABUSE CASES

The pre-trial procedures discussed in the previous two sections can be replaced in respect of serious and complex fraud cases by arrangements under the Criminal Justice Act 1987.[36] This Act was passed following the Report of the Committee on Fraud Trials, chaired by Lord Roskill,[37] although it differs in some important respects from the Committee's recommendations.[38]

The first modification to normal procedures is that normal transfer procedure can be replaced by a special notice of transfer procedure.[39] This can be put into effect where a person has been charged with an indictable offence, and, in the opinion of the "designated authority"[40] or one of its officers, the evidence would be sufficient for proceeding for transfer and reveals a case of fraud of such seriousness and complexity that it is appropriate for its management to be taken

---

[30] See J. Baldwin and F. Feeney, "Defence Disclosure in the Magistrates' Courts" (1986) 49 M.L.R. 593.

[31] Baldwin (1985), Chap. 7

[32] "Pre-Trial Reviews in the Magistrates' Court: Guidance for Defence Solicitors" (1983) 80 L. S. Gaz. 2330.

[33] J. Baldwin, (1987) 151 J. P. N. 611. The schemes in some areas were discontinued. A recent survey showed that 43 of 218 magistrates' courts that responded operated a formal PTR system while a further 30 conducted them on an informal or *ad hoc* basis: A. Mulcahy, I. Brownlee and C. Walker, "An evaluation of Pre-Trial Reviews in Leeds and Bradford Magistrates' Courts" (1993) 33 H.O.R.B. 10, 11. See also Brownlee, Mulcahy and Walker, (1994) 158 J. P. N. 234, 250.

[34] J. Baldwin, *op. cit.*, at p. 613.

[35] See Mulcahy *et al.*, *op. cit.*

[36] See the annotations to this Act by I. Leigh in *Current Law Statutes Annotated 1987*.

[37] HMSO, 1986. See M. Levi, (1986) 13 J. L. S. 117.

[38] In particular, the government rejected a recommendation that trial by jury be replaced in some cases by trial by a fraud trials tribunal: see below, pp. 908–910.

[39] 1987 Act, ss.4–6, as amended by the Criminal Justice Act 1988, s.144 (the amendments are explained by H.O. Circular 84/1988: (1988) 152 J.P.N. 700), and to be amended by the Criminal Procedure and Investigations Bill 1996, cl.44.

[40] The D.P.P., the Director of the Serious Fraud Office, the Commissioners of Inland Revenue, the Commissioners of Customs and Excise or the Secretary of State.

over by the Crown Court without delay. A "notice of transfer" must be served on the magistrates' court in whose jurisdiction the offence has been charged, not later than the time at which the prosecution would be required to serve a notice of the prosecution case. The court's functions thereupon cease, except in respect of such matters as bail, legal aid and witness orders.[41] The notice must specify the proposed place of trial and the charge or charges, and a copy of the notice and (copies of the documents containing the evidence including oral evidence) on which the charge or charges are based must be given to the defendant and to the Crown Court.[42]

A decision to give notice of transfer "shall not be subject to appeal or liable to be questioned in any court," but any person to whom the notice relates may apply to the Crown Court for any charge to be dismissed on the ground that the evidence disclosed would not be sufficient for a jury properly to convict him or her of it.[43] Applications may be made orally or in writing, but oral evidence may only be given with the leave of the judge, and leave is only to be granted if it appears to him or her that the interest of justice so requires. A discharge has the same effect as a refusal by a magistrates' court to commit for trial, except that no further proceedings on a charge may be brought except by a voluntary bill of indictment.[44] There is no right of appeal at the interlocutory stage against a refusal to dismiss a charge, but judicial review may be granted in exceptional circumstances.[45]

The other major modification is that there are formal arrangements for "preparatory hearings" in place of the arrangements that exist for pre-trial reviews in the Crown Court.[46] The aims of such a hearing are (a) identifying issues likely to be material to the jury's verdict; (b) assisting its comprehension of such issues; (c) expediting proceedings before the jury; or (d) assisting the judge's management of the trial. A judge of the Crown Court may order a preparatory hearing where it appears that substantial benefits are likely to accrue, on the application of prosecution or defence or of his or her own motion. They are not confined to cases which have been the subject of a notice of transfer. The judge has power to order the prosecution to prepare and serve a "case statement" setting out the principal facts, names of witnesses, exhibits and propositions of law that the prosecution will be relying upon. The prosecution should also indicate any documents or other matters that in their view should be agreed by the defendant. On compliance with such an order, the judge may order the defendant to prepare and serve a written statement setting out in general terms the nature of the defence, and to indicate any objections to the case statement, any point of law which he or she wishes to take, and the extent to which documents or other matters specified by the prosecution are agreed.[47] The defendant need not,

---

[41] See The Magistrates' Courts (Notice of Transfer) Rules 1988 (S. I. 1988 No. 1701).

[42] The Criminal Justice Act 1987 (Notice of Transfer) Regulations 1988 (S. I. 1988 No. 1691).

[43] 1987 Act, s.6, substituted by the Criminal Justice Act 1988, s.144; The Criminal Justice Act 1987 (Dismissal of Transferred Charges) Rules 1988 (S. I. 1988 No. 1695). This is the *Galbraith* test (below, p. 869): *R. v. X* [1989] Crim.L.R. 726, Henry J., Southwark Crown Court.

[44] Above, pp. 749–750.

[45] *R. v. Central Criminal Court, ex p. Director of the Serious Fraud Office* [1993] 1 W.L.R. 946.

[46] 1987 Act, ss.7–10; The Criminal Justice Act 1987 (Preparatory Hearings) Rules 1988 (S.I. 1988 No. 1699).

[47] The judge has no power to prohibit the prosecution from reinterviewing witnesses in the light of the defence statements or to control such further interviews: *R. v. Nadir, R. v. Turner (John)* [1993] 1 W.L.R. 1322.

however, disclose who will give evidence[48] or serve the case statement on a co-defendant.[49] The process is similar to the exchange of pleadings and other documents in civil litigation.

The preparatory hearing is regarded as part of the trial and not as a preliminary to it, and accordingly starts with the arraignment[50] of the defendant.[51] The hearing is conducted by the judge who is to preside at the trial proper,[51] and counsel briefed to appear at the trial should take part in the hearing. The judge has the same powers to order disclosure as exist before the hearing, and there is a general duty on each party to inform the court of any significant matter which might affect the proper and convenient trial of the case. More importantly, the judge may determine any question as to the admissibility of evidence and any other question of law relating to the case.[52] Any such order or ruling will take effect at the trial, subject to two qualifications. First, an appeal against the order or ruling can be taken forthwith to the Court of Appeal (Criminal Division), but only with the leave of the judge or the Court of Appeal.[53] The preparatory hearing can continue meanwhile, but the jury cannot be sworn until after the appeal is determined or abandoned. Secondly, the order or ruling can be varied or discharged by the judge at the trial.

The requirement that the defence disclose its case at the preparatory hearing was controversial, in that this was required before the prosecution had proved its case.[54] In the Act's final form, the defendant is only required to set out the nature of the defence in general terms, and need not disclose the names of defence witnesses. Moreover, no part of the defence case revealed at the preparatory hearing can be disclosed at the trial proper, unless either the defendant consents, or there has been a departure from the case as indicated at the hearing. Either party is at liberty to depart from the case disclosed at the hearing, but if there is such a departure, or a failure to comply with a requirement imposed at the hearing, the judge (or any other party, with the leave of the judge) may comment, and "the jury may draw such inference as appears proper."[55]

There are reporting restrictions in respect of applications for dismissal, preparatory hearings and related interlocutory appeals, analogous to those for committal proceedings.[56]

The Criminal Justice Act 1991[57] introduced similar arrangements for transfer in respect of offences of a violent or sexual nature where there is a child witness (who may be the victim, or someone who witnessed the commission of the

---

[48] Except in relation to an alibi or expert evidence: see p. 756.

[49] *Re Tariq* [1991] 1 W.L.R. 101.

[50] See p. 748, n. 42.

[51] This must be so other than in exceptional circumstances such as the death or illness: *R. v. Southwark Crown Court, ex p. Customs and Excise Commissioners* [1993] 1 W.L.R. 764.

[52] But only questions that accord with the specified aims of preparatory hearings, not, *e.g.* a question whether proceedings should be dismissed as an abuse of process: *Re Gunawardena, Harbutt and Banks* [1990] 1 W.L.R. 703; and questions of law, not the exercise of discretion: *R. v. Smithson* [1994] 1 W.L.R. 1052.

[53] The Criminal Justice Act 1987 (Preparatory Hearings) (Interlocutory Appeals) Rules 1988 (S.I. 1988 No. 1700). See *Case Statements made under section 9 of the Criminal Justice Act 1987* (1993) 97 Cr. App. R. 417.

[54] I. Leigh, *op. cit* n. 36 above, pp. 38–21—38–23.

[55] 1987 Act, s.10(1). A new s.10 is to be substituted by the Criminal Procedure and Investigation Bill 1996, Sched. 2, para. 5.

[56] *ibid.*, s.11, *cf.* above, p. 747. A new s.11 is to be substituted by the 1996 Bill, Sched. 2, para. 6.

[57] s.53 and Sched. 6, to be amended by the Criminal Procedure and Investigations Bill 1996, cl. 44.

offence). There is no provision for preparatory hearings. Finally, the War Crimes Act 1991[58] provides for a transfer procedure in respect of charges under the Act.

J. OBTAINING LEGAL ADVICE AND REPRESENTATION

We stressed the importance of legal aid and advice in civil proceedings by dealing with it at the beginning of the civil procedure chapter. Its availability may determine whether the case goes ahead at all. In criminal proceedings it is not relevant to that issue, but must be made available as a way of ensuring that defendants have what specialist help they need in the presentation of their defence. Different criteria are obviously required for the grant and administration of criminal legal aid.[59]

Legal advice and professional assistance may be required by defendants at two quite different stages. They will initially have to deal with the police and face interrogation by them, the results of which are likely to have a considerable influence on their case at trial. They may wish to be advised how to conduct themselves to the best advantage at this stage of the procedure. Then, if charged, they will want assistance in the preparation and presentation of their case at and before the trial. The extent to which lawyers are involved in these two distinct situations is different. Almost all those charged with serious offences are represented at trial, many fewer are "represented" during interrogation at the police station.

1. LEGAL ADVICE AT THE POLICE STATION

As we have seen, the Police and Criminal Evidence Act 1984 strengthens the right of those being interviewed by the police to have access to legal advice, and the courts have emphasised the importance of these rights in excluding evidence of confessions obtained in breach of them.[60]

The legal advice scheme can be used for the purpose of securing the services of a solicitor at the police station and the eligibility of the accused and the extent of any financial contribution are calculated according to the figures set out earlier in our discussion of the scheme.[61] In theory, the accused has the opportunity, the means and the motive to ensure that he or she is properly advised on the most advantageous way to conduct him- or herself at the police station. In practice, only a minority of accused persons receive that advice.

Prior to the introduction of the Police and Criminal Evidence Act 1984, a number of surveys showed that a minority of suspects at the police station asked

---

[58] Sched. 1, Pt. I. (not in force).
[59] It was only in 1980 that both schemes were put under the aegis of the same government department. Formerly, criminal legal aid was the responsibility of the Home Office.
[60] See above, pp. 681–688.
[61] See above, pp. 491–510.

to see a solicitor, and most such requests were refused.[62] The requirement in the Administrative Directions that accompanied the Judges' Rules that persons in custody should be informed orally of the rights and facilities available to them was not widely observed.[63] The police were also criticised for simple obstruction of those who got as far as asking to be allowed to contact a solicitor. The Royal Commission on Criminal Procedure took note of these criticisms in their final recommendations,[64] on which the relevant provisions in PACE were based. The RCCP recognised that the provision of information alone does not ensure that the right to have a lawyer is exercised. This was illustrated by American experience after the decision in *Miranda v. Arizona*[65] required every suspect to be told of his or her right to consult a lawyer, and have the lawyer present during interrogation. Studies carried out in the United States still revealed surprisingly small numbers of suspects getting legal advice.[66]

The early indications of the impact of PACE on access to legal advice at the police station[67] were that (1) there was a significant increase in the number of suspects seeking legal advice; (2) that they still only constituted a minority; (3) that a variety of ploys were used by the police to discourage exercise of the right to see a lawyer; (4) that only a small proportion of suspects had a lawyer with them during police interrogation; (5) that there might have been a rise in the number of suspects who refused to make admissions during interrogation.

Brown's study[68] showed that 25 per cent of all detainees asked for a solicitor while at the police station, although there was considerable variation (14 per cent to 41 per cent) from station to station. As might be expected, take-up rates were higher for more serious offences, again with considerable variations for individual stations.[69] The police contacted a solicitor on behalf of 22 per cent of detainees, and 21 per cent had some form of consultation with one whilst at the police station. In over three-quarters of these cases, the solicitor attended in person; otherwise, advice was given over the telephone.[70] In 80 per cent of cases in which solicitors attended advice was given prior to any police interview, but solicitors attended only 12 per cent of all police interviews with suspects. Fifty per cent of those who requested a solicitor saw one within the hour and nearly

---

[62] M. Zander, [1972] Crim.L.R. 342 (11 per cent of 134 appellants to the Court of Appeal had contacted a solicitor; a further 32 per cent had asked to speak to a solicitor and had been refused); J. Baldwin and M. McConville, [1979] Crim.L.R. 145 (31 per cent of 352 defendants at Crown Court had asked to see a solicitor, over three-quarters of these requests being refused; P. Softley, *Police Interrogation: An Observational Study in Four Police Stations*, RCCP Research Study No. 4 (HMSO, 1980) (requests from 12 per cent of 168 suspects being interrogated at a police station, with one-third refusals).

[63] Softley (1980), p. 65.

[64] RCCP Report, paras.4.81 ff.

[65] 348 U.S. 436 (1966).

[66] See, *e.g.* M. Wald, *et al.*, "Interrogation in New Haven: the Impact of Miranda" 76 Yale L.J. 1519 (1967).

[67] See D. Brown, *Detention at the Police Station under the Police and Criminal Evidence Act 1984* (H.O. Research Study 104, 1989), Chap. 3 and "PACE and the right to legal advice" (H.O.R.P.U. Bulletin 26:26); A. Sanders, *et al., Advice and Assistance at Police Stations and the 24 Hour Duty Solicitor Scheme* (L.C.D., 1989), summarised at (1990) 140 N.L.J. 85, and [1990] Crim.L.R. 494; B. L. Irving and I. K. McKenzie, *Police Interrogation* (1989), pp. 53–59, 113–115, 157–164, 199–200.

[68] Above. Based on a sample of over 5,500 custody records from 32 police stations in 10 forces.

[69] See further, Sanders, *et al.* (1989), Chap. 3.

[70] The research by Sanders, *et al.* showed a higher proportion of cases where telephone advice was given, particularly by duty solicitors: *ibid.* Chap. 6.

80 per cent within two hours, but some detainees had to wait much longer. Duty solicitors gave over one third of all advice and assistance provided at police stations.[71] A superintendent permitted access to a lawyer to be delayed in 4 per cent of cases in which legal advice was requested.

Research by Sanders, et al. sought to examine the factors behind the low take-up rates.[72] These include failure in a small proportion of cases to inform suspects of the right to legal advice, either orally or by Home Office notice;[73] failure in a much larger number of cases to inform the suspect that legal advice would be free, under the 24-hour scheme;[74] the use by the police of a wide variety of ploys to discourage exercise of the right of access;[75] "unwillingness of suspects to add to their length of detention; fatalism (legal advice will not help them out of trouble); confidence (legal advice is not needed because their innocence is obvious); triviality of the alleged offence; their feelings about the police; dislike of lawyers."[76] It was suggested that take-up rates will always be low because many suspects are fatalistic, confident or view a quick escape from custody as an overriding priority. However, they might well rise considerably if rights were explained properly, and if PACE required a positive decision to *refuse* legal advice to trigger section 58.

A number of steps have been taken in response to such findings as these. Thus the provisions of PACE Code C have been tightened. The 1991 and 1994 revisions added a number of requirements.[77] Accordingly, "all people in police detention" must be informed that they may at any time consult and communicate privately with a solicitor, "and that independent legal advice is available free of charge from the duty solicitor."[78] A poster advertising the right to legal advice must be prominently displayed in the charging area of every police station.[79] "No police officer shall at any time do or say anything with the intention of dissuading a person in detention from obtaining legal advice."[80] Whenever legal advice is requested, and unless the right to such advice can properly be delayed, "the custody officer must act without delay" to secure its provision to the person concerned.[81] A person who declines to speak to a solicitor in person must be expressly informed of the right to have advice by telephone. A person who still declines legal advice must be asked for the reasons, and any reasons given must be recorded in the custody record.[82] Reminders of the right to free legal advice must be given at various stages, including immediately prior to the commencement or re-commencement of any interview at a police station.[83] A report by Brown et al. following the introduction of the 1991 version

---

[71] *ibid.* p. 42.

[72] *ibid.* Chap. 4.

[73] Contrary to the requirements of Code C.3.1 and C.3.2: and see above p. 764.

[74] Custody Officers were asked in a Note for Guidance (*3E*) to provide suspects with a Law Society leaflet explaining the scheme.

[75] *e.g.* the incomplete or incomprehensible reading of rights; emphasis on delay; "sign here, here and here", with no information given; "you don't want a solicitor do you?"

[76] Sanders, *et al.* (1989), p. 72.

[77] The 1995 revision incorporated a number of recommendations by the RCCJ (Report, Cm. 2263, pp. 35–39). See D. Wolchover and A. Heaton-Armstrong, [1995] Crim.L.R. 356.

[78] Code C.6.1, added by the 1995 revision.

[79] Code C.6.3, added by the 1991 revision.

[80] Code C.6.4, reworded in the 1995 revision. The 1991 version stated that "no attempt should be made to dissuade the suspect from obtaining legal advice."

[81] Code C.6.5, first added to para. 6.2 of the 1991 revision.

[82] *ibid.*, added by the 1994 revision.

[83] *ibid.*, added by the 1991 revision.

of Code C revealed an increase in the proportion of suspects requesting legal advice from 24 per cent to 32 per cent; 25 per cent of suspects having a legal consultation compared with 18 per cent, two-thirds being seen in person; but legal advisers less often remaining to attend police interviews with their clients.[84]

The research of Sanders, *et al.* also raised doubts about the quality of service provided to suspects in police stations, more particularly by duty solicitors, given the high proportion of telephone advice, often perceived as less satisfactory by suspects, and the low rate of attendance at interrogations.[85] A further point, explored by McConville and Hodgson.[86] is that in a very high proportion of cases, suspects see a clerk and not a qualified solicitor. Such clerks may be trainees, retired police officers, or even wholly inexperienced clerical staff. McConville and Hodgson found overall[87] that many advisers lacked adequate legal knowledge and confidence, and that advisers made no attempt to obtain information from the investigating officers, in 45 per cent of cases routinely failed to discover important material known to the client or to examine the legal position with care, and made no intervention in the interview in 78 per cent of cases.[88] The RCCJ found these findings to be "disturbing", noted that it had brought the problems to the attention of the Law Society and the Legal Aid Board, and encouraged improvements in training. More significantly, they recommended that steps should be taken to make "own solicitors" and their representatives subject to the same standards as duty solicitors and their representatives.[89] From 1995, payments for police station work are restricted to qualified and trainee solicitors, approved "duty solicitor" representatives, and other representatives accredited under a new Law Society and Legal Aid Board scheme; representatives may, however, be registered as "probationary" pending accreditation.[90]

The actual impact of advice is uncertain. Sanders *et al.* found that suspects confess less often when they have advice, but that the differences are not dramatic. It might be that solicitors persuade suspects to remain silent or deny the offence or simply that they help suspects to hold firm to their existing intentions to do so. Most officers claimed that advice had little or no effect. Sanders *et al.* suggested, however, that many suspects who do not receive advice could have been greatly assisted, and found that the police manage to circumvent

---

[84] *Changing the Code* (H.O.R.S. No.129, HMSO, 1992). See further, below pp. 503–504.

[85] Sanders *et al.* (1989), Chap. 6. See further, below pp. 504–506.

[86] *Custodial Legal Advice and the Right to Silence* (RCCJ Research Study No.16, HMSO, 1993). This research was based on the practices of 17 solicitors' firms and three agencies to whom solicitors' firms had delegated custodial advice work. 180 cases were studied. See also M.McConville, *et al., Standing Accused* (1994). The proportion of "own solicitor" (rather than duty solicitor) cases in which a clerk is used was found to have risen to 75 per cent (16 per cent articled clerks, 31 per cent other clerks, 21 per cent former police officers). Other studies have found a lower proportion: see discussion by McConville and Hodgson, pp. 15–16.

[87] As summarised by the RCCJ, Cm. 2263, pp. 37–38.

[88] John Baldwin found that advisers said nothing in 66 per cent of the cases and actively intervened in only 9 per cent (*The Role of Legal Representatives at the Police Station*, RCCJ Research Study No.3, HMSO, 1992; based on analysis of a sample of audio- and video-recordings of interviews).

[89] Cm. 2263, p. 38.

[90] See the Legal Aid Board Legal Advice and Assistance at Police Stations Register Arrangements 1994. L. Bridges and J. Hodgson, "Improving Custodial Legal Advice" [1995] Crim.L.R. 101 for a critique of the scheme and the associated training packages; they point to the "loopholes" that exempt "own" solicitors, trainee solicitors and duty solicitor representatives, and note that its impact is likely to be over time and not immediate.

solicitors in various ways, such as by questioning during the journey to the police station, during processing, and while the suspect is alone in the cell.[91] They also emphasised that solicitors do not only provide legal advice: they can provide less tangible assistance such as by protecting suspects from real or imaginary danger from the police, explaining to suspects what is happening to them, and making representations to the police about charge or bail, or alleged mistreatment.[92] Overall, effort needed to be put into securing more wholehearted police compliance with PACE and the Code of Practice; and equal effort into securing better responses from solicitors.[93]

2. ADVICE AND REPRESENTATION AFTER CHARGE

The primary vehicle for the provision of publicly funded legal assistance in criminal cases is the criminal legal aid scheme. Apart from this, however, an accused person may obtain advice and assistance from his or her own solicitor under the green form scheme,[94] or from a duty solicitor at the magistrates' court under the Legal Aid Board Duty Solicitor Arrangements.[95] Apart from receiving legal advice the accused may, for example, be assisted in applying for a legal aid order. Assistance may also include assistance by way of representation (ABWOR).[96] This can cover a bail application; making a plea in mitigation for an accused in custody who pleads guilty; representing a person who is to be dealt with for failure to obey a court order and who may be imprisoned; and representation for any other person not in custody who in the solicitor's opinion, requires it.[97] However, ABWOR is not available for oral hearings of applications for dismissal under section 6 of the Magistrates' Courts Act 1980[98] or proceedings in which the client pleads not guilty, or, unless the solicitor considers the circumstances exceptional, in connection with a non-imprisonable offence.[99] It is also the case that ABWOR for a hearing can be provided by a solicitor in the precincts of the court at the court's request; the court must be satisfied that the hearing should proceed on the same day and that the party would not otherwise be represented.[1] Where advice and assistance is provided under the Duty Solicitor Arrangements, there is no limit on the cost of advice and assistance, it is available without regard to the client's resources, and the solicitor claims remuneration under the Arrangements.[2] Otherwise, it is funded through the green

---

[91] Sanders, *et al* (1989), pp. 150–151.

[92] *ibid.* p. 186.

[93] *ibid.* p. 192.

[94] Above, pp. 491–510.

[95] Above, pp. 496–497, 502–507.

[96] Above, pp., 495–496. Legal advice and ABWOR for criminal cases in the magistrates' courts is provided for by the Legal Advice and Assistance (Scope) Regulations 1989 (S.I. 1989 No. 550), regs. 6, 7, and the Legal Advice and Assistance Regulations 1989 (S.I. 1989 No. 340), esp. regs. 4–13, 22–27; Legal Aid Board Duty Solicitor Arrangements 1994, Parts VII and VIII.

[97] Scope Regulations, reg. 7(2); Duty Solicitor Arrangements 1994, para. 50.

[98] See above, p. 746.

[99] Respectively, reg. 7(3), as amended by S.I. 1995 No. 1987, and para. 51(1).

[1] Scope Regulations, reg. 7(1)(b). This provision is not confined to criminal proceedings. However, the solicitor must not be in the precincts of the court for the purpose of providing ABWOR.

[2] S.I. 1989 No. 340, regs. 4(2)(b), 7(3), 8(2); Legal Advice and Assistance (Duty Solicitors) (Remuneration) Regulations 1989 (S.I. 1989 No. 341), as amended.

form scheme, and subject to that scheme's cost limits and conditions of eligibility.[3]

The principles upon which legal aid is granted, and the obligations of the recipient, are established by the Legal Aid Act 1988[4] and the regulations made thereunder.[5] The present system attempts to ensure that every person charged with a serious offence, or an offence which may have particularly serious consequences for him or her, is provided with sufficient professional assistance to allow the case to be properly prepared and presented, subject to a contribution towards the cost according to means.

An application for criminal legal aid is normally made to the magistrates' court, although the Crown Court also has the power to grant it and even the appellate courts in appropriate circumstances.[6] There is also a role for the area committees, appointed by the Legal Aid Board, which administer the civil legal aid scheme, since they constitute the criminal legal aid committees with functions under the Criminal Legal Aid regulations.

In all cases, representation can only be granted to persons if it appears to the court that their financial resources are such as under the regulations make them eligible.[7] If it does, then legal aid is *mandatory* in cases of murder trials; where the prosecutor is seeking to appeal to the House of Lords; where the accused is brought before a magistrates' court in custody, is liable to be remanded in custody, and wishes to be represented; and where the accused is kept in custody after conviction for medical or other reports.[8] In all other cases, the court may make an order for legal aid for a defendant "... where it appears desirable to do so in the interests of justice...."[9] Any doubts are to be resolved in the defendant's favour.[10]

A single legal aid order may be made by a magistrates' court to cover the committal proceedings, the trial on indictment (if committed), and advice and assistance as to an appeal (if convicted).[11] There is little disagreement about legal aid for trials in the Crown Court and the statistics show a remarkable degree of consistency. All but a handful of applications for legal aid for trial at the Crown Court are granted and the proportion of legally aided defendants in the Crown Court has risen from 93 per cent. (in 1972) 97 per cent (in 1994)[12].

---

[3] S.I. 1989 No. 340, reg. 9. The prior approval of the Legal Aid Board is necessary for ABWOR under reg. 7(2) of the Scope Regulations, but not under reg. 7(1)(b): S.I. 1989 No. 340, reg. 22.

[4] The Legal Aid Act 1982, s.1, provided for these schemes to be put on a statutory basis under Legal Aid Act 1974, s.15.

[5] Legal Aid in Criminal and Care Proceedings (General) Regulations 1989 (S.I. 1989 No. 344),as amended. See generally, A. Samuels, "Criminal Legal Aid: The Issues of Principle" [1983] Crim.L.R. 223, especially the materials noted on p. 223; H. Levenson, "Contributions and the new criminal legal aid" [1984] *Legal Action* 37, and "Appeals and reviews in criminal legal aid" [1984] *Legal Action* 49.

[6] Legal Aid Act 1988, s.20.

[7] *ibid.* s.21(5). The court must require a statement of means from applicants, with supporting documentary evidence, unless they are incapable of furnishing one by reason of their physical or mental condition, or they have already submitted one and their financial circumstances have not changed, or the applicant (or his or her spouse or "common law spouse") is on income support, family credit or disability working allowance: 1989 Regulations, regs.11 and 23, as amended.

[8] *ibid.* s.21(3).

[9] *ibid.* s.21(2).

[10] *ibid.* s.21(7).

[11] *ibid.* s.19(2).

[12] *Criminal Statistics England and Wales 1982*, Cmnd. 9048, Chap. 9; *Judicial Statistics 1994* Cm. 2891, Chap. 10.

The statutory condition that legal aid should be granted where it is in the interests of justice has been amplified by the "Widgery criteria"[13], now set out in section 22 of the 1988 Act. If a case exhibits one or more of the following factors, there are grounds for thinking that representation is desirable:

"(a) That the charge is a grave one in the sense that the accused is in real jeopardy of losing his liberty or suffering serious damage to his reputation;

(b) that the charge raises a substantial question of law;

(c) that the accused is unable to follow the proceedings and state his own case because of his inadequate knowledge of English, mental illness or other mental or physical disability;

(d) that the nature of the defence involves the tracing and interviewing of witnesses or expert cross-examination of a witness for the prosecution;

(e) that legal representation is desirable in the interest of someone other than the accused as, for example, in the case of sexual offences against young children where it is undesirable that the accused should cross-examine the witness in person."[14]

There is rarely any difficulty in establishing that an offence to be tried on indictment can be fitted into one or other of the categories.

The problems in the criminal legal aid scheme have related to the application of these principles in magistrates' courts when a defendant seeks legal aid in respect of a summary offence or an either-way offence to be tried summarily. An application for legal aid in magistrates' court proceedings may be made orally to the court (who may then refer it to the justices' clerk to be dealt with) or in writing direct to the justices' clerk.[15] The clerk or the court may grant or refuse the application. If it is refused, the applicant may either renew it or, in certain cases, apply for review to the appropriate area legal aid committee. Only the court (or a justice of the peace to whom the matter has been referred by the justices' clerk) can refuse a renewed application; either the court (or justice of the peace) or the justices' clerk can grant it.[16] The role of the clerk in administering legal aid led to some disquiet about the rate of refusal in certain courts, particularly where it appeared that the clerks were acting vigorously to implement undisclosed policies or Government directives on cost-saving.[17] The review procedure, originally instituted by the Legal Aid Act 1982, was an attempt to meet some of those criticisms in relation to committal proceedings and the trial of either-way offences. The cases in which legal aid must be granted in the magistrates' court are very few. Such statistics as there are suggest that very few defendants charged with summary offences receive legal aid, although

---

[13] Contained in para. 180 of *Legal Aid in Criminal Proceedings* (Cmnd. 2934, 1966) the report of a Departmental Committee chaired by Widgery J., as he then was.

[14] These criteria are incorporated, in the form of questions, into the application form for criminal legal aid which is prescribed by S.I. 1989 No. 344, as amended.

[15] The term "justices' clerk" includes a court official authorised by the clerk to act on his or her behalf: S.I. 1989 No. 344, reg. 3.

[16] S.I. 1989 No. 344, regs.11–17

[17] L.C.D. Circular 81(3), reproduced in (1981) 131 N.L.J. 359, and see H. Levenson, (1978) 128 N.L.J. 52; (1979) 129 N.L.J. 375; *LAG Bulletin*, January 1980, April 1980, May 1981. Especial attention was paid to Waltham Forest: "What a difference a clerk makes", *LAG Bulletin*, March 1982.

a significant number of defendants tried for either-way offences do.[18] The magistrates' court, however, does not have an easy task. It has been suggested that the Widgery criteria do not work well because they are complex, imprecise and open to a wide range of interpretations.[19] This inevitably leads to substantial variations in the grant of legal aid, and the refusal figures are further distorted by the unwillingness of solicitors even to apply for aid to courts where they know that the application is likely to be unsuccessful.

The reasons for the variations in approach have been analysed in recent research.[20] They are to be explained not by the composition of the case load but by different policies adopted by different magistrates' courts and clerks. Some take too broad a view of "offence seriousness"; nearly all underestimate the need for legal skills before the magistrates. Fresh guidance on the "interest of justice test" was issued in May 1994 jointly by the L.C.D., the Justices' Clerks' Society and the Legal Aid Board.[21] It is too early to gauge the effect.

What matters to a defendant is the refusal to grant aid, and the possibility of having such a decision reviewed depends upon the type of offence charged. In the case of a *summary* offence, he or she may make a further application, for the court has power to grant aid at any stage of the proceedings,[22] or may seek judicial review in the High Court.[23] Neither course of action is likely to be successful in the majority of cases.[24] In the case of an *either-way* offence which is to be tried summarily, he or she may seek a review by the criminal legal aid committee[25] so long as the application for review is made after the first refusal of legal aid, *and* the refusal was based on lack of merits, *and* the application for legal aid had been made at least 21 days before the date fixed for the trial of the offence.[26] On a review, the criminal legal aid committee may make an order subject to the contribution conditions that will already have been fixed by the court or the justices' clerk.[27] As an alternative to the review, the defendant may renew the application for legal aid or seek judicial review[28] as above. When the magistrates refuse legal aid for a *trial on indictment* the simplest course will be to make a fresh application to the Crown Court.[29]

Legal aid in criminal cases may be made subject to a contribution from the

---

[18] 5 per cent of defendants in summary trials and 71 per cent of defendants in the trial of either-way offences in the magistrates' court receive legal aid: *Judicial Statistics 1989*, Cm. 1154, Table 10.8. These figures are no longer available.

[19] The Royal Commission on Legal Services described the evidence to this effect as "compelling": R.C.L.S., Vol. 1, para. 14.7.

[20] R. Young, T. Moloney and A. Sanders, *In the Interest of Justice? The Determination of Criminal Legal Aid Applications* (Legal Aid Board, 1992), discussed by R. Young, [1993] Crim.L.R. 336.

[21] The guidance is reproduced in the annual *Legal Aid Handbook*. For criticism, see E. Cape, *Legal Action*, September 1994, p. 19: "it is clear that a primary purpose of the guidance is to discourage the granting of legal aid and, on the whole, the guidance gives a narrow and restrictive interpretation of the relevant criteria."

[22] S.I. 1989 No. 344, reg. 10.

[23] See pp. 969–976, below.

[24] See, *e.g.*, *R. v. Macclesfield JJ., ex p. Greenhalgh* (1979) 144 J.P. 142; *cf. R. v. Brigg JJ., ex p. Lynch* (1983) 148 J.P. 214.

[25] The area committees functioning under the civil legal aid scheme are designated for this additional purpose: S.I. 1989 No. 344, reg. 9.

[26] *ibid.*, reg. 15.

[27] As the court has no discretion to vary the stipulated contribution, neither does the committee.

[28] Again, this is unlikely to be successful: *e.g. R. v. Cambridge Crown Court, ex p. Hagi* (1979) 144 J.P. 145.

[29] Legal Aid Act 1988, s.20(2).

defendant. Prior to the Legal Aid Act 1982, the amount of contributions actually collected was not significant when set against the overall cost of criminal legal aid,[30] but the contribution system was then restyled.[31]

The effect of this provision is to require a means test which leads to a fixed contribution. The court appears to have no discretion over whether to order a contribution or over the amount.[32] In applying the means test, the regulations provide for a calculation closely linked to that made in the grant of civil legal aid[33] which results in the assessment of disposable income and disposable capital. In respect of disposable income the defendant must contribute a weekly amount (determined by reference to the Fourth Schedule of the regulations)[34] for the duration of the legal aid order,[35], and in respect of disposable capital, the whole of the amount in excess of £3,000.[36] In any event, the contribution shall not exceed the actual costs of the defence and any excess will be refunded.[37] In addition, the court has a discretion to remit the contribution where a defendant is acquittted or an appeal against conviction is allowed.[38]

This new system came into operation on March 1, 1984, but does not seem to have led to a significant increase in the level of contributions.[39] It is very different from that proposed by the Royal Commission on Legal Services, which would have involved a statutory right to legal aid save for summary offences and the abolition of contribution orders in magistrates' court proceedings.[40]

The Legal Aid Act 1988[41] gives the Lord Chancellor power to direct the Legal Aid Board to assume responsibility for granting criminal legal aid.

While its initial position was that it was not able to match the current levels of service,[42] it subsequently recommended that it should have that responsibility.[43] However, this recommendation was not accepted, given further steps taken to promote consistency in the grant of legal aid and the recovery of contributions.[44]

---

[30] In 1982, the total amount spent on criminal legal aid was £108,000,000. Contributions amounted to £1,540,000, collected from 24,000 out of 478,000 defendants who were granted aid: *Criminal Statistics 1982, op. cit.*, Chap. 9, Table 9.5.

[31] See H. Levenson, "Contributions and the new criminal legal aid" [1984] *Legal Action* 37.

[32] Legal Aid Act 1988, s.23.

[33] S.I. 1989 No. 344, regs.26, 27 and Sched. 3, as amended by S.I. 1990 No. 489, S.I. 1992 No. 720 and S.I. 1993 No. 789.

[34] The weekly instalment of contribution is £1 for each £3 or part of £3 by which the average weekly disposal income exceeds £48, with no contribution payable if the income does not exceed £49: S.I. 1989 No. 344, Sched. 4, as amended by S.I. 1993 No. 789 and S.I. 1996 No. 646.

[35] Prior to changes effected by S.I. 1993 No. 789 as part of the general cut in legal aid eligibility limits (see above, p. 578) contributions were payable for up to six months.

[36] *ibid.* Sched. 4.

[37] *ibid.* reg. 39.

[38] *ibid.* reg. 35, as substituted by S.I. 1993 No. 789.

[39] In 1993, an estimated 30,586 of the 560,459 applications granted in all courts had contribution orders attached: *Judicial Statistics 1993*, Tables 10.2–10.4, 10.9. In 1994, payments in respect of criminal legal aid totalled £518,344,693 and receipts totalled £4,164,164: *Judicial Statistics 1995*, Table 10.7.

[40] R.C.L.S.; Vol. 1, paras.14.9 and 14.30–31. Abolition of contribution orders is supported by the Legal Action Group: *Legal Action*, August 1992, p. 3.

[41] s.3(4).

[42] *Legal Aid Board: Report to the Lord Chancellor* (Cm. 680, 1989), pp. 17–18.

[43] *Legal Aid Board: Report 1992–93* (1992–93 H.C. 735), pp. 26–30. This was conditional on changes to the system.

[44] *Legal Aid Board: Report 1993–94* (1993–94 H.C. 435), p. 41; reaffirmed in early 1996 (L.C.D. Press Notice, January 30, 1996).

The Consultation Paper, *Legal Aid–Targetting Need*[45] suggests four options for applying the interests of justice test: (1) leaving the decision with the courts, but only if there is "a very marked improvement, very soon" in the way in which they carry out their functions; (2) assessment by the contracted solicitor; (3) assessment by the Legal Aid Board, although it is "difficult to see how this could work efficiently" because of the comparative inaccessibility of the Board's offices; (4) developing a simpler set of criteria.[46]

Finally, recent research on the quality of service provided by crimnal defence practices has shown that the very significant expansion in the extent of representation under the auspices of the legal aid and advice schemes

"does not appear to have been accompanied by an improvement or transformation in the quality of representation."[47]

While a minority of firms studied corresponded to "classical,"[48] "managerial"[49] or "political"[50] models, the majority—the "typical" or "routine" firms—tended to display such characteristics as poor working conditions; lawyers' low status and renumeration; lack of stability and cohesion; extensive delegation to paralegals; and lack of continuity in the representation of individual clients.[51] Almost all the respondents (from a sample of trainee solicitors)

"came to see criminal defence practices as geared, in co-operation with the other elements of the system, towards the routine production of guilty pleas."[52]

This tended to be conferred by observation of the poor quality advice at the police station and of the investigation into and preparation of the defence case in contested proceedings.[53] Too often advisers appear to share the police assumption that their clients were guilty and that a guilty plea was an appropriate outcome.

K. EVALUATIONS

At this point we seek to identify some themes underlying the legal structures we have set out in the chapter.

---

[45] Cm. 2854, 1995, pp. 70–75. Something had to be done in view of the qualification attached to the L.C.D'.s Legal Aid Accounts from 1990–91 that there is "significant and material uncertainty as to the propriety and regularity of the substantial sums of criminal legal aid expenditure": see National Audit office, *The Administration of Legal Aid in England and Wales* (1992–93 H.C. 90), pp. 18–19, Appendix C.

[46] They might be deemed to be met for indictable and either-way offences, where the applicant may be unable to understand the proceedings or state his or her own case because of inadequate knowledge of English, mental illness or disability, or there is an allegation of a serious abuse of power by the police. Further criteria would be specified for summary offences.

[47] M. McCorville *et al.*, *Standing Accused* (1994), p. 273.

[48] Solicitor-centred; high degree of internal cohesion and stability; relatively low volume of cases.

[49] Firm's activities systematised to reduce administration and delay through the introduction of routine procedures; management of the delegation of work.

[50] Commitment to client embraced as the firm's basic organising framework.

[51] McConville *et al.* (1994), Chap. 2.

[52] *ibid.* p. 71 and, generally, Chap. 3.

[53] *ibid.*, Chaps.4–10.

1. THEORETICAL APPROACHES

The latest major official reviews in the area of criminal procedure were undertaken by the Royal Commission on Criminal Procedure[54] (RCCP) and the Royal Commission on Criminal Justice[55] (RCCJ). The former's term of reference were to examine whether changes were needed in England and Wales, in:

"(i) the powers and duties of the police in respect of the investigation of criminal offences and the right and duties of suspects and accused persons, including the means by which these are secured;

(ii) the process of and responsibility for the prosecution of criminal offences; and

(iii) such other features of criminal procedure and evidence as relate to the above."

The latter's terms of reference were

"to examine the effectiveness of the cirminal justice system in England and Wales in securing the conviction of those guilty of criminal offences and the acquittal of those who are innocent, having regard to the efficient use of resources"

and in particular to consider whether changes were needed in eight specific areas.[56] Many features of pre-trial criminal procedure and practice flow from the recommendations of these bodies, modified as they have been in important respects by the government. The RCCP Report led to the Police and Criminal Evidence Act 1984 and the Prosecution of Offences Act 1985. The RCCJ Report has led to changes introduced by the Criminal Justice and Public Order Act 1994 and the Criminal Appeal Act 1995,[57] with a Criminal Procedure and Investigations Bill under consideration in the 1995-96 session of Parliament. At the same time many changes have been introduced simply as a matter of government policy.[58] The former approach provides the opportunity for fundamental theoretical issues to be addressed, in a way that the latter does not. Whether the opportunity is seized is a separate matter.

[54] *Report* (Cmnd. 8092, 1981); *The Investigation and Prosecution of Criminal Offences in England and Wales: The Law and Procedure,* (Cmnd. 8092–1, 1981). Twelve Research Studies were commissioned.

[55] Report (Cm. 2263, 1993). The extensive literature on the RCCJ includes the following: M.McConville and L.Bridges (eds.), *Criminal Justice in Crisis* (1994); S. Field and P. Thomas (eds.), "Justice and Efficiency? The Royal Commission on Criminal Justice" (1994) 21 J.L.S. 1–164 (special issue); Symposium, [1993] Crim.L.R. 808 ff., L. Bridges and M. McConville, (1994) 57 M.L.R. 75; M. Zander, *ibid.,* p. 264; reply by Bridges and McConville, *ibid.,* p. 267; R. Young and A. Sanders, (1994) 14 O.J.L.S. 435.

[56] (i) the conduct and supervision of police investigations; (ii) the role of the prosecutor and the disclosure of material to the defence; (iii) the role of experts; (iv) the arrangements for the defence of accused persons, access to legal advice and expert evidence; (v) the "right to silence"; (vi) the powers of the court in directing proceedings and the courts' duty in considering evidence; (vii) the role of the Court of Appeal and (viii) arrangements for considering and investigating allegations of miscarriages of justice.

[57] See below, pp. 923–931, 936–939.

[58] See, *e.g.,* changes in sentencing, below, p. 886–888, and in the organisation of the police and the courts, *e.g.* above, pp. 60–63 (Magistrates' courts).

(a) The "fundamental balance" in the criminal process

In formulating its recommendations in respect of the matters within its terms of reference, the RCCP was required to have regard "both to the interests of the community in bringing offenders to justice and to the rights and liberties of persons suspected of crime," and to take into account the "need for the efficient and economical use of resources."

The RCCP regarded the task of reviewing the criminal process with what it termed the "fundamental balance' between the interests of the community and the rights and liberties of individual citizens in mind as the "central challenge" which faced it.[59] Previous official reports on aspects of criminal justice[60] had made no or only passing reference to the concept, although the debate that followed the Eleventh Report of the Criminal Law Revision Committee had revealed the main schools of thought on the nature and role of a possible balance in pre-trial criminal procedure. The most controversial of the recommendations in the Eleventh Report involved the restriction of the suspect's right of silence when interrogated by the police. The supporters of the change took a utilitarian approach: "the law should be such as will secure as far as possible that the result of the trial is the right one."[61] The many improvements in criminal law, procedure and trial over the previous century justified the removal of safeguards that appeared unduly to favour the defence. Leading opponents took a libertarian stance, and argued that

> ". . . in reality the right of silence formed a vital issue in the whole constitutional relationship in a free society between the individual and the state. . . . Each step in the criminal process, . . . including the right of silence, must be judged not only as a means to the goal of reaching a reliable verdict, but also, and equally important, for its coherence with a liberal understanding of how free persons, including suspects in the police station, at all stages ought to be treated."[62]

A third, distinct, approach was to regard some, although not necessarily all, of the individual's rights in pre-trial procedure as negotiable, provided that appropriate checks and safeguards were introduced. Thus a minority of the Criminal Law Revision Committee was prepared to modify the right of silence only if statutory provision was made for the use of tape recorders.[63] In general terms it was the third approach that the RCCP purported to adopt, although not simply as a series of compromises between the other main schools of thought. Some commentators on the Report took the view that an appropriate balance had not been struck[64]: others were less sceptical.[65]

---

[59] RCCP Rep., p. 4.
[60] Royal Commission on Police Powers and Procedure (Cmd. 3297, 1929); Royal Commission on the Police (Cmnd. 1728, 1962); Eleventh Report of the Criminal Law Revision Committee on Evidence (General) (Cmnd. 4991, 1972).
[61] Eleventh Report, p. 15.
[62] RCCP Rep., pp. 9, 10.
[63] ibid. pp. 10, 11.
[64] e.g. D. McBarnet, [1981] Crim.L.R. 445 (noting the wider powers to be given to the police, the removal of traditional safeguards, the weakness and vagueness of the safeguards proposed in their place, and that the research was heavily dependent on police sources, and even then selectively ignored); M. McConville and J. Baldwin, (1982) 10 Int. Jo. Sociology of Law 287.
[65] (albeit with particular reservations): L. H. Leigh (1981) 44 M.L.R. 296; B. Smythe [1981] P.L. 184, 481.

By contrast with the RCCP, the Royal Commission on Criminal Justice did not even attempt to explore theoretical issues in any depth. The approach of the RCCJ was to examine the separate elements set out in the terms of reference,[66] and make such detailed, practical recommendations as they thought appropriate. They noted that it could be argued that

"there is a potential conflict between the interests of justice on the one hand and the requirement of fair and reasonable treatment for everyone involved, suspects and defendants included, on the other."[67]

They accepted that these would not be reconcilable throughout the system in the eyes of all those involved. However,

"we do believe that the fairer the treatment which all the parties receive at the hands of the system the more likely it is that the jury's verdict, or where appropriate the subsequent decision of the Court of Appeal, will be correct."[68]

This discussion is both curious and revealing. The Commission's conception of the "interests of justice" was not explained, but the contrast drawn with the fair treatment of individuals suggests that it is "the conviction of those guilty of criminal offences and the acquittal of those who are innocent" (taking words from the terms of reference). This suggests a return to utilitarianism. The possibility that an individual's right to fair treatment might itself be a fundamental value that requires respect in its own terms, irrespective of whether it promotes or diminishes the "correctness" of verdicts is not recognised or explored. Ultimately the Commission attempted to by-pass the issue with its claim that

"when taken as a whole our recommendations serve the interests of justice without diminishing the individual's right to fair and reasonable treatment."[69]

However, the cautionary "when taken as a whole" suggests that the Commission accepted that some particular recommendations might be prejudicial to individual rights.

Both the RCCJ's refusal to address theoretical issues directly, and the implicit theoretical approach that was discerned from its recommendations were the subject of much adverse comment.[70] Commentators criticised the RCCJ's elevation of the resources issue to "co-equal status" with the traditional concerns of convicting the guilty and acquitting the innocent[71] and its

"uncritical acceptance of the theory of criminal justice implicit in a liberal

---

[66] Above, p. 773.
[67] Cm. 2263, p. 8.
[68] ibid.
[69] ibid.
[70] See M. McConville and L. Bridges (eds.), *Criminal Justice in Crisis* (1994), Part I, especially Chaps. 1–5 by, respectively, Bridges and McConville, McConville, Lacey, Nobies and Schiff and Wells. *Cf.* the defence of the RCCJ on this point by one of its members, M. Zander, (1993) N.L.J. 1364.
[71] Bridges and McConville, *op. cit.*, above, p. 11.

reading of its terms of reference—terms which place efficiency on all fours with justice, and which construct the conviction of the innocent as no more important than the acquittal of the guilty.''[72]

In the event, its recommendations seemed mostly to be directed at improvements in the efficient management of the system at the expense of the presumption of innocence. Most had

"no bearing whatsoever on the cultural and structural features of the system which led to miscarriages of justice, and some of those which do are likely to exacerbate those underlying causes rather than the reverse.''[73]

(b) Theoretical models

The Royal Commission on Criminal Procedure characterised the "two main opposing groups" in the right of silence debate as "those who gave paramountcy to the principles of the presumption of innocence and the burden of proof, and those who saw the purpose of the criminal justice system as being a means to the end of bringing the guilty to justice.''[74] The identification by the Royal Commission of these two major schools of thought echoes the two theoretical models of the criminal process proposed by Herbert L. Packer as an aid to the evaluation of the criminal justice system in the United States, the Due Process Model and the Crime Control Models.[75] These models represented

"an attempt to abstract two separate value systems that compete for priority in the operation of the criminal process. Neither is presented as either corresponding to reality or representing the ideal to the exclusion of the other.''[76]

Moreover, they did not represent the difference between the law as it should be ("law in the books") and the law as in fact it operated ("law in action"). They were extremes, and reality lay at some point on the spectrum between them. Indeed, there was some common ground in the two models: assumptions (1) that the functions of defining conduct that may be treated as criminal is separate from and prior to the process of identifying and dealing with persons as criminals; (2) that when it appears that a crime has been committed and that there is a reasonable prospect of apprehending and convicting its perpetrator, criminal process ought ordinarily to be invoked; (3) that there are limits to the powers of government to investigate and apprehend persons suspected of committing crimes (*e.g.* the security and privacy of the individual may not be invaded at will); (4) that accused persons may, if they wish, force the operators of the process to demonstrate to an independent authority (the court) that they are guilty. Differences between the models lay in part in the strength and content of these assumptions, particularly the fourth.

Under the Crime Control Model, the most important function of the criminal process is the repression of criminal conduct. To fulfil this purpose, the system

---

[72] Lacey, *op. cit.* n. 70 above, pp. 31–34.
[73] *ibid.*, pp. 40–41.
[74] RCCP Rep., p. 11.
[75] H. L. Packer, *The Limits of the Criminal Sanction* (1969), Part II.
[76] *ibid.* p. 153.

must operate efficiently. It must have the capacity to apprehend, try, and convict a high proportion of offenders whose offences become known, and to do so with speed and finality. This leads to an emphasis on informality and uniformity, and on minimising the occasions for challenge. Extra-judicial processes are preferred to judicial: the expertise of police and prosecutors is relied upon to screen out those who are probably innocent; those who are left in should be processed as speedily as possible, preferably with a plea of guilty at the trial stage.

> "The image that comes to mind is an assembly-line conveyor belt down which moves an endless stream of cases, never stopping, carrying the cases to workers who stand at fixed stations and who perform on each case as it comes by the same small but essential operation that brings it one step closer to being a finished product. . . ."[77]

By contrast, the Due Process Model resembles an obstacle course. "Each of its successive stages is designed to present formidable impediments to carrying the accused any further along in the process."[78] This model stresses the dangers of error in informal, non-adjudicative fact finding: people are notoriously unreliable observers of disturbing events and confessions to the police may be induced by physical or psychological coercion. Formal, adjudicative, adversary fact finding processes, in which the case is heard by an impartial tribunal and the accused has a full opportunity to challenge the case against him or her, are necessary to reduce the dangers of error. Mistakes (convicting the innocent, setting the guilty free) should be eliminated to the fullest extent possible. (Under the Crime Control Model, such mistakes are acceptable in so far as they do not interfere with the repression of crime, (e.g. by allowing too many guilty people to escape)). Apart from the question of reliability, there is also a concern to prevent official oppression of the individual, and emphasis on the presumption of innocence and on securing compliance with the procedural rules governing the criminal process, perhaps with the exclusion of illegally obtained evidence or reversal of convictions where the rules are breached. On the assumption that the resources made available for the operation of the criminal process are limited, a preference for Due Process values over Crime Control values will lead to a reduction in the quantitative output of the system.

Writing in the late 1960s, Packer concluded that the criminal process as it actually operated in the large majority of cases in the United States probably approximated to the Crime Control Model. On the other hand, judicial decisions based on the U.S. Constitution were pushing the law nearer to the Due Process Model.[79] For McConville and Baldwin, writing in 1981, the English system too in many ways conformed to the Crime Control Model. Although the police-suspect encounter was one of the key exchanges in the criminal process, the safeguards available to suspects in custody were virtually non-existent. Similarly, there was a lack of Due Process safeguards surrounding pleas of guilty, and connected procedures such as plea bargaining; almost 90 per cent of all

[77] ibid. p. 159.
[78] ibid. p. 163.
[79] ibid. p. 239. Major cases included *Miranda v. Arizona* 384 U.S. 436 (1966) (suspects in custody must be advised of their rights, which include the right of access to a lawyer before interrogation); *Mapp v. Ohio* 367 U.S. 643 (1961) (rule excluding illegally obtained evidence applicable to state as well as federal prosecutions); *Gideon v. Wainwright* 372 U.S. 325 (1963) (state must provide counsel for defendants financially unable to provide their own).

defendants charged with serious offences pleaded guilty, and trial by jury (the epitome of the Due Process Model) was used by only 5 per cent of those eligible to be so tried. The function of the jury was thus "largely symbolic—to uphold due process values in the occasional show trial."[80] Another commentator, D. J. McBarnet, stressed the point that it would not be correct to regard the substance of the law as reflecting Due Process values which are then subverted "by policemen bending the rules, by lawyers negotiating adversaries out of existence, by out-of-touch judges or biased magistrates. . . ." In reality "the law governing the production, preparation and presentation of evidence does not live up to its own rhetoric. . . . Police and court officials need not abuse the law to subvert the principles of justice; they need only use it."[81]

Developments since the early 1980s have, like the system as a whole, reflected both Due Process and Crime Control values. However, the latter have tended to predominate.[82] Thus as regards pre-trial procedure, the introduction of the PACE regime has seen the significant extension of police powers of arrest, stop-search, detention and evidence-gathering. While many of these powers are comparatively rarely used, the numbers of arrest and stop-searches have rocketed.[83] The requirement of "reasonable suspicion" does not seem to be a practical constraint,[84] supervision of police officers on the street is minimal, and powers are used disproportionately against "the young, male, working class and black."[85]

By contrast, the increased regulation of the interrogation process, including the right of access to legal advice, and the enforcement of that regulation by judicial decisions to exclude confession evidence certainly reflect both the rhetoric and practice of Due Process. However, the limits must be noted: most suspects are interrogated without a lawyer present; the quality of much of the legal advice is poor; and there is no rule that illegally obtained evidence is inadmissible.[86] These Due Process-based developments have nevertheless been used to justify attenuation of the "right of silence", itself an embodiment of Due Process values.[87] The inherently coercive interrogation process remains in police hands and convictions may still be based solely on a confession. While interrogations in serious cases should now be tape-recorded, confessions may be influenced by off-the-record deals made outside the police station, in police cells or while the tape-recorder is switched off.[88] The crucial need for a change

---

[80] M. McConville and J. Baldwin, *Courts, Prosecution and Conviction* (1981), pp. 3–7.

[81] *Conviction* (1981), pp. 154–157. See also McBarnet, "False Dichotomies in Criminal Justice Research" in J. Baldwin and A. K. Bottomley, *Criminal Justice: Selected Readings* (1978), Chap. 2. *Cf.* McConville *et al.*, *The Case for the Prosecution* (1991), Chap. 9, criticising McBarnet's approach in so far as it would focus attention on the law (and the judicial and political elites who made it) and regard the practice of "the system's low-level officials such as the police" as relatively unimportant; and for its assumption that legal rhetoric does not form part of the law itself.

[82] See R. Sanders and A. Young, *Criminal Justice* (1994).

[83] See above, pp. 669–671.

[84] Indeed arrests of persons in fact guilty of an arrestable offence are lawful: see above, p. 667.

[85] A. Sanders and R. Young, "The Rule of Law, Due Process and Pre Trial Criminal Justice" (1994) C.L.P. 125, 137. *Cf.* R. Reiner in R. Morgan and R. Reiner (eds.), *The Oxford Handbook of Criminology* (1994), p. 727 (cited by Sanders and Young) referring to a study that confirmed "that the weight of adversarial policing falls disproportionately on young men in the lower socio-economic and least powerful social group."

[86] See above, pp. 503–504, 684–688, 766.

[87] Above, pp. 688–691.

[88] Above, pp. 682–683, 686, n. 76.

in attitude so that the police approach investigations (and interviews) with an open mind is to be addressed only as a matter for police (re) training.[89]

Another Due Process development, the disclosure requirements imposed by the judges in the context of miscarriage of justice cases, is to be modified by statute, and accompanied by new requirements as to defence disclosure.[90] Here the government's Crime Control objective, seeking to maximise the efficiency with which cases are despatched, can be seen clearly. The effect of the Crown Prosecution Service as an antidote to these trends is uncertain, given its normal dependence on the case as presented to it by the police. While much of the criticism here is that too few cases are discontinued, the government seems more inclined to respond to police complaints that cases are dropped unnecessarily, possibly by weakening the evidential requirements.[91]

The predicted consequence of these moves towards Crime Control is an increase in miscarriages of justice, where the innocent are convicted. If this is so, the new arrangements for investigating alleged miscarriages[92] will be seriously tested.

Finally, while evaluation of the criminal justice process from the standpoints of Due Process and Crime Control is in our view helpful, it should be noted both that the dichotomy has its critics[93] and that other models have been proposed.[94]

2. FUNDAMENTAL RIGHTS

The trend towards Crime Control summarised in the preceding section has generated increasing interest in the extent to which fundamental rights are identified and protected by standards of international law within which the domestic law of the criminal justice process must function. Furthermore, the European Convention on Human Rights and the International Covenant on Civil and Political Rights has been drawn on by Ashworth in proposing a "general framework of

---

[89] Above, p. 688.
[90] cf. above, pp. 706–707.
[91] Above, pp. 753–758.
[92] Below, pp. 936–939.
[93] See A. Ashworth, *The Criminal Process* (1994), pp. 28–29, criticising (1) a lack of a clear explanation of the relationship between the two models; (2) the assumption that there was a significant relationship between the system of pre-trial justice and the crime rate; (3) the underestimation of the importance of resource management; (4) the absence of allowance for victim-related matters; and (5) internal inconsistencies (e.g. the emphasis on speed in only the Crime Control model).
[94] See A. B. Bottoms and J. D. McClean, *Defendants in the Criminal Process* (1976), pp. 226–232, and M. King. *The Framework of Criminal Justice* (1981), Chap. 2. Bottoms and McClean identify a third, Liberal Bureaucratic Model, based on the viewpoint of the "enlightened courts administrator': this purports to prefer Due Process values to Crime Control values, but imposes pressures (*e.g.* in support of summary trials and guilty pleas) to make the system workable, and in so doing in practice reinforces Crime Control. King analyses in models, three based on the perspectives of typical participants: (i) Due Process (defence lawyers), (ii) Crime Control (police), and (iii) Medical (probation officers: emphasis on reabilitation); and three based on the work of social theorists: (iv) Bureaucratic (emphasising the management of crime and criminals), (v) Status Passage (emphasising the public degradation of the defendant) and (vi) Power (emphasising the maintenance of class domination).

ethical principles'' for the criminal process.[95] Accordingly, he has identified[96] the right to be treated with humanity and without degradation;[97] the right of victims to compensation;[98] the right of innocent persons not to be convicted;[99] the right to be treated fairly and without discrimination;[1] the right to be presumed innocent;[2] the principle of legality (*i.e.*, "the law should state clearly and in advance the body of rules and exceptions relating to the rights and powers that may be taken over individuals during the criminal process'');[3] reasonable grounds for arrest and detention;[4] the right to be brought before a court;[5] the right to prepare a proper defence;[6] the right of the victim to respect in the criminal process;[7] the right to trial within reasonable time;[8] and the principle of equality of arms between defence and prosecution.[9]

The Government has consistently maintained that U.K. law complies with international standards,[10] subject to derogations in respect of the Prevention of Terrorism (Temporary Provisions) Act 1989.[11] Claims in the context of the criminal justice process in England and Wales of breaches of the ECHR have generally failed, outside the particular context of prisoners' rights.[12] Nevertheless, recourse to the ECHR may become increasingly fruitful in the light of current trends. Furthermore, the development of ethical principles from these international standards may have added value in informing the training (and retraining) of the professional groups operating within the criminal justice process. Indeed, measures such as training and better lines of accountability,

> "espoused in various forms by such politically disparate groups as the 1993 Royal Commission on Criminal Justice . . . and by Michael McConville, Andrew Sanders, and Roger Leng at the end of their sharply critical research reports on police and prosecution services,[13] are now recognised to be far more promising than mere changes in legal rules."[14]

---

[95] A. Ashworth, *The Criminal Process* (1994), Chap. 3; S. H. Bailey, "Rights in the Administration of Justice" in D. J. Harris and S. Joseph (eds.), *The ICCPR and United Kingdom Law* (1995), Chap 6.

[96] *ibid.*, pp. 57–67. As to derogation, see *ibid.* p. 67–71.

[97] Cf. Art. 3, ECHR, art.7, ICCPR, prohibiting the use of torture or inhuman or degrading treatment or punishment. These obligations are non-derogable.

[98] See below, pp. 988–990.

[99] Reflected in a number of the rights that follow.

[1] Art.14, ECHR; arts.2(1) and 26, ICCPR.

[2] Art.6(2), ECHR; art.14(2), ICCPR.

[3] Cf. the prohibition of retrospective criminal laws: art.7, ECHR; art.15, ICCPR.

[4] Art.5(1)(c), ECHR; *cf.* art.9(1)(3), ICCPR.

[5] Art.5(3), ECHR; art.9(3), ICCPR.

[6] Art.6(3), ECHR; art.14(3), ICCPR.

[7] Below, pp. 781–782.

[8] Art.6(1) ECHR; art.14(3)(c), ICCPR.

[9] Derived from the requirement that trials be fair: art.6(1), ECHR; art.14(1), ICCPR.

[10] See e.g. Periodic Reports of the UK under the ICCPR.

[11] Section 14 authorises detention for questioning without judicial authority for up to 7 days. The European Court of Human Rights held that this contravened art.5(3), (5), ECHR, in *Brogan* v. *United Kingdom* (1988) 11 E.H.R.R. 117: The subsequent notice of derogation was upheld in *Brannigan and McBride* v. *United Kingdom* (1993) 17 E.H.R.R. 539.

[12] See above, p. 112.

[13] *The Case for the Prosecution* (1991), Chap. 10.

[14] Ashworth (1994), p. 84.

Codes of ethics

"must . . . play an important part in the dynamics of change."[15]

3. THE ROLE OF THE VICTIM

In recent years, increased attention has been paid to the role of the victim. Two paradoxes have been noted.[16] First, there is the contradiction that the victim has a crucial role to play in reporting the offence to the police and as the major agent in detecting the offender, but that little account is taken of the victim's attitudes and experiences by the professionals involved in the criminal justice system. Second, "major projects aimed at fulfilling victims' needs have been set up without regard to, or even investigation into, victims' expressed needs."[17] These projects include the Criminal Injuries Compensation Scheme (a state scheme for compensating the victims of violent crime[18]), schemes for compensation or reparation by offenders,[19] victim support schemes[20] and mediation or conciliation schemes.[21] While such schemes provide some assistance to victims, much more could be done.[22] The police seem to have been rather more responsive to the needs of victims than have magistrates' courts.[23] The government has responded by strengthening the compensation provisions, and by issuing a Victims' Charter which sets out the "rights and entitlements" of crime victims.[24] Among its features are the duty of the police to keep victims informed of all important stages in a case; the duty of the C.P.S. to ensure that full details of injuries or losses have been established before trial and to advise prosecutors

---

[15] ibid., pp. 86–88.
[16] J. Shapland, J. Willmore and P. Duff, Victims in the Criminal Justice System (1985), Chap. 10. See, generally, S. Walkate, Victimology (1989).
[17] ibid. p. 178.
[18] Established under the royal prerogative in 1964; to be reconstituted as a statutory scheme by the Criminal Injuries Compensation Act 1995 (cf. above, p. 46). The scheme is administered by the Criminal Injuries Compensation Board. See T. Newburn The Settlement of Claims at the Criminal Injuries Compensation Board (H.O. Research Study No. 112, 1989).
[19] Criminal courts have power to make compensation orders under the Powers of Criminal Courts Act 1973, ss.35–38, as amended or substituted by the Criminal Justice Act 1988, ss.104, 105. The defendant's means have to be taken into account, and orders have been made less frequently than they could be: see Shapland et al. (1985), Chap. 8; T. Newburn, The Use and Enforcement of Compensation Orders in Magistrates' Courts (H.O. Report Study No. 102, 1988). A court must now give reasons if it fails to make an order.
[20] Schemes whereby volunteers visit victims and offer emotional and practical support. The reactions of both victims and police are generally positive: T. Newburn, (1989) 26 H.O.R.B. 22; and see M. Maguire and C. Corbett, The Effects of Crime and the Work of Victims Support Schemes (1987); D. Trust, Help for Victims of Crime and Violence (1989); M. L. Gill and R. I. Mawby, Volunteers in the Criminal Justice System (1990), Chap. 5. Schemes to help victims and witnesses attending the Crown Court have also been established on a number of centres.
[21] See T. F. Marshall and S. Merry, Crime and Accountability: Victim/Offender Mediation in Practice (HMSO, 1990); M. Wright, [1995] Crim. L.R. 187.
[22] See Shapland et al. (1985), Chap. 10.
[23] J. Shapland and D. Cohen, "Facilities for Victims: the Role of the Police and the Courts" [1987] Crim.L.R. 28. See also T. Newman and S. Merry, Keeping in Touch (H.O. Research Study No. 116, 1990).
[24] The Times, February 23, 1990. The Charter is published by the Home Office. See D. Miers, (1992) 55 M.L.R. 482; H. Fenwick, [1995] Crim. L.R. 843. A new edition was published in 1996.

to correct statements made in court which denigrate a victim's character; the right of the families of murder victims to be consulted about the timing of the killer's release and whether restrictions should be placed on where he or she lives and works. This all, however, falls short of giving the victim a formal role in the criminal justice process as a party to the prosecution, which some argue is necessary for the problems to be cured.[25]

---

[25] But *cf*. A. Ashworth, *The Criminal Process* (1994), pp. 34–37, arguing that decisions as to prosecution, bail or custody and punishment should be taken in the public interest and not according to the personal views of the victim. On the development of victim inpact statements in other jurisdictions, see A. Ashworth, [1993] Crim.L.R. 498.

CHAPTER 14

THE CIVIL TRIAL

FROM the variety of different civil proceedings we take the action in the Queen's Bench Division as our example, as we did in the chapter on pre-trial civil procedure.[1] However, we shall also make reference to the county court and the resolution of issues in that court by the arbitration process.

It is arguable that very little time should be spent considering the civil trial, since so much effort is expended on resolving the case prior to that stage.[2] The alternative resolution of disputes is an approach supported by Lord Woolf's Inquiry into the Civil Justice System. Indeed discussion of the trial stage is almost incidental to the Woolf Report.[3] However, the civil trial is important not only in being the final point for the resolution of disputes, but also as it is only at trial in the High Court or on appeal from a trial that precedents may be set which will clarify and develop the law.[3a] Without decisions of such a nature the law would stagnate, failing to address the many existing and future problems which society presents.

A. ADVERSARIAL PROCEDURE

Adversarial procedure is the fundamental, characteristic feature of English civil justice.[4]

> "You have two adversaries in every civil dispute—someone asserting a right, someone denying it. Someone contending for one thing, someone contending against it."[5]

The trial procedure reflects this view of the conduct of civil cases, as well as the principles of judicial neutrality and unpreparedness. Lord Woolf, whilst not recommending the abandonment of the adversarial principle,[6] identified it as a major cause of many of the problems associated with the civil justice system.[7] What he recommends is the retention of the best aspects of the adversarial

---

[1] See Chap. 11.

[2] See above, pp. 555–566.

[3] Lord Woolf, *Access to Justice* (1995) (hereafter, Woolf Report (1995)).

[3a] See also above, pp. 421–446 and N. Armstrong, "Making Facts", in A. A. S. Zuckerman and R. Cranston (eds.) *Reforming Civil Procedure* (1995), pp. 99–100.

[4] Sir Jack I. H. Jacob, *The Fabric of English Civil Justice* (1987), p. 5. Adversarial procedure can be compared with the inquisitorial system, see *ibid.* pp. 5–19. See also N. Andrews, *Principles of Civil Procedure* (1994), Chap. 3 and Woolf Report (1995), p. 29.

[5] Sir Jack I. H. Jacob, "The Adversary System of Civil Litigation" (1983) City of London Law Review 17, 18.

[6] Woolf Report (1995), p. 29.

[7] *ibid.*, pp. 7–8 and 15; and see above, pp. 592, 597–600, and 626–633.

approach with a more interventionist management role for the courts.[8] This has most significance for the pre-trial stage,[9] but has implications also for the trial stage.

Judicial unpreparedness is not necessarily conducive to effectiveness and efficiency. The Civil Justice Review recommended that judges should read case papers before the hearing.[10] It is currently the function of the parties, normally through counsel,[11] to bring the evidence and argue the law which will win the case.[12] It is with the litigant and lawyer control of the process with which Lord Woolf is in profound disagreement; this is why he wishes to see the introduction of effective court management of cases.[13]

As a consequence of the Civil Justice Review, some important changes have already been introduced which have an impact on the trial stage. There is a move towards controlling the excessive use of documents,[14] and a review of the hearsay rule in civil proceedings leading to its abolition.[15] The latter reflects the reality that "the rules of evidence play an almost insignificant part in the civil trial process."[16]

The consequence of Lord Woolf's reforms would be that the case would be much better prepared for the trial.[17] In consequence, Lord Woolf was able to recommend that, on the fast track,[18] trials would be confined to not more than three hours; no oral evidence would be admitted from experts;[19] there would be "limited oral evidence from witnesses of fact, supplemented as necessary by written submissions and written evidence"; "use of the period of time allocated to parties would be a matter for their discretion although normally a claimant would not be expected to open his [or her] case. Citation of authorities or reliance upon written reports would involve no more than giving the reference and identifying the passages relied on (preferably in advance of trial). Short written submissions on the law would be accepted"; there would be "short judicial reasons for the decision" which would merely involve an indication of the judge's approach rather than a detailed discussion of the law and an identification of the evidence which the judge accepted.[20] On the multi-track, for more weighty cases,[21] there would be less change to the trial procedure because of the nature of the cases, but case management and pre-trial review[22] would involve the clearer identification of the issues for trial and matters which could be resolved prior to trial would be so dealt with, thus there might be a form of

---

[8] *ibid.*, p. 29.

[9] See above, Chaps.10 and 11.

[10] *Civil Justice Review, Report of the Review Body on Civil Justice* (Cm. 394, 1989), paras.261–265.

[11] The frequency of litigants in person is increasing, see above, p. 630.

[12] This is consequent upon the adversarial approach and is reflected from the stage of pleadings onwards; see Chap. 11.

[13] See above, pp. 597–600.

[14] See C.C.R. Ord. 17, r.12.

[15] *Civil Justice Review* (1989), paras.266–270; Law Commission, *The Hearsay Rule in Civil Proceedings* (L.C. Consultation Paper No. 117, 1991); and the Civil Evidence Act 1995.

[16] Jacob (1987), p. 266. For an introduction to the law of evidence in civil trials, see J. O'Hare and R. N. Hill, *Civil Litigation* (6th ed., 1993), Chap. 19.

[17] See above, pp. 628–629.

[18] See above, pp. 597–600 and 629–630. See also Woolf Issue Paper, *Fast Track Project* (1996).

[19] See below, p. 633 and see Woolf Issue Paper, *Expert Evidence* (1996).

[20] Woolf Report (1995), p. 43.

[21] See above, p. 63.

[22] This could set a programme, timetable and budget for the trial: Woolf Report (1995), p. 50.

"rolling adjudication" up to and including a trial. There would be a fixed date for the trial.[23]

At the beginning of a trial, the *opening speech* is made on behalf of the plaintiff. The object of the opening speech is to outline the case with reference to the evidence that is to be called. The opening may be briefer in a civil case than in a criminal case since there will not normally be a jury and counsel will not have to explain such matters as the burden and standard of proof to the judge. Counsel has not been able to assume that the judge has any familiarity with the papers in the case[24] so his or her job has been summarised as being: ". . . to explain the whole case to the judge: to read the pleadings, the letters and other documents . . ., to summarise what all the witnesses he is calling will say, and how his client views the issue."[25] Normally any agreed reports or other documentary evidence are put in evidence in the opening speech.[26] If the judge has had the opportunity to read the relevant papers, it may be indicated to counsel that there is no need to cover all the points in the opening speech; indeed there may be no opening speeches.[27] This illustrates the advantage of trial by judge alone—the judge can move counsel on where matters are understood or undisputed without the constraint of ensuring that the jury have grasped the issue, and if the judge is prepared, considerable time and cost can be saved during the trial. At the conclusion of the opening speech for the plaintiff, the first witnesses are called.

It is no accident that there are witnesses *for* the plaintiff and witnesses *for* the defendant. The parties are free to choose the people who can give evidence to support their contentions and the witnesses line up behind the "litigant gladiators",[28] clearly identified with one side or the other.

Counsel for the plaintiff will call each witness in turn.[29] A witness is questioned to extract testimony which is expected to be favourable to the plaintiff. The plaintiff's solicitor will have prepared in advance a statement of the evidence already given by the witness and counsel will use this "proof of evidence" as the basis of his or her questions. The questioning of a witness by the counsel "on the same side" is termed *examination in chief*.[30] Counsel must observe two rules during the examination. Leading questions[31] must not be asked and the witness's evidence given in court must not be contradicted by reference

---

[23] *ibid.*, pp. 49–51.

[24] But see now the expectation that judges will have to read case papers, as in the Commercial Court.

[25] *Going to Law* (1974), a report by JUSTICE, at para. 16. See also D. Barnard, *The Civil Court in Action* (2nd ed., 1985), p. 200.

[26] *e.g.* medical reports or the reports of other experts.

[27] R.S.C. Ord. 35, r.7; C.C.R. Ord.22, r.5A; and see O'Hare and Hill (1993), p. 527.

[28] A phrase taken from Jacob (1983). Note the concerns about expert witnesses in the Woolf Report (1995), see above, p. 633.

[29] Subject to the acceptance of witness statements instead, see O'Hare and Hill (1993), p. 527 and see above for problems associated with such statements, at pp. 632–633.

[30] As to the judge's role in examining witnesses for both the plaintiff and the defence, see p. 794, below.

[31] A leading question is one which suggests to the witness the answer which counsel expects. "What time did the accident occur?" is a proper question. "The accident occurred at 7.30 p.m. did it not?" is a leading question and, therefore, prohibited. It is commonly agreed between counsel that a witness may be "led" on non-contentious issues to save time.

to a conflicting statement of that witness in the proof of evidence.[32] Because the Code of Conduct prevents a barrister from discussing a case or the evidence to be given with a potential witness other than the lay client, a character witness or an expert witness[33] (makes the interests of the lay client require it and after a proper proof of the evidence of that witness has been supplied)[34] and because the "coaching" of witnesses by counsel is forbidden,[35] it is quite possible that there may be variations in testimony when the witness is under examination.

At the conclusion of the examination-in-chief of each witness for the plaintiff, counsel for the defendant is given the opportunity to *cross-examine* in an attempt to shake the testimony of the witness or to extract information useful to the defendant's case. In cross-examination, counsel is at liberty to exploit contradictory statements made by the witness but counsel does not have available the witness's proof of evidence which is the property of the other side.

The case for the defendant is put in exactly the same way with an opening speech and the examination of witnesses.[36] After the defence evidence has been heard, counsel for the defendant may make a closing speech summarising his or her view of the evidence and the law, to which counsel for the plaintiff may reply. Again, the judge has a discretion to indicate to counsel that argument on a particular point which may already have been decided or which is considered to be irrelevant need not be recited. At any point in the proceedings the judge may decide to look at the place in which the events in issue took place.[37] The judge would normally be accompanied at a "view" by the parties and their legal representatives.[38]

Ultimately, the judge is required to give a reasoned judgment, stating the conclusions on the factual issues in dispute and the legal implications of those findings of fact.[39]

There are variations to the above procedure.[40] First, the judge may sit with assessors.[41] Secondly, there are a few cases where the judge may sit with a

---

[32] It is, of course, open to counsel to ask a witness to think again about an answer, but the discrepancy between the answer and the earlier statement may not be suggested. In an extreme case, counsel might seek to have the earlier statement put in as evidence at the end of the examination-in-chief: Civil Evidence Act 1968, s.2(2).

[33] *Code of Conduct for the Bar of England and Wales* (1990), para. 607.1.

[34] *ibid.*, para. 607.2.

[35] *ibid.*, para. 607.3; *Written Standards for the Conduct of Professional Work; General Standards*, para. 6.1.

[36] Defence counsel is only permitted an opening speech if he or she is actually calling witnesses: R.S.C. Ord. 35, r.7(4) . In the county court, defence counsel must normally choose between an opening and a closing speech: O'Hare and Hill (1993), p. 528. Before proceeding to case presentation, defence counsel may submit that the plaintiff has failed to make out a case to which a response is required. A judge is unlikely to be prepared to accept such a submission, because the defendant has to agree to give evidence in the event of the submission being rejected: *Alexander v. Rayson* [1936] 1 K.B. 169; O'Hare and Hill (1993), p. 528.

[37] R.S.C., Ord. 35, r.8. The viewing is not necessarily restricted to places, although that is most common. The rule provides for an inspection of "any place or thing with respect to which any question arises." In *Line v. Taylor* (1862) 3 F. & F. 731 it had to be determined whether a dog was vicious. Serjeant Ballantine proposed that the dog be brought into court in the charge of his keeper. His opponent, Chambers, objected "as the experiment would be useless, while the dog was under the control of his keeper, and perilous, if he were not so." The dog was produced; the jury decided it was not vicious.

[38] *Goold v. Evans* [1951] T.L.R. 1189; *Salsbury v. Woodland* [1970] Q.B. 324.

[39] See below p. 794.

[40] See Andrews (1994), p. 438.

[41] See below, p. 793.

jury.[42] Thirdly, the court may order separate trials of liability and quantum of damages.[43] Finally, preliminary questions of fact and law can be heard before the main trial.[44]

B. WITNESSES AND EXPERT EVIDENCE

Witnesses may well be under pressure in giving evidence. It will be for counsel to decide who to call, taking account, for example, of whether they will provide evidence that is convincing enough to be a valuable aid to the presentation of the case.

The pressures on an expert witness will be less, particularly since such a witness will have had time to reflect upon the evidence to be given. In many civil trials part of the evidence is likely to be given by such witnesses. Expert evidence is opinion evidence,[45] and opinion evidence is admissible from an expert, though not from an ordinary witness.[46] Experts are not limited to giving opinion evidence. They may:

"(a) assist a party to establish the facts and to assess the merits of a case and with its preparation; (b) give to the court, as evidence, their expert opinion where opinion evidence apart from that of an expert would not be strictly admissible; (c) give factual evidence on a subject, where because of their expertise, their evidence will have greater weight than that of an unqualified witness. Evidence as to foreign law will fall into this category. So does the evidence which surveyors sometimes give, in addition to their opinion evidence, as to measurements they have made or examinations which they have carried out; (d) conduct inquiries on behalf of the court and report to the court as to their findings; and (e) sit as assessors with judges to assist the court to understand the technical evidence which the court has to consider."[47]

The right of the parties to adduce expert evidence is somewhat restricted by the Civil Evidence Act 1972[48] and the Rules of the Supreme Court[49] and provision is made for pre-trial disclosure of such evidence in most cases. The object of such disclosure is to save expense, where possible, by discovering whether there is a real dispute between the parties and to avoid either party being taken by surprise on a technical matter and being forced to seek an adjournment. A party will not normally be allowed to call expert evidence at trial unless the disclosure procedure has been followed or unless the other party agrees.[50] It is,

---

[42] See below, pp. 789–793. In this case, the judge does not give judgment, but gives a direction to the jury.

[43] R.S.C. Ord. 33, r.4.

[44] R.S.C. Ord. 33, r.3.

[45] Which would not normally be admissible as evidence.

[46] See C. Tapper, *Cross and Tapper on Evidence* (8th ed., 1995), Chap. 13.

[47] Woolf Report (1995), p. 181.

[48] s.2.

[49] Ord. 38, Part IV.

[50] Ord. 38, r.36.

therefore, possible for the parties to make an explicit agreement that each side may call what expert evidence it wishes at trial, thus getting round the disclosure provisions, but the prospect of savings in time and money both before and at trial may well be a powerful inducement to disclose.

The expert witness may be different from an "ordinary" witness in that evidence is being given on matters within a field of knowledge, often after a prolonged examination. However, the expert witness is examined and cross-examined in just the same way. More importantly, the expert witness is just as much the "property" of one party. There is a temptation for parties to indulge in a battle of experts in court, sometimes hoping to win the point by the sheer volume of evidence or by the eminence of their witness(es). Some have argued[51] that it is unedifying to see leading members of the same profession being forced to disagree under skilful cross-examination, that such disagreement may serve to confuse rather than clarify the issues for the court, and that additional costs are unnecessarily incurred by taking evidence from two or more people on the same point. However, this is an almost inevitable consequence of the adversarial system of procedure and the power of the parties to adduce what relevant evidence they wish.

There is a power in the court to alleviate some of these problems by appointing an independent expert in any matter which is to be tried by judge alone.[52] This may seem to present an ideal solution to the problem of the battle of experts but it is subject to a serious limitation. The court may only make such an order on the application of a party to the action. The *Supreme Court Practice* notes that such applications have been very few in number.[53] Perhaps the court should be given the power to appoint an independent expert on its own authority even though that would begin to erode the adversarial system.

An additional power, which could be useful in this context, is contained in the Supreme Court Act 1981, s.70, which allows the appointment of assessors or scientific advisers to assist in the hearing and disposal of the action. These are people who sit with the judge at the trial of the action and their role is considered more fully later in this chapter.

The subject of expert witnesses has been discovered to be a major concern to those with an interest in the civil justice system.[54]

> "The need to engage experts was a source of excessive expenses, delay and, in some cases, increased complexity, through the excessive or inappropriate use of experts. Concern was also expressed as to their failure to maintain their independence from the party by whom they have been instructed."[55]

In making recommendations for reform, Lord Woolf distinguished between the fact-finding and opinion-giving roles; aimed to increase the independence of experts; desired to encourage the use of experts to narrow, not widen, the issues; intended to reduce the delay and cost engendered by their use; and

---

[51] See, *e.g.* A. Kenny, "The Expert in Court" (1983) 99 L.Q.R. 197.

[52] R.S.C., Ord. 40, r.1.

[53] *The Supreme Court Practice 1995*, p. 698. There has been some judicial encouragement for the appointment of a court expert but this has obviously not had any significant effect: *Re Saxton* [1962] 1 W.L.R. 968, *per* Lord Denning M.R. at p. 973.

[54] Woolf Report (1995), p. 181.

[55] *ibid.*

desired to reduce the inconvenience to experts of their involvement in civil procedures.[56] Thus he made the following proposals:

"(1) the calling of expert evidence should be subject to the complete control of the court; (2) the court should have discretion, with or without the agreement of the parties, to appoint an expert to report or give evidence to the court; (3) the court should have wide power to appoint assessors; (4) experts should be given clear guidance that, when preparing their evidence or actually giving evidence to a court, their first responsibility is to the court and not their client; (5) any report prepared for the purposes of giving evidence to a court should be addressed to the court; (6) such a report should end with a declaration that it includes everything which the expert regards as being relevant to the opinion which he [or she] has expressed in his [or her] report and that he [or she] has drawn to the attention of the court any matter which would affect the validity of that opinion; (7) if experts instructed by the parties meet at the direction of the court, it should be unprofessional conduct for an expert to be given or to accept instructions not to reach agreement. If the experts cannot reach agreement on an issue they should specify their reasons for being unable to do so; (8) once an expert has been instructed to prepare a report for the use of a court, any communication between the expert and the client or his [or her] advisers should no longer be the subject of legal privilege; (9) codes of practice providing guidance as to the practice in relation to experts should be drawn up jointly by the appropriate professional bodies representing the experts and the legal profession; (10) unless the plaintiff is relying on the doctor by whom he [or she] is being treated, the defendant should be told whom the plaintiff intends to instruct and invited to make any comments as to the proposed instructions; (11) before a doctor reports on behalf of a plaintiff or defendant, the opposing party should have the opportunity to give instructions to that doctor; (12) if more than one doctor is to be instructed in a case on the fast track, the doctors should be instructed at the same time with a view to producing a joint report; (13) every effort should be made by the court to avoid doctors having to attend court, or if they have to attend court, to reduce the inconvenience this involves. Video technology should be used for this purpose."[57]

C. THE USE OF THE JURY IN CIVIL CASES

Jury trial is wholly exceptional and confined to a handful of cases. The erosion in the use of juries has been gradual. It appears to have begun with the introduction of the discretionary use of juries in all but six causes of action in 1833,[58]

---

[56] *ibid.*, pp. 181–182.
[57] *ibid.*, pp. 192–193.
[58] Rules of the Supreme Court 1883, Ord. XXXVI. The causes of action in which there was a right to jury trial were: libel, slander, malicious prosecution, false imprisonment, seduction and breach of promise of marriage. These provisions formed the basis of the statutory reform in 1933. An analysis of the decline in the use of the jury, on the basis of statistics then available, is contained in R. M. Jackson, "The Incidence of Jury Trial during the Past Century" (1937) 1 M.L.R. 132.

and was continued by the temporary suspension of jury trial beginning during the First World War and ending in 1925.[59]

The current position, now found in section 69 of the Supreme Court Act 1981, was first established in 1933.[60] Section 69 provides, first, for a qualified right to jury trial in some cases, and, secondly, for a discretion to order jury trial in other cases.

The qualified right to jury trial applies in cases of fraud,[61] libel, slander, malicious prosecution and false imprisonment.[62] Jury trial is to be granted unless "the court is of the opinion that the trial requires any prolonged examination of documents or accounts or any scientific or local examination which cannot conveniently be made with a jury. . . ."[63] This qualified right is exercised most frequently in defamation actions (that is libel and slander). The decision whether to permit jury trial depends upon a balance of the desire to grant trial by jury where requested and the need to take a realistic view about the material with which juries can deal in a trial and the length of time which a trial is expected to take or, put another way, the efficient administration of justice.[64] After considerable debate about the outcome of a number of celebrated libel actions,[65] the Court of Appeal now has the power either to order a new trial on the ground that damages awarded by jury are excessive or inadequate or, without the agreement of the parties, to substitute for the sum awarded by the jury such sum as appears to the court to be proper.[66] As the jury's control over award of damages lessens, it is possible that jury trial will become less attractive to plaintiffs.

Further, the court has a discretion to order jury trial in other cases.[67] Jury trial should be ordered only in exceptional cases[68] and it will be very difficult to persuade a judge to exercise the discretion to order trial by jury. The factors

---

Jackson does not advance the view that the 1883 Rules were significant in reducing the number of jury trials, but the figures seem to support that contention. See also, M. G. Buckley, "Civil Trial by Jury" (1966) 19 C.L.P. 63. A good chronological account is provided by Bankes L.J. in *Ford v. Blurton* (1922) 38 T.L.R. 801, at pp. 802–803.

[59] The Juries Act 1918 provided for trial by judge alone unless the court ordered otherwise, subject to the right to jury trial in a category of cases slightly wider than that in the 1883 Rules. This provision was continued by the Administration of Justice Act 1920, but repealed by the Administration of Justice Act 1925.

[55] The Administration of Justice (Miscellaneous Provisions) Act 1933, s.6. The number of jury trials declined sharply after 1933.

[61] The meaning of fraud in this context was considered by Sir Robert Megarry V.-C. in *Stafford Winfield Cook v. Winfield* [1981] 1 W.L.R. 45. In criminal trials, it has been debated whether jury trials in (complex) fraud cases should be retained, see pp. 908–910, below.

[62] Or any other questions or issues prescribed: Supreme Court Act 1981, s.69(1)(c).

[63] Supreme Court Act 1981, s.69(1).

[64] *Beta Construction Ltd v. Channel Four Television Co. Ltd*, [1990] 1 W.L.R. 1042. The national importance of the issues may render jury trial appropriate even if there is considerable documentary evidence: *Rothermere v. Times Newspapers* [1973] 1 W.L.R. 448. The case concerned an article written by Bernard Levin in *The Times*, March 19, 1971, entitled "Profit and dishonour in Fleet Street." However, due care must be taken not to overburden the jury, as may have occurred in *Orme v. Associated Newspapers Group*, March 31, 1981 (unreported) (Q.B.D.); December 20, 1982 (unreported) (C.A.), where the trial, involving alleged defamation of the Moonies, lasted more than five months and 117 witnesses were called. Lawyers are required to take great care in estimating the length of trials so as to avoid hardship for potential jurors: *Practice Direction (Juries: Length of Trials)* [1981] 1 W.L.R. 1129.

[65] *e.g.* the cases brought by Jeffrey Archer, Koo Stark, Sonia Sutcliffe and Elton John.

[66] Courts and Legal Services Act 1990, s.8 and R.S.C., Ord. 59, r.11.

[67] Supreme Court Act 1981, s.69(3).

[68] *Ward v. James* [1966] 1 Q.B. 273, *per* Lord Denning M.R., at p. 303. In the event, this case was sent for jury trial but the court was influenced by factors peculiar to it. The point was emphasised in *Williams v. Beasley* [1973] 1 W.L.R. 1295, *per* Lord Diplock at p. 1299H.

to be taken into account are: the need for uniformity in the award of damages in personal injury cases, the jury being ignorant of the conventional figures in comparable cases;[69] that in such cases the severity[70] or unusual[71] nature of the injuries are not exceptional circumstances, but if they are unique or nearly so,[72] jury trial may be appropriate; the possibility of dishonesty[73] or deliberate lying; the fact that the honour and integrity of the person applying for jury trial may be at stake;[74] the fact that trial without a jury is speedier and less expensive;[75] the proposition that, in the circumstances, trial by judge alone is "more likely to achieve a just result than trial by jury."[76] Further, Lord Diplock indicated that jury trial should not be ordered either simply because there might be a conflict of evidence, since many cases will involve issues of credibility and that is not a sufficient reason to depart from the "usual rule" of trial by judge alone[77] or simply because a party has "the mistaken belief ... that judges as a class are likely to be biased against him or in favour of his opponent" since to decide on that basis would provide such beliefs with credence, whereas the system is based upon "an impartial judiciary."[78]

If a jury trial does take place it, as in criminal proceedings, is controlled by the provisions of the Juries Act 1974. The qualification for service of jurors, the procedure for summoning, the compilation of panels, the ballot and swearing of jurors, and the right to challenge for cause are all exactly the same for civil and criminal trials.[79] Majority verdicts may be accepted in civil cases, although there is greater flexibility than in criminal matters since the parties to the action may proceed by agreement with an incomplete jury.[80] The discretion to exclude a juror from service which may be exercised by the appropriate officer or by the court[81] is likely to be exercised more freely in civil matters where there may be considerable hardship or inconvenience caused by a long trial.[82]

SHOULD THE JURY BE RETAINED IN CIVIL CASES?

If the debates on the Supreme Court Bill 1981 are any guide, this is, indeed, an academic question. Parliament showed itself unwilling to countenance any further restriction on the right to jury trial, let alone its abolition.[83]

The disadvantages of jury trial appear to be the additional time, and conse-

---

[69] *Ward v. James* [1966] 1 Q.B. 273, *per* Lord Denning M.R. at pp. 296–300, 303.
[70] *Sims v. William Howard and Son Ltd* [1964] 2 Q.B. 409.
[71] *Watts v. Manning* [1964] 1 W.L.R. 623.
[72] *Hodges v. Harland and Wolff Ltd* [1965] 1 W.L.R. 523. In this highly unusual case the plaintiff was injured whilst using a diesel-driven air compressor. The spindle of the machine caught in his trousers and avulsed his penis and scrotal skin. Jury trial was ordered. The observations of Davies L.J. at pp. 1087–1088 are helpful in setting out the difficulties of jury trial.
[73] *Sims v. William Howard and Son Ltd* [1964] 2 Q.B. 409, *per* Pearson L.J. at p. 419.
[74] *Ward v. James* [1966] 1 Q.B. 273, *per* Lord Denning M.R. at p. 295; *Williams v. Beasley* [1973] 1 W.L.R. 1295, *per* Lord Diplock at p. 1298H.
[75] *Williams v. Beasley* [1973] 1 W.L.R. 1295, *per* Lord Diplock at p. 1299H.
[76] *ibid. per* Lord Diplock at p. 1299H.
[77] *ibid. per* Lord Diplock at p. 1298–9.
[78] *ibid.* p. 1299H.
[79] See below, pp. 890–900.
[80] Juries Act 1974, s.17.
[81] Juries Act 1974, s.9(2), (4).
[82] *Practice Direction (Juries: Length of Trial)* [1981] 1 W.L.R. 1129.
[83] Jacob (1987), pp. 156–160.

quent additional expense, of a jury trial, the variability of jury verdicts, the potential hardship and inconvenience suffered by individual jurors in lengthy cases, the unrealistic expectations that lay people should listen to and comprehend complex and extensive evidence, the unpredictability of jury verdicts and the reluctance of the Court of Appeal to interfere with jury awards, and the additional burden which may be placed on counsel and judge where complex questions of law are in issue.[84]

These reasons are sound pragmatic grounds for the proposition that jury trial is not the "best" mode of trial for all civil actions and that trial by judge alone would normally be preferable. But are any of the reasons sufficiently strong to support the view that trial by jury should not be permissible?

The Faulks Committee on Defamation[85] recommended restrictions on the use of juries in defamation actions whilst rejecting arguments for their total abolition. The Committee concluded that in defamation cases the court should have the same discretion to order jury trial as in other civil cases and that the function of the jury should be limited to deciding issues of liability, leaving the assessment of damages to the judge.[86] The following summarises the view of the Committee:

> "We believe that much of the support for jury trials is emotional, and derives from the undoubted value of juries in serious *criminal* cases, where they stand between the prosecuting authority and the citizen. But the true function of the civil jury is to weigh facts impersonally and recompense the claimant for an injury that he may have sustained—tasks for which the judge is trained by many years of experience and for which jurors have no training at all."[87]

Is it right to describe the support for the jury as "emotional"? Various distinguished judges have declared the constitutional importance of the right to jury trial. For example, Atkin L.J. in *Ford v. Blurton* describe jury trial as "the bulwark of liberty, the shield of the poor from the rich and the powerful."[88] Although, the argument of Atkin L.J. may appear to be more

---

[84] These defects of the jury as a mode of trial are culled from various sources including: M.G. Buckley, "Civil Trial by Jury" (1966) 19 C.L.P. 63; W.R. Cornish, *The Jury* (1968), Chap. 8; P. Devlin, *Trial by Jury* (1956), pp. 130–135; *Hodges v. Harland and Wolff Ltd* [1965] 1 W.L.R. 523; *Ward v. James* [1966] 1 Q.B. 273; and the *Report of the Committee on Defamation* (Cmnd. 5909, 1975) (The Faulks Committee). Some of the disadvantages of jury trial are illustrated by *Orme v. Associated Newspapers Ltd* (see n.59 above), a case involving the alleged defamation of the director of The Holy Spirit Association for the Unification of World Christianity. The trial began in October 1980 and lasted until the end of March 1981. 117 witnesses were called. Very many documents had to be considered. The closing speeches lasted several days. The original estimate of the length of the trial was six to seven weeks. This case lead to the proposal of an, ultimately unsuccessful, amendment to the Supreme Court Bill which would have meant that trial by jury could be denied where the length of the trial would make it inconvenient for a jury to try the action.

[85] *Report of the Committee on Defamation* (Cmnd. 5909, 1975), Chap. 17 gives a very good account of the role of the jury in defamation actions.

[86] *ibid.* paras.455–457.

[87] *ibid.* para. 496.

[88] (1922) 38 T.L.R. 801 at 805. See also, to similar effect, Bankes L.J. in the same case. The same point was made by Mr Frank Dobson M.P. in the debates on the Supreme Court Bill when he said: "Jury service is more important to the preservation of individual liberty and the preservation of our judicial system than all the scurvy race of lawyers put together."

suited to the jury in criminal trials, there is some truth in it in relation to civil trials. However, if judges are independent of the state and other vested interests,[89] perhaps the argument has lost much of its force. A different argument is that it is desirable to involve as many people as possible in the administration of justice[90] and that the jury stands between the judges and the person in the street to ensure that ordinary standards are applied in the doing of justice.[91]

Even if there may be criticism of the distinction between the five specified causes of action and other civil cases, trial by jury is unlikely to be abolished in civil matters, but responsibility lies with the judges for ensuring that the worst features of jury trial are not often evident.

D. THE ROLE OF THE JUDGE

In civil matters the judge normally sits alone to determine the outcome of the action. The incidence of jury trial has already been explained, but there are a number of situations in which the judge may have the assistance of others sitting with him or her. The composition of the Employment Appeal Tribunal,[92] with lay members and High Court judges, exemplifies the formal introduction of lay expertise into the judicial process, but there is a general power vested in the High Court to call in the aid of one or more assessors or scientific advisers in particular cases.[93]

Assessors are used especially in admiralty proceedings in the Queen's Bench Division,[94] but there is nothing to prevent a judge using an assessor in other cases. It may cause expense and inconvenience to the parties if the hearing has to be adjourned so that the judge may find and appoint an appropriate expert, but there is strong support for that course of action,[95] in preference to obtaining assistance from an expert after the hearing has concluded and before judgment is given.[96]

Scientific advisers may be appointed in an action for the infringement of a patent and will render similar assistance to the judge.[97] The role of both assessor and scientific adviser is to listen to the evidence and give the judge such assistance as may be required in formulating the judgment and, if an opinion is given on the outcome, that opinion and the reasons for it may be taken into account by the Court of Appeal in the event of an appeal.[98]

---

[89] See above, pp. 239–249.

[90] See, *e.g.*, the evidence of Sir Peter Rawlinson Q.C. and Viscount Dilhorne given to the Faulks Committee (1975), para. 477.

[91] On a pragmatic level, Lord Denning M.R. supported the jury for the protection of a person's honour and integrity or to discover when one party may be lying: *Ward v. James* [1966] 1 Q.B. 273, at p. 295.

[92] See pp. 66–67 above.

[93] Supreme Court Act 1981, s.70 and R.S.C., Ord. 33, r.6.

[94] Where the assessor is normally one or more of the Elder Brethren of Trinity House.

[95] From Devlin J. in *Esso Petroleum Co. Ltd v. Southport Corporation* [1956] A.C. 218 at pp. 222–223. His view was supported by the House of Lords in the same case.

[96] *ibid.* at p. 223.

[97] Supreme Court Act 1981, s.70. See also *Supreme Court Practice 1995*, p. 597.

[98] *Hettersley and Sons v. G. Hodgson Ltd* (1905) 21 T.L.R. 178.

In a civil action it may prove difficult for the judge to refrain from intervening with questions and observations. However, the judge does not have to attain the standards of objectivity and neutrality as appertain in a criminal trial, since usually no jury is present. The procedure is relatively flexible in a civil trial and the absence of the jury enables the judge to take a more positive line over matters which may be considered to be irrelevant or uncontentious. However, the judge must not take such an active part in the case that it appears that counsel is deprived of the conduct of the action. Denning L.J. put the judge's role as follows:

> "The judge's part . . . is to hearken to the evidence, only himself asking question of witnesses when it is necessary to clear up any point that has been overlooked or left obscure; to see that the advocates behave themselves seemly and keep to the rules laid down by law; to exclude irrelevancies and discourage repetition; to make sure by wise intervention that he follows the points that the advocates are making and can assess their work; and at the end to make up his mind where the truth lies."[99]

If sitting alone, a judge may take time to decide where the truth lies or, more accurately, whether the plaintiff has satisfied the burden of proof,[1] and give a reserved judgment at a later date, or an extempore judgment may be given at the conclusion of the hearing. If sitting with a jury, the judge must sum up the evidence and direct on the law as would be done in a trial on indictment.[2] Ultimately judgment will be given.

E. THE JUDGMENT AND REMEDIES

A judgment is a reasoned decision in which the judge will normally set out the facts of the case as he or she has decided, and give the conclusions on the law applicable to them.[3] Some of the arguments put by counsel may be rehearsed so as to set the decision in context,[4] and an opinion is likely to be given on all matters relating to the action which might be relevant if the losing party were to appeal. In particular, there may be findings of fact which are not crucial to the judgment given at first instance but which might become relevant if the Court of Appeal were to take a different view of the law. The trial judge will be attempting to avoid the expense and difficulty of a new trial if the appellate court changes a part of the judgment.[5]

---

[99] *Jones v. National Coal Board* [1957] 2 Q.B. 55 at p. 64.

[1] *i.e.* whether the plaintiff has proved his or her case on a balance of probabilities.

[2] See below pp. 881–886.

[3] As to the desire to limit what the judge will say in fact track cases, see above, p. 630.

[4] Because it is the responsibility of the parties to advance argument on the issues which they wish to be decided it is always important to know whether a particular line of argument has been canvassed or not when assessing a judgment. In respect of appellate decisions reported in the Law Reports series, the major arguments of counsel are normally set out as part of the report.

[5] *e.g.*, although a judge may find against a plaintiff on the question of the defendant's liability in negligence, the quantum of damages will be determined lest the Court of Appeal reverses on the liability point. If no finding had been made on quantum the issue would have to be the subject of another trial.

The remedies available in civil proceedings are various, dependent upon the action being sought by the plaintiff.[6] There is an important adage worthy of repetition. It states that where there is a legal right there is, or ought to be, a legal remedy and where there is no remedy there is no right. There is an extensive range of remedies, which may be added to or varied[7] by judicial decision or the Rules Committee establishing the Rules of the Supreme Court.[8] The remedies that were available varied according to whether the action was one in the High Court or the county court. However, section 3 of the Courts and Legal Services Act 1990 provides that county courts may make the same remedial orders as the High Court.[9] Damages is the most likely remedy sought in an action in the Queen's Bench as considered here and in Chapter 11, but students should be aware that other remedies are available. In particular, the plaintiff may be seeking the recovery or restitution of property,[10] one of the many equitable remedies, such as an order for specific performance,[11] or an injunction,[12] or a declaration.[13]

Damages is the common law term for an order requiring payment of money. An award of damages may be made in relation to a vast range of wrongs and indebtedness.[14] The traditional division of damages is into liquidated and unliquidated damages: liquidated where the plaintiff specifies a set sum of money as owed at law in the original claim; unliquidated where the court must calculate the sum to be paid if liability is established, unless there is agreement on the quantum of damages between the parties. The method by which unliquidated damages are assessed is of most concern.

Damages can be claimed primarily on a contract or tort claim, and the basis for awarding damages will be slightly different dependent upon the action. The basic theory of damages for contract is that they should provide a sum that will, financially at least, fulfil the claimant's expectation under the promise made. The basic theory of tort damages is that the claimant, so far as money can, should be returned to the position before the wrong was done. However, it would appear that, despite the theoretical differences, modern law is taking a more pragmatic attitude.

In practice, High Court judges are most commonly called upon to assess damages in cases where the defendant has negligently inflicted personal injuries

---

[6] See, generally, F. H. Lawson, *Remedies of English Law* (2nd ed., 1980) and M. Tilbury, M. Noone and B. Ketcher, *Remedies* (1988) (this is an Australian work drawing on considerable English material).

[7] If a new remedy affects the substantive law, it can only be created by Act of Parliament.

[8] See Jacobs (1987), pp. 170–172.

[9] County courts do not have the power to order mandamus, certiorari or prohibition or orders of kinds to be prescribed by the Lord Chancellor.

[10] As to recovery of land, see Lawson (1980) and A. M. Prichard, *Squatting* (1981). Specific recovery of chattels is possible, although an order may provide the defendant with an option of retaining the property and paying its value instead.

[11] Available to enforce contractual obligations.

[12] The prime form of injunction is prohibitory since it forces a defendant to desist from wrongful conduct or forbids wrongful conduct when it has not even started, *i.e. the quia timet* injunction. A mandatory injunction requires the doing of some act.

[13] R.S.C., Ord. 15, r.16.

[14] Whilst the chapter concentrates on actions in contract and tort, an award of damages can be made in relation to an action in quasi-contract, in certain equity actions, *e.g.*, where recission is allowed for innocent misrepresentation, or where a trustee commits a breach of trust. Further, certain tribunals may also make awards of compensation, *e.g.*, an industrial tribunal for unfair dismissal.

upon the plaintiff.[15] Damages are usually awarded in a lump sum[16] and, as the action lies in tort, are designed to compensate the plaintiff for his or her losses. There are normally two basic aspects of an award: (i) compensation for non-pecuniary losses, and (ii) compensation for pecuniary or economic losses. Under the first head there may be damages for pain and suffering and loss of amenity[17] or, where the part of a body injured has no apparent function, the injury itself.[18] Damages for loss of amenity are awarded roughly in accordance with a tariff dependent on the seriousness of the injury or injuries.[19] Under the second head fall damages for such items as lost earnings[20] and medical expenses.

For example, in *Lim Poh Choo v. Camden and Islington Area Health Authority*[21] the plaintiff, an N.H.S. registrar, suffered serious brain damage after a minor operation. She was ultimately awarded £229,298.64. This included £20,000 for pain and suffering and loss of amenities; £3,956 for expenses to the date of trial; £16,500 for the cost of care in Malaysia; £1,923 for travelling expenses; £4,226.64 for the cost of care in the United Kingdom to date; £14,213 for loss of earnings to the date of trial; £76,800 for the cost of future care; and £92,000 for the loss of future earnings including pension rights.

At the end of the judgment, counsel for the successful party must ask formally for judgment to be entered for the client in the terms which the judge has indicated. Counsel may ask for "judgment for the plaintiff for £229,298.64", or "judgment for the defendant and that the plaintiff's claim be dismissed". At this stage the question of any interest payable on a money judgment will be raised by counsel, who will also ask for costs.[22] Traditionally, money judgments were expressed in sterling, but since 1975 it has been possible for a court to give judgment in a foreign currency.[23]

The final responsibility rests with the successful party, who relies upon his or her solicitor. He or she must draw up the terms of the judgment on a special form and have it entered in the judgment book kept in the Judgment Office.[24] Having obtained judgment, the successful party must go on to enforce it. Con-

---

[15] See W. V. H. Rogers, *Winfield and Jolowicz on the Law of Tort* (14th ed., 1994), Chap. 23; M. A. Jones, *A Textbook on Torts* 4th ed., 1993 pp. 403–426. See also above, pp. 558–560 and 562.

[16] *ibid.* There are exceptions to this general rule: (1) provisional damages may be awarded in personal injuries actions where there is a possibility that there will be a serious deterioration in the plaintiff's condition, thus a sum can be awarded without regard to that eventuality but, if it occurs, the plaintiff may return to court, see s.32A of the Supreme Court Act 1981 and Jones (1993), pp. 410–411; (2) a "structured settlement" that is payment for damages in periodic payments, which can take account of related losses as they occur, either for a fixed period of time or until the death of the plaintiff, see Jones (1993), p. 412, the Finance Act 1995 and the Damages Act 1996.

[17] *e.g*, damages for the loss of a leg, which may be increased where the plaintiff was a keen sports player whose enjoyment of life is thus substantially impaired.

[18] *e.g.*, a spleen: *Forster v. Pugh* [1955] C.L.Y. 741.

[19] Details of damages awarded in personal injury cases are given in *Kemp and Kemp on the Quantum of Damages* (looseleaf).

[20] In the most serious cases there will be the difficult task of estimating the loss of earnings in the future.

[21] [1980] A.C. 174.

[22] See pp. 530–533 above.

[23] *Miliangos v. George Frank (Textiles) Ltd* [1976] A.C. 443, not following the previous authority, *Re United Railways of Havana and Regla Warehouses Ltd* [1961] A.C. 1007. On the precedent implications of this decision, see above pp. 931–933.

[24] R.S.C., Ord. 42, r. 5. See *Supreme Court Practice 1995*, pp. 719–721.

trary, perhaps, to expectations, that party's troubles may only just be beginning![25]

F. ENFORCING JUDGMENT: EXECUTION[26]

(a) Introduction

"[T]he machinery of the enforcement of the judgments and orders of the court constitute the very foundation of the judicial process. It represents the coercive power of the court in the exercise of its judicial authority. It expresses the will of the state to buttress the judiciary . . . and makes their judgments and orders authoritative and obligatory, binding and conclusive."[27]

If judgment is obtained, the order of the court may be declaratory or constitutive[28] and nothing more need be done. In most instances, however, the order will require the performance of some further act or acts or the abstention from acts. The law appears to lean heavily in favour of inducement rather than direct compulsion. The form of the court order will frequently demonstrate this: thus the normal order in an action for damages requires the defendant to pay the plaintiff the specified figure.[29]

Many defendants obey court orders out of law-abiding motives. Others will be influenced by the appreciation that practical procedures exist to secure performance or obedience. These procedures might be said to form a system of enforcement, which Jacob, however, has described as being

"an unplanned, unsystematic, haphazard, complex system. It operates, especially in relation to money judgments, largely on a hit-or-miss basis. In relation to both money and non-money judgments, it is in part effective, but in part it is ineffective, inefficient, somewhat random and sometimes oppressive."[30]

The procedures that exist are variously derived from the common law, equity and statute. They are primarily aimed at specific forms of judgment, but they

---

[25] One of the considerations which a plaintiff must have in mind at the commencement of an action is whether the defendant will be able to satisfy any judgment that may be given against him or her.

[26] Jacob (1987), pp. 185–210; Sir Jack I. H. Jacob, "The Enforcement of Judgment Debts" in *The Reform of Civil Procedural Law* (1982); O'Hare and Hill, (1993), Chaps.24, 25. As to the enforcement of foreign judgments and the enforcement of judgments outside England and Wales, see O'Hare and Hill (1993), pp. 602–604 and Andrews (1944), pp. 530–538.

[27] Jacob (1987), pp. 185–186; and see Andrews (1994), p. 514.

[28] "Constitutive" orders are extremely various and extend across many areas of law. Examples in the civil law are: adoption and legitimation orders, award of custody and guardianship, divorces, appointment of trustees, dissolution of partnerships, liquidation of companies, adjudication in bankruptcy. Sometimes the order merely records a fact, an example being the declaration that a seeming marriage was in fact always null and void. See Lawson (1980), Chap. 17.

[29] R.S.C., Appendix A, Forms Nos. 43, 45, 49. In the ordinary procedure for recovering land, the modern formula is that the defendant "do give" possession to the plaintiff: R.S.C., Appendix A, Form 42 and C.C. Form 134.

[30] Jacob (1987), p. 188.

are capable of being used for any type of judgment if they can be effective. Thus sequestration, authorising the seizure of all or any property of the defendant within the jurisdiction, imposition of a fine and committal to prison are all drastic sanctions suitable for flagrant breaches of orders such as injunctions, but in extreme circumstances they can be used to enforce other types of judgment where there has been a civil contempt of court.[31] Imprisonment for a few civil debts may also be imposed, separately from a finding of contempt of court.[32]

A brief description of the main execution orders available follows, but prior to seeking such an order it may be necessary to discover the debtor's means. This can be achieved by an oral examination of the judgment debtor in the High Court or a county court.[33]

(b) Enforcement of money judgments[34]

(i) Fieri facias or warrant of execution

These forms of enforcement operate against the debtor's chattels and goods. The High Court form is the writ of *fieri facias*. This writ is issued to the sheriff of the county where the defendant's goods are located and the sheriff's officers enforce the writ by seizing goods sufficient to cover in value the amount owed under the judgment, the costs of execution and expenses.

The county court form is the warrant of execution which requires the court bailiff to carry out the order. The seized goods must be expected to cover only the amount owed under the judgment and the costs of execution.

Where the sum to be enforced is £5,000 or more, proceedings must be taken in the High Court, regardless of in which court the trial was heard. Where the sum is less than £2,000, enforcement must be through the county court. For sums in between, enforcement may be through either court.[35]

The exercise of this concurrent jurisdiction is vast. In 1995, 63,814 writs of *fieri facias* were issued and 895,301 warrants of execution were issued.[36] It has been suggested that the debtor's goods "which are exempt from seizure in

---

[31] *ibid.*, pp. 205–210.

[32] *ibid.* pp. 198–202. Since the Administration of Justice Act 1970, s.11, imprisonment, through the issue of a judgment summons, has been retained only for debtors on maintenance orders, debtors for the payment of taxes and certain specified statutory contributions and liabilities: see O'Hare and Hill (1993), p. 602 and R. Blackford, *County Court Practice Handbook* (9th ed., 1989), Chap. 23. The *Report of the Committee on One-Parent Families* (Cmnd. 5629, 1974) recommended that imprisonment for maintenance defaulters be abolished. Jacob recommends that imprisonment for all classes of debt should be abolished ((1987), p. 202) although it appears that some Circuit judges would welcome the restoration of imprisonment for civil debt (*ibid.*, p. 250, n. 7).

[33] See O'Hare and Hill (1993), pp. 588–589 and Blackford (1989), pp. 143–145. See also Andrews (1944) pp. 523–525 concerned with procuring information, avoiding the dissipation of assets, preventing the debtor leaving the jurisdiction, and preserving documents.

[34] R.S.C. Ord.45, 46, 47; C.C.R. Ord.26. See O'Hare and Hill (1993), Chap. 24 and Blackford (1989), Chaps.20, 22 and 24. Note the importance of ensuring enforcement action is taken before the onset, if any, of the defendant's insolvency; see Andrews (1994), pp. 521–523.

[35] High Court and County Courts Jurisidiction Order 1991, art.8; and see Andrews (1994), p. 515 and O'Hare and Hill (1993), p. 590. This change was consequent upon the *Civil Justice Review*.

[36] *Judicial Statistics 1995* (Cm. 3290, 1996), Table 3.12 and 4.16 respectively.

execution are woefully inadequate both in their description and their value."[37] The Courts and Legal Services Act has since amended the list.[38]

(ii) Garnishee proceedings[39]

By these proceedings, the successful party, the judgment creditor, obtains the judgment debt by "attachment" of a debt owed to the judgment debtor by a third party, *i.e.* a debt owed to the judgment debtor by a third party is automatically paid to the judgment creditor. In 1995, 557 garnishee orders were made absolute in the High Court,[40] that is the third party was required to pay the debt to the judgment creditor. Using a slightly different procedure, 5,425 garnishee summonses were issued in the county courts.[41]

(iii) Attachment of earnings[42]

A garnishee order is not available with regard to earnings. The Attachment of Earnings Act 1971 for the first time empowered the courts to enforce employers to make deductions from the earnings of employees to be paid into court to satisfy the employees' debts. This is primarily a jurisdiction of the county court, the High Court only having power to attach for payment of maintenance orders, and not judgments generally.[43] In 1995, 70,034 orders were made to secure the payment of a judgment debt.[44]

(iv) Charging orders[45]

Charging orders are statutory orders whereby charges are created on property.[46] The judgment creditor becomes in effect an equitable chargee with rights to

---

[37] Jacob (1987), p. 196.

[38] s.15, following the recommendations of the *Report on the Enforcement of Judgment Debts* (Cmnd. 3909, 1969), para. 675, has provided a new list of goods which are exempt from seizure: "(i) such tools, books, vehicles and other items of equipment as are necessary to that person for use personally by him in his employment, business or vocation; (ii) such clothing, bedding, furniture, household equipment and provisions as are necessary for satisfying the basic domestic needs of that person and his family." See D. Greenberg, "Enforcement Law and the Courts and Legal Services Act 1990" (1990) 140 N.L.J. 1794.

[39] R.S.C. Ord.49; C.C.R. Ord.30.

[40] *Judicial Statistics 1995*, Table 3.12.

[41] *ibid.*, Table 4.16.

[42] C.C.R. Ord.27.

[43] Attachment of Earnings Act 1971, s.1. The procedural amendments introduced by the Courts and Legal Services Act 1990, Sched. 17, will make collection arrangements more flexible and may pave the way for this procedure to be handled by one central office: see Greenberg (1990).

[44] *Judicial Statistics 1995*, Table 4.17. In the same year 2,252 orders were made in the county court to secure the payment of maintenance: *ibid.*

[45] R.S.C. Ord. 50; C.C.R. Ord. 31.

[46] Charging Orders Act 1979, s.1; R.S.C., Ord. 50; C.C.R., Ord. 31. County court orders must be sought where the sum in question is less than £5,000.

recoup his or her debt from income of the property or from its sale in due course. Consequently, the debtor cannot, for example, sell the property without satisfying the debt or having the order transferred to other property. The principal property so chargeable is land or any interest in land, and the charge is registrable under the Land Charges Act 1972. Government and company stocks, dividends and interest on such stock, and moneys in court may also be subjected to a charging order.[47] An application for a charging order must be made in a county court, unless the judgment debt exceeds £5,000, in which case the application may be made in the High Court.[48] In 1995, 23,581 charging orders were issued.[49]

(v) Equitable execution: appointment of a receiver

Where none of the other means of execution is likely to be effective, it is possible for a receiver to be appointed to take income due to the judgment debtor and apply it towards the debt owed to the judgment creditor.[50] Because of the effectiveness of the other means of execution and since it is cumbersome, this is a rarely used means of enforcement.

(c) Possession orders[51]

(i) Land

The normal procedure is to apply for a writ of possession in the High Court[52] or a warrant for possession in the county court.[53] The bailiffs acting under the writ clear all people from the premises, whether they were parties to the action or not. This is a very important procedure, because it may well be dangerous for a successful party otherwise to attempt to occupy land which has been awarded by the court. In 1995, 1,355 possession writs were issued by the High Court and 51,096 county court warrants for possession of land were executed.[54]

(ii) Goods

Judgments for delivery of goods may or may not contain an option in the defendant to pay the value instead of giving up the goods. Where there is no such

---

[47] Charging Orders Act 1979, s.2; R.S.C., Ord. 50; C.C.R., Ord. 31.

[48] Charging Orders Act 1979, s.1(1) and (2); and see Andrews (1994), at p. 518.

[49] *Judicial Statistics 1995*, Tables 3.12 and 4.16 of which 21,584 were made in a county court: *ibid.* Table 4.12.

[50] R.S.C., Ord. 51; C.C.R., Ord. 32. See O'Hare and Hill (1993), p. 601; Blackford (1989), p. 176 and Andrews (1994), pp. 520–521.

[51] See O'Hare and Hill (1993), pp. 607–608 and Blackford (1989), pp. 140–147.

[52] R.S.C., Ord., 45(3). Special rules under Ord. 88 apply to a mortgage action.

[53] C.C.R., Ord. 25.

[54] *Judicial Statistics 1995*, Tables 3.12 and 4.16. The county court issued 117,301 warrants for possession of land.

option, execution is by way of writ of delivery in the High Court which instructs the sheriff to cause the goods to be delivered to the plaintiff.[55] In the county court a similar procedure is undertaken through the warrant of delivery.[56] In 1995, the High Court issued 48 writs for delivery and 8,549 county court warrants for delivery of goods were issued.[57]

(d) Mandatory and prohibitory order[58]

(i) Specific performance

A failure by a seller to execute an instrument in response to a judgment for specific performance may be overcome by the appointment of someone else (usually a Chancery Master or a district judge) to execute it in the seller's stead.

(ii) Injunction

The injunctions that may be imposed as a means of execution are the same as those that may be imposed as a remedy consequent upon the trial.[59]

(e) Conclusion

Such enforcement procedures form the largest component of the work of the civil courts, amounting for a substantial proportion of their resources.[60] This is reflected in the figures quoted above from the *Judicial Statistics 1994*. For this reason, and for the long expressed concern about the enforcement system, debt enforcement procedures were examined as a part of the Civil Justice Review.[61] As a consequence of the factual study,[62] the Review identified the following considerations which should form the basis of any system of debt recovery through the courts:

"(i) The system should aim to recover as much as possible of the debt quickly, cheaply and simply.
(ii) Creditors should be able to obtain adequate information about debtors' circumstances.
(iii) Maximum information should be available about debtors on public files.
(iv) There should be machinery for bringing together multiple debts.
(v) The period for repayment should not last indefinitely and a debtor should be restored to full economic status as soon as possible.

---

[55] R.S.C., Ord. 45.
[56] C.C.R., Ord. 26.
[57] *Judicial Statistics 1995*, Tables 3.12 and 4.16.
[58] O'Hare and Hill (1993), pp. 608–609 and Blackford (1989), Chap. 33.
[59] See above p. 795.
[60] *Civil Justice Review* (1988), para. 534(i).
[61] *ibid.* Chap. 9. "Debt enforcement" is not limited to the enforcement of judgment debts: *ibid.*, para. 534.
[62] *Civil Justice Review*, Consultation Paper No. 4 (1986).

(vi) Debtors and their families should not be subjected to unwarranted hardship, fear or humiliation."[63]

Based on these considerations, a series of recommendations was made, including: changing the responsibility for executing county court judgments; improving the county court bailiff system by changing its management, particularly by integrating it into the court service, and by redefining its duties; creating a manual setting out the duties of a county court bailiff which should be made publicly available; inviting detailed reform of the law relating to the High Court enforcement officers; and introducing plain English into the terminology.[64] The possibility of requiring all claims to start in the county court was not pursued.[65]

Whilst these reforms, if introduced, would go a considerable way to solving some of the problems with enforcement, they do not address Jacob's central demand which is that the system is so confusing, complex and unfair that radical reform is called for in the form of the creation of a Central Enforcement Authority.[66] Such a system would have the attributes of simplicity and speed, efficiency and effectiveness. The Authority "would operate as an integrated system for the enforcement of judgments and would enjoy exclusive jurisdiction for this purpose and thus it would produce uniformity and equality of treatment for all judgments and eliminate procedural anomalies and differences between the different courts that enforce judgments at present. It would provide the mechanism for enforcing through one office, attached to each of the county courts throughout the country, all the judgments of the civil courts and tribunals."[67]

G. ARBITRATION IN THE COUNTY COURT

The arbitration procedure in small claims in the county court is very significant. In 1994, 88,170 cases were disposed of by arbitration and 24,477 by trial.[68]

The situations in which a small claim will reach arbitration in the county court and the standard terms of reference for the arbitration have been set out in Chapter 11.[69] We only need to remind ourselves at this point of the particular features of the arbitration which distinguish it from the trial procedure we have been considering in this chapter.

The strict rules of evidence do not apply to the hearing and it is intended to

---

[63] *Civil Justice Review* (1988), para. 620.

[64] *ibid.* paras.627–651.

[65] *ibid.* paras.612–3. At present all applications for charging orders when the judgment debt is within the monetary jurisdictional limits of the county court must be made in the county court and not in the High Court: Charging Orders Act 1979, ss.1(2) and 7, see Jacob (1987), p. 193, which Sir Jack regarded as a model principle to apply to all processes for the enforcement of money judgments and see above.

[66] *ibid.* pp. 271–273. This proposal builds on that of an Enforcement Office made by the Payne Report (1969). So complex are the issues that Andrews provides guidance on "tactical considerations", see Andrews (1994), pp. 525–526.

[67] Jacob (1987), p. 271.

[68] *Judicial Statistics 1995*, Table 4.7.

[69] See above, pp. 593–594.

be informal.[70] In order to afford a fair and equal opportunity to each party to present their case, the arbitrator is free to adopt whatever form of procedure is thought to be appropriate.[71] This clearly marks a substantial deviation from the adversarial procedure of trial, although quite how flexibly the procedures are operated will depend upon the district judge who is likely to be the arbitrator.[72] Lord Woolf discovered that district judges take seriously the responsibility to ensure that proceedings are informal and that they have thought deeply about it.[73] For the Woolf Inquiry, Professor Baldwin interviewed district judges and discovered that there are four different approaches to the conduct of hearings: "(a) 'going for the jugular' (identifying the central issues at an early stage and sticking to them); (b) 'hearing the parties' (allowing the parties greater latitude to develop their arguments in their own way); (c) 'passive' (talking to each of the parties like a solicitor interviewing clients); and (d) 'mediatory' (encouraging the parties to agree their own solution)."[74] Lord Woolf took the view that this variety was unacceptable, since not only is the judge the adjudicator, his or her decision being effectively final because of the very limited availability of an appeal, but he or she is also "a key safeguard of the rights of both parties", being often "a substitute for a legal representative."[75] Lord Woolf also noted that "the most crucial element affecting litigants' perceptions of small claims schemes is their treatment by the judge."[76] Lord Woolf, therefore, proposed that "all district judges and deputy district judges should be trained in handling small claims to ensure a more consistent approach."[77] In order to save costs and time, Lord Woolf also proposed that the option of paper arbitration should be encouraged by more effective publicity.[78]

In one respect the rules for the arbitration seem to be narrower than the rules in the High Court. There is a power given to the arbitrator to consult an expert, or call for an expert report, or invite an expert to attend the hearing as an assessor, *but only with the consent of the parties*.[79] As against the power of the High Court to appoint an assessor of its own volition,[80] this is a surprising limitation and, although the arbitrator's own initiative may be used in suggesting expert evidence (in the High Court it must be on the application of a party[81]), either party may frustrate the arbitrator's objective. It is presumably to prevent additional cost being forced on the parties that the arbitrator does not have the power to call evidence of his or her own motion, but that problem might be circumvented by a requirement that the arbitrator gain the agreement of the parties to a reasonable fee for the evidence, rather than to the obtaining of the

---

[70] Unless the court on making the reference to arbitration determines otherwise: C.C.R., Ord. 19, r.7(3).
[71] The arbitrator, if appropriate, may put questions to witnesses and parties, and may explain legal terms and expressions: C.C.R. Ord. 19, 1.4.
[72] C.C.R. Ord. 19, r.5. and see above, p. 596.
[73] Woolf Report (1995), p. 107.
[74] *ibid.*, pp. 107–108. Baldwin also discovered differences in the way district judges dealt with evidence and the substantive law: *ibid.*, p. 109.
[75] *ibid.*, p. 108.
[76] *ibid.*
[77] *ibid.*, pp. 108–110 and 118.
[78] *ibid.*, pp. 111–112 and 118.
[79] This power may be exercised at any time before the decision of the arbitrator is given, and either before or after the hearing: C.C.R., Ord. 19, r.7(6).
[80] Supreme Court Act 1981, s.70; see p. 793 above.
[81] R.S.C., Ord. 40, r.6.

evidence. In response to this issue and recognising the likelihood of an increased need of experts because of a proposed increase in jurisdiction, Lord Woolf proposes that district judges be more ready to exercise their powers, such as they are; that the cost of the assessor would be recoverable from the unsuccessful party; and that a court should be prepared to exercise the jurisdiction of appointing an expert arbitrator.[82]

---

[82] Woolf Report (1995), p. 113.

PART IV

THE HEARING

CHAPTER 15

THE TRIBUNAL HEARING

At the hearing, the chairman of the tribunal has the difficult task of ensuring that a sufficient level of informality is achieved so that the parties do not feel inhibited in putting their respective cases, whilst maintaining some procedural and evidentiary safeguards so that the rights of the parties are not prejudiced in an unacceptable way.

We made the point in the previous chapter on tribunals that it is scarcely possible to choose a "typical" tribunal and the observations hereafter draw on a variety of sources. However, just as there are common problems to be solved in devising an appropriate pre-hearing procedure, so there are common problems in the conduct of hearings. What procedural rules, if any, should be followed? What evidence will be admitted? What role should the chairman play and what responsibilities does he or she have? What sort of representation, if any, should be permitted/encouraged, and how should it be funded?

A. PROCEDURE

Differing approaches to the achievements of procedural fairness may be observed, but in most tribunals much is left to the chairman in determining the form of the hearing. Three illustrations may demonstrate that the amount of guidance given by the appropriate rules is often minimal.

1. The Social Security Appeal Tribunal

The procedural regulations for Social Security Appeal Tribunals provide that:

"Subject to the provisions of the Administration Act and of these Regulations—. . . in the case of a tribunal . . . the procedure shall be such as the chairman shall determine."[1]

This general power is qualified in certain respects by other provisions. Representation is permitted;[2] witnesses may be called;[3] every person who has the right to be heard shall be given an opportunity of putting questions directly to any witnesses called at the hearing and of addressing the tribunal;[4] the hearing

[1] Social Security (Adjudication) Regulations 1995, (S.I. 1995, No. 1801), reg. 2(1)(a). The "Administration Act" is the Social Security Administration Act 1992.
[2] *ibid.*, reg. 2(1)(b).
[3] *ibid.*, reg. 4(9).
[4] *ibid.*, reg. 4(9).

shall be in public unless the claimant requests a private hearing or the chairman directs that the hearing shall be private on the grounds that intimate personal or financial circumstances may have to be disclosed or that public security is involved[5]; any party to the proceedings is entitled to be present and to be heard.[6]

It is the chairman who decides how these requirements should be fulfilled and it is to be expected that there will be variations in procedure from chairman to chairman. There is, however, a guide which sets out general principles.[7] The Social Security Commissioners[8] may correct procedural irregularities on appeal, but it will be apparent that the provisions are so widely drafted that such an irregularity will have to be very serious before it will be regarded as material.[9]

The standard procedure[10] is for the claimant (or his or her representative) to state the case and call witnesses[11]; the claimant and his witnesses may then be questioned by the chairman, and/or the members, and/or the presenting officer[12]; the presenting officer then makes a submission and is subject to questioning; the claimant is asked for any final observations. The *Guide to Procedure* makes it clear, however, that

"There is ... no hard and fast rule about this and it may be courteous, and help to dispel any feeling on his part that matters have been taken out of his hands, to offer the choice of sequence to the claimant or his representative."[13]

At the conclusion of the hearing, the members of the tribunal consider their decision in private.[14]

The parties to the proceedings must be informed, in writing, of the decision

[5] *ibid.*, reg. 4(4).

[6] *ibid.*, reg. 4(5). "Party to the proceedings" is defined in reg. 1(2), and in the case of appeals to an appeal tribunal includes the claimant, the adjudication officer (the D.S.S. Officer whose job is to make the original decision on entitlement to benefit), the Secretary of State and any other person appearing to the chairman to be interested in the proceedings.

[7] *Social Security Appeal Tribunals: a guide to procedure* (HMSO, 2nd ed., 1988).

[8] See above, p. 70. The Commissioners constitute an appeal body from the decisions of Social Security Appeal Tribunals.

[9] In practice the most important ground of appeal is failure to state the reasons for a decision adequately: N. J. Wikeley, *Ogus, Barendt and Wikeley's The Law of Social Security* (4th ed., 1995), p. 678.

[10] Suggested in the *Guide to Procedure*, pp. 24–25. However, it is not just the order of events which is significant but the attitude and appearance of the tribunal members. One of the original authors, representing a nervous claimant at a N.I.L.T., had been at pains to explain in advance the informality of the procedure and distinguish it from court procedure as seen in "Crown Court" on television. The opening remarks of the chairman of the tribunal were, "Good afternoon, I must warn you, Mrs X, that you must tell the truth in these proceedings—we are just like a court." If the claimant had been unrepresented, the niceties of procedure would have mattered little after that!

[11] This assumes that the claimant attends or is represented. The tribunal has a discretion to proceed with the hearing in the absence of the claimant: Adjudication Regulations, reg. 4(3); and if a claimant fails to attend without giving a reasonable explanation "it will usually be right to proceed with the hearing": *Guide to Procedure*, p. 18.

[12] The presenting officer is an officer of the D.S.S. specifically assigned to present cases before tribunals. Some presenting officers, therefore, become very experienced "advocates" and well known to their local tribunal. This job may not, however, occupy all the time of an officer, in which case he or she may also carry out the duties of an adjudication officer.

[13] At p. 24.

[14] The clerk to the tribunal is permitted to remain with the members during their deliberations: Adjudication Regulations, reg. 2(2).

as soon as may be practicable after the case has been decided.[15] The written decision must include a statement of the reasons for the decision, a record of the material facts found and, where the decision is not unanimous, that one of the members dissented and the reasons for that dissent.[16]

The role of the presenting officer in the procedure of the S.S.A.T. is interesting in that he or she is expected to put forward the view of the officer who made the decision against which the claimant is appealing, but is also expected to exercise individual judgment and assist the tribunal in reaching a proper resolution of the case.[17] This may require him or her to advance arguments on behalf of the appellant if he or she thinks that they should be brought to the attention of the tribunal, although there have been differing views expressed about the enthusiasm with which presenting officers have fulfilled that function.[18] The tribunal and the claimant may be assisted insofar as it is unlikely that a presenting officer will be defending at a hearing his or her own decision on an original claim and objectivity may be easier to display in those circumstances.[19] The unusual practice of allowing adjudication officers to defend their own decisions as presenting officers is likely to emphasise the adversarial nature of the proceedings at the expense of the inquisitorial.

It is legitimate to ask to what extent an inquisitorial mode is adopted in the hearing. It is true that the tribunal members are more involved in the direct questioning of both sides than a judge would be, and the informal structure of the proceedings allows particular points, once raised, to be followed through to a conclusion immediately if that appears convenient.[20] The functions of the statutory authorities (adjudication officer, tribunal, Commissioner) have been described as

"investigatory or inquisitorial. A social security appeal tribunal is exercising quasi-judicial functions and forms part of the statutory machinery for

[15] Adjudication Regulations, reg. 23(3).
[16] ibid. reg. 23(2).
[17] For a lawyer's analysis of this role, see Diplock L.J. in R. v. Deputy Industrial Injuries Commissioner, ex p. Moore [1965] 1 Q.B. 456 at p. 486. A claimant would not necessarily take the same view, even if he knew what was meant by lis inter partes and amicus curiae.
[18] M. Herman, Administrative Justice and Supplementary Benefits (1972); K. Bell, Research Study on Supplementary Benefit Appeal Tribunals, Review of Main Findings: Conclusions: Recommendations (D.H.S.S. 1975). The Adjudication Officers' Guide (Vol. 1, para. 05328) states that "The role of the AO is that of amicus curiae . . . and not an advocate. The AO should not put questions to any claimant or witness in a hostile manner and it is entirely inappropriate for the AO to think in terms of 'winning' the case." Despite this, during observations of hearings for the study by Genn and Genn (1989) "many Presenting Officers were seen to argue their cases forcefully and to display pleasure when their decision was ultimately confirmed" (p. 161). Baldwin, Wikeley and Young (Judging Social Security (1992), Chap. 7), found that while most of the POs interviewed seemed to have a reasonable grasp of the amicus curiae concept, the role adopted most often in practice was neutral and reactive (in 20 per cent of cases, the PO appeared to adopt the full amicus curiae role; in 8 per cent an adversarial position was taken) (pp. 184–185).
[19] The Adjudication Officers' Guide states (Vol. 1, para. 05310) that "The AO who made the decision under appeal can attend the hearing and present the case personally. However, more often the AO will be represented by the presenting officer."
[20] One of the original authors experienced a N.I.L.T in which he was interrupted in the midst of representations by comments from the claimant's husband who was attending the hearing as a "member of the public" and was sitting at the back of the room. The chairman encouraged him to speak up and proceeded to deal with the point he raised by questioning both the claimant and the insurance officer. Having dealt with it to his satisfaction the chairman asked if the husband had any further observations . . .

investigating claims. . . . Its investigatory function has as its object the ascertainment of the facts and the determination of the truth. . . .''[21]

As an aspect of this

"It is open to a tribunal and indeed it is the members' duty, whenever they identify a point in favour of the claimant, notwithstanding that it has not been taken by the claimant, to consider it and to reach their decision in the light of it.''[22]

Moreover, the presenting officer should attempt to present a balanced view. However, there are limits. A tribunal is not expected to question facts presented by a claimant just in case after further investigation they might prove to be materially different in the claimant's favour, especially where there is no suggestion that the claimant is unsure of the facts as presented.[23]

". . . [T]he primary duty for making out his case falls on the claimant,[24] and he must not expect to rely on the tribunal's own expertise. We would be slow to convict a tribunal of failure to identify an uncanvassed factual point in favour of the claimant in the absence of the most obvious and clear cut circumstances.''[25]

Moreover, exhortations that an inquisitorial approach should be adopted do not necessarily reflect the actual practice.[26]

An example of a Form AT3, which records the proceedings at a particular S.S.A.T. hearing, is reproduced in Chapter 12.[27]

2. The Industrial Tribunal

The rules of procedure for a hearing at an Industrial Tribunal are, in some respects, more explicit. The objectives to be attained at the hearing are included as part of the rules. In respect of the S.S.A.T., we noted that the normal provision is simply for the chairman to determine the procedure, for the Industrial Tribunal, the rules specify that:

"The tribunal shall, so far as it appears to it appropriate, seek to avoid formality in its proceedings and shall not be bound by any enactment or

---

[21] R.(S) 1/87, pp. 6–7 (Commissioner V. G. H. Hallett); *Guide to Procedure*, p. 8.

[22] R.(SB) 2/83, p. 557 (Tribunal of Commissioners).

[23] *ibid.*, p. 558. It was contended on behalf of the claimant that the local tribunal should, of its own motion, have investigated the origin and nature of funds in a personal account in a building society, in order to determine whether they truly represented business assets and not personal monies. That contention was rejected.

[24] But see pp. 814–815, on the burden of proof in S.S.A.T.s.

[25] R.(SB) 2/83, p. 558.

[26] The study by Genn and Genn (1989) found that while S.S.A.T. chairs consistently expressed the belief that proceedings were inquisitorial, this was denied by many experienced representatives, whose views were "often based on the perception that tribunals did not have the time to delve in sufficient detail into appellants' cases:" pp. 159–163.

[27] See above, pp. 651–652.

rule of law relating to the admissibility of evidence in proceedings before the courts of law. The tribunal shall make such enquiries of persons appearing before it and witnesses as it considers appropriate and shll otherwise conduct the hearing in such a manner as it considers most appropriate for the clarification of the issues before it and generally to the just handling of the proceedings."[28]

Although those may be the implicit objectives of other tribunals, it is interesting that they should be explicit for the Industrial Tribunal, and consequently ironic that the Industrial Tribunal is generally reckoned to be one of the more formal and legalistic of the tribunals.

The hearing takes place in public unless the tribunal is of the opinion that a private hearing is appropriate on the grounds of national security or other specified grounds[29]; any person entitled to appear at the hearing is entitled to give evidence, call witnesses, question any witness and address the tribunal.[30] If a party has failed to attend the hearing, the tribunal must consider the originating application or notice of appearance, any written representations submitted and any written answer[31] received, but subject to that provision, the hearing may proceed or may be adjourned, or the application may be dismissed, at the discretion of the tribunal.[32]

The order of events at a hearing is likely to differ with the nature of the claim.[33] In the ordinary unfair dismissal case the burden of proof lies with the employer to show that the dismissal was not unfair and the employer will normally be called on first. If the employee alleges constructive dismissal, or the employer otherwise disputes the fact of dismissal, then it will be for the employee to begin and make out his or her case. Whoever has the first word, the procedure thereafter is, in form, similar to court procedure with the calling, examination and cross-examination of witnesses leading to final statements on both sides. The chairman and members of the tribunal may ask more questions and become more involved in the proceedings than a judge would, and the rules about the correct form of examination and cross-examination are relaxed along with the rules of evidence,[34] but an observer at a hearing would receive a strong impression of adversarial procedure and formality.

3. RENT ASSESSMENT COMMITTEES

The Rent Assessment Committee[35] exercises jurisdiction of three main kinds. It receives and determines objections against the fixing and registration (or

---

[28] The Industrial Tribunals (Constitution and Rules of Procedure) Regulations 1993 (S.I. 1993 No. 2687), Rules of Procedure, r.9(1).

[29] *ibid.*, r.8(2), (3).

[30] *ibid.*, r.9(2).

[31] See above, pp. 645–646.

[32] *ibid.*, rr.8(5), 9(3).

[33] For Industrial Tribunal procedure generally, see I. T. Smith and Sir John C. Wood, *Industrial Law* (5th ed. 1993), pp. 309–324; *Sweet & Maxwell's Encyclopedia of Employment Law*, Parts I.A.7 and 5; *Tribunal Practice and Procedure* (I.D.S. Handbook Series 2 No. 4, 1994).

[34] See pp. 811–822 below for further discussion.

[35] See generally R. E. Megarry, *The Rent Acts* (1988), Vol. 1, Chaps.24 and 25, Vol. 3, Chaps.16 and 17; J. C. Martin, *Residential Security* (2nd ed., 1995), Chaps.10 and 14.

confirmation) of a fair rent by a rent officer[36]; it fixes the rent of an assured
tenancy where the landlord proposes a rent increase[37]; and, when exercising the
powers of a rent tribunal, it controls rent and security of tenure in respect of
"restricted contracts."[38] Some potential confusion was created by the Housing
Act 1980 in the abolition of the rent tribunal and the reallocation of its functions
to a Rent Assessment Committee[39] but we shall attempt to distinguish the two
by reference to R.A.C. and R.A.C. (R.T.).

The R.A.C. and R.A.C. (R.T.) share a feature which distinguish them from
the other tribunals we have so far considered, in that they do not need to hold
a hearing. The obligation lies on the landlord and the tenant to request the
opportunity to make oral representations and there are provisions for the disposal
of the matter on written representations in the absence of an application for a
hearing.[40] It should be emphasised that the absence of a hearing does not relieve
the tribunal of considering the matter, indeed it points up the inquisitorial role
because the committee then have an obligation to make such inquiry as they
think fit and consider any information supplied or representation made by the
parties.[41] This demonstrates the necessity for procedural safeguards throughout
the determination of an issue—they are not confined to a hearing.

If the landlord or tenant requests the opportunity to make oral representations
then the R.A.C. or the R.A.C. (R.T.), as appropriate, will arrange a hearing. For
the hearing, the procedural rules are slightly different in respect of the R.A.C.
and R.A.C. (R.T.) but it is unlikely that the formal differences are reflected in
the actual procedure adopted by the chairman.

The R.A.C. rules provide that, ". . . the parties shall be heard in such order,
and . . . the procedure shall be such as the committee shall determine" and "a
party may call witnesses, give evidence on his own behalf and cross-examine
any witnesses called by the other party."[42] Each party may be heard in person
"or by a person authorised by him in that behalf," whether or not a solicitor
or barrister.[43] The rules specify that the hearing shall be in public unless the
committee decide otherwise "for special reasons."[44]

In respect of the R.A.C. (R.T.), "the procedure at a hearing shall be such as the
rent tribunal may determine" and a party may appear in person or be represented

---

[36] Under the provisions of the Rent Act 1977, Pt. IV.
[37] Under the Housing Act 1988, Pt. I.
[38] As defined in Rent Act 1977, ss.19–21.
[39] s.72. The provisions of the section are, at first sight, so startling that they may properly be set
out in full:
  (1) Rent tribunals, as constituted for the purposes of the 1977 Act, are hereby abolished and
      section 76 of the 1977 Act (Constitution, etc. of rent tribunals) is hereby repealed.
  (2) As from the commencement of this section the functions which, under the 1977 Act, are
      conferred on rent tribunals shall be carried out by rent assessment committees.
  (3) A rent assessment committee shall, when constituted to carry out functions so conferred,
      be known as a rent tribunal."
The object appears to be to achieve a uniformity of appointment for the two bodies, without
diminishing their functions.
[40] Rent Act 1977, Sched. 11, paras.6, 7(1)(b), 9 and Rent Assessment Committee (England and
Wales) Regulations 1971 (S. I. 1971 No. 1065), reg. 6 (R.A.C.s); Rent Act 1977 s.28(1), (2);
Rent Assessment Committees (England and Wales) (Rent Tribunal) Regulations 1980 (S. I. 1980
No. 1700), reg. 4 (R.A.C. (RT)).
[41] 1977 Act, Sched. 11, paras.7(1)(a), 9(1) (R.A.C.s); Rent Act 1977, s.78(2) (R.A.C. (RT)).
[42] S. I. 1971 No. 1065, reg. 4.
[43] Rent Act 1977, Sched. 11, para. 8.
[44] S. I. 1971 No. 1065, reg. 3(1).

by anyone he or she wishes.[45] The tribunal may if they think fit, and at the request of either party shall, unless for some special reason they consider it undesirable, allow the hearing to be held in public.[46] There is no specific provision for the calling of witnesses, giving of evidence, or cross-examination.

These formal differences may not actually affect the *style* of the hearing but it is odd that there should be discrepancies in the procedural rules, particularly where the same members are involved in each type of hearing. The R.A.C. (R.T.) rules are the later and there are echoes in them of the rules which have been developed in social security tribunals, yet the allocation of the functions of the rent tribunal to the R.A.C. in 1980 ought to have provided an opportunity for standardisation. If there can be no accepted procedural criteria in this case, what hope is there for establishing uniform procedure across the wide range of tribunals?

B. EVIDENCE

In civil and criminal trials there are clear rules about the sort of evidence which may be given; the location of the burden of proof; and the standard of proof. Such clear rules are not to be found in tribunal adjudication. In the adversarial procedure of the civil or criminal trial the burden of proof is normally readily identified, but where there is an inquisitorial atmosphere in tribunals it is more difficult to locate. Some of the rules which render relevant evidence inadmissible at a trial rely heavily for their justification on the inability of a jury to decide the proper weight to be given to potentially prejudicial evidence. An experienced tribunal chairman, it is said, ought to be able to attribute the correct amount of weight to almost every piece of relevant information. Further, it is always argued that the absence of "strict" rules of evidence enhances the informality of tribunal procedure and makes it more comprehensible to the lay person.

However, a balance needs to be maintained between the requirements of informality and the interests of the parties to the tribunal. It may be assumed that some rules of evidence are specifically designed to prevent a conclusion being reached on unreliable information,[47] so that it would not be acceptable to abandon the principles of evidence altogether in tribunal adjudication. We shall hope to illustrate how tribunals cope with the problems of onus and standard of proof, relevance and admissibility.

1. GENERAL PRINCIPLES[48]

There is an important difference between courts and tribunals in that many tribunals rely on the expertise of the chairmen and members in determining

---

[45] S. I. 1980 No. 1700, regs. 6, 7(1).

[46] *ibid.*, reg. 7(1).

[47] The exclusion of hearsay evidence is based mainly on its potential unreliability, and such evidence is treated with considerable caution in tribunal proceedings although it is admissible, see pp. 816–817, below.

[48] There is little available material about the use of evidence in tribunals, but see R. E. Wraith and P. G. Hutchesson, *Administrative Tribunals* (1973), pp. 265–273; J. Fulbrook, *Administrative Justice and the Unemployed* (1978), pp. 268–276; C. Yates, [1980] J. S. W. L. 273 (supplementary benefit appeals) and [1980] Conv. 136 (rent tribunals); J. G. Logie and P. Q. Watchman, (1989) 8 C. J. Q. 109 (S. S. A. T. s); P. J. Rowe, (1994) 1 Jo. of Social Security Law 9.

questions of fact.[49] It is interesting to note that the jury, at its inception, was intended to rely upon the collective knowledge of its members, although such knowledge could now constitute a reason for excusal or challenge.[50] The justification for tribunal adjudication rests partly on the expertise of the adjudicators in the appropriate field, and there is ample authority for the proposition that they may rely on their own specialist knowledge to interpret evidence given to them by the parties or to fill in gaps where evidence has not been given.[51] Were this not the case there would be no possibility of an appeal succeeding in a social security matter where the appellant chose not to appear, was unrepresented and made no written representations. The chances of success for such an appellant are slender but they do exist.[52]

Those tribunals which are not merely administrative bodies but exercise a judicial function are bound to conform to the rules of natural justice.[53] The way in which a tribunal deals with evidence must accord with those rules which require, broadly, that the proceedings must be fair in all the circumstances. In respect of the giving of evidence it seems that every party to a hearing must be given an opportunity to put his or her case and to call relevant evidence in support.[54] That right is supported by the rules of procedure of some tribunals[55] and although there was a discretion on the part of the chairman of Supplementary Benefit Appeal Tribunals to exclude evidence which was clearly irrelevant or immaterial, that discretion had to be exercised with care and with a due regard to the necessity of allowing justice to be seen to be done.[56] In the Industrial Tribunal it has been suggested that there is no discretion to exclude evidence which would be admissible; there is clearly a discretion to include evidence which would be inadmissible.[57] Such a discretion is often referred to as a discretion to disregard the "strict" rules of evidence:[58]

---

[49] Indeed, expertise is a criterion for the appointment of members in many tribunals, see above, pp. 215–216.

[50] See below, pp. 889, 896–899.

[51] J. A. Smillie, "The Problem of 'Official Notice'—Reliance by Administrative Tribunals on the Personal Knowledge of their Members" [1975] P. L. 64.

[52] There are reported instances in K. Bell *et al.*, "National Insurance Local Tribunals: A Research Study" (1975) 4 *Journal of Social Policy* 1.

[53] See Sir William Wade and C. F. Forsyth, *Administrative Law* (7th ed., 1994), Chap. 15. All the tribunals we have so far considered have a judicial function.

[54] *R. v. Hull Prison Board of Visitors, ex p. St Germain (No. 2)* [1979] 1 W. L. R. 1401.

[55] See above, pp. 805–811.

[56] Although this proposition is taken from R(SB) 6/82 and related to Supplementary Benefit Appeal Tribunals, it is likely to have wider application as an expression of one of the requirements of natural justice. The dilemma for a tribunal chairman is that he or she may not be able to take a view about the relevance of evidence until it has been heard.

[57] *Rosedale Mouldings Ltd v. Sibley* [1980] I.C.R. 816. The first part of the proposition was doubted in *Snowball v. Gardner Merchant Ltd* [1987] I.C.R. 719, where the E.A.T. suggested that an industrial tribunal might properly "decide not to admit evidence which would be admissible under the strict rules of evidence, if, for example, it considered it to be unfair to do so or, as in the field of criminal law, its prejudicial effect outweighed its probative value" (p. 722).

[58] This is a significant phrase because it embodies the notion that some basic rules of evidence must still apply, even in tribunals. The phrase is also to be found in the standard terms of reference to arbitration under the small claims procedure in the county court, see above, pp. 802–804.

2. The Standard of Proof and the Burden of Proof

Proof beyond reasonable doubt is the standard adopted in the trial of criminal matters, and in civil cases the party bearing the burden of proof must establish the case on a balance of probabilities.[59] It is the latter standard that is adopted in tribunal proceedings, although some writers suggest that in particular tribunals the chairman and members may not always identify the standard as clearly as that.[60] The standard of proof is closely linked in reported decisions of tribunals with the question of the burden of proof and who bears it. In an early decision of a National Insurance Commissioner the formulation of Lord Birkenhead L.C. in *Lancaster v. Blackwell Colliery Co.*[61] was adopted:

"If the facts which are proved gave rise to conflicting inferences of equal degrees of probability, so that the choice between them is a mere matter of conjecture, then of course the applicant fails to prove his case, because it is plain in these matters the onus is on the applicant. But where the known facts are not equally balancing probabilities as to their respective value, and where a reasonable man might hold that the more probable conclusion is that for which the applicant contends, then the arbitrator is justified in drawing an inference in his favour."

The question of which party, if any, bears the burden of proof in tribunal proceedings really needs to be examined in respect of each individual tribunal,[62] starting from the assumption that it will normally be the party making the assertion who must prove it. That assumption, which derives from the position in the civil or criminal trial,[63] may not be appropriate where the proceedings are conducted on a truly inquisitorial basis with the tribunal reaching an evaluation of the information presented, yet it exercises a powerful influence.

It may not, of course, be necessary to rely on an assumption. Provision may have been made by statute,[64] or by procedural rules,[65] or in the decisions of

---

[59] For a full consideration of the standard of proof in civil and criminal matters, see C. Tapper, *Cross and Tapper on Evidence* (8th ed., 1995), pp. 158–175.

[60] There was particular doubt about S.B.A.T.s.: J. Fulbrook, *Administrative Justice and the Unemployed* (1978), p. 272. There are isolated examples where a higher standard of proof has been required, *e.g. Judd v. Minister of Pensions and National Insurance* [1966] 2 Q.B. 580, where the Divisional Court held that the Minister must establish his or her case beyond reasonable doubt in certain matters before the Pensions Appeal Tribunal.

[61] (1919) 12 B.W.C.C. 400 at p. 406, cited in C.I. 401/50.

[62] We have already made the point that it is impossible to generalise about tribunals. The examples which follow are from tribunals which we have described elsewhere.

[63] See C. Tapper, *Cross and Tapper on Evidence* (8th ed., 1995), pp. 119–155.

[64] Employment Rights Act 1996, 2 ss. 210(5), 163(2), providing that on a reference to a tribunal a person's employment during any period shall be deemed to have been continuous unless the contrary is proved, and that a dismissal shall be presumed to have been on account of redundancy, unless the contrary is proved. *Cf. Secretary of State for Employment v. Globe Elastic Thread Co. Ltd* [1980] A.C. 506. See also, Jobseekers Act 1995, s.14(1), excusing from disqualification for jobseeker's allowance those who can prove that they were not directly interested in the relevant trade dispute, and Employment Rights Act 1996 s. 98(4), which is interpreted as imposing no burden of proof on either party in respect of the reasonableness of a dismissal: *Post Office (Counters) Ltd v. Heavey* [1990] I.C.R. 1.

[65] *e.g.* The Immigration Appeals (Procedure) Rules 1984 (S.I. 1984 No. 2041), r.31, which deals specifically with the burden of proof and locates it on the appellant or the Secretary of State depending on the fact in issue.

particular tribunals,[66] stipulating where the burden of proof will lie. Where the jurisdiction of the tribunal is original, rather than appellate, it will also usually be clear where the burden lies, even if it may shift during the hearing. In the Industrial Tribunal, for example, when the applicant alleges that he or she has been unfairly dismissed it will be for the *employer* to prove that the dismissal was not unfair. If the employer disputes that there has been a dismissal the onus lies with the *employee* to prove that there has.[67]

In respect of some tribunals, no importance attaches to the question of burden of proof because the tribunal is arriving at a valuation rather than establishing a right or claim. The Rent Assessment Committee provides an example in that it is the obligation of the committee to arrive at its own judgment of a fair rent in the light of any representations made by the landlord and/or tenant.[68] Neither has the burden of proof—the committee must make its own decision which may not reflect the contentions of either party.

As regards Social Security Appeal Tribunals, the general position appears to be[69] that it is for the claimant to make out his or her entitlement[70]; that where there are exceptions from basic entitlements it is for those who assert that the exceptions apply to prove that they do[71]; and that once a decision has been made awarding benefit for a particular period, the onus of proving that grounds exist for reviewing the decision lies on those who assert that the existing decision is wrong.[72] However, the basic principle that it is for the claimant to establish entitlement is modified to the extent that the tribunal conforms to the rhetoric of adopting an inquisitorial rather than accusatorial approach.[73]

Thus, in *R. v. National Insurance Commissioner, ex p. Viscusi*,[74] which concerned a claim for industrial disablement benefit, Buckley L.J. had this to say:

"As regards the burden of proof, as Lord Denning M.R. has pointed out, these are not adversary proceedings: they are inquisitorial proceedings; and in such proceedings questions of burden of proof do not arise in the same way in which they would in proceedings between parties in a law suit. It is for the medical board or the medical appeal tribunal, as the case may

---

[66] *e.g.* The decision of the National Insurance Commissioner that the burden of proof on the allegation of cohabitation should lie with the insurance officer, R(G) 1/53. This decision has been consistently followed.

[67] See above, p. 809.

[68] See above, pp. 809–811.

[69] See J. Mesher in A. Kiralfy (ed.), *The Burden of Proof* (1987), Chap. 11, "Social Security Law". Before amalgamation, the position was less clear in S.B.A.T.s than N.I.L.T.s: see C. Yates, [1980] J.S.W.L. 273, 274–276.

[70] *R. v. National Insurance Commissioner, ex p. Hudson and Jones* [1970] 1 Q.B. 477; *R. v. National Insurance Commissioner, ex p. Viscusi* [1974] 1 W.L.R. 646; see also, *e.g.* R.(1) 32/61; R.(S.B.) 15/81; R.(S.B.) 8/84 ("It is for the claimant to establish his title to a single payment ..." (p. 882)).

[71] *e.g.* disqualifications for unemployment benefit under: the Social Security Contributions and Benefits Act 1992, s.28: R.(U) 2/60 (for the insurance officer (now adjudication officer) to prove that the claimant lost her job through misconduct); R.(U) 20/64 (for the insurance officer to prove that claimant left employment voluntarily; if this is done, it is for the claimant to prove that he or she did not leave without just cause): Mesher (1987), pp. 220–222. See now the Jobseekers Act 1995, s.19. Another example is discontinuance of benefit on the ground of cohabitation: R.(SB) 17/81; *Crake v. Supplementary Benefits Commission* [1982] 1 All E. R. 498.

[72] R. (I) 1/71; Mesher (1987), pp. 225–227.

[73] Mesher (1987), pp. 214–218. See above, pp. 807–808.

[74] [1974] 1 W.L.R. 646.

be, to investigate the case inquisitorially and to decide whether the claimant is entitled to benefit under the Act. But, of course, the fact remains that the medical board or the medical appeal tribunal, as the case may be, must be satisfied that the claimant is entitled to benefit: and so, in a sense, and subject to such statutory assumptions as are prescribed by the Act itself, it does rest with the claimant in the end to make out his claim.''

3. RELEVANCE AND ADMISSIBILITY

Detailed exclusionary rules have been developed in civil and criminal matters which render certain evidence inadmissible on the grounds that it would be unduly prejudicial or unreliable. Inevitably, the operation of such rules can lead to the exclusion of evidence which is highly relevant to the facts in issue. In tribunal proceedings the test of *relevance* is given priority with the consequence that very little evidence is likely to be excluded altogether from consideration. It may be that particular sorts of evidence are treated with some circumspection by the chairman and members, but it is expected that they will be able to assess the value and reliability of the evidence given and accord it appropriate weight in their deliberations. Many of the strict exclusionary rules of evidence result from a fear that a jury will be unable to judge satisfactorily how much significance to attach to inherently unreliable or prejudicial evidence,[75] and that fear should not be present when it is tribunal members who are adjudicating. Consequently, the strict rules of evidence are normally disregarded in favour of a much wider test of admissibility:

"... technical rules of evidence, however, form no part of the rules of natural justice. The requirement that a person exercising quasi-judicial functions must base his decision on evidence means no more than it must be based upon material which tends logically to show the existence or non-existence of facts relevant to the issue to be determined, or to show the likelihood or unlikelihood of the occurrence of some future event the occurrence of which would be relevant. It means that he must not spin a coin or consult an astrologer, but he may take into account any material which, as a matter of reason, has some probative value in the sense mentioned above. If it is capable of having any probative value, the weight to be attached to it is a matter for the person to whom Parliament has entrusted the task of deciding the issue.[76]"

This statement of Diplock L.J. has been cited with approval on a number of occasions and applied to different adjudications. The judge was actually dealing with the decision of a deputy Industrial Injuries Commissioner on a claim for industrial injury benefit, but his words have also been held to apply to an appeal to the Minister under the Town and Country Planning Act 1962[77]; an

---

[75] That is why the rules are stricter in criminal cases, but have been relaxed in civil cases where it is now highly unusual to have a jury, see pp. 789–793, above.
[76] *R. v. Deputy Industrial Injuries Commissioner, ex p. Moore* [1965] 1 Q.B. 456 at p. 488.
[77] *T. A. Miller Ltd v. Minister of Housing and Local Government* [1968] 1 W.L.R. 992.

adjudication by a prison Board of Visitors under the Prison Rules 1964[78]; and a formal investigation of a complaint of unlawful discrimination under the Race Relations Act 1976.[79] This general rule, that evidence is admissible in tribunal proceedings if it is of some "probative value", even though it would be inadmissible in court, has been embodied in procedural rules[80] and adopted in tribunal decisions.[81] It would appear that probative means relevant.

This rule of admissibility has been formulated in the context of the principles of natural justice and it is still the case that there is an obligation to ensure that each party has a full and fair hearing. In the Industrial Tribunal the general rule has been expressed in a slightly modified way to permit the exclusion of evidence where its admission, ". . . could in some way adversely affect the reaching of a proper decision in the case."[82] In social security tribunals the general rule was followed and many reported decisions expressed the power of the tribunals to admit any relevant evidence.[83] Indeed in Case R(IS) 5/93, the Social Security Commissioner (V. G. H. Hallett) held that the tribunal had erred in law in refusing to listen to hearsay evidence simply because it could not be tested by cross-examination.

The weight that is to be attached to relevant evidence is a matter for the tribunal and it is instructive to consider the approach of various tribunals in respect of hearsay evidence—the sort of evidence which tribunals have most often been invited to exclude.

4. HEARSAY

A hearsay statement is one which is made, orally or in writing, by a person other than the witness testifying and which is offered to prove a fact asserted in the statement.[84] An adjudication officer, investigating the question of whether a person in receipt of unemployment benefit (now jobseeker's allowance) is actually working, states that he has interviewed the claimant's next door neighbours who have told him that they saw the claimant leave his house every morning with a bag of tools, and that the claimant has admitted to them that he is "making a bit on the side". The statement of the adjudication officer, when put to the tribunal by the presenting officer at the hearing of the claimant's appeal against disqualification from benefit, would constitute hearsay.

The rules restricting the admissibility of hearsay evidence in civil courts and documentary evidence in criminal courts are much less stringent than they

---

[78] *R. v. Hull Prison Board of Visitors, ex p. St. Germain (No. 2)* [1979] 1 W.L.R. 1401.

[79] *R. v. Commission for Racial Equality, ex p. Cottrell* [1980] 1 W.L.R. 1580.

[80] *e.g.* The Immigration Appeals (Procedure) Rules 1984 (S.I. 1984 No. 2041) r.29 "An appellate authority may receive oral, documentary or other evidence of any fact which appears to the authority to be relevant to the appeal, notwithstanding that such evidence would be inadmissible in a court of law."

[81] See below, n. 84.

[82] *Coral Squash Clubs Ltd v. Matthews* [1979] I.C.R. 607, at p. 611. The Employment Appeal Tribunal in that case held that it was ". . . clear that an Industrial Tribunal is not bound by the strict rules of evidence but should exercise its good sense in weighing matters which come before it" (*ibid*)

[83] *e.g.* R.(I) 36/61, R.(I) 13/74, R.(U) 12/56, R.(U) 5/77.

[84] This is a very abbreviated definition. Interested students should consult C. Tapper, *Cross and Tapper on Evidence* (8th ed., 1995), Chap. XIII.

were,[85] but the rules concerning oral hearsay statements in criminal matters remain strict and their justification is said to be that hearsay evidence cannot properly be tested in court because of the absence of the maker of the statement; and depends upon the potentially inaccurate repetition of the statement by the witness.[86] Set against those difficulties is the undeniable fact, recognised by tribunals, that, "If tribunals were obliged to reject hearsay evidence . . . many claimants would find it quite impossible to establish their claims."[87]

In the Industrial Tribunal the policy merely seems to be to require the members of the tribunal to consider carefully what *weight* to attach to admitted hearsay evidence. In *Coral Squash Clubs Ltd v. Matthews*,[88] the Industrial Tribunal had refused to admit hearsay evidence about alleged licensing offences by the manager of a squash club, on the grounds that where the allegation was of a criminal offence and where the witnesses could have been located and produced the strict rule of exclusion should be applied. Their decision was reversed by the Employment Appeal Tribunal who ruled the evidence to be admissible, holding that the question of criminality was not in issue before the tribunal and that the failure to produce witnesses merely went to the weight of the evidence. The E.A.T. stated that a tribunal should, ". . . exercise its good sense in weighing the matters that come before it."[89]

Social security tribunals have taken much the same view. In an early decision, a Commissioner warned that the value of evidence which would be inadmissible in a court of law must be carefully considered and may be of very little weight,[90] and that phrasing has been adopted in subsequent decisions.[91] A particular type of hearsay which social security tribunals have been unwilling to accept is the statements of claimants' representatives. The Commissioner has said that such statements are not evidence and that where questions of fact are in issue on which a claimant or other qualified witness can speak they should be called to give evidence.[92] It has indeed been suggested that

"In practical terms, the result would seem to be that the use of hearsay is so severely restricted that it is virtually inadmissible. Indeed there is no reported case known to the authors in which a Commissioner has upheld the decision of an appeal tribunal which acted solely or principally on the basis of hearsay evidence."[93]

What is lacking is a clear policy on the criteria to be applied in determining the admissibility and reliability of hearsay evidence.

---

[85] Reforms were effected by the Civil Evidence Acts 1968 and 1995 and the Criminal Justice Act 1988.
[86] See Law Reform Committee, 13th Report, *Hearsay Evidence in Civil Proceedings* (Cmnd. 2964, 1966); Criminal Law Revision Committee, 11th Report, *Evidence (General)* (Cmnd. 4991, 1972), pp. 132–154.
[87] R.(U) 12/56.
[88] [1979] I.C.R. 607.
[89] *ibid.*, at p. 611.
[90] C.I. 97/49.
[91] R.(G) 1/51; R.(U) 12/56; R.(U) 5/77.
[92] R.(I) 36/61. The same principle applies to the adjudication officer's representative: R.(SB) 10/86.
[93] J. G. Logie and P. Q. Watchman, (1989) 8 C.J.Q. 109, 116.

5. WITNESSES

The requirement of natural justice that a party should be given a fair hearing is normally taken to comprehend the right to put his or her own case and correct or contradict statements that have been made by the other party.[94] This is likely to be achieved by the calling of witnesses. The right to call witnesses is set out in the procedural rules for the tribunals we have so far considered in detail.[95] However, the right appears to be subject to the discretion of the chairman. The chairman's obligation is to ensure a fair hearing, but he or she is not required to hear every witness that one of the parties might wish to call.

The position in social security tribunals was stated by a Commissioner in R(SB)6/82. The decision related to a S.B.A.T., but the principles are presumably equally applicable to the S.S.A.T.s. In that decision, the chairman of a S.B.A.T. had refused to hear a witness whom the claimant wished to call. On the facts, the Commissioner concluded that there had been an error of law since the witness appeared to have relevant and material evidence to give, and the case was remitted for re-hearing. On the general point the Commissioner said:

> "Tribunals are not bound to hear evidence which is clearly irrelevant or immaterial, whether it be from a witness actually giving evidence before the tribunal or from a proposed witness. The discretion to stop or curtail such evidence should, however, always be exercised with care, and in its exercise due regard should in my view always be paid to the necessity of allowing justice to be seen to be done."[96]

Industrial Tribunals would, no doubt, adopt similar criteria. Other aspects of the law of evidence relating to witnesses have been held to be applicable to tribunal adjudications, including the principles that a witness's testimony can be accepted even though not corroborated,[97] and that a witness's answers to questions concerning his or her credibility must be accepted as final (to avoid undue preoccupation with side-issues).[98]

C. THE ROLE OF THE CHAIRMAN

The references to the chairman in the last two sections of this chapter will already have demonstrated the significance of his role. The task of any chairman, whatever the nature of the tribunal, is to ensure that:

> ". . . the proceedings are conducted with scrupulous fairness to all parties and that the proper balance is struck between formality and informality. In particular, he must make sure at the outset that the parties fully understand

---

[94] See generally Sir William Wade and C.F. Forsyth *Administrative Law* (7th ed., 1994), Chap. 15.
[95] See above, pp. 812.
[96] R.(SB) 6/82, para. 5, a decision of Mr J. S. Watson.
[97] R.(I) 2/51; R.(SB) 33/85; R.(SB) 12/89 (social security tribunals).
[98] *Aberdeen Steak Houses Group plc v. Ibrahim* [1988] I.C.R. 550, E.A.T. (Industrial Tribunals); cf. *Snowball v. Gardner Merchant Ltd* [1987] I.C.R. 719, E.A.T.

the issue, especially when they are not legally represented; and he must ensure that they have an opportunity to present their cases adequately."[99]

Different chairmen may quite properly take different views about how to conduct tribunal hearings whilst pursuing the objectives referred to in the preceding paragraph, and the chairman's discretion is substantial. Since so much depends on the chairman it is important briefly to examine three issues—the appointment and qualification of chairmen; training provision; the adequacy of judicial and other safeguards intended to ensure procedural fairness.

1. APPOINTMENT AND QUALIFICATION

The formal position on appointment and qualification is set out in Chapter 4.[1] The involvement of the Lord Chancellor in the appointment of the majority of tribunal chairmen is intended to demonstrate, and preserve, their independence of the relevant government department. As to qualification, the controversy is over the desirability of requiring that a chairman should be legally qualified.

The inherent difficulty in tribunal adjudication will by now have become apparent. It is desirable to achieve a high standard of decision-making coupled with demonstrable procedural fairness, whilst retaining the informality, cheapness and speed which are meant to be the hallmarks of the tribunal. Lawyer-chairmen seem to have less difficulty in achieving the former than the latter. Two examples will suffice.

When the Industrial Tribunal was created, the procedural rules specifically required the chairman, in setting the procedure, to seek to avoid formality so far as it was appropriate to do so.[2] All chairmen of Industrial Tribunals are lawyers of not less than seven years' standing[3] and the appellate body is presided over by a High Court judge.[4] The Industrial Tribunal has become formal, with predictable procedure and a large body of case-law.[5] That can hardly be a coincidence.

The Supplementary Benefit Appeal Tribunal was accustomed to non-lawyer chairmen. There was no prohibition on the appointment of lawyers but by 1980, after 14 years of existence,[6] only one chairman in four was legally qualified.[7]

---

[99] *Report of the Council on Tribunals 1959*, p. 6.
[1] Above, pp. 214–215.
[2] See above, pp. 808–809.
[3] Above, p. 215, n. 84.
[4] For the composition of the Employment Appeal Tribunal, see above, pp. 66–67.
[5] It has attracted both judicial and academic criticism on that account. The criticism reflects a particular view of the functions of an I.T. See the observations of Lord Denning M.R. in *Walls Meat Co. Ltd v. Khan* [1979] I.C.R. 52, at p. 56; Lawton L.J. in *Clay Cross (Quarry Services) Ltd v. Fletcher* [1979] I.C.R. 1, at p. 8; Ormrod L.J. in *National Vulcan Engineering Insurance Group Ltd v. Wade* [1978] I.C.R. 800, at p. 808; Dunn L.J. in *Methven v. Cow Industrial Ltd* [1980] I.C.R. 463, at p. 470.
[6] S.B.A.T.s were created by the Ministry of Social Security Act 1966 as the successor to national assistance appeal tribunals.
[7] N. Harris, "The Appointment of Legally Qualified Chairmen for S.B.A.T.s" (1982) 132 N.L.J. 495.

Kathleen Bell's research.[8] published in 1975, was not especially complimentary to the existing chairmen:

> "... generally speaking, they did not fully comprehend the complexities of the work ... too often proceedings were unsystematic, inconsistent and over-influenced by sympathy or otherwise. Separate deliberations were frequently non-existent when the appellant was absent, and in other instances were quite often somewhat rambling and of rather poor quality. We examined a large number of official Reports of Proceedings, the majority of which did not adequately record a reasoned decision."[9]

This view was supported by other commentators.[10] Following the Bell Report there was a determined effort to appoint more lawyers as S.B.A.T. chairmen. Following the merging of S.B.A.T.s and N.I.L.T.s into Social Security Appeal Tribunals,[11] the chairmen of the S.S.A.T.s are all lawyers of at least five years' standing,[12] and a regional and national structure of full-time chairmen has been created.[13]

S.S.A.T.s are obviously more closely modelled on the N.I.L.T. than the S.B.A.T., and expected to achieve the standards set by the N.I.L.T. The N.I.L.T. certainly achieved a reputation as one of the best models of an informal tribunal with a qualified chairman.[14] In the view of Professor Lewis, who had some harsh criticism of S.B.A.T.s, N.I.L.T.s [were] "... usually a model of balancing informal expertise with order and legality."[15]

The debate over the desirability of lawyer-chairmen involves many of the same arguments that are deployed in respect of legal representation at tribunals.[16] The skills of the lawyer are thought to lie in order, objectivity and procedure rather than speed, informality and expertise. The Franks Committee were early advocates of the legally-qualified chairman. "Objectivity in the treatment of cases and the proper sifting of facts are most often best secured by having a legally qualified chairman."[17] The Committee also noted that there had been substantial agreement on this matter among witnesses. Later writers have advanced further arguments[18]: the ability of lawyers to uphold basic legal principles in the field of administrative adjudications[19]; the maintenance of firm

---

[8] *Research Study on Supplementary Benefit Appeal Tribunals, Review of Main Findings: Conclusions: Recommendations* (HMSO, 1975).

[9] *ibid.*, at p. 6.

[10] A. Frost and C. Howard, *Representation and Administrative Tribunals* (1977); M. Herman, *Administrative Justice and Supplementary Benefits* (1972); N. Lewis, "Supplementary Benefits Appeal Tribunals" [1973] P.L. 257.

[11] Above, p. 68. These arrangements came into effect in April 1984 and there were transitional provisions which have now eliminated all non-lawyer chairmen.

[12] *ibid.* The period was formerly seven years.

[13] There is a President of the Independent Tribunal Service and a number of Regional Chairmen with supervisory and training responsibilities.

[14] There appears to have been no specific requirement that chairmen of N.I.L.T.s should be qualified lawyers, but it was an almost unbroken rule of practice.

[15] N. Lewis, "Supplementary Benefit Appeal Tribunals" [1973] P.L. 275.

[16] See below, pp. 822–835.

[17] Report of the Committee on Administrative Tribunals and Enquiries (Cmnd. 218, 1957), para. 55.

[18] They are collected and analysed by J. Fulbrook, *Administrative Justice and the Unemployed* (1978), pp. 215–219.

[19] H. W. R. Wade, *Towards Administrative Justice* (1963), p. 43.

control over tribunals bred out of confidence and expertise[20]; the natural inclination of lawyers to control bias and prejudice in the presentation of cases; and
the grasp of legal questions which is relevant in most areas of tribunal work.[21]

These views have not gone unopposed,[22] and even the advocates of lawyer-
chairmen have not usually gone so far as to suggest that chairmanship should
be the exclusive province of lawyers,[23] yet the recent developments have been
along that line. It is unfortunate that other very suitable people may be excluded
from chairmanship. The presence of a lawyer-chairman is certainly no guarantee
of good chairmanship; a recent survey found that in one of every six S.S.A.T.
hearings observed, "the chairman's conduct of the case was in our view open
to serious criticism", citing particular examples of cases where the chairman
was "accusatory in approach", "too dominant" or "maintained a severe, stern
tone of voice throughout."[24]

2. TRAINING

Arrangements for the training of tribunal chairman and (especially) members
have long been recognised to be inadequate. In recent years steps have been
taken to improve the position, but the matter is yet to receive the attention and
the resources that are necessary.[25]

3. CORRECTION OF PROCEDURAL IRREGULARITIES

In the major tribunals we have so far considered there is a provision for a
right of appeal to an appellate body who have the power to correct procedural
irregularities.[26] Where there is no appellate body[27] or where the appeal does not
properly deal with the defect alleged judicial review may be sought. That remedy
is considered in Chapter 17.[28] Both the existence of the appellate body and the
ultimate oversight of the courts provide the safeguard against the wrongful exercise of chairman's considerable discretion.

---

[20] H. L. Elcock, *Administrative Justice* (1969), pp. 50–53.
[21] Especially in the Industrial Tribunals, and in the determination of claims in respect of industrial injuries.
[22] R. M. Titmuss, "Welfare 'Rights', Law and Discretion" (1971) 42 *Political Quarterly*, pp. 113–132.
[23] The Franks Committee (above, n. 17) recommended that, ". . . the appointment of persons without legal qualification should not be ruled out when they are particularly suitable." (para. 55).
[24] Baldwin, Wikeley and Young, *Judging Social Security* (1992), pp. 115–119.
[25] See above, pp. 216–217.
[26] The Employment Appeal Tribunal for Industrial Tribunals, and the Social Security Commissioners for S.S.A.T.s.
[27] *e.g.* there "may be" no appeal from the Immigration Appeal Tribunal.
[28] pp. 964–972.

D. THE ROLE OF THE "WING" MEMBERS

It is a distinctive feature of the tribunal system that it gives considerable scope for lay participation in adjudication. Some of the alleged disadvantages of lawyer-chairmen may be moderated by the presence of lay people as members of the tribunal.

The appointment of the lay members has already been described,[29] and there is comparatively little in the way of research work into how the laymen approach their task and the nature of their relationship with the chairman.[30] At least in relation to social security tribunals there is doubt about the extent of their participation in the hearing and the adjudication, although it is recognised that a lack of participation may result from the absence of training and guidance. Indeed, a recent survey found that few wing members said very much, that two-thirds of those members who remained silent were entirely passive and that many "can be said to have given the appearance of being seriously out of their depth." Furthermore it appeared that members frequently failed to participate actively in the deliberations.[31]

E. REPRESENTATION BEFORE TRIBUNALS

". . . it is desirable that every applicant before any tribunal should be able to present his case in person or to obtain representation."[32]

In order to achieve this objective, the Royal Commission on Legal Services asserted that tribunal procedure would need to be simplified wherever possible; the existing schemes for representation by lay persons would need to be developed and funded; and legal aid would need to be made available for certain cases.[33] These findings were based on a significant amount of evidence received by the Commission[34] which was in addition to the published research already available.[35] An important study was more recently commissioned by the Lord Chancellor's Department, covering Social Security Appeal Tribunals, Industrial Tribunals, Mental Health Review Tribunals and Immigration Adjudicators.[36] The

---

[29] Above, pp. 215–216.
[30] See J. Fulbrook, *Administrative Justice and the Unemployed* (1978), pp. 226–229; J. Baldwin, N. Wikeley and R. Young, (1992), pp. 143–153.
[31] Baldwin, Wikeley and Young (1992), pp. 146–147.
[32] R.C.L.S. Vol. 1 para. 15.11, p. 169.
[33] *ibid.*
[34] The Commission received evidence from both lawyers and non-lawyers active in the tribunal representation field. Its own research is contained in Vol. 2. Section 4, pp. 91–101.
[35] Notably the studies carried out by Professor Kathleen Bell, *Research Study on Supplementary Benefit Appeal Tribunals, Review of Main Findings: Conclusions: Recommendations* (D.H.S.S. 1975): "National Insurance Local Tribunals," *Journal of Social Policy*, Vols.3.4 and 4.1 (1974/5). Other studies include R. Lawrence *Tribunal Representation* (1980); E. Kessler *et al.*, *Combatting Poverty; C.A.Bx., Claimants and Tribunals* (NACAB Occasional Paper No. 11, 1980); R. Lawrence, "Solicitors and Tribunals" [1980] J.S.W.L. 13; *Tribunal Assistance, the Chapeltown experience* (NACAB Occasional Paper, No. 14, 1982).
[36] H. Genn and Y. Genn, *The Effectiveness of Representation at Tribunals* (L.C.D., 1989), discussed by R. Young, (1990) 9 C.J.Q. 16 and T. Mullen, (1990) 53 M.L.R. 230.

whole question of tribunal representation is one which has continued to attract much attention, especially because of the large numbers of cases currently being determined by tribunals.[37]

In this section we consider six related issues, the first three relating to the present position and the second three to possible future provision of representation. What are the rules about representation? Who are the representatives? What do they do? Should lawyers be involved in representation less often, more often, or not at all? Should legal involvement be funded under the Legal Aid Scheme? In what way, if at all, should schemes of representation by lay persons be developed?

1. THE RULES

Whether or not there is an absolute right to legal representation protected by the principles of natural justice,[38] it is rare for such a right to be specifically denied by tribunal rules.[39] However, a right to legal representation is only useful if the applicant has sufficient funds to pay a lawyer[40]; can find one who is competent in the field; and if the case is one in which the skills of a lawyer will be significant. As we shall see, representation by lawyers in tribunals is not generally common.

Some tribunals place restrictions on representation by persons other than lawyers,[41] but the usual provision is for an unfettered right to representation.[42] The ability of the applicant to select an appropriate representative has resulted in the appearance before tribunals of a wide variety of representatives.

2. WHO ARE THE REPRESENTATIVES?

Some distinctions must be made between the different tribunals in that they attract different representatives.

The study by Genn and Genn showed that Citizens Advice Bureaux were the most frequent representatives at S.S.A.T.s (closely followed by family or friends); the U.K.I.A.S. before Immigration Adjudicators; lawyers and trade unions at Industrial Tribunals; and solicitors at M.H.R.T.s.[43] The proportion of all appellants represented at the hearing varied considerably. 16 per cent of

---

[37] See Chap. 2, pp. 52–56.
[38] See Sir William Wade and C. F. Forsyth, *Administrative Law* (7th ed., 1994), at p. 540.
[39] The only exception seems to be the service committee to the Family Health Services Authority which hears complaints against general practitioners made by their patients. Before that Tribunal paid representation by a lawyer is not permitted, he or she may only appear as a "friend" and not address the Committee or put questions to witnesses: National Health Service (Service Committees and Tribunal) Regulations 1992 S(4). (S.I. 1992 No. 664), Sched. 4, para. 5(4).
[40] Save in exceptional circumstances, see p. 825, below.
[41] For example, representation by non-lawyers is only permitted at the discretion of the Performing Rights Tribunal, the Lands Tribunal and the Commons Commissioners, see R.C.L.S. Vol. 1, para. 15.3.
[42] See the procedural rules of the tribunals considered at pp. 805–811, above.
[43] Genn and Genn (1989), pp. 19, 33, 46, 58. R.C.L.S. Vol. 2, Section 4, Tables 4.7; Bell, *Research on S.B.A.T.s*, at pp. 15–16 (see n. 35, above).

S.S.A.T. appellants were represented, but only 12 per cent by agencies or individuals with experience of representation or with any special expertise.[44] In contrast, 90 per cent of appellants at immigration hearings, 58 per cent of applicants and 73 per cent of respondents at Industrial Tribunals, and 61 per cent of applicants at M.H.R.T.s were represented by someone other than a relative or friend.[45]

Although there will always be some who defy categorisation, it is possible to discern five groupings from amongst those people who undertake representation.

First, there are those who represent at tribunals as a result of a *professional interest in their members or clients.* Lest that definition would appear to include lawyers we would stress that we are referring here principally to trade union representatives, employers' organisation representatives and social workers who go to a tribunal with a client. Representation has been a significant feature of the legal services supplied by trade unions to their members,[46] and this is particularly marked in the field of national insurance, industrial injuries and employment issues. This has resulted in the trade unions taking a cautious view over the future development of lay or legal representation. They appear not to be anxious to have competitors providing alternative services to their members.[47] Social workers have been involved in the work of S.B.A.T.s and S.S.A.T.s. This group of representatives should be in a position to offer effective representation as a result of skill and experience acquired in particular tribunals.

The second group consists of representatives provided by *voluntary organisations* for the benefit of their members. The Benson Commission noted the work done by the Royal British Legion in Pensions Appeal Tribunals,[48] and the Claimants' Unions have specialised in the area of social security tribunals.[49]

The third group consists of representatives provided by *generalist or specialist advice agencies* for the benefit of anyone who wishes to consult the agency and accept an offer of help. The Citizens Advice Bureaux have provided such a service to the public,[50] and there are other examples of advice agencies becoming involved in representation as an incidental part of their general service. Specialist agencies, like the Child Poverty Action Group, provide representation in their own field.[51] The United Kingdom Immigration Advisory Service (U.K.I.A.S.) provides an interesting example of a specialist agency set up with public funds to deal with enquiries on a particular topic. It was described by the Benson

---

[44] Genn and Genn (1989), pp. 19–22.

[45] *ibid.*, pp. 32–35, 43–53, 56–59.

[46] G. Latta and R. Lewis, "Trade Union Legal Services" (1974) *XII British Journal of Industrial Relations* 561; R. Lewis and G. Latta, "Union Legal Services" (1973) 123 N.L.J. 386.

[47] See G. Bindman, "Trade Unions and Legal Services" *LAG Bulletin*, March 1979, 56.

[48] R.C.L.S., Vol. 1, para. 15.16.

[49] On the role of the Claimants' Unions, see H. Rose, "Who Can de-label the Claimant," in M. Adler and A. Bradley, *Justice, Discretion and Poverty* (1976).

[50] Although it is fair to point out that much has depended on the ability and willingness of volunteers in a particular bureau to undertake the task of representation, and there is considerable pressure and CABx resources. The coverage has consequently been patchy. A majority of CABx provide a representation service of some sort, although not necessarily for more than the occasional case: interview with a NACAB representative cited by J. Baldwin, (1989) 8 C.J.Q. 24, 36. By 1995, in 86 per cent of bureaux, advisers undertook representation themselves: NACAB Annual Report 1994–95, p. 21.

[51] CPAG can take up a limited number of more complex cases such as appeals to the Commissioners, and then only if referred by local advisers: *National Welfare Benefits Handbook* 1995–96, p. 421.

Commission as, "... a unique counselling and advocacy service dealing with one field of tribunal work and manned by a full time salaried staff."[52]

The fourth group consists of representatives provided by various specific *tribunal representation projects*. The C.A.B. service has been associated with major schemes in Birmingham, Leeds, Sheffield, Newcastle and Wolverhampton and has also provided the stimulus for other local initiatives.[53] The Free Representation Unit provides representation before tribunals in London and is staffed by young barristers and bar students.[54] The various tribunal representation schemes have come under close scrutiny, since they may provide a model for the development of lay representation. They are all organised on a different basis and attract funds from different sources but this variety may prove fruitful in the evaluation of alternative models. We consider their organisation further, at a later point in this chapter.

The fifth group consists of *lawyers*. We have already noted that lawyers do provide some representation in tribunals, but this is normally at the expense of the client. Very few tribunals have rules as to costs which would allow the recovery of legal expenses.[55] Some representation is funded publicly but it is exceptional. Legal aid is available for representation before the Lands Tribunal, the Commons Commissioners and the Employment Appeal Tribunal, and the legal advice scheme is available for representation at Mental Health Review Tribunals—assuming that the applicant can satisfy the general criteria of eligibility.[56] The legal advice scheme may be used to fund preparatory work for tribunal hearings and to pay for a solicitor to "assist" a client at the hearing.[57] Assistance short of representation can no doubt prove very irritating for the tribunal and it appears that solicitors may have been remunerated for assistance which has spilled over into representation.

There must inevitably be a composite group of "everybody else." Particularly in S.B.A.T.s, the category of friends and relatives as representatives was significant. As we shall shortly demonstrate, the role of a "representative" can be very restricted, and it may be sufficient that his attendance has ensured the attendance of the applicant. That job can be done as well (possibly better) by a friend as by an advocate.

3. What do Representatives do?

This may seem to be an odd question. However, we use it to demonstrate that the assistance offered by a representative may range more widely than simply putting the applicant's case at a hearing.

From the outset, the representative is likely to be involved in an advice-giving role whether he or she is an expert in the field or not.[58] It is obvious that those

---

[52] R.C.L.S. Vol. 1 para. 15.17: See further, p. 835, below.
[53] See further, below, pp. 834–835.
[54] See above, p. 641.
[55] See above, p. 539.
[56] For legal aid, see pp. 568–580 above; for advice by way of representation (ABWOR) see pp. 495–496 above.
[57] See above, p. 493. The legal advice scheme only covers representation if regulations so provide: Legal Aid Act 1988, s.8(2); ABWOR is only available in a limited range of situations.
[58] Even the next-door neighbour might be asked whether or not to appeal!

experienced representatives who have gained a thorough knowledge of their subject are able to evaluate the merits, and likely success, of the applicant's case and can act accordingly. This advisory role is significant because it may operate to exclude the weak and unmeritorious cases at an early stage.[59] If the effect of this screening is to allow the representative only to pursue those cases believed to be worthwhile, he or she gains an enhanced reputation with the tribunal in respect of the cases that are pursued through to a hearing. Moreover, the scarce resources of advice agencies and the like should not be used to support hopeless cases.

There are some reservations expressed about the validity of this advisory role, not least because the adviser may be constituting him- or herself as the adjudicator rather than the tribunal, and coming between the applicant and the tribunal. It is argued that applicants should be given the confidence and expertise to use the system themselves rather than experience the "interference" of another expert who would come to some tidy arrangement with the tribunal leaving the claimant as isolated as ever.[60] This is a minority view, however, and most of the representation schemes that have been established place emphasis on the provision of advice by an "expert" at an early stage.[61] There is also the reservation expressed by some about

"doing the Government's job for them. You are telling someone to leave the country or not to . . . claim a benefit. You are the soft police."[62]

A second function of a representative may be to act as a negotiator on behalf of the applicant with a view to effecting a settlement of the problem.[63] We noted the importance of settlements in the civil process in Chapter II[64]—they also have their place in the tribunal process. The intervention of a third party on behalf of an applicant may produce a change in the decision which satisfies the claimant. This might be called anti-representation since it has the effect of preventing a tribunal hearing, but it benefits both the applicant and the tribunal.[65]

A third function of representation may be simply to ensure the attendance of the applicant. This is sometimes referred to as a "hand-holding exercise."[66] The published figures demonstrate that an applicant has a higher chance of success at a tribunal if he or she attends, whether or not represented, than if he or she does not attend.[67] Claimants who receive an unfavourable decision on their claim

---

[59] See Genn and Genn (1989), pp. 134–135.
[60] The Claimants' Union recognises a "right" to be represented whatever the merits of the case might appear to be. See generally, R. Lawrence, *Tribunal Representation* (1980), p. 18; H. Rose, "Who Can De-Label the Claimant?" in M. Adler and A. Bradley, *op. cit.*
[61] Some of the tribunal representation schemes operate on a "consultancy" basis whereby volunteer lay representatives themselves receive help and guidance at the early stages of a possible appeal (see, for example, the West Midlands project—*Combatting Poverty*, n. 35 above). Others give a direct service to the claimant but rely heavily on the expertise of the representatives.
[62] Quotation from a Law Centre, cited by Genn and Genn (1989), pp. 134–135.
[63] *ibid.*, pp. 135–138.
[64] Above, pp. 554–563.
[65] One of the arguments advanced in favour of the extension of representation is its effect in diminishing the caseload of tribunals.
[66] Particularly by the Citizens Advice Bureaux. See the NACAB Administrative Circular (1974), cited in R. Lawrence, *Tribunal Representation* (1980), p. 59. This circular is no longer current, but the function remains the same.
[67] K. Bell, *op. cit.* (above, n. 35); Genn and Genn (1989), p. 68 (S.S.A.T.s); this is not a surprising finding. Attendance at least allows the tribunal the possibility of questioning the claimant.

may immediately give notice of appeal without giving thought to how to pursue the appeal.[68] On receipt of the appeal papers they decide not to go along to the hearing because the case is not arguable, or they are frightened, or ignorant of the process, or no longer interested. If they seek advice at all, they may simply need the reassurance that someone will attend the tribunal with them and help them through the procedure—not necessarily as an advocate but as a friend. Once at the hearing, with the presence of a supporter they are able to respond sufficiently to the tribunal to allow the case fully to be considered.

A fourth function is that of preparing the case for the hearing, good preparation being fundamental to the success of appeals. This includes interviewing the client, collecting documentary evidence, arranging for witnesses to attend and researching the law. Most appellants and applicants are likely to have difficulty in identifying the facts relevant to the case and securing the necessary evidence.[69]

This may seem quite a late stage to be arriving at the representative's job of representing. At the hearing, the function of the representative is to put forward the applicant's case without coming completely between the applicant and the tribunal. The representative should not forget that the tribunal will be interested to hear from the applicant directly.[70] The need to marshal the arguments for the benefit of the tribunal will be dictated partly by the complexity of the subject matter and partly by the procedure adopted.[71] The skills required are not necessarily those of the advocate—but it helps the tribunal if the representative can present a logical, orderly, relevant analysis of the issues and the evidence. Statistics show that the represented claimant is better off at a tribunal.[72] This point is confirmed by the study by Genn and Genn,[73] which also indicates that specialist representatives have the greatest effect on the probability of success.[74]

Finally, the expertise gained by the representative and his or her familiarity with the system may be used for the benefit of others in the exchange of information and pressure for reform. In the informal world of tribunals the shared experience is invaluable. This sharing may be formal, through publications,[75] or informal, through word of mouth but it is undoubtedly a factor in the increasing success of lay representatives.

Much of this section has been directed towards the less formal tribunals and the experience of the Industrial Tribunal is somewhat different. There, the actual representation at the hearing takes on the major significance and the other

---

[68] This does not mean that a high proportion of the recipients of adverse D.S.S. decisions appeal: see Genn and Genn (1989), pp. 130–134.

[69] Genn and Genn (1989), pp. 138–147.

[70] The Social Security Commissioner has, on occasion, criticised a representative who appears to have dominated the hearing to the exclusion of the applicant. (See R.(I) 36/61).

[71] In the Industrial Tribunal, for example, the representative has his or her job defined by the adoption of a fairly standard, adversarial procedure. See pp. 808–809 above.

[72] Although there are some reservations about the interpretation of the evidence: R. Lawrence, *Tribunal Representation* (1980), pp. 19–20.

[73] Genn and Genn (1989), Chap. 3. Other factors independently associated with success were the type of case, number of witnesses, geographical location (S.S.A.T.s) and the identity of the chair or the adjudicator (S.S.A.T.s, I.T.s, Immigration hearings).

[74] Welfare rights centres, tribunal units and law centres for social security appeals, U.K.I.A.S. and lawyers for immigration hearings.

[75] For example, information is disseminated through NACAB and CPAG literature (*e.g.*, respectively, through *The Adviser* and the *Welfare Rights Bulletin*), and other periodicals.

functions are consequently diminished.[76] It is not surprising that with considerable lawyer representation the emphasis has been placed upon advocacy.

Overall it was the clear conclusion of the study by Genn and Genn that representation of appellants and applicants increases the accuracy of tribunal decision-making and improves the fairness of the process by which decisions are reached.[77] Arguments that tribunals proceedings are informal and simple, and that representation is accordingly unnecessary and undesirable, are ill-founded.[78] The view of tribunals, representatives and presenting officers in the four areas studied

> "was that much of the law with which they were concerned was complex and the adjudicative function of tribunals was often a highly technical forensic process."[79]

Moreover,

> "the experience of unrepresented appellants and applicants indicates that, even in the most informal hearings, they have difficulty in expressing themselves; they do not understand the relevance of the rules and regulations that are quoted to them; and when they lose, frequently leave in a state of disappointment and frustration."[80]

It was the unanimous belief of representatives interviewed that "no matter how well-intentioned tribunals might be, it was impossible to compensate for lack of representation"; on the other hand, the majority of chairs of S.S.A.T.s and industrial tribunals believed that they could compensate for lack of representation. The observation of hearings for the purpose of the study tended to confirm the former view.[81]

Finally, some fears have been expressed about the extent to which an involvement with representation will inevitably result in a commitment to reform of the system, an over-identification with the position of the applicants, or an engagement in political activity.[82] How objective/disinterested can a representative remain? This anxiety has been examined and answered effectively by David Bull, whose analysis of the range of advocacy and its implications for the representatives is very convincing.[83]

4. SHOULD LAWYERS BE INVOLVED MORE? LESS? AT ALL?

The answer to this particular question depends upon the skills which lawyers bring to tribunal representation and the effect that the deployment of those skills

---

[76] The negotiation function is, to some extent, undertaken by the conciliation officers of A.C.A.S., see above, p. 646.
[77] Genn and Genn (1989), pp. 247–248.
[78] *ibid.*
[79] *ibid.*, p. 244; and generally Chap. 4.
[80] *ibid.*, pp. 246–247; and generally Chap. 7.
[81] *ibid.*, pp. 215–216.
[82] This has been a particular fear of NACAB who are very sensitive about allegations of political involvement and campaigning.
[83] D. Bull, "The Anti-Discretion Movement in Britain: Fact or Phantom?" [1980] J.S.W.L. 65.

is likely to have on the style and procedure of tribunals. It further depends upon the objectives which a system of tribunals seeks to achieve, and upon the complexity of the law which is being administered, the nature of the particular tribunal under consideration and upon the nature of the particular case under consideration, for there may be especial circumstances which warrant the attention of a lawyer.

Given all these variables it is difficult to formulate a single answer. Perhaps the convenient starting-point is to ask whether lawyers have a place in tribunal representation at all. Against the proposition that a citizen should have a right to legal representation in all forms of judicial or quasi-judicial proceedings[84] may be put the assertion that lawyers "spoil" tribunal adjudication by detracting from those qualities which tribunals are alleged to display, namely speed, informality, cheapness and expertise.[85] In particular, it has been argued that, in respect of areas in which discretion is an important element, the introduction of "legalism" is likely to hinder the operation of discretion to the disadvantage of the claimant.[86] These arguments have not prevailed[87] and there is, apparently, only one example of a tribunal which positively prohibits legal representation.[88] It would certainly be difficult now to make a case for a blanket prohibition on legal representation, and it is generally accepted that lawyers have *some* part to play.

The more difficult question is the *extent* to which lawyer-representation is desirable. In practice, this question is closely linked with the possibility of providing public funds for such representation, for without funding the likelihood that an applicant will be able to pay for the services of a lawyer is slim.[89] However, until a positive case has been made for legal representation, funds will not be made available. What is the strength of the case?

There has been comparatively little evidence of the extent to which lawyers are involved in tribunal work or, incidentally, of their likely response if money were to be made available to allow them to undertake more.[90] Statistics from the research studies that have been done demonstrate the very low proportion of cases in social security tribunals which have lawyer representatives[91] and although the proportion is much higher in Industrial Tribunals[92] there is little to indicate whether a few firms provide representation as a specialist service or

---

[84] See above, p. 823.
[85] For the virtues (alleged) of tribunal adjudication, see above, pp. 44–45. It is interesting to note that in the county court small claims procedure (see above, pp. 802–804.) legal representation is not prohibited but it is discouraged because of the no-costs rule. Some commentators would have argued for a complete ban on lawyers.
[86] R. M. Titmuss, "Welfare 'Rights', Law and Discretion," (1971) 42 *Political Quarterly*, pp. 113–132. The subject is discussed fully in J. Fulbrook, *Administrative Justice and the Unemployed* (1978), pp. 276–293.
[87] Indeed, in the social security field benefits (first supplementary benefit, now income support) have become rule—rather than discretion-based and there is no longer a right of appeal to a tribunal in respect of the main remaining discretion-based benefit (social fund payments).
[88] The service committees of the Family Health Services Authority, see p. 823, n. 39, above.
[89] This is especially the case in social security tribunals where there is likely to be only a relatively small amount of money at stake. Costs are not normally awarded by tribunals, see p. 539, above.
[90] R. Lawrence, "Solicitors and Tribunals" [1980] J.S.W.L. 13; N. Harris, "Solicitors and Supplementary Benefit Cases" (1983) 34 N.I.L.Q. 144.
[91] K. Bell, *op. cit.* below, n. 44; R.C.L.S. Vol. 2, Section 4; Genn and Genn (1989), p. 20.
[92] R.C.L.S. Vol. 2, Section 4, Tables 4.7, 4.8; Genn and Genn (1989), pp. 44–45, 50.

whether most firms will undertake this type of work.[93] If the Industrial Tribunal is any guide the presence of lawyer representatives is likely to formalise procedure and reinforce the adversarial style of the proceedings. This fear has been expressed also in respect of social security tribunals, not least because the criticisms levelled at such tribunals by lawyers tend to focus on the failure to follow a consistent and clear judicial process in adjudication.[94] The lawyers' response to such a failure is normally to formulate procedural rules and safeguards to be operated by lawyers.

The research conducted by Professor Bell indicated that there was no great enthusiasm amongst appellants for professional advocates; rather they were anxious to see the tribunal play a more *enabling* role thereby improving the opportunity for appellants to put their own case.[95] Few among the tribunals and representatives interviewed for the study by Genn and Genn believed that lawyers were necessarily best equipped to conduct tribunal representations; the most common view was that specialisation and experience were the most important qualifications.[96]

Despite fears that lawyerly skills may frustrate some of the objectives of tribunal adjudication, the prevailing view is that legal representation is desirable in particular circumstances. This view is based mainly upon the combined arguments of legal complexity in certain fields and the importance of the issues to the individual claimant. The Royal Commission on Legal Services was content merely to state, ". . . there are cases when a denial of legal aid for representation by a lawyer will put the applicant at a disadvantage. We have in mind, for example, cases before Supplementary Benefit Appeal Tribunals which involve allegations of cohabitation or dishonesty, and some of the claims before Industrial Tribunals which involve difficult problems of law and fact."[97] The study by Genn and Genn concluded that while the main development should be in the direction of increased funding to lay agencies, this would not provide the complete answer. There might be a need for skilled legal representation before the explicitly adversarial Industrial Tribunals, and to fill gaps left by the uneven geographical coverage of lay advice and representation agencies.[98]

The Benson Commission had considered much evidence on the provision of legal representation in tribunals and concluded that there are *some* cases before *all* tribunals in which it was necessary. The identification of those cases is problematic, but some indication of the factors which might necessitate legal representation is given by the tests formulated to govern the granting of legal aid. The assumption seems to have been made that legal representation will only really be available when legal aid is available[99] and we discuss in the next section the criteria which might be adopted in determining eligibility.

---

[93] R. Lawrence, *op. cit.* n. 35 above, inclines to the former view.

[94] K. Bell, *Research Study on Supplementary Benefit Appeal Tribunals. Review of Main Findings: Conclusions: Recommendations*, (DHSS, 1975), at pp. 19–20.

[95] *ibid.*, p. 18.

[96] Genn and Genn (1989), p. 245; generally pp. 171–178, 193–198, 210–215.

[97] R.C.L.S. Vol. 1 para. 15.24.

[98] Genn and Genn (1989), pp. 249–250.

[99] This is why the two issues of whether lawyers should be involved, and whether they should be paid out of the Legal Aid Fund are extremely difficult to disentangle. When they are needed, they should be paid for . . . See the evidence of The Law Society in *R.C.L.S. Memorandum No. 3* (1978). Evidence to the same effect was received from the Council on Tribunals, the President of Industrial Tribunals and other individuals. This view was supported by the Lord Chancellor's Advisory Committee on Legal Aid.

5. WHEN SHOULD LEGAL AID BE AVAILABLE FOR TRIBUNALS?

There is no serious dispute that it would be inadvisable for legal aid to be made immediately available for all cases in all tribunals. Different reasons would be given by different people. The expense; the inappropriateness; the difficulty of applying the "merits" test[1]; the availability of skilled lay representation; the possible lack of interest amongst the solicitors' profession[2] would all be reasons used to reject the extension of legal aid to all cases. There is an equal measure of agreement about the need to extend legal aid to *some* tribunal cases, but two difficulties arise. First, it is difficult to agree the criteria which would establish eligibility; second, the advocates of the development of lay representation would not wish the extension of legal aid to be viewed as an alternative to funding better organised and more comprehensive schemes of lay representation.

The Council on Tribunals has consistently advocated the extension of legal aid,[3] and its view has been supported by the Lord Chancellor's Advisory Committee,[4] by the President of Industrial Tribunals[5] and by other groups and individuals. It was the formulation of the test of eligibility submitted by the Council on Tribunals which won the approval of the Benson Commission, subject to some additions. The Council proposed in their evidence to the Commission that an applicant for legal aid should show ". . . that in the particular circumstances of his case he reasonably requires the services of a lawyer, and the certifying committee shall in this respect have regard to the suitability and availability of any other forms of assistance." The Council instanced several situations where representation by a lawyer might be regarded as appropriate—

"(i) where a significant point of law arises,
  (ii) where evidence is likely to be so complex or specialised that the average layman could reasonably wish for expert help in assembling and evaluating the evidence and in its testing or interpretation,
 (iii) where a test case arises,
  (iv) where deprivation of liberty or the ability of an individual to follow his occupation is at stake."[6]

To these situations the Commission added three others: where the amount at stake is significant *to the claimant*; where suitable lay representation is

---

[1] This is the standard test for legal aid—"Would a solicitor advise a private client to pursue or defend the action?"—see above, p. 571. The test is almost unworkable in relation to many tribunals because of the lack of correlation between the amount at stake and the cost of legal representation.

[2] See R. Lawrence, "Solicitors and Tribunals" [1980] J.S.W.L. 13, at pp. 19–25.

[3] *e.g. Annual Reports*, 1976–77, p. 6; 1987–88, pp. 17–21; 1994–95, p. 7. The Franks Committee had made such a recommendation in 1958: *Report*, para. 89.

[4] This subject was first considered at length in the *24th Report of the Law Society on Legal Aid and Advice*, 1973/74, pp. 47–55. Thereafter it recurred in the *33rd Legal Aid Annual Reports* [1982–83], pp. 194–209; the *35th Reports* [1984–85], pp. 232–243; *38th Reports* (1987–88), pp. 103–105; *39th Reports* (1988–89), pp. 112–114.

[5] In his evidence to the Royal Commission on Legal Services, referred to in R.C.L.S. Vol. 1, at para. 15.28.

[6] *ibid.*, para. 15.28; endorsed by the Lord Chancellor's Advisory Committee on Legal Aid: *33rd Legal Aid Annual Reports* [1982–83], at p. 205. These criteria were endorsed in the Council's Annual Report for 1994–95, p. 9.

unavailable; where the special circumstances of the individual make legal representation desirable.[7]

These criteria, it is suggested, would be applied by the appropriate legal aid committee[8] and used to determine whether the "merits" tests for legal aid had been satisfied. An alternative view, that legal aid should be granted or recommended by the chairman of the appropriate tribunal,[9] was not supported by the Benson Commission.

It is evident that these criteria were formulated upon the assumption that there would be an adequate lay representation service available, and the supporters of such a service feared that these might be regarded as alternative, rather than complementary, developments. This dilemma confronts the reformer who wishes to advance the cause of tribunal representation but takes the view that the more important use of public funds is in the training and organisation of lay representatives. To oppose the extension of legal aid may appear to be siding with the forces of darkness; to support it, with limited funds available, may be reducing the possibility of more general improvement.

The Government's response to the Benson Commission was not encouraging[10]; it noted that all those involved in tribunal proceedings were already eligible, subject to means, for legal advice and assistance[11] and that assistance by way of representation was available for proceedings in mental health review tribunals.[12] "Extensions of assistance by way of representation and legal aid are made where it is shown to be necessary and resources allow."[13]

The Lord Chancellor's Advisory Committee on Legal Aid subsequently recommended that legal aid should be extended as a matter of priority to bail applications to the immigration appellate authorities, and to the Immigration Appeal Tribunal, the Social Security Commissioners, Industrial Tribunals and the Vaccine Damage Tribunal.[14] The Government's position was to reiterate its response to the Benson Royal Commission. Indeed, it was stated that, pending the outcome of the research project on the effectiveness of representation, "the Government does not intend that there should be any general extension of publicly funded tribunal representation."[15] Given that outcome, noted at a number of points in the chapter, it is likely that any future development will be in the area of lay representation. This position was supported by the Legal Aid Efficiency Scrutiny[16] and the Legal Aid Board,[17] but their respective suggestions that the extension of representation might be funded by restricting the scope of

---

[7] *ibid.*, The Commission's additions were criticised and rejected by the Lord Chancellor's Advisory Committee: *33rd Annual Reports* [1982–83], at p. 205.

[8] Now the Area Director, see p. 510, above.

[9] See, for example, R. Micklethwait, *The National Insurance Commissioners* (1976), at p. 56.

[10] *The Government Response to the Report of The Royal Commission on Legal Services*, (Cmnd. 9077, 1983).

[11] See above, pp. 491–510.

[12] Introduced in December 1982, see above, p. 495.

[13] *Response*, above n. 10, p. 18.

[14] *33rd Legal Aid Annual Reports* [1982–83], pp. 194–209; *35th Annual Reports* [1984–85], pp. 236–242 (adding the Vaccine Damage Tribunal to the list). The Council on Tribunals' list of priorities is longer, and includes M.H.R.T.s, Medical Appeal Tribunals and Immigration Adjudicators (see Annual Report for 1987–88 (1988–89 H.C. 102), p. 18).

[15] White Paper on *Legal Aid in England and Wales, A New Framework* (Cm. 118, 1987), para. 30.

[16] (L.C.D. 1986), Vol. 2, Part IV. See further above pp. 515–517.

[17] *Second Stage Consultation on the Future of the Green Form Scheme* (1989), para. 12.

the green form scheme were widely criticised as unrealistic and undesirable.[18]

The Lord Chancellors' Consultation Paper, *Legal Aid—Targeting Need* [19] returned to the issues. While *legal* representation before tribunals should not be norm, given that their procedures "are in general less formal and more simple than court proceedings", not all cases are straightforward and "in such cases it sometimes might be in the interests of both the individual and the tribunal that representation should be available." A pilot scheme could be run under the proposed block contracting system[20] to test the effect of the grant of legal aid on the efficiency of the proceedings, the value for money spent on legal aid and the appropriate criteria for grant.[21] Furthermore, it was proposed that contracts for work in the area of social welfare law would be available to solicitors, agencies employing solicitors and non-solicitor agencies covering (i) initial fact-gathering and problem diagnosis; (ii) basic advice and assistance; and (iii) (except in the case of non-solicitor agencies) more detailed problem resolution including court proceedings, representation and ADR. However, representation before certain tribunals would be covered as part of element (ii).[22]

6. How Should Lay Representation be Developed?

"If agencies which provide advice and representation before tribunals are to give an adequate service, they should have enough money to provide training for staff, an up-to-date information service and proper administrative support . . . we recommend that public funds should be made available to approved agencies to assist in the training of tribunal representatives."[23]

"[The recommendation is] accepted in principle subject to further consideration being given to timing and the availability of resources."[24]

If the Government were to make available resources to implement the Benson Commission recommendation, then consideration would have to be given to the most effective method of organising schemes of lay representation. There is a variety of schemes already in existence which might provide a guide for national development.

Lawrence[25] distinguished three types of scheme which could be observed amongst the 16 or so existing tribunal units. He characterised these types as *referral agencies, advice bureau based* and *support units*.[26]

The *referral agencies* accept tribunal cases at the hearing stage from another agency which has done all the preparatory work and got the case ready for the tribunal. The representatives attached to such agencies operate purely as

---

[18] *e.g.* responses to the Legal Aid Board by the Lord Chancellor's Advisory Committee (*39th Legal Aid Annual Reports* (1988–89), p. 96), the Law Society (Response, p. 28) and NACAB (Response, p. 7).
[19] Cm. 2854, 1995; see pp. 519–525.
[20] Above, p. 522.
[21] Cm. 2854, pp. 61–62.
[22] *ibid.*, pp. 58–61.
[23] R.C.L.S. Vol. 1, paras.15.20, 15.21.
[24] *Response*, above n. 10, at p. 18.
[25] R. Lawrence, *Tribunal Representation* (1980).
[26] *ibid.*, at p. 84.

advocates and will send the applicant back to the original agency if there is any follow-up work to be done after the hearing has taken place. Typical of this kind of organisation of specialist advocates is the Free Representation Unit which draws its members from amongst Bar students and young barristers.[27] Such a unit normally relies heavily on the initial competence of some other agency[28] to prepare the case in such a way that it is ready for a hearing.

Advice bureau based units operate from or alongside established agencies, often CABx, with particular responsibility for taking on the tribunal representation work of that agency. This is, in some ways, the easiest unit to develop since it can emerge from the expertise of workers in the bureau in response to a perceived need for the work.[29] The Newcastle Tribunal Assistance Unit[30] exemplifies that process, and the Chapeltown unit in Leeds is similarly bureau-based.[31] These units have a wider role because of the close connection with a bureau and find themselves involved in formal and informal training of bureau workers as well as advice and representation. The value of having a unit attached in this way is the effect it has of raising the general level of advice-giving in the host agency. It is clear that the tendency at first is for the agency to push *all* problems in the subject area of the unit onto the unit, including perfectly routine enquiries. After an initial period, however, the general competence to handle such enquiries increases and the work of the agency is consequently strengthened.[32]

Support units are those which are not intended directly to offer representation, but rather to train, inform, advise and assist other representatives in the area which is served by the unit. The NACAB/EEC Tribunal Project in the West Midlands[33] operated in this way from the outset although the staff found the need to deal with some casework in order to retain their own expertise in representation. Of course, such units depend on their ability to stimulate interest in representation amongst agencies in the area and it can be difficult to break down reluctance on the part of volunteers.[34] The task is less easy for support units than for bureau-based services with their constant contact with both workers and clients.

. This categorisation does not take account of all the units presently in operation[35] but it may offer some guidance for future development. The Citizens Advice Bureaux network would seem to provide a good basis for bureau-based units. However, geographical coverage is still incomplete and it might prove hopelessly expensive to provide bureau-based units in rural areas where there

---

[27] Above, p. 825.

[28] This may be an unsatisfactory feature of such a scheme. The particularly fruitful parts of the other two types of scheme depend on the contact between representative and adviser and the building up of the general level of advice-giving.

[29] The drawback of this type of unit is that it relies heavily on the skills of few people. Holidays, illness, pressure of work can then disrupt the representation service quite significantly.

[30] Established in 1974 with the support of the Newcastle CAB. It experienced a rapid rise in workload and subsequently attracted work from a wide area.

[31] See *Chapeltown CAB, Leeds, Tribunal Assistance Unit Progress Report—First Two Years Aug. 1976—Aug. 1978* (NACAB Occasional Paper No. 6, 1979); *Tribunal Assistance, The Chapeltown experience* (NACAB Occasional Paper No. 14, 1982).

[32] R. Lawrence, *op. cit.*, esp. Chap. 5; *Tribunal Assistance* (above, n. 31), pp. 56–58.

[33] *Combatting Poverty: CABx, Claimants and Tribunals* (NACAB Occasional Paper No. 11, 1980); above, p. 826, n. 61.

[34] *ibid.*, pp. 47–56.

[35] R. Lawrence, *op. cit.* at p. 85.

is relatively less work to do. Support units are not directly effective and seem to take longer to stimulate a reliable service. In the longer term, however, they have a much broader effect on the area they serve.

A further kind of service, commended by Genn and Genn,[36] is the single-purpose agency, exemplified by the former United Kingdom Immigration Advisory Service. It is, however, doubtful that it would be practicable to extend this model generally to all tribunals in which there is a representation problem.[37]

The Lord Chancellor's Advisory Committee advocated the development of a strong voluntary lay representation service, possibly based on the CABx, utilising the skills of "resource lawyers." Such a scheme would complement legal representation funded by legal aid in difficult cases and would be closest to the *support units* of the models we have discussed.[38]

7. Procedural Reform

The preceding sections have all made one important assumption: that the tribunal system will continue in much the same way, becoming, if anything, rather more legalistic. The need for improved representation is based on that assumption.

The Benson Commission recommended a review of the procedures of tribunals in order to ensure that applicants in person are able to conduct their own cases whenever possible.[39] Such a review might have an effect on the need for representation, but would raise again the fundamental principles of tribunal adjudication. In the end, the question, "What kind of representation do we need?" is linked inextricably with the question, "What kind of tribunals do we want?" As we have seen, the study by Genn and Genn strongly reinforces the view that the idea that procedures can be simplified, given the great complexity of much of the law dealt with by tribunals, is unduly optimistic.

---

[36] Genn and Genn (1989), pp. 193–198, 250.
[37] See T. Mullen, (1990) 53 M.L.R. 230, 234–235. The responsibilities of U.K.I.A.S. were themselves split in 1992 between the Refugee Legal Centre and the Immigration Appeals and Advisory Service.
[38] *3rd Annual Legal Aid Reports* [1982–83], pp. 201–203; 35th Reports [1984–85], pp. 235–236.
[39] R.C.L.S., Vol. 1., paras.15.12, 15.13.

CHAPTER 16

THE CRIMINAL TRIAL

THIS chapter examines the criminal trial. It should be read taking a critical approach, bearing in mind Packer's two models of criminal justice.[1] The crime control model emphasises the importance of the repression of criminal behaviour in the most efficient manner. There is a requirement for high rates of arrest and conviction, and a major interest in speed and finality in the system. There is, therefore, a reliance on informal, routine procedures, relying heavily on the work of the police to determine guilt. Consequently, whatever procedures are used presume guilt. The due process model stresses the need to protect the accused against error. Whereas the crime control model looks like a conveyor-belt approach to criminal justice, the due process model looks more like an obstacle course. Every stage in the due process model assumes the innocence of the accused and requires formidable impediments to be overcome to establish guilt. Essential, therefore, to the due process model is the trial stage.

The rhetoric of the English criminal justice system reflects the due process model, as will be indicated by this chapter. Examples to consider are the presumption of innocence, reflected in the prosecution having the burden of proof in a criminal trial, and the rules relating to the admissibility of evidence. However, as White and Sanders and Young make clear,[2] it is inappropriate quickly to dismiss the crime control model since, for example, many cases are diverted from trial, the police, it is alleged, have on occasion violated the rules governing their powers and many, perhaps too many, guilty pleas are entered.[3] The crime control model plays a greater role, induced an increasing role, in the English criminal justice system than would at first appear.

It may also be of some value in reading this chapter to consider that there is a difference between methods of establishing the truth and the procedure in the criminal trial.[4] At the criminal trial, it is for the prosecution to establish its case against the accused to the satisfaction of the magistrates or jury beyond a reasonable doubt through an adversarial procedure. Considerable efforts are made to ensure "fairness" in the procedure, so the court cannot take account of all

---

[1] See H. L. Packer, *The Limits of the Criminal Sanction* (1968). Packer's models are discussed more fully in relation to pre-trial criminal procedure at pp. 776–779 above, where also attention is drawn to the "fundamental balance" between the interests of the community and the rights and liberties of individual citizens considered by the Royal Commission on Criminal Procedure. For a summary of Packer's models, see R. C. A. White, *The Administration of Justice* (1985), Chap. 7, esp. pp. 113–114. For the enthusiastic student, M. King, *The Framework of Criminal Justice* (1981) provides a method of examining the criminal justice system by building more models on to those created by Packer. A summary of King's work is also to be found in White (1985), pp. 114–116. A. Sanders and R. Young adopt the Packer models approach throughout their *Criminal Justice* (1994).

[2] White (1985), p. 114; Sanders & Young (1994).

[3] As to diversion from trial, see above pp. 709–718 and the fixed penalty notice scheme noted briefly below at p. 839; the Police and Criminal Evidence Act 1984 is now preventing what may have been regular violations, see above Chap. 13; as to the debate concerned with "plea bargaining" see pp. 856–858, 862–865, 867–869, 876–878 below.

[4] See, further, Z. Bankowski, "The Jury and Reality" in M. Findlay and P. Duff (eds.), *The Jury Under Attack* (1988) and works referred to there.

possible forms of evidence. Outside the criminal trial, judgments as to the truth of a matter are likely to be made, not by adversarial methods, but inquisitorial; not so as to be satisfied beyond reasonable doubt, but as more likely than not; not by evidence which passes the rules of legal admissibility, but on any reliable evidence. It is not the objective of the criminal trial to establish the truth of what happened, although it is presumably believed that the criminal trial will produce results which closely resemble the truth of the matter.

A. SUMMARY TRIAL[5]

Whilst the bulk of the work of magistrates' courts concerns minor offences, their powers of sentencing are limited and their decisions create no legal precedents, they do deal with the vast majority of criminal cases[6] and they constitute the tribunal most likely to be encountered by the "ordinary" person. Thus the manner in which they perform their function is of considerable significance.

We have already considered the ways in which the appearance of a person accused of a summary offence or an offence triable either way can be secured.[7] We have also explained the procedure adopted by the court in selecting the mode of trial of an offence triable either way.[8] If summary trial is the appropriate way of determining liability for the offence charged, the first formal step is for the magistrates' clerk to read the information to the accused or the defendant (these terms are used inter-changeably), and secure a plea.

---

[5] The body of literature on the summary trial is increasing. The practitioners works are *Stone's Justices Manual* and *Blackstone's Criminal Practice*, both published annually. The main books relied on in this chapter are A. E. Bottoms and J. D. McLean, *Defendants in the Criminal Process* (1976); E. Burney, *J.P., Magistrate, Court and Community* (1979); P. Carlen, *Magistrates' Justice* (1976); A. P. Carr, *Criminal Procedure in Magistrates' Court* (1983); P. Darbyshire, *The Magistrates' Clerk* (1984); J. Gregory, *Crown Court or Magistrates' Court?* Office of Population Censuses and Surveys (HMSO 1976); B. Harris, *The Criminal Jurisdiction of Magistrates* (11th ed., 1988); H. Parker, M. Sumner and J. Jarvis, *Unmasking the Magistrates* (1989); J. W. Raine, *Local Justice* (1989); P. J. Rowe and S. J. Knapp, *Evidence and Procedure in Magistrates' Courts* (3rd ed., 1989); R. Tarling, *Sentencing Practice in Magistrates' Courts*, Home Office Research Study No. 56 (1981), J. Vennard, *Contested Trials in Magistrates' Courts*, R.C.C.P. Research Study No. 6 (1980); J. Vennard, *Contested Trials in Magistrates' Courts*, Home Office Research Study No. 71 (1981); C. Hedderman and B. Noxon, *Magistrates Courts or Crown Court? Mode of Trial Decisions and Sentencing*, Home Office Research Study No. 125 (1992). For a brief summary of the work of the Home Office Research and Planning Unit, see D. Moxon, "Current Research Bearing on the Work of Magistrates' Courts" (1984) 148 J.P.N. 634.

[6] In 1994, 1,947,000 defendants were proceeded against at magistrates' courts, of whom 102,000 were aged between 10 and 17; 26 per cent of these proceedings were for indictable offences; 30 per cent for summary, non-motoring offences; and 44 per cent for summary motoring offences: *Criminal Statistics 1994* (Cm. 3010, 1995), Table 6.1. In the same year, 402,100 defendants were proceeded against in the Crown Court, of whom 2,800 were aged between 10 and 17. A further 3,400 appeared in the Crown Court for sentence after summary conviction (of whom 100 were aged between 10 and 17), because the magistrates' sentencing powers were not sufficient in the circumstances: *ibid.* Table 6.5.

[7] See pp. 728–731, above.

[8] See pp. 723–726, above.

1. THE INFORMATION

The information is the formal document containing the allegation(s) against the accused.[9] Unlike an indictment it does not contain a separate statement of the alleged offence and then the particulars alleged to constitute the offence.[10] It merely contains a statement which combines the essential facts and the alleged offence. It is sufficient if the accused is given reasonable notice of the charge to be met and the way in which it is alleged the offence was committed.[11] The use of plain, non-technical language is intended to simplify matters for the accused. Specimen informations[12] relating to criminal damage, theft and carrying an offensive weapon follow:

(i) Henry Frederick Smailey on the 1st day of March 1996 did without lawful excuse damage a motor vehicle, namely a Ford Escort number ABC 123, belonging to John Smith intending to damage the property or being reckless as to whether that property would be damaged; contrary to section 1(1) of the Criminal Damage Act 1971

(ii) Henry Frederick Smailey on the 1st day of March 1996 stole £15 belonging to John Smith; contrary to sections 1 and 7 of the Theft Act 1968.

(iii) Henry Frederick Smailey on the 1st day of March 1996 without lawful authority or reasonable excuse had with him in a public place, namely the Victoria Shopping Centre, Nottingham, an offensive weapon namely a bayonet; contrary to section 1(1) of the Prevention of Crime Act 1953.

2. PRESENCE OF THE ACCUSED

At a trial on indictment, the accused must be in court to enter a plea and is normally present through the whole trial.[13] Summary trial is different in that provision is made for guilty pleas to be made by post and also, where the accused fails to appear at the appointed time and place, for trial in the absence of the accused. Both these procedures are designed to spare the time and expense of the participants where there is no real intention to defend the charge, but they are hedged with certain safeguards to ensure that injustice does not result.

Written pleas of guilty made by post may be entered only if the offence is a summary offence punishable by not more than three months' imprisonment. The safeguards ensuring no injustices result are that the accused must be served with a statement of the facts alleged by the prosecution and an explanatory note, in addition to the usual summons; a wish not to be present must be made clear by the accused in writing; the statement of facts, the plea and anything which the accused has written in relation to mitigation or personal financial circum-

---

[9] For the full form of an information, see p. 728, above.

[10] Specimen indictments are set out at pp. 848–849, below.

[11] The rules relating to the drafting of an information are contained in the Magistrates' Courts Rules 1981 (S.I. 1981, No. 552). The most informal style permitted is to be found in rule 100.

[12] The prescribed full form of information is to be found in the Magistrates' Courts (Forms) Rules 1981 (S.I. 1981, No. 553), Form 1.

[13] See p. 855, below.

stances must be read out in court by the clerk; and no information is given to the court by the prosecution other than that contained in the documents.[14] This procedure is very strict and any deviation will result in the proceedings being a nullity.[15] This procedure may now also be used even where the defendant is present, provided he or she consents.[16]

A magistrates' court has a discretion to proceed with a trial in the absence of the accused[17] where the right to be present has been voluntarily waived. The right is voluntarily waived by the accused, for example, abusing it as a consequence of indecent, outrageous or unseemly behaviour, or ceasing to claim it by deliberately jumping bail. In any case, the court must exercise its discretion with great reluctance, never for anyone's convenience, but solely in the interests of the administration of justice.[18]

Note should also be made of the fixed penalty notice system, used not only for parking offences, but also, for example, for speeding, not wearing a seat belt or crash helmet and violating a red light. The motorist is issued a ticket giving brief particulars of the offence and the name of the clerk to whom payment of a fixed sum must be made. This system produces an end result similar to that where the full court system is used, but there are significant time and costs savings for all involved.[19]

3. THE PLEA

A plea is usually only sought to the general issue, that is, the accused is asked to plead guilty or not guilty. However, preliminary points may be raised; for example, whether the court has jurisdiction to try the accused or whether the information charges more than one offence. If it is successfully raised, the trial cannot continue.[20]

In a summary trial where the accused is present, the information is read out by the magistrates' clerk. The accused is asked to plead guilty or not guilty. The accused's plea must be freely made and unambiguous, and should normally

---

[14] Magistrates' Courts Act 1980, s.12. The option is made available at the discretion of the prosecution: *Blackstone's Criminal Practice 1996*, para. D17.13.

[15] See *R. v. Epping and Dugar JJ., exp. Breach* [1987] R.T.R. 233 and *Blackstone's Criminal Practice 1996*, para. D17.13.

[16] Magistrates Courts Act 1980, s.12A (added by the Criminal Justice and Public Order Act 1994) and see *Blackstone's Criminal Practice 1996*, para. D17.13.

[17] Under the Magistrates Courts Act 1980, s.11. A plea of not guilty is entered on behalf of the the accused and the prosecution evidence is heard. Service of the summons must be proved. The accused may show, within 21 days after finding out about the proceedings, that he or she did not know of the summons or proceedings until after their commencement in which case the conviction would be set asider under the Magistrates Courts Act 1980, s.14. See J. Sprack, *Emmins on Criminal Procedure* (6th ed., 1995), pp. 176–177 and see *Blackstone's Criminal Practice 1996*, para. D17.11–D17.12.

[18] Harris (1988), p. 242.

[19] See Emmins (1995), pp. 15–16.

[20] Special pleas may be entered as those in response to an indictment: see pp. 850–852, below, although technically the pleas of autrefois acquit and autrefois convict only apply to indictments. The same effect is achieved in magistrates' courts by dealing with the matter on a plea of not guilty. See *Blackstone's Criminal Practice 1996*, paras D17.17 and Harris (1988), pp. 243–254.

be made personally.[21] The accused's response determines the remainder of the procedure.

There is, however, no specific procedure to deal with the situation where the accused does not reply. The procedure available in the Crown Court to consider fitness to plead is not available to a magistrates' court.[22] The possibilities are either to discontinue the proceedings, and perhaps contact the social services department; or to commit the accused for trial in the Crown Court if the offence can be tried on indictment; or to enter a plea of not guilty, and then determine whether the accused did the act or made the omission charged and, if so, impose a hospital order without convicting the accused.[23]

4. THE GUILTY PLEA

If the accused enters a guilty plea, the court can proceed to hear the facts of the case from the prosecution, including any further offences which the accused wishes to have taken into consideration and any previous convictions. These facts are not usually elicited from witnesses unless there is some substantial disagreement,[24] but are presented by the prosecutor concerned. The procedure before sentence is increase. The same as that in the Crown Court (see below).[25]

In certain circumstances social inquiry reports are required, for example, before a community service order can be imposed, and it is normal for a case to be adjourned if such a report is necessary or desirable.[26] The probation service is responsible for compiling a report and it will be available to the bench at the adjourned hearing, when the defence will have the opportunity of seeing and commenting upon it. With or without a report, the bench will listen to anything that may be said by the defence by way of mitigation of sentence.

Where the defendant pleads guilty, there is a sentencing discount as in the Crown Court (see below).[27]

5. THE NOT GUILTY PLEA

A plea of not guilty normally results in an immediate adjournment to an agreed date so that the prosecution and defence can assemble their witnesses and court

---

[21] *R. v. Wakefield JJ., exp. Butterworth* [1970] 1 All E.R. 1181; *R. v. Gowerton JJ., exp. Davies* [1974] Crim. L. R. 253; *R. v. Kingston upon Thames Magistrates' Court, ex p. Davey* (1985) 149 J.P. 744.

[22] *R. v. Metropolitan Stipendiary Magistrate Tower Bridge, ex p. Aniifowosi* (1985) 149 J.P. 748. As to "fitness to plead" see below pp. 859–860.

[23] Mental Health Act 1983, s.37(3); see *R. v. Lincoln (Kesteven) JJ., ex p. O'Connor* [1983] 1 W.L.R. 335; M. Wasik, "Hospital Orders without Trial" (1983) 147 J.P.N. 211 and *Blackstone's Criminal Practice 1996*, paras. D17.17 and D17.23.

[24] Magistrates' Courts Act 1980, s.9(3).

[25] See *Blackstone's Criminal Practice 1996*, para. D19.12.

[26] Magistrates Courts Act 1980, s.10(3) and see *Blackstone's Criminal Practice 1996*, para. D19.11.

[27] The other options open to the prosecution are to withdraw a summons or to offer no evidence; see *Blackstone's Criminal Practice 1996*, paras. D17.20–D17.21. Magistrates have no discretion not to try an information, except where inordinate delay has lead to an abuse of process: *ibid.*, para. D17.25.

time can be allocated.[28] At the adjourned hearing the procedure will follow the normal adversarial lines. The prosecution is entitled to address the court through an opening speech and will then lead evidence through witnesses who will be subject to examination in chief, cross-examination and, perhaps, re-examination.[29] If the case is not especially difficult, the prosecution will often start with witnesses, since, with an experienced bench, there is no need to stress general points which might be necessary at a trial on indictment.[30]

At the close of the prosecution case, the defence may submit that there is no case to answer. The magistrates stop the hearing if they find that no reasonable tribunal could convict on the prosecution evidence, either because an essential element of the offence has not been proved or because the evidence has been discredited on cross-examination.[31] The magistrates must not say whether *they* would convict on the evidence so far presented, merely whether a reasonable bench *could* convict. If the submission is accepted, the accused is discharged. If it is rejected, the right of the defence to call witnesses and build a defence is not prejudiced.

At the close of the defence case, the defence is entitled to make a closing speech to the bench. Exceptionally, the prosecution may be permitted to speak again and, if so, the defence will be given a second opportunity;[32] the defence is entitled to the last word.

The rules of evidence are the same for summary trial as for trial on indictment. A particular problem in summary trial exists when there is a challenge to the admissibility of an item of evidence.[33] It is for the magistrates to decide, for example, whether a confession is admissible in accordance with the Police and Criminal Evidence Act 1984.[34] They must obviously be informed of the accused's confession. If they decide it is not admissible, they must attempt to determine the guilt of the accused without taking account of the confession. Such a task is extraordinarily difficult, but is nevertheless essential where the deciders of fact and law are one (or three) and the same.[35]

---

[28] See M. Wasik and A. Turner, "Sentencing Guidelines for Magistrates' Courts" [1993] Crim. L.R. 345, at p. 355.

[29] Magistrates Court Rules 1981, r.13, and see *Blackstone's Criminal Practice 1996*, paras. D18.1–D18.7 and Harris (1988), pp. 257–261. The order of proceedings is similar to that in trial on indictment, see pp. 850–854, below.

[30] *e.g.*, the burden and standard of proof, the need to listen carefully to the evidence, etc.

[31] The criteria are contained in a *Practice Note* [1962] 1 All E.R. 448 (criticised by E. C. J. McBride, (1990) 154 J.P.N. 99) and see *Blackstone's Criminal Practice 1996*, para. D18.8. Justices are warned against forming a view without hearing the whole of the evidence save in the two cases mentioned in the text.

[32] Magistrates' Courts Rules 1981, r.13.

[33] See Rowe and Knapp (1989), pp. 76–79 and *Blackstone's Criminal Practice 1996*, para. D18.6.

[34] In magistrates' courts the dual function of the justices as judges of both fact and law generally renders the "trial within a trial" an unnecessary sophistication, though one must be held where the admissibility of a confession is in issue: *R. v. Liverpool Juvenile Court, ex parte R.* [1988] Q.B. 1. See *Blackstone's Criminal Practice 1996*, para. D18.6 (esp. p. 1424) and R. Pattenden, *Judicial Discretion and Criminal Litigation* (2nd ed., 1990), pp. 313–314. As to the admissibility of confessions, see pp. 878–880, below.

[35] See also p. 51, above, and for the situation in a trial on indictment, p. 880.

6. THE UNREPRESENTED DEFENDANT

It has so far been assumed that the accused who appears[36] at a magistrates' court is represented. The availability of legal aid[37] and the existence of duty solicitor schemes at magistrates' courts[38] means that representation is more readily available than in the past. However, many defendants in magistrates' courts are unrepresented, and this is not likely to change for the foreseeable future.[39] At least when pleading not guilty, the lack of representation is a major disadvantage.[40] The difficulties for an unrepresented defendant include ignorance of procedure; the pressure imposed by a bewildering situation; an inability to understand, or even hear, what is going on; and the difficulty of putting forward one's own case sensibly, clearly and intelligibly.[41] The willingness of the clerk to assist an unrepresented defendant as far as pressure of business and the responsibility to the justices permit may ameliorate, but cannot eliminate these difficulties.[42] Any inequality of resources between prosecution and defence strikes deep at the heart of an adversarial system: when a significant imbalance exists, the system does not work fairly.[43]

7. THE VERDICT

The magistrates normally retire to consider their decision. Where the trial is before a bench of lay magistrates, rather than a stipendiary magistrate, a majority[44] must be satisfied beyond reasonable doubt that the charge is proved before they can convict. The magistrates decide questions of both fact and law. On matters of practice and procedure, law and mixed law and fact relating to the charge they will have the benefit of advice from their clerk, which, in prac-

---

[36] For trial in the absence of the accused, see p. 838, above. Legal aid would not be granted for such work, but legal advice and assistance might.

[37] As to the granting of legal aid, see pp. 767–772, above.

[38] See above, pp. 500–507 and 763–767, and Emmins (1995), pp. 457.

[39] See H. Astor, "The Unrepresented Defendant: A Consideration of the Role of the Clerk in Magistrates' Courts" (1986) 13 J.L.S. 225, at 237.

[40] One study showed that of 111 defendants who pleaded not guilty at a magistrates' court, 30 per cent of those unrepresented were acquitted, whereas 64 per cent of those represented by lawyers were acquitted: M. Zander, "Unrepresented Defendants in Magistrates' Courts" (1972) 122 N.L.J. 1041. On the other hand, a study by the Lord Chancellor's Department suggested that acquittal rates did not vary on the basis of representation: Lord Chancellor's Department, *Report of a Survey of the Grant of Legal Aid in Magistrates' Courts* (1983), Table 17, quoted in M. Zander, *Cases and Materials on the English Legal System* (6th ed., 1993), p. 346 (hereafter Zander, *Cases and Materials* (1993)).

[41] See S. Dell, *Silent in Court* (1971) and Carlen (1976), both quoted in Zander, *Cases and Materials* (1993), pp. 344–352.

[42] Astor (1986), p. 238. See, further, Darbyshire (1984), pp. 170–181.

[43] See A. Sanders and R. Young, *Criminal Justice* (1994), p. 258 and J. Jackson, "Trial Procedures" in C. Walker and K. Starmer (eds.) *Justice in Error* (1993), p. 131. See also Article 68 the European Connection on Human Rights.

[44] Which is the reason why magistrates normally sit in threes, see p. 51, above. The chairperson has no casting vote so that if a two person court is divided the case must be retried.

tice, they accept.[45] The clerk is also able to offer advice on sentencing. The clerk must not appear to be influencing the magistrates' decision on the facts when giving legal advice.[46]

The appellate courts have been quick to establish that justice must be seen to be done in magistrates' courts. It is improper for a third party to be with the magistrates in the retiring room whilst they consider their verdict. Even the briefest of interventions may raise doubts about what has transpired between an outsider and the magistrates, and so is strictly forbidden.[47] A similar rule is imposed to preserve the inviolability of the deliberations of a jury.[48]

There is, however, a difference between a jury engaged in fact-finding and the position of magistrates. The jury have already received instruction on the law from the judge in a summing-up. The magistrates will receive advice if they ask for it from the clerk, which they may seek in the course of their deliberations. The influence a clerk has over the magistrates is a matter of conjecture. Speculation that the clerk may have played too substantial a role in the verdict can be fuelled by his or her presence in the retiring room for a substantial period. The courts will quash a conviction if the clerk visits the retiring room where there is no good reason for doing so.[49] The best approach is for legal advice, including not only advice on questions of law and practice and procedure but also refreshing the magistrates' memory as to matters of evidence and principles of sentencing, to be given in open court, when the advocates on both sides can contribute to the advice being proffered.[50] However, if it is thought that the magistrates have retired to consider their verdict having been misinformed as to the law, the clerk may inform them of the correct position.[51]

On returning to court the magistrates give their verdict of guilty or not guilty without giving any reason.[52] If the verdict is guilty the procedure will follow the same course as after a plea of guilty. If not guilty, the accused will be discharged.

8. Sentencing

Not only is it the function of the magistrates to determine guilt, but they must also impose a sentence upon the offender. Maximum sentences are laid down

---

[45] The advice from the clerk is regulated by *Practice Direction* [1981] 1 All E.R. 1163. For a fuller consideration of the status and role of the clerk, see pp. 205–210, above. As to the practice of accepting that advice, see *R. v. Jones-Nicks* [1977] R.T.R. 72 and see Emmins (1995), p. 196 and *Blackstone's Criminal Practice 1996*, para. D17.30.

[46] *Practice Note (Justices' Clerks)* [1953] 1 W.L.R. 1416 and see *Blackstone's Criminal Practice 1996*, para D17.31.

[47] *R. v. Stratford upon Avon JJ., ex p. Edmonds* [1973] R.T.R. 356.

[48] See pp. 902–903, below.

[49] In *R. v. Guildford JJ., ex p. Harding* (1981) 145 J.P. 174 the conviction was quashed because the clerk had retired with the magistrates to advise them when the case was absolutely straightforward.

[50] See, *Practice Direction* [1981] 1 W.L.R. 1163, para. 3; *Blackstone's Criminal Practice 1996*, para. D17.30.

[51] See Justices of the Peace Act 1979, s.28(3) and *R. v. Uxbridge JJ., ex p. Smith* [1985] Crim. L.R. 670 and commentary by D. J. Birch.

[52] Juries are similarly excused from explaining the basis of their decisions: see p. 901, below. However, magistrates may be required to record their findings of fact and the principles of law upon which they reach their decision, if required by the convicted defendant to state a case for consideration by the Divisional Court: see pp. 920–921, below.

in respect of each offence. Some offences can be punished by imprisonment (with or without a fine); some by a fine, or lesser sentence, alone. Where the offence is one triable summarily only, magistrates may not at present impose a term of imprisonment greater than six months for any single offence. The maximum fine is laid down by reference to the standard scale of fines which was introduced in 1982. It has five levels. Currently level 1 imposes a maximum fine of £200, level 2 a maximum fine of £500, level 3 a maximum fine of £1,000, level 4 a maximum fine of £2,500 and level 5 (otherwise known as the statutory maximum) a maximum fine of £5,000. Where the offence is triable either way and is being tried summarily, magistrates still cannot impose a term of imprisonment more than six months, but the maximum fine they may impose is at least £5,000 and is greater if the statute so provides.[53]

Rarely would the maximum term of imprisonment or fine be imposed. In addition, it is not necessarily the case that imprisonment, for example, will be imposed when it is available as a sentencing option. Indeed a major question for the magistrates is whether to impose a custodial sentence or not. The range of non-custodial sentences available includes, not only imposing a fine, but also placing someone on probation, ordering attendance at an attendance centre, suspending or partially suspending a sentence of imprisonment, ordering someone to do community service or granting an absolute or conditional discharge, as well as specific options available for young people.[54]

There has been considerable disquiet about the disparity in magistrates' sentencing.[55] The obstacles in the way of achieving uniformity of approach were identified by Wasik and Turner as being: (a) little authority assisting magistrates in their sentencing jurisdiction; (b) the size and diversity of the magistracy militated against a consistent approach; (c) the independence of the magistracy might militate against the acceptance of guidelines.[56] This has been addressed by the implementation of the principled approach of the Criminal Justice Act 1991[57] and the introduction of the Magistrates Association *Sentencing Guidelines* in 1992, which were both a development of an earlier approach[58] and a means of fulfilling the approach of the 1991 Act. It seems likely that the *Guidelines* will be both welcomed and followed by magistrates since the previous guidance had been used by them.[59] The *Guidelines* aim ''to improve 'consistency of approach' and

---

[53] If the magistrates' court finds that their powers of sentence are not sufficient for an offence triable either way, they may commit the offender to Crown Court for sentence: Magistrates' Courts Act 1980, s.38, see Emmins (1995), pp. 209–214 and see *Blackstone's Criminal Practice 1996*, paras. D19.13–18.

[54] As to sentencing in magistrates' courts, see Emmins (1995), pp. 193–195 (for offences triable summarily only) and pp. 246–247 (for offences triable either way).

[55] See M. Wasik and A. Turner, ''Sentencing Guidelines for the Magistrates' Courts'' [1993] Crim. L.R. 345, at pp. 347–348, and see Raine (1989), pp. 86–94 and 97–98 and Parker, Summer and Jarvis (1989).

[56] Wasik and Turner (1993), pp. 345–346. The ''bench effect'' has been described as a significant factor in sentencing decisions, that is a particular bench of magistrates adopting a general approach; see Tarling (1981) and Raine (1989), pp. 94–100.

[57] See below, pp. 886–888.

[58] The Magistrates Association began producing *Suggestions for Road Traffic Offences* in 1966 and the *Sentencing Guide for Criminal Offences (other than Road Traffic)* in 1989; see Wasik and Turner (1993), pp. 346–347.

[59] See Wasik and Turner (1993), pp. 346–348.

[they] identif[y] the central task of the sentencer to be 'how to assess the relative *seriousness* of each case and how to arrive at a *commensurate penalty.* ''[60]

9. DO MAGISTRATES REACH THE RIGHT RESULT?

The answer to this question, as with the question whether juries arrive at the right result,[61] depends upon what is meant by "right result" and may well be impressionistic. Care must be taken with assertions either that magistrates or that juries acquit too many people. The rate of acquittals in 1994 in both magistrates' courts and the Crown Court were close.[62] However, this simple approach hides a more interesting point, as indicted in a study by Vennard,[63] that for "contested either way cases, the chances of acquittal were substantially higher in the Crown Court (57 per cent) than in the magistrates' courts (30 per cent)."[64] Even so, there are many different beliefs, about summary trial, including that an accused has a greater chance of acquittal before a jury, that magistrates' impose lighter sentences in circumstances where the Crown Court and magistrates have the same sentencing powers, that judges impose lighter sentences in the same circumstances, and that magistrates' courts are biased in favour of the prosecution.[65] Further, there is some evidence that the criminal fraternity lack confidence in magisterial decision-making:[66] "Defendants do not expect justice to be done in the magistrates' court."[67] Is that because magistrates get decisions wrong, or because they get them right?

Vennard's study of contested trials in the magistrates' court[68] gives some support to the view that magistrates weigh evidence carefully and reach a verdict which is broadly in line with identifiable features of the evidence heard. The criticism that is most frequently made of magistrates is that they place too much credibility on the evidence of police officers and are generally too "prosecution-minded".[69] This criticism emanates not only from the accused who opt for trial by jury because it is "fairer," or because magistrates are amateurs who cannot be expected to get it right, or because they estimate that there is a better chance of acquittal,[70] but also from amongst those individuals and organisations who

---

[60] *Sentencing Guidelines* at p. ii, quoted in Wasik and Turner (1993), at pp. 348–349.

[61] See pp. 906–908, below.

[62] 26 per cent of defendants were acquitted at magistrates' courts, compared with 20 per cent at the Crown Court: *Criminal Statistics 1994* (Cm. 3010, 1995), Tables 8.6, 8.9.

[63] J. Vernard, "The Outcome of Contested Trials" in D. Moxon (ed.), *Managing Criminal Justice* (1985).

[64] Sanders and Young (1994), p. 299.

[65] Bottoms and McLean (1976), Chap. 4; Parker, Sumner and Jarvis (1989), p. 60; and D. Riley and J. Vennard, "Triable-either-way cases: Crown Court or magistrates' court?" (1988) 25 *Home Office Research Bulletin* 31, at p. 34.

[66] Riley and Vennard (1988), p. 34.

[67] Saunders and Young (1994), p. 299.

[68] Vennard (1980); Vennard (1981) and J. Vennard, "Acquittal Rates in Magistrates' Courts" (1981) 11 *Home Office Research Bulletin* 21.

[69] See, *e.g.*, evidence to the James Committee, *The Distribution of Criminal Business Between the Crown Court and the Magistrates Court* (Cmnd. 6323, 1975); B. Wootton, *Crime and Penal Policy* (1978).

[70] Gregory (1976).

gave evidence to the James Committee.[71] The research study undertaken by Vennard had as its aims:[72]

> (i) to appraise and itemise for contested cases the substance of the evidence presented by the prosecution and the defence, and attempt to quantify weaknesses and strengths in that evidence—such as whether or not the credibility of witnesses was impugned; and
>
> (ii) to attempt to explain trial outcome in contested cases in relation to the type of evidence presented by both parties and to criteria pertaining to witness credibility.

On somewhat limited evidence Vennard concluded that her findings indicated that "... magistrates' decisions whether to convict or acquit are strongly associated with a few quantifiable indices of the evidence adduced by the parties and the credibility of witnesses."[73] Strong associations were detected between direct evidence implicating the accused given by the prosecution witnesses whose credibility was not impugned and conviction. Conversely there was a strong association between acquittal, the prosecution witnesses' lack of credibility, and the lack of direct evidence. These findings are not startling but they may reassure critics that magistrates are generally operating along rational lines.

For one other view, which relies partly upon different work by Vennard on acquittal rates, one may look at King's response[74] to proposals by the Justices' Clerks Society[75] that more trials should be diverted into the magistrates' court. King was dismissive of claims that magistrates offer a better quality of justice than juries and argued vigorously against proposals to reduce the right to jury trial.[76] Further, Sanders and Young, having reviewed the research evidence, are satisfied that the perception of defendants as to the unfairness of magistrates' court trial is an accurate one.[77] They identify a number of possible explanations for the higher acquittal rate at Crown Court than magistrates' court: (a) more people have to be convinced in the Crown Court (at least 10 out of 12 rather than two out of three; (b) the social composition of the magistrates[78] as compared with juries[79] militates more in favour of conviction at a magistrates' court; (c) magistrates become "case-hardened" whereas juries come fresh to the criminal justice system; (d) lower court procedures place defendants at a greater disadvantage because of the lack of disclosure requirements,[80] the magistrates are aware of inadmissible evidence (*e.g.*, confessions), and justices' clerks have a

---

[71] See n. 69, above.

[72] Vennard (1981), p. 4.

[73] *ibid.* p. 20.

[74] M. King, "Against Summary Trial" *LAG Bulletin*, April 1982, p. 14.

[75] "A Case for Summary Trial—Proposals for a Redistribution of Criminal Business" published by the Justices' Clerks Society.

[76] It was certainly the experience of the James Committee (1975) that its proposals to remove the right to trial by jury for minor thefts brought an outraged response, not least in the House of Commons. The proposal, originally incorporated in the Criminal Law Bill 1977, disappeared during the Bill's progress through Parliament. The opposition was, it is true, based more on a commitment to jury trial than on an antipathy to magisterial justice. See p. 721, above.

[77] Sanders and Young (1994), pp. 299–304.

[78] See above, pp. 196–201.

[79] See below, pp. 890–893.

[80] As to disclosure in the Crown Court, see above, pp. 750–756.

significant impact.[81] They conclude that it "is no exaggeration to say that magistrates' courts are crime control courts overlaid with a thin layer of due process icing. At every twist and turn in the process, defendants are saddled with handicaps which undermine their willingness or ability to stand on their rights in court."[82] In consequence, they are surprised that the Royal Commission wished to reduce the right to jury trial, especially since no research was commissioned to examine justice in the lower courts.[83]

B. TRIAL ON INDICTMENT

If the proceedings are transferred from a Magistrates' court for trial in the Crown Court, those proceedings are begun by the "preferment of a bill of indictment". This procedure simply involves sending the bill of indictment[84] to the appropriate officer of the Crown Court for signature.[85] Once it is signed, the accused may be brought before the court.[86] Then the accused must be asked to plead to the indictment, in a process known as arraignment.

The indictment is the formal statement of the charge(s) against the accused and should contain the statement of the offence, that is a description of the offence, and the particulars of the offence, that is a brief statement of the essential facts which constitute the offence. The statement of the offence should be precise, using the recognisable common law name,[87] the statutory name and derivation,[88] or sufficient details of a statutory offence.[89] The particulars must give "reasonable information as to the nature of the charge,"[90] so that the accused knows the details of the charge and the prosecution may not shift its ground during the trial.[91] Three specimen indictments follow: a common law offence, a precise statutory description and a statutory offence for which there is no short description. They are taken from decided cases and reflect particular difficulties of those cases. Simpler cases will produce simpler indictments.

---

[81] Sanders and Young (1994), pp. 299–301.

[82] *ibid.* (1994), p. 304.

[83] *ibid.* (1994), pp. 302–303.

[84] Ultimate responsibility for this lies with counsel for the prosecution (*Blackstone's Criminal Practice 1996*, para. D8.3) but in most cases it is now the responsibility of the Crown Prosecution Service to draft and determine the form of an indictment: Procedural Notice issued by the Crown Prosecution Service and the Lord Chancellor's Department: (1989) 139 N.L.J. 188.

[85] The appropriate officer retains for the time being the responsibility for signing indictments: *ibid.*

[86] Where the accused has been committed for trial, the bill of indictment must be preferred within 28 days of the date of notice of transfer, unless that period is extended: Indictment (Procedure) Rules 1971 (S.I. 1971 No. 2084), r.5, as amended. The time limit is not mandatory: *R. v. Urbanowski* (1976) 62 Cr.App.R. 229, C.A.; *R. v. Soffe* (1982) 75 Cr.App.R. 133, C.A. Delay in bringing proceedings may be regarded as an abuse of process and thus cause criminal proceedings to be stopped, see Pattenden (1990), pp. 33–38.

[87] *e.g.*, murder; manslaughter; blasphemy; conspiracy to corrupt public morals.

[88] *e.g.*, theft, contrary to s.1 of the Theft Act 1968; robbery, contrary to s.8(1) of the Theft Act 1968; arson, contrary to s.1(1) and (3) of the Criminal Damage Act 1971.

[89] *e.g.*, removing an article from a place open to the public, contrary to s.11(1) of the Theft Act 1968; sexual intercourse with a girl under 13, contrary to s.5 of the Sexual Offences Act 1956.

[90] Indictment Rules 1971 (S.I. 1971 No. 1253), r.5(1).

[91] The accused, if he or she requests, is entitled to a copy of the indictment free of charge: *ibid.* r.10(1).

(i) *Shaw v. D.P.P.*[92]

STATEMENT OF OFFENCE

Conspiracy to corrupt public morals

PARTICULARS OF OFFENCE

Frederick Charles Shaw on divers days between the 1st day of October 1959 and the 23rd day of July 1960 within the jurisdiction of the Central Criminal Court, conspired with certain persons who inserted advertisements in issues of a magazine entitled "Ladies' Directory" numbered 7, 7 revised, 8, 9, 10 and a supplement thereto, and with certain other persons whose names are unknown, by means of the said magazine and the said advertisements to induce readers thereof to resort to the said advertisers for the purposes of fornication and of taking part in or witnessing other disgusting and immoral acts and exhibitions, with intent thereby to debauch and corrupt the morals as well of youth as of divers other liege subjects of Our Lady the Queen and to raise and create in their minds inordinate and lustful desires.

(ii) *R. v. Miller*[93]

STATEMENT OF OFFENCE

Arson, contrary to section 1(1) and (3) of Criminal Damage Act 1971

PARTICULARS OF OFFENCE

James Miller on a date unknown between August 13 and 16, 1980, without lawful excuse, damaged by fire a house known as No. 9, Grantham Road, Sparkbrook, intending to do damage to such property or reckless as to whether such property would be damaged.

(iii) *R. v. Markus*[94]

STATEMENT OF OFFENCE

Conniving at a corporation fraudulently inducing the investment of money contrary to sections 13(1)(b) and 19 of the Prevention of Fraud (Investments) Act 1958

PARTICULARS OF OFFENCE

Edward Jules Markus between August 25, 1970, and January 15, 1971, within the jurisdiction of the Central Criminal Court being a director of Agricultural Investment Corporation S.A. of the First National Investment Corporation S.A. and of Agri-International S.A. and of Agri-International

---

[92] [1962] A.C. 220.
[93] [1983] 2 A.C. 161.
[94] [1976] A.C. 35.

(U.K.) Ltd connived at the fraudulent inducement of Agricultural Investment Corporation S.A., through its agents First National Investment Corporation S.A. and Agri-International S.A. and Agri-International (U.K.) Ltd
of Dr Hermann Schlick and Mrs Theodoline Schlick to take part in an
arrangement to invest $1038.32 in Agri-Fund (the said investment being
an arrangement with respect of property other than securities, the purpose
or pretended purpose of which was to enable the said Dr Hermann Schlick
and the said Mrs Theodoline Schlick to participate in the profits alleged to
be likely to arise from the holding of Agri-Fund) by representations that
Agricultural Investment Corporation S.A. was genuinely carrying on an
honest business and that moneys invested in Agri-Fund were immediately
redeemable at the option of the investor which representations both he and
the said corporation knew to be misleading false and deceptive.

These examples satisfy the requirements that an indictment should include
such information as to the time and place of the offence as to indicate to the
accused the acts which are alleged to constitute the offence,[95] a reasonably clear
description of any property involved,[96] the identity of any "victim" or a description reasonable so as to be identifiable,[97] any factual circumstances necessary
to the offence,[98] and any special mental element required by the offence which
is not inherent in the statement of the offence.[99]

Indictments may contain more than one offence provided they are founded
on the same facts or for part of a series of offences of the same or a similar
character, but the charges must be separated and are then known as "counts".[1]

1. HEARING IN OPEN COURT

It is often regarded as essential to the administration of justice that hearings
take place in open court.[2] Public trials and media reporting are essential to the

---

[95] An allegation as to time may be made in ordinary language, and the dates between which the
offence may be quite a long way apart, as in Shaw's indictment. It is only in a few cases that
either time or place is of the essence of the offence, in which case greater particularity is required.

[96] In Miller's indictment, No. 9 Grantham Road, Sparkbrook. The name of the owner of the property
is unnecessary in most cases.

[97] In Markus' indictment, Dr Herman Schlick and Mrs Theodoline Schlick.

[98] e.g., in an indictment for theft, the particulars must state that the property in question belonged
to another, but does not have to state who that other was.

[99] e.g., the particulars on an indictment for an offence under s.18 of the Offences Against the Person
Act 1861 should allege an intent to do grievous bodily harm to the victim or to resist or prevent
lawful apprehension, as appropriate. The particulars of an indictment for arson under s.1(1) and
(3) of the Criminal Damage Act 1971 must allege either an intent to destroy or damage another's
property, or recklessness as to whether such property would be destroyed or damaged.

[1] See p. 000, below.

[2] e.g. Art. 6(1) of the European Convention on Human Rights provides: "In the determination of
. . . any criminal charge against him, everyone is entitled to a fair and public hearing within a
reasonable time by an independent and impartial tribunal established by law. Judgment shall be
pronounced publicly but the press and public may be excluded from all or part of the trial in
the interests of morals, public order, or national security in a democratic society, where the
interests of juveniles or the protection of the private life of the parties so require, or to the extent
strictly necessary in the opinion of the court in special circumstances where publicity would
prejudice the interests of justice." Art. 10 and 13 may also be relevant. See D.J. Harris, M.
O'Boyle and C. Warbrick, *Law of the European Convention on Human Rights* (1995), chaps. 6,
11 and 14.

administration of justice.[3] Nevertheless, there are some occasions on which either or both may be restricted.[4] Concern about the number of cases taking place out of the eye of the public was so great that a right of appeal against orders restricting or preventing reports of or restricting access to trials on indictment was introduced by section 159 of the Criminal Justice Act 1988.[5] *Blackstone's Criminal Practice 1996* points out that courts[6] have the common law powers to sit *in camera* where (a) there is the possibility of disorder, (b) a witness would refuse to testify publicly, (c) the effect of a public hearing on possible future prosecutions would be too damaging.[7] In addition, there are statutory powers under the Official Secrets Act 1920 and the Children and Young Persons Act 1933.[8] As regards media reporting, the media has a general freedom to report, subject primarily to liability for contempt of court. Section 4 of the Contempt of Court Act 1981 allows for postponing reporting where that is necessary to avoid "a substantial risk of prejudice to the administration of justice".[9]

2. THE ORDER OF PROCEEDINGS

We shall consider the proceedings at trial in some detail in this chapter and see them from the point of view of the various parties to the trial: the accused, counsel, witnesses, the judge and the jury. At the outset it is useful to set out the chronology of the trial from the first appearance of the accused until he or she leaves the court.[10]

(a) The arraignment[11]

The accused is brought to the bar of the court and the indictment is read out and a plea in respect of each count is sought. The plea may be to the "general issue", that is a plea of "guilty" or "not guilty". Alternatively, a plea of a

---

[3] See *Attorney-General v. Leveller Magazine* [1979] A.C. 440, Art. 6(1) of the European Convention on Human Rights (emphasising the need for a "fair and public hearing" and that judgment is to "be pronounced publicly") and *Blackstone's Criminal Practice 1996*, para. D2.47.

[4] Allowance for this is made in the European Convention: "but the press and public may be excluded from all or part of the trial in the interests of morals, public order, or national security in a democratic society, where the interests of juveniles or the protection of the private life of the parties so require, or to the extent strictly necessary in the opinion of the court in special circumstances where publicity would prejudice the interests of justice:" Art. 6(1).

[5] Much of the credit for the creation of this provision is due to Tim Crook and the National Union of Journalists, see, *e.g., R. v. Central Criminal Court, ex p. Crook, The Times,* November 8, 1984.

[6] Both Crown Court and a magistrates' court, even though s.121(4) of the Magistrates' Courts Act 1980 obliges magistrates' courts to sit in open court; see *Blackstones Criminal Practice 1996*, para. D2.53 and Archbold, *Criminal Pleading, Evidence and Practice 1995*, para. 4–2.

[7] *Blackstone's Criminal Practice 1996*, para. D2.49.

[8] *See Blackstone's Criminal Practice 1996*, para. D2.50.

[9] *See Blackstone's Criminal Practice 1996*, para. D2.52 and S. H. Bailey, D. J. Harris and B. L. Jones, *Civil Liberties: Cases and Materials* (4th ed., 1995), pp. 392–399. Reporting is also limited by the need to comply with general rules relating to contempt of court to protect the trial from being prejudged or prejudiced and also by other statutory rules, such as s.11 of the Contempt of Court Act 1981 on withholding of names and various provisions to protect the identity of children and victims of sexual offences.

[10] See also D. Barnard, *The Criminal Court in Action* (4th ed., 1994).

[11] See *Blackstone's Criminal Practice 1996*, paras. D9.1–D9.4.

special nature may be entered. This is the point of the trial where issues such as double jeopardy, the jurisdiction of the court to try the accused and errors in the indictment may be raised.[12]

(i) Double jeopardy

A basic principle is that no person should be tried twice for the same offence. Consequently "the unwarranted harassment of the accused by multiple prosecutions" is avoided.[13] The principle is established in English law by the availability of the special pleas in bar: the pleas of *autrefois acquit*; of *autrefois convict*; and of pardon.[14] These pleas are rarely used in practice, because the accuracy of court records ensures that people are rarely prosecuted for the same offence twice.[15]

(1) *Autrefois acquit and autrefois convict*.[16] The appropriate plea, depending upon whether the accused has already been acquitted (*autrefois acquit*) or convicted (*autrefois convict*) of the same offence, or substantially the same offence, is normally made in writing before the beginning of the trial, although it may be made at any stage. After such a plea, it is for the judge without a jury to decide whether the plea is successful.[17]

The circumstances in which either plea will be available were explored in *Connelly v. D.P.P.*.[18] The House of Lords, mainly through the speech of Lord Morris, indicated that the pleas are not limited to circumstances where an accused has been charged with exactly the same offence arising out of the same set of circumstances. A person previously acquitted or convicted of an offence cannot be tried again for that same offence or a substantially similar offence or an offence which was a proper alternative.[19] A proper alternative offence is one of which the accused could have been found guilty at the earlier trial instead of that named in the indictment. So, for example, if Fred is acquitted of murdering Ann, he cannot later be charged with her murder, even if there is fresh evidence, nor can he be charged with her manslaughter or causing her death by reckless driving or causing her grievous bodily harm with intent. Further, if the accused has previously been acquitted of an offence which, as a matter of fact, is essential to establish guilt of the offence charged, he or she cannot be tried

---

[12] As will be seen in the relevant passage, these issues can also be raised at other points in the sequence of the trial.

[13] See M. L. Friedland, *Double Jeopardy* (1969), pp. 3–4.

[14] The possibility of similar questions arising through issue estoppel must be recognised, although such an argument is probably inapplicable to the criminal law: *D.P.P. v. Humphrys* [1977] A.C. 1. The more likely method of raising these questions is through the inherent power of the judges to prevent oppression of an accused where there is an abuse of process. Abuse of process is a claim being considered by the courts much more frequently in recent years, see Pattenden (1990), pp. 32–38.

[15] See Emmins (1995), p. 95.

[16] For a full treatment of the law, see *Blackstone's Criminal Practice 1996*, paras. D9.28–D9.37; Archbold (1995), paras.4–101 to 4–130; Emmins (1995), pp. 95–98.

[17] Criminal Justice Act 1988, s.122.

[18] [1964] A.C. 1254.

[19] The power to enter an alternative verdict is provided by the Criminal Law Act 1967, s.6, which has been widely interpreted by the House of Lords in *R. v. Wilson*; *R. v. Jenkins and another* [1984] A.C. 242; see *Blackstone's Criminal Practice 1996*, paras. D15.20, D15.21 and D15.30.

for that lesser offence later.[20] However, the plea of autrefois convict does not operate to prevent a person being tried on a charge which is more serious than the one of which he or she has originally been convicted. So, for example, if Dorothy attacks and seriously injures Michael she may be convicted of causing grievous bodily harm with intent. If Michael dies after the trial from the injuries, Dorothy may be tried for murder, provided Michael's death takes place within a year and a day of the attack.[21]

(2) *Pardon.* The plea is that the accused has already been pardoned for the offence.[22]

(ii) Jurisdiction

The plea is that the court has no jurisdiction to try the accused for the relevant offence.[23]

(iii) Errors in the indictment

There are many technical rules about the drafting of indictments, primarily concerned with the requirements that indictments must be (a) positive and (b) not duplicitous. The rules are discussed in the works on criminal procedure.[24] Such errors perceived by the accused may be raised for consideration through a number of avenues, but primarily by applying to the judge to quash the indictment[25] or by an abuse of process claim. These are not pleas as such. It is most unlikely that the almost obsolete demurrer will be used to object to the wording of the indictment.[26]

(b) The empanelling and swearing of the jury

If a plea of not guilty is entered, a jury of twelve people will be empanelled and, after an opportunity for challenges, sworn. The indictment will be read to

---

[20] Consequently, an earlier acquittal of theft precludes a trial for robbery on the same facts, because theft is an essential element in proving robbery, see Theft Act 1968, ss.1 and 8.

[21] See *R. v. Dyson* [1908] 2 K.B. 454 and J. C. Smith and B. Hogan, *Criminal Law* (7th ed., 1992), pp. 327–350, esp, p. 330.

[22] Pardons now always follow convictions, so the plea has become obsolete, see *Blackstone's Criminal Practice 1996*, para. D9.40.

[23] The plea is concerned with the territorial jurisdiction of the court. The Crown Court can, as a general rule, only try crimes committed in England and Wales, see *Blackstone's Criminal Practice 1996*, para. D1.72. Jurisdiction issues relating to crimes of fraud and dishonesty will be covered by the Criminal Justice Act 1993 when implemented; *ibid.*, paras. D1.73–D1.76. As to exceptions to the general rule, see *ibid*, paras, D1.77–D1.84.

[24] *Blackstone's Criminal Practice 1996*, Archbold (1995), Emmins (1995).

[25] As to a motion to quash the indictment and the errors that may be raised, see *Blackstone's Criminal Practice 1996*, para. D8.39; Archbold (1995), paras.1–1 to 1–273; Emmins (1995), Chap. 6.

[26] Archbold (1995), para. 4–99.

the jury which will be told of its obligation to listen to the evidence and to determine guilt or innocence.

(c) The opening speech

Counsel for the prosecution addresses the jury. The function of the opening is to explain to the jury the basic elements of the prosecution case, the evidence that is to be called and the burden and standard of proof. Even allowing for the fact that any mistakes may ultimately be corrected by the judge in the summing-up, it is vital that prosecution counsel does not claim more than can be proved for it may eventually be difficult for the jury to remember whether allegations made in the speech were actually substantiated by the evidence.[27] Equally counsel must not refer to any evidence which is inadmissible,[28] or which defending counsel has indicated will be challenged as inadmissible.

(d) The prosecution case

Witnesses called by the prosecution give their evidence in turn (examination-in-chief) and may be subjected to questioning by the defence (cross-examination). Counsel for the prosecution may have the final word with each witness (re-examination) but must ask questions only on matters raised in the course of cross-examination. The way in which and the sort of questions counsel asks and whether evidence is admissible are both decided upon by the judge alone.[29]

(e) Defence submission of no case to answer

At the close of the prosecution case the defence may ask the trial judge to direct the jury to acquit the accused because there is no case to answer. If this submission is accepted, the trial ends and the accused is acquitted.

(f) Defence opening speech

Defence counsel is only entitled to make an opening speech to the jury if at least one witness (other than the accused) is to be called as to the *facts* of the case. Otherwise, counsel must simply start to call evidence.

(g) The defence case

Witnesses called by the defence are examined. They may be cross-examined by prosecution counsel and re-examined by defence counsel.

---

[27] A particular example of the dangers is to be found in the trial of James Hanratty, where a vital piece of evidence was referred to in the opening speech but never proved in evidence; see L. Blom-Cooper, *The A6 Murder*. In any event, it may be tactically more sensible to pitch the opening on a relatively low key lest the jury should later be disappointed with the prosecution witnesses.

[28] The opening of such evidence will not automatically lead to the quashing of a subsequent conviction: *R. v. Jackson* [1953] 1 W.L.R. 591. The normal course would be for the judge to discharge the jury and recommence the trial if the defendant has been seriously prejudiced.

[29] See pp. 865–866 and 878, below.

(h) Closing speeches

Both counsel may address the jury at the close of the evidence. The prosecution goes first and the defence has the last word. In the closing speech prosecution counsel may review the evidence and emphasise alleged strengths in the prosecution case and weaknesses in the defence. The jury is likely to be reminded once again of the burden and standard of proof.

(i) The summing-up

The trial judge must sum up the evidence to the jury, directing it as to the law and explaining its function.

(j) The verdict

The jury retire to consider its verdict. Only very exceptionally is evidence admitted after the retirement of the jury. An unanimous verdict is the first objective, but a majority verdict may eventually be acceptable. The verdict of the jury is announced by the person known as the "foreman" in open court.

(k) Information for sentencing

Since not all the necessary information is provided during the trial to enable an appropriate sentence to be imposed, after conviction an information gathering exercise is often undertaken, which includes the possibility of a plea in mitigation being made by either defence counsel or the accused in person.

(l) Sentence

The judge passes sentence on the accused.

3. THE ACCUSED

Historically, the accused laboured under a considerable disadvantage in the criminal trial. The Criminal Law Revision Committee, considering the rules of evidence in criminal cases identified the following difficulties which had hindered the accused:[30]

(i) The "indecent haste" with which trials were conducted, in a potentially unfair manner.[31] Representation, legal aid and judicial unwillingness to curtail trials now ensure that there are few complaints of brevity. If anything, now the complaint is that trials go on too long.

---

[30] Criminal Law Revision Committee, *Eleventh Report, Evidence (General)* (Cmnd. 4991, 1972), pp. 10–12.
[31] Mr Justice Hawkins described one 1840's Old Bailey Trial which lasted two minutes 53 seconds as "a high example of expedition," and stated that trials after dinner lasted on average four minutes: Hawkins, *Memoirs*, cited in the C.L.R.C. 11th Report (1972), p. 11.

   (ii) Legal representation was severely restricted before 1836.[32] The arrival
       of legal aid has ensured representation in at least all serious cases,
       although the accused may occasionally still be unrepresented.[33]
  (iii) The accused was not permitted to give evidence on oath in all cases.
       The Criminal Evidence Act 1898 provided the accused with this right
       in all cases.[34]
  (vi) There was only rarely a right to appeal against conviction. A general
       right of appeal was provided by the Criminal Appeal Act 1907.[35]

Since all these obstacles to a fair trial have been removed, and, according to
the C.L.R.C., because of the improved quality of juries and magistrates, it has
been suggested that the accused is in a very strong position in the criminal trial.[36]
This view is not accepted by all commentators. McBarnet,[37] on completion of
a critical examination of the criminal justice system, concluded that the "process
of conviction is easier than the rhetoric of justice would have us expect—and
easier still the lower the status of the defendant."[38] Whilst the law appears to
provide considerable protection for the accused, there are many exceptions to
that law, which reduce the protection in reality. At the time she was writing,
McBarnet was able to point to the fact that the actual operation of the right to
silence does not guarantee that the accused need not incriminate himself or
herself; and whilst there is in many cases a formal right to jury trial, the vast
majority of cases are tried without a jury.[39] Since then the right to silence has
been abolished and other changes have meant that even the rhetoric of justice
is viewed by many commentators as unconvincing.[40]

    The first procedural question concerns the attendance of the accused at court.
If in custody, the accused is brought to court from prison; if on bail, the accused
is informed of the time and date of the trial and told to attend. The accused
must attend court so as to answer in person when the indictment is put, because
no-one else may enter a plea.[41] Whilst needing to be present at the arraignment,
the accused may be absent for the trial, although that will happen only in exceptional cases, because the accused needs to be present in order to "hear the case
against him and have the opportunity . . . of answering it."[42] Such cases include

---

[32] Prior to the Trials for Felony Act 1836, the defence counsel in felony trials was limited to
arguments on points of law and giving advice to the defendant on how he or she should conduct
his or her case.

[33] As to the availability of legal aid, see above, pp. 767–772.

[34] The accused could only make an unsworn statement from the dock, which would carry little
credibility with the jury: see M. Cohen, "The Unsworn Statement from the Dock" [1981] Crim.
L.R. 224.

[35] As to criminal appeals, see pp. 923–944, below.

[36] C.L.R.C. Eleventh Report (1972), pp. 10–12.

[37] D. J. McBarnet, *Conviction: Law, the State and the Construction of Justice* (1981).

[38] *Ibid.*, p. 155.

[39] *Ibid.*, pp. 154–155.

[40] See, e.g. Sanders and Young (1994) and below.

[41] *R. v. Heyes* [1951] 1 K.B. 29 and see *Blackstone's Criminal Practice 1996*, para. D9.18. In some
circumstances, the failure of the accused to plead personally to the indictment results in a mistrial:
R. v. Boyle [1954] 2 Q.B. 292; *R. v. Ellis* (1973) 57 Cr. App. R. 571. However, if the trial had
proceeded as though a "not guilty" plea had been recorded no material irregularity had necessarily occurred: *R. v. Williams* [1978] Q.B. 373 and see *Blackstone's Criminal Practice 1996*, paras.
D9.6, D9.2 and D9.14. As to the position in summary trials, see pp. 838–839, above.

[42] *R. v. Lee Kun* (1916) 11 Cr. App. R. 293, 300, *per* Lord Reading. See *Blackstone's Criminal
Practice 1996*, paras. D11.26–D11.29, *R. v. Howson* (1982) 74 Cr. App. R. 172 and G. Zellick,
"The Criminal Trial and the Disruptive Defendant" (1980) 43 M.L.R. 121, 284.

those where the accused is violent or disorderly,[43] is ill,[44] or absconds from the trial.[45] An accused who is likely to intimidate a witness may be removed from the presence of the witness, but not out of hearing.[46]

The second procedural question relates to the accused's response on arraignment after the indictment has been read. The accused is required to answer to every count on the indictment and each plea will be recorded. In the great majority of cases the plea will be "guilty" or "not guilty," although there are several other possibilities.[47]

(a) The plea of guilty

This acknowledgment of guilt must be unmistakeable. It must be made freely by the accused in person who must have knowledge of the elements of the offence.[48] The accused must not be under undue pressure from counsel or the court. It is quite proper for defence counsel to advise the accused, perhaps in very forceful terms, that a plea of guilty could be advantageous in securing a lesser sentence and/or that the evidence seems to point strongly to guilt. Counsel must also stress that a guilty plea should only be entered if the accused has actually committed the alleged offence.[49]

The importance attached to the accused's freedom to enter the plea desired is reflected in the "plea bargaining" cases where it was suspected that unfair pressure had been placed on the accused.[50] "Plea bargaining ... describes the practice whereby the accused enters a plea of guilty in return for which he will be given some consideration that results in a sentence concession."[51]

---

[43] See *Blackstone's Criminal Practice 1996*, para. D11.27. It is possible to handcuff or restrain an accused, but only if there is a danger of escape or violence, and whether such restraint is justified should be investigated in court without the jury, see *R. v. Vratsides* [1988] Crim. L.R. 251. See also *R. v. Berry* (1897) 104 L. T. Journ. 110, where the accused performed an impromptu striptease on the clerk's table.

[44] *R. v. Orton* (1873), cited in Archbold (1995), para. 3–47; *R. v. Howson* (1981) 74 Cr. App. R. 172, where it was indicated that the discretion must not be exercised if the accused's defence could be prejudiced by his or her absence and see *Blackstone's Criminal Practice 1996*, para. D11.29.

[45] *R. v. Jones (No. 2)* [1972] 1 W.L.R. 887 and see *Blackstone's Criminal Practice 1996*, para. D11.28.

[46] *R. v. Smellie* (1919) 14 Cr. App. R. 128. As to the statutory extension of this power in relation to the use of live television links, especially in child abuse cases, see pp. 871–872 below.

[47] See pp. 850–852, above.

[48] *R. v. Golathan* (1915) 11 Cr. App. R. 79. For the dangers of pleas entered by counsel, see *Ellis* (1973) 57 Cr. App. Rep. 571 and *Blackstone's Criminal Practice 1996*, para. D9.18.

[49] See *ibid.*, para. D9.24 on involuntary pleas and see below, p. 868 on the obligations of defence counsel.

[50] The particular pressure that gives rise to concern is where it appears to the accused that the judge has indicated to counsel that an unsuccessful plea of not guilty will attract a heavier sentence: *R. v. Turner* [1970] 2 Q.B. 321, see pp. 876–878, below.

[51] J. Baldwin and M. McConville, *Negotiated Justice* (1977), p. 19. This research study is a prerequisite for any detailed study of the subject of plea bargaining. See also, P. Thomas, "Plea Bargaining and the Turner Case" [1970] Crim. L.R. 559; A. Davis, "Sentences for Sale: A New Look at Plea Bargaining in England and America" [1970] Crim. L.R. 150 and 218; R. Purves, "That Plea-Bargaining Business" [1971] Crim. L.R. 470; S. McCabe and R. Purves, *By-Passing the Jury* (1972); Bottoms and McLean (1976); J. Baldwin and M. McConville, "Plea Bargaining: legal carve-up or legal cover-up" (1978) 5 B.J.L.S. 228, "Plea Bargaining and the Court of Appeal" (1979) 6 B.J.L.S. 200, "The Influence of the Sentencing Discount in Inducing Guilty Pleas" in J. Baldwin and A. K. Bottomley (eds.), *Criminal Justice: Selected Readings*, "Preserving the Good Face of Justice: Some Recent Plea Bargain Cases" (1978) 128 N.L.J. 872 and *Court, Prosecution and Conviction* (1981); S. Moody and J. Tombs, "Plea Negotiations and

The first method is by a plea arrangement made between prosecuting and defence counsel whereby a plea of guilty to a lesser charge on the indictment is accepted in return for the prosecution not proceeding with the more serious charges.[52] The second method by which the sentence concession is obtained is a plea of guilty to the offence charged. A guilty plea attracts a lighter sentence.[53] The amount of discount can be substantial.[54] In some cases the discount will operate not only to reduce the severity of a particular form of sentence but also to alter the type of sentence from, for example, custodial to non-custodial.

The value of a guilty plea in the criminal process is that it reduces the time and money spent on achieving convictions, it obviates the need for a trial and the inherent difficulties of proof, it spares the witnesses an experience which can be both unpleasant and distressing,[55] and it is alleged to demonstrate an attitude of contrition and remorse on the part of the accused. The advantages to the prosecution of offering concessions or inducements to persuade the accused to plead guilty are the certainty and economy thereby secured. These advantages must be balanced against the need to ensure that offenders are convicted of offences only when they are actually guilty and which properly represent the seriousness of their behaviour.[56]

For the truly guilty defendant and the prosecution, a plea bargain represents a mutually beneficial compromise. A guilty plea is obtained and so is a sentence concession. However, these concessions also operate (intentionally) as inducements and create pressure on the accused. There are, however, significant problems both with charge-bargaining and with the sentence discount. Although the research of McCabe and Purves suggested that the guilty pleas obtained were justified in the light of the evidence and the benefit to the criminal justice system,[57] subsequent research has largely demonstrated that the change of plea, especially when late, was based upon the advice of the lawyers[58] and was contrary to the actual wishes of the accused, resulting in the supposed imprisonment of innocent people.[59] Having noted the inability of the judiciary to control this problem,[60] Sanders and Young conclude that charge bargaining has the "potential to undermine adversarial due process and to increase the risk that innocent

Scotland" [1983] Crim. L.R. 297; S. Moody and J. Toombs, *Prosecution in the Public Interest* (1982); Sanders and Young (1994), pp. 334–338.

[52] See pp. 863–865, below. This is also known as charge-bargaining, see Sanders and Young (1994), pp. 269–271 and 301–318.

[53] See D. A. Thomas, *Current Sentencing Practice*, para. A8.2(b) and see *R.v. Cain* [1976] Q.B. 496. See Sanders and Young (1994), pp. 318–339.

[54] *Current Sentencing Practice*, at para A8.2(c), suggests that the extent of the reduction is between one quarter and one third of what would otherwise have been the sentence and see *Blackstone's Criminal Practice 1996*, para. E1.18. The discount now has statutory recognition, see Criminal Justice and Public Order Act 1994, s.48 which also requires reasons to be given for the reduction (s.48(2)); see B. Davies and G. Dingwall, "Defendants' guilty pleas and Section" 48 (1966) *Legal Action*, February, 8.

[55] This may be a particularly significant factor where the charges include sexual offences: *R. v. Grice* (1977) 66 Cr. App. R. 167.

[56] See below, pp. 863–864 for the obligations of prosecuting counsel.

[57] S. McCabe and R. Purves, *By-passing the Jury* (1972) and see Sanders and Young (1994), pp. 307–308.

[58] See below, pp. 863–865 and 867–869 as to the role of the lawyers.

[59] A. Bottoms and J. McClean, *Defendants in the Criminal Process* (1976) and J. Baldwin and M. McConville, *Negotiated Justice* (1977); and see Sanders and Young (1994), pp. 308–309. However, the Crown Court Survey discovered that few innocent people were persuaded to plead guilty; see Zander and Henderson (1993), pp. 96–98.

[60] See below, pp. 876–878.

persons will plead guilty"[61] and yet they point out that the Royal Commission merely stated that "We see no objection to such discussions, but the earlier they take place the better; consultation between counsel before the trial would often avoid the need for the case to be listed as a contested trial."[62] The concern of the Commission was with the wastage of resources of the "cracked trial", that is the trial which was believed to be contested, but at which the accused pleads guilty.[63] The specific dangers associated with the sentence discount also surround the possibility of innocent people pleading guilty.

> "[The] sentencing discount, by encouraging defendants to convict them-selves through a guilty plea, reduces the effect of the due process principle that the burden of proof rests on the prosecution. The prosecution of cases involving no more than vague allegations and other potential misuses of state prosecutorial power may be left unchecked. Moreover, the high guilty plea rate to which the sentence discount contributes means that there is little incentive for the prosecuting authorities to ensure that only properly prepared cases are brought to trial. . . . A further problem is that the dis-count principle penalises those who stand on their right to put the pros-ecution to proof."[64]

If a guilty plea is made in error by the accused, it may be withdrawn, and the trial judge may permit a change of plea at any time before sentence.[65]

(b) The plea of not guilty

This plea occasions little difficulty. It constitutes a denial of the prosecution's allegations and requires them to prove all the elements of their case, except those facts admitted by the defence.[66] The plea must be entered by the accused personally.[67]

A plea of not guilty may be changed during the trial with the leave of the judge.[68] There are many reasons for a change of plea, including a realisation of the effect of sentence discount when there has been a guilty plea and the pos-sibility of an unwelcome outcome of the trial if the plea of not guilty is maintained.[69]

The prosecution does not have to proceed to trial but could (a) offer no evi-dence or (b) let counts lie on the file.[70]

---

[61] Sanders and Young (1994), p. 318.

[62] RCCJ, Report (1993), p. 114 quoted in Sanders and Young (1994), at p. 318.

[63] In fact not all parties are disappointed; the C.P.S., whilst recognising the resources wastage, also appreciated the guilty plea, especially when the prosecution was not convinced that it would get a conviction: Zander and Henderson (1993), p. 156.

[64] Sanders and Young (1994), p. 322.

[65] S. v. Manchester Recorder [1971] A.C. 481. Late changes of plea may well be made when the accused indicates that his or her original plea was made as a result of threats, see e.g., R. v. Dodd, Pack and others (1982) 74 Cr.App.R. 50.

[66] Admissions may be made at various stages of criminal proceedings in accordance with the Crimi-nal Justice Act 1967, s.10: see Emmins (1995), pp. 134–135.

[67] For instances where a plea of not guilty is entered on behalf of the accused, see below.

[68] As to the procedure to be adopted on change of plea, see R. v. Ellis (1973) 57 Cr. App.R. 571.

[69] In R. v. Sullivan [1984] A.C. 156 the accused changed his plea to guilty, because when he raised the claim that he assaulted someone when in an epileptic fit it was made clear that he was raising the defence of insanity which would result in his being sent to a mental hospital.

[70] Blackstone's Criminal Practice 1996, paras. D9.16 and D9.17.

(c) The accused not pleading

The expectation is that the accused will be able, with legal representation, to plead. However, the accused may "stand mute", that is make no reply or no intelligible reply, when the charge is put. A jury must be empanelled[71] to determine whether the accused is "mute of malice" or "mute by visitation of God". The issue is tried like any other jury matter by the bringing of evidence, examination of witnesses, summing-up and verdict. If the accused is found to be mute of malice (the prosecution having proved it beyond a reasonable doubt) a plea of not guilty is formally entered on behalf of the accused.[72] If found to be mute by visitation of God the question arises as to whether the accused is fit to plead to the charge at all. If found fit to plead, a not guilty plea is entered.

(d) Fitness to plead

The question of fitness to plead may arise not only where the accused has remained silent on arraignment and been found mute by visitation of God, but also where there is a defence submission of unfitness or the prosecution bring the matter to the judge's attention. The question is "whether the accused is under a disability, that is to say under any disability such that . . . it would constitute a bar to his being tried. . . ."[73] This issue is determined by a jury[74] considering the evidence and reaching a verdict in the normal way.[75] If the jury finds the accused unfit to plead, it must then determine whether he or she "did the act or made the omission charged against him as the offence" and, if so, make such a finding.[76] If not so satisfied, the jury must acquit the accused.[77] This procedure should avoid the criminal justice system detention of innocent, but mentally unfit, people in hospital.[78]

If the matter goes to the jury, they must determine whether or not the accused can instruct a solicitor and counsel, plead to the indictment, that is understand the charge and the significance of a plea, challenge jurors, understand the evidence, and give evidence.[79]

Because it is desirable that a person charged with a criminal offence should stand trial if possible and should have the chance to show that the prosecution case is inadequate, the question of fitness to plead may be deferred until the opening of the defence case, at the discretion of the trial judge.[80] The onus of proving the question of fitness lies with the party raising it. If raised by the

---

[71] In the normal way, see pp. 893–895, below.

[72] Criminal Law Act 1967, s.6(1) and the *Blackstone's Criminal Practice 1996*, para. D9.11.

[73] Criminal Procedure (Insanity) Act 1964, s.4(1).

[74] If a jury has found the accused mute by visitation of God the same jury may be resworn to try the issue of fitness, or a new jury may be used.

[75] Criminal Procedure (Insanity) Act 1964, s.4(5). There must be written oral evidence of two doctors: s.4(6).

[76] Criminal Procedure (Insanity) Act 1964, s.4A(2) and (3).

[77] *Ibid.*, s.4A(4).

[78] See *Blackstone's Criminal Practice 1996*, para. D9.8. The person might still be admitted to hospital, but through the non-criminal procedures within the Mental Health Act 1983, Part II. See R. D. Mackay, "Mental Condition Defences in the Criminal Law" (1995).

[79] *R. v. Pritchard* (1836) 7 C. & P. 303; *R. v. Robertson* [1968] 1 W.L.R. 1767. See, generally, *Blackstone's Criminal Practice 1996*, para. D9.7; Archbold (1995), paras.4–114 to 4–120; Emmins (1995), pp. 89–90; and Smith and Hogan (1992), pp. 182–185.

[80] Criminal Procedure (Insanity) Act 1964, s.4(2). The same process then applies: s.4A(5).

defence it must be proved on a balance of probabilities; if raised by the prosecution or the judge it must be proved beyond reasonable doubt.[81]

At one time, the mandatory consequence of such a finding was that the person had to be transferred to a mental hospital. This was the case even if the individual had no (treatable) mental disorder, which is not a requirement for the finding.[82] However, the changes introduced to the procedure by the Criminal Procedure (Insanity and Unfitness to Plead) Act 1991 will alleviate some of these problems by avoiding the finding affecting someone who did not commit the act or make the admission. In addition, that Act made significant changes to the consequences that flow from a finding of unfitness. Under the amended Criminal Procedure (Insanity) Act 1964, s.5, the court may make an admission order to such hospital as the Secretary of State specifies, make a guardianship order under the Mental Health Act 1983, make a supervision and treatment order, or make an order for the accused's absolute discharge.

(e) Right to silence

It was always the case that a judge had to be particularly careful in addressing the jury where the accused had made no answer to the police and/or had not disclosed a defence until trial,[83] and when the accused had exercised the right to give evidence at trial. The "right to silence" was predicated on the propositions that the accused should not be required to provide any evidence which might be incriminating and is entitled to make the prosecution prove its case without answering questions before or at the trial. Some comment could be made by the judge. It was safest for the judge not to comment on the accused's failure to disclose a defence until trial or to answer questions before trial, with some exceptions.[84] Where the accused failed to testify, the accepted comment was that established by Lord Parker C.J. in *R. v. Bathurst*[85]:

> " ... the accused is not bound to give evidence, that he can sit back and see if the prosecution have proved their case, and that, whilst the jury have been deprived of the opportunity of hearing his story tested in cross-examination, the one thing that they must not do is to assume that he is guilty because he has not gone into the witness box."

What the judge could not do was to suggest to the jury that guilt could be assumed from silence. Proposals for change had been made, controversially, by the Criminal Law Revision Committee in 1972,[86] but only limited changes were

---

[81] The question of the onus and standard of proof is considered in *R. v. Podola* [1960] 1 Q.B. 325, which is of general interest on the question of fitness to plead.

[82] See C. Emmins, "Unfitness to Plead: Some Thoughts Prompted by Glenn Pearson's Case" [1986] Crim. L.R. 604.

[83] There are number of relatively long standing obligations on the accused: (1) pre-trial disclosure in fraud cases: Criminal Justice Act 1987, s.2 and see *Blackstone's Criminal Practice 1996*, para. D1.59; (2) notice of an alibi defence: Criminal Justice Act 1967, s.11 and see *ibid.*, para. D13.4; (3) notice of the intended use of expert evidence: Police and Criminal Evidence Act 1984, s.81 and see *ibid.*, para. F10.3.

[84] See *Blackstone's Criminal Practice 1996*, paras. F19.2–F19.3.

[85] [1968] 1 All E.R. 1175, at p. 1178. See also *R. v. Martinez-Tobon* [1994] 1 W.L.R. 388 and *Blackstone's Criminal Practice 1996*, para. F19.11.

[86] *Eleventh Report: Evidence (General)* (Cmnd. 4991).

recommended by the Royal Commission on Criminal Justice.[87] However, major changes, restricting the right to silence in terms of testifying at trial, have been introduced by the Criminal Justice and Public Order Act 1994. The right to keep silent is not abolished but greater risks are now run by the accused who maintain that position.

Section 34[88] provides that where an accused, before charge, when questioned under caution or after charge, "failed to mention any fact relied on in his defence" in criminal proceedings and that fact was one "which in the circumstances existing at the time the accused could reasonably have been expected to mention when so questioned, charged or informed" then the judge (or magistrates) may "draw such inferences from the failure as appear proper."[89] There can be no conviction on silence alone,[90] and the inference that may be drawn is "to allow the conclusion that the fact is untrue; in other words the provision goes only to the credit to be given to the evidence of the particular fact."[91] The requirement to mention facts must, it has been argued,

"make allowance: (a) for the personal characteristics of the accused (e.g., mental handicap/illness) to be taken into account in deciding what he should reasonably be expected to have mentioned; (b) for the extent of the accused's knowledge of the case against him (e.g., if he is not told when an offence is supposed to have occurred he cannot reasonably be expected to mention an alibi)."[92]

As regards the failure to testify, section 35 provides that at a trial[93] and at the conclusion of the prosecution case (so it would appear that the matter does not arise where there is no case to answer[94]) if the accused does not give evidence or then answer questions (without good cause), "it will be permissible for the court or jury to draw such inferences as appear proper from his failure to give evidence or his refusal, without good cause, to answer any question." Whilst the accused is not compelled to give evidence,[95] the risks in failing to give evidence are enhanced, since the inference which the court may draw is that the accused is guilty of the offence charged.[96] However, the accused cannot be

---

[87] RCCJ, Report (1993), pp. 54–55. The majority recommended that "it is when but only when the prosecution has been fully disclosed that defendants should be required to offer and answer to the charges made against them at the risk of adverse comment at trial on any new defence they then disclose or on any departure from the defence which they previously disclosed."

[88] s.36 and 37 are concerned with the failure to account for objects, substances, marks and presence; see *Blackstone's Criminal Practice 1996*, paras. F19.8–F19.9.

[89] Criminal Justice and Public Order Act 1994, s.34(1) and (2).

[90] *Ibid.*, s.38.

[91] *Blackstone's Criminal Practice 1996*, para. F19.4. What inferences may be drawn will depend upon the particular circumstances of the case; see *Haw Tua Tau v. Public Prosecutor* [1982] A.C. 136 and see *Blackstone's Criminal Practice 1996*, para. F19.7.

[92] *Blackstone's Criminal Practice 1996*, para. F19.7.

[93] If the accused's guilt is not in issue or "it appears to the court that the physical or mental condition of the accused makes it undesirable for him to give evidence", the provisions do not apply: s.35(1).

[94] *Blackstone's Criminal Practice 1996*, para. F19.13.

[95] s.35(4).

[96] s.35(3), see *Murray v. D.P.P.* [1994] 1 W.L.R. 1 (on the existing Northern Ireland provisions) and *Blackstone's Criminal Practice 1996*, para. F19.13.

convicted solely on an inference drawn from silence,[97] and inferences of guilt will not be drawn where the prosecution has a weak case.[98]

These changes may be regarded as a significant infringement in the existing rights of the accused, and may reflect a move towards the crime control model.[99]

There are other procedural matters concerning the accused as well as his or her attendance and arraignment, particularly the extent to which character and antecedents can be referred to and the extent to which the credibility of prosecution witnesses can be attacked. These matters are dealt with in discussing the roles of other participants in the trial.

4. Representation and the Obligations of Counsel

The availability of legal aid[1] ensures that it is very unusual to find an unrepresented accused in the Crown Court. Those who are unrepresented have normally chosen to conduct their own defence.[2] Both prosecution and defence counsel are under obligations to behave in a particular manner in the course of the trial and we shall examine some examples. Counsel should always act in accordance with the rules and etiquette of the Bar.[3] "A practising barrister has an overriding duty to the Court to ensure in the public interest that the proper and efficient administration of justice is achieved: he must assist the court in the administration of justice and must not deceive or knowingly or recklessly mislead the court."[4] The latter principle is of the utmost importance and impinges upon the task of counsel at several points in the trial.

(a) Prosecuting counsel

The Standards Applicable to Criminal Cases annexed to the Code of Conduct for the Bar of England and Wales state that:

> "Prosecuting counsel should not attempt to obtain a conviction by all means at his command. He should not regard himself as appearing for a party. He should lay before the Court fairly and impartially the whole of the facts which comprise the case for the prosecution and should assist the Court on all matters of law applicable to the case."[5]

---

[97] s.38.

[98] *Murray v. D.P.P.* [1994] 1 W.L.R. 1; *Waugh v. The King* [1950] A.C. 203; and see *Blackstone's Criminal Practice 1996*, para. F19.14.

[99] See, further, below, p. 914.

[1] See pp. 767–772, above.

[2] If the defendant is unrepresented, the judge is under an obligation to ensure the proper conduct of the trial: Archbold (1995), paras.4–315 to 4–316.

[3] *Code of Conduct for the Bar of England and Wales* (5th ed., 1990), as amended. "The general purpose of this Code is to provide the standards of conduct on the part of barristers which are appropriate in the interests of justice in England and Wales . . .": *ibid.* para. 102 and see above, Chap. 3.

[4] *ibid.* para. 202. A barrister's other duties include the obligation to act honestly and with proper regard to the public confidence in the profession, to exercise independent, professional judgment and to promote fearlessly the client's best interests: *ibid.* paras.203, 205, 206.

[5] *ibid.* Annex H, para. 10.1 *et seq.* (hereinafter, *Standards in Criminal Cases*). See also the Report of Mr. Justice Farquharson's Committee on the Role of Prosecuting Counsel (1986), set out in Archbold (1995), paras.4–72 to 4–80.

This view has found judicial expression at various times and prosecuting counsel have even been described as "ministers of justice assisting in the administration of justice."[6] A distinguished Old Bailey judge, who had been Senior Prosecuting Counsel at that court, warned a prosecutor against feeling pride or satisfaction in the mere fact of success, or boasting of the percentage of convictions secured over a period of time. It is, he said, ". . . no rebuff to his prestige if he fails to convince the tribunal of the prisoner's guilt."[7] It is highly undesirable for prosecuting counsel to use unnecessarily emotive language which can only excite sympathy for the victim or prejudice against the accused.[8]

What is required of prosecuting counsel is an element of objectivity in conducting the trial process. This will often be difficult to achieve.

Three broad areas may be identified which necessitate careful consideration and the exercise of judgment by counsel: the desirability and propriety of a plea arrangement; the nature and presentation of the prosecution case at trial; the amount of assistance which needs to be given to the defence or the judge.

(i) The plea arrangements

Where there are a number of counts in the indictment or where one count contains alternative charges or where the jury might convict of a lesser charge, it is not uncommon for the defence to offer or the prosecution to seek a plea of guilty to a lesser charge in return for an agreement from the prosecution to offer no evidence on the more serious charge. This is a form of plea bargaining. In a sense, there is a double advantage in these circumstances. Assume that the accused is charged on one indictment containing two separate counts of rape and one count of indecent assault. If, in return for an agreement to accept not guilty pleas to the counts of rape, the accused agrees to plead guilty to the other count he will render himself liable to a less severe sentence on the lesser charge and also receive credit for a guilty plea. Clearly, the offer of a plea arrangement creates a certain amount of pressure on the accused.[9] Sanders and Young suggest that barristers acting for the prosecution have a number of reasons, other than the client's best interests, for seeking to settle a case, including that they are expected to seek bargains since that is, for example, in the interests of the administration of justice, and the comity of the Bar; and the fact that a barrister may do both prosecution and defence work which encourages agreements.[10]

The advantages of a guilty plea for the prosecution are obvious: there is a saving of time and money; witnesses are spared the experience of testifying; the inevitable uncertainty of the trial is exchanged for the certainty of a plea. On the other hand, "a Crown Prosecutor must never accept a guilty plea just because it is convenient."[11] Justice demands first that the offence in the indict-

[6] *R. v. Puddick* (1865), set out in Archbold (1995), paras.4–72 to 4–80.
[7] C. Humphreys, "The Duties and Responsibilities of Prosecuting Counsel" [1955] Crim. L.R. 739.
[8] Archbold (1995), para. 4–264.
[9] For a consideration of the pressures on the accused, see pp. 856–858, above.
[10] Sanders and Young (1994), pp. 313–315.
[11] Code for Crown Prosecutors, para. 9.1. See also the Home Affairs Committee Fourth Report for Session 1989–90, *Crown Prosecution Service* H.C. 118–1, paras.36–44.

ment should be prosecuted where the evidence supports the charge,[12] unless there are exceptional factors suggesting otherwise, and secondly that the court should be able to pass a sentence that matches the seriousness of the offending.[13]

Defence counsel will merely be negotiating for an "offer" which can be put to the client, whilst reminding the client that a plea of guilty should be entered only if he or she is actually guilty. The vigour with which defence counsel commends the arrangement which has been negotiated may be related to factors other than the strength of the evidence and the story of the client.[14]

The arrangement of pleas is a common feature of the trial on indictment and it is alleged that it can be improperly facilitated by "overcharging" the accused at the outset. If more serious charges are included on the indictment when the evidence is, at best, equivocal, prosecuting counsel has more to bargain with. The Code for Crown Prosecutors discourage a proliferation of charges and prohibits proceeding with a more serious charge "just a defendant to plead guilty to a less serious one."[15]

There are two constraints on plea arrangement. First, prosecuting counsel exercise no significant formal influence over sentence.[16] No bargain is directly permissible about the length of sentence on particular charges, but is permissible about the charges to be proceeded with.

Secondly, consideration must be given to the role of the judge. The respective roles of prosecuting counsel and judge have not been clearly defined, but it would seem that counsel has the right to offer no evidence on the indictment as a whole or to offer no evidence on a particular count. It is also the responsibility of the prosecution to decide whether to drop a particular charge.[17] The Court of Appeals has accepted the approach propounded by the Farquharson Committee on the Role of Prosecuting Counsel[18] that the decision is for prosecuting counsel subject to three important qualifications:

(1) If counsel seeks the approval of the judge, in particular where it is desirable to reassure the public at large that the course proposed is a proper one, counsel must abide by the judge's decision.[19]

(2) Where the judge takes a view on the basis of the information available that counsel is taking the wrong decision, the judge may decline to pro-

---

[12] Whilst this is based upon *R. v. Soanes* (1948) 32 Cr. App. R. 136, which, in part, whilst not representing the present position, as will be seen from the following discussion in the text, does represent a commonly held view.

[13] Code for Crown Prosecutors, para. 9.1.

[14] See further, pp. 867–869.

[15] Code for Crown Prosecutors, para. 7.2.

[16] Prosecuting counsel is limited, in effect, to rehearsing the facts about the previous record of the defendant. See G. Zellick, "The Role of Prosecuting Counsel in Sentencing" [1979] Crim. L.R. 493; M. King, "The Role of Prosecuting Counsel in Sentencing—What about Magistrates' Courts?" [1979] Crim. L.R. 775 and *Standard in Criminal Cases*, para. 11.8.

[17] *R. v. Grafton* (1993) 96 Cr. App. R. 156.

[18] A copy of the Report is to be found in Archbold, 1995 paras.4–72 to 4–80. On the basis of that Report, Sir Thomas Hetherington, the previous D. P. P., considers the relationship between the prosecution and the courts: *Prosecution and the Public Interest* (1989), pp. 169–171. See also Crown Prosecution Service, *The Crown Court: A Guide to Good Practice for the Courts* (1990).

[19] This proposition is supported by *R. v. Broad* (1978) 68 Cr. App. R. 281. In the Yorkshire Ripper case, the judge was asked whether he would accept the agreement between the prosecution and the defence to accept a plea by Peter Sutcliffe of guilty of manslaughter by diminished responsibility when charged with murder. The judge refused to accept the agreement, presumably because the public interest demanded a trial for murder.

ceed with the case until counsel has consulted with the Director of Public Prosecutions on whether to proceed in the light of the judge's comments. In the final analysis, the judge has no right to prevent counsel proceeding as decided.[20]

(3) Where a decision has to be made on whether to proceed during the course of the trial, that decision is to be made by counsel. The prosecution cannot discontinue proceedings after the end of its case without the leave of the judge.

None of this guidance relates to the power of the Attorney-General to enter a nolle prosequi to end the proceedings, which may be done at any stage.

(ii) The presentation of the prosecution case

Apart from planning the general strategy of the prosecution case, counsel[21] has four specific tasks in its presentation. Opening and closing speeches are made, prosecution witnesses are examined and defence witnesses are cross-examined. In each of these tasks rules of conduct as well as rules of procedure and evidence must be observed.

The *opening speech* to the jury is of the utmost importance. The greatest level of concentration and understanding is likely to be exhibited at the beginning and end of a trial. Jurors, especially, are likely to be taking their duties very seriously at the outset of the trial and the opening speech is bound to have considerable impact. It is highly undesirable that prosecuting counsel should open the case with unnecessarily emotive language, and where the offences charged are likely to excite particular sympathy for the victim or prejudice against the accused counsel should warn the jury not to be influenced by such emotions in weighing the evidence.[22]

In *examination-in-chief* of prosecution witnesses, counsel must obey the

---

[20] See also the Guidelines to Prosecution Counsel given by the Bar Committee of the Senate of the Four Inns of Court and the Bar (1984), as approved in *R v. Jenkins* (1986) 83 Cr. App. R. 152. In *R. v. Renshaw* [1989] Crim. L. R. 811, the Court of Appeal, referring to the Farquharson Report (1986), emphasised that it is important for the judge to listen to the reasons of counsel for offering no evidence, in particular since counsel may well have information not available to the judge, otherwise the judge is not in a position to decide whether to approve or disapprove counsel's proposed course of action.

[21] Counsel is not employed by the Crown Prosecution Service, whose lawyers do not yet have the right of audience in the Crown Court for trials (see above, pp. 128–129). The relationship between the instructing lawyer from C.P.S. and counsel was considered by the Farquharson Report (1986) and quoted in the *Standards in Criminal Cases*: para. 11.6 deals with some of the difficult cases: "(a) where counsel has taken a decision on a matter of policy with which his [or her] professional client has not agreed, it would be appropriate for him [or her] to submit to the Attorney-General a written report of all the circumstances, including his [or her] reasons for disagreeing with those who instructed him [or her]; (b) when counsel has had an opportunity to prepare his [or her] brief and to confer with those instructing him [or her], but at the last moment before trial unexpectedly advises that the case should not proceed or that pleas to lesser offences should be accepted, and his [or her] professional client does not accept such advice, counsel should apply for an adjournment if instructed to do so; (c) subject to the above, it is for prosecuting counsel to decide whether to offer no evidence on a particular count or on the indictment as a whole and whether to accept pleas to a lesser count or counts."

[22] Archbold (1995), para. 4–264. See also the Farquharson Report (1986).

golden rule of sticking to the facts in issue. Counsel should not use leading questions[23] (except on uncontentious matters and with the agreement of the defence[24]) and there are certain other constraints on the lines of questioning.[25] Whether a question is a leading one is a matter for the judge to decide.

In *cross-examination* of defence witnesses, prosecuting counsel is entitled to test their evidence fully and fairly subject to the normal constraints on the line of questioning.[26] Counsel may ask leading questions. If prosecuting counsel does choose to question the accused, there are statutory restrictions upon the putting of questions about the criminal past and bad character of the accused.[27]

(iii) Assisting the other participants—the defence and the judge

Prosecuting counsel has an obligation to assist the defence by the disclosure of certain evidence. The disclosure provisions are considered more fully else-where,[28] but in brief the prosecution must inform the defence of the name and address of any person who has made a statement related to the prosecution but is not to be called as a witness; of the existence of statements made previously by a prosecution witness which are inconsistent with evidence given at trial by the witness; and of the previous convictions, if any, of prosecution witnesses which are known to the prosecution. These disclosures may materially assist the defence case and further assistance requested by the defence may be rendered by the prosecution at their discretion.[29]

The obligation to assist the judge is made clear in the Code of Conduct. Not only must counsel assist by arguments on point of law or procedure arising during the trial, but it is also "the duty of prosecuting counsel to assist the court at the conclusion of the summing-up by drawing attention to any apparent errors or omissions of fact or law."[30] Needless to say, this duty has to be discharged with considerable tact.

Influencing the court with regard to sentence is not part of the duties of prosecuting counsel, although the prosecution may now request that the Attorney-General seek a review by the Court of Appeal of a sentence believed to be unduly lenient.[31]

---

[23] *i.e.* a question which by its form suggests the desired answer. "You saw the defendant take the jewellery and put it in his pocket, didn't you?"

[24] There are other exceptions to the general rule, *e.g.*, when the witness called for the prosecution turns out to be hostile, *i.e.*, deliberately obstructive, the Criminal Procedure Act 1865, s.3, permits the use of leading questions to cross-examine the witness to elicit the expected information; see J. A. Andrews and M. Hirst, *Criminal Evidence* (2nd ed., 1991), paras.7.06ff.

[25] *e.g.*, questions about previous inconsistent statements may not generally be put (unless the witness is hostile), nor questions impugning the witness's credit. Counsel must not vilify, insult or annoy any witness: *Code of Conduct*, para. 610(e).

[26] That is it should be directed to an issue in the case or to the credit of a witness. Questions can be put about previous inconsistent statements, see the Criminal Procedure Act 1865, ss.4 and 5.

[27] See Criminal Evidence Act 1898, s.1(f).

[28] See pp. 750–760 above.

[29] See *Standards in Criminal Cases*, para. 114(c) and (d) and Sanders and Young (1944), pp. 340–341.

[30] *Standards in Criminal Cases*, para. 11.7

[31] *ibid.* para. 11.8. As to the review of sentencing, see the Criminal Justice Act 1988, s.36, and pp. 932–935, below.

(b) Defence counsel

Counsel defending a client in a criminal case may face conflict between the duty to the court and the duty to the client. It may be asked how counsel can act as advocate for someone who is "obviously guilty", or put forward a defence or a mitigation which appears to be based on the slenderest of evidence. The answer given by the Bar is that, consistent with counsel's duty not knowingly to deceive or mislead the court,[32] every accused person has a right to have the prosecution case tested and their own case put.[33] In a statement following the case of *R. v. McFadden*,[34] in which the trial judge had criticised counsel for wasting time, the Chairman of the Bar said[35]:

> "It is the duty of counsel when defending an accused on a criminal charge to present to the court, fearlessly and without regard to his personal interests, the defence of that accused. It is not his function to determine the truth or falsity of that defence, nor should he permit his personal opinion of that defence to influence his conduct of it. . . . Counsel also has a duty to the court and to the public. This duty includes the clear presentation of the issues and the avoidance of waste of time, repetition and prolixity. In the conduct of every case counsel must be mindful of this public responsibility."[36]

The "cab-rank" principle is intended to ensure that every accused can engage an advocate.[37] Counsel must ". . . endeavour to protect his client from conviction except by a competent tribunal and upon legally admissible evidence sufficient to support a conviction for the offence charged."[38] Counsel should "ensure that the defendent is never left unrepresented at any stage of his trial."[39] Counsel's opinion of the weight of evidence and the credibility of any defence being suggested by the client will obviously be factors in the advice which defence counsel gives.

(i) Advising on plea and the accused's confession

Counsel cannot leave a client unaware of the concessions to be gained from a sentence discount[40] or plea arrangement.[41] However, it must be made clear to

---

[32] *Code of Conduct*, para. 202.

[33] This is one of the fundamental principles of the Bar: see *Standards in Criminal Cases*, Responsibilities of Defence Counsel and p. 149, above.

[34] (1976) 62 Cr.App.R. 187.

[35] Melford Stevenson J. had taken a very dim view of the length of the trial in which the evidence had occupied over 30 days, and the closing speeches for the defence six and a half days. There were seven defendants, but the judge thought that counsel had behaved improperly and took the unusual course of inviting the taxing master to look carefully at the fees allowed counsel on legal aid taxation.

[36] (1976) 62 Cr.App.R. 193. The complaints against defending counsel were investigated by the Professional Conduct Committee of the Bar, and rejected.

[37] See pp. 149–151, above.

[38] *Standards in Criminal Cases*, para. 12.1.

[39] *ibid.*, para. 16.2.1.

[40] See pp. 856–858, above, and p. 888, below.

[41] See pp. 863–865, above.

the accused that there is complete freedom of choice of plea and that the accused has complete responsibility for it.[42] In practice the advice and attitude of defence counsel can be crucial, as the study of Baldwin and McConville[43] demonstrates. For example, 48 accused people gave as their reason for their changing plea the advice that they had received from counsel. It is difficult to offer advice which will inevitably carry great weight whilst leaving the accused free to make up his or her mind. In 21 out of 121 cases there was evidence that the advice given was not fair or proper.

Counsel may give an assessment of the strength of the prosecution case and the likelihood of acquittal, the details of any plea arrangement which has been or might be negotiated, the possible range of sentence and the discount for a guilty plea, the credibility of any defence which may be advanced, and the dangers of attempting to discredit prosecution witnesses, especially the police. Also important is counsel's attitude and demeanour. If the accused is given the impression that counsel has no hope or confidence of an acquittal or appears indifferent to the accused's protestations of innocence, the pressure on the accused will be further increased.

The Court of Appeal, considering defence counsel's obligations to advise a client, said that if need be the advice may be in strong terms, but that counsel must emphasise that the accused should only plead guilty if actually guilty.[44] If defence counsel deprives the accused of the freedom of plea, a guilty plea would be a nullity.[45] However, such cases are rare since the advice needs to be couched in extreme terms to contravene the guidelines.

If an innocent client decides to plead guilty, counsel must continue to represent the client, "but only after he has advised what the consequences will be and that what can be submitted in mitigation can only be on the basis that the client is guilty."[46]

Sanders and Young suggest that the defence barrister may not always be acting in the best interests of her or his client. This, they suggest, is because of the barrister's obligation to the court and the administration of justice as well as to the client,[47] the low standard fees for legal aid work encourage the barrister to seek late guilty pleas, barristers are under considerable pressure of work thus often receiving briefs shortly before seeing the client so they are often ill-prepared and "ill-disposed to fight on a defendant's behalf", and many criminal barristers are not of particularly high quality.[48]

Counsel may discover that the client is guilty of the offence charged. This may emerge from the client in clear terms in the form of a confession or as a result of inconsistent statements or from supposition on the part of counsel. A conflict then arises between the duty to the client and the duty to the court. If the discovery is based upon inconsistent statements or counsel's suspicions or speculations, no general guidance is provided by the Code of Conduct since it all depends on the actual circumstances of the particular case.[49] If the discovery is based upon a confession, it is made clear that counsel is not prevented from

---

[42] *ibid.*
[43] *Negotiated Justice* (1977), Chap. 3.
[44] *R. v. Turner* [1970] 2 Q.B. 321, 326. See also *Standards in Criminal Cases*, para. 12.3.
[45] *R. v. Peace* [1976] Crim.L.R. 119; *R. v. Inns* (1975) 60 Cr.App.R. 231.
[46] *Standards in Criminal Cases*, para. 12.5.
[47] See above, p. 149.
[48] Sanders and Young (1994), pp. 309–312.
[49] *ibid.*, para. 13.6.

appearing in the accused's defence, nor does it release counsel from "his imperative duty to do all that he honourably can for his client."[50] However, a confession limits what counsel may do. Counsel "must not assert as true that which he knows to be false. He may not connive at, much less attempt to substantiate, a fraud."[51] Counsel may not suggest that someone else committed the crime or call any evidence known to be false. Counsel may take objections to the competency of the court, to the form of the indictment, to the admissibility of evidence and to the evidence admitted. "In other words, a barrister must not . . . set up an affirmative case inconsistent with the confession made to him."[52] Further, since the issue in a criminal trial is whether or not the accused is guilty and the burden of proof lies on the prosecution, counsel may test the prosecution evidence and may argue that the case against the accused has not been established.[53]

(ii) Correcting defects

The conflict between the duty to the client and the duty to the court may also arise with regard to defence counsel's obligations in respect of procedural error, or factual or legal errors made by the court, not noticed by the prosecution.[54] One view, proceeding partly from the conception of the trial as a game in which the underdog (the accused) is entitled to the benefit of any errors, is that defence counsel is under no obligation to correct the judge. The Code of Conduct, however, requires counsel to bring all authorities, that is all relevant statutes and cases, and any procedural irregularity to the attention of the court before the summing up has begun.[55] Points of procedural irregularity must not be reserved so as to form the basis of an appeal.[56]

(iii) The conduct of the defence

If, at the end of the prosecution presentation, defence counsel believes that a case has not been established against the accused, a submission of no case to answer may be made which, if successful, results in the acquittal of the accused. The judge must decide whether or not the prosecution have adduced evidence on which a jury, properly directed, could convict in accordance with the law.[57] If the Crown Prosecution Service carefully consider whether or not to prosecute there should be relatively few successful submissions, unless, for example, the

---

[50] *ibid.* para. 13.2. It is also important to bear in mind: "(a) that every punishable crime is a breach of common or statute law committed by a person of sound mind and understanding; (b) that the issue in a criminal trial is always whether the defendant is guilty of the offence charged, never whether he is innocent; (c) that the burden of proof rests on the prosecution."

[51] *ibid.* para. 13.1.

[52] *ibid.* para. 13.3.

[53] *ibid.* para. 13.4.

[54] *ibid.* para. 13.5.

[55] If they are noticed by the prosecution, they should be raised with the judge: see p. 149, above. *Code of Conduct*, para. 610(c).

[56] *ibid.*

[57] *R. v. Galbraith* [1981] 1 W.L.R. 1039 and see Emmins (1995), pp. 129–131.

prosecution witnesses fail to appear or do not support the case for the prosecution.[58]

The formal procedure for the defence case, if the case proceeds, will be the same as for the prosecution, with an opening speech, witnesses and a closing speech, but it is the tactical conduct of the case which gives rise to greater difficulties. A major problem will often be the extent to which prosecution witnesses can be attacked without allowing the prosecution to place in evidence details of the (bad) character of the accused, including any previous convictions.

The normal rules of evidence prevent evidence being given by prosecution witnesses about the accused's character[59] and also forbid cross-examination of the accused on that subject.[60] Such cross-examination may, however, be permitted where the defence has sought to establish the accused's good character or cast imputations upon the character of the prosecutor or prosecution witnesses.[61] It is this latter rule which creates the problem, for the dividing line between an emphatic denial of guilt and an allegation of lies or misconduct by prosecution witnesses (particularly police officers) may be a very narrow one.[62] Counsel, if instructed by the accused to allege that the whole of the prosecution case is a "put-up job", will have to advise on the consequences of running that particular defence. To assist counsel, the trial judge will usually give a warning when a line of cross-examination is being used which may expose the accused to cross-examination as to character.[63]

(iv) After the verdict

Defence counsel, after a plea or verdict of guilty, will usually make a plea in mitigation of sentence on behalf of the client. As favourable a view as possible is put on the client's circumstances and suggestions may be made as to why particular sentences would or would not be appropriate. Care must be taken in referring to third parties during mitigation, for they will have no opportunity to contest any assertions. No allegation may be made which is ". . . merely scandalous, or intended or calculated to villify insult or annoy a . . . person."[64]

Save in exceptional circumstances, it is defence counsel's duty to see the client after conviction and sentence.[65] Counsel may give initial advice on appeal or the existence of grounds of appeal.[66]

---

[58] However, see above, Chap. 13.

[59] See below n. 23.

[60] See generally, C. Tapper, *Cross and Tapper on Evidence* (8th ed., 1995)), chaps. 6 and 7.

[61] Criminal Evidence Act 1898, s.1(f).

[62] See *R. v. Tanner* (1977) 76 Cr.App.R. 56 and the discussion in Archbold (1995), para. 4–360. The most helpful dictum is that of Lord Hewart C.J. in *R. v. Jones* (1924) 17 Cr.App.R. 117, 120: It is ". . . one thing to deny that he had made the confession, but it is another thing to say that the whole thing was a deliberate and elaborate concoction on the part of the inspector: that seems to be an attack on the character of the witness." General guidance is to be found in a decision of the House of Lords, *Selvey v. D.P.P.* [1970] A.C. 304.

[63] *ibid.* at p. 342A; *R. v. Cook* [1959] 2 Q.B. 340, 348.

[64] *Code of Conduct*, para. 610(e).

[65] *Standards in Criminal Cases*, para. 17.2.

[66] As to appeals in criminal cases, see pp. 923–944, below esp. p. 923.

5. WITNESSES

In most contested trials witness evidence will be called by either or both the prosecution and the defence.[67] People who might be witnesses may be unwilling to appear or there may be some doubt about their capacity to give evidence. Whether a witness satisfies the legal requirements to give evidence is a matter of law for the judge. Prosecuting and defence counsel exercise considerable discretion in who they will call. They must bear in mind not only the legal requirements but also the practical consideration that there is no point in calling someone who will not "come up to proof", that is, someone who will not be able to provide a convincing and consistent story in court, particularly under cross-examination. In certain cases it may be necessary to call expert witnesses.

(a) Competence of witnesses

"Competence" in this respect is used in two different ways. First, it raises the question of whether the accused and the accused's spouse are allowed to give evidence. The accused has been allowed to give evidence on his or her own behalf since the Criminal Evidence Act 1898, s.1. The accused's spouse has been competent for the defence since the 1898 Act,[68] but only became generally competent for the prosecution by virtue of the Police and Criminal Evidence Act 1984, s.80.[69]

Secondly, it raises the question of whether a person will be capable of giving evidence. A person must be competent both to take the oath or to affirm and to give evidence. Competence in this question may arise where the witness is a child or someone suffering from a mental disorder. Where the child is aged 14 or more, her or his competence will be determined in the same way as that of an adult. The matter is one for the judge, who must determine whether the proposed witness has the capacity to understand the solemnity of the proceedings and the special obligation to tell the truth.[70] The law as regards children under 14 has changed significantly, largely in response to the recognition of child abuse and the need to enable children, who are often the only witnesses, to give evidence. By virtue of the Criminal Justice Act 1988, s.33A, a child's evidence is given unsworn and it is to "be received unless it appears to the court that the child is incapable of giving intelligible testimony."[71] The Court of Appeal has stated that this means that the test of a child's competence is "whether the child was able to understand the questions put to him or her, to communicate, and to give a coherent and comprehensible account of the matters

---

[67] Some cases, *e.g.*, can be proved on scientific evidence alone.

[68] See now the Police and Criminal Evidence Act 1984, s.80(1)(b).

[69] Police and Criminal Evidence Act 1984, s.80(1)(a). He or she is not competent if jointly charged with the accused: *ibid.* s.80(4). As to both the competence and compellability of spouses, see P. Creighton, "Spouse Competence and Compellability" [1990] Crim. L.R. 34 and *Blackstone's Criminal Practice 1996*, paras. F4.11–F4.16.

[70] *R. v. Bellamy* [1986] Crim. L.R. 54, and see *Blackstone's Criminal Practice 1996*, para. F4.19. A person with a mental disorder is not necessarily incapable of giving evidence: *R. v. Hill* (1851) 2 Den. 254.

[71] If a child may be of "unsound mind", the same principles apply as to adults; see Criminal Justice Act 1991, s.52(2) and *Blackstone's Criminal Practice 1996*, para. F4.17.

in relation to which he or she was giving evidence. Built into that concept was an ability to distinguish between truth and fiction or between fact and fantasy.''[72]

(b) Compellability of witnesses

Most people can be compelled to be witnesses, with the exception of the accused and the accused's spouse. However, the accused's spouse is compellable on behalf of the accused generally, and for the prosecution and co-accused in cases of assault or worse offences on the spouse witness or people under 16 and sexual offences committed against the spouse witness or someone under 16.[73]

(c) Giving evidence

A witness gives evidence initially in response to questions from counsel by whom he or she was called.[74] "Leading" questions must be avoided.[75] The witness is then available to counsel for the other side for cross-examination, where the object will be to elicit evidence favourable to the cross-examiner's case and to discredit unfavourable evidence. Finally, counsel who called the witness is entitled to re-examine the witness, but must not raise any new issues.[76]

Giving evidence in court is a trying experience.[77] Consequently, counsel has to be aware of the possibility of the witness not coming up to proof. What is meant here is the capacity of the witness not only to retell the story convincingly when responding to examination-in-chief, but also to be able to stick to that story when subject to cross examination.

For some witnesses, the trauma of a court appearance will be particularly severe. This has been made graphically apparent in child sexual abuse cases. Many of these cases have not been prosecutions of the alleged abuser, but child care cases where the rules of evidence are less stringent. However, if a prosecution is instituted, it will be necessary to consider whether the victim can give evidence. As has already been seen, the first hurdle is whether or not the child is competent to give evidence. If so, it has to be considered whether the child will be able to give evidence in the daunting atmosphere of the court under the gaze of the alleged abuser. The court has always had the power to screen the

---

[72] *R. v. D* (1995), *The Times*, November 15. This may all mean that very young children, *e.g.*, under five, can rarely be in a position to give evidence: *R. v. Z* [1990] 2 Q.B. 355, esp. 359–360 and *Blackstone's Criminal Practice 1996*, para. F4.17.

[73] A spouse is not compellable where jointly charged with the accused: the Police and Criminal Evidence Act 1984, s.80(4) and see Creighton (1990) and *Blackstone's Criminal Practice 1996*, paras. F4.11–F4.14.

[74] Usually, the witness will be giving evidence in conformity with the case which counsel is putting; however, as to the position if the witness turns out to be hostile, see p. 866, above. As to the usual rule of the inadmissibility of out-of-court statements which are to the same effect as the in-court evidence, see *Fox v. G.M.C.* [1960] 3 All E.R. 225; usually, a witness may not refresh memory in court but must speak from their own recollection of the events, but there is an exception in that a witness may refer to a contemporaneous note of the matters to which the testimony relates. Witnesses are encouraged to refresh their memories out of court by reference to their original witness statements, and in some cases may interrupt their testimony in order to do so, see *R. v. Da Silva* (1990) 90 Cr.App.R. 233. There are rules which provide that the prosecution must tell the defence if their witnesses have seen their statements prior to giving evidence, see *Blackstone's Criminal Practice 1996*, paras. F6.6–F6.12.

[75] See p. 866, above.

[76] *R. v. Harman* [1985] Crim.L.R. 326.

[77] See Royal Commission on Criminal Justice, *Report* (Cm.2263, 1993), p. 128.

witness from the gaze of the accused, although the witness must be open to the view of the court.[78] The Criminal Justice Act 1988 added to this by providing for the possibility of children in certain cases their evidence through a live television link.[79] The Criminal Justice Act 1991 introduced a further significant change[80] by allowing for the admissibility as evidence in chief of a pre-recorded interview between an adult and a child.[81] This may well reduce the trauma faced by a child witness,[82] but he or she must still be available for cross-examination, which can be through the live television link.

(d) Expert witnesses

The function of an expert witness in a criminal trial is to assist the jury in matters outside the jury's competence or normal knowledge.[83] For example an expert may prove, from scientific tests, that the accused has handled explosives[84] or, from DNA testing, that the accused had sexual intercourse with the victim[85] or, from examining a vehicle, that a road traffic accident was caused by brake failure. Expert evidence will not be admitted to resolve a question on which the jury can bring their own experience to bear, for example, on a defence of provocation, the effect on an ordinary man of discovering that his girlfriend was pregnant by another man[86] or, on a prosecution for publishing an obscene book, the effect it may have on an ordinary person likely to read it.[87]

Problems with forensic science and other expert evidence have been partly to blame for some of the recently identified miscarriages of justice. The Royal Commission on Criminal Justice made a number of recommendations to address

---

[78] *R. v. Smellie* (1919) 14 Cr.App.R. 128 and *R. v. X.* (1990) 91 Cr.App.R. 36.

[79] Criminal Justice Act 1988, s.32, and see J. R. Spencer and R. Flin, *The Evidence of Children* (1990).

[80] s.54 added s.32A to the Criminal Justice Act 1988.

[81] Great care has to be taken with these interviews, see the *Memorandum of Good Practice on Video Recorded Interviews with Child Witnesses for Criminal Proceedings*, G. Davies, C. Wilson, R. Mitchell and J. Milsom, *Videotaping Children's Evidence: An Evaluation* (1995) and *Blackstone's Criminal Practice 1996*, para. F16.25.

[82] See Davies *et al.* (1995), which discovered, however, that there is much scepticism as to the value of the procedure for the interests of justice and the children themselves.

[83] See *Cross and Tapper on Evidence* (1995), pp. 555–559. As to the work of such experts, see I. R. Freckleton, *The Trial of the Expert* (1987), D. J. Gee, "The Expert Witness in the Criminal Trial" [1987] Crim.L.R. 307, P. Roberts and C. Willmore, *The role of forensic science evidence in criminal proceedings* (RCCJ Research Study No.11, 1993), RCCJ Report, Chap. 9, R. Stockdale and C. Walker, "Forensic Evidence" in C. Walker and K. Starmer (eds.), *Justice in Error* (1993).

[84] Care must, of course, be taken in what tests are used and what they establish and in presenting the evidence accurately, reliably, fairly and credibly. Failure in these respects was part of the reason for the interim report on the Maguire case concluding that their convictions for taking part in IRA explosions were unsafe, see Sir John May, *Interim Report on the Maguire Case* (1990). The Court of Appeal, quashed the convictions.

[85] See K. F. Kelly, J. J. Rankin and R. C. Wink, "Method and Application of DNA Finger-printing: A Guide for the Non-Scientist" [1987] Crim.L.R. 105, R. M. White and J. J. D. Greenwood, "DNA fingerprinting and the law" (1988) 51 M.L.R. 145 and T. Burke *et al.* (eds.) *DNA Fingerprinting: Approval and Applications* (1991). DNA fingerprinting, otherwise known as genetic fingerprinting, played a crucial role in the arrest and conviction of Colin Pitchfork for the murder of two young girls, see J. Wambaugh, *The Blooding* (1989).

[86] See *R. v. Turner* [1975] Q.B. 834.

[87] See *R. v. Anderson* [1972] 1 Q.B. 304. By contrast, if the question was the effect a publication would have on a child, expert evidence might be admissible, see *D. P. P. v. A & BC Chewing Gum Ltd* [1968] 1 Q.B. 159.

some of the identified problems. A major problem has been that the forensic laboratory services have been available largely only to the prosecution and have become prosecution-minded, such that there can be a failure to exercise true scientific objectivity in dealing with the evidence and a failure to pass on information and interpretations of value to the defence rather than the prosecution.[88] In consequence, the Royal Commission recommended that the forensic science facilities should be available to the defence as well as the prosecution,[89] though its efficacy will depend upon legal aid being available for the purpose.[90] Quality control was also obviously at fault, and the Royal Commission makes a raft of proposals intended to address this problem.[91] At the end of the day, of course, quality control relies upon the individuals wishing and being able to act independently and honestly and not wishing to assist in "case construction" rather than case assessment.

6. THE ROLE OF THE JUDGE[92]

The characterisation of the judge as the umpire or referee in our adversarial system is not entirely appropriate in the context of the trial on indictment. It is true that the judge should apply the rules, allow counsel to present the case without undue hindrance, not intervene unduly and that ultimately the decision on matters of fact belongs to the jury. However, it is equally true that the judge exercises a very considerable discretion in respect of many aspects of the trial and it is reasonably clear that the way in which that discretion is exercised may have a significant bearing on the outcome. Indeed, in certain circumstances, the judge's ruling will determine the case. In considering the extent of the judge's discretion and the possible effects of its exercise we should bear in mind the relationship between judge and jury.

The separation of functions between the judge and the jury is that the judge is to deal with matters of law and the jury with matters of fact. It is the judge's function to determine certain procedural matters; to consider any plea bargaining; to decide upon the admissibility of evidence; to sum up on the law and the evidence for the benefit of the jury; and to pass sentence. It will be seen that the distinction between matters of law and matters of fact is often blurred, and that the judge, in any case, has considerable influence in the determination of matters of fact.

Whilst the judge has a significant impact in some areas, in other areas, he or she has very little influence. For example, in relation to plea bargaining, the judge has little influence, and yet it might be thought that greater judicial

---

[88] See P. Roberts and C. Willmore, *The role of forensic science evidence in criminal proceedings* (RCCJ Research Study No. 11, 1993) and J. Rozenberg, "Miscarriages of Justice" in E. Stockdale and S. Casale (eds.), *Criminal Justice Under Stress* (1992).

[89] RCCJ Report, p. 149.

[90] See Sanders and Young (1994), p. 264.

[91] RCCJ Report, Chap. 9.

[92] See *Jones v. National Coal Board* [1957] 2 Q.B. 55, discussed by Lord Denning in *The Due Process of Law* (1980), pp. 58–62, see p. 000, above. See P. Devlin, *The Judge* (1979) and, for a unique account by the judge of a criminal trial, P. Devlin, *Easing the Passing* (1985). See also Pattenden (1990); A. Samuels, "Judicial Misconduct and the Criminal Trial" [1982] Crim. L.R. 221.

involvement would be more likely to protect the interests of the defendant, as well as paying adequate respect to the administration of justice.[93] There is clearly a dilemma in considering to what extent to involve the judge. There is a clear desire to see jury involvement, although their role in the criminal justice system is in fact minimal.[94] There does not appear to be a public desire to see judicially controlled criminal justice, if only because of suspicions about what judges might do. Set against this is the ability of the judge to exercise independent judgment. This dilemma can be considered by noting the recommendations of the Royal Commission to introduce a form of judicial management of cases. This reflects a lack of confidence in the parties adequately to progress a case, so the Commission recommends that "wherever practicable in complex cases judges should take on responsibility for managing the progress of a case, securing its passage through the various stages of pre-trial discussion to preparatory hearing and trial and making sure that the parties have fulfilled their obligations both to each other and to the court."[95] This goes much further than the administrative responsibilities currently lying with presiding and resident judges.[96] The danger of making such changes is that the delicate balance necessitated within an adversarial approach is affected without due consideration given to whether it has had an inappropriate effect upon the rights of the defendant.

(a) Procedural matters

From the outset, the judge has control over the progress of the trial and the administrative and procedural problems that may arise. The judge must decide questions relating to the form of the indictment and any necessary amendment to it;[97] the taking of the plea from the accused and its acceptability;[98] whether a special plea of *autrefois acquit* or *autrefois convict* has been successfully raised by the accused; the determination of preliminary points raised by counsel; and the desirability of separate trials.[99] Whilst these may be classed as procedural questions, their importance should not be underestimated. In some cases the determination of the procedural point may settle the whole issue.

The empanelling and swearing of the jury is subject to judicial control. The judge will settle any question over challenges.[1] Once sworn, with the case pro-

---

[93] See below, pp. 913–914.

[94] See below, pp. 914–915.

[95] RCCJ Report (1993), p. 142.

[96] *ibid.*

[97] As to questions relating to the form of the indictment, for example, whether the indictment discloses any offence, see Archbold (1995), paras.1–115 to 1–158. Under the Indictments Act 1915, s.5 the judge may allow amendment to the indictment at any stage of a trial provided there will be no injustice in all the circumstances. See Archbold (1995), para. 1–158 to 1–165 and *R. v. Nelson* (1977) 65 Cr.App.R. 119, which is also instructive on the obligations of defence counsel to draw irregularities to the notice of the court, *cf.* p. 869, above.

[98] For the role of the judge in relation to prosecuting counsel's obligations in plea arrangements, see p. 864 above. In *R. v. Winterflood* (1978) 68 Cr.App.R. 291, the trial judge appears to have taken the initiative in suggesting the addition of a charge to the indictment to which the accused might plead guilty.

[99] The practice is to join several charges together on one indictment where they are founded on the same facts or form part of a series of offences of the same or similar character and so have one trial: Indictment Rules 1971, r.9. See *Blackstone's Criminal Practice 1996*, paras. D8.24–D8.26 and C. Yates, "How Many Counts to an Indictment?" [1976] Crim.L.R. 428.

[1] See pp. 897–898 below.

ceeding, the jury may be discharged by the judge for a variety of reasons.[2] The effect of discharging the jury is not to acquit the accused—he or she may be remanded for a second trial.[3]

It is also the judge's responsibility to maintain order in court. The judge has powers of punishment for contempt where there is misbehaviour.[4]

Although counsel for the prosecution and the defence must conduct their respective cases in accordance with the Code of Conduct, the judge has a significant role in controlling the questioning of witnesses by counsel[5] and in restraining counsel from improper practices. Control should be discreet and the judge must resist the temptation to take over the questioning or to criticise counsel's conduct to such an extent that the jury might thereby be prejudiced.[6]

(b) Plea bargaining[7]

The judge has to be very careful in playing any role in plea arrangements, although he or she is now obliged to state that there was a reduction in open court as required by the Criminal Justice and Public Order Act 1994, s. 48. The extent to which it is proper for the judge to indicate the nature of the sentence discount[8] appropriate in a particular case if the accused enters a guilty plea gives rise to difficulties. Whilst the benefit to the accused is tangible when the prosecution offers an arrangement, it is not precisely quantifiable. When the judge indicates a view about sentence, the inducement is precise and the pressure greatly increased.

The Court of Appeal considered the matters of principle involved in judicial intervention in the case of *R. v. Turner*.[9] Turner had pleaded not guilty on a charge of theft. During an adjournment he was advised by counsel to change his plea. Turner knew that counsel had seen the judge and thought that counsel

---

[2] See pp. 900–901, below.

[3] *R. v. Randall* [1960] Crim.L.R. 435. In this case the jury was discharged after returning verdicts of not guilty, which were then stated to be majority verdicts. (Majority verdicts were not at that time acceptable). The plea of autrefous acquit at the second trial was rejected.

[4] There is a summary power to punish contempts "in the face of the court" which exists to maintain the dignity and authority of the judge and to ensure a fair trial and which applies in a magistrates' court: Contempt of Court Act 1981, s.12. See *Balogh v. Crown Court at St Albans* [1975] 1 Q.B. 73, discussed in Lord Denning, *The Due Process of Law* (1980), pp. 12–18. The accused was apprehended before he livened up court proceedings by introducing "laughing gas" into the ventilating system at St Albans Crown Court. See also, *Morris v. Crown Office* [1970] 2 Q.B. 114 (group of students breaking up a libel trial); *R. v. Aquarius* [1974] Crim.L.R. 373 (disruptive behaviour of defendant); *R. v. Logan* [1974] Crim.L.R. 609 (outburst by defendant after sentence); *Lecointe v. Courts Administrator of the Central Criminal Court* (1973, unreported) (distribution of leaflets at the Old Bailey inciting people to picket the court); *R. v. Powell* (1994) 98 Cr.App.R. 224 (member of public wolf-whistled at a female juror from the public gallery). See S. H. Bailey, D. J. Harris and B. L. Jones, *Civil Liberties: Cases and Materials* (4th ed., 1995), pp. 428–440. Judge Pickles sentenced a witness to five days imprisonment for her failure to give evidence against her ex-boyfriend. The Court of Appeal in *R. v. Renshaw* [1989] Crim.L.R. 811 quashed the finding of contempt because the trial was not fair, but made clear that a person who refuses without adequate excuse to give evidence to the court may be punished, which will usually mean imprisonment.

[5] The line of questioning must be relevant and material and witnesses should be treated courteously.

[6] *R. v. McFadden* (1976) 62 Cr.App.R. 187, and see Samuels (1982), p. 223.

[7] As to the position of the accused, and prosecuting and defence counsel, see pp. 856–858, 863–865, 867–869, above.

[8] As to the reduction in sentence in response to a guilty plea, see p. 858, above.

[9] [1970] 2 Q.B.321.

was relaying the views of the judge when he said that a guilty plea was likely to result in a non-custodial sentence, whereas a finding of guilty would bring a custodial sentence. Turner was repeatedly told that the choice of plea was his. He changed his plea to guilty and later appealed on the ground that he did not have a free choice in retracting his original plea.

The appeal was allowed on the basis that the accused may have felt that the views expressed were those of the trial judge and might, therefore, have been deprived of his freedom of plea.[10] On the general issue Lord Parker C. J. made four observations.[11]

(i) Counsel must give the best advice he or she can, in strong terms if need be, including the advice that a plea of guilty is a mitigating factor which may allow the court to pass a lesser sentence. The accused must be told not to plead guilty unless he or she has committed the offence charged.[12]

(ii) The accused must have freedom of choice of plea.[13]

(iii) There must be freedom of access between counsel and judge in order that matters which cannot be mentioned in open court may be communicated. Counsel for the defence and the prosecution should both be present as well as the defence solicitor, if he or she so wishes. Any such meetings should only take place when really necessary and the judge should only treat them as private where necessary.[14]

(iv) A judge should never indicate the sentence he or she is minded to impose, save that counsel may be told that whatever the plea, he or she is minded to impose a particular type of sentence, *e.g.*, probation, or a fine, or a custodial sentence. A judge should never say that on a finding of guilt a more severe sentence would be passed, nor should it be indicated that on a guilty plea he or she would pass a particular sentence, lest it be thought that a more severe sentence would result after a finding of guilt. Any discussion on sentence should be communicated by counsel to the accused.

Those observations appear to have limited the judicial role substantially and established a clear code of procedure, but they contain one major difficulty. The judge is told never to indicate that a sentence passed after a conviction would be more severe than a sentence passed after a guilty plea. Given the generally acknowledged rule that guilty pleas lead to sentence discounts, how can this principle be observed? The judge is not permitted to say what everyone knows.

---

[10] This is the basic question which the court will consider in all cases of this kind—"Has the plea been made freely and voluntarily?" *cf. R. v. Inns* (1975) 60 Cr.App.R. 251; *R. v. Peace* [1976] Crim.L.R. 119.

[11] [1970] 2 Q.B.321, pp. 326–327.

[12] See, further, p. 868, above.

[13] See p. 856, above.

[14] The necessity to limit the discussions in the judge's room has been emphasised by the Court of Appeal in *R. v. Smith* [1990]1 W.L.R. 1311, drawing attention to the words of Mustill L.J. in *R. v. Harper-Taylor* (1988) 138 N.L.J. 80 where the requirement that justice be done in public for all to see and hear was emphasised. Thus, whilst the jury may have to be required to withdraw, rarely should meetings take place outside the courtroom. If such meetings do take place, there must be a shorthand note-taker present, as stated in *R. v. Smith*, in part to avoid the sort of unseemly dialogue between judge and counsel which took place at the end of Smith's trial. See also *R. v. Pitman, The Times*, October 31, 1990.

The Court of Appeal in *R. v. Cain*[15] subsequently acknowledged this difficulty, but the authority of *R. v. Turner* was strengthened by a subsequent *Practice Direction*[16] which reaffirmed the procedure set out by Lord Parker.

To sum up, the judicial role should be limited to the consideration of arrangements negotiated between counsel, although the ultimate decision on plea arrangements lies with counsel,[17] and to the indication of the particular type of sentence whether the sentence follows a guilty plea or conviction after a not guilty plea. Once the judge becomes involved in indicating alternative sentences any accused is likely to be under the same pressure as Turner and, " . . . once he felt that this was an intimation emanating from the judge, it is really idle in the opinion of this court to think that he really had a free choice in the matter."[18]

(c) Admissibility of evidence

One of the functions of the trial judge is to control the input of material upon which the jury will ultimately base its decision. This the judge does by applying the complex body of rules which make up the law of evidence.[19]

(i) Relevance and admissibility

The evidence a jury hears must be both relevant and admissible. Evidence is relevant if it is logically probative or disprobative of some matter which requires proof, *i.e.* if it makes that matter more or less probable.[20] Thus when a person is accused of murder it is relevant to prove that he or she had a motive to kill the victim, that he or she was seen in possession of the murder weapon, and that he or she was unwilling to account for his or her movements at the time the murder was committed. None of these matters would, standing alone, be likely to establish beyond reasonable doubt that the accused committed the offence, but the proof of each tends to render guilt more probable, which is all that is required.

Not all evidence which is relevant is also admissible. Relevant evidence may have various deficiencies, the most common of which are that it may be unreliable or prejudicial to a fair trial. Rules of exclusion have therefore developed to prevent such evidence being given. Thus the hearsay rule operates to exclude statements not made in court as evidence of the truth of the facts stated, since statements which are not made while giving evidence are considered insufficiently *reliable* to be acted upon by a jury.[21] Thus, for example, it would be

---

[15] [1976] Q.B. 496.

[16] [1976] Crim. L.R. 561.

[17] See p. 863, above.

[18] [1970] 2 Q.B. 321, 326B, *per* Lord Parker C.J.

[19] See generally *Cross and Tapper on Evidence* (1995); Andrews and Hirst (1991) and *Blackstone's Criminal Practice 1996*, Section F.

[20] *Per* Lord Simon in *D.P.P. v. Kilbourne* [1973] A.C. 729, 756, H.L.

[21] "[Hearsay evidence] is not the best evidence and it is not delivered on oath. The truthfulness and accuracy of the person whose words are spoken to by another witness cannot be tested by cross-examination, and the light which his demeanour would throw on his testimony is lost": *Teper v. R.* [1952] A.C. 480, 486, *per* Lord Normand. For proposals to reform the law relating to hearsay, see the Law Commission, *Evidence and Criminal Proceedings: The Hearsay Rule*

inadmissible hearsay for a police officer to give evidence that a person interviewed during the investigation told the police officer that the accused had committed the crime. It would be a different matter if the person concerned came to court and made the same accusation on oath.[22] An example of a rule which operates to exclude *prejudicial* evidence is that which prohibits the giving of evidence of the accused's bad character, including previous convictions. If the jury heard such evidence, it is feared that it would be so incensed that it would give it undue weight in assessing the case against the accused.[23]

The rules of exclusion are seldom absolute and the judge must be familiar with the various exceptions which exist and under which evidence may be received. Exceptions are frequently made in respect of evidence which is not subject to the deficiency against which the rule of exclusion is designed to guard. Thus a confession made by an accused person, though hearsay, may be given in evidence, as it is a statement which goes against the interest of the person making it and so is unlikely to be unreliable.[24] Exceptions may also be made where the need to prevent the giving of certain evidence is outweighed by other factors. Thus evidence of the bad character of the accused may be received where it is of particular value in proving the case against him or her; for instance where a man is charged with drowning his wife in the bath and it is proved that his previous wives drowned in similar circumstances.[25]

Exceptions to the rules of exclusion are generally hedged about with conditions to prevent the admission of undesirable evidence. Thus, for example, where it is proposed to rely upon a confession made by an accused person, the prosecution must, by virtue of section 76 of the Police and Criminal Evidence Act 1984, be able to prove beyond reasonable doubt that it was not obtained either:

"(a) by oppression of the person who made it; or
 (b) in consequence of anything said or done which was likely, in the circumstances existing at the time, to render unreliable any confession which might be made by him in consequence thereof."[26]

---

and Related Issues (L.C. Consultation Paper No. 138, 1995) and A. A. S. Zuckermann, "The futility of Hearsay" [1996] Crim. L.R.4; D. C. Ormerod, "' The Hearsay Exceptions" [1996] Crim. L.R. 16; J. R. Spencer, "Hearsay Reform: A Bridge Not Far Enough?" [1996] Crim. L.R. 29.

[22] When evidence is presented directly to the court in this way, not only is it subject to the sanction of the oath, but also the reliability of the evidence can be tested by cross-examination, and the witness's demeanour seen by the jury.

[23] Such evidence is not necessarily devoid of probative value: *D.P.P. v. Kilbourne* [1973] A.C. 729, 757, *per* Lord Simon. But a jury might think it proved more than it does: in other words, the probative value of the evidence is outweighed by its prejudicial effect, see *Boardman v. D.P.P.* [1975] A.C. 421, 456, *per* Lord Cross.

[24] Numerous other exceptions to the hearsay rule exist. Much documentary hearsay is admissible under Part II of the Criminal Justice Act 1988, for example, while oral statements made by participants in events in the heat of the moment and before they have had time to concoct anything to their advantage are admissible at common law, see *R. v. Andrews* [1987] A.C. 281. For a more complete statement of the exceptions see Andrews and Hirst (1991), Chaps. 18–20.

[25] *R. v. Smith* (1915) 11 Cr.App.R. 229.

[26] Police and Criminal Evidence Act 1984, s.76(2).

(ii) Determining admissibility

Where the admissibility of an item of evidence, such as a confession, is contested, it would obviously be inadvisable for argument to take place in front of the jury, which would then hear that a confession had been made, even if it were subsequently ruled to be inadmissible. There is therefore a special procedure whereby matters relating to the admissibility of evidence may be determined in the absence of the jury,[27] and this is known as the trial within a trial or *voir dire*. Witnesses may be called in the usual way,[28] and legal argument heard, after which the judge makes his or her ruling.[29]

(iii) Discretionary exclusion

Where the strict rules of evidence might operate unfairly, a trial judge has various discretionary powers to exclude from the jury's consideration evidence which is both relevant and admissible.[30] The best known and most frequently exercised power is to be found in section 78 of the Police and Criminal Evidence Act 1984, which provides that the judge:

> "may refuse to allow evidence on which the prosecution proposes to rely to be given if it appears to the court that, having regard to all the circumstances, including the circumstances in which the evidence was obtained, the admission of the evidence would have such an adverse effect on the fairness of the proceedings that the court ought not to admit it."

An example of the use of this power might be in respect of a confession which, though it was not obtained in circumstances rendering it inadmissible under section 76 of the 1984 Act,[31] was nevertheless procured in breach of the rules governing interrogation in such a way that it would be unfair to admit it.[32] In addition to the power conferred by section 78, the trial judge may exclude evi-

---

[27] For the difficulties presented to magistrates, see p. 841 above.

[28] Although a special oath is used, which is known as the *"voire dire"* ', and from which the procedure takes its name: "I swear I will true answer make to all such questions as the court shall demand of me."

[29] The trial within a trial may form a significant, and sometimes lengthy, part of the proceedings. When the "Birmingham Six" came to trial, a "trial within a trial" was held to determine the admissibility of confessions made by the accused, which lasted eight days, at the end of which the statements were admitted by the judge, Bridge J., who gave a reasoned decision covering 15 pages: *McIlkenny v. Chief Constable of West Midlands Police Force* [1980] Q.B. 283, 314, *per* Lord Denning M.R.

[30] See generally Pattenden (1990), Chap. 7.

[31] See above.

[32] See, *e.g., R. v. Samuel* [1988] Q.B. 615 in which the accused confessed to robbery after having been denied access to his solicitor in breach of s.58 of the Police and Criminal Evidence Act 1984. The court regarded this denial of "one of the most important and fundamental rights of a citizen" as sufficient justification for exclusion of the confession under s.78.

dence by virtue of the discretion vested in him or her by the common law[33] and by various statutes.[34]

(d) Summing up

The other major matters of law which are the responsibility of the judge are those which must be explained to the jury so that it can reach a proper decision. The judge will deal with these matters in the summing up, telling the jury that it must accept his or her direction on issues of law.

Lord Hailsham, at the time the Lord Chancellor, emphasised the judge's obligations in summing up:

> "The purpose of a direction to a jury is not best achieved by a disquisition on jurisprudence or philosophy or a universally applicable circular tour round the area of law affected by the case. The search for universally applicable definitions is often productive of more obscurity than light. A direction is seldom improved and may be considerably damaged by copious recitations from the total content of a judge's notebook. A direction to a jury should be custom-built to make the jury understand their task in relation to a particular case. Of course, it must include references to the burden of proof and the respective role of jury and judge. But it should also include a succinct but accurate summary of the issues of fact as to which a decision is required, a correct but concise summary of the evidence and arguments on both sides and a correct statement of the inferences which the jury are entitled to draw from their particular conclusions about the primary facts."[35]

Achieving such a summing up may well be difficult, especially in the case of long and complex trials.[36] It would seem proper to suggest that many of the problems might be avoided if judges were careful to ensure that the language they use is that which a jury is likely to understand[37] and that the length of time taken to deliver a summing up is as little as possible consistent with clarity.[38]

A summing up usually consists of the following elements.[39]

---

[33] The judge has power at common law to exclude evidence at his or her discretion where the prejudicial effect of prosecution evidence outweighs its probative value, and (in certain cases) where evidence has been improperly obtained, see *R. v. Sang* [1980] A.C. 402.

[34] See, *e.g.*, Criminal Justice Act 1988, s.25: power to exclude admissible documentary evidence where not in the "interests of justice" to admit it.

[35] *R. v. Lawrence* [1982] A.C. 510. See also *R. v. McVey* [1988] Crim.L.R. 127.

[36] See pp. 908–910, below for consideration of whether the jury should be involved in long complex cases, especially fraud cases.

[37] The point is made, *e.g.*, by R. Harding, "Jury Performance in Complex Cases" in Findlay and Duff (1988), Chap. 5; by M. Levi, "The Role of the Jury in Complex Cases" in Findlay and Duff (1988), Chap. 6; and by Edward Griew, "Summing Up the Law" [1989] Crim.L.R. 768, who supports his argument, at p. 773, with American research which suggests "that a good many vocabulary items freely used in jury instructions are incomprehensible to an alarming percentage of jurors. . . ." In the Crown Court Survey, it was found that most jurors perceived no difficulties with legal jargon in understanding their case: Zander and Henderson (1993), at p. 212. Very few jurors had difficulty with the judge's direction on the law: *ibid.*, pp. 216–217.

[38] Many jurors, in the Crown Court Survey, were of the view that they could have coped without the judge summing up on the facts, although fewer took this view with the longer cases: *ibid.*, pp. 214–215.

[39] Always to include all these elements is likely to be unnecessary and, sometimes, very confusing, see Griew (1989) and Pattenden (1990), pp. 177–212.

(i) A direction as to the respective tasks of judge and jury

The jury is told that it is for the judge to decide upon matters of law and for it to decide upon matters of fact and that it should not be influenced by any judicial opinions expressed about the evidence; it is for the jury to decide what facts have been proved.[40] It would be naive to think, however, that the views of the judge, if expressed, have no bearing on the jury's decision.[41]

(ii) A direction as to the burden and standard of proof

The judge should tell the jury about the burden and standard of proof.[42] Prosecuting counsel may have done so in the opening speech and it may have been referred to during the trial. The judge tells the jury that the burden of proving the guilt of the accused lies on the prosecution save in the case of the common law defence of insanity,[43] and subject to any statutory exception.[44] The standard that must be satisfied is proof beyond a reasonable doubt.[45] So if, for example, Vera, a defendant, raises the issue by stating that an apparent attack was carried out in self-defence, it is for the prosecution to prove beyond reasonable doubt that she was not acting in self defence, rather than on Vera to prove on a balance of probabilities that she was so acting.

---

[40] *R. v. Bradbury* (1920) 15 Cr.App.R. 76; *R. v. Mason* (1924) 18 Cr.App.R. 131. See Emmins (1995), p. 143. The jury may decide upon a verdict which may appear to be "perverse" despite this statement, provided it realises it has that opportunity: see p. 906, below. There are also some rare circumstances in which the judge may direct a conviction, see below, p. 885.

[41] At its lowest, the position of the summing-up at the end of the trial must give it significance. Add to that the respect accorded to a professional's view by lay people and their natural tendency to rely on the judge's analysis and the judge's influence is clear.

[42] If a case gets to the stage of a summing-up, Griew has doubted whether talk of the burden of proof is appropriate, since the prosecution must by then have established a prima facie case, otherwise a submission of no case to answer would have succeeded; and, in reality, the jury must rely on all the evidence, not just that provided by the prosecution, but also that provided by the defence: Griew (1989). If the jury ask for further guidance, the judge should use similar words to that used in the original direction: *R. v. Milligan, The Times*, March 11, 1989.

[43] As established in *M'Naghten's Case* (1843) 10 Cl. & F. 200 and see *Blackstone's Criminal Practice 1996*, para. F3.3.

[44] Such exceptions may be express, see, *e.g.*, the defence of diminished responsibility in the law of murder, Homicide Act 1957, s.3(2) and see *Blackstone's Criminal Practice 1996*, para. F3.4; or implied, see *R. v. Hunt* [1986] A.C. 352, H.L. and see *Blackstone's Criminal Practice 1996*, para. F3.5. The possibility that the burden may be imposed on the accused impliedly by statute and how it can be decided that the burden is so imposed have been vigorously criticised by P. Mirfield in "The Legacy of Hunt" [1988] Crim.L.R. 19. D.J. Birch in "Hunting the Snark: the Elusive Statutory Exception" [1988] Crim.L.R. 221, arguing against Mirfield, suggests that *R. v. Hunt* is in fact helpful in determining when the burden is impliedly imposed on the accused by statute.

[45] If the burden lies upon the defence, the standard is the lower one of the balance of probabilities: *R. v. Carr-Briant* (1943) 29 Cr.App.R. 76. As to the prosecution standard, the actual formulation of the direction to the jury has varied. "Satisfied so that you feel sure" has its supporters: *Walters v. The Queen* [1960] 2 A.C. 26; *R. v. Summers* (1952) 36 Cr.App.R. 14. So does, "satisfied beyond all/any/a reasonable doubt": *D.P.P. v. Woolmington* [1935] A.C. 462; *R. v. Lawrence* [1982] A.C. 510. For the judge who wishes to be doubly safe, the direction, ". . . satisfied beyond reasonable doubt so that you feel sure of the defendant's guilt" has also been approved: *Ferguson v. The Queen* [1979] 1 W.L.R. 94.

The judge directs that the jury must be satisfied of the accused's guilt. This has not been thought to create any problems. It has been observed, however, to cause some difficulties in cases where the crime can be established on the basis of a number of different, mutually exclusive grounds. If, for example, six jurors are satisfied as to one ground for a conviction, and the other six as to a different, mutually exclusive ground, how can the jury really be satisfied as to the guilt of the accused?[46]

(iii) A direction as to the definition of the offence charged and the facts which have to be proved before there can be a conviction

The judge must explain to the jury the legal requirements of the offence charged and the facts of which the jury must be convinced before it can convict. This often is not easy. In a case of theft, for example, the judge should say that the property stolen must have belonged to someone else and must have been appropriated by the accused, who must have been dishonest and intending to deprive the other person permanently of the property.[47] Yet there are already difficulties. What is an appropriation? What amounts to dishonesty? What if the property has been "borrowed," to be returned at some (distant) future date?[48] Some difficulties may be resolved by judges relying on model directions created by the courts[49] and specimen directions produced by the Judicial Studies Board with the approval of the Lord Chief Justice.[50] On the other hand, it might be questioned whether use of such directions may not introduce excess rigidity[51] and, in particular, whether it might not confuse the jury both by using overly complex (lawyerly) language and by introducing superfluous law.[52]

The example of theft raises starkly the problem of the distinction between matters of law and matters of fact when considering what to say about words like "dishonesty". The judge must direct the jury on issues of law. The problem that arises is the tendency that the courts have to regard at least some words appearing in criminal offences as words of the ordinary English language whose meaning is not, therefore, a question of law.[53] This was the approach taken with regard to "dishonesty" by the Court of Appeal in *R. v. Feely*,[54] which was trenchantly criticised largely on the ground that it was leaving to the jury a

---

[46] See J. C. Smith, "Satisfying the Jury" [1988] Crim.L.R. 335.

[47] Theft Act 1968, s.1.

[48] All these questions give rise to considerable difficulty in the law of theft as will immediately be apparent from a perusal of J. C. Smith, *The Law of Theft*, paras.18–53; 120–129; 138–141.

[49] See, *e.g.*, the model direction as to the meaning of "recklessness" in the offences under the Criminal Damage Act 1971 established by Lord Diplock in *Commissioner of Police for the Metropolis v. Caldwell* [1982] A.C. 341, 354.

[50] *Judicial Studies Board Report for 1991–1995*, para. 4.22.

[51] See Lord Hailsham's statement in *R. v. Lawrence*, n. 45 above.

[52] Griew (1989), who points out that there may be a temptation amongst trial judges to provide too much legal information in order to make their directions unappealable.

[53] See Lord Reid in *Brutus v. Cozens* [1973] A.C. 854 (on the meaning of the word "insulting" in the Public Order Act 1936, s.5, since repealed); Lawton L.J. in *W. v. L.* [1974] Q.B. 711 (on the meaning of "mental illness" in the Mental Health Act 1959).

[54] [1973] Q.B. 530.

decision which was properly that of the judge.[55] This approach is still adopted in the interpretation of some words, although judges usually provide definitions where possible.[56] Of course, the greater the number of issues of law upon which the judge gives a direction, the fewer the opportunities for the exercise of discretion or common sense by the jury and the greater is the control of the judge.[57]

As to "dishonesty", the Court of Appeal in *R. v. Ghosh*[58] has decided not to leave the matter entirely to the jury, which would mean that the jury could in effect apply its own standards.[59] Neither has the court provided a detailed legal definition, which would perhaps be impossible to achieve. Instead it has indicated that, as a matter of law, the accused will be dishonest if the jury decides: (i) that what was done was dishonest by the standards of ordinary, decent people; and (ii) that the accused must have realised that what was being done was by those standards dishonest.[60]

(iv) A direction as to evidential points

It may be necessary for the judge to give directions about the evidence which the jury has heard. The jury may have to be warned of the legal requirements in relation to certain evidence lest it rely upon that evidence too readily in deciding questions of fact. The judge again exercises control over the jury.

An example is where the defence is one of mistaken identity, since eyewitness evidence may be based on a fleeting glimpse. Rarely would, for example, a by-passer have more than a swift glimpse of the bank robber running out of a bank to the getaway car. In such circumstances it is possible for witnesses genuinely and honestly to be convinced that they are right. They may, in fact, be mistaken. The jury must be informed of the problems which can arise. Before the summing up, the judge may withdraw the evidence from the jury if it is "poor" and the prosecution should inform the defence of any material discrepancies between the description originally given and the accused's actual appearance. In the summing-up, the judge should warn the jury of the need for caution; the circumstances in which the identification took place should be drawn to the attention of the jury, in particular the length of time the observation could have lasted and the conditions; the judge should remind the jury of any weaknesses that have become apparent and point out to the jury that evidence of recognition of someone known can be relied upon more satisfactorily than identification of a stranger.[61]

---

[55] See, *e.g.*, D. W. Elliott, "Law and Fact in Theft Act Cases" [1976] Crim.L.R. 707; G. Williams, "Law and Facts" [1976] Crim.L.R. 472, 537; E. J. Griew, *Dishonesty and the Jury* (1974); A. Briggs, "Judges, Juries and the Meaning of Words" (1985) 5 L.S. 314.

[56] No definition of the meaning of "intention" has been provided by the courts in a series of recent cases, see Smith and Hogan (1992), at pp. 53–59.

[57] The jury will usually follow such a direction by the judge, and thus the exercise of discretion is limited. The jury is, of course, permitted to exercise discretion outside the judge's direction, which some might describe as not legitimate or perverse, see p. 000, below.

[58] [1982] 2 Q.B. 1053. See commentary at [1982] Crim.L.R. 608, and D. W. Elliott, "Dishonesty in Theft: A Dispensable Concept" [1982] Crim.L.R. 395.

[59] *R. v. Feely* [1973] Q.B. 530, C.A. See Smith, para. 127.

[60] *R. v. Ghosh* [1982] 2 Q.B. 1053, 1064.

[61] *R. v. Turnbull* [1977] 2 Q.B. 224 for a comprehensive listing of the rules relating to evidence of identification, see *Blackstone's Criminal Practice 1996*, paras. F18.1–F18.29.

(v) A summary of the evidence in the case

It is for the judge to put the case before the jury which, in particular in a complex case, will involve a substantial amount of the evidence being rehearsed for the jury's benefit.[62] Whether this is really an appropriate function, especially as it may be unnecessary, may provide the judge with too much influence over the jury, and may make it appear as though the prosecution is being supported by the judge, is doubtful.[63]

Whilst the determination of matters of fact is for the jury, the judge is entitled to comment on matters arising out of the evidence,[64] including the strength of the respective cases,[65] the demeanour and quality of witnesses,[66] the credibility of evidence and the quality of any argument. Comment may be in strong terms provided that, overall, it is not unfair[67] and the jury is reminded clearly and forcefully that they have the ultimate responsibility for deciding issues of fact.[68] Comments may be other than verbal: gesture, tone of voice and facial expression can all speak volumes in indicating the judge's view of the merits, and such matters do not appear in the transcript.[69] The Court of Appeal appears to be unwilling to interfere with a conviction on the ground that the judge has over-stepped the permissible limits of comment unless the summing-up is very defective.[70] An informal constraint on the extent of judicial comment is the possibility that the jury will react against a very strong direction to convict and, out of

---

[62] R. v. Attfield (1961) 45 Cr.App.R. 309. The judge keeps a note of the evidence—a process which has a significant effect on the speed of the criminal trial—and will remind the jury of it in the summing-up. However, merely reading out such notes, especially in complex cases, was criticised by the Court of Appeal in R. v. Charles (1979) 68 Cr.App.R. 334, see Emmins (1995), p. 145. The judge must also be careful to put the defence case fully and properly, see R. v. Tillman [1962] Crim.L.R. 261; R. v. Hamilton [1972] Crim.L.R. 266. For a particularly abbreviated summing-up consisting almost entirely of a low, prolonged whistle, see Pie-powder, by a circuit tramp (1911), p. 70, cited in Samuels (1982). For an incisive consideration of the function of summing up, see Griew (1989).

[63] D. Wolchover, "Should Judges Sum Up on the Facts?" [1989] Crim.L.R. 781 and the findings of the Crown Court Survey for the Royal Commission on Criminal Justice.

[64] See R. v. Evans (1990) 91 Cr.App.R. 173. For an interesting account of the summing up in the Oz case, see T. Palmer, The Trials of Oz (1971). There was a great deal of comment contained in that summing-up which was the subject of appeal: R. v. Anderson [1972] 1 Q.B. 304.

[65] "[I]n O'Donnell (1917) 12 Cr.App.R. 219 a conviction was upheld where the judge said that the prisoner's story was a 'remarkable' one and contrary to previous statements he had made, but in Canny (1945) 30 Cr.App.R. 143 repeatedly telling the jury that the defence was 'absurd' and that there was no foundation for defence allegations amounted to a direction to find the case against the accused proved. The conviction was therefore quashed.": Emmins (1995), p. 145.

[66] "I thought he was a jolly good witness. He wasn't prepared to whitewash all of Oz like some of the other so-called experts and I can't say fairer than that": per Judge Argyle, quoted in Palmer (1971), p. 252.

[67] R. v. Middlesex Justices, ex p. D.P.P. [1952] 2 Q.B. 758; R. v. O'Donnell (1917) 12 Cr.App.R. 219; R. v. Canny (1945) 30 Cr.App.R. 143.

[68] R. v. West (1910) 4 Cr.App.R. 179; R. v. Beeby (1911) 6 Cr.App.R. 138; R. v. Frampton (1917) 12 Cr.App.R. 202. The following is an example of such a direction: "... if I now express an opinion and you agree, well, that's alright. If not, you can disagree. You do not have to do what I tell you. What I think is irrelevant. You have to decide": per Judge Argyle: Palmer (1971), p. 239.

[69] See Wolchover (1989).

[70] cf. R. v. Anderson [1972] 1 Q.B. 304. Such defects will occur where the judge usurps the jury's function, as in R. v. Canny (1945) 30 Cr.App.R. 143, see n.65 above. This issue may also overlap with the question of whether a judge can direct a conviction, see text below.

perversity or sympathy for the accused or some other motivation, bring in a verdict of acquittal.

Although there have been cases which suggest that a judge may direct a conviction,[71] the current position of the Court of Appeal is that such a direction should never be given.[72]

(e) Sentencing[73]

Once the jury have found the accused to be guilty of an offence or after the accused has pleaded guilty, it is for the judge to pass sentence on the offender. The judge must have the necessary information available about the offence and the offender. If this is available, sentencing may occur immediately; if not, there may be an adjournment.

(i) Information for sentencing[74]

The judge must be provided with the facts of the offence. Where the accused has pleaded guilty, these facts will not as yet have been set out. They are now given by the prosecutor, unless disputed, in which case there may be a "Newton" hearing at which the prosecutor is obliged to prove them.[75]

A police officer will then provide evidence as to the offender's "antecedents," that is previous convictions, educational history, employment record, home circumstances and resources. The defence may challenge the evidence, in which case the prosecutor must prove it. Further information may be contained in a variety of reports, in particular a social inquiry report, prepared by either a probation officer or a social worker, considering the factors leading to the offence and a recommendation as to appropriate sentence. Other reports include medical and psychiatric reports and reports from places where a person has been held, such as a remand centre or prison when on remand in custody.

The defence may then make a plea in mitigation.[76]

Finally, an offender may have other cases taken into consideration. This clears up outstanding offences and the offender is likely to get a substantial sentencing reduction for those offences so as to reward honesty.

---

[71] See, *e.g., R v. Ferguson* (1970) 54 Cr. App. R. 410.

[72] *R v. Gent* (1988) 89 Cr. App. R. 247, *R v Gordon* (1991) 92 Cr. App.R. 50 and see Archbold (1995), paras.4–422 to 4–423. The possibility of a judge being able to direct a jury where there is no evidence for a matter where the burden is on the defence is argued both in Archbold (1995) at para. 4–423a and by J. C. Smith in the Commentary to *R. v. Wright* [1992] Crim. L.R. 596.

[73] For a brief description of the sentencing function of magistrates, see pp. 000–000 above. See D. A. Thomas, *Current Sentencing Practice* (looseleaf); A. Ashworth, *Sentencing and Criminal Justice* (2nd ed. 1995); M. Wasik *Emmins on Sentencing* (2nd ed. 1993); Emmins (1995); C. Harding and L. Koffman, *Sentencing and the Penal System: Text and Materials* (2nd ed. 1995); E. Stockdale and K. Devlin, *Sentencing* (1987); N. Walker, *Sentencing: Theory, Law and Practice* (1985); M. Wasik and C. Munro, *Sentencing judicial discretion and training* (1992); A. Ashworth and A. van Hirsch, *Principled Sentencing* (1992).

[74] See Emmins (1995), Chap. 15.

[75] So-called after the decision of the Court of Appeal in *R. v. Newton* (1983) 77 Cr.App.R. 13.

[76] See also p. 870, above.

(ii) What sentence is imposed?[77]

A sentence is laid down for each offence.[78] For a very limited range of offences the penalty is fixed by law. Murder is the main example, since the judge is obliged to impose a sentence of life imprisonment. If the offence is a common law offence, the sentence is a maximum of life imprisonment or a fine. If the offence is a statutory offence, the statute will lay down the punishment.

Any sentence laid down is a maximum and that maximum is rarely imposed. The judge has a wide range of possible sentences from which to choose. Broadly speaking, for people over 21,[79] these fall into the non-custodial and the custodial options. The non-custodial option includes fines, probation, community service orders and an absolute or conditional discharge. Further, there are a variety of other orders, such as an order to pay costs to the prosecution or compensation to the victim, which, whilst not being sentences, have much the same effect as a fine as far as the offender is concerned. The custodial option is imprisonment, which may be suspended or partly suspended.

The judge must choose an appropriate sentence. For many years, the Court of Appeal had been developing a tariff approach to sentencing by the setting of guidelines in an endeavour to ensure consistency in sentencing. Parliament decided to develop a principled approach by introduction of the Criminal Justice Act 1991.[80] The objective is to ensure that the sentence fits the seriousness of the offence, that imprisonment is only used where necessary, and that reasons are given for the sentences imposed. So, *e.g.*, s.1 creates statutory criteria for the imposition of a custodial sentence and states, at s.1(2), that "the court shall not pass a custodial sentence on the offender unless it is of the opinion—(a) that the offence, or the combination of the offence and one or more offences associated with it, was so serious that only such a sentence can be justified for the offence; or (b) where the offence is a violent or sexual offence, that only such a sentence would be adequate to protect the public from serious harm from him." S. 1(4) goes on to impose the obligation to give reasons, in open court, why either (a) or (b) are satisfied, and to explain why a custodial sentence is imposed. S. 2 imposes principles for the determination of the length of a particular sentence. It provides, in s.2(2), that

"the custodial sentence shall be—

(a) for such term (not exceeding the permitted maximum) as in the opinion of the court is commensurate with the seriousness of the offence, or the combination of the offence and one or more offences associated with it; or

---

[77] See Emmins (1995), Chaps.16, 17 and 18. A number of additional options are open where an offender is under 21.

[78] If the offender has been committed by the magistrates to trial on indictment for an offence triable either way and also a related summary offence within s.41 of the Criminal Justice Act 1988, the Crown Court has the sentencing powers which the magistrates' court would have had on conviction at summary trial.

[79] The sentences available where the offender is under 21 are different, see Emmins (1995), pp. 258, 277–282 and Chap. 18 *passim*.

[80] There were many problems with the details of the scheme introduced, but a significant number have been resolved by subsequent statutory amendment.

(b) where the offences is a violent or sexual offence, for such longer term
(not exceeding that maximum) as in the opinion of the court is necessary
to protect the public from serious harm from the offender.''

Longer sentences than those suggested by the seriousness of the offence must
be explained in open court.[81] Within the statutory framework, appellate guidance
still operates on the meaning of the terms of the 1991 Act and how that operates
in the context of particular offences. It seems, therefore, that certain developed
principles continue to apply, *e.g.*, that the shortest possible prison sentence
should be imposed where one is to be imposed at all.[82] A similar principled
approach is introduced for the imposition of other offences.

The approach imposed by the Criminal Justice Act 1991 are consistent with
the principles developed for imposing a life sentence rather than a determinate
sentence.[83] The principles are that such a sentence may be imposed only where

''(a) The offence or offences are in themselves grave enough to require a very
long sentence.
(b) It appears from the nature of the offences, or from the accused's history,
that he is a person of mental instability who, if at liberty, would probably
re-offend and present a grave danger to the public.
(c) The accused will remain unstable and a potential danger for a long and/
or an uncertain period.''[84]

Where the offender has a mental disorder, a hospital order may be imposed
under the Mental Health Act 1983.[85]

7. THE JURY[86]

(a) Historical background[87]

The decision of the Fourth Lateran Council in 1215 to withdraw the support of
the Roman Catholic Church from the process of trial by ordeal is generally
recognised as the factor which prompted the adoption of the jury system for the

---

[81] s.2(3). This also applies to a custodial sentence for an indeterminate period, *i.e.* discretionary life
imprisonment: s.2(4).
[82] The principle derives from *Bibi* [1980] 1 W.L.R. 1193, but seems still to apply; see *Blackstone's
Criminal Practice 1996*, para. E1.11. It was assumed that the sentencing discount (see above,
pp. 000–000) continued to apply, and this is now confirmed by the Criminal Justice and Public
Order Act 1994, s.48.
[83] See *Attorney-General's Reference (No. 34 of 1992)* (1994) 15 Cr. App. R. (S.) 167 and *Blackstone's Criminal Practice 1996*, para. E1.23.
[84] *ibid.*, para. E1.23.
[85] See Emmins (1995), pp. 308–310 and *Blackstone's Criminal Practice 1996*, Section E20.
[86] Much material is available. That to which we shall particularly be referring in this section
includes: W. R. Cornish, *The Jury* (1971); Lord Devlin, *Trial by Jury* (1956); N. Walker with
A. Pearson (ed.), *The British Jury System* (1975); J. Baldwin and M. McConville, *Jury Trials*
(1979); M. McConville and J. Baldwin, *Courts, Prosecution and Conviction* (1981); M. D. A.
Freeman, "The Jury on Trial" (1981) 34 C.L.P. 65; M. Findlay and P. Duff (eds.), *The Jury
Under Attack* (1988).
[87] Sir Frederick Pollock and F. W. Maitland, *History of English Law* (2nd ed., 1898), Vol. II, pp.
618–650; W. S. Holdsworth, *History of English Law* (3rd ed., 1922), Vol. 1, pp. 312–350; J. H.
Baker, *An Introduction to English Legal History* (3rd ed., 1990), Chap. 5.

determination of criminal cases. That the jury was in existence before 1215 is undisputed, since it would have been almost the only means of collecting information in administrative as well as judicial matters.[88] In addition to determining issues which were relevant to the king, juries came to be used for determining issues of interest to private individuals and were available to replace trial by battle.[89] When trespass was alleged, including the allegation of a breach of the king's peace, a writ of *venire facias* went to the sheriff who summoned a group of twelve[90] men to meet and give a verdict on the allegation. On the demise of trial by ordeal the jury was used to determine the guilt of alleged criminals.[91]

In the beginning, the role of the jury was unclear.[92] Were the twelve individuals to deliberate and deliver a verdict to the judge, or was the judge to treat them as witnesses, examine them and then come to a decision? The resolution of this question shaped the future of the jury and the future of criminal procedure.[93] In the event, the collective deliberative role of the jury prevailed and the transition from knowledge to ignorance as the primary characteristic of a juror began. The landmarks are well known. By 1367 it had become established that the verdict had to be unanimous.[94] Witnesses began to give evidence and the jury were prevented from talking to any outsider until they reached a verdict.[95] In *Bushell's* case it was established that the jury had the right to give a verdict according to its conscience.[96] By the eighteenth century it was finally established that a juror should not take part in a case of which he had personal knowledge. Now a juror should be excused where he or she is personally concerned in the facts of the case or is closely connected with a party or prospective witness.[97]

(b) The role of the jury

The jury has been described as having three functions.[98] First, it is the jury that is to decide the facts and it is on those facts which it then determines guilt. The jury is to arrive at its verdict by considering whether it is satisfied that the prosecution has proved its case solely on the evidence presented at the trial and in accordance with the direction of the judge as to the law.[99] Secondly, the jury adds certainty to the law, since it gives a general verdict. The jury merely states that the accused is either guilty or not guilty, and gives no reasons. The decision is not open to dispute. Thirdly, the jury represents the ''just face'' of the criminal

---

[88] The practice of getting a group together and putting them under oath to tell the truth had been highly effective for the Normans.

[89] Under Henry II two assizes existed: the grand assize and the petty assize. It was the petty assize which evolved into the jury.

[90] Why twelve? The answer is unknown, although it is the same number as the Apostles of Christ and the ancient tribes of Israel.

[91] C. Wells, ''Instructions given by Henry III to Itinerant Justices 1219'' (1914) 30 L.Q.R. 97.

[92] Pollock and Maitland (1898), pp. 622 ff.

[93] Guiding procedure into the adversarial system and away from the inquisitorial system with its emphasis on judicial involvement.

[94] Baker (1990), p. 90.

[95] *ibid.*, p. 89.

[96] *R. v. Sheriffs of London, ex p. Bushell* (1670) Vaughn 135.

[97] *Practice Direction* (1988) 87 Cr.App.R. 294.

[98] See P. Duff and M. Findlay, ''The Jury in England: Practice and Ideology'' (1982) 10 International Journal of the Sociology of Law 253. See also, M. Findlay, ''The Role of the Jury in a Fair Trial'' in Findlay and Duff (1988), Chap. 10.

[99] As to the respective roles of judge and jury, see pp. 874, 878–881, 881–886, above and as to the obligation upon the prosecution, see p. 866, above.

justice system, since it can arrive at its unchallengeable decision on any basis it chooses. In particular, it is proper for the jury to arrive at an acquittal according to its conscience,[1] even if a conviction is clearly required according to the relevant law.

Whilst the jury has these functions, it is not all that should be said about its role, particularly since they could be performed by other bodies. Jury service is described as an important public duty.[2] It has been suggested that the jury satisfies the constitutional role that no-one should be tried apart from judgment by one's peers. Whilst this claim is frequently made, however, it does not follow that the phrase "judgment by one's peers" has a consistent meaning. Marshall suggests that it can mean one, or more, of the following:

1. A claim to the judgment of one's peers, or equals or neighbours
2. A claim to the judgment of a body of fair-minded persons
3. A claim to judgment by an independent or impartial body of persons
4. A claim to the judgment of a randomly chosen body of persons
5. A claim to the judgment of a representative body of persons."[3]

In fulfilling its functions and its constitutional role, there are a number of qualities which enable a jury to perform effectively. Thus a jury, it is said, should be independent, impartial and representative, and it should be randomly selected. It is not the case that these qualities are always consistent; for example, a representative jury may be partial[4] and random selection does not necessarily produce fairness in the trial.[5]

(c) Qualification for jury service and selection

To *qualify* for selection as a juror, a person must be aged between 18 and 70,[6] registered as a parliamentary or local government elector, and have been ordinarily resident in the United Kingdom for any period of at least five years since the age of 13.[7] In addition, a person must not fall into the categories of people disqualified or ineligible by Schedule 1 of the Juries Act 1974.

The people *disqualified* are those who (1) at any time have been sentenced in the United Kingdom to life imprisonment, custody for life, or a term of five years or more imprisonment or youth custody, or to be detained during Her Majesty's pleasure or (2) at any time in the last ten years have in the United Kingdom served any part of a sentence of imprisonment, youth custody or detention, or had imposed a suspended sentence of imprisonment or order for detention or a community service order; or (3) at any time in the last five years has

---

[1] As established in *Bushell's Case*, see n. 96, above. See also T. A. Green, *Verdict According to Conscience, 1200–1800* (1985) for a history of the jury in this role.

[2] *Practice Direction* (1988) 87 Cr.App.R. 294.

[3] G. Marshall, "The judgement of one's peers: some aims and ideal of jury trial" in Walker with Pearson (1975), p. 5.

[4] See M. Findlay with P. Byrne, "Introduction" in Findlay and Duff (1988).

[5] See Sanders and Young (1994), p. 358. This is a particular problem when faced with issue of the racial mix of a jury; see below, p. 892.

[6] People who are aged more than 65 are entitled, if they wish, to be excused from jury service: Juries Act 1974, s.9, Sched. 1, Part III, as amended by the Criminal Justice Act 1988, s.119(2). As to excusal from jury service, see p. 895, below.

[7] Juries Act 1974, s.1, as amended by the Criminal Justice Act 1988, s.119(1).

been placed on probation in the United Kingdom; or (4) are on bail in criminal proceedings.[8]

The people who are *ineligible* for jury service fall into four categories:[9] (1) the judiciary,[10] (2) others concerned with the administration of justice, including barristers (and their clerks), solicitors and trainees, the staff of the Crown Prosecution Service, authorised advocates or litigators, court staff, prison officers and prison custody officers, police officers and forensic scientists, (3) the clergy,[11] and (4) mentally disordered persons.[12]

The objectives of disqualification and ineligibility are first to exclude from participation people who are or have been intimately concerned with the administration of justice, presumably on the basis either that a jury with lawyers on it will not decide according to the judge's direction but might use its own knowledge of the law, or that current or previous involvement in the criminal justice system will deprive the jury of its impartiality. The second objective is to exclude from participation those who are demonstrably incompetent. There is at least an implicit assumption that a basic level of intellectual ability is necessary for a person to be able to be involved in the performance by the jury of its various functions.[13] Inevitably a number of people are excluded who might make very good jurors, and exclusions mean that the jury is not representative of the whole of society.

The qualifications for jury service were revised in 1972,[14] when the requirement that a juror should be an occupier of a house with a prescribed rateable value was abolished, and the electoral register adopted as the basis of qualification. There had been growing criticism of the composition of the jury, and its unrepresentative nature.[15] Since the adoption of the new qualification, research has demonstrated[16] that the composition of juries has changed pro-

---

[8] Juries Act 1974, Sched. 1, Part II, as amended by the Juries (Disqualification) Act 1984. This amending legislation significantly increased the number of people who were consequently disqualified from jury service. Category (4) was added by the Criminal Justice and Public Order Act 1994. Whether offenders should be disqualified is a matter of debate, particularly as people on bail are innocent until proved guilty; see, for a related argument, Sanders and Young (1994), pp. 362–363.

[9] Juries Act 1974, Sched. 1, Part I, as amended.

[10] The "judiciary" includes not only the holders of high judicial office, but also, amongst others, Circuit judges, recorders, Masters of the Supreme Court and J.P.s.

[11] Including vowed members of a religious order living in a religious community.

[12] The Juries Act 1974 as amended by the Mental Health (Amendment) Act 1982 and the Mental Health Act 1983.

[13] Such reasoning does not explain the exclusion of the clergy, but may explain the exclusion of monks and nuns who choose to live in a religious community removed from everyday life. See further the Report of the Departmental Committee on Jury Service, Chair: Lord Morris (Cmnd. 2627, 1965); White (1985), p. 78. As to the discharge of people who cannot understand a case, see p. 900 below.

[14] By the Criminal Justice Act 1972, which implemented some of the recommendations of the Morris Committee (1965).

[15] In Lord Devlin's oft-quoted phrase, the property qualification produced a jury which was, "... predominantly male, middle-aged, middle-minded and middle-class": *Trial by Jury*, p. 20. It is reported that when Bernard Rothman and others were tried at Derby Assizes in 1932 on charges relating to a mass trespass on private land near Kinder Scout in the Peak District, the jury consisted of two brigadier-generals, three colonels, two majors, three captains and two aldermen: *The Guardian*, January 18, 1982.

[16] *Jury Trials*, pp. 94–99.

foundly. Juries are less middle class[17] and much younger than before,[18] but there is still an under-representation of women and members of ethnic minorities.[19] Indeed, two-thirds of all juries are white and defence barristers are often concerned with the racial mix of a jury.[20] The failure to ensure a representative jury[21] has been explained by Bohlander as being that "there exists the distinct possibility that the different life style, mentality and experience arising from membership of an ethnic minority will not be taken sufficiently into account in trials where members of such a minority are the defendants."[22]

Trial judges have a discretion to discharge a juror to prevent scandal and perversion of justice, and this may permit the exclusion of someone who is, for example, completely deaf.[23] However, the discretion does not extend to securing the establishment of a representative jury. The Court of Appeal in *R. v. Ford*[24] decided that a trial judge has no power to interfere with the composition of the jury or the jury panel in order to produce a multiracial jury and that there is no principle that a jury should be racially balanced. The argument in favour of racially balancing the jury is to avoid partiality as, for example, in the trial of Rose, a black man accused of murder, where the judge had asked potential jurors to disqualify themselves if they had strong views against black people or supported the extreme Right or the extreme Left.[25] This would not, however, now be appropriate in the light of *R. v. Ford*. The Royal Commission on Criminal Justice has responded by proposing a very limited proposal for engineering a racially mixed jury, but only in cases with "unusual and special features".[26] Sanders and Young have pointed out that "cases with such features are likely

---

[17] *ibid*. Table 10, p. 95.
[18] *ibid*. Table 11, p. 96. 27 per cent of jurors empanelled in Birmingham in 1975 and 1976 were under 30.
[19] The Crown Court Survey discovered that more men than in the general population serve on juries (53 per cent on juries and 48 per cent in the general population); that most juries had a wide spread of ages; that most jurors were working fulltime (69 per cent); that there was a slight over-representation of clerical workers and under-representation of skilled manual workers; and that there were more people who left school later than in the general population: Zander and Henderson (1993), pp. 234–241. Ethnic mix is considered in the text following.
[20] Zander and Henderson (1993), p. 241 as referred to in Sanders and Young (1994), p. 359.
[21] For further consideration in the context of the abolition of the defence right of peremptory challenge, see below, pp. 896–900.
[22] M. Bohlander, " 'By a jury of his peers'—The Issue of Multi-racial Juries in a Polyethnic Society" (1992) XIV(1) Liverpool L.R. 67, as quoted in Sanders and Young (1994), p. 359.
[23] R. Buxton, "Challenging and Discharging Jurors—1" [1990] Crim.L.R. 225. The judicial power to discharge jurors is considered further at pp. 900–901 below.
[24] [1989] 3 All E.R. 445. The court's reasons for rejecting the power were that it would interfere with random selection, that the power would have to be granted by statute and that it interferes with the responsibility of the Lord Chancellor's Department to summon jurors, *ibid*. pp. 448–449.
[25] This, and other examples, are to be found in M. Zander, *A Matter of Justice* (1988), at pp. 222–226. See also *R. v. Broderick* [1970] Crim.L.R. 155, where the Court of Appeal had said that the trial judge could go no further than ascertaining whether there was a coloured juror on the panel. This possibility is now questionable in the light of the decision in *R. v. Ford*; see also *R. v. Danvers* [1982] Crim.L.R. where the judge, Mr. Recorder Cowley Q.C. at Nottingham Crown Court, rejected a challenge to the array (*i.e.* the whole panel), on the ground that it was unrepresentative, holding that it was no requirement in law that there should be a coloured member of a jury or a jury panel, approved in *R. v. Ford*. See Baldwin and McConville (1979), pp. 97–98; A. Dashwood, "Juries in a Multi-racial Society" [1972] Crim.L.R. 85; the commentary to *R. v. Danvers* by G. W. Hoon at [1982] Crim.L.R. 681; and Buxton, [1990] Crim.L.R. 225, 234–235.
[26] R.C.C.J., Report (1993), pp. 133–134, as quoted in Sanders and Young (1994), p. 359.

to be rare."[27] Further consideration should be given to a proposal by the Commission for Racial Equality for "a special procedure to be available where the case is believed to have a racial dimension which results in a defendant from an ethnic minority community believing that he or she is unlikely to receive a fair trial from an all-white jury."[28] Simply relying upon random selection, and failing to address real concerns about jury composition is not likely to satisfy the deep concerns held about the criminal justice system by many people from an ethnic minority.

Selection of jurors from the electoral register used to be a matter for individual summoning officers. Since February 1981, random selection by computer has been utilised.[29] A number is allotted to every person on the electoral register, and a random number programme is then run through the computer to produce the jury list. It is not possible to challenge the summoning officer on the basis that the jury panel is not representative, because no black person is on the panel, although if bias or other impropriety could be shown then a challenge could be founded.[30]

(d) Summons, empanelling and vetting

The people selected for jury service receive a summons requiring them to attend at the Crown Court at a specified time.[31] Accompanying the summons are a form, which is intended to identify those ineligible or disqualified, and a set of notes, which explains something of the procedure of jury service and the functions of the juror.[32] A failure to attend the Crown Court can result in a fine, as can unfitness for service through drink or drugs after attendance.[33] Again, the implicit assumption is that a person must be competent in order to act as a juror. This principle, in the circumstances, permits derogation from the requirement that the jury be randomly selected.

Those summoned for service constitute the jury panel and from the panel the jury for an individual case will be selected.[34] The panel may be divided into parts relating to different days or sittings.[35] The jury list contains the names,

---

[27] ibid.

[28] R.C.C.J., Report (1993), p. 133.

[29] See Zander, A Matter of Justice (1988), p. 217; see also, R. Tarling, "The Random Selection of Jurors", Home Office Research Bulletin No. 13 (1982) and Lord Chancellor's Department, The Crown Court: A Guide to Good Practice for the Courts (1990), paras.9.1–9.2.

[30] R. v. Ford [1989] 3 All E.R. 445, 450. As to challenge, see below pp. 896–900.

[31] The power to summon is granted to the Lord Chancellor by the Juries Act 1974, s.2, who delegates it to such officers. In so summoning jurors, the officer is required to have regard to the convenience of the persons summoned and where they live, in particular to the desirability of selecting jurors within reasonable daily travelling distance of the place where they are to attend: ibid. s.2(2). See Lord Chancellor's Department (1990), paras.9.3–9.5.

[32] The notes assist the juror in the task by dealing with the swearing-in and challenges, trial procedure, the verdict, secrecy, taking notes, etc.

[33] Juries Act 1974, s.20, as amended. The person summonsed must attend and not someone standing in for them. In response to claims of juror personation (see, S. Enright, "Britain's reluctant jurors" (1989) 138 N.L.J. 538), the Lord Chancellor's Department has emphasised that it is a criminal offence for any person to impersonate a juror, and as a matter of routine court staff will check on identity: (1989) 138 N.L.J. 758.

[34] See p. 896 below. The Lord Chancellor's Department has set targets and introduced management controls to monitor and review the number of jurors who are summoned to attend court each day against the number who actually sit on trials: Lord Chancellor's Department (1990), para. 9.6.

[35] Juries Act 1974, s.5.

addresses and dates for attendance of the panel. The parties to the case and their lawyers are entitled to inspect the list before or during the trial.[36] Such information may assist counsel in deciding whether to challenge any of the jurors but, since the occupation of jurors is no longer provided, there is very little on which defence counsel may rely for a challenge for cause.[37]

The controversial subject of *jury vetting* surfaced in 1978 as a result of the trial of a soldier and two journalists (Aubrey, Berry and Campbell) on charges under the Official Secrets Act 1911. It became apparent during the trial that the jury panel had been investigated[38] and, in the ensuing public debate, the Attorney-General published the guidelines under which the vetting had been carried out.[39]

The guidelines make clear that vetting may involve the search of criminal records for the purpose of ascertaining whether or not a member of the panel is a disqualified person,[40] or the limited further investigation of members of the panel (a) in security or terrorist cases[41] with the object of revealing political beliefs which are so biased that they might interfere with the juror's fair assessment of the facts or lead a juror to exert improper pressure on fellow jurors, or (b) in security cases alone with the object of discovering whether a juror might be in danger of making improper use of evidence given *in camera*.[42] A further investigation is made, on the personal authority of the Attorney-General, using the records of Police Special Branches and, with regard to the cases in (b), the security services, and is known as an "authorised check." No checks other than with these sources and no general enquiries may be made except to the limited extent that they may be needed to confirm the identity of a juror. The information gleaned from an authorised check is sent to the Director of Public Prosecutions, who decides what information ought to be provided to prosecuting counsel. Consequently, a juror may be asked to stand by for the Crown[43] provided it is appropriate to exercise that power in the circumstances,[44] but the

---

[36] *ibid.* s.5(2), (3).

[37] See below, pp. 896–898. In 1973 the occupation of jurors was removed from the list by the Lord Chancellor in the exercise of powers, under the Courts Act 1971, s.32, now the Juries Act 1974, s.5(1), to determine the information included on the list; see H. Harman and J. Griffith *Justice Deserted: The Subversion of the Jury* (1979). Such information would be of considerable assistance to counsel in deciding whether to exercise the right of challenge, see p. 897, below.

[38] In the first trial, defence counsel made an application to have the jury discharged. One of the accused said so on television with the result that the first trial was stopped and the jury discharged. This gave the opportunity for the matter to be raised directly at the beginning of the second trial. The Attorney-General's Guidelines were first published during the course of the second trial on October 11, 1978.

[39] The current full text is to be found at (1989) 88 Cr. App. R. 124 and in *Blackstone's Criminal Practice 1996*, at pp. 2241–2243. For the original text before the 1986 amendement, see (1981) 72 Cr. App. R. 14.

[40] The Annex to the Guidelines contains the Recommendations of the Association of Chief Police Officers with regard to the carrying out of checks on the previous convictions of the jury panel to ensure that disqualified persons do not sit on a jury. For the full text, see (1989) 88 Cr.App.R. 125.

[41] These are cases described as being exceptional types of cases of public importance for which the provisions as to majority verdicts and the disqualification of jurors may not be sufficient to ensure the proper administration of justice. Jury vetting is thus a further safeguard in (a) security cases, defined as cases in which national security is involved and part of the evidence is likely to be heard *in camera*, and (b) terrorist cases, of which no definition is provided: Attorney-General's Guidelines (1989) 88 Cr.App.R. 124.

[42] *ibid.*

[43] See below, p. 899.

[44] As to the guidance on the exercise of the power of stand by as a consequence of jury vetting, see the Attorney-General's Guidelines, paras. 9, 10, 11 and 12.

prosecution is under duty to ask a juror to stand by where he or she might be biased against the defendant.[45]

The legality of the original guidelines was contested in *R. v. Sheffield Crown Court, ex p. Brownlow*, where a majority of the Court of Appeal (Civil Division) said *obiter* that they were unconstitutional.[46] The point was not strictly in issue since the court decided, in any event, that it had no jurisdiction to review an order made by a Crown Court judge, but the condemnation of the practice was clear. However, in the Criminal Division of the Court of Appeal the point was argued in *R. v. Mason*[47] and the court had no hesitation in upholding the legality of vetting, although the judgment is specifically restricted to the use of vetting for the purpose of ascertaining convictions. The Court confirmed the propriety of vetting the panel for convictions, passing the information to the prosecution, using it to exercise the right to stand by and passing the information to defence counsel if it would be fair so to do. Whether jury vetting in security and terrorist cases is acceptable remains to be argued.

The practice of jury vetting is alleged to undermine the jury as a random selection of fellow citizens assembled for the purpose of determining guilt[48] and so represent a dangerous move to grant excessive power to the State in favour of the 'crime control model.[49]

On the other hand, exclusion of people within the Attorney-General's Guidelines may prevent partiality on the part of the jury, and prevent the verdict of the jury being unduly swayed by the prejudices of one particular member, consequently maintaining public confidence in the general verdict.[50]

It is not known how widespread jury vetting is. As Sanders and Young point out, "the secrecy surrounding the practice is itself a denial of due process values."[51]

(e) Excusal and discretionary deferral

Any member of a jury panel may be excused service on the basis of previous service,[52] or on showing entitlement to be excused,[53] or, at the discretion of the appropriate officer, for good reason.[54]

---

[45] Sanders and Young (1994), pp. 356–357. The prosecution is only obliged to give a (general) indication of why a juror may be inimical to their interests: Attorney-General's Guidelines, para. 11.

[46] [1980] Q.B. 530, Lord Denning M.R. and Shaw L.J. Brandon L.J. expressed serious doubts about the practice.

[47] [1981] Q.B. 881.

[48] See Harman and Griffith (1979); A. Nicol, "Official Secrets and Jury Vetting" [1979] Grim. L.R. 284; Zander *Cases and Materials* (1993), pp. 432–438; Freeman (1981).

[49] Sanders and Young (1994), pp. 359–360.

[50] See, further, A. Freiberg, "Jury Selection in Trials of Commonwealth Offences" in Findlay and Duff (1988), Chap. 7 and Zander, *A Matter of Justice* (Revised ed. 1989), pp. 227–228.

[51] Sanders and Young (1994), p. 356.

[52] Juries Act 1974, s.8. People summoned who have served or attended to serve on a jury in the preceeding two years or been excused jury service for a period which has not finished are entitled to be excused.

[53] *ibid.* s.9(1) and Sched. 1, Part III, as amended by the Criminal Justice Act 1988, s.119(2). Those entitled to be excused include people aged more than 65, peers and peeresses entitled to attend the House of Lords, M.P.s, M.E.P.s, members of the armed forces and members of the medical and other similar professions.

[54] *ibid*, s.9(2). If the appropriate officer refuses to excuse a person from jury service an appeal to the court may be made: *ibid.* s.9(3). Any person who so appeals must be given an opportunity to make representations in support of the appeal: *Practice Direction* (1988) 87. Cr.App.R. 294. See *R. v. Guildford Crown Court, ex p. Siderfin* [1990] 2Q.B. 683 and *Blackstone's Criminal Practice 1996*, para. D10.3 and Archbold (1995), para. 4–211.

The first two provisions are straightforward, but the discretion to excuse from service is not one which is widely known. The notes which accompany the jury summons make no mention of excusal. The discretion is exercised in accordance with a *Practice Direction*[55] which makes clear that the normal presumption where a person is not entitled to be excused as of right is in favour of requiring a person to serve when summoned, because

> "jury service is an important public duty which individual members of the public are chosen at random to undertake. . . . There will however be circumstances where a juror should be excused, for instance where he or she is personally concerned in the facts of the particular case or is closely connected with a party or prospective witness. He or she may also be excused on grounds of personal hardship or conscientious objection to jury service. Each application should be dealt with sensitively and sympathetically."[56]

A person's attendance may be deferred, if it is shown to the appropriate officer that there is good reason for it.[57]

(f) Ballot, challenges and swearing in

From the jury panel, the jury for a particular case is selected by ballot in open court.[58] The clerk of the court has the names of all members of the panel. The names are put on cards, the cards are shuffled and the clerk reads out the names from the pile of cards. Hence, a random selection should be achieved from a randomly-selected panel.

On entering the jury box to be sworn, each juror may be challenged by the prosecution or the defence.[59] The defence has only the right to challenge for cause. The prosecution has the right to challenge for cause or to require a juror to stand by.

Challenge for cause has been fairly unusual,[60] but the abolition of peremptory challenge and the imposition of restrictions on the prosecution's right to stand by[61] "have given new practical importance to what had been thought to be [this] largely obsolescent institution."[62] It is possible to challenge the panel,[63] but the most likely use of challenge is to individual jurors. Challenge can be on statutory grounds, that is on the basis of ineligibility or disqualification, or common law

---

[55] (1988) Cr. App. R. 294.
[56] Concern has been expressed that the frequency of the grant of excusal adversely affects the representativeness of the jury, see *The Times*, October 25, 1988 and more recently by the Labour Parts (1995).
[57] Juries Act 1974, s.9A, inserted by the Criminal Justice Act 1988, s.120.
[58] Juries Act 1974, s.11.
[59] The prosecution's power is from the Juries Act 1825, s.29) and that of the defence from the Juries Act 1974, s.12(1). See R. Buxton, "Challenging and Discharging Jurors—1" [1990] Crim.L.R. 225.
[60] In a survey of 3, 165 cases the defence challenged for cause in 39 cases, *i.e.* 1 per cent and the prosecution challenged for cause in 25 cases, *i.e.* 1 per cent: J. Vennard and D. Riley, "The Use of Peremptory Challenge and Stand by of Jurors and their Relationship to Trial Outcome" [1988] Crim.L.R. 731.
[61] See below.
[62] Buxton (1990), p. 225.
[63] *ibid.* pp. 225–226.

grounds.[64] There are four possible forms of common law challenge all still properly known by their Latin titles:

   (i) propter honoris respectum, that is privilege of peerage;
   (ii) propter delictum, that is past criminal conviction;
   (iii) propter defectum, that is lack of requisite qualification;
   (iv) propter affectum, that is presumed or actual bias in the juror.

Of these grounds of challenge, the first three are relatively straightforward, since they refer back to ineligibility and disqualification.[65] Bias requires further consideration. In this context it means "whether the individual juror will be able to, and will, be loyal to his oath to give a true verdict according to the evidence."[66] Buxton classifies bias into three headings:

   (a) Connection with the case[67] or with the parties,[68] and if there is a connection, bias is in effect assumed;
   (b) Knowledge of the accused's character[69] and if there is knowledge, bias is also in effect assumed;
   (c) General hostility,[70] in this case, bias is not assumed but must be established.

It follows from the meaning of bias that the fact that a juror is of a particular race or holds a particular religious belief cannot be the basis of a challenge for cause on the grounds of bias (or any other ground).[71]

Jurors cannot be questioned before being challenged to ascertain whether there is ground for it, consequently basing a challenge on heads (iii) and (iv) may be particularly difficult, especially since the defence only has information as to the juror's name and address and not as to occupation.[72] If a challenge is

---

[64] As to ineligibility for and disqualification from jury service, see pp. 890–892 above. On statutory challenge, see Buxton (1990) *op. cit.*, p. 227 and on common law challenge, see *ibid.* pp. 227–234 and Archbold (1995), para. 4–231 to 4–234 (1990); and *Blackstones Criminal Practice 1996*, paras. D10.8-D10.12.

[65] See Buxton (1990), pp. 228–229. Buxton, at p. 228, points out that, whilst not all criminal convictions can ground a challenge for cause as such, nevertheless a criminal conviction might ground a challenge on some other basis such as bias, as indicated by the Court of Appeal in R. *v. Mason* [1981] Q.B. 881.

[66] Buxton (1990), pp. 229–230.

[67] *e.g.*, that the juror is personally connected with the facts of the particular case, see *ibid.*, p. 230.

[68] *e.g.*, that the juror is related to one of the parties, see *ibid.*

[69] Personal knowledge is intended here, not that gained through the media, which may, though, in exceptional circumstances be sufficient, see *ibid.*, pp. 231–232.

[70] *e.g.*, the holding of political opinions, the Court in R. *v. Swain* (1838) 2 M. & Rob. 112 emphasised the need to establish more than mere general hostility. In that case two jurors' active opposition to the Poor Law Act 1834 founded such a challenge, see Buxton (1990)., p. 232.

[71] R. *v. Ford* [1989] 3 ALL E.R. 445, 449 and see above, pp. 891–893.

[72] The restriction on questioning is imposed by R. *v. Dowling* (1845) 7 St. Tr. (N.S.) 381; R. *v. Stewart* (1845)1 Cox C. C. 174; Buxton (1990), p. 226. Compare the very different position in the United States where potential jurors may be questioned to ascertain whether they might be prejudiced. In one case it took four months to question 1,035 people before a jury could be sworn. See Harman and Griffith (1979), pp. 26–27 and M. George, "Jury selection, Texas style" (1988) 138 N.L.J. 438. Buxton (1990)., p. 227, n. 15 points out that the recommendation of the Roskill Committee on Fraud Trials to re-instate the provision of a juror's occupation has not been implemented.

made, it is tried by the trial judge.[73] The burden of proof lies on the party
challenging. Witnesses may be called to support or defeat the challenge, but a
prima facie case must be made before the challenged juror may be cross-
examined, upon which fairly stringent limits are placed.[74]

In 1988 the defence right of peremptory challenge was abolished. This right
had meant that the defence could exclude, without reason, up to three[75] members
of the jury. Abolition of the right was proposed by the Roskill Committee[76] in
fraud trials. The call for complete abolition appears to have followed on from
the acquittal of the accused in the "Cyprus Secrets" trial.[77]

The main objection to this form of challenge was that it interfered with the
random selection of a jury and that the effect of this unacceptable possibility
would be heightened where in a trial involving more than one accused they
combine their challenges and consequently radically alter the composition of
the jury. The other objections were that the use of a challenge would lead either
to juries being more likely to acquit or to juries being more likely to convict,
and that the form of challenge brought the criminal justice system into disrepute.

TABLE 3

Number of Peremptory Challenges Used Per Defendant					
Number of	Peremptory challenges per defendant				Trials
defendants	0	>0 to 1	>1 to <3	3 (max)	
1	80%	8%	6%	6%	2611
2	71%	18%	10%	1%	411
3	62%	23%	14%	1%	93
4 or more	46%	46%	8%	0%	50
				TOTAL	3165[78]

However, the evidence suggested that the peremptory challenge was not
excessively used. In a survey of 3,165 cases undertaken by Vennard and Riley
the peremptory challenge was used in 704 cases, *i.e.* 22 per cent. More detailed
figures show its use in relation to the number of accused people, which suggests
that "there was no evidence of the widespread pooling of challenges which is
often thought to alter the balance of the jury in multidefendant cases."

The evidence also suggested that the peremptory challenge did not have a
significant effect on the rate of acquittals. Indeed the number of convictions was
higher where the right of challenge had been exercised! Further, the available
evidence suggests that the composition of the jury has little effect upon verdict.[79]

---

[73] Juries Act 1974, s.12(1). The judge may order that the hearing of a challenge for cause be *in
camera* or in chambers: Criminal Justice Act 1988, s.118(2).

[74] See Archbold (1995), para. 9–235.

[75] Until the Criminal Law Act 1977, s.43, it had been possible to challenge seven jurors.

[76] *Report of the Departmental Inquiry on Fraud Trials* (HMSO, 1986), para. 7.38.

[77] The accused pooled their peremptory challenges. Consequently they were able to alter the composition of the jury. For a survey of the recent history to the abolition of the peremptory challenge,
see Zander (1989), pp. 217–222.

[78] Vennard and Riley (1988), pp. 735, 736, 738.

[79] See Vennard and Riley (1988), p. 738, referring to the review of research by Hastie and Penrod:
R. Hastie and S. Penrod, *Inside the Jury* (1983). The same conclusion is arrived at by Baldwin
and McConville—(1979), pp. 104–105; by Zander (1989), p. 226 and by J. J. Gobert "The
Peremptory Challenge—An Obituary" [1989] Crim.L.R. 528.

This evidence, however, was only addressed to the question of the practical use and effect of the challenge and not to the question of principle whether such interference with random selection adversely affecting the impartiality of the jury should be permitted.

The case for retaining the challenge included the argument that the peremptory challenge assisted in the obtaining of a non-biased jury by excluding people having the characteristics believed by experienced defence lawyers to predispose them to fail to decide a case in accordance with the evidence.[80] On the other hand, peremptory challenge was one of the few, admittedly limited, ways in which the accused could attempt to achieve a representative jury in terms of race[81] and sex and thus a jury which would more likely be impartial.[82] It will be noted that both sides were able to argue that their proposal more satisfactorily provided for the impartiality of the jury.[83]

The prosecution still retains the right to stand by for the Crown, which is similar to the peremptory challenge.[84] The prosecution has the right to require someone not to sit on the jury (stand by) unless there are not enough members of the panel left from which to produce a jury.[85] Any challenges thereafter have to be for cause. Whilst this right of stand by still exists, its use has been limited through the issuing of guidelines by the Attorney-General which specifically state that the abolition of the peremptory challenge means that "the Crown should assert its right to stand by only on the basis of clearly defined and restrictive criteria."[86] These criteria do not include the right to influence the overall composition of the jury nor should the right be exercised with a view to tactical advantage,[87] but the right may be used in connection with jury vetting or where a juror is manifestly unsuitable and the defence agree with the exercise of the power.[88]

A juror, having entered the jury box and remained unchallenged, is then sworn[89] in. The juror's oath makes no reference to the possibility of deciding according to conscience:

---

[80] Whether the views of the lawyers as to who will be biased and who will not are accurate is doubtful, but a challenge means that lawyers may give full vent to their sad experiences of jurors not deciding cases according to the evidence, see Gobert (1989).

[81] Since there is no power in the judge to achieve such a jury by exercise of the power of discharge, according to the Court of Appeal in R. v. Ford [1989] 3 All E.R. 445, the racial composition of a jury is a matter purely of chance; and see above, pp. 000–000.

[82] See N. Blake, "The Case for the Jury" in Findlay and Duff (1988), Chap. 9; Zander (1989), pp. 217–222 and Gobert (1989).

[83] As to the arguments for and against the peremptory challenge, see Blake in Findlay and Duff (1988) and Zander (1989), pp. 217–222.

[84] The prosecution had a right of peremptory challenge until 1305. The constitutionality of the right to standby was confirmed in R. v. McCann (1991) 92 Cr.App.R. 239.

[85] Technically, the Crown is exercising a challenge for cause but the trial of the cause is postponed until the panel is exhausted: R. v. Parry (1837) 7 C. & P. 836; R. v. Casement [1917] 1 K.B. 98. See also, J. F. McEldowney, "Stand By for the Crown: an Historical Analysis" [1979] Crim.L.R. 272.

[86] (1989) 88 Cr.App.R. 123, para. 3.

[87] ibid. para. 1.

[88] The power, therefore, can be used where it becomes apparent that a juror selected to try a complex case is illiterate: ibid. para. 5. The limitation on the right of stand by would not entirely satisfy Gobert, who argued that peremptory challenge did not need to be abolished, but that any perceived problems should have been resolved by less drastic methods, e.g., a rule not to permit the aggregation of challenges, in a multi-defendant trial: Gobert (1989).

[89] Some jurors may wish to affirm, either because of having a faith which will not permit them to swear on the New or Old Testament, or having no faith.

"I swear by Almighty God that I will faithfully try the defendant[s] and give a true verdict[s] according to the evidence."[90]

When 12 have been sworn the accused may be "given in charge" to the jury and the trial can begin.[91]

(g) Discharge[92]

The judicial power to discharge[93] the jury or individual jurors once the trial has begun is closely related to the challenge for cause considered above. Consequently, there is no power to discharge a jury because it is not racially mixed.[94] A judge's decision to discharge a jury or juror is unchallengeable, whereas if the judge decides not to discharge, that decision may be challenged on appeal against conviction by the accused on the basis that the conviction is to be regarded as unsafe and unsatisfactory because there was no discharge.[95]

If doubt arises about the capacity to act as a juror because of physical disability or insufficient understanding of English, an individual juror may be discharged. It may also be appropriate to accommodate a juror by exercising the discharge power, for example, on the death of a spouse.[96]

The discharge power enables the judge to deal with irregularities and improprieties before and after the retirement of the jury to consider its verdict. Before retirement, the sort of matters which may lead the judge to discharge a juror are: drunkenness; inattention to the proceedings; frivolous behaviour; acquisition of information which ought not to be available to a juror, such as existing knowledge of the accused's bad character; or contact with someone outside the jury which in the circumstances is an irregularity rather than acceptable conduct and which may interfere with the course of justice.[97] In view of the nexus between challenge and discharge, an important ground for discharge is bias in a juror becoming apparent later than the time for challenge. In some cases the bias of an individual juror may lead to the discharge of the jury as a whole, since the accused's right to a fair trial has been prejudiced.[98]

A long trial can place a considerable strain on the jury and there are provisions which allow the discharge of individual jurors in the course of a trial in the

---

[90] Oaths Act 1978, ss.1, 4; *Practice Direction* [1984] 3 All E.R. 528. An alternative form is provided for jurors who wish to affirm.

[91] This is not an essential part of trial procedure. At the end of the swearing-in, the clerk may read the indictment to the jury and tell them that it is their "charge" to say whether the accused is guilty or not.

[92] See R. Buxton, "Challenging and Discharging Jurors—2" [1990] Crim.L.R. 84, and Archbold (1995) at paras.4–243 to 4–252a and *Blackstone's Criminal Practice 1996*, paras. D10.18–D10.23.

[93] Juries Act 1974, s.16. This power is exercisable in any trial except when it is for an offence punishable with death: *ibid.*, s.16(1)(2) as amended by the Criminal Justice Act 1988, s.121.

[94] *R. v. Ford* [1989] 3 All E.R. 445, and see p. 892 above.

[95] Buxton, (1990–I), 284–285.

[96] *ibid.* p. 285. The power must be exercised by a High Court or Circuit judge or recorder.

[97] *ibid.* pp. 286–287.

[98] *ibid.* pp. 287–288, commenting on *R. v. Spencer* [1987] A.C. 128 where the House of Lords decided that the failure to discharge the jury after three of them had been in discussion with a biased, discharged juror who may well have influenced them, meant that the conviction had to be quashed as being unsafe. For the test of bias, see *R. v. Gough* [1993] A.C. 646 and Archbold (1995), paras.4–246 to 4–249.

event of illness or other good reason.[99] So long as the jury does not fall below nine members, the trial can proceed.[1]

After retirement, the jury must not separate or speak to anyone.[2] If there is any such separation or communication the jury will normally be discharged.[3]

(h) The trial, the summing up and the deliberations

During the course of the trial the members of the jury sit together in the jury box and listen to the evidence and the speeches of counsel. Jurors are entitled to take notes if they wish.[4] Such notes taken are subject to the same restrictions of secrecy as the jurors' deliberations. Jurors may also ask questions.[5] At an early stage of the trial, probably at the first adjournment, the jurors will be warned not to discuss the case with anyone except amongst themselves, and then only in the jury room. This instruction is designed to prevent outside influences on jurors[6] and may be reinforced by a reminder not to come to a view about the case until all the evidence and arguments have been heard.[7]

The contents of the summing up have been noted in the preceding section, as well as the significant place it has in the sequence of the trial. The initial direction on verdict will be that unanimity should be achieved, and although the jurors will know from the notes provided that a majority verdict is possible, the object of the deliberations should be unanimity. At the end of the summing up the jury retires to the jury room to consider its verdict and are kept together privately until a verdict is reached or it is discharged.[8] The jury bailiff must ensure that no one comes into contact with the jury except by leave of the court.[9] In particularly difficult cases it may be necessary to provide overnight hotel accommodation for the jurors under the close supervision of the court. If the jury requires further information from the judge to explain a point in the

---

[99] Juries Act 1974, s.16, provides that a juror can be discharged when incapable of continuing to act through illness or for any other reason. The power to discharge should be exercised generously. Trial by jury depends upon the willing co-operation of the public and, in any event, an aggrieved and inconvenienced juror is not likely to be a good one: *R. v. Hambery* [1977] Q.B. 924.

[1] Juries Act 1974, s.16(1). The number required for a majority verdict is adjusted accordingly: see p. 903, below.

[2] As to other aspects of the secrecy of the jury room, see below pp. 902–903.

[3] Buxton, (1990–I) 288–291. Permission may be granted under the Juries Act 1974, s.13, which, since the amendment of the Criminal Justice and Public Order Act 1994, includes the period after retirement of the jury.

[4] Although some have doubted the value of this (see Cornish (1971), pp. 50–51), the Royal Commission has recommended that the judge should explain in the opening remarks that they may make notes: R.C.C.J., Report (1993), p. 134. This was based upon the discovery that jurors frequently found notes helpful: Zander and Henderson (1993), pp. 201–212.

[5] They rarely do so: Zander and Henderson (1993), pp. 213–214.

[6] Not necessarily sinister influences: the juror must give a verdict according to the evidence adduced in court and not on any other basis.

[7] This instruction may not always be heeded. The anonymous juror in the Thorpe trial revealed that the jury had decided on acquittal on the first day of the trial: see "Thorpe's trial: how the jury saw it" *New Statesman*, July 27, 1979.

[8] Circumstances are now somewhat less primitive than when juries were locked up without refreshment to encourage them to concentrate. Juries are now allowed refreshment at their own expense: Juries Act 1974, s.15.

[9] Juries Act 1974, s.13. This rule is enforced very strictly and any breach of it is likely to lead to the discharge of the jury or the later quashing of any conviction: *R. v. Prime* (1973) 57 Cr.App.R. 632; *R. v. Goodson* [1975] 1 W.L.R. 549; *R. v. Davis* (1960) 44 Cr.App.R. 235.

summing up, or if guidance is required, the normal practice is for counsel to be consulted and the jury, if necessary, brought back into court. The judge then tries to resolve the problem and may, if appropriate, remind the jury of the evidence.

The jurors will select a person known as a "foreman" to speak for the jury on all matters and, ultimately, to deliver the verdict. An important aspect of the role of the foreman is to chair the jury's deliberations. Consequently, he or she has the possibility of significantly influencing the decision.[10] The method of selection is a matter for the jury.[11]

The deliberations of the jury are kept secret. Jurors are told that what is said in the jury room should not be disclosed to anyone even after the trial is over.[12] There have been examples of this instruction being ignored and some of what is known about the jury and the way in which it approaches its task emanates from the published experiences of individual jurors.[13] Statute makes it contempt of court to obtain, disclose or solicit any particulars of statements made, opinions expressed, arguments advanced or votes cast by members of a jury in the course of their deliberations in any legal proceedings.[14]

The secrecy of the jury room is said to be the basis on which trial by jury continues to exist. The arguments in favour of secrecy have been stated by Mr Justice McHugh:[15] (1) it is necessary to ensure freedom of discussion in the jury room; (2) it protects jurors from outside influences; (3) if the public knew how juries reached decisions, the jury would lose its place in the public esteem; (4) without it citizens would be reluctant to serve as jurors; (5) it is necessary to ensure the finality of the verdict; (6) it protects the community satisfaction which flows from a unanimous verdict; (7) it enables juries to bring in unpopular verdicts; (8) it prevents unreliable disclosures by jurors and prevents verdicts being misunderstood; (9) it protects the privacy of the individual juror and prevents harassment; (10) it protects jurors from pressure to explain their reasons for a verdict; (11) it prevents vendettas against jurors; (12) it prevents enormous public pressures being placed on jurors.

The arguments against secrecy and in favour of disclosure have been stated by the same author:[16] (1) it will make juries more accountable; (2) it will enable injustices to be cured; (3) it could lead to inquiries into the reliability of convictions; (4) it could lead to worthwhile reforms of the legal system; (5) it may have an educational effect on the public; (6) it is necessary to ensure that jury trial can be properly examined to see if it is working;[17] (7) it is required by each juror's freedom of expression.

---

[10] J. Baldwin and M. McConville, "Juries, Foremen and Verdicts" (1980) 20 Brit.J.Criminol. 35.
[11] The question apparently often put is, "Has anybody been on a jury before?" A juror who admits to experience often becomes foreman.
[12] As they are informed in the notes accompanying the jury summons.
[13] E. Devons, "Serving as a Juryman in Britain" (1965) 28 M.L.R. 561; D. Barber and G. Gordon (ed.), *Members of the Jury* (1976).
[14] Contempt of Court Act 1981, s.8(1). Such proceedings for contempt may only be brought by, or with the permission of, the Attorney-General, or on the motion of a competent court: s.8(3). A competent court for this purpose is one which has jurisdiction to deal with the alleged contempt.
[15] "Jurors' Deliberations, Jury Secrecy, Public Policy and the Law of Contempt" in Findlay and Duff (1988), pp. 62–65.
[16] *ibid.* pp. 65–67.
[17] Jury research is not made impossible, but is made much harder, by the secrecy requirement; see S. McCabe, "Is Jury Research Dead"? in Findlay and Duff (1988), Chap. 2, and see pp. 906–908, below.

"The one recommendation of the [Royal] Commission that has received unequivocal support from the academic community is that s.8 of the Contempt of Court Act 1981 should be amended so as to permit proper research into jury decision-making."[18]

(i) Majority verdicts[19]

The requirement that the verdict be unanimous, which had stood since the thirteenth century, was abandoned by the Criminal Justice Act 1967, which introduced the majority verdict. The governing provision is now the Juries Act 1974, s.17:

"(1)   ... the verdict of a jury in proceedings in the Crown Court or the High Court need not be unanimous if—
  (a) in a case where there are not less then eleven jurors, ten of them agree on a verdict; and
  (b) in a case where there are ten jurors, nine of them agree on a verdict.
...
  (3) The Crown Court shall not accept a verdict of guilty by virtue of subsection (1) above unless the foreman of the jury has stated in open court the number of jurors who respectively agreed to and dissented from the verdict.
  (4) No court shall accept a verdict by virtue of subsection (a) ... unless it appears to the court that the jury have had such period of time for deliberation as the court thinks reasonable having regard to the nature and complexity of the case; and the Crown Court shall in any event not accept such a verdict unless it appears to the court that the jury have had at least two hours for deliberation."

At the outset the jury is directed to reach an unanimous verdict[20] and no mention should normally be made of the majority verdict procedure.[21] However, as has been mentioned, the jurors know of the procedure from the notes accompanying the jury summons.

A *Practice Direction*[22] sets out the procedure which ensures that the safeguards contained in the Act (a minimum period of deliberation and a statement in open court of the majority) are observed. The stages are as follows:

---

[18] Sanders and Young (1994), p. 390. As to the evaluation of the performance of juries, see below pp. 906–910.

[19] See generally, Archbold (1995), paras.4-440 to 4-444; Emmins (1995), pp. 162–163; and *Blackstone's Criminal Practice 1996*, paras. D15.12–D15.17. At a summary trial, there is normally a bench of three magistrates and conviction is by majority, see p. 842, above.

[20] See p. 901, above.

[21] *R. v. Thomas* [1983] Crim.L.R. 745. The fact that the judge told the jury in the summing-up that he was entitled to take a majority verdict after at least two hours was held not to be such a significant irregularity that there was the risk of a miscarriage of justice. The fear is of "inviting" the jury to disagree from the start: see also *R. v. Modeste* [1983] Crim.L.R. 746.

[22] [1967] 1 W.L.R. 1198, as clarified by *Practice Direction* [1970] 1 W.L.R. 916.

1. If the jury returns[23] within two hours,[24] only a unanimous verdict is acceptable. If there is no unanimity the jury is sent back for further deliberation.
2. If the jury returns after two hours ten minutes[25] have elapsed it is asked if a verdict has been reached. If it is not unanimous and the judge considers that the jury has had a reasonable time for deliberation and having regard to the nature and complexity of the case the judge will direct it that a majority verdict is acceptable, although they should still try to reach unanimity.
3. When the jury finally returns, a precise set of questions is asked:
   (i) Have at least ten (or nine as the case may be) of you agreed upon your verdict? If "Yes",
   (ii) What is your verdict? Please answer only "Guilty" or "Not Guilty".
   (iii) (a) If "Not Guilty"—accept the verdict without more ado.
   (b) If "Guilty"—is that the verdict of you all or by a majority?
   (iv) If "Guilty" by a majority, how many of you agreed to the verdict and how many dissented?

The foreman must state in open court the number of jurors who agreed to and dissented from the verdict before the judge can properly accept a guilty verdict, but there is no requirement that the precise words of the *Practice Direction* be used so long as it is clear to the ordinary person how the jury divided.[26] The formulation of the questions in the *Practice Direction* is intended to prevent anyone (other than the jurors) knowing whether or not a guilty verdict was reached by a majority.[27]

Before the introduction of the majority verdict, it was the case that if a jury failed to reach a unanimous verdict it was discharged and the accused might or might not be retried at the discretion of the prosecution. The majority verdict was introduced because fears of jury "nobbling" had been expressed and it was argued that the unanimity rule made it too easy for professional criminals to threaten or intimidate one member of a jury into holding out for a not guilty verdict.[28] However, the evidence to support these arguments put forward by the Government to support the majority verdict was at best scanty.[29] The Government mentioned also the argument that the reform would save resources in avo-

---

[23] "Returns" in the context of the Practice Direction includes being sent for by the judge who may be wondering how the deliberations are progressing.
[24] The statutory requirement that not less than two hours should be allowed for the initial deliberation is mandatory: *R. v. Barry* [1975] 1 W.L.R. 1190. The initial period may be such longer time as the judge thinks reasonable. A complicated case is an instance where a longer period is to be expected: Juries Act 1974, s.17(4); *R. v. Bateson* (1969) 54 Cr.App.R. 11; *R. v. Thornton, R. v. Stead* (1989) 89 Cr.App.R. 54.
[25] *Practice Direction* [1970] 1 W.L.R. 916. The period that has elapsed since the last member of the jury left the jury box must be stated in open court before the jury is asked for its verdict. The extra ten minutes allows for the practical necessities of returning from the jury room to the court room: Emmins (1995), p. 163.
[26] *R. v. Pigg* [1983] 1 W.L.R. 6.
[27] Thus avoiding a sort of second-class acquittal. See *R. v. Adams* [1969] 1 W.L.R. 106.
[28] See P. Duff and M. Findlay, "The Politics of Jury Reform" in Findlay and Duff (1988), Chap. 13, at pp. 212–215 and N. Blake in *ibid.*, p. 143. See also, P. Byrne, "Jury Reform and the Future" in *ibid.*, Chap. 12, at p. 191.
[29] See, *e.g.* Blake, *op. cit.* and Sanders and Young (1994), pp. 361–364.

iding the consumption of time for the police and others involved in a second trial, although little importance was attached to this argument.[30]

It has been suggested that there are very strong arguments against the use of majority verdicts since the unanimity principle rather than the majority verdict reduces the risk of convicting the innocent, unanimous verdicts command greater community acceptance and thus the public has greater confidence in the criminal justice system, and the evidence suggests that the rate of hung juries, that is where the jury is discharged after being unable to agree, has not been much affected by the introduction of the majority verdict.[31] Further, Freeman has argued that the introduction of the majority verdict weakens the effect of the requirement that the prosecution must prove its case beyond a reasonable doubt, since if one member of a jury of twelve people is not satisfied of the guilt of the accused that is a clear indication that there is a reasonable doubt as to the prosecution's case and so the accused should be acquitted.[32] Maher has pointed out that this argument rather assumes that proof beyond a reasonable doubt is a concept which can be described in terms of probability. However, "it can be said that insisting on an unanimity rule is not always necessary in order to show that the principle of proof of the guilt of the accused beyond reasonable doubt is being taken seriously. For if a jury is large in size and is also representative of the community or society in general, then some relaxation of the rule may not frustrate the purpose of the principle which is to give the accused a right not to be convicted of a charge unless the case against him has been made out at a level of practical certainty. The rule of unanimity may also be relaxed where this right receives adequate protection by other means. . . . But it can be said that if no such safeguards exist for an accused then jury verdicts must be unanimous, or be near to unanimity, if the accused's right to proof of his guilt at the level of practical certainty is to be upheld."[33]

The introduction of majority verdicts and the consequent debate is an example of an instance where the Packer models may be helpful. The Government appears to have been aware that most of its arguments in favour of majority verdicts were crime control model arguments, which may be why emphasis was placed on the change to majority verdicts improving fairness to the accused by preventing jury nobbling. This approach emphasises a value of the due process model.[34] Further, Maher's argument for accepting the majority verdict is conditional upon true respect being granted to the principles of due process.

(j) Is the jury competent to make decisions?

Is the jury actually competent to perform its functions?[35] It has been asserted that the jury acquits too many people accused of crime.[36] The evidence to support such a claim is, at best, equivocal.[37]

---

[30] See Duff and Findlay in Findlay and Duff (1988), p. 213.

[31] D. Brown and D. Neal, "Show Trials: The Media and the Gang of Twelve" in *ibid.*, Chap. 8, at p. 134.

[32] Freeman (1981). See also Brown and Neal in Findlay and Duff (1988), p. 134.

[33] G. Maher, "The Verdict of the Jury" in *ibid.*, Chap. 3 at pp. 45–49, esp. p. 49.

[34] Duff and Findlay in *ibid.*, pp. 212–215.

[35] As to the functions of the jury, see pp. 889–890, above.

[36] See, in particular, Sir R. Mark, "Minority Verdicts" (1973), extracted in M. Zander, *Cases and Materials on the English Legal System* (6th ed., 1993), pp. 471–475 and see Sanders and Young (1994), pp. 370–379 for a particularly telling critique.

[37] See the statistics referred to at p. 845, n. 62, above, which do not distinguish between pleas of guilty and not guilty; S. Butler, "Acquittal Rates" and J. Vennard, "The Outcome of Contested

The question, further, raises doubts, first, whether it is proper for juries to decide cases on whatever grounds it chooses, regardless of the direction on the law by the judge, and, secondly, whether the jury is capable of understanding the evidence and making decisions in complex cases. These doubts may be regarded as an attack on the independence of the jury since some would argue that the very arbitrariness and prejudice of which complaint is made proves that independence.[38]

(i) Do juries arrive at "perverse" verdicts?

There are two aspects of the question whether juries reach "perverse" verdicts: first, whether a jury's decisions according to conscience should be permitted, and, secondly, what the function of the jury is when matters of conscience are not raised.

(1) *"Perverse" verdicts and the conscience of the jury.* If the value of trial by jury lies in the involvement of the public in the criminal process, thus permitting the exercise of "community conscience" and providing the "just face" of the law,[39] the jury, it can be argued, must be entitled to arrive at decisions which appear to be contrary to the law. Thus the jury's acquittal of Clive Ponting of charges under the section 2 of the Official Secrets Act 1911 may be viewed as the jury exercising its constitutional role to arrive at a decision according to its conscience.[40]

Ponting had passed to Tam Dalyell M. P. documents relating to the sinking of the Argentinian battleship, the *General Belgrano*, by a British submarine during the Falklands War in 1982. These documents were clearly covered by section 2, and the judge directed the jury that, on his understanding of section 2, Ponting had no authorisation to pass them to someone such as Dalyell and there was no other lawful justification for Ponting's act. Nevertheless the jury acquitted him.

On the other hand, it can be argued that permitting juries to decide according to their conscience is completely inappropriate in "enlightened times."[41] Thus, the acquittal of Ponting may be regarded as wholly improper. If the law is wrong, the proper means of challenge and change is through the democratic process.

(2) *"Perverse" verdicts and jury decision-making.* Whatever view is taken as to the acceptability of the jury acting according to its conscience, there may be

---

Trials" in D. Moxon (ed.), *Managing Criminal Justice* (1985); Zander (1993), pp. 475–476. Sir Robert Mark's other grounds of complaint such as the professional criminal being let off too frequently, and the activities of crooked lawyers are responded to by Zander (1993) at pp. 475–478. See for a vigorous critique of Mark's argument: Sanders and Young (1994), pp. 370–379.

[38] See, *e.g.*, Brown and Neal in Findlay and Duff (1988); and Mr Justice McHugh in *ibid.*

[39] As to this function of the jury, see p. 890, above.

[40] C. Ponting, *The Right to Know: The Inside Story of the Belgrano Affair* (1985). See also N. MacCormick, "The Interest of the State and the Rule of Law" in P. Wallington and R. M. Merkin, *Essays in Memory of Professor F. H. Lawson* (1986).

[41] The phrase is that of Jeremy Bentham in *Draught of a Code for the Organisation of the Judicial Establishment in France* (1790), quoted in G. Marshall, "The judgement of one's peers: some aims and ideal of jury trial" in Walker with Pearson (1975), p. 1.

an argument about "perverse' verdicts in a different sense. Whether juries' verdicts may be described as "perverse" on a more general basis depends upon what the role of the jury in decision-making is perceived to be. If a narrow approach is taken, a verdict is right if it is reached by the jury after an honest, careful and reasonable attempt to apply the law (as explained by the judge in the summing up) to the facts as it finds them, taking no other circumstances into account.[42] What is then achieved is both greater certainty in the outcome of trials and greater consistency in juries' decisions.[43] A broad approach might perceive a verdict to be right where it is a verdict of acquittal, say, after a consideration of the evidence which indicated guilt or even without any consideration of the evidence at all, provided it nevertheless results from a reasonable exercise of discretion in favour of the accused reflecting the jury's sympathy, clemency or disapproval of the prosecution.

The narrow approach will view more acquittals as perverse verdicts and hence leads to the argument that reform of the jury is necessary. Jury research has been undertaken to attempt to consider whether juries do arrive at "perverse verdicts." Because of the limitations imposed upon researchers, the methods employed to analyse and explain the decision-making process and the verdicts reached in particular cases have necessarily been indirect.[44] One approach has been to compare the verdict of the jury in selected cases with the "verdict" of the professional participants in the trial; the other has been to arrange for a "mock" or "shadow" jury to listen to a case and then observe its deliberations when required to give a verdict. Both methods have their drawbacks but the results are illustrative of different features of jury decisions.

Two major English studies have been conducted which take account of the views of the professionals.[45] The first, by McCabe and Purves,[46] dealt with 475 accused tried on indictment over a two-year period, concentrating solely on the 115 who were acquitted by the jury. The second, by Baldwin and McConville,[47] dealt with 2,406 accused who appeared in the Birmingham Crown Court over an eighteen month period, concentrating on the 500 accused who contested their cases. The latter study is, therefore, of wider significance since it looks at all jury verdicts and not solely acquittals. There were some differences of methodology but both studies sought to explain the relevant verdicts by reference to the views of counsel,[48] solicitors, the judge and police officers.[49]

The first study attempted to categorise the 115 acquittals[50] according to the views of the professionals. It appeared that only 15 of the 115 acquittals were based on a deliberate decision to go against the evidence. All the others were explicable on the grounds of weakness in the prosecution case, the failure of prosecution witnesses or the credibility of the accused's explanation. Many of

---

[42] The argument is not denying the jury's function to be the decider of the facts.

[43] See, e.g., on the general point about consistency, Lord Devlin, The Judge (1979), Chap. 5; also E.J. Griew, Dishonesty and the Jury (1974) and G. Williams, The Proof of Guilt (1963), Chap. 10.

[44] See McCabe in Findlay and Duff (1988). See also R. Eldin, "A Juror's Tale" (1988) 138 N.L.J. 37.

[45] Reference should also be made to M. Zander, "Are Too Many Professional Criminals Avoiding Conviction?—A Study of Britain's Two Busiest Courts" (1974) 37 M.L.R. 28.

[46] S. McCabe and R. Purves, The Jury at Work (1972).

[47] J. Baldwin and M. McConville, Jury Trials (1979).

[48] The Bar did not co-operate in the Birmingham survey.

[49] The police did not co-operate in the Oxford survey.

[50] In the Oxford study there were a further 58 cases in which the accused was acquitted on the direction of the judge.

the acquittals were regarded as correct by the professionals and the proportion of perverse verdicts was established as low in relation to acquittals[51] and very low in relation to all contested cases.[52]

In the second study, Baldwin and McConville concluded that it was not possible to determine an overall pattern in the cases where the outcome was regarded as questionable. Those cases included convictions as well as acquittals and so doubts are raised about the conventional wisdom that the accused gets the benefit of the doubt from the jury. A similar proportion of wayward verdicts occurred in this study[53] and the authors agreed that it was a tiny fraction of all cases that pass through the criminal courts, yet they pointed out the serious nature of the cases tried by the jury and concluded that trial by jury is ". . . an arbitrary and unpredictable business."[54] The authors recognised that the significance of their research was limited to an assessment of the accuracy of verdicts and that the political and constitutional issues were also very important. They believed, however, that the political and constitutional debate should be informed by as much knowledge as possible about the veracity of jury verdicts.

In sum, the English evidence[55] demonstrates that there is an identifiable, if relatively small, number of cases in which juries reach perverse verdicts, although views differ on whether these deviations can be explained on any particular basis.

In the course of the Oxford study,[56] McCabe and Purves also utilised the "shadow" jury technique. In 30 cases, a second "jury" was installed in the court to listen to the proceedings and then to deliberate and reach a verdict. This method has the drawback that the degree of pressure which exists when a jury is dealing with the fate of an accused is lacking in mock deliberations, but the main conclusions pointed to the care and determination of the jurors to go about their task methodically, discount their prejudices and look for evidence on which to base their verdict.[57] This would suggest that in real cases the jury is likely to display the same, or an even greater, degree of conscientiousness and application. On the other hand, some evidence suggests that jury trial is a lottery when considering the competence of jurors to follow and remember evidence and think through the issues raised logically and carefully.[58]

(ii) The jury in complex cases

A similar debate is encountered when considering the role of the jury in complex cases. The debate relies more upon the nature of the trials, such as fraud trials and trials involving scientific evidence, which, it is suggested, means that the

---

[51] One verdict in eight amongst the jury acquittals, and one verdict in eleven amongst all acquittals.
[52] One verdict in thirty-two amongst the accused dealt with in the period of the study.
[53] *Jury Trials*, Chaps. 4 and 5.
[54] *ibid.* p. 132.
[55] There has been more extensive research in America, starting with H. Kalven and H. Zeisel, *The American Jury* (1966) (The Chicago Jury Project); see McCabe in Findlay and Duff (1988). In England, Zander's conclusions are broadly in line with the other studies.
[56] S. McCabe and R. Purves, *The Shadow Jury At Work* (1974). See also, A. P. Sealy, "What Can Be Learned from the Analysis of Simulated Juries?" in Walker with Pearson (1975).
[57] *ibid.* p. 61.
[58] See *The Times*, October 24, 1988.

jury cannot competently arrive at proper decisions. The inherent complexity of some cases was part of the argument that led to the abolition of the jury in most civil cases.[59] In the context of criminal cases, the Roskill Committee on Fraud Trials concluded that "we do not find trial by a random jury a satisfactory way of achieving justice in cases as long and complex as [many fraud trials]. We believe that many jurors are out of their depth."[60] Consequently, the Committee recommended that for complex fraud cases, the jury should be abolished and trial should take place before a Fraud Trials Tribunal.[61] This conclusion was reached even though the Committee stated that it was unable to obtain accurate evidence to suggest "that there has been a higher proportion of acquittals in complex fraud cases than in fraud cases or other criminal cases generally."[62] Indeed the Roskill Committee appears to have based its view, in so far as it was based on any evidence, at least in part on the conclusions of the study by Baldwin and McConville.[63] However, Baldwin and McConville had concluded that none of the questionable acquittals that they reported had been in a complex fraud case. In fact the jury had convicted in six of the eight cases which involved complex fraud issues and the two acquittals appeared to have been regarded as broadly justified.[64]

On that basis one author has suggested that the assertion of the Roskill Committee about the incompetence of the jury is really an article of faith.[65] Similar doubts about jury competence have been raised in cases involving scientific evidence.[66] The research on the decision-making of juries[67] suggests that juries are competent to make decisions, including decisions in complex cases. It has been suggested that the real fault in complex cases lies not with the jury, but rather with other participants in the criminal trial.[68]

Levi concluded that jury performance would be considerably improved if "greater care were devoted to the instruction of the jury on points of evidence and on the method to be followed when assessing it."[69] In particular there appears to be a tendency for judges to attempt to make their decisions to the jury "appeal proof" by full, undifferentiated reference to all the relevant law and any guideline judgments that exist, without taking sufficient care to empha-

---

[59] See pp. 789–793, above.
[60] *Fraud Trials Committee: Report*; Chair: Lord Roskill (1986), para. 8.35.
[61] *ibid.* para 8.51.
[62] *ibid.* para 8.35.
[63] J. Baldwin and M. McConville, *Jury Trials* (1979), see above.
[64] *ibid.* pp. 61–62.
[65] R. Harding, "Jury Performance in Complex Cases" in Findlay and Duff (1988), p. 77. Mr Merricks, a member of the Roskill Committee, felt that the case for change was not made out, partly because of the evidence and partly because most people making submissions were in favour of the jury. See also, M. Zander, "The Report of the Roskill Committee on Fraud Trials" [1986] Crim.L.R. 423.
[66] See, *e.g.*, Harding in Findlay and Duff (1988), pp. 82–90, concentrating on the Australian criticism of jury performance in such cases as the *Chamberlain* case. See also the criticisms of jury competence considered in M. Levi, "The Role of the Jury in Complex Cases" in Findlay and Duff, (1988), Chap. 6; and Lord McCluskey, *Law, Justice and Democracy* (1986) (Reith Lectures).
[67] See above.
[68] As pointed out by both Harding in Findlay and Duff, and Levi in *ibid.*
[69] Levi *op. cit.*, p. 109. The Roskill Committee recognised this problem and, in fraud cases where there was still to be jury trial, made a number of recommendations to improve jury comprehension, including the use of visual aids and proper preparation of documentation: *Fraud Trials Committee* (1986), Chap. 9. The same point is made with regard to the judge's responsibility in summing up to the jury, see pp. 881–886, above.

sise simply and only those matters necessary for the decision of the jury on the facts of the particular case and in response to the actual issues raised by counsel.[70]

(k) Replacing the jury?[71]

Questions have been raised about the role and efficacy of the jury. Although not frequently suggested, replacement of the jury by some other method of determining facts in criminal matters must be considered. There would appear to be four options.[72]

(i) The single judge[73]

Most civil trials are conducted by a judge alone[74] deciding both fact and law. In criminal matters the stipendiary magistrate has the same function. The role of the stipendiary is somewhat restricted because of the lesser degree of seriousness of the offences tried and also because any appeal against conviction is by way of rehearing, so that there would be significant differences in merely translating a stipendiary to the Crown Court.

The advantages of this option include time-saving at trials through not having to explain so many matters to the jury which it then decides, the reduction in the likelihood of decision-making being affected by outside influences,[75] and the reduction in the likelihood of verdicts not in accordance with the law.

The disadvantages of this option include the lack of community participation, the loss of the independence and impartiality of the jury, and the possibility that the judge would become case-hardened or prosecution-minded. Further, there would be little protection against eccentricity, and decisions on guilt being taken by one person might be too onerous a burden.[76]

(ii) The bench of judges

Some of the disadvantages of the single judge option, such as the possibility of becoming prosecution-minded or making eccentric decisions, might be avoided by a bench of three or five judges. The disadvantages of this option include that

---

[70] *ibid.* pp. 109–111. The same point is made by E. Griew, "Summing Up the Law" [1989] Crim.L.R. 768. See also p. 883, above.

[71] See, W. R. Cornish, *The Jury* (1968), Chap. 10.

[72] Assuming that we are considering alternative types of tribunal rather than adjustment to the jury, such as the reduction of the number of jurors to six.

[73] See J. Jackson and S. Doran, *Judge without Jury* (1995).

[74] See p. 790, for the significance of the jury in civil trials.

[75] The judge may be more immune to threats. This line of reasoning lay behind the introduction of single judge courts in certain trials in Northern Ireland in 1973 as a result of the Diplock Report (Report of the Commission to Consider Legal Procedures to Deal with Terrorist Activities in Northern Ireland, Cmnd. 5185, 1972), see now, the Northern Ireland (Emergency Provisions) Act 1978.

[76] See, *e.g.*, S. Greer and A. White, "Restoring Jury Trial to Terrorist Offences in Northern Ireland" in Findlay and Duff (1988), Chap. 11.

it would be enormously expensive and recruitment might be difficult and that the nature of the judiciary would be transformed because a considerable increase in the number of judges would allegedly weaken the bench. There would be considerable implications for the legal profession if a career judiciary were necessitated.

Many of the disadvantages associated with decision-making by professionals remain, in particular the absence of community participation in trial. The dislike of such decision-making will not have been lessened by the willingness of benches of judges of the Court of Appeal to permit convictions to stand where new evidence has emerged after the trial which might cause a jury to entertain reasonable doubt.[77]

(iii) The composite tribunal

On certain appeals from the magistrates' court, a Crown Court judge sits with two lay magistrates.[78] Some European jurisdictions[79] rely heavily upon the composite tribunal of lay people and judge and one observer, at least, has professed himself to be impressed by the system.[80]

The advantages would include the probability that trials would be speedier because the judge would be involved in all discussions, and that the lay people involved would be able to outvote the judge thus maintaining the overriding influence of representatives of the community.

Possible disadvantages would include whether the judge would have too large a say in most cases and whether decision-making would still be independent and impartial so as to preserve a fair trial. The lay people might have to be trained which could mean that they would no longer be representatives of the community.

(iv) The special jury

The special jury is an option which seeks to satisfy the demand for community participation and independence, but to ensure competence through training. Thus a jury is still selected from non-lawyers, but the only people eligible to serve on such a jury are those who have been trained for jury service. Consequently, the objective of random selection may be defeated and trial would be in the hands of a select group of people, albeit not all lawyers.

---

[77] A development initiated by the decision of the House of Lords in *Stafford v. D.P.P.* [1974] A.C. 878. It is heavily criticised in Lord Devlin, *The Judge* (1979) at pp. 148–176.

[78] See pp. 210–211, above. It used to be possible for lay magistrates to sit with a judge at a trial on indictment, but that was unusual and they did not take part in the decision: Supreme Court Act 1981, s.8(1).

[79] Described in Cornish (1968).

[80] Cornish was particularly complimentary about the Scandinavian system: *ibid.* Chap. 10.

C. EVALUATIONS

Critical analysis of the criminal trial is essential. It may be that the Packer's two model system[81] will help students to think through the many issues in relation to the criminal trial. For example, it might be suggested that the crime control model, emphasising the necessity to reduce criminal conduct and requiring that the system operate efficiently, helps to explain why it has been proposed that more offences be tried summarily where the accused does not need to be present, why plea bargaining is permitted, why the right to silence has been restricted and why proposals for jury reform are made, especially in relation to the alternatives to the jury, and on particular aspects such as the majority verdict, jury vetting and jury composition.[82] On the other hand, it could be suggested that the due process model helps to explain certain developments with regard to the criminal trial, for example, the developments as to the exclusion of evidence under the Police and Criminal Evidence Act 1984 and the end of the mandatory collaboration warning for several offences under the Criminal Justice and Public Order Act 1994.[83]

However, Packer's models are intended to be extremes, recognising that systems actually adopt a balance,[84] as the Royal Commission on Criminal Procedure set out to achieve in its "fundamental balance"[85] and which the Royal Commission on Criminal Justice recognised.[86] It is also necessary, therefore, to consider whether that balance is actually being achieved, or whether too much emphasis is being placed on the desire to control crime or on the desire to ensure that the accused gets a fair trial.

An approach on the basis of these models or the fundamental balance can be undertaken on any of the topics in this chapter, but attention might, for example, be drawn to the following arguments:

(a) Magistrates' court or Crown Court trial?

Frequently suggestions are made to increase the number of offences triable in the magistrates' courts. The arguments in favour tend to be based upon efficiency since magistrates trials will be cheaper and will not last as long, there is the possibility of written pleas of guilty, the trial may proceed in the absence of the accused and magistrates may be less likely to acquit.[87]

These appear to be arguments founded on the concept of crime control.[88] However, that does not necessarily make them bad or wrong, if adequate protections for the accused are provided. It is this side of the balance which may be

---

[81] For a description of these models, see above, pp. 776–779 and p. 836.

[82] See P. Duff and M. Findlay, "The Politics of Jury Reform" in Findlay and Duff (1988), Chap. 13. See generally Sanders and Young (1994).

[83] See I. H. Dennis, "The Criminal Justice and Public Order Act 1994: The Evidence Provisions" [1995] Crim.L.R. 4, at pp. 6–9.

[84] See p. 836, above.

[85] See pp. 774–776, above.

[86] The Royal Commission was, however, required to pay significant attention to efficiency and cost and it failed to make clear its basic approach for which it has been criticised, see, *eg.*, Sanders and Young (1994).

[87] See p. 895, n. 62.

[88] See also Sanders and Young (1994), p. 361.

missing, in view of the poor levels of legal representation[89] and the need of the magistrates to decide matters of both law and fact.[90]

A move towards magistrates' court trial may, of course, be thought to be fundamentally inappropriate if, for example, there is a belief that jury trial is an essential element in a fair trial or that only jury trial represents the essential requirement of community participation.

(b) Plea bargaining[91]

In the course of this chapter two forms of plea bargaining have been considered from the perspective of the various participants in the criminal trial, not least the accused. They are the plea arrangement between counsel for the accused to plead guilty to a lesser charge, otherwise known as charge bargaining,[92] and the sentencing discount available on a plea of guilty by the accused.[93]

If the crime control model is thought to be the proper model to adopt, plea bargaining has much to say for it in encouraging the guilty to plead guilty, and in saving considerable resources by having fewer contested trials.

However, it seems generally to be accepted that the inducements to plead guilty, if they are regarded as legitimate at all, should not be such that they create a substantial danger of the innocent pleading guilty. The pressures exerted by defence counsel giving advice to the accused "in strong terms" were identified by Baldwin and McConville in their research study which concentrated on 121 Crown Court defendants who made late changes of plea from not guilty to guilty.[94] The criticisms made of the attitude and performance of counsel caused the publication of the research to be surrounded with controversy, but the conclusions of the study were that the sentencing discount and the rules governing the interrogation of suspects by the police were primarily responsible for any deficiencies exposed, rather than the conduct of the participants in the criminal process.[95]

Although lip-service is paid to the notion that the discount is based on the expression of remorse, the primary justification for the inducements to plead guilty is administrative expediency. In a system which places so much emphasis upon the assumed innocence of the accused and the right to require the prosecution to prove their case, the existence of strong pressures to plead guilty may appear quite contradictory. The evidence currently available allows no complacency and suggests that more attention needs to be focused on those who plead guilty and, as a result, do not participate in the elaborate procedures described in the rest of this chapter.[96]

---

[89] See pp. 767–772, above.

[90] See pp. 842–843, above.

[91] See Sanders and Young (1994), pp. 269–273 and 307–338.

[92] See pp. 856, 863–866, 867–869, above.

[93] See pp. 857–858, 864–866, above.

[94] *Negotiated Justice* (1977). The research technique involved detailed interviews with defendants accused of serious crimes. The interviews were conducted soon after the trial had finished and it is inevitable that the particular sample might be inclined to protest innocence and exaggerate the pressures involved. Nevertheless, it would appear that the number of people wrongly convicted after a guilty plea may be underestimated.

[95] *ibid.* Chap. 6.

[96] See further, S. Dell, *Silent in Court* (1971); S. McCabe and R. Purves, *By-Passing the Jury* (1972); Bottoms and McClean (1976). See also McBarnet (1981).

(c) **Right to silence**

The restrictions on the right to silence[97] may well be argued to be an example of the move towards the crime control model, since they make the task of the prosecution slightly easier and deprive the accused of the adversarial system right to make the prosecution prove its case without assistance from the defence. It is almost impossible to find anyone, other than the Government and the police, in support of the restrictions imposed on the right prior to trial. As Dennis[98] points out, the case for reform when examined is not strong. The arguments are: (1) that "in practice the right to silence has been relied upon mainly by groups such as suspected terrorists, professional criminals suspected of serious crimes such as armed robbery, and businessmen and others suspected of sophisticated offences of serious fraud",[99] but the evidence does not support such conclusions; (2) "that silence on the part of such suspects is evidentially significant; it is though to be a generally reliable indicator of a consciousness of guilt",[1] but reasons for silence are not simply guilty, but also protection of others and systemic reasons; (3) "silence in the police station decreases the chance of prosecution and increases the chance of acquittal at trial if there is a prosecution",[2] but again the evidence fails to support the reason.

The restrictions on the right of silence at trial have not been so unanimously condemned, even though they strike at the heart of the adversarial system, that the prosecution must prove its case. This is because the accused retains the right of silence, but at greater risk,[3] and, as Dennis points out,[4] "at trial the accused will usually be legally represented. . . . He [or she] will know the case against him [or her], and . . . will have had a full opportunity to hear and test the evidence against him [or her]. The trial takes place in public before an impartial judge and jury." Is this perspective convincing?

(d) **Jury reform**

If crime control were the dominant motive in jury reform, arguments for abolition of the jury would be anticipated, since juries are inefficient and may acquit too many people, their decisions are unpredictable, and there is no appeal against an acquittal. In fact, proposals for the abolition of the jury are very rarely put forward, perhaps because of the popular support the jury receives through an ingrained belief that it is a constitutional protection against improper action by the State or simply that it is every person's right to be tried by one's peers.

The arguments are actually concerned with what crimes should be tried by the jury.[5] Many advocates of the jury are firmly of the view that it is under

---

[97] See above, pp. 860–862.
[98] I. H. Dennis, "The Criminal Justice and Public Order Act 1994: The Evidence Provisions" [1995] Crim. L. R. 4, pp. 11–14. He draws upon research including JUSTICE, *Right of Silence Debate: The Northern Ireland Experience* (1994); R. Leng, *The Right to Silence in Police Interrogation: A Study of Some of the Issues Underlying the Debate* (RCCJ Research Study No. 10, 1993); and M. McConville and J. Hodgson, *Custodial Legal Advice and the Right to Silence* (RCCJ Research Study No. 16, 1993).
[99] Dennis (1995), p. 11.
[1] *ibid.*, p. 12.
[2] *ibid.*, p. 13.
[3] See above, pp. 860–862.
[4] *ibid.*, p. 18.
[5] See above.

attack, but that the attack is not direct or frontal against the institution of the jury itself.[6] Some advocates take the view that the attack is predicated on the basis of the crime control model. This model explains, it is argued, the move in favour of majority verdicts,[7] the change in disqualification conditions excluding a considerable number of potential jurors,[8] and the acceptance of jury vetting.[9] On the other hand, it might be suggested that the recent alterations are merely redressing the balance from a position where too many of the provisions were far too favourable to the accused.

---

[6] See, *e.g.* P. Duff and M. Findlay, "The Politics of Jury Reform" in Findlay and Duff (1988), Chap. 13; Freeman (1981); Lord Devlin, *Trial by Jury* (1956); Lord Devlin, "Trial By Jury for Fraud" (1986) 6 O. J.L.S. 311.

[7] See pp. 903–905, above and see Sanders and Young (1994), pp. 361–364.

[8] See pp. 890–891, above.

[9] See pp. 894–895, above and see Sanders and Young (1994), pp. 355–360.

CHAPTER 17

APPEALS AND JUDICIAL REVIEW

A. INTRODUCTION

IN this chapter we consider the various mechanisms for correcting errors in, and otherwise reviewing, the decisions of courts and tribunals. There are two basic kinds of legal procedure that are available for these purposes. An *appeal* may be provided by statute: indeed it will only be available if a statute has so provided, as the common law does not recognise any rights of appeal as such. The common law has provided only for the *review* of decisions either on the ground that the body which made the decision had no jurisdiction in the matter, or on the ground that the formal record of proceedings revealed that there had been some error of law. Where the body was an inferior body of limited jurisdiction, the appropriate remedy was a writ of certiorari to remove the proceedings into the Court of King's Bench: if the decision was shown to be defective it would be quashed. If such a body was proposing to act outside the jurisdiction in the future, a writ of prohibition would lie to prevent it from so acting; if it failed to perform a duty, the appropriate remedy was a writ of mandamus. These "prerogative" remedies would be available to challenge, for example, the decisions of justices of the peace in summary criminal proceedings or in civil cases. Where, however, the decision was that of one of the superior courts, or followed a criminal trial on indictment at the assizes or quarter sessions, the remedy was a writ of error, closely analogous to certiorari.[1] There were also informal devices whereby matters could be adjourned so that the views of other judges could be obtained[2] and special procedures for the review of decisions in the Court of Chancery.[3]

In the nineteenth and early twentieth centuries, writs of error were replaced by statutory appeals. The prerogative writs continued to be available in respect of the courts of summary jurisdiction, but now in parallel to statutory appeals. They were also increasingly used to correct the decisions of local authorities, government departments and statutory tribunals. In 1938 they became prerogative "orders" rather than writs,[4] and in 1978 they came to be exclusively available on a new procedure termed an "application for judicial review".[5]

Apart from these basic options there are various other avenues for the redress of grievances, some of which are enshrined in statute (*e.g.* references by the Home Secretary to the Court of Appeal (Criminal Division)), some dependent on an exercise of the royal prerogative (*e.g.* the prerogative of mercy) and some informal.

There are two basic functions fulfilled by mechanisms for appeal or review.

---

[1] See above, p. 38.
[2] *ibid.*
[3] *ibid.*
[4] Administration of Justice (Miscellaneous Provisions) Act 1938, s.7.
[5] See below, pp. 969–976.

The first is that of the correction of errors of fact, substantive law or procedure made by the court or tribunal below. The second is that of the harmonious development of the law. Appellate courts commonly comprise a number of judges whereas trial courts and tribunals normally have a single judge or legally-qualified chairman, sitting alone or with a jury or lay members. Appellate judges tend to be of greater experience and seniority than trial judges and their case load tends to be smaller, giving greater time for consideration; these factors become more pronounced the higher one moves up the courts hierarchy. In limited circumstances fresh evidence may be admitted before the reviewing court. Appellate courts may also correct divergences of approach among different courts of first instance.[6]

B. VARIABLE FACTORS IN APPEAL AND REVIEW MECHANISMS

There are a number of factors which must be taken into account when considering any legal procedure for redressing a grievance:

(1) Who can institute an appeal?[7]
(2) Can the appeal be brought as of right or only by the leave of a court or other body?
(3) What are the permissible grounds for an appeal?
(4) What is the time limit within which an appeal must be brought?
(5) To which court or tribunal does the appeal lie?
(6) What material may the appellate body consider?
(7) Who may appear as parties on the appeal?
(8) What are the powers of the appellate court?

C. APPEALS

In this section we consider appeals from courts and tribunals.[8] We concentrate on appeals in basic civil and criminal cases: in addition a vast number of rights of appeal have been created in special cases which cannot be covered in detail.[9] The appeals are presented in four groups:

(1) Summary criminal proceedings and civil proceedings originating in magistrates' courts;
(2) Criminal proceedings on indictment;
(3) Civil cases originating in a county court or the High Court;
(4) Appeals in administrative law matters.

---

[6] e.g. the Court of Appeal in *Froom v. Butcher* [1976] Q.B. 286 settled the difference between judges who held that failure to wear a seat belt in a car would normally constitute contributory negligence and those who did not: the former approach was approved.
[7] For convenience this is to be taken here to include "seek review".
[8] As to the constitution and functions of appellate courts, see Chap. 2.
[9] A list may be found in D. Price, *Appeals* (1982).

The basic principles governing rights of appeal from a court seem to be that: (1) there should be one chance to appeal on the facts or merits and a series of opportunities to take points of law up the hierarchy of the courts; (2) there should be one chance to appeal as of right, with further appeals being dependent upon obtaining leave; and (3) that an acquittal by a jury in a criminal case should be regarded as final. Appeals from tribunals or public authorities tend to be limited to points of law.

1. APPEALS FROM MAGISTRATES' COURTS

A person aggrieved by a decision of a magistrates' court in a criminal case, or in certain civil cases, has the option of (1) appealing on fact or law to the Crown Court or (2) appealing on a point of law alone direct to the High Court, by way of "case stated." If the first option is chosen, an appeal lies thereafter to the High Court as in (2). In family cases, the appeal lies only to the High Court.

Once a case reaches the High Court, further appeals in criminal cases lie only to the House of Lords, and further appeals in civil cases lie on the same basis as in other civil cases determined by the High Court. In a criminal case, where the magistrates commit a convicted person to the Crown Court for sentence, the appeal thereafter lies to the Court of Appeal (Criminal Division).[10]

(a) Appeals from magistrates' courts to the Crown Court

The defendant in a criminal case may appeal to the Crown Court, as of right, (a) if he or she pleaded guilty,[11] against sentence; or (b) if he or she did not plead guilty, against the conviction or sentence.[12] "Sentence" includes any order made on conviction other than an order for costs and certain other orders.[13] Similarly, a person may appeal against an order for contempt of a magistrates' court[14] or an order binding him or her over to keep the peace or to be of good behaviour.[15] The prosecutor or complainant may not appeal against an acquittal or a refusal to make an order.[16]

---

[10] Criminal Appeal Act 1968, s.10: see below, p. 933.

[11] If the plea of guilty was "equivocal" the defendant may appeal to the Crown Court to set aside the conviction and remit the case to the magistrates with a direction to enter a plea of "not guilty" and try the case summarily: the magistrates' court is obliged to comply with the direction provided that there has been a proper inquiry by the Crown Court and sufficient evidence from which it could find that the plea had been equivocal: *R. v. Plymouth JJ., ex p. Hart* [1986] Q.B. 950. A plea is equivocal where something emerges during the trial which throws doubt on it, *e.g.* "guilty, but I took it by mistake." See *R. v. Durham Quarter Sessions, ex p. Virgo* [1952] 2 Q.B. 1. The Crown Court should seek affidavit evidence from the chairman of the bench or the clerk before sending it back: *R. v. Rochdale JJ., ex p. Allwork* [1981] 3 All E.R. 433. The Crown Court may also remit a case where it subsequently transpires that a plea of guilty was made under duress: *R. v. Huntingdon Crown Court, ex p. Jordan* [1981] Q.B. 857.

[12] Magistrates' Courts Act 1980, s.108(1).

[13] *ibid.*, s.108(3). Probation orders and orders for conditional discharge were formerly excluded: see now the Criminal Justice Act 1982, s.66(2).

[14] Contempt of Court Act 1981, s.12(5).

[15] Magistrates' Courts (Appeals from Binding Over Orders) Act 1956, s.1.

[16] Such a right may be expressly conferred, *e.g.* the Customs and Excise Management Act 1979, s.147: offences under the Customs and Excise Acts.

Notice of appeal must be given within 21 days after the day on which the decision or sentence appealed against was given.[17] The notice must state the grounds for appeal. The Crown Court may extend the time for giving notice of appeal either before or after it expires.[18] If the defendant is legally aided, the clerk to the justices must supply a copy of his or her notes[19]; if the defendant is not, the clerk should view requests for notes sympathetically.[20]

The appeal is treated as a complete rehearing,[21] and the procedure is exactly the same as at a summary trial in the magistrates' court. The appeal can be heard notwithstanding the absence of the appellant,[22] even where he or she has not instructed counsel to appear on his or her behalf.[23] The relevant witnesses will attend the court and give evidence as at the original trial. The parties are not, however, confined to the evidence placed before the magistrates. Where the appeal is against sentence only, it is usual for the prosecution merely to put forward facts which had been admitted or found by the magistrates, although there is no technical reason why sworn evidence should not be given.[24]

The powers of the Crown Court are as follows.[25] It may correct any error or mistake in the order or judgment against which the appeal is brought, and at the end of the hearing may:

(a) confirm, reverse or vary any part of the decision appealed against, including a determination not to impose a separate penalty in respect of an offence;[26]

(b) remit the matter with its opinion thereon to the authority whose decision is appealed against; or

(c) make any order in the matter as it thinks just and exercise any power which that authority might have exercised.

---

[17] Crown Court Rules 1982 (S.I. 1982 No. 1109), r.7.

[18] *ibid.*

[19] Legal Aid in Criminal and Care Proceedings (General) Regulations 1989 (S.I. 1989 No. 344), reg. 42.

[20] *R. v. Clerk to Highbury Corner JJ., ex p. Hussein* [1986] 1 W.L.R. 1266, following *R. v. Clerk to Lancaster JJ., ex p. Hill* (1983) 148 J.P. 65, in preference to *dicta* in *Hill v. Wilson* (1984) 149 J.P. 252.

[21] See *Drover v. Rugman* [1951] 1 K.B. 380; *Northern Ireland Trailers v. Preston Corporation* [1972] 1 W.L.R. 203; *Hughes v. Holley* (1986) 86 Cr. App. R. 130: these cases show that the court must, however, consider the state of affairs existing at the time the order was appealed against. Appeals against binding-over orders are to be conducted as a rehearing: *Shaw v. Hamilton* [1982] 1 W.L.R. 1308.

[22] *R. v. Croydon Crown Court, ex p. Clair* [1986] 1 W.L.R. 746 (the Crown Court had refused to hear the appeal in the appellant's absence: mandamus was granted requiring them to do so).

[23] *R. v. Crown Court at Guildford, ex p. Brewer* (1987) 87 Cr. App. R. 265 (the appellant's counsel was present, but, following refusal of an application for an adjournment, took no further part in the proceedings as he had no instructions to do so). The Crown Court has power to set aside its own order dismissing an appeal, *e.g.* where the appellant is absent as the result of a misunderstanding: *R. v. Knightsbridge Crown Court, ex p. Johnson* [1986] Crim. L.R. 803.

[24] *Paprika Ltd v. Board of Trade* [1944] K.B. 327; *Shaw v. Hamilton* [1982] 1 W.L.R. 1308; *Williams v. R.* (1983) 77 Cr. App. R. 329; *R. v. Telford JJ., ex p. Darlington* (1987) 87 Cr. App. R. 194.

[25] Supreme Court Act 1981, s.48, as amended by the Criminal Justice Act 1988, s.156.

[26] Prior to the enactment of s.156 of the 1988 Act, the subsection merely referred to a power to vary "the decision appealed against", the Divisional Court in *Dutta v. Westcott* [1987] Q.B. 291 gave the words a strained interpretation in holding that the Crown Court was empowered to vary the penalty imposed for another offence dealt with by the magistrates on the same occasion, but which was not appealed against: the amendment gave express authority for this.

These powers are subject to any limit or restriction imposed by any other enactment. A punishment in a criminal case may be more or less severe than that awarded by the magistrates' court, provided that it could have been imposed by that court.[27] The court must give reasons for its decision.[28]

In civil matters, appeals lie to the Crown Court in respect of a variety of licensing matters.[29]

(b) Appeals from magistrates' courts to the High Court by "case stated"

Any person who was party[30] to any proceedings before a magistrates' court or who is "aggrieved"[31] by its decision may question the decision on the ground that it is wrong in law or in excess of jurisdiction by applying to the justices for them to state a case for the opinion of the High Court.[32] An application may not be made following committal proceedings,[33] at an interlocutory stage in a summary hearing,[34] to challenge a decision by the magistrates declining jurisdiction,[35] where there is otherwise a right of appeal to the High Court or where the decision is said by an enactment to be "final".[36] The application must be made within 21 days, and any right to appeal to the Crown Court is lost when this is done.[37] The justices may refuse to state a case if they are of opinion that the application is "frivolous",[38] but may not do so where the application is made by or under the direction of the Attorney-General. If they do exercise their power to refuse, the applicant may seek an order of mandamus from the High Court to compel them to state a case, and the High Court has a discretion whether to make an order.

The procedure for stating a case is regulated by the Magistrates' Courts Rules 1981.[39] The application is made to the clerk to the justices. Unless the application is refused, a draft case must be sent to the parties, and it may be amended

---

[27] See *Arthur v. Stringer* (1986) 84 Cr. App. R. 361.

[28] *R. v. Harrow Crown Court, ex p. Dave* [1994] 1 W.L.R. 98.

[29] See, *e.g.* Licensing Act 1964, ss.21, 50, 81B, 146, 154.

[30] *e.g.* defendant *or prosecutor* in a criminal case: *R. v. Newport (Salop) JJ., ex p. Wright* [1929] 2 K.B. 416.

[31] This covers a person who is not a party but whose legal rights are affected by the decision: *Drapers Company v. Holder* (1892) 57 J.P. 200, *e.g.* the owner of stolen goods who seeks a restitution order.

[32] Magistrates' Courts Act 1980, s.111(1).

[33] *Atkinson v. United States Government* [1971] A.C. 197; *Cragg v. Lewes District Council* [1986] Crim. L.R. 800.

[34] *Streames v. Copping* [1985] Q.B. 920 (to challenge a disputed ruling that the magistrates had jurisdiction). *Cf. Loade v. D. P. P.* [1990] 1 Q.B. 1052 (Divisional Court has no jurisdiction in a criminal case to entertain an appeal by case stated at an interlocutory stage of an appeal to the Crown Court); there is such a jurisdiction in civil cases, but justices should exercise their power only in exceptional circumstances (*R. v. Chesterfield JJ., ex p. Kovacs* [1992] 2 All E.R. 325).

[35] *Pratt v. A. A. Sites Ltd* [1938] 2 K.B. 459: the remedy here is to apply for judicial review: see *Streames v. Copping*, at p. 928 (May L.J.).

[36] 1980 Act, s.111(4).

[37] *ibid.*, s.111(4). See *P. & M. Supplies (Essex) Ltd v. Hackney London Borough Council* (1990) 154 J.P. 814. An appeal by case stated against conviction will not debar an appeal to the Crown Court against sentence, and vice versa: an appeal by case stated on both matters debars the appeal to Crown Court completely: *R. v. Winchester Crown Court, ex p. Lewington* [1982] 1 W.L.R. 1277.

[38] This term includes cases where the argument on the point of law cannot succeed, *e.g.* where the law has been authoritatively stated in a superior court.

[39] S.I. 1981 No. 552, as amended, rr.76–81.

by the justices in the light of any representations received. The case must state the facts found and the questions of law or jurisdiction on which guidance is sought. It must specify any finding of fact which is claimed to be unsupported by evidence, but it may not otherwise contain a statement of evidence. In practice it is normally prepared by the clerk.

In criminal cases the appeal is heard by a Divisional Court of the Queen's Bench Division; otherwise, it is normally heard by a single judge. Where the appeal relates to the enforcement of a maintenance order, the appeal lies to the Family Division.[40] The appellant must lodge the case in the Crown Office or the Principal Registry of the Family Division within 10 days of receiving it, and must serve a copy on the respondent within four days of so lodging it. The High Court may return the case for amendment.[41]

On an appeal, the High Court may reverse, affirm or amend the decision or remit it to the justices for their reconsideration in the light of the court's opinion, or make such other order as the court thinks fit.[42] Apart from the obvious power to correct errors of law, such as the misinterpretation of a statute, the court will treat any decision unsupported by the evidence, or otherwise one which no reasonable magistrates could reach, as erroneous in law.[43] The court may take the view that in the light of its ruling on the law in a criminal case the defendant is clearly guilty or clearly innocent, in which event it will direct the magistrates to convict or acquit as the case may be. Otherwise the matter will be left to the magistrates. However, the Divisional Court may only order the magistrates' court to make an appropriate order or otherwise to complete unfinished proceedings: it may not order a retrial.[44] Appeal against sentence should normally be directed to the Crown Court.[45]

(c) Appeals from magistrates' courts to the High Court in family cases

In certain family matters an appeal lies to the Family Division of the High Court. These include the making or refusal of orders under the Domestic Proceedings and Magistrates' Courts Act 1978[46] and varations of maintenance orders[47]. The appeal can raise matters of fact or law and is not by case stated. A notice of motion must be served and the appeal entered within six weeks of the decision challenged.[48] The court may receive further evidence (but in practice does so only in exceptional circumstances), draw its own inferences of fact and may make any order that the magistrates might have made and any other order that the case might require, or may remit the matter with its opinion for

---

[40] R.S.C., Ord. 56, r.5. An appeal is normally heard by a single judge unless the court directs that it should be heard by a Divisional Court.
[41] Supreme Court Act 1981, s. 28A, inserted by the Statute Law (Repeals) Act 1993, Sched. 2, para. 9.
[42] *ibid.*
[43] *Bracegirdle v. Oxley* [1947] 1 K.B. 349. This is significantly narrower than the appeal on the merits to the Crown Court: see section (a) above.
[44] *Rigby v. Woodward* [1957] 1 W.L.R. 250; *Maydew v. Flint* (1984) 80 Cr. App. R. 49.
[45] *R. v. Ealing JJ., ex p. Scrafield* [1994] R.T.R. 195 (application for judicial review rejected).
[46] Other than interim maintenance orders, against which no appeal lies. Appeals as to the *enforcement* of maintenance orders lie by case stated: see section (b), above.
[47] Maintenance Orders Act 1958, s.4(7).
[48] Family Proceedings Rules 1991 (S.I. 1991 No. 1247, as amended), r.8.2. This appeal regime is distinct from that under the Children Act 1989 (see below): *P. v. P. (Perodical Payments)* [1995] 1 F.L.R. 563.

rehearing by the magistrates.[49] Appeals from the making of or refusal to make an order under the Children Act 1989 also lie from the magistrates' court to the Family Division.[50] Notice of appeal must normally be served within 14 days. Appeals are heard by a judge of the Family Division at the nearest convenient High Court centre.[51] On an appeal the High Court may make such orders as may be necessary to give effect to its determination of the appeal.[52]

(d) Appeals from the Crown Court to the High Court

Where there has been an appeal from a magistrates' court to the Crown Court, any party to the proceedings[53] may appeal by case stated on a point of law or jurisdiction to the High Court.[54] The procedure is similar to that for such appeals from the magistrates' court direct to the High Court.[55] The same right of appeal is available in respect of any other decision of the Crown Court[56] except one relating to trial on indictment and in certain licensing matters.[57]

(e) Appeals from the High Court to the House of Lords

In civil cases which have reached the High Court on appeal, further appeals lie on the same bases as in other civil matters determined by the High Court.[58] Until 1960 there was, however, no further right of appeal in a criminal case, and the Divisional Court of the Queen's Bench Division was the final authority on many matters concerning summary offences.[59] Under the Administration of Justice Act 1960[60] either the prosecutor or the defendant may appeal to the House of Lords on a point of law of public general importance. Leave must be obtained from either the Divisional Court or the House of Lords: the Divisional

---

[49] R.S.C., Ord. 55, r. 7.

[50] Children Act 1989, s.94. See Family Proceedings Rules 1991, r.4.22.

[51] *Practice Direction (Appeals from Magistrates' Courts)* [1992] 1 W.L.R. 261.

[52] 1989 Act, s.94(4). The principles of *G. v. G (Minors: Custody Appeal)* [1985] 1 W.L.R. 647 (below, p. 957) broadly apply to appeals under s.94: *Re M (Section 94 appeals)* [1995] 1 F.L.R. 546, C.A. Fresh evidence will only be received in exceptional circumstances: *Croydon London Borough Council v. A* [1992] Fam. 169; *cf. S v. Merton London Borough Council* [1994] 1 F.C.R. 186.

[53] *i.e.* in a criminal case, either prosecutor or defendant.

[54] Supreme Court Act 1981, s.28. Through an oversight the powers of disposal available in respect of appeals from the magistrates court (n. 42 above) are not available in respect of appeals from the Crown Court; the Law Commission has recommended that they should be: Report on *Administative Law: Judicial Review and Statutory Appeals* (Law Com. No. 226, 1994), p. 105.

[55] Crown Court Rules 1982, (S.I. 1982 No. 1109), r.26, and *cf.* above pp. 920–921.

[56] *e.g.* matters such as firearms licensing where an appeal lies direct to the Crown Court: see P. J. Clarke and J. W. Ellis, *The Law Relating to Firearms* (1981), pp. 104–111; *Kavanagh v. Chief Constable of Devon and Cornwall* [1974] Q.B. 624.

[57] Supreme Court Act 1981, s.28(2) *cf.* s.29(3), below p. 976. As to appeals in relation to trials on indictment, see below, pp. 923–944, and on the relationship between appeals by case stated and applications for judicial review, see below, p. 976. The Law Commission (*op. cit.*, n. 54 above), has recommended that no new case stated appeals be created and that appeals on a point of law are to be preferred: p. 106.

[58] See below, pp. 945–959.

[59] For example, there was no right to appeal against the unsatisfactory decisions in *Thomas v. Sawkins* [1935] 2 K.B. 249 and *Duncan v. Jones* [1936] K.B. 218: see S. H. Bailey, D. J. Harris and B. L. Jones, *Civil Liberties: Cases and Materials* (4th ed., 1995), pp. 248–251, 259–264.

[60] ss.1–9.

Court must certify that a point of law of general public importance is involved,[61] and it must appear either to that court or to the House of Lords[62] that the point ought to be considered by the House. On the appeal, the House may exercise any of the powers of the Divisional Court or may remit the case to it.

2. APPEALS FOLLOWING TRIAL ON INDICTMENT

(a) Appeals from the Crown Court to the Court of Appeal (Criminal Division)

An acquittal by a jury in a criminal case is regarded as sacrosanct: the prosecutor has no right of appeal however perverse the verdict of the jury.[63] However, persons convicted[64] of an offence on indictment may appeal to the Court of Appeal (Criminal Division).[65] The powers of the Court of Appeal were remodelled by Part I of the Criminal Appeal Act 1995, following recommendations of the Royal Commission on Criminal Justice.[66]

(i) Appeals against conviction

(1) *Grounds and procedure.* The person convicted may only appeal if either (a) a certificate from the trial judge that the case is fit for appeal or (b) leave of the Court of Appeal (Criminal Division) is obtained.[67]

The appellant must either serve the trial judge's certificate on the appropriate officer of the Crown Court with a notice of appeal, or serve notice of application for leave to appeal.[68] The notice must be served within 28 days of conviction, although the time limit may be extended by the court.[69] The grounds of the appeal or application must be stated,[70] but may be varied or amplified within

---

[61] There is no right to appeal against the refusal of a certificate: *Gelberg v. Miller* [1961] 1 All E.R. 618n, H.L.

[62] The application for leave is made first to the Divisional Court and only if that court refuses to the House of Lords.

[63] The Attorney-General may refer cases where there has been an acquittal to the Court of Appeal (Criminal Division), but not so as to affect the defendant: see below, pp. 939–940. Furthermore, the High Court is to be given power to quash acquittals tainted by interference with or intimidation of a juror or witness: Criminal Procedure and Investigations Bill 1996, cl.38–41.

[64] This includes a person who pleaded guilty; *R. v. Lee (Bruce)* [1984] 1 W.L.R. 578; *R. v. Swain* [1986] Crim.L.R. 480; and where a verdict has been returned, but the judge has postponed sentence: *R. v. Drew* [1985] 1 W.L.R. 914.

[65] See above, pp. 95–96; Criminal Appeal Act 1968; Criminal Appeal Rules 1968 (S.I. 1968 No. 1262, as amended) (hereafter "C.A.R."); *Guide to Proceedings in the Court of Appeal Criminal Division* [1983] Crim.L.R. 415; (1983) 77 Cr.App.R. 138; P, O'Connor, [1990] Crim.L.R. 615.

[66] Cm. 2263, 1993, Chap. 10. See Sir John Smith, [1995] Crim.L.R. 920.

[67] 1968 Act, s.1(2), as substituted by the Criminal Appeal Act 1995, s.1. Prior to this change, the person convicted could appeal as of right on any ground which involved a question of law alone.

[68] *ibid.*s.18(1); C.A.R. 1968, r.2(1). The Crown Court forwards the notice to the Criminal Appeal Office with the trial documents and any others which may be required: *Practice Direction (Crime: Notices of Appeal)* [1988] 1 W.L.R. 34.

[69] 1968 Act, s.18(2). Leave may be granted some years later. See *e.g. R. v. Foster* [1985] Q.B. 115, where F. was convicted of rape in 1977, following a plea of guilty. Another man confessed to and was convicted of the offence in 1981. F. was granted a free pardon in 1982 (see below, p. 987), and leave to appeal in 1984, when the conviction was quashed.

[70] C.A.R. 1968, r.2(2)(a).

such time as the court may allow.[71] The appellant may apply for bail,[72] and be present at the hearing.[73]

If it appears to the Registrar of Criminal Appeals that the notice of appeal or of application for leave to appeal does not show any substantial ground he or she may refer the appeal or application to the court for summary determination, and the court, if it considers the appeal to be frivolous[74] or vexatious may dismiss the appeal summarily.[75]

The defendant at the trial should be seen by his or her solicitor and counsel in the event of conviction or sentence and advised on whether there appear to be reasonable grounds for an appeal.[76] The defendant may only pursue an appeal under sections 1 and 2 of the 1968 Act once, even where he or she seeks to adduce fresh evidence on the second occasion.[77] An appeal abates on the death of the appellant.[78]

Applications for leave to appeal are normally dealt with by a single judge who examines the papers and may grant leave, refuse it, or refer the case to the court. If leave is refused an application may be renewed to the court within 14 days.[79] The court will hold a hearing, which may be combined with the hearing of the appeal on the merits. Legal aid may be granted for further advice and assistance and for representation before the single judge or the court.[80] The

---

[71] C.A.R. 1968 r.2(2)(c). This may be after the 28-day period.

[72] Bail may be granted by the Crown Court (Supreme Court Act 1981, s.81(1)(f) and (1A) to (1G), inserted by the Criminal Justice Act 1982, s.29(1)) or the Court of Appeal (Criminal Division) (Criminal Appeal Act 1968, s.19, as substituted by the 1982 Act, s.29(2)(b)). See *Practice Direction (Crown Court: Bail Pending Appeal)* [1983] 1 W.L.R. 1292.

[73] *ibid.*, s.22. He or she is entitled to be present except in four cases where the leave of the court is necessary: (1) the appeal is on a point of law alone; (2) for an application for leave to appeal; (3) for an ancillary application; (4) where he or she is in custody after a verdict of not guilty by reason of insanity or of a finding of disability.

[74] *e.g.* the ground of appeal could not possibly succeed on argument: *R. v. Taylor* [1979] Crim.L.R. 649.

[75] Criminal Appeal Act 1968, s.20, as substituted by the Criminal Justice Act 1988, s.157. The original form of s.20 made this procedure available only in respect of appeals involving a question of law alone.

[76] *Guide to proceedings in the Court of Appeal Criminal Division* (1983) 77 Cr.App.R. 138. See also M. Zander, [1972] Crim.L.R. 132, [1975] Crim.L.R. 364 and *Practice Note* [1974] 2 All E.R. 805. This work should be covered by any trial legal aid order: see the Legal Aid Act 1988, s.2(4), which provides that a grant of representation in a criminal case includes "advice and assistance as to any appeal." The RCCJ was very critical of the quality of legal advice given at this stage, and the arrangements for access to advice from prison: Cm. 2263, pp. 164–167, based on J. Plotnikoff and R. Woolfson, *Information and Advice for Prisoners about Grounds for Appeal and the Appeals Process* (RCCJ Research Study No.18, 1993).

[77] *R. v. Pinfold* [1988] Q.B. 462; *R. v. Berry* [1991] 1 W.L.R. 125: there are two apparent exceptions: where the decision on the original appeal is a nullity and where, owing to some defect in procedure, the appellant on the first appeal being dismissed suffered an injustice, (*e.g.* the appellant has not been notified of the hearing of the appeal, or counsel has been unable to attend (*ibid.*)). A case may also be referred back to the Court of Appeal by the Criminal Cases Review Commission (a power previously exercised by the Home Secretary), see below, pp. 936–939.

[78] *R. v. Kearley (No.2)* [1994] 2 A.C. 414.

[79] An extension to the initial 28-day period will readily be granted if reasonable grounds are shown; however, the time limit of 14 days for a renewal application will be enforced strictly and only extended in exceptional circumstances: *R. v. Towers* (1984) 30 Cr.App.R. 231.

[80] Legal Aid Act 1988, ss.19(1)(c)(2), 20(1)(2). Where an application is made before the giving of notice of appeal or an application for leave to appeal, the grant of legal aid may be limited to advice on whether there appear to be reasonable grounds of appeal, and assistance in the preparation of the notice or application: *ibid.*, s.21(8). Legal aid may be granted by the Court of Appeal, a single judge, or the Registrar, who may specify the stage at which it shall commence: see the Legal Aid in Criminal and Care Proceedings (General) Regulations 1989 (S.I. 1989 No.

single judge and the court have power, when refusing an application for leave to appeal, to direct that part of the time during which a person has been in custody after lodging his application should not count towards sentence.[81] In both 1970 and 1980 the then Lord Chief Justice issued a reminder of the existence of this power in view of the delay caused to the hearing of meritorious appeals by the lodging of huge numbers of hopeless applications.[82] In the two years after 1970 the number of applications for leave to appeal was cut by a half, although the problem subsequently recurred. In the 1980 Direction, it was stated a direction for loss of time "will normally be made unless the grounds are not only settled and signed by counsel, but also supported by the written opinion of counsel." Counsel should only so act where he or she considers that the proposed appeal is properly arguable. Moreover, a direction will also normally be made where an application is renewed to the court after the single judge has refused it as wholly devoid of merit: here, whether or not the grounds have been settled and signed by counsel.[83]

The administrative tasks in relation to appeals are performed by the Criminal Appeal Office, headed by the Registrar of Criminal Appeals. The documents in the case, including, if appropriate, a transcript, are assembled by the office.[84] If leave is granted, a lawyer on the staff of the office then prepares a descriptive "summary" of the facts and grounds of appeal to assist the full court. This should usually be available to counsel.[85]

(2) *Evidence.*[86] The court, under section 23(1) and (3) of the Criminal Appeal Act 1968[87], *may* "if they think it necessary or expedient in the interests of justice": (a) order the production of any document, exhibit or other thing connected with the proceedings; (b) order the examination of any witness who would have been a compellable witness at the trial, whether or not he or she was called; and (c) receive any evidence which was not adduced in the proceedings from which the appeal lies.[88]

In considering whether to receive any evidence, the Court of Appeal must have regard in particular to

---

344), reg. 22. An order granted by the court may be limited to representation by counsel only: *ibid.*, reg. 44(4).

[81] Criminal Appeal Act 1968, s.29(1), as amended by the Criminal Justice Act 1988, Sched. 15, para. 27. Thus a direction may not be made if leave is granted, or where there is a certificate under ss.1 or 11(1A) of the 1968 Act, or s.81(1B) of the Supreme Court Act 1981.

[82] Lord Parker C.J.: (1970) 54 Cr.App.R. 280; Lord Widgery C.J.: (1980) 70 Cr.App.R. 186.

[83] *R. v. Gayle, The Times*, May 28, 1986.

[84] Criminal Appeal Act 1968, s.32; C.A.R., rr.18–20. The Registrar may determine that only a "short transcript" is necessary, covering charges, pleas, summing-up and evidence after verdict. The appellant here may obtain a full transcript at his or her own expense. In practice, a transcript of evidence is rarely needed: *R. v. Campbell, The Times*, July 21, 1981.

[85] *Practice Direction (C.A.) (Criminal Division) (Criminal Appeal Office Summaries, The Times,* October 7, 1992.

[86] See R. Pattenden, *Judicial Discretion and Criminal Litigation* (2nd ed., 1990), pp. 355–358.

[87] As amended by the Criminal Appeal Act 1995, s.4(1).

[88] The court may examine such material as it thinks fit in deciding whether to order production of documents or the attendance of witnesses at the hearing of the appeal: it is not confined to material relating to the trial and the documents placed before the court by the parties: *R. v. Callaghan* [1988] 1 W.L.R. 1, a pre-appeal review in the Birmingham pub bombers' case: the appellants sought to prevent the judges reading documents relating to other litigation and police inquiries arising out of the case, unless raised by the parties; the court held that its *jurisdiction* was not so confined, but acceded to the appellants' request in the exercise of its discretion.

"(a) whether the evidence appears to the court to be capable of belief;

  (b) whether it appears to the court that the evidence may afford any ground for allowing the appeal;

  (c) whether the evidence would have been admissible in the proceedings from which the appeal lies on an issue which is the subject of the appeal[89]; and

  (d) whether there is a reasonable explanation for the failure to adduce the evidence in those proceedings."[90]

Between 1966 and 1995, section 23(2) of the 1968 Act provided for a *duty* of the court to receive evidence which was "likely to be credible", and which would have been admissible in the proceedings from which the appeal lay on an issue which was the subject of the appeal, and the court was satisfied that there was a reasonable explanation for the failure to adduce it at trial. The RCCJ thought that the "likely to be credible" test, which was interpreted as "evidence well capable of belief",[91] imposed too high a threshold.[92]

In *R. v. Lattimore and others*[93] the Court of Appeal emphasised that the conditions limiting the old section 23(2) duty were not to be read as limiting the discretion under section 23(1).[94] This case arose out of the killing of Maxwell Confait, which was shortly followed by a fire at the house where he lived. Two youths were convicted of killing him (one for murder, one manslaughter) and those two and another were convicted of arson, solely on the basis of their own confessions. Three years later the Home Secretary referred the cases to the Court of Appeal (Criminal Division).[95] The court, acting under section 23(1), received the evidence of three expert witnesses who had given evidence at the trial (two fire experts and a pathologist) and two further medical witnesses who gave evidence as to the time of death. However, they refused to admit evidence of persons who sought to throw light on the killer's identity, as they doubted its credibility and admissibility and in any event did not need to rely upon it. In addition, the Crown was permitted to call a fire expert and a forensic pathologist who had given evidence at the trial. The court held that this evidence showed that the lapse of time between the killing and the fire was much greater than had originally been thought and it threw sufficient doubt on the confessions for the homicide and arson convictions to be quashed. Scarman L.J. stated that the medical evidence was presented to the Court of Appeal "in a much sharper focus than it was at the trial."[96] In other cases under the original version of

---

[89] *i.e.* the issue must have been raised first at the trial: *R. v. Melville* [1976] 1 W.L.R. 181.

[90] 1968 Act, s.23(2), as substituted by the Criminal Appeal Act 1995, s.4(1). Under (d) the test is whether evidence could with "reasonable diligence" have been obtained for use at the trial: *R. v. Beresford* (1971) 56 Cr.App.R. 143: B had failed to mention his presence at the "Poco a Poco Club" until he sought leave to introduce an alibi witness on the appeal. The court held that he had not used reasonable diligence and in any event disbelieved the witness.

[91] *per* Edmund Davies L.J. in *R. v. Stafford and Luvaglio* (1968) 53 Cr.App.R.1, 3.

[92] Cm. 2263, p. 174.

[93] (1975) 62 Cr.App.R. 53.

[94] *ibid.*, p. 56.

[95] See below, pp. 936–937.

[96] *ibid.* p. 60. The events were subsequently the subject of an Inquiry by Sir Henry Fisher: 1977–78 H.C. 90, which concluded that "on a balance of probabilities" all three were involved in the arson and that two (excluding one of the two originally convicted for it) were involved in the killing. The report made a number of recommendations concerning the interrogation process and other aspects of the case.

s.23 fresh evidence was admitted where another person confessed to the crime for which the appellant was convicted,[97] where prosecution witnesses subsequently made statements inconsistent with their testimony[98] or had subsequently been found to have fabricated confessions attributed to suspects in other cases,[99] and where it was claimed that there was an irregularity at the trial.[1] Exceptionally, fresh evidence could be admitted following an unequivocal plea of guilty,[2] or where an arguable line of defence was not pursued at trial.[3]

Under the current version of section 23, the discretion under section 23(1) is now structured by reference to the conditions set out in subsection (2) and there is no longer a *duty* to receive evidence in specified circumstances. However, it will be noted that the court ultimately retains a discretion to receive evidence even where there is no reasonable explanation for the lack of adduction at trial. The RCCJ urged "that in general the court should take a broad, rather than a narrow, approach" to their powers to receive evidence.[4] Accordingly, the old cases remain as useful illustrations of the receipt of evidence; indeed, if anything, the approach of the court should now be broader.

(3) *Disposition.* Section 2 of the Criminal Appeal Act 1968 as originally enacted provided that:

"2(1)—Except as provided by this Act, the Court of Appeal shall allow an appeal against conviction if they think—

(a) that the verdict of the jury should be set aside on the ground that under the circumstances of the case it is unsafe or unsatisfactory; or

(b) that the judgment of the court of trial should be set aside on the ground of a wrong decision of any question of law; or

(c) that there was a material irregularity in the course of the trial,

and in any other case shall dismiss the appeal:

Provided that the Court may, notwithstanding that they are of the opinion that the point raised in the appeal might be decided in favour of the appellant, dismiss the appeal if they consider that no miscarriage of justice has actually occurred.

(2) In the case of an appeal against conviction the Court shall, if they allow the appeal, quash the conviction."

---

[97] *R. v. Ditch* (1969) 53 Cr. App. R. 627.

[98] *R. v. Conway* (1979) 70 Cr. App. R. 4.

[99] *R. v. Williams, The Times,* January 27, 1994.

[1] *R. v. Leggett and others* (1969) 53 Cr. App. 51: interruptions by the Chairman of Quarter Sessions (*e.g.* when it appeared that an address by counsel to the jury would be protracted "he observed in a loud voice, 'Oh, God,' and then laid his head across his arm and made groaning noises": p. 56). Appeal dismissed.

[2] *R. v. Lee* (*Bruce*) [1984] 1 W.L.R. 578; *R. v. Foster* [1985] Q.B. 115 (F. had received a free pardon for offences of which another had now been convicted); *R. v. Swain* [1986] Crim. L.R. 480 (evidence that there was a risk that D's mind was affected by LSD when he changed his plea to guilty).

[3] *R. v. Ahluwalia* [1992] 4 All E.R. 889. The court did, however, emphasise that it required much persuasion to allow a defence to be raised for the first time on appeal if the option had been exercised at trial not to pursue it; here a contemporary report on D stated that she suffered from "endogenous depression" at the time she killed her husband: D was not consulted about the report and it was unclear why it had not been pursued as the basis of a diminished responsibility defence. The court ordered a retrial.

[4] Cm. 2263, p. 174.

These grounds for intervention were somewhat wider than those that were open to the Court of Criminal Appeal under the Criminal Appeal Act 1907.[5] The RCCJ criticised the drafting of section 2 as "confusing".[6] For example, the grounds overlapped in that an error of law or an irregularity at trial might cause the court to think that the original conviction was unsafe or unsatisfactory; it was doubtful whether there was any difference between "unsafe" and "unsatisfactory"; the wording of the proviso appeared difficult to reconcile with (a) and (b). Accordingly, they recommended (by a majority) that section 2 be redrafted to provide a single broad ground of appeal, that a conviction "is or may be unsafe". If it was unsafe, the appeal would be allowed outright; if it might be, the conviction would be quashed and (normally) a retrial ordered.

Section 2 now provides that

"(1) Subject to the provisions of this Act, the Court of Appeal—
(a) shall allow an appeal against conviction if they think that the conviction is unsafe; and
(b) shall dismiss such an appeal in any other case."

Under the original version of section 2, verdicts were set aside as unsafe and unsatisfactory where, for example, there had been a misdirection as to the ingredients of the offence charged or the burden of proof, the judge had improperly withdrawn an issue from the jury or failed to put a line of defence to them, evidence was wrongfully admitted or excluded or, exceptionally, where counsel's decision not to call the defendant "was taken either in defiance of or without proper instructions, or when all the promptings of reason and good sense pointed the other way."[7] Decisions on some of these points could also amount to a wrong decision on a point of law under section 2(1)(b). The "material irregularity" ground in section 2(1)(c) was designed to cover procedural irregularities,[8] although other defects were sometimes so described. Under this head the Court of Appeal could interfere with an exercise of discretion[9] by the judge where he or she had "erred in principle or there is no material on which he could properly have arrived at his decision,"[10] or the court thought that the judge's ruling might have resulted in injustice to the defendant.[11]

---

[5] The court could allow an appeal if they thought that the verdict was unreasonable, or could not be supported by the evidence or otherwise there was an error of law or a miscarriage of justice. The wider grounds were first enacted in the Criminal Appeal Act 1966.

[6] Cm. 2263, pp. 167–169. See also R. J. Buxton, (1993) 109 L.Q.R. 66.

[7] R. v. Clinton [1993] 4 All E.R. 998, 1005. The question was not the extent of counsel's ineptitude but the effect on the trial according to the (then) terms of the 1968 Act, s.2(1)(a). Cf. R. v. Goutam [1988] Crim. L.R. 109 and R. v. Ensor [1989] 1 W.L.R. 497, discussed in Clinton. In suggesting in Ensor that the court would only intervene in cases of "flagrantly incompetent advocacy", the court was only giving "general guidelines" as to the correct approach and was not intending to derogate from the wording of s.2(1)(a).

[8] per Lord Salmon in D.P.P. v. Shannon [1975] A.C. 717, 773.

[9] e.g. to sever counts in an indictment, to permit cross-examination of a defendant on his or her previous convictions or to discharge a jury.

[10] Devlin J. in R. v. Cook (1959) 43 Cr.App.R. 138, 147.

[11] R. v. McCann (1991) 92 Cr.App.R. 239: the court held that the trial judge should have ordered a retrial of the three charged with conspiracy to murder Mr Tom King, following public statements made by Mr King and Lord Denning concerning the proposal to change the law on the right to silence.

The approach to section 2(1)(a) was described as follows by Widgery L.J. in *R. v. Cooper*[12]:

"[I]n cases of this kind the court must in the end ask itself a subjective question, whether we are content to let the matter stand as it is, or whether there is not some lurking doubt in our minds which makes us wonder whether an injustice has been done. This is a reaction which may not be based strictly on the evidence as such; it is a reaction which can be produced by the general feel of the case as the court experiences it."

Indeed, a conviction could be quashed as unsafe and unsatisfactory where the specific grounds of appeal were rejected.[13]

While the new single ground of appeal appears to comprehend only part of one of the original grounds specified in section 2,[14] Parliament was assured by the Home Secretary that

"in substance it restates the existing practice of the Court of Appeal and I am pleased to note that the Lord Chief Justice has already welcomed it."[15]

According to the Minister of State, the Lord Chief Justice and the senior judiciary believed that "the new test re-states the existing practice of the Court of Appeal".[16] Accordingly, the RCCJ's unanimous view that the Court of Appeal "should be readier to overturn jury verdicts that it has shown itself to be in the past"[17] does not appear to have been reflected in the new drafting of section 2,[18] although it may find its way into the court's approach in practice.[19]

Where fresh evidence is admitted, the question for the court is still whether, in the light of the evidence overall, the verdict is unsafe (formerly, unsafe and unsatisfactory[20]). This point was made by the House of Lords in *Stafford v. D.P.P.*[21] After referring to the concept of the "lurking doubt" mentioned in *R. v. Cooper*[22] Viscount Dilhorne continued, "That this is the effect of section

---

[12] [1969] 1 Q.B. 267, 271. The case was one of alleged mistaken identification and another man of similar appearance had admitted to a witness that he had committed the crime: even though all the evidence had been before the jury, the conviction was quashed. For other examples of "lurking doubts" see *R. v. Pattinson* (1973) 58 Cr.App.R. 417; *R. v. Spencer* [1987] A.C. 128.

[13] *R. v. Bracewell* (1978) 68 Cr.App.R. 44.

[14] See Sir John Smith, [1995] Crim. L.R. 920, 923–925.

[15] Vol.256 H. C. Deb., March 6, 1995, col. 24, cited by Smith, *op.cit.*

[16] Standing Committee B, March 21, 1995, col. 26, cited by Smith, *op.cit.*

[17] Cm. 2263, p. 162.

[18] The words "or may be" in the RCCJ's recommendation for s.2 were thought by some to send this signal; however, given that a conviction is "unsafe" if there is merely a "lurking doubt" (see above), it is difficult to see what of substance was added by those words: see Smith, *op.cit.* n.14 above, pp. 921–922.

[19] The RCCJ's wish to see a broader approach to incompetent advocacy, noting that a conviction may be unsafe even where incompetence is not "flagrant" (Cm. 2263, p. 174) seems already to be reflected in the Court of Appeal decision in *R. v. Clinton* (above, p. 928, n.7).

[20] The fresh evidence would not reveal an error of law or constitute a "material irregularity" under s.2(1)(b) and (c) of the Criminal Appeal Act 1968 as originally drafted.

[21] [1974] A.C. 878. Followed in *R. v. Callaghan* (1988) 88 Cr.App.R. 40 (the first reference to the Court of Appeal in the Birmingham pub bombing case); *R. v. Byrne* (1988) 88 Cr.App.R. 33.

[22] Above.

2(1)(a) is not to be doubted,''[23] although he also emphasised that the Court of Appeal should not place any fetter or restriction on its power under section 2. The court was not bound to ask in a case where new evidence was admitted whether that evidence "might . . . have led to the jury returning a verdict of not guilty?'': if *it* was satisfied that there was no reasonable doubt about the guilt of the accused the conviction should not be quashed even though the jury might have come to a different view.

This approach to "fresh evidence" cases has been roundly criticised by Lord Devlin[24] on the basis that it is wrong in principle for judges rather than juries to determine whether the appellant is guilty; the proper course of action where the fresh evidence *could* have made a difference to the verdict[25] would be for the court to order a new trial.[26] The first verdict should be regarded as unsatisfactory simply on the ground that it was not given upon the whole of the evidence.[27] Given that the appeal in *Stafford v. D.P.P.* was dismissed, the appellants were thereafter imprisoned on the basis of the verdict of the judges.

Given that the matter is to be tested by reference to the views of the appeal court judges rather than the views of a hypothetical jury, a further question arises whether that is so in all fresh evidence cases. In particular, should the judges determine issues as to whether the oral testimony of a new or re-examined witness is credible?[28] In a number of cases the court has ordered a new trial,[29] but in *R. v. Cooper and McMahon*[30] the court determined such a question itself. The case is one of the most publicised examples of a miscarriage of justice, and came before the Court of Appeal on no less than five occasions. Three men, Cooper, McMahon and Murphy, were convicted of the murder of a Luton subpostmaster during an unsuccessful robbery. They were identified by a professional criminal, Mathews, who admitted taking part in the robbery but denied involvement in the murder. He turned Queen's evidence and the men were convicted solely on his testimony. They appealed without success to the Court of Appeal. Mathews subsequently received part of the reward offered by the Post Office. In 1973 Murphy's conviction was quashed by the Court of Appeal following the discovery of a fresh alibi witness. This naturally threw doubt on Mathews' identification of Cooper and McMahon and the Home Secretary referred the case to the Court of Appeal on three further occasions. On the first of these in 1975, the court refused to permit Mathews to be recalled for further cross-examination, indicated that the jury "could" have acquitted Murphy and convicted the others, and dismissed the appeal. The court refused leave to appeal to the House of Lords, reaffirming that in the light of *Stafford v. D.P.P.*[31] it was "not a necessary function of this Court, when considering fresh evidence, to evaluate the effect which it would have on the jury at the

---

[23] [1974] A.C. p. 892.
[24] *The Judge* (1979), pp. 133–135, 148–176.
[25] This was in effect the same test as that for applying the proviso: see *Stirland v. D.P.P.* (1944) 30 Cr.App.R. 40, 46–47.
[26] See below, p. 931. Indeed, until 1989 the court could *only* order a new trial in fresh evidence cases.
[27] See counsel's argument in *Stafford v. D.P.P.* [1974] A.C. 878, 884C.
[28] The test for admissibility is merely whether the fresh evidence is *capable* of belief: see above, p. 926.
[29] See Devlin (1979), pp. 165–166.
[30] See Devlin (1979), pp. 166–173; L. Kennedy (ed.), *Wicked Beyond Belief* (1980).
[31] [1974] A.C. 878.

trial."[32] On the second, in 1976, Mathews was recalled and cross-examined: the judges concluded from their observations that he was telling the truth on the "vital part of his story" although other parts were discredited (a "cock and bull story"). This self-evidently surprising result did not inspire confidence in trial (or at least partial trial) by judges alone. The final reference by the Home Secretary (of the case of McMahon alone) was unsuccessful on the ground that the fresh alibi evidence sought to be tendered was not likely to be credible, and even if believed would be insufficient to afford a ground for allowing the appeal.[33] In 1980, following the publication of a book on the case edited by Ludovic Kennedy (*Wicked Beyond Belief*), the Home Secretary, William White-law, ordered the release of Cooper and McMahon[34]: the case was "wholly exceptional" and there was a "widely felt sense of unease about it" which he shared. He was not to be taken as criticising his predecessors, who had "acted with scrupulous regard to the constitutional conventions in referring each piece of alleged new evidence to the Court of Appeal and in acting in accordance with the court's judgment. Any general departure from that rule would clearly be disastrous." His action was not to be take as a precedent.

The RCCJ[35] endorsed Lord Devlin's criticism insofar as it concerned a decision by the court to hear and evaluate itself the fresh evidence and despite it to reject the appeal. In their view, the proper approach once the court has decided to receive fresh evidence that is relevant and capable of belief, and which could have affected the outcome of the case, is that it should quash the conviction and order a retrial. However, if a retrial was not practicable or desirable, the court should decide the matter itself in accordance with *Stafford*, and not simply allow the appeal automatically. The Criminal Appeal Act 1995 did not address this question.

Other possibilities that may be open to the Court of Appeal are the substitution of a conviction for an alternative offence, where the jury would have found the defendant guilty of that offence and it appears to the court that the jury must have been satisfied of facts which proved him or her guilty of it,[36] and the substitution of a finding of insanity or of unfitness to plead.[37]

(4) *New Trials*. Where the Court of Appeal allows an appeal against conviction, it may order that the appellant be retried where it appears that this is required by the interests of justice.[38] The appellant may only be retried for the offence in respect of which the appeal was allowed, an offence of which he or she could have been convicted at the original trial on an indictment for that offence or an offence charged in an alternative count of the indictment at the trial on which the jury were discharged from giving a verdict.[39]

Prior to the amendment made by section 43 of the Criminal Justice Act 1988,

---

[32] (1975) 61 Cr.App.R. 215.

[33] *R. v. McMahon* (1978) 68 Cr.App.R. 18: criticised in Kennedy (1980), pp. 132–135.

[34] Vol. 988 H. C. Deb., July 18, 1980, written answers, cols. 719–720.

[35] Cm. 2263, p. 175.

[36] Criminal Appeal Act 1968, s.3. The sentence may not be higher than that originally passed.

[37] *ibid.*, s.6, Sched. 1.

[38] 1968 Act, s.7(1), as amended by the Criminal Justice Act 1988, s.43(2). See Pattenden (1990), pp. 366–370. For the procedure on retrial see s.8 and Sched. 1. Any sentence passed after a retrial may not be longer than the original one.

[39] *ibid.*, s.7(2). For the analogous power to award a *venire de novo*, see below, p. 941. This can only be done where the original trial is a nullity.

the Court of Appeal could only order a retrial where fresh evidence was received under section 23 of the Criminal Appeal Act 1968.[40] This limitation was cogently criticised, and the case for its removal powerful.[41] In particular, in a number of cases where (1) the appellant appeared to have a good argument in law but little or none on the merits, but (2) the case was not suitable for an application of the proviso,[42] the Court of Appeal or House of Lords succumbed to the temptation to "bend" the law to enable the appeal to be dismissed. Justice appeared to be done in the case itself but at the expense of the development of the law in a consistent, coherent and principled way.[43] Unfortunately, the change can still be criticised as not going far enough,[44] in that the power does not extend to ordering a retrial for an offence which arises out of the same facts, but which is different from those charged in the original indictment. Such a power might well be necessary where there is a flaw in the indictment which is not so serious as to render the trial a nullity (in which case a *venire de novo* may be ordered). This could arise where the defendant is convicted of the wrong or a non-existent offence,[45] and the indictment contains no suitable alternative count. The omission was drawn to the Government's attention, but the position was defended on the basis that

"It is one thing to legislate for the differing interpretations of the law by higher and lower courts, but quite another to build into the law the assumption that the prosecution will occasionally blunder. And in addition there might be difficulties in principle in conferring on the Court of Appeal what might appear to be prosecutorial function if it was to have a role in specifying the charges on which a retrial could be based."[46]

A wider retrial power exists in Scotland.[47]

Where a retrial is ordered, arrangements must normally take place within two months. Thereafter, if the prosecution wishes to proceed, it must apply to the Court of Appeal for leave; conversely, the defendant may apply to the Court of Appeal to set aside the retrial order and enter a verdict of acquittal of the offence for which he or she was ordered to be retried. On either application, the court may grant leave, but may only do so if it is satisfied that the prosecution has acted with due expedition, and that there is a good and sufficient cause for a retrial in spite of the lapse of time since the retrial order was made.

(ii) Appeals against sentence and reviews of sentencing

A person who has been convicted of an offence on indictment may appeal to the Court of Appeal (Criminal Division) against any sentence[48] passed on him

---

[40] See above, pp. 925–927.
[41] See the first edition of this book at pp. 712–714.
[42] See above.
[43] J. R. Spencer, "Criminal law and criminal appeals" [1982] Crim.L.R. 260.
[44] J. R. Spencer, "Retrials and tribulations" (1988) 138 N.L.J. 315.
[45] *e.g.* "anal rape": *R. v. Gaston* (1981) 73 Cr.App.R. 164.
[46] Home Office letter in response to Spencer: (1988) 138 N.L.J. 641.
[47] Criminal Procedure (Scotland) Act 1995, s.185.
[48] This includes any order made by the court when dealing with an offender including a hospital order under the Mental Health Act 1983, a recommendation for deportation, a confiscation order under the Drug Trafficking Act 1994 (other than one made by the High Court) or Part VI of the

or her for the offence, except where the sentence is fixed by law.[49] Leave to appeal must be obtained from the Court of Appeal, or the judge who passed the sentence must certify that the case is fit for appeal,[50] and the procedure is essentially the same as in appeals against conviction. The court, if it considers that the appellant should be sentenced differently, may quash any sentence or order which is the subject of the appeal and substitute any other sentence or order that it thinks appropriate, provided that it would have been within the jurisdiction of the court below. The appellant may not, however, be dealt with more severely than by the court below,[51] except that the court may bring a suspended sentence into effect.[52]

The court will interfere with an exercise of discretion as to sentence where the sentence is not justified by law, where matters are improperly taken into account or improperly ignored, where fresh matters are to be taken into account, or where the sentence is manifestly excessive or wrong in principle. One of the accepted functions of the Court of Appeal is that of laying down guidelines for sentencing.[53]

The court has the same powers to deal with sentences imposed in cases where a person convicted after summary trial is committed to the Crown Court for sentence,[54] or where a person previously made the subject of a conditional discharge, a probation order, a community service order, combination order, curfew order, attendance centre order or suspended sentence is further dealt with by the Crown Court for the offence.[55] However, an appeal in such a case only lies if the sentence of imprisonment or youth custody is for six months or more,[56] or the sentence is outside the power of the court which convicted him or her, or the court recommends deportation, orders disqualification from driving, activates a suspended sentence or imposes a restriction order or makes a declaration of relevance under the Football Spectators Act 1989.[57]

Part IV of the Criminal Justice Act 1988[58] introduced a new procedure

Criminal Justice Act 1988 (or variations thereof), a probation order or an absolute or conditional discharge: Criminal Appeal Act 1968, s.50, as amended. Apart from the orders expressly mentioned in s.50, the section covers such matters as driving disqualifications, costs orders, compensation orders: see *R. v. Hayden* [1975] 1 W.L.R. 852. It also includes binding-over orders contingent on a conviction: *R. v. Williams (Carl)* [1982] 1 W.L.R. 1398, but not a recommendation as to the minimum period that a person convicted of murder should serve (Murder (Abolition of Death Penalty) Act 1965, s.1(2)): *R. v. Aitken* [1966] 1 W.L.R. 1076; *R. v. Bowden and Begley* (1983) 77 Cr. App. R. 66; or an order to contribute toward legal aid costs: *R. v. Hayden* [1975] 1 W.L.R. 852; *R. v. Raeburn* (1981) 74 Cr.App.R. 21.

[49] Criminal Appeal Act 1968, s.9(1). He or she may also appeal against any sentence passed for a summary offence dealt with by the Crown Court under s.41 of the Criminal Justice Act 1988 (above, p. 727); 1968 Act, s.9(2), inserted by the 1988 Act, Sched. 15, para. 21.

[50] 1968 Act, s.11 as amended by the Criminal Justice Acts 1982, s.29(2)(a), and 1988, Sched. 15, para. 23.

[51] *ibid.* A hospital order with an indefinite restriction order was held not to be more severe than a sentence of three years' imprisonment in *R. v. Bennett* [1968] 1 W.L.R. 980. The court may add a recommendation for deportation.

[52] 1968 Act, s.11(4), substituted by the Criminal Justice Act 1988, Sched. 15, para. 24.

[53] See generally, *R. v. Newsome and Browne* [1970] 2 Q.B. 711, and above, pp. 887–888.

[54] Not in cases where the defendant *appeals* to the Crown Court.

[55] 1968 Act, s.10, as amended by the Criminal Justice Acts 1982, Sched. 14, para. 23, 1988, Sched. 15, para. 22 and 1991, Sched. 11, para. 3.

[56] Two sentences are treated as a single sentence if they are passed on the same day, or expressed by the court to be a single sentence, or are consecutive sentences.

[57] 1968 Act, s.10(3), as amended.

[58] ss.35, 36: in force from February 1, 1989. See also Sched. 3 and the Criminal Appeal (Reviews of Sentencing) Rules 1989 (S.I. 1989 No. 19). See the notes by I. Leigh in *Current Law Statutes Annotated 1988*, A. Green, (1990) 43 C.L.P. 55. and R. Henham, [1994] Crim L.R. 499.

whereby the Attorney-General may refer certain sentences[59] to the Court of Appeal (Criminal Division). It is available in respect of cases of a description specified by statutory instrument made by the Secretary of State, or in which sentence is passed on a person for an offence triable only on indictment or for an offence of a description specified by statutory instrument.[60] The power may be exercised where "it appears to the Attorney-General that the sentencing of a person in a proceeding in the Crown Court has been unduly lenient." Without prejudice to the generality of this, the condition may be satisfied if it appears that the judge erred in law as to his or her powers of sentencing.[61] The Attorney-General must apply for leave to refer a case within 28 days of the passing of the sentence. The Court of Appeal may quash any sentence passed on the defendant, and in place of it pass such sentence (including a heavier sentence[62]) as it thinks appropriate and as the court below had power to pass when dealing with him or her. When the Court of Appeal has concluded its review, the Attorney-General or the defendant may refer a point of law to the House of Lords. The Court of Appeal must certify that it is a point of law of general public importance, and the leave of either the Court of Appeal or the House of Lords is necessary.

The Government had previously proposed a procedure analogous to the Attorney-General's reference procedure, in which the Court of Appeal would have had power to give guidance as to sentencing principles but no power to vary the sentence in question. This had been included in the Prosecution of Offences Bill 1985, but had been defeated in the House of Lords.[63] The present procedure gives the Court of Appeal power to increase or otherwise vary the sentence in question. The Home Secretary indicated that he did not expect the procedure to be employed frequently, suggesting a dozen cases a year as the probable number of such references.[64] The arguments in favour of the new procedure were marshalled by J. R. Spencer,[65] who wrote that under-sentencing: (i) blunts the deterrent effect of the criminal law; (ii) causes outrage to the victim; (iii) is demoralising to the police; (iv) causes injustice to those who were appropriately sentenced; (v) undermines public confidence in the administration of justice and the authority of the courts; (vi) may cause public danger; and (vii) hinders development of a rational sentencing policy by the Court of Appeal. The main[66] contrary argument is that the procedure offends the principle against double jeopardy, in particular the need "to prevent the state . . . abusing its power and control over the prosecution process in order to harass and oppress

[59] The term has the same meaning as in the Criminal Appeal Act 1968, except that it does not include an interim hospital order under Part III of the Mental Health Act 1983: 1988 Act, s.35(6). It includes a deferred sentence: *Attorney General's Reference (No. 22 of 1992)* [1994] 1 All E.R. 105.

[60] 1968 Act, s.35(3)–(5), as amended by the Criminal Justice and Public Order Act 1994, Sched 9, para. 34. The Criminal Justice Act 1988 (Review of Sentencing) Order 1994 (S.I. 1994 No.119) extended the procedure to cover offences of indecent assault, threats to kill, cruelty to a person under 16, and attempts to commit or inciting the commission of those offences. It is intended to extend the procedure to cases of serious or complex fraud (Standing Committee B, February 24, 1994, cols. 988–990).

[61] 1988 Act, ss.36(1)(a), (2).

[62] *Attorney-General's Reference (No. 4 of 1989)* [1990] 1 W.L.R. 41.

[63] See J. R. Spencer, (1985) 149 J.P.N. 262.

[64] Standing Committee H, February 23, 1988, col. 219, cited by Leigh, *op. cit.* The decision is, however, the Attorney-General's and not the Home Secretary's.

[65] "Do we need a prosecution appeal against sentence?" [1987] Crim.L.R. 724.

[66] Others are summarised, and dismissed by Spencer, *ibid.*, pp. 729–736.

an individual or minority."[67] While it is "virtually unthinkable" that the government would seek to abuse its powers in this way, the risk should nevertheless be recognised.[68] One weakness in the new procedure is that no provision is made for the comprehensive review of sentences: the possible, undesirable, consequence is that it will be sentences that happen to attract adverse comment in the media that will be referred.[69]

The Court of Appeal has stated that an application will not be granted unless there was some error of principle in the judge's sentence and that public confidence would be damaged if the sentence was not altered.[70]

(iii) Appeals against findings of insanity

A person in whose case a verdict of not guilty by reasons of insanity[71] is returned may appeal to the Court of Appeal on the same grounds as against a conviction.[72] The powers of the court are similar. However it may dismiss the appeal if none of the grounds for allowing it relates to the question of the appellant's insanity under the *M'Naghten* rules and, but for that insanity, the proper verdict would have been that he was guilty of some other offence.[73] In appropriate cases, the court may substitute a conviction for an offence, or a verdict of acquittal[74]: in the former case it has power to pass an appropriate sentence or make a hospital or other order, in the latter it may order that the appellant be admitted to hospital for assessment.[75]

Similar provisions govern appeals against findings that a person is under a disability and did the act or made the omission charged against him.[76] If the court allows an appeal against a finding of disability, the appellant may then be tried for the offence, and the court may order that pending the trial the appellant may be kept in custody, released on bail or detained under the Mental Health Act 1983. If, otherwise, the court allows an appeal against a finding that the appellant did the act or made the omission, the court must direct a verdict of acquittal to be recorded.

---

[67] S. Seabrooke, "Two-timing the double jeopardy principle" [1988] Crim.L.R. 103, 104. Spencer takes a narrower view of the double jeopardy principle: [1987] Crim.L.R. 724, 735, as meaning (1) that it is wrong to punish a person twice for the same offence; and (2) that a person must not be put in peril of conviction twice.

[68] Seabrooke, [1988] Crim.L.R, 103.

[69] Spencer, [1987] Crim.L.R. 724, 730; A. Heaton-Armstrong, (1988) 152 J.P. 278.

[70] *Attorney-General's Reference (No. 5 of 1989) (R. v. Hill-Trevor)* (1990) 90 Cr.App. R. 358 (custodial sentence substituted for a fine for causing death by reckless driving); *Attorney-General's Reference (No.4 of 1989)* [1990] 1 W.L.R.41. The first was *Attorney-General's Reference (No. 1 of 1989)* (1989) 90 Cr.App.R. 141, which set guidelines for sentencing for incest.

[71] "Insanity" here means insanity under the *M'Naghten* rules, which do not cover all cases of mental disorder and do cover some situations where there is no mental disorder: see generally J. C. Smith and B. Hogan, *Criminal Law* (7th ed., 1992), pp. 192–210.

[72] 1968 Act, ss.12, 13, as amended by the Criminal Appeal Act 1995, s.2. See above, p. 928.

[73] *ibid.*, s.13(3).

[74] *ibid.*, s.13(4).

[75] *ibid.*, ss.14, 14A, as substituted by the Criminal Procedure (Insanity and Unfitness to Plead) Act 1991, s.4, and Sched. 1 to the 1991 Act.

[76] *ibid.*, ss.15, 16, as amended by the 1991 Act, Sched. 3, paras. 2, 3.; *cf.* above, p. 859.

(iv) Appeals against conviction on special verdict

If the Court of Appeal considers that the trial judge has drawn an incorrect conclusion from a special verdict entered by a jury, it may substitute the correct conclusion, and pass any sentence that may be authorised by law.[77]

(v) References by the Criminal Cases Review Commission

Where a person was (1) convicted on indictment or (2) tried on indictment and found not guilty by reason of insanity or (3) found by a jury to be under a disability, the Home Secretary formerly had power to refer the case to the Court of Appeal.[78] Two kinds of reference were possible. The first was a reference of the whole case, in which event the reference was treated as an appeal.[79] The court was not limited to the grounds mentioned in the Home Secretary's letter of reference.[80] A further appeal could then lie to the House of Lords. The other possibility is that a particular point might be referred for the opinion of the court.[81] The court gave what was essentially only an advisory opinion, with any further action to be taken by the Home Secretary.[82] This form of reference was uncommon.[83]

The Home Secretary preferred to refer a case to the Court of Appeal rather than to recommend the exercise of the prerogative to grant a pardon or remit a sentence[84]: it was thought that persistent use of the power to recommend a pardon would undermine the distinction between the functions of the executive and of the judiciary.[85] Indeed it was, in part, dissatisfaction with the review by the Home Office of criminal convictions that led to the establishment of the Court of Criminal Appeal. The Home Secretary's approach was summarised in a memorandum to the Home Affairs Committee[86]:

"In considering convictions on indictment, the Home Secretary . . .
  (a) will not normally intervene where normal avenues of appeal to the Court of Appeal have not been exhausted;
  (b) will, where the normal avenues are not available and intervention seems justified, consider using his power of reference to enable the Court to hear the case;
  (c) will consider recommending the exercise of the Royal Prerogative where intervention seems justified but for some reason (*e.g.* lapse of time,

---

[77] 1968 Act, s.5.
[78] 1968 Act, s.17.
[79] *ibid.*, s.17(1)(a).
[80] *R. v. Chard* [1984] A.C. 279; followed in *R. v. Callaghan* [1988] 1 W.L.R. 1.
[81] 1968 Act, s.17(1)(b).
[82] See *Thomas (Arthur) v. The Queen* [1980] A.C. 125, where the Privy Council held that advice given to the Governor-General under an identically worded provision was not binding on him, and could not be the subject of an appeal to the Privy Council.
[83] See, *e.g. R. v. O'Neill* (1948) 33 Cr. App.R. 19; *R. v. McCartan* (1958) 42 Cr. App. R. 262; *R. v. McMahon* (1978) 68 Cr. App. R. 18.
[84] See below, pp. 987–990.
[85] 1981–82 H.C. 421, 6th Report on *Miscarriages of Justice*, p. 2.
[86] *ibid.*

inadmissibility as evidence of salient new facts) a resort to the judicial appeal process would not be appropriate.''

However, the Home Secretary would not intervene on the basis of evidence already considered by the courts. A case would only be referred where there was some new evidence or new consideration of substance which had not been before the courts and which appeared to cast doubt on the safety of the conviction.[87] Moreover, if a case was referred to the Court of Appeal and the conviction was upheld, the Home Secretary would only intervene thereafter if the case was wholly exceptional.[88]

A further point is that it is only the Court of Appeal that can quash a conviction: a pardon does not have that effect.[89] Thus, in a number of cases the reference procedure was been used to secure the formal quashing of a conviction[90] or a sentence[91] that fell outside the powers of the trial court, often for reasons of some technicality. Indeed, it was uncommon for the Court of Appeal to quash a conviction, following a reference, on the basis of its doubts about the merits of the conviction.[92] "Judicial distaste for the whole reference procedure has verged at times upon open hostility."[93] A decision of the Home Secretary to refuse to refer a case to the Court of Appeal could be challenged on an application for judicial review; such challenges were generally unsuccessful.[94] However, in *R. v. Secretary of State for the Home Department, ex p. Hickey (No. 2)*[95] the Divisional Court held that where the Secretary of State ordered inquiries to be made following receipt of a petition, he was obliged as a matter of fairness to disclose the outcome of those inquiries to the petitioner before deciding whether to refer a case under section 17.

The exercise of the section 17 reference power, particularly in the context of

---

[87] *ibid.* In a number of cases the courts rejected applications for judicial review of decisions not to make s.17 references, holding that this policy was not applied inflexibly: *R. v. Secretary of State for the Home Department, ex p. Pegg (Kenneth Stephen)* [1991] C.O.D. 47; *R. v. Secretary of State for the Home Department, ex p. McCallion* [1993] C.O.D. 148.

[88] *e.g. R. v. Cooper and McMahon*, above, p. 930. The previous Home Secretaries had firmly taken the view that they should not override the court's decision: see L. Kennedy, (ed.), *Wicked Beyond Belief* (1980), pp. 130, 159–160, 169.

[89] *R. v. Foster* [1985] Q.B. 115: see above, p. 923, n. 69, below, p. 987, n. 20.

[90] *R. v. Davies* (1981) 76 Cr. App. R. 120 (following D.'s extradition, a new count was added to the indictment with D.'s agreement, but contrary to the Extradition Act 1870, s.19).

[91] *e.g. R. v. Bardoe* [1969] 1 W.L.R. 398 (youth of 17 wrongly sentenced to life imprisonment); *R. v. McKenna* (1985) 7 Cr. App. R.(S) 348; *R. v. Seafield, The Times,* May 17, 1988 (suspended sentence supervision order wrongly attached to six month and three month sentences, neither being a sentence of "more than six months").

[92] Widely publicised rejections of appeals included the Cooper and McMahon case, above, p. 930; the Birmingham pub bombing case (*R. v. Callaghan* (1988) 88 Cr. App. R. 40; C. Mullin, *Error of Judgment* (Rev. ed., 1990); the Carl Bridgwater murder case (see P. Foot, *Murder at the Farm* (1988)). By contrast, the Court of Appeal allowed an appeal in case of the Guildford Four (*R. v. Richardson, The Times,* October 20, 1989) although here the prosecution felt itself unable to support the convictions (see G. McKee and R. Franey, *Time Bomb* (1988); S. Edwards (1989) 139 N. L. J. 1449). It also ultimately allowed an appeal in the case of the Birmingham six: *R. v. Mcllkenny* [1992] 2 All E. R. 417 and the Maguire seven: *R. v. Maguire* [1992] 2 All E. R. 433.

[93] P. O'Connor, [1990] Crim. L.R. 615, 617.

[94] *R. v. Secretary of State for the Home Department, ex p. Cleeland* (unreported, October 8, 1987); *R. v. Same ex p. Ewing* (unreported, July 28, 1988); *R. v. Same ex p. Garner* [1989] C. O. D. 461; the cases cited in n. 87 above, *R. v. Secretary of State for the Home Department, ex p. Ram* [1995] C.O.D. 250.

[95] [1995] 1 W.L.R. 734.

the high profile miscarriage of justice cases, generated much controversy. The RCCJ found that the power was not often exercised,[96] noting the self-imposed limitations adopted by the Home Office. It concluded that the Home Secretary's role was "incompatible with the proper separation of powers as between the courts and the executive" and recommended the establishment of a new independent Criminal Cases Review Authority to consider alleged miscarriages of justice, to supervise further inquiries (if needed) and to refer cases to the Court of Appeal.[97] This recommendation was implemented by Part II (ss.8–25) of the Criminal Appeal Act 1995.

The 1995 Act establishes the Criminal Cases Review Commission as a body corporate, independent of the Crown, with not fewer than 11 members appointed by the Queen on the recommendation of the Prime Minister. Members may be full-time or part-time and are appointed for five years (renewable to a maximum of 10 years). At least one-third of the members must be legally qualified, and at least two-thirds must be persons who appear to the Prime Minister to have knowledge or experience of any aspect of the criminal justice system (of whom one must have knowledge etc. of the Northern Ireland system).[98] Where a person has been convicted of an offence on indictment, the Commission may at any time refer the conviction to the Court of Appeal and (whether or not they refer the conviction) any sentence (not fixed by law) imposed in relation to the conviction. The reference is to be treated as an appeal under sections 1 or 9 of the 1968 Act.[99] On a reference, the Commission may give notice that any other conviction on the indictment in question is to be treated as referred. The Commission also has power to refer a verdict of not guilty by reason of insanity, and findings that a person is under a disability and did the act or made the omission charged; these are to be treated as appeals under sections 12 and 15 of the 1968 Act, respectively.[1] The Commission also has power to refer summary convictions and sentences to the Crown Court.[2] References may not be made unless

"(a) the Commission consider that there is a real possibility that the conviction, verdict, finding or sentence would not be upheld were the reference to be made,
(b) the Commission so consider—
    (i) in the case of a conviction, verdict or finding, because of any argument, or evidence, not raised in the proceedings which led to it or on any appeal or application for leave to appeal against it, or
    (ii) in the case of a sentence, because of an argument on a point of law, or information, not so raised, and
(c) an appeal against the conviction, verdict, finding or sentence has been determined or leave to appeal against it has been refused."[3]

---

[96] 36 cases (48 appellants) between 1981 and 1988, 28 (49 appellants) between 1989 and 1992. The Home Office received between 700 and 800 "petitions" each year: Cm. 2263, p. 181.
[97] *ibid.*, pp. 182–187. See K. Malleson, (1994) 21 J.L.S. 151.
[98] 1995 Act, s.8 and Sched. 1.
[99] Above, pp. 923, 933.
[1] 1994 Act, s.9 and (on ss.12, 15 of the 1968 Act) see above, p. 935.
[2] *ibid.*, s.11. The Crown Court may grant bail to a person whose conviction or sentence is referred.
[3] *ibid.*, s.13(1).

However this is not to prevent the making of a reference

"if it appears to the Commission that there are exceptional circumstances which justify making it."[4]

Notwithstanding the view of the RCCJ that the approach of the Home Office was unduly restrictive,[5] these provisions appear to enshrine the previous policy.

Other points are that references may be made with or without an application having been made by the person to whom it relates; the Commission must take account of any application or representations made to it by or on behalf of the person concerned, any other representations made to it and any other matters which appear to it to be relevant; the Commission may refer a particular point to the Court of Appeal for its opinion; where a reference is treated as an appeal, the appeal may be on any ground whether or not related to the Commission's reason for making the reference; where an application is made for a reference, the Commission must give reasons to the applicant for deciding not to make one.[6] The Commission may be directed to make an investigation by the Court of Appeal and may be asked by the Home Secretary to consider a matter arising in the consideration of whether to recommend the exercise of the prerogative of mercy.[7] The Commission has powers to obtain documents and to require the appointment of investigating officers from a police force or (if appropriate) another public body, who must undertake such inquiries as the Commission may from time to time reasonably direct. There is also a general power to take any steps which they consider appropriate for assisting them in the exercise of any of their functions, including undertaking or arranging for others to undertake inquiries, and obtaining, or arranging for others to obtain, statements, opinions and reports.[8]

These developments are to be welcomed, particularly as the new Commission is to be better resourced than the sections of the Home and Northern Ireland Offices that it replaces.[9] However, its effectiveness will depend on the criteria it establishes for deciding which cases should be the subject of further inquiries, and on the attitude of the Court of Appeal to cases referred.[10]

(vi) Attorney-General's References.[11]

Section 36 of the Criminal Justice Act 1972 introduced a procedure whereby the Attorney-General may refer a point of law to the Court of Appeal where the defendant in a trial on indictment has been acquitted. The point must actually

[4] *ibid.*, s.13(2).
[5] Above, p. 938.
[6] 1995 Act, s.14.
[7] *ibid.*, ss.15, 16. The Commission statement is conclusive of the matter referred. The Commission may also give a reasoned opinion to the Home Secretary that he or she should consider whether to recommend exercise of the prerogative of mercy.
[8] *ibid.*, ss.17–22. For restrictions on the disclosure of information by members or employees of the Commission, see ss.23–25.
[9] See K. Malleson, [1995] Crim.L.R. 929, 930–931, noting, however, that an increase in workload was also anticipated.
[10] *ibid.*, pp. 932–936. *Cf.* above, p. 929.
[11] See J. Jaconelli, [1981] Crim.L.R. 543.

have arisen in the case. The court gives its opinion and may thereafter refer the point to the House of Lords. The Attorney-General may appear in person or be represented by counsel: the acquitted person may be represented by counsel, or with leave may appear in person.[12]

The reference has no effect on the trial or the acquittal. No mention must be made in the reference of the proper name of any person or place which is likely to lead to the identification of the acquitted person.[13] His or her identity must not be disclosed during the proceedings except with consent.

The aim of this procedure is to ensure that an erroneous direction by a trial judge on the law is corrected at the earliest opportunity and without the need for legislation. Whereas the defendant may appeal where such a direction leads to an erroneous conviction, the prosecution has no right to appeal against an erroneous acquittal in a trial on indictment. The sanctity of an acquittal by a jury is maintained by the provisions designed to secure that the reference procedure cannot operate to the detriment of the person acquitted.

In general, judges have resisted the introduction of procedures whereby matters may be referred to them for an advisory opinion.[14] One of the grounds for refusing in the exercise of their discretion to grant a declaration on a disputed matter of law is that the dispute is hypothetical rather than real.[15] However, the opinions under the reference procedure relate to a real case, and, moreover, one in which an opinion has already been expressed by the trial judge. The exact status of the opinions as precedent is, however, uncertain: as they have no actual effect on the outcome of the case as far as the defendant is concerned, it is arguable that they are not binding, either on trial judges or on the Court of Appeal itself; however, they are obviously of strong persuasive force.

The reference procedure has been characterised as "problematic"[16] in view of the doubts as to precedental status and the fact that the defendant often has little interest in contesting the case.[17] Nevertheless, the procedure has been of value in providing authoritative guidance in a number of areas of criminal law, most notably that of conditional intention to steal, where the Court of Appeal's decision on a reference put an end to a line of argument that had led to a large number of undeserved acquittals.[18]

---

[12] In practice, however, the defendant is normally not represented and counsel for the Attorney-General is opposed by counsel appearing as *amicus curiae*, instructed by the Treasury Solicitor. In *Attorney-General's References (Nos. 1 and 2 of 1979)* [1980] Q. B. 180, the Law Commission, who had instigated the references in order to secure clarification of the law concerning conditional intention to steal, submitted a memorandum for the assistance of the court.

[13] Criminal Appeal (Reference of Points of Law) Rules 1973 (S. I. 1973 No. 1114), r.3.

[14] There was weighty judicial opposition to clause 4 of the Rating and Valuation Bill 1928, which would have enabled the Minister of Health to seek advisory opinions from the High Court on questions of rating law: the clause was dropped: see Lord Hewart, *The New Despotism* (1929) Chap. 7; E. C. S. Wade, (1930) 46 L.Q.R. 169 and (1931) 47 L.Q.R. 58; C. K. Allen, (1931) 47 L.Q.R. 43, 60.

[15] *e.g. Blackburn v. Att.-Gen.* [1971] 1 W.L.R. 1037, where the court declined to make a declaration on the hypothetical question whether by signing the Treaty of Rome, Her Majesty's Government would irreversibly surrender in part the sovereignty of Parliament.

[16] J. Jaconelli, *op. cit.*

[17] The Supreme Court of the United States refuses to consider "moot" points even where they arise out of real and not hypothetical situations.

[18] *Attorney-General's References (Nos. 1 and 2 of 1979)* [1980] Q.B. 180. See *R. v. Bayley and Easterbrook* [1980] Crim.L.R. 503.

(vii) Venire de novo

Where there has been a "mistrial", in the sense either that the trial has never been validly commenced or the jury has not validly returned a verdict, the Court of Appeal may order the issue of a writ of *venire de novo* for a "new" trial: the first "trial" is treated as a nullity.[19] This may be done, for example,[20] where proceedings have not been properly instituted,[21] where the court is not properly constituted,[22] where the defendants although separately indicted are tried together,[23] where there is an equivocal plea of guilty which should not have been accepted as such,[24] where the jury is not properly constituted,[25] where the jury is improperly discharged before giving a verdict,[26] or the verdict is ambiguous.[27] It is open to the Court of Appeal simply to quash a conviction without ordering a retrial.[28] Moreover, there may be a rule that the court may not order a *venire de novo* where the "mistrial" led to an acquittal.[29]

In *R. v. Rose*[30] the House of Lords emphasised that the power to order a *venire de novo* was not available where there was an irregularity in the course of the trial occurring between the time that it had been validly commenced and the discharge of the jury after returning a verdict. Here, the judge had applied improper pressure on the jury to reach a verdict by imposing a time limit: the House held that the Court of Appeal had no alternative but to quash the conviction under section 2 of the Criminal Appeal Act 1968, and had no jurisdiction to order a *venire de novo*.[31]

---

[19] This jurisdiction, formerly exercised by the Court for Crown Cases Reserved, was preserved for the Court of Criminal Appeal (*Crane v. D.P.P.*·[1921] 2 A.C. 299) and is now exercised by the Court of Appeal under the Supreme Court Act 1981, s.53(2).

[20] See R. B. Cooke, (1955) 71 L.Q.R. 100; M. Knight, *Criminal Appeals* (1970), pp. 216–219.

[21] *R. v. Angel* (1968) 52 Cr.App.R. 280: the consent of the D.P.P. was necessary but had not been obtained; *R. v. Newland* [1988] Q.B. 402: the indictment was a nullity as it joined disparate offences (*cf. R. v. O'Reilly* (1989) 90 Cr.App.R. 40).

[22] *R. v. Cronin* (1940) 27 Cr.App.R. 179: trial presided over by a person unqualified to act as a deputy recorder.

[23] *Crane v. D.P.P.*, n.19 above.

[24] See above, p. 918, n. 11; see, *e.g. R. v. Baker* (1912) 7 Cr.App.R. 217, 252.

[25] *e.g.* where a juror was personated by his bailiff, who was neither on the jury panel nor qualified to be so: *R. v. Wakefield* (1918) 13 Cr.App.R. 56, or where the defendant is denied his right of challenge: *R. v. Williams* (1925) 19 Cr.App.R. 67; *R. v. Gash* (1967) 51 Cr.App.R. 37.

[26] *R. v. Hancock* (1931) 100 L.J.K.B. 419: the defendant changed his pleas from not guilty to guilty, but the jury did not formally return a guilty verdict.

[27] *R. v. Lewis* (1988) 87 Cr.App.R. 270: the way the verdicts were taken left it unclear whether they were unanimous or majority.

[28] See, *e.g. R. v. Golathan* (1915) 11 Cr.App.R. 79; *R. v. Lewis* (1988) 87 Cr.App.R. 270. It is not clear whether it is open to the prosecution to recommence proceedings: if the court is simply regarded as holding the decision of the "first" trial to be a nullity, it seems that there could be such proceedings; if, however, the conviction is quashed under the Criminal Appeal Act 1968, s.2, the position is as if there had been a judgment and verdict of acquittal and fresh proceedings could be met by a plea of *autrefois acquit*.

[29] *R. v. Middlesex Quarter Sessions, ex p. D.P.P.* [1952] 2 Q.B. 758. An alternative ground for the decision was that the irregularity was not such as to cause a mistrial. There may be exceptions to the supposed rule where the defendant is party to the irregularity or is tried by a court with no jurisdiction over charges of the kind in question: R. B. Cooke, (1955) 71 L.Q.R. 100, 116.

[30] [1982] A.C. 822.

[31] The position is the same where the defendant changes his or her plea to guilty in reliance on the judge's ruling on a point of law that is subsequently shown to be erroneous: *R. v. Hunt* [1986] Q.B. 125, 132 (an appeal was allowed by the House of Lords, but this point was not dealt with: [1987] A.C. 352.)

The court of trial may direct a *venire de novo* where the jury is discharged before giving a verdict, for example where they fail to agree or there is an irregularity in the conduct of proceedings.[32]

(b) Appeals from the Court of Appeal (Criminal Division) to the House of Lords)

An appeal lies from the Court of Appeal (Criminal Division) to the House of Lords at the instance of either the defendant or the prosecutor.[33] The Court of Appeal must certify that a point of law of general public importance is involved.[34] In addition, leave must be obtained from either the Court of Appeal or the House of Lords and this can only be granted where it appears that the point is "one which ought to be considered by the House.''[35] If leave is granted, the House may in its discretion allow a point to be argued that is not connected with the point certified.[36]

An application for leave to appeal is normally made immediately after the Court of Appeal's decision, but may be made in writing within 14 days.[37] The point is normally formulated by counsel for the applicant, sometimes with the assistance of counsel for the other side. If a certificate is refused the matter may not be taken any further: the refusal is not itself a decision that may be subject to appeal.[38] Reasons are not normally given for refusing a certificate.[39] Where a certificate is granted, the application for leave should be made first to the Court of Appeal, and only if leave then is refused by that court, to the House of Lords, within 14 days.[40] The Court of Appeal may grant bail[41] and legal aid.[42]

Where the prosecutor is granted leave to appeal or gives notice of intention to apply for leave, and but for the decision of the Court of Appeal the defendant would be liable to be detained, the Court of Appeal may make an order for his or her detention or direct that he or she is not to be released except on bail so long as the appeal is pending.[43] An order under the Mental Health Act 1983 may be continued.[44] A defendant who is detained may apply to the Court of Appeal or House of Lords to be present at the hearing of the appeal of prelimi-

---

[32] See R. B. Cooke, *op. cit.* pp. 120–125; Juries Act 1974, s.21(4).

[33] Criminal Appeal Act 1968, s.33(1). Where a point of law is referred to the Court of Appeal by the Attorney-General under the Criminal Justice Act 1972, s.36 (see above, p. 939) the court may thereafter refer the point to the House of Lords.

[34] The RCCJ recommended that this requirement be dropped: Cm. 2263, p. 178.

[35] 1968 Act, s.33(2).

[36] *Att.-Gen. for Northern Ireland v. Gallagher* [1963] A.C.349. Where, however, the certificate relates to conviction only the House will not deal with matters of sentence: *Jones v. D.P.P.* [1962] A.C. 635.

[37] Criminal Appeal Act 1968, s.34. The time limit may be extended: *ibid.*

[38] *cf.* in relation to appeals to the House of Lords from the Divisional Court, *Gelberg v. Miller* [1961] 1 W.L.R. 459, above, p. 923, n. 61.

[39] *R. v. Jones* (1975) 61 Cr.App.R. 120; *R. v. Cooper, R. v. McMahon* (1975) 61 Cr.App.R. 215.

[40] Criminal Appeal Act 1968, s.34. The time limit may be extended.

[41] *ibid.*, s.36.

[42] Legal Aid Act 1988, s.19(1)(d), 20(3): legal aid may be granted by the Registrar or the single judge, but not the House of Lords. If the prosecutor appeals or applies for leave to appeal legal aid must be granted if the defendant's means warrant it: *ibid.*, s.20(3)(b).

[43] Criminal Appeal Act 1968, s.37(2). The order ceases to have effect if leave is refused, or the application for leave is not made within the due time, or the appeal is determined, or the liability for detention otherwise ceases, as the case may be: *ibid.*, ss.34(3), 37(3).

[44] *ibid.*, s.37(4)(4A).

nary or incidental matters.[45] If no order for continued detention is made, or the defendant is released or discharged before the appeal is disposed of, the defendant cannot be detained again as the result of the decision of the House of Lords on the appeal.[46]

The rules governing petitions to the House of Lords for leave to appeal and petitions of appeal are prescribed by the House of Lords Directions as to Procedure applicable to Criminal Appeals.[47] The former are heard by an Appeal Committee, the latter by the House itself or an Appellate Committee.[48] If leave is granted by the Court of Appeal there is no statutory time limit for lodging the petition of appeal although the Procedure Directions state that this must be done within three months: if leave is granted by an Appeal Committee, the committee may set a time limit.[49] Statement(s) of facts and issues, an Appendix of Documents and cases must be lodged on a similar basis to that for civil appeals.[50] If any of the parties intend to invite the House to depart from one of its own previous decisions, this intention must be clearly stated.

The House in disposing of an appeal may exercise any of the powers of the Court of Appeal or remit the case to that court.[51] Any sentence substituted by the House of Lords runs from the time when the other sentence would have begun to run, unless the House otherwise directs.[52] Any time spent on bail pending hearing of the appeal does not count towards the sentence.[53]

Until 1960, an appeal could only be taken from the Court of Criminal Appeal to the House of Lords if the Attorney-General granted a *fiat* or certificate that a point of law of exceptional public importance was involved and that it was in the public interest that a further appeal be brought.[54] Between 1907 and 1960 there were 23 successful applications for a *fiat*. The exercise of the Attorney-General's discretion to grant or refuse a *fiat* was in certain instances highly controversial. The Administration of Justice Act 1960[55] introduced the present arrangements which, *inter alia*, brought an end to the involvement of the Attorney-General. The number of criminal appeals to the House of Lords has, accordingly, increased. However, it has been debated whether, on balance, the increased involvement of the House in criminal law matters has proved beneficial. In his commentary on *R. v. Caldwell*,[56] Professor J. C. Smith noted that the "House of Lords has a dismal record in criminal cases. All too often their

---

[45] *ibid.*, s.38.
[46] *ibid.*, s.37(5). See *D.P.P. v. Merriman* [1973] A.C. 584, 606; *U.S. Government v. McCaffery* [1984] 1 W.L.R. 867, 873; *R. v. Hollinshead* [1985] A.C. 975, 998–999, *per* Lord Roskill, who stated that an order should be made unless there were strong reasons for not so doing.
[47] See the *Supreme Court Practice 1995*, para. 16–117, ff.
[48] See above, pp. 98–101.
[49] House of Lords Directions as to Procedure applicable to Criminal Appeals 1992, Dirs. 8, 9; *Practice Direction (House of Lords: Procedure Amendments)* [1996] 1 W.L.R. 450.
[50] See below, p. 962.
[51] Criminal Appeal Act 1968, s.35(3). Where the House of Lords hears an appeal, but it turns out that points not disposed of by the Court of Appeal are relevant to whether a conviction should stand, the House may remit the matter to the Court of Appeal or itself exercise the powers of the Court of Appeal in relation to those points: *R. v. Mandair* [1995] 1 A.C. 208, H.L. The Court of Appeal may not otherwise itself relist the case to consider the unresolved grounds: *R. v. Berry (No.2)* [1991] 1 W.L.R. 125 and *R. v. Berry (No.3)* [1995] 1 W.L.R. 7, C.A.
[52] *ibid.*, s.43(2).
[53] *ibid.*, s.43(1).
[54] See "Appeals to the House of Lords" [1957] Crim.L.R. 566.
[55] See D. G. T. Williams, [1961] Crim.L.R.87.
[56] [1982] A.C. 341.

Lordships' decisions have to be reversed by legislation."[57] His criticisms were echoed by Professor Glanville Williams,[58] who remarked that the average age of Law Lords is higher than that of members of the Court of Appeal, and that "old men" are "often fixed in their opinions" and "tend to ignore the opinions of others". He noted that a further drawback was the breadth of the House's jurisdiction: "It is particularly inapt that a Chancery judge should have the casting vote in the House of Lords in a criminal case, as Lord Cross did in *Hyam*."[59]

After a survey of the record of the House in criminal cases between 1960 and 1984, Professor A. T. H. Smith concluded that appeals by the Crown in such cases should be abolished, and replaced by the Attorney-General's Reference procedure. Decisions from the Divisional Court could go to the Court of Appeal (Criminal Division), but no further.[60]

3. APPEALS IN CIVIL CASES

In this section we consider appeals in civil cases originating in the county court or the High Court. Appeals in civil cases originating in the magistrates' court or Crown Court have already been discussed.[61]

(a) Appeals from the county court to the Court of Appeal (Civil Division)

In general, a person dissatisfied with a decision of a county court may appeal to the Court of Appeal.[62] In certain cases, however, the appeal is expressly excluded[63]:

— questions of fact arising in certain actions by a landlord for possession of the premises;
— an order extending the time for appealing;
— an order expressed by statute to be final[64];
— a decree absolute of divorce or nullity of marriage, by a party who, having had time and opportunity to appeal from the decree nisi, has not done so;
— where the parties have agreed in writing that the judge's decision shall be final.

In certain cases an appeal may only be brought with the leave of the county

---

[57] [1981] Crim.L.R. 393.

[58] *ibid.*, pp. 581–582.

[59] [1975] A.C. 55.

[60] "Criminal Appeals in the House of Lords" (1984) 47 M.L.R. 133.

[61] See above, pp. 920–922.

[62] County Courts Act 1984, s.77(1). Until 1934 the appeal lay first to a Divisional Court and thereafter to the Court of Appeal. In bankruptcy cases the appeal lies to a Divisional Court of the Chancery Division; an appeal lies from that court to the Court of Appeal with the leave of either, and the decision of the Court of Appeal is final: Insolvency Act 1986, s.375(2).

[63] County Courts Act 1984, s.77(6); Supreme Court Act 1981, s.18(1)(b)(c)(d); 1984 Act, s.79(1).

[64] A final order may be set aside if procured by fraud: *cf. Lazarus Estates Ltd. v. Beasley* [1956] 1 Q.B. 702, and in matrimonial cases, a final order may be set aside if there is fraud, mistake or material non-disclosure: *Robinson v. Robinson (Practice Note)* [1982] 1 W.L.R. 786.

court judge or the Court of Appeal: the classes prescribed[65] include those where the claim or counter-claim (according to which is the subject of the appeal) is for an amount not exceeding £5,000 (contract, tort and analogous cases) or where the value of the property does not exceed £15,000 (equity, probate and analogous cases) or the value of the appeal is unquantifiable, and where the decision of the county court judge is made in an appellate capacity. However, no leave is required where the court's determination includes or preserves an injunction or concerns the upbringing of a child.[66]

In other cases, an appeal lies as of right.

Appeals may be based on questions of fact, discretion or law.[67] The procedure for appealing and the powers of the Court of Appeal are discussed in the section on appeals from the High Court.[68]

Appeals lie from decisions of a District judge to the county court judge.[69] In interlocutory matters, the judge considers the issue *de novo*, and may substitute his or her view for that of the District judge. Where the appeal is from a judgment or final order, the role of the county court judge is analogous to that of the Court of Appeal on appeals from decisions of the judge.[70] Accordingly, he or she may only order a new trial in the same circumstances as the Court of Appeal,[71] and may only interfere with a discretionary decision if no reasonable District judge could have so decided.[72]

(b) Appeals from the High Court to the Court of Appeal (Civil Division)

(i) When does an appeal lie?

Appeals normally lie from any judgment or order of the High Court to the Court of Appeal (Civil Division).[73] In some circumstances, the appeal may be direct to the House of Lords.[74] Generally, there is a right to appeal. In respect of some matters, however, the appeal is expressly excluded by statute:
— any criminal cause or matter[75];

---

[65] By the Lord Chancellor under the County Courts Act 1984, s.77(2)–(4): the County Court Appeals Order 1991 (S.I. 1993 No. 1877). See also the general requirements as to leave imposed by R.S.C. Ord.59 r.1B,. made under the Supreme Court Act 1981, s.18(1A) (inserted by the Courts and Legal Services Act 1990, s.7).

[66] S.I. 1991 No. 1877, art. 3.

[67] The circumstances in which the Court of Appeal will consider a point of law not raised in the county court are now the same as for appeals from the High Court to the Court of Appeal (below, p. 953): *Pittalis v. Grant* [1989] Q.B. 605. Formerly, a more restrictive approach was adopted.

[68] See below, pp. 945–959.

[69] County Court Rules 1981, Ord. 13 r.1(10) (interlocutory matters) and Ord. 37, r.6 (final orders or judgments).

[70] See below, pp. 953–959.

[71] *Devenish v. P.D.I. Homes (Hythe) Ltd* [1959] 1 W.L.R. 1188.

[72] *Woodspring District Counci v. Taylor, The Times* May 15, 1982.

[73] Supreme Court Act 1981, s.16(1).

[74] See below, pp. 960–961.

[75] Supreme Court Act 1981, s.18(1)(a). Here, the appeal lies to the House of Lords under the Administration of Justice Act 1960: see above, pp. 922–923.

— any order allowing an extension of time for appealing[76];
— any decision expressed by statute to be final[77];
— a decree absolute of divorce or nullity of marriage, by a party who, having had time and opportunity to appeal from the decree nisi, has not done so[78];
— any decision of the High Court on an appeal under section 1 of the Arbitration Act 1979 on a question of law arising out of an arbitration award, or under section 2 of the Act on a question of law arising in the course of a reference, other than as provided by the 1979 Act[79];
— a judgment or order of the High Court sitting as a Prize Court[80];
— an order refusing leave to a vexatious litigant to institute or continue legal proceedings.[81]

In other cases an appeal only lies if leave is obtained[82]:

(a) a determination by a Divisional Court of any appeal to the High Court[83];
(b) orders made with the consent of the parties or relating only to costs which are by law left to the court's discretion[84];
(c) an order granting or refusing any relief made at the hearing of an application for judicial review;
(d) orders which include the giving or refusing of possession of land;
(e) orders including the grant or refusal of a new tenancy under Part II of the Landlord and Tenant Act 1954;
(f) interlocutory orders,[85] except in the following case:
  (i) where the liberty of the subject is concerned;
  (ii) in the case of a decree nisi in a matrimonial cause;
(g) an order made on an appeal to a judge from any order of a Master, the Admiralty Registrar or a District Judge of the Family Division or a District Registry;
(h) orders under section 42(1) of the Supreme Court Act 1981 (restriction of vexatious legal proceedings);
(i) orders relating to the existence, position, form, extent or course of a boundary or the existence or terms of an easement.

---

[76] 1981 Act, s.18(1)(b). An appeal lies from a refusal to make such an order: *Rickards v. Rickards* [1990] Fam. 194.
[77] *ibid*, s.18(1)(c).
[78] *ibid.*, s.18(1)(d).
[79] *ibid.*, s.18(1)(g).
[80] *ibid.*, s.16(2). An appeal lies to the Privy Council.
[81] *ibid.*, s.42(4).
[82] s.18 (1A) of the Supreme Court Act 1981 (inserted by the Courts and Legal Services Act 1990, s.7) enables leave requirements to be imposed by rules of court. See R.S.C. Order 59, r.1B, added by S.I. 1993 No. 2133, and amended by S.I. 1995 No. 2206.
[83] *e.g.* in civil cases: *cf.* above. p. 921.
[84] R.S.C. Ord. 59 r.1B (1)(b). An order that a solicitor is personally liable for costs does not fall within r.1B (1)(b): *cf. Thompson v. Fraser* [1986] 1 W.L.R. 17 (under the forerunner to this provision).
[85] The distinction between final and interlocutory orders caused much uncertainty and gave rise to a large body of case law: see, *e.g. Salter Rex & Co. v. Ghosh* [1971] 2 Q.B. 597, 601; *White v. Brunton* [1984] Q.B. 570. A classification is now provided by R.S.C. Ord. 59 r.1A, inserted by S.I. 1988 No. 1340, r.7.

Leave may be given by the court below[86] or the Court of Appeal.

The application for leave must be made first to the court below, unless there are special circumstances which make that impossible or inappropriate,[87] and if leave is refused, then to the Court of Appeal. In the latter event the application may be determined by a single judge of the Court of Appeal[88] on paper; if leave is refused, the application may be renewed in open court before two Lords Justices[89]: the single judge may, if he or she thinks fit, refer the application to a full court.[90] If leave is granted other than after a hearing *inter partes*, the respondent may apply to have the matter reconsidered by two Lords Justices.[91]

Even where leave to appeal is not necessary, the Court of Appeal may decline to entertain an appeal where, for example, the issue is or has become hypothetical,[92] or the parties have agreed not to appeal.[93]

(ii) Who may appeal?

Where in principle an appeal lies, any party to proceedings in the court below and any person on whom notice of the order or judgment is served[94] may appeal. In addition, any person who *could* have been made a party to the action may appeal, provided he or she obtains leave from the Court of Appeal.[95]

(iii) Procedure for appealing

The appellant must serve a "notice of appeal" on all parties to the proceedings in the court below who are directly affected by the proceedings,[96] and any other person directed by the Court of Appeal, the single judge or the Registrar of Civil Appeals.[97] The notice may be given in respect of the whole or a specified part of the judgment or order of the court below. For example in a personal injuries case there might be an appeal against the quantum of damages only. The notice must specify the grounds of the appeal and the precise form of the order which the appellant proposes to ask the Court of Appeal to make: the appellant will need leave to rely on any ground or apply for any relief at the hearing not specified in the notice of appeal.[98]

---

[86] An application may be made to any judge of the High Court, not necessarily the judge who heard the case: *Warren v. T. Kilroe & Sons Ltd.* [1988] 1 W.L.R. 516 (decided under s.18(1)(h) of the 1981 Act (now repealed)).

[87] R.S.C. Ord. 59, r.14(4).

[88] 1981 Act, s.54(6). See *Practice Direction (Court of Appeal: Single Judge)* [1985] 1 W.L.R. 739.

[89] R.S.C. Ord. 59, r.14(2A); *Carter (R.G.) Ltd v. Clarke* [1990] 1 W.L.R. 578.

[90] R.S.C. Ord. 59, r.14(10).

[91] *ibid.* r.14(2B); *The Iran Nabuvat* [1990] 1 W.L.R. 1115.

[92] *e.g. Sutch v. Burns* [1944] K.B. 406; *Sun Life Assurance Co. of Canada v. Jervis* [1944] A.C. 111.

[93] *Jones v. Victoria Graving Dock Co.* (1877) 2 Q.B.D. 314.

[94] R.S.C. Ord. 44, r.2.

[95] *per* Jessel M.R. in *Crawcour v. Salter* (1882) 30 W.R. 329; *Re B (an infant)* [1958] 1 Q.B. 12.

[96] R.S.C. Ord. 59, r.3(5).

[97] *ibid.*, r.8.

[98] *ibid.*, r.3(2)(3).

The notice must normally be served within four weeks from the date on which the judgment or order of the court below was sealed or otherwise perfected.[99] The exceptions are (1) where a certificate is granted for an appeal direct to the House of Lords, but the House refuses leave, where the four week period runs from the date of refusal,[1] and (2) social security appeals, where there is a six week time limit.[2] The time limit may be extended or abridged by the court below, provided that the application for extension or abridgment is made within the specified period,[3] or by the Registrar of Civil Appeals, the single judge, or the Court of Appeal.[4] Where, however, the time limit for appealing has expired, an extension will only be granted in exceptional cases[5]: a more liberal exercise of this discretion would be unfair to the other party or parties. The court has an inherent jurisdiction to strike out a notice of appeal if it is hopeless or an abuse of process.[6]

A respondent who is served with a notice of appeal may, within 21 days,[7] serve a "respondent's notice" on the appellant and all parties to the proceedings in the court below directly affected. This must be done where the respondent wishes to contend that the decision of the court below, in respect of the cause of action related to the notice of appeal,

(a) should be varied; or
(b) should be affirmed on grounds other than those relied upon by that court; or
(c) was wrong in whole or in part.

The notice must specify the grounds of the respondent's contention, and, in cases (a) and (c), the precise form of the order which he or she proposes to ask the court to make: the respondent will need leave to apply for any relief not specified in the notice or to rely upon any ground which is either not specified in the notice or relied upon by the court below.[8]

Where the respondent is dissatisfied with the decision of the court on a *separ-*

---

[99] R.S.C. Ord. 59, r.4(1), as amended.
[1] R.S.C. Ord. 59, r.4(2): see below, pp. 960–961.
[2] R.S.C. Ord. 59, r.21.
[3] R.S.C. Ord. 59, r.15.
[4] R.S.C. Ord. 3, r.5. Where leave to appeal is required and granted by the Court of Appeal, time for serving notice of appeal is automatically extended by seven days from the grant of leave, provided the application for leave was made within the four week time limit: R.S.C. Ord. 59, r.4(3).
[5] *Practice Note (Court of Appeal: New Procedure)* [1982] 1 W.L.R. 1312 (Sir John Donaldson, M.R.). See, *e.g. Palata Investments v. Burt & Sinfield* [1985] 1 W.L.R. 942 (extension granted where there was a very short delay (three days) and an acceptable excuse); *cf. Norwich & Peterborough Building Society v. Steed* [1991] 1 W.L.R. 449 (court in its exercise of discretion should consider the length of delay and the reasons for it, the degree of prejudice to the respondent if leave were granted, and the prospective appeal's chance of success; delay of 6½ months while legal aid was sought excusable); *cf. Mallory v. Butler* [1991] 1 W.L.R. 458 (no excuse for 3½ month delay and no arguable case).
[6] *Burgess v. Stafford Hotel Ltd* [1990] 1 W.L.R. 1215; *Barclay's Bank v. Khaira* [1993] 1 F.L.R. 343.
[7] The time can be extended: Ord. 59, r.6(3); Ord. 3, r.5(4): see *V.C.S. v. Magmasters* [1984] 1 W.L.R. 1208.
[8] R.S.C. Ord. 59, r.6.

ate cause of action from that raised in the notice of appeal, the proper course is to serve a separate notice of appeal.[9]

The notice of appeal or respondent's notice may be amended without leave before the date on which the appeal appears in the List of Forthcoming Appeals, and, thereafter, with the leave of the Court of Appeal, the single judge or the Registrar.[10]

The purpose of the notice of appeal is to:

"define and confine the area of controversy on the hearing of the appeal, thus saving both time and expense to the parties. It is intended that wherever possible the members of the court will have read the notice of appeal and any respondent's notice and the reasons for the judgment under appeal before the appeal is called on, and a properly drawn notice of appeal will enable counsel to come at once to the central issues without any prolonged opening."[11]

The same principles apply to a respondent's notice.[12] The grounds should be stated shortly and simply: these notices are not designed to be as elaborate as pleadings.[13]

Within seven days of the later of (1) service of the notice of appeal or (ii) the date on which the judgment or order of the court below was sealed or otherwise perfected, or within such further time as may be allowed by the Registrar of Civil Appeals,[14] the appellant must leave a copy of the judgment or order appealed from and two copies of the notice of appeal with the Registrar. The Registrar thereupon causes the appeal to be entered in the court records and assigned to the proper list of appeals[15]: there is a series of lists depending on the court or tribunal from which the appeal is taken.[16]

The next stage is the appearance of the appeal in the "List of Forthcoming Appeals". The appellant then has 14 days to lodge copies of a series of specified documents, including the notice of appeal, any respondent's notice, the judgment or order of the court below, the pleadings, a record of the judge's reasons, relevant parts of the transcript or judge's note of evidence and relevant affidavits and exhibits.[17] An expedited hearing may be ordered in appropriate cases.[17a]

At any time after an appeal has been set down in the appropriate list of appeals the Registrar may give:

---

[9] *National Society for the Distribution of Electricity by Secondary Generators v. Gibbs* [1900] 2 Ch. 280.

[10] R.S.C. Ord. 59, r.7. Applications for leave are made first to the Registrar, who will require good reasons why the amendment was not made earlier and to be satisfied that the application is made at the earliest possible moment: *Practice Note (Court of Appeal: New Procedure)* [1982] 1 W.L.R. 1312, 1313–14.

[11] *ibid.*, p. 1312.

[12] *ibid.*, pp. 1313–14.

[13] *Sansom v. Sansom (Practice Note)* [1956] 1 W.L.R. 945.

[14] See *C.M. Van Stillevoldt BV v. El Carriers Inc.* [1983] 1 W.L.R. 297; *Hollis v. R. B. Jenkins, The Times*, January 31, 1984.

[15] R.S.C. Ord. 59, r.5, as amended by S.I. 1986 No. 1187 and S.I. 1991 No. 1884

[16] *Practice Note (Court of Appeal: New Procedure)* [1982] 1 W.L.R. 1312, 1313. See the *Supreme Court Practice 1995* Vol. 1, para. 59/3/7. The papers are vetted by a lawyer in the Civil Appeals Office: *Practice Statement (Civil Appeals: Setting down)* [1990] 1 W.L.R. 1436.

[17] R.S.C. Ord. 59, r.9(1) (2) (2A); *Practice Direction (Court of Appeal: procedure)* [1995] 1 W.L.R. 1191, Part II. Documents central to the appeal must also be included in a "core bundle".

[17a] *Unilever plc v. Chefaro Properties Ltd. (Practice Note)* [1995] 1 W.L.R. 243.

"... such directions in relation to the documents to be produced at the appeal, and the manner in which they are to be presented, and as to other matters incidental to the conduct of the appeal, as appear best adapted to secure the just, expeditious and economical disposal of the appeal."[18]

This was described as "perhaps the most important single change in the rules."[19] The hope was expressed that as experience of the new system built up the rate of disposal of appeals could be increased without detriment to, and even with an improvement in, the quality of the justice which was administered.[20] Possible time-saving devices included "perfected grounds of appeal," which refer to the key authorities and the relevant portions of the summing-up and evidence or the provision of a skeleton outline of the argument annotated by reference to the documents and authorities. Notice has also been given that time limits will be strictly enforced unless there are good grounds for granting an extension.[21] Doubts have, however, been expressed:

"[T]here prevails at present an emphasis on efficiency, time saving and expedition, which tends to undermine the English system of appeal (which is predicated upon the advocate's right to conduct the appeal in the way most beneficial to his client's interests) and to assimilate it to American and continental procedure. For all practical purposes this has dispensed with oral presentation and leaves the conduct of a very short hearing to the court rather than Counsel, while in England tradition entitles Counsel to be to a large extent 'in possession of the court.' "[22]

Notwithstanding such doubts, the Court of Appeal has reinforced the emphasis in question, while denying that the effect has been deleterious in the way suggested.[23] From June 6, 1989, skeleton arguments have been compulsory in all cases, except where appeals are heard as a matter of great urgency and in any individual case where the court otherwise directs. They must normally be lodged not less than 14 days before the expected date of the hearing.[24] The appellant's skeleton argument must be accompanied by a chronology of events. Counsel must certify time estimates for the length of the appeal hearing and check periodically that the estimate is correct.[25] At the oral hearing, counsel are normally expected to proceed direct to the grounds of and issues in the appeal without any preamble. Oral argument in support of applications for leave to appeal and renewed applications for judicial review are expected to be completed within 20 and 30 minutes, respectively; limits may also be set for oral arguments on appeals.[26]

---

[18] *ibid.*, r.9(3).

[19] *Practice Note (Court of Appeal: New Procedure)* [1982] 1 W.L.R. 1312, 1315.

[20] *ibid.*

[21] *Practice Direction (Court of Appeal: Procedure)* [1995] 1 W.L.R. 1191, para. 49 (skeleton arguments) and Part II (documentation).

[22] F. A. Mann, (1983) 2 C.J.Q. 320, 322–325, at p. 325.

[23] *Practice Direction (Court of Appeal: Presentation of Argument)* [1989] 1 W.L.R. 281: Introduction (pp. 281–284). This followed a working party, chaired by Purchas L.J. This Direction was superseded by *Practice Direction (Court of Appeal: Procedure)* [1995] 1 W.L.R. 1191.

[24] In heavy or complex cases the court is likely to direct that skeleton arguments should be exchanged earlier (starting within 28 days after entry of the appeal in the List of Forthcoming Appeals): *Practice Direction (Court of Appeal: Procedure)* [1995] 1 W.L.R. 1191, para. 41.

[25] *ibid.*, paras. 14–19.

[26] *ibid.*, paras. 9, 11, 19.

(iv) Interlocutory applications

Interlocutory applications, for example for a stay of execution,[27] for leave to adduce fresh evidence,[28] or for security for the costs of appeal, are heard by a single judge or the Registrar: only the judge, however, may deal with matters concerning an injunction or a stay of execution.[29] The Court of Appeal has all the powers and duties as to amendment and otherwise of the High Court.[30]

An appeal lies respectively from the Registrar to the single judge and from the single judge to the Court of Appeal, by means of a fresh application brought within 10 days. However, an appeal does not lie to the Court of Appeal without leave of that court in respect of a determination of the Registrar which has been reviewed by the single judge.[31] No appeal lies from the determination by the judge of an application for leave to appeal.[32]

(v) Evidence in the Court of Appeal (Civil Division)

An appeal to the Court of Appeal is expressed to be "by way of rehearing".[33] This is not a rehearing in the same sense as appeals from magistrates' courts to the Crown Court[34] but a rehearing "on the documents". The court has power:

—"to draw inferences of fact and to give any judgment and make any order which ought to have been given or made, and to make such further or other order as the case may require;"[35]

and

—"to make any order, on such terms as the Court thinks just, to ensure the determination on the merits of the real question in controversy between the parties."[36]

The court should take account of any new authorities and of any relevant, retrospective, legislation. For example, in *Attorney-General v. Vernazza*,[37] Mr

---

[27] R.S.C. Ord. 59, r.13: an appeal does not operate as a stay of execution unless directed by the court below, a single judge of the Court of Appeal or the court itself.

[28] See below, pp. 952–953.

[29] R.S.C. Ord. 59, r.10(9).

[30] R.S.C. Ord. 59, r.10(1).

[31] R.S.C. Ord. 59, r.14(11) and (12). The judge must consider the matter afresh and use his or her own discretion: *C.M. Van Stillevoldt BV v. E.L. Carriers Ltd* [1983] 1 W.L.R. 207; thereafter, the Court of Appeal will only interfere where the single judge has erred in principle: *Kloeckner & Co. SA v. Gatoil Overseas Inc.* [1990] 1 Lloyd's Rep. 177; *Wren v. Braunston Canal Services, The Times*, November 23, 1990.

[32] *ibid.*, r.14(12); Supreme Court Act 1981, s.54(6): see *Daisystar Ltd v. Town & Country Building Society* [1992] 1 W.L.R. 390.

[33] R.S.C. Ord. 59, r.3(1).

[34] See above, pp. 919–920.

[35] R.S.C. Ord. 59, r.10(3). This power may be exercised notwithstanding that the relevant point is not covered by a notice of appeal or respondent's notice: r.10(4).

[36] R.S.C. Ord. 59, r.10(4).

[37] [1960] A.C. 965.

Vernazza was declared to be a vexatious litigant and prohibited by the High
Court from *instituting* legal proceedings without leave. By the time his appeal
was heard by the Court of Appeal, the High Court had been given a new statutory power to prohibit vexatious litigants from *continuing existing* proceedings
without leave. The House of Lords held that the new legislation, as it affected
procedural and not substantive rights, was retrospective, should have been
applied to Mr Vernazza by the Court of Appeal, and should be applied to him
now. Where there are new authorities or legislative provisions which are relevant
to a decision of the High Court, leave to appeal out of time will be granted if
it is just to do so.[38]

Similarly, the court should take account of any material changes in the facts
since the trial. For example, in *Murphy v. Stone-Wallwork (Charlton) Ltd*[39] an
action was brought by an employee against his employers for breach of statutory
duty. The judge and the Court of Appeal assessed the damages on the assumption that the plaintiff would continue to be employed by the defendants on
lighter work. A fortnight after the decision in the Court of Appeal, the plaintiff
was dismissed because of his incapacity. The House of Lords[40] held that even
though it did not appear that the employers had acted in bad faith or oppress-
ively, evidence of the change of circumstances was admissible, as the basis on
which the case had been conducted on both sides had been suddenly and materially falsified. It should, however, be noted that the change occurred within the
time limit for appealing: it is unlikely that a leave to appeal out of time would
be granted in such circumstances, in view of the need for finality in litigation,
unless, perhaps, there was bad faith or oppression.

Where a party to an appeal seeks to adduce fresh evidence concerning matters
other than events that have occurred since the trial, a more restrictive approach
is adopted. Where judgment has been given after trial or hearing of the cause
or matter on the merits,[41] such fresh evidence is only admitted on "special
grounds".[42] Three conditions were laid down by Denning L.J. in *Ladd v.
Marshall*[43]:

(1) It must be shown that the evidence could not have been obtained with
    reasonable diligence for use at the trial.
(2) The evidence must be such that, if given, it would probably have an
    important influence on the result of the case, although it need not be
    decisive.

---

[38] *In Re Earl of Berkeley, Borrer v. Berkeley* [1945] Ch. 1; *Anns v. Walcroft Property Co. Ltd*
[1976] Q.B. 882; *Property and Reversionary Investment Corporation Ltd v. Templar* [1977] 1
W.L.R. 1223.

[39] [1969] 1 W.L.R. 1023. See also *Mulholland v. Mitchell* [1971] A.C. 666; *Hughes v. Smith, The
Times*, April 21, 1989. Evidence concerning post-hearing developments is "readily admitted" in
cases concerning the welfare of children: *G. v. G. (Minors: Custody Appeal)* [1985] 1 W.L.R.
647, 654, *per* Lord Fraser. See, *e.g. M. v. M. (Minor: Custody Appeal)* [1987] 1 W.L.R. 404;
A. v. A. (Custody Appeal: Role of Appellate Court)) [1988] 1 F.L.R. 193; *Re A. (A. Minor)
(Abduction)* [1989] 1 F.L.R. 365.

[40] The same principle would have applied by the Court of Appeal if the change had occurred after
the trial.

[41] This includes summary judgment under R.S.C. Ords.14 or 86: *Langdale v. Danby* [1982] 1
W.L.R. 1123.

[42] R.S.C. Ord. 59, r.10(2).

[43] [1954] 1 W.L.R. 1489, 1491: approved by the House of Lords in *Skone v. Skone* [1971] 1 W.L.R.
812 and *Langdale v. Danby*, above.

(3) The evidence must be such as is presumably to be believed, or, in other words, must be apparently credible, though it need not be incontrovertible.[44]

These conditions may be relaxed where the welfare of a child is at stake,[45] or on appeals concerning applications for judicial review,[46] or appeals against committal orders.[47]

The Court of Appeal similarly adopts a restrictive approach to points not taken at the trial and presented for the first time in the Court of Appeal. The court will not decide in favour of an appellant on a new point unless it is satisfied beyond doubt (1) that it has before it all the facts bearing upon the new contention as completely as if it had been raised at the trial, and (2) that no evidence could have been adduced at the trial which by any possibility could prevent the point from succeeding.[48] Accordingly it may permit a new question to be raised on the construction and application of a regulation where the facts are not disputed.[49]

(vi) Decision-making in the Court of Appeal

The approach of the Court of Appeal varies according to whether the appeal concerns (1) questions of fact; (2) awards of damages; (3) exercises of judicial discretion; and (4) questions of law.

(1) *Questions of fact.* In the vast majority of cases, the trial will have been conducted by a judge sitting without a jury. The findings of fact will be set out in the judgment. On an appeal, a distinction will be drawn by the Court of Appeal between findings of "primary fact" and inferences of fact drawn from

---

[44] See, *e.g. Roe v. Robert McGregor & Sons* [1968] 1 W.L.R. 925; *Williams v. Reason* (Note) [1988] 1 W.L.R. 96; *Mason v. Mason* [1986] 2 F.L.R. 212 and *Krywald v. Krywald* [1988] 2 F.L.R. 401 (financial provision); *Ferguson v. Welsh* [1987] 1 W.L.R. 1553; *Sutcliffe v. Pressdram Ltd* [1991] 1 Q.B. 153. The points that a large sum of money is at stake and that a foreign element is involved do not justify relaxing the requirements: *The Gudermes* [1984] 1 Lloyd's L.R. 5.

[45] *M. v. M. (Minor: Custody Appeal)* [1987] 1 W.L.R. 404, 409; *cf.* Sheldon J. in *Devon County Council v. C.* [1985] F.L.R. 619, and *Re G. (A Minor) (Wardship: Access)* [1988] 1 F.L.R. 305. It has, however, been suggested that such a relaxation could only be effected by the House of Lords or by legislation: Latey J. in *P. v. P. (Minors: Custody Appeal)* [1984] F.L.R. 99, 113.

[46] *R. v. Secretary of State for the Home Department, ex p. Momin Ali* [1984] 1 W.L.R. 663, 669–670 (Sir John Donaldson M.R.: the principles underlying *Ladd v. Marshall* were applicable "subject always to the discretion of the court to depart from them if the wider interests of justice so require"), and 673 (Fox L.J.). On the facts, the principles did apply, and fresh evidence which could have been placed before the judge was excluded.

[47] *Irtelli v. Squatriti*, The Times, March 2, 1992.

[48] See Lord Herschell in *The Tasmania* (1890) 15 App.Cas. at p. 225 and Jessell M.R. in *Ex p. Firth, re Cowburn* (1882) 19 Ch.D. 419, 429; *Ashcroft v. Mersey Regional Health Authority* [1985] 2 All E.R. 96; *Transcontainer Express Ltd v. Custodian Security Ltd* [1988] 1 Lloyd's L.R. 128.

[49] *Donaghey v. P. O'Brien & Co.* [1966] 1 W.L.R. 1170, 1180; on appeal: *Donaghey v. Boulton & Paul Ltd* [1968] A.C. 1, 14, 23, 31; *cf. Jones v. Department of Employment* [1989] Q.B. 1 (Court of Appeal willing to entertain a new argument on a point of law on an appeal against striking out, where the facts are assumed).

those primary facts (sometimes termed "secondary facts").[50] The Court of
Appeal is most reluctant to disturb findings of primary fact where they are based
on the testimony of witnesses who have been seen by the judge, and who, in
accordance with the practice of the Court of Appeal, will not be seen in person
on the appeal.[51] The judge's findings will normally have been based, at least in
part, on his or her observations of manner and demeanour, and this advantage
is denied to the Court of Appeal. In exceptional cases, the court may find that
the trial judge has "failed to use or has palpably misused his advantage."[52] The
judge's impression of the witnesses' demeanour "should be carefully checked
by a critical examination of the whole of the evidence."[53] A judgment:

> "... may be demonstrated ... to be affected by material inconsistencies
> and inaccuracies or [the trial judge] may be shown to have failed to appreci-
> ate the weight or bearing of circumstances admitted or proved or otherwise
> to have gone plainly wrong."[54]

The court is a little less reluctant to interfere with findings based upon expert
evidence.[55]

On the other hand, the Court of Appeal is much more willing to draw inferences from the primary facts different from those drawn by the trial judge: it
is generally in as good a position as the judge to draw such inferences.[56]

The role of the Court of Appeal in appeals on questions of fact was considered
in *Whitehouse v. Jordan*.[57] The trial judge held a senior hospital registrar to
have been negligent in the course of delivering a baby by pulling too hard and
too long on obstetric forceps, causing brain damage. This finding was based on
a combination of expert evidence, a report by the consultant professor who was
the registrar's head of department, and the testimony of the mother. This finding
was reversed by the Court of Appeal (Lord Denning M.R. and Lawton L.J.,
Donaldson L.J. dissenting). The majority held that the expert evidence against
the registrar was defective in certain respects, and could not stand up against
the expert evidence in his favour; that the judge had acted incorrectly in interpreting a crucial word in the report in its dictionary sense rather than in that
now stated by the professor to be the sense intended; and that as the judge had
disbelieved most of the mother's evidence, he ought not to have relied upon
any of it. The mother had testified that force had been applied to the extent that
her hips had been lifted off the table. The judge accepted that this could not
literally have been true, but held that it showed that she "could" have been
pulled towards the bottom of the delivery bed. On this last point, Lawton L.J.
said that this was one of the rare cases where the appeal court was entitled to
disregard the trial judge's assessment of the reliability of a witness. He had
"palpably misused his advantage" in seeing the witness by turning her account
of what had happened, which physically could not have taken place, into one

---

[50] See above, p. 11.
[51] *SS. Hontestroom (Owners) v. SS. Sagaporack (Owners)* [1927] A.C. 37; *Powell v. Streatham
Manor Nursing Home* [1935] A.C. 243; *Watt or Thomas v. Thomas* [1947] A.C. 484.
[52] *per* Lord Summer in *SS. Hontestroom v. SS. Sagaporack*, above, at p. 47.
[53] *per* Lord Greene M.R. in *Yuill v. Yuill* [1945] P. 15, 22.
[54] *per* Lord Macmillan in *Watt or Thomas v. Thomas* [1947] A.C. 484 at p. 491.
[55] *Joyce v. Yeomans* [1981] 1 W.L.R. 549 (medical witnesses).
[56] *Benmax v. Austin Motor Co. Ltd* [1955] A.C. 370.
[57] [1981] 1 W.L.R. 246.

which could. The House of Lords unanimously endorsed the conclusion of the majority of the Court of Appeal. They stressed the point that apart from the mother's testimony, the issues concerned inferences from the primary facts in the sense of the evaluation of testimony accepted to have been honestly given.[58] As to the mother's testimony, the House agreed unanimously that the judge's "reconstruction" of it should be disregarded.

Where the trial is conducted with a jury, the powers of the Court of Appeal are more limited. A verdict will be set aside if the evidence was such that no jury properly directed could reasonably have returned it.[59]

(2) *Awards of damages.* The Court of Appeal will not vary an award of damages merely because the judges sitting on the appeal would have awarded a different figure. It will only do so:

"... if satisfied that the judge has acted on a wrong principle of law or has misapprehended the facts, or has, for those or other reasons, made a wholly erroneous estimate of the damage suffered."[60]

In practice, the Court of Appeal is much more likely to interfere with an award of damages than a finding of fact, especially where, as with large personal injuries awards, complex calculations are necessary.

Where damages were assessed by a jury, the Court of Appeal was only prepared to interfere with an award where it was "so excessive or so inadequate that no 12 reasonable jurors could reasonably have awarded it."[61] The consequence of this cautious approach was that awards of significantly different amounts in similar cases were permitted to stand. This was one of the factors in the move away from trial by jury in civil cases.[62] In *Ward v. James*,[63] Lord Denning M.R. said[64]:

"In future this court will not feel the same hesitation as it formerly did in upsetting an award of damages by a jury. If it is out of all proportion to the circumstances of the case' (that is, if it is far too high or far too low), this court will set it aside."

This approach appears to bring the position closer to that applied to awards by judges. In *Sutcliffe v. Pressdram Ltd*[65] the Court of Appeal set aside a libel award of £600,000 to the wife of the so-called "Yorkshire Ripper". The traditional approach was followed, and it was not regarded as having been changed by *Ward v. James*.[66]

The Court of Appeal may substitute an award of damages for that made by a judge. If the award was made by a jury the position formerly was that the

---

[58] See Lord Wilberforce, *ibid.* pp. 249–250; Lord Fraser of Tullybelton, *ibid.*, p. 263.
[59] See below, p. 958.
[60] *per* Morris L.J. in *Scott v. Musial* [1959] 2 Q.B. 429, 437.
[61] *ibid.*, pp. 437–8.
[62] See above, pp. 789–793.
[63] [1966] 1 Q.B. 273.
[64] *ibid.*, p. 301.
[65] [1991] 1 Q.B. 153.
[66] n. 63 above. A majority of the Court of Appeal regarded the jury in the *Sutcliffe* case as having wrongly included an award of exemplary damages. Mrs Sutcliffe settled the case for £60,000.

Court of Appeal could only vary an award with the consent of the parties[67]: otherwise it had to order a new trial, which could be by judge alone. However, there is now power to make rules of court enabling the Court of Appeal in specified cases to substitute an award for that made by the jury.[68] Accordingly, it is now provided that in any case where the Court of Appeal has power to order a new trial on the ground that damages awarded by a jury are excessive or inadequate, the court may instead of so ordering substitute such sum as appears to it to be proper.[69]

(3) *Exercises of discretion.* On many matters, a decision may be left to an exercise of the judge's discretion. This is commonly so in interlocutory matters such as pleading, discovery, venue and mode of trial. Here, the matter will normally have been considered first by a master or registrar, and then, by way of a fresh application to the judge. At this stage the judge will consider the matter afresh and may substitute his or her discretion for that of the master. However, if the matter is then taken to the Court of Appeal, that court will only interfere with the judge's exercise of discretion if he or she has erred in law, applied an incorrect principle, misapprehended the facts, taken irrelevant matters into consideration or ignored relevant considerations, or if the court is satisfied that the decision was wrong.[70] This is not regarded as enabling the Court of Appeal to interfere merely because the judges sitting on the appeal would have exercised the discretion differently.[71] An example is *Charles Osenton & Co. v. Johnston,*[72] where the House of Lords reversed an order for trial by an official referee on the ground that the judge had not given sufficient weight to the point that the professional reputation of surveyors was at stake.

In addition, modern statutes commonly leave decisions on substantive as distinct from procedural matters to the discretion of judges. Examples include awards under the Inheritance (Provision for Family and Dependants) Act 1975, financial provision after divorce and decisions concerning custody of and access to children. The same principles have been applied to the role of the Court of Appeal here,[73] and it has been stressed that the court should be particularly unwilling to interfere where the exercise of discretion is based on the impression made by a person in the witness box.[74]

However, in custody cases there has been a difference between: (1) those

---

[67] R.S.C. Ord. 59, r.11(4). Where a head of damages has been erroneously included or excluded the only consent required is that of the person entitled to receive or the person liable to pay the damages, as the case may be: *ibid.*

[68] Courts and Legal Services Act 1990, s.8.

[69] Ord. 59 r.11(4), as substituted by S.I. 1990 No. 2599. See *Rantzen v. Mirror Group Newspapers Ltd* [1994] Q.B. 670, where the C.A. reduced a libel award from £250,000 to £110,000, the court noting that it should scrutinise large awards of damages more closely than hitherto in the context of the protection of freedom of expression by Art. 10, ECHR; and *John v. Mirror Group Newspapers Ltd.* [1996] 2 All E.R.35, where the C.A. reduced an award of £350,000 to £75,000, and held that in future juries could be referred by way of comparison to the conventional compensation scales in personal injury cases, as well as previous libel awards, and both judge and counsel could indicate to the jury the level of award they thought appropriate.

[70] *Evans v. Bartlam* [1937] A.C. 473. This is regarded as broader than the tests applied by the court in reviewing exercises of administrative discretion under the principles stated in the *Wednesbury case* (see below, p. 971, n. 9): *Tsai v. Woodworth, The Times,* November 30, 1983.

[71] *per* Viscount Simon L.C. in *Charles Osenton & Co. v. Johnston* [1942] A.C. 130, 138.

[72] *ibid.*

[73] See, *e.g. In re Thornley, Decd.* [1969] 1 W.L.R. 1037; *Preston v. Preston* [1982] Fam. 17.

[74] *B. v. W. (Wardship: Appeal)* [1979] 1 W.L.R. 1041.

who take the view that the appellate court should only interfere where the judge has erred in law, taken some irrelevant matter into account or failed to take some relevant matter into account, or where the decision is "plainly wrong" in the sense that no reasonable judge could have so decided[75]; and (2) those who take the view that, in addition, the appellate court may interfere on the ground that the judge's decision is "plainly wrong" as a consequence of erring in the course of balancing the relevant factors.[76] The House of Lords in *G. v. G. (Minors: Custody Appeal)*[77] clearly endorsed the second school of thought. It expressly rejected as too narrow the "no reasonable judge" formulation: this was based on the "*Wednesbury* unreasonableness" principle[78] applicable to judicial control over the decision of an administrative body, and was not the appropriate test here. The distinction between the tests was admittedly "a fine one". Furthermore, it was clear that even under the less restricted approach approved by the House of Lords, the Court of Appeal would only exceptionally interfere with a decision where it could not point to an error of law or to a particular factor that should (or should not) have been taken into account: *i.e.* only in a case where the judge had "exceeded the generous ambit within which a reasonable disagreement is possible."[79]

A further point made by the House of Lords in *G. v. G. (Minors: Custody Appeal)*[80] was that the principles set out are generally applicable to all judicial exercises of discretion: appeals concerning the welfare of children do not form a special category.[81] The principles have subsequently been cited in connection with financial provision after divorce,[82] the award of costs[83] and the grant of injunctions.[84] The adherents of both schools were agreed that the Court of Appeal may not interfere merely because the members of that court would have exercised the discretion differently.[85]

If an appellate court wishes to vary a discretionary order, it may either substitute an appropriate order, remit the case to the judge (or to another judge) or, in exceptional cases, hear evidence in order to resolve any doubts.[86]

---

[75] Stamp L.J. dissenting, in *Re F (A Minor) (Wardship: Appeal)* [1976] Fam. 238, 249–255; Sir John Arnold P. in *Clode v. Clode* (1982) 3 F.L.R. 360, 363.

[76] *Re O (Infants) (Wardship: Appeal)* [1971] Ch. 748; Browne and Bridge L.JJ. in *Re F (A Minor) (Wardship: Appeal)* [1976] Fam. 238; *B. v. W. (Wardship: Appeal)* [1979] 1 W.L.R. 1041; *D. v. M. (Minor: Custody Appeal)* [1983] Fam. 33.

[77] [1985] 1 W.L.R. 647. See J. Eekelaar, (1985) 48 M.L.R. 704; C. Forder and R. Ward, "Child custody appeals: the search for principle" [1987] C.L.J. 489; S. P. de Cruz, (1986) 130 S.J. 563.

[78] Below, p. 971.

[79] *per* Lord Bridge at [1985] 1 W.L.R. 647, 656.

[80] *per* Lord Fraser at p. 652, based on Asquith L.J. in *Bellenden (formerly Satterthwaite) v. Satterthwaite* [1948] 1 All E.R. 343, 345. The point that this formulation should not apply where there is an error of law or principle is emphasised by Eekelaar, and by Forder and Ward, *op. cit.* n. 77 above. Most of the post-*G. v. G.* cases in which an appeal has been allowed have been characterised as involving errors of principle, rather than errors in balancing the relevant factors.

[81] *ibid.*, p. 651, *per* Lord Fraser.

[82] *Morris v. Morris* [1985] 1 F.L.R. 1176; *Mason v. Mason* [1986] 2 F.L.R. 212; *Allen v. Allen* [1986] 2 F.L.R. 265; *Whiting v. Whiting* [1988] 1 W.L.R. 565.

[83] *Hawkins v. Dhawan* [1987] 2 E.G.L.R. 157.

[84] *Att.-Gen. v. Guardian Newspapers Ltd* [1987] 1 W.L.R. 1248.

[85] *Re F (A Minor)*, n. 76 above, at pp. 250 (Stamp L.J.); 257–258 (Browne L.J.); *Clarke-Hunt v. Newcombe* (1983) 4 F.L.R. 482, 486–487 (Cumming-Bruce L.J.).

[86] *per* Lord Scarman in *B. v. W.*, n. 76 above, at p. 1055, in relation to custody orders.

(4) *Questions of law.* Here, the Court of Appeal may simply substitute its opinion for that of the court below.

(vii) Applications for a new trial

Section 17 of the Supreme Court Act 1981 provides that applications for a new trial must normally be directed to the Court of Appeal. However, rules of court may prescribe cases or classes of cases where applications are to be made to the High Court: such cases can only be those where trial was by a judge alone and no error of the court at the trial is alleged.[87] The procedure for applications to the Court of Appeal for a new trial is virtually the same as for an appeal.[88]

Where a case is tried by judge alone, the proper course for a dissatisfied party is normally[89] to appeal. On an appeal, the Court of Appeal may, as we have noted, correct any error of fact or law and may vary the judgment. However, in some cases it may be appropriate for the Court of Appeal to order a new trial.[90] This may be so where, for example, the essence of the complaint is that there has not been a fair trial. For example, a party may be "taken by surprise" where a case is called on for hearing unexpectedly, or develops in a wholly unexpected manner. Similarly, a new trial may be ordered where fresh evidence is discovered,[91] or a witness confesses that his or her evidence was false,[92] or in cases of misconduct by the judge[93] or counsel.

Where a case is tried by a judge sitting with a jury, the proper course for a party dissatisfied is to apply for a new trial. The grounds for such applications mentioned above in relation to trial by judge alone will also be relevant here. In addition, there are a number of grounds related particularly to jury trial, including misdirection of the jury, the improper admission or rejection of evidence, and claims that there was no evidence to go to the jury, that the verdict was against the weight of evidence or that the damages are excessive or inadequate.[94] However, the court is not bound to grant a new trial on the ground of misdirection, or the improper admission or rejection of evidence, or because the verdict of the jury was not taken upon a question which the judge at the trial was not asked to leave to them, unless the Court of Appeal is of the opinion that this caused some "substantial wrong or miscarriage".[95] In other words, there will be no new trial in these circumstances if the court is satisfied that the jury, if rightly directed, would still have returned the same verdict.[96]

A verdict supported by no evidence is regarded as erroneous in law: if it is

---

[87] *e.g.* where judgment has been obtained in the absence of a party: Ord. 35, r.2(1) (see *Re Edwards' Will Trusts, Edwards v. Edwards* [1982] Ch. 30).
[88] R.S.C. Ord. 59, r.2.
[89] *i.e.* unless an application must be made to the High Court: n. 87 above.
[90] Jurisdiction to do so is conferred by R.S.C. Ord. 59, r.11(1).
[91] See above, p. 952. *Meek v. Fleming* [1961] 2 Q.B. 366 (court misled by concealment of material evidence).
[92] *Piotrowska v. Piotrowski* [1958] 1 W.L.R. 798.
[93] *Jones v. National Coal Board* [1957] 2 Q.B. 55, above, p. 237, n. 89.
[94] See above, p. 956.
[95] R.S.C. Ord. 59, r.11(2).
[96] *Rowell v. Pratt* [1938] A.C. 101, 116.

claimed, however, that a verdict is against the weight of evidence, it will only be set aside if it was one that no reasonable jury could have found.[97]

A new trial may be ordered on one particular aspect of a case, without affecting the other aspects.[98] For example, there may be a new trial on a question of damages without prejudice to a finding of liability.

(viii) Appeals from masters, district judges and referees

Generally speaking, an appeal lies from the decision of a High Court master or a District judge of the High Court, to a judge of the appropriate division sitting in chambers.[99] The judge will rehear the matter and is not fettered by the decision of the master or District judge.[1] An appeal lies from a decision of a judge in chambers, whether or not the matter has previously been before a master or District judge, to the Court of Appeal, subject to the restrictions applicable generally to appeals to that court.[2]

In certain cases, an appeal lies with leave direct from a master of the Queen's Bench or Chancery Divisions to the Court of Appeal.[3] These are (a) cases where a matter has been tried by the master or referred to him or her for a final decision, and (b) decisions on an assessment of damages or of the value of goods, or an assessment of interest.[4]

An appeal lies from a decision of an official referee[5] to the Court of Appeal:

(1) on a point of law; or, when section 18(1)(f) of the Supreme Court Act 1981[6] does not apply, on a question only of costs;

(2) with the leave of the official referee or the Court of Appeal, on a question of fact, or, when section 18(1)(f) does apply, on a question only of costs;[7]

(3) where he or she has made or refused to make an order of committal for contempt of court.[8]

---

[97] *Metropolitan Ry. Co. v. Wright* (1886) 11 App. Cas.152; *Mechanical Inventions Co. Ltd v. Austin* [1935] A.C. 346. If it is obvious that no verdict for the plaintiff on all the available evidence could be supported, the court may save the waste of time in ordering a new trial by ordering judgment to be entered for the defendant: *Mechanical Inventions Co. Ltd. v. Austin, ibid.*

[98] R.S.C. Ord. 59, r.11(3).

[99] R.S.C. Ord. 58, rr.1(1), 3.

[1] *Evans v. Bartlam* [1937] A.C. 473, 478. All relevant evidence should be considered, including evidence that was not but could have been adduced before the registrar: *Wales Tourist Boards v. Roberts, The Times,* January 10, 1987. A narrower approach is adopted of the appeal is only against a costs order: *Hoddle v. C.C.F. Construction Ltd* [1992] 2 All E.R. 550.

[2] See above, pp. 945–947; and see also R.S.C. Ord. 58, r.6, substituted by S.I. 1988 No. 298, r.4.

[3] R.S.C. Ord. 58, r.2, as amended. Where a decision under (b) involves the determination of some other matter, an appeal also lies to the Court of Appeal in relation to that matter.

[4] Under, respectively, R.S.C. Ord. 36, r.11 and Ord. 37.

[5] See above, pp. 92–93.

[6] See above, p. 946, r. 18(1)(b). s.18(1) (f) has been repealed and replaced by R.S.C. Ord. 59.

[7] R.S.C. Ord. 58, r.4., substituted by S.I. 1988 No. 1340, r.6. Formerly, an appeal on a question of fact lay only if it related to a charge of fraud or breach of professional duty. On the principles governing the grant of leave to appeal on questions of fact, see *Virgin Group Ltd. v. De Morgan Group plc, The Times,* March 9, 1994.

[8] Administration of Justice 1960, s.13(2)(b).

(c) Appeals from the High Court to the House of Lords

In certain circumstances an appeal in a civil case may be taken directly from the High Court (whether a single judge or a Divisional Court) to the House of Lords, "leap-frogging" the Court of Appeal. The conditions are prescribed by Part II of the Administration of Justice Act 1969.[9]

Any of the parties to civil proceedings[10] in the High Court may apply to the trial judge[11] for a certificate to the effect that he is satisfied:

(1) that the "relevant conditions" are fulfilled in relation to his decision in the proceedings;
(2) that a sufficient case for a "leap-frog" appeal has been made out to justify an application for leave to appeal; and
(3) that all the parties consent to the grant of a certificate.[12]

Where apart from the provisions of Part II of the 1969 Act no appeal would lie to the Court of Appeal without the leave of the trial judge or the Court of Appeal, the judge is not to grant a certificate unless it appears to the judge that apart from those provisions "it would be a proper case for granting leave."[13]

The "relevant conditions" are:

(1) that a point of law of general public importance is involved in the decision; and
(2) that the point of law either—

"(a) relates wholly or mainly to the construction of an enactment or of a statutory instrument, and has been fully argued in the proceedings and fully considered in the judgment of the judge in the proceedings, or
(b) is one in respect of which the judge is bound by a decision of the Court of Appeal or of the House of Lords in previous proceedings, and was fully considered in the judgments given by the Court of Appeal or the House of Lords (as the case may be) in those previous proceedings."[14]

No certificate can be granted if by virtue of any enactment no appeal would lie from the High Court to the Court of Appeal or from the Court of Appeal to the House of Lords, or if the decision or order of the judge was made in the exercise of jurisdiction to punish for contempt of court.[15]

Otherwise, the judge has a discretion whether to grant a certificate,[16] and no

---

[9] This possibility was recommended by the Evershed Committee on Supreme Court Practice and Procedure, Final Report (Cmd. 8878, 1953), paras.483–503. The Law Lords at the time were not in favour of the proposal, but attitudes had changed by the late 1960s. See L. Blom-Cooper and G. Drewry, *Final Appeal* (1972), pp. 149–151.

[10] *i.e.* "proceedings other than proceedings in a criminal cause or matter": Administration of Justice Act 1969, s.12(8).

[11] Or Divisional Court, as the case may be: *ibid.*

[12] 1969 Act, s.12(1).

[13] *ibid.* s.15(3).

[14] *ibid.* s.12(3).

[15] *ibid.* s.15(1)(2)(4).

[16] *I.R.C. v. Church Commissioners for England* [1975] 1 W.L.R. 1383.

appeal lies from a refusal.[17] The application for a certificate should normally be made at the hearing but may be made within 14 days.[18]

If a certificate is granted any party may apply within one month to the House of Lords for leave to appeal directly.[19] No hearing is held. The House may grant leave "if ... it appears ... to be expedient to do so," whereupon no appeal will lie to the Court of Appeal.[20] Moreover, no appeal will lie to the Court of Appeal once a certificate is granted until either the time for an application for leave has expired or, where an application is made, until it has been determined by the House.[21]

The "leap-frog" procedure is used in comparatively few cases,[22] although it does enable there to be a significant saving in time and expense if a case is destined for the House of Lords. One of the problems is that it may be difficult for a trial judge to perceive that a case is so destined: it may only become so in the light of the decision in the Court of Appeal.[23]

(d) Appeals from the Court of Appeal to the House of Lords

An appeal lies from any judgment or order of the Court of Appeal to the House of Lords, provided that leave is obtained from either court.[24] No appeal lies from a decision of the Court of Appeal to refuse leave for an appeal to itself; such a refusal does not constitute a "judgment or order".[25] An application for leave is made first to the Court of Appeal, normally immediately after judgment. It is only if leave is refused that a petition for leave may be made to the House.

Among grounds commonly given by the Court of Appeal for refusing leave to appeal are that the point concerns an interlocutory matter, the point is one of fact rather than law, the subject matter is trivial, the matter has become of academic interest only to one or both of the parties[26] and that the Court of Appeal was unanimous and not divided. On the other hand, leave is normally granted in revenue cases.[27]

Petitions to the House of Lords for leave are heard by an Appeal Committee of three Law Lords,[28] and must be lodged within one month from the date of the order of which complaint is made.[29] The committee considers the petition, and if all three members are unanimously of the opinion that it is not admissible

---

[17] 1969 Act s.12(5).

[18] *ibid.* s.12(4).

[19] The House may grant an extension of time: *ibid.* s.13(1).

[20] *ibid.* s.13(2).

[21] *ibid.* s.13(5).

[22] The early practice is reviewed by G. Drewry in "Leapfrogging—And a Lord Justices' Eye View of the Final Appeal" (1973) 89 L.Q.R. 260.

[23] *e.g.* as in *Cassell & Co. Ltd v. Broome* [1972] A.C. 1027: see above, pp. 425–426. The Lord Chancellor suggested that in view of the doubts raised about the direction in *Rookes v. Barnard* [1964] A.C. 1129, the proper course would have been to wait for a case in which the point was directly raised and suggest that the parties take *that* case directly to the House of Lords: *ibid.*, p. 1053.

[24] Appellate Jurisdiction Act 1876, s.3; Administration of Justice (Appeals) Act 1934, s.1.

[25] *Lane v. Esdaile* [1891] A.C. 210; *Whitehouse v. The Board of Control* [1960] 1 W.L.R. 1093; *cf. Geogas S.A. v. Trammo Gas* [1991] 1 W.L.R. 776 (no appeal against grant of leave by C.A.).

[26] *cf. Ainsbury v. Millington* [1987] 1 W.L.R. 379, where the House refused to hear arguments on this ground in a case in which leave had been granted.

[27] See L. Blom-Cooper and G. Drewry, *Final Appeal* (1972), pp. 146–149.

[28] See above, p. 100 and L. Blom-Cooper and G. Drewry, *Final Appeal* (1972), Chap. VII.

[29] House of Lords Practice Directions applicable to Civil Appeals (July 1994 ed.), Dir. 2.

it is dismissed without a hearing. If a petition is admissible, the Appeal Committee considers whether leave should be given. If it is unanimously of the opinion that leave should be refused, it is dismissed without a hearing. If the Appeal Committee takes the provisional view that leave should be given, or given on terms, the respondents are invited to lodge objections. If having considered those objections, the Appeal Committee's opinion remains the same, leave is granted without a further hearing. In any case in which the members are not unanimous, the petition is referred for an oral hearing by the committee.[30] The parties may appear in person or may be represented by solicitors (known as "agents" on appeals to the House) or counsel. In the case of "leapfrog" appeals from the High Court[31] the petition for leave must be lodged within one month from the date on which the necessary certificate was granted: the time can be extended. The petition is considered by the Appeal Committee without a hearing.[32] No reasons are normally given for refusing leave. Conditions may be attached to a grant of leave: this is commonly done on appeals by the Inland Revenue in tax cases, where leave is only granted if the Revenue undertake to pay the costs of the appeal for the respondent in any event. If a condition is imposed by the Court of Appeal, the applicant may treat this as a refusal and apply for leave to the House of Lords.

Where an application for leave to appeal has been refused, it is nevertheless possible, in exceptional cases, for a fresh application to be made and granted.[33]

An appeal must be lodged in the House of Lords within three months of the date of the order appealed from, unless the House or the court below otherwise orders, or a different period is fixed by statute.[34] Leave to appeal out of time may be obtained. Unless legal aid has been granted, or the appellant is in an appeal under the Child Abduction and Custody Act 1985 or a minister or government department, or the respondent agrees to waive the requirement, the appellant must give security for costs in the sum of £18,000.[35]

The appeal is normally considered by an Appellate Committee of five Law Lords.[36] The parties may appear in person or be represented by counsel. Wherever possible, a "statement of the facts and issues involved in the appeal" should be agreed by the parties; otherwise, each must submit their own. An appendix of documents should also be prepared. The statement and appendix must be lodged within six weeks of the presentation of the appeal. The parties must also each lodge a "case", "being a succinct statement of [their] argument in the Appeal", in the form of the heads of argument counsel proposes to submit.[37] All members of the Appellate Committee will have read the statement(s) and case and the judgments in the court below in advance of the hearing.

The House has noted and deprecated a tendency to expand the written cases

---

[30] ibid., Dir. 4.

[31] See above, pp. 960–961.

[32] Practice Directions applicable to Civil Appeals, Dir. 6.

[33] See Buttes Gas v. Hammer [1982] A.C. 888 (leave to appeal from [1975] Q.B. 557 in the light of related proceedings: but note the criticisms of F. A. Mann, (1983) 2 C.J.Q. 320, 325–326); R. v. Home Secretary, ex p. Khera [1984] A.C. 74, (the House of Lords invited the appellant to re-apply for leave following their Lordships' decision to review R. v. Home Secretary, ex p. Zamir [1980] A.C. 930).

[34] Practice Directions applicable to Civil Appeals, Dir. 8.

[35] ibid., Dir.11.

[36] See above, p. 100.

[37] See above, p. 100. Practice Directions applicable to Civil Appeals, Dir. 16.

to incorporate and develop in them detailed written arguments, supported by lengthy citations and references to numerous authorities:

"... much on the same lines as the written 'briefs' submitted by the parties in appeals to appellate courts in the United States, which have resulted in oral argument playing a relatively insignificant role in the decision-making process adopted by appellate courts in that country."[38]

The pre-reading was, it was emphasised, not intended to reduce the part played by oral argument in the decision-making process. Cases should include the *heads* of argument on each issue, and only *key* authorities should be mentioned.

It has, however, been doubted whether all members of the Committee do always read all the papers in advance, and whether all the members always come to a hearing without at least a provisional conclusion in mind.[39] It would obviously be undesirable for preconceived opinions to be based on limited information. Indeed, it has been suggested that changes in the practice of both the Court of Appeal[40] and the House of Lords may inevitably transform the nature of oral argument:

"... which is bound to lose its force where it is no longer a dialogue in the traditional sense, but an attempt to dislodge or fortify an existing impression, however provisional it may be said to be. . . .
[T]he introduction of radical changes under the heading of practice and procedure is outside the province of judges."[41]

The respective approaches of the House to question of fact, discretion and law are similar to that taken by the Court of Appeal.[42] The House "may determine what of right, and according to the law and custom of this realm, ought to be done" in relation to the appeal. Where the House reverses or varies an order of the court below, or orders anything to be done by the court below, the order of the House of Lords must be made an order of the High Court[43]: the House itself has no machinery for enforcement.

4. APPEALS IN ADMINISTRATIVE LAW MATTERS

(a) Introduction

No neat classification is possible of the vast range of functions performed by administrative authorities. Neither is it possible to discern any clear pattern in the availability of rights of appeal from administrative decisions.[44]

---

[38] *M.V. Yorke Motors v. Edwards* [1982] 1 W.L.R. 444, 446–448; reaffirmed in *G. v. G. (Minors: Custody Appeal)* [1985] 1 W.L.R. 647. These principles now apply to the statement(s) of facts and issues: Dir. 12.

[39] F.A. Mann, (1983) 2 C.J.Q. 320, 327–328, 334–335.

[40] See above, pp. 97–98, 949–950.

[41] F. A. Mann, above, pp. 953–958.

[42] See above, pp. 953–958.

[43] See R.S.C. Ord. 32, r.10.

[44] See S.A. de Smith and R. Brazier, *Constitutional and Administrative Law* (7th ed., 1994), pp. 587–589; Law Commission Report, *Administrative Law: Judicial Review and Statutory Appeals* (Law Com. No. 226), Part XII.

The Franks Committee[45] noted that:

"... over most of the field of public administration no formal procedure is provided for objecting or deciding on objections. ... Of course the aggrieved individual can always complain to the appropriate administrative authority, to his Member of Parliament, to a representative organisation or to the press. But there is no formal procedure on which he can insist. ... It may be thought that in these cases the individual is less protected against unfair or wrong decisions [than where there is provision for a formal procedure involving a tribunal or inquiry]."[46]

Such decisions were outside the committee's terms of reference, although it did express "much sympathy" with the proposal by Professor W. A. Robson that there should be a general administrative appeal tribunal, with jurisdiction to hear not only appeals from tribunals and from ministers after a public inquiry, "but also appeals against harsh or unfair administrative decisions in that considerable field of administration in which no special tribunal or enquiry procedure is provided."[47] The committee, however, felt that it had to consider the proposal in relation to its limited terms of reference, and that, viewed from that standpoint, the proposal was to be rejected.

Since then, the problem noted by the Franks Committee has been partly met by the establishment of "Ombudsmen" of various kinds. The Parliamentary Commissioner for Administration and Local Commissioners have power to investigate complaints that there has been injustice consequent on "maladministration" in central and local government.[48] The concept of "maladministration" covers such matters as corruption, bias, unfair discrimination, giving misleading advice, failure to explain the reasons for a decision, losing correspondence and unreasonable delay. The relevant defects are mostly procedural, although where a decision is "thoroughly bad in quality" maladministration may be inferred, and in certain circumstances authorities may be required to reconsider a rule that has caused hardship. The commissioners may not, however, question the merits of a discretionary decision taken without maladministration,[49] and may not entertain a complaint in respect of which there is a right of appeal to a tribunal or a remedy by way of proceedings in a court of law, unless it is not reasonable to expect the complainant to utilise those possibilities.[50]

As to the availability of statutory appeals against administrative decisions, the late Professor de Smith noted[51] that there is in general no appeal against discretionary decisions of central government involving questions of national policy or the allocation of scarce resources, against decisions of public corporations or against most discretionary decisions of local authorities on the allocation of limited resources.

[45] See above, pp. 40–41.
[46] Cmnd. 218, pp. 2–3.
[47] Cmnd. 218, p. 28.
[48] See generally, de Smith and Brazier (1994), Chap 33; Sir William Wade and C.F. Forsyth, *Administrative Law* (7th ed., 1994), pp. 79–106, 141–143; P. P. Craig, *Administrative Law* (3rd ed., 1994), pp. 127–141. There is also an office of National Health Service Commissioner (held by the P.C.A.) and there are two Commissioners in Northern Ireland.
[49] Parliamentary Commissioner Act 1967, s.12(3); Local Government Act 1974, s.34(3).
[50] *ibid.* ss.5(2) and 26(6) respectively.
[51] de Smith and Brazier (1994), pp. 587–588.

However, in certain other areas of public administration, particularly where no sensitive issue of policy is involved, where questions of law may loom large or where a decision has a significant impact on individual rights of liberty or property there may be provision for an appeal.

(b) Particular areas

(i) Regulatory functions

Many activities are subjected to state regulation for such purposes as the protection of public health and welfare. Certain activities are prohibited by law. Others are permitted provided that those who participate in them register with a public authority.[52] Yet others require a specific permission or licence from a public authority: the ease with which a licence may be obtained, and the grounds upon which a licence may be refused are almost infinitely variable.

Control may also be exerted by procedures for inspection. For example, health and safety inspectors may inspect factory premises, offer advice on safety matters, issue notices requiring the cessation of dangerous activities, and, in the last resort, bring criminal proceedings for breaches of the law.

Decisions made in the course of regulatory procedures of this kind are commonly subject to a statutory right of appeal to a tribunal,[53] the Crown Court,[54] a county court[55] or, most commonly, a magistrates' court.[56]

In a small number of cases, such as decisions of the Director-General of Fair Trading concerning consumer credit licensing and the supervision of estate agency work, an appeal lies to a minister, in these examples the Secretary of State for Trade and Industry.

It is normal for it to be possible on such appeals to challenge a decision on the merits as well as on any point of law. This may be so even where it is expressly stated that the decision is "at the discretion" of the authority in question. For example, a grant of a permit for amusements with prizes[57] is "at the discretion of the local authority."[58] An appeal lies to the Crown Court. In *Sagnata Ltd v. Norwich Corporation*,[59] the Court of Appeal held that the recorder at quarter sessions (now the Crown Court) had been correct to go into the merits of a refusal of a permit afresh on appeal, although this did not mean that he "ought not to pay great attention to the fact that the duly constituted and elected

---

[52] Registration requirements may also be imposed to raise revenue.

[53] *e.g.* appeals to an Industrial Tribunal against an improvement or prohibition notice served by a health and safety inspector.

[54] *e.g.* decisions of a chief officer of police in relation to firearms certificates and the registration of firearms; refusal of a permit for the commercial provision of amusements with prizes and many decisions of justices of the peace in administrative matters: see D. Price, *Appeals* (1982), pp. 37–40.

[55] *e.g.* a person aggrieved by a notice requiring him or her to carry out works of repair, by a demand for the recovery of expenses where the authority has acted in default or by a demolition or closing order: Housing Act 1985, ss.191, 269, and Sched. 10, para. 6; Price (1982), pp. 46–49.

[56] *e.g.* revocation of a pilot's licence; refusal of a pet shop licence; refusal of registration of a nursery, child minder, or nursing home: Price (1982), pp. 53–60.

[57] *e.g.* fruit machines.

[58] Lotteries and Amusements Act 1976, Sched. 3. para. 7(1)(a).

[59] [1971] 2 Q.B. 614.

local authority have come to an opinion on the matter, and ought not lightly to reverse their opinion.''[60]

(ii) Welfare benefits

Another important sphere of state activity is that of the provision of many kinds of welfare benefits. Here, it is common for rights of appeal to be granted to a tribunal[61] or, in a few cases,[62] a minister.

(iii) Tribunals

Where a decision-making function has been entrusted to a tribunal, it is normal for there to be a further appeal on points of law, either to a special appellate tribunal such as the Social Security Commissioners or the Employment Appeal Tribunal,[63] to the High Court or to the Court of Appeal.[64] For example, the Tribunals and Inquiries Act 1992 provides[65] for a right of appeal on a point of law to the High Court from the decisions of over 10 tribunals,[66] and there are several others for which similar provision is made by specific statutes. Appeals from tribunals to the High Court on points of law may be required to be made by means of a case stated procedure. Most lie to the Queen's Bench Division, but some, such as those against decisions of the Commons Commissioners and the Special and General Commissioners of Income Tax, lie to the Chancery Division. Appeals are generally heard by a single judge, unless the High Court's decision will be final, in which case the appeal will normally be heard by a Divisional Court.[67]

(iv) Land use

Given the traditional concern of the law for the protection of property rights it is perhaps not surprising that statutory rights to appeal figure prominently in respect of governmental decisions that infringe or affect property rights. Two

---

[60] per Lord Goddard C.J. in *Stepney Borough Council v. Joffe* [1949] 1 K.B. 599, 603, endorsed by Edmund Davies L.J. in *Sagnata*, n. 59 above, at p. 637. See also *Darlington Borough Council v. Paul Wakefield* (1988) 153 J.P. 481.

[61] See above, pp. 67–71.

[62] *e.g.* on questions whether contribution conditions for benefits have been satisfied: Social Security Administration Act 1992, s.17.

[63] See above, pp. 66–67, 70.

[64] *e.g.* from the Lands Tribunal and the Foreign Compensation Commission.

[65] s.11. The appeal must be brought by a ''party'' to proceedings: *i.e.* a litigant and not merely a beneficiary of the litigation: *S. (a minor) v. Special Educational Needs Tribunal* [1996] 1 W.L.R. 382).

[66] *e.g.* Industrial Tribunals (for certain matters), Rent Assessment Committees and Pension Appeal Tribunals.

[67] The procedure on ordinary appeals is regulated by R.S.C. Ord. 55 and on appeals by case stated by Ord. 56. R.S.C. Ord. 57 makes further provision for appeals to Divisional Courts.

kinds of procedure require special mention here. First, planning permission is generally necessary for "the carrying out of building, engineering, mining or other operations in, on, over or under land" or "the making of any material change in the use" of buildings or land.[68] Applications for permission are made to the local planning authority and an appeal on merits, fact or law lies against a refusal to the Secretary of State for the Environment. An appeal may involve a hearing by way of a public local inquiry conducted by an inspector appointed by the Secretary of State, unless the appellant wishes simply to make written representations. The inspector may make the decision personally, except in the 30 per cent or so of larger-scale applications, where the decision is taken by the Secretary of State. An appeal thereafter lies on a point of law to the Queen's Bench Division.[69]

Secondly, there are many powers which authorise the compulsory acquisition of land. The typical procedure provides for a compulsory purchase order to be made by a local authority, subject to confirmation by a minister. If there are objections, a hearing before an inspector must be held on behalf of the minister. If the minister confirms the order, the typical provision[70] governing further appeals enables a person aggrieved by the order to apply within six weeks to the High Court for the order to be quashed on the ground either:

(1) that it is "not within the powers of the Act"; or
(2) that the applicant has been substantially prejudiced by failure to comply with a requirement of the Act.

The order may not otherwise be challenged: thus the person aggrieved may not, for example, seek to challenge an order by applying for judicial review[71] whether within the six week period or not.[72]

The first limb of the grounds of challenge purports to approximate to judicial review under the *ultra vires* doctrine,[73] although it has been given a wider interpretation by the courts. The correct approach was stated as follows by Lord Denning M.R. in *Ashbridge Investments Ltd v. Minister of Housing and Local Government*[74]:

"The court can only interfere on the ground that the Minister has gone outside the powers of the Act or that any requirement of the Act has not been complied with. Under this section it seems to me that the court can

---

[68] Town and Country Planning Act 1990, s.55.

[69] Similar arrangements apply in respect of enforcement notices issued following a breach of planning control. In *Bryan v. U.K.*, *The Times*, December 8, 1995, the European Court of Human Rights held that they did not infringe Art. 6, ECHR. While the inspector appointed by the Secretary of State could not be an "independent and impartial tribunal" as required by Art. 6, given that the Secretary of State could revoke the inspector's power to determine an appeal at any time, the review available on a subsequent appeal to the High Court was sufficient to provide the guarantees of Art. 6.

[70] *e.g.* Acquisition of Land Act 1981, ss.23–25; Housing Act 1985, Sched. 22, para. 7; Town and Country Planning Act 1990, ss.287, 288.

[71] See below, pp. 968–974.

[72] See *Smith v. East Elloe R.D.C.* [1956] A.C. 736; *R. v. Secretary of State for the Environment, ex p. Ostler* [1977] Q.B. 122.

[73] See below, pp. 969–972.

[74] [1965] 1 W.L.R. 1320, 1326. Applied by the Court of Appeal in *Coleen Properties Ltd v. Minister of Housing and Local Government* [1971] 1 W.L.R. 433, and subsequent cases.

interfere with the Minister's decision if he has acted on no evidence; or if he has come to a conclusion to which on the evidence he could not reasonably come; or if he has given a wrong interpretation to the words of the statute; or if he has taken into consideration matters which he ought not to have taken into account, or vice versa; or has otherwise gone wrong in law. It is identical with the position when the court has power to interfere with the decision of a lower tribunal which has erred in point of law."

This would appear to extend the grounds of challenge to include errors of law not of a kind to cause the authority to act *ultra vires*.

(v) Appeals from ministers

In a small number of situations where ministers have to determine questions which may have a significant legal content, there is a further right of appeal on a point of law (or analogous grounds) to the High Court. These include the procedures mentioned in the previous section, decisions of the Secretary of State for Trade and Industry on appeals from the Director-General of Fair Trading, decisions of the Secretary of State for Social Security on national insurance contribution conditions and deportation decisions.[75]

(vi) Immigration

The impact on individual liberty of decisions to refuse entry to or to deport persons who have no legal right to enter or remain in the United Kingdom is such that a special appellate structure has been established.[76] The decisions of immigration officers or the Home Secretary, whether discretionary or not, may normally be the subject of an appeal to an Immigration Adjudicator, and then to the Immigration Appeal Tribunal.[77] An appeal then lies, with leave, on a point of law, to the Court of Appeal.[78] Where a deportation order is made on the ground that it is conducive to the public good "as being in the interests of national security or of the relations between the United Kingdom and any other country or for other reasons of a political nature", there is no appeal, but representations may be made to "three advisors", who may advise the Home Secretary but may not make a binding decision.[79]

D. APPLICATIONS FOR JUDICIAL REVIEW

An appeal will only lie if expressly provided by statute. Apart from, but parallel to, any appellate structure is the control exercised by the High Court over the

---

[75] See below.
[76] Immigration Act 1971, Part II.
[77] In certain cases, the appeal lies directly to the I.A.T.
[78] Asylum and Immigration Appeals Act 1993, s.9.
[79] Immigration Act 1971, s.15(3). See *R. v. Secretary of State for the Home Department, ex p. Hosenball* [1977] 1 W.L.R. 766.

decisions of any statutory authority[80] with a limited jurisdiction or area of power. This "judicial" control is exercised on the basis of two doctrines. By far the more significant is the *ultra vires* doctrine. The other is the power of the High Court to quash any decision within the reach of the prerogative order of certiorari if an error of law is apparent on the face of the decision-making body's record of proceedings: for this purpose it is immaterial whether the error of law is such as to cause the body to act *ultra vires*.[81] There is not the space here to give more than a very brief account of the *ultra vires* doctrine, and the procedures for seeking judicial review.[82]

1. THE ULTRA VIRES DOCTRINE

Public authorities are normally given a circumscribed area of authority by Parliament. The function of the courts is to ensure that such authorities, whether inferior courts, tribunals, ministers or local authorities, do not exceed any of the limits expressly set by Parliament, and that they perform any statutory duties. If that were all to be done, the *ultra vires* doctrine would simply be an exercise in statutory interpretation, and more or less straightforward as the case might be. However, the courts have in addition read certain implied limitations into governmental powers aimed at ensuring that those powers are not abused, and that decision-making processes are fair procedurally. It is assumed that these limitations are to be observed unless Parliament expressly provides otherwise.

If express or implied limits are exceeded, the body in question is said to have acted "*ultra vires*" *i.e.* beyond its powers: if they are not, the body has acted "*intra vires*". Where a decision is judicial rather than administrative[83] the term "jurisdiction" is used rather than "power", but the difference is one of terminology rather than substance. For convenience of exposition a number of different *ultra vires* situations are commonly distinguished.

(a) Straightforward situations

In some cases a question may arise whether a particular activity falls within the scope of existing statutory authority. For example, in *Attorney-General v. Fulham Corporation*[84] the establishment of a municipal laundry was held not to be within the corporation's statutory powers to provide wash-houses. The courts, however, accept that authority may be "reasonably implied" from the

---

[80] Or bodies established under the royal prerogative: *R. v. Criminal Injuries Compensation Board, ex p. Lain* [1967] 2 Q.B. 864; or otherwise performing public functions: *R. v. Panel on Take-Overs and Mergers, ex p. Datafin plc.* [1987] Q.B. 815.

[81] *R. v. Northumberland Compensation Appeal Tribunal, ex p. Shaw* [1952] 1 K.B. 338. This doctrine is in practice obsolete.

[82] The leading works include de Smith, Woolf and Jowell, *Judicial Review of Administrative Action* (5th ed. 1995); Sir William Wade and C. F. Forsyth, *Administrative Law* (7th ed., 1994); P. P. Craig, *Administrative Law* (3rd ed., 1994). For a briefer account see S. A. de Smith and R. Brazier, *Constitutional and Administrative Law* (7th ed., 1994), Chaps.29, 30. On the application for judicial review, see R. J. Gordon, *Judicial Review: Law and Procedure* (2rd ed., 1995); G. Aldous and J. Alder, *Applications for Judicial Review* (2rd ed., 1994); R. J. Gordon, *Crown Office Proceedings* (1990).

[83] These categories represent each end of a spectrum rather than two discrete categories.

[84] [1921] 1 Ch. 440.

express provisions of a statute,[85] and, furthermore, that matters "reasonably incidental" to activities expressly or impliedly authorised will also be held to be
intra vires.[86]

(b) Jurisdiction over fact and law

In many situations, a body may only act where it is first established that a given
state of affairs exists. For example, a court or tribunal may only have jurisdiction
over a certain geographical area; a rent tribunal may only have jurisdiction in
respect of "leases" of "furnished" premises; there may be a monetary limit to
jurisdiction. In these examples, the "preliminary", "collateral" or "threshold"
question is clearly distinguishable from the "main" question the court or tribunal has to determine. Moreover, the former is determinable at the commencement of that body's hearing. The superior courts have taken the view that
inferior courts and tribunals may not extend their jurisdiction by erroneous determinations of these "preliminary", "collateral" or "jurisdictional" issues,
whether or not the error is one of fact or law.[87] If challenged, decisions on these
points will be redetermined by the High Court on an application for judicial
review.

In other cases, however, the distinction between "preliminary" and "main"
questions is less easy to draw. This is particularly so where it is alleged that a
tribunal with jurisdiction at the commencement of an inquiry has "wandered
outside its designated territory" by misconstruing the statute which gives it
power to act. This area of administrative law has been the subject of much
sophisticated analysis: it has, however, been doubted whether there is any clear
cut or convincing test to distinguish "jurisdictional" questions from others. It
may be that in the last resort the classification applied by a reviewing court
turns more on whether that court wishes to intervene than on the application of
any clear principle.

The decision of the House of Lords in *Anisminic Ltd v. Foreign Compensation
Commission*[88] was widely regarded as broadening significantly the range of
errors of law that would be regarded as causing a tribunal to exceed its
jurisdiction.

In *Pearlman v. Keepers and Governors of Harrow School*[89] Lord Denning
M.R. said that the traditional distinction between jurisdictional and non-
jurisdictional errors should be discarded and replaced by a rule that all errors
of law, as distinct from errors of fact, should be regarded as jurisditional. This
view has been broadly endorsed by certain members of the House of Lords, but
not in respect of courts whose decisions are in law "final".[90]

(c) Discretion

The courts under the *ultra vires* doctrine ensure that bodies entrusted with a
discretion do not fetter it unlawfully by developing rigid rules which preclude

---

[85] *Baroness Wenlock v. River Dee Co.* (1885) 10 App.Cas.354, 362.
[86] *Att.-Gen. v. Great Eastern Railway Co.* (1880) 5 App.Cas.473, 478.
[87] See, *e.g. R. v. City of London, etc. Rent Tribunal, ex p. Honig* [1951] 1 K.B. 641.
[88] [1969] 2 A.C. 147.
[89] [1979] Q.B. 56.
[90] *In Re Racal Communications Ltd* [1981] A.C. 374 *per* Lord Diplock and Lord Keith; *R. v. Hull
University Visitor, ex p. Page* [1993] A.C. 682.

a genuine consideration of each case on its merits or by entering contracts or other agreements incompatible with a proper exercise of discretion. Similarly, a body may not be estopped from exercising a statutory discretion and may not delegate the exercise of a discretion without express or implied statutory authority.

Furthermore, an administrative body may not "abuse" its discretion by exercising powers in bad faith or for an improper purpose, by taking account of irrelevant considerations or ignoring relevant considerations, or by making a decision that is so unreasonable, no reasonable authority could make it.[91]

(d) Natural justice

There are two basic principles of natural justice. The first, the *nemo judex in sua causa* rule, provides that no person should be a judge in his or her own cause, and is applied to judicial or quasi-judicial decisions. The rule is breached where the adjudicator has a direct financial interest[92] or has acted both as prosecutor and judge, or where there is a real danger of bias.[93]

The other, the *audi alteram partem* rule, applies to a wider range of decision-making functions and requires prior notice to be given of a decision adverse to individual interests together with an opportunity to make representations. The detailed content of this rule varies from the rigorous procedural standards expected of courts to the minimal standards of "fairness" required in respect of purely administrative decisions: the content in any given case will depend on the court's appraisal of what is appropriate in the circumstances.[94]

(e) Procedural ultra vires

The procedure to be adopted for a particular decision-making process may be expressly prescribed by statute or statutory instrument. However, the consequences of failure to observe a particular step are not commonly spelled out. The courts draw a distinction between *mandatory* and *directory* requirements: failure to observe a mandatory step renders the ultimate decision *ultra vires*; failure to observe a directory step does not have this effect, although in some cases "substantial compliance" may be necessary. Important safeguards such as an obligation to consult[95] or to inform a person of rights of appeal[96] are normally held to be mandatory: trivial typographical errors which do not mis-

---

[91] These principles were expounded by Lord Greene M. R. in *Associated Provincial Picture Houses Ltd v. Wednesbury Corporation* [1948] 1 K.B. 223.

[92] *e.g. Dimes v. Grand Junction Canal Proprietors* (1852) 3 H.L.Cas.759 (decision of Lord Cottenham L.C. set aside by the House of Lords on the ground that he held shares in the plaintiff company).

[93] *R. v. Gough* [1993] A.C. 646.

[94] See, *e.g. Ridge v. Baldwin* [1964] A.C. 40 (dismissal of a chief constable without prior notice and a proper hearing held to be void); *R. v. Commission for Racial Equality, ex p. Cottrell & Rothon* [1980] 1 W.L.R. 1580, 1586–7 (emphasising the variable content of the *audi alteram partem* rule and the duty to act fairly); *R. v. Secretary of State for the Home Department, ex p. Doody* [1994] 1 A.C. 531 (fairness may require reasons to be given for a decision).

[95] *Agricultural etc. Training Board v. Aylesbury Mushrooms Ltd* [1972] 1 W.L.R. 190.

[96] *London & Clydeside Ltd v. Aberdeen District Council* [1980] 1 W.L.R. 182.

lead[97] are normally regarded as directory matters, although the distinction is not always easy to draw.[98]

2. THE METHODS OF OBTAINING JUDICIAL REVIEW

(a) Introduction

Judicial review of judicial and administrative decisions and delegated legislation may be sought "directly" or "collaterally". A direct challenge may be made either:

(1) by an "application for judicial review" in the Queen's Bench Division where the court may award one or more of a number of remedies: namely, certiorari, mandamus, prohibition, an injunction, a declaration and damages; or

(2) in an ordinary action in the Queen's Bench or Chancery Divisions for an injunction, a declaration, or damages.

A challenge is made collaterally where the argument that an act or decision, such as a bye-law, is *ultra vires* is raised as a defence to enforcement proceedings or prosecution.[99]

The new, unified, procedure for an application for judicial review was introduced in 1978. In 1982, the House of Lords held that as a general rule it will be contrary to public policy and an abuse of the process of the court for a plaintiff complaining of a public authority's infringement of his or her "public law rights" to seek redress by an ordinary action rather than an application for judicial review.[1] Private law claims against public authorities, such as actions for damages, may still be brought by ordinary proceedings.[2] The distinction between public law and private law matters can, however, be very difficult to draw. After some hesitation,[3] it has been held that the principle of *O'Reilly v. Mackman*[4] does not prevent a defendant in criminal proceedings for breach of a bye-law raising the validity of the bye-law collaterally by way of defence at the trial.[5] Similarly, in a civil case, matters of *vires* may be raised in defence of private law rights, where those rights are not dependent upon a public law decision.[6]

---

[97] *e.g. R. v. Dacorum Gaming Licensing Committee* [1971] 3 All E.R. 666.

[98] Lord Hailsham in the *London & Clydeside* case, n. 95 above, suggested *obiter* that the courts should adopt a more flexible approach to this issue: this view is beginning to find favour: see, *e.g.* the Court of Appeal in *R. v. Lambeth Borough Council, ex p. Sharp* [1987] J.P.L. 440.

[99] See, *e.g. Kruse v. Johnson* [1898] 2 Q.B. 91.

[1] *O'Reilly v. Mackman* [1983] 2 A.C. 237.

[2] *Davy v. Spelthorne Borough Council* [1984] A.C. 262.

[3] *Quietlynn Ltd v. Plymouth City Council* [1988] Q.B. 114, D.C. (pet.dis. [1987] 1 W.L.R. 1090, H.L.).

[4] n. 99 above.

[5] *R. v. Reading Crown Court, ex p. Hutchinson* [1988] Q.B. 384, D.C. (pet.dis. [1988] 1 W.L.R. 308). The challenge was ultimately successful: *D.P.P. v. Hutchinson* [1990] 2 A.C. 783.

[6] *Wandsworth London Borough Council v. Winder* [1985] A.C 461 (council tenant entitled to raise in defence to an action for arrears of rent that the council's decision to raise the rent was an *ultra vires* abuse of discretion under the *Wednesbury* principles: the argument ultimately failed: *Wandsworth London Borough Council v. Winder* (No. 2) (1988) 20 H.L.R. 400). In *Roy v. Kensington and Chelsea and Westminster Family Practitioner Committee* [1992] 1 A.C. 624, the

(b) Procedure on applications for judicial review

The procedure on applications for judicial review is prescribed by section 31 of the Supreme Court Act 1981 and R.S.C. Order 53. An application for mandamus, prohibition or certiorari, or for an injunction restraining a person from acting in an office in which he or she is not entitled to act, *must* be brought under Order 53. An application for a declaration or injunction (other than of the kind just mentioned) *may* be brought under Order 53,[7] and such a remedy may be granted where the court considers it just and convenient so to do, having regard to the nature of the matters in respect of which, and the persons and bodies against whom, mandamus, prohibition or certiorari may be granted, and all the circumstances of the case.

On an application for judicial review, the applicant may claim any one or more of the remedies listed above, and may be awarded damages if there is a good cause of action. The procedure is in two stages. The applicant must first obtain leave from a High Court judge of the Queen's Bench Division. Where the application for leave is refused, the applicant may renew it by applying, in a criminal case, to a Divisional Court, and in a civil case, to a judge sitting in open court. The applicant must specify the relief sought and the grounds for his claim and file an affidavit verifying the facts relied on. He or she may be allowed to amend his claim on such terms, if any, as the court thinks fit.

The court may not grant leave unless it considers that the applicant has a "sufficient interest" in the matter (*locus standi*): it is not necessary, however, for him or her to show that his or her legal rights are affected.[8]

Once leave is granted, the application is made to a judge sitting in open court, unless the court directs that it be made to a judge in chambers or a Divisional Court: criminal cases are, however, always heard by a Divisional Court. The court may entertain interlocutory applications for orders such as those for discovery, interrogatories and cross-examination on affidavits. Evidence is given in affidavit form,[9] and leave to cross-examine is in practice rarely granted.

An application must be made promptly, and in any event within three months from the date when grounds for the application first arose, unless the court considers there are good grounds for extending the period.[10]

All the remedies are discretionary, and may be refused, for example, where the applicant is actuated by improper motives or on the ground of undue delay.[11]

House of Lords held that a doctor was entitled to enforce his private law rights to remuneration (whether contractual or statutory) by an ordinary action. In *Mercury Communications Ltd. v. Director General of Telecommunications* [1996] 1 W.L.R. 48, Lord Slynn emphasised that flexibility should be retained in determining the limits of "public law" and "private law."

[7] Subject to the principle expressed in *O'Reilly v. Mackman*, n. 99 above.

[8] *Inland Revenue Commissioners v. National Federation of Small Businesses* [1982] A.C. 617.

[9] As to the principles governing the admission of fresh evidence, see *R. v. Secretary of State for the Environment, ex p. Powis* [1982] 1 All E.R. 788, 797–798.

[10] Ord. 53, r.4, as amended by S.I. 1980 No. 2000, and S.I. 1987 No. 1423, r.63, Sched. See *R. v. Stratford-upon-Avon District Council, ex p. Jackson* [1985] 1 W.L.R. 1319; *R. v. Dairy Produce Quota Tribunal for England and Wales, ex p. Caswell* [1990] 2 A.C. 738.

[11] The Supreme Court Act 1981, s.31(6) provides that where the court considers there has been undue delay, it may refuse to grant leave to apply, or any relief sought, "if it considers that the granting of the relief sought would be likely to cause substantial hardship to, or substantially prejudice the right of any person or would be detrimental to good administration." This is regarded as complementing Ord. 53, r.4: *ex p. Jackson* and *ex p. Caswell*, above.

(c) A comparison with ordinary actions

It should be noted that in ordinary actions for a declaration or injunction there is no requirement of leave, the limitation period is normally six years, although a remedy may still be refused on the ground of undue delay, and the applicant is not required to swear an affidavit in support of his or her factual allegations. Moreover, it is the more useful procedure where it is necessary for a witness to give evidence orally. However, a person will only have *locus standi* to be granted a declaration or injunction in an ordinary action if his or her legal rights are affected or he or she has suffered special damage.[12] Otherwise, that person must either apply for judicial review under Order 53, where the test for *locus standi* is less strict, or seek the consent of the Attorney-General for "relator proceedings." Here, the Attorney-General is the nominal plaintiff, although the proceedings are taken at the expense of the applicant (or "relator").[13] The Attorney-General's decision to grant or refuse consent may not be challenged.[14]

(d) The remedies

(i) Mandamus

The prerogative[15] order of mandamus[16] lies to compel performance of a public (not necessarily statutory) duty. For example, it may be granted where a tribunal wrongfully declines to hear a matter that does in fact lie within its jurisdiction, or, where there has been an *ultra vires* abuse of discretion, to ensure that the matter is reconsidered according to law.[17]

(ii) Prohibition and certiorari

The prerogative orders of prohibition and certiorari[18] are similar in scope. Prohibition lies to restrain a tribunal or other authority where it is about to act *ultra vires* or to complete an *ultra vires* act already begun. Certiorari lies to quash[19] a decision already made where:

    (1) it is *ultra vires*; or
    (2) it has been obtained by fraud[20]; or
    (3) there is an error of law apparent on the face of the record of proceedings.

---

[12] *Boyce v. Paddington Corporation* [1903] 1 Ch. 109; *Gouriet v. Union of Post Office Workers* [1978] A.C. 435.
[13] See, *e.g. Att.-Gen ex rel. McWhirter v. Independent Broadcasting Authority* [1973] Q.B. 629.
[14] *Gouriet v. Union of Post Office Workers*, n. 12 above.
[15] So called because the writ replaced by the modern order was thought to be especially associated with the Crown.
[16] Normally pronounced "mandaymus".
[17] *e.g. Padfield v. Minister of Agriculture* [1968] A.C. 997.
[18] Normally pronounced "sersheeorair'eye".
[19] Not "squash," "quosh" or "gnash" (*cf. R. v. Pressick* [1978] Crim.L.R. 377).
[20] See *R. v. Wolverhamptom Crown Court, ex p. Crofts* [1983] 1 W.L.R. 204.

These orders were formerly confined to decisions in respect of which there was a duty to act judicially, but they may now be sought in respect of any judicial or administrative[21] (but not legislative) act.

(iii) Declarations and injunctions

A person may obtain a declaration on a disputed matter of law, or an injunction, whereby a party to an action is required to do or refrain from doing a particular thing.[22] These were in origin private law remedies but are today frequently sought in respect of the decisions of public authorities.

(iv) Habeas corpus[23]

The prerogative writ of *habeas corpus ad subjiciendum* lies to secure a person's release from wrongful imprisonment. An *ex parte* application for a writ must be made to a Divisional Court of the Queen's Bench Division or, if no such court is sitting, to a single judge of any Division of the High Court, and takes precedence over other business. In an emergency, an application may be made to a judge out of court, for example, at home at night. If prima facie grounds are shown by an affidavit by or on behalf of the prisoner matter is normally adjourned to a Divisional Court for a full hearing. In exceptional cases the writ may be issued forthwith to the custodian, requiring that the prisoner be produced to the court at the time specified for the full hearing. It either event, the burden of justifying the detention lies on the custodian: if he or she fails, the prisoner's release is ordered.

The grounds for granting a writ of habeas corpus are essentially the same as for an application for judicial review. An appeal lies in civil cases as of right of the Court of Appeal and then with leave to the House of Lords. In criminal cases, no appeal can lie from an order made by a single judge,[24] but an appeal does lie from the Divisional Court to the House of Lords, with the leave of either.[25] An appeal may be taken from a refusal to discharge the prisoner or an order of release: in the latter event the person's right to remain at large cannot be affected by the outcome of the appeal.[26] After a refusal to grant habeas corpus no further application may be made on the same grounds and evidence.[27]

An application for habeas corpus is the standard method of challenging extradition decisions.

---

[21] *R. v. Hillingdon London Borough Council, ex p. Royco Homes Ltd* [1974] Q.B. 720.

[22] See further above, p. 795.

[23] See R. J. Sharpe, *The Law of Habeas Corpus* (2nd ed., 1989); deSmith, Woolf and Jowell, *Judicial Review of Administrative Action* (5th ed., 1995), pp. 672–681; R.S.C. Order 54.

[24] Administration of Justice Act 1960, s.15(2): a single judge may only grant an application: the matter must otherwise be referred to a Divisional Court: *ibid.*, s.14(1).

[25] *ibid.*, ss.1, 15(3).

[26] *ibid.*, s.15(1)(4). In criminal cases an order may be made providing for the continued detention of the defendant or directing that he or she shall not be released except on bail: *ibid.*, s.5.

[27] *ibid.*, s.14(2).

(e) Relationship between applications for judicial review and appeals

The remedies available on an application for judicial review are discretionary, and will not be awarded if there is some equally convenient and beneficial remedy such as a right of appeal. However, an appeal to a minister against a planning condition will not, for example, be regarded as convenient as certiorari where the issue is purely one of law.[28] Indeed, it has sometimes been stated that an application for judicial review must be made where a challenge is based on the *ultra vires* doctrine, rather than exercising a right to appeal on a point of law.[29]

Conversely, an application for judicial review will be less appropriate than an appeal by case stated where complicated findings of fact are involved,[30] and will not be entertained in respect of points arising in the course of trials or committal proceedings[31]: such proceedings must be concluded before any challenge can take place, whether by appeal or application for judicial review.

Statutory provisions may purport to exclude or restrict judicial review. For example, the Crown Court is made amenable to the supervisory jurisdiction of the High Court in respect of matters other than those relating to trial on indictment.[32]

An application for judicial review may be made to challenge a sentence or order on the ground that it is harsh or oppressive.[33]

E. REFERENCES TO THE EUROPEAN COURT OF JUSTICE[34]

One of the major functions of the Court of Justice of the European Communities[35] is that of ensuring consistency in the decision making of national courts

---

[28] *R. v. Hillingdon London Borough Council, ex p. Royco Homes Ltd* [1974] Q.B. 720.

[29] *Metropolitan Properties Co. v. Lannon* [1968] 1 W.L.R. 815; *Chapman v. Earl* [1968] 1 W.L.R. 1315; *Henry Moss Ltd v. Customs and Excise Commissioners* [1981] 2 All E.R. 86, 90 (*per* Lord Denning M.R.), criticised by A. W. Bradley [1981] P.L. 476; *contra, Elliott v. Brighton Borough Council* (1980) 79 L.G.R. 506.

[30] *R. v. Crown Court at Ipswich, ex p. Baldwin* [1981] 1 All E.R. 596.

[31] *R. v. Wells Street Stipendiary Magistrate, ex p. Seillon* [1978] 1 W.L.R. 1002 (committal proceedings); *R. v. Rochford JJ. ex p. Buck* (1978) 68 Cr.App.R. 114. (summary trial).

[32] Supreme Court Act 1981, s.29(3); *R. v. Sheffield Crown Court, ex p. Brownlow* [1980] Q.B. 530; jury vetting order held to relate to trial on indictment; J. Kodwo Bentil, (1988) 152 J.P.N. 323. See also above, p. 367.

[33] *R. v. St Albans Crown Court, ex p. Cinnamond* [1981] Q.B. 480; *R. v. Tottenham JJ., ex p. Joshi* [1982] 1 W.L.R. 631. It has been suggested that *Cinnamond* was wrongly decided (Watkins L.J. in *Arthur v. Stringer* (1986) 84 Cr.App.R. 361, 368), or should at least be confined to cases where the sentence is "truly astonishing" (Watkins L.J. in *R. v. Crown Court at Croydon, ex p. Miller* (1986) 85 Cr.App.R. 152 (decided before *Arthur v. Stringer*)). The court may, however, refuse in the exercise of its discretion to entertain an application for judicial review if a right to appeal against sentence has not been exercised: *R. v. Battle Magistrates' Court, ex p. Shepherd* (1983) 5 Cr.App.R. (S.) 124.

[34] D. W. K. Anderson, *References to the European Court* (1995); L. Collins, *European Community Law in the United Kingdom* (4th ed., 1990), Chap. 3; T. C. Hartley, *The Foundations of European Community Law* (4th ed., 1994), Chap. 9; L. N. Brown and T. Kennedy, *The Court of Justice of the European Communities* (4th ed., 1994), Chap. 10; H. G. Shermers, *et al.* (eds.), *Article 177 EEC: Experiences and Problems* (1987); A. Arnull, "The Use and Abuse of Article 177 EEC" (1989) 52 M.L.R. 622 and "References to the European Court" (1990) 15 E.L. Rev. 375.

[35] See above, pp. 103–109.

in community law matters. The governing provision in the EC Treaty is Article 177[36]:

"(1) The Court of Justice shall have jurisdiction to give preliminary rulings concerning:
    (a) the interpretation of this Treaty;
    (b) the validity and interpretation of acts of the institutions of the Community and of the European Central Bank;
    (c) the interpretation of the statutes of bodies established by an act of the Council, where those statutes so provide.
(2) Where such a question is raised before any court or tribunal of a Member State, that court or tribunal may, if it considers that a decision on the question is necessary to enable it to give judgment, request the Court of Justice to give a ruling thereon.
(3) Where any such question is raised in a case pending before a court or tribunal of a Member State, against whose decisions there is no judicial remedy under national law, that court or tribunal shall bring the matter before the Court of Justice."

The equivalent provision in the European Coal and Steel Community Treaty (Art. 41) is more narrowly drawn:

"The Court shall have sole jurisdiction to give preliminary rulings on the validity of acts of the High Authority and of the Council where such validity is in issue in proceedings brought before a national court or tribunal."

Thus it would appear that only questions of *validity* can be referred. However, the Court has held that it does have jurisdiction to give preliminary rulings on the interpretation of the ECSC Treaty and of acts of the Commission and the Council adopted under it.[37] It should be noted, moreover, that within these narrower limits the jurisdiction of the court is exclusive: the label "preliminary" ruling is in this context misleading.

It should be noted that the reference procedure is not strictly an appeal: the decision to refer is taken by the national court and not a party and the court will only rule on the point of Community law raised and remit the case to the national court to apply the law to the facts of the case. The remainder of this discussion will relate to the EC and Euratom. We now examine the elements of Article 177 in more detail.

1. THE MATTERS THAT MAY BE REFERRED

The Court may give rulings concerning (1) the interpretation of Treaty provisions[38]; and (2) the interpretation and validity of acts of the Community insti-

---

[36] The equivalent provision in the Euratom Treaty (Art. 150) is virtually identical.

[37] Case C-221/88, *Busoni* [1990] E.C.R. I-495.

[38] Art. 177(1)(a) EC covers the EC Treaty and all Treaties amending or supplementing it: subsidiary conventions are not covered: Case 44/84, *Hurd v. Jones (Inspector of Taxes)* [1986] E.C.R. 29 (agreement between the Member States setting up European Schools in Community Countries not within Art. 177): see L.N. Brown, (1986) 23 C.M.L. Rev. 895; Case 152/83, *Demouche v.*

tutions (certainly the Council[39] and Commission and probably the Parliament and the Court itself[40]). Where, however, the act of the Council in question is the "statute" regulating the operation of an institution or body established by the Council, the court may only give a ruling if the statute so provides,[41] and the ruling may only concern interpretation, not validity.[42] The task of "interpretation" is taken to include that of determining whether a provision is directly effective.[43] A question of validity *must* be referred as the European Court has the exclusive jurisdiction to rule on such a question.[44]

2. "Any Court or Tribunal"

Article 177(2) of the EC Treaty provides that "any court or tribunal" may refer a question if the conditions stated are applicable. In the United Kingdom, procedural rules have been made governing references from the High Court and the Court of Appeal (Civil Division),[45] the Court of Appeal (Criminal Division),[46] the Crown Court[47] and county courts.[48] However, it is clear that magistrates' courts[49] and statutory tribunals[50] have power to refer matters to the Court of Justice even though no procedural rules have been made. The meaning of the expression "court or tribunal" will in the last resort be determined by the Court of Justice, and the title of an institution and its status in national

---

Fonds de Garantie Automobile [1987] E.C.R. 3833 (agreement between national bureaux of motor vehicle insurers not within Art. 177, notwithstanding that it implemented a Council Directive). The Court may also interpret the final provisions of the Maastricht Treaty, and those parts that amend other treaties (Art.L/TEU); accordingly it does not generally have jurisdiction in respect of the provisions establishing the European Union or the Common Foreign and Security Policy and Justice and Home Affairs pillars of the EU.

[39] The Court has asserted jurisdiction under Art. 177 to interpret agreements between the Community and non-Member States, concluded on behalf of the Community by the Council: Case 181/73, *Haegeman v. Belgium* [1974] E.C.R. 449 (Association Agreement between the EEC and Greece); or even agreements involving Member States to which the Community is not formally a party: Cases 267–269/81, *SPI* [1983] E.C.R. 801 (General Agreement on Tariffs and Trade). For criticism, see Hartley (1994), pp. 271–274.

[40] Although a preliminary ruling is not itself an act that can be questioned on an application for a further preliminary ruling: Case 69/85, *Wunsche Handelsgesellschaft v. Germany* [1986] E.C.R.947: see G. Bebr, (1987) 24 C.M.L. Rev. 719; this does not prevent the national court making a subsequent reference in the same proceedings: *ibid.*; Case 14/86, *Pretore di Salo v. Persons Unknown* [1989] 1 C.M.L.R. 71.

[41] Under Art. 150/Euratom, rulings concerning "statutes" may be given "save" where those statutes provide otherwise."

[42] Art. 177(1)(c)/EC.

[43] See above, pp. 314–324.

[44] This is expressly provided by Art. 41/ECSC, and the same position has been reached as regards the EC by the Court in Cases 314/85, *Firma Foto Frost v. Haupzollant Lübeck-Ost* [1988] 3 C.M.L.R. 57, applied in *R. v. Ministry of Agriculture, Fisheries and Food, ex p. FEDESA* [1988] 3 C.M.L.R. 661.

[45] R.S.C. Ord. 114.

[46] Criminal Appeal (References to the European Court) Rules 1972 (S.I. 1972 No. 1786).

[47] Crown Court Rules 1982 (S.I. 1982 No. 1109), r.29.

[48] County Court Rules 1981, Ord. 19, r.11.

[49] See, *e.g. R. v. Plymouth JJ., ex p. Rogers* [1982] Q.B. 863.

[50] By 1989 references had been made by the Employment Appeal Tribunal, a National Insurance Commissioner, Social Security Commissioners, Special Income Tax Commissioners, Value Added Tax Tribunals and a Northern Ireland industrial tribunal.

law is not decisive.[51] It seems that any institution which exercises judicial or quasi-judicial functions and which has at least "a measure of official recognition"[52] will be included, and not, therefore, bodies whose functions are advisory,[53] investigatory, conciliatory, legislative or executive,[54] and not arbitrators[55] or (probably) domestic tribunals which exercise jurisdiction solely by virtue of a contractual arrangement between the parties.[56] Where a court or tribunal performs both judicial and non-judicial functions in respect of particular proceedings, (e.g. as examining magistrate and public prosecutor), the Court of Justice will accept a reference from it in the first of those capacities.[57] The expression "court or tribunal of a Member State" extends to the courts of dependent territories to which at least the general institutional provisions (and possibly any provisions) of the EC Treaty apply.[58]

3. THE POWER TO REFER

Where any "question" within the scope of the preliminary rulings procedure is "raised before" any national court or tribunal that body may, "if it considers that a decision on the question is necessary to enable it to give judgment", refer the question to the European Court.

(a) "Question ... raised before"

The question can be raised by a party or by the court itself.[59] Moreover, it is immaterial that the parties take the same position on the point of Community law.[60] The question for reference will be formulated by the national court, although the Court of Justice will confine itself to ruling on matters of *interpretation* and *validity*: it will not rule on the *application* of Community law to the

---

[51] See W. Alexander and E. Grabandt, (1982) 19 C.M.L.Rev. 413; Case 61/65, *Vaassen* [1966] E.C.R. 261; Case 36/73, *Nederlandse Spoorwegen* [1973] E.C.R. 1299; Case 138/80, *Borker* [1980] E.C.R. 1975; Case 246/80, *Broekmeulen* [1981] E.C.R. 2311; Case 102/81, *Nordsee v. Reederei Mond* [1982] E.C.R. 1095.

[52] *e.g.* supervision or regulation by a minister: *Vaassen* and *Broekmeulen*, above.

[53] The fact that functions are technically advisory will not prevent the institution from being regarded as a "court or tribunal" if in reality it operates as a judicial body; accordingly, the Dutch *Raad van State* (Council of State), in practice the supreme administrative court, has been held to be within Article 177: *Nederlandse Spoorwegen*, n. 51 above. By contrast, the *commissione consultiva per la infrazioni valutarie* (Consultative Commission for Currency Offences), which gives reasoned opinions to the Italian Treasury on sanctions to be imposed for foreign exchange violations, was held not to fall within Art. 177 in Case 318/85, *Criminal proceedings against Undterweger* [1986] E.C.R. 955: its opinions were not binding on the Treasury minister.

[54] *e.g.* the professional association of the Paris Bar: *Borker*, n. 51 above.; or the Luxembourg Director of Taxation: Case C-24/92, *Corbiau v. Administration des Contributions* [1993] E.C.R.I-1227 (although entertaining a complaint against tax authorities, the Director was not an independent third party).

[55] *Nordsee*, n. 51 above: See G. Bebr, (1985) 22 C.M.L.Rev. 489; C. M. Schmitthoff, (1987) 24 C.M.L.Rev. 143.

[56] Hartley (1994), pp. 276–279.

[57] Case 14/86, *Pretore di Salo v. Persons Unknown* [1987] E.C.R. 2545.

[58] Case C-355/89, *Barr and Montrose Holdings* [1991] E.C.R. I-3479 (courts of the Isle of Man).

[59] See, *e.g.* R.S.C. Ord. 114, r.2(1).

[60] Advocate General Slynn in Case 244/80, *Foglia v. Novello (No. 2)* [1981] E.C.R. 3045, 3071–3072.

facts or the compatibility of national law with Community law even if requested
to do so. The Court will reformulate questions put too widely, and may even
formulate the question for itself if the national court fails to do so.[61]

(b) "A decision on the question is necessary to enable it to give judgment"

This wording makes it clear that the material issue is whether a *decision* on the
point of Community law is necessary and not whether a *reference* is necessary.
The Court of Justice will not normally review the decision of the national court
that a reference should be made,[62] although in exceptional circumstances it may
decline to accept a reference on the ground that the matter has not arisen in
real, genuine, litigation: it is not willing to render advisory opinions, of academic
interest only, on "general or hypothetical questions".[63] Accordingly, the Court
has now said that the national court should state in its order for reference the
reasons for which it considers it necessary to obtain a preliminary ruling, unless
these can be clearly deduced from the file on the case.[64] Furthermore, the Court
will not rule on questions clearly irrelevant to the issues before the national
court.[65]

Essentially, the decision to refer is for the national court or tribunal. However,
in the *Rheinmuhlen* cases the Court of Justice held that: (1) "a rule of national
law whereby a court is bound on points of law by the rulings of a superior court
cannot deprive the inferior courts of their power to refer . . . questions" to the
Court,[66] but that (2) Article 177 does not preclude a decision of an inferior court
to refer a question "from remaining subject to the remedies normally available
under national law."[67] This suggests that any attempt to fetter the discretion of
a court under Article 177(2) will be contrary to Community law. Nevertheless,
in *Bulmer v. Bollinger*[68] Lord Denning M.R. laid down certain "guidelines,"
which have been relied upon in a number of cases since, but which have also,
in some respects, been the subject of widespread criticism, not least on the basis

---

[61] This was done in Case 6/64, *Costa v. E.N.E.L.* [1964] E.C.R. 585; however, the Court may be
unable to do so: Case 14/86, *Pretore di Salo v. Persons Unknown* [1987] E.C.R. 2545, where
the Court could not make anything of a very general question posed by the Italian court.

[62] *ibid.*; Cases 98, 162 and 258/85, *Bertini v. Regione Lazio* [1986] E.C.R. 1885.

[63] Case 104/79, *Foglia v. Novello (No. 1)* [1980] E.C.R. 745; Case 244/80, *Foglia v. Novello (No.
2)* [1981] E.C.R. 3045: see A. Barav, (1980) 5 E.L. Rev. 443, G. Bebr, (1980) 17 C.M.L.Rev.
525 (*Foglia No. 1*); D. Wyatt, (1981) 6 E.L. Rev. 449, G. Bebr, (1982) 19 C.M.L.Rev. 421
(*Foglia No. 2*). It should be noted that this litigation was between private parties in Italy but was
in reality directed at the alleged incompatibility of a French law with Community law. *Cf.* Cases
98, 162 and 258/85, *Bertini*, above.

[64] *Foglia v. Novello (No. 2)*, above, at p. 3062.

[65] Case C-83/91, *Meilicke* [1992] E.C.R. I-4871 and Case 343/90, *Lourenço Dias v. Director da
Alfândega do Porto* [1992] E.C.R. I-4673; see T. Kennedy, (1993) 18 E.L. Rev.121.

[66] Case 166/73, *Rheinmühlen-Düsseldorf v. EVSt (No. 1)* [1974] E.C.R. 33: the lower court was,
under German law, bound on points of law by decisions of a superior court; the Court of Justice
held that this could not take away the lower court's power to refer under Art. 177(2). See also
Case 106/77, *Italian Minister for Finance v. Simmenthal* (No. 2) [1978] E.C.R. 629.

[67] Case 166/73, *ibid.* (No. 2) [1974] E.C.R. 139. The court rejected the suggestion by A. G. Warner
that the existence of a right to appeal against an order referring a question to the Court was
contrary to Community law: see [1974] E.C.R. 33, 43–44.

[68] [1974] Ch. 401, 422–425.

that they may constitute "fetters" which are contrary to Community law.[69] His Lordship set out the guidelines in two groups: (1) guidelines as to whether a decision is "necessary"; and (2) guidelines as to the exercise of the "discretion" to refer. He regarded the question of "necessity" as a condition precedent to the exercise of the discretion and, presumably, as raising matters of law or jurisdiction rather than discretion.[70] However, it seems that his Lordship erroneously thought that it was the *reference* that had to be "necessary," whereas Article 177(2) makes it clear that the significant point is whether a *decision* by the national court on the point is "necessary".[71] Accordingly, two of the matters mentioned by Lord Denning M.R. in relation to "necessity" should have been placed with the other group: the presentation here has been revised accordingly.

(i) Jurisdiction to refer: is a decision "necessary?"

(1) *"The point must be conclusive"* and (2) *"find the facts first".* According to Lord Denning M.R. the point must be conclusive in the sense that a decision one way must lead to judgment for one party and a decision the other way to judgment for the other. Where the point would only be conclusive if decided one way, and the trial would have to go its full course in respect of the contested issues of fact or of English law if decided the other, then, according to Lord Denning M.R., a reference might be "desirable" or "convenient" but could not be "necessary". Moreover, "[a]s a rule you cannot tell whether it is necessary to decide a point until all the facts are ascertained. So in general it is best to decide the facts first."[72]

It seems to be generally agreed that this is too narrow, and that the correct view is that it may be appropriate to refer a point where there are still matters outstanding which will have to be determined should the decision of the Court of Justice go one way rather than another.[73] This broader view has been adopted by Ormrod L.J. in the Court of Appeal,[74] by the Divisional Court[75] and by Bingham J. in the High Court.[76] These cases suggest, however, that while there is jurisdiction to refer at an early stage, the facts should normally be found first.[77] A difficulty here is that it may not be clear which facts are relevant for

[69] See, *e.g.* F. G. Jacobs, (1974) 90 L.Q.R. 486; J.D.B. Mitchell, (1974) 11 C.M.L.Rev. 351; E. Freeman, [1975] C.L.P. 176; Collins (1990), pp. 176–183. In *Bulmer v. Bollinger*, Stephenson L.J. (with whom Stamp L.J. agreed) stated that judges should "bear in mind" the considerations set out by Lord Denning M.R. ([1974] Ch. 401, 430) but was also conscious of the requirement that the discretion must not be fettered (*ibid.*, p. 431).

[70] Collins (1990), p. 179.

[71] *ibid.* p. 177.

[72] [1974] Ch. 401 at p. 422, 423.

[73] R.S.C. Ord. 114, r.2(1) provides that an order for reference may be made at any stage.

[74] *Polydor Ltd v. Harlequin Record Shops Ltd* [1980] 2 C.M.L.R. 413, 428: "necessary" to mean "reasonably necessary" and not "unavoidable."

[75] *R. v. Plymouth JJ., ex p. Rogers* [1982] Q.B. 863, 867–870.

[76] *Customs and Excise Commissioners v. ApS Samex* [1983] 1 All E.R. 1042, 1054.

[77] Templeman L.J. in *Polydor*, n. 73 above, at p. 426; Lord Lane C.J. in *R. v. Plymouth JJ.*, n. 74 above, at p. 182; Bingham J. in *Samex*, above at p. 1056c. See also Lord Diplock in *R. v. Henn and Darby* [1981] A.C. 850, 904. In *R. v. Plymouth JJ.* and *Samex* the matters outstanding were not significant in extent; a reference was, however, made at an early stage by Taylor J., with the agreement of both sides, in *R. v. Ministry of Agriculture, Fisheries and Food, ex p. Agegate Ltd*

the purposes of Community law until after the reference has been made. On the other hand, it has also been stressed by English courts that it may be impossible to formulate the questions to be referred until after a case has been argued.[78]

A further point is that it is not necessary that the whole of a case be affected by Community law for a decision to be necessary: it is sufficient if a particular aspect, such as the measure of damages or the terms of a court order should be so affected.

The move away from Lord Denning M.R.'s attempt to formulate a narrow, clear-cut rule in this context means that the matter is so much one for the appreciation of the court itself that it would be artificial to seek to perpetuate the supposed distinction between "necessity" and "discretion": the approach of an appellate court is in practice likely to be similar in each case.

(ii) Exercise of the discretion to refer

(1) *Previous ruling. In Da Costa v. Nederlandse Belastringadministratie*[79] the Court of Justice stated that where it has given a ruling on a particular question of interpretation, and the same question arises in a subsequent case before a national court of last resort, the earlier ruling may "deprive the obligation [under Art. 177(3)] of its purpose and thus empty it of its substance."[80] There would thus be no *obligation* to refer, although the Court also stressed that a national court still had a *discretion* to refer the question. In *Bulmer v. Bollinger*[81] Lord Denning M.R. noted that the Court of Justice was not bound by its own previous decisions and said that an English court should only refer a case in such circumstances if it thinks the earlier ruling to be wrong or if there are new factors which ought to be brought to the notice of the Court of Justice.

(2) *Acte clair.* It has been a matter of much controversy whether a national court, whether a court of last resort or not, may decline to refer a question to the Court of Justice on the ground that, notwithstanding the absence of any prior ruling on the point by the Court of Justice, the point is clear and so no "question" arises. Commentators, both academic and judicial, have argued against the *acte clair* doctrine on the basis that there is a real risk that the national courts of different countries may each regard a question as "clear" but in fact decide it differently.[82] Conversely, national courts in Several Member States

---

[1987] 3 C.M.L.R. 939, and by Henry J. in *R. v. Ministry of Agriculture, Fisheries and Food, ex p. FEDESA* [1988] 3 C.M.L.R. 661; a reference was made notwithstanding that there was an unresolved conflict on some factual matters, and over the objections of one party, by the Court of Appeal in *R. v. Pharmaceutical Society of Great Britain, ex p. Association of Pharmaceutical Importers* [1987] C.M.L.R. 951.

[78] *Church of Scientology v. Customs and Excise Commissioners* [1981] 1 All E.R. 1035, 1039 (Brightman L.J.); *Lord Bethell v. SABENA* [1983] 3 C.M.L.R. 1 (Parker J.).

[79] Cases 28, 29 and 30/62, [1963] E.C.R. 31.

[80] *ibid.* p. 38. The same effect may be produced where previous decisions of the court have already dealt with the point of law in question "irrespective of the nature of the proceedings which led to those decisions, even though the questions at issue are not strictly identical": Case 283/81, *CILFIT v. Ministry of Health* [1982] E.C.R. 3415,3429.

[81] [1974] Ch. 401, 422.

[82] See, *e.g.* Judge Pescatore in M. E. Bathhurst *et al.* (eds.), *Legal Problems of an Enlarged European Community* (1972), pp. 27–46 (but *cf.* M. Lagrange, (1971) 8 C.M.L.Rev. 313); A. G. Capotorti in Case 283/81, *CILFIT v. Ministry of Health* [1982] E.C.R. 3415; G. Bebr, (1981) 18 C.M.L.Rev. 475, 484–489.

have endorsed and relied upon the doctrine. In *Bulmer v. Bollinger*[83] Lord Denning M.R. stated that there was no need to refer a question if the point is considered to be "reasonably clear and free from doubt."[84] Rather to everyone's surprise, in *CILFIT v. Ministry of Health*[85] the Court of Justice approved the doctrine, although not in nearly so broad a formulation as Lord Denning's: thus, there is no *obligation* to refer if:

". . . the correct application of Community law is so obvious as to leave no scope for possible doubt. The existence of such a possibility must be assessed in the light of the specific characteristics of Community law, the particular difficulties to which its interpretation gives rise and the risk of divergences in judicial decisions within the Community."

In practice in United Kingdom courts the *acte clair* issue has arisen in courts other than of last resort, which accordingly have a discretion to refer.[86] There appears to have been a variation in approach depending on the context. Thus, the unwillingess of judges to refer possible defences arising under Community law to actions for breach of intellectual property rights has been contrasted with an apparent willingness to refer questions concerning equal pay and sex discrimination in employment law.[87] Points regarded by judges as clear turn out on closer examination by commentators to be at least arguable. The dangers of a reluctance to refer questions have been stressed by the House of Lords in *R. v. Henn and Darby*,[88] where Lord Diplock noted the different approaches to statutory interpretation adopted respectively by the Court of Justice and English courts[89] and the point that each of the (then) six texts of Community law was of equal authority. His Lordship said that English judges should not be "too ready to hold that because the meaning of the English text . . . seems plain to them no question of interpretation can be involved."[90] However, where the point was one "to which an established body of case law plainly applies" an English court might properly take the view that no real question of interpretation was involved.[91]

---

[83] [1974] Ch. 401. See also the decision of the Conseil d'Etat in *Cohn-Bendit* [1980] 1 C.M.L.R. 543; G. Bebr, (1983) 20 C.M.L.Rev. 439.

[84] *ibid.*, p. 423.

[85] [1982] E.C.R. 3415. See D. Wyatt, (1983) 8 E.L.Rev. 179; N. P. Gravells, (1983) 99 L.Q.R. 518; H. Rasmussen, (1984) 9 E.L. Rev. 242.

[86] But *cf. S.A. Magnavision v. General Optical Council (No.2)* [1987] 2 C.M.L.R. 262, below, p. 986.

[87] A. Arnull, "Article 177 and the Retreat from Van Duyn" (1983) 8 E.L. Rev.365. See also A. Dashwood and A. Arnull, "English Courts and Article 177 of the EEC Treaty" (1984) 4 Y.E.L. 255, L. W. Gormley, "The Application of Community Law in the United Kingdom, 1976–1985" (1986) 23 C.M.L.Rev 287, 288–303.

[88] [1981] A.C. 850.

[89] See above, pp. 404–412.

[90] [1981] A.C. 850 at p. 906. See also Lord Diplock's speech in *Garland v. British Rail Engineering Ltd* [1983] 2 A.C. 751; *cf.* Bingham J. in *Customs and Excise Commissioners v. Ap S Samex* [1983] 1 All E.R. 1042: on three of four points the judge held clear views, but accepted that each was not so clear as to be *acte clair*; the Court of Appeal in *R. v. Pharmaceutical Society of Great Britain, ex p. Association of Pharmaceutical Importers* [1987] 3 C.M.L.R. 951, *per* Kerr L.J. at pp. 969–970; and McCullough J. in *R. v. Dairy Produce Quota Tribunal, ex p. Hall & Sons (Dairy Farmers) Ltd* [1988] 1 C.M.L.R. 592 (discussed by Arnull, (1989) 52 M.L.R. 622, 628–631).

[91] [1981] A.C. 850, 906. Lord Diplock thought that the interpretation of Art. 30 was clear in this sense, but as the Court of Appeal had taken a different view, the point was referred to the Court

Lord Diplock's views were echoed by Sir Thomas Bingham M.R. in *R. v. International Stock Exchange of the U.K. and the Republic of Ireland Ltd, ex p. Else (1982) Ltd*[92]:

> "I understand the correct approach in principle of a national court (other than a final court of appeal) to be quite clear: if the facts have been found and the Community law issue is critical to the court's final decision, the appropriate course is ordinarily to refer the issue to the Court of Justice unless the national court can with complete confidence resolve the issue itself. In considering whether it can with complete confidence resolve the issue itself the national court must be fully mindful of the differences between national and Community legislation, of the pitfalls which face a national court venturing into what may be an unfamiliar field, of the need for uniform interpretation throughout the Community and of the great advantage enjoyed by the Court of Justice in construing Community instruments. If the national court has any real doubts, it should ordinarily[93] refer."

While this should "no more be read as a statute than Lord Denning's original guidelines"[94] this does reflect a "*communitaire* approach consistent with the spirit of judicial co-operation that is needed if the Article 177 system is to do its job of ensuring uniform interpretation of Community law throughout the Community."[95]

(3) *Other points.* Other factors identified by Lord Denning M.R. in *Bulmer v. Bollinger*[96] as relevant to the exercise of a court's discretion included: (1) the time to get a ruling; (2) the need not to overload the Court of Justice; (3) the need to formulate the question clearly, which was another reason for finding the facts first; (4) "Unless the point is really difficult and important, it would seem better for the English judge to decide it himself"; (5) expense; and (6) the wishes of the parties:

> "If both parties want the point to be referred to the European Court, the English court should have regard to their wishes, but it should not give them undue weight. The English court should hesitate before making a reference against the wishes of one of the parties, seeing the expense and delay which it involves."

The tenor of Lord Denning's judgment was obviously restrictive: references

---

of Justice. See also *R. v. Secretary of State for Social Services, ex p. Bomore Medical Supplies Ltd* [1986] 1 C.M.L.R. 228 (and other cases, discussed by Arnull, (1989) 52 M.L.R. 622, 631–636).

[92] [1993] Q.B.534, 545: see Walsh, (1993) 56 M.L.R. 881 and E. Szyszczak, (1995) 20 E.L.Rev. 214. Applied by Leggatt L.J. in *R. v. Secretary of State for the National Heritage, ex p. Continental Television BV* [1993] 2 C.M.L.R. 333, 346.

[93] Not *necessarily*: see *R. v. Ministry of Agriculture, Fisheries and Food, ex p. Portman Agrochemicals Ltd* [1994] 3 C.M.L.R. 18, where while the judge did have doubts as to the meaning of Community law, the issue would become academic by the time the response to an Art.177 reference would be received.

[94] S. Weatherill and P. Beaumont, *EC Law* (2nd ed., 1995), p. 297.

[95] *ibid.*

[96] [1974] Ch. 401, 423–425.

should only be made in exceptional cases, and (possibly) only by the House of Lords. The possibility that the guidelines may, to an extent, conflict with Community law has already been noted.[97] However, the breadth of the discretion to refer has also been noted:

"The matters referred to by Lord Denning are specifically stated only to be guidelines and, as Lord Denning himself said, when referring to the guidelines laid down by the House of Lords in *The Nema*,[98] with reference to applications for leave to appeal in matters of arbitration, 'guidelines may be stepped over, and are flexible.' I take it that he would apply the same standard to his own guidelines. At all events, it is perfectly clear that, where a discretion is conferred upon the court, that discretion cannot be fettered."[99]

One point not stressed expressly in *Bulmer v. Bollinger*[1] is whether references should normally only be made by appellate courts. It has since been suggested that references should only exceptionally be made by trial judges in the Crown Court[2] and by magistrates' courts.[3] It is, however, often argued that an early reference may save time and expense.

4. THE OBLIGATION TO REFER

Article 177(3) of the EEC Treaty provides that where a decision on a question of Community law is necessary to enable a court or tribunal to give judgment in a pending case, and that court or tribunal is one "against whose decisions there is no judicial remedy under national law," an *obligation* to refer arises. The points discussed above concerning "necessity," previous rulings and the *acte clair* doctrine are equally applicable here: indeed the decision in *CILFIT v. Ministry of Health*[4] arose in respect of Article 177(3).

In addition, there is the question as to which courts are covered by Article 177(3). The wording of the paragraph suggests that it applies only to courts from which an appeal never lies.[5] The view more widely favoured, however, is that it applies to any court from which an appeal or other "judicial remedy" does not lie in the case in question.[6] One difficulty that has not been settled is whether the remedy has to be available as of right. In *Hagen v. Fratelli D. &*

---

[97] See above, pp. 980–981.

[98] [1980] 2 Lloyd's Rep. 83.

[99] *per* Parker J. in *Lord Bethell v. SABENA* [1983] 3 C.M.L.R. 1, 4. *Cf.* Sir Thomas Bingham in *ex p. Else (1982)* Ltd, n. 92 above, p. 984.

[1] [1974] Ch. 401.

[2] *R. v. Henn and Darby* [1981] A.C. 850, 906: Lord Diplock regarded this as equivalent to referring before the facts are found. The Crown Court is presumably not so inhibited when dealing with an appeal from the magistrates in a summary criminal case: *cf. Charles Robertson (Developments) Ltd v. Caradon District Council* [1988] 1 C.M.L.R. 293.

[3] *R. v. Plymouth JJ., ex p. Rogers* [1982] Q.B. 863, 870–871.

[4] Above, pp. 982–983.

[5] This was stated to be the correct view by Lord Denning M.R. *obiter* in *Bulmer v. Bollinger* [1974] Ch. 401: the other members of the Court of Appeal expressed no view on the matter.

[6] See the Court of Justice, *obiter*, in Case 6/64, *Costa v. E.N.E.L.* [1964] E.C.R. 585, 592.

G. Moretti S.N.C.[7] Buckley L.J. stated that the "ultimate court of appeal" in this country "is either [the Court of Appeal] if leave to appeal to the House of Lords is not obtainable, or the House of Lords."[8] It is not clear whether "obtainable" means "obtainable ever" or "obtainable in the particular case" but the latter interpretation seems more likely. In *S.A. Magnavision NV v. General Optical Council (No. 2),*[9] it was argued that once the Divisional Court, on an appeal by case stated from a magistrates' court in a criminal matter, had refused to certify a point of law of general public importance, it fell within Art. 177(3). The refusal of the certificate would block any further appeal (to the House of Lords) and could not itself be challenged on appeal.[10] The Divisional Court sidestepped the argument, holding (1) that as it had already dismissed the appeal, it was *functus officio,*[11] notwithstanding that the order had not yet been drawn up and (2) that in any event the point of Community law was clear and the *acte clair* doctrine applicable. It is also uncertain whether the availability of the remedy of certiorari, which may only be sought if leave to apply is obtained, counts as a "judicial remedy".[12]

The fact that an interlocutory order may not be the subject of an appeal does not render it final for the purposes of Article 177(3) provided that the decision is subject to review in the main or subsequent proceedings from which a reference may be made.[13]

5. PROCEDURE

As mentioned above, procedural rules have been made for county courts, the Crown Court, the High Court and the Court of Appeal.[14] All references from these courts must be channelled through the Senior Master of the Queen's Bench Division.

An appeal lies against a decision or refusal to refer in the ordinary way. An order for reference by the High Court is deemed to be a final order and so an appeal lies without leave.[15] Notice of appeal must be served within 14 days and the order is not transmitted until this time limit has expired, and, if an appeal

---

[7] [1980] 3 C.M.L.R. 253.

[8] *ibid.* p. 255, *cf.* Kerr L. J. (for a unanimous Court of Appeal) in *R. v. Pharmaceutical Society of Great Britain, ex p. Association of Pharmaceutical Importers* [1987] 3 C.M.L.R. 951, 969: "A court or tribunal below the House of Lords can only fall within [Art. 177(3)] where there is no possibility of any further appeal from it." In *Chiron Corp. v. Murex Diagnostics (No. 8)* [1995] F.S.R. 309 the Court of Appeal held that an application to the House of Lords for leave to appeal constituted a "judicial remedy" for the purposes of Art. 177.

[9] [1987] 2 C.M.L.R. 262.

[10] See above, p. 923.

[11] "having performed his function": *i.e.* the function of the judge is exhausted: D. M. Walker, *The Oxford Companion to Law* (1980), p. 508. *cf. Chiron Corp. v. Murex Diagnostics,* n. 87 above.

[12] It was so held by Mr J. G. Monroe in *Re a Holiday in Italy* [1975] 1 C.M.L.R. 184 (decision of a National Insurance Commissioner) but see F. G. Jacobs, (1977) 2 E.L. Rev. 119.

[13] Case 107/76, *Hoffman-La Roche v. Centrafarm* [1977] E.C.R. 957: see F. G. Jacobs, (1977) 2 E.L. Rev. 354; Cases 35 and 36/82, *Morson v. Netherlands; Jhanjan v. Netherlands* [1982] E.C.R. 3723: see N. P. Gravells, (1983) 8 E.L. Rev. 250.

[14] See above, p. 978.

[15] See *R. v. International Stock Exchange of the U.K. and the Republic of Ireland Ltd, ex p. Else (1982) Ltd.* [1993] Q.B. 534, where the Court of Appeal set aside a reference by the High Court.

is lodged, until after it has been disposed of.[16] Leave is necessary to appeal against refusal of an order for reference.[17]

F. THE ROYAL PREROGATIVE OF MERCY

The Crown has retained certain of its prerogative powers as "fountain of justice" in the field of the administration of justice. One such area is the prerogative of mercy exercised by the Crown on the advice of the Home Secretary. This may take one of three forms[18]:

"(i) A Free Pardon, the effect of which is that a conviction is to be disregarded, so that, so far as is possible, the person is relieved of all penalties and other consequences of the conviction; or

(ii) A Conditional Pardon, which excuses or varies the consequences of the conviction subject to conditions—this power has been used primarily to commute a sentence of death to one of life imprisonment, a purpose which it still serves in respect of sentences in the Isle of Man and Jersey; or

(iii) Remission of all or part of the penalty imposed by the Court."

The power to recommend special remission is normally used for reasons unconnected with the merits of the conviction, for example, to reward assistance to the prison authorities or to release a dying prisoner. Occasionally it may be used where new information casts doubt on the rightness of a conviction but the case is not suitable for reference to the Court of Appeal.[19]

A free pardon[20] is

"normally only recommended when there are not merely doubts about the defendant's guilt but convincing grounds for thinking that he was innocent"; and this means "morally as well as technically innocent. This 'clean

---

[16] R.S.C. Ord. 114, rr.4, 5, 6.

[17] Bulmer v. Bollinger [1974] Ch. 401, 420–421, 430–431, cf. BLP Group v. Customs and Excise Commissioners [1994] S.T.C. 41.

[18] Sixth report from the Home Affairs Committee of the House of Commons (1981–82, H.C. 421), Home Office Memorandum, p. 1. The Criminal Cases Review Commission (previously the Home Secretary) may refer cases to the Court of Appeal (Criminal Division): see above, pp. 936–939. The following summary is based on this Memorandum. See also the comprehensive survey by A. T. H. Smith, [1983] P.L. 398, and the works cited therein; C. H. Rolph, The Queen's Pardon (1978); C. H. W. Gane, 1980 J.R. 18.

[19] Home Office Memorandum, pp. 2–3.

[20] There is much confusion over the exact implications of a "free pardon": see A. T. H. Smith, op. cit., pp. 417–422. It seems to depend on the exact terms of the pardon in question. The terminology is clearly inappropriate where a person has been pronounced to be innocent. In New Zealand it has been held to be technically no more than an indication that the person concerned was wrongfully convicted: Re Royal Commission on Thomas [1980] 1 N.Z.L.R. 602, and in R. v. Foster [1985] Q.B. 115, the Court of Appeal (Criminal Division) held that the effect of a free pardon was to remove from the subject of the pardon all pain, penalties and punishments ensuing from the conviction but not to eliminate the conviction. (The court proceeded to quash the conviction: see A. Wolfgarten and A. N. Khan, (1986) 130 S.J. 157.) Compare the current Home Office view, above.

hands' doctrine implies that the Home Secretary must be satisfied . . . that in the incident in question the defendant had no intention of committing an offence and did not in fact commit one.''[21]

In practice the prerogative is more freely used in respect of cases tried summarily than tried on indictment.

A person who is acquitted on a criminal charge or whose conviction is quashed on appeal normally has no legal right to compensation.[22] However, for many years it has been the normal practice of the Home Secretary to offer *ex gratia* compensation where a person is granted a free pardon, or, following the emergence of new evidence, has had his or her conviction quashed on appeal out of time or after the Home Secretary has referred the case to the Court of Appeal. A payment may also be made where there has been misconduct or default by the police or some other agency of the criminal justice system and in other, exceptional, cases. Payments are not, however, made simply because there has been an acquittal or a quashed conviction. The amount of compensation is fixed on the recommendation of an independent assessor (in practice the chairman of the Criminal Injuries Compensation Board) whose advice is always accepted.[23] The assessor takes account of pecuniary losses, damage to character or reputation and physical hardship. The offer is made without admission of liability, and while the claimant is free to accept or refuse, if he or she accepts any legal claim must be waived.[24]

In 1985, the Home Secretary stated that he would pay compensation

(1) wherever that was required by the United Kingdom's international obligations; the provision in point was article 14.6 of the International Covenant on Civil and Political Rights, which provides:

"When a person has by a final decision been convicted of a criminal offence and when subsequently his conviction has been reversed or he has been pardoned on the ground that a new or newly discovered fact shows conclusively that there has been a miscarriage of justice, the person who has suffered punishment as a result of such conviction shall be compensated according to law, unless it is proved that the nondisclosure of the unknown fact in time is wholly or partly attributable to him.''

He remained willing to pay compensation in two further situations:

---

[21] *ibid.* p. 3. In *R. v. Secretary of State for the Home Department, ex p. Bentley* [1993] 4 All E.R.442, the Divisional Court invited the Home Secretary to reconsider his decision not to recommend a posthumous free pardon for Derek Bentley, who was hanged in 1953 for the murder of a police officer; his decision was flawed in that he had failed to consider the possibility of a posthumous conditional pardon reflecting not that B was "morally and technically innocent" (the criteria for a full (or free) pardon, which in the Home Secretary's view were not fulfilled), but simply that B ought to have been reprieved.

[22] It is difficult to establish a cause of action for malicious prosecution: it is necessary to prove, *inter alia*, that the prosecution lacked reasonable and probable cause and that the defendant acted maliciously: W. V. H. Rogers, *Winfield and Jolowicz on Tort* (14th ed., 1994), pp. 572–580.

[23] The procedure was set out in H.C. Deb, 29 July 1976, written answers, cols.328–330.

[24] Between 1972 and 1981 there were 47 *ex gratia* payments: 16 of £10,000 or more and three of £20,000 or more: *Home Office Memorandum*, Appendix A(4). In 1983, £77,000 was paid to a man convicted of murder in 1973 on the basis of evidence of a Home Office scientist subsequently discredited. In 1984 Patrick Meehan accepted an offer of £50,500 after seven years in prison: he had previously rejected an offer of £7,500 and the amount was reassessed by an Edinburgh advocate: *Daily Telegraph*, February 2, 1984.

(2) to people who did not fall within the terms of the preceding paragraph but who had spent time in custody following a wrongful conviction or charge, where he was satisfied that it had resulted from serious default on the part of a member of a police force or of some other public authority;

(3) in other, exceptional, circumstances; in particular where facts emerged at trial or on appeal within time that completely exonerated the accused person (and not merely where the prosecution had been unable to sustain the burden of proof beyond reasonable doubt). The Home Secretary also stated that he would regard any recommendation as to amount made by the assessor as binding upon him.[25]

A further step was taken by section 133 of the Criminal Justice Act 1988, which enacted a statutory right to compensation in situation (1) above. The right follows the terms of Article 14.6, except that it must be shown "beyond reasonable doubt" (not "conclusively") that there has been a miscarriage of justice. The compensation is paid to the accused person or, if he or she is dead, to the personal representatives. Whether there is a right to compensation is determined by the Secretary of State; the amount by an assessor appointed under Schedule 12 to the 1988 Act.[26] The assessor must in particular have regard to the seriousness of the offence and the severity of the punishment, the conduct of the investigation and prosecution and any other conviction of the person and any punishment resulting from them.[27]

Cases for the exercise of the prerogative of mercy and requests for compensation are considered by the Home Office's Criminal Department.[28] The relevant papers are scrutinised, and, if it is thought to be necessary, further inquiries are commissioned.

The working of the system has been considered in recent reports by the Home Affairs Committee and JUSTICE.[29] The Home Affairs Committee thought that cases should continue to be processed by the Home Office, but noted that decisions were often presented in such a way as to seem arbitrary: delays should be explained and reasons given for a refusal to take action normally given. However, there should be an independent review body to advise the Home Secretary on the exercise of the prerogative of mercy. This body should be able to take into account a wider range of matters than those currently considered by the Home Office, including evidence which was known to counsel or the police but not put before the jury, for example for tactical reasons that turn out to have

---

[25] Vol. 87 H. C. Deb, November 29, 1985, written answers, cols.691–692: see P. Ashman, (1986) 136 N.L.J. 497.

[26] An assessor must be a lawyer who possesses a seven-year general qualification under the Courts and Legal Services Act 1990, s.71, or an advocate or solicitor in Scotland or a Northern Ireland barrister or solicitor of seven years standing, a person who holds or has held judicial office in any part of the United Kingdom, or the chairman or a member of the Criminal Injuries Compensation Board: Criminal Justice Act 1988, Sched. 6, para. 2, as amended by the 1990 Act, Sched. 10, para. 72(1).

[27] 1988 Act, s.133 (4A), added by the Criminal Appeal Act 1995, s.28.

[28] See the Devlin Report on Evidence of Identification in Criminal Cases, 1975–76 H.C. 338, pp. 55–56, 142–145; Home Office Memorandum, pp. 4–5.

[29] 1981–82 H.C. 421; JUSTICE Report, Compensation for Wrongful Imprisonment (1982); JUSTICE Report, Miscarriages of Justice (1989). See also the JUSTICE Report, Home Office Reviews of Criminal Convictions (1968); B. Woffinden, Miscarriages of Justice (1987); and, on the compensation issue, G.H.L. Fridman, (1963) 26 M.L.R. 481; C. Shelbourn, [1978] Crim. L.R. 22.

been misguided. It should also be able to advise the exercise of the royal prerogative where its investigation has shown the verdict to be unsafe and unsatisfactory: it should not be necessary for the convicted person to prove his or her innocence. The committee were impressed by Sir David Napley's statement that he was unable from his own experience to recall "a single case where the Home Office has, as a result of its own investigations, felt able to recommend a pardon or any other recognition that a conviction was necessarily wrongful." On the other hand officials had expressed disquiet about certain cases where the courts had refused to interfere with a verdict.[30]

The government rejected most of the Committee's proposals, apart from those concerning matters of presentation.[31] The Home Secretary indicated that he would in future be prepared to exercise his power of reference more readily and the Lord Chief Justice that there was scope for the Court of Appeal to be more ready to exercise its powers to receive evidence or order a retrial.

The JUSTICE Committee considered the issue of compensation. It thought that persons given a free pardon and those whose convictions are quashed after a reference by the Home Secretary should have a *right* to compensation. Other persons whose convictions are quashed on appeal should be entitled to apply for compensation although that compensation could be refused or reduced in the light of the claimant's conduct or if the conviction was quashed on a technicality. In certain circumstances compensation should be paid to persons committed for trial in custody and acquitted or discharged, and persons who have had part of their sentence remitted. Claims should be dealt with by an Imprisonment Compensation Board established on the lines of the Criminal Injuries Compensation Board. The recent reforms constitute only a partial move in this direction.[32]

JUSTICE returned to these matters in its 1989 Report on *Miscarriages of Justice*. It summarised its own case work in connection with alleged miscarriages of justice, and examined the reasons why such miscarriages occur. Many of its recommendations concern the investigation, trial and appeal stages of the criminal process. As regards the post-appeal stage, it took the view that the government's response to the Home Affairs Committee's report had not met the criticisms, and that there had been no discernible change in the practice of the Home Office and the Court of Appeal since then.

The changes introduced by the Criminal Appeal Act 1995[33] do not affect directly the exercise of the royal prerogative of mercy. However, the RCCJ was of the view that it would normally only be appropriate to exercise the prerogative, in a miscarriage of justice case where that was shown by evidence that would be inadmissible in court.[34] The CCRC has express power to give assistance to the Secretary of State in connection with the prerogative of mercy,[35] and the investigation of cases will be supervised by them rather than the Home Office.

---

[30] 1981–82 H.C. 421, p. x.

[31] *Government Reply to the Sixth Report from the Home Affairs Committee Session, 1981–82* H.C. 421 (Cmnd. 8856, 1983).

[32] JUSTICE described the details of the scheme as "disappointing": 31st Annual Report of JUSTICE, pp. 27–28.

[33] Above, pp. 923–932.

[34] Cm. 2263, p. 184.

[35] Above, p. 939.

INDEX